DATE DUE

NO 28 '05			

DEMCO 38-296

The Left Guide

A Guide to Left-of-Center Organizations

Edited by Derk Arend Wilcox

Economics America, Inc.
Ann Arbor, Michigan

While every attempt has been made to ensure the accuracy of the information in this publication, Economics America, Inc. does not guarantee that all information herein is correct. The publisher accepts no payment for listing; and inclusion in this publication does not imply endorsement of the organization.

This publication is designed to provide authoritative information. It is sold with the understanding that the publisher is not engaged in rendering legal, accounting, or other professional service. If legal advice or other expert assistance is required, the services of a competent professional should be sought.

Corrections brought to the attention of the publisher, once verified, will be included in future editions.

This publication is a creative work fully protected by all applicable copyright laws, as well as missappropriation, trade secret, unfair competition, and other state, federal, and international laws. The authors and editors have added economic and intellectual value to the underlying factual material. That added value includes but is not limited to: classification, selection, coordination, expression, and organization. In addition, no information from this work may be entered into any database for any purpose.

The copyright holder will rigorously defend, protect and litigate all of its rights in this publication.

The paper used in this publication is acid free and meets the minimum requirements of American Standard for Information Sciences--Permanence of Paper for Printed Materials, ANSI Z39.48-1984.

Printed in the United States by Braun-Brumfield, Inc.

TABLE OF CONTENTS

Organizations in <u>The Left Guide</u>

The distinction between the Left and Right began as a reference to seating arrangements of the French Assembly in the 1790's. The monarchists sat on the right, and the republicans on the left. Modern usage of Left and Right usually breaks down into liberals and conservatives. Unfortunately, the connotations of liberal and conservative have not remained consistent in modern times, especially the word "liberal." To avoid confusion, <u>The Left Guide</u> avoids using the term "liberal" altogether. Organizations in <u>The Left Guide</u> are usually referred to as Civil Libertarians, Progressives, Leftists, Socialists, and Radicals.

How were organizations selected? <u>The Left Guide</u> was produced with the help and cooperation of most of the listed organizations. The organizations knew the focus and the title of the <u>Guide</u>, and they wanted to be listed. Others were reluctant. A familiar refrain (also one that we frequently encountered when producing the companion directory, <u>The Right Guide</u>) was that "we are neither Left nor Right, we are just sensible." This was especially common with organizations that seek to represent large numbers of people and actively seek the greatest membership. Reluctant organizations were also groups that receive significant government funds, either through contracts or grants. Since most of the organizations listed in <u>The Left Guide</u> take positions on current issues, it is relatively easy to match positions with their place on the political spectrum. If we were in doubt, we referred to published material from Americans for Democratic Action and The American Conservative Union. Both organizations monitor votes of members of Congress on key issues and scales the votes on what most people would call the Left and the Right. Of course, neither organization necessarily agrees with our classifications.

Organizations listed in <u>The Right Guide</u> tend to be dominated by policy organizations that rely on analytic economic and social studies. They promote their agenda via these studies; focusing on lobbyists, spokesmen, friendly media outlets, and to a much smaller extent, the general public. With the notable exception of the Religious Right and the Gun Lobby, the Right does not rely on coalition building, grassroots involvement, and political power. Organizations listed in <u>The Left Guide</u> rely heavily on these methods. It is not uncommon for an organization in <u>The Left Guide</u> to produce no academic-style studies, but to use political power as their sole means of influence. Through grassroots organizations, labor unions, religious groups, college students, community activists, and coalitions of these components, the Left influences policy. A new trend is the increasing output of Left-oriented economic and social studies to advance its agenda.

Before the <u>Left Guide</u> there was not a unified source of information on left-of-center organizations. It was difficult for private citizens, journalists, students or scholars to understand the extent and impact of Left-oriented organizations in America. <u>The Left Guide</u> is part of a seven-year continuing effort to make the work of both the Left and the Right more widely available. It is a comprehensive and independent source of information on organizations that promote and advance the principles and objectives of the Left.

Ideas for further improvement are welcome. We would appreciate any corrections, additions or deletions. Please send names and addresses of organizations that should be listed and we will do our best to evaluate them for listing in the next edition. Inclusion does not imply agreement or association with any other organization listed in <u>The Left Guide</u>. There is no charge to be listed, and we accept no financial contributions. Our one source of funds for the project is the sale of the <u>Guide</u>.

The Editor
<u>The Left Guide</u>
Economics America, Inc.
612 Church St.
Ann Arbor, MI 48104

HOW TO USE THE LEFT GUIDE

Most users will probably turn to the **Profiles** section and find the information they need. Only if they cannot find the organization or information they need will they read this section.

PROFILE SUBJECT INDEX

The **Profile Subject Index** is designed to help researchers locate organizations by an area of interest rather than by a specific organization's name. It is especially useful when researchers are dealing with a new subject matter.

PROFILES

This section contains information on most of the active left-of-center organizations in the United States. Information in the **Profiles** is organized as follows:

SAMPLE PROFILE

Environmental Action Foundation (EAF)
6930 Carroll Ave., Suite 600
Takoma Park, MD 20912   **Phone:**   (301) 891-1100   **E-Mail:** eaf@igc.apc.org
USA   **Fax:**   (301) 891-2218   **Web-Page:** http://www.cconct.apc.org/eaf/

Contact Person: Margaret Morgan-Hubbard, Executive Director. **Officers or Principals:** Margaret Morgan-Hubbard, Executive Director ($45,474); Nancy Hirsh, Secretary ($36,705); Andrew Stevenson, President ($0); James Overton, Treasurer.
Mission or Interest: Environmental organization founded in 1970 "to ensure a grassroots voice in national environmental debates....Our work is guided by the knowledge that creating environmental sustainability is inextricably linked to achieving social justice."
Accomplishments: In 1994 EAF was the first national environmental group to interject sustainable energy issues into preparations for the 1995 U.N.'s World Summit for Social Development. In a partnership with the Department of Energy, EAF staff traveled to New England and the Midwest to facilitate the inclusion of various interest groups into the federal government's energy policy-making process. EAF testified at a March hearing that took a "giant step forward in ensuring that renewable energy providers are able to ship clean power to the market." In the fiscal year ending September 1994 EAF spent $156,125 on its Energy Project. $134,021 was spent on Energy Conservation projects. $74,842 was spent on the Waste and Toxic Substances project that provides public education on the community's right to know about toxic substances, and legal assistance to "toxic victims."
Net Revenue: FY ending 9/94 $590,494 ($17,665, or 3%, from government grants)
Net Expenses: $746,448 84%/6%/10% **Net Assets:** (-$120,199) **Citations:** 3:222
Products or Services: Educational materials, grassroots coordination, information, testimony and lobbying. EAF spent $1,248 on lobbying; $198 on grassroots lobbying and $1,050 on the direct lobbying of legislators. This was up from $826 the previous year, but down from $3,783 two years prior.
Tax Status: 501(c)(3) **Annual Report:** Yes. **Employees:** 14
Board of Directors or Trustees: Scott Bernstein (Center for Neighborhood Technology), Maurice Sampson (Inst. for Local Self-Reliance).
Periodicals: *Environmental Action* (quarterly magazine).
Internships: Yes, for those with skills such as researching and writing.
Other Information: Environmental Action Foundation was founded by the organizers of the original Earth Day in 1970. It was affiliated with the 501(c)(4) Environmental Action, until EA was merged with EAF on July 1, 1994. Now the functions of both are carried out under the 501(c)(3) incorporation of EAF. Before the merger, the two separate organizations had combined net revenues of $801,268, net expenses of $929,640, and net assets of (-$119,108). Margaret Morgan Hubbard received compensation from both organizations totaling $51,535. EAF prides itself on remaining grassroots. To that end they raise funds through a growing canvassing operation and maintain a mailing list valued at $140,442. The Foundation received $513,578, or 87% of revenue, from gifts and grants from foundations, businesses, affiliates and individuals. (These grants included $70,000 from the Joyce Mertz-Gilmore Foundation, $42,159 from the Environmental Federation of America, $35,000 from the Rockefeller Family Fund, $20,000 from the Beldon Fund, $15,000 from the Tides Foundation, $15,000 from the Compton Foundation, and $15,000 from the Town Creek Foundation.) $17,665, or 3%, from government grants. $15,418, or 3%, from interest on savings and temporary cash investments. $12,170, or 2%, from consulting fees. The remaining revenue came from other program services, membership dues, rental income, and miscellaneous sources.

We selected this profile because it not only has an entry in every category, but it also has additional information that needs explaining. Some of the organizations do not have an entry for one or more of the categories. This is due to the inability of the staff and editors to ascertain that particular information. We included all pertinent information that we were able to obtain.

Name: The organization's official name is given, along with an acronym if they commonly use one. "The" is excluded if it is the first word in the name. Some names have been modified slightly to make them easier to find. For example; the Maine affiliate of the American Civil Liberties Union (ACLU) is called the Maine Civil Liberties Union Foundation. To make it easier to find this organization, it is listed with all of the other ACLU affiliates as "American Civil Liberties Union, Maine Foundation." In situations where there are numerous affiliates, such as the ACLU and Planned Parenthood, the national headquarters are listed first, followed by the affiliates in alphabetical order. If researchers cannot find the organization they are looking for, it is best to check the **Keyword Index** under various words in the organization's name.

Address: The official address is always used. Sometimes small groups use the home or office address of a key official. We use this address if it is the only one provided.

Phone: The voice phone is listed with its area code.

Fax: The facsimile number is provided when available. If the number is listed as "same," it is the same as the voice number. It is always best to call first and get permission before sending something via fax.

E-Mail: The number to reach the organization via computer is provided when available.

Web-Page: The web-page is a computer address that many organizations have. Unlike an e-mail address, the web-page is not used for two-way communications, although that option is sometimes available. The web-page contains various pre-set information and graphics about the group, and often includes access to its studies, reports, and activities. Organizations find this a very cost-effective and immediate way to inform members and interested parties, so these web sites are becoming more common. Even if there is no address listed here, it is recommended that you call the voice number and ask if they have a web site.

Contact Person: The person listed is usually best suited to answer researchers' questions quickly. Most questions can be referred to specialists or the chief official if needed.

Officers or Principals: Lists some of the key officials associated with the organization. These are usually people who are directly involved in the day-to-day operation of the organization. Under this listing we include the salary and compensation for the three highest-paid employees of the *nonprofit* organizations. If one or more of the three highest-paid employees is not paid anything then it is listed as ($0). It is not uncommon for only one, two, or even none, of the officers or staff to be paid. If there is no amount listed in parentheses for the first three officers or principals, then we were unable to locate their compensation; it does not necessarily mean they were unpaid. If there are more than three who earn over $100,000, we will include more than just the three highest paid. Disclosure laws differ for organizations with various IRS tax statuses. Notably, organizations with 501(c)(4) or (c)(5) status are only required to disclose the compensation of its officers, while 501(c)(3) nonprofits must disclose officers' compensation *and* the five highest-paid employees who are paid more than $50,000. (See **Tax Status** below for more information.) Unless otherwise noted, the amounts given are for the year listed under **Total Revenue**.

Mission or Interest: A brief statement of objectives. Some organizations have many detailed goals and others express their aspirations in more abstract or ethereal terms. Whenever the organization's own words seem to capture their essence best, we put these in quotes.

Accomplishments: Lists what the organization or The Left Guide's editors believe to be the organization's most significant or interesting results. Space usually limits the information that can be presented. How the organization spent its revenues is typically listed here. This is where the recipients of philanthropic foundations' grants are listed.

Total Revenue: Includes "Contributions, Gifts, Grants, and Similar Amounts Received" for 501(c) organizations. This does not include the value of services donated by volunteers. The amount listed here is for a single fiscal year. Some organizations do not end their fiscal year December 31. For these organizations we have listed them as FY (for Fiscal Year), and then whatever month their fiscal year ended. So an organization whose total revenue was $590,494, and whose fiscal year ended December 31, 1994, is listed simply as "1994 $590,494." If that same organization ended their fiscal year in September, as does the Environmental Action Foundation, it will be listed as "FY ending 9/94 $590,494." Many organizations receive government grants. These grants usually come from the federal government, but many receive grants from state and local governments as well. Government grants are listed by total amount and percentage of net revenue that this constitutes. In our example - "$17,665, or 3%, from government grants." More detailed information on these government grants, when available, is listed under **Other Information**. Listed information reflects the latest data on file with the Internal Revenue Service. For more information on what constitutes revenue, consult "Instructions for Form 990" from the IRS.

Total Expenses: "Program Services, Management and General, and Fundraising Expenses" for 501(c) organizations. This is how much the organization spent to operate in the given fiscal year. The fiscal year for **Total Expenses** is the same as for the period listed in **Total Revenues**. The three percentages following the expenses constitutes the breakdown of expenses by Program Services/Management and General/Fundraising Expenses - in our example, "84% / 6% / 10%." These percentages should add up to 100%; however, in some cases rounding-off may cause discrepancies. In some instances, payments to affiliates is a substantial expense, and is not reflected by these three percentages, causing a large difference between the sum and 100%. It should be noted that there is often crossover between these categories. (For example, the publication of a newsletter will fall under the heading of "Program Services," but this newsletter will also usually contribute to fundraising efforts.) For more information on what constitutes expenses, consult "Instructions for Form 990" from the IRS.

Net Assets: "Net Assets or Fund Balances, end of year." The net assets include the current year's excess (or deficit) of revenue over expenses plus the net assets (or deficit) carried over from the previous fiscal year. Grant-making private foundations' net assets are listed at their market value, as opposed to their book value. Rather than accumulating assets, some organizations are net debtors at the end of the fiscal year. The Left Guide lists net debt in parentheses, with a negative sign, like this: (-$120,199). This is unlike standard accounting procedures, where either a negative sign or parentheses denotes negative value, and both together would signify a positive value. We hope this does not cause confusion among users of the Guide familiar with accounting procedures. However, most users of the Guide will probably not be familiar with standard accounting procedures, and for that reason we used both a negative sign and parentheses to make it easier to determine at a glance that the organization is a net debtor at the end of that fiscal year. If the Environmental Action Foundation had net assets, it would have been listed as "$120,199." For more information on what constitutes net assets, consult "Instructions for Form 990" from the IRS.

Citations: The Left Guide, using a database and search procedures provided by DataTimes®, searched the full text and abstracts of over 2,000 daily newspapers nationwide for citations of the 285 largest organizations, as determined by yearly expenditures. Grant-making foundations, labor unions, and professional associations were omitted from this number. A small number of organizations that should have been included in the largest 285 were not because their financial information was received after the search had been conducted. The search covered the calendar year beginning on August 1, 1995, and ending August 27, 1996. The listing for the citations includes two numbers separated by colons. For example, the listing for the Environmental Action Foundation looks like this; **"Citations: 3:222"** The first number "3" is the total number of citations found for that group. The second number, "222," is the rank, out of the 285 groups. The Environmental Action Foundation had the 222nd most citations out of the 285 groups that were searched. In some cases where an organization has two divisions and the name of one division is included in the name of the other, usually a research/education division and a lobbying division, such as People for the American Way Action Fund (lobbying) and People for the American Way (research and education), a search for one would find citations for the other. Since the affiliates work together anyway, both organizations will be listed with the same citation count and rank. Not all organizations seek the public's attention, so the number of citations may not reflect those groups' influence or ability. Affiliates also make the measurement of citations difficult. The American Civil Liberties Union has dozens of affiliates nationwide, and a citation counted may pertain to a specific local affiliate rather than the national office, to whom the citations are being attributed. Others names' could easily be confused with a common phrase when searching text; for example, "Common Cause" is the name of a group and a common phrase. Because of this, the citation count *may* be high. Despite these qualifications the editors and publisher find these measures informative, and a useful guide to the relative influence of the various organizations.

Products and Services: Includes tangible activities and objects produced or offered by the organization. **Periodicals** are listed separate from this heading. Lobbying expenditures are listed here. There are typically two types of lobbying, grassroots lobbying and direct lobbying. Grassroots lobbying refers to the organization's efforts to generate interest on the part of the general public regarding a specific piece of legislation. This might include postcard- and letter-writing campaigns, rallies, demonstrations, billboards, or newspaper and magazine ads that urge you to call or write your representative. Direct lobbying is either face-to-face contact between the organization's lobbyist and the legislator, or direct contact by the organization with the legislator or his office through phone calls or letters.

Tax Status: Many organizations are for-profit businesses that maintain operations based on the sale of their goods or services. They are listed as simply "For profit." The most frequently listed nonprofit tax status is 501(c)(3). Briefly, this means that contributions to the organization are considered charitable donations and thus deductible for taxpayers who itemize. A 501(c)(3) organization may engage in educational activities, but may not directly try to influence a particular piece of legislation. That is, they may publish a nonpartisan analysis of particular legislation, but they may not come directly out and say this legislation should not be enacted. To do so would be considered lobbying. There are exceptions to this rule. 501(c)(3) organizations may spend approximately 15% to 20% of their expenses on lobbying without paying a penalty, depending on the amount of their expenses. The second most frequently listed tax status is 501(c)(4). These are also nonprofit; however, individuals may not (in general) deduct payments to these groups, but in some cases businesses can deduct payments to them as ordinary and necessary expenses. A 501(c)(4) organization may lobby on behalf of, or against, specific legislation if it is to promote the general social welfare, and not the benefit of a single industry. Another common tax status is 501(c)(6) which is granted to business leagues. These organizations represent a common business interest and may lobby on behalf of that interest. In general, donations to 501(c)(6) organizations are not deductible, although a portion of membership fees may be. Labor unions are 501(c)(5). Social clubs are 501(c)(7). Political action committees, or PACs, are not tax exempt. PACs may contribute directly to campaigns for political office. We have made no attempt to verify all the organizations' tax status with the IRS, and users of The Left Guide should verify this information and obtain qualified tax counsel in all cases. There are many other forms of tax-exempt status. Researchers are referred to IRS Publication 557, "Tax-Exempt Status for your Organization," for more information.

Report: Indicates the availability of an annual report from the organization.

Employees: Usually includes full-time staff. However, some probably list part-time and volunteers too. Researchers should recognize that many organizations have a tiny or nonexistent full-time staff but have extensive programs. Some accomplish their goals through unpaid volunteers and others use consultants, leased, temporary and contract personnel.

Internships: Indicates if the organization has an active interest in obtaining summer or temporary interns. Sometimes the interns receive a modest stipend. Students who are knowledgeable about the organization's interests, the subject areas that interest the organization, and who have skills such as word processing, spread sheets and office procedures have the best chance at these openings. Others should inquire about unpaid internships. Most organizations would consider an application for an unpaid summer internship from a college student.

Periodicals: Lists regularly produced publications. Books, pamphlets, papers and studies are listed under **Products and Services**.

Board of Directors or Trustees: Lists members of the board. Many organizations have a long list of distinguished board members, but only a partial list is included here due to space limitations. In private enterprise, board members are usually paid for service. Nonprofit board members are usually significant donors, high-level employees of major corporations, or leaders of other advocacy organizations. Many organizations now have a separate board of academic advisors for intellectual guidance. Sometimes these academic advisors are listed under this heading or else under **Other Information**.

Other Information: This section includes information that does not fit under the other headings. It also includes information that the organizations or the editors think would help researchers to understand what these organizations do. More detailed information regarding sources of funding is included here, including contributing foundations. Details regarding assets are often given here. Background information on the organization, key employees, or founders is often included here.

STATUS UNKNOWN

This section contains an alphabetical list of groups identified as left-of-center, a fact the editors of The Left Guide have been unable to confirm. Despite written requests for information, we received no response. Some of these groups are in operation, but uninterested in appearing in the Guide, or the organization is defunct and the mail was not returned to us. We list the last known address, phone number and contact person we have. Be aware that these groups may be less responsive to your interest. We, of course, welcome any information on these organizations that would be of value to researchers.

NO FORWARDING ADDRESS

This section lists organizations believed to be left-of-center or progressives, but mail sent to the address listed was returned as "no forwarding address." Whether these organizations are still functioning at other addresses or are suitable for listing is unknown. The last known addresses for these groups are listed. The editors earnestly solicit information about these organizations for future editions.

DEFUNCT

These organizations, unlike those in **Status Unknown** and **No Forwarding Address**, have been confirmed to no longer operate. We provide the last known address for purposes of identification and to assist researchers who may study the life cycle of these groups. The political Left has been creating organizations and coalitions for over six decades. It would not be possible to list all that have disbanded. The organizations listed here have become defunct in the last few years. The editors welcome information on other groups that have ceased operations or that are successors to the ones listed in this section.

PERIODICALS

This section contains an alphabetical list of the serial publications produced by the organizations listed in the **Profiles** section, whether they are members-only newsletters, or magazines and newspapers available at your local newsstand.

OTHER INFORMATION SOURCES

The Left Guide is the most comprehensive guide to left-of-center organizations. However, there are other publications of a specialized nature that cover other aspects of the progressive movement, or that would interest users of The Left Guide. We include these sources so that researchers have, in a single source, the most complete guide to the Left.

GEOGRAPHIC LIST

This section includes the organizations from the **Profiles** section listed geographically by the 50 states and the District of Columbia. This section does not include page numbers. Researchers can use this section to find local organizations, or to study the distribution of advocacy organizations.

KEYWORD INDEX

Keyword indices may be unfamiliar to those who do not regularly use library reference materials. This index lists groups not only alphabetically by the first word in its name, but also by all other key words in the organization's name (words such as the, of, for, etc., are not indexed). For more complete information on how to use it, see the **Keyword Index** title page immediately preceding the keyword index.

PROFILE SUBJECT INDEX

The organizations in the **Profiles** section are listed in alphabetical order by name. The **Profile Subject Index** lists organizations by subject so that researchers who are not looking for a particular group, but rather are looking for information on a particular topic, can find a variety of organizations dedicated to that area of interest. For example, researchers looking for information on toxic waste will find groups who focus on public policy surrounding this issue in the **Environmental Organizations** section, under the subsection **Health and Toxins**, in the **Profile Subject Index**.

MULTI-CATEGORY

Organizations under this heading have a very wide range of interests. Researchers can contact these groups about any of the areas listed in the Profile Subject Index, although none have programs in all areas. Because of their wide-ranging interests, organizations listed here are good first contacts in researching either established or new subject areas.

ABORTION AND REPRODUCTIVE RIGHTS

These organizations advocate unfettered access to abortion procedures, including publicly funded abortions. They typically also advocate publicly funded contraceptive materials and information. Reasons for support differ. Some advocate abortion as a means of controlling population growth and therefore aiding or improving the environment, some see it as a means of alleviating poverty, while others see it as central to sexual freedom and liberation from traditional roles. All agree, however, that it is a fundamental right of a woman to terminate her pregnancy.

AIDS/HIV POLICY

These organizations promote public policies that devote more resources to research into the causes and treatment of the Acquired Immune Deficiency Syndrome (AIDS) and its associated virus, the Human Immunodeficiency Virus (HIV). Also advocate rights for those who suffer from the syndrome, and typically promote homosexuals' rights and the acceptance of homosexuality. (See **HOMOSEXUALITY AND SOCIETY** for more homosexuals' rights organizations.)

ANARCHISTS

Anarchists oppose all forms of government and authority. Many are influenced by Karl Marx, but unlike socialists, do not see government ownership of the means of production as a necessary precursor to communism. Rather, they typically believe that in the absence of government, society will organize itself into voluntary communal units.

ARTS, CULTURE, AND ENTERTAINMENT

These organizations critique current culture - the arts, entertainment, popular culture, literature - and its effects on society. Many of them see underlying cultural influences as more important to the shaping of our society than any current partisan fight. They often see traditional American culture as racist, patriarchal, capitalistic, misogynist, and biased against homosexuals, and seek to expose and criticize these facets. Some actively produce their own materials that challenge and undermine existing culture, or build up another one that they see as more open and inclusive.

ATHEISTS

While there is nothing inherently political about atheism, these organizations attribute their leftism to being the logical result of denial in the belief of a divine being.

CHILDREN AND PUBLIC POLICY

These organizations advocate the rights of children and seek increased public welfare for children and on their behalf. They often favor a legal standing for children equal to that of adults before the courts. Positions vary, however. Some see children as in need of complete protection and provision by government agencies, while others see children as deserving complete rights, free of government and parental restraints. Others offer programs, such as environmental, directed by or for children.

CIVIL RIGHTS AND LIBERTIES

These organizations advocate the protection and expansion of legal rights. Some support general rights for the entire population, while others focus on special constituencies, such as African-Americans, Latinos, women, homosexuals, the disabled, and others.

COMPUTER NETWORKS

Many organizations now have web pages and e-mail. These networks, in addition to providing access to these web pages and e-mail, serve a variety of functions including; posting information and studies, legislative alerts, on-line fax services, automatic e-mail updates, and other services.

CONSUMER ADVOCACY AND SAFETY

These organizations believe that individuals in the market place are unnecessarily exposed to risks that threaten buyers with financial, health, and environmental harm. They advocate greater government control over products and the exchange of goods.

ECONOMIC POLICY

These organizations advocate economic policies that rely more on governmental decision making than on markets to carry out functions of economic organization such as the determination of prices, income distribution, and the nature and quantity of goods and services produced. Emphasis is frequently placed on policies that result in a re-distribution of wealth, and increasingly, on policies that favor environmental conservation over economic growth. Often these organizations are a good source for current and historic economic data, as well as academic-style studies and analysis.

EDUCATION

The listed organizations are all concerned with education and the education system, although their approaches vary. All favor the protection and expansion of publicly-funded education, and tend to oppose 'school choice' and 'voucher' systems. Some are professional organizations that seek to shape and direct what is taught and how it is taught. Most advocate the teaching of 'diversity.' That is, they promote an emphasis on teaching the traditions and history of other cultures, and de-emphasize or criticize the traditions and history of Western culture. Others represent certain stances (i.e. environmentalists or peace groups) and conduct outreach efforts to students and educators.

ENVIRONMENTAL ORGANIZATIONS

ANIMAL RIGHTS

These organizations see animals as deserving of many if not all of the same protections and rights accorded to humans. They typically disavow the use of animals for food, clothing, medical testing, and labor. Many are opposed to the ownership of animals by humans for pets. Although animal rights advocates are often in disagreement with environmentalists, who consider animal testing for toxicology essential to their efforts, they typically share a common outlook with environmentalists - the view that non-human aspects of the natural world should be considered on a higher or equal basis with humans, and that the use of a natural resource for human consumption is not an inherent right.

CONSERVATIONISTS

There is nothing inherently political about the conservation of natural resources, what makes the difference is methods and emphasis. The organizations listed here have all proposed solutions or advocated legislation that relies on governmental control of private property or markets. They typically downplay or disavow the right to private property, and oppose 'takings' laws which would compensate land owners for the prohibition of the use of their land as the landowner sees fit.

GENERAL

These are the organizations that make up the environmental, or 'green' movement. Their approaches and goals vary, but they maintain a common core: Most make a clear distinction between the 'natural' environment, as it might exist in the absence of humans, and the environment created by humans, specifically following the industrial revolution. These organizations see the latter as a direct threat to the former. Furthermore, these organizations believe that the use of natural resources for human consumption upsets the ecological balance and that this human action must be controlled, curtailed or stopped. These threats vary from local pollution and discrete health risks, to perceived global changes and threats.

HEALTH AND TOXINS

These organizations focus on the health aspects of man-made or accumulated toxins in our environment. Emphasis is on chemical by-products of industrial production, pesticides, nuclear energy and waste, and the harmful effects of substances we intentionally ingest, such as tobacco products or food.

POPULATION

These organizations seek to reduce or slow the growth of the human population worldwide. Concerns of these groups are numerous. Of utmost concern is the reduction of natural resources due to humans' consumption, especially non-renewable resources. This reduction of resources causes poverty and ultimately starvation. Humans' consumption creates byproducts that threaten the natural environment, including industrial pollution, 'greenhouse gasses,' and ozone depleting chemicals. Increasing population raises population density to levels that reduce the quality of life. Population increases alter and increase patterns and rates of immigration, especially from under-developed to the developed nations, causing dislocation and social disturbances. Most advocate voluntary birth control and governmental incentives to reduce birthrates, but some favor more coercive measures.

FEMINISTS

These organizations all pursue a change in the status of women in society. Most see women as long-time victims of males in a patriarchal society. Some challenge perceived gender differences. Others endorse gender differences by asserting that society is based on 'masculine characteristics,' such as competition and conflict. These groups typically seek a society based more on 'feminine characteristics,' such as cooperation.

FOREIGN POLICY

ARMS CONTROL

These organizations seek the eradication of weapons of mass destruction. In pursuit of this goal they seek intermediary steps that will limit the production and distribution of weapons.

GENERAL

These organizations focus on the United States' foreign policy. Unlike their counterparts on the Right, they generally are less reliant on the use of military force. When they do advocate the use of military force, it is generally as part of a "peace keeping" action, and generally part of a multi-national effort. These organizations typically support an increased role for multi-national organizations and institutions, such as the United Nations, in the development and execution of the United States' foreign policy. These organizations also focus on the international development organizations, such as the World Bank and International Monetary Fund.

INTERNATIONAL CONCERNS

These organizations focus not only on the United States' and international agencies' policy towards a specific country or region, but also on other facets of these countries or regions. Although the United States' foreign policy is a concern of theirs and they seek to influence that policy, their focus does not always center around that policy. Often they maintain extensive contacts with organizations and individuals these countries.

FOUNDATIONS

These are the philanthropic foundations that award grants to the organizations listed in The Left Guide, and the organizations that monitor and aid them. For some, leftist public policy organizations are the sole focus of their awards, for others it is a small portion of their grant budget. There are two kinds of foundations, though both are 501(c)(3). Some foundations are endowed and make grants from an existing pool of assets, which grows with little or no new funds from the public. Others rely on yearly donations from the public or government, and have little in the way of accumulated assets. (Public disclosure rules are different for the two kinds of foundations, so for example, endowed foundations' **Net Expenses** will not be followed by a percentage breakdown of spending.)

GRASSROOTS AND COMMUNITY ORGANIZING

These organizations build political coalitions in a given community to petition, advocate, and mobilize for government programs, organized labor, and social change. Many of these organizations are influenced by, or are direct descendants of, the methods advocated by Saul Alinsky, the author of <u>Rules for Radicals</u> and founder of the Industrial Areas Foundation. Most of these organizations focus on urban racial and ethnic minority neighborhoods, but increasingly, rural areas are organizing as well, especially in the South. A typical coalition consists of labor unions, local government officials, the religious community, social activists and increasingly, environmentalists.

GOVERNMENT REFORM AND ACCOUNTABILITY

These organizations focus on the workings of the federal government, and sometimes state and local governments. In general, they want a more responsive government and elected officials. They are typically against the role of private and corporate money in campaigns, and document the way that this money influences the political process. Many advocate a federally funded campaign system. Others advocate a more open government, and easier access to government documents and information.

GUN CONTROL

These organizations attempt to restrict or prohibit the ownership and use of firearms in the hands of private citizens. They typically see the ownership of firearms as a cause of violence and disorder in society.

HEALTH CARE

These organizations advocate reformation of the delivery of medical services in the United States. Reform measures typically depend on governmental action, rather than markets, to set prices and mandate care. Funding would typically come from increased taxes or employer mandates. Some advocate a single-payer 'Canadian style' health care system. Others focus on mental health treatment and patients rights.

HOMELESSNESS AND PUBLIC POLICY

These organizations focus on policy involving people who lack adequate shelter due to economic circumstance, mental illness, substance abuse, or choice. These groups typically advocate increased public funding for housing and promote the legal rights of the homeless. Many of these groups also provide social services for the homeless, such as shelter or health care, that have no direct political component; however, all of the organizations listed here focus, to some degree, on public policy and legislation.

HOMOSEXUALITY AND SOCIETY

These organizations focus on the status of homosexuals in society. There are many different perspectives. Groups focus on legal rights, cultural status, homosexuals and HIV/AIDS, and some on political activism. All promote homosexuality as equal to and deserving of the same rights and status as heterosexuality. (For more information on organizations focusing on AIDS, see **AIDS/HIV POLICY**.)

HUMAN RIGHTS

These organizations promote human rights worldwide (for a listing on those who focus on human rights domestically, see **CIVIL RIGHTS AND LIBERTIES**). Definitions and origins of human rights vary, but most see certain activities as sacrosanct, immutable, and in need of protection from various institutions, usually governments. While most across the political spectrum recognize human rights, there is disagreement over which ones take precedence, and whether some exist at all. These particular organizations are included in The Left Guide because of their emphasis on not only rights that are almost universally agreed upon, such as free speech, the right of political dissent, and free assembly, but also on rights such as women's rights, economic rights, homosexuals' rights, and environmental rights. At the same time they de-emphasize or dispute rights considered essential in American tradition, such as the right to private property or the right to keep and bear arms.

HUNGER AND PUBLIC POLICY

These organizations advocate policies that are intended to alleviate hunger, both domestically and internationally. Many provide direct, non-political, social services, such as food distribution, but all of the organizations listed here focus on public policy.

IMMIGRATION

These organizations focus on immigration and public policy. Most favor an open-border policy and complete legal rights and access to social services for legal and illegal immigrants. Some, however, are opposed to immigration based on overpopulation and environmental concerns.

LABOR UNIONS

These organizations are either labor unions with a 501(c)(5) tax status, or are nonprofit organizations that work for and with these unions. Other organizations advocate labor policy, or focus on the rights of workers. The Left Guide does not include all labor unions, however it does attempt to include the major labor unions, and focuses on their political activities. Many would argue that organized labor is inherently a political activity; but including every union, and especially the thousands of union locals, is beyond the scope of The Left Guide.

LEGAL

These organizations use the United States' court system to change public policy. Some perform research and others litigate cases that they feel are in the public's interest, choosing cases that will set precedent and have a maximum impact on the legal system. Others monitor the court system for biases, and advocate changes to rectify these biases.

MEDIA

These organizations monitor the major news and entertainment industries. Generally concerned with corporate ownership and monopolization of the media. Most seek greater inclusion of leftist points of view, and a change in the way the media reports stories on the environment, military, economy, and minority groups. Often these groups support a greater role for advocacy in media and news presentations. (For left-of-center groups that are creating their own media outlets, please see **RADIO AND TELEVISION PROGRAMMING, COMPUTER NETWORKS, PUBLISHING,** and **ARTS, CULTURE, AND ENTERTAINMENT.**)

PARTISAN POLITICS

Most of the groups in this guide are political in nature, but the groups here are directly involved in electoral politics. Many are either themselves direct advocates of, or closely associated with a political party, are in some way connected to the process of electing candidates or passing legislation, or are constant observers of the process. Some of these organizations focus on political and electoral reform.

PEACE, ANTI-WAR, ANTI-MILITARISM

These organizations advocate a conflict-free world, and consider wars unnecessary and unproductive. Approaches to achieving this goal vary. Many are against all forms of violence, even in self defense, and advocate passive resistance, often modeled after Mahatma Gandhi and the Rev. Martin Luther King Jr. Some blame the presence of weapons, armies, and depictions of violence as the obstacles to peace, and pursue the eradication of these. Others blame the existence of nation-states and seek their abolition. Other approaches include reliance on religious practices and dictates.

PUBLISHERS

While most of the organizations listed in <u>The Left Guide</u> publish something, such as a newsletter or report, these organizations' primary purpose is the publication of journals, magazines, or books. Some of these publications are small, low-circulation newsletters and magazines, frequently called " 'zines." These 'zines are often more visual and graphics-oriented, as opposed to text.

RACE AND ETHNICITY-BASED PUBLIC POLICY

These organizations advocate public policy and social change that focuses on racial discrimination and conflict. Some advocate policies based on the specific needs of, or benefiting, a specific race or ethnic group.

RADIO AND TELEVISION PROGRAMMING

These organizations produce radio or television programming. Although many of the organizations produce or host a single show in a single market, these groups broadcast nationwide, or are syndicated and can be heard nationwide or in several major markets.

RELIGION AND PUBLIC LIFE

These organizations could be, but rarely are, referred to as 'the Religious Left.' These are left-of-center organizations that draw from religious teachings and traditions to promote their policies.

SENIOR CITIZENS AND PUBLIC POLICY

These organizations support public policy that specifically benefits seniors. Central to these efforts is the preservation and expansion of the Social Security and Medicare systems. Other goals include the creation of a universal, government-controlled, health-care system.

SOCIALISTS

These organizations have many variants, including adherents of Lenin, Stalin, and Soviet-style communism; Maoists and Chinese-style communism; and democratic variants. However, they all have roots in the philosophy of Karl Marx and Friedrich Engels. Their common world view is that there are two classes of people, capitalists who own the means of production, and workers who exchange their labor for wages. According to socialists, the value of all goods produced is determined by the amount of labor that goes into its production. Since the capitalists keep a portion of what the goods sell for - therefore depriving the workers of the full return on their labor - they are exploiting the laborers. This ongoing exploitation is the driving force behind social and historic change, and is the source of inequity, poverty, imperialism, and war. Socialists seek to transfer the ownership of the means of production to the workers through government control using democracy, or violence if necessary. Later, according to Marx, the government will wither away, leaving all ownership directly in the hands of the workers. This final stage is communism. Most of the organizations listed in The Left Guide are influenced to some degree by the ideas and goals of socialists, but these organizations advocate uncompromising and direct socialism.

WELFARE AND SOCIAL WORK PROVISION

These organizations promote policies that increase the amount of social services and goods that are provided for recipients by the taxpayers through government agencies. Some of these organizations represent the professionals who provide and manage the social services.

WORLD GOVERNANCE AND MULTI-NATIONAL ORGANIZATION

These organizations advocate a greater, or complete, role for multi-national or supra-national organizations in the governance of the United States and other nations. Some support the current United Nations, while others seek a more powerful body. Some of these organizations seek a world-wide federalist system, while others advocate the complete elimination of nation-states.

PROFILES

This section contains information obtained from various reliable sources, including the organizations themselves. Where a quotation appears, unless otherwise attributed, it indicates that the statement comes directly from the organization. The **Profiles** section presents the basic information most researchers need; the organization's mission, accomplishments, key personnel, address, phone and fax numbers. We also included more in-depth and difficult to obtain information in many of the **Profiles**; financial information, salaries, and sources of funding. While we have listed the major areas of interest, most organizations have more interests then could be listed in the profile. Almost all of the organizations will respond to telephone or written inquiries. Most organizations are pleased to help, especially if you mention The Left Guide as your contact.

50 Years is Enough: U.S. Network for Global Economic Justice

1025 Vermont Ave., N.W., Suite 300
Washington, DC 20005   **Phone:**   (202) 463-2265   **E-Mail:** wb50years@igc.apc.org
USA   **Fax:**   (202) 879-3186

Contact Person: Njoki Njehu.   **Officers or Principals:** Lisa McGowan.
Mission or Interest: "A network of 170 U.S. organizations working for fundamental reform at the World Bank and International Monetary Fund." Specifically, opposed to privatization of government-run industries and austerity measures as conditions of help from these international lenders. A project of the International Rivers Network (see separate listing).
Accomplishments: "We are the U.S. network of a global coalition of activists and NGO's who have been working for economic justice at the World Bank and IMF since the institutions' 50th anniversary in 1994." Organized a Washington, DC rally for "Gender Justice" to call attention to the fact that "International Financial Institutions, multinational corporations, governments, and even social justice organizations exclude women in economic decision making."
Products or Services: 50 Years is Enough Resource Guide and Directory.
Annual Report: No. **Employees:** 2   **Internships:** Yes.
Other Information: Members of the Network include Development GAP, Food First, Friends of the Earth, Institute for Policy Studies, Global Exchange, Maryknoll Justice and Peace Office, Nicaragua Network, Student Environmental Action Coalition, Washington Peace Center, and others.

A. Philip Randolph Educational Fund

1444 I St., N.W., Suite 300
Washington, DC 20005   **Phone:**   (202) 289-2774
USA

Contact Person: Norman Hill, President.
Officers or Principals: Clayola Brown, Vice President ($0); Leon Lynch, Treasurer ($0); Edgar Romney, Secretary ($0).
Mission or Interest: "To encourage the expansion of black political participation at the state, local, and national levels of government by registering voters, organizing non-partisan get-out-the vote drives and voter education."
Accomplishments: In the fiscal year ending August 1994, the Fund spent $265,559 on its programs. The largest program, with expenditures of $131,880, was grants awarded to various organizations, including local chapters, and $17,237 for the AFSCME union. $65,978 was spent on the "APR Cooperative Craft Union Cooperative Project" which "employs dislocated black bricklayers in Los Angeles in the short term, and later other discriminated-against workers in California." $21,200 was spent on a national outreach program that "implements and coordinates outreach and placement activities, as directed by the International Masonry Fund, of minorities and women to broaden participation in training programs offered under this demonstration program."
Net Revenue: FY ending 8/94 $265,559 ($21,200, or 8%, from government grants)
Net Expenses: $283,562 91%/9%/0% **Net Assets:** (-27,771)
Tax Status: 501(c)(3)
Board of Directors or Trustees: Dr. Bernard Anderson, Sandra Feldman, Ernest Green, Dorothy Height (Leadership Conference on Civil Rights), Norman Hill (National Committee on Pay Equality), Leon Lynch (Leadership Conference on Civil Rights), Dr. Ray Marshall, Lenore Miller (Retail, Wholesale, and Department Store Union), Rep. Eleanor Holmes Norton (D-DC), Arch Puddington, Edgar Romney (Intl. Ladies Garments Workers Union), Dr. William Julius Wilson (Center for Public Integrity).
Other Information: Asa Philip Randolph was an American labor leader. Affiliated with the 501(c)(4) A. Philip Randolph Institute. The Fund received $234,359, or 88% of revenue, from gifts and grants awarded by foundations, businesses, and individuals. $21,200, or 8%, from a contract with the International Masonry Institute, funded by the U.S. Department of Education. $10,000, or 4%, from a grant "to support a technical assistance program to promote economic and social development in African-American neighborhoods."

Aaron and Martha Schecter Private Foundation

1060 N. Northlake Dr.
Hollywood, FL 33019   **Phone:**   (305) 921-6111
USA

Contact Person: Aaron Schecter, Trustee.
Officers or Principals: Martha Schecter, Trustee ($0); Laurie Schecter, Trustee ($0); Julie Schecter, Trustee ($0).
Mission or Interest: Philanthropy that includes leftist policy organizations in its grant making.
Accomplishments: In the fiscal year ending September 1995 the Foundation awarded $139,036 in grants. Recipients of the largest grants included: $25,000 for the Funding Exchange, $12,500 for the Center for International Policy, $10,000 for the Haymarket People's Fund, $5,200 for Planned Parenthood, $5,000 each for the Piedmont Peace Project, ACLU Foundation, Ploughshares Fund, and Peace Development Fund. Other recipients included: The Feminist Majority Foundation, People's Rights Fund, Sierra Club Legal Defense Fund, Center for Defense Information, Center for Investigative Reporting, Center for Social Research and Education, People for the American Way, Public Citizen Foundation, Institute for Democratic Socialism, ACLU Foundation of Florida, Americans for Peace Now, Amnesty International, Center for Constitutional Rights, Greenpeace, Commonwealth Coalition, Share the Wealth Project, Natural Resources Defense Council, Union of Concerned Scientists, and Peace and Justice Education Fund.
Net Revenue: FY ending 9/95 $176,809 **Net Expenses:** $157,575 **Net Assets:** $2,592,032
Tax Status: 501(c)(3)
Other Information: The Foundation received $128,803, or 73%, from dividends and interest from securities. $48,006, or 27%, from capital gains on the sale of securities.

Abelard Foundation

c/o White & Case
115 Avenue of the Americas
New York, NY 10036
USA

Contact Person: Malcolm Edgerton, Jr., Secretary.
Officers or Principals: George Wells, President ($0); Kristen Wells, Frances and David Magee, Adele Bernhardt, Peter Neufeld, Vice Presidents ($0); Charles and Christine Schreck, Treasurer; Albert Schreck, Assistant Treasurer.
Mission or Interest: Grant-making foundation. Awards grants to environmental, gay rights, feminist, and other organizations pursuing progressive goals.
Accomplishments: In 1994 the Foundation awarded $346,650 in grants. Recipients of the largest grants included: $18,000 to the Tides Foundation, $12,000 to the Grantee Exchange Fund, $11,000 to the Santa Cruz Barrios Unidos, and $10,000 each to the Black Awareness Community Development Organization, Catholic Community Services, Coalition for Human Dignity, Immigrant and Refugee Rights and Services, Powder River Basin Resource Council, Silicon Valley Toxics Coalition, Western Colorado Congress, Women's Economic Agenda Project.
Net Revenue: 1994 $478,521 **Net Expenses:** $467,419 **Net Assets:** $2,498,493
Tax Status: 501(c)(3)
Board of Directors or Trustees: Albert Wells, Susan Wells, Melissa and Michael Blessing, Joel Schreck, Thomas and Celeste Schreck, Daniel Schreck, Teresa Juarez, Steven and Sheryl Bernhard, Michael and Nancy Berhard, Susan and Donald Collins, Andrew Heineman, Jr, Lewis Butler, George Gnoss, Patricia Hewitt.
Other Information: The Foundation received $308,000, or 64% of revenue, from gifts and grants awarded by foundations, businesses, and individuals. $91,377, or 19%, from dividends and interest from securities. $77,300, or 16%, from capital gains on the sale of securities. The remaining revenue came from other miscellaneous sources. The Foundation held most of its assets, 61%, in corporate stocks.

Abortion Rights Mobilization (ARM)

175 5th Ave., Suite 814
New York, NY 10010   **Phone:** (212) 673-2040
USA

Contact Person: Lawrence Lader, President. **Officers or Principals:** Lana C. Phelan, Executive Vice President ($0); Barbara Seaman, Vice President ($0); Joseph T. Skehan, Ph.D., Secretary/Treasurer ($0).
Mission or Interest: "To implement and guarantee a woman's right to legal abortion as decreed by the U.S. Supreme Court...To engage in legal, social and informational aspects of abortion and birth control. This includes research on use of alternative abortion options."
Accomplishments: In 1994 ARM spent $28,754 on its programs.
Net Revenue: 1994 $69,317 **Net Expenses:** $30,343 95%/5%/0% **Net Assets:** $145,813
Tax Status: 501(c)(3)
Board of Directors or Trustees: Edith Tiger (Nat'l. Emergency Civil Liberties Comm.), Dr. Vicki Alexander, Fran Avallone, Caroline Bird, Sey Chassler, Denise Fuge, Rev. David Garcia, Hon. Ross Graham, Rev. Robert Hare (Scarborough Presbyterian Church), Hon. Babette Joseph, Jennie Lifrieri, Joseph O'Rourke, Hon. Charles Porter, Hon. Percy Sutton (Inter City Broadcasting).
Other Information: ARM is affiliated with the ARM Research Council. ARM received $62,100, or 90% of revenue, from gifts and grants awarded by foundations, businesses, and individuals. $6,872, or 10%, from dividends and interest from securities. The remaining revenue came from interest on savings and temporary cash investments, and other miscellaneous sources.

Acid Rain Foundation

1410 Varsity Dr.
Raleigh, NC 27606   **Phone:** (919) 828-9443
USA

Contact Person: Harriett S. Stubbs, Executive Director.
Mission or Interest: Promotes public awareness of acid rain.
Net Revenue: 1993 $15,962   **Tax Status:** 501(c)(3)

Action for Corporate Accountability

129 Church St., Suite 703
New Haven, CT 06510   **Phone:** (203) 787-0061
USA

Contact Person: Idrian Resnick, Executive Director. **Officers or Principals:** Idrian Resnick, Executive Director ($40,288).
Mission or Interest: Promotes the "Infant Health Campaign" and "informing the public about corporate misinformation regarding infant formula."
Accomplishments: In 1992 the organization spent $161,517 on its efforts.

Net Revenue: 1992 $108,274   Net Expenses: $191,505   84%/11%/5%   Net Assets: (-$15,925)
Tax Status: 501(c)(3)
Board of Directors or Trustees: Doug Clement, Lisa Fleishman, Douglas Johnson, Rodney Leonard, Janice Mantell, William Mills, Leslye Orloff, Mark Ritchie.
Other Information: The organization received $107,536, or 99% of revenue, from gifts and grants awarded by foundations and individuals. $738, or 1%, from interest on savings and temporary cash investments.

Action for Grassroots Empowerment and Neighborhood Development Alternatives (AGENDA)
2826 S. Vermont Ave., Suite 11
Los Angeles, CA 90007   Phone: (213) 730-4950
USA

Contact Person: Anthony Thigpen, Chairman.
Mission or Interest: According to a funding source it was "Founded after the 1992 rebellion in South Central Los Angeles to help communities develop models for leadership development, grassroots organizing, and policy intervention...establishment of a multi-cultural alliance around the themes of social, economic and environmental justice."
Accomplishments: Conducts the Environmental and Economic Justice Project.
Tax Status: 501(c)(3)
Other Information: In 1994, AGENDA received $35,000 from the Jessie Smith Noyes Foundation.

Action on Smoking and Health (ASH)
2013 H St., N.W.
Washington, DC 20006   Phone: (202) 659-4310
USA   Fax: (202) 833-3921   Web-Page: http://ash.org/ash/

Contact Person: John F. Banzaf, III, Executive Director.
Officers or Principals: Martin Adam Jacobs, Chairman; Alfreda Winnings, Prince Joli Quentin Kansil, Vice Chairpersons.
Mission or Interest: "Legal action and education on the hazards of smoking, protecting the rights of the non-smoking majority."
Accomplishments: ASH was key in the banning of cigarette commercials on radio and TV, and in creating first non-smoking areas and then a ban on smoking in airlines, trains and busses. Use lawsuits and government regulations to reduce and ban smoking. In 1994 ASH brought suit against the federal Occupational Safety and Health Administration (OSHA), arguing that "OSHA had not only unreasonably delayed action on the issue of ETS (second-hand smoke), but had also acted illegally in violating its own regulations which require that the regulation of suspected carcinogens (such as ETS) be treated in separate fast-track proceedings." ASH claims that if the FDA announced that it had jurisdiction over cigarettes, as the FDA has stated it may do, it will be relying on a legal principle established in an action brought by ASH, ASH v. Harris. ASH has filed complaints using the Americans with Disabilities Act. "ASH also provided a nonsmoking father's attorney with research and advice needed to overturn an order granting custody of his children to their smoking mother although the children had asthma, otitis media and sinusitis. The new order granted custody to the father...In addition, ASH conducted legal research suggesting that in some instances it might be appropriate for a non-parent (e.g. a doctor) to file a complaint of child abuse/neglect/endangerment with the proper child-care authority if a child's health was being threatened by exposure to tobacco smoke." ASH supported a bill introduced by Henry Waxman (D-CA) which proposed to ban smoking in virtually all non-residential buildings; the bill, H.R. 3434 was called the "Smokefree Environment Act of 1993." In 1994 ASH spent $1,429,282 on its programs.
Net Revenue: 1994 $1,317,609   Net Expenses: $1,429,282   80%/6%/13%   Net Assets: $2,216,813
Tax Status: 501(c)(3)
Board of Directors or Trustees: Dr. Margaret New, Ethel Wells.
Periodicals: ASH Smoking and Health Review (bimonthly newsletter).
Other Information: In 1994 ASH received $1,126,312, or 85% of revenue, from gifts and grants awarded by foundations, businesses, and individuals. (These grants included $250 from the Haymarket People's Fund, $100 from the One World Fund, and $100 from the Compton Foundation.) $172,247, or 13%, from investment income. $13,861, or 1%, from mailing list rentals. The remaining revenue came from the sale of educational materials and other miscellaneous sources.

Activists for Animals
409 E. 118th St.
New York, NY 10035   Phone: (212) 807-0300
USA

Contact Person: Catherine Kubic, President.
Officers or Principals: Richard Kubic, Vice President ($0); Donald Scalia, Secretary ($0); Kathleen Brady, Treasurer ($0).
Mission or Interest: "Public demonstrations to educate the public, publicize organization's goals, and to prevent cruelty to animals."
Accomplishments: In its first year, 1992, the organization spent $2,393 on its programs.
Net Revenue: 1992 $5,634   Net Expenses: $4,249   Net Assets: $1,385   Tax Status: 501(c)(3)
Other Information: The organization received 100% of revenue from gifts and grants.

Advocacy Institute
1707 L St., N.W., Suite 400
Washington, DC 20036   **Phone:**   (202) 659-8475
USA

Contact Person: David Cohen, Chairman.   **Officers or Principals:** Kathleen Sheeky, Director ($71,840); Michael Pertschuk, President ($71,840); David Cohen, Chairman ($71,840); Maureen Burke, Training Director; Phillip Wilbur, Media Advocacy Director; Barry Rubin, General Council; Brian Carney, CFO.
Mission or Interest: Provides training and information for effective public policy advocacy.
Accomplishments: In the fiscal year ending September 1994, the Institute spent $1,788,481 on its programs. The largest program, with expenditures of $902,410, was leadership training to "strengthen the public interest by providing leadership training, workshops, seminars, counseling, internships, training and written guides on advocacy skills." $692,584 was spent researching and advocating policies that revolve around tobacco products. $121,034 was spent to "strengthen the public awareness of the importance of automobile fuel efficiency by providing a network and materials."
Net Revenue: FY ending 9/94 $1,926,703 **Net Expenses:** $2,084,846 86%/10%/4% **Net Assets:** $160,970
Citations: 4:217
Products or Services: SAFETYnet, an interactive computer database to link groups and individuals "committed to preventing gun violence." Lobbying - the Institute spent $653 on grassroots lobbying. This was a decrease of 88% from $5,349 the year before.
Tax Status: 501(c)(3)
Board of Directors or Trustees: Patricia Bauman (Bauman Family Foundation), Helene Brown, Roger Craver, Elise Garcia (Dir. of Communications and Development, St. Mary's Univ., School of Law), Peter Kovlar, Terry Lierman, Richard Paisner, Leroy Ritchie (Chrysler Corp.), Jack Sheehan (United Steelworkers of America), Linda Tarr-Whelan (National Center for Policy Alternatives), Dr. Reed Tuckson (Pres., Charles R. Drew Univ. of Medicine and Science), Fred Wertheimer (Common Cause), Arthur White, Kenneth Young.
Other Information: Formerly the Institute for Public Policy Advocacy. The Institute received $1,381,990, or 72% of revenue, from gifts and grants awarded by foundations, businesses, and individuals. (These grants included $250,000 over two years from the Ford Foundation,$125,000 from the Joyce Foundation, $100,000 from the Florence and John Schumann Foundation, $27,920 from the Henry J. Kaiser Family Foundation, $25,000 from the Bauman Family Foundation, $10,000 from the Barbra Streisand Foundation, and $2,500 from the Beldon Fund.) $529,697, or 27%, from contracts, services, workshops and seminars. The remaining revenue came from interest on savings and temporary cash investments, and other miscellaneous sources.

Advocate: The National Gay & Lesbian Newsmagazine
6922 Hollywood Blvd., Suite 1000
Los Angeles, CA 90028   **Phone:** (213) 871-1225   **E-Mail:** info@advocate.com
USA   **Fax:**   (213) 467-6805   **Web-Page:** http://www.advocate.com

Contact Person: Jeff Yarbrough, Editor in Chief.
Officers or Principals: Gerry Kroll, Editor; Michael W. Elkins, Managing Editor; Sam Watters, Publisher.
Mission or Interest: *The Advocate* is a leading magazine covering the homosexual community and their political advocacy efforts. Focus on the entertainment business and politics.
Accomplishments: Circulation of 76,000. *The Advocate* has won many awards for articles, art direction, and general excellence. The average Advocate reader is male, 39 years old, has a household income of $72,440, and attended college.
Tax Status: For profit.
Periodicals: *The Advocate: The National Gay & Lesbian Newsmagazine* (biweekly magazine).
Other Information: Published by Liberation Publications at the same address. Published since 1967.

Advocates for Children and Youth
300 Cathedral St., Suite 500
Baltimore, MD 21201   **Phone:**   (410) 547-9200
USA

Contact Person: Donna C. Talliert, Executive Director. **Officers or Principals:** Charlene Uhl, RAF Director ($49,455); Claudette Brown, Schoolhouse Legislative Director ($48,195); Amy Blank, "Vote Kids" Director ($45,780); Anne Price, "Kids Count" Director; Marci Abell, President; K. C. Burton, Vice President; William Stulginsky, Treasurer; Janice M. Flynn, Secretary.
Mission or Interest: Public policy organization focusing on the "health and well-being of the children of Maryland who have special needs, including children who are handicapped, abused neglected, educationally deprived or delinquent."
Accomplishments: In the fiscal year ending June 1994, the organization spent $1,084,335 on its programs.
Net Revenue: FY ending 6/94 $1,143,162 ($74,003, or 6%, from government grants)
Net Expenses: $1,182,010 92%/8%/0% **Net Assets:** (-$21,981) **Citations:** 210:78
Products or Services: Public policy and lobbying. The Advocates spent $20,851 on the direct lobbying of legislators. This was a 53% increase over the previous year.
Tax Status: 501(c)(3)
Board of Directors or Trustees: Raymond Bank, George Barrett, John Baum, Leigh Stevenson Cobb, Timothy Doran M.D., Judge Ellen Hollander (Circuit Court of Baltimore), James Kramon, Traci Lerner, Cheri Wyron Levin, Prof. Susan Leviton (Univ. of Maryland at Baltimore School of Law), Peggy Mainor (Child Advocacy Network), Sally Millemann, Terry Rubenstein, David

Sawtelle (V.P., NationsBank), Rosalie Streett, Brian Weese (Encore Books), Robin Weiss M.D. (Sheppard Pratt Hospital).
Other Information: Advocates for Children and Youth received $1,024,678, or 90% of revenue from direct and indirect public support in the form of gifts and grants awarded by foundations, affiliates, businesses, and individuals. $74,003, or 6%, from government grants. $40,649 net, or 4%, from special fund-raising events. The remaining revenue came from interest on savings and temporary cash investments.

Advocates for Highway and Auto Safety

777 N. Capital St., N.E., Suite 410
Washington, DC 20002   **Phone:**   (202) 408-1711
USA   **Fax:**   (202) 408-1699

Contact Person: Judith Lee Stone, President.   **Officers or Principals:** Judith Lee Stone, President ($121,656); Stephen Brobeck, Secretary ($0); Lawrence M. Zippen, Treasurer ($0); D. Richard McFerson, Andrew McGuire, Co-Chairs.
Mission or Interest: Promotes safer highways through legislation of tougher standards at the federal level. Opposed to raising the speed limit. At the state level they advocate tougher drunk driving, motorcycle helmet and seat belt laws.
Accomplishments: In 1993 they spent $873,700 on their programs.
Net Revenue: 1993 $1,323,544 **Net Expenses:** $1,313,290 67%/33%/0% **Net Assets:** $903,299 **Citations:** 202:82
Products or Services: Legislative monitoring and lobbying. "Saved by the Air Bag" program to document the efficacy of air bags.
Tax Status: 501(c)(4)
Board of Directors or Trustees: Stephen Brobeck (Consumer Federation of America), Rebecca Brown (Mothers Against Drunk Driving), Joan Claybrook (Public Citizen), Clarence Ditlow (Center for Auto Safety), Donald Friedman (MCR Technology), Jay Halfon (NY Public Interest Research Group), Stephen Hargarten, M.D. (American College of Emergency Physicians), Ralf Hotchkiss (San Francisco State Univ.), Stephen Teret (American Public Health Assoc.), Hubert Williams (Police Foundation), August Alegi (GEICO), Patricia Browski (Nat. Association of Insurance Agents), Herman Brandau (State Farm Insurance), Len Brevik (Independent Insurance Agents of America), John Conners (Liberty Mutual Insurance), Dale Hammond (The Travelers), Sonja Larkin-Thorne (ITT Hartford Insurance Group), Rodgers Lawson, Ph.D. (Alliance of American Insurers), Gerald Maatman (Kemper National Insurance), Robert Vagley (American Insurance Assoc.), Marie van Luling (Aetna Life and Casualty).
Other Information: Advocates received $1,285,750, or 97% of revenue, from grants awarded by foundations, companies and individuals. $37,794, or 3%, from interest on savings and temporary cash investments.

Advocates for the Disabled

1314 N. 3rd St., Suite 116
Phoenix, AZ 85004-1749   **Phone:**   (602) 256-9673
USA   **Fax:**   (602) 256-5060

Contact Person: Sue Schaafsma, Executive Director.
Officers or Principals: Susan Schaafsma, Executive Director ($38,796); Ruth Wooten, Supervisor ($33,618); Linda Lund-Wyatt, Chair ($0); Sheryl Sacry, Vice Chair; Richard Nolan, Secretary; Judy Longmeyer.
Mission or Interest: Assist low-income disabled people to prove eligibility for SSI and disability benefits. Assists them in managing benefits.
Accomplishments: In 1994 Advocates for the Disabled assisted 1,851 clients. The organization claims clients were 99.2% successful and received $11,957,285 in benefits. In the past they have helped 12,380 clients receive over $108 million in benefits. 30% of clients were awarded Social Security Disability Insurance, 38% were awarded Supplemental Security Income, and 30% received both. The largest portion of those helped, 54%, had mental disorders, another 16% had musculoskeletal impairments, 7% had circulatory disorders, 5% had "ill-defined" conditions. The rest had various impairments. The average client was a 42 year old white male with some high school education who had a mental disorder. Most clients, 89%, had previously been denied disability claims. In the fiscal year ending June 1994 Advocates spent $863,074 on programs.
Net Revenue: FY ending 6/94 $953,187 ($872,021, or 92%, from government grants)
Net Expenses: $896,441 96%/4%/0% **Net Assets:** $357,000 **Citations:** 388:48
Products or Services: Social work, legal advocacy, expert testimony, training manual, and special sessions for professional social workers.
Tax Status: 501(c)(3) **Annual Report:** Yes. **Employees:** 18
Board of Directors or Trustees: Millie Hines, David Lee, Richard Childress, Linda Czarnecki, Lawrence Groth, Ken Jacuzzi, Chuck Johnson, Elaine Josephs, Marcos Morales.
Internships: Yes, for Arizona State University students at bachelor and masters of social work levels.
Other Information: Founded in 1970. Advocates for the Disabled received $872,021, or 92% of revenue, from government grants. $34,047, or 4%, from the Arizona Bar Foundation. $28,058, or 3%, from gifts and grants awarded by foundations, companies and individuals. $5,197, or 1%, from dividends and interest from securities. The remaining revenue came from court-awarded attorney's fees, sales of manuals, and interest on savings and temporary cash investments.

Advocates for the Homeless

P.O. Box 475
Frederick, MD 21701   **Phone:**   (301) 662-2003
USA

Contact Person: Ann Ryan, Executive Director.   **Officers or Principals:** Ann Ryan, Executive Director ($34,000); Gary Hughes,

President ($0); Carolyn Barranca, Vice President ($0); Richard Menconeri, Secretary.
Mission or Interest: Social services for the homeless, eviction prevention and intervention, and advocacy and community education. Focus on Frederick County in Maryland.
Accomplishments: In 1994 the organization spent $135,189 on its programs. The largest program, with expenditures of $92,668, provided transitional housing for the homeless. $33,024 was spent on eviction prevention and intervention. $9,497 was spent on advocacy and community education.
Net Revenue: 1994 $169,130 ($43,196, or 26%, from government grants) **Net Expenses:** $176,765 76%/19%/5%
Net Assets: $8,383   **Tax Status:** 501(c)(3)
Board of Directors or Trustees: Ruth Ann Offutt, Jack Burdette, Dr. Barbara Hetrick, Helen Rossi, Kathleen Costlow, Mike Catron, David Stauffer, Ruth Roney, Karen Spain.
Other Information: Advocates for the homeless received $94,544, or 56% of revenue, from gifts and grants awarded by foundations, businesses, and individuals. $43,196, or 26%, from government grants. $25,196 net , or 15%, from special fund-raising events. $6,057 net, or 4%, from rental income. The remaining revenue came from dividends and interest from securities.

Advocates for Youth
1025 Vermont Ave., N.W., Suite 210
Washington, DC 20005   **Phone:**   (202) 347-5700
USA

Contact Person: Margaret Pruitt Clark, Executive Director. **Officers or Principals:** Margaret Pruitt Clark, Executive Director ($82,402); Marijke Velzeboer, Deputy Director ($66,385); Asha Mohamud, Director of International Programs ($55,702); Abigail English, J.D., Chair; Margaret Booth, Vice Chair; David Kaplan, M.D., Secretary; Daniel Pellegrom, Treasurer; Pamela Haughton-Denniston, Director of Public Affairs; Sandra Villareal, Director of Finance; Jennifer Daves, Director of Media Projects.
Mission or Interest: Advocates for Youth (formerly the Center for Population Options) advocates birth control, the right to have an abortion, HIV/AIDS prevention, and population control. Special focus on teenagers and the third world.
Accomplishments: In the fiscal year ending March 1994, the organization spent $1,397,735 on its programs. The largest program, with expenditures of $307,709, was the international efforts. These efforts included $53,791 in grants to foreign agencies. $202,813 was spent on public education in the form of "articles, publications and resources compiled, written and edited for distribution to the public." $199,489 was spent on HIV/AIDS education, which "provides education to youth on the causes and prevention of AIDS." $176,997 was spent on the Media Project to "work with major Hollywood writers, producers, actors and industry executives to increase prime time sexual programming on issues of responsible teenage sexuality and contraceptive use." $172,176 was spent on public policy projects that "monitors legislative and administrative activities on issues of family planning and abortion for public education purposes and advocates unrestricted teenage access to contraceptive education." $145,775 was spent to "support school-based clinics." $132,715 was spent on sexuality education that "designs and provides training and technical assistance to organizations working with or reaching young people both nationally and internationally."
Net Revenue: FY ending 3/94 $1,915,317 ($223,998, or 12%, from government grants)
Net Expenses: $1,870,151 75%/19%/6% **Net Assets:** $25,811 **Citations:** 186:85
Products or Services: Articles and publications, other educational efforts. In the past the organization has engaged in lobbying. In 1991 the organization spent $1,264 on lobbying.
Tax Status: 501(c)(3)
Board of Directors or Trustees: Jane Delano Brown, Ph.D. (School of Journalism, Univ. of NC), Holly Delany Cole, Robin Elliott, Mary Draper Janney, Robert Johnson, M.D. (New Jersey Medical School), Opia Mensah Kumah (Population Communication Services, Johns Hopkins Univ.), Felicia Lynch, Henrietta Marshall, Patricia O'Brien, Alberto Rizo, M.D., Vicki Sant (Summit Found.), Trudi Schutz, Rev. Kenneth Smith (Theological Seminary), Leo Morris, Ph.D. (Center for Disease Control and Prevention), Norissa Johnson, William Johnson.
Other Information: Advocates for Youth received $1,468,017, or 77% of revenue, from gifts and grants awarded by foundations, businesses, and individuals. (These grants included $300,000 over three years from the John D. and Catherine T. MacArthur Foundation, $190,000 over two years from the Carnegie Corporation, $50,000 from the Robert Sterling Clark Foundation, $50,000 from the John Merck Fund, $30,000 from the Henry J. Kaiser Family Foundation, $20,000 from the General Service Foundation, $15,000 from the Compton Foundation, $500 from the Stewart R. Mott Charitable Trust. In 1995, $3,190 from the Rockefeller Foundation.) $223,998, or 12%, from government grants. $205,724, or 11%, from program service fees and the sale of publications. The remaining revenue came from dividends and interest from securities, interest on savings and temporary cash investments, capital gains on the sale of assets, and other miscellaneous sources. Net revenue was decreased by the loss of $8,872 on the sale of assets.

Affinity Group of Evolutionary Anarchists
P.O. Box 1402
Lawrence, KS 66044-8402
USA

Contact Person: Ed Stamm.
Mission or Interest: An address exchange group linking individuals who favor "education and self-organization as the preferred methods of achieving a voluntary, egalitarian and cooperative society." Supports and organizes anarchists.
Accomplishments: Currently 23 participants in their network.
Products or Services: "Consent or Coercion: An Anarchist Case for Social Transformation and Answers to Questions About Anarchism," pamphlet.
Tax Status: No formal status.   **Periodicals:** *Meander Quarterly* (quarterly journal).
Other Information: "Anarchy is freedom, not disorder. It's the absence of order, but a consensual order without hierarchy or coercion. Anarchy is the opposite of totalitarianism."

Africa Faith and Justice Network
401 Michigan Ave., N.E., Suite 230
Washington, DC 20017   **Phone:**   (202) 832-3412
USA

Contact Person: John Murray, President.   **Officers or Principals:** John Murray, President ($0); Maria Homung, Vice President ($0); John Schneider, Secretary/Treasurer ($0).
Mission or Interest: Religious organization focusing on Africa. Educational activities include workshops and conferences dealing with "economic justice," human rights, democracy, and other issues facing Africans.
Accomplishments: In 1994 the Network spent $109,015 on its programs. The annual conference was attended by ninety people. Workshops were attended by 26 members and guest Africans. These workshops ended with visits to the U.S. Treasury and the World Bank.
Net Revenue: 1994 $115,285 **Net Expenses:** $123,563 88%/9%/3% **Net Assets:** $55,836
Products or Services: Publications, conferences, workshops, electronic bulletin board.
Tax Status: 501(c)(3)
Board of Directors or Trustees: Joan Mumaw, James Ferguson, William Dyer, Mark Weber, Mara Frundt, Margaret Rogers, Edward Dougherty (Maryknoll Fathers), Janice McLaughlin (Maryknoll Sisters).
Periodicals: *Country Reports* (bimonthly).
Other Information: The Network received $73,870, or 64% of revenue, from gifts and grants awarded by foundations, businesses, and individuals. $33,813, or 29%, from membership dues. $5,997, or 5%, from conferences and workshops. The remaining revenue came from interest on savings and temporary cash investments.

Africa Fund
17 John St., 12th Floor
New York, NY 10038   **Phone:**   (212) 962-1210
USA

Contact Person: Adrena Ifill, Associate Director.   **Officers or Principals:** Jennifer Davis, Executive Director ($30,871); Adrena Ifill, Associate Director ($18,563); Tilden LeMelle, Chairperson ($0); Marsha Bonner, Vice Chairperson; Marvin Rich, Treasurer.
Mission or Interest: Promotion of human rights in Africa. Aid to refugees and support of political prisoners. Support trade unions in Africa.
Accomplishments: In 1993 the Fund spent $483,497 on its projects. The largest project, with expenditures of $434,262, was research, education and dissemination on African issues. Programs included $136,239 in grants awarded to organizations in the U.S. and Africa. Many of the grants and programs focused on apartheid in South Africa.
Net Revenue: 1993 $447,098 **Net Expenses:** $561,408 86%/7%/7% **Net Assets:** $200,505
Tax Status: 501(c)(3)
Board of Directors or Trustees: Owen Bieber (UAW), Robert Boehm, Hon. William Booth (ret., NY City Judge), Elizabeth Calvin (United Methodist Church), George Houser (American Committee on Africa), John L.S. Holloman Jr. M.D., Margaret Marshall (V.P., Harvard Univ.), Rose Milligan (Peace Development Fund), Frank Montero, Andrew Norman, Venita Vinson (Vice Chair, CO State Democratic Party), Peter Weiss.
Other Information: Affiliated with the 501(c)(4) American Committee on Africa at the same address. The two affiliates had combined net revenues of $537,107, net expenses of $635,294, and net assets of $232,331. Jennifer Davis served as executive director of both and received a combined $38,337, Adrena Ifill served as associate director for both, and received $20,626. The Fund received $431,648, or 97% of revenue, from gifts and grants awarded by foundations, businesses, and individuals. $8,605, or 2%, from interest on savings and temporary cash investments. $6,845, or 1%, from literature sale.

African-American Institute
833 United Nations Plaza
New York, NY 10017   **Phone:**   (212) 350-2952
USA

Contact Person: Vivian L. Derryck, President.
Officers or Principals: Vivian Lowery Derryck, President ($147,624); Frank Ferrari, Vice President ($138,976); Pamela McCloud, Project Director ($91,508); Maurice Tempelsman, Chairman; Roger Wilkins, Vice Chairman.
Mission or Interest: Human rights, economic development, and organized labor in Africa.
Accomplishments: In the fiscal year ending September 1993, the Institute spent $8,520,814 on its programs. The largest program, with expenditures of $6,439,497, assisted African development by providing educational opportunities for African students to study in the United States or Africa, and then fill "high-level manpower needs in African universities or serve in African civil services." $1,945,690 was spent strengthening African-American relations by exchanging short-term visitors in the fields of media, business, and labor. Also publishes *Africa Report* magazine.
Net Revenue: FY ending 9/93 $11,475,780 ($8,852,989, or 77%, from government sources)
Net Expenses: $11,392,365 75%/24%/1% **Net Assets:** $10,179,083 **Citations:** 63:129

Tax Status: 501(c)(3)

Board of Directors or Trustees: Dr. Dolly Desselle Adams (Women's Missionary Society, African Methodist Episcopal Church), Yvonne Braithwaite Burke (Los Angeles County Board of Supervisors), Dr. William Cotter (Pres., Colby College), Kerry Kennedy Cuomo (Exec. Dir., Robert F. Kennedy Memorial Center for Human Rights), Dr. Francis Deng (Brookings Inst.), Harold Doley Jr., Thomas Donahue (AFL-CIO), Dr. Peggy Dulany (Synergos Inst.), Nadine Hack (NYC Commission for the United Nations Consular Corps. & International Business), Jon Hagler, Bernard Harleston (Harvard Univ.), William Hayden (Senior Managing Director, Bear, Stearns & Co.), Robert Hoen (US/South Africa Leadership Exchange Program), Prof. Walter Kamba (Univ. of Zimbabwe), George Lindsay (Debevoise & Plimpton), James Lowry, William Lucy (AFSCME, Coalition of Black Trade Unionists), Richard Matzke (Pres., Chevron Overseas Petroleum), Hon. Donald McHenry (School of Foreign Service, Georgetown Univ.), Harriet Michel (Natl. Minority Supplier Development Council), Dr. Randolph Nugent (United Methodist Church), Hon. Olusegun Obasanjo (former Head of State, Nigeria), Nancy Clark Reynolds, Loren Ross (Treasurer, Russell Sage Found.), D.E.I. Smyth (V.P., Corporate Affairs, H.J. Heinz Co.), Dr. John Spencer (Middlebury College), Carl Ware (Pres., Africa Group, Coca-Cola Intl.), Thomas Winship (Center for Foreign Journalism).

Periodicals: *Africa Report* (magazine).

Other Information: The Institute received $8,852,989, or 72% of total revenue, from government grants. $2,294,681, or 19%, from gifts and grants awarded by foundations, affiliates, businesses, and individuals. (In 1995 these grants included $15,000 from the Rockefeller Foundation.) $532,354, or 4%, from capital gains on the sale of securities. $425,542, or 3%, from dividends and interest from securities. The remaining revenue came from magazine subscriptions, and interest on savings and temporary cash investments.

African-American Labor Center

1925 K St., N.W., Suite 300
Washington, DC 20006   **Phone:**   (202) 778-4600
USA

Contact Person: Patrick J. O'Farrell, Executive Director.

Officers or Principals: Patrick J. O'Farrell, Executive Director ($149,886); David Brombart, Deputy Director ($125,657); Michael Lescault, Program Director ($109,418); Gebreselassie Gebremariam, Regional Director ($106,967); Joseph W. Davis, Director of Education ($106,012); Lane Kirkland, President; Thomas Donahue, Secretary/Treasurer.

Mission or Interest: "Free democratic trade union and cooperative education programs conducted in various African countries." Affiliated with the AFL-CIO and the Free Trade Union Institute.

Accomplishments: In 1994 the Center spent $8,539,597 on its programs.

Net Revenue: 1994 $10,048,738 ($9,698,335, or 97%, from government grants)

Net Expenses: $10,145,331 84%/16%/0% **Net Assets:** $386,104 **Citations:** 1:240

Tax Status: 501(c)(3)

Other Information: The Center received $9,698,335, or 97% of revenue, from government grants. $332,257, or 3%, from affiliates. The remaining revenue came from interest on savings and temporary cash investments.

Agenda

220 S. Main St.
Ann Arbor, MI 48104   **Phone:**   (313) 996-8018
USA

Contact Person: Ted Sylvester, Editor.   **Officers or Principals:** Laurie Wechter, Editor; Phyllis Engelbert, Eric Jackson, Associate Editors; Jennifer Hall, Business Manager.

Mission or Interest: A leftist tabloid distributed in the Ann Arbor, Michigan and University of Michigan area. Covers national and local events, as well as the arts and politics.

Accomplishments: Over 20,000 copies of each issue are distributed each month.

Tax Status: For profit.

Periodicals: *Agenda: Ann Arbor's Alternative Newsmonthly* (monthly tabloid).

Other Information: The *Agenda* was founded in 1986, making its ten-year run the longest alternative journal in Ann Arbor.

Agent Orange Victims International

P.O. Box 2465
Darien, CT 06820   **Phone:**   (203) 656-0003
USA

Contact Person: Frank McCarthy, President.   **Officers or Principals:** Pat Carstens, Treasurer ($29,615); James Spallow, Vice President ($28,442); Philip Kraft, Secretary ($27,462).

Mission or Interest: "Identify and assess the needs of, and provide assistance to veterans and their families. Major focus is children of Vietnam veterans afflicted with medical problems."

Accomplishments: In 1993 the organization spent $210,405 on its programs, providing financial aid to over 150 children.

Net Revenue: 1993 $407,978 **Net Expenses:** $399,171 53%/15%/32% **Net Assets:** $128,487

Tax Status: 501(c)(3)

Other Information: Agent Orange Victims International received $407,502, or 99.9% of revenue, from gifts and grants awarded by foundations, businesses, and individuals. The remaining revenue came from interest on savings and temporary cash investments.

AIDS Action Committee of Massachusetts

131 Clarendon St.
Boston, MA 02116 **Phone:** (617) 437-6200
USA

Contact Person: Cheryl Schaffer, Deputy Executive Director.
Officers or Principals: Lawrence Kessler, Executive Director ($83,300); Cheryl Schaffer, Deputy Executive Director ($60,462); Valerie Langbehn, Director of Development ($56,225); Robert Greenwald, Director of Public Policy; Mary Ann Kowalski, Director of Administration; Gary Bailey, President; Rhoda Creamer, Clerk; Stephen Weiner, Treasurer; Mark Walsh, Vice President.
Mission or Interest: Research and educational service agency working to raise public awareness about AIDS, affect public policy concerning AIDS, and help those afflicted with the disease.
Accomplishments: In the fiscal year ending April, 1994, the Committee spent $5,348,862 on its programs. The largest project was AIDS education, spending $2,377,853, conducting workshops, conferences and other educational forums to raise AIDS awareness among several targeted audiences. $2,090,261 was spent on client services, both direct assistance and client referrals. Awarded $750,000 in grants to other organizations. Recipients of the largest grants included $30,000 for the AIDS Action Council, and $25,000 each for: Asociacion San Martin de Porres, Brockton Area Multi-Service, Dimock Community Center, Fenway Community Center, Gay and Lesbian Advocates and Defenders, Haitian Community AIDS Outreach Project, Hispanic Office of Planning and Evaluation, North Shore AIDS Health Project, Pine Street Inn, Positive Directions, Social Justice for Women, Strongest Link AIDS Services, Women Inc. And the Boston Living Center.
Net Revenue: FY ending 4/94 $7,607,979 ($1,892,389, or 25%, from government grants)
Net Expenses: $7,855,471 68%/17%/20% **Net Assets:** $2,246,615 **Citations:** 16:180
Products or Services: Social services, grants, educational materials, more. Lobbying - in the fiscal year ending April 1994, they spent $39,000 on lobbying, conducted by Mary Ann Walsh. The lobbying efforts were directed toward researching and advising various AIDS-related bills in Massachusetts.
Tax Status: 501(c)(3)
Other Information: The Committee received $1,892,389, or 25% of revenue, from government grants. Special events raised $3,731,336, or 49%. $1,804,396, or 24%, came from grants made by foundations, companies and individuals. (These grants included $11,350 from the Haymarket People's Fund.) Educational programs accounted for $95,875, or 1%. The remainder came from interest on savings and temporary cash investments.

AIDS Action Council

1875 Connecticut Ave., N.W., Suite 700
Washington, DC 20009 **Phone:** (202) 986-1300
USA

Contact Person: Christine Lubinski, Deputy Executive Director.
Officers or Principals: Christine Lubinski, Deputy Executive Director ($80,436); Daniel Bross, Executive Director ($50,732); Mario Cooper, Chairman ($0); Craig Miller, Vice Chair; Jimmy Loyce, Secretary.
Mission or Interest: Lobbies to promote "research into the HIV virus and promote Public Awareness about the infection and to clarify and establish federal HIV policies."
Accomplishments: In 1994 the Council spent $655,375 on its programs.
Net Revenue: 1994 $775,042 **Net Expenses:** $775,900 84%/4%/12% **Net Assets:** $814 **Citations:** 147:95
Tax Status: 501(c)(4)
Board of Directors or Trustees: Birch Bayh, Charles Bremer, Pat Christen, Leah Daughtry, Thomas Dunlap, Sandra Estepa, Anne Hill, David Hollander, Larry Kessler, Chuck Kuehn, Lulu Lopez, Jeffery Morris, Douglas Nelson, Jeff Richardson, Judy Stanfield, Terry Stone, Lorraine Teel, Michael Weinstein, David Wexler, James Williams, Phill Wilson.
Other Information: Affiliated with the 501(c)(3) AIDS Action Foundation at the same address. The two affiliates had combined net revenues of $1,697,838, net expenses of $1,749,336, and net assets of $105,024. Deputy Executive Director Christine Lubinski held that position with both affiliates and was paid $115,250, and Executive Director Daniel Bross held that position with both and was paid $72,990. The Council received $729,951, or 94% of revenue, from membership dues. $38,964, or 5%, from gifts and grants awarded by affiliates, foundations, businesses, and individuals. (These grants included $15,000 from the AIDS Action Foundation. In 1993, the Council received $200,000 from Gay Men's Health Crisis.) $6,127, or 1%, from interest on savings and temporary cash investments.

AIDS Action Foundation

1875 Connecticut Ave., N.W., Suite 700
Washington, DC 20009 **Phone:** (202) 986-1300
USA

Contact Person: Christine Lubinski, Deputy Executive Director.
Officers or Principals: Christine Lubinski, Deputy Executive Director ($34,814); Daniel Bross, Executive Director ($22,258); Timothy Boggs, Chairman ($0); Thomas G. Dunlap, Vice President/Treasurer; Lili Rundback, Secretary.
Mission or Interest: "To conduct and promote educational, charitable, and scientific activities related to the AIDS epidemic."
Accomplishments: In 1994 the Foundation spent $788,736 on its programs. The Foundation awarded a grant of $15,000 to its

501(c)(4) affiliate, the AIDS Action Council.
Net Revenue: 1994 $922,796 **Net Expenses:** $973,436 81%/1%/18% **Net Assets:** $104,210 **Citations:** 6:210
Products or Services: Educational activities and coordination.
Tax Status: 501(c)(3)
Board of Directors or Trustees: Alvan Fisher M.D., Hartina Flournoy, Phillip Lacy, Craig Miller, David Wexler.
Other Information: Affiliated with the 501(c)(3) AIDS Action Foundation at the same address. The two affiliates had combined net revenues of $1,697,838, net expenses of $1,749,336, and net assets of $105,024. Deputy Executive Director Christine Lubinski held that position with both affiliates and was paid $115,250. Executive Director Daniel Bross held that position with both and was paid $72,990. The Foundation awarded the Council a $15,000 cash grant and reimbursed it $459,604 for underwritten program activity expenses. The Foundation received $889,665, or 96% of revenue, from direct and indirect public support in the form of gifts and grants awarded by foundations, affiliates, businesses, and individuals. (These grants included $100,000 from the Joyce Mertz-Gilmore Foundation, $5,000 from Gay Men's Health Crisis.) $27,309, or 3%, from special fund-raising events, specifically a premier of the movie "Philadelphia" and a New Year's Gala. $5,822, or 1%, from interest on savings and temporary cash investments.

AIDS Action League

3463 Ramona St.
Sacramento, CA 95826   **Phone:** (916) 737-1381
USA

Contact Person: Karolyn MacDiarmid, Executive Director. **Officers or Principals:** Karolyn MacDiarmid, Executive Director ($37,200); Marc Keyser, President ($35,000); Donna Gaffney-Baker, Vice President ($0); Pat Leonard, Secretary/Treasurer.
Mission or Interest: Promotes AIDS awareness and provides services for people with AIDS.
Accomplishments: In 1994 the League spent $231,108 on its programs. Community awareness was the largest program, costing $180,715 and reaching approximately 150,000 people in Northern California through the "Grass Roots Awareness Program." $40,963 was spent to house three families and one individual with AIDS. $6,545 was spent to send employees and volunteers to various organizations and schools for AIDS education.
Net Revenue: 1994 $338,998 **Net Expenses:** $350,348 66%/26%/8% **Net Assets:** $4,325
Products or Services: Educational materials.
Tax Status: 501(c)(3)
Other Information: They are affiliated with the 501(c)(4) Taxpayers for Justice. The League received $335,253, or 99% of revenue, from grants awarded by foundations, companies and individuals. $2,471 net came from the sale of assets other than inventory, and the remaining $1,274 came from membership dues.

AIDS Coalition to Unleash Power (ACT-UP!)

135 W. 29th St., 10th Floor
New York, NY 10001   **Phone:** (212) 564-2437
USA   **Fax:** (212) 594-5441

Contact Person: Walt Wilder, Director.
Mission or Interest: Organization representing people with AIDS and the HIV virus that uses confrontational tactics to advocate changes in government spending and policies, and in the policies of pharmaceutical and health care companies. Homosexuals' rights.

AIM: America's Intercultural Magazine

7308 S. Eberhart
Chicago, IL 60619   **Phone:** (312) 874-6184
USA   **Fax:** (206) 543-2746

Contact Person: Myron Apilado. **Officers or Principals:** Ruth Apilado, Mark Boone.
Mission or Interest: "To purge racism from the human bloodstream by way of the written word." Publish short stories, articles and poetry.
Accomplishments: Publishing since 1974.
Products or Services: Yearly Short Story Contest for "well-written stories with lasting social significance, proving that people from different backgrounds are more alike than different. The Stories should not moralize. Maximum length is 4,000 words. Winners are published in the fall issue."
Tax Status: Unincorporated nonprofit. **Employees:** All volunteer.
Periodicals: *AIM: America's Intercultural Magazine* (quarterly).
Other Information: "Dr. Myron Apilado, present editor, is Vice President of Minority Affairs at the University of Washington in Seattle. His mother, Ruth Apilado, after teaching in the Chicago Schools for 40 years, started the magazine. Myron has promised to continue publishing after her death.

Alan Guttmacher Institute (AGI)

120 Wall St., 21st Floor
New York, NY 10005   **Phone:** (212) 248-1111   **E-Mail:** 102127.1701@compuserve.com
USA   **Fax:** (212) 248-1952

Contact Person: Beth Fredrick, Director of Communications.
Officers or Principals: Jeanie I. Rosoff, President ($156,266); Jacqueline D. Forrest, Vice President/Director of Research and Planning ($112,572); Cory L. Richards, Vice President/Director of Public Policy ($103,136); Donald L. Mullare, Director of Finance and Administration; Olivia Nordberg, Director of Publications; Alma T. Young, Chair; Alan E. Guttmacher, Senior Vice Chair; Kenneth C. Edelin, Vice Chair; Paul S. Sperry, Treasurer; Renee Jenkins, Secretary.
Mission or Interest: Promotes publicly funded, universal family planning services including abortion and contraception. Produces and disseminates research that promotes this goal. The Institute has recently begun research and education projects "designed to assess the availability and equitable provision of infertility services, genetic screening, and prenatal diagnosis and care."
Accomplishments: Recently published Hopes and Realities: Closing the Gap Between Women's Aspirations and Their Reproductive Experiences. The Institute distributed the publication worldwide to 35,000 individuals and organizations. The publication was timed to coincide with the Beijing Conference on Women. In 1994 the Institute spent $1,442,057 on domestic policy research and $602,432 on international policy research. That same year they spent $1,194,993 on domestic public and professional education, and $538,300 on international.
Net Revenue: 1994 $4,983,627 ($856,613, or 17% of revenue, from government grants)
Net Expenses: $4,841,785 78%/19%/3% **Net Assets:** $1,247,033 **Citations:** 482:42
Products or Services: Numerous studies, reports, factbooks, databases. Lobbying - in 1994 the Institute spent $74,063 on the direct lobbying of legislators.
Tax Status: 501(c)(3) **Annual Report:** Yes. **Employees:** 50
Board of Directors or Trustees: Includes: Taunya Banks (Univ. of Baltimore School of Law), Sarah Brown, M.P.H. (Senior Study Dir., Inst. of Medicine, National Academy of Sciences), Prof. R. Alta Charo, J.D. (Univ. of Wisconsin), Robert Diamond, M.D. (Exec. V.P., Biothink), Prof. Lee Lee Doyle (Univ. of Arkansas for Medical Sciences), Robin Chandler Duke (Chair., Population Action Intl.), Prof. Noreen Goldman (Demography and Public Affairs, Princeton Univ.), Renee Jenkins, M.D., F.A.A.P. (Howard Univ. Hospital), Judith Jones, M.S. (National Center for Children in Poverty, Columbia Univ.), Daniel Pellegrom (Pres., Pathfinder Intl.), David Perlman (science editor, *San Francisco Chronicle*), many others.
Periodicals: *Family Planning Perspectives* (bimonthly journal), *International Family Planning Perspectives* (quarterly journal), *Washington Memo* (10 issues/year newsletter), *State Reproductive Health Monitor* (quarterly newsletter).
Internships: No formal program, although they have hired interns in the past.
Other Information: Dr. Alan Guttmacher was a former president of Planned Parenthood. They have a Washington, DC office, 1120 Connecticut Ave., N.W., Suite 460, Washington, DC 20036, voice (202) 296-4012, fax (202) 223-5756. AGI was formed in 1968 and was originally called the Center for Family Planning Program Development. It was then a part of the Planned Parenthood Federation of America. In 1977 the name changed to the Alan Guttmacher Institute and it became separately incorporated, although it is still affiliated with Planned Parenthood. The Institute has a reputation as "the most reliable source for data on family planning issues, contraception and teen pregnancy." They are a frequently cited source, and are even quoted by those who oppose their goals. The Institute has a stated policy of publishing all research - even when the data does not support AGI's advocacy efforts. The Institute received $3,768,845, or 76% of revenue, from gifts and grants awarded by foundations, companies, and individuals. (These grants included $1,086,000 from the William and Flora Hewlett Foundation, $292,000 from the Robert Wood Johnson Foundation, $253,228 from the Henry J. Kaiser Family Foundation, $75,000 from the Robert Sterling Clark Foundation, $35,000 from the General Services Foundation, $34,691 from the American Foundation for AIDS Research, $7,500 from the Ms. Foundation, $1,000 from the Stewart R. Mott Charitable Trust. In 1995, $127,500 from the Rockefeller Foundation.) $856,613, or 17%, came from government grants. $129,524, or 3%, from journal subscriptions. $120,037, or 2%, from the sale of publications. $53,592, or 1%, from interest on savings and temporary cash investments. The remaining revenue came from advertising income, royalties, and other miscellaneous income.

Alaska Public Interest Research Group (PIRG)

P.O. Box 220411
Anchorage, AK 99522
USA

Contact Person: Hugh Fleischer, President.   **Officers or Principals:** Rex Butler, Secretary/Treasurer ($0).
Mission or Interest: Alaska affiliate of Public Interest Research Group. Focus on consumer protection, nuclear and toxic waste.
Accomplishments: In the fiscal year ending June 1994, the Group spent $45,055 on its programs.
Net Revenue: FY ending 6/94 $59,214 **Net Expenses:** $56,748 79%/16%/5% **Net Assets:** $21,990
Tax Status: 501(c)(3)
Board of Directors or Trustees: Don May, Matt Nicolai.
Periodicals: *AK PIRG Advocate* (quarterly newsletter).
Other Information: Affiliated with the AK PIRG Lobby. The Group received $28,184, or 47% of revenue, from gifts and grants. $24,480, or 41%, from telephone canvassing. $1,460, or 2%, from a special fund-raising event, the "AK PIRG Follies." The remaining revenue came from interest on savings and temporary cash investments, membership dues, conference fees, and the sale of publications.

Alliance for Acid Rain Control

444 N. Capitol St., Suite 602
Washington, DC 20001   **Phone:**   (202) 624-7709
USA

Contact Person: Ned Helme, Executive Director.   **Officers or Principals:** Ned Helme, Executive Director ($31,354); Hon. Mike

Sullivan, Gov. Tommy Thompson (R-WI), Co-Chairmen ($0).

Mission or Interest: Provide information and support to state governors and legislators regarding acid rain and energy issues.

Accomplishments: In the fiscal year ending June 1994, the Alliance spent $258,614 on its programs. The largest program, with expenditures of $62,783, was membership services that included regulation and legislation updates at both the federal and state levels. $41,855 was spent on "governmental support to provide state governors and legislators information regarding acid rain and energy impact analysis of proposed legislation and assistance in the drafting of effective legislation. The Alliance also awarded a grant of $153,976 to its affiliate, the Center for Clean Air Policy.

Net Revenue: FY ending 6/94 $76,395 **Net Expenses:** $303,460 85%/12%/2% **Net Assets:** $1,221

Products or Services: Analysis, publications, model legislation, more.

Tax Status: 501(c)(4)

Board of Directors or Trustees: Hon. Cecil Andrus (former governor of Idaho, Democrat), Gov. Roy Romer (D-CO), Richard Abdoo, Hon. Tony Earl (former governor of Wisconsin, Democrat), Hon. Tom Kean (former governor of New Jersey, Republican), Sen. Gaylord Nelson, Dr. Paul Portney, Marilynne Roberts, Hon. Mario Cuomo (former governor of New York, Democrat), William Davis, Victoria Tachinkel, Gov. John Waihee (former governor of Hawaii, Democrat).

Other Information: The Alliance for Acid Rain Control is affiliated with the 501(c)(3) Center for Clean Air Policy at the same address. As executive director of both organizations, Ned Helme received a combined compensation of $124,575. The Alliance received $72,500, or 95% of revenues, from membership dues. The remaining revenue came from interest on savings and temporary cash investments.

Alliance for Animals (AFA)

661 Massachusetts Ave.
Arlington, MA 02174   **Phone:** (617) 648-6822
USA

Contact Person: Donna Bishop, Executive Director.   **Officers or Principals:** Donna Bishop, Executive Director ($14,179); Mary Axelrod, Esq., President ($0); Elisabeth Carr-Jones, Secretary ($0); Carol Ann Piantedosi, Treasurer. (Salaries from 1995.)

Mission or Interest: "To alleviate animal suffering, foster a humane ethic and raise the status of animals in our community, and promote public awareness of the needs of animals, through public education and the direct delivery of needed services...Bring about a reduction in the use of animals in areas of experimentation, agriculture, fashion, and provide for better animal care."

Accomplishments: In 1992 the Alliance spent $17,826 on its programs. It is the "only organization in the metropolitan Boston area" providing low-cost services such as spay/neutering and a "no-kill" animal shelter.

Net Revenue: 1992 $21,830 **Net Expenses:** $18,475 96%/4%/0% **Net Assets:** $11,375

Products or Services: Low-cost services to reduce pet overpopulation, public education on the right of animals.

Tax Status: 501(c)(3)

Board of Directors or Trustees: Susan Baldomar, Deborah Dutton, Andrew Tangborn Ph.D.

Periodicals: *ALLY* (quarterly newsletter).

Other Information: The Alliance received $8,431, or 39%, from membership dues. $8,015, or 37%, from fees for veterinarian care. $5,343, or 24%, from gifts and grants awarded by foundations, businesses, and individuals. The remaining revenue came from interest on savings and temporary cash investments.

Alliance for Environmental Education

51 Main St.
The Plains, VA 22171   **Phone:** (703) 838-8171
USA

Contact Person: Duane A. Cox, President.   **Officers or Principals:** Duane A. Cox, President ($0).

Mission or Interest: Educational organization that combines businesses, labor, environmentalists, grassroots organizations, teachers and others to promote the environment. Works to establish centers at colleges and universities.

Accomplishments: Over 35 member organizations which represent 15 million people. In the fiscal year ending June 1993 the organization spent $6,814,963 on its programs.

Net Revenue: FY ending 6/93 $6,566,953 ($269,479, or 4%, from government grants)

Net Expenses: $6,814,963 100%/0%/0% **Net Assets:** $72,346 **Citations:** 6:210

Tax Status: 501(c)(3)

Board of Directors or Trustees: Dr. Agni Arvanitis (Pres., Biopolitics Intl. Organization), Carey Crane, Dr. Henry Hooper (Assoc. V.P., Academic Affairs, Northern AZ Univ.), Thomas Lambrix (Union Camp Corp.), Dr. Stephen Buckles (Pres., National Council on Economic Education), George Foote Jr., Tracy Kay (Rye Nature Center), Dr. Harvey Olem (Center for Watershed Protection), Clair Ghylin, Steven Kussman (Dir., Communications Programs, American Gas Assoc.), John Padalino (Pres., Pocono Environmental Education Center).

Other Information: The Alliance received $6,155,273, or 94% of revenue, from 'in-kind contributions.' $269,479, or 4%, from government grants. (These grants included $242,689 from the Environmental Protection Agency, and $20,790 from the Tennessee Valley Authority.) $78,926, or 1%, from gifts and grants awarded by foundations, businesses, and individuals. The remaining revenue came from special fund raising events, membership dues, and interest on savings and temporary cash investments.

Alliance for Justice

1601 Connecticut Ave., N.W., Suite 610
Washington, DC 20009   **Phone:** (202) 332-3224   **E-Mail:** HN5866 handsnet.org
USA   **Fax:** (202) 265-2510

Contact Person: Nan Aron, President.

Officers or Principals: Nan Aron, President ($66,755); Carol Seifert, Deputy Director ($58,539); Nancy Register, Development Director ($40,369), James Weill, Chair, Gail Harmon, Treasurer, Mark Silbergeld, Secretary.

Mission or Interest: The Alliance for Justice "works to advance the cause of justice for all Americans, to strengthen the public interest community's ability to influence public policy, and to foster the next generation of advocates." The Alliance is composed of members from other leftist advocacy organizations (see Board of Directors and their affiliations for a list).

Accomplishments: Alliance for Justice led the opposition to the nominations of Robert Bork and Clarence Thomas to the Supreme Court. In 1994 they spent $148,377 on their annual First Monday luncheon which is broadcast to dozens of law schools and promotes public interest law. They spent $95,774 on their Advocacy Forum, providing technical assistance to encourage nonprofits to engage in advocacy. $66,934 was spent on civic training for youth engaged in national service - the first participants were from the AmeriCorps program. $39,095 was spent to counter property rights advocates who would erode "the ability of the government to safeguard the environment, consumer safety, and public health." $38,562 was spent on their Judicial Selection Review. In 1994 they reviewed Clinton's picks for the federal judiciary and praised the president's nomination of almost 60% women and minorities. Their report on Supreme Court Justice Stephen Breyer during his nomination was widely cited in the media including "Washington Week in Review," *The Washington Times*, and *The Los Angeles Times*. Another $62,622 was spent to monitor and research "justice issues."

Net Revenue: 1994 $521,408 **Net Expenses:** $550,297 84%/7%/8% **Net Assets:** $488,304 **Citations:** 193:84

Products or Services: Publications, videos, other reports and materials. Lobbying - in 1994 the Alliance spent $5,856 directly lobbying public officials. This was more than double what they spent the year before. They produce Myth v. Fact - Foundation Support of Advocacy, a guide encouraging charitable giving to advocacy organizations reviewed by Nancy Fellner (Assoc. Counsel, Ford Foundation Legal Dept.) and John Edie (General Counsel, Council on Foundations) as well as others.

Tax Status: 501(c)(3) **Annual Report:** Yes. **Employees:** 10

Board of Directors or Trustees: Leonard Rubenstein (Bazelon Center for Mental Health Law), Alex Polikoff (Business & Professional People for the Public Interest), Louise Trubek (Center for Public Representation), James Weil (Children's Defense Fund), Alan Houseman (Center for Law and Social Policy), Carlyle Hall (Center for Law in the Public Interest), Mark Silbergeld (Consumers Union), Janet Stotland (Education Law Center), Joan Graff (Employment Law Center), Nancy Davis (Equal Rights Advocates), Rob Fersh (Food Research and Action Center), Gail Harmon, Douglas Parker (Inst. For Public Representation at Georgetown Univ. Law Center), Robert Schwartz (Juvenile Law Center), Antonio Hernandez (Mexican American Legal Defense and Education Fund), Michael Edwards (National Education Association), Terisa Chaw (National Employment Lawyers Assoc.), Johanna Wald (Natural Resources Defense Council), Joel Thomas (National Wildlife Federation), Marcia Greenberger (National Women's Law Center), Bob Peregoy (Native American Rights Fund), Sarah Parnell (NOW Legal Defense and Education Fund), Joan Vermeulen (NY Lawyers in the Public Interest), Armando Menocal (Public Advocates), Buck Parker (Sierra Club Legal Defense Fund), Rick Hoppe (Wilderness Society), Linda Wharton (Women's Law Project), Donna Lenhoff (Women's Legal Defense Fund).

Internships: Yes.

Other Information: The Alliance received $491,878, or 94% of revenue, from direct and indirect public support in the form of gifts and grants awarded by foundations, companies, and individuals. (These grants included $50,000 from the Florence and John Schumann Foundation, $25,000 from the Rockefeller Family Fund, $15,000 from the New-Land Foundation, $500 from the Stewart R. Mott Charitable Trust.) $21,753, or 4%, from interest on savings and temporary cash investments. $7,777 or 1%, from publication sales.

Alliance for Survival

200 N. Main St., Suite M-2
Santa Ana, CA 92701   **Phone:** (714) 547-6282
USA   **Fax:** (714) 547-6322

Contact Person: Marion Pack, Executive Director. **Officers or Principals:** Marion Pack, Executive Director ($1,758); Jean Bernstein, President ($0); Alan Seman, Secretary ($0); Bob Anderson, Treasurer ($0).

Mission or Interest: Environmental organization focusing on radioactive waste and other problems. Also concerned with the arms race and conflict resolution..

Accomplishments: Gave testimony to the San Bernardino Board of Supervisors on nuclear waste. Went to Washington, DC, and met with representatives about low-level nuclear waste. Participated in "Hiroshima/Nagasaki Remembered." In 1993 the Alliance spent $21,376 on its programs. Programs included; Opposition to a nuclear waste dump in Ward Valley. "High School Environmental Legislative Network." Speakers bureau.

Net Revenue: 1993 $26,441 **Net Expenses:** $26,068 **Net Assets:** (-$669)

Tax Status: 501(c)(4)

Board of Directors or Trustees: Joanna Schermer, Marc Nedleman, Bill Strahan.

Other Information: The Alliance received $26,441, or 100% of revenue, from gifts and grants awarded by foundations, businesses, and individuals.

Alliance to End Childhood Lead Poisoning

227 Massachusetts Ave., N.E., Suite 200
Washington, DC 20002   **Phone:** (202) 543-1147
USA

Contact Person: Don Ryan, Executive Director. **Officers or Principals:** Don Ryan, Executive Director ($84,472); James K. W. Rochow, Project Director ($68,656); Anna M. Guthrie, Director ($61,871); Bailus Walker, Jr., Ph.D., Chairman; Ellen Silbergeld, Ph.D., Vice Chair; Richard M. Cooper, Secretary; Charles A. Hurley.

Mission or Interest: "The Alliance's mission is to frame the national agenda, formulate innovative approaches and bring scientific and technical knowledge, public policy, economic forces, other organizations and community leaders to prevent childhood lead poisoning."

Accomplishments: In 1994 the Alliance spent $1,357,699 on its programs. The largest program, with expenditures of $506,189, was a national conference. $363,354 was spent on developing and implementing prevention strategies. Other programs worked at coalition building, public policy development, and public education and outreach.

Net Revenue: 1994 $1,534,452 ($711,186, or 46%, from government grants) **Net Expenses:** $1,472,587 92%/8%/0%

Net Assets: $505,506 **Citations:** 12:191

Products or Services: Conferences, brochures and publications, research, and lobbying. The Alliance spent $14,888 on grassroots lobbying. This was an increase of 69% over the previous year.

Tax Status: 501(c)(3)

Board of Directors or Trustees: Cushing Dolbeare, Walter Farr, Jr., Alvaro Garza, M.D., Stephanie Pollack, David Hall, M.D., Ph.D., Knut Ringen, Ph.D., Robert Bullard, Ph.D., Teresa Heinz, Maurci Jackson, Rudolph Jackson, Philip Landrigan, M.D., Agnes Lattimer, M.D., Charles Lee, David Maxwell, Julia Moore, John Norquist.

Other Information: The Alliance hired the firms of Birch & Davis Associates of Silver Spring, MD, and the Western Consortium for Public Health of Berkeley, CA, for consulting. The companies were paid $76,171 and $100,000 respectively. The Alliance received $711,186, or 46% of revenue, from government grants. $605,792, or 39%, from gifts and grants awarded by foundations, businesses, and individuals. $186,367, or 12%, from conference registration fees. $12,878, or 1%, from dividends and interest from securities. The remaining revenue came from the sale of publications, honoraria, rental income, and other miscellaneous sources.

Alternative Media Information Center

39 West 14th St., Suite 403
New York, NY 10011   **Phone:** (212) 929-2663
USA

Contact Person: Donald Derosby, Executive Director. **Officers or Principals:** David Meieren, Filmmaker ($37,490); Donald Derosby, Executive Director ($33,600); Reginald Woolery, Blanca Vazquez, Amy Chen, Co-Chairs ($0).

Mission or Interest: Sponsors independent filmmakers, reviews films and videos addressing "AIDS, women's issues, poverty, environment." Trains educators and activists to use film and videos in the classroom and neighborhood. Litigates freedom of expression legal issues.

Accomplishments: Feminists for Free Expression Project. In 1993 the Center spent $3,284,341 on its programs. The largest expenditure, $3,120,829 supported independent filmmakers. $84,344 was spent to train educators and community workers on how to use film and video. $49,189 was spent on publications; 6,400 copies of the Media Guide were distributed and 2,500 copies of a newsletter exploring the relationship between the media and social change were distributed.

Net Revenue: 1993 $3,922,880 ($400,298, or 10%, from government grants) **Net Expenses:** $3,328,074 99%/1%/1%

Net Assets: $882,842 **Citations:** 0:255

Products or Services: Publications, sponsorship of independent filmmakers.

Tax Status: 501(c)(3)

Board of Directors or Trustees: Lumumba Bendele, Hye Jung Park, Barbara Joseph, Mimi Rosenberg, Marlin Adams, Carol Roman.

Other Information: The Center received $3,245,713, or 83% of revenue, from gifts and grants awarded by foundations, companies and individuals. (These grants included $20,000 from the J. Roderick MacArthur Foundation, $5,000 from the New World Foundation.) $400,298, or 10%, from government grants. $211,089, or 5%, from program services including the sale of tapes and publications. $49,042 net, or 1%, from fund-raising events. The remaining revenue came from interest on savings and temporary cash investments, and dividends and interest from securities.

Alternative Press Center

1443 Gorsuch Ave.
Baltimore, MD 21218   **Phone:** (410) 243-2471
USA

Contact Person: Richard Wilson, President. **Officers or Principals:** Richard Wilson, President ($24,588); Leslie Wade, Secretary ($14,610); Mary Ann Barrett, Treasurer ($4,821).

Mission or Interest: Provides library services to the general public and publishes a directory of alternative periodicals of the left and radical left.

Accomplishments: In 1993 the Center spent $22,010 on its programs. These included library services open to the public twenty-five hours each week.

Net Revenue: 1993 $49,940 **Net Expenses:** $44,960 **Net Assets:** $33,974

Products or Services: Library collection, directories.

Tax Status: 501(c)(3)

Periodicals: *Alternative Press Index* (quarterly magazine), lists periodicals and contains book, film, and musical recording reviews.

Other Information: The Center received $49,408 net, or 99% of revenue, from the sale of inventory. The remaining revenue came from investment income.

Alternatives to Militarism

175 5th Ave., Suite 2135
New York, NY 10010   **Phone:**   (212) 679-2250
USA   **Fax:**   (212) 679-2252

Contact Person: Thomas Ensign, President.   **Officers or Principals:** Thomas Ensign, President ($19,239); Ken Cunningham, Francine Smilen, Louis Font, Michael Uhl, Directors ($0).
Mission or Interest: "Works against the pervasive growth of militarism within our society. We believe that the military institution must be strictly subject to civilian control and that the idea that military means provide 'solutions' to the complex problems facing our society is fundamentally unsound. We support those in uniform who oppose military illegality or raise the standard of international law."
Accomplishments: Citizen Soldier project "has provided legal defense to GI's who were prosecuted for refusing military orders based on international law. Examples are: Dr. Huet-Vaughn, M.D., who based her refusal to serve in the Persian Gulf on international law; Capt. Larry Rockwood, who reported human rights violations while serving with the U.S. Army in Haiti; and Sgt. Daniel Cobos, who refused to fly further 'spy' missions in support of the Contras who attacked Nicaragua." Advocate benefits for veterans who have "been harmed by atomic bomb testing, Agent Orange in Vietnam and Persian Gulf syndrome." Offers programs to help soldiers leave the service. Monitors the links between the military and private militias. In 1994 the organization spent $41,794 on its programs.
Net Revenue: 1994 $75,574 **Net Expenses:** $74,290 56%/21%/22% **Net Assets:** (-$1,959)
Products or Services: <u>Addicted to War</u> cartoon book explaining why the U.S. is continually involved in wars and other activities abroad.
Tax Status: 501(c)(3) **Annual Report:** Yes. **Employees:** 2
Periodicals: *On Guard* (newsletter) provided free to GI's at military bases.
Internships: No.
Other Information: Founded in 1975. The organization received 100% of revenue from gifts and grants awarded by foundations, businesses, and individuals. (These grants included $4,000 from the North Star Fund.)

Aluminum, Brick and Glass Workers International Union

3362 Hollenberg Dr.
Bridgeton, MO 63044   **Phone:**   (314) 739-6142
USA   **Fax:**   (314) 739-1216

Contact Person: Ernest J. LaBaff, President.   **Officers or Principals:** Ernest J. LaBaff, President ($76,725); Harvey Martin, Secretary/Treasurer ($73,798); Roy Albert, Vice President ($69,726).
Mission or Interest: "International union that represents its members who are principally employed in the aluminum, brick, tile, clay, glass, and ceramic industries in the United States and Canada." Represents approximately 44,000 members. Member of the AFL-CIO.
Accomplishments: 320 locals. In the fiscal year ending March 1995, the Union spent $5,467 on legislative expenses, and conducted only in-house lobbying with expenses of less than $2,000.
Net Revenue: FY ending 3/95 $8,334,720 **Net Expenses:** $7,027,839 **Net Assets:** $5,496,021
Tax Status: 501(c)(5)
Periodicals: *ABG Light* (bimonthly newsletter).
Other Information: The Union received $8,199,150, or 98% of total revenue, from membership dues. $170,710, or 2%, from dividends and interest from securities. The remaining revenue came from interest on savings and temporary cash investments, and other miscellaneous sources.

Amalgamated Clothing and Textile Workers Union (ACTWU)

1710 Broadway
New York, NY 10019   **Phone:**   (212) 242-0700
USA   **Fax:**   (212) 255-8169

Contact Person: Jack Sheinkman, President.   **Officers or Principals:** Jack Sheinkman, President ($141,591); Arthur Loevy, Secretary/Treasurer ($117,803); Bryce Raynor, Vice President ($114,844).
Mission or Interest: Union representing approximately 260,000 members. Member of the AFL-CIO.
Accomplishments: The Union spent $2,914 on public affairs, and conducted only in-house lobbying with expenses of less than $2,000.
Net Revenue: 1994 $26,024,168 **Net Expenses:** $27,197,311 **Net Assets:** $10,353,186
Tax Status: 501(c)(5)
Board of Directors or Trustees: Gary Bonadonna, Edward Clark, Anthony Costanza, Olga Diaz, Bruce Dunton, Mark Fleischman, John Fox, Arthur Hoover, John Hudson, Amanda Jackson, James Johnson, Richard MacFadyen, Andrew Mattey, Frank Nicholas, Carmen Papale, Joan Suarez, Pat Sullivan, others.
Periodicals: *Labor Unity* (monthly newsletter).
Other Information: ACTWU recently merged with the International Ladies Garment Workers Union (ILGWU) to form the Union of Needle Trades, Industrial and Textile Employees (UNITE). The three officers also received compensation from the affiliated Amalgamated Bank of New York, Sheinkman received $17,000, and Loevy and Raynor received $13,000 each.

American Anti-Vivisection Society (AAVS)

801 Old York Rd., Suite 204
Jenkintown, PA 19046   **Phone:**   (215) 887-0816   **E-Mail:** AAVSONLINE@AOL.COM
USA   **Fax:**   (215) 887-2088

Contact Person: Tina Nelson, Executive Director.   **Officers or Principals:** Margaret B. Eldon, President ($58,429); Sue Leary, Secretary ($2,400); James A. Clark, Treasurer ($2,400); Eleanor Cave, Vice President.
Mission or Interest: "The mission of the American Anti-Vivisection Society is to end experiments on animals and oppose all other forms of cruelty to animals." Opposition to animal testing, hunting, omnivorous diets (for humans), animal farming and captive animals used for entertainment.
Accomplishments: In 1994 AAVS spent $724,774 on their educational efforts. These included the "Animalearn" education program directed at children, which *Newsweek* magazine cited for its effectiveness. The Outreach program resulted in letters to the editor being published in *The Wall Street Journal, Philadelphia Inquirer, Washington Times* and others. AAVS's literature was presented at almost 20 national conventions, including the National Association of Biology Teachers and the National Science Teachers Association. Successfully campaigned for the elimination of a "dog lab" at the University of Pennsylvania medical school. Medical students had practiced injections and intravenous techniques on dogs before the dogs were euthanized.
Net Revenue: 1994 $1,103,515 **Net Expenses:** $980,701 74%/20%/6% **Net Assets:** $6,661,180 **Citations:** 4:217
Products or Services: Grassroots activism and networking support. Lobbying. Educational materials, especially those produced for children and the educational establishment.
Tax Status: 501(c)(4) **Annual Report:** Yes. **Employees:** 10
Board of Directors or Trustees: Douglas Barr, Joseph Donahue, Joseph Ludwig, Margaret Dawson, George Flannery, Mrs. James McCracken, Richard Torpey, Esq.
Periodicals: *The AV Magazine* (bimonthly magazine), *ActiVate For Animals* (monthly newsletter).
Other Information: They are affiliated with the 501(c)(3) Alternatives for Research and Development Foundation which awards grants for alternatives to animal research. The Society received $533,216, or 48% of revenue, from gifts and grants awarded by foundations, companies and individuals. $444,863, or 40%, from dividends and interest on securities. $65,336 net, or 6%, from the sale of assets other than inventory. $23,279, or 2%, from membership dues. The remaining revenue came from the reimbursement of costs incurred for educational materials.

American Association of Retired Persons (AARP)

601 E St., N.W.
Washington, DC 20049   **Phone:**   (202) 434-2277
USA   **Fax:**   (202) 434-2320

Contact Person: Horace B. Deets, Executive Director.
Officers or Principals: Horace B. Deets, Executive Director ($342,965); Richard A. Henry, Chief Operating Officer ($157,996); Eugene I. Lehrmann, President ($0); Robert P. Shreve, Ed.D., Chairman; Lena L. Archuleta, Vice Chairman; Joseph S. Perkins, Vice President; Beatrice S. Braun, M.D., Secretary; C. Keith Campbell, Treasurer.
Mission or Interest: Founded in 1958 "To enhance the quality of life for older persons; to promote independence, dignity, and purpose for older persons; to lead in determining the role and place of older persons in society; and to improve the image of aging." Originally founded to assist older persons in buying insurance. In 1963 the Colonial Penn Group was founded to take over the AARP's insurance business. Due to complaints from the insurance industry about competing with a tax-exempt organization, the insurance business was sold off to Prudential in 1979. Questions about the AARP using its tax-exempt status to unfairly compete in insurance, pharmaceuticals, and other areas continue today; most recently, Senate hearings were held on these matters in 1995. Although fairly new to lobbying, the AARP has become a political force due to its 33 million members. The AARP has been very successful in preserving and expanding programs for seniors, including Social Security and Medicare. However, the AARP has been less successful in helping to create new programs. In 1988 the AARP was a major force behind the passage of the Catastrophic Health Insurance Bill, but was unable to save it when seniors attacked the program and Congressmen who supported it, based on the fact that it did not cover long-term care and imposed a high marginal tax rate on seniors. During the health care reform debate of 1993-94 initiated by President Clinton's plan, the AARP put forth its own plan for national health insurance (a long-standing goal), but it was never seriously considered and it caused public dissention in the AARP's membership.
Accomplishments: Approximately 33 million members and 4,000 chapters. Considered by most to be one of, if not *the*, most powerful lobbying forces in Washington, DC. Its membership journal, *Modern Maturity*, has the highest circulation of any magazine in the country. In 1994 the AARP spent $247,345,893 on its programs. The largest program, with expenditures of $99,856,278, was the production and distribution of *Modern Maturity* and the *AARP Bulletin*. $75,937,463 was spent on the administration of government grants (see **Other Information** for details) that benefit seniors. $5,165,219 was spent on legal counsel for the elderly. $4,629,448 was spent on "Work Force" programs. Other programs included tax help, consumer affairs, health advocacy, criminal justice services, "Women's Initiative," and minority affairs.
Net Revenue: 1994 $441,968,796 ($75,937,463, or 17%, from government grants) **Net Expenses:** $426,286,641 58%/42%/0%
Net Assets: $43,298,564 **Citations:** 6,846:2
Products or Services: Service for senior citizens, including federal jobs training and placement programs.
Tax Status: 501(c)(4) **Employees:** Total payroll of $62,795,745.
Board of Directors or Trustees: John Lione, M.D., Ann Miller, Jane Pang, Ruth Scarborough, Thomas Shanley, Ph.D., Marle Sanderman, Allan Tull, Esther Cinja, Helen Boosalis, Allen Buckingham, Bernice Shepard, Howard Shumway, Merle Wilson, Ed.D.
Periodicals: *Modern Maturity* (bimonthly magazine), *AARP Bulletin* (monthly newsletter), *Highlights* (bimonthly newsletter).

Other Information: The AARP owns 100% of the for profit AARP Financial Services Corp., which provides insurance and other financial services. The Corp. was valued at $13,628,012. The AARP received $145,741,908, or 32% of total revenue, from membership dues. $101,659,095, or 23%, from "insurance plan allowance." $75,937,463, or 17%, from government grants. (These grants included $47,977,604 from the U.S. Department of Labor, $23,622,818 from the EPA, $3,060,370 from the IRS, $616,511 from the U.S. Department of Health and Human Services, $313,510 from the District of Columbia Office of Aging, $194,530 from the U.S. Department of Housing and Urban Development, $137,751 from the U.S. Department of Justice, and $10,374 from the Corporation for National Community Service.) $47,930,874, or 11%, from advertising. $37,054,954, or 8%, from royalties. $32,483,353, or 7%, from dividends and interest from securities. $9,787,625, or 2%, from miscellaneous program revenue. The remaining revenue came from gifts and grants, and interest on savings and temporary cash investments. The AARP lost $8,195,370 on the sale of assets, and $540,560 on certain program services, including the operation of a cafeteria and asset retirement. The AARP held $185,893,891, or 63% of assets, in securities. $30,438,651, or 10%, in buildings and equipment. Other assets included $9,636,450 in software development.

American Atheist General Headquarters
7215 Cameron Rd.
Austin, TX 78752-2973   **Phone:**   (512) 458-1271
USA

Contact Person: Orin "Spike" Tyson, Director.   **Officers or Principals:** Jon J. Murray, President ($56,705); Robin Murray O'Hair, Secretary ($26,556); Madalyn O'Hair, Treasurer ($0); Don Sanders, Vice President.
Mission or Interest: Promotion of atheism and the separation of religion and public life.
Accomplishments: In 1993 the Headquarters spent $338,759 on its programs. Produced and distributed the American Atheist Television Forum, a half-hour educational news/talk show broadcast on over 140 community access cable television systems.
Net Revenue: 1993 $384,345 **Net Expenses:** $389,088 87%/10%/0% **Net Assets:** $16,244
Products or Services: Publications, conference, television programming.
Tax Status: 501(c)(3)
Board of Directors or Trustees: Reynold Bourquin.
Other Information: Madelyn Murray O'Hair's lawsuit led to the 1963 Supreme Court ruling that prohibited organized prayer and Bible reading in public schools. As of August 1996, Madalyn O'Hair, her son Jon, and her daughter Robin, have been missing since the fall of 1995. Former vice president Arnold Via says "My theory is that they were kidnaped and are being held prisoner somewhere in this country...Off the wall, I claim the Vatican did it...the Vatican or the CIA. Someone with enough clout to cover it up." Madelyn Murray O'Hair's other son, William, abandoned atheism for fundamentalist Christianity. Affiliated with the 501(c)(3) American Atheists at the same address. The two affiliates had combined net revenues of $774,905, net expenses of $822,590, and net assets of $47,378. The General Headquarters received $368,626, or 96% of revenue, from gifts and grants awarded by foundations, businesses, and individuals. $14,661, or 4%, from a convention. The remaining revenue came from publication sales and interest on savings and temporary cash investments.

American Atheists
7215 Cameron Rd.
Austin, TX 78752-2973   **Phone:**   (512) 458-1244
USA

Contact Person: Jon G. Murray, President.
Officers or Principals: Madalyn O'Hair, Treasurer ($0); Robin Murray O'Hair, Secretary ($0).
Mission or Interest: Organization promoting atheism and the separation of religion and public life.
Accomplishments: In 1993 the organization spent $135,351 on its programs. It also paid $298,151 to its affiliates, $201,772 for the American Atheist General Headquarters, and $96,379 for the Society of Separationists.
Net Revenue: 1993 $390,560 **Net Expenses:** $433,502 31%/0%/0% **Net Assets:** $31,134
Products or Services: Publications, periodicals, and other merchandise.
Tax Status: 501(c)(3)
Board of Directors or Trustees: Arnold Via, Henry Scmuck.
Other Information: (For more information on the O'Hairs, see the profile for the American Atheist General Headquarters.) Affiliated with the 501(c)(3) American Atheist General Headquarters at the same address. The two affiliates had combined net revenues of $774,905, net expenses of $822,590, and net assets of $47,378. The organization received $260,203, or 67% of revenue, from gifts and grants awarded by foundations, businesses, and individuals. $77,791, or 20%, from membership dues. $35,198, or 9%, from the sale of books. $6,553, or 2%, from the sale of merchandise. $6,500, or 2%, from a convention. $3,557, or 1%, from subscription sales. The remaining revenue came from interest on savings and temporary cash investments.

American Civil Liberties Union, National (ACLU)
132 W. 43rd St.
New York, NY 10036   **Phone:**   (212) 944-9800
USA   **Fax:**   (212) 730-4652

Contact Person: Ira Glasser, Executive Director.   **Officers or Principals:** Ira Glasser, Executive Director ($130,250); Alma Montclair, Assistant Secretary/Treasurer ($101,200); Nadine Strossen, President; George Forman, Controller.

Mission or Interest: National office of the ACLU. Lobbying to protect and expand civil liberties and constitutional rights.

Accomplishments: In 1994 the ACLU spent $2,988,795 on its programs. The largest program, with expenditures of $1,577,653, was public education. $915,808 was spent examining and influencing legislation. $495,334 was spent formulating policies related to civil liberties. The national ACLU awarded $3,989,449 to affiliates. The ACLU has 49 501(c)(4) affiliates nationwide. In 1994 the 501(c)(4) affiliates had total revenues, expenses, and assets of $4,150,240, $4,160,402, and $1,964,148.

Net Revenue: 1994 $10,068,882 **Net Expenses:** $9,512,114 31%/6%/21% **Net Assets:** $3,718,781 **Citations:** 8,932:1

Tax Status: 501(c)(4)

Board of Directors or Trustees: Frank Askin (Rutgers Law School), Alice Bendheim, Judith Bendich, Jeffrey Bramlett, James Crawford, Liz Dodd (Sierra Club Legal Defense Fund), Dan Edwards, James Ferguson II, Jeremiah Gutman, James Hall Jr., David Harris, Olivia Henry, Susan Herman (Brooklyn Law School), William Hinkle, Woody Kaplan, Robert Kapp, Mary Ann Lamanna (Univ. of NE, Omaha), Denise LeBoeuf (Loyola Death Penalty Resource Center), Stephen Lee, Roslyn Litman, Joan Mahoney (Western New England College School of Law), Nancy Maihoff, Elizabeth McGeever, Michael Meyers (New York Civil Rights Coalition), Scott Morrison, Wendy Nakamura, Rolland O'Hare, Susan Park, Robert Remar, Edmund Robinson, David Rudovsky, Margaret Russell (Santa Clara Univ. School of Law), Raymond Schowers, Frank Susman, Catherine Travis, Charles Watts (Vanderbilt University Law School), David Waxse, Richard Zacks, as well as representatives of the ACLU's state affiliates.

Other Information: Affiliated with the 501(c)(3) American Civil Liberties Union Foundation at the same address. The ACLU received $9,798,997, or 97% of revenue, from gifts and grants awarded by foundations, businesses, and individuals. $139,719, or 1%, from mailing list rentals. $86,737, or 1%, from interest on savings and temporary cash investments. The remaining revenue came from the sale of literature and dividends and interest from securities.

American Civil Liberties Union, National Foundation (ACLU)

132 W. 43rd St.
New York, NY 10036   **Phone:** (212) 944-9800
USA   **Fax:**   (212) 730-4652

Contact Person: Ira Glasser, Executive Director

Officers or Principals: Alvin Bronstein, Project Director ($101,570); John A. Powell, Legal Director ($88,680); Sandra Sedacca, Development Director ($88,409); Steven Shapiro, Legal Director; Marcia Lowry, Project Director; Jim Calaway, Treasurer.

Mission or Interest: National headquarters of the ACLU. Educational and legal activities to promote, protect, and expand civil liberties and Constitutional rights.

Accomplishments: In 1993 the Foundation spent $8,681,481 on its programs. $6,920,103 on legal services and litigation, and $1,761,378 on educational activities. The Foundation's litigation brought it $1,927,832 in court-awarded attorney's fees.

Net Revenue: 1993 $13,553,346 **Net Expenses:** $11,635,338   **Net Assets:** $14,091,266 **Citations:** 8,932:1

Products or Services: Litigation, public education, and lobbying. In 1993 the Foundation spent $217,800 on lobbying; $2,000 on grassroots lobbying, and $215,000 on the direct lobbying of legislators. This was down 23% from the year before.

Tax Status: 501(c)(3)

Board of Directors or Trustees: Frank Askin (Rutgers Law School), Alice Bendheim, Judith Bendich, Vivian Berger, James Ferguson II, Diane Geraghty, Susan Herman (Brooklyn Law School), Woody Kaplan, Gara LaMarche, Micki Levin, Michael Meyers (New York Civil Rights Coalition), Robert Remar, Nadine Strossen (New York Law School).

Other Information: Affiliated with the 501(c)(4) national American Civil Liberties Union at the same address. In addition, the ACLU has 49 501(c)(4) affiliates nationwide. In 1994 the 501(c)(4) affiliates had total revenues, expenses, and assets of $4,150,240, $4160,402, and $1,964,148. The Foundation received $10,660,417, or 79% of revenue, from gifts and grants awarded by foundations, businesses, affiliates and individuals. (These grants included $300,000 over three years from the John D. and Catherine T. MacArthur Foundation, $130,000 from the Robert Sterling Clark Foundation, $35,000 from the J. Roderick MacArthur Foundation, $30,000 from the Joyce Mertz-Gilmore Foundation, $25,000 from the New World Foundation, $15,000 from the American Foundation for AIDS Research, and $5,000 from the Aaron and Martha Schecter Foundation. In 1994, $200,000 from the Joyce Mertz-Gilmore Foundation, $5,000 from the Stewart R. Mott Charitable Trust.) $1,927,832, or 14%, from court-awarded attorney's fees. $449,410, or 3%, from dividends and interest from securities. $96,446, or 1%, from the sale of literature. $63,568 net, or less than 1%, from capital gains on the sale of securities. The remaining revenue came from rental income, interest on savings and temporary cash investments, and royalties. In 1994 the Foundation received $25,000 from the Rockefeller Family Fund.

American Civil Liberties Union, Colorado Foundation (ACLU)

400 Corona St.
Denver, CO 80218   **Phone:** (303) 777-5482
USA   **Fax:**   (303) 777-1773

Contact Person: James Joy, Executive Director.   **Officers or Principals:** David Miller, Legal Director ($64,239); James Joy, Executive Director ($60,160); Gwen Thomas, Chair ($0); Joel Ehrlich, Vice Chair; Darold Killmer, Secretary/Treasurer.

Mission or Interest: Protection and expansion of civil rights and constitutional rights.

Accomplishments: In 1994 the Foundation spent $266,766 on its programs. $184,405 was spent on litigation. The Foundation receives approximately 10,000 calls each year and selects 125 that are referred to volunteer lawyers. Approximately 50 cases per year go to litigation. ACLU Foundation of Colorado received $274,744 in court-awarded attorney's fees in 1994. $82,361 was spent on educational activities.

Net Revenue: 1994 $461,704 **Net Expenses:** $428,471 62%/15%/23% **Net Assets:** $26,940

Products or Services: Litigation, conferences, programs for lawyers, public speakers, more.

Tax Status: 501(c)(3)
Board of Directors or Trustees: Karen Ashby, Kathy Bonham, Alan Chen, Amy Divine, Sandra Goldman, Harold Hagan, Barbara Kelley, David Lane, Amanda O'Neill, Ed Ramey, William Reynolds, Ron Rossi.
Other Information: They are affiliated with the 501(c)(4) ACLU of Colorado. The Foundation received $274,744, or 60% of revenue, from court-awarded attorney's fees. $157,784, or 34%, from gifts and grants awarded by foundations, companies, and individuals. $20,456 net, or 4%, from special events. The remaining revenue came from miscellaneous sources.

American Civil Liberties Union, Delaware Foundation (ACLU)
702 King St., Suite 600-A
Wilmington, DE 19801   **Phone:** (302) 654-3966
USA

Contact Person: Judith Mellen, Executive Director.   **Officers or Principals:** Judith Mellen, Executive Director ($38,370); Max S. Bell, President ($0); Richard Cohen, Harry Hamermesh, Vice Presidents ($0); Jeffrey Raffel, Secretary; Ann Tansey, Treasurer.
Mission or Interest: Support for civil liberties and constitutional rights.
Accomplishments: In 1994 the Foundation spent $63,311 on its programs. The largest expenditure was public education, at $31,849. Legal activities cost $28,549, and lobbying expenditures were $2,913.
Net Revenue: 1994 $80,517 **Net Expenses:** $84,648 **Net Assets:** $72,346
Tax Status: 501(c)(3)
Board of Directors or Trustees: Mary Aber, Keith Booker, Phyllis Bookspan, James Carter, Bruce Dresbach, Darian Harris, Henry Heiman, Minerva Marrero, Elizabeth McGeever, Grace Messner, Norman Monhait, Jamal Mubdi-Bey, Elisabeth Poole, Dan Rosenthal, John Schuenemeyer, Robert Stewart, James Welch.
Other Information: Affiliated with the 501(c)(4) American Civil Liberties of Delaware. The Foundation received $43,388, or 54% of revenue, from grants awarded by foundations, companies and individuals. $35,515 net, or 44%, came from special events. The remaining revenue came from investment income.

American Civil Liberties Union, Eastern Missouri Fund (ACLU)
4557 Laclede Ave.
St. Louis, MO 63108   **Phone:** (314) 361-2111
USA

Contact Person: Joyce Armstrong, Executive Director.
Officers or Principals: Joyce Armstrong, Executive Director ($56,569); Mark Sableman, President ($0); Milly Cohn, Alberta Slavin, Brad Pierce, Vice Presidents ($0); John Gamache, Secretary; Norman Gilbert, Treasurer.
Mission or Interest: Protection and advancement of civil liberties and Constitutional rights.
Accomplishments: In 1994 the Fund spent $132,825 on its programs; $66,776 for legal assistance and $66,049 for public education. The Fund received $61,895 in court-awarded attorneys' fees.
Net Revenue: 1994 $176,281 **Net Expenses:** $160,510 **Net Assets:** $425,427
Products or Services: Litigation and public education.
Tax Status: 501(c)(3)
Other Information: Affiliated with the 501(c)(4) ACLU of Eastern Missouri. The Fund received $61,895, or 35% of revenues, from court-awarded attorneys' fees. $58,914, or 33%, from gifts and grants awarded by foundations, businesses, and individuals. $28,202, or 16%, from special fund-raising events, mostly from a "Bill of Rights Day Dinner & Entertainment." $13,966, or 8%, from dividends and interest from securities. $4,205, or 2%, from capital gains on the sale of securities. The remaining revenue came from miscellaneous sources.

American Civil Liberties Union, Florida Foundation (ACLU)
10729 S.W. 104th St.
Miami, FL 33176   **Phone:** (305) 576-2336
USA

Contact Person: Robyn Blumner, Executive Director.   **Officers or Principals:** Robyn Blumner, Executive Director ($20,048); James K. Green, President ($0); Raymond Arsenault, Vice President ($0); Lorie Fridell, Secretary.
Mission or Interest: Protection of civil liberties and constitutional rights in Florida.
Accomplishments: In 1993 the Foundation spent $157,013 on its programs. This included $131,702 on litigation and $25,311 on educational services.
Net Revenue: 1993 $756,709 **Net Expenses:** $232,283 68%/13%/19% **Net Assets:** $778,564
Tax Status: 501(c)(3)
Board of Directors or Trustees: Francisco Arcura, Jon Asfour, Jeanne Baker, Randall Berg, Barry Butin, Gwen Galloway, Illen Cantor, Pamela Chamberlin, Henry Comiter, Richard Cooper, Larry Corman, Alan Ehrlich, Tim Feeney, Bill Galagher, Stacey Gillman, Sidney Goetz, Jill Hanson, Paul Joseph, Warren Keiner, Ronald Lauria, Stanley Marable, Siobhan McLaughlin, Jim Mullins, Mary Onkka, Steve Phillippy, Paul Pohlman, Denise Prescod, Gilbert Raiford, Rochelle Reback, Ren Rieur, Larry Roberts, Valentin Rodriguez, Virginia Rosen, Roger Sanderson, Sol Silverman, Nadine Smith, Larry Spalding, Carl Stephanus, Allan Terl, Fran Tetunic, Mark Tietig, Carl Trough, Dwight Wells, Therese Westerfield, Linda Wisniewski.
Other Information: Affiliated with the 501(c)(4) ACLU of Florida. The Foundation received $728,786, or 96% of revenue, from grants awarded by foundations, companies and individuals. $27,923, or 4%, came from dividends and interest from securities.

American Civil Liberties Union, Hawai'i Foundation

P.O. Box 3410
Honolulu, HI 96801
USA

Phone: (808) 522-5900
Fax: (808) 522-5909

Contact Person: Vanessa Chong, Executive Director.   **Officers or Principals:** Vanessa Chong, Executive Director ($36,303);
Collin M. Fritz, President ($0), Pamela Lichty, Vice President ($0), Patrick Taomae, Treasurer.
Mission or Interest: Education and litigation to promote civil liberties with an emphasis on federal and Hawai'ian constitutional
rights. Litigation and lobbying to support same-sex marriages.
Accomplishments: In 1993 the Foundation spent $55,406 on educational programs and $55,407 on litigation. They received
$44,265 in court-awarded attorney's fees.
Net Revenue: 1993 $231,250 **Net Expenses:** $190,517 58%/27%/15% **Net Assets:** $41,597
Products or Services: Litigation, essay contest, speakers bureau, news releases, more. Pamphlets in English, Samoan, and
Hawai'ian.
Tax Status: 501(c)(3) **Annual Report:** No. **Employees:** 3
Other Information: Affiliated with the 501(c)(4) American Civil Liberties Union of Hawai'i. The Foundation received $160,616,
or 69% of revenue, from grants awarded by foundations, companies and individuals. $44,265, or 19%, came from court-awarded
attorney's fees. $25,116 net, or 11%, came from fund-raising events. The reminder came from interest and dividends from securities
and literature sales.

American Civil Liberties Union, Louisiana Foundation (ACLU)

234 Loyola Ave., Suite 925
New Orleans, LA 70112
USA

Phone: (504) 522-0628

Contact Person: Madlyn Bagneris, President.
Officers or Principals: Joseph F. Sheley, Secretary; Frederick Stielow, Vice President, Finance; J.R. Wiltberger, Treasurer.
Mission or Interest: Legal action and education to protect and expand civil liberties and constitutional rights.
Accomplishments: In 1994 the Foundation spent $49,128 on its programs.
Net Revenue: 1994 $85,499 **Net Expenses:** $67,644 73%/19%/8% **Net Assets:** $5,556
Tax Status: 501(c)(3)
Board of Directors or Trustees: Denise LeBoeuf, Charles Delbaum, M. Michele Fournet, Alan Gerson, Rodney Grunes, Nadine
Henneman, Martha Kegel, Rose Ledet, Patricia Morris, Steven Rittvo, Henry Walker.
Other Information: The Foundation received $85,410, or 99.9% of revenue, from gifts and grants awarded by foundations,
businesses, and individuals. The remaining revenue came from interest on savings and temporary cash investments.

American Civil Liberties Union, Maine Foundation (ACLU)

97A Exchange St.
Portland, ME 04101
USA

Phone: (207) 774-5444

Contact Person: Sally Sutton, Executive Director.   **Officers or Principals:** Sally Sutton, Executive Director ($37,026);
Patricia Peard, President ($0); Nonny Soifer, Vice President ($0); Hugh Calkins, Treasurer; Calien Lewis, Secretary.
Mission or Interest: Litigation and education to protect and expand civil liberties and rights.
Accomplishments: In 1994 the Foundation spent $69,721 on its programs. The Foundation received $12,156 in court-awarded
attorneys fees for its litigation.
Net Revenue: 1994 $128,393 **Net Expenses:** $166,126 42%/19%/22% **Net Assets:** (-$8,475)
Products or Services: Litigation, educational materials, lobbying. The Foundation spent $1,061 on the direct lobbying of
legislators. The Foundation paid $19,212 to the national ACLU, and $9,086 to its 501(c)(4) affiliate, the American Civil Liberties
Union of Maine.
Tax Status: 501(c)(3)
Other Information: Affiliated with the 501(c)(4) American Civil Liberties Union, Maine, at the same address. The Foundation
received $98,373, or 77% of revenue, from gifts and grants awarded by foundations, businesses, and individuals. $17,521 net, or
14%, from special fund-raising events including; the Justice Louis Scolnik Award Dinner, an annual meeting, and a reception co-
sponsored with the Gay and Lesbian Advocates and Defenders (GLAD) to support legal work in the area of homosexuals' rights.

American Civil Liberties Union, Michigan Fund (ACLU)

1249 Washington Blvd., Suite 2910
Detroit, MI 48226
USA

Phone: (313) 961-7728

Contact Person: Howard Simon, Executive Director.
Officers or Principals: Paul Denenfeld, Attorney ($47,810); Howard Simon, Executive Director ($26,404).
Mission or Interest: "Defense and advancement of the Bill of Rights, civil rights and civil liberties."

Accomplishments: In 1993 the Fund spent $158,558 on its projects; $50,147 on education and $108,411 on litigation. The Fund received $100,754 in court-awarded attorney's fees.
Net Revenue: 1993 $341,719 **Net Expenses:** $213,407 74%/13%/12% **Net Assets:** $327,132
Products or Services: Litigation, educational activities.
Tax Status: 501(c)(3)
Other Information: Affiliated with the 501(c)(4) American Civil Liberties Union of Michigan. The Fund received $214,894, 63% of yearly revenue, in grants from foundations, companies and individuals. Court-awarded attorney's fees contributed another $100,754, or 29%. $9,416, or 3%, from an affiliate's subsidy, and the remainder came from the sale of inventory and interest on savings and temporary cash investments.

American Civil Liberties Union, National Capital Area Fund

1400 20th St., N.W., Suite 119
Washington, DC 20036   **Phone:** (202) 457-0800
USA

Contact Person: Mary Jane DeFrank, Executive Director.
Officers or Principals: Mary Jane DeFrank, Executive Director ($59,516); Arthur B. Spitzer ($57,240); Emilio Cividanes, Chairperson; Robert Plotkin, Vice Chair; Cynthia Harrison, Secretary; Felice Levine, Treasurer.
Mission or Interest: Promotes civil liberties and constitutional rights.
Accomplishments: In 1993 the Fund spent $120,973 on litigation. $34,549 was spent on public education.
Net Revenue: 1993 $258,170 **Net Expenses:** $222,924 70%/20%/10% **Net Assets:** $118,547
Products or Services: Litigation, lectures, public statements, annual awards dinner, more.
Tax Status: 501(c)(3)
Board of Directors or Trustees: Adrienne Barth, H. Stewart Dunn , Jr., Eugene Fidell, Jocelyn Frye (Women's Legal Defense Fund), Judith Harris, Elinor Horwitz, David Joseph, Fred Joseph, Dan Rapoport, Paul Siegel, Tom Schneider, Helene Toiv, Claudia Withers (Fair Employment Council).
Other Information: Affiliated with the 501(c)(4) American Civil Liberties Union of the National Capital Area. The Fund received $210,725, or 82% of revenue from direct and indirect support in the form of gifts and grants awarded by foundations, companies, affiliates, and individuals. $45,755 net, or 18%, from the Annual Awards Dinner. The remaining revenue came from interest on savings and temporary cash investments, and dividends and interest from securities.

American Civil Liberties Union, New Jersey (ACLU)

2 Washington Place
Newark, NJ 07102   **Phone:** (201) 642-2084
USA

Contact Person: Edward Martone, Executive Director.   **Officers or Principals:** Edward Martone, Executive Director ($46,200); Fran Farber-Walter, President ($0); Fred Clever, Ron Chen, Vice Presidents ($0).
Mission or Interest: Litigation and education supporting civil and constitutional rights.
Accomplishments: In 1994 the Union spent $77,329 on its programs. Received $74,075 in court-awarded attorney's fees.
Net Revenue: 1994 $205,407 **Net Expenses:** $197,359 39%/31%/29% **Net Assets:** $88,579
Products or Services: Litigation, lobbying and educational services.
Tax Status: 501(c)(4)
Other Information: Affiliated with the Civil Liberties Education and Action Fund. In 1994 $129,252, or 62% of revenue, came from grants awarded by affiliates, foundations, and individuals. $74,075, or 38%, came from court-awarded attorney's fees. The remaining revenue came from interest on savings and temporary cash investments.

American Civil Liberties Union, Northern California (ACLU)

1663 Mission St., Suite 460
San Francisco, CA 94103   **Phone:** (415) 621-2493
USA

Contact Person: Milton Estes, Chair.   **Officers or Principals:** Joanne A. Lewis, Nancy Pemberton, Davis Riemer, Margaret M. Russell, Vice Chairs ($0); Ephraim Margolin, Charles Marson, Advisory Counsel; Stephen Bomse, General Counsel.
Mission or Interest: Lobbies for the purpose of "sustaining and promoting the Bill of Rights through education of the General Public and legislative activity."
Accomplishments: In the fiscal year ending March 1994, the Union spent $493,851 on its programs.
Net Revenue: FY ending 3/94 $855,645 **Net Expenses:** $727,471 68%/23%/10% **Net Assets:** $655,012
Citations: 46:141 **Tax Status:** 501(c)(4)
Board of Directors or Trustees: Harry Ainsgard, Abby Abinanti, James Blume, Barbara Brenner, Leonard Bronstein, Luz Buitrago, David Bunnell, Angelo Butler, Robert Capistrano, William Carpmill, Helen Chang, Marna Cohen, Marlene De Lancie, Kathleen Dooley, Eleanor Eisenberg, Theresa Friend, Dick Grosboll, Janet Haley, Christina Huskey, Lawrence Jensen, Len Karpman, Ethel Long-Scott, Susan Mizner, Charis Moore, Herbert Nelson, Maria Ontiveros, David Oppenheimer, Rachel Richman, Marcelo Rodriguez, Louise Rothman Riemer, Andrew Rudiak, Zona Sage, Alberto Saldmando, Ethan Schulman, Frances Strauss, Michelle Welsh, Dona Yamashiro.

Other Information: Affiliated with the 501(c)(3) American Civil Liberties Union Foundation of Northern California at the same address. The two affiliates had combined net revenues of $2,742,255, net expenses of $2,649,979, and net assets of $1,509,833. The Union received $440,195, or 51% of revenue, from gifts and grants awarded by foundations, businesses, and individuals. $280,536, or 33%, from membership dues. $117,176, or 14%, from expense reimbursements from affiliates. $17,738, or 2%, from interest on savings and temporary cash investments.

American Civil Liberties Union, Northern California Foundation (ACLU)

1663 Mission St., Suite 460
San Francisco, CA 94103   **Phone:** (415) 621-2493
USA

Contact Person: Jean Hom.   **Officers or Principals:** Alan Schlosser, Staff Attorney ($81,494); Margaret Crosby, Staff Attorney ($80,720); Cheri Bryant, Associate Director ($50,605); Milton Estes, Chair; James B. Blume, Treasurer; Davis Reimer, Development Chair; Joanne Lewis, Field Director; Nancy Pemberton, Legislative Policy; Margaret Russell, Legal Committee.
Mission or Interest: Protection of civil liberties and constitutional rights. Focus on Northern California.
Accomplishments: In the fiscal year ending March 1994, the Foundation spent $1,080,703 on its programs. For its litigation, the Foundation received $650,708 in court-awarded attorney's fees.
Net Revenue: FY ending 3/94 $1,886,610 **Net Expenses:** $1,922,508 56%/14%/19% **Net Assets:** $854,821
Citations: 46:141
Tax Status: 501(c)(3)
Other Information: The Foundation is affiliated with the 501(c)(4) American Civil Liberties Union of Northern California at the same address. The two affiliates had combined net revenues of $2,742,255, net expenses of $2,649,979, and net assets of $1,509,833. The Foundation made a payment of $217,069 to the National ACLU Foundation, as part of a pre-determined support quota. The Foundation received $1,107,588, or 58% of revenue, from direct and indirect public support in the form of gifts and grants awarded by foundations, businesses, affiliates and individuals. (These grants included $75,000 from the Rosenberg Foundation, $20,000 from the Wallace Alexander Gerbode Foundation, $10,000 from the Rex Foundation, and $100 from the Compton Foundation.) $650,708, or 34%, from court-awarded attorney's fees. $74,485, or 4%, from educational programs contributions. $52,342, or 3%, from interest on savings and temporary cash investments. The remaining revenue came from various expense reimbursements and other miscellaneous sources.

American Civil Liberties Union, Ohio Foundation

1226 W. 6th St., Suite 200
Cleveland, OH 44113   **Phone:** (216) 781-6277
USA   **Fax:** (216) 781-6438

Contact Person: Christine Link, Executive Director.   **Officers or Principals:** Christine Link, Executive Director ($0); Nancy Walters, President; Scott Greenwood, Vice President; Marc Williams-Young, Treasurer; Sue Carter, Secretary.
Mission or Interest: "To expand the rights and liberties guaranteed by the constitution and bill of rights through public education and litigation."
Accomplishments: The Foundation won a case before the U.S. Supreme Court that allowed the Klu Klux Klan to erect a cross for public display in Columbus's Capitol Square. In 1994 they spent $355,951 on the Foundation's programs. The Foundation received $350 in court-awarded fees. The Foundation set aside $19,320 for an "African-American payroll position" in 1996.
Net Revenue: 1994 $415,798 **Net Expenses:** $426,409 83%/16%/1% **Net Assets:** $151,329
Products or Services: Litigation, public education.
Tax Status: 501(c)(3)
Board of Directors or Trustees: Eliot Kalman, Julia Davis, Tanya Poteet, Bob Umholtz, Scott Greenwood, Spencer Neth, Jean Braucher (Univ. of Cincinnati School of Law), Ben Sheerer, Ray Vasvari, Max Wohl, Noreen Willhelm (Planned Parenthood of Dayton), Carol Ganzel, Jeff Gasmo, Louise Lefkort, Shirley Johnson, Peter Levin, Alice Malin, Gwendolyn McFarlin, Nancy Pierce, Sue Carter, Tim Downing, Peter Joy, Marc Williams-Young.
Periodicals: *ACLU News* (quarterly newsletter).
Internships: Yes, unpaid law clerks and summer interns for special projects.
Other Information: Affiliated with the 501(c)(4) American Civil Liberties Union of Ohio. The Foundation received $306,904, or 74% of revenue, from grants awarded by foundations, companies and individuals. $86,987, or 21%, came from a transfer of funds. The remaining revenue came from; the sale of books and literature, interest and dividends, conferences and other special events.

American Civil Liberties Union, Oklahoma Foundation

600 N.W. 23rd St., Suite 104
Oklahoma City, OK 73103   **Phone:** (405) 525-3831
USA   **Fax:** (405) 524-2296

Contact Person: Joann Bell, Executive Director.
Officers or Principals: Joann Bell, Executive Director ($29,814); Dorothy Alexander, General Counsel ($0); Mark Henrickson, President ($0); Randall Coyne, Vice President; Kenneth Ford, Treasurer; Larry Prater, Secretary; Michael Camfield, Development Director; Lois Chiles-Braver, Affirmative Action Officer; William Hinkle, National Board Representative.
Mission or Interest: Protection of civil liberties and constitutional rights.
Accomplishments: In 1993 the Foundation spent $38,961 on its programs. $21,445 was spent on litigation and $17,516 on public education.

Net Revenue: 1993 $62,083 **Net Expenses:** $80,727 48%/20%/32% **Net Assets:** $25,622
Products or Services: Litigation, literature, speakers, more.
Tax Status: 501(c)(3)
Board of Directors or Trustees: Joanne Duke, Rex Friend, Joan Luxenburg, Keith Myers, Marge Farwell, Philip Gate, Larry Hochhaus, Brian Marcum, Lloyd Owens, Con Hood, Scott Kayla Morrison, Marjorie Ramana, Kay Swift Samaripa, Betsy Tonihka, Esther Reiner, Barbara Santee, Carolyn Torrence, Wayne Robinson, Susan Spencer, Shirley Wiegand.
Other Information: The Foundation received $54,273, or 87% of revenue, from gifts and grants awarded by foundations, companies and individuals. $4,034, or 6%, from dividends and interest from securities. $3,776 net, or 6%, from special fund-raising events.

American Civil Liberties Union, Oregon Foundation (ACLU)

310 S.W. 4th Ave., Suite 705
Portland, OR 97204   **Phone:**   (503) 227-6928
USA

Contact Person: David J. Fidangue, Executive Director.
Officers or Principals: Joan Biggs, President ($0); Pete Dorn, Secretary ($0); Fran Storrs, Vice President, Education ($0); Cathy Travis, Vice President, Legislation ($0); Cory Streisinger, Vice President Policy; Floreid Walker, Treasurer.
Mission or Interest: Education and litigation to protect civil liberties and constitutional rights.
Accomplishments: In 1994 the Foundation spent $146,594 on its programs, $73,776 on education and $72,818 on litigation. For the litigation activities the Foundation was awarded $1,940 in court-awarded attorney's fees. The Foundation hosted syndicated columnist Molly Ivins for a lecture.
Net Revenue: 1994 $249,271 ($12,833, or 5%, from government grants) **Net Expenses:** $191,627 76%/7%/17%
Net Assets: $72,853
Products or Services: Litigation, meetings, educational activities.
Tax Status: 501(c)(3)
Board of Directors or Trustees: David Allen, George Bell, Melinda Eden, Jeanne Goodrich, Emilio Hernandez, Laurie Inacy, Arnold Ismach, Annabelle Jaramillo, Bernie Jolles, Stuart Kaplan, Carol Lewis, Wendy Madar, Katherine McDowell, Lynn Nakamoto, Tom Potter, Joan Rich, Jean Tate, Mary Turner, Patti Zembrosky-Barkin.
Other Information: The Foundation received $210,693, or 85% of revenue, from gifts and grants awarded by foundations, companies, affiliates, and individuals. $12,833, or 5%, from government grants. $11,195 net, or 5%, from special fund-raising events, including a Molly Ivins lecture. $7,792, or 3%, from interest on savings and temporary cash investments. The remaining revenue came from other investments, court-awarded attorney's fees, and other miscellaneous sources.

American Civil Liberties Union, Pennsylvania Foundation (ACLU)

125 S. 9th St., Suite 701
Philadelphia, PA 19105   **Phone:**   (215) 592-1513   **E-Mail:** aclupubed@aol.com
USA   **Fax:**   (215) 592-1343

Contact Person: Toby Venier.   **Officers or Principals:** Stefan B. Presser, Legal Director ($52,921); Deborah Leavy, Executive Director ($40,611); Gary Kalman, Development Director ($23,800); James Crawford, President; Michael Louik, Vice President; Annette Brenner, Secretary/Treasurer. (Salaries are from 1993.)
Mission or Interest: Protection of civil and constitutional rights.
Accomplishments: In 1995 the Foundation honored Lani Guinier for her civil rights work. Guinier is the lawyer perhaps best known for her controversial, and failed, nomination as President Clinton's Assistant Attorney General for Civil Rights. In 1994 the Foundation spent $1,377,630 on its activities; this included $1,287,691 on litigation expenses and $89,939 on public education. The Foundation received $60,542 in court-awarded attorney's fees.
Net Revenue: 1994 $1,625,745 **Net Expenses:** $1,556,943 88%/5%/7% **Net Assets:** $444,770
Products or Services: Litigation and public education.
Tax Status: 501(c)(3)
Board of Directors or Trustees: Karl Baker, Diane Bass, Nolan Bowie, Raymond Bradley, Burton Caine, Hiram Carmona, Spencer Coxe, William Davidon, S. Gordon Elkins, Robert Fiebach, Kenneth Frazier, Sue Frietsche, Nancy Gellman, Gloria Gilman, Sally Gordon (Univ. of Pennsylvania, Law School), Howard Harrison, Cassandra Jones Harvard, Teri Himebaugh, Babaette Josephs, Arthur Kaplan, Sam Klein, Nancy Knauer, Seth Kreimer, Eleanor Myers, Michael Nutter, Edward Posner, Dr. Katalin Eve Roth, David Rudovsky (Penn Law School), Susan Shenkin, Leslie Seymore, Kenneth Shropshire (Wharton School), Muriel Morisey Spence (Temple Law), Liz Werthan.
Other Information: The Foundation received $1,449,601, or 89% of revenue, from gifts and grants awarded by foundations, affiliates, businesses, and individuals. $98,430 net, or 6%, from special fund-raising events. $60,542, or 4%, from court-awarded attorneys' fees. The remaining revenue came from interest and other miscellaneous sources.

American Civil Liberties Union, San Diego and Imperial Counties Foundation (ACLU)

1202 Kettner Blvd., Suite 600
San Diego, CA 92101   **Phone:**   (619) 232-2121
USA

Contact Person: Linda Hills, Executive Director.   **Officers or Principals:** Linda Hills, Executive Director ($52,316); Jordan Budd, Legal Director ($33,474); E. Wally Miles, President; Michael Marrinan, First Vice President; Candace Carroll, Second Vice President; Belle Granich, Secretary; Roberta Spoon, Treasurer.
Mission or Interest: Promotes civil liberties and constitutional rights.
Accomplishments: In 1993 they spent $72,955 on research and education projects and $99,223 on litigation services. Litigation included: Murphy v. Bilbray, brought suit against the county of San Diego because of the maintenance of a large cross on Mt. Helix at a county-owned park. The cross and a small parcel of land was given to the San Diego Historical Society by the county, but both sides maintained the case should still be heard; the ACLU because it maintained that the gift of the cross and land was a violation of the California Constitution, and the County because of the importance of the case. Ellis v. City of La Mesa, the ACLU sought and won the change of the La Mesa police emblem, which depicted the cross on Mt. Helix mentioned in Murphy v. Bilbray, on the police uniforms, cars, etc. American Friends Service Committee, et al. v. United States of America alleges that systematic human rights abuses are carried out by U.S. Immigration and Naturalization Services and Border Patrol.
Net Revenue: 1993 $209,777 **Net Expenses:** $253,257 68%/22%/10% **Net Assets:** $89,218
Products or Services: Litigation and educational activities.
Tax Status: 501(c)(3)
Board of Directors or Trustees: Charles Bird, Marco Lopez, Roberto Martinez, John Murphy, Wendy Nakamura, Elisabeth Semel.
Other Information: Affiliated with the 501(c)(4) ACLU of San Diego and Imperial Counties. The Foundation received $166,637, or 79% of revenue, from gifts and grants awarded by foundations, companies, affiliates and individuals. $22,169, or 11%, from special fund-raising events. $12,808, or 6%, from dividends and interest from securities. $7,822, or 4%, from capital gains on the sale of securities. The remaining revenue came from program services, including seminar fees, the sale of literature, etc.

American Civil Liberties Union, South Carolina Foundation (ACLU)

1338 Main St., Suite 800
Columbia, SC 29201   **Phone:**   (803) 799-5151
USA

Contact Person: Steven J. Bates, Executive Director.   **Officers or Principals:** Steven J. Bates, Executive Director ($34,000); Kevin Alexander Gray, President ($0); Pamela Robinson, Treasurer ($0); David Kennison, Secretary.
Mission or Interest: Legal defense and public education on behalf of civil rights and constitutional liberties.
Accomplishments: In 1994 the Foundation spent $30,706 on its programs.
Net Revenue: 1994 $59,361 **Net Expenses:** $62,327 49%/50%/1% **Net Assets:** $253,060
Tax Status: 501(c)(3)
Other Information: Affiliated with the 501(c)(4) ACLU of South Carolina at the same address. The Foundation received $51,876, or 87% of revenue, from direct and indirect public support in the form of gifts and grants awarded by affiliates, foundations, businesses, and individuals. $7,450, or 13%, from interest on savings and temporary cash investments. The remaining revenue came from literature sales.

American Civil Liberties Union, Southern California Foundation (ACLU)

1616 Beverly Blvd.
Los Angeles, CA 90026   **Phone:**   (213) 977-9500
USA

Contact Person: Ramona Ripston, Executive Director.   **Officers or Principals:** Paul Hoffman, Legal Director ($81,957); Mark Rosenbaum, General Counsel ($78,855); Ramona Ripston, Executive Director ($78,083); Lee Masters, Chair; Danny Goldberg, President; Susan Adelman, Alan Bergman, Madeline Goodwin, Bob Johnson, Eve Slaff, Peg Yorkin, Vice Presidents; Louis Colen, Treasurer; Irma Colen Secretary; Lloyd Smith, Assistant Secretary/Treasurer.
Mission or Interest: Southern California office of the American Civil Liberties Union. Advocates and litigates civil liberties and constitutional rights.
Accomplishments: In 1993 they litigated a total of 109 active cases. Among these were: Wiener v. FBI, this suit would require the FBI to turn over documents regarding FBI surveillance of the late musician, John Lennon. American-Arab Anti-Discrimination Committee v. Thornburgh challenged the constitutionality of a law which authorized the deportation of aliens who "advocate""world communism" or who are "members" or "affiliates" of organizations which distribute literature advocating "world communism." Greenpeace v. City of Glendale challenging the city's requirement that door-to-door canvassers be fingerprinted - Greenpeace and the ACLU maintained that this was a violation of privacy. Curran v. Mt. Diablo Council of the Boy Scouts of America challenging the Boy Scouts policy of barring participation by lesbians and gay men. Filed an amicus brief In the Matter of Joshua Richard supporting a 'hate-crimes' law on the basis that it is not punishing thought, but rather the action. In 1993 they spent $1,818,265 on their legal services program. They received $373,311 in court-awarded attorneys' fees.
Net Revenue: 1993 $1,893,081 **Net Expenses:** $2,216,890 82%/13%/5% **Net Assets:** $5,253,425 **Citations:** 13:188
Tax Status: 501(c)(3)
Board of Directors or Trustees: Ruth Abraham, Lucy Adelman, Marilyn Bergman, Jay Boberg (IRS Records), Thomas Carter, Barbara Corday (New World Television), Richard Dreyfuss, Jane Egly, Joyce Fisk, Leo Frumkin, Sherry Frumkin, Mary Ellen Gale (Whittier College School of Law), Alan Gleitsman, Elyse Grinstein, Stanley Grinstein, Joshua Grode, Susan Grode, Barry Hirsch, Dorothy Jonas, Jimi Kaufer, Leonard Kaufman, Shari Leinwand, Irving Lichtenstein, M.D., Marty Longbine, Mark Magidson, Shirley Magidson, Gary Mandinach, Steven Markoff, Faye Nuell Mayo, Robin Meadow, Trisha Murakawa, Lucille Ostrow, Max Palevsky, Sarah Jessica Parker, Judy Balaban Quine, Andrea Rich, Dolores Robinson, Richard Rosenzweig (Playboy Enterprises), Marc Seltzer, Bob Shafer, Alan Sieroty, Robert Smith (Geffen Records), Fred Specktor, Barbra Streisand (Barbra Streisand Found.), Kate Summers, Florence Temkin, June Tyre, Paula Weinstein (Spring Creek Productions, Warner Bros.), JoAnne Widzer, Irwin Winkler, Larry Winokur, Chic Wolk, Beatrice Zeiger.

Other Information: They are affiliated with the 501(c)(4) ACLU of Southern California. The Foundation received $1,122,879, or 59% of revenue, from gifts and grants awarded by foundations, companies, and individuals. (These grants included $77,000 from the Barbra Streisand Foundation, $25,000 from the North Star Fund, $2,500 from the Liberty Hill Foundation.) $373,311, or 20%, from court-awarded attorney's fees. $198,378, or 10%, from dividends and interest from securities. $172,727, or 9%, from special fund-raising events. The remaining revenue came from net income on rental properties.

American Civil Liberties Union, Tennessee Foundation (ACLU)

P.O. Box 120160
Nashville, TN 37212   **Phone:**   (615) 320-7142
USA

Contact Person: Hedy Weinberg, Executive Director. **Officers or Principals:** Hedy Weinberg, Executive Director ($17,470); David Wiley, President ($0); Valerie Traub, Vice President ($0); Patricia Mock, Secretary; Donald O. Peterson, Treasurer.
Mission or Interest: Promotion of civil liberties and constitutional rights.
Accomplishments: In 1994 the Foundation spent $34,310 on its programs. $17,737 on litigation and $16,674 on public education. The Foundation received $2,614 in court-awarded attorney's fees.
Net Revenue: 1994 $64,494 **Net Expenses:** $68,000 50%/24%/26% **Net Assets:** $172,693
Tax Status: 501(c)(3)
Board of Directors or Trustees: Bruce Barry, Tom Bibler, Glenn Carter, Donald Davis, Dan Einstein, Mona Frederick, Barbara Futter, Ruth Gove, Edward Hart, Stacy Hickox, Jill Jackson, Bruce Kramer, Sheri Lipman, Susan Martin, Ellen McPherson, Victor Pestrak, Joe Rader, Bob Rasmussen, Betsy Schwartz, Charles Sienknecht, Terrence Sjoreen, Stanton Smith, Martha Stovall, Joe Sweat, Chuck Watts.
Other Information: The Foundation received $28,524, or 44% of revenue, from gifts and grants awarded by foundations, affiliates, businesses, and individuals. $21,050, or 33%, from a special fund-raising event, the Bill of Rights Dinner. $12,008, or 19%, from dividends and interest from securities. The remaining revenue came from court-awarded attorney's fees, and other miscellaneous sources.

American Civil Liberties Union, Utah Foundation (ACLU)

Boston Bldg., Suite 715
Salt Lake City, UT 84111   **Phone:**   (801) 521-9862
USA

Contact Person: Carol Gnade, Executive Director.
Officers or Principals: Carol Gnade, Executive Director ($42,866); Kathryn Kendall, Attorney ($39,840).
Mission or Interest: Protection and advancement of civil liberties and constitutional rights.
Accomplishments: In 1994 the Foundation spent $137,271 on its programs; $118,480 on litigation relating to "prison treatment, abortion, school prayer, etc.," and $18,791 on public education. The foundation received $109,441 in court-awarded legal fees.
Net Revenue: 1994 $246,401 **Net Expenses:** $170,067 81%/7%/12% **Net Assets:** $65,354
Products or Services: Litigation, speakers, bulletins, advertisements, lectures, more.
Tax Status: 501(c)(3)
Other Information: The Foundation received $148,572, or 57% of total revenue, from direct and indirect public support in the form of gifts and grants awarded by foundations, affiliates, companies and individuals. $109,441, or 42%, from court-awarded attorney's fees. $2,552, or 1%, from interest on savings and temporary cash investments. Revenue was partially offset by a large net loss, $14,360, from special events.

American Civil Liberties Union, Vermont Foundation (ACLU)

110 E. State St.
Montpelier, VT 05602   **Phone:**   (802) 223-6304
USA

Contact Person: Andrea Warnke, Associate Director.
Officers or Principals: Leslie Williams, Executive Director ($30,040); Andrea Warnke, Associate Director ($24,035); Valerie White, President ($0); John Shullenberger, Vice President; Marion Kellogg, Treasurer; Ben Stein, Secretary; Richard Axelrod, National Board Representative.
Mission or Interest: Protection and advancement of civil and constitutional rights.
Accomplishments: In 1994 the Foundation spent $58,205 on its programs. This included $1,824 in litigation expenses.
Net Revenue: 1994 $80,409 **Net Expenses:** $72,759 80%/10%/10% **Net Assets:** $999
Tax Status: 501(c)(3)
Board of Directors or Trustees: Margie Pulaski, Richard Axelrod, Sally Conrad, William Dorsch, Trudy Seeley, Laura Fishman, Bern Friedelson, Carla Hochschild, Peggy Hyde, Ralph O'Mara Garcia, Holly Perdue, Caroline Bergh, James Lee, Sandra Nall, Daniel Krymkowski, David Williams, Peter Lawrence, Gordon Miwa.
Other Information: Affiliated with the 501(c)(4) ACLU of Vermont. The Foundation received $80,001, or 99.5% of revenue, from direct and indirect public support in the form of gifts and grants awarded by foundations, affiliates, businesses, and individuals. The remaining revenue came from interest on savings and temporary cash investments.

American Civil Liberties Union, Virginia (ACLU)

6 North 6th St., Suite 400
Richmond, VA 23219   **Phone:**   (804) 644-8022
USA

Contact Person: Kent Willis, Executive Director.   **Officers or Principals:** Kent Willis, Executive Director ($29,485); Chuck Rust-Tierney, President ($0); Jayne Barnard, Barbara Ziony, Sebastian Graber, Vice Presidents ($0); John Cochrane, Treasurer; Kate Wertheim, Secretary; John Levy, Chair, Legal Panel.
Mission or Interest: Protection of civil liberties with an emphasis on the Bill of Rights.
Accomplishments: In 1994 the Union spent $43,081 "to inform members of the Virginia General Assembly on important civil liberties issues." $36,975 was spent to educate and influence the public, and $21,380 was spent on litigating civil liberties and voting rights cases.
Net Revenue: 1994 $490,207 **Net Expenses:** $110,695 92%/6%/2% **Net Assets:** $582,208
Products or Services: Lobbying, litigation, public education forums.
Tax Status: 501(c)(4)
Board of Directors or Trustees: Frank Feibelman, Gene Hulbert, Beatrice Mook, Doug Mook, Beth Garrett, Gladstone Hill, Phil Caminer, Norman Fuller, John Cochrane, David Drachsler, Peter Gavian, Ron Hall, David Kaufman, Steve Levinson, Paula Kaiser, Betsy Brinson, Stew Dunn, Sebastian Graber, Jay Hamby, John Levy, Shelly Latin, Stephen Lenton, Wade Mann, George Smith.
Periodicals: Legislative newsletter.
Other Information: They are affiliated with the 501(c)(3) American Civil Liberties Union Foundation of Virginia at the same address. At the two affiliates combined, Kent Willis, who splits his time as Executive Director of both, is compensated with $49,142. The Union received $390,323, or 80% of the year's revenue, from the national office in New York. $86,796, or 18%, came from membership dues, $5,210 from interest and temporary cash investments, and the rest came from the sale of newsletters and literature.

American Civil Liberties Union, Virginia Foundation (ACLU)

6 North 6th St., Suite 400
Richmond, VA 23219   **Phone:**   (804) 644-8022
USA

Contact Person: Kent Willis, Executive Director.   **Officers or Principals:** Stephen B. Penshing, Legal Director ($37,141); Kent Willis, Executive Director ($19,657); Chuck Rust-Tierney, President ($0); Jayne Barnard, Barbara Ziony, Sebastian Graber, Vice Presidents; John Cochrane, Treasurer; Kate Wertheim, Secretary; John Levy, Chair, Legal Panel.
Mission or Interest: Research and litigation to protect civil liberties and constitutional rights.
Accomplishments: In 1994 the Foundation spent $142,254 on its programs. $86,838 was spent on litigation. The Foundation was awarded $18,450 in court-awarded attorney's fees for its litigation. $55,416 was spent on public education activities.
Net Revenue: 1994 $209,668 **Net Expenses:** $157,097 91%/5%/4% **Net Assets:** $6,745
Products or Services: Litigation and educational activities and materials.
Tax Status: 501(c)(3)
Other Information: The Foundation is affiliated with the 501(c)(4) American Civil Liberties Union of Virginia at the same address. At the two affiliates combined, Kent Willis, who splits his time as Executive Director of both, was compensated with $49,142. The Foundation received $189,481, or 90% of revenue from direct and indirect public support; that is grants awarded by foundations, individuals, and affiliates. $18,450, or 9%, came from court-awarded attorney's fees. The remaining revenue came from interest on savings and temporary cash investments.

American Civil Liberties Union, Washington Endowment Fund (ACLU)

705 2nd Ave., Suite 300
Seattle, WA 98104-1799   **Phone:**   (206) 624-2184
USA

Contact Person: Kathleen M. Taylor, Executive Director.
Officers or Principals: Kathleen M. Taylor, Executive Director ($0); Paul Lawrence, President ($0); Judy Porterfield, 1st Vice President ($0); Karen Boxx, 2nd Vice President; Beth Andrus, Secretary; David Griffith, Treasurer.
Mission or Interest: Endowment fund supporting the American Civil Liberties Union of Washington and the ACLU national office.
Accomplishments: In 1993 the Fund payed its Washington state Foundation affiliate $68,000 and the national office $2,060.
Net Revenue: 1993 $71,520 **Net Expenses:** $72,302 0%/3%/0% **Net Assets:** $729,534
Products or Services: Funding for affiliates.
Tax Status: 501(c)(3)
Board of Directors or Trustees: Judy Bendich, Susan Loitz, Monica Zucker.
Other Information: Affiliated with the 501(c)(4) ACLU of Washington, and the 501(c)(3) American Civil Liberties Union of Washington Foundation at the same address. $48,326, or 68% of revenue came from dividends and interest from securities. $27,483, or 38%, came from direct and indirect public support in the form of grants from foundations, affiliates, and individuals. (This support included $2,242 from their affiliate, the ACLU of Washington Foundation.) Revenues were partially offset by a loss of $4,289 on the sale of securities.

American Civil Liberties Union, Washington Foundation

705 Second Ave, Suite 300
Seattle, WA 98104-1799   **Phone:**   (206) 624-2184
USA

Contact Person: Kathleen M. Taylor, Executive Director.
Officers or Principals: Julya Hampton, Legal Programs Director ($45,430); Randy Balogh, Development Director ($38,435); Douglas S. Honig, Public Education Director ($37,735); Kathleen M. Taylor, Executive Director; Paul Lawrence, President; Judy Porterfield, First Vice President; Karen Boxx, Second Vice President; Beth Andrus, Secretary; David Griffith, Treasurer.
Mission or Interest: Public education and litigation to protect civil liberties and the Bill of Rights.
Accomplishments: In 1993 the Foundation spent $378,008 on its programs, $228,170 on litigation and $149,838 on education programs. The Foundation paid $71,772 to the National ACLU as part of a revenue-sharing agreement, and $2,243 to the ACLU Washington Endowment Fund for services provided.
Net Revenue: 1993 $693,648 **Net Expenses:** $552,138 68%/6%/13% **Net Assets:** $381,731
Products or Services: Litigation and educational programs.
Tax Status: 501(c)(3)
Board of Directors or Trustees: Judy Bendich, Susan Loitz, Monica Zucker.
Other Information: The Foundation received $640,155, or 92% of revenue, from direct and indirect public support in the form of gifts and grants awarded by foundations, affiliates, companies and individuals. (These grants included $68,000 from the ACLU of Washington Endowment Fund.) $43,615 net, or 6%, from the sale of Bill of Rights calendars. $8,604, or 1%, from dividends and interest from securities. The remaining revenue came from other miscellaneous sources, including the sale of books, posters, t-shirts, and speech honoraria.

American Civil Liberties Union, Western Missouri Foundation (ACLU)

706 W. 42nd St., Suite 108
Kansas City, MO 64111   **Phone:**   (816) 756-3113
USA   **Fax:**   (816) 756-0945

Contact Person: Dick Kurlenbach, Executive Director.
Officers or Principals: Jay Barrish, President ($0); Doug Kingsbury, Vice President ($0); Martin Levit, Vice President ($0); Roberta Eveslage, Secretary; Larry Denny, Treasurer; David Waxse, General Counsel; Janice Ownes, Affirmative Action Officer.
Mission or Interest: Protection and expansion of civil rights and constitutional rights.
Accomplishments: In 1994 the Foundation spent $81,090 on its programs, including a $77,290 transfer of funds to an affiliate organization.
Net Revenue: 1994 $93,261 **Net Expenses:** $83,580 **Net Assets:** $98,584
Tax Status: 501(c)(3)
Board of Directors or Trustees: Leslie Bissell, Erika Fox, Angela Keck, Rich Kowalewski, Sandy Krigel, Renee Marlin, Thomas McMorris, Linda McNicholas, Harris Mirkin, Rick Newhouse, Susan Perry, Roger Preston, Gordon Risk, Linda Rostenberg, John Swomley.
Other Information: The Foundation received $67,052, or 72% of revenue, from gifts and grants awarded by foundations, businesses, and individuals. $20,486, or 22%, from membership dues. $5,171, or 5%, from a dinner honoring of the Executive Director. The remaining income came from miscellaneous sources.

American Civil Liberties Union, Wisconsin Foundation (ACLU)

933 N. Mayfair Rd., Suite 111
Milwaukee, WI 53226   **Phone:**   (414) 272-4032
USA   **Fax:**   (414) 272-0182

Contact Person: Dianne Greenley, President.   **Officers or Principals:** Dianne Greenley, President ($0); Loretta Webster, Vice President ($0); William Lynch, Secretary/Treasurer ($0).
Mission or Interest: Protection and advancement of civil liberties and constitutional rights.
Accomplishments: In 1994 the Foundation spent $206,863 on its programs. The Foundation averages ten new cases each year, with an average of ten cases active at all times.
Net Revenue: 1994 $179,102 **Net Expenses:** $242,893 85%/10%/5% **Net Assets:** $62,043
Tax Status: 501(c)(3)
Board of Directors or Trustees: Janice Baudin, Ruth Conniff, Luis Garza, James Hall, Diane Legomsky, David Luce, A. Steven Porter, John Quinlan, Walter Rattan, Athan Theoharis, Frieda Webb.
Other Information: The Foundation received $127,556, or 71% of revenue, from direct and indirect public support, in the form of gifts and grants awarded by foundations, businesses, and individuals. $43,123 net, or 24%, from special fund-raising events. $4,638, or 3%, from court awarded attorney's fees. $3,785, or 2%, from dividends and interest from securities.

American Committee on Africa (ACOA)

17 John St., 12th Floor
New York, NY 10038   **Phone:**   (212) 962-1210
USA

Contact Person: Jennifer Davis, Executive Director.
Officers or Principals: Jennifer Davis, Executive Director ($7,466); Adrena Ifill, Associate Director ($2,063); William H. Booth, President ($0); Wyatt Tee Walker, David Scott, Vice Presidents; Frederick B. Williams, Treasurer.
Mission or Interest: Lobbying affiliate of the Africa Fund. Works to influence foreign policy regarding Africa. Concerned about peace and justice issues, political prisoners, human rights, racism, and more.
Accomplishments: In 1993 the Committee spent $61,046 on its programs.
Net Revenue: 1993 $90,009 **Net Expenses:** $73,886 83%/8%/9% **Net Assets:** $31,826
Tax Status: 501(c)(4)
Board of Directors or Trustees: Jon Chapman (Presbyterian Church USA), Imani Countess (Washington Office on Africa), Ralston Deffenbaigh Jr. (Lutheran Immigration and Refugee Service), Bill Henning (V.P., CWA), M. William Howard (Pres., NY Theological Seminary), Elizabeth Landis (ret., Senior Political Affairs Officer, Office of the United Nations Commissioner for Namibia), Tilden LeMelle (Pres., Univ. of DC), Edgar Romney (Intl. Ladies Garment Workers Union), Jean Sindab (Natl. Council of Churches), Timothy Smith (Interfaith Center on Corporate Responsibility), Doreen Tilghman (United Methodist Church), Stephanie Urdang.
Periodicals: *ACOA Action News* (bi-annual newsletter).
Other Information: Affiliated with the 501(c)(3) Africa Fund at the same address. The two affiliates had combined net revenues of $537,107, net expenses of $635,294, and net assets of $232,331. Jennifer Davis served as executive director of both and received $38,337 in combined compensation. Adrena Ifill served as associate director for both, and received $20,626. The Committee received $48,822, or 54% of revenue, from program services. $40,085, or 44%, from gifts and grants awarded by foundations, businesses, and individuals. The remaining revenue came from interest on savings and temporary cash investments, and honoraria and travel fees.

American Conservation Association

30 Rockefeller Plaza, Room 5600
New York, NY 10112   **Phone:**   (212) 649-5819
USA

Contact Person: Carmen Reyes, Treasurer.   **Officers or Principals:** Carmen Reyes, Treasurer ($34,389); Charles M. Clusen, Executive Director ($0); Laurence Rockefeller, President ($0); R. Scott Greathead, Secretary.
Mission or Interest: Grant-making organization that awards money to environmental and conservation organizations. Also conducts its own educational activities.
Accomplishments: In 1994 the Association awarded $531,500 in grants. Recipients of the largest grants included: $75,000 for the Natural Resources Defense Council, $50,000 for the Sierra Club Legal Defense Fund, $50,000 for the Wilderness Society, $25,000 for Scenic America, and $20,000 each for the National Audubon Society, Scenic Hudson, and the Catskill Center for Conservation and Development. $818,967 was spent on educational activities. The largest program, with expenditures of $442,462, was the Children's Earth Fund, an educational program that works through teachers "designed to help children take action to save the planet." Students pledge to "save one ton of carbon dioxide (the primary greenhouse gas) at home during the year," and "joined in asking the President to make the U.N. Earth Summit succeed by pledging to cut back U.S. carbon dioxide emissions." Approximately 500,000 children took the carbon dioxide pledge. In cooperation with cable television station Nickelodeon, the Association developed "Pennies for the Planet," a program that persuades children to raise funds for items such as tree seeds, solar cookers, and water purification. $125,740 for the Northern Forest Lands Project, a coalition of twenty-two organizations, to "promote healthy, well-managed private forest lands and develop strong, diverse sustainable economies" in a region across northern New England and New York. Other programs include protection for Alaskan wilderness, solar energy promotion, urban gardening, and other conservation efforts.
Net Revenue: 1994 $1,783,449 **Net Expenses:** $1,720,028 **Net Assets:** $244,250
Tax Status: 501(c)(3)
Board of Directors or Trustees: John Adams (Natural Resources Defense Council), Frances Beinecke, Nash Castro, William Conway (Wildlife Conservation Society), Henry Diamond, Red Kent III (Project for Open Spaces), George Lamb, William McHenry, Patrick Noonan (Conservation Fund), Story Clark Resor, David Sampson, Gene Setzer, Cathleen Douglas Stone (Office of the Mayor, Boston), Russell Train (World Wildlife Fund), William Whyte Jr.
Other Information: The Association received $1,769,061, or 99% of revenue, from gifts and grants awarded by foundations, businesses, and individuals. (These grants included $1,250,000 from the Jackson Hole Preserve, $120,000 from Earth Force, $117,500 from the Pew Charitable Trust, and $15,000 from the Skerryvore Foundation.) $17,813, or 1%, from interest on savings and temporary cash investments. The Association lost $3,425 on the sale of assets.

American Educational Trust (AET)

P.O. Box 53062
Washington, DC 20009   **Phone:**   (202) 989-6050   **E-Mail:** wrmea@aol.com
USA   **Fax:**   (202) 232-6754

Contact Person: Dokhi Fassihian, Business Manager.   **Officers or Principals:** Richard H. Curtiss, Executive Director ($30,000); Andrew I. Killgore, President ($30,000); Humphrey Walz, Chairman ($0).
Mission or Interest: "Educate the American public about the politics of the Middle East and U.S. foreign policy toward the Middle East."

Accomplishments: The Trust claims that its monthly magazine, the *Washington Report on Middle East Affairs*, has "the largest individually paid circulation of any Middle East-related publication in the U.S. or Canada. In 1992 the Trust spent $1,021,803 on its programs. $681,894 was spent on publishing and distributing the *Washington Report*. $209,647 was spent on the production and dissemination of books about the Middle East. $107,508 was spent collecting and distributing news clipping and television reports via fax and video tape. $22,754 was spent on disseminating translations of articles from the Hebrew press.
Net Revenue: 1992 $1,301,159 **Net Expenses:** $1,187,695 86%/13%/1% **Net Assets:** $137,543 **Citations:** 1:240
Products or Services: Publications, news distribution, and lobbying.
Tax Status: 501(c)(4) **Annual Report:** No. **Employees:** 6
Periodicals: *Washington Report on Middle East Affairs* (monthly magazine).
Internships: Yes, help with administration and research.
Other Information: Affiliated with 501(c)(3) AET Literary Endowment. The *Washington Report* has been published by retired foreign service officers since 1982. AET does not take "partisan domestic political positions." As a solution to the Palestinian-Israeli conflict, AET endorses the United Nations Security Council Resolution 242, the "land-for-peace formula." The *Washington Report* is frequently critical of Israel, and of the Israeli lobby in the United States. In 1992 it cost $681,894 to publish the *Washington Report*, and subscriptions and advertising brought in $326,740 in revenue; so publication and distribution required a subsidization of $355,154. In 1992 the Trust received $576,963, or 44% of revenue, from gifts and grants awarded by foundations, businesses, and individuals. $319,430, or 25%, from subscriptions. $207,190, or 16%, from book sales. $154,800, or 12%, from the sale of faxed news clippings. The remaining revenue came from the sale of other information services, advertising, and interest on savings and other temporary cash investments.

American Federation of Labor and Congress of Industrial Organizations (AFL-CIO)

815 16th St., N.W.
Washington, DC 20006   **Phone:**   (202) 637-5000
USA   **Fax:**   (202) 637-5058

Contact Person: John Sweeney, President.
Officers or Principals: Lane Kirkland, former President ($183,260); Thomas R. Donahue, former Secretary/Treasurer ($155,760); John Sweeney, President; Richard Trumka, Secretary/Treasurer; Linda Chavez-Thompson, Executive Vice President.
Mission or Interest: "The AFL-CIO is a federation of affiliated national and international labor unions, trade and industrial departments, state and local central bodies and directly affiliated local unions." Approximately 13,300,000 members and about 620 local groups.
Accomplishments: In 1995 there was a major change in AFL-CIO leadership. The AFL-CIO elected John Sweeney president. Sweeney was previously president of the Service Employees International Union. He is known for his aggressive and confrontational tactics, and effective recruiting methods. Richard Trumka from the United Mine Workers, who was the choice of many 'labor progressives', was elected secretary/treasurer. This was the Federation's first contested election. Steve Rosenthal was named as the Federation's new political director. Rosenthal was formerly with the Communications Workers of America, and a key supporter of the advocacy organization, Jobs With Justice. Lately Rosenthal was a deputy for Labor Secretary Robert Reich. Bob Wages, president of the Oil, Chemical and Atomic Workers Union, and an advocate of forming a labor party, was elected to the Federation's Executive Council. Sweeney promised to increase funding for the Federation's Organizing Institute, which trains union organizers (in 1994 the Organizing Institute spent $1,949,000). This coincides with Linda Chavez-Thompson's assignment of building stronger alliances between locals and the Federation. Sweeney proposed the creation of a "Strategic Action Center" to focus on new strategies and techniques, especially in the face of the declining effectiveness of striking. The Federation pledged to spend $35 million dollars, funded by a special dues collection, to help Democrats in the November 1996 elections. In 1996 the Union hosted the "Union Summer" which brought hundreds of students and workers on organizing campaigns and political projects. In 1994 the AFL-CIO spent $3,599,065 to promote a national health care system and support President Clinton's health care plan. The Union spent $80,536 on the anti-NAFTA campaign, the free-trade agreement that was extended to Mexico and ratified during the previous year. The Union awarded $15,385,930 in grants, most going to labor education, organizing, and other support groups. $1,739,399 went to "state political education activity."
Net Revenue: 1994 $71,962,525 **Net Expenses:** $68,083,700 **Net Assets:** $85,367,911
Products or Services: Collective bargaining and labor organizing. Annual George Meany Human Rights Award for international human rights and Murray-Green-Meany Award for distinguished service to America.
Tax Status: 501(c)(5)
Board of Directors or Trustees: Executive Council members in 1994 included: Morton Bahr, John Barry, George Becker, Owen Bieber, Moe Miller, Marvin Boede, William Bywater, Ron Carey, Linda Chavez-Thompson, Arthur Coia, Douglas Dority, Robert Georgine, Wayne Glenn, Edward Hanley, Francis Hanley, James Hatfield, Frank Hurt, Gloria Johnson, John Joyce, George Kourpias, Sigurd Lucassen, Gerald McEntee, Jay Mazur, Lenore Miller, James Norton, Michael Sacco, Albert Shanker, Jack Sheinkman, Vincent Sombrotto, John Sturdivant, Richard Trumka, Eugene Upshaw.
Periodicals: *AFL-CIO News* (biweekly newsletter).
Other Information: Founded in 1952. The AFL-CIO received $64,988,834, or 90% of revenue, from membership dues. $2,982,512, or 4%, from interest on savings and temporary cash investments. $1,579,139, or 2%, from affiliates. $1,182,858 net, or 2%, from rental income. $1,121,344, or 2%, from affiliates, members, and other unions to pay for health care reform activities. The remaining revenue came from subscriptions, sales of educational materials, dividends and interest from securities, and other miscellaneous sources. The Union had a net loss of $783,245 on the sale of securities. In the fiscal year ending June 1994, the AFL-CIO and its affiliates received approximately $2,038,000 in federal funding.

American Federation of State, County and Municipal Employees (AFSCME)

1625 L St., N.W.
Washington, DC 20036   **Phone:**   (202) 429-1000
USA

Contact Person: Gerald W. McEntee, President.
Mission or Interest: Union representing government employees. Member of the AFL-CIO.
Accomplishments: Approximately 1,300,000 members.
Tax Status: 501(c)(5)
Periodicals: *AFSCME Leader* (weekly newsletter), *Public Employee Newspaper* (eight times a year).
Other Information: In the year between July 1993 and June 1994, AFSCME received $148,000 in federal funding.

American Federation of Teachers (AFT)

555 New Jersey Ave., N.W.
Washington, DC 20001   **Phone:**   (202) 879-4400
USA   **Fax:**   (202) 238-1133

Contact Person: Albert Shanker, President.
Officers or Principals: Albert Shanker, President ($226,380); Edward McElroy, Secretary/Treasurer ($165,277).
Mission or Interest: Union representing teachers and other education employees. Member of the AFL-CIO.
Accomplishments: Approximately 625,000 members. Awarded $911,205 in grants to other unions and nonprofit organizations.
Net Revenue: FY ending 6/95 $74,833,299 **Net Expenses:** $67,849,600 **Net Assets:** $49,853,773
Tax Status: 501(c)(5)
Periodicals: *AFT Action* (weekly newsletter), *American Educator* (quarterly magazine), *American Teacher* (eight times a year newsletter).
Other Information: Founded in 1916. Affiliated with the 501(c)(3) American Federation of Teachers Educational Foundation at the same address. The union received $67,094,552, or 90% of revenue, from membership dues. $3,706,452, or 5%, from insurance premiums. The remaining revenue came from interest on savings and temporary cash investments, advertising, and other sources.

American Federation of Teachers Educational Foundation

555 New Jersey Ave., N.W.
Washington, DC 20001   **Phone:**   (202) 879-4470
USA

Contact Person: Edward J. McElroy, Secretary/Treasurer.
Officers or Principals: Albert Shanker, President ($0); Thomas Hobart, Albert Fondy, Directors ($0).
Mission or Interest: Research and educational organization affiliated with the American Federation of Teachers and the AFL-CIO. "Seeks to assist educators in their efforts to introduce and expand democratic civic education within the formal educational system, in order to help foster the development of a democratic culture."
Accomplishments: In the fiscal year ending June 1994, the Foundation spent $1,286,298 on its programs. These programs included assistance for the Centers for Disease Control by setting up pilot sites to help with and evaluate the American Federation of Teachers' HIV/AIDS prevention efforts. Also awarded grants of $66,933 to the Smith Richardson Foundation for project Freedom House, and $80,919 for the Free Trade Union Institute for distribution to foundations in Poland, Hungary, Romania, Bulgaria, and the Czech Federation. Another grant of $33,000 was awarded for the Lincoln Memorial Project, an exhibit in the lower lobby of the Lincoln memorial.
Net Revenue: FY ending 6/94 $1,286,167 ($1,158,465, or 90%, from government grants)
Net Expenses: $1,286,298 100%/0%/0% **Net Assets:** $4,961
Products or Services: Grants and educational programs.
Tax Status: 501(c)(3)
Other Information: The Foundation received $1,158,465, or 90% of revenue, from government grants. $115,701, or 9%, from gifts and grants awarded by foundations, businesses, and individuals. The remaining revenue came from interest on savings and temporary cash investments. The Foundation reimbursed the American Federation of Teachers $488,650 for expenses. The officers are full-time employees of the American Federation of Teachers, AFL-CIO, and are compensated by that union.

American Federation of Television and Radio Artists (AFTRA)

260 Madison Ave.
New York, NY 10016   **Phone:**   (212) 532-0800
USA   **Fax:**   (212) 921-8454

Contact Person: Herta Suarez.   **Officers or Principals:** Herta Suarez ($48,353).
Mission or Interest: Union representing approximately 75,000. Member of the AFL-CIO.
Accomplishments: The Union spent only $2,000 or less on in-house lobbying.
Net Revenue: FY ending 4/94 $524,726 **Net Expenses:** $827,393 **Net Assets:** $0
Tax Status: 501(c)(5)
Periodicals: *AFTRA Magazine* (quarterly).
Other Information: The union received 100% of its revenue from membership dues.

American Foundation for AIDS Research (AmFAR)

733 3rd Ave, 17th Floor
New York, NY 10017   **Phone:**   (212) 682-7440
USA

Contact Person: Paul Corser, Program Officer.   **Officers or Principals:** Ellen Cooper, M.D., M.P.H., Vice President ($146,667); Jerome Radwin, Senior Vice President ($133,333); Rico E. Viray, Program Development ($103,334); Peter Minichiello, Vice President ($100,000); Elizabeth Taylor, Founding National Chairman; Mathilde Krim, Ph.D., Chairman; Mervin F. Silverman, M.D., M.P.H., President; Wallace Sheft, C.P.A., Treasurer; Rt. Rev. William E. Swing, Secretary.
Mission or Interest: "To identify unmet needs in the fight against HIV/AIDS and to act as a catalyst in initiating, promoting and funding deserving projects in HIV/AIDS-related basic biomedical and clinical research, as well as psychosocial research, community-based clinical testing of potential treatments for HIV/AIDS, education for HIV/AIDS prevention, and the development of sound HIV/AIDS-related public policy. AmFAR acts as a major source of up-to-date and objective information on the HIV/AIDS pandemic and its impact on society and seeks to educate this country and the international community about issues of AIDS prevention treatment, and public policy, stressing the global nature of the epidemic and the threat it represents to all people."
Accomplishments: In the fiscal year ending June 1994, the Foundation spent $18,268,670 on its programs. $9,708,937 of this is distributed in grants to other organizations. The majority of these grants go to medical institutions for research and treatment, and to community-based treatment centers such as Gay Men's Health Crisis. Some of theses grants go to public policy organizations, these included: $100,000 for the Foundation for Human Understanding, $80,350 for the Coalition for Immigrant and Refugee Rights, $35,000 for the Black Leadership Coalition on AIDS, $34,691 for the Alan Guttmacher Institute, $25,000 for the American Association of Physicians for Human Rights, $26,531 for Rural Empowerment Research, $16,357 for the Drug Policy Foundation, $15,000 for the ACLU Foundation, $12,472 for the North Carolina Lesbian and Gay Health Project, $10,000 for Youthwave, $8,750 for the Research Foundation for Mental Hygiene, $6,158 for the Physicians Forum for Family Planning, $5,167 for the Women's Project, $5,000 for the American Civil Liberties Union, $5,000 for the Center for Policy Studies, $4,991 for the Hetrick-Martin Institute, $4,982 for the National Conference of State Legislatures, $4,259 for the Pink Triangle Foundation, and $2,500 for the Center for Urban Action.
Net Revenue: FY ending 6/94 $22,692,952 **Net Expenses:** $25,468,829 72%/5%/23% **Net Assets:** $809,175
Citations: 298:57
Products or Services: Grants, educational information, and lobbying. The Foundation spent $107,866 on lobbying, $27,957 on grassroots lobbying and $79,909 on the direct lobbying of legislators. This was down 46% from the previous year.
Tax Status: 501(c)(3)
Board of Directors or Trustees: Arlen Andelson, John Breglio, Robert Burkett, Jonathan Canno, Kenneth Cole, Mrs. Michael Eisner, Harvey Fineberg, M.D., Ph.D., Michael Fuchs, Jerome Groopman, M.D., Robert Guillaume, Beatrix Hamburg, M.D., James Hormel, Arnold Klein, M.D., Jay Levy, M.D., Jonathan Mann, M.D., M.P.H., Maurice Marciano, Kenneth Mayer, M.D., Lincoln Moses, Ph.D., Declan Murphy, Jane Nathanson, Thomas Stoddard, Nathaniel Ward Stout, Rosemary Tomich.
Other Information: AmFAR was founded by the merger of the AIDS Medical Foundation and the National AIDS Research Foundation. AmFAR hired the Los Angeles firm Whitney Associates for fundraising, and the San Francisco firm Mervyn Silverman & Associates for consulting. The two firms were paid $263,633 and $173,850 respectively. The Foundation received $16,877,135, or 74% of total revenue, from gifts and grants awarded by foundation, businesses, and individuals. (These grants included $50,000 from the F.M. Kirby Foundation.) $5,615,403 net, or 25%, from special fund raising events. The remaining revenue came from interest on savings and temporary cash investments, rental income, and other miscellaneous sources. The Foundation lost $11,068 on the sale of assets.

American Friends Service Committee (AFSC)

1501 Cherry St.
Philadelphia, PA 19102   **Phone:**   (215) 241-7000   **E-Mail:** LLove@afsc.org
USA   **Fax:**   (215) 864-0104

Mission or Interest: "A Quaker organization supported by individuals of different faiths who care about social justice, humanitarian service, and peace. Its work is based on a Quaker belief in the dignity and worth of every person, and faith in the power of love and nonviolence to bring about change." Concerns include: Ant-militarism and non-violence, homosexual and lesbian rights with an emphasis on youth, community building, prisoners rights, hunger and homelessness, economic justice, and the environment.
Accomplishments: AFSC operates 104 programs domestically and worldwide.
Products or Services: Hear Our Voices: A Resource Directory of Immigrant & Refugee Women's Projects.
Citations: 414:46   **Tax Status:** 501(c)(3)
Other Information: In 1993 the Committee received $10,000 from the Town Creek Foundation. In 1994 the Committee received $50,250 from the Ruth Mott Fund, $25,000 from the Joyce Mertz-Gilmore Foundation, $21,000 from the Haymarket People's Fund, $16,919 from the Tides Foundation, $6,500 from the Abelard Foundation, $6,000 from the South Coast Foundation, $650 from the Vanguard Public Foundation, and $600 from the Compton Foundation.

American Humanist Association (AHA) / *The Humanist*

7 Harwood Drive
P.O. Box 1188
Amherst, NY 14266   **Phone:**   (716) 839-5080
USA   **Fax:**   (716) 839-5079

Contact Person: Ed Doerr, President.   **Officers or Principals:** Frederick Edwards, Managing Editor; Valerie White, Senior Editor.

Mission or Interest: Leftist organization that "applies humanism - a naturalistic and democratic outlook informed by science, inspired by art, and motivated by compassion - to broad areas of social and personal concern." Secular and anti-religious the Association focuses on calling attention to the activities of the Religious Right. Publishes *The Humanist*.

Accomplishments: Founded in 1941. *The Humanist* has featured contributors that included: Dan Rather, Betty Friedan, Noam Chomsky, Faye Wattleton and Kurt Vonnegut. Science fiction author Isaac Asimov was president of the Association until his death in 1992. The Association presents annual Humanist Awards. 1996 winners included film-maker Oliver Stone, biologist Richard Dawkins (author of The Selfish Gene), Riane Eisler, Martha Hardman, Annette van Howe. The AHA is a affiliated with the ACLU and is a Nongovernmental Organization of the United Nations.

Products or Services: Books, pamphlets, speakers bureau, video and audio tapes. *Humanism: Making Bigger Circles*, a film narrated by Isaac Asimov.

Board of Directors or Trustees: *The Humanist*'s editorial board includes: Andre Bacard, Joseph Barnhart, H.J. Blackham, Bette Chambers, Beverly Earles, Albert Ellis, Edward Ericson, James Farmer, Betty Friedan, Edna Ruth Johnson, Marty Klein, Marvin Kohl, Jean Kotkin, Gerald Larue, Lester Mondale, Lloyd Morain, Mary Morain, Maxine Negri, Suzanne Paul, Howard Radest, James Randi, Ward Tabler.

Periodicals: *The Humanist* (bimonthly magazine).

Other Information: The AHA is a successor to the Humanist Press Association established in 1935, which was in turn a successor to the Humanist Fellowship organized at the University of Chicago in 1927.

American Indian Law Center

P.O. Box 4456
Albuquerque, NM 87196   **Phone:**   (505) 277-5462
USA

Contact Person: Philip S. Deloria, Executive Director.

Officers or Principals: Philip S. Deloria, Executive Director ($61,790); Toby F. Grossman, Staff Attorney ($59,875); Heidi Estes, Staff Attorney ($37,171); Nancy Tuthill, Secretary/Treasurer; Robert Lewis, Executive Officer.

Mission or Interest: Prepare American-Indian students for law school and "to strengthen Indian tribal governments by focusing on the needs of Indian communities and tribal governments and providing broad-based services to tribes and other governments."

Accomplishments: In the fiscal year ending June 1994, the Center spent $337,681 on its programs. $263,783 spent on a pre-law school summer institute that serves up to 30 students.

Net Revenue: FY ending 6/94 $473,016 ($288,593, or 61%, from government grants) **Net Expenses:** $469,355 72%/28%/0%

Net Assets: (-$78,715) **Citations:** 6:210

Tax Status: 501(c)(3)

Other Information: The Center received $288,593, or 61% of revenue, from government grants. $78,330, or 17%, from reimbursed program expenses. $52,239, or 11%, from a forgiven rental debt. $40,823, or 9%, from a private grant. $11,200, or 2%, from gifts and grants awarded by foundations, companies and individuals. The remaining revenue came from interest on savings and other temporary cash investments, sale of publications, and other miscellaneous sources.

American Institute for Free Labor Development

1925 K St., N.W., Suite 400
Washington, DC 20006   **Phone:**   (202) 659-6300
USA   **Fax:**   (202) 872-0618

Contact Person: Jesse A. Friedman, Deputy Executive Director.

Officers or Principals: William C. Doherty, Executive Director ($140,358); Jesse A. Friedman, Deputy Executive Director ($115,529); Michael A. Donovan, Regional Director ($110,506); Michael F. Verdu, Country Program Director ($100,454); David Jessup, Director of Human Rights; Kevin F. Shaver, Director of Finance and Administration; Lane Kirkland, President; Thomas Donahue, Secretary/Treasurer; Albert Shanker, Vice President.

Mission or Interest: "Development of Latin American (and Caribbean) trade union organizations along the lines of enlightened and responsible trade union leadership." Conducts trade union development in Latin America through joint projects with the AFL-CIO and the U.S. Government. During the Cold War the Institute was known as a staunch opponent of Communist unions abroad.

Accomplishments: In 1994 the Institute spent $9,081,771 on its programs. These programs included approximately 1,300 seminars and the training of approximately 32,000 students.

Net Revenue: 1994 $12,127,349 ($10,385,431, or 86%, from government grants and cooperative agreements)

Net Expenses: $12,136,623 75%/25%/0% **Net Assets:** $1,025,694

Tax Status: 501(c)(3)

Board of Directors or Trustees: Morton Bahr (Communication Workers of America), Owen Bieber (UAW), William Bywater (Intl. Union of Electrical Workers), Linda Chavez-Thompson (AFL-CIO), Douglas Dority (United Food and Commercial Workers Intl. Union), Robert Georgine (AFL-CIO), Charles Gray (AFL-CIO), James Hatfield (Glass, Molders, Pottery, Plastics and Allied Workers Intl. Union), Gloria Johnson (Coalition of Labor Union Women), John Joyce (Intl. Union of Bricklayers), Jay Mazur (Intl. Ladies' Garment Workers Union), John Sturdivant (American Federation of Government Employees), John Sweeney (Service Employees Intl. Union).

Other Information: The Institute received $10,385,431, or 86% of revenue, from "grants and cooperative agreement" with the U.S. Government. $1,235,539, or 10%, from "grants with the Free Trade Institute." $250,293, or 2%, from the AFL-CIO. $220,724, or 2%, from other grants. The remaining revenue came from interest on savings and temporary cash investments.

American Library Association (ALA)

50 E. Huron St.
Chicago, IL 60611
USA

Phone: (312) 944-6780
Fax: (312) 440-0901

Contact Person: Peggy Sullivan, Executive Director.
Officers or Principals: Peggy Sullivan, Executive Director ($113,167); Ernest Martin, Associate Executive Director ($96,128); Margaret Barber, Associate Executive Director ($94,769); Betty Turock, President; Ann Symons, Treasurer.
Mission or Interest: "The American Library Association is a charitable and educational institution organized for the purpose of serving libraries and librarianship. Its programs include publishing of books, periodicals, pamphlets, and graphic arts materials designed to assist librarians, libraries, and other information service organizations to effectively serve the general public and specialized users." Committed to openness and diversity. Opposed to any form of censorship. The Association has various membership divisions, two of the most recently formed being the ALA Black Caucus and the Gay and Lesbian Task Force.
Accomplishments: In the fiscal year ending August 1994, the ALA spent $23,108,290 on its programs. The largest program, with expenditures of $13,260,107, was general activities. This included general programs, conferences, and publications. $6,433,717 was spent on divisional activities. The ALA awarded $119,686 in grants to other organizations and individuals.
Net Revenue: FY ending 8/94 $26,923,167   **Net Expenses:** $27,029,582   85%/15%/0%   **Net Assets:** $11,466,566
Citations: 978:23
Products or Services: Publications, videos, conferences, technical information, and lobbying. The ALA spent $46,038 on the direct lobbying of legislators. This was down 2% from the previous year. The ALA lobbies against censorship and perceived restrictions, and on behalf of increased funding for libraries.
Tax Status: 501(c)(3)
Board of Directors or Trustees: Betty Blackman, Nancy Bolt, Cesar Caballero, Bruce Daniels, Charles Beard, Mary Somerville, Nancy Kranich, Evie Wilson-Lingbloom.
Periodicals: *American Libraries* (monthly magazine), and *Booklist* (bimonthly magazine).
Other Information: The ALA received $5,484,437, or 20% of total revenue, from conference fees. $5,336,378, or 19%, from membership dues. $4,265,384, or 15%, from magazine subscriptions. $3,671,822, or 13%, from advertising revenue. $3,068,315, or 11%, from the sale of books. $1,752,482, or 7%, from government grants. $1,563,836, or 6%, from gifts and grants awarded by foundations, businesses, and individuals. $1,319,198, or 5%, from graphics and videos. $510,085, or 2%, from dividends and interest from securities. $402,366 net, or 1%, from capital gains on the sale of securities. The remaining revenue came from rental income and other miscellaneous sources. The ALA realized a loss of $734,665 on investments.

American Medical Student Association (AMSA)

1902 Association Dr.
Reston, VA 22091
USA

Phone: (703) 620-6600
Fax: (703) 620-5873

E-Mail: amsapr@aol.com
Web-Page: http://medamsa.bu.edu/

Contact Person: Shawn Taylor Zelman, Director of Public Relations.   **Officers or Principals:** Paul R. Wright, Executive Director ($93,350); Lydia Vaias, M.D., President; Andrew Nowalk, Vice President; Denise DeNoble, Treasurer.
Mission or Interest: "AMSA is committed to improving health care and healthcare delivery to all people, promoting active improvement in medical education, involving its members in social, moral and ethical obligations of the profession of medicine, assisting in the improvements and understanding of world health problems, contributing to the welfare of medical students, interns, residents, and post MD/DO trainees, and advancing the profession of medicine...When you join AMSA, you become part of a vital force of future physicians who believe that health professionals and patients are partners in the management of health, and that access to high-quality health care is a right and not a privilege. At AMSA, activism is a way of life. Student idealism is transformed into meaningful public services, innovation and institutional change." The Association has various task forces and standing committees that contribute to the work of AMSA. These include Aging, AIDS, Bioethics, Health Through Peace, Humanistic Medicine, Legislative Action, Lesbian, Gay & Bisexual People in Medicine, Minority Affairs, and Women in Medicine. AMSA joined Handgun Control's "Campaign to Protect Sane Gun Laws." Opposed to reducing public funds for abortion and family planning, supports fetal tissue research, supports guidelines that require medical schools to offer abortion training to OB/GYN students, and opposed to the ban on late term D&X, 'partial birth' abortions. Supports affirmative action.
Accomplishments: Founded in 1950. More than 150 local chapters.
Net Revenue: FY ending 4/94 $2,720,523   **Net Expenses:** $2,205,038   **Net Assets:** $1,427,435
Products or Services: Programs, publications, benefits, educational materials, and more for medical students.
Tax Status: 501(c)(6)   **Annual Report:** Yes.   **Employees:** 35
Board of Directors or Trustees: Jeff Brown, M.D., Helen Burstin, M.D., M.P.H., Pierre Rouzier, M.D.
Periodicals: *New Physician* (monthly magazine), *Task Force Quarterly* (quarterly magazine).
Internships: Yes, including State Health Policy Fellowship Programs and Washington Health Policy Fellowship Programs.
Other Information: AMSA president Lydia Vaias, M.D., warns, "Shift to the 1992 Republican Convention. Pat Buchanan is given high-visibility air time to advertise his hate-filled vision of 'family values' for America...presidential candidate Phil Gramm introduces legislation to do away with affirmative action because it gives minorities and women preference over more qualified white males...physicians David Gunn and John Britton are killed by pro-life advocates because they perform abortions...The political, economic and social conditions that allowed the insidious rise of the Nazi party exist in American society today. The flag-waving nationalism and political maneuvering exhibited today by the extreme right is chillingly familiar." The Association is affiliated with the 501(c)(3) American Medical Student Association Foundation. The two affiliates had combined net revenues of $4,561,729, net expenses of $4,615,049, and net assets of $2,048,567. Paul Wright served as executive director of both and was paid a combined $155,584. AMSA received $1,560,994, or 57% of revenue, from royalties. $425,780, or 16%, from advertising. $300,743, or 11%, from membership dues. $222,370, or 8%, from conventions, exhibits, etc. $69,072, or 3%, from gifts and grants awarded by foundations, businesses, and individuals. The remaining revenue came from rental income, publication sales, subscriptions, interest on savings and temporary cash investments, and other miscellaneous sources.

American Medical Student Association Foundation

1902 Association Dr.
Reston, VA 22091
USA

Phone: (703) 620-6600
Fax: (703) 620-5873

E-Mail: amsapr@aol.com
Web-Page: http://medamsa.bu.edu/

Contact Person: Paul R. Wright, Executive Director.   **Officers or Principals:** Paul R. Wright, Executive Director ($62,234); K. Westpheling, Director, Health Promotion and Disease Protection ($54,129); J. Hedgecock, Associate Director, Program Development ($44,944); Valerie E. Stone, M.D., M.P.H., President.

Mission or Interest: Research and education affiliate of the American Medical Student Association. Provides services for medical students and promotes medical care for under-served populations.

Accomplishments: In the fiscal year ending April 1994 the Foundation spent $2,410,011 on its programs. The largest program, with expenditures of $1,529,996, was the Health Promotion and Disease Prevention Program designed to "interest students in medical practices in the inner city and rural communities." Other programs encouraged interest in medical practices in Africa, promoted community awareness about alcohol and substance abuse, the well-being of medical students with a focus on alcohol and drug abuse prevention, health care public policy and more. Stipends are paid to students who participate in these programs.

Net Revenue: FY ending 4/94 $2,563,803 ($2,160,872, or 84%, from government grants)
Net Expenses: $2,410,011 80%/20%/0% **Net Assets:** $621,132 **Citations:** 10:198
Tax Status: 501(c)(3)
Board of Directors or Trustees: Helen Burstin M.D., M.P.H., Jeff Brown, M.D., Pierre Rouzier, M.D.
Other Information: The Association is affiliated with the 501(c)(6) American Medical Student Association. The two affiliates had combined net revenues of $4,561,729, net expenses of $4,615,049, and net assets of $2,048,567. Paul Wright served as executive director of both and was paid a combined $155,584. The Foundation received $2,160,872, or 84% of revenue, from government grants. $280,038, or 11%, from gifts and grants awarded by foundations, businesses, and individuals. $69,049, or 3%, from royalties. $17,069, or 1%, from interest on savings and temporary cash investments. The remaining revenue came from membership dues and other miscellaneous sources.

American Postal Workers Union

1300 L St., N.W.
Washington, DC 20005
USA

Phone: (202) 842-4215

Contact Person: Morris Biller, President.   **Officers or Principals:** William Burrus, Executive Vice President ($123,249); Douglas C. Holbrook, Secretary/Treasurer ($123,249); Robert Tunstall, Clerk Division Director ($120,514); Morris Biller, President ($114,502); Roy Braunstein, Legislation Director ($119,830); James McCarthy, Clerk Division Assistant Director ($113,533); Frank Romero, Organization Director ($113,127); James Lingberg, Maintenance Division Director ($112,672); Cliff Guffey, Assistant Director, Clerk Division ($112,235); Mike Reid, Legislative Aid ($112,099); Joyce Robinson, Research and Education Director ($109,223); Malcolm T. Smith, National Representative ($105,821); Edgar Williams, Maintenance Division Assistant Director ($104,714); Randle Sutton, Maintenance Division Assistant Director ($104,714); Sidney Brooks, Human Relations Director ($104,511); Donald Ross, Motor Vehicle Division Director ($104,511); George McKeithen, Special Delivery Messenger Division Director ($104,511); Thomas Thompson, Clerk Division Assistant Director ($104,511).

Mission or Interest: Union representing 330,000 workers for the U.S. Postal Service. Member of the AFL-CIO. Monitors and lobbies on behalf of legislation affecting their workers. Educational activities.

Accomplishments: In 1994 the Union spent $40,207,192 on its activities. $14,258,184, or 35% of expenditures, went to salaries, wages, pension plans and other benefits for union officials. The Union spent only $2,000 or less on in-house lobbying activities.

Net Revenue: 1994 $38,585,340 **Net Expenses:** $40,207,192 **Net Assets:** $20,795,966
Tax Status: 501(c)(5)
Other Information: The Union received $34,487,310, or 89% of revenue, from membership dues. $2,420,779, or 6%, from health plan service fees. $1,007,826, or 3%, from interest on savings and temporary cash investments. The remaining revenue came from publication sales and subscriptions, rental income, royalties, health plan reimbursements, and other miscellaneous sources.

American Public Welfare Association

810 First St., N.W.
Washington, DC 20002-4205
USA

Phone: (202) 682-0100

Contact Person: A. Sidney Johnson, Executive Director. **Officers or Principals:** A. Sidney Johnson, Executive Director ($162,424); Linda Wolf, Associate Executive Director ($122,467); Beverly Vanich, Project Manager ($99,913).

Mission or Interest: "The Association contracts to manage research and demonstration projects for federal and state governments, and private foundations."

Accomplishments: In 1993 the Association spent $2,873,900 on its programs. Most, $2,748,436, was spent on research and demonstration projects. The remainder was spent on "Welfare Professional Membership Services," such as publications and conferences for individual and state and local agency members.

Net Revenue: 1993 $3,557,773 ($273,381, or 8%, from government grants) **Net Expenses:** $3,474,287
Net Assets: $1,682,277 **Citations:** 72:120
Tax Status: 501(c)(3)

Other Information: The Association received $1,484,280, or 42% of revenue, from membership dues. $1,232,712, or 35%, from gifts and grants awarded by foundations, businesses, and individuals. $383,791, or 11%, from the sale of publications. $273,381 or 8%, from government grants. (In the year between July 1993 and June 1994, the Association received $350,000 in grants from the U.S. Department of Health and Human Services.) $117,422, or 3%, from conferences. The remaining revenue came from interest on savings and temporary cash investments, advertising, sale and rental of mailing list labels, and other miscellaneous sources. Net revenue was reduced by a loss of $31,653 on the sale of assets other than inventory.

American Solar Energy Society (ASES)

2400 Central Ave., Unit G-1
Boulder, CO 80301   **Phone:** (303) 443-3130   **E-Mail:** beckych@csn.net
USA   **Fax:**   (303) 443-3212 **Web-Page:** http://www.engr.wisc.edu/centers/sel/ases/ases2.ktml

Contact Person: Larry Shirley, Chair.   **Officers or Principals:** Ingrid Melody, Secretary; Rebecca Vories, Treasurer.
Mission or Interest: "Formed in 1954 as a nonprofit organization to provide a forum for scientific exchange in the field of solar energy."
Accomplishments: Accredited as a Non-Governmental Organization with the United Nations Economic and Social Committee. More than 4,000 members in more than 105 countries worldwide.
Tax Status: 501(c)(3) **Employees:** 5
Board of Directors or Trustees: Donald Aitken, Christine Donovan, Helen English, Yogi Goswami, Mark Kelley III, Frank Kreith, Susan Luster, Vicki Mastaitis, Fred Morse, Joan Ogden, Donald Osborn, Sharon Stine, Mary Tucker, Carl Weinberg.
Periodicals: *Solar Energy* (journal), *SunWorld* (quarterly magazine), *ISES News* (semiannual newsletter), *Solar Today* (bimonthly magazine).
Internships: No.
Other Information: ASES's 1996 annual conference was sponsored by the U.S. Department of Energy.

American-Arab Anti-Discrimination Committee (ADC)

4201 Connecticut Ave., N.W., Suite 500
Washington, DC 20008   **Phone:** (202) 244-2990   **E-Mail:** adc@adc.org
USA   **Fax:**   (202) 244-3196

Contact Person: Ghada Khouri, Editor.   **Officers or Principals:** Hamzi Moghrabi, Chairman; Abdeen Jabara, Vice Chairman; Dr. Safa Rifka, Treasurer/Secretary; Albert Mokhiber, President.
Mission or Interest: "Civil rights organization dedicated to fighting anti-Arab discrimination, stereotyping and defamation."
Accomplishments: In 1993 the ADC persuaded Disney to change the lyrics of a song in the movie "Aladdin" for its video release. Conducted a "sensitivity seminar" for CBS news executives. ADC's president was interviewed in *Z Magazine*. The ADC's 1993 national convention featured keynote speakers Secretary of State Warren Christopher, Senator George McGovern, and Haitian President Jean-Bertrande Aristide. 60 Minutes' Mike Wallace moderated a "Media Criticism Panel" which included *Rolling Stone's* William Greider, and Saul Landau of the Institute for Policy Studies. The ADC, in cooperation with eleven other civil rights groups (Coalition Against Police Abuse, National Lawyers Guild, Committee in Solidarity with the People of El Salvador, International Jewish Peace Union, American Indian Movement, National Association of Arab Americans, National Conference of Black Lawyers, Palestine Solidarity Committee, Association of Arab-American University Graduates, and the Bay Area Anti-Apartheid Network), filed a civil rights lawsuit against the Anti Defamation League of B'nai B'rith. The ADC alleged that the Anti-Defamation League engaged in an "illegal, nationwide spy operation...(that) focused on Arab-Americans, anti-apartheid activists and others." The ADC et al charged the Anti-Defamation League with paying for confidential police information, going through the plaintiffs' trash, and infiltrating the plaintiffs' organizations in conjunction with "its spying activity." Police raided the Anti-Defamation League's San Francisco and Los Angeles offices and seized documents and evidence. The League settled criminal allegations "by agreeing to pay a $75,000 fine to the city of San Francisco." The civil lawsuit is still not resolved.
Tax Status: 501(c)(4) **Annual Report:** Yes.
Board of Directors or Trustees: Terry Ahwal, Naila Asali, Naim Assed, Halim Awde, Naim Ayoub, Cheryl Faris, Dr. Farouk Hamouda, Hamzi Moghrabi, Dr. Adnan Mourany, Norma Odeh, Smar Sakakini, Harold Samhat, Dr. Suad Shuber, Dr. George Younan. The National Advisory Committee included: Rep. John Conyers (D-MI), Rep. Patricia Danner (D-MO), Rep. Nick Joe Rahall (D-WV), Muhammad Ali, Hon. Toney Anaya, Hon. George Bashara, Noam Chomsky, Hon. Ramsey Clark (U.S. Attorney General, 1967-69), Hon. George Crockett, Archbishop John Elya, Hon. Paul Findley, Casey Kasem, Hon. Paul McCloskey Jr., Hon. Herb Mocol, Hon. Mary Rose Oakar, Archbishop Philip Saliba.
Periodicals: *ADC Times* (monthly newsletter).
Internships: Yes.
Other Information: The ADC has regional offices in Jordan, and Detroit, MI: 220 Bagley, Michigan Bldg., Suite 502, Detroit, MI 48226, (313) 965-7680.

Americans for Democratic Action (ADA)

1625 K St., N.W., Suite 210
Washington, DC 20005   **Phone:** (202) 785-5980
USA

Contact Person: Amy Isaacs, Director.   **Officers or Principals:** Amy Isaacs, Director ($56,227); Sen. Paul Wellstone, President ($0); Bill Markus, Treasurer ($0); Roberta Weiner, Secretary; Winn Newman, Counsel.

Mission or Interest: Research, education, and lobbying organization that provides services, technical support, and information to members.
Accomplishments: The ADA is one of the oldest liberal advocacy organizations, operating since 1947. They are well-known for their ratings of elected officials based on voting records. These ADA ratings are widely used, and are frequently used in conjunction with the American Conservative Union's ACU ratings. In 1993 the ADA spent $408,314 on its programs.
Net Revenue: 1993 $625,640 **Net Expenses:** $670,827 61%/39%/0% **Net Assets:** $670,827 **Citations:** 216:77
Products or Services: Seminars, technical support, lobbying, more.
Tax Status: 501(c)(4)
Board of Directors or Trustees: Michael Peil, Dan Press, Henry Berger, Rep. John Lewis (D-GA), Margie Bernard, Dean Levitan, Joanne Rising.
Periodicals: *ADA Today* (quarterly journal).
Other Information: The ADA received $261,323, or 42% of revenue, from membership dues. $165,735, or 26%, from gifts and grants awarded by foundations, businesses, and individuals. $92,131, or 15%, from event income. $29,127, or 5%, from banquet revenue. $24,272, or 4%, from expense reimbursements. $17,871, or 3%, from mailing list rentals. The remaining revenue came from subscriptions, convention registration, interest on savings and temporary cash investments, and other miscellaneous sources.

Americans for Peace Now

27 W. 20th St., 9th Floor
New York, NY 10011   **Phone:** (212) 645-6262
USA

Contact Person: Gary E. Rubin, Executive Director.   **Officers or Principals:** Linda Gaal Pressberg, Director of U.S. Operations ($53,934); Ahavia Scheindlin, National Director, Development and Planning ($51,000); Gail Pressberg, Director, Center for Israeli Peace and Security ($48,792); Richard Gunther, Linda Heller Kamm, Co-Presidents; Shifra Bronznick, Gerald Bubis, Co-Chairs; David A. Guberman, Treasurer; Michael Walzer, Secretary.
Mission or Interest: Organization pursuing peace in the Middle East with a focus on Israel.
Accomplishments: In 1993 Americans for Peace Now spent $1,012,697 on its programs. $339,521 was spent on approximately 260 educational meetings and forums. $220,060 was spent producing and distributing publications. $69,162 was spent on approximately 350 film, video, and slide show presentations. The organization awarded $383,954 in grants; $382,500 for the Peace Now Education Fund in Jerusalem, Israel, and $1,484 for For the Record.
Net Revenue: 1993 $1,588,874 **Net Expenses:** $1,342,480 75%/10%/15% **Net Assets:** $127,008 **Citations:** 66:127
Tax Status: 501(c)(3)
Board of Directors or Trustees: Elaine Attias, Richard Dreyfuss, Sara Ehrman, Laurel Eisner, Max Factor III, Nanette Falkenberg, Daniel Fleshler, Robert Freedman, Theodore Friedman, Florence Galkin, Rabbi Laura Geller, Alan Gleitsman, Rachel Golden, Rabbi Susan Harris, Kenneth Klothen, James Klutznick, Victor Kovner, Mark Kramer, Rabbi Joy Levitt, Daniel Mayers, Hava Mendelberg, Jo-Ann Mort, Letty Cottin Pogrebin, Rabbi Sanford Ragins, Esther Leah Ritz, Leonard Rogoff, Irwin Rosenblum, Max Samson, Renata Manasse Schwebel, Mark Seal, Rabbi Chaim Seidler-Feller, Sidney Shapiro, Stanley, Sheinbaum, Rabbi Joshua Stampfer, Albert Stern, Daniel Thursz, Philip Warburg, Rabbi Bruce Warshal, Peter Weiss, Edward Witten, Eliot Zashin.
Other Information: Americans for Peace Now received $1,588,853, or 100% of revenue, from gifts and grants awarded by foundations, businesses, and individuals. (These grants included $30,000 from the Hauser Foundation, $25,000 from the Naomi and Nehemiah Cohen Foundation, $6,000 from the Foundation for Middle East Peace, $5,300 from the Peace Development Fund, $1,500 from the Liberty Hill Foundation, $1,000 from the Norman Lear Foundation. 1994 grants included $50,000 from the Nathan Cummings Foundation, $35,000 from the Bydale Foundation.) The remaining revenue came from dividends and interest from securities.

Americans for Religious Liberty

P.O. Box 6656
Silver Springs, MD 20906   **Phone:** (301) 598-2447
USA

Contact Person: Ed Doerr, Executive Director.
Officers or Principals: Ed Doerr, Executive Director ($22,156); John M. Swomley, Jr., President.
Mission or Interest: Education and litigation to "Preserve the American tradition of religious, intellectual and personal freedom in a secular and democratic state."
Accomplishments: In 1993 the organization spent $118,918 on its activities.
Net Revenue: 1993 $150,860 **Net Expenses:** $119,018 **Net Assets:** $145,058
Tax Status: 501(c)(3)
Periodicals: *The Voice of Reason* (quarterly newsletter).
Other Information: The organization received $146,741, or 97% of revenue, from gifts and grants awarded by foundations, businesses, and individuals. $4,119, or 3%, from interest on savings and temporary cash investments.

Americans for the Environment (AFE)

1400 16th St., N.W.
Washington, DC 20036   **Phone:** (202) 797-6665
USA

Contact Person: Roy Morgan, Executive Director.   **Officers or Principals:** Roy Morgan, Executive Director ($51,038); Johannah Bary, Chair ($0); Connie Mahan, Treasurer ($0); Ron Tipton, Secretary.

Mission or Interest: An educational institute that "serves as the electoral skills training arm of the environmental community."
Accomplishments: In 1994 AFE spent $194,411 on its programs. These programs included training grassroots organizations in voter contact, volunteer organization, media targeting, get-out-the-vote activities, and fundraising.
Net Revenue: 1994 $221,579 **Net Expenses:** $242,202 80%/18%/2% **Net Assets:** (-$38,808)
Products or Services: Organizing and lobbying. AFE spent $3,000 on lobbying.
Tax Status: 501(c)(3)
Board of Directors or Trustees: Chuck Paquette (National Wildlife Federation), Dianne Russell (Inst. for Conservation Leadership), Thomas Atkins (Environmental Action Found.), Peter Coppelman (Greenfield Environmental), Peter Harnik (Rails-to-Trails Conservancy), Stella Koch (Audubon Naturalist Society), John McComb (World Conservation Monitoring Centre), Lisa Metcalfe (National Wildlife Federation), Beth Olderman (Vanguard Communications), Sumner Pingree (Global Environment Fund), Chuck Savitt (Island Press), Alice Walker (Concerned Citizens of Brentwood), Peter Williams (Washington Council of Agencies), Reid Wilson (Sierra Club).
Other Information: AFE received $218,978, or 98% of revenue, from gifts and grants awarded by foundations, businesses, and individuals. (These grants included $20,716 from the Environmental Federation of America.) $3,281, or 1%, from training and education fees. The remaining revenue came from interest on savings and cash investments. In 1994 AFE received $111,766 from the Environmental Federation of America, and $669 from the Environmental Federation of California.

Americans United for Separation of Church and State

1816 Jefferson Place, N.W.
Washington, DC 20036   **Phone:**   (202) 466-3234
USA   **Fax:**   (202) 466-2587

Contact Person: Barry Lynn, Executive Director.
Officers or Principals: Barry Lynn, Executive Director ($112,841); Susan Green, Associate Executive Director ($97,774); Rudolph Bush, Associate Executive Director ($70,826); Rev. Calvin Didier, President; Robert Lipshutz, Vice President; Bert Beach, Secretary; Donald Erickson, Treasurer; Steven Green, Legal Director; Joseph Conn, Editor; Kim Yelton, Legislative Director.
Mission or Interest: Advocating and fighting to maintain "the separation of church and state." Litigation in support of that goal. Opposed to the Religious Right's agenda.
Accomplishments: Founded in 1947, the organization currently "represents more than 52,000 individuals, as well as 3,000 cooperating churches and other religious bodies." Opposed school voucher programs where vouchers paid parochial school tuition. In the fiscal year ending September 1994, the organization spent $994,234 on its programs. The largest program, with expenditures of $464,625, was the production and distribution of publications and other educational materials. $223,525 was spent on Field Services that maintain contacts with government leaders and church officials nationwide and keep members alerted regarding proposed legislation. Legal expenses were $200,198.
Net Revenue: FY ending 9/94 $1,968,817 **Net Expenses:** $2,049,147 49%/26%/25% **Net Assets:** $4,409,838
Citations: 378:50
Products or Services: Litigation, publications and lobbying. Americans United spent $21,564 on lobbying, specifically on mailings to members, legislators, and the general public in the attempt to influence legislation.
Tax Status: 501(c)(3)
Board of Directors or Trustees: Dr. Bert Beach, T. Scott Bunton (Director of Legislation & Policy, Sen. John Kerry, D-MA), Elder Robert Dale, Dr. James Dunn (Exec. Dir., Baptist Joint Committee on Public Affairs), Donald Erickson, Dr. C. Welton Gaddy, Bruce Hunter (American Association of School Administers), Robert Lipshutz, Robert Nixon, Linda Rogers-Kingsbury, Edward Tabash, Thomas Upchurch (Pres., Georgia Partnership for Excellence in Education), Albert Walker, Sarah Weddington.
Periodicals: *Church and State* (monthly newsletter).
Other Information: Affiliated with the 501(c)(3) Americans United for Church and State Fund and Americans United Research Foundation. The Fund had receipts of $1,323. Americans United and the Foundation had combined net revenues of $2,151,144, net expenses of $2,136,356, and net assets of $6,041,927. Americans United for the Separation of Church and State received $1,598,507, or 81% of revenue, from gifts and grants awarded by foundations, businesses, and individuals. $211,745, or 11%, from dividends and interest from securities. $150,680, or 8%, from capital gains on the sale of securities. The remaining revenue came from miscellaneous sources. Net revenue was decreased by a loss from rental properties.

Americans United Research Foundation

1816 Jefferson Place, N.W.
Washington, DC 20036   **Phone:**   (202) 466-3234
USA   **Fax:**   (202) 466-2587

Contact Person: Dr. Jimmy R. Allen, President.   **Officers or Principals:** Dr. Roy Valentine, Vice President ($0); Rev. Calvin Didier, Secretary ($0); Dr. James Langley, Treasurer ($0); Elder Melvin Adams, Assistant Treasurer.
Mission or Interest: Research and education affiliate of Americans United for Separation of Church and State.
Accomplishments: In the fiscal year ending September 1994, the Foundation spent $50,000 on its programs.
Net Revenue: FY ending 9/94 $182,327 **Net Expenses:** $87,209 57%/43%/0% **Net Assets:** $1,632,089
Tax Status: 501(c)(3)
Other Information: Affiliated with the 501(c)(3) Americans United for Church and State Fund and the 501(c)(4) Americans United for Separation of Church and State. The Fund had receipts of $1,323. Americans United and the Foundation had combined net revenues of $2,151,144, net expenses of $2,136,356, and net assets of $6,041,927. The Foundation received $108,000, or 59% of revenue, from gifts and grants awarded by foundations, businesses, and individuals. $66,343, or 36%, from dividends and interest from securities. $7,509, or 4%, from capital gains on the sale of securities. The remaining revenue came from the sale of literature.

Amnesty International of the U.S.A. (AIUSA)
322 Eighth Ave.

New York, NY 10001-4808	**Phone:** (212) 807-8400
USA	**Fax:** (212) 627-1451

Contact Person: William F. Schulz, Executive Director.
Officers or Principals: John Healey ($279,178); Curtis Goering ($101,203); William Schulz, Executive Director ($72,848); Mary W. Gray, Chair; Alicia Partnoy, Vice Chair; Mort Winston, Treasurer; Judy Patterson, Secretary; Phil Villers, Ombudsperson.
Mission or Interest: "Providing assistance to and working toward the release of persons who, in violation of the provisions of the Universal Declaration of Human Rights, are imprisoned, detained, restricted or otherwise subjected to physical coercion or restriction by reasons of their political, religious or other conscientiously held beliefs or by reason of their ethnic origin, color, sex or language (provided that they have not used or advocated violence). Further, it supports and works for the right of fair and prompt trials for all political prisoners and an end to the use of torture and executions for all prisoners." Opposed to the death penalty in all cases.
Accomplishments: Amnesty's Freedom Writers campaign writes letters on behalf of political prisoners and has approximately 45,000 volunteer writers. Amnesty draws support from many on all sides of the political spectrum. In the fiscal year ending September 1994, Amnesty spent $15,658 on its programs.
Net Revenue: FY ending 9/94 $23,231,513 **Net Expenses:** $21,396,132 73%/9%/18% **Net Assets:** $5,908,889
Citations: 3,280:9
Products or Services: Publications, letter writing, organizing, and lobbying. AIUSA spent $64,256 on lobbying, $1,533 on grassroots lobbying and $62,723 on the direct lobbying of legislators.
Tax Status: 501(c)(3)
Board of Directors or Trustees: Kathi Anderson-Rivera, Enriqueta Bauer, Anita Bela Bohm, Glenn Church, Louisa Coan (Natl. Endowment for Democracy), Sandra Coliver (Article 19), Sandy Elster, Dave Flockhart, Rick Halperin, Ronald Hampton, Reza Jalali, Philip Kent (Turner Home Entertainment), Marianne Philbin (Chicago Foundation for Women), Miraan Sa, Nomgcobo Sangweni, Kim Marie Thorburn, Amy Voege, Heather Wiley.
Periodicals: *Amnesty Action* (bimonthly newspaper).
Other Information: Amnesty International U.S.A. is affiliated with the international body, Amnesty International, in London. The U.S. body awarded a grant of $5,109,554 for the international body. Also affiliated with the 501(c)(3) Concerts for Human Rights. Amnesty International U.S.A. used Public Interest Communications of Falls Church, VA for telemarketing fundraising. Public Interest Communications was compensated with $876,479. Cravers, Matthews, Smith of Falls Church, VA, was used for fundraising consulting and received $804,228. Public Interest Data of Falls Church, VA, was used for list maintenance service and received $311,445. Amnesty International U.S.A. received $22,676,581, or 98% of revenue from direct and indirect public support in the form of gifts and grants awarded by foundations, affiliates, businesses, and individuals. (These grants included $7,500 from the Tides Foundation, $7,500 from the Middle Passage Foundation, $5,000 from the Bydale Foundation, $2,500 from the Barbra Streisand Foundation,$1,000 from the Peace Development Fund, $1,000 from the New Prospect Foundation, $1,000 from the Compton Foundation, $1,100 from the Stewart R. Mott Charitable Trust, $1,000 from the Aaron and Martha Schecter Foundation, and $750 from the Vanguard Public Foundation.) $227,830, or 1%, from mailing list rentals. The remaining revenue came from literature sales, interest on savings and temporary cash investments, conference fees, and other miscellaneous sources.

Angelina Fund
186 Sachems Head Rd.
Guilford, CT 06437
USA

Contact Person: Samuel G. Wiener, Jr., President.
Officers or Principals: Sara M. Wiener, Director ($0); Richard Healy, Director ($0).
Mission or Interest: Grant-making foundation that funds a number of leftist organizations.
Accomplishments: In 1994 the Fund awarded $756,000 in grants. The recipients of the largest grants included $102,500 to the New World Foundation, $25,000 each to the American Civil Liberties Union Foundation, Labor Education Research Project, and the Vanguard Public Foundation, and $20,000 each to the Center for Media Education, Center for Public Integrity, Teamster Rank and File Education, Fairness and Accuracy in Reporting, Southerners for Economic Justice, and others.
Net Revenue: 1994 $313,301 **Net Expenses:** $792,319 **Net Assets:** $2,925,318
Tax Status: 501(c)(3)
Other Information: The Fund received $308,591, or 78% of total revenue, from capital gains on the sale of assets. $49,008, or 12%, from interest on savings and temporary cash investments. $37,124, or 9%, from dividends and interest from securities. The Foundation held $1,650,086, or 56% of assets, in corporate stock. $801,320, or 27%, in corporate bonds.

Animal People
P.O. Box 205

Shushan, NY 12873	**Phone:** (518) 854-9436	**E-Mail:** ANMLPEOPLE@aol.com
USA	**Fax:** (518) 854-9601	

Contact Person: Merritt Clifton, Editor.
Officers or Principals: Merritt Clifton, Editor ($12,000); Kim Bartlett, Publisher ($12,000); Patrice Greanville, Director.
Mission or Interest: "*Animal People* provides independent professional coverage of the entire field on animal protection, from animal control to zoological conservation. We have no alignment or affiliation with any advocacy group or ideology." Opposed to the use of animals for medical testing and hunting.

Accomplishments: "We've been first to expose many forms of animal abuse that subsequently became national causes, e.g. the treatment of horses in the production of Premarin. We are probably best known, however, for our annual resume of the budgets, assets, and salaries paid by the 50-60 leading national animal and habitat protection groups (as well as some of the leading opposition groups.)" Publishes financial information, including its own, and other measures of an organization's effectiveness. Has published information on animal rights groups making money from stock in companies that use animals for product safety testing. Writes on how to read direct mail, and find out which programs are worth supporting. Also publishes financial information on "opposition" groups-hunters organizations such as Ducks Unlimited and medical research groups such as Americans for Medical Progress. In 1994 *Animal People* spent $84,897 on its programs.
Net Expenses: 1994 $105,052 **Net Assets:** $14,593
Tax Status: 501(c)(3) **Employees:** 2
Periodicals: *Animal People* (monthly tabloid).
Other Information: Kim Bartlett and Merritt Clifton are wife and husband. "Our emphasis is on reporting, accuracy, and fair treatment of all. We don't just echo the claims of advocacy groups; rather, we look to see what's true."

Animal Rights Coalition
3255 Hennepin Ave., S., Suite 30
Minneapolis, MN 55408   **Phone:**   (612) 822-6161
USA   **Fax:**   (612) 822-0469

Contact Person: Heidi Greger, Ph.D., President.   **Officers or Principals:** Nicholas Atwood, Vice President.
Mission or Interest: "Dedicated to ending the suffering, abuse, and exploitation of non-human animals through education, activism, and intervention."
Accomplishments: "Initiated and won a lawsuit against the University of Minnesota to force disclosure of records pertaining to animal research...University Records Project to examine university records...Organized and won campaign to end 'dog labs' at the university."
Tax Status: 501(c)(3) **Annual Report:** Yes. **Employees:** All volunteer.
Periodicals: *Animal Rights Coalition News* (quarterly newsletter).

Animal Rights Foundation of Florida (ARFF)
P.O. Box 841154
Pembroke Pines, FL 33084   **Phone:** (954) 968-7622   **E-Mail:** ARFF MAIN@aol.com
USA   **Fax:**   (954) 979-6415   **Web-Page:** http://envirolink.org/arrs/index/html

Contact Person: Nanci Alexander, President.   **Officers or Principals:** Nan Vollbracht, Secretary Treasurer ($0); Caren Lesser, Vice President ($0); Laura Strickland, Newsletter Editor.
Mission or Interest: "To eliminate animal abuse and exploitation in all forms by educating the public with demonstrations, ads, speakers, and brochures."
Accomplishments: "ARFF assisted in the introduction of legislation in the state to ban the Youth Deer Hunt, to provide humane working conditions for carriage horses, to prohibit dogs from riding in the back of pickup trucks, to ban canned hunts...ARFF stopped the forced participation by local college students in animal dissection, stopped a condo association from poisoning raccoons, stopped the greased pig contest at the Martin County Fair, stopped a chicken plucking contest, stopped numerous live animal displays." Carried a banner saying "Liberate Lab Animals" at a demonstration at the University of Miami. Urged people to skip pet shops and buy animals from shelters. Held a candlelight vigil for greyhounds who died mysteriously at a kennel. In 1994 the Foundation spent $79,455 on its programs.
Net Revenue: 1994 $101,255 **Net Expenses:** $88,113 90%/8%/2% **Net Assets:** $167,333
Products or Services: Speakers, pamphlets on subjects such as Disney's treatment of animals, petting zoos, and lobbying. In 1994 the Foundation spent approximately $3,000 on lobbying.
Tax Status: 501(c)(3) **Annual Report:** Yes. **Employees:** 2
Board of Directors or Trustees: Board of Advisors included: Rep. Peter Deutsch (D-FL), Cathleen Anderson (City Commissioner, Hollywood, and Pres. Animal Birth Control), Stedman Carr D.V.M., Doris Day (Pres., Doris Day Animal League), Priscilla Feral (Friends of Animals), Jay Ferber D.V.M., Scott Fuerst, Alex Hershaft Ph.D. (Farm Animals Reform Movement), D. Paul Mack D.V.M., Cleveland Amory (Fund for Animals), Alex Pacheco (People for the Ethical Treatment of Animals), Barry Silver, Tom Regan (Culture and Animal Foundation).
Periodicals: *ARFF News* (bimonthly newsletter).
Internships: Yes.
Other Information: ARFF was established in 1989.

Animal Rights International (AIR)
P.O. Box 214, Planetarium Station
New York, NY 10024   **Phone:**   (212) 873-3674
USA

Contact Person: Henry Spira, President.
Officers or Principals: Henry Spira, President ($19,796); Sonia Corts, Vice President ($0); Linda Petrie, Secretary ($0).
Mission or Interest: Animal rights organization working to "phase out the use of animals in testing, education and research." Sees the largest abuse of animals occurring in the raising of animals for food. "Our ideal is a non-violent dinner table. Wouldn't we all rather stroll through apple orchards than stumble through slaughter-houses? We actively and urgently encourage the public to upgrade to a meatless diet for ethical reasons."

Accomplishments: Australian animal rights activist says of AIR president, Henry Spira, "probably you've been the most successful activist in the United States." Spira is well known for his tactical approach and many successes. We is willing to work with his opponents, and goes after partial solutions in the short term. Spira's actions convinced Revlon to stop animal testing. AIR's campaign against U.S. Department of Agriculture practices that require cattle imported from Mexico to be branded on the face resulted in, first a scaling back of the policy, then a reversal of it in 1994. In 1994 AIR spent $163,160 on its programs.
Net Revenue: 1994 $137,452 **Net Expenses:** $168,941 97%/2%/2% **Net Assets:** $168,941
Tax Status: 501(c)(3)
Board of Directors or Trustees: Palmer Wayne.
Periodicals: *Coordinator's Report* (quarterly newsletter).
Other Information: Animal Rights International received $136,294, or 99% of revenue, from direct and indirect public support in the form of gifts and grants awarded by foundations, affiliates, businesses, and individuals. $1,158, or 1%, from interest on savings and temporary cash investments.

Animal Rights Law Clinic
Rutgers University
15 Washington St.
Newark, NJ 07102   **Phone:** (201) 648-5989
USA   **Fax:** (201) 648-1249

Contact Person: Anna Charlton.   **Officers or Principals:** Dr. Gary Francione
Mission or Interest: Legal advocacy on behalf of animals' rights and animals' rights advocates.
Other Information: During the fiscal year ending July 1994, the Clinic received $71,100 from People for the Ethical Treatment of Animals.

Animal Rights Mobilization
P.O. Box 6989
Denver, CO 80206   **Phone:** (303) 388-7120
USA

Contact Person: Robin Duxbury, President.   **Officers or Principals:** Robin Duxbury, President ($28,500); Mary Robbins, Secretary/Treasurer ($1,857); Jim Mason, Vice President ($0); George Edwards.
Mission or Interest: To inform the public and eliminate animal exploitation and abuse.
Accomplishments: Launched an eight-month campaign against a proposed marine park in Denver to prevent the park from exhibiting captive dolphins. The marine park management changed its minds and said it would not include dolphins. The organization claims to be the only animal rights group to force a researcher to rescind her grant money from the National Institutes of Health that was to be used for animal experimentation. In 1993 the organization spent $47,281 on its programs.
Net Revenue: 1993 $135,391 **Net Expenses:** $97,859 48%/47%/5% **Net Assets:** $13,493
Products or Services: Publications and advocacy.
Tax Status: 501(c)(3) **Annual Report:** Yes. **Employees:** 2
Internships: Yes, in the fall.
Other Information: Formerly called Trans-Species Unlimited. The organization received $135,391, or 100% of revenue, from gifts and grants awarded by foundations, companies, and individuals.

Animal Rights Network / *The Animals' Agenda*
3201 Elliott St.
Baltimore, MD 21224   **Phone:** (410) 675-4566   **E-Mail:** 75543.331@compuserve.com
USA   **Fax:** (410) 675-0066   **Web-Page:** http://www.envirolink.org/arrs/aa/

Contact Person: Peter Gerard, President.   **Officers or Principals:** Peter Gerard, President; Kim W. Stallwood, Editor in Chief; Davy Davidson, Vice President; Gene Bauston, Secretary; Evelyn Kimber, Treasurer.
Mission or Interest: Animal rights organization and publisher of *The Animals' Agenda*.
Accomplishments: *The Animals' Agenda* is considered to be the leading journal of the animal rights movement.
Tax Status: 501(c)(3)
Board of Directors or Trustees: Pamelyn Ferdin, Len Mitchell, Simone Aviva Petterson, Ken Shapiro Ph.D. (Psychologists for the Ethical Treatment of Animals), Doug Stoll. Advisors include: Cleveland Amory (Fund for Animals), Batya Bauman (Feminists for Animal Rights), Rev. Prof. Andrew Linzey, Jim Mason (author, An Unnatural Order), Jim Motavalli (*E Magazine*), Belton Mouras (United Animal Nations - USA), Farley Mowat (author, Never Cry Wolf), Melanie Roberts (Sumerlee Found.), Pete Singer Ph.D. (author, Animal Liberation), Alice Walker (author, The Color Purple).
Periodicals: *The Animals' Agenda* (bimonthly magazine).

Animal Welfare Institute (AWI)
P.O. Box 3650
Washington, DC 20007   **Phone:** (202) 337-2332
USA

Contact Person: Cathy Liss, Executive Director.   **Officers or Principals:** Cathy Liss, Executive Director ($29,900); Christine Stevens, President ($0); Cynthia Wilson, Vice President ($0); Roger Stevens, Treasurer; Freeborn G. Jewett, Jr., Secretary.

Mission or Interest: "Promotes the welfare of all animals and seeks to reduce the sum total of pain and fear inflicted on animals by humans."

Accomplishments: In the fiscal year ending June 1994, the Institute spent $664,378 on its programs. Of that, $210,383 was spent on a special "Save the Whales" program. The Institute awarded $64,105 in grants to other organizations. The largest grant, $55,000, went to the Environmental Investigation Agency. Other recipients included The Netherlands Greenpeace, People for the Ethical Treatment of Animals, and Earth Island Institute.

Net Revenue: FY ending 6/94 $692,158 **Net Expenses:** $711,334 85%/12%/3% **Net Assets:** $544,821 **Citations:** 8:207

Tax Status: 501(c)(3)

Board of Directors or Trustees: Madeline Bemelmans, David Hill, Ailgen Train, Jean Wallace Douglas.

Other Information: The Institute is affiliated with the Society for Animal Protective Legislation. The Institute received $607,804, or 88% of revenue, from gifts and grants awarded by foundations, businesses, and individuals. (These grants included $5,000 from the Wallace Genetic Foundation. In 1995 they included $19,106 from the Tides Foundation.) $31,450, or 5%, from interest on savings and temporary cash investments. $21,493, or 3%, from membership dues. $20,664 net, or 3%, from capital gains on the sale of securities. $6,767, or 1%, from dividends and interest from securities. The remaining revenue came from the sale of inventory, and other miscellaneous sources.

Animals' Agenda
(see the Animal Rights Network)

Anti Defamation League Foundation (ADL)
823 United Nations Plaza
New York, NY 10017   **Phone:** (212) 490-2525
USA   **Fax:**   (212) 867-0779

Contact Person: Naomi A. Lax, Associate Director, Endowments and Planned Giving.

Officers or Principals: Daniel E. Weinberg, Director, Endowments and Giving ($86,706); Stanlee Stahl ($67,375); Izhak Weintraub ($62,122); Burton Levinson, President; Melvin Salberg, Executive Vice President; Maxwell E. Greenberg, Secretary; Robert H. Naftaly, Treasurer; Arnold Forster, General Counsel.

Mission or Interest: Assists the Anti Defamation League of B'nai B'rith in its objectives and encourages and administers endowments and other gifts. "The organization leases property, loans money and extends credit to the Anti Defamation League of B'nai B'rith."

Accomplishments: In the fiscal year ending June 1994, the Foundation spent $1,692,376 on its programs. It also distributed $3,594,689 to its affiliates.

Net Revenue: FY ending 6/94 $2,665,478 **Net Expenses:** $6,957,338 24%/20%/4% **Net Assets:** $14,587,744

Citations: 2,246:9   **Tax Status:** 501(c)(3)

Board of Directors or Trustees: Barbara Balser, Tommy Baer, Howard Berkowitz, Kenneth Bialkin, Meyer Eisenberg, Thomas Homburger, Charles Kriser, Douglas Krupp, Glen Lewy, Allan Margolis, I. Barry Mehler, George Moss, Alvin Rockoff, Milton Schneider, George Stark, Gerald Stempler, Robert Sugarman, Glen Tobias.

Other Information: Affiliated with the 501(c)(3) Anti-Defamation League of B'nai B'rith at the same address. The two affiliates had combined net revenues of $38,608,134, net expenses of $42,383,465, and net assets of $15,414,742. The Foundation received $2,556,209, or 78% of total revenue, from gifts and grants awarded by foundations, businesses, and individuals. $635,401, or 19%, from dividends and interest from securities. $59,978, or 2%, from capital gains on the sale of securities. $37,214, or 1%, from interest on savings and temporary cash investments. The Foundation lost $623,324 on properties rented to affiliates.

Anti Defamation League of B'nai B'rith (ADL)
823 United Nations Plaza
New York, NY 10017   **Phone:** (212) 490-2525
USA   **Fax:**   (212) 867-0779

Contact Person: Mark D. Medin, Assistant to the National Director.   **Officers or Principals:** Abraham H. Foxman, National Director ($200,000); Stuart Tauber, Development ($160,000); Peter T. Willner, Chief Operating Officer ($125,000); Bobbie Arbesfeld, Finance and Administration ($105,000); Jess N. Hordes, Washington Representatives ($105,000); Jeffrey P. Sinensky, Civil Rights ($104,000); Kenneth Jacobson, Program and International Affairs ($103,000); Ann Tourk, Community Service ($100,000); Mark A. Feldman, Marketing and Communications ($100,000); David H. Strassler, National Chair; Howard P. Berkowitz, Chair, National Executive Committee; Robert H. Naftaly, Treasurer; Irving Shapiro, Secretary.

Mission or Interest: "The Anti-Defamation League of B'nai B'rith is a nonprofit organization formed in 1913 for the purpose of defending democratic ideals and eliminating anti-Semitism and bigotry around the world, while providing knowledgeable leadership for the American Jewish Community on a national level."

Accomplishments: The ADL recently released publications about the 'Religious Right' and the militia movement that received substantial media attention. In the fiscal year ending June 1994, the ADL spent $26,019,180 on its programs. The largest program, with expenditures of $13,549,428, was community service cooperating with regional and local chapters. $4,578,464 was spent on national affairs. This included "research, library files and investigation relating to anti-Semitism, anti-Semitic trends, bigotry and hate movements. Develops programs of counteraction regarding all facets of bigotry and anti-Semitism in the United States." $4,311,337 was spent producing publications, audio-visual materials, and press releases. $1,068,351 was spent on education that included, "teacher training and intergroup education programs on human relations for private and public schools, school systems, colleges, universities and industry and includes costs related to ADL's A World of Difference Institute." Other programs include litigation in civil rights and church-state matters, interreligious programs, leadership training, national affairs, foreign affairs, and issues pertaining to Israel and the Middle East. The ADL awarded $50,860 in grants.

Net Revenue: FY ending 6/94 $35,942,656 **Net Expenses:** $35,426,127 73%/9%/18% **Net Assets:** $826,998
Citations: 2,500:10
Products or Services: Publications, conferences, educational materials, grants, and lobbying. The League spent $238,797 on lobbying.
Tax Status: 501(c)(3)
Board of Directors or Trustees: Meyer Eisenberg, Thomas Homburger, Judi Krupp, Allan Margolis, Lester Pollack, Joel Sprayregen, Barbara Balser, David Rose, Ronald Sobel, Sydney Iarkow, Lawrence Atler, others.
Other Information: In 1993 the ADL was accused of spying on Arab-Americans, anti-apartheid activists and others. According to the American-Arab Anti-Discrimination Committee (ADC), the ADL received confidential information from police sources, went through the trash of people under observation, and infiltrated various organizations, including the ADC. Police raided the ADL's San Francisco and Los Angeles offices, and seized documents and evidence. The ADC, and eleven other organizations (including the Coalition Against Police Abuse, National Lawyers Guild, Committee in Solidarity with the People of El Salvador, International Jewish Peace Union, American Indian Movement, National Association of Arab-Americans, National Conference of Black Lawyers, Palestine Solidarity Committee, Association of Arab-American University Graduates, and the Bay Area Anti-Apartheid Network) as well as seven individuals, brought a civil rights law suit against the ADL. The ADL settled criminal allegations by paying a fine of $75,000 to the City of San Francisco. The civil lawsuit is still unresolved. The ADL is affiliated with the 501(c)(3) Anti-Defamation League Foundation at the same address. The two affiliates had combined net revenues of $38,608,134, net expenses of $42,383,465, and net assets of $15,414,742. The League received $35,491,563, or 99% of total revenue, from gifts and grants awarded by foundations, businesses, and individuals. $415,058, or 1%, from the sale of publications. The remaining revenue came from interest on savings and temporary cash investments, dividends and interest from securities, and other miscellaneous sources. The ADL lost $30,857 on the sale of securities.

Appalachia Science in the Public Interest (ASPI)
P.O. Box 298
Livingston, KY 40445   **Phone:** (606) 256-0077
USA   **Fax:**   (606) 256-0083

Contact Person: Al Fritsch, Executive Director.
Mission or Interest: "Making science and technology responsive to the needs of the people of Central Appalachia." Emphasis on environmentalism.
Accomplishments: Conducted eight projects under the Appalachian Sustainable Forest Center. Produces numerous "Environmental Resource Assessments."
Products or Services: Books, research papers, "Earth Healing" videotapes, technical papers, study guides, more.
Tax Status: 501(c)(3)

Appalachian Community Fund
517 Union Ave., Suite 206
Knoxville, TN 37902   **Phone:** (615) 523-5783   **E-Mail:** appafund@aol.com
USA   **Fax:**   (615) 523-1896

Contact Person: Wendy Johnson.
Officers or Principals: Barbara Banks, Chair ($0); Don Manning-Miller, Treasurer ($0); Benita Whitman, Secretary ($0).
Mission or Interest: "An activist-controlled foundation committed to supporting progressive social change in the central states of Appalachia which include east Kentucky, east Tennessee, West Virginia and southwest Virginia."
Accomplishments: In the fiscal year ending June 1995, the Fund awarded $258,399 in grants. Recipients included: $7,500 each to the Coalition for Jobs and the Environment, Southern Appalachian Labor School, Virginia Black Lung Association, Appalachia Research and Defense Fund of Kentucky, Livingston Economic Alternatives in Progress, Ohio Valley Environmental Coalition, Appalachian Women's Alliance, Harlan County Open Governance Project, and Women's Initiative Networking Groups, $7,000 each to the Workers of Rural Kentucky, Southern Organizing Committee, Tennessee Industrial Renewal Network, West Virginia Economic Justice Project, and the Citizens Coal Council.
Net Revenue: FY ending 6/95 $368,972 **Net Expenses:** $409,859 75%/12%/13% **Net Assets:** $400,783
Tax Status: 501(c)(3)
Board of Directors or Trustees: Emanuel Bailey, Jim Branson, Stephen Fisher, Nancy Hilsbos, Aisha K, Peter Reilly, Beth Roberts, Franki Patton Rutherford, Marcus Wilkes.
Other Information: A member of the Funding Exchange Network. The Fund received $338,749, or 92% of revenue, from gifts and grants awarded by foundations, businesses, and individuals. $22,597, or 6%, from interest on savings and temporary cash investments. The remaining revenue came other miscellaneous sources.

Appalachian Peace Education Center (APEC)
211 W. Main St.
Abingdon, VA 24210
USA

Mission or Interest: Creative conflict resolution, race relations, Central America, women's issues, and migrant workers' issues.
Other Information: In 1994 the Center received $4,000 from the Appalachian Community Fund.

Aquarian Research Foundation

5620 Morton St.
Philadelphia, PA 19144
USA

Phone: (215) 849-3237

Contact Person: Art Rosenblum, Director.
Mission or Interest: Peace and justice issues based on cooperation and communalism.
Net Revenue: less than $25,000   **Tax Status:** 501(c)(3)
Periodicals: *Aquarian Alternatives* (newsletter).

Archives on Audio

P.O. Box 170023
San Francisco, CA 94117-0023
USA

Phone: (415) 346-1840   **E-Mail:** archives@igc.apc.org
Web-Page: http://www.cygnus/kfjc/emory

Contact Person: Paul Korntheuer.
Mission or Interest: A mail order company that sells the audio cassette recordings of political researcher David Emory's radio show. "Mr. Emory's broadcasts focus on the U.S. military and intelligence community's historical involvement with international fascism."
Accomplishments: Emory's broadcasts have been featured on the Pacifica radio stations in Los Angeles (WPFK), New York (WBAI), and other smaller stations.
Products or Services: Audio tapes featuring subjects such as; "The CIA, the Military & Drugs", "AIDS: Epidemic or Weapon of War?", "Mind Control & the U.S. Intelligence Agencies", "The Fascist '3rd Position' - The Far Right and Their Attempt to Co-opt Progressive Forces", and many others.
Tax Status: For profit. **Annual Report:** No. **Employees:** 2

Ark Trust

5461 Noble Ave.
Sherman Oaks, CA 91411
USA

Phone: (818) 786-9990   **E-Mail:** arktrust@earthlink.net

Contact Person: Michael Giannelli, Ph.D., Executive Director.
Mission or Interest: Animal rights group that monitors how animals are portrayed in the media.
Accomplishments: Conducted the first ever "Animal Issues in the Media: A Ground Breaking Report" which documented the portrayal of animals in the media and resulted in a cover story in *The Animal's Agenda*. The study found that: 1) Violence toward animals is "rampant" on Saturday morning cartoons, even more so than in prime-time programming. 2) Animals are more likely than humans to be presented as perpetrators of violence. 3) Wild animals are portrayed as more violent, or victims of violence, more often than domestic animals. 4) Animals are more likely than humans to be treated as villains, either violent or merely troublesome. 5) Animal rights activists are mostly depicted as violent. The study was conducted by George Gerbner, Ph.D., Dean Emeritus of the Annenberg School for Communications at the University of Pennsylvania. Dr. Gerbner is considered a "pioneer in the field" of media violence. The Ark Trust gives awards for positive portrayal of animals, the Genesis Awards, and "Foe Paws" for negative portrayals.

Arkansas Coalition for Choice

P.O. Box 23013
Little Rock, AR 72221
USA

Other Information: In the fiscal year ending June 1994, the Coalition received $17,500 from the Ms. Foundation for Women.

Arkansas Institute for Social Justice

1024 Elysian Fields Ave.
New Orleans, LA 70117
USA

Phone: (504) 943-5954

Contact Person: Pat House, President.   **Officers or Principals:** Pat House, President ($0); James Lynch, treasurer ($0).
Mission or Interest: Provides assistance to low income residents, and advocates public policy that benefits them. Focus on home ownership and financial institutions, and schools.
Accomplishments: In 1993 the Foundation spent $1,574,160 on its programs. Programs included loan counseling to assist low-income people in becoming homeowners, the Financial Democracy Project which included lobbying to "restructure the nation's financial system," leadership training to empower low-income persons to "challenge various government entities such as school boards to improve their effectiveness," and neighborhood revitalization.
Net Revenue: $1,974,068 80%/20%/1% **Net Expenses:** $1,556,260 **Citations:** 0:255
Products or Services: Lead screening for children, loan counseling, lobbying. The Institute spent $14,960 on lobbying; split evenly between holding rallies and demonstrations, and the direct lobbying of legislators.

Tax Status: 1993 $2,182,076
Other Information: Affiliated with several nonprofit and for-profit organizations, Association for Community Organization Now (ACORN), ACORN Housing Corp., Affiliated Media Foundation, Elysian Fields Corp., ACORN Services, Citizen Consulting, Labor Links, and Service Employee's International Union, AFL-CIO Local 100. The Institute awarded $812,553 in grants to these organizations. The Institute received $2,065,268, or 95% of revenue, from gifts and grants awarded by foundations, businesses, and individuals. (These grants included $326,250 from the U.S. Catholic Confrence Campaign for Human Development, $250,000 from the Florence and John Schumann Foundation, $221,280 from North Shore, $191,050 from the W.K. Kellogg Foundation, $75,000 from the Aaron Diamond Foundation, $50,000 from the Joyce Foundation, $45,000 from the Discount Foundation, $35,000 from the Arca Foundation, two grants totaling $31,000 from the New York Community Trust, $25,000 from the John D. And Catherine T. MacArthur Foundation, two grants totaling $25,000 from the New York Foundation, $15,000 from the New World Foundation, and $15,000 from the Surdna Foundation.) $64,389, or 3%, from interest on a note payable. $36,744, or 2%, from interest on savings and temporary cash investments. The remaining revenue came from training fees, and other miscellaneous sources.

Arms Control Association
1726 M St., N.W., Suite 201
Washington, DC 20036   **Phone:**   (202) 463-8270
USA   **Fax:**   (202) 463-8273

Contact Person: Spurgeon M. Keeny, Jr., President.   **Officers or Principals:** Spurgeon M. Keeny, Jr., President ($81,806); Jack Mendelson, Director ($74,750); John Schulz, Director ($50,600).
Mission or Interest: Research and dissemination of research on topics pertaining to peace, international security, arms control, non-proliferation, disarmament, and defense policy.
Accomplishments: John Holum, President Clinton's director of the U.S. Arms Control and Disarmament Agency (ACDA), told the Arms Control Association during a speech that "the relationship between the ACDA director and the Arms Control Association very nearly approximates that between a junior executive and the corporate board." In the fiscal year ending June 1994, the Association spent $676,324 on its projects. The largest project, with expenditures of $331,399, was the publication and distribution of *Arms Control Today*. $155,553 was spent on media programs, including press conferences and staff contacts with members of the media. $128,502 on educational programs, $33,443 on membership services, and $27,427 on public policy research and the maintenance of a library.
Net Revenue: FY ending 6/94 $772,072 **Net Expenses:** $747,319 91%/3%/6% **Net Assets:** $130,095 **Citations:** 83:114
Tax Status: 501(c)(3)
Board of Directors or Trustees: McGeorge Bundy, George Bunn (Center for International Security & Arms Control), Maj. Gen. William F. Burns (Ret.), Antonia Chayes, William Coleman Jr., Susan Eisenhower (Center for Post-Soviet Studies), Randall Forsberg, Raymond Garthoff (Brookings Inst.), J. Bryan Hehir (Center for International Affairs), Thomas Hughes (Carnegie Endowment for International Peace), Henry Kendall (MIT), Michael Klare (Hampshire College), Harold Homgju Koh (Yale Law School), Betty Lall, James Leonard, Robert McNamara (Secretary of Defense, 1961-1968), Saul Mendlovitz (World Order Models Project), Julia A. Moore, Janne Nolan (Brookings Inst.), Frank Press (Carnegie Inst.), Lt. Gen. Robert Pursley (Logistics Management Inst.), Stanley Resor, John Rhinelander, John Steinbruner (Brookings Inst.), Jeremiah Sullivan, Paul Warnke.
Periodicals: *Arms Control Today* (ten times a year journal).
Other Information: The Association received $683,730, or 89% of revenue, from gifts and grants awarded by foundations, businesses, and individuals. (These grants included $200,000 over two years from the Carnegie Corporation, $20,000 from the Ploughshares Fund, $15,000 from the Winston Foundation. In 1995, $50,000 from the Rockefeller Foundation.) $58,212, or 8%, from membership dues. $18,290, or 2%, from "fundraising." The remaining revenue came from dividends and interest from securities, the sale of books and publications, mailing list rentals, advertising, and other miscellaneous sources.

Asia Pacific Center for Justice and Peace
110 Maryland Ave., N.E., Box 70
Washington, DC 20002   **Phone:**   (202) 543-1094
USA

Contact Person: Katherine Johnson, Executive Director.   **Officers or Principals:** Roger Rumpf, former Executive Director ($18,528); D. Luce, President ($0); S. Benson, Vice President ($0); M. Cohen, Treasurer; K. Ramanathan, Secretary.
Mission or Interest: "Information and resources on human rights situations and labor rights in South East Asian countries."
Accomplishments: In 1993 the Center spent $136,256 on its programs.
Net Revenue: 1993 $137,624 **Net Expenses:** $146,938 93%/7%/0% **Net Assets:** $30,407
Tax Status: 501(c)(3)
Board of Directors or Trustees: B. Inversin, C. Numi, H. Ohta, P. Pinkerton, J. Pulcini, L. Worthington.
Other Information: The Center absorbed the Asia Resource Center. (The financial information listed is for the Asia Resource Center.) The Center received $115,665, or 84% of revenue, from gifts and grants received by foundations, businesses, and individuals. $17,718, or 13%, from program service fees, including tour fees, product sales, rental fees, and honoraria. $3,490, or 2%, from investment income. The remaining revenue came from interest on savings and temporary cash investments.

Asian American Legal Defense and Education Fund (AALDEF)
99 Hudson St., 12th Floor
New York, NY 10013   **Phone:**   (212) 966-5932
USA

Contact Person: Margaret Fung, Executive Director.   **Officers or Principals:** Margaret Fung, Executive Director ($39,840); Stanley Mark, Program Director ($36,749); Elizabeth Ouyang ($33,812); Lillian Ling Huang, Assistant Director.
Mission or Interest: Litigation and education to promote the rights of Asian Americans.
Accomplishments: In the fiscal year ending June 1994, the Fund spent $344,609 on its programs. The largest program, with expenditures of $102,326, was legal education. This program educated Asian Americans about their legal rights through seminars, pamphlets, workshops, and free legal advice clinics. $80,989 was spent on voting rights activities, including litigation and voter registration. $59,672 was spent on litigation and education to combat anti-Asian violence. $35,496 for immigrants rights projects. Other programs included labor and employment rights, "environmental justice," and reparations for Japanese Americans. The fund received $6,000 in court-awarded attorney's fees for successful litigation.
Net Revenue: FY ending 6/94 $407,763 ($3,060, or 1%, from government grants) **Net Expenses:** $406,808 85%/8%/7%
Net Assets: $127,573
Products or Services: Publications, litigation, voter registration, and lobbying. AALDEF spent $1,925 lobbying in the areas of "civil rights, immigration, anti-Asian violence, redress for Japanese Americans, voting rights, and labor rights."
Tax Status: 501(c)(3)
Board of Directors or Trustees: Michael Shen, Vivian Cheng-Khanna, Grace Hwang, Harsha Murthy (GE Capital), Cao O (Asian American Federal of NY), Joan Washington, Haywood Burns (National Lawyer's Guild Foundation), Eduardo Capulong, Nicholas Chen, Noland Cheng, Ira Glasser (ACLU), Jack Greenberg (Columbia Law School), Peter Lederer, Chanwoo Lee (Legal Aid Society), Donald Liu (U.S. Health Care), JoAnn Lum (Chinese Staff and Workers Assoc.), Fay Chew Matsuda (Chinatown History Museum), Alex Moon, Karen Sauvigne (CUNY Law School), Arthur Soong, Ko-Yung Tung, Susan Ching Wong, Napoleon Williams Jr., Gail Wright-Sirmans.
Other Information: The Fund received $313,402, or 77% of revenue, from direct and indirect public support in the form of gifts and grants awarded by foundations, affiliates, businesses, and individuals. (These grants included $20,000 from the Norman Foundation, $100 from the Ruth Mott Fund.) $83,455, or 20%, from special fund-raising events, including an annual dinner and a theater party. $6,000, or 1%, from court-awarded attorney's fees. $3,060, or 1%, from government grants. The remaining revenue came from the sale of publications, interest on savings and temporary cash investments, and other miscellaneous sources.

Asian Immigrant Women Advocates

310 8th St., Suite 301
Oakland, CA 94607   **Phone:**   (510) 268-0192
USA

Mission or Interest: Works to organize labor in the garment industry.
Accomplishments: Orchestrated the boycott of products by fashion designer Jessica McClintock.
Other Information: In the fiscal year ending June 1994 the Advocates received $40,000 from the Rosenberg Foundation, $15,000 from the Joyce Mertz-Gilmore Foundation, $12,000 from the McKay Foundation, and $2,500 from the Ms. Foundation for Women. In 1995 they received $1,000 from the Tides Foundation.

Asian-American Free Labor Institute

1925 K St., N.W., Suite 301
Washington, DC 20006   **Phone:**   (202) 778-4500
USA

Contact Person: Kenneth P. Hutchinson, Executive Director.   **Officers or Principals:** Kenneth P. Hutchinson, Executive Director ($135,441); Lane Kirkland, President ($0); Thomas R. Donahue, Secretary/Treasurer ($0).
Mission or Interest: Affiliated with the AFL-CIO. Works with union officials to provide them with knowledge and skills. Special focus on union-to-union contacts between U.S. unions and their counterparts in Asia.
Accomplishments: In 1994 the Institute spent $3,771,481 on its programs. It sponsored 603 seminars, workshops, conferences, and symposia for the benefit of 47,348 trade unionists.
Net Revenue: 1994 $5,039,725 ($2,673,525, or 53%, from government grants) **Net Expenses:** $5,007,572 75%/25%/0%
Net Assets: $598,927
Tax Status: 501(c)(5)
Board of Directors or Trustees: Morton Bahr (Communication Workers of America), John Barry (Intl. Brotherhood of Electrical Workers), Arthur Coia (Laborer's Intl. Unions of N. America), Douglas Dority (Food & Commercial Workers Intl. Union), Frank Hanley (Intl. Union of Operating Engineers), Gloria Johnson (Coalition of Labor Union Women), Jay Mazur (Intl. Ladies' Garment Workers Union), Gerald McEntee (AFSCME), Lenore Miller (Retail, Wholesale & Department Store Union), Albert Shanker (American Federation of Teachers), John Sturdivant (American Federation of Government Employees), John Sweeney (Service Employees Intl. Union), Richard Trumka (United Mine Workers of America), Lynn Williams (United Steel Workers of America), Frank Hurt (Bakery, Confectionary & Tobacco Workers Intl. Union).
Other Information: The Institute received $2,673,525, or 53% of revenue, from government grants. $2,366,200, or 47%, from indirect public support in the form of gifts and grants from affiliates and foundations. The remaining revenue came from interest on savings and temporary cash investments.

Assassination Archives and Research Center

(see Coalition on Political Assassinations)

Association for Gay, Lesbian, and Bisexual Issues in Counseling (AGLBIC)

P.O. Box 216
Jenkintown, PA 19046   **Phone:** (503) 753-6074   **E-Mail:** tge@hopewest.com
USA   **Fax:**   (503) 758-1445

Contact Person: Tom Eversole, Secretary.
Officers or Principals: Bob Barret, Colleen Logan, Co-Chairs; Robert Rhode, Treasurer.
Mission or Interest: Member of the American Counseling Association. "To educate and sensitize the members of the American Counseling Association to issues of concern to sexual minorities; to advocate for issues of concern to sexual minorities and their counselors; to provide support for gay, lesbian and bisexual counselors, and to develop and publish resources for counselors dealing with sexual minority clients."
Accomplishments: "AGLBIC has been a voice for lesbian, gay and bisexual counselors and other concerned professionals within the American Counseling Association since 1974. AGLBIC has sponsored ACA resolutions, assisted ACA staff, contributed journal articles, and presented convention programs concerning sexual minority issues."
Annual Report: No.
Periodicals: *AGLBIC Newsletter* (quarterly).
Internships: No.
Other Information: The Association was formerly called the National Caucus of Gay and Lesbian Counselors, and the Association for Gay and Lesbian Issues in Counseling Association.

Association for Union Democracy (AUD)

500 State St., 2nd Floor
Brooklyn, NY 11217   **Phone:** (718) 855-6650
USA   **Fax:**   (718) 855-6799

Contact Person: Carl Biers, Executive Director.   **Officers or Principals:** Susan Jennik, former Executive Director ($31,385); Herman Benson, Secretary/Treasurer ($10,000); Judith R. Schneider, President.
Mission or Interest: "AUD recognizes that the labor movement, an indispensable defender of the American standard of living, can be a great force for democracy and social progress...For the movement to fulfill its potential it must be thoroughly democratic in its own internal life. Toward that end, (union members) must have the right to free speech, the right to criticize their officials without penalties, the right to support or oppose candidates for union office, to fair hiring and grievance procedures free of intimidation or favoritism."
Accomplishments: Filed suits and briefs in the U.S, Supreme Court and lower courts. Developed an international network of union democracy lawyers and activists.
Net Revenue: 1994 $193,606 **Net Expenses:** $152,201 83%/9%/8% **Net Assets:** $150,410
Products or Services: Classes in union democracy and work-place rights for rank and file union members. Numerous books and publications. Conferences. Special projects focusing on: Federal employees, women, and minority workers. In 1994 they spent $126,714 on these projects.
Tax Status: 501(c)(3) **Annual Report:** Yes. **Employees:** 3 full-time, 1 part-time.
Board of Directors or Trustees: Arthur Fox, John Harold, Barbara Harvey, Prof. Alan Hyde (Rutgers University Law School), Prof. William Kornblum (CUNY), Paul Alan Levy (Public Citizen Litigation Group), James McNamara, Antonio Ramirez, Prof. Emeritus Ruth Spitz (Harry VanArsdale School of Labor Studies), Prof. Clyde Summers (Univ. of Pennsylvania Law School).
Periodicals: *Union Democracy, $50+ Club News,* (bimonthly newsletters).
Internships: Yes, unpaid internships for pre-law and law students.
Other Information: The Association received $133,834, or 69% of revenue, from gifts and grants awarded by foundations, affiliates, companies and individuals. (These grants included $150 from the Ruth Mott Fund.) $56,994, or 29%, from program services. The remaining revenue came from dividends and interest from securities.

Association of Community Organizations for Reform Now (ACORN)

523 W. 15th St.
Little Rock, AR 72202   **Phone:** (501) 376-7151   **E-Mail:** poldirect@acorn.org
USA   **Fax:**   (501) 376-3952

Contact Person: Maude Hurd, President.   **Officers or Principals:** Wade Rathke, Organizer.
Mission or Interest: Developing leaders and organizations in low-income communities. Advocates for more social programs and governmental assistance. In 1990 ACORN added the following planks to its "People's Platform," 1) Low-cost energy and protection from utilities, 2) Health care for all regardless of ability to pay, 3) Guaranteed affordable housing, 4) Jobs and job training for all, and childcare for workers, 5) Rural issues such as preserving the family farm, 6) Community-based development and control over private development 7) Banking reform, 8) Tax wealth and base all taxes on ability to pay, 9) Environmental protection with a focus on hazardous waste in communities, 10) Secure neighborhoods safe from rape and violence against women, and protect against drug trade violence, 11) Civil rights enforcement, 12) Communications; greater control of the media by low and moderate income people, 13) Education, and 14) more Democracy in community decisions.
Accomplishments: Approximately 75,000 member families. Over 26 state-based affiliates. In March of 1995, ACORN activists disrupted a meeting between House Speaker Newt Gingrich and the National Association of Counties by banging on lunch trays and shouting "Nuke Newt!" ACORN took the lead in the "Squatters' Rights" movement, advocating the occupation of abandoned inner city housing.
Net Revenue: 1993 est. $3,000,000 **Citations:** 4:217

Products or Services: ACORN Members Handbook.
Tax Status: 501(c)(4)
Periodicals: *United States of ACORN* (occasional newspaper), and *Homesteader* (quarterly newsletter).
Other Information: Established in Arkansas in the early 1970's. Emerged from the organization of the National Welfare Rights Organization. ACORN members are approximately 70% black and Latino, and 70% female. Affiliated with the 501(c)(3) Institute for Social Justice. In 1994 Various ACORN affiliates recieved a total of $436,000 from the Campaign for Human Development. ACORN's national office is located at: 739 8th St., S.E., Washington, DC 20003, (202) 547-2500.

Association of Flight Attendants (AFA)
1625 Massachusetts Ave., N.E., Suite 300
Washington, DC 20036   **Phone:**   (202) 328-5400
USA   **Fax:**   (202) 328-5424

Contact Person: Devona Maki, President.   **Officers or Principals:** Devona Maki, President ($75,087); R. Frederick Casey, Vice President ($74,985); Sharon E. Madigan, Secretary/Treasurer ($69,771).
Mission or Interest: Union representing approximately 36,000 flight attendants. Affiliated with the AFL-CIO.
Net Revenue: 1994 $13,628,771 **Net Expenses:** $12,087,780 **Net Assets:** $1,740,829
Tax Status: 501(c)(5)
Periodicals: *Flightlog* (bimonthly journal).
Other Information: The Association received $13,542,177, or 99% of revenue, from membership dues. The remaining revenue came from interest on savings and temporary cash investments, advertising revenue from publications, dividends and interest from securities, and other miscellaneous sources. In 1993 the AFL-CIO loaned $250,000 to the Association at the below-market rate of 4.62%.

Association of Forest Service Employees for Environmental Ethics
P.O. Box 11615
Eugene, OR 97440-9958
USA

Tax Status: 501(c)(3)
Other Information: In 1993 the Association received $10,000 from the Town Creek Foundation. In 1994, $20,000 from the Rockefeller Family Fund, $7,500 from the New-Land Foundation, $250 from the One World Fund, $200 from the Compton Foundation.

Association of Trial Lawyers of America (ATLA)
1050 31st St., N.W.
Washington, DC 20007   **Phone:**   (202) 965-3500
USA

Contact Person: Thomas H. Henderson, Executive Director.   **Officers or Principals:** Thomas H. Henderson, Executive Director ($243,292); Alan Parker, Senior Director ($175,863); Michael Starr, General Counsel ($163,769); Madelyn Appelbaum, Senior Director ($103,221); J. Robert Carr, Senior Director ($102,631); Barry J. Nace, President; Pamela Anagnos Liapakis, Vice President; Howard L. Nations, Secretary; Richard D. Hailey, Treasurer; Richard H. Middleton, Jr., Parliamentarian.
Mission or Interest: Provides research, assistance, and advocacy on behalf of product liability lawyers. Opposed to caps on punitive damage awards, tort reform, product liability reform, and 'loser pays' laws. Operates through a number of divisions and caucuses, including the Minority Caucus, New Lawyers, Women Trial Lawyers, Litigation Group, and representatives in each state as well as some international.
Accomplishments: The Association of Trial Lawyers of America's Political Action Committee contributed $2.2 million to political campaigns in 1994, making it the sixth largest PAC. 94% of the contributions went to Democrats. In the fiscal year ending July 1994, the Association held two conventions, each attended by over 2,000 lawyers, published a magazine, conducted legal research at the request 10,000 lawyers, and conducted public affairs including legislation monitoring at the state and local level. Successfully helped defeat various reforms in tort law and product liability reform. The Association spent $31,776 on liaison efforts with consumer advocacy groups. $14,556 was spent on state legislative liaison. Other expenses included $922,537 on consultants, $1,254,819 on marketing and promotion, $18,557 on "insurance and actuarial research", $1,037,072 on "preservation of adversary system", $860,156 on state activity support, and $252,073 on "public service relations."
Net Revenue: FY ending 7/94 $15,972,637 **Net Expenses:** $16,157,491 **Net Assets:** $3,282,344
Products or Services: Annual directory of members, research, conferences, and lobbying. The Association spent $937,834 on lobbying and political expenditures.
Tax Status: 501(c)(6)
Board of Directors or Trustees: Donald Walker, Margie Lehrman, Ann Casso. At least two members from each state, as well as the various caucuses, sit on the Board of Governors.
Periodicals: *Trial* (monthly magazine), *Advocate* (monthly magazine).
Other Information: Affiliated with the 501(c)(3) Association of Trial Lawyers of America Education Fund. The two affiliates had combined net revenues of $18,891,401, net expenses of $18,789,174, and net assets of $1,881,044. The Association received $9,705,650, or 61% of revenue, from membership dues. $1,782,292, or 11%, from the annual and midwinter conventions. $1,585,275, or 10%, from the legal research exchange. $1,473,967, or 9%, from magazine advertising revenues. $582,800, or 4%, from royalties. $424,297, or 3%, from mailing list rentals. $223,339, or 1%, from interest on savings and temporary cash investments. The remaining revenue came from magazine subscriptions, sales of the membership directory, endorsements, and rental income.

Association of Trial Lawyers of America Education Fund

1050 31st St., N.W.
Washington, DC 20007   **Phone:**   (202) 965-3500
USA

Contact Person: Gerry Miller, Assistant Dean.   **Officers or Principals:** Margie Lehrman, Dean ($61,808); Liane E. Leshne, Editor-in-Chief ($51,050); Peter Quinn, Managing Editor ($43,475); Barry J. Nace, President; Pamela Anagnos Liapakis, Vice President; Howard L. Nations, Secretary; Richard D. Hailey, Treasurer; Richard H. Middleton, Jr., Parliamentarian.
Mission or Interest: Research and education affiliate of the Association of Trial Lawyers.
Accomplishments: In the fiscal year ending July 1994, the Fund spent $1,994,735 on its programs. The largest program, with expenditures of $1,251,079, was seminars and colleges held to provide continuing education for trial lawyers. $743,656 was spent publishing *Law Reporter*, a monthly case reference periodical, *Products Liability* and *Professional Negligence Law Reporter*.
Net Revenue: FY ending 7/94 $2,918,764 **Net Expenses:** $2,631,683 76%/22%/2% **Net Assets:** (-$1,401,300)
Citations: 0:255
Products or Services: Publications, seminars, video and audio tapes.
Tax Status: 501(c)(3)
Board of Directors or Trustees: Same as the Association of Trial Lawyers of America.
Periodicals: *Law Reporter, Products Liability*, and *Professional Negligence Law Reporter* (monthly journals).
Other Information: Affiliated with the 501(c)(6) Association of Trial Lawyers of America at the same address. The two affiliates had combined net revenues of $18,891,401, net expenses of $18,789,174, and net assets of $1,881,044. The Education Fund received $1,363,387, or 44% of total revenue, from direct and indirect public support in the form of gifts and grants awarded by foundations, affiliates, businesses, and individuals. $1,078,551, or 35%, from fees from colleges and seminars. $552,670, or 18%, from the sale and subscriptions to publications. $80,661, or 3%, from library service fees. The remaining revenue came from the interest on savings and temporary cash investments. The Fund lost $156,952 on the sale of inventory.

Association on Third World Affairs

1629 K St., N.W.
Washington, DC 20006   **Phone:**   (202) 331-8455
USA   **Fax:**   (202) 785-3607

Contact Person: Dr. Lorna Hahn.   **Officers or Principals:** Prof. Luanne Feik.
Mission or Interest: "Provide pertinent information, promote constructive activities, regarding important and controversial issues."
Accomplishments: "Helping bring change to South Africa, helping to free Cambodia, helping to get assistance for deserving governments and people. Much of this accomplished through Capitol Hill conferences with ambassadors, congresspersons."

Astraea National Lesbian Action Foundation

116 E. 16th St., 7th Floor
New York, NY 10003   **Phone:**   (212) 529-8021   **E-Mail:** ANLAF@aol.com
USA   **Web-Page:** http://imageinc.com/astraea/

Contact Person: Katherine Acey, Executive Director.   **Officers or Principals:** Maxine Blake, Jeanette Martinez, Co-Chairs; Ivy J. Young, Program Director; Karen Zelermyer, Development Director; Di Eckerle, Executive Assistant.
Mission or Interest: Astraea awards grants and sponsors film, book, and other cultural projects that "directly address issues related to heterosexism, homophobia, and sexism. Organizations must demonstrate an understanding of the connections among oppressions and be working actively to eliminate all forms of oppression - based on sexual orientation, gender, class, race, ethnicity, age, physical and mental ability, national identity, and religious affiliation." Provides technical assistance and leadership training to other activist groups. "It is our job to raise the money needed to purchase the 'building materials,' to raise consciousness about the importance of giving to ourselves, and to provide the technical assistance necessary to create structures that endure."
Accomplishments: Executive Director Katherine Acey attended the Fourth World Conference on Women in Beijing as part of a delegation funded by the Ms. Foundation for Women. In the fiscal year ending June 1995 the Foundation awarded $244,770 in grants. Recipients included; the Center for Nonwhite Lesbians, International Gay and Lesbian Human Rights Commission, Kitchen Table: Women of Color Press, DYKE-TV, Lavender Youth Recreation and Information Center, Lesbian Fat Activist Network, National Center for Lesbian Rights, Sistah-to-Sistah, Women's Project, Lesbian Avengers, Esperanza Peace and Justice Center, Gay and Lesbian Media Coalition, the Women's Funding Network, and many others.
Products or Services: Directory of foundations funding homosexual organizations. Annual writers awards, Sappho Award of Distinction, and Margot Karle Scholarships for a "woman student within the City University of New York system who demonstrates a commitment to social activism."
Tax Status: 501(c)(3)
Board of Directors or Trustees: Mary Andes, Cynthia Dames, Carolina Cordero Dyer, Mari Keiko Gonzalez, Amber Hollibaugh, Mai Kiang, Toni Long, Kathleen Morris, Rita Zimmer.

Periodicals: *Astraea Bulletin* (quarterly newsletter).
Other Information: Founded in 1977 by "a multi-racial, multi-class group of feminists." In 1994 the Foundation received $267,000 from the Joyce Mertz-Gilmore Foundation (part of a multi-year $400,000 grant), $21,000 from the Ms. Foundation for Women, $2,280 from the Stewart R. Mott Charitable Trust. $6,000 from the Vanguard Public Foundation, $3,000 from the Haymarket People's Fund.

Bailey Communications / *Second Stone*

P.O. Box 8340
New Orleans, LA 70182   **Phone:** (504) 891-7555   **E-Mail:** secstone@aol.com
USA   **Fax:**   same

Contact Person: Jim Bailey, Publisher.
Mission or Interest: Publications for gay Christians. *Second Stone* is "a national ecumenical Christian social justice news journal with a specific outreach to sexual orientation minorities."
Accomplishments: Publishing since 1988. "*Second Stone* has informed and inspired thousands of gay and lesbian Christian readers around the world and has provided a voice against injustice directed toward this community by church and society."
Tax Status: For profit. **Annual Report:** No. **Employees:** 2
Periodicals: *Second Stone* (bimonthly newspaper). **Internships:** No.

Bakery, Confectionery and Tobacco Workers International Union

10401 Connecticut Ave.
Kensington, MD 20895   **Phone:** (301) 933-8600
USA   **Fax:**   (301) 946-8452

Contact Person: Frank Hurt, President.   **Officers or Principals:** Frank Hurt, President ($149,480); Eugene McDonald, Secretary/Treasurer ($139,880); David Durkee, Executive Vice President ($127,137).
Mission or Interest: An international labor union representing approximately 116,000 members. Formed in 1978 by the merger of the Tobacco Workers International Union and the Bakery and Confectionery Workers' Union.
Accomplishments: During 1994 the Union sanctioned and supervised eight strikes involving 16,685 worker-days lost. Assisted unorganized labor groups in uniting. Helped arrange 39 National Labor Relations Board elections, resulting in 769 potential members.
Net Revenue: 1994 $10,753,703 **Net Expenses:** $12,239,999 **Net Assets:** $21,826,998
Products or Services: Labor organizing and representation. Scholarships.
Tax Status: 501(c)(5)
Board of Directors or Trustees: Carmine D'Angelo, Lillian Gainer, Earl Jaggers, James Lair, Herbert Marx, Danny Murphy, Paul Pannell, Frelan Patrick, Lurlean Plump, Robert Ray, William Sprandel, Jerry Sprouse, James Sutton, Ginnette Theriault, John Truckenmiller, William Walton, William Anderson, Avron Bergman.
Periodicals: *BCT News* (nine times a year).
Other Information: The Union is affiliated with the AFL-CIO. The Union received $9,181,886, or 85% of revenue, from membership dues. $796,087, or 7%, from rental income received from affiliated health benefit and pension funds. $733,126, or 7%, from dividends and interest from securities. The remaining revenue came from the sale of supplies and other miscellaneous sources. Net revenue was decreased by a loss of $74,826 on the sale of securities and other assets.

Bank Information Center (BIC)

2025 I St., N.W., Suite 400
Washington, DC 20006   **Phone:** (202) 466-8191
USA

Contact Person: Chad Dobson, Secretary/Treasurer.
Officers or Principals: Chad Dobson, Secretary/Treasurer ($50,000); Robin Belly, Vice President ($0).
Mission or Interest: Monitors and provides information on the activities of the World Bank, Development Bank, the Inter-American Development Bank. Opposes the actions of these banks which they feel are harmful to the environment, to indigenous people, and to social progress through the support of privatization. Works with non-governmental organizations throughout the world, concentrating on Latin America.
Accomplishments: In 1994 the Center spent $457,133 on its programs. This included $17,209 for grants awarded to various individuals and organizations, most of them in Latin America. Grants are for the monitoring of activities funded by these multilateral development banks and for organizational activities.
Net Revenue: 1994 $432,189 **Net Expenses:** $457,133 100%/0%/0% **Net Assets:** $41,931
Products or Services: Library, databases on banks and environmental issues.
Tax Status: 501(c)(3)
Other Information: The Center received $432,085, or 99.9% of revenue, from gifts and grants awarded by foundations, businesses, and individuals. (These grants included $20,000 from the J. Roderick MacArthur Foundation.) The remaining revenue came from interest on savings and temporary cash investments.

Barbra Streisand Foundation

1460 4th St., Suite 212
Santa Monica, CA 90401   **Phone:**   (310) 395-3599
USA   **Fax:**   (310) 395-9676

Contact Person: Rachel Donaldson, Program Officer.
Officers or Principals: Margery Tabankin, Executive Director ($65,000); Barbra Streisand, Director ($0).
Mission or Interest: Philanthropic foundation created by entertainer Barbra Streisand that funds national organizations supporting, "civil liberties for all populations; women's issues including choice, pay equity and health-related issues; civil rights with an emphasis on race relations between African-Americans and Jews. AIDS research, advocacy, service and litigation; children's and youth-related issues with a focus on the economically disadvantaged."
Accomplishments: In 1993 the Foundation awarded $842,485 in grants. The recipients of the largest grants were: $100,000 for the Arkansas Cancer Research Center, $77,000 for the American Civil Liberties Union (California), $50,000 each for the Environmental Defense Fund, Hollywood Policy Center, and the U.S. Holocaust Memorial Museum, $27,800 for the AIDS Project, Los Angeles, $25,000 each for the Museum of Tolerance and Friends of Peace Now, $20,000 each for Citizens Fund and the Natural Resources Defense Council, $16,000 for Education First, and $15,000 each for Inform, Lighthawk, Alliance for Justice, Center for Reproductive Law & Policy, Fairness and Accuracy in Reporting and Project NIMSA.
Net Revenue: 1993 $570,727   **Net Expenses:** $927,086   **Net Assets:** $3,012,182
Tax Status: 501(c)(3)
Board of Directors or Trustees: Richard Baskin, Alan Bergman, Marilyn Bergman, Dr. Marvin Goldberger, Jason Gould, Page Jenkins, Stanley Sheinbaum.
Internships: No.
Other Information: Although the Foundation stresses that it funds only <u>national</u> organizations, and the only health-related organizations it funds focus on AIDS, the largest grant in 1993, $100,000, went to the Arkansas Cancer Research Center. The Foundation received most of its yearly revenue $221,692, or 39%, from royalty income. $168,733 from dividends and interest from securities, and $164,802 from the net sale of assets. The Foundation's assets were held primarily in corporate stocks worth $1,162,313 at fair market value, or 39% of assets. Corporate bonds worth $757,625 fair market value, or 25% of assets. Government bonds worth $744,420 fair market value, or 25% of assets. The remaining assets were held in non-interest bearing cash, interest on savings and temporary cash investments, and office equipment.

Bauman Family Foundation

2040 S. St., N.W.
Washington, DC 20009   **Phone:**   (202) 328-2040
USA   **Fax:**   (202) 328-2003

Contact Person: Patricia Bauman, President.
Officers or Principals: Patricia Bauman, President ($135,840); John Bryant, Jr., Director ($114,880); Irene Crow, Director ($0).
Mission or Interest: Grant-making foundation that primarily funds environmental organizations.
Accomplishments: In 1996 the Bauman Family Foundation played a key role in establishing the Preamble Center for Public Policy. In the fiscal year ending June 1995, the Foundation awarded $1,759,824 in grants. The recipients of the largest grants included: $105,000 to the Focus Project, $80,000 to the Institute for Agriculture and Trade Policy, $75,000 each to the Labor / Community Strategy Center, New World Foundation, and the National Center for Economic Alternatives, $65,000 to the National Religious Partnership for the Environment, $60,000 to the Poverty and Race Research Council, $52,500 to Native Action, $45,000 to the U.S. PIRG Education Fund, and $40,000 to the Government Accountability Project.
Net Revenue: FY ending 6/95 $2,321,861   **Net Expenses:** $2,041,920   **Net Assets:** $32,456,469
Tax Status: 501(c)(3)
Other Information: The Foundation received $1,759,824, or 71% of total revenue, from investment partnerships, which included corporate stock. $520,949, or 21%, from dividends and interest. $125,716, or 5%, from rental income. $60,000, or 2%, from gifts and grants awarded by foundations, businesses, and individuals. The remaining revenue came from interest on savings and temporary cash investments. The Foundation lost $144,701 on the sale of securities. The Foundation held $15,194,723, or 47% of assets, in investment partnerships which included corporate stock. $6,901,607, or 21%, in corporate stock.

Bay Area Bisexual Network (BABN)

2404 California St., Box 24
San Francisco, CA 94115   **Phone:**   (415) 703-7977   **E-Mail:** gswitch@igc.atc.org
USA

Contact Person: Matthew LeGrant, Co-Chair.   **Officers or Principals:** Lani Ka'ahumann, Co-Chair.
Mission or Interest: Umbrella group for bisexual organizations and persons in the Bay Area. Publishes *Anything That Moves: The Magazine for the Uncompromising Bisexual*, a magazine featuring articles, essays, letters, fiction, poetry and more - with graphical sexual content.
Accomplishments: *Anything That Moves* is the only full-length feature magazine for and by bisexuals. It is in its sixth year of publication.
Products or Services: Speakers bureau and resource hotline.
Tax Status: Nonprofit status pending.   **Annual Report:** No.   **Employees:** All volunteer.

Board of Directors or Trustees: Jim Frazin, Maggi Rabenstein, Mark Silver.
Periodicals: *Anything That Moves.*
Internships: No.
Other Information: Affiliated with the Bisexual Network of the United States.

Bay Area Physicians for Human Rights

4111 18th St., Suite 6
San Francisco, CA 94114   **Phone:** (415) 558-9353
USA   **Fax:**   (415) 558-0466

Contact Person: Lisa Capadini, Chair.
Officers or Principals: John Gilmore, Vice Chair ($0); Toby Duner, Treasurer ($0); Charles Meltzer, Secretary ($0).
Mission or Interest: Physicians promoting lesbian and gay rights and AIDS awareness.
Accomplishments: In 1993 the organization spent $55,894 on its programs. The largest program, with expenditures of $33,315, was grants for other organizations. $22,579 was spent on community AIDS education.
Net Revenue: 1993 $418,846 **Net Expenses:** $89,843 62%/38%/0% **Net Assets:** $811,363
Tax Status: 501(c)(3)
Other Information: The organization received $338,050, or 81% of revenue, from direct and indirect public support in the form of gifts and grants awarded by foundations, businesses, affiliates, and individuals. $34,425, or 8%, from dividends and interest from securities. $24,240, or 6%, from membership dues. $13,590, or 3%, from educational programs that inform "health professionals about gay/lesbian health needs and concerns." $10,503, or 3%, from interest on savings and temporary cash investments. The Physicians lost $2,187 on the sale of securities.

Beauty Without Cruelty

175 W. 12th St., Suite 16G
New York, NY 10011
USA

Contact Person: Ethel Thurston, Ph.D., Chair.
Mission or Interest: Animal rights organization that focuses on the cosmetics industry.
Net Revenue: 1994 $7,364   **Tax Status:** 501(c)(3)

Beldon Fund

2000 P St., N.W., Suite 410
Washington, DC 20036   **Phone:** (202) 293-1928   **E-Mail:** beldon@igc.apc.org
USA   **Fax:**   (202) 659-3897

Contact Person: Mercede Graham, Program Associate.
Officers or Principals: Judy Donald, Former Secretary/Treasurer ($46,816); Diane Ives, Secretary/Treasurer ($28,770); John R. Hunting, President ($0); R. Malcolm Cumming, Assistant Secretary/Treasurer.
Mission or Interest: The Beldon Fund awards grants to environmental organizations at the state and local level. "One outcome of the last election (1994) is that many environmental battles are shifting from federal to state and local levels. Thus it will be even more imperative that the Beldon Fund continue its longtime support of state-based environmental organizations...A larger and even more long-term aftershock is that we may be moving closer to a corporate state. If so, there will be a new focus for environmental foundations in the offing: documenting and challenging the pervasive power of unfettered (and thus, environmentally destructive) capitalism."
Accomplishments: In the fiscal year ending November 1994, the Fund awarded $489,550 in grants. Recipients of the largest grants included: two grants totaling $35,000 for American Environment, two grants totaling $30,000 for the Clean Water Fund, $20,000 for the Environmental Action Foundation, $15,000 for Arizona Toxics Information, and $12,500 for the Natural Resources Defense Council.
Net Revenue: FY ending 11/94 $678,922 **Net Expenses:** $667,269 **Net Assets:** $23,116
Tax Status: 501(c)(3)
Other Information: Affiliated with the Beldon II Fund at the same address. The Fund received $669,999, or 99% of revenue, from gifts and grants awarded by foundations, businesses, and individuals. The remaining income came from interest on savings and temporary cash investments, and other miscellaneous sources.

Berkeley Community Law Center

3130 Shattuck Ave.
Berkeley, CA 94705   **Phone:** (510) 548-4040
USA

Contact Person: J. Marley, Development Director. **Officers or Principals:** Bernida Reagan, Executive Director ($57,396); Peter McAweeney, Chair ($0); Margot Rosenberg, Treasurer ($0).
Mission or Interest: "The Center is a clinical placement program for law students at the University of California, Berkeley, Boalt Hall School of Law, serving the low-income communities of Berkeley, Emeryville and Oakland, California. Under the supervision of staff attorneys and members of the Boalt Hall faculty, the students offer free advise, counseling and representation to low-income clients with problems in the areas of public benefits, housing and AIDS-related law."

Accomplishments: In the fiscal year ending June 1995, the Center spent $487,723 on its programs.
Net Revenue: FY ending 6/95 $631,953 ($459,748, or 73%, from government grants) **Net Expenses:** $590,222 83%/12%/5%
Net Assets: $240,464 **Citations:** 2:231
Products or Services: Legal services for low-income clients. The Center awards scholarships to law students at UC Berkeley, funded from the interest on the Huey P. Newton Scholarship Fund. The Fund is named after the Black Panther Party founder and Minister of Defense. In his lifetime, Newton had been charged with a number of murders, including that of Oakland policeman John Frey for which he was convicted (the conviction was later overturned on appeal due to a technical error in the judge's instructions to the jury). Newton was later killed during a drug deal.
Tax Status: 501(c)(3)
Board of Directors or Trustees: Carolyn Patty Blum (Immigration Studies, Boalt Hall School of Law, UC Berkeley), Henry Hewitt, Anthony Iton M.D. J.D., Michael Loeb, Renee Maria Saucedo (La Raza Centro Legal), Kathryn Seligman, Andrew Shagrin, Laura Stein (Legal Services Dept., The Clorox Co.), Prof. Stephen Sugarman (Boalt Hall School of Law, UC Berkeley), Hon. Claudia Wilken (Judge, U.S. District Court, Northern District of CA).
Internships: Yes, summer internships for law students. It is a clinical internship for the Boalt Hall School of Law.
Other Information: The Center received $459,748, or 73% of revenue, from government grants. (These government grants included $133,000 from the Department of Education, $89,545 from the city of Berkeley, $42,450 from the County of Almeda, and $12,674 from the City of Oakland.) $150,829, or 24%, from gifts and grants awarded by foundations, corporations and individuals. (These grants included $182,079 from the Ryan White Foundation, $50,000 from the University of California, Boalt Hall, $13,897 from the United Way, and $8,350 from the Legal Services Corporation.) $4,066, or 1%, from interest on savings and temporary cash investments. The remaining revenue came from miscellaneous sources.

Berkeley Journal of Sociology (BJS)

458A Barrows Hall / Department of Sociology
Berkeley, CA 94705   **Phone:** (510) 642-2771
USA   **Fax:** (510) 642-0659

Contact Person: Christy Getz. **Officers or Principals:** Editorial Board: Anne Beard-Liikala, Beth Bernstein, Kim DaCosta, Linus Huang, Stacy Lawrence, Steve Lopez, Katherine Ogburn, Amy Schalet, Nathaniel Silva, Scott Stumbo, Eddy U, Ann Wood.
Mission or Interest: Publish the work of radical/leftist/unorthodox scholars, including students and untenured faculty.
Accomplishments: "Forty years as one of the only student-run journals in the country." Articles are indexed in *Sociological Abstracts* and the *Alternative Press Index*.
Tax Status: Unincorporated nonprofit association at the Univ. of California, Berkeley. **Annual Report:** No. **Employees:** 1
Board of Directors or Trustees: Advisory Board: Richard Apostle (Dalhousie Univ.), Elaine Draper (Univ. of Southern CA), Samuel Fraber (Brooklyn College), Seth Fisher (Univ. of CA, Santa Barbara), John Foran (Univ. of CA, Santa Barbara), Dair Gillespie (Univ. of UT), Jerome Himmelstein (Amherst College), Paul Lichterman (Univ. of WI, Madison), Ivan Light (UCLA), Michael Kimmel (SUNY, Stony Brook), Kinuthia Macharia (Harvard Univ.), Gary Marx (Univ. of CO, Boulder), Greg MacLauchlan (Univ. of Southern CA), Thomas Scheff (Univ. of CA, Santa Barbara), Gay Seidman (Univ. of WI, Madison), Lyn Spillman (Univ. of Notre Dame), Mary Waters (Harvard Univ.), Christine Williams (Univ. of TX, Austin), Jim Wood (San Diego State Univ.).
Periodicals: *Berkeley Journal of Sociology* (annual academic journal).
Internships: No.

Between the Lines: For Lesbians, Gays, Bisexuals & Friends

1632 Church St.
Detroit, MI 48216   **Phone:** (313) 961-4862   **E-Mail:** Between.The.Lines@um.cc.umich.edu
USA   **Fax:** (313) 961-5285

Contact Person: Shannon Rhoades, Editor-in-Chief. **Officers or Principals:** Julie R. Enzer, Chair.
Mission or Interest: "*Between the Lines* is dedicated to serving the lesbian, gay, bisexual, and transgendered communities in Michigan through a forum of public dialogue and communication. We strive to create a publication with thoughtful political, social, economic, and personal analysis and provide a voice to our communities." Between the Lines offers "a vision of justice and equality, compassion and fairness. While extremists bait people of color, women, lesbians and gay men as wanting special rights; we know that we all simply want justice. The right to keep a job, the right to work with dignity, the right to housing, the right to access to public accommodations. We are seeking equity."
Accomplishments: Features the comic strip "Dykes to Watch Out For."
Tax Status: For profit.
Board of Directors or Trustees: John Burchett, Carla Gillard, Crystal Muldrow, Matt Ostrander, Tim Retzloff, Shannon Rhoades, Cheryl Troup, Patrick Yankee, Charlotte Young.
Periodicals: *Between the Lines* (monthly tabloid).

Black Veterans for Social Justice

686 Fulton St.
Brooklyn, NY 11217   **Phone:** (718) 935-1116
USA

Contact Person: Job Mashariki, Executive Director. **Officers or Principals:** Job Mashariki, Executive Director ($75,500); Lawrence Smith, Chair Person ($0); Muslimah Toliver, Secretary ($0); John Carter, Treasurer.

Mission or Interest: Works for solutions to problems facing black veterans. Focus on problems of homelessness, HIV/AIDS, racism, job counseling, and leadership training.
Accomplishments: In 1994 the organization spent $572,555 on it programs. The largest program, with expenditures of $156,559, was for homeless veterans, providing outreach services, housing searches, and counseling. $85,344 was spent on HIV/AIDS counseling. Other programs included various types of counseling and assistance, "Stop the Violence" campaign, and community leadership training.
Net Revenue: 1994 $633,504 ($472,339, or 75%, from government grants) **Net Expenses:** $661,641 87%/10%/4%
Net Assets: $15,578 **Citations:** 2:231
Tax Status: 501(c)(3)
Board of Directors or Trustees: Philip Jones, Herbert Tibbs, Pete Carter, Oronde Takuma, Na Sha, George Johnson, Tyrone Williams.
Periodicals: *Black Vet* (bimonthly newsletter).
Other Information: Black Veterans for Social Justice received $472,339, or 75% of revenue, from government grants. $88,215, or 14%, from gifts and grants awarded by foundations, businesses, and individuals. (These grants included $3,000 from the North Star Fund.) $71,242, or 11%, from program services. The remaining revenue came from interest on savings and temporary cash investments.

Blue Ridge Environmental Defense League

P.O. Box 88
Glendale Springs, NC 28629   **Phone:**   (910) 982-2691
USA

Contact Person: Janet M. Hoyle, Executive Director.
Officers or Principals: James A. Johnson, Sam Tesh, Co-Presidents ($0); Carol Bradley, Jean Colston, Fred Dye, Pam Jopson, Claude Ward, Vice Presidents ($0); Marian Wallin, Secretary; Jennifer Smith, Treasurer.
Mission or Interest: "Promote education on environmental issues to the general public and grassroots organizations."
Accomplishments: In 1994 the League spent $107,431 on its programs.
Net Revenue: 1994 $121,114 **Net Expenses:** $116,585 92%/0%/8% **Net Assets:** $105,365
Tax Status: 501(c)(3)
Board of Directors or Trustees: Joann Almond, Mark Barker, Willie Bazemore, Paulette Blair, Mickii Carter, Richard Crowe, Bill Evans, Mark Flomenhoft, Jody Friedman, Gene Holt, Mike Hughes, Charles Jackson, Geneva Johnson, Gayl Knox, Chuck Lieberman, Dr. Richard Maas, Mamie Moore, Edward Parker, Brenda Remmes, Leisa Roberts, Lenora Rose, Ron Shackelford, Charles Tillery, Susan Whiteside, Ann Willardson.
Other Information: The League received $101,607, or 84% of revenue, from gifts and grants awarded by foundations, businesses, and individuals. (These grants included $15,000 from the Ruth Mott Fund, $6,000 from the Jessie Smith Noyes Foundation. The League was awarded $150,000 from the Florence and John Schumann Foundation, but the grant was rescinded.) $9,410, or 8%, from special fund-raising events. $3,559 net, or 3%, from the sale of inventory. $3,382, or 3%, from membership dues. The remaining revenue came from interest on savings and temporary cash investments, and the sale of recyclables.

Body Politic, The

P.O. Box 2363
Binghamton, NY 13902   **Phone:**   (607) 648-2760
USA

Mission or Interest: Feminist newsletter. Coverage of abortion rights and gender issues.
Periodicals: *The Body Politic* (newsletter).

Boston Reproductive Rights Network

P.O. Box 686
Cambridge, MA 02130   **Phone:**   (617) 494-1161   **E-Mail:** rcaap@aol.com
USA   **Fax:**   same

Contact Person: Rosemary.
Mission or Interest: Abortion rights organization focusing on Massachusetts. Operates the Abortion Access Project, "the project is addressing the crisis of decreasing services with proactive strategies to increase the number of abortion providers and the availability of accessible abortion services."
Accomplishments: "Increased the number of hospitals in Massachusetts providing abortions, established a program for Ob-Gyn residents in one residency program, added reproductive health curriculum at one medical school." Paid for signs on busses and trains in the Boston area that say "Abortion Access: Without it you've got no choice."
Net Revenue: Less than $50,000
Products or Services: Directory of abortion services in Massachusetts, fact sheets.
Tax Status: 501(c)(3)
Periodicals: *AAP* (quarterly newsletter), *Reproductive Rights Network Newsletter* (tri-annual newsletter).
Other Information: In 1994 the Network received $10,000 from the Ms. Foundation.

Bound Together Books

1369 Haight St.
San Francisco, CA 94117   **Phone:**   (415) 431-8355
USA

Contact Person: Tom, Tet, Rad or Joey.
Mission or Interest: "All volunteer, collectively run anarchist bookshop...emphasis on anarchism but a range of other alternative titles (i.e. gay-lesbian, women's, small press titles, etc.)."
Accomplishments: Started the "Prisoners' Literature Project." Helped organize the 1989 Without Borders Festival - an anarchist conference. In honor of their twentieth anniversary in 1996 they hosted the first Bay Area Anarchist Book Fair. Speakers included Robert Anton Wilson, Susie Bright, and Jello Biafra of the "Dead Kennedys" band.
Products or Services: Books, posters, pamphlets, videos and occasional events.
Tax Status: For profit.

Bread and Roses Community Fund

1500 Walnut St., Suite 1305
Philadelphia, PA 19102   **Phone:**   (215) 731-1107
USA   **Fax:**   (215) 731-0453

Contact Person: Judy Claude, Executive Director.   **Officers or Principals:** Judy Claude, Executive Director ($38,763).
Mission or Interest: Grant-making foundation that focuses on grassroots organizations.
Accomplishments: In the fiscal year ending July 1994, the Fund awarded $189,543 in grants. The Fund awards grants to organizations that fit into various categories. Of these categories, women's rights received the most, followed by (in order), youth organizing, community organizing, AIDS and health activism, lesbian and gay rights, arts and social change, economic justice, peace and justice international, worker's rights, human rights and civil liberties, and resources for organizing. Recipients of the largest grants included: three grants totaling $11,500 for the Greater Philadelphia Women's Medical Fund, four grants totaling $10,450 for the Women's Law Project, four grants totaling $10,000 for ACT UP!, $5,000 each for the Greater Camden County Reinvestment Corp., Kensington Joint Action Council, Training Center Workshops, and the University City New School, $4,000 each for the AIDS Law Project of Pennsylvania, Philadelphia Independent Film/Video Assoc., the Police-Barrio Relations Project, Women Against Abuse, CATA Farmworkers United, Asian American United, and the Future Leaders Network.
Net Revenue: FY ending 7/94 $431,672 **Net Expenses:** $349,500 71%/17%/12% **Net Assets:** $236,192
Products or Services: Grants and technical assistance.
Tax Status: 501(c)(3)
Board of Directors or Trustees: Cynthia Fowler, John Hellebrand, Jenny Anne Horst-Martz, Elaina Johnson, Gary Kalman, Suzanne Lashner, Jonathan Lax, Ervin Miller, L. Glen Scott, Betty Shabazz, Audrey Tucker, Richard Baron, Linda Berman, Karen Claiborne, Peggy Curchack, John Fong.
Other Information: A member of the Funding Exchange Network. The Fund received $377,791, or 88% of revenue, from direct and indirect public support in the form of gifts and grants awarded by foundations, businesses, affiliates, and individuals. (These grants included $10,000 from the Rex Foundation, $6,000 from the Vanguard Public Foundation, and $3,500 from the Tides Foundation.) $34,183 net, or 8%, from special fund-raising events, including a "Tribute to Change" luncheon, ad book, and auction. $10,897, or 3%, from program service income. The remaining revenue came from interest on savings and temporary cash investments.

Brethren Peace Fellowship

P.O. Box 455
New Windsor, MD 21776   **Phone:**   (410) 775-2254
USA

Contact Person: Dale Aukerman.   **Officers or Principals:** Wilbur Wright Jr., President.
Mission or Interest: "Renewal and spread of Christian peace witness in the Church of the Brethren and beyond; peacemaking grounded in the Lordship of Jesus Christ."
Accomplishments: Handed out leaflets at Billy Graham crusades in Baltimore and Washington. Held vigils outside a tank factory near York, PA, and at the Army War College at Carlisle, PA.
Tax Status: 501(c)(3) **Annual Report:** No. **Employees:** All volunteer.
Periodicals: Newsletters, one for the Mid-Atlantic region, and one for the Atlantic-Northeast region.
Other Information: Founded in 1967.

Brookings Institution

1775 Massachusetts Ave., N.W.
Washington, DC 20036   **Phone:**   (202) 797-6000
USA   **Fax:**   (202) 797-6004

Contact Person: Michael H. Armacost, President.
Officers or Principals: Bruce K. MacLaury, Former President ($240,192); John M. Hills, Vice President ($182,632); Henry J. Aaron, Program Director ($149,213); Lawrence J. Korb, Program Director ($145,636); John D. Steinbruner, Program Director ($145,204); Thomas E. Mann, Program Director ($140,721); Charles L. Schultze, Senior Fellow ($137,504); Julie I. Englund, Treasurer ($133,324); James A. Johnson, Chairman; Michael H. Armacost, President.

Mission or Interest: Centrist to liberal-left research and public policy institution. "To promote, carry on, conduct and foster scientific research, education, training and publication in the broad fields of economics, government administration, and the political and social sciences generally, involving the study, determination, interpretation and publication of economic, political and social facts and principles relating to questions of local, national or international significance; to promote and carry out these objects, purposes and principles without regard to and independently of the special interests of any group in the body politic, either political, social or economic."

Accomplishments: Brookings is one of the first, and most prominent of Washington, DC, think tanks. In the fiscal year ending June 1994, the Institution spent $12,942,306 on its programs. The largest program, with expenditures of $3,701,982, was economic studies. $3,438,684 was spent on foreign policy studies, $2,937,100 on the Center for Public Policy and Education, and $1,486,257 on governmental studies. Other programs included the Brookings Fellowship program, Social Science Computer Center, and a public affairs office.

Net Revenue: FY ending 6/94 $23,093,046 ($404,928, or 2%, from government grants)

Net Expenses: $16,845,948 77%/17%/6% **Net Assets:** $120,669,168 **Citations:** 2,246:12

Products or Services: Numerous publications, reports, fellowships, conferences, symposiums, and more. Books published by the Brookings Press. MacLaury Chair and Friedman Fellowships for scholars.

Tax Status: 501(c)(3)

Board of Directors or Trustees: Leonard Abramson (Pres., U.S. Healthcare), Ronald Arnault (CFO, ARCO), Dr. Elizabeth Bailey (Wharton School), Barton Biggs (Chair, Morgan Stanley Asset Management), Frank Cary (retired Chairman & CEO, IBM), A.W. Clausen (retired Chairman & CEO, BankAmerica Corp.), Prof. Kenneth Dam (Univ. of Chicago Law School), Robert Erburu (Chair, Times Mirror Co.), William Gray III (Pres., United Negro College Fund), Vartan Gregorian (Pres., Brown Univ.), Teresa Heinz (Chair, Heinz Family Philanthropies), Prof. Samuel Hellman M.D. (Dept. of Radiation and Cellular Oncology, Univ. of Chicago), Hon. Roy Huffington, Joseph James (Pres., Council on Foundations), Nannerl Keohane (Pres., Duke Univ.), Thomas Labercque (Chair, Chase Manhattan Corp.), Hon. Jim Lynn, Hon. Donald McHenry (School of Foreign Service, Georgetown Univ.), Robert McNamara (Secretary of Defense, 1961-1968), Dr. Mary Patterson McPherson (Pres., Bryn Mawr College), Constance Berry Newman (Under Secretary, Smithsonian Inst.), David Rockefeller Jr., (Chair, Rockefeller Financial Services), Ralph Saul (CIGNA Corp.), Henry Schacht (Chair., Cummins Engine Co.), Michael Schulhof (Pres., Sony Corp. of America), Robert Smith Brookings, and many others from the world of business, law, academia, and government.

Periodicals: *Brookings Review* (quarterly magazine).

Other Information: Brookings traces its roots back to 1916, and is named in honor of business entrepreneur and philanthropist Robert Brookings. The Institution received $11,170,750, or 48% of revenue, from gifts and grants awarded by foundations, businesses, and individuals. (These grants included $200,000 from the William and Flora Hewlett Foundation. In 1995, $241,700 from the Rockefeller Foundation.) $4,499,390, or 19%, from dividends and interest from securities. $3,662,727, or 16%, from capital gains on the sale of securities. $3,291,455, or 14%, from conference fees. $404,928, or 2%, from government grants. The remaining revenue came from interest on savings and temporary cash investments, rental income, other investment income, and other miscellaneous sources. The Institution lost $935,054 on the sale of inventory.

Bulletin of Concerned Asian Scholars

3239 9th St.
Boulder, CO 80304   **Phone:**   (303) 449-7439   **E-Mail:** doub@csf.colorado.edu
USA

Contact Person: John Livingston, President. **Officers or Principals:** Bill Doub, Publisher.
Mission or Interest: Publication devoted to peace, the environment and anti-imperialism with a focus on South East Asia.
Net Revenue: 1994 $65,602 **Net Expenses:** $64,601 **Net Assets:** $29,355
Tax Status: 501(c)(3)
Periodicals: *Bulletin of Concerned Asian Scholars* (quarterly journal).
Other Information: Established in 1968 in opposition to the war in Vietnam.

Bulletin of the Atomic Scientists
(see the Educational Foundation for Nuclear Science)

Bullitt Foundation

1212 Minor Ave.
Seattle, WA 98101   **Phone:**   (206) 343-0807   **E-Mail:** bullittfdn@aol.com
USA   **Fax:**   (206) 343-0822

Contact Person: Emory Bundy, Administrative Manager. **Officers or Principals:** Denis Hayes, President ($134,215); Emory Bundy, Administrative Manager ($87,867); Kathleen Becker, Program Officer ($43,920); Marilyn Fike, Director of Administration; Harolynne Bobis, Assistant to the President; Lois Brown, Administration Assistant.
Mission or Interest: Philanthropy that awards grants to preserve, protect, and restore the environment of the Pacific Northwest. Their awards are aimed at protecting the environment, reducing population to 'carrying capacity' levels, and supporting government planning of development and resource allocation.
Accomplishments: In 1993 they awarded $4,471,661 in grants. The recipients of the largest grants were: $170,000 for the People for Puget Sound, $150,000 for the Natural Resources Defense Council, $130,000 for the Washington Environmental Council, $125,000 for the National Audubon Society, $110,000 for the Wilderness Society, $100,000 for the Sierra Club Legal Defense Fund and the Alaska Conservation Foundation, $90,000 for 1000 Friends of Washington, $80,000 for Long Live the Kings, and $75,000 each for American Rivers, Environmental Defense Fund, and Warm Springs Tribe. In 1994 they also gave a $5,000 grant to the free-market oriented Foundation for Research on Economics and the Environment for a project called "Writers on the Range" that is expected to result in a book.

Net Revenue: 1993 $8,562,223 **Net Expenses:** $5,688,669 **Net Assets:** $94,606,156
Products or Services: Grants, meetings, conferences and other public events.
Tax Status: 501(c)(3) **Annual Report:** Yes. **Employees:** 6
Board of Directors or Trustees: Harriet Bullitt, Katherine Bullitt, Stimson Bullitt, Priscilla Collins, B. Gerald Johnson, Hubert Locke, Darlene Madenwald, Douglass Raff.
Internships: Yes.
Other Information: The Bullitt Foundation employs The Rockey Company in Seattle for public relations. In 1993 they were paid $44,604 for services. The Foundation received $5,071,818, or 59% of revenue, from the sale of assets. $3,025,179, or 35%, from interest on savings and temporary cash investments. $355,698, or 4%, from dividends and interest on securities. The remaining income came from royalties and "partnership income." The Foundation held most of its assets, 94%, in corporate and U.S. government securities.

Business and Professional People for the Public Interest

17 E. Monroe St., Suite 212
Chicago, IL 60603   **Phone:** (312) 641-5570
USA

Contact Person: Alexander Polikoff, Executive Director.
Mission or Interest: A public interest law firm addressing the issues of 'social and economic justice.'
Other Information: In 1994 the organization received $149,500 from the Joyce Foundation, $45,000 from the New Prospect Foundation, $5,000 from the Wieboldt Foundation.

Bydale Foundation

11 Martine Ave.
White Plains, NY 10606   **Phone:** (914) 428-3232
USA

Contact Person: Milton D. Solomon, Vice President.
Mission or Interest: Grant-making foundation that primarily funds leftist organizations.
Accomplishments: In 1994 the Foundation awarded $440,750 in grants. The recipients of the largest grants included: $35,000 for Americans for Peace Now, $20,000 each for the Foundation for Economic Trends, Greenhouse Crisis Foundation, and North Carolina Center for Peace Education, $15,000 for Fairness and Accuracy in Reporting, $12,500 each for the Institute for Research and Education on Human Rights, and the National Abortion and Reproductive Rights Action League Foundation, $12,000 for the Planned Parenthood League of CT, and $10,000 each for the Center for Democratic Renewal, Emergency Need Pool for Israel-Palestinian Project, Israel Union for Environmental Defense, Institute for Social Justice, National Public Radio, Parliamentarians Global Action, Teachers and Writers Collaborative, and Young Audiences Inc.
Net Revenue: 1994 $532,177 **Net Expenses:** $569,554 **Net Assets:** $9,943,380
Tax Status: 501(c)(3)
Other Information: The Foundation received $487,119, or 87% of revenue, from dividends and interest from securities. $75,558, or 13%, from interest on savings and temporary cash investments. The Foundation lost $30,500 on the sale of securities. The Foundation held $5,026,558, or 51% of its assets, in corporate bonds. $3,406,377, or 34%, in corporate stocks.

C.S. Fund

469 Bohemian Highway
Freestone, CA 95472   **Phone:** (707) 874-2942
USA

Contact Person: Roxanne Turnage, Deputy Director.
Officers or Principals: Martin Teitel, Executive Director ($79,717); Roxanne Turnage, Deputy Director ($48,838); Marise Meynet Stewart, Trustee ($2,250); Maryanne T. Mott, President; Herman E. Warsh, Secretary/Treasurer.
Mission or Interest: Grant-making foundation that focuses on the environment, peace, and the media.
Accomplishments: In the fiscal year ending October 1994, the Fund awarded $782,500 in grants. The recipients of the largest grants included: $50,000 for the Foundation on Economic Trends, $37,000 for Institute for Agriculture and Trade Policy, $30,000 each for the Center for Investigative Reporting, Data Center, Government Accountability Project, $25,000 each for the JSI Research and Training Institute, Antarctica Project, Defenders of Wildlife, Rural Advancement Foundation, Center for Constitutional Rights, Council for Responsible Genetics, and Commission on Religion in Appalachia.
Net Revenue: FY ending 10/94 $1,237,417 **Net Expenses:** $1,316,687 **Net Assets:** $456,897
Tax Status: 501(c)(3)
Board of Directors or Trustees: Michael Warsh.
Other Information: The Fund received $1,266,773, or 99% of gross revenue, from gifts and grants awarded by foundations, businesses, and individuals. (These grants included $56,843 from the Warsh-Mott Legacy.) The remaining income came from interest on savings and temporary cash investments, and other miscellaneous income. The Fund had a loss of $41,646 on the sale of securities. The Fund held most of its assets, $318,933, or 70%, in land, buildings, and equipment. $105,418, or 23%, held in savings and temporary cash investments.

California Women's Law Center

6024 Wilshire Blvd.
Los Angeles, CA 90036   **Phone:** (213) 935-4101
USA

Contact Person: Jenifer McKenna, Director.   **Officers or Principals:** Abby J. Liebman, Executive Director ($67,000); Roberta Ikemi, Attorney ($40,786); Sharon Seto, Administrator ($33,482); Dr. Diane Bonta, President; Angela Oh, Vice President; Beatriz Olvera-Stotzer, Treasurer; June Baldwin, Secretary.
Mission or Interest: "Provides legal and technical assistance to legal service providers and other attorneys throughout California to advance the rights of women."
Accomplishments: In the fiscal year ending June 1994, the Center spent $337,706 on its programs.
Net Revenue: FY ending 6/94 $382,386 **Net Expenses:** $384,172 88%/8%/4% **Net Assets:** $30,252
Products or Services: Legal services, lobbying. The Center spent $5,955 on various methods of lobbying.
Tax Status: 501(c)(3)
Board of Directors or Trustees: Barbara Faye Waxman, Natalie Sanders M.D., Billie Heller, Janice Kamenir-Reznik, Sheila James Kuehl, Feelie Lee Ph.D., Christine Littleton, June Sale, Carla Sanger, Dorothy Jonas, Carla Barboza, Emily Levine.
Other Information: The Center was co-founded by Sheila James Kuehl, who is currently the first openly lesbian representative elected to California's state assembly. The Center received $326,681, or 85% of revenue, from gifts and grants awarded by foundations, businesses, and individuals. $35,815 net, or 9%, from the "Just a Taste" special fundraising event. $17,352, or 5%, from training seminar fees. The remaining revenue came from the sale of publications and interest on savings and temporary cash investments.

Calumet Project for Industrial Jobs

4012 Elm St.
East Chicago, IN 46312   **Phone:** (219) 398-6393
USA

Contact Person: Juanita Williams, President.   **Officers or Principals:** Juanita Williams, President ($0); Jim Hornak, Vice President ($0); Rev. Dr. Barbara Edgecombe, Secretary ($0); Anna Flores Martell, Treasurer.
Mission or Interest: Promotion of labor relations with local industries.
Accomplishments: In the fiscal year ending June 1994, the Project spent $52,445 on its programs.
Net Revenue: FY ending 6/94 $183,749 **Net Expenses:** $101,711 52%/48%/0% **Net Assets:** $67,415
Tax Status: 501(c)(3)
Board of Directors or Trustees: Aaron Anderson, Lorenzo Crowell, Barbara Edwards, Nancy Jones, Willie Moore, Charles Pettersen, Kerry Taylor, Bennie Bailey, Raymond Kottka, Londale Micou, Prof. Bruce Nissen (Indiana Univ., Northwest), Rose Rodriguez, Rev. Doug Witt.
Other Information: The Project received $179,441, or 98% of revenue, from direct and indirect public support in the form of gifts and grants awarded by foundations, affiliates, businesses, and individuals. (These grants included $30,000 from the Florence and John Schumann Foundation, $10,000 from the Ms. Foundation for Women.) $2,229 net, or 1%, from special fund-raising events. $2,079, or 1%, from interest on savings and temporary cash investments.

Campaign for a Sustainable Milwaukee

1726 N. 1st St., Suite 202
Milwaukee, WI 53212   **Phone:** (414) 372-7175
USA

Contact Person: Bill Dempsey.
Mission or Interest: Grassroots community organization focusing on job creation, 'a living wage,' community reinvestment, labor rights, and labor equity.

Campaign for Human Development (CHD)

(see the United States Catholic Conference)

Campaign for Peace and Democracy

P.O. Box 1640, Cathedral Station
New York, NY 10025   **Phone:** (212) 666-5924   **E-Mail:** camppeacedem@igc.apc.org
USA   **Fax:**   (212) 662-5892

Contact Person: Jennifer Scarlott, Associate Director.   **Officers or Principals:** Joanne Landy, President ($39,562); Jennifer Scarlott, Associate Director ($36,032); Thomas Harrison, Associate Director ($0).
Mission or Interest: "Dedicated to promoting a new, progressive, and non-militaristic U.S. foreign policy - one that renounces power politics and uses cooperation, aid, and political support to encourage democratization and social change throughout the world. The campaign brings together members of the peace movement, environmentalists, trade unionists, feminists, gay and minority rights activists, academics, journalists, and independent scholars."

Accomplishments: Nominated for the *Utne Reader* award for international reporting. Held protests and demonstrations supporting the lifting of the arms embargo imposed against Bosnia (1993), supporting abortion rights in Poland (1992), against Soviet violence in Lithuania (1991), against the U.S. invasion of Panama (1990), others. Took out an ad in a December 1985 *New York Times* protesting President Reagan's Nicaragua policies. In 1994 the Campaign spent $126,571 on its activities.
Net Revenue: 1994 $200,742 **Net Expenses:** $171,265 74%/19%/7% **Net Assets:** $52,267
Products or Services: Conferences, seminars, rallies, protests and publications. Sends fact-finding delegations.
Tax Status: 501(c)(3) **Employees:** 2
Board of Directors or Trustees: Don Bacheller, Lynn Chancer, Margaret Crane, Manuela Dobos, John Feffer, Todd Gitlin, Judith Hempfling, Andrea Imredy, John Miller, Carlos Pabon, Grace Paley, Stephen Shalom, Michael Simmons, Bill Smith, Ann Snitow, Dorie Wilsnack, Kent Worcester.
Periodicals: *Peace & Democracy* (quarterly magazine).
Internships: Yes, unpaid.
Other Information: Founded in 1982. The campaign received $200,742, or 100% of revenue, from grants awarded by foundations, businesses and individuals. (These grants included $27,500 from the Joyce Mertz-Gilmore Foundation, $8,250 from the Winston Foundation for World Peace, $1,000 from the North Star Fund.)

Campaign for U.N. Reform
713 D St., S.E.
Washington, DC 20003   **Phone:** (202) 546-3956
USA

Contact Person: Eric Cox, Executive Director. **Officers or Principals:** Eric Cox, Executive Director ($25,368); Floyd Ramp, President ($0); Ray Short, First Vice President ($0); Rosemary Young, Second Vice President.
Mission or Interest: Advocacy and lobbying on behalf of a stronger and more effective United Nations. "Global Statesmanship" ratings that rate Congressmen and Senators on their votes pertaining to U.N. funding and international cooperation.
Accomplishments: In 1994 the Campaign spent $36,418 on its programs.
Net Revenue: 1994 $50,354 **Net Expenses:** $52,026 **Net Assets:** $7,527
Products or Services: Publications, lobbying, voters' guides, campaign contributions, more.
Tax Status: 501(c)(4)
Board of Directors or Trustees: Capt. Tom Hudgens, Carlyn Kaiser Stark, William Fisher, Kermit Rhode, Barbara Rhode, B. Gerard Cordelli, Howard Taylor, Hugh Stier, John Dale Jr., Charles Guettel.
Periodicals: *UN Reform Campaigner* (newsletter).
Other Information: The Campaign received $50,044, or 99% of revenue, from gifts and grants awarded by foundations, businesses, affiliates, and individuals. The remaining revenue came from investment income.

Carnegie Corporation of New York
437 Madison Ave.
New York, 10022   **Phone:** (212) 371-3200
USA

Contact Person: Dorothy Wills Knapp, Secretary.   **Officers or Principals:** David A. Hamberg, President; Barbara Denning Finberg, Executive Vice President; Newton Norman Minow, Chairman; Eugene H. Cota-Robles, Vice Chairman; Jeanmarie Conte Grisi, Treasurer; Patricia L. Rosenfield, Program Chair, Human Resources in Developing Countries; David C. Speedie, III, Program Chair, Preventing Deadly Conflict; Vivien Stewart, Program Chair, Education and Youth Development.
Mission or Interest: "The advancement and diffusion of knowledge and understanding." Current focus on education and development of children, strengthening human resources in developing countries, and preventing deadly conflict. Most spending goes to international programs with an emphasis on the United Nations.
Accomplishments: In the fiscal year ending September 1993 the Corporation awarded $51,870,145 in grants. The recipients of the largest grants included (many of these grants cover multiple years, and are not disbursed in one lump-sum payment): $800,000 for the Carnegie Endowment for International Peace, $700,000 for the Children's Defense Fund, $675,000 for the Tides Foundation, $555,000 for the NAACP Legal Defense and Education Fund, $450,000 for the Puerto Rican Legal Defense and Education Fund, $250,000 for the NAACP Special Contributions Fund, $200,000 each for the Center for Responsive Politics, Arms Control Association, Gorbachev Foundation USA, and Parliamentarians for Global Action, $185,700 for the United Nations Economic Commission on Africa, $150,000 each for the United Nations Institute for Training and Research, and Wisconsin Project on Nuclear Arms Control, and $100,000 each for the African American Institute, Center for Governmental Studies, Center for Policy Alternatives, Economic Policy Institute, Human Rights Watch, Lawyers Committee for Human Rights, United Nations (for the Fourth World Conference on Women in Beijing), and the World Health Organization.
Net Assets: FY ending 9/93 $1,170,000,000
Tax Status: 501(c)(3) **Annual Report:** Yes.
Board of Directors or Trustees: Richard Beattie, Richard Celeste, James Pierpont Comer (Assoc. Dean, Yale Univ., School of Medicine), Caryl Parker Haskins, Maria Teresa Thierstein Simoes-Ferreira Heinz (Howard Heinz Endowment), James Johnston (Chair/CEO, Federal National Mortgage Assoc.), Helene Lois Kaplan (Chair, Barnard College), Thomas Kean (World Wildlife Fund), Shirley Malcolm, Laurence Alan Tisch (Tisch Found.), Wilma Tisch (Tisch Found.).
Other Information: The Corporation was founded with money from Andrew Carnegie, founder of the Carnegie Steel Company which he sold to J. P. Morgan for $400 million.

Carnegie Council on Ethics and International Affairs

170 E 64th St.
New York, NY 10021   Phone: (212) 838-4120
USA

Contact Person: Joel Rosenthal, President. **Officers or Principals:** Robert Myers, former President ($113,345); Joel Rosenthal, President ($79,200); Chris Sigur ($63,357); Russel Hardin, Treasurer.
Mission or Interest: "Increased understanding on ethics and international affairs."
Accomplishments: In the fiscal year ending June 1995, the Council spent $1,255,523 on its programs. The largest program, with expenditures of $570,363, conducted educational activity and produced pamphlets on topics such as human rights, religion, and economics. $538,153 was spent on Asian programs that examined "the continued development of the economic, political, and social institutions that strengthen the foundations of democracy in the region. Other programs included conferences, the "Carnegie Conversations," that bring together experts and "specially invited groups of people from corporations."
Net Revenue: FY ending 6/95 $998,142 **Net Expenses:** $2,032,972 62%/38%/0% **Net Assets:** $22,688,883
Citations: 1:240   **Tax Status:** 501(c)(3)
Board of Directors or Trustees: Bruce Bent, Phyllis Collins, Edward Cox, Thomas Donaldson, Malcolm Gudis, Allison Halaby, Charles Kegley Jr., Ethel Lefrak, Donald Mariarity, Joseph O'Hare, Ann Phillips, Robert Pines, Julius Scott Jr., Michael Smith, Maurice Spanbock, Harrison Steans, Paula Stern, Merry White, John Bennett, Charles Judd, Eiji Uehiro.
Other Information: The Council received $656,987, or 50% of total revenue, from gifts and grants awarded by foundations, businesses, affiliates, and individuals. $610,986, or 47%, from dividends and interest from securities. $22,627, or 2%, from interest on savings and temporary cash investments. $17,732, or 1%, from the sale of publications. The Council lost $310,190 on the sale of securities. The Council held $19,403,941, or 83% of total assets, in corporate stock.

Carnegie Endowment for International Peace / *Foreign Policy*

2400 N St., N.W.
Washington, DC 20037   **Phone:** (202) 797-6400
USA   **Fax:**   (202) 862-2610

Contact Person: Morton I. Abramowitz, President.
Officers or Principals: Morton I. Abramowitz, President ($196,125); Larry L. Fabian, Secretary ($112,964); Charles W. Maynes, III ($111,633); Leonard Spector, Senior Associate ($108,020); Robert Carswell, Chairman; James C. Gaither, Vice Chairman.
Mission or Interest: Private Foundation that, rather than making grants, funds its own projects promoting world peace. Publishes *Foreign Policy*.
Accomplishments: In the fiscal year ending June 1994, the Endowment spent $2,075,681 on its programs, or about 23% of expenses. The largest program, with expenditures of $855,191, was the publication of *Foreign Policy*. *Foreign Policy* is "widely regarded as one of the most influential affairs journals in the world, (it) was launched in 1970 to encourage fresh and more vigorous debate on the vital issues confronting U.S. foreign policy...cited and watched by U.S. government officials, world leaders, influential figures in corporate and labor circles, and students of foreign relations, this award-winning journal was picked by the 1992 *Mediaguide* as one of the most influential magazines in the United States...Many now-prominent authors published their first journal article in *Foreign Policy*. A current example is Anthony Lake, National Security Advisor in the Clinton Administration, who first published with *Foreign Policy* in the early 1970's." $528,612 was spent on the Immigration Policy Institute. "Unless managed firmly but thoughtfully, migration will pose critical challenges for democratic order and for international peace and stability...Program staff work with numerous governments, other leading nongovernmental institutions in the United States and abroad, international organizations, and various United Nations agencies." The Immigration Policy's core funding came from the Ford Foundation. $367,828 was spent on the Nuclear Non-Proliferation Project. The Project includes analyzing and publishing on various related issues, and monitoring and reporting on situations, such as North Korea's nuclear activities. $321,050 was spent on the Moscow Office, which works on U.S.-Russian relations, and many of the same programs as the other projects, but in Moscow.
Net Revenue: FY ending 6/94 $15,819,926 **Net Expenses:** $9,036,135 **Net Assets:** $113,077,898
Tax Status: 501(c)(3)
Board of Directors or Trustees: Charles Bailey II, Harry Barnes (Critical Languages & Area Studies Consortium), Gregory Craig, Richard Debs (Advisory Dir., Morgan Stanley & Co.), William Donaldson (Chair./CEO, New York Stock Exchange), John Douglas, Henry Fowler (Goldman Sachs & Co.), Prof. Douglas Fraser (Wayne State Univ.), Marion Fremont-Smith, Leslie Gelb (*New York Times*), Robert Goheen (Pres. Emeritus, Princeton Univ.), Ernest Gross, Lawrence Hafstad (former V.P., GM), Shirley Huftstedler, Thomas Hughes (Pres. Emeritus), James Johnson (Chair/CEO, Fannie Mae), Prof. Milton Katz (Suffolk Univ. Law School), Prof. Donald Kennedy (Stanford Univ.), Prof. Robert Legvold (Harriman Inst., Columbia Univ.), Wilbert LeMelle, Stephen Lewis Jr. (Pres. Carleton College), George Lindsay, Prof. George Lodge (Harvard Univ., Graduate School of Business), William Macomber, Jessica Mathews (V.P. World Resources Inst.), Prof. Barbara Newell (Florida State Univ.), Olara Otunnu (Pres., International Peace Academy), Howard Petersen, Wesley Posvar (Univ. of Pittsburgh), Norman Ramsey (Pres. Emeritus, Universities Research Association), Edson Spencer, Donald Straus (Pres. Emeritus, American Arbitration Assoc.), Leonard Woodcock, Charles Zwick.
Periodicals: *Foreign Policy* (quarterly journal).
Other Information: The Endowment received $9,327,394, or 59% of revenue, from capital gains from the sale of securities. $4,294,958, or 27%, from dividends and interest from securities. $1,541,463, or 10%, from gifts and grants awarded by foundations, businesses, and individuals. (These grants included $800,000 over two years from the Carnegie Corporation.) $653,343, or 4%, from program services, including publication sales, advertising revenue, mailing list rentals, royalties, and use of the conference center. The remaining revenue came from interest on savings and temporary cash investments, and other miscellaneous sources. $82,199,080, or 73% of the Endowment's assets, was held in corporate stocks and bonds. $26,269,072, or 23%, was held in government obligations.

Carrying Capacity Network (CCN)
1325 G St., N.W., Suite 1003
Washington, DC 20005-3104   **Phone:**   (202) 879-3044   **E-Mail:** CCN@igc.apc.org
USA   **Fax:**   (202) 879-3019

Contact Person: John Jacobson, Development Coordinator.
Officers or Principals: Monique Miller, Executive Director; David Durham, Chair.
Mission or Interest: The social, environmental, and economic consequences of population growth. Focus on natural population growth as well as immigration. "'Carrying Capacity' refers to the number of individuals who can be supported without degrading the natural, cultural, and social environment, i.e. without reducing the ability of the environment to sustain the desired quality of life over the long term." Board member and newsletter editor (and former Senior Economist in the Environmental Department of the World Bank) Herman E. Daly states that economic growth cannot continue indefinitely. He proposes very heavy taxation on resource extraction and energy to hold back the growth of the economy. Because of its emphasis on restricting immigration, 1) to preserve the quality of life in the immigrants' would-be destination and 2) because it serves as an outlet to allow the country of origin to avoid dealing with population issues, the Network often works with those on the Right as well.
Accomplishments: Carrying Capacity's research has been featured on NBC Nightly News, the BBC, *Washington Post, Los Angeles Times, New York Times*, NPR, The Donahue Show, *U.S. News and World Report, Wall Street Journal, San Francisco Chronicle, Christian Science Monitor, USA Today*, CBS Radio, *Newsweek* and others.
Products or Services: Educational materials, research, and lobbying.
Tax Status: 501(c)(3)
Board of Directors or Trustees: Virginia Abernethy, Albert Bartlett, Herman Daly (former Senior Economist, Environmental Dept., World Bank), K.R. Hammond, Edith Lavin, David Pimentel, Ieda Siqueira Wiarda. Advisory Board includes: Robert Costanza, Kingsley Davis, Anne Ehrlich, Paul Ehrlich (author, The Population Bomb), Brock Evans, William Griffiths, Robert Kaufman, L. Hunter Lovins (Rocky Mountain Institute), Daniel Luten, Hon. Gaylord Nelson, Nancy Sue Pearlman, Marcia Pimental, Claudine Schneider, Edgar Wayburn.
Periodicals: *Clearinghouse Bulletin* (monthly newsletter), *Focus* (quarterly journal).

Carter Center
One Copenhill
Atlanta, GA 30307   **Phone:**   (404) 331-3900
USA

Contact Person: Carrie Harmon, Director of Public Information.
Officers or Principals: Pamela Wuichet, Director of Development ($81,925); Jim Brasher, Special Assistant to President Carter ($79,761); Carrie Harmon, Director of Public Information ($62,031); Pres. James E. Carter, Chairman; Rosalyn Carter, Vice Chairman; Charles Kirbo, Treasurer; Bob J. Lipshutz; Bill Foege, Executive Director.
Mission or Interest: "Organization created by Jimmy Carter to facilitate scholarly research and concerted action programs by providing staff, administrative management, housing, and operational support to the organizations located at its facilities in Atlanta, Georgia. At present, these organizations include Global 2000, Inc., The Task for Child Survival, The Carter-Menil Rights Foundation, and The Carter Center of Emory University." These organizations focus on international cooperation and conflict resolution, third world development, and poverty in the U.S.
Accomplishments: In the fiscal year ending August 1994, the Center spent $16,797,808 on its programs. Most of this, $14,593,839, went to grant awards. These grants were: $10,814,191 for The Atlanta Project, $2,957,712 for Global 2000, and $821,936 for the Carter Center of Emory University.
Net Revenue: FY ending 8/94 $38,566,781 **Net Expenses:** $19,873,079 85%/8%/8% **Net Assets:** $52,906,610
Tax Status: 501(c)(3)
Board of Directors or Trustees: Terry Adamson, Iris Frank, John Hardman.
Other Information: The center used the consulting services of James Martin Brasher of Washington, DC for fund raising and paid him $65,320. The Center received $35,445,674, or 92% of total revenue, from gifts and grants awarded by foundations, businesses, and individuals. (These grants included $1,650,000 from the John D. and Catherine T. MacArthur Foundation. In 1995, $185,000 from the Rockefeller Foundation.) $1,849,847, or 5%, from program service revenues, including reimbursed fees from affiliated organizations. $1,285,021, or 3%, from interest on savings and temporary cash investments.

Catholic Worker, The
36 E. 1st St.
New York, NY 10003   **Phone:**   (212) 777-9617
USA

Contact Person: Brian Harte, Managing Editor.   **Officers or Principals:** Frank Donovan, Jane Sammon, Editors.
Mission or Interest: Newspaper of the Catholic Worker Movement founded by Dorothy Day (1897-1980), and Peter Maurin (1877-1949). "Working directly to alleviate the immediate sufferings of the poor and other victims of injustice, by offering a critique of the causes of poverty and oppression, and by proposing ways to eliminate these causes -- in order to build, in the words of Peter Maurin, 'a world where it is easier to be good'."
Products or Services: Numerous books by Dorothy Day, Peter Maurin, and others.
Tax Status: For profit. "We have never sought tax-exempt status since we are convinced that justice and the works of mercy should be acts of conscience which come at a sacrifice, without governmental sanction, regulation or reward."
Periodicals: *The Catholic Worker* (bimonthly newspaper).

Catholics for a Free Choice (CFFC)

1436 U St., N.W., Suite 301
Washington, DC 20009   **Phone:** (202) 986-6093
USA

Contact Person: Frances Kissling, President.
Officers or Principals: Frances Kissling, President ($88,700); Denise Shannon, Executive Vice President ($55,790); Gregory Lebel, Vice President, Public Policy ($55,333); Eileen Moran, Chair; Stephen Collins, Treasurer; Mary Hunt, Secretary.
Mission or Interest: Abortion rights organization that "was organized for the purpose of educating the general public about the Catholic perspective on a woman's right not to bear children against her will."
Accomplishments: In 1994 the organization spent $1,705,539 on its programs. The largest program, with expenditures of $299,289, was the Latin America Program, which "concentrated on educational activities for health care and religious workers." This program included $142,632 in grants. $262,269 was spent on research and publications. Other projects included education and communication, and building a grassroots network.. CFFC awarded a total of $347,833 in grants to groups in Latin America and the United States. Recipients of these grants included $47,100 for the Latina Center for Reproductive Health, $10,000 for the Religious Consultation on Ethics, $551 for Hoyas for Choice, $500 for Vermont Catholics for a Free Choice, and $50 for the National Coalition of American Nuns. The remaining recipients were in Latin America.
Net Revenue: 1994 $1,908,134 **Net Expenses:** $1,705,539 91%/5%/4% **Net Assets:** $919,606 **Citations:** 380:49
Products or Services: Education, speaking engagements, publications, lobbying. CFFC spent $68,417 on lobbying, $6,580 on grassroots lobbying and $61,837 on the direct lobbying of legislators. This was an increase of 645% over the previous year.
Tax Status: 501(c)(3)
Board of Directors or Trustees: Angela Bonavoglia, Silvia Cancio, Mary Gordon, Daniel Maguire, Giles Milhaven, Marysa Navarro-Aranguren, Rosemary Radford Ruether, Flora Rodriguez Russel, Marcela von Vacano, Peter Wilderotter, Susan Wysocki.
Periodicals: *Conscience* (quarterly newsletter).
Other Information: CFFC hired the Mill Valley, CA, firm of Martin & Glantz for management and media services. The firm was paid $65,800. CFFC received $1,855,244, or 97% of revenue, from direct and indirect support in the form of gifts and grants awarded by foundations, affiliates, businesses, and individuals. (These grants included $60,000 from the Robert Sterling Clark Foundation, $55,000 from the Deer Creek Foundation, $40,000 from the Compton Foundation, $15,000 from the General Service Foundation, $3,800 from the Jessie Smith Noyes Foundation, $2,000 from the Ruth Mott Fund, and $1,000 from the Stewart R. Mott Charitable Trust.) $40,568, or 2%, from interest on savings and temporary cash investments. The remaining revenue came from the sale of subscriptions, the sale of inventory, and honoraria. In 1993 the organization received $525,000 over three years from the John D. and Catherine T. MacArthur Foundation.

Center for a New Democracy (CND)

410 7th St., S.E.
Washington, DC 20003   **Phone:** (202) 543-0773
USA   **Fax:**   (202) 543-2591

Mission or Interest: Supports community organizing projects. Works on campaign reform with ACORN and Public Interest Research Group (PIRG) affiliates.
Tax Status: 501(c)(3)
Other Information: In 1994 the Center received $80,000 from the Florence and John Schuman Foundation, and $10,000 from the New World Foundation.

Center for Alternative Mining Development Policy

210 Avon St., Suite 4
La Crosse, WI 54603-3097   **Phone:** (608) 784-4399
USA   **Fax:**   same

Contact Person: Al Geddicks.
Mission or Interest: "To provide information and technical assistance to Indian Tribes and rural communities in the Lake Superior region about the social, economic and environmental impacts of metallic sulfide mining."
Accomplishments: "Assisted the Sokaogon Chippewa and others to stop Exxon's ecologically destructive metallic sulfide mining at the headwaters of the Wolf River in 1986."
Net Revenue: 1994 under $25,000.
Products or Services: Educational materials, videos and books. The New Resource Wars: Native and Environmental Struggles Against Multinational Corporations (South End Press, 1993).
Tax Status: 501(c)(3) **Annual Report:** No.
Board of Directors or Trustees: Roscoe and Evelyn Churchill (Rusk County Citizens Action Group), Walt Bresette (Lake Superior Greens).
Other Information: Affiliated with the Watershed Alliance Toward Environmental Responsibility and the Wisconsin Resources Protection Council.

Center for Campus Organizing (CCO)

P.O. Box 748
Cambridge, MA 02142   **Phone:** (617) 354-9363   **E-Mail:** cco@igc.apc.org
USA   **Fax:**   (617) 547-5067   **Web-Page:** http://envirolink.org/orgs/cco

Contact Person: Rich Cowan, Clearinghouse Coordinator. **Officers or Principals:** Nicole Newton, Right Wing Educator and Field Organizer; Michelle Persard, Office Coordinator; Jeremy Smith, Publications Coordinator.
Mission or Interest: "A national clearinghouse which promotes progressive activism and investigative journalism on campus." Organizational assistance and coalition building. Researches the activities of the Right on colleges campuses. "Part of the problem is to highlight the present lived experience of racism and sexism, and to describe the history of white and male supremacy in the U.S. While it is good to accumulate facts and figures as evidence...nothing can be as powerful as 'telling it like it is,' to raise consciousness by establishing the painful human consequences of racism and injustice."
Accomplishments: In 1996 CCO inaugurated its Annual Campus Progressive Journalism Awards. These cash prizes are awarded in categories such as best campus-based alternative newspaper, reporting, humor, opinion writing, and hell raising. Judges include Norman Solomon of Fairness and Accuracy in Reporting, Patti Wolter of *Mother Jones*, and Jeremy Smith of the Center for Alternative Journalism. Coordinated protests on more than 100 campuses for the "National Days of Campus Action against the Contract with America" in March 1995. Received coverage in *The New York Times*, *Washington Post*, MTV News, NPR, *Z Magazine*, *The Nation*, *Rolling Stone*, *Chronicle of Higher Education*, and *San Francisco Chronicle*.
Net Revenue: FY ending 9/95 $121,820 **Net Expenses:** $89,760
Products or Services: Guide to Uncovering the Right on Campus, Guide for Campus Alternative Journalists, and Organizing Guide for Peace and Justice Groups. Activist resources, including legal, accounting, computer, and graphic art assistance. Books, videos, flyers.
Tax Status: 501(c)(3) **Annual Report:** Yes. **Employees:** 7
Board of Directors or Trustees: Dina Carreras, Ken Cunningham, Prof. Jean Douthwright (RIT), Prof. Matt Green (Union College), Prof. Henry Linschitz (Brandeis Univ.), Dion Thompson. Advisors include: Dr. Jean Hardisty (Political Research Associates), Prof. Michio Kaku (City College), Prof. Mel King (MIT), Prof. Frances Fox Piven (CUNY), Loretta Ross (Center for Human Rights Education), Prof. Charles Schwartz (Berkeley), Prof. Joni Seager (Univ. of VT), Prof. George Wald (Harvard Univ.).
Periodicals: *Infusion* (quarterly magazine).
Internships: Yes.
Other Information: Formerly called the University Conversion Project.

Center for Clean Air Policy
444 N. Capitol St., Suite 602
Washington, DC 20001   **Phone:** (202) 624-7709
USA

Contact Person: Ned Helme, Executive Director. **Officers or Principals:** Ned Helme, Executive Director ($93,221); Mark Popovich ($64,859); David Festa ($61,740); Hon. Tony Earl, Chairman.
Mission or Interest: Works with state, local, and even foreign governments, to provide research and analysis on issues related to energy and the environment, and the reduction of "ozone and global warming emissions."
Accomplishments: In the fiscal year ending June 1994, the Center spent $1,215,012 on its programs. The largest program, with expenditures of $336,993 was the State Energy and Environment Exchange Program which provided "technical expertise to Czechoslovakia." $282,441 was spent to study Transportation and Global Warming, and produce an "aggressive action plan for the Milwaukee region." Other projects deal with utilities, energy conservation "Northern Bohemia Air Quality Initiative," and other subjects.
Net Revenue: FY ending 6/94 $1,431,736 ($464,498, or 32%, from government grants) **Net Expenses:** $1,274,508 95%/4%/1% **Net Assets:** $8,759 **Citations:** 14:185
Tax Status: 501(c)(3)
Board of Directors or Trustees: Hon. Hugh Carey (former governor of New York, Democrat), Dr. Mark Levine, Jim Maddy, John Palmisano, B.B. Blevins, Gov. Ben Nelson (D-NE), Gov. Roy Romer (D-CO), Richard Abdoo, Hon. Tony Earl (former governor of Wisconsin, Democrat), Hon. Tom Kean (former governor of New Jersey, Republican), Sen. Gaylord Nelson, Paul Portney, Marilynne Roberts, Hon. Mario Cuomo (former governor of New York, Democrat), William Davis, Victoria Tachinkel, Hon. John Waihee (former governor of Hawaii, Democrat).
Other Information: Affiliated with the 501(c)(4) Alliance for Acid Rain Control at the same address. As executive director of both organizations, Ned Helme received a combined $124,575 in compensation. The Center received $958,961, or 67% of revenue, from gifts and grants awarded by foundations, affiliates, businesses, and individuals. (These grants included a transfer of $153,976 from the affiliated Alliance for Acid Rain Control, $80,000 from the Joyce Foundation, $75,000 from the Pew Charitable Trusts, and $50,000 from the Joyce Mertz-Gilmore Foundation.) $464,498, or 32%, from government grants. The remaining revenue came from dividends and interest from securities.

Center for Community Advocacy
9 W. Gabilan St., Suite 12
Salinas, CA 93901   **Phone:** (408) 753-2324
USA

Contact Person: Vanessa W. Vallarta. **Officers or Principals:** Hon. Lydia M. Villarreal, President ($0); Federico Melgoza, Vice President ($0); Katherine E. Stoner, Secretary ($0); Rev. Thomas B. Woodward, Treasurer.
Mission or Interest: "Educational programs and legal services provided to farm workers at labor camps throughout the Salinas Valley."
Accomplishments: In 1994 the Center spent $161,616 on its programs. These "improved the living conditions of over 3,000 people." The Center received $1,850 in court-awarded attorney's fees for a settlement "pertaining to improving living conditions for farm-worker housing."

Net Revenue: 1994 $256,211 **Net Expenses:** $220,802 73%/9%/17% **Net Assets:** $136,743
Tax Status: 501(c)(3)
Board of Directors or Trustees: Armando Ascencio, Rabbi Bruce Kadden, Martin Marroquin, Bonnie Hurtington, Olga Camacho, Basil Mills, Hon. Sam Karas (Board of Supervisors, Monterey), John Staples, Ricardo Islas, Edmundo Leal, Robert Graham, Serafin Rodriguez, Maria Concepcion Ramirez, Jesus Madrid, Morley Brown.
Other Information: Center president Lydia Villarreal is a Municipal Court Judge in the County of Monterey. The Center received $247,748, or 97% of revenue, from gifts and grants awarded by foundations, businesses, and individuals. (These grants included $70,000 from the Rosenberg Foundation, $35,000 from the Campaign for Human Development, $17,000 from the McKay Foundation.) $4,500, or 2%, from fees paid for services by other nonprofit organizations. $1,913, or 1%, from interest on savings and temporary cash investments. The remaining revenue came from dividends and interest from securities, and speaking fees.

Center for Community Change
1000 Wisconsin Ave., N.W.
Washington, DC 20007   **Phone:**   (202) 342-0519
USA   **Fax:**   (202) 342-1132

Contact Person: Pablo Eisenberg, President.
Officers or Principals: Pablo Eisenberg, President ($112,426); Andrew H. Mott, Vice President ($101,490); Othello W. Poulard, Vice President ($98,390); John Carr, Chair; Bruce Hanson, Treasurer; Leonard Lesser, Secretary.
Mission or Interest: Gives financial and technical support to community nonprofit organizations.
Accomplishments: In the fiscal year ending September 1993 the Center spent $4,606,710 on its programs. The Center spent $1,949,953 on technical assistance and awarded $2,656,757 in grants. The recipients of the largest awards were: $721,720 for the National Committee for Responsive Philanthropy, $415,155 for the National Community Reinvestment Coalition, $218,552 for the Neighborhood and Family Initiative, $179,000 for the Mott Foundation Small Grants Project, $175,503 for HUD Technical Assistance, $163,055 for the National Coalition on Human Needs, $137,990 for the Neighborhood Revitalization Project, and $100,324 for the Public Housing Initiative. Other, smaller grants went to: the United Community Housing Coalition, Northwest Organizing Project, Association of Street Vendors, Korean Immigrant Workers Advocates, HUD Tenants Coalition of Newark, Latino Community Land Trust, Task Force for Historic Preservation and the Minority Community, Watts Century Latino Organization, Minority Community Organizing Internship, First Environment Project, Rural Justice Center, Spirituality of Struggle, and others.
Net Revenue: FY ending 9/93 $6,081,715 ($158,655, or 3%, from government grants)
Net Expenses: $5,602,215 82%/16%/2% **Net Assets:** $367,382 **Citations:** 67:125
Products or Services: Software for analyzing Home Mortgage Disclosure Act data. Grants, publications, and technical assistance. Lobbying - the Center spent $14,764 on lobbying, $3,972 on grassroots lobbying and $10,792 on the direct lobbying of legislators or government officials. This was down 26% from the year before.
Tax Status: 501(c)(3) **Annual Report:** Yes. **Employees:** 45
Board of Directors or Trustees: Rebecca Doggett (Auditor General, State Dept. of Education, NJ), Michael Ansara (SHARE Systems), Polly Baca (CO Inst. For Hispanic Education & Economic Development), Harriet Barlow (Blue Mountain Center), Marie Kirkley-Bey, Julian Bond, Edwin Booth (Cummins Electronics), Arthur Brazier, John Carr (U.S. Catholic Conference), Roger Clay Jr., Gordon Chin (Chinatown Neighborhood Improvement Resource Center), Michael Clark (Management Assistance Project), Patricia Dinner, Jane Fox (Nature Conservancy), Douglas Fraser, Carolyn Garland, Irma Gonzales, Ronald Grzywinski (ShoreBank Corp.), Wade Henderson (NAACP), Andrew Hernandez (Southwest Voter Registration and Education Project), Gracia Hillman (League of Women Voters), John Lewis (Inter-Tribal Council of AZ), Prof. Burke Marshall (Deputy Dean, Yale Law School), Ginny Montes, Mary Mountcastle, Janice Petrovich, Benson Roberts, Ron Shiffman (Pratt Inst.), Hon. Linda Yanez (Justice, 13th Court of Appeals).
Periodicals: *The CRA Reporter* (quarterly newsletter covering developments associated with the Community Development Act), *Community Change* (quarterly magazine).
Other Information: The Center has an office in San Francisco: 160 Sansome St., 7th Floor, San Francisco, CA 94104, voice (415) 982-0346, fax (415) 956-6880. The Center is affiliated with the Fund for the Center for Community Change at the same address. The Center received $5,873,711, or 97% of revenue, from grants awarded by foundations, companies and individuals. (These grants included $1,022,500 from the Charles Stewart Mott Foundation, $425,000 from the Fund for the Center for Community Change, $30,000 from the Rosenberg Foundation, $25,000 from the Joyce Mertz-Gilmore Foundation, $20,524 from the Wallace Alexander Gerbode Foundation, $10,000 from the McKay Foundation, $7,500 from the Ruth Mott Fund, and $2,000 from the Lucius and Eva Eastman Fund. In 1995, $125,000 from the Rockefeller Foundation.) $158,655, or 3%, from government grants. The remaining revenue came from dividends and interest from securities.

Center for Constitutional Rights (CCR)
666 Broadway
New York, NY 10012   **Phone:**   (212) 614-6464
USA

Contact Person: Andrea Kincannan, Administrative Director. **Officers or Principals:** Miriam Thompson, former Executive Director ($38,925); Margaret Carey, Attorney ($38,336); Audrey Seniors, Legal Worker ($34,481); Nancy Scerbo, Development Director; Andrea Kincannan, Administrative Director; Robert Boehm, Chairman; Arthur Kinoy, Vicki Alexander, Co-Presidents; Haywood Burns, Rhonda Copelon, Peter Weiss, Vice Presidents; Judy Lerner, Secretary/Treasurer.

Mission or Interest: Litigation and education to protect and expand civil rights. Founded by Arthur Kinroy, Peter Weiss, and the late William Kunstler and Ben Smith. Works on behalf of radicals and "political prisoners."

Accomplishments: The Center worked with the Feminist Women's Health Center in charging anti-abortion protestors with violating racketeering (RICO) laws. In 1994 the Center lobbied against the Omnibus Violent Crime Control and Prevention Act, on the basis that it would "execute more people or lock them up for longer periods of time, disregarding Constitutional protection, without having any appreciable effect on crime in our society...Given the already disproportionate treatment of African American and Hispanic males in the criminal justice system, this bill can particularly be viewed as an attack on people of color."

Net Revenue: 1993 $1,659,483 **Net Expenses:** $1,531,594 72%/13%/15% **Net Assets:** $1,897,376 **Citations:** 132:101

Products or Services: In 1993 the Center spent $1,104,812 on its programs. The center received $297,034 in court-awarded attorney's fees.

Tax Status: 501(c)(3)

Other Information: Founding attorney William Kunstler made a career out of defending terrorists, bombers, murders, and robbers in the U.S. and worldwide who used political justification for their crimes. According to Kunstler, "The thing I'm most interested in is keeping people on the street who will forever alter the character of this country: the revolutionaries...I'm really interested only in spending my talents and any assets I have to keep the revolutionaries functioning." The Center paid $39,208 to Riptide, Inc. for public relations. Riptide is a subsidiary of the Center. The Center received $1,333,479, or 80% of revenue, from gifts and grants awarded by foundations, businesses, and individuals. (These grants included $40,000 from the New World Foundation, $25,000 from the C.S. Fund, and $500 from the Aaron and Martha Schecter Private Foundation.) $297,034, or 18%, from court-awarded attorney's fees. $14,702 net, or 1%, from special fund-raising events. The remaining revenue came from interest on savings and temporary cash investments, and other miscellaneous sources.

Center for Cuban Studies

124 W. 23rd St.
New York, NY 10011   **Phone:** (212) 246-0559
USA

Contact Person: Sandra Levinson, Director. **Officers or Principals:** Sandra Levinson, Director ($29,248).

Mission or Interest: Research, analysis, seminars and conferences focusing on Cuba and the Caribbean.

Accomplishments: In 1993 the Center spent $180,612 on its programs.

Net Revenue: 1993 $244,778 **Net Expenses:** $244,349 74%/22%/4% **Net Assets:** $43,345

Tax Status: 501(c)(3)

Periodicals: *Cuba Update* (bimonthly newsletter).

Other Information: Founded in 1978. The Center received $77,020, or 31% of revenue, from gifts and grants awarded by foundations and individuals. (These grants included the Tides Foundation and the Funding Exchange.) $52,046, or 21%, from educational programs. $37,879, or 15%, from membership fees. $37,502 net, or 15%, from the sale of inventory. $32,821, or 13%, from international exchange program fees. The remaining revenues came from other miscellaneous sources.

Center for Defense Information (CDI)

1500 Massachusetts Ave., N.W.
Washington, DC 20005   **Phone:** (202) 862-0070   **E-Mail:** cdi@igc.apc.org
USA   **Fax:** (202) 862-0708   **Web-Page:** http://www.cdi.org

Contact Person: Rear Admiral Gene R. La Rocque, USN (Ret.), President. **Officers or Principals:** Rear Adm. Gene R. La Rocque, USN (Ret.), President ($51,251); Stephen R. Paschke, Vice President ($44,000); Arthur Berliss, Jr., Cpt., USNR (Ret.), Secretary ($0); Edward H. R. Blitzer, Treasurer; Lt. Colonel Piers M. Wood, USAR (Ret.), Chief of Staff; Vice Admiral John J. Shanahan, USN (Ret.), Director; Rear Admiral Eugene J. Carroll, USN (Ret.), Deputy Director.

Mission or Interest: "Founded in 1972, (CDI) is an independent monitor of the military, conducting research and analyzing military spending, policies and weapons systems."

Accomplishments: In 1994 CDI spent $1,258,285 on its programs. The largest program expenditure, $732,772, was on research, analysis, and public education activities which are made available to the public, journalists, congress and policy makers. $374,161 was spent on the production and distribution of "America's Defense Monitor," a weekly TV program that appears on PBS and cable stations nationwide. $79,542 was spent on producing and distributing *The Defense Monitor*, a journal published ten times yearly with a circulation of 50,000, including members of congress, the State Department, all military academies, colleges and universities, national organizations, and others. $71,810 was spent studying the economic and foreign policy implications of international arms trading. CDI claims that its military library is second only to the Pentagon's in completeness.

Net Revenue: 1994 $1,429,553 **Net Expenses:** $1,636,565 77%/15%/8% **Net Assets:** $4,944,602 **Citations:** 259:63

Products or Services: Television programing, publications, public speaking, radio commentary, and lobbying. In 1994 CDI spent $53,207 on lobbying; $7,954 on grassroots lobbying and $45,253 on the direct lobbying of lawmakers.

Tax Status: 501(c)(3) **Employees:** 30

Board of Directors or Trustees: Doris Bato, David Horowitz, Alan Kay, John Rockwood, Philip Straus.

Periodicals: *Defense Monitor* (ten times yearly journal), *CDI Military Almanac* (annual).

Internships: Yes.

Other Information: The Center for Defense Information was originally a project of the Fund for Peace. The Center has consistently opposed U.S. intervention abroad. It opposed most of the U.S.'s new weapon systems, including the stealth bomber and Strategic Defense Initiative (Star Wars). Center president Gene La Rocque served in the Navy from 1941 to 1972. He and CDI were denounced in two full-page ads taken out in *The Washington Times* in 1983. The ads were paid for and signed by 424, and then 575, retired admirals who denounced La Rocque as "Injurious to the best interests of our country" for his appearance on Soviet television criticizing President Reagan's arms control efforts. CDI received $1,060,674, or 74% of revenue, from gifts and grants awarded by foundations, businesses, and individuals. (These grants included $30,000 from the Compton Foundation, $25,000 from the Ruth Mott Fund,$10,000 from the Deer Creek Foundation, and $2,500 from the Aaron and Martha Schecter Foundation.) The Center does not seek or accept money directly from the government, or from the military industry. $160,935, or 11%, from dividends and interest from securities. $150,983, or 11%, from capital gains on the sale of securities. $47,791, or 3%, from program service revenues, including honoraria, subscriptions, fees, etc. The remaining revenue came from interest on savings and cash investments.

Center for Democratic Renewal and Education

P.O. Box 50469
Atlanta, GA 30302   **Phone:**   (404) 221-0025
USA

Contact Person: Beni Ivey, Executive Director.   **Officers or Principals:** Beni Ivey, Executive Director ($38,880); Loretta Ross, Staff ($33,750); Harvey Kahn, Director ($14,125); Rev. C.T. Vivian, Chairperson.
Mission or Interest: "Provide general and specific information and education to communities, groups and individuals with positive responses to hate group activities." Focus on groups considered racist, misogynist, and anti-homosexual.
Accomplishments: The Center, along with the National Council of Churches, was the driving force behind the summer of 1996 stories regarding the burning of churches with predominantly black congregations. In March of 1996 the Center released a study asserting that racist-related arson attacks on black churches has been increasing in recent years. (Many sources contradict these claims, showing that fires are actually decreasing and that arson and race appear to be a factor in only a small percentage of fires. Ironically, however, since the claims were made, 'copycat' fires seem to have increased from the coverage of the "increase" in racially-based arsons.) Chairperson Rev. C.T. Vivian, blaming conservatives, said, "There's only a slippery slope between conservative religious persons and those that are really doing the burning." In the fiscal year ending June 1994, the Center spent $398,844 on its programs. These programs included $68,715 in grants to local community organizations.
Net Revenue: FY ending 6/94 $568,868 **Net Expenses:** $538,022 74%/21%/5% **Net Assets:** $40,711 **Citations:** 363:51
Products or Services: Research manuals, community organizing, videos, other publications.
Tax Status: 501(c)(3)
Board of Directors or Trustees: Rev. Mac Charles Jones, Anne Braden, Marilyn Clement, Jan Douglas, Jean Hardisty (Political Research Associates), Harvey Kahn, Vernice Miller, Rev. David Ostendorf, Ralph Paige, Othello Poulard, Rudy Ryser, Mab Segrest, Hilary Shelton, Tom Turnipseed, Consuelo Urquiza, Lucius Walker, Joanne Watson, Leah Wise.
Other Information: The Center for Democratic Renewal has a Southern California affiliate, People Against Racist Terror (see separate listing). The Center was previously called the National Anti-Klan Network. The Center received $532,363, or 94% of revenue, from gifts and grants awarded by foundations, businesses, and individuals. (These grants included $20,000 from the New World Foundation, $20,000 from the Norman Foundation, and $10,000 from the Bydale Foundation.) $19,845, or 3%, from the sale of manuals and literature. $7,675, or 1%, from membership dues. The remaining revenue came from interest on savings and temporary cash investments, and other miscellaneous sources.

Center for Economic Conversion

222 View St., Suite C
Mountain View, CA 94041   **Phone:**   (415) 968-8798   **E-Mail:** action@wti.org
USA

Contact Person: Jeanne Lewis, Office Manager.   **Officers or Principals:** Ralph Austin, President ($0); Dave Offen, Secretary ($0); Tom Thomas, Treasurer ($0); Carol Webb, Vice Chair; Bruce Allen, Communications Director.
Mission or Interest: To encourage and aid in the conversion of military spending to domestic spending. Communications Director Bruce Allen refers to the 1995 Republican budget bills as "a formal declaration of economic war on the poor, the sick, the elderly, students, workers (both currently employed and laid off), and the environment." which are a result of "the forces of neo-fascism currently ravaging the nation."
Accomplishments: In the fiscal year ending September 1994, the Center spent $245,618 on its programs. The largest program, with expenditures of $206,320, went toward "educational speakers, organizing assistance to conversion activists, technical assistance to workers, managers and public officials confronting military cutbacks." $39,298 was spent on "Community Data Processing" providing computer services and technical assistance to nonprofit advocacy organizations.
Net Revenue: FY ending 9/94 $347,042 **Net Expenses:** $348,827 70%/23%/7% **Net Assets:** $71,511
Tax Status: 501(c)(3)
Board of Directors or Trustees: Ed Becks, Mo Hourmanesh, Larissa Keet, Edie Norton, Dave Offen, Jay Siegel, Tim Such, Emily Weinstein, Tom Wright.
Periodicals: *Positive Alternatives* (quarterly journal).
Other Information: The Center received $261,370, or 75% of revenue, from gifts and grants awarded by foundations, businesses, and individuals. (These grants included $82,500 from the Peace Development Fund, $10,000 from the Town Creek Foundation, $2,500 from the New Prospect Foundation, $1,036 from the Progressive Way, $500 from the Compton Foundation, and $500 from the Vanguard Public Foundation.) $47,970, or 14%, from fees for computer and technical services. $9,665, or 3%, from honoraria. $8,977 net, or 3%, from special fund-raising events. $5,800, or 2%, from consulting fees. The remaining revenue came from educational service fees, the sale of inventory, interest on savings and temporary cash investments, and other miscellaneous sources.

Center for Economic Democracy / *Boycott Quarterly*

P.O. Box 30727
Seattle, WA 98103   **E-Mail:** BoycottGuy@aol.com
USA

Contact Person: Zachary D. Lyons, Editor and Publisher.
Mission or Interest: Publishes *Boycott Quarterly*, a publication that lists a wide spectrum of boycotts currently being undertaken against various companies, and even states based on objectional activities. Most of the listed boycotts are for activities more objectionable to those on the Left, but the Quarterly includes the boycotts undertaken across the political spectrum, such as the conservative American Family Association's boycotts. Also publishes articles related to "Economic Democracy", which is Lyons' term for using personal expenditures to influence policy and society.
Accomplishments: "*Boycott Quarterly* is regularly cited by North America's largest papers as the boycott authority."
Annual Report: No.
Periodicals: *Boycott Quarterly* (quarterly journal).
Other Information: In 1994 *Boycott Quarterly*, then called *Boycott Monthly*, absorbed the *National Boycott News*.

Center for Environmental Information

50 W. Main St.
Rochester, NY 14614   **Phone:**   (716) 262-2870
USA   **Fax:**   (716) 262-4156

Contact Person: William Wagner, Executive Director.   **Officers or Principals:** Alan J. Knauf, Chairman ($0); S. Ram Shrivastava, Vice Chairman/Treasurer ($0); Rev. Rheanolte LeBarbour, Secretary ($0).
Mission or Interest: Environmental education and to serve as a mediator between businesses and the public.
Accomplishments: In 1994 the Center spent $174,658 on its programs. The largest program, with expenditures of $89,400 was publication and distribution of a "Global Climate Change Directory." $59,279 was spent producing educational seminars attended by 200. $25,979 for contract work mediating between businesses and the public.
Net Revenue: 1994 $262,244 ($34,000, or 13%, from government grants) **Net Expenses:** $225,416 77%/23%/0%
Net Assets: (-$15,701)
Tax Status: 501(c)(3)
Board of Directors or Trustees: James Atwater, David Huddleston, Dr. Haines Lockhart Jr. (Dir., Corporate Environment, Eastman Kodak), Terry Richman, Carolie Simone, Elizabeth Thorndike, James White.
Other Information: The Center received $94,634, or 36% of revenue, from gifts and grants awarded by foundations, businesses, and individuals. $75,159, or 29%, from publishing and marketing sales. $34,000, or 13%, from government grants. $29,223, or 11%, from seminar registration fees. $18,003, or 7%, from membership dues. The remaining revenue came from interest on savings and temporary cash investments, and other miscellaneous sources.

Center for Gulf South History and Culture

1539 Crete St.
New Orleans, LA 70119   **Phone:**   (504) 944-4823
USA

Contact Person: Dennis Formento, Editor.
Officers or Principals: Eric Bookhardt, William Lavender, Arthur Pfister, Susan Ferron, Editor.
Mission or Interest: "To explore bioregions, georegions, psychoregions, through the marriage of bioregional culture and surrealism." Publishes *Mesechabe: A Journal of Surre(gion)alism*.
Accomplishments: *Mesechabe* has included "Pulitzer Prize winning poet Gary Snyder, Andrei Codrescu, Diane DiPrima (poets); bioreginalist Peter Berg, satirist Max Cafard, and even hot sex tips from the unlovable David Duke." Poet Gary Snyder said "*Mesechabe* is the kind of journal a place like the Lower Mississippi deserves; unpredictable, funny, masqued, suave, indulgent, elegantly anarchic, and slyly informative. I have admired it from the first."
Tax Status: 501(c)(3) **Annual Report:** No. **Employees:** All volunteer.
Periodicals: *Mesechabe* (periodic journal).
Other Information: "*Mesechabe* (pronounced Mes-sa-cha-bey) is derived from the original name for the Mississippi River." The journal accepts art, graphics, poetry and prose.

Center for Immigrants Rights (CIR)

48 St. Marks Place
New York, NY 10003   **Phone:**   (212) 505-6890
USA   **Fax:**   (212) 995-5876

Contact Person: Roseann Micallef.
Officers or Principals: Reynaldo Guerrero, Executive Director ($33,362); Jackson Chin, Staff Attorney ($31,150); Lourdes I. Santiago, Esq., Chair ($0); Karen C. Wagner, Treasurer; Azalia Torres, Esq., Secretary; Sonia Bu, Vice Chair.
Mission or Interest: "To defend and expand the rights of immigrants, regardless of their status, through education, advocacy and community organizing."

Accomplishments: For 15 years the Center has been instrumental in organizing immigrant workers in New York City.
Net Revenue: FY ending 6/94 $275,265 ($127,423, or 46%, from government grants) **Net Expenses:** $339,584 38%/62%/0%
Net Assets: $7,069
Products or Services: Conferences, seminars, informational materials.
Tax Status: 501(c)(3) **Employees:** 9 full-time, 2 part-time.
Board of Directors or Trustees: Lorinda Chen (New York Health and Hospital Corp.), Martha Davis, Esq. (NOW Legal Defense Fund), Alejandro Duhalde (Natl. Health & Human Services), Andrew Fair, Esq., Christie Huh, Howard Jordan (Inst. For Puerto Rican Policy), Marla Kamiya (Committee Against Anti-Asian Violence), Peter Lin (Chinese Staff & Workers Assoc.), Stan Mark, Esq. (Asian American Legal Defense Fund), Rev. Hector Navas (United Baptist Church), Estela Vasquez (Natl. Health & Human Services), Jean Vernet (Trust for Public Land), Allan Wernick, Esq.
Periodicals: *CIR Reports* (quarterly).
Internships: Yes.
Other Information: CIR is part of the National Network for Immigrants and Refugee Rights. "CIR remains committed to working with all immigrants - which is becoming increasingly more difficult with the rise in anti-immigrant legislation and climate." The Center received $136,279, or 50% of revenue, from gifts and grants awarded by foundations, companies, and individuals. (These grants included two grants totaling $40,000 from the Joyce Mertz-Gilmore Foundation, $20,000 from the J. Roderick MacArthur Foundation, $17,500 from the Ms. Foundation, $11,000 from the Vanguard Public Foundation, $7,259 from the North Star Fund, $4,983 from the Peace Development Fund, $1,000 from the Vanguard Public Foundation.) $127,423, or 46%, from government grants. $10,471, or 4%, from training session fees. The remaining revenue came from interest on savings and temporary cash investments.

Center for International Environmental Law (CIEL)

1621 Connecticut Ave., N.W., Suite 200
Washington, DC 20009   **Phone:**   (202) 332-4840
USA

Contact Person: Frederick R. Anderson, Chairman.
Officers or Principals: Durwood J. Zaelke, President ($67,623); David Downes, Staff Attorney ($36,099); Donald Goldberg, Staff Attorney ($35,247); Barbara L. Shaw, Vice President, Finance; J. Vance Hughes, Vice Chairman.
Mission or Interest: Works with nonprofit organizations and non-governmental organizations (NGO's) in other countries to promote international environmental laws that apply to trade, commerce, and other activities.
Accomplishments: In the fiscal year ending June 1994, the Center spent $705,065 on its programs. The largest program, with expenditures of $231,298, was the Trade and Environment Program. This included working with congress, nonprofit organizations, and NGO's to "strengthen the environmental provisions of NAFTA and GATT. Worked with the International Standards Organization to help set standards for environmental management, packaging, and labeling standards. Assisted in the design of a new environmental program at the United Nations Environment Programme in Geneva. $149,099 was spent on the Central and East European Program. This included working with NGO's in these countries to promote environmental laws pertaining to development and privatization. Funding for these projects came from the Charles Stewart Mott Foundation, Foundation for Deep Ecology, Rockefeller Brothers Foundation, and U.S. AID subgrants through the World Wildlife Fund, University of Minnesota, and the World Resources Institute. $113,603 was spent on the Biodiversity and Wildlife Program. This included advising citizen groups, government agencies, NGO's, and nonprofit organizations. Played a major role in organizing the Biodiversity Action Network. These projects were funded by the John D. and Catherine T. MacArthur Foundation, Jenifer Altman Foundation, and the Moriah Fund. Other programs worked with the Americas and Caribbean, Ozone Action (which they funded), and the Climate Action Network (which they provided with legal advice on global warming).
Net Revenue: FY ending 6/94 $755,446 ($142,468, or 19%, from government grants) **Net Expenses:** $746,188 94%/5%/1%
Net Assets: $65,186 **Citations:** 9:202
Products or Services: Trade and the Environment: Law, Economics, and Policy (1993, Island Press), other books and publications, consulting, organizational services, legal advice.
Tax Status: 501(c)(3)
Board of Directors or Trustees: Harry Barnes Jr., Christopher Stone, Wilton Lawrence Wallace.
Other Information: The Center received $590,758, or 78% of revenue, from gifts and grants awarded by foundations, businesses, and individuals. (These grants included $150,000 from the Florence and John Schumann Foundation.) $142,468, or 19%, from government grants. $12,266, or 2%, from fees paid by other nonprofits for services. The remaining revenues came from publication sales, fees from international institutions, and interest on savings and temporary cash investments.

Center for International Policy (CIP)

1755 Massachusetts Ave., N.W., Suite 312
Washington, DC 20036   **Phone:**   (202) 232-3317   **E-Mail:** cip@igc.apc.org
USA   **Fax:**   (202) 232-3440   **Web-Page:** http://www.us.net/cip/index.htm

Contact Person: Alexandra Trombley, Executive Assistant. **Officers or Principals:** Hon. Robert E. White, President; William Goodfellow, Executive Director; Hon. Donald M. Fraser, Sen. Tom Harkin, Co-Chairmen; James Morrell, Director of Research.
Mission or Interest: Founded in the "wake of the Vietnam War, to promote a foreign policy that reflected democratic values." Focus on Latin America.
Accomplishments: Initiated a campaign to link foreign aid to human rights. Promoted the 1987 Arias peace plan for Central America in Congress. President Robert White, a former ambassador to El Salvador, became one of Haitian President Aristide's closest advisors during Aristide's exile in the United States. White led five congressional delegations to Haiti and presented recommendations to President Clinton. CIP staff were also present at the negotiations that led to Aristide's return to Haiti. Programs to normalize relations with Cuba. In 1995 the Center launched a program to review and recommend changes in the CIA.

Tax Status: 501(c)(3) **Annual Report:** No. **Employees:** 12
Board of Directors or Trustees: Thomas Asher, Mario Baeza, Hon. Michael Barnes (former Rep., D-MD), Lowell Blankfort (newspaper publisher, San Diego), William Butler (Chair, Intl. Commission of Jurists), Adrian DeWind, Samuel Ellsworth, Prof. Richard Falk (Princeton Univ.), Gerald Gilmore (former consultant on the third world, World Council of Churches), Susan Horowitz (Office of the Public Advocate, NY), Sally Lilienthal (Ploughshares Fund), Prof. Cynthia McClintock (George Washington Univ.), Luis Mendez, Stewart R. Mott (Fund for Constitutional Government), Maurine Rothschild (Radcliffe College), Paul Sack, Linda Storrow (former associate publisher, *The Nation*), Prof. Dessima Williams (Brandeis Univ., former Ambassador of Grenada to the Organization of American States).
Periodicals: *International Policy Report* (monthly newsletter).
Internships: Yes, unpaid internships are available during the fall, spring, and summer.
Other Information: Founded in 1975. In 1994 the Center received grants of $31,290 from the General Service Foundation, $12,500 from the Aaron and Martha Schecter Private Foundation, $3,000 from the Stewart R. Mott Charitable Trust.

Center for Investigative Reporting (CIR)
568 Howard St., 5th Floor
San Francisco, CA 94105   **Phone:** (415) 543-1200   **E-Mail:** CIR@igc.apc.org
USA   **Fax:**   (415) 543-8311

Contact Person: James Curtiss, Communications Director. **Officers or Principals:** Sharon Tiller, Director ($40,625); Sarah Henry, Reporter ($31,725); Eve Pell, Reporter ($30,592); Dan Noyes, Executive Director; Jerome E. Dougherty, President; Elizabeth Eudey, Vice President; Elizabeth Pike, Secretary/Treasurer; Steve Katz, Development Director.
Mission or Interest: "Conducts research on important political and economic issues and distributes the information through the production of manuscripts, magazines, newspaper articles, books, transcripts, and video documentaries...CIR is the country's only independent, non-profit organization established to do investigative reporting."
Accomplishments: "CIR's award-winning stories, the result of some 400 investigations over the past 18 years, have helped spark Congressional hearings and legislation, U.N. resolutions, public-interest law suits and charges in the activities of multinational corporations, governmental agencies and public figures." CIR reports have won awards from Columbia University, the National Educational Film and Video Festival, Council on International Non-theatrical Events, American Bar Association, Native American Journalists Association, and *E Magazine*. Reports have been published or aired on PBS, NPR, *Los Angeles Times Magazine*, *San Francisco Chronicle*, *New York Daily News*, *Ms.*, *California Lawyer*, and others. Many co-productions with PBS's Frontline. In 1993 the Center spent $815,083 on its programs.
Net Revenue: 1993 $1,048,781 **Net Expenses:** $1,048,781 78%/15%/7% **Net Assets:** $114,642 **Citations:** 12:192
Tax Status: 501(c)(3) **Annual Report:** Yes. **Employees:** 8
Board of Directors or Trustees: Nancy Campbell, Cynthia Gorney, Herb Gunther, Jules Kroll, Frank McCulloch, Dan Noyes, Maureen O'Neill, Raul Ramirez, Kirby Walker, David Weir. Advisors include: Lowell Bergman (producer, 60 Minutes), Sylvia Chase (ABC's Prime Time Live), Osborn Elliott (former dean, Columbia University Journalism School), Seymour Hersh (author-journalist), Bill Moyers (PBS host), Daniel Schorr (NPR), Susan Stamberg (NPR), Mike Wallace (60 Minutes), Judy Woodruff (MacNeil/Lehrer NewsHour), more.
Periodicals: *Muckraker* (monthly newsletter).
Internships: Yes. CIR's intern program was included in the Princeton Review's 1994 <u>America's Top 100 Internships</u>.
Other Information: CIR receives Public Broadcasting System (PBS) contracts to produce programming. The Center received $538,781, or 51% of revenue, from gifts and grants awarded by foundations, businesses, and individuals. (These grants included $500,000 over two years from the John D. and Catherine T. MacArthur Foundation, $30,000 from the C.S. Fund, $15,000 from the Town Creek Foundation, $1,500 from the New World Foundation, $1,500 from the Wallace Alexander Gerbode Foundation, $1,000 from the Vanguard Public Foundation, and $250 from the Aaron and Martha Schecter Foundation.) $455,514, or 43%, from contract revenue for services and information sold. $37,844, or 4%, from royalties and speaking fees. $15,952, or 2%, from publication sales. The remaining revenue came from interest on savings and temporary cash investments.

Center for Law and Social Policy
1616 P St., N.W., Suite 150
Washington, DC 20036   **Phone:** (202) 328-5140
USA

Contact Person: Alan Houseman, Executive Director. **Officers or Principals:** Alan Houseman, Executive Director ($62,466); Mark H. Greenberg, Senior Staff Attorney ($60,375); Paula Roberts, Senior Staff Attorney ($60,375); Karen Schussler, Developer; Jodie Levin-Epstein, Senior Policy Advocate; Linda Perle, Senior Staff Attorney; Joseph Onek, Chair.
Mission or Interest: The Center for Law and Social Policy develops "strategies, training, and materials for use by local advocates to pursue economic independence and support for lower income families headed by women...Representation on block grant programs and tax issues affecting the poor...ensure that people with disabilities have equal opportunity to obtain meaningful employment, decent housing, adequate health care and access to free, appropriate education...preserve the federal legal services program...engage in research and representation to assure that poor people, minorities and the disabled have access to adequate, high quality and cost-effective health care."
Accomplishments: In the fiscal year ending June 1994 the Center spent $981,568 on its programs.
Net Revenue: FY ending 6/94 $1,100,721 ($15,548, or 1%, from government grants) **Net Expenses:** $1,141,359 86%/6%/8%
Net Assets: $401,807 **Citations:** 157:91

Products or Services: Research, legal action, conferences, publications, and lobbying. In the fiscal year ending June 1994 the Center spent $3,990 on lobbying; $391 on grassroots lobbying and $3,599 on the direct lobbying of legislators.
Tax Status: 501(c)(3)
Board of Directors or Trustees: Brooksley Born, Thomas Ehrlich (Indiana Univ.), Irv Garfinkel (Columbia Univ.), Lawrence Latto, Sylvia Law (New York Univ. Law School), Simon Lazarus, Margaret Miller, Irma Neal (IBM), Joseph Onek, Marion Pines (Johns Hopkins Univ.), Marna Tucker.
Other Information: The Center received $1,012,349, or 92% of revenue, from gifts and grants awarded by foundations, companies and individuals. (These grants included $100,000 from the Joyce Foundation, $95,000 from the Rosenberg Foundation and $10,000 from the Center on Budget and Policy Priorities.) $43,467, or 4%, from interest on savings and temporary cash investments. $24,399, or 2%, from the sale of publications. $15,548, or 1%, from government grants. The remaining income came from conferences and other miscellaneous sources.

Center for Law in the Public Interest
5750 Wilshire Blvd., Suite 561
Los Angeles, CA 90036   **Phone:**   (310) 470-3000
USA

Contact Person: Jack Nicholl, Executive Director.   **Officers or Principals:** Jack Nicholl, Executive Director ($19,320, for contracted services); Brent N. Rushforth, President ($0); Tracy Westen, Secretary ($0).
Mission or Interest: Public interest legal advocacy group.
Accomplishments: In the fiscal year ending November 1993, the Center spent $285,079 on its activities. The largest portion of this, $224,424, was paid for contracted attorneys' services. For these activities, the Center received $318,130 in court-awarded attorney's fees. Cases involved in included Citizens Against Gated Enclaves v. City of Los Angeles, Coalition for Los Angeles County Planning in the Public Interest v. County of Los Angeles, Friends of Ballona Wetlands v. California Coastal Commission, Citizens Committee to Save Our Village v. City of Claremont, and others.
Net Revenue: FY ending 11/93 $469,128 **Net Expenses:** $317,048 90%/8%/2% **Net Assets:** $408,942 **Citations:** 172:89
Tax Status: 501(c)(3)
Board of Directors or Trustees: Kirk Dillman, Norm Emerson, Annie Gilbar, Carolyn Mannon Haber, Frances Hrobak, Elisa Leyva, Wesley Marx, Gladys Meade (American Lung Assoc.), Peter Mieras, Josephine Powe, Cynthia Robbins, Paul Rubenstein, Brent Rushforth, Stanley Sheinbaum, Robert Strickland, Gail Title, Tracy Westen (CA Commission on Campaign Financing), Francis Wheat, Robert Wolfe.
Other Information: The Center received $318,130, or 68% of revenue, from court-awarded attorney's fees. $103,309, or 22%, from gifts and grants awarded by foundations, businesses, and individuals. $42,751, or 9%, from capital gains on the sale of securities. $4,938, or 1%, from interest on savings and temporary cash investments.

Center for Legal Advocacy
455 Sherman St.
Denver, CO 80203   **Phone:**   (303) 722-0300
USA

Contact Person: Mary Anne Harvey, Executive Director.   **Officers or Principals:** Mary Anne Harvey, Executive Director ($54,755); Chester R. Chapman, Director, Legal Services ($53,935); Kristen A. Kutz, Supervising Attorney ($42,868); Mary Cook, President; George B. Curtis, Vice President; Brian W. Klepinger, Ph.D., Secretary; Judith Fouret Alexander, Treasurer.
Mission or Interest: Legal advocacy organization that uses litigation to press for the rights of those with developmental disabilities and mental illness, older Americans, and other disabled persons.
Accomplishments: In the fiscal year ending September 1994, the Center spent $1,067,694 on its programs.
Net Revenue: FY ending 9/94 $1,115,491 ($765,198, or 69%, from government grants)
Net Expenses: $1,146,121 93%/2%/5% **Net Assets:** $30,491 **Citations:** 12:191
Tax Status: 501(c)(3)
Board of Directors or Trustees: Martha Aguilar, Harry Almy, Gerald Bader Jr., Mary Baum, Mark Caldwell, James Carder, Dale Coski, Jane Grogan, David Henninger, Dawn Howard, Donald MacDonald, Patrick Schilken, Terry Wasley.
Other Information: The Center received $765,198, or 69% of revenue, from government grants. $327,137, or 29%, from direct and indirect public support in the form of gifts and grants awarded by foundations, businesses, affiliates, and individuals. $6,105, or 1%, from client fees. The remaining revenue came from workshop fees, publications, income from special fund-raising events (including an AIDS Walk), interest on savings and temporary cash investments, and other miscellaneous sources.

Center for Media Literacy (CML)
1962 S. Shenandoah St.
Los Angeles, CA 90034   **Phone:**   (310) 559-2944   **E-Mail:** cml@earthlink.net
USA   **Fax:**   (310) 559-9396   **Web-Page:** http://www.earthlink.net/~cml

Contact Person: Sally Mishkind, Operations.   **Officers or Principals:** Rosalind Silver, Editor ($36,926); Elizabeth Thoman, Executive Director ($22,750); Clive M. Bridgewater, Chair ($0).
Mission or Interest: "Help children and adults prepare for living and learning in a global media culture by translating media literacy research and theory into practical information." Focus on issues such as: the influence of advertising, media violence, media images of gender roles, bias in the news, and more.

Accomplishments: "CML is the largest publisher and distributor of media literacy teaching materials." Active membership of over 2,000. Materials and lesson plans used by educators throughout the U.S.

Net Revenue: 1993 $505,057 **Net Expenses:** $484,492 69%/20%/11% **Net Assets:** (-$49,728) **Citations:** 29:158

Products or Services: Media Literacy Workshop Kits curriculum materials. These Kits contain lesson plans, materials, discussion topics and other tools for classroom use. Topics include: "Break the Lies that Bind: Sexism in the Media," "News for the 90's: How to Analyze the News," "Citizenship in a Media Age: Building the Common Good," and others. They also promote media critiques from other sources such as Fairness and Accuracy In Reporting and Common Courage Press,

Tax Status: 501(c)(3) **Annual Report:** No. **Employees:** 5

Board of Directors or Trustees: Ron Austin (Geronimo Productions), Martha Coleman (All Saints Episcopal Church), Beverly Davis, CPA (Korn/Ferry Intl.), Phyllis de Pocciotto (Santa Barbara Film Festival), Sara Miller McCune (McCune Found.), Joanne Wycoff (Cox Cable).

Periodicals: *Connect* (quarterly).

Internships: Yes, unpaid, minimum of three months or 250 hours during the school year.

Other Information: Prior to 1994 they were known as Center for Media and Values. The Center received $237,807, or 47% of revenue, from gifts and grants awarded by foundations, companies and individuals. (These grants included $20,000 from the C.S. Fund, and $1,000 from the Norman Lear Foundation.) $124,532, or 25%, from program services, including the sale of publications, subscriptions, and workshop kits. $119,835, or 24%, from membership dues. $15,221, or 3%, from conferences. The remaining revenue came from interest on savings and temporary cash investments, and miscellaneous sources.

Center for Medicare Advocacy

791 South Main St.
South Windham, CT 06266   **Phone:**   (203) 456-7790
USA

Contact Person: Charles Hulin, Co-Director.   **Officers or Principals:** Charles Hulin, Co-Director ($118,382); Judith Stein Hulin ($118,382); Brad Plebani, Staff Attorney ($118,356); Walter Keenan, Staff Attorney ($112,340); Marion Russotto, President; Sonia Colby, Treasurer; Constance Neal, Secretary.

Mission or Interest: Informs Medicare recipients of their rights, and provides legal services and litigation for individuals who are denied benefits. Provides consulting services for other Medicare advocates and advocacy programs.

Accomplishments: In the fiscal year ending June 1994, the Center spent $1,563,002 on its programs.

Net Revenue: FY ending 6/94 $1,557,325 ($1,575,331 from government grants, see **Other Information**)

Net Expenses: $1,563,002 100%/0%/0% **Net Assets:** $766,113 **Citations:** 13:188

Products or Services: Educational materials, litigation and legal counseling, and consulting.

Tax Status: 501(c)(3)

Other Information: The Center received $1,575,331 from government grants. These government grants exceeded net revenue because net revenue was reduced by a loss of $95,748 from unrealized depreciation and realized losses on the sale of securities. Other sources of revenue included $62,403 from interest on savings and temporary cash investments, $13,595 from consulting fees and other forms of representation, and $1,744 from gifts and grants awarded by foundations, businesses, and individuals.

Center for Neighborhood Technology (CNT)

2125 W. North Ave.
Chicago, IL 60647   **Phone:**   (312) 278-4800   **E-Mail:** info@cnt.org
USA   **Fax:**   (312) 278-3840   **Web-Page:** http://www.cnt.org

Contact Person: Patricia Abrams, Executive Director. **Officers or Principals:** Scott Bernstein, President; Jeremy Warburg Russo, Chair; Bliss Williams Browne, Vice Chair; Peter Manikas, Secretary; Elizabeth Densmore, Treasurer.

Mission or Interest: Community investment and building. Grassroots organizing. Focus on transportation, energy, and housing policies.

Accomplishments: CNT has pioneered new sources of funding for community reinvestment. For example, the federal Intermodal Surface Transportation Efficiency Act of 1991 set up funds for Congestion Mitigation and Air Quality. CNT showed that community reinvestment in areas around public transportation (in this case Chicago's elevated train), led to increased ridership, moving people out of their automobiles and decreasing congestion and improving air quality. "This sets the precedent for access by other communities around the country to this $1.1 billion fund." CNT worked with the Natural Resource Defense Council on a study which demonstrated that families living near public transportation saved "$396 a month in transit-rich areas compared with locations that are transit poor." The implications being that those who live near public transportation should be approved for larger mortgages because of decreased transportation expenses. "The location-efficient mortgage has been adopted by the President's Council on Sustainable Development and the White House Dialogue on Greenhouse Gas Reductions as an innovative solution to urban and environmental problems." CNT received a federal grant to give communities access to information regarding affordable housing, and economic development as part of the Clinton Administration's information superhighway initiative. The network allows communities to identify "discriminatory lending practices and enable them to mount effective bank challenges under the Community Reinvestment Act. The on-line project is in partnership with OMB Watch and its computer network, RTKNET. CNT's magazine *The Neighborhood Works* has won several awards, including the *Utne Reader's* 1994 Alternative Press Award for Service Journalism, and one of the 1993 Top Ten Media Heroes from AlterNet and the Institute for Alternative Journalism.

Net Revenue: 1994 $1,443,411 (CNT received government grants) **Net Expenses:** $1,374,645

Net Assets: $1,115

Tax Status: 501(c)(3)
Board of Directors or Trustees: Joe Block, Ramiro Borja, Jonathan Boyer, Dorreen Carey, Ric Gudell, Joanna Hoelscher, Leon Jackson, Nancy Juda, Susan Kaplan, Katherine Laing, William Moorhead, Jerrold Much, Mary Nelson, Barack Obama, Art Perez, Michael Perlow, Juan Rivera, Kris Ronnow, Angelo Rose, David Saltzman, Rev. P.D. Saunders, Faith Smith, Kathryn Tholin, Robert Weissbourd, Wanda White.
Periodicals: *The Neighborhood Works* (bimonthly magazine), *Place Matters* (quarterly newsletter).
Other Information: CNT received $913,641, or 63% of revenue from foundations. (These grants included $200,000 from the Joyce Foundation, $100,000 from the Nathan Cummings Foundation, $50,000 from the Joyce Mertz-Gilmore Foundation, $16,500 from the Wieboldt Foundation.) $378,043, or 26%, from fees for services and consulting. $78,024, or 5%, from gifts and grants awarded by government, businesses, and individuals. $21,106, or 1%, from subscriptions and sales of publications. $12,795, or 1%, from special fund-raising events. The remaining revenue came from interest on savings and temporary cash investments, and other miscellaneous sources.

Center for New Creation
845 North Lincoln St.
Arlington, VA 22201
USA

Contact Person: Marie Dennis Grosso, President.   **Officers or Principals:** Marie Dennis Grosso, President ($0); Margaret Schellenberg, Secretary ($0); Joan Urbanczyk, Treasurer ($0).
Mission or Interest: Education and organization to promote; affordable housing, women's issues, immigration issues, labor and trade issues, awareness about homelessness, the "role of the middle class in the new world order," spirituality, art and social conscience, popular economics, human rights, and other "justice issues."
Accomplishments: In the fiscal year ending November 1993, the Center spent $21,000 on its programs. The Center's newsletter reaches more than 1,100 people per issue.
Net Revenue: FY ending 11/93 $26,868 **Net Expenses:** $25,034 **Net Assets:** $16,126
Products or Services: Publications and workshops.
Tax Status: 501(c)(3)
Periodicals: Quarterly newsletter.
Other Information: The Center received $20,388, or 76% of revenue, from gifts and grants awarded by foundations, companies, and individuals. $4,010, or 15%, from membership dues. $1,265 net, or 4%, from special fund-raising events. The remaining revenue came from program services, the sale of goods, and investment income.

Center for Policy Alternatives
1875 Connecticut Ave., N.W., Suite 710
Washington, DC 20009   **Phone:**   (202) 387-6030
USA

Contact Person: Linda Tarr-Whelan.   **Officers or Principals:** Jeffrey Tyrens, President.
Mission or Interest: Policy center focusing on change at the state and local level.
Accomplishments: Published "A Matter of Simple Justice: Women's Rights are Human Rights - A Report to American Women & Men on the Occasion of the UN 4th World Conference on Women."
Products or Services: Reports, video tapes.
Tax Status: 501(c)(3)
Other Information: In 1993 the Center received $100,000 from the Carnegie Corporation, and $15,000 from the Town Creek Foundation. In 1994, $40,000 from the Robert Sterling Clark Foundation, $10,000 from the Ms. Foundation for Women, $5,000 from the Joyce Mertz-Gilmore Foundation, $3,000 from the Bauman Family Foundation, $250 from the Stewart R. Mott Charitable Trust.

Center for Political Ecology
P.O. Box 8467
Santa Cruz, CA 95061   **Phone:**   (408) 459-4541   **E-Mail:** CNS@CATS.VCSC.EDU
USA   **Fax:**   (408) 459-3518

Contact Person: James O'Connor, Chairperson.   **Officers or Principals:** Barbara Laurence, Secretary/Treasurer ($13,854).
Mission or Interest: Environmental organization focusing on the links between culture and ecology. Publishes *Capitalism, Nature, Socialism: A Journal of Socialist Ecology*, "the only international theoretical and political journal of socialist ecology - including ecological Marxism and feminism."
Accomplishments: Articles from *Capitalism, Nature, Socialism* have been reprinted in *Political Affairs* (the journal of the Communist Party USA) and in other publications.
Net Revenue: FY ending 6/95 $19,550 **Net Expenses:** $22,364 **Net Assets:** $95,758
Products or Services: Meetings, conferences, books, videos and pamphlets.
Tax Status: 501(c)(3) **Annual Report:** No. **Employees:** 1 paid, 6-10 volunteers.
Board of Directors or Trustees: Daniel Faber (Northeastern Univ.), Roberto Marotto, Dennis Van-Tassel.
Periodicals: *Capitalism, Nature, Socialism* (quarterly journal), available in English, Spanish and Italian.
Internships: Yes. Interns work on producing the journal, community outreach, local ecology history projects, more.

Other Information: The Center received $10,632, or 54% of revenue, from gifts and grants awarded by foundations, companies and individuals. $6,692, or 34%, from investment income. The remaining income came from program services, and there was a loss on the sale of securities.

Center for Popular Economics (CPE)

P.O. Box 785
Amherst, MA 01004   **Phone:** (413) 545-0743   **E-Mail:** cpe@acad.umass.edu
USA   **Fax:**   (415) 545-2921

Contact Person: Lisa Nelson, Executive Director.
Mission or Interest: "U.S. economic priorities do not reflect the needs and rights of the majority of people in this country and throughout the world. The well-being of the planet and much of its population have long been sacrificed to the profits of corporations, banks, and the people who own them...The Center for Popular Economics is a non-profit collective of political economists." CPE offers week-long intensive institutes "designed for activists, organizers and educators...No previous economics training is needed." Offers institutes in the U.S. and international economies.
Accomplishments: Programs included the "Project on the Urban Economic Crisis," workshops and conferences, and publications. A union district director said "I returned from the week-long seminar exuberant. It was exciting to be so stimulated and to learn a vast amount of concentrated information in such as short period of time. The instructors were excellent and thought provoking. I will continue to recommend the Institute to my friends and fellow union members."
Products or Services: The New Field Guide to the U.S. Economy, The War Against the Poor: A Defense Manual, other books and pamphlets.
Tax Status: 501(c)(3) **Annual Report:** No. **Employees:** 40
Other Information: In 1995 the Center received $1,000 from Resist.

Center for Public Integrity

1634 I St., N.W., Suite 902
Washington, DC 20006   **Phone:** (202) 783-3900   **E-Mail:** ctrforpi@essential.org
USA   **Fax:**   (202) 783-3906   **Web-Page:** www:http://ww.essential.org/cpi

Contact Person: Charles Lewis, Executive Director.   **Officers or Principals:** Charles Lewis, Executive Director ($103,258); Allen Pusey, Treasurer ($0); Charles Piller, Secretary ($0); Alejandro Benes, Managing Director.
Mission or Interest: "Informing and educating the public about critical issues of integrity in the American political process." The Center was established in 1989 "to create a mechanism through which important, national issues can be investigated and analyzed by talented, responsible journalists over a period of months and the written material can be presented in full form without the traditional time and space limitations. Published Center studies then become resources for reporters, community groups and academics." Although the Center's Board of Advisors is slanted towards the Left, the Center remains nonpartisan, and its work is critical of both Democratic and Republican politicians. Study's focus on campaign financing, lobbying, and financial connections of policy makers and their advisors.
Accomplishments: The Center gained wide-spread media attention in February 1996 when, during the Republican presidential primary, it called attention to the fact that candidate Pat Buchanan's campaign co-chairman Larry Pratt had links to militia organizations and had spoken at events that had neo-Nazi and white supremacist representation. Other studies have called attention to the monied interests who were given access to President Clinton and the late Commerce Secretary Ron Brown's international trade missions after donating funds to the President's campaign or the Democratic Party. In 1994 the Center spent $477,797 on its programs.
Net Revenue: 1994 $575,016 **Net Expenses:** $567,032 84%/5%/11% **Net Assets:** (-$29,892) **Citations:** 499:41
Products or Services: Research, press releases, and publications.
Tax Status: 501(c)(3)
Board of Directors or Trustees: Josie Goytisolo, Bill Hogan, Susan Loewenberg, Charles Piller, Marianne Szegedy-Maszak, Paula Walker. The Center's Board of Advisors includes: James David Barber, Owen Bieber (UAW), James MacGregor Burns, Hodding Carter (Assistant Sec. of State for Public Affairs, 1977-1980), Gustavo Godoy, Colin Greer, Herbert Hafif, Rev. Theodore Hesburgh, Molly Ivins (syndicated columnist), Kathleen Hall Jamieson, Sonia Jarvis, Lane Kirkland (AFL-CIO), Bill Kovach, Prof. Charles Ogletree (Harvard School of Law), Arthur Schlesinger Jr. (historian), William Schneider, Pearl Stewart, William Julius Wilson.
Periodicals: The Public I (monthly newsletter).
Other Information: The Center received $473,778, or 82% of revenue, from gifts and grants awarded by foundations, businesses, and individuals. (These grants included $300,000 from the Florence and John Schumann Foundation, $57,472 from the Joyce Foundation, $30,000 from the Deer Creek Foundation, $20,000 from the Angelina Fund.) $79,750, or 14%, from contract fees, including a contract with "a major news organization" to provide investigative information. $11,075, or 2%, from consulting fees, including, again, a "major news organization." $5,876, or 1%, from subscriptions and the sale of publications. The remaining revenue came from honoraria.

Center for Public Representation

22 Green St.
Northampton, MA 01060   **Phone:** (413) 586-6024
USA

Contact Person: Steven J. Schwartz, Executive Director.   **Officers or Principals:** Steven J. Schwartz, Executive Director ($140,521); Cathy E. Costanzo, Assistant Director ($105,847); Robert V. Agoglia, Program Director ($66,314); Stephen Arons, President; William Breitbart, Treasurer; Robert D. Fleischner, Associate Director; David Engle, Attorney; Elizabeth A. Coombs.
Mission or Interest: "Legal assistance counsel and representation to institutionalized and low-income handicapped persons at no charge."
Accomplishments: In the fiscal year ending June 1994, the Center spent $1,080,061 on its programs.
Net Revenue: FY ending 6/94 $1,315,305 ($177,091, or 13%, from government fees and contracts)
Net Expenses: $1,200,808 90%/10%/0% **Net Assets:** $1,569,380 **Citations:** 38:146
Products or Services: Legal counsel and litigation.
Tax Status: 501(c)(3)
Board of Directors or Trustees: Robert Riedel, Judith Souweine, Rebecca Macauley, William Newman, Judi Chamberlin, Jose Melina.
Other Information: The Center received $335,097, or 25% of revenue, from the Disability Law Center. $329,318, or 25%, from attorney's fees and consultations. $232,241, or 18%, from the Massachusetts Legal Assistance Corporations. $177,091, or 13%, from fees and contracts from government agencies. $78,917, or 6%, from training revenue. $75,769, or 6%, from dividends and interest from securities. $27,165, or 2%, from capital gains on the sale of securities. $25,125, or 2%, from the National Association of Protection and Advocacy. $14,306, or 1%, from the Massachusetts Bar Foundation. The remaining income came from interest on savings and temporary cash investments, and other miscellaneous sources.

Center for Public Representation, Wisconsin

121 S. Pinckney St.
Madison, WI 53703   **Phone:**   (608) 251-4008
USA

Contact Person: Michael Pritchard, Executive Director.   **Officers or Principals:** Robert Peterson, Program Manager ($41,917); Michael Pritchard, Executive Director ($38,200); Michael Rust, Program Manager ($34,215); Jay Grenig, President; Adrian Cohen, Treasurer; Nancy Rottier, Secretary; Carla Wright, Vice President.
Mission or Interest: "Group and individual representation before administrative, legislative and judicial agencies" for low income persons. Provides training for law students, attorneys, and others to act as advocates.
Accomplishments: In the fiscal year ending June 1994, the Center spent $1,100,924 on its programs.
Net Revenue: FY ending 6/94 $1,216,250 ($966,786, or 79%, from government grants) **Net Expenses:** $1,271,649 87%/11%/2% **Net Assets:** $50,773
Products or Services: Advocacy and advocacy training, conferences, publications, health services for low income families, and lobbying. The Center spent $19,023 on lobbying, $825 on grassroots lobbying and $18,198 on the direct lobbying of legislators.
Tax Status: 501(c)(3)
Board of Directors or Trustees: Prof. Peter Carstensen (Univ. of WI Law School), Robert Harris, Judi McMullen (Marquette Univ. Law School), Arthur Phillips, Susan Rosenberg, John Walsh, Daphne Webb, Ruth Westmont.
Other Information: The Center received $966,786, or 79% of revenue, from government grants. $94,096, or 8%, from training and publication contracts. $64,584, or 5%, from direct and indirect public support in the form of gifts and grants awarded by foundations, businesses, affiliates, and individuals. $44,595, or 4%, from training and conference fees. $21,077, or 2%, from the sale of publications and royalties. The remaining revenue came from honoraria, interest on savings and temporary cash investments, and other miscellaneous sources.

Center for Reflection on the Second Law (CFRSL)

8420 Camellia Dr.
Raleigh, NC 27613   **Phone:**   (919) 847-5819   **E-Mail:** jimber1@aol.com
USA   **Fax:**   (919) 676-5895

Contact Person: James F. Berry, Director.
Mission or Interest: "CFRSL accuses the modern corporation of practices which will bring on certain failure to the Earth system and with it the failure of the human enterprise. Corporations exploit Earth and people. They take; they never give back...Corporations poison the sea, the water and the air, they strip Earth of its trees and wilderness. Their insanity is evident everywhere, in every country, every forest, at every shopping mall, at the super highways at every beltway...They strip people of their right to a decent wage and to work that has meaning and value for themselves and for society...Executives who administer the affairs of the corporations are not executives at all; they are courtiers dancing attendance on a royal fiction called a corporation; a deathless 'legal person' without a soul or heart, with a one-track robot brain, a Frankenstein-like monster."
Accomplishments: In 1995 the Center held its eleventh annual conference, "The Context for Human Survival." The conference featured former executive director of Greenpeace, Richard Grossman speaking on "Disempowering and Dismantling the Modern Corporation" and the founder/director of the Earth Community Center, Jane Blewett speaking on "Women and the Corporate World."
Net Revenue: 1992 $4,809
Products or Services: Audio and video tapes of the annual conferences.
Tax Status: 501(c)(3) **Annual Report:** No. **Employees:** All volunteer.
Board of Directors or Trustees: Acasia, Stephanie Bass, Peter Berg, Anne Berry, Margaret Berry, Thomas Berry, Wendell Berry, Hal Crowther, Michael Dowd, David Haenke, Hazel Henderson, Bill Holman, Evelyn Mattern, Charles Mulholland, John Papworth, Zach Ralston, Sallie Ricks, Kirkpatrick Sale (author, Human Scale), Jane Sharp, Charlene Spretnak, Clay Stalmaker, Brian Swimme.
Periodicals: Periodic circular.

Center for Reproductive Law and Policy

120 Wall St.
New York, NY 10005   **Phone:**   (212) 514-5534
USA

Contact Person: Janet Benshoof, President.
Mission of Interest. Legal work at the national and local level to advance abortion rights.
Accomplishments: Fought to make sure that abortion rights were at the forefront of issues at the 1994 United Nations conference on population in Cairo.
Tax Status: 501(c)(3)
Other Information: Founded in 1992. In 1994 the Center received $115,000 from the Robert Sterling Clark Foundation, $50,000 from the Henry J. Kaiser Family Foundation, $40,000 from the General Service Foundation, $30,000 from the Jessie Smith Noyes Foundation, $30,000 from the New-Land Foundation, $20,000 from the Deer Creek Foundation, $15,000 from the Ms. Foundation for Women, $15,000 from the Tides Foundation, $2,500 from the Stewart R. Mott Charitable Trust. The Kaiser Family Foundation awarded the Center another $31,050 for 1994, but had not paid it by the end of the year. In 1993 the Center received $100,000 from the John Merck Fund.

Center for Responsive Politics

1320 19th St., N.W., Suite 700
Washington, DC 20036   **Phone:**   (202) 857-0044   **E-Mail:** info@crp.org
USA   **Fax:**   (202) 857-7809   **Web-Page:** http://www.crp.org

Contact Person: Ellen Miller, Executive Director.   **Officers or Principals:** Ellen S. Miller, Executive Director ($89,300); Larry Makinson,Program Director ($67,925); Margaret Engle, Communications Director ($51,900); Thomas R. Asher, Chair.
Mission or Interest: To study the influence of money on politics, "aimed at creating a more involved citizenry and a more responsive Congress." Operates through several projects; The Open Secrets project which monitors and analyzes contributions to congress. State Open Secrets which operates at the state level. National Library on Money and Politics database. Soft Money Research that monitors the unlimited contributions made to the political parties by corporations, unions, and individuals. Other projects monitor the Federal Election Commission's compliance activities, host conferences and seminars, and serve as a media resource.
Products or Services: Open Secrets: The Encyclopedia of Congressional Money and Politics by Larry Makinson and Joshua Goldstein. Numerous other books, how-to guides and publications.
Net Revenue: 1995 $1,249,593 **Net Expenses:** $1,307,599 **Net Assets:** $904,730 **Tax Status:** 501(c)(3)
Board of Directors or Trustees: Martha Angle, Hon. Dick Clark, Paul Hoff, Sonia Jarvis, Peter Kovler, John Murphy, Whitney North Seymour Jr., Paul Thomas, Robert Weinberger.
Periodicals: *Capital Eye* (bimonthly newsletter).
Other Information: In 1994 the Center received $445,000 from the Florence and John Schumann Foundation, $91,500 from the Joyce Foundation, $30,000 from the Rockefeller Family Fund, $7,500 from the New World Foundation, and $500 from the Jessie Smith Noyes Foundation. In 1993, $200,000 over two years from the Carnegie Corporation.

Center for Science in the Public Interest (CSPI)

1875 Connecticut Ave., N.W.
Washington, DC 20009   **Phone:**   (202) 332-9110
USA   **Fax:**   (202) 265-4954

Contact Person: Michael F. Jacobson, Secretary.   **Officers or Principals:** Michael F. Jacobson, Secretary ($90,704); Dennis Bass, Deputy Director ($77,721); Bruce Silverglade, Legal Director ($73,846); Kathleen O'Reilly, President; James Sullivan, Treasurer; George Hacker, Project Director; Stephen Schmidt, Editor in Chief; Bonnie Liebman, Nutrition Director.
Mission or Interest: Public education about health and nutrition. Pursues changes in U.S. health policy, including changes in labeling, marketing, and pesticide use.
Accomplishments: Well known for their work on the health affects and fat content of fast foods, Mexican foods, Italian foods, Chinese foods, movie theater popcorn, restaurant breakfasts, and sea food. In the fiscal year ending June 1994, the Center spent $7,759,389 on its programs. The largest program, with expenditures of $3,797,403, was the production and distribution of public education materials such as charts, books, booklets, pamphlets, and brochures. $2,831,229 was spent on production and distribution of a newsletter to approximately 650,000 subscribers. $1,130,757 was spent on special projects, such as the previously mentioned exposes of fat content in food. The Center made $2,707,871 in payments to affiliates.
Net Revenue: FY ending 6/94 $12,420,505 **Net Expenses:** $11,163,969 70%/1%/5% **Net Assets:** $2,062,253
Citations: 1,751:15
Products or Services: Books, brochures, educational materials, conferences, press conferences, and lobbying. The Center spent $178,475 on lobbying, $11,061 on grassroots lobbying, and $167,414 on the direct lobbying of legislators. This was an increase of 27% over the previous year.
Tax Status: 501(c)(3)
Board of Directors or Trustees: Robert Haft, David Hensler, Marvin Scheiderman, Deborah Szekely, Anne Bancroft.
Periodicals: *Nutrition Action Healthletter* (ten issues per year journal).
Other Information: Affiliated with the Center for the Study of Commercialism at the same address. The Center received $10,858,104, or 87% of revenue, from direct and indirect support in the form of gifts and grants awarded by foundations, affiliates, businesses, and individuals. (These grants included $500 from the Compton Foundation.) $1,102,515, or 9%, from the sale of publications. $424,798, or 3%, from royalties. The remaining revenue came from interest on savings and temporary cash investments, and other miscellaneous sources.

Center for Socialist History

2633 Etna St.
Berkeley, CA 94704   **Phone:**   (510) 549-3908
USA

Contact Person: Ernest Haberkeen, Executive Director.
Officers or Principals: Jacki Ruby, Secretary/Treasurer ($0); Arthur Lipow, Director ($0); Stephen F. Diamond, Director ($0).
Mission or Interest: Public library and research institution focusing on the history of socialism.
Accomplishments: Serves approximately 25 people annually. In 1994 the Center spent $11,163 on its programs.
Net Revenue: 1994 $25,040 **Net Expenses:** $11,163 **Net Assets:** $88,700
Products or Services: Library services, books and periodicals.
Tax Status: 501(c)(3)
Other Information: The Center received $23,000, or 92% of revenue, from gifts and grants awarded by foundations, businesses, and individuals. $1,957, or 8%, from investment income. The remaining revenue came from the sale of assets other than inventory.

Center for Teaching Peace

4501 Van Ness St., N.W.
Washington, DC 20016   **Phone:**   (202) 537-1372
USA

Contact Person: Mavoureen McCarthy, Vice President. **Officers or Principals:** Mavoureen McCarthy, Vice President ($29,833); Colman McCarthy, President ($10,000); James McCarthy, Secretary/Treasurer ($0).
Mission or Interest: "To teach the philosophy and practice of non-violence as a way of resolving conflicts."
Accomplishments: In the fiscal year ending May 1995, the Center spent $106,241 on its programs. The largest program, with expenditures of $33,755, was "Teaching Peace in the Classroom" in District of Columbia classrooms. Other programs combine baseball leagues with peace education and literacy tutoring, develop curriculum, and peace programs at correctional facilities.
Net Revenue: FY ending 5/95 $122,076 **Net Expenses:** $119,029 89%/11%/0% **Net Assets:** $93,555
Tax Status: 501(c)(3)
Other Information: The Center received $111,695, or 91% of revenue, from gifts and grants awarded by foundations, businesses, and individuals. (In the fiscal year ending May 1994, grants included $100,000 from the Florence and John Schuman Foundation, $15,000 from the Barbra Streisand Foundation, $10,000 from the Joyce Foundation, and $7,500 from the Helen Sperry Lea Foundation.) $8,274, or 7%, from programs services, including lecture fees, course tuition, and materials. $2,107, or 2%, from interest on savings and temporary cash investments.

Center for the Study of Commercialism (CSC)

1875 Connecticut Ave., N.W., Suite 300
Washington, DC 20009   **Phone:**   (202) 332-9110
USA

Contact Person: Michael F. Jacobson, Secretary/Treasurer. **Officers or Principals:** Ronald Collins, President ($0).
Mission or Interest: "Influences public opinion and the media on the excesses of commercialism in American culture by waging educational campaigns about over commercialization." Promotion of a more environmentally and psychologically sound way of living.
Accomplishments: In the fiscal year ending June 1994, the Center spent $59,068 on its programs. The largest program, with expenditures of $28,234, was general education which included various informational activities and a "clearinghouse on commercialism for reporters." $27,921 was spent on the "Marketing Madness Project" that produced a book "that will teach the public about the effects of commercialism on society." $2,913 was spent producing a quarterly newsletter.
Net Revenue: FY ending 6/94 $64,177 **Net Expenses:** $66,253 89%/6%/4% **Net Assets:** $26,242
Tax Status: 501(c)(3)
Board of Directors or Trustees: Joan Claybrook, Nicholas Johnson, Larry Kirstein, James Weill.
Periodicals: *Advice* (quarterly newsletter).
Other Information: Affiliated with the Center for Science in the Public Interest. $42,572, or 66% of revenue, from gifts and grants awarded by foundations, businesses, and individuals. $20,779 net, or 32%, from the sale of inventory. $825, or 1%, from interest on savings and temporary cash investments.

Center for Third World Organizing (CTWO)

1218 E 21st St.
Oakland, CA 94606   **Phone:** (510) 533-7583   **E-Mail:** ctwo@igc.apc.org
USA   **Fax:**   (510) 533-0923

Contact Person: Johanna Harding. **Officers or Principals:** Francis Calpotura, Co-Executive Director ($25,000); Rinku Sen, Co-Executive Director ($23,000); Mark Toney, President ($0); Luissa Blue, Vice President; Tim Sampson, Secretary/Treasurer.
Mission or Interest: "CTWO work nationally in communities of color to build direct-action membership organization."
Accomplishments: In 1994 they spent $304,615 on organizing projects in Oakland, Sacramento and Denver, and two national coordinating projects. They spent $194,615 on "A New Collaboration for Hands-On Relationships" (ANCHOR), a project bringing together leaders in immigrant and refugee communities with leaders in established communities of color. $110,001 was spent on the Minority Activist Apprenticeship Program (MAAP) which trained 20 interns to work on local community issues.

Net Revenue: 1994 $649,955 **Net Expenses:** $961,992 88%/11%/1% **Net Assets:** $171,466 **Citations:** 0:255
Products or Services: Connects activists with religious funders. Publications, networking and organizational activities.
Tax Status: 501(c)(3) **Annual Report:** Yes. **Employees:** 15
Board of Directors or Trustees: Gary Delgado, Her Chao Gunther, Maria Jimenez, Alicia Sanchez, Scot Nakagawa.
Periodicals: *Third Force* (bimonthly magazine).
Internships: Yes, the Minority Activist Apprenticeship Program and others.
Other Information: The Center received $581,471, or 89%, from gifts and grants awarded by foundations, companies, and individuals. (These grants included $50,000 from the Florence and John Schumann Foundation, $45,000 from the New World Foundation, $32,946 from the Rosenberg Foundation, $15,000 from the McKay Foundation, $8,000 from the Abelard Foundation, $5,000 from the Chinook Fund, $4,000 from the Vanguard Public Foundation, $2,000 from the Tides Foundation.) $20,747, or 3%, from technical assistance fees. $18,790, or 3%, from publication sales. $9,580, or 1%, from rental income. The remaining revenue came from training fees, membership dues, interest on savings and temporary cash investments, dividends and interest from securities, and other miscellaneous sources.

Center for War / Peace Studies
218 East 18th St.
New York, NY 10003   **Phone:**   (212) 475-1077
USA   **Fax:**   (212) 260-6384

Contact Person: Richard Hudson, Executive Director.   **Officers or Principals:** Richard Hudson, Executive Director ($36,000); Harrison B. W. Hoffman, Chairman ($0); Oscar Israel, Vice Chairman ($0); Mel Dubin, Secretary.
Mission or Interest: Pursues global government to establish a world governed by international law, not force. Advocates a system called the "Binding Triad." "The world has tried to deal with its crises under an obsolete international political system based on full sovereignty of almost 200 nation-states, with no assignment of authority to their collective entity...The Binding Triad is, in essence, a weighted voting system which would make General Assembly decision-making acceptable to the world's diverse array of nations...the United Nations already has three of the four critical elements essential to a system of effective, democratic global governance." The Binding Triad would make General Assembly decisions binding by passing resolutions by a majority, based on votes weighted by three factors, 1) one-nation-one-vote, 2) population, 3) contributions to the U.N. Budget. The Center thinks that, given assigning weighted votes based on these three factors, nations would concede some of their national sovereignty and conform to these binding resolutions.
Accomplishments: Albert Einstein once wrote a letter to executive director Richard Hudson, saying "it seems to me that you may be able to write an effective popular book to convince people of the necessity of World Government." More recently, folk singer Pete Seger has been advocating the Binding Triad, and has joined the Center's Board of Sponsors.
Net Revenue: FY ending 6/95 $78,977 **Net Expenses:** $65,620 **Net Assets:** (-$7,542)
Products or Services: Publications.
Tax Status: 501(c)(3)
Board of Directors or Trustees: Michael Erlanger, Benjamin Ferencz, Myron Kronisch, Betty Lall, Miles Pennybacker, Charles Price III, Joan Warburg, Hannah Wasserman, Paul Szasz.
Periodicals: *Global Report* (quarterly newsletter).
Other Information: The Center received $77,709, or 98% of revenue, from gifts and grants awarded by foundations and individuals. (These grants included $2,500 from the Bydale Foundation.) $1,184, or 1%, from mailing list rentals. The remaining revenue came from investment income.

Center for Women Policy Studies (CWPS)
2000 P St., N.W., Suite 508
Washington, DC 20036   **Phone:**   (202) 872-1770
USA

Contact Person: Jennifer Tucker, Deputy Director.   **Officers or Principals:** Leslie R. Wolfe, President ($76,929); Jennifer Tucker, Deputy Director ($63,064); Irene Natividad, Secretary ($0).
Mission or Interest: Center for Women Policy Studies "was founded in 1972 as a feminist policy research and advocacy institution, concentrating especially on the issues of women and race and class bias in society. The Center's programs address: educational equity, work/family and workplace diversity policies, economic opportunity for low income women, violence against women, girls and violence, women's health, reproductive rights and health, women and AIDS, and leadership development."
Accomplishments: The Center has been actively supporting the "Contract With American Women" created by Bella Abzug and the Women's Environment and Development Organization. The Contract calls for, among other things, "equal pay for work of comparable value" and strengthening affirmative action. In 1994 the Center spent $682,773 on its programs. The largest program expenditure, $217,291, was for "Women's Health Decision Making," a program that studied "barriers to women's access to respectful and effective health care." The second largest, $107,803, was the "Chilly Classroom Project," that studied females' status in the classroom. $105,884 was spent on an AIDS Project. $99,748 was spent on focus groups of women of color to explore how they "define and experience work/family issues." Other projects included; $9,516 for Educational Equity Policy Studies, and $24,622 for studying SAT's and the Gender Gap.
Net Revenue: 1994 $665,238 ($78,900, or 12%, from government grants) **Net Expenses:** $716,694 95%/1%/5%
Net Assets: $32,210 **Citations:** 69:123
Products or Services: Research, publications, videos, conferences, more.

Tax Status: 501(c)(3)
Board of Directors or Trustees: Felicia Lynch, Rayna Green (Smithsonian Inst.), Charlotte Bunch, Jean Hardisty (Political Research Assoc.), Jessie Bernard, Irene Lee, Stephen Moskey (Aetna Life).
Other Information: The Center received $558,208, or 84% of revenue, from gifts and grants awarded by foundations, companies and individuals. (These grants included $20,000 from the Ms. Foundation.) $78,900, or 12%, from government grants. $28,130, or 4%, from the sale of publications. $10,277, or 2%, from interest on savings and temporary cash investments. The remaining revenue came from dividends and interest from securities. Revenue was partially offset by a net $5,271 loss on the sale of assets other than inventory, and a net loss of $7,451 from the "Wise Women Awards."

Center for Women's Economic Alternatives

P.O. Box 1033
Ahoskie, NC 27910
USA

Other Information: In 1994 the Center received $30,000 from the Campaign for Human Development, $15,000 from the New World Foundation, $7,500 from the Ms. Foundation for Women.

Center on Budget and Policy Priorities

777 N. Capitol St., N.E., Suite 705
Washington, DC 20002   **Phone:**   (202) 408-1080
USA

Contact Person: Robert Greenstein, President.   **Officers or Principals:** Robert Greenstein, President ($106,873); Iris Lav, Associate Director ($89,400); Andrew Krepnevich, Project Director ($80,750); Elise Saltzberg, Secretary.
Mission or Interest: Focus on the federal budget (and, to a lesser degree, state budgets) and advocacy of reduced military spending and increased social welfare spending for low-income citizens.
Accomplishments: In 1994 the Center spent $3,171,709 on its programs. The largest program, with expenditures of $664,050, was research and analysis of public policy issues. $648,607 was spent on state fiscal issues, "analysis of state budget and tax policy in order to obtain adequate resources for efforts to reduce poverty and assist low and moderate-income households." $575,748 was spent researching welfare reform. Welfare reform activities included $44,000 in grants; $12,000 each for the National Council of La Raza and the Joint Center for Political and Economic Studies, and $10,000 each for the Center for Law and Social Policy and the Children's Defense Fund. $516,868 was spent to research and promote strategies to help the working poor. These included advocacy of the Earned Income Tax Credit expansion, and $130,000 in grants awarded to other organizations. These grants included $65,000 each for the Local Initiatives Support Corporation and The Enterprise Foundation. $389,593 was spent on child and maternal health projects, such as advocating improving maternal and child health through the Supplemental Food Program. Other projects included defense economics, policy, and budget.
Net Revenue: 1994 $3,958,060   ($48,629, or 1%, from government grants)   **Net Expenses:** $3,913,849   81%/11%/8%
Net Assets: $1,329,556   **Citations:** 617:35
Products or Services: Research, analysis, publications, and lobbying. The Center spent $42,511 on lobbying, $14,650 on grassroots lobbying and $27,861 on the direct lobbying of legislators. This was a decrease of 53% from the year before.
Tax Status: 501(c)(3)
Board of Directors or Trustees: Henry Aaron (Brookings Inst.), Rebecca Blank, David de Ferranti, Marian Wright Edelman (Children's Defense Fund), Dr. Arthur Flemming, James Gibson, John Kramer, Rep. Eleanor Holmes Norton (D-DC), Marion Pines (Johns Hopkins Univ.), Susan Sechler, Juan Sepulveda Jr., Jeffrey Smith, Dr. William Wilson, William Woodside.
Periodicals: *WIC Newsletter* (a newsletter covering the federal Women, Infants and Children program, including legislative and regulatory matters).
Other Information: The Center received $3,644,324, or 92% of revenue, came from gifts and grants awarded by foundations, businesses, affiliates, and individuals. (These grants included $80,510 from the Henry J. Kaiser Family Foundation, $76,218 from the Nathan Cummings Foundation, $66,085 from the Rosenberg Foundation, $50,000 from the Joyce Foundation, $50,000 from the Deer Creek Foundation, $20,000 from the Ruth Mott Fund, and $15,000 from the James C. Penney Foundation. In 1993, $175,000 from the Charles Stewart Mott Foundation, and in 1995, $450,000 from the Rockefeller Foundation.) $67,543, or 2%, from subscriptions. $61,343, or 2%, from dividends and interest from securities. $38,341, or 1%, from interest on savings and temporary cash investments. $31,830, or 1%, from capital gains on the sale of securities. The remaining revenue came from the sale of publications, conference registration fees, honoraria, and consulting fees.

Center on National Labor Policy

5211 Port Royal Road, Suite 103
North Springfield, VA 22151   **Phone:**   (703) 321-9180
USA

Contact Person: Michael E. Avakian, Vice President.   '
Officers or Principals: Michael E. Avakian, Vice President ($62,360); Louis E. Weiss, Chairman/President ($0); Vernon L. Williams, Secretary ($0); Robert D. Love, Treasurer; Stephen O. Goodrick, Executive Vice President.
Mission or Interest: Litigation activities, legal defense, information services and reports to set labor policies.
Accomplishments: In the fiscal year ending October 1994, the Center spent $106,671 on its programs. Involved in ten lawsuits at various stages of hearings and appeals. Most cases involve a union or the National Labor Relations Board.

Net Revenue: FY ending 10/94 $171,761   **Net Expenses:** $133,566   80%/10%/10%   **Net Assets:** $49,952
Tax Status: 501(c)(3)
Board of Directors or Trustees: Charles Sligh.
Other Information: The Center received $170,056, or 99% of revenue, from gifts and grants awarded by foundations and individuals. $1,528, or 1%, from interest on savings and temporary cash investments. The remaining revenue came from dividends and interest from securities.

Center on War and the Child

P.O. Box 487
35 Benton St.
Eureka Springs, AR 72632   **Phone:**   (501) 253-8900
USA   **Fax:**   (501) 253-7149

Contact Person: Dr, Richard Parker, Director.
Mission or Interest: To promote violence as a major public health policy issue. To confront the portrayal of violence in the media which presents or glorifies violence as an acceptable form of conflict resolution. To counteract militarism and the effects of militarism.
Products or Services: Workshops and forums to educate and counter violent culture. Offers the Kids Without Violence Program, which consists of three workshops, Violent Culture - Violent Kids, Raising Peaceful Children in a Violent Society, and Kids Without Violence.
Tax Status: 501(c)(3)
Other Information: Founded in 1987.

Center to Prevent Handgun Violence

1225 I St., N.W., Suite 1100
Washington, DC 20005   **Phone:**   (202) 289-7319
USA

Contact Person: Nancy Gannon, Director of Education.
Officers or Principals: Dennis Hennigan, Director of Legal Affairs ($77,280); Nancy Gannon, Director of Education ($53,664); Richard Aborn, President ($43,992); Sarah Brady, Chair; Alan Bennett, Secretary; Mark Ingram, Treasurer.
Mission or Interest: Research and education affiliate of Handgun Control.
Accomplishments: In 1994 the Center spent $1,911,890 on its programs. The largest program, with expenditures of $1,341,670, was public education, including "school based programs to increase awareness and build skills to reduce gun injuries and gun deaths among children, teens and their families." $433,924 was spent on litigation to "create a body of law to reduce gun violence." This includes legal action against the manufacturers of guns and ammunition, holding them responsible for crimes committed with their products. $136,296 for membership services.
Net Revenue: 1994 $2,795,620   **Net Expenses:** $2,410,268   79%/4%/17%   **Net Assets:** $1,847,273   **Citations:**   194:83
Tax Status: 501(c)(3)
Board of Directors or Trustees: Jack Corderman, James Brady, Kevin Chavous, Roscoe Dellums, Judy Soto, Harry Kahn, Stan Foster, Mary Lewis Grow, Frank Hartmann, John Phillips, Alice Darnell Lattal, Ron David, M.D., Lucy Norman DeSanchez.
Other Information: Affiliated with the 501(c)(4) Handgun Control, Inc. at the same address. The two affiliates had combined net revenues of $9,080,816, net expenses of $8,520,139, and net assets of $3,079,176. Richard Aborn served as president of both and received combined compensation of $122,768. The Center received $2,718,162, or 97% of revenue, from direct and indirect public support in the form of gifts and grants awarded by foundations, affiliates, businesses, and individuals. (These grants included $40,500 from the Joyce Foundation, $30,000 from the Ruth Mott Fund, $500 from the Compton Foundation, $250 from the Vanguard Public Foundation, and $250 from the Haymarket People's Fund.) $81,291, or 3%, from dividends and interest from securities. The remaining revenue came from interest on savings and temporary cash investments, and other miscellaneous sources.

Central America Education Fund

1151 Massachusetts Ave.
Cambridge, MA 02138   **Phone:**   (617) 492-8699
USA

Contact Person: Julia Hurst, President.   **Officers or Principals:** James O'Brien, Treasurer ($0); Douglas Matthews, Clerk ($0).
Mission or Interest: Social justice and peace in Central America. Focuses on the United States involvement in that area. Offers classes in the Spanish language, and cultural events.
Accomplishments: In 1994 the Fund spent $172,120 on its programs. The largest program, with expenditures of $98,933, was the hosting of cultural and educational events. $62,247 was spent on Spanish classes. $10,940 on the production and distribution of a newsletter.
Net Revenue: 1994 $261,140   **Net Expenses:** $258,457   67%/9%/24%   **Net Assets:** $34,416
Tax Status: 501(c)(3)
Periodicals: Newsletter.
Other Information: The Fund received $187,951, or 72% of revenue, from gifts and grants awarded by foundations, businesses, and individuals. $72,809, or 28%, from Spanish language classes fees. The remaining revenue came from translation fees. The Fund held an account receivable valued at $29,951 from an agreement with a former employee to make periodic payments in partial restitution of misappropriated funds.

Central Committee for Conscientious Objectors

1515 Cherry St.
Philadelphia, PA 19146   **Phone:**   (215) 545-4626
USA

Contact Person: Lou Ann Merkle.
Officers or Principals: Walter Luan, Chair ($0); Jim Feldman, Peter Goldman, Jon Landau, Board Members ($0).
Mission or Interest: Pacifism and anti-militarism. Provides information on draft and military avoidance. Provides counseling and legal aid for conscientious objectors.
Accomplishments: In the fiscal year ending August 1994, the Committee spent $150,907 on its programs. $124,886 was spent on counseling, training and outreach, and $26,021 on periodicals.
Net Revenue: FY ending 8/94 $156,652 **Net Expenses:** $220,977 68%/18%/14% **Net Assets:** $100,607
Tax Status: 501(c)(3)
Periodicals: *CCCO News Notes* (quarterly newsletter), *Objector* (nine times a year).
Other Information: The Committee received $136,065, or 87% of revenue, from gifts and grants awarded by foundations, businesses, and individuals. $10,861 net, or 7%, from special fund-raising events. $2,489, or 2%, from dividends and interest from securities. $2,452 net, or 2%, from the sale of inventory. The remaining revenue came from honoraria, rental income, and other miscellaneous sources.

Cesar E. Chavez Foundation

P.O. Box 62
Keene, CA 93531   **Phone:**   (805) 822-5571   **E-Mail:** chavezfdtn@igc.apc.org
USA

Mission or Interest: Foundation dedicated to preserving the memory of Cesar Chavez (1928-1993), the founder of the United Farm Workers union.
Accomplishments: Chavez's family lost their homestead farm when he was ten. After that they became migrant laborers. He later worked as an urban organizer for the Community Service Organization. In 1962 he began to organize farm laborers, and founded the union that was to become the United Farm Workers. In 1965 the union found its most effective tool, a consumer boycott of grapes, to force a collective bargaining agreement with growers. The newly formed Foundation to preserve his memory and works has, to date, begun construction of the Cesar E. Chavez Plaza, and assisted in the production of "The Cesar Chavez Story", an hour-long documentary on Chavez's life. The Foundation is working with Prof. Richard Jensen of the University of Nevada, Las Vegas' Greenspun School of Communications, to produce a book analyzing Chavez's speeches.
Products or Services: "Common Man, Uncommon Valor - The Cesar Chavez Story", video documentary and an accompanying study guide.
Tax Status: 501(c)(3)
Other Information: Affiliated with the 501(c)(5) United Farm Workers at the same address.

Chardon Press

P.O. Box 11607
Berkeley, CA 94702   **Phone:**   (510) 704-8714   **E-Mail:** Chardn@aol.com
USA   **Fax:**   (510) 649-7913

Contact Person: Kim Klein, Owner. **Officers or Principals:** Stephanie Roth, Owner.
Mission or Interest: Publishes the *Grassroots Fundraising Journal*. "Writing publishing and distributing information about fundraising for small nonprofits dedicated to social justice."
Accomplishments: Have sold over 12,000 copies of their book, Fundraising for Social Change, now in its 3rd edition.
Tax Status: For profit. **Annual Report:** No. **Employees:** 3
Periodicals: *Grassroots Fundraising Journal* (bimonthly journal).
Other Information: Founded in 1982.

Charles Stewart Mott Foundation

1200 Mott Foundation Bldg.
Flint, MI 48502-1851   **Phone:**   (810) 238-5651
USA   **Fax:**   (810) 766-1753

Contact Person: Judy Y. Samelson, Vice President, Communications.
Officers or Principals: William Samuel White, President/Chairman; Richard Kent Rappleye, Vice President/Secretary/Treasurer; Jim L. Krause, Assistant Treasurer; Maureen H. Smyth, Vice President, Programs; Robert E. Swaney, Jr., Chief Investment Officer.
Mission or Interest: Grant-making philanthropy that concentrates on community organizing.
Accomplishments: In 1993 the Foundation awarded $49,031,475 in grants. Grant recipients included; $1,022,500 for the Center for Community Change, $300,000 for Independent Sector, $270,000 for the National Training and Information Center, $242,000 for Accion International, $228,603 for the National Council of La Raza, $200,000 each for the Low-Income Housing Information Service, and Friends of the Earth, $180,000 for the Natural Resource Defense Council, $175,000 each for the Center on Budget and Policy Priorities, and the Women's Self Employment Project, $150,000 for the Seventh Generation Fund, $125,000 for the Nature Conservancy, $120,000 for the Union Institute, $100,891 for the Earth Action Network, and $100,000 for the Citizen's Clearinghouse for Hazardous Wastes.

Net Assets: 1993 $49,031,475
Products or Services: People of Color Environmental Groups: 1994-95 Directory.
Tax Status: 501(c)(3)
Board of Directors or Trustees: Webb Franklin Martin, Charles Harding Mott II, Ruth Rawlings Mott, Douglas Xavier Patino, William Piper, Willa Player, John Wilson Porter, Judy Samelson, Maureen Smyth, Robert Swaney Jr., George Whyel.
Periodicals: *Mott Exchange* (quarterly newsletter).

Chicago Animal Rights Coalition

6 Willow Springs
Plano, IL 60545   **Phone:**   (708) 552-7872
USA

Contact Person: Steven O. Hindi, President.
Officers or Principals: Steven O. Hindi, President ($0); Terri L. Campbell, Secretary/Treasury ($0).
Mission or Interest: "To reduce and eliminate the exploitation, abuse and killing of animals. To educate the public to alternatives to the use of animals, to heighten public awareness of the use and abuse of animals."
Accomplishments: In 1994 the Coalition spent $4,078 on its programs.
Net Revenue: 1994 $9,641 **Net Expenses:** $4,512 90%/10%/0% **Net Assets:** $5,129
Tax Status: 501(c)(3)
Board of Directors or Trustees: Gregory Campbell.
Other Information: The Coalition received $9,506, or 99% of revenue, from gifts and grants awarded by foundations and individuals. The remaining revenue came from the sale of inventory.

Chicago Coalition for the Homeless

1325 S. Wabash, Suite 205
Chicago, IL 60605   **Phone:**   (312) 435-4548
USA

Contact Person: John A. Donahue, Executive Director.   **Officers or Principals:** John A. Donahue, Executive Director ($55,000); Ellyn S. Harris, Director of Development ($45,750); Les Brown, Program Coordinator ($41,100); Alexander Sharp, President; Bernard Lacour, Vice President; Sharon Schaff, Secretary; Oliver Prince, Jr., Treasurer.
Mission or Interest: "Organized to research, create and implement programs to reverse the decline in low-income housing and to address the problem of homelessness in Chicago...increase awareness about the problem of homelessness."
Accomplishments: In the fiscal year ending June 1995 the Coalition spent $489,179 on its programs.
Net Revenue: FY ending 6/95 $776,765 **Net Expenses:** $830,404 59%/13%/28% **Net Assets:** $140,458 **Citations:** 52:138
Tax Status: 501(c)(3)
Board of Directors or Trustees: Michelle Saddler, Julie Biehl.
Other Information: The Coalition received $701,040, or 90% of revenue, from gifts and grants awarded by foundations, businesses, and individuals. (These grants included $10,000 from the Wieboldt Foundation, and $4,000 from the New Prospect Foundation.) $20,786 net, or 3%, from special fund-raising events. $8,805, or 1%, from interest on savings and temporary cash investments. The remaining revenue came from membership dues and other miscellaneous sources.

Children's Alliance for Protection of the Environment

P.O. Box 307
Austin, TX 78767
USA

Contact Person: Patricia Scharr, Executive Director.
Officers or Principals: Patricia Scharr, Executive Director ($29,377); Ingrid Kavanagh, Director of Outreach ($15,448); Gary Hagood, Chairman ($0); Jane Capron, Secretary; Frederick Cruiser Roland, Treasurer.
Mission or Interest: "Enhanced environmental awareness and initiated action on conservation, preservation and restoration activities for young people worldwide."
Accomplishments: In 1994 the Alliance spent $78,721 on its programs.
Net Revenue: 1994 $95,505 **Net Expenses:** $100,964 **Net Assets:** $13,510
Tax Status: 501(c)(3)
Board of Directors or Trustees: Erica Chan, Kathy Hooper, Mark Hooper, Janis Terry, Mike Terry.
Other Information: The Alliance received $92,902, or 97% of revenue, from gifts and grants awarded by foundations, businesses, and individuals. $1,152, or 1%, from program service revenues. The remaining revenues came from royalties and other miscellaneous sources.

Children's Defense Fund (CDF)

25 E St., N.W.
Washington, DC 20001   **Phone:** (202) 662-3622
USA   **Fax:**   (202) 662-3550

Contact Person: Marian Wright Edelman, President.

Officers or Principals: Marian Wright Edelman, President ($93,600); James D. Weill, General Counsel ($80,177); Clifford M. Johnson, Director of Programming and Policy ($77,875); David Hornbeck, Chair; Reynald Latortue, Treasurer; Sarah Jones, Development Director; Marylee C. Allen, Development Director; Paul Smith, Director of Child Welfare.

Mission or Interest: Research and development of policy intended to benefit the health and well-being of children. Encourages government funded programs to deal with "health care, family income support, adolescent pregnancy prevention, child care, etc."

Accomplishments: CDF's past chairs have included First Lady Hillary Rodham Clinton and Health and Human Services Secretary Donna Shalala. The Fund organized the June 1996 "Stand for Children" march on Washington, DC that attracted 200,000 participants. In 1994 the Fund spent $11,732,262 on its programs. The largest program, with expenditures of $3,387,101, was the administration of government and community affairs, "monitoring of federal and state programs for children, providing technical assistance to local child advocates and service providers." $3,273,195 was spent to develop public policy and programs, including the collection of data on the status of children. $2,701,508 was spent on the "Black Community Crusade for Children" to "connect and galvanize black leadership around specific goals of children and to identify, train, and empower an new generation of black servant-leaders on behalf of children." $2,370,458 was spent on public education and publications.

Net Revenue: 1994 $16,435,439 **Net Expenses:** $14,448,745 81%/12%/7% **Net Assets:** $14,052,372 **Citations:** 25:165

Products or Services: Annual Health of America's Children, public policy research, publications, data collection, and lobbying. The Fund spent $386,205 on lobbying, $97,356 on grassroots lobbying and $288,849 on the direct lobbying of legislators. This was an increase of 73% over the previous year, and an increase of 309% over 1992.

Tax Status: 501(c)(3)

Board of Directors or Trustees: Nancy Abraham (Senior Vice Pres., Investments, Shearson Lehman Bros.); Maureen Cogan (*Art & Auction Magazine*), Leonard Coleman Jr. (Pres., National Baseball League), John Deradourff, Thomas Draper, Winifred Green (Pres., Southern Coalition for Educational Equality), Henry Hampton, Dorothy Height (Pres., National Council of Negro Women), James Joseph (Pres., Council on Foundations), Marylin Levitt DSW (New York Univ. Medical Center), Eileen Norton (Forum on Children's Issues), Dennis Rivera, Susan Thomases, Thomas Troyer, Bailus Walker Jr., Ph.D., M.P.H. (Dean of Public Health, Univ. of Oklahoma), Suzanne Weil, Abigail Wexner.

Periodicals: *CDF Reports* (monthly newsletter).

Other Information: CDF's President, Marion Wright Edelman, has received over 100 honorary degrees and the Albert Schweitzer Humanitarian Prize. Recently the Fund closed local offices in Mississippi, Texas, and the District of Columbia. According to a May 28, 1996 *Wall Street Journal* article, "CDF has been losing credibility. Its once-vaunted policy research is less respected, say congressional and administrative staffers...The Republican takeover of Congress in 1994 didn't help the CDF's influence, of course, but the decline began earlier." Edelman describes these events as "a turning point" and that "this is just the beginning of the next phase of the movement." The article noted that the Fund's "unrivaled access to corporate dollars" has not changed. The Fund received $15,088,261, or 92% of revenue, from direct and indirect public support in the form of gifts and grants awarded by foundations, businesses, affiliates, and individuals. (These grants included $1,000,000 from the Florence and John Schumann Foundation, $166,000 from the Joyce Foundation, $101,814 from the Henry J. Kaiser Family Foundation, $25,000 from the Ruth Mott Fund, $10,000 from the Center on Budget and Policy Priorities, $3,000 from the Crestar Foundation, $2,600 from the New Prospect Foundation and $1,000 from the Compton Foundation. In 1993, $700,000 over three years from the Carnegie Corporation, and in 1995, $1,000,000 from the Rockefeller Foundation.) $823,887, or 5%, from the sale of publications and products. $398,264, or 2%, from a national conference. $131,424, or 1%, from honoraria. The remaining revenue came from interest on savings and temporary cash investments, and other miscellaneous sources. The Fund lost $117,039 on special fund-raising events, and $25,952 from the sale of securities.

Chinese for Affirmative Action

17 Walter U. Lim Place
San Francisco, CA 94108   **Phone:**   (415) 274-6765
USA

Contact Person: Henry Derr, Executive Director.   **Officers or Principals:** Henry Derr, Executive Director ($43,864).

Mission or Interest: Promotes rights for Asian and Chinese-Americans. Supports affirmative action, bi-lingual services, access to taxpayer funded programs.

Accomplishments: In the fiscal year ending July, 1994, they spent $188,225 to promote their civil rights services. They spent $115,612 on their Employment Fund that facilitates employment opportunities for low-income, limited English speaking immigrants and other minorities. $72,907 was spent on the Office of Community Development that assists Chinese-Americans in entering the construction industry. Filed an amicus brief supporting the Clinton Administration's Solicitor General's argument that in the case of U.S. v. The Commonwealth of Virginia, (concerning the admission of females to the Virginia Military Institute), the Supreme Court should apply "strict scrutiny" to the question of whether gender discrimination has occurred. "Strict scrutiny," rather that "intermediate scrutiny," is usually applied to race discrimination cases, and has never been applied before to gender discrimination cases.

Net Revenue: FY ending 7/94 $444,948 ($81,350, or 18%, from government grants) **Net Expenses:** $448,900 84%/16%/0%

Net Assets: $1,022,024

Products or Services: Litigation, educational services, and job development services.

Tax Status: 501(c)(3)

Other Information: The organization received $156,278, or 35% of revenue, from grants awarded by foundations, affiliates, and individuals. $138,474 net, or 31%, came from fund-raising special events. $81,350, or 18%, came from government grants. $26,489, or 6%, came from membership dues. $15,033, or 3%, came from interest on savings and temporary cash investments. The remaining revenue came from dividends and interest from securities, rents, and net profits on the sale of inventory.

Chinese Progressive Association
123 Waverly Place
San Francisco, CA 94108   **Phone:**   (415) 391-6986
USA

Contact Person: Gordon Mar, Director.
Officers or Principals: Gordon Mar, Director ($21,915); Angela Chu, Linda Li, Co-Chairs ($0); Chris Oei, Treasurer ($0).
Mission or Interest: Promotes and provides services for Chinese-Americans.
Accomplishments: In 1994 the Association spent a total of $42,857 on its programs. The largest program, costing $36,945, was the Chinatown Environmental Action Project. This project educated 3,000 low-income immigrants about environmental issues. In 1994 they organized two rallies, set up street-corner information tables, and hosted a community forum opposing California's Proposition 187. Proposition 187 would deny public social services to illegal immigrants - it passed by about a two-to-one margin.
Net Revenue: 1994 $72,610   ($4,237, or 6%, came from government grants) **Net Expenses:** $55,458   77%/19%/3%
Net Assets: $17,265
Products or Services: Environmental education, youth activities, leadership training, citizenship and language programs for immigrants, and lobbying.
Tax Status: 501(c)(3)
Other Information: The Association received $54,240, or 75% of revenue, from grants awarded by foundations, businesses and individuals. (These grants included $408 from Progressive Way.) Program services brought in $8,056, or 11%. $4,237, or 6%, came from government grants. $2,645, or 4%, from membership dues. $2,250 net, or 3%, came from rental income. $1,161, or 2%, came from fund-raising events.

Chinook Fund
2412 W. 32nd Ave.
Denver, CO 80211   **Phone:**   (303) 455-6905   **E-Mail:** chinookfun@aol.com
USA   **Fax:**   (303) 477-1617

Contact Person: Mike Roque, Executive Director.   **Officers or Principals:** Mike Roque, Executive Director ($26,074); Patrick Jackson, President ($0); Virginia Martinez, Vice President ($0); Lucy Loomis, Secretary; Robin Stephens, Treasurer.
Mission or Interest: Grant-making foundation supporting community-based activist organizations.
Accomplishments: In the fiscal year ending June 1994, the Fund spent $141,410 on its programs, and $106,735 was awarded in grants. The recipients of the largest grants included: Four grants totaling $8,080 for the Rocky Mountain Peace Center, two grants totaling $9,000 for Ground Zero, and $5,000 each for the Center for Third World Organizing and the Northeast Denver Housing Center.
Net Revenue: FY ending 6/94 $215,914 **Net Expenses:** $186,932   76%/14%/11% **Net Assets:** $122,135
Tax Status: 501(c)(3)
Board of Directors or Trustees: Brad Armstrong, Anne Byrne, Steff Clothier, Wendy Emrich, John Hickenlooder, Kat Morgan, Douglas Remington, Brian Underhill, Roslyn Washington.
Other Information: The Chinook Fund is a member of the Funding Exchange. The Fund received $212,125, or 98% of revenue, from direct and indirect public support in the form of gifts and grants awarded by foundations, affiliates, businesses, and individuals. (These grants included $3,000 from the Vanguard Public Foundation, $1,000 from the Compton Foundation.) $3,078, or 2%, from interest on savings and temporary cash investments. The remaining revenue came from returned grants and other miscellaneous sources.

CHOICE
1233 Locust St., 3rd Floor
Philadelphia, PA 19107   **Phone:**   (215) 985-3355
USA   **Fax:**   (215) 985-3369

Contact Person: Lisa Shulock, Executive Director.
Officers or Principals: Lisa Shulock, Executive Director ($50,645); Marilyn Lucas, President ($0).
Mission or Interest: Provides family planning, AIDS referral services, and social services such as prenatal care and child care for low income women. "To provide information and referrals on human sexuality, sexually transmitted diseases and other reproductive health issues to low income families."
Accomplishments: In the fiscal year ending June 1994, CHOICE spent $1,046,147 on its programs. The largest program, with expenditures of $352,966, was maternal and child care. $283,651 was spent on child care and referral services. $201,382 was spent on AIDS information referrals. $161,478 on family planning services.
Net Revenue: FY ending 6/94 $1,109,310   ($935,184, or 84%, from government grants)
Net Expenses: $1,134,509   92%/8%/0% **Net Assets:** $71,709 **Citations:** 205:80
Tax Status: 501(c)(3)
Board of Directors or Trustees: Amy Brantz Bedrick, Jacquelynn Brinkley, Nancy Brodie, Shirley Coker, Denise Colliers, Julia Dutton Ph.D., Ron Francis, Jarma Frisby, Oscar Garcia-Vera, Gail Dinter-Gottlieb Ph.D., Gail Hawkins, Janis Holloway, Brenda Hudson, Margaret Myers, Kathy Nicholson, Sandra Pollard, Sara Robins, Maris Savard M.D., Linda Schleifer, Stella Tsai, Jean Young.
Other Information: CHOICE received $935,184, or 84% of revenue, from government grants. $144,209, or 13%, from direct and indirect public support in the form of gifts and grants awarded by foundations, businesses, affiliates, and individuals. (These grants included $63,000 from Women's Way, and $2,000 from the Bread and Roses Community Fund.) $16,961, or 2%, from day care service fees. $8,175 net, or 1%, from special fund-raising events. The remaining revenue came from other miscellaneous sources.

Christic Institute

P.O. Box 845
Malibu, CA 90265
USA

Contact Person: Daniel Sheehan, President.   **Officers or Principals:** Daniel Sheehan, President ($27,000); Sara Nelson, Vice President ($27,000); William Davis, Secretary/Treasurer ($25,000); Margaret Johnson.
Mission or Interest: An organization using investigative procedures and legal action to call public attention to covert action, perceived cover-ups, and illegalities.
Accomplishments: The Christic Institute brought suit against a nuclear power plant on behalf of Karen Silkwood's estate for her wrongful death after, they believe, she discovered negligence at the plant. The case was won by the Christic Institute, who was represented by lawyer Gary Spence, however the jury's verdict was overturned by the presiding judge. The judge's verdict was appealed, and the plant settled out of court, assuming that it would be cheaper than a prolonged legal battle. In 1986 the Institute filed a Federal Racketeering Act Civil Suit and Common Law Assault complaint against 29 individuals. The basis was a bomb that exploded at a press conference called by a dissident Nicaraguan Contra leader, Eden Pastora, in La Penca, Nicaragua. The explosion injured two American journalists, Tony Avirgan and Martha Honey, on whose behalf the suit was brought. The suit charged American expatriate John Hull and "Mr Hull's Central American 'Contra' associates and North and South American weapons and cocaine suppliers in an illegal 'off-the-shelf' weapons and cocaine supply operation indirectly coordinated by Lt. Colonel Oliver North of the American National Security Council." The Miami Federal District Court Judge, James Lawrence King, ruled against the Institute and ordered them to pay $1,218,000 to the defendants for filing a frivolous lawsuit "they were never going to be able to prove." The Institute appealed, and was again ruled against and fined. The Institute sold its National Offices in Washington, DC, and mortgaged the Washington residence of its staff to pay the fines. The Institute maintains that the final report of Iran/Contra Special Prosecutor Lawrence Walsh concurred with their opinion that Lt. Colonel Oliver North et al supplied John Hull and the Contras with C-4 explosives like those used in the bombing. They also maintain that the government of Costa Rica has charged Hull and his associates for the bombing. Fenton Communications was used by the Institute for publicity. In 1993 the Institute spent $367,966 on its programs. The largest program, with expenditures of $278,430, was litigation. Other programs included public education, grassroots organizing and public outreach, handling requests from the media, and conducting investigations.
Net Revenue: 1993 $435,711 **Net Expenses:** $484,194 76%/23%/1% **Net Assets:** $34,874
Tax Status: 501(c)(3)
Other Information: The Institute received $335,845 net, or 77% of revenue, from the sale of the National Office. $98,985, or 23%, from gifts and grants awarded by foundations, businesses, and individuals. The remaining revenue came from the sale of inventory, and interest on savings and temporary cash investments.

Church Women United (CWU)

110 Maryland Ave., N.E.
Washington, DC 20002   **Phone:**   (202) 544-8747   **E-Mail:** CWU_WASHINGTON.PARTI@ECUNET.ORG
USA   **Fax:**   (202) 543-1297

Contact Person: Nancy Chupp, Director.   **Officers or Principals:** Ann Baker Garvin, President; Van Lynch, First Vice President; Shirley Nilsson, Second Vice President; Rhoda Ikiko Iyoya, Secretary/Treasurer.
Mission or Interest: "To help clarify the moral issues at stake in public policy and to express those concerns to the appropriate person in government in a responsible and timely way. We equip women of faith to become informed public policy advocates in our priority areas: health care and economic justice for women and children in poverty. In addition, we advocate directly on these issues to the U.S. Congress and the Administration. To accomplish our goals we publish bimonthly legislative updates; activate phone calls and letter-writing campaigns on timely legislative proposals; and participate in issue briefings on Capitol Hill."
Products or Services: 'Women and Children First: A Faith-Based Perspective on Welfare Reform," video and study guide. Lobbying.
Tax Status: 501(c)(3) **Annual Report:** Yes. **Employees:** 2
Periodicals: *Church Women ACT* (bimonthly legislative update), *INFORM* (bimonthly legislative update), *Churchwoman Magazine* (quarterly magazine).
Other Information: CWU also has a New York office. "We are supported by the African Methodist Episcopal Church, African Methodist Episcopal Zion Church, American Baptist Churches USA, Disciples of Christ, Christian Methodist Episcopal Church, Church of God, Church of the Brethren, Church of the New Jerusalem, Council of Hispanic American Ministries, Episcopal Church, Evangelical Lutheran Church in America, Greek Orthodox Church of North and South America, International Council of Community Churches, Korean American Church Women United, Mennonite Church, Moravian Church in North and South America, National Baptist Convention USA, Presbyterian Church USA, Progressive National Baptist Convention, Reformed Church in America, Religious Society of Friends, Reorganized Church of Jesus Christ of Latter Day Saints, United Church of Christ, United Methodist Church."

CIABASE

P.O. Box 5022
Herndon, VA 22070   **Phone:**   (703) 437-8487   **E-Mail:** rmcgehee@igc.apc.org
USA   **Fax:**   same

Contact Person: Ralph McGehee.

Mission or Interest: "To provide a research resource for serious scholars and journalists, regardless of their political leanings on the CIA."
Accomplishments: Reviews of the database include: "An outstanding job," - Seymour Hersh. "A tremendously useful tool for any reporter or researcher." - *The Nation*. "A powerful tool that includes obscure sources and a comprehensive cross-index." - *The Progressive*. "CIABASE is owned by most major media organizations, by top-ranking academic institutions, professors and activists."
Products or Services. Computer database that currently consists of over 32,000 annotated entries in over 9MBs of information.
Tax Status: For profit. **Employees:** 1
Other Information: Ralph McGehee served 25 years in the CIA, 14 years overseas as an operations officer and 11 years at its headquarters. Upon leaving the CIA he wrote the book Deadly Deceits and began to compile CIABASE.

Cineaste
200 Park Ave., S., Suite 1601
New York, NY 10003   **Phone:** (212) 982-1241
USA   **Fax:** same

Contact Person: Gary Crowdus, Editor-in-Chief.
Officers or Principals: Dan Georgakas, Roy Grundmann, Cynthia Lucia, Richard Porton, Leonard Quart, Editors.
Mission or Interest: Quarterly magazine on the art and politics of the cinema.
Accomplishments: Featured interviews with numerous top movie directors, actors, and producers. *Film Quarterly* says of *Cineaste*, "it is the balance between the psychological and the political on the levels of both life and art that keeps *Cineaste* interviews on the cutting edge of film criticism."
Tax Status: 501(c)(3) **Annual Report:** No. **Employees:** All volunteer.
Board of Directors or Trustees: Associates include: Prof. Tom Doherty (Brandeis Univ.), Pat Dowell (film critic, NPR), John Fried, Guy Hennebelle (editor, *CinemAction*), Prof. Andrew Horton (Loyola Univ.), Wendy Lidell (Dir., Intl. Film Circuit), Prof. Louis Menashe (Polytechnic Univ.), Prof. Brian Neve (Univ. of Bath), Gerald Peary (film critic, *The Improper Bostonian*), Jesse Rhines, Miriam Rosen, Prof. Robert Sklar (NY Univ.), Prof. Dennis West (Univ. of ID).
Periodicals: *Cineaste* (quarterly).

Cinema Guild
1697 Broadway, Suite 506
New York, NY 10019   **Phone:** (212) 246-5522   **E-Mail:** thecinemag@aol.com
USA   **Fax:** (212) 246-5525

Contact Person: Gary Crowdus.
Officers or Principals: Philip Hobel, Mary-Ann Hobel, Co-Chairs; Gary Crowdus, General Manager.
Mission or Interest: Film, video and multimedia distribution. Many of the films and videos feature political content, including histories of protest movements, labor organizing, gay rights activism, and the persecution of minorities in the United States.
Accomplishments: Many award winning films available.
Products or Services: Catalog.
Tax Status: For profit. **Annual Report:** No. **Employees:** 5   **Internships:** Yes.

Citizen Action
1730 Rhode Island, N.W., Suite 403
Washington, DC 20036   **Phone:** (202) 775-1580
USA   **Fax:** (202) 296-4054

Officers or Principals: Cathy Hurwitt, Legislative Director.
Mission or Interest: Consumer and environmental organization.
Accomplishments: Three million members nationwide. Published research on the connections between campaign contributions and public policy. Opposed reforming Medicare with a voucher-based system.
Tax Status: 501(c)(4)
Other Information: Affiliated with the 501(c)(3) Citizens Fund.

Citizen Alert
P.O. Box 1681
Las Vegas, NV 89125   **Phone:** (702) 796-5662   **E-Mail:** niel@nevada.edu
USA   **Fax:** (702) 796-4886

Contact Person: Richard Nielson, Executive Director.
Officers or Principals: Chris Brown, Executive Director ($26,367); Tracie Lindeman, Executive Director ($6,200); Bob Fulkerson, Executive Director ($3,091); JoAnne Garrett, President; Helen Jones, Secretary; Keith Tierney, Secretary.
Mission or Interest: Builds alliances among ranchers, miners, Native Americans, peace activists, and environmentalists to address important national nuclear, military and environmental concerns.

Accomplishments: In 1994 Citizen Alert spent $218,320 on its programs. Although Citizen Alert did not lobby in 1994, it has in the past. $4,156 was spent on lobbying in 1992.

Net Revenue: 1994 $263,604 Net Expenses: $272,489   80%/20%/0%   Net Assets: $1,297

Tax Status: 501(c)(3) **Annual Report:** Yes. **Employees:** 4
Board of Directors or Trustees: Bill Rosse, Steve Alastuey, Raven.
Periodicals: *Citizen Alert Newsletter.*
Internships: Yes.
Other Information: Founded in 1975. Citizen Alert received $249,315, or 93% of total revenue, from direct and indirect public support in the form of gifts and grants awarded by affiliates, foundations, businesses, and individuals. (These grants included $25,000 from the Jessie Smith Noyes Foundation, $17,600 from the Peace Development Fund, $10,000 from the Beldon Fund, and $600 from the Vanguard Public Foundation.) $19,605, or 7%, from membership dues. The remaining revenue came from interest on savings and temporary cash investments. The organization lost $3,247 on special fund-raising events.

Citizens Clearinghouse for Hazardous Waste (CCHW)

119 Rowell Ct.
Falls Church, VA 22040   **Phone:**   (703) 237-2249   **E-Mail:** cchw@essential.org
USA   **Fax:**   (703) 237-8389

Contact Person: Barbara Sullivan. **Officers or Principals:** Lois Marie Gibbs, President ($43,200); Stephen Lester, Treasurer ($41,040); Holly Gibson, Secretary ($0); Dr. Kenneth Miller, Vice President.
Mission or Interest: Environmental organization dedicated to educating the public about the dangers of toxins in our everyday surroundings.
Accomplishments: CCHW was founded in 1981 by Lois Gibbs, leader of the campaign at Love Canal. CCHW "is the only national environmental organization started and led by grassroots organizers." CCHW has worked with over 8,000 community based groups nationwide. "The federal Superfund program, established in 1980 to clean up waste cites, was a direct outgrowth of CCHW President Lois Gibbs' work with her neighbors at Love Canal." CCHW was at the front of the 'environmental justice' movement, "exposing the Cerrell report and other studies that document the deliberate siting of unsafe facilities in communities in which most residents are people of color, low-income, rural, Catholic, elderly, and/or without college education." In 1994 the Clearinghouse spent $562,539 on its programs. The main focus of their efforts was on educational programs warning of the hazards of dioxins and hazardous wastes. CCHW awarded $94,140 in grants to local environmental organizations. Top recipients of these grants included; $5,000 for Dine Citizens Against Ruining the Environment, $4,665 for the East River Community Development Association, $3,000 each for the Gateway Green Corporate Committee, Tonatierra Community Development, and the Pennsylvania Environmental Network.
Net Revenue: 1994 $687,767 **Net Expenses:** $687,767 82%/9%/10% **Net Assets:** $119,278 **Citations:** 27:162
Products or Services: Publications, community organizing, educational events, grants, Dying from Dioxin (1995, South End Press) book, more.
Tax Status: 501(c)(3) **Annual Report:** Yes. **Employees:** 10
Board of Directors or Trustees: Dr. Murray Levine (SUNY), Hon. Clyde Foster (former mayor, Triana, AL), Vilma Hunt (EPA Health Assessment Group), Luella Kenny (Love Canal Homeowners Assoc.), Pame Kingfisher (Native Americans for a Clean Environment), Dr. Ken Miller (AFL-CIO), Dr. Beverly Paigen (Jackson Laboratories), Suzi Ruhl (Legal Environmental Assistance Found.), Alonso Spencer (Save Our County).
Periodicals: *Everyone's Backyard* (quarterly magazine), *Environmental Health Monthly* (monthly journal).
Internships: Yes.
Other Information: CCHW received $590,777, or 86% of revenue, from gifts and grants awarded by foundations, corporations ("CCHW does not accept money from the government or corporations that pollute"), and individuals. (These grants included $30,000 from the Jessie Smith Noyes Foundation, $25,000 from the Bauman Family Foundation, $10,061 from the Environmental Federation of America, $6,250 from the New World Foundation, $547 from the Environmental Federation of California, and $500 from the Aaron and Martha Schecter Private Foundation. In 1993, $100,000 from the Charles Stewart Mott Foundation.) $43,868, or 6%, from membership dues. $18,197, or 3%, from the sale of publications. $13,036, or 2%, from travel reimbursements from local groups CCHW helps with organizational or technical assistance. The remaining revenue came from interest on savings and temporary cash investments, training fees, and event registration fees.

Citizens for a Better Environment

407 S. Dearborn, Suite 1775
Chicago, IL 60605   **Phone:**   (312) 939-1530
USA

Contact Person: Marilyn Goris, Secretary. **Officers or Principals:** Marilyn Goris, Secretary ($33,000); Susan Mudd, Vice president ($23,244); Dorothy Lagerroos, Chairman ($0); Michael Finn, Vice Chair; P.W. Parker, Treasurer.
Mission or Interest: Research, complaint referrals, and other informational activities related to toxins.
Accomplishments: In 1994 the organization spent $1,152,033 on its activities.
Net Revenue: 1994 $1,636,761 **Net Expenses:** $1,680,992 69%/7%/25% **Net Assets:** (-$88,646) **Citations:** 66:128
Tax Status: 501(c)(3)
Board of Directors or Trustees: Sally Benjamin, Elizabeth Black, Thomas Crawford, Michael Finn, Bill Taylor, Richard Tworek.
Other Information: Citizens for a Better Environment received $1,636,761, or 98% of revenue, from gifts and grants awarded by foundations, businesses, and individuals. (These grants included $233,941 from the Joyce Foundation and $10,000 from the Wallace Alexander Gerbode Foundation, $5,000 from the Wieboldt Foundation.) $18,004, or 1%, from legal fees recovered from law suits. The remaining revenue came from interest on savings and temporary cash investments, and other miscellaneous sources.

Citizens for Environmental Justice

P.O. Box 1841
Savannah, GA 31401   **Phone:**   (912) 233-0907
USA

Contact Person: Mildred McClain, Project Coordinator.
Mission or Interest: To increase the participation of blacks in the environmental and anti-nuclear power movement in Georgia and South Carolina. Concerned with the future of the Savannah River nuclear weapons facility.
Tax Status: 501(c)(3)
Other Information: Founded in 1991. In 1994 the organization received $15,000 from the Ploughshares Fund, $15,000 from the Jessie Smith Noyes Foundation, $5,000 from the Peace Development Fund.

Citizens for Tax Justice

1313 L St., N.W.
Washington, DC 20005   **Phone:**   (202) 626-3780
USA

Contact Person: Ira Arlook, President. **Officers or Principals:** Gerald W. McEntee, Vice President ($0); Lawrence Smedley, Secretary ($0); John J. Sweeney, Treasurer ($0).
Mission or Interest: Public policy organization that advocates and lobbies for steeply 'progressive' taxes (higher tax rates on higher incomes).
Accomplishments: In 1994 the organization spent $330,113 on its programs.
Net Revenue: 1994 $318,389 **Net Expenses:** $330,113 100%/0%/0% **Net Assets:** $36,468
Tax Status: 501(c)(4)
Other Information: Citizens for Tax Justice has strong ties with organized labor. Vice president Gerald McEnlee is the president of AFSCME, and treasurer John Sweeney is president of the AFL-CIO. The organization received $316,177, or 99% of revenue, from gifts and grants awarded by foundations, businesses, and individuals. $2,212, or 1%, from the sale of publications.

Citizens for Truth About the Kennedy Assassination

(see Coalition on Political Assassinations)

Citizens Fund

1730 Rhode Island, N.W., Suite 403
Washington, DC 20036   **Phone:**   (202) 775-1580
USA   **Fax:**   (202) 296-4054

Tax Status: 501(c)(3)
Other Information: Affiliated with Citizen Action. In 1993 the Fund received $20,000 from the Barbra Streisand Foundation. In 1994 it received $78,500 from the Tides Foundation, $35,000 from the Joyce Foundation, $25,000 from the Joyce Mertz-Gilmore Foundation, $15,000 from the Ruth Mott Fund, $10,400 from Friends of the Earth, and $10,000 from the Beldon II Fund.

Citizens to End Animal Suffering and Exploitation (CEASE)

P.O. Box 44-456
Somerville, MA 02144   **Phone:**   (617) 628-9030
USA

Contact Person: Karen Bunting, President.
Officers or Principals: Lauretta Woods, Director ($20,100); Diana Cartier, Secretary/Treasurer ($0).
Mission or Interest: "Protection of wildlife and domestic animals from hunting and trapping" through protests and pickets, lawsuits, and education. Also opposed to vivisection, the treatment of circus animals, and pet over-population.
Accomplishments: In the fiscal year ending September 1994 CEASE spent $48,169 on its programs.
Net Revenue: FY ending 9/94 $62,780 **Net Expenses:** $104,614 46%/23%/31% **Net Assets:** $4,221
Products or Services: Leaflets, publications, video tapes, advertising, litigation, and lobbying. CEASE spent $3,967 on lobbying, $2,795 on grassroots lobbying and $1,172 on the direct lobbying of lawmakers, a 112% increase over the previous year.
Tax Status: 501(c)(3)
Other Information: CEASE received $34,036, or 54% of revenue, from gifts and grants awarded by foundations, businesses, and individuals. $27,357, or 44%, from membership dues. The remaining revenue came from interest on savings and temporary cash investments, sale of inventory, and other miscellaneous sources.

City Limits Community Information Service / *City Limits*

40 Prince St.
New York, NY 10012   **Phone:**   (212) 925-9820
USA   **Fax:**   (212) 966-3407

Contact Person: Andrew White, Editor.
Officers or Principals: Andrew White, Editor ($29,167); Andrew Reicher, Chairman ($0); Beverly Chevvront, Secretary ($0).

Mission or Interest: Publishes *City Limits*, a magazine of urban community development and activism. Focuses on housing, health care, child care, job creation, feminism, education, demographics, and community reinvestment.
Accomplishments: In the fiscal year ending June 1994 the Service spent $220,025 on publishing and distributing *City Limits*.
Net Revenue: FY ending 6/94 $170,080 **Net Expenses:** $221,225 99%/1%/0% **Net Assets:** $66,667
Tax Status: 501(c)(3)
Periodicals: *City Limits* (ten times a year magazine).
Other Information: The Service received $96,475, or 57%, from gifts and grants awarded by foundations, businesses, and individuals. (These grants include $15,000 from the Joyce Mertz-Gilmore Foundation, $10,000 from the Robert Sterling Clark Foundation, and $4,500 from the North Star Fund.) $37,049, or 22%, from subscriptions. $31,140, or 18%, from advertising. $3,938, or 2%, from miscellaneous sales. $1,478, or 1%, from interest on savings and temporary cash investments. The magazine cost $220,025 to produce and brought in $72,127 in revenue, requiring subsidization of $147,898.

Clean Water Action
1320 18th St., N.W.
Washington, DC 20036   **Phone:**   (202) 457-1286
USA

Contact Person: David Zwick, President.
Officers or Principals: Sue Sargent-Spitz, Secretary ($0); Michael Gravitz, Treasurer ($0).
Mission or Interest: Promotes public policies relating to clean water and the environment.
Accomplishments: In 1994 the Foundation spent $6,837,537 on its programs. $6,700,786 was spent on citizens education and community involvement, and $136,751 was spent on "lobby outreach to organizations and education relating to water and the environment."
Net Revenue: 1994 $9,886,381 **Net Expenses:** $9,875,267 69%/6%/25% **Net Assets:** $346,272 **Citations:** 204:81
Tax Status: 501(c)(4)
Board of Directors or Trustees: Sophi Ann Aoki Robertson (Friends of the Future), William Fontenot, David Grubb (West Virginia Citizen Action Group), Lewis Helm, Peter Lockwood, Robert Loring, Dr. James Marti, Patricia Schifferle, Terry Reuther, Paul Twerdowsky, David Tykulsker.
Other Information: Affiliated with the 501(c)(3) Clean Water Fund at the same address. Clean Water Action received $9,699,286, or 98% of revenue, from gifts and grants awarded by foundations, businesses, and individuals. (These grants included $8,000 from Friends of the Earth, $2,000 from the Haymarket People's Fund.) $135,991, or 1%, from membership dues. The remaining revenue came from the sale of assets, interest on savings and temporary cash investments, and other miscellaneous sources.

Clean Water Fund
1320 18th St., N.W.
Washington, DC 20036   **Phone:**   (202) 457-1286
USA

Contact Person: Jonathan Scott, Associate Development Director.
Officers or Principals: Barbara Schecter, Development Director ($60,309); Jonathan Scott, Associate Development Director ($34,741); Peter Lockwood, President ($0); David Zwick, Executive Vice President; Larry Wallace, Treasurer.
Mission or Interest: Protection and restoration of clean water. Works against pollution, both industrial and agricultural, that threatens water supplies and wetland habitats.
Accomplishments: In 1993 the Fund spent $1,140,477 on its programs. The largest program, with expenditures of $483,752, was targeted for land and water resources protection and conservation. $380,786 was spent on pollution prevention, including scientific and technical assistance for citizens groups. $154,239 for initiatives related to making the economy more environmentally friendly. $121,700 for research, training, outreach and education.
Net Revenue: 1993 $1,675,725 ($36,422, or 2%, from government grants) **Net Expenses:** $1,567,761 73%/13%/14% **Net Assets:** $191,493 **Citations:** 59:131
Tax Status: 501(c)(3)
Board of Directors or Trustees: Sophie Ann Aoki Robertson (Friends of the Future), David Borden (Victoria Intl.), Louise Dunlap, Peter Lockwood, Patricia Schifferle.
Other Information: Affiliated with the 501(c)(4) Clean Water Action at the same address. The Fund received $1,632,424, or 97% of revenue, from direct and indirect public support in the form of gifts and grants awarded by foundations, businesses, affiliates, and individuals. (These grants included $76,062 from the Environmental Federation of America, $30,000 from the Beldon Fund, $25,000 from the Ruth Mott Fund, $20,000 from the Cary Charitable Trust, $15,000 from the Town Creek Foundation, and $1,550 from the Environmental Federation of California.) $36,422, or 2%, from government grants. The remaining revenue came from interest on savings and temporary cash investments, membership dues, and the sale of products.

Climate Institute
324 4th St., N.E.
Washington, DC 20002   **Phone:**   (202) 547-0104
USA

Contact Person: John C. Topping, Jr., President
Officers or Principals: Dr. Ata Qureshi, Director ($45,000); John C. Toppings, Jr., President ($42,187); Dan Power, Vice President ($18,462); Sir Crispin Tichell, Dr. Stephen Leatherman, Co-Chairmen; John P. Bond, Treasurer.

Mission or Interest: Activities linking researchers and policy makers, the public, and the press "intended to speed policy makers responses to global environmental issues."

Accomplishments: In 1993 the Institute spent $563,558 on its programs. These programs included: An Asia-Pacific Seminar on Climate Change. National workshops in India, Pakistan, Malaysia, Indonesia, Viet Nam, Sri Lanka, and the Philippines. Assembled an Advisory Committee to review and approve definitions and methodologies for addressing the issue of "Environmental Refugees." Assisted with the organizing of municipal symposiums in Portland, OR, and Chicago, IL. Convened a scientific briefing on climate change and ozone depletion for the city council and chamber of commerce of Chattanooga, TN.

Net Revenue: 1993 $692,192 ($25,000, or 4%, from government grants) **Net Expenses:** $682,820 83%/16%/2% **Net Assets:** $49,980 **Citations:** 15:182

Tax Status: 501(c)(3)

Board of Directors or Trustees: Dr. Noel Brown, Joseph Cannon, Dr. H. Nuzhet Dalfes, Lynne Edgerton, Dr. Tom Gale, Mark Goldberg, Quim Luis Manuel Guerra, Lee Huebner, Dr. Gordon MacDonald, Dr. Jim McCulloch, Dr. Shuzo Nishioko, Dr. Martin Parry, Paul Pritchard, Hon. Tom Roper, Dr. Hind Sadek, Hon. Claudine Schneider, Dr. Stephen Schneider, Pier Vellinga.

Periodicals: *Climate Alert* (newsletter).

Other Information: The Institute received $389,847, or 56% of revenue, from contract services. $276,661, or 40%, from gifts and grants awarded by foundations, businesses, and individuals. $25,000, or 4%, from government grants. The remaining revenue came from other miscellaneous sources.

Coalition for Basic Human Needs (CBHN)

54 Essex St.
Cambridge, MA 02139   **Phone:** (617) 497-0126
USA   **Fax:**   (617) 492-8101

Contact Person: Kevin Rudolph.   **Officers or Principals:** Della Marie Morrison, President; Mary Quinn, Director; Elisa Jeannette Huezo, Organizer; Karen Jeffreys, Statewide Campaign Coordinator.

Mission or Interest: A welfare rights organization focusing on Massachusetts. "We base our mission on a social welfare system for all citizens. Our Family Grant Proposal is to guarantee health care, income, day care and education for all Americans."

Accomplishments: "Numerous welfare grant increases; rent supplement for AFDC families; defeat of a proposal to create a mandatory, segregated, and inferior health care system for Boston's AFDC population; institution of $150 yearly clothing allowance for AFDC children." In 1995, on the occasion of CBHN's 17th anniversary, the organization received numerous accolades, including: "Northeastern Law School applauds CBHN for vigorous and visionary articulation of the rights of welfare mothers." "Here's to years of fighting media battering of poor families," (Media Research and Action Project). "We count on your voice, you can count on ours," (National Association of Social Workers, MA).

Products or Services: Fighting for Women's Voice awards.

Employees: 5

Board of Directors or Trustees: Donna Arlington, Patricia Bailey, Lori Cairns, Anna Engley, Thia Hadge, Marla Justice, Heidi Keezer, Aida Marcial, Dellamarie Rezendes, Karen Rock, Josefina Serrano, Sue Shurtleff, Gina Thompson, Vicki Woodard.

Periodicals: *Talkin' Basics* (monthly newsletter).

Internships: Yes, for sociology, social work, law, public administration, and political science majors.

Coalition for Clean Air

901 Wilshire Blvd., Suite 350
Santa Monica, CA 90401   **Phone:** (310) 260-4770
USA

Contact Person: Dennis Zane, Executive Director.   **Officers or Principals:** Dennis Zane, Executive Director ($45,000); Tom Soto, President ($0); Ralph Perry, Vice President ($0); Abby Arnold, Treasurer.

Mission or Interest: "Restoration of air quality through monitoring compliance with air pollution legislation; providing technical resources, and public education." Focus on California.

Accomplishments: In the fiscal year ending June 1994, the Coalition spent $171,985 on its programs.

Net Revenue: FY ending 6/94 $250,067 **Net Expenses:** $226,233 76%/11%/13% **Net Assets:** (-$2,830)

Tax Status: 501(c)(3)

Board of Directors or Trustees: Juliette Anthony (Clare Found.), Wil Baca, Ed Begley Jr. (actor), Howard Brody, Kelly Candaele, Tayni Chase (Center for Environmental Education), Jack Novack, Ward Elliot (Claremont McKenna College), Cliff Gladstein, Cindy Harrell-Horn, Anne Smith, Steve Sullivan, Linda Waade.

Other Information: The Coalition received $246,709, or 99% of revenue, from direct and indirect public support in the form of gifts and grants awarded by foundations, affiliates, and individuals. (These grants included $36,886 from the Environmental Federation of California.) $3,118, or 1%, from membership dues. The remaining revenue came from interest on savings and temporary cash investments.

Coalition for Environmentally Responsible Economies (CERES)

711 Atlantic Ave.
Boston, MA 02111   **Phone:** (617) 451-0927
USA

Contact Person: Joan Bavaria, Co-Chair

Mission or Interest: Coalition of national and regional environmental organizations, social investors, church and public pension funds, labor, and public interest groups.

Accomplishments: In 1989 CERES developed the "Valdez Principles," guidelines for corporate practices that promote "sustainable development."

Tax Status: 501(c)(3)

Other Information: In 1993 the Foundation received $10,000 from the Town Creek Foundation. In 1994 the Coalition received $23,000 from the Jessie Smith Noyes Foundation.

Coalition for Free and Open Elections
P.O. Box 20263, London Terrace Station
New York, NY 10011   **Phone:**   (212) 691-0776   **E-Mail:** ban@igc.apc.org
USA   **Fax:**   (415) 441-4268   **Web-Page:** Ann Rosenhaft, Chair

Officers or Principals: Improve the legal environment for third parties and independent political candidates.
Mission or Interest: "Coordinated lobbying in state legislatures from 1985 to the present which resulted in easier ballot access for new parties or independent candidates in Arizona, Colorado, Connecticut, Georgia, Hawaii, Idaho, Kansas, Kentucky, Missouri, Montana, Nevada, Oregon, Rhode Island, South Dakota, Texas, Utah, Virginia and Wyoming."
Other Information: West Coast office in San Francisco: P.O. Box 470296, San Francisco, CA 94147, (415) 922-9779, contact Richard Winger.

Coalition for Human Dignity
P.O. Box 40344
Portland, OR 97240   **Phone:**   (503) 281-5823
USA

Contact Person: Jonathan Mozzochi, Executive Director.   **Officers or Principals:** Jonathan Mozzochi, Executive Director ($15,604); Steve Gardiner, Secretary/Treasurer/Research Director ($12,482); Patricia McGuire, President ($0).
Mission or Interest: Research, analysis, and dissemination of information on the "tactics and threat of racist and anti-democratic groups, with the goal of devising effective opposition strategies."
Accomplishments: Conducted technical training for the American Jewish Committee, Communities Against Hate, Northwest Coalition Against Malicious Harassment, Northwest Labor Council, Planned Parenthood, and the Washington Education Association. Presented information at over 50 workshops, conferences, and public meetings. In 1994 the Coalition spent $60,000 on its programs.
Net Revenue: 1994 $95,525 **Net Expenses:** $85,366 **Net Assets:** $8,998
Products or Services: Several publications including, Northwest Imperative, Almost Heaven, Patriot Games, and others.
Tax Status: 501(c)(3)
Board of Directors or Trustees: Leslie Abbott, Stew Albert, Abby Layton, Jonny Mayoral, Cecil Prescod, Eric Ward, Steven Wasserstrom.
Periodicals: *Dignity Report.*
Other Information: The Coalition received $79,370, or 81% of gross revenue, from gifts and grants awarded by foundations, businesses, and individuals. (These grants include $10,000 from the C.S. Fund, $10,000 from the Abelard Foundation, and $7,500 from the Bydale Foundation.) $18,682, or 19%, from program services. The Coalition lost $2,527 on the sale of inventory.

Coalition for New Priorities
202 S. State St., Suite 1500
Chicago, IL 60604   **Phone:**   (312) 362-0500
USA

Contact Person: Bernice Bild, Executive Director.
Mission or Interest: Working to redirect the federal budget toward social spending.
Other Information: In 1994 the Coalition received $7,500 from the Wieboldt Foundation. In 1995, $1,000 from Resist.

Coalition for the Homeless
87 Chambers St.
New York, NY 10007   **Phone:**   (212) 964-5900
USA

Contact Person: Mary Brosnanan, Executive Director.
Officers or Principals: Mary Brosnanan, Executive Director ($63,000); Marylee Diamond, Administrative Director ($50,118); Alan Mucatel, Development Director ($44,250); Jack Doyle, Chairman; Ellen Baxter, Vice Chairman; Steven Coe, Treasurer; Allen Bromberger, Terry Andreas, Secretaries; Ann Nortz, State Policy Director; Lisa Daugaard, Legal Director.
Mission or Interest: Social services and public policy advocacy on behalf of the homeless.
Accomplishments: In the fiscal year ending June 1994 the Coalition spent $3,068,182 on its programs. The largest set of programs, with expenditures of $2,211,461, went for social services including housing, support for AIDS sufferers, summer camps for homeless children, job training and other emergency services. $476,732 was spent on a mobile food distribution program. $379,989 was spent on public policy advocacy including litigation, rally organizing, policy analysis, and "strategy to eradicate the systemic roots of homelessness."

Net Revenue: FY ending 6/94 $3,571,530 ($1,772,667, or 50%, from government grants) **Net Expenses:** $3,695,529 83%/9%/8% **Net Assets:** $2,460,535 **Citations:** 764:26 (this figure includes the citations for the D.C. Coalition for the Homeless.) **Tax Status:** 501(c)(3)
Other Information: The Coalition owns 100% of an investment in low-income housing, the Bridge Building Management Co. The Coalition received $1,772,667, or 50% of revenue, from government grants. $1,663,011, or 47%, from gifts and grants awarded by foundations, businesses, and individuals. $111,711, or 3%, from rental income. The remaining revenue came from interest on savings and other temporary cash investments, dividends and interest from securities, and other miscellaneous sources.

Coalition for the Homeless
1234 Massachusetts Ave., N.W., Suite C-1015
Washington, DC 20005   **Phone:**   (202) 347-8870
USA

Contact Person: Judith Dobbins, Executive Director.   **Officers or Principals:** Judith Dobbins, Executive Director ($72,278); Samuel Trevino, Director of Finance ($47,832); Lawrence M. Zippin, Chairman ($0); J. Rene Carter, Vice Chair; Matthew S. Galvez, Treasurer; Robert B. Pender, General Counsel; Alice Vetter, Secretary.
Mission or Interest: "To provide emergency shelter for the homeless and to address underlying problems that keep people homeless." Housing and social services for the homeless.
Accomplishments: In 1994 the Coalition spent $3,174,887 on its programs.
Net Revenue: 1994 $3,596,897 ($3,406,059, or 95%, from government grants) **Net Expenses:** $3,649,970 87%/12%/1%
Net Assets: $1,634,229 **Citations:** 764:26 (this figure includes the citations for the NYC Coalition for the Homeless.)
Tax Status: 501(c)(3)

Coalition of Black Trade Unionists
P.O. Box 66268
Washington, DC 20035-6268   **Phone:**   (202) 429-1203
USA

Contact Person: Wilburn Duncan, Executive Director.   **Officers or Principals:** Wilburn Duncan, Executive Director ($0); William Lucy, President ($0); Cleve Robinson, Executive Vice President ($0); Willie L. Baker, First Vice President; Connie Bryant, Second Vice President; Ernest Lofton, Secretary; William Simons, Treasurer.
Mission or Interest: Promoting the benefits of organized labor membership, with a focus on black workers. "Providing a voice in determining the terms and conditions of employment."
Accomplishments: Conferences and conventions.
Net Revenue: 1994 $229,628 **Net Expenses:** $252,307 **Net Assets:** $9,087
Tax Status: 501(c)(5)
Other Information: The Coalition received $179,814, or 78% of revenue, from conference registration fees. $28,196, or 12%, from membership dues. $15,000, or 7%, from a grant. $6,618, or 3%, from contributions received at the convention.

Coalition of California Welfare Rights Organizations
1901 Alhambra Blvd., 2nd Floor
Sacramento, CA 95816   **Phone:**   (916) 736-0616
USA   **Fax:**   (916) 736-2645

Contact Person: Elisa James, President.
Officers or Principals: Merkel Harris, Vice President ($0); Debra Roman, Secretary ($0); Cynthia Anderson, Treasurer ($0).
Mission or Interest: "To protect and promote the rights of low income families."
Accomplishments: In the fiscal year ending June 1994 the organization spent $111,980 on its programs.
Net Revenue: FY ending 6/94 $195,595 ($106,082, or 54%, from government grants) **Net Expenses:** $143,924 78%/22%/0%
Net Assets: $55,622   **Tax Status:** 501(c)(3)
Board of Directors or Trustees: Nancy Berlin, Linda Lemaster, Benny Sanchez, Joanne Sanchez, Victoria Yanez.
Other Information: The Coalition received $106,082, or 54% of revenue, from government grants. $89,265, or 46%, from reimbursed attorney's fees. The remaining revenue came from interest on savings and temporary cash investments, and other miscellaneous sources.

Coalition of Labor Union Women (CLUW)
1126 16th St., N.W.
Washington, DC 20036   **Phone:**   (202) 296-1200
USA

Contact Person: Gloria T. Johnson, President.   **Officers or Principals:** Chrystl Lindo-Bridgeforth ($36,000); Yvonne Cohen, Office Manager ($33,000); Samantha Burke, Administrative Assistant ($13,000); Winn Newman, General Counsel; Lela Foreman, Treasurer; Clara Day, Executive Vice President; Pat Scarcelli, Recording Secretary; Anna Padia, Corresponding Secretary.
Mission or Interest: Focuses on issues of concern to union women. Advocates abortion rights and national health care.

Accomplishments: In 1994 CLUW observed its 20th anniversary, held conferences, and conducted three meetings bringing together over 350 women at each.
Net Revenue: 1994 $293,491 **Net Expenses:** $249,945 **Net Assets:** $292,041
Tax Status: 501(c)(5)
Board of Directors or Trustees: Eleanor Bailey (NY Metro), Lula Binns, Evelyn Dubrow (Intl. Ladies' Garment Workers' Union), Carolyn Forrest (UAW), Jean Hervey, Josephine LeBeau, Margaret Shelleda, Barbara VanBlake, Gwen Wells, Marsha Zakowski.
Periodicals: *CLUW News* (bimonthly).
Other Information: CLUW received $152,661, or 52% of revenue, from gifts and grants awarded by foundations, unions, and individuals. (These grants included $25,000 from the Jessie Smith Noyes Foundation, $10,000 from the Ms. Foundation for Women.) $64,791, or 22%, from membership dues. $57,502 net, or 20%, from special fund-raising events, $8,576, or 3%, from interest on savings and temporary cash investments. The remaining revenue came from the sale of inventory, and other miscellaneous sources.

Coalition on Homelessness (COH)

126 Hyde St., Suite 102
San Francisco, CA 94102   **Phone:**   (415) 346-3740
USA   **Fax:**   (415) 775-5639

Contact Person: Paul Boden, Secretary. **Officers or Principals:** Anna D'Amato, President ($0); Laura Ware, Treasurer ($0).
Mission or Interest: "The Coalition on Homelessness was organized in 1987 to garner the active participation of poor people on both the design and critique of public policy and non-profit services that result in permanent solutions to poverty." Programs include: support for undocumented (illegal) homeless immigrants, a legal division to end civil rights abuses of homeless people, creating an alliance between the homeless and low income parents, and support programs to help provide mental health, income assistance, and other social programs.
Accomplishments: In 1994 the Coalition spent $257,422 on its programs. COH advocated and designed The McMillan Center, a drop-in center for substance abusers that has reduced street deaths. Helped set up a grievance procedure whereby shelter residents can appeal disciplinary actions through an impartial process. Advocated the policy, now enacted, of Department of Social Services contracts with shelters to include target hiring quotas of between 5%-50% homeless and low-income individuals. Advocated a policy, now enacted, of a formerly homeless advocate, funded by the city, who ensures that shelter residents are not unfairly evicted from shelters and are treated in an unbiased manner.
Net Revenue: 1994 $308,714 **Net Expenses:** $299,328 86%/8%/6% **Net Assets:** $71,514
Products or Services: Advocation and education of policies devised by, and on behalf of, homeless and low-income individuals.
Tax Status: 501(c)(3) **Annual Report:** No. **Employees:** 8
Board of Directors or Trustees: Ali Riker (Center for Juvenile and Criminal Justice), Margarita Chavez (Family Rights and Dignity), Arnette Watson (Client Advocate), Tyrone Jackson (A Women's Place), Greg Winter (Hamilton Family Shelter), Brian Russell (General Assistance Rights Union), Kym Valadez (Swords to Plowshares), Richard Marquez (AYUDA), September Jarrett (Low-Income Housing Fund).
Periodicals: *Street Sheet* (monthly tabloid published and distributed by the homeless).
Internships: Yes.
Other Information: COH received $308,307, or 99% of revenue from gifts and grants awarded by foundations, companies, and individuals. (These grants included $2,000 from the Vanguard Public Foundation, $1,620 from Progressive Way.) The remaining income came from interest on savings and temporary cash investments and dividends and interest from securities.

Coalition on Homelessness and Housing in Ohio (COHHIO)

1066 N. High St.
Columbus, OH 43201   **Phone:**   (614) 291-1984
USA   **Fax:**   (614) 291-2009

Contact Person: Susan Francis, Communications Coordinator. **Officers or Principals:** William Faith, Executive Director ($34,000); Jim Cain, Associate Director; Matt Penrod, Housing Policy Director; Carolyn Steele, AmeriCorps Project Coordinator.
Mission or Interest: COHHIO was formed as a result of a merger between the Ohio Coalition for the Homeless and the Ohio Housing Coalition. (NOTE: The financial information here comes from the pre-merger Ohio Coalition for the Homeless.) "Committed to ending homelessness and to promoting decent, safe, affordable housing for all...Identifying and advocating for immediate and long-term solutions to homelessness...Informing and raising awareness of the public and policy makers about homelessness and Ohio's housing needs."
Accomplishments: "Successfully advocated for the restoration of over $7 million in the Family Emergency Assistance through the Ohio Department of Human Services. Successfully pushed for enactment of HB 321, Ohio's new Fair Housing legislation (1992). Implemented the AmeriCorps Houses the Homeless project, which placed over 30 AmeriCorps members in 22 direct service organizations around the state to assist homeless Ohioans to secure and maintain their own housing." Created and distributed over 75,000 pieces of the "Homeless Children Education Literature" to schools, children's programs, and shelters. Hosted a statewide conference attended by over 350 people. In 1993 the Ohio Coalition for the Homeless spent $195,718 on its programs.
Net Revenue: 1993 $213,600 ($100,534, or 47%, from government grants) **Net Expenses:** $228,033 86%/9%/5%
Net Assets: $32,943
Products or Services: Publications, organization, conferences, and lobbying. In 1993 the Coalition spent $5,800 on lobbying at the federal and state level.

Tax Status: 501(c)(3) **Annual Report:** Yes. **Employees:** 7 full time, 34 AmeriCorps workers.
Board of Directors or Trustees: Barbel Adkins, Tom Albanese, Ruth Arden Beshalske, Patricia Barnes, Caren Bauer, Nora Bethea, Phyllis Beyers , Lee Blons, Rose Ann Braniff, Chip Bromley, James Butler, Susan Coccia, Ed Deering, Carol Duncan, Cynthia Flaherty, Barbara Flexter, Mike Fontana, Buddy Gray, Nancy Hoge, Martin Jarret, Kathleen Kennedy, Roy Lowenstein, Brenda Martin, Roger McCauley, Phil McKinney, Kay Monter, Cheryl Moreno, David Pacetti, Sharon Parries, Sr. Loretta Rafter, Barbara Reiter, Sr. Margaret Scheetz, Linda Stallworth, Marguerite Turnbull, Margy Waller, Lynne Wortham, Kalpana Yalamanchili.
Periodicals: *Breaking Ground* (quarterly newsletter).
Internships: No.
Other Information: The Ohio Coalition for the Homeless received $100,534, or 47% of revenue, from government grants. $93,510, or 44%, from gifts and grants awarded by foundations, companies, and individuals. $16,035, or 7%, from conference and workshop fees. The remaining revenue came from interest on savings and temporary cash investments, rental income, and other miscellaneous sources.

Coalition on Political Assassinations

P.O. Box 772
Washington, DC 20044   **Phone:** (202) 785-5299   **E-Mail:** nisbco@igc.apc.org
USA   **Fax:** (202) 293-3218

Contact Person: John Judge, President. **Officers or Principals:** John Judge, President ($12,680); Daniel S. Alcorn, Esq., General Counsel ($0); Dr. Cyril Wecht, Chairman ($0).
Mission or Interest: Pursues the complete release of all government documents pertaining to assassinations. In particular, they seek "resolution of major U.S. political murders - John F. Kennedy, Robert F. Kennedy, Martin Luther King, Jr. and others."
Accomplishments: Two national conferences, legislative and grassroots support for John F. Kennedy Assassination Records Review Board. Their Advisory Board includes Academy Award winning director Oliver Stone.
Net Revenue: FY covering 3/15/94 through 12/94 $70,053 **Net Expenses:** $58,240 70%/2%/28% **Net Assets:** $11,812
Products or Services: Research, conferences, video and audio tapes, and other information on political assassinations and the government cover-ups.
Tax Status: 501(c)(4) **Annual Report:** No. **Employees:** 0
Board of Directors or Trustees: Gary Aguiler, M.D., Walter Brown, Ph.D., James DiEugenio, Patrick Fourmy, James Lesar, Philip Melanson, Ph.D., Jerry Policoff, Janette Rainwater, Ph.D., Peter Dale Scott, Ph.D.
Periodicals: *Open Secrets* (monthly newsletter) and *Prologue* (Monthly newsletter).
Internships: No.
Other Information: The Coalition is composed of three member organizations; the Assassination Archives and Research Center, Citizens for Truth About the Kennedy Assassination, and Committee for an Open Archives. The Coalition received $39,630, or 47% of revenue, from membership dues. $29,101, or 41%, from program services. $1,052, or 2%, from grants awarded by foundations, companies and individuals. The remaining revenue came from interest on savings and temporary cash investments.

Coalition to Preserve Choice: 2 to 1

P.O. Box 5863
Providence, RI 02903   **Phone:** (401) 455-0755
USA

Mission or Interest: "To provide education about the need to preserve reproductive choice in the U.S. and Rhode Island."
Accomplishments: In the fiscal year ending June 1994, the Coalition spent $20,680 on its programs.
Net Revenue: FY ending 6/94 $20,625 **Net Expenses:** $21,191 **Net Assets:** $161
Tax Status: 501(c)(3)
Board of Directors or Trustees: Edie Ajello, Jane Argentieri, Trina Barnes, Jane Cerilli, Barbara Fields, David Heckman, Bob Lee, Cathy Lewis, Martha Marteney, Patrice Pop, Mary Riley, Kim Rose, Marti Rosenberg.
Other Information: The Coalition received $18,809, or 91% of revenue, from gifts and grants awarded by foundations, businesses, and individuals. $1,816 net, or 9%, from special fund raising events.

Coalition to Stop Gun Violence

100 Maryland Ave., N.E.
Washington, DC 20002   **Phone:** (202) 544-7190
USA

Contact Person: Michael Beard.
Officers or Principals: Joel Kanter, Chairman ($0); Rev. James Atwood, Secretary ($0); Hillary Shelton, Treasurer ($0).
Mission or Interest: To reduce and end violence involving guns through the restriction and prohibition of gun ownership.
Accomplishments: In 1994 the Coalition spent $1,013,076 on its programs. The largest program, with expenditures of $898,805, developed educational materials and events. $68,461 was spent on research. $33,173 was spent advocating legislation "which would ban handguns from importation, manufacture, sales, transfer, ownership, possession and use by the general public." $12,637 was spent disseminating their programs and research. This included $6,701 in grants that were awarded to: $2,951 for their 501(c)(3) affiliate, $2,500 for the Committee for a Better Milwaukee, $1,000 for the Free Speech Coalition, $100 each for Marylanders Against Handgun Violence and the Fraternal Order of Police, and $50 for The Phoenix School.

Net Revenue: 1994 $990,659 **Net Expenses:** $1,461,056 69%/7%/23% **Net Assets:** $44,728 **Citations:** 35:153
Products or Services: Films, pamphlets, forums, lectures, lobbying.
Tax Status: 501(c)(4)
Board of Directors or Trustees: Robert Alpern (Unitarian Universalist Assoc.), Stephanie Arellano (U.S. Students Assoc.), Bernice Balter (Women's League for Conservative Judaism), Alan Berman (American Assoc. of Suicidiology), Herb Blinder (American Ethical Union), Dr. William Burman (Pan American Trauma Assoc.), Michael Casserly (Council of Great City Schools), Aileen Cooper (B'nai B'rith Women), Jay Cutler (American Psychiatric Assoc.), Evelyn Dubrow (ILGWU), Dr. Amitai Etzioni (Communitarian Network), Darryl Fagin (Americans for Democratic Action), Ruth Flower (Friends Committee on National Legislation), David Frank (North American Federation of Temple Youth), Rich Gilbert (American Public Health Association), Dr. Eleanor Hinton Hoytt (National Council of Negro Women), Pat Kenoyer, Fr. Peter Klink (Jesuit Conference), Rev. Kathy Lancaster (Presbyterian Church USA), Rabbi Lynne Landsberg (Union of American Hebrew Congregations), Jay Lintner (United Church of Christ), Katherine Mainzer (Citizens for Safety), Robert McAlpine (National Urban League), Tim McElwee (Church of the Brethren), Rabbi Paul Menitoff (Central Conference of American Rabbis), Sammie Moshenberg (National Council of Jewish Women), Edward Muir (United Federation of Teachers), Mark Pelavin (American Jewish Congress), Karabelle Pizzigati (Child Welfare League), Clayton Ramey (Fellowship of Reconciliation), Lenny Rubin (Jewish Community Center Assoc.), Bob Schwartz (Disarm Education Fund), Ken Sehested (Baptist Peace Fellowship of North America), Karl Shelly (Mennonite Central Committee), Victoria Stanhope (National Assoc. of School Psychologists), Beverly Stripling (YWCA of the USA), Rev. Wesley Wakefield (Bible Holiness Movement), Laura DeKoven Waxman (U.S. Conference of Mayors), Jeffrey Weintraub (American Jewish Committee), Don Weisman (United Synagogues of America).
Other Information: The Coalition is affiliated with the 501(c)(3) Educational Fund to End Gun Violence at the same address. The two had combined net revenues, expenses, and assets of $1,205,241, $1,660,117, and $105,419. The Coalition received $965,680, or 97% of revenue, from gifts and grants awarded by foundations, businesses, and individuals. The remaining revenue came from "overhead contribution," rental reimbursement from their affiliate, mailing list rentals, and interest on savings and temporary cash investments.

Colorado Coalition for the Homeless

2100 Broadway
Denver, CO 80205   **Phone:** (303) 293-2217
USA

Contact Person: John Parvensky, Executive Director.
Officers or Principals: John Parvensky, Executive Director ($50,880); Mary Helen Sandoval, President ($0); Susan Brown, Karen Musikka, Gerry McCafferty, Vice Presidents ($0); Rebecca Martinez, Secretary.
Mission or Interest: Provide social services for the homeless, works to inform the public about the problem of homelessness, and advocates public policy to alleviate these problems.
Accomplishments: In 1994 the Coalition spent $3,295,531 on its programs. The Health Care Project was the largest program, at $1,702,339. This program provided medical care, mental health and dental services. The Coalition has accrued approximately $508,000 in Medicaid reimbursements (spending of these funds is budgeted for future years). Housing projects expenditures of $1,427,009 assisted indigent persons in finding temporary and permanent housing, and a transitional living facility for mentally ill women. $166,183 went to education and advocacy projects.
Net Revenue: 1994 $3,942,397 ($2,396,239, or 61%, from government grants) **Net Expenses:** $3,631,527 91%/8%/2%
Net Assets: $6,533,222 **Citations:** 42:142
Products or Services: Social services, educational activities, and policy advocacy. Although the Coalition did not engage in lobbying in 1994, they have in the past; the most the Coalition spent was $4,814 in 1991.
Tax Status: 501(c)(3)
Board of Directors or Trustees: Arthur McFall, Kenneth Barela (Pikes Peak Mental Health Center), Terry Benjamin (Emergency Family Assistance), Joy Blue Bird, Lance Cheslock, Natalie Funk (Samaritan Inst.), Leana Long, Steve Speer, Mark Taylor (Natl. Development & Finance Corp.).
Other Information: The Coalition received $2,396,239, or 61% of revenue, from government grants. These government grants were federal, state and local, including; $1,044,902 from Public Health Service, $584,513 from Housing and Urban Development, $318,206 from local government, $242,667 from Health and Human Services; $83,675 from the U.S. Department of Agriculture, and $12,402 from the Federal Emergency Management Agency. $1,237,908, or 32%, from direct and indirect public support in the form of gifts and grants awarded by foundations, companies, affiliates and individuals. $286,598, or 7%, from program services, including revenues from the shelters and clinics they work with. The remaining revenue came from dividends and interest on securities, and net income from special events. The Coalition also received deferred revenue for future periods from numerous sources including many of the government agencies. In addition, other deferred revenue was received, including; $9,563 from Comic Relief, $212,523 from the city of Denver, and $5,516 from the Colorado Department of Education.

Columbia Foundation

One Lombard St., Suite 305
San Francisco, CA 94111   **Phone:** (415) 986-5179
USA

Contact Person: Susan Clark Silk, Executive Director
Officers or Principals: Madeline Haas Russell, President; Charles Phillips Russell, Vice President; Christine Haas Russell, Treasurer; Alice Cornella Russell-Shapiro, Secretary.
Mission or Interest: Grant-making foundation that focuses on the San Francisco area.

Accomplishments: In the fiscal year ending May 1994, the Foundation awarded $2,841,311 in grants. Recipients of these grants included; three grants totaling $157,600 for the Natural Resources Defense Council, $30,000 each for the Greenbelt Alliance, Federation of American Scientists Fund, and the Tides Foundation, $25,000 each for the Center for National Independence in Politics, Earth Island Institute, and Mothers and Others for a Livable Planet, and $20,000 each for the Center for the Study of Law and Politics, Gay and Lesbian Alliance Against Defamation, and the Environmental Protection Information Center.
Net Assets: FY ending 5/94 $43,600,381
Tax Status: 501(c)(3) **Annual Report:** Yes.
Other Information: The Columbia Foundation was established in 1940 by president Madeline Haas Russell. President Russell is a member of the Haas family, the owners of Levi-Strauss and Co. Ms. Russell has been active in California Democratic politics.

Committee Against Registration and the Draft
P.O. Box 262
Madison, WI 53701-0262
USA

Mission or Interest: Peace organization against the military and against draft registration.

Committee for National Health Insurance
1757 N St., N.W., 5th Floor
Washington, DC 20036   **Phone:** (202) 23-9685
USA

Contact Person: Melvin A. Glasser, President. **Officers or Principals:** Melvin A. Glasser, President ($0); Douglas A. Fraser, Chairman ($0); Thomas R. Donahue, Secretary/Treasurer ($0).
Mission or Interest: Organized labor-led research and educational organization advocating a federal health-care system.
Accomplishments: In the fiscal year ending April 1994, the Committee spent $100,617 on its programs. These included grants of $65,000 for the Families USA Foundation, and $25,000 for Jobs with Justice.
Net Revenue: FY ending 4/94 $29,531 **Net Expenses:** $150,459 72%/28%/0% **Net Assets:** $547,349
Tax Status: 501(c)(3)
Board of Directors or Trustees: Owen Beiber (UAW).
Other Information: Affiliated with the 501(c)(4) Health Security Action Council at the same address. The two affiliates had combined net revenues of $129,182, net expenses of $339,784, and net assets of $760,555. The Committee received $22,395, or 76% of revenue, from interest on savings and temporary cash investments. $7,000, or 24%, from gifts and grants awarded by foundations and individuals. The remaining revenue came from reimbursed expenses.

Committee for Nuclear Responsibility (CNR)
P.O. Box 421993
San Francisco, CA 94142   **Phone:** (415) 776-8299
USA

Contact Person: Egan O'Connor, Executive Director. **Officers or Principals:** Egan O'Connor, Executive Director ($29,800).
Mission or Interest: Anti-nuclear weapons and power, concerned with environmental toxins. "CNR's single program service is the generation and distribution of educational material about sources and health effects of ionizing radiation...CNR is deeply involved in original research and analysis, and in public education about the basic rules of scientifically credible epidemiological research."
Accomplishments: In 1994 the Committee spent $44,433 on its programs. CNR produced and published a book on breast cancer.
Net Revenue: 1994 $73,457 **Net Expenses:** $53,235 83%/6%/10% **Net Assets:** $252,491
Products or Services: Books and documents. **Tax Status:** 501(c)(3)
Board of Directors or Trustees: June Allen M.ed., Hon. Ramsey Clark (former U.S. Attorney General, 1967-69), Prof. Paul Ehrlich (author, The Population Bomb), Frances Farenthold (Inst. for Policy Studies), Franklin Gage, Dr. John Gofman, Prof. David Inglis, Dr. Eloise Kailin, Prof. Ian McHarg (Univ. of PA), Prof. George Wald (Harvard Univ.).
Other Information: The Committee received $62,591, or 85% of revenue, from gifts and grants awarded by foundations, businesses, and individuals. (These grants included $1,000 from the Joyce Mertz-Gilmore Foundation.) $8,530, or 12%, from interest on savings and temporary cash investments. $1,590, or 2%, from the sale of books. The remaining revenue came from dividends and interest from securities.

Committee for Open Archives
(see Coalition on Political Assassinations)

Committee for Truth in Psychiatry
P.O. Box 1214
New York, NY 10003   **Phone:** (212) 473-4786   **E-Mail:** andrel@pie.org
USA

Contact Person: Linda Andre, Director.
Officers or Principals: They have a representative in each state.

Mission or Interest: Working for informed consent to electro-shock therapy (ECT). Support a complete ban on the procedure. The Committee is comprised of people who have been treated with electroshock therapy.
Accomplishments: The Committee has given testimony before state legislators and has worked with Congressional representatives and aides, federal agencies, and the FDA. "We are recognized nationally as an authority on the effects of ECT."
Products or Services: Research and educational activities.
Tax Status: 501(c)(3) status is pending.
Periodicals: Newsletter (2-3 times a year).
Other Information: They currently operate on a very small budget but are applying for 501(c)(3) status and are looking to expand.

Committee in Solidarity with the People of El Salvador (CISPES)
19 W. 21st St.
New York, NY 10010   **Phone:**   (212) 229-1290
USA

Contact Person: Diane Green, Executive Director.
Officers or Principals: Michael Zielinski, Secretary ($0); Cherenne Horzuk, Treasurer ($0).
Mission or Interest: Focuses on problems in El Salvador, and the United State's role in the affairs of that country. Opposed to the United States' military support for the government of El Salvador.
Accomplishments: Opposition to the foreign policies of Presidents Reagan and Bush. Supported the Marxist FMLN (Frente Farabundo Marti de Liberacion Nacional) guerillas during that country's civil war. Opposed military aid to the government. In 1993 CISPES spent $383,925 on its programs. These programs included $95,981 to send a delegation to El Salvador. $76,785 was spent for peaceful demonstrations in support of democracy and human rights in El Salvador. $76,785 was spent on educational materials and publications. $57,588 was spent providing human rights information. $38,393 was spent training community leaders and working with local community organizations. $38,393 was spent on humanitarian aid for projects in El Salvador. CISPES also awarded $27,338 in grants.
Net Revenue: 1993 $774,513 **Net Expenses:** $671,368 57%/12%/31% **Net Assets:** (-$34,538) **Citations:** 17:178
Tax Status: 501(c)(4)
Board of Directors or Trustees: Geoff Herzog, Sarah Lewton, Michael Prokosch, Gina Olaon.
Periodicals: *ALERT: Focus on Central America* (monthly newsletter).
Other Information: CISPES has been accused of being created by the Marxist FMLN guerillas in El Salvador and the Communist Party USA, as a United States lobbying and funding network - a charge CISPES denies. These charges were made by, among others, former FMLN leader Alejandro Montenegro. CISPES is affiliated with the 501(c)(3) CISPES Education Fund. The Committee received $571,332, or 74% of revenues, from foundations, and individuals. (These grants included $1,000 from the Vanguard Public Foundation.) $126,515, or 16%, from the CISPES Education Fund. $57,668, or 7%, from the sale of merchandise. The remaining revenue came from advertising, membership dues, dividends and interest from securities, special fund-raising events, and other miscellaneous sources.

Committee to Bridge the Gap (CBG)
1637 Butler Ave., Suite 203
Los Angeles, CA 90025   **Phone:**   (310) 478-0829
USA

Contact Person: Daniel Hirsch, President.   **Officers or Principals:** Daniel Hirsch, President ($43,492); Sheldon C. Plotkin, Secretary ($0); Mildred Plotkin, Treasurer ($0); Pauline Saxon, Vice President; Rev. H. Mike Fink, Assistant Secretary.
Mission or Interest: Concerned with issues relating to the proliferation of "nuclear technologies," nuclear power and the environment.
Accomplishments: In 1994 the Committee spent $122,792 on its programs. The largest program, with expenditures of $58,424, provided "technical analyses of proliferation issues associated with emerging nuclear technologies." $46,972 was spent on the Ward Valley Project, providing analyses of environmental issues associated with the Ward Valley Nuclear Project. $12,396 was spent performing analyses on policy options for improving reactor safety in the former Soviet Union and Eastern Europe. $5,000 was spent providing technical assistance to communities near Department of Energy nuclear facilities.
Net Revenue: 1994 $172,052 **Net Expenses:** $143,527 86%/7%/7% **Net Assets:** $88,228
Products or Services: Technical analyses and assistance, lobbying. The organization spent $7,803 on lobbying, $419 on grassroots lobbying and $7,384 on the direct lobbying of legislators. This was a 367% increase over the previous year.
Tax Status: 501(c)(3)
Other Information: The Committee received $169,431, or 98% of revenue, from gifts and grants awarded by foundations, businesses, and individuals. (The Committee has received substantial support from the W. Alton Jones Foundation. The Committee received $20,000 from the Ploughshares Fund, $10,000 from the Deer Creek Foundation.) $2,621, or 2%, from interest on savings and temporary cash investments.

Common Cause
2030 M St.
Washington, DC 20036   **Phone:**   (202) 833-1200   **E-Mail:** commoncaus@aol.com
USA   **Fax:**   (202) 659-3716

Contact Person: Anne McBride, President.

Officers or Principals: Fred Wertheimer, Former President ($80,589); Ann McBride, President ($76,079); Dominic Ucci, Vice President ($72,470); Edward Cabot, Chairman; Dorothy Cecelski, Secretary; Susan Kinnecome, Treasurer; Randy Huwa, Deborah Baldwin, Susan Manes, Michael Mawby, Jane Mentinger, Jay Hedlund, Vice Presidents.

Mission or Interest: "The organization has helped to achieve national and state reforms in the areas of campaign financing, open meetings, lobby disclosure, government ethics, civil rights, and the federal budget process." Lobbies for campaign reform, and supports publicly financed campaigns.

Accomplishments: Approximately 250,000 members. The organization awards annual Public Service Achievement awards. In 1995 the four winners were Janelle Goetcheus, M.D., medical director for Health Care for the Homeless, Ralph Neas, executive director of the Leadership Conference on Civil Rights, Eddie Staton, founder of Men Against Destruction-Defending Against Drugs and Social Disorder (MAD DADS), and Jane Yarn, founder of Georgia's first environmental lobbying organization, Save America's Vital Environment. In 1994 Common Cause spent $5,882,879 on its programs. The largest program, with expenditures of $2,789,231, provided "National Lobbying, Issue Management and Communication" which included "staff and volunteers who maintain contact with members of Congress; monitor federal executive branch activity; communicate and interpret information on Common Cause issues to state and Congressional Districts. $2,272,687 was spent on "State Lobbying, Issues Management and Communications" with programs similar to the national efforts. $820,961 was spent on program development and management. This included policy formation and litigation.

Net Revenue: 1994 $10,314,311 **Net Expenses:** $10,226,716 58%/27%/15% **Net Assets:** $1,062,980 **Citations:** 5,904:3

Tax Status: 501(c)(4)

Board of Directors or Trustees: Barbara Bader Aldave (Dean, St. Mary's University School of Law), Prof. Deborah Arnesen (New England College), Prof. William Avery (Uinv. of Nebraska), Rebecca Avila (Los Angeles Ethics Commission), David Beaulieu (Minnesota Commissioner of Human Rights), Prof. Peter Brown (Univ. of Maryland), Peter Butzin (Pres., Datamaster), Prof. Paulette Caldwell (New York Univ.), David Campbell, Sarah Chandler, InChul Choi (Korean American Community Services), Nicholas Johnson (former FCC Commissioner), Asst. Prof. David King (Harvard Univ.), Prof. Susan Lederman (Kean College of New Jersey), Prof. Hubert Locke (Univ. of Washington), Andy Loewi (former counsel, U.S. Senate Ethics Committee), Norma Mayfield (Public Interest Advocate), Robert Meier, Ruth Milburn, Prof. Robert Moore (Columbia College), Roger Morris, Jonathan Motl, Hon. Mary Lou Munts (former WI State Rep.), Asst. Prof. Candice Nelson (American Univ.), Prof. Jeanne Noble (CUNY), Bradley Phillips.

Periodicals: *Common Cause* (magazine).

Other Information: Common Cause states that it does not accept grants from governments, businesses, or foundations. (This is not unusual for a 501(c)(4) organization. Since contributions are not tax deductible, businesses and foundations do not usually contribute anyway.) Support comes from membership dues and gifts or grants from members. The organization received $6,164,831, or 60% of revenue, from gifts and grants awarded by members. This comes out to approximately $25 from each member. $3,925,658, or 38%, from membership dues. $175,844, or 2%, from royalties and mailing list rentals. The remaining revenue came from interest on savings and temporary cash investments, the sale of publications, and other miscellaneous sources.

Common Courage Press

P.O. Box 702
Monroe, ME 04951   **Phone:** (207) 525-0900
USA   **Fax:**   (207) 525-3068

Contact Person: Flic Shooter. **Officers or Principals:** Greg Bates.

Mission or Interest: Publisher of books with a strongly leftist view.

Accomplishments: "In the age of Republican monsters and spineless Democrats, Common Courage continues to expand. More importantly, our books continue to aid a variety of political projects." Publishes several books by Noam Chomsky. Rebellion from the Roots: Indian Uprising in Chiapas by Pacifica Radio commentator John Ross won the 1995 American Book Award from the Before Columbus Foundation. Other recent titles include: Race for Justice: Mumia Abu-Jamal's Fight Against the Death Penalty by defense counsel Leonard Weinglass, Toxic Sludge is Good for You: Lies, Damn Lies and the Public Relations Industry by John Stauber, Bridge of Courage by Jennifer Harbury, White Lies, White Power: The Fight Against White Supremacy and Reactionary Violence by *People Against Racist Terror* editor Michael Novick, Timber Wars, by Earth First! member Judi Bari (who was injured when a pipe bomb exploded in her car), and many others.

Products or Services: Book catalog, books.

Tax Status: 501(c)(3) **Annual Report:** No. **Employees:** 4

Internships: Yes, positions in all aspects of small press publishing.

Common Giving Fund

666 Broadway, 5th Floor
New York, NY 10012
USA

Contact Person: Ron Hanft, Secretary.

Mission or Interest: Philanthropic foundation whose funds are managed by the Funding Exchange, and whose sole recipient (during the fiscal year ending April 1995) was the North Star Fund.

Accomplishments: In the fiscal year ending April 1995 the Fund awarded $766,046 to the North Star Fund.

Net Revenue: FY ending 4/95 $780,624 **Net Expenses:** $920,358 **Net Assets:** $10,930,622

Tax Status: 501(c)(3)

Other Information: Located at the same address as the Funding Exchange and North Star Fund. The Funding Exchange was paid $50,000 for managing the Common Giving Fund. The Common Giving Fund received $465,327, or 60% of revenue, from dividends and interest from securities. $315,297, or 40%, from capital gains on the sale of securities. The Fund held $6,090,855, or 56% of assets, in corporate stock. $2,901,235, or 27%, from government obligations. $1,560,839, or 14%, in corporate bonds.

Commonweal Foundation / *Commonweal*

15 Dutch St.
New York, NY 10038   **Phone:**   (212) 732-0800
USA

Contact Person: Edward Skillin, President.
Officers or Principals: Paul D. Baumann, Associate Editor ($49,423); Patrick Jordan, Managing Editor ($37,538); Richard Haas, Business Manager ($37,062); Margaret O. Steinfels, Secretary/Treasurer; James O'Gara, Vice President.
Mission or Interest: Publishes a monthly magazine, "To create an informed, spiritually grounded, doctrinally sophisticated American Catholic laity, committed to democracy and social justice, capable of realizing Catholic and American ideals personally and in the public forum...to combine respect for papal authority with awareness of its limits."
Accomplishments: Rembert Weakland, archbishop of Milwaukee, says of *Commonweal*, "To know what is going on in the Catholic intellectual world, there is no better place than *Commonweal*." In the fiscal year ending September, 1994, they spent $592,024 on publication and distribution. Circulation is about 18,000.
Net Revenue: FY ending 9/94 $829,837 **Net Expenses:** $823,102 72%/28%/0% **Net Assets:** $85,553 **Citations:** 183:87
Products or Services: Monthly magazine. Awards the Graymoor prize.
Tax Status: 501(c)(3)
Board of Directors or Trustees: Sidney Callahan, Richard Sexton, Daniel Murtaugh, Dennis O'Brien.
Periodicals: *Commonweal* (monthly magazine).
Other Information: The Foundation received $697,408, or 84% of revenue, from publishing *Commonweal*. This includes subscriptions ($569,492), advertising ($75,477), royalties ($17,901), mailing list rentals ($14,340),and other sources. $130,326, or 16%, from grants awarded by foundations, companies and individuals. The remaining revenue came from interest and dividends. *Commonweal* cost $592,024 to publish and distribute, and provided $697,408 in revenue - a net gain of $105,384. It is uncommon for a magazine of opinion to make net gains.

Communist Party USA (CPUSA)

235 W. 23rd St.
New York, NY 10011   **Phone:**   (212) 989-4994   **E-Mail:** cpusa@rednet.org
USA   **Fax:**   (212) 229-1713   **Web-Page:** pww@igc.apc.org

Contact Person: Esther Davis, National Organizing Department.
Officers or Principals: Gus Hall, National Chairman; George Meyers, Chair, National Labor Commission; Sam Webb, Secretary, National Labor Commission; National Labor-Community Relations Director; Victor Perlo, Chair, Economics Commission; Jarvis Tyner, Chair, Legislative and Electoral Commission; Terrie Albano, National Coordinator, Young Communist League; Debbie Bell, Chair, National Teacher's Commission; Judith LeBlanc, Chair, Jobs and Equality Task Force; Tony Monteiro, Chair, African American Equality Commission; Tim Wheeler, Editor, *People's Weekly World*; Joe Sims, Editor, Political Affairs; James West, International Secretary.
Mission or Interest: United States political party advocating revolutionary communism.
Accomplishments: CPUSA celebrated its 75th anniversary in 1994. Anniversary speakers and well-wishers included Rev. Lucius Walker, the founder of Pastors for Peace, John Randolph, a Tony award-winning actor, Hon. George Crockett (D-MI), as well as other labor leaders and community activists. Produced a booklet on the environment called "People and Nature Before Profits." The booklet was hailed by folk singer Pete Seeger, the secretary of the Seattle Audubon Society, Hazel Wolf, and the president of the National Association for Public Health Policy, Terrence E. Carroll.
Products or Services: Hosts the Young Communists League. Numerous pamphlets and publications. Speaker's bureau. "History's Challenge" video.
Board of Directors or Trustees: Lee Dlugin, Lorenzo Torres. Elena Mora, Dee Myles.
Periodicals: *Political Affairs* (monthly theoretical journal), *People's Weekly World* (weekly tabloid),
Other Information: Gus Hall was a prominent labor organizer in the steel-working industries and a founder of the United Steelworkers of America. He was elected party secretary in 1959, and chairman in 1986. Hall has run for president of the U.S.A. three times, in 1972, 1976, and 1980. Chair of the Party's Economics Commission, Victor Perlo, was an economist in the Roosevelt administration and, according to the recently released "Venona Intercepts" (communications between Soviet agents in the U.S. and their superiors in the Soviet Union that were intercepted and deciphered by U.S. intelligence agencies), he was the head of a spy network operating in the War Production Board, Treasury Department, and other government agencies. Communist Party publications are printed by Long View Publishing Co. at the same address.   An alternative e-mail address is "communistpty@igc.apc.org". The Young Communist League is located at the same address.

Communist Voice Organization

P.O. Box 13261, Harper Station
Detroit, MI 48213-0261
USA

Contact Person: Joseph Green, Editor.
Mission or Interest: Publishes *Communist Voice*. "The Communist Voice Organization is a group of comrades spread over a few cities...We are dedicated to helping put Marxism-Leninism on a firm anti-revisionist basis, thus paving the way for communism to take its place once again as the ideology of the militant proletariat in its struggle for a new world. We oppose the state-capitalist regimes falsely calling themselves 'communist', whether the Soviet Union of yesterday or Cuba, China, N. Korea, etc. today, and we oppose both Stalinism and its twin brother Trotskyism."

Annual Report: No. **Employees:** All volunteer.
Periodicals: *Communist Voice.*   **Internships:** No.
Other Information: "We regard that the *Communist Voice* is the successor to the *Workers Advocate* because we continue the anti-revisionist cause to which the *Workers Advocate* was dedicated. The WA was founded in 1969 with the aim of rebuilding a genuine communist party in the U.S. For a quarter of a century, the WA firmly opposed the pro-Soviet 'Communist' Party and other opportunist organizations as revisionist travesties of Marxism and betrayers of the cause of the working class. From 1980 to 1993, the WA was the national voice of the Marxist Leninist Party (MLP). In Nov. 1993 the 3rd Congress of the MLP dissolved the party and killed the WA. The CVO stems from those comrades who opposed the demoralization of the 5th Congress majority. The Communist Voice continues, in different form, with fewer resources, and with more focus on the theoretical task, the struggle of the WA to contribute to the organization of a revolutionary proletarian party."

Communities for a Better Environment

500 Howard St., Suite 506
San Francisco, CA 94105   **Phone:** (415) 243-8373   **E-Mail:** cbesf@igc.apc.org
USA

Contact Person: Emily Scot. **Officers or Principals:** Michael Belliveau, Executive Director ($40,002); Margaret Williams, Finance Director ($29,048); Nora Chorover, Legal Director ($28,928); Nick Arguimbau, Secretary; Richard Blades, Treasurer; Stephanie Pincetl, President; Gary Patton, Vice President.
Mission or Interest: Environmental organization seeking to "transform a vision of a healthy, sustainable future into effective advocacy and citizen action that prevents pollution and reduces environmental health hazards in urban communities."
Accomplishments: Pioneered the use of emergency planning and the "Community Right To Know Act." Received $203,666 in court-awarded attorney's fees. Won a precedent-setting "Good Neighbor Agreement" from a local Unocal refinery. The agreement included; independent safety audits, 143 tons of air pollution reductions, $238,000 for an independent health study of chemical spill victims, $3 million for community projects over a fifteen-year period and more. A similar agreement with a Chevron refinery resulted in Chevron agreeing to; pay $5 million to community programs, provide skilled job training for 100 people, install leakless valves and more. Filed suite against RECLAIM, a smog trading program in Southern California, on the grounds that it allowed more pollution than previous Air Quality Management Plans. In 1994 they spent $696,587 on these programs and initiatives.
Net Revenue: 1994 $1,055,345 ($14,783, or 1% of revenue from governmental sources)
Net Expenses: $1,053,769 66%/14%/20% **Net Assets:** $80,013
Products or Services: Publications, studies, legal action, more. Lobbying - in 1994 they spent $11,109 on lobbying, $1,566 on grassroots lobbying and $9,543 on the direct lobbying of legislators. This represented a 230% increase over the previous year.
Tax Status: 501(c)(3) **Annual Report:** Yes. **Employees:** 19
Board of Directors or Trustees: Ken Finney, Bryan Ford, Gilda Haas, Marianne Brown, Joanne Marlow, Jill Ratner, Libbie Agran; Katheryn Knight.
Internships: Yes, legal and program internships.
Other Information: They were formerly called Citizens for a Better Environment. They also have a Los Angeles office: 605 W. Olympic Blvd., Suite 850, Los Angeles, CA 90015, (213) 486-5114. The organization received $824,669, or 78% of revenue, from direct and indirect public support in the form of gifts and grants awarded by foundations, companies, affiliates and individuals. (These grants included $40,000 from the Florence and John Schumann Foundation, $38,290 from the Environmental Federation of California, $22,500 from the Liberty Hill Foundation, $6,000 from the Vanguard Public Foundation, $5,000 from the Compton Foundation.) $203,666, or 19%, from court-awarded attorney's fees. $14,783, or 1%, from government grants. The remaining income came from the sale of publications, net income from special events, interest on savings and temporary cash investments, and other miscellaneous sources.

Community for Creative Non-Violence

425 2nd St., N.W.
Washington, DC 20001   **Phone:** (202) 393-1909
USA

Contact Person: Lonnie Robertson, President. **Officers or Principals:** Keith Mitchell, Vice President ($0); Lois Mitchell, Treasurer ($0); Willis Partington, Secretary ($0).
Mission or Interest: Homeless activist organization founded by the late Mitch Snyder. Provides issue activism and service for the homeless and hungry.
Accomplishments: Mitch Snyder produced and popularized the claim that there are 3.5 million homeless individuals in America. In the fiscal year ending June 1994 the organization spent $240,147 on its programs. All of this went toward providing assistance and services for the homeless and the hungry, including food, shelter, and referral services.
Net Revenue: FY ending 6/94 $324,996 **Net Expenses:** $325,373 74%/26%/0% **Net Assets:** $12,370,251
Tax Status: 501(c)(3)
Other Information: The organization received $324,996, or 100% of revenue, from gifts and grants awarded by foundations, businesses, and individuals.

Compton Foundation

545 Middlefield Rd., Suite 178
Menlo Park, CA 94025   **Phone:** (415) 328-0101
USA

Contact Person: Edith Eddy, Executive Director. **Officers or Principals:** Edith Eddy, Executive Director ($15,646).

Mission or Interest: Grant-making foundation that awards money to organizations pursuing peace and world order (25%), the environment (24%), over-population concerns (19%), general education (11%), art and culture (10%), equal educational opportunity (6%), social services for children (1%), community welfare (1%), and general and mental health (less than 1%) and other miscellaneous.

Accomplishments: In 1994 the Foundation awarded $4,065,153 in grants. The recipients of the largest grants were: thirteen grants totaling $593,955 for various Planned Parenthood affiliates, nine grants totaling $582,770 for the Fund for Peace, two grants totaling $255,000 for the American Youth Foundation, four grants totaling $70,000 for the Nature Conservancy affiliates, $60,000 for the Population Council, $40,000 each for Catholics for a Free Choice and Population Action International, $38,430 for the Tides Foundation, $35,000 for International Women's Health Coalition, and $30,000 each for the Educational Foundation for Nuclear Science, Centre for Development and Population Activities, Global Fund for Women, Pathfinder International, and the Environmental Defense Fund.

Net Revenue: 1994 $5,398,006 **Net Expenses:** $4,817,249 **Net Assets:** $67,733,938

Tax Status: 501(c)(3)

Other Information: The Foundation received $3,369,505, or 62% of revenue, from capital gains on the sale of securities. $1,924,048, or 36%, from dividends and interest from securities. $104,453, or 2%, from interest on savings and temporary cash investments. The Foundation held $50,971,183, or 75% of assets, in corporate stock.

Computer Professionals for Social Responsibility (CPSR)

P.O. Box 717
Palo Alto, CA 94302   **Phone:** (415) 322-3778   **E-Mail:** CPSR@cpsr.org
USA   **Fax:**   (415) 322-4748   **Web-Page:** http://www.cpsr.org/home .html

Contact Person: Audrie Krause, Executive Director.   **Officers or Principals:** Marc Rotenberg, Office Director ($39,130); Eric Roberts, President ($0); Doug Shuler, Chair ($0); Steve Dever, Secretary; Tom Thornton, Treasurer.

Mission or Interest: "A national public-interest alliance of computer professionals and computer users concerned about the impact of computer technology on society." According to the "Computer and Information Technologies Platform" of the CPSR Berkeley chapter's Peace and Justice Working Group, "As a society, we possess the technical know-how to resolve homelessness, illiteracy, the absence of privacy, the skewed distribution of information and knowledge, the lack of health care, environmental damage, and poverty. These problems exist only because of the way we prioritize research and development, implement technologies, and distribute our social wealth...(this) is a political problem." To address this political problem, as computer professionals, they focus on the uses of computer technology to alleviate these problems. To this end they advocate: Universal access to education and technology, including the subsidization of computers, modems, and databases. Preservation of civil liberties. Guaranteed income for workers displaced by changes in the economy. Environmentally safe manufacturing. International cooperation. Research priorities redirected toward the 'public good.'

Accomplishments: Created the "Seattle Community Network Project" which linked community activists, educators, environmentalists, librarians and others. Their "Privacy and Civil Liberties Project" works to ensure that new technologies do not infringe on privacy rights. They have been vigorous opponents of the federal government's key-escrow encryption proposal, better known as the Clipper Chip Initiative. Instrumental in getting government information available on public databases. CPSR representatives have appeared on PBS's McNeill-Lehrer News Hour and NPR. In June of 1993 the CPSR board of directors had a chance to talk to the Clinton Administration's science policy team and congressional staff members working on science and technology.

Net Revenue: FY ending 6/94 $295,693 **Net Expenses:** $342,902 85%/10%/3% **Net Assets:** $14,581

Products or Services: Research, education, publications, and policy roundtables. Lobbying - in the fiscal year ending June 1994, they spent $18,644 on lobbying; $15,537 on grassroots efforts and $3,107 on the direct lobbying of legislators.

Tax Status: 501(c)(3) **Annual Report:** Yes. **Employees:** 3

Board of Directors or Trustees: Mary Connors, Ph.D. (Research Psychologist, NASA), Jim Davis, Hans Klein, Ph.D. (George Mason Univ.), Assoc. Prof. Blaise Liffick (Millersville Univ.), Steve Miller (author, Civilizing Cyberspace, Addison-Wesley), Aki Namioka, Doug Schuler (Community Network Movement), Prof. Terry Winograd (Stanford Univ.), Marsha Cook Woodbury (Assoc. Dir. of Education, Sloan Center, Univ. of IL, Urbana-Champaign).

Periodicals: The CPSR Newsletter (quarterly). **Internships:** Yes.

Other Information: CPSR has 22 chapters nationwide. The organization received $180,671, or 61% of revenue, from gifts and grants awarded by foundations, companies and individuals. (These grants included $29,000 from the Markle Foundation, $25,000 from the Millstream Fund, $20,000 from the J. Roderick MacArthur Foundation, $20,000 from the John D. and Catherine T. MacArthur Foundation, $15,000 from Interval Research, $10,000 from Apple Computer, $10,000 from the National Science Foundation, and $8,000 from the Telecommunications Education Trust.) $97,306, or 33%, from membership dues. $15,315, or 5%, from fund-raising conferences. The remaining revenue came from interest on savings, dividends and interest on securities, and other miscellaneous sources.

Concern

1794 Columbia Rd., N.W., Suite 6
Washington, DC 20009   **Phone:** (202) 328-8160
USA

Contact Person: Susan F. Boyd, Executive Director. **Officers or Principals:** Susan F. Boyd, Executive Director ($18,299); Burks B. Lapham, Chairman ($0); Suzanne T. Humpstone, Secretary ($0); Mary Louise Slayton, Treasurer.

Mission or Interest: "The development, publication and distribution of community action guides on timely environmental issues."
Accomplishments: In the fiscal year ending June 1994, Concern spent $73,995 on its programs. The largest of these, with expenditures of $29,277, was Community Outreach. This included responses to requests for information from the general public, and from teachers at the elementary, secondary, undergraduate and graduate levels for use in the classroom and for exhibits. $24,715 was spent on the Sustainable Communities program that "is building public awareness about new planning processes that link environmental, economic and social issues." Other projects included energy, water, waste, and pesticides.
Net Revenue: FY ending 6/94 $84,888 **Net Expenses:** $84,863 **Net Assets:** $86,691
Products or Services: Global Warming and Energy Choices, Drinking Water and Groundwater, Pesticides in our Community, and other publications.
Tax Status: 501(c)(3)
Board of Directors or Trustees: Susan Boyd, Beverly Carter, Augusta Field, Linda Graham, Cynthia McGrath, Joan Martin-Brown, Dorothy Michael, Beret Moyer, Ravida Preston, Rosalind Rockwell.
Other Information: Concern received $79,058, or 93% of revenue, from gifts and grants awarded by foundations, businesses, and individuals. (These grants included $10,000 from the Town Creek Foundation.) $3,724, or 4%, from program service revenues. $2,106, or 3%, from investment income.

Concerned Citizens for Racially Free America
P.O. Box 320497
Birmingham, AL 35232   **Phone:** (205) 836-4055   **E-Mail:** RAP507@AOL.COM
USA   **Fax:** same

Contact Person: Richard A. Peters, Director.
Mission or Interest: Civil rights organization promoting the advancement of African-Americans. "The African American community is angry with the Dominate, Capitalistic, Violent, White Male Society we are subjected to and particularly the defending of this society. Why? Clearly our white society (as a whole) is racist to the core."
Accomplishments: Their newsletter publishes the status of various discrimination cases settled by the Equal Employment Opportunity Commission (EEOC). They conclude that cases involving a white litigant are settled much faster. "'We've been had, hoodwinked, bamboozled.' Our Justice system is hard at work. However, is this 'Justice, or Just Us'?"
Tax Status: 501(c)(3) **Employees:** All volunteer.
Periodicals: Concerned Citizen (quarterly).
Other Information: Their motto is, "We're doing something." "The black youth of today firmly believe in freedom and liberty for all, or no freedom and liberty at all...They do NOT fear death. As a black child, they feel they were born in jail. The jail is Racism through the process of discrimination in America. -- All of our larger cities are held in hostage! WHY? White America condones racism; And Black people look the other way...The ball is in your court white America."

Concerts for Human Rights Foundation
322 8th Ave.
New York, NY 10001   **Phone:** (212) 807-8400
USA

Contact Person: John G. Healy, President.
Officers or Principals: Suriya S. Sandersham, Secretary ($0); Stephen King, Treasurer ($0).
Mission or Interest: Affiliated with Amnesty International, USA. Promotes concerts and raises funds for human rights.
Accomplishments: In the fiscal year ending March 1994, the Foundation undertook no projects, and all expenses were for management and general administration.
Net Revenue: FY ending 3/94 $40,225 **Net Expenses:** $40,225 **Net Assets:** $0
Tax Status: 501(c)(3)
Other Information: Affiliated with Amnesty International USA at the same address. The Foundation received $39,004, or 97% of revenue, from program services. $973, or 2%, from the sale of videos. $248, or 1%, from investment income.

Concord Feminist Health Center / *WomenWise*
38 S. Main St.
Concord, NH 03301   **Phone:** (603) 225-2739
USA   **Fax:** (603) 228-6255

Contact Person: Luita Spangler.   **Officers or Principals:** "Collective organization - no officers."
Mission or Interest: Nonprofit women's health clinic that provides abortion services. In addition, it is actively involved in community and national politics. "We are a group of concerned women involved in the struggle for reproductive rights which include abortion rights, gay and lesbian liberation, freedom from sterilization abuse, and freedom from chemical, nuclear and occupational hazards. We also take an active role in protecting the civil rights of all people and are often a leading voice on issues of oppression." The Center is a member of the National Abortion Federation, National Coalition of Abortion providers, and the American Public Health Association. They are coalition participants with the NH Women's Lobby, the Health Care Coalition, the Reproductive Rights Coalition, and the Martin Luther King Coalition. The Center publishes *WomenWise*.
Accomplishments: Won the 1992 New Hampshire Civil Liberties Union's Bill of Rights Award, the 1981 New Hampshire Women's Health Network's Health Advocate of the Year, and the 1980 New Hampshire Susan B. Anthony Award.
Tax Status: 501(c)(3) **Annual Report:** No. **Employees:** 10
Periodicals: *WomenWise* (quarterly tabloid).   **Internships:** Yes, working on *WomenWise*.

ConflictNet
(see the Institute for Global Communications)

Congress of Independent Unions
303 Ridge St.
Alton, IL 62002   **Phone:**   (618) 462-2447
USA

Contact Person: Richard Davis, President .
Officers or Principals: Richard Davis, President ($71,638); Paul Seiberaugh, Executive Vice President ($69,828); John Flach, Secretary/Treasurer ($67,528); Daniel F. Gretemon, National Vice President; Truman Davis, National President Emeritus.
Mission or Interest: "To continue to promote, preserve and defend the rights of employees to organize and bargain collectively with their employers through representatives of their choice; to increase wages and to impose conditions of employment; to secure equitable retirement plans, health insurance, workman's compensation and unemployment insurance laws and other conditions that tend to make employees and their families more secure and to assist and cooperate with other organizations where mutual benefits maybe derived."
Net Revenue: FY ending 10/94 $523,877 **Net Expenses:** $540,206 **Net Assets:** $823,547
Tax Status: 501(c)(5)
Other Information: The Congress received $470,146, or 90% of revenue, from membership dues. $37,207, or 7%, from interest on savings and temporary cash investments. $16,961, or 3%, from reimbursement for the personal use of automobiles.   The remaining revenue came from dividends and interest from securities.

Constitutional Rights Foundation
601 S. Kingsley
Los Angeles, CA 90005   **Phone:**   (213) 487-5590
USA

Contact Person: Todd Clark, Executive Director. **Officers or Principals:** Todd Clark, Executive Director ($102,838); Jo Ann Burton ($70,806); Harold Ellis, Director of Finance ($68,895); Knox M. Cologne, III, President; William J. Bogaard, Hon. Haley J. Fromholz, Richard S. Kolodny, Stephen Meier, Vice Presidents; Marvin Sears, Secretary.
Mission or Interest: Civil liberties and civil rights organization that focuses on students. "A community based organization which develops programs and materials to educate students about the rights and responsibilities of effective citizenship and offers technical assistance, teacher training and various other services in the subject matter areas of law and government, business and society and civic participation."
Accomplishments: In 1994 the Foundation spent $3,289,931 on its programs. The largest program, with expenditures of $2,814,591, was meeting the expenses allocated to programs funded by grants from the Office of Juvenile Justice and Delinquency Prevention, and the State Department of Education. $475,340 was spent on classroom educational activities, including mock trials.
Net Revenue: 1994 $4,123,534 ($2,534,718, or 61%, from government grants) **Net Expenses:** $4,045,605   81%/13%/5%
Net Assets: $996,162 **Citations:** 27:163
Tax Status: 501(c)(3)
Periodicals: *Bill of Rights in Action* (quarterly newsletter).
Other Information: The Foundation received $2,534,718, or 61% of revenue, from government grants. $1,370,825, or 33%, from direct and indirect public support in the form of gifts and grants awarded by foundations, affiliates, businesses, and individuals. $102,054, or 2%, from sales of inventory. $67,995, or 2%, from fees from mock trials. $37,618, or 1%, from History Day fees. The remaining revenue came from interest on savings and temporary cash investments, and capital gains on the sale of securities.

Consumers Union / *Consumer Reports*
101 Truman Ave.
Yonkers, NY 10703-1057   **Phone:**   (914) 378-2000
USA

Contact Person: Rhoda H. Karpatkin, President.   **Officers or Principals:** Rhoda H. Karpatkin, President ($237,021); James Davis, Vice President, Marketing ($177,176); Conrad Harris, Vice President/Chief Financial Officer ($165,524); R. David Pittle, Vice President ($165,161); Jeffrey Asher ($153,888); Louis Milani ($148,834); Joel Gurin, Vice President/Editor ($148,681); Josephine Lerro, Vice President/Administration ($143,019); Eileen Denver ($142,193); Simon Aronin ($136,484); Edward Groth ($134,261); Jan Liss, Senior Director, Planning ($109,826). (289 other employees are paid more than $50,000).
Mission or Interest: "Consumers Union advances the interests of consumers by providing information and advice about products and services and about issues affecting their welfare, and by advocating a consumer point of view." Publishes *Consumer Reports* magazine. The Union has consistently supported a national health care system, and during the debate of the Clinton health care plan, advocated a Canadian-style, or single-payer, system.
Accomplishments: In the fiscal year ending May 1995 the Union spent $113,290,624 on its programs. The largest program, with expenditures of $112,959,624, was the production and publication of consumer information. This included the publication and distribution of *Consumer Reports*. This also included $856,500 in grants for other organizations. These grants included: $538,000 for IOCU, $128,000 for the Paul H. Douglas Consumer Research Center, $37,000 for the Consumer Federation of America, $20,000 each for Public Voice in Food and Health Policy, and NY Citizens Utility Board, and $15,000 each for the Public Policy Education Fund of NY, and the National Consumer Law Center. $331,000 was spent on "intervention in California class action suits in order to protect the interests of California consumers." This intervention into California "insurance proceedings" produced $330,695 in revenue from fees.

Net Revenue: FY ending 5/95 $129,244,533   **Net Expenses:** $130,702,706   87%/11%/3%   **Net Assets:** $31,622,000
Citations: 2,078:14
Products or Services: Publications, legal intervention, and lobbying. The Union spent $556,685 on lobbying. These lobbying efforts included grants of $22,500 for the Alliance for Non-Profit Mailers, and $10,500 for the Consumers Federation of America.
Tax Status: 501(c)(3)
Board of Directors or Trustees: Robert Adler, Carol Barger, Christine Bjorklund, Dr. Jean Bowers, Joan Claybrook (Public Citizen), Dr. John Crum, Clarence Ditlow (Center for Auto Safety), Jean Ann Fox, Betty Furness, James Quest, Michael Jacobson, Dr. Leonard L.D. Morse, Sharon Nelson, Joel Nobel, Dr. Milton Pressley, Peter Sullivan, Dr. Julian Waller.
Periodicals: *Consumer Reports* (monthly magazine).
Other Information: Consumers Union and the City of Yonkers Industrial Development Agency have issued "Civic Facility Revenue Bonds" in 1989, 1991, and 1994. These bond issues were for $20,000,000, $10,000,000, and $15,000,000. The proceeds from these bonds went to finance the acquisition and renovation of the Union's National Testing Center and headquarters, acquire an adjacent parcel of land, and finance capital costs on the construction of a 75,000 square foot addition to the research and testing center. The bonds bear interest at a variable rate, which, as of May 1995, was 3.45% for the 1989 and 1991 bonds, and was 3.25% on the 1994 bonds. As of 5/95 the amount due on these bonds was listed as a liability of $43,900,000. The Union received $115,814,279, or 89% of total revenue, from subscriptions to *Consumer Reports*. $5,329,546, or 4%, from gifts and grants awarded by foundations, and individuals. (These included $20,000 from the Joyce Mertz-Gilmore Foundation.) $5,175,795, or 4%, from dividends and interest from securities. $2,955,798 net, or 2%, from special fund-raising events, specifically raffles. The remaining revenue came from fees collected from the California class action suit, interest on savings and temporary cash investments, and other miscellaneous sources. Consumers Union lost $460,458 on the sale of securities. The Union held $73,582,000, or 42% of total assets, in U.S. Government obligations. $57,575,000, or 33%, in land, buildings and equipment.

Context Institute / *IN CONTEXT*

P.O. Box 11470
Bainbridge Island, WA 98110   **Phone:** (206) 842-0216   **E-Mail:** CI@context.org
USA   **Fax:**   (206) 842-5208

Contact Person: Kathryn True.
Officers or Principals: Robert C. Gilman, Founding Editor ($24,000); Diane A. Gilman, Associate Publisher ($23,149); Sarah van Gelder, Editor; Rick Jackson, President; Danaan Parry, Vice President; Fred Noland, Treasurer.
Mission or Interest: Publishes *IN CONTEXT*, which "explores the building of a culture that is environmentally and social sustainable over the long run, while meeting the pressing needs of the people of today. It investigates the full range of human concerns - environmental, social, economical and spiritual - into a long-term, whole-system, solution oriented perspective."
Accomplishments: *IN CONTEXT* was named the *Utne Reader*'s 1994 winner for "best coverage of emerging issues." During 1994 the Institute printed 16,000 copies of each issue, and immediately distributed approximately 11,000 copies of each. In 1994 the Institute spent $300,412 on its programs. $294,012 went to publishing and distributing *IN CONTEXT*, other programs included speaking, presentations, and consulting.
Net Revenue: 1994 $342,922   **Net Expenses:** $315,036   95%/5%/0%   **Net Assets:** (-$69,575)
Tax Status: 501(c)(3)   **Employees:** 5
Board of Directors or Trustees: Sharif Abdullah, David Korten (People Centered Development Forum), Jagoda Perich-Andersen, Elizabeth Pinchot, Gifford Pinchot.
Periodicals: *IN CONTEXT* (quarterly journal).
Internships: Yes, unpaid.
Other Information: The Institute received $188,100, or 55% of revenue, from the sale of publications. $128,394, or 37%, from gifts and grants awarded by foundations, businesses, and individuals. (These grants included $6,000 from the Bullitt Foundation.) $25,161, or 7%, from honoraria. The remaining revenue came from interest on savings and temporary cash investments.

Council for a Livable World Education Fund

110 Maryland Ave., N.E.
Washington, DC 20002   **Phone:** (202) 543-4100
USA   **Fax:**   (202) 543-6297

Contact Person: John Isaacs, President.   **Officers or Principals:** T. Caramone, Director, Conventional Arms Project ($39,500); M. Fonte, Development Director ($39,500); John Isaacs, President ($28,500).
Mission or Interest: Founded by scientists in 1962 to warn of the dangers of nuclear weapons. Provides research and technical information on various issues including conventional arms sales, UN peacekeeping, nuclear weapons, and other subjects related to peace and disarmament.
Accomplishments: In 1994 the Fund spent $300,595 on its programs. The largest program, with expenditures of $75,864, was the publication of a newsletter sent to 1,600 people concerning the conventional arms trade. $71,975 was spent on the UN Project, which included coalition building, press briefings, speaking engagements, and a briefing book distributed to 4,000 people. $68,040 was spent on a nuclear non-proliferation educational campaign which included the distribution of 10,000 briefing books.
Net Revenue: 1994 $351,260   **Net Expenses:** $448,076   67%/17%/16%   **Net Assets:** $143,908
Products or Services: Briefing books, speaking engagements, publications, and lobbying. The Fund spent $65,063 on lobbying, $1,001 on grassroots lobbying and $63,672 on the direct lobbying of legislators. The amount spent on lobbying has increased over the years. 1994's lobbying expenses were 16% more than 1993, 23% more than 1992, and 54% more than 1991.

Tax Status: 501(c)(3)
Board of Directors or Trustees: Robert Drinan (Georgetown Univ. Law Center), Jerome Grossman, Dudley Herschbach (Harvard Univ.), John Polanyi (Univ. of Toronto), Edward Purcell (Harvard Univ.), George Rathjens (MIT, Center for Int. Studies), Carl Sagan (Cornell Univ.), Jane Sharp (Center for Defence Studies), Paul Warnke (Fund for Peace).
Other Information: Affiliated with the 501(c)(4) Council for a Livable World. The Education Fund received $337,732, or 96% of revenue, from gifts and grants awarded by foundations, businesses, and individuals. (These grants included $10,000 from the New World Foundation, $2,000 from the Stewart R. Mott Charitable Trust, $1,000 from the Compton Foundation, and $500 from the New Prospect Foundation.) $10,848, or 3%, from reimbursed expenses. $2,680, or 1%, from interest on savings and temporary cash investments.

Council for a Livable World

110 Maryland Ave., N.E.
Washington, DC 20002   **Phone:**   (202) 543-4100
USA   **Fax:**   (202) 543-6297

Mission or Interest: Lobbies for peace.
Products or Services: Press briefing book on multilateral peace operations.
Tax Status: 501(c)(4)
Other Information: Affiliated with the 501(c)(3) Council for a Livable World Education Fund. In 1994 the Council received $45,000 from the Ploughshares Fund, $25,000 from the Winston Foundation.

Council on Economic Priorities

30 Irving Place, 9th Floor
New York, NY 10003-2386   **Phone:**   (212) 420-1133
USA   **Fax:**   (212) 420-0988

Contact Person: Alice Tepper Marlin, Executive Director.
Officers or Principals: Alice Tepper Marlin, Executive Director ($103,800); Sheila Ratner, Administrative Director ($72,011); Deborah Leipziger, Department Head ($30,000); Lee B. Thomas, Chair.
Mission or Interest: Encourages greater corporate responsibility in such areas as the environment and defense projects.
Accomplishments: Encouraged international banks to link aid to demilitarization. Alice Tepper Marlin won the "Right Livelihood Award." In 1994 the Council spent $863,978 on its programs. The largest program, with expenditures of $328,527, was "Social Responsibility." $310,723 was spent on environment and energy projects, $113,297 on national security programs, and $111,431 on public education.
Net Revenue: 1994 $1,186,907 **Net Expenses:** $1,185,931 73%/16%/11% **Net Assets:** $4,127 **Citations:** 135:100
Products or Services: Numerous guides to socially-conscious shopping and investing. Produced a teacher's guide for their publications with the Council on International and Public Affairs.
Tax Status: 501(c)(3)
Board of Directors or Trustees: Sanford Cloud Jr. (National Conference), E. Tyna Coles, John Connor Jr., Phoebe Eng, Edith Everett, Lew Franklin, Robert Heilbroner, Jacob Imberman, Mary Gardner Jones (Consumer Interest Research), Greg Lewin, Henry Morgan, Carole Robbins, Arthur Rosenfeld, Jack Sheinkman (Amalgamated Clothing & Textile Workers Union), Beth Smith, Michaela Walsh, George Wallerstein.
Periodicals: *Council on Economic Priorities Research Report.*
Other Information: Founded in 1970. The Council employed the New York city firm of Hemming & Gillman for fund raising. The firm was paid $37,500. In 1994 the Council received $806,119, or 68% of revenue, from gifts and grants awarded by foundations, businesses, and individuals. (These grants included $30,000 from the Joyce Mertz-Gilmore Foundation, $25,000 from the Winston Foundation for World Peace, $17,500 from the Deer Creek Foundation, $5,000 from the Jessie Smith Noyes Foundation, $1,000 from the Stewart R. Mott Charitable Trust, and $500 from the Compton Foundation.) $159,171 net, or 13%, from a special fund-raising event, the annual awards dinner. $117,652, or 10%, from the sale of studies. $96,065, or 8%, from subscriptions. The remaining revenue came from interest on savings and temporary cash investments.

Council on Foreign Relations (CFR) / *Foreign Affairs*

58 E. 68th St.
New York, NY 10021   **Phone:**   (212) 734-0400
USA

Contact Person: Leslie H. Gelb, President.   **Officers or Principals:** Leslie H. Gelb, President ($233,897); James Hoge, Editor ($174,000); Alton Frye, Senior Vice President ($173,568); Kenneth H. Keller, Senior Vice President ($168,138); Henry Siegman, Senior Fellow ($162,500); Larry L. Fabian, Senior Vice President ($140,000); Jessica Mathews, Senior Fellow ($130,000); Michael Clough, Senior Fellow ($127,530); David Kellogg, Publisher ($117,993); Nicholas X. Rizopoulos, Vice President, Studies ($116,605); David Woodbridge, Treasurer ($115,480).
Mission or Interest: Influential foreign policy association. Although non-partisan, it has long been considered centrist to left. Although the Council does not officially take positions on issues, its membership and articles published in *Foreign Affairs* tended to represent non-intervention in military actions against communism, but supports intervention for peace-keeping or as part of a multi-national force. Following the Reagan and Bush presidencies, and their more conservative cabinets and advisors, more conservative Republicans have joined in recent years, including Jeane Kirkpatrick and former Defense Secretary, Dick Cheney.

Accomplishments: Since its founding in 1919, the Council has attracted a membership of some of the most influential members in politics, the judiciary, foreign service, and national media, including Presidents Bush and Clinton. In the fiscal year ending June 1994, the Council spent $10,112,201 on its programs. The largest portion of this, $3,779,400, went to the publication and distribution of the journal *Foreign Affairs*. $3,194,400 went to study programs, including study groups, workshops, symposia, and seminars. $1,256,400 was spent holding forums for the discussion of international affairs. Other programs included the publication of books, membership services, public education, and maintaining their library.

Net Revenue: FY ending 6/94 $18,255,544 **Net Expenses:** $13,905,044 73%/20%/7% **Net Assets:** $64,364,900

Citations: 1,076:21

Tax Status: 501(c)(3)

Board of Directors or Trustees: Paul Allaire (Xerox Corp.), Robert Allen (AT&T), John Bryson, James Burke (Partnership for a Drug-Free America), Hon. Richard Cheney (AEI, former Defense Secretary), John Clensin (Bellsouth Corp.), William Cohen, Richard Cooper (Harvard Univ., Center for Intl Affairs), E. Gerald Corrigan (Goldman Sachs & Co.), Kenneth Dam (Univ. of Chicago Law School), Thomas Donahue (AFL-CIO), Robert Erburu (Times Mirror Co.), Thomas Foley (former Congressional Speaker of the House), Maurice Greenberg (American Intl Group), Rita Hauser (Hauser Found.), Robert Hormats (Goldman Sachs Intl), Karen Horn (Bank One), James Houghton (Corning Inc.), Karen Elliott House (Dow Jones & Co.), Charlayne Hunter-Gault (MacNeil-Lehrer NewsHour), Jeane Kirkpatrick (AEI, former Ambassador to the U.N.), Joshua Lederberg (Rockefeller Univ.), Peter Peterson (Blackstone Group), Theodore Sorensen, Garrick Utley (ABC News), Paul Volker (former Federal Reserve Chairman).

Periodicals: *Foreign Affairs* (bimonthly journal).

Other Information: The Council on Foreign Relations is a frequent target of the populist-Right in the United States. Organizations such as the John Birch Society cite the CFR's enthusiasm for international governing institutions, and the socialist leanings of some of its founders and subsequent members. The CFR is criticized by the radical Left as well, with both the Left and Right taking issue with the amount of influence the CFR holds. Almost every Secretary of State in the last 50 years has held membership, as well as other top foreign-policy officials. Several Supreme Court Justices are members, as well as leaders of the House and Senate. CFR received $7,772,200, or 43% of revenue, from the gifts and grants awarded by foundations, businesses, and individuals. (These grants included $234,000 over two years from the Ford Foundation, and $150,900 from the Hauser Foundation. In 1995, $30,000 from the Rockefeller Foundation.) $4,259,600, or 23%, from income related to the publication and circulation of *Foreign Affairs*. $2,435,000, or 13%, from dividends and interest from securities. $1,705,900, or 9%, from membership dues. $1,284,782, or 7%, from capital gains on the sale of securities. $330,800, or 2%, from the sale of books. $236,600, or 1%, from local forums. The remaining revenue came from the sale of assets (other than securities), interest on savings and temporary cash investments, and other miscellaneous sources.

Council on International Public Affairs

777 U.N., Plaza, Suite 3C
New York, NY 10520   **Phone:** (212) 972-9877   **E-Mail:** cipany@igc.apc.org
USA   **Fax:** (212) 972-9878

Contact Person: Ward Morehouse, President.

Officers or Principals: Donald Harrington, Chairman; William Cowan, Vice Chairman; Winthrop R. Munyan, Secretary/Treasurer.

Mission or Interest: Seeks global change through the redistribution of wealth, labor organizing, and environmental justice. "Only with widespread political mobilization of working people will it be possible to strip away the enormous powers and privileges of major corporations and reclaim the American Dream."

Accomplishments: The Council works through various programs. The Policy Studies Associates publishes "materials for college and pre-college students that develop policy studies and citizenship skills." The Associates worked jointly with the Council on Economic Priorities (CEP) to produce a teacher's guide for CEP's new publication, Students Shopping for a Better World. The Policy Studies Associates worked with the League of Women Voters on a book about New York state government. Another program, the Center for International Training and Education, seeks "to help internationalize the school and college curriculum in the U.S." The Apex Press program publishes "books providing critical analyses of and new approaches to significant economic, social, and political issues in the U.S. and throughout the world. It has a special focus on economic and social justice issues and the impact of technology on contemporary society. The Press collaborates with the Labor Institute. The Program on Economic Democracy focuses on "social and environmental justice issues, including economic and social rights." This program produces an annual reference source, "The Underbelly of the U.S. Economy Project."

Net Revenue: 1994 $389,330 **Net Expenses:** $374,715

Products or Services: Catalog of books from Apex Press. Other publications and videos.

Tax Status: 501(c)(3) **Annual Report:** Yes. **Employees:** 10

Board of Directors or Trustees: David Denbo, Dorothy Goodman (Friends of International Education), Betty Lall (Council on Economic Priorities), Prof. Michael O'Leary (Syracuse Univ.), Betty Ramey, Robert Richter.

Internships: No.

Other Information: Received financial support from the North Shore Unitarian Universalist Veatch Program.

CovertAction Quarterly (CAQ)

1500 Massachusetts Ave., N.W., Suite 732
Washington, DC 20005   **Phone:** (202) 331-9763   **E-Mail:** caq@igc.apc.org
USA   **Fax:** (202) 331-9751   **Web-Page:** http://www.worldmedia.com/caq

Contact Person: Phillip Smith, Associate Editor.

Officers or Principals: Terry Allen, Editor; Louis Wolf, Research Director; Ellen Ray, Bill Schaap, Publishers.

Mission or Interest: Quarterly magazine of investigative reporting focusing on the intelligence community.
Accomplishments: Publishing since July 1978. *CAQ* stories have won *Utne Reader* and Project Censored awards. Recently featured authors such as: Mumia Abu-Jamal, Chip Berlet, Allen Ginsberg, the late William Kunstler, and Howard Zinn.
Tax Status: District of Columbia nonprofit. **Employees:** 4
Periodicals: *CovertAction Quarterly*.
Other Information: In 1993 the publication received $2,000 from the Peace Development Fund.

Crossroads Fund
3411 W. Diversey Ave., Suite 20
Chicago, IL 60647-1245   **Phone:**   (312) 227-7676   **E-Mail:** croadfund@igc.apc.org
USA   **Fax:**   (312) 384-3904

Contact Person: Alice Cottingham, Executive Director.
Officers or Principals: Alice Cottingham, Executive Director ($35,625); Lucretia Smith, Assistant Director ($34,001); Kimberly Grimshaw, President; Karin Candelaria, Administrative Assistant; Chris D'Arpa, Development Director.
Mission or Interest: Grant-making philanthropy focusing on grassroots organizations in the Chicago area. Priority interests are, "low-income communities, civil and human rights (e.g., women, lesbian and gay), workers' rights, the environment, multi-racial efforts, and international solidarity work." Grants up to $7,000 are made to organizations with annual budgets less than $100,000.
Accomplishments: In fifteen years of grant-making they have awarded $1.6 million. In the fiscal year ending June 1994, they awarded $137,121 in grant money. Top recipients included: $12,441 for the New World Resource Center, $7,000 each for the Networking for Democracy for Palestine Solidarity Committee, Lesbian and Gay Community Center of Chicago, Canfield/Austin Interfaith Action Network, Robbins Recreation/Training Center, Union of Palestinian Women's Association, $6,000 for Insight Arts, $5,900 for the Funding Exchange, $5,000 each for the Peace and Justice Radio Project, Women in the Director's Chair, CCISSA, Pintig Cultural Group, and the Prison Action Group.
Net Revenue: FY ending 6/94 $283,142 **Net Expenses:** $288,663 73%/12%/14% **Net Assets:** $38,771
Products or Services: Grants, conferences, and workshops.
Tax Status: 501(c)(3) **Annual Report:** No. **Employees:** 4
Board of Directors or Trustees: Bennie Bailey, Kay Berkson, Sarah Bradley (Ounce of Prevention Fund), Anne Christopherson (Women & Children First Bookstore), Steven Feuerstein, Mabbie Gibbs, Prof. Kirk Harris, Dale Hayes, Maha Jarad (Exec. Dir., Union of Palestinian Women's Assoc.), Dubra Lazard, Cherie Lockett, Nancy Myers, Jose Navarro (Lawyers Committee for Civil Rights), Esther Nieves (Erie Neighborhood House), Francisco Ramos (Centro San Bonifacio), Jill Rhode, Dave Spencer, Carlos Vega (Prison Action Committee), Dave Spencer, Marie Villanueva (Asian American Inst.), Stan West.
Periodicals: *Crossroads Fund* (biannual newsletter).
Internships: Yes, minimum three months commitment.
Other Information: Jean Hardisty of Political Research Associates was a former President of the Crossroads Fund. They are a member of the Funding Exchange. The Fund received $253,320, or 89% of revenue, from gifts and grants awarded by foundations, companies and individuals. (These grants included $6,000 from the Vanguard Public Foundation, $1,000 from the New Prospect Foundation, and $1,000 from the Rex Foundation.) $24,998 net, or 9%, from a special fund-raising event, "Dancin' with the Grass." The remaining revenue came from interest on savings and temporary cash investments, and miscellaneous sources.

Cuba Information Project
198 Broadway, Suite 800
New York, NY 10038   **Phone:**   (212) 227-3422   **E-Mail:** infocuba@igc.apc.org
USA   **Fax:**   (212) 227-4859

Contact Person: Leslie Cagan.
Mission or Interest: "To nurture a national movement working to end the economic blockade against Cuba and to normalize relations with our neighbor, Cuba." The project believes that the economic blockade hurts the Cuban people, not Castro, and since other countries ignore the embargo, it is the United States who will be isolated in the world community.
Accomplishments: "Our organizing materials have helped local groups get organized; we help people around the country get involved; provide up-to-date information on developments in U.S. policy; and have helped send millions of dollars of humanitarian aid to the Cuban people."
Products or Services: Directory of organizations working to change U.S. policy toward Cuba, organizing materials, legislative updates, videos, more.
Tax Status: 501(c)(3) **Annual Report:** No. **Employees:** 2
Periodicals: *Cuba Action* (newsletter).
Other Information: In 1995 the Project received $1,000 from Resist.

Cultural Survival
46 Brattle St.
Cambridge, MA 02138   **Phone:**   (617) 441-5400
USA   **Fax:**   (617) 441-5417   **Web-Page:** http://csinc@cs.org

Contact Person: Kevin Kinsella, Membership Coordinator.
Officers or Principals: Alexander See, Manager ($46,224); Theodore MacDonald, Project Director ($45,063); Dominique Irvine, Manager ($44,509); David Maybury-Lewis, President; Cheryl Abbott, Director.
Mission or Interest: "Nonprofit Human Rights organization specializing in the human rights of indigenous people and ethnic minorities."

Accomplishments: Its publication, *Cultural Survival Quarterly*, has won awards. Recently held a conference at Harvard University on Native American Gaming - a first on this topic anywhere. In the fiscal year ending August 1994, the organization spent $858,229 on its programs. The largest program, with expenditures of $423,187, "imports sustainably harvested non-timber forest products, the sales from which protect endangered rain forests worldwide. Funds generated from these sales support indigenous peoples to be economically stable." $361,010 was awarded in grants.
Net Revenue: FY ending 8/94 $1,370,037 ($158,360, or 12%, from government grants)
Net Expenses: $1,307,571 66%/33%/1% **Net Assets:** (-$222,108) **Citations:** 125:105
Products or Services: Publications and reports.
Tax Status: 501(c)(3) **Annual Report:** Yes. **Employees:** 8
Board of Directors or Trustees: Lawrence Fouraker, Joseph Schmidt, Prof. S. James Anaya (College of Law, Univ. of IA), Barbara Ettinger, Rueben Shohet, John Terborgh (Center for Tropical Conservation, Duke Univ.), Lester Anderson, David Smith (Vice Dean, Harvard Law School), Leon Eisenburg (Dean, Harvard Medical School), Marguerite Robinson.
Periodicals: *Cultural Survival Quarterly* (quarterly journal).
Internships: Yes, contact Pia Maybury-Lewis.
Other Information: Cultural Survival received $459,560, or 34% of revenue, from program services, including payments from businesses promoting Cultural Survival's products. $352,700, or 26%, from gifts and grants awarded by foundations, businesses, and individuals. (These grants included $2,000 from the Aaron and Martha Schecter Charitable Foundation, $1,250 from the Compton Foundation, and $250 from the Vanguard Public Foundation.) $311,278 net, or 23%, from the sale of inventory. $158,360, or 12%, from government grants. $55,741 net, or 4%, from special fund-raising events. The remaining revenue came from interest on savings and temporary cash investments. Among its assets, Cultural Survival held a farm valued at $5,600.

DataCenter
464 19th St.
Oakland, CA 94612
USA

Phone: (510) 835-4692

Contact Person: Fred Setterberg, President.
Officers or Principals: Kim Klein, Vice President ($0); Eric Leenson, Secretary/Treasurer ($0); Fred Geoff, Executive Director.
Mission or Interest: Maintains a library and provides informational services. Collects articles and information and files it topically under such categories as labor, economics, third world, media, Central America, corporate responsibility, and more.
Accomplishments: In 1994 the DataCenter spent $440,630 on its programs. Approximately 570 patrons used the library in person. Other clients used its customized clipping services. Other projects include monitoring plant closings and layoffs, and publishing the information in the *Plant Shutdowns Monitor*, that had 12 subscribers. A bibliographic newsletter on culture, diversity, and freedom of expression issues, *CultureWatch*, that had 175 subscribers. A monthly collection of newspaper clippings from Latin America called *Information Services Latin America*, that had 248 subscribers. *Third World Resources* that publishes information related to third world regions and had 1,500 subscribers. Many of the DataCenter's clients and users are educators and other nonprofit organizations, so DataCenter reaches an audience much larger than its subscription base and patron count.
Net Revenue: 1994 $570,914 **Net Expenses:** $566,170 78%/13%/9% **Net Assets:** $51,174 **Citations:** 7:209
Products or Services: Third World Resources Directory (1994, Orbis Books), clipping services, publications, library and informational services.
Tax Status: 501(c)(3)
Board of Directors or Trustees: Dean Emeritus Ben Bagdikian (Graduate School of Journalism, UC Berkeley), Elizabeth Farnsworth (correspondent & producer, MacNeil/Lehrer NewsHour), Isao Fujimoto (UC Davis), Dan Geiger (Vanguard Foundation).
Periodicals: *Plant Shutdowns Monitor* (monthly report), *CultureWatch* (monthly newsletter), *Information Services Latin America* (monthly collection of news clippings), *Third World Resources* (quarterly journal).
Other Information: The DataCenter received $350,484, or 61% of revenue, from gifts and grants awarded by foundations, businesses, and individuals. (These grants included $82,250 from the John D. and Catherine T. MacArthur Foundation, $40,000 from the Public Welfare Foundation, $40,000 from the Unitarian Universalist Veatch Program, $20,000 from the Tides Foundation, $20,000 from the Winston Foundation for Peace, $20,000 from the C.S. Fund, $20,000 from the Jessie Smith Noyes Foundation, $15,000 from the Deer Creek Foundation, $15,000 from the Funding Exchange, $15,000 from the HKH Foundation, $10,000 from the Wallace Alexander Gerbode Foundation, $10,000 from the McKay Foundation, $10,000 from the Warsh-Mott Legacy, $6,000 from the Cook Brothers Educational Fund, $5,000 from the Ottinger Foundation, $5,000 from the South Coast Foundation, $5,000 from the Tides Foundation, $5,000 from CarEth Foundation, $3,500 from the Angelina Fund, and $1,000 from the Compton Foundation.) $212,493, or 37%, from publications, research, and library-use fees. $4,882, or 1%, from interest on savings and temporary cash investments. $3,055, or 1%, from rental income.

Daughters of Sarah
3801 N. Keeler
Chicago, IL 60641
USA

Contact Person: Barbara Daly, President.
Officers or Principals: Barbara Daly, President ($0); Patti Manglis, Secretary ($0); Leslie Lewis, Treasurer ($0).
Mission or Interest: "To promote the cause of Christian feminism, primarily by the publication and distribution of a magazine, *Daughters of Sarah*, and other related literature."
Accomplishments: *Daughters of Sarah* has approximately 5,000 subscribers. In June 1993, the organization spent $117,973 on its programs.

Net Revenue: FY ending 6/93 $132,636 **Net Expenses:** $129,847 91%/7%/2% **Net Assets:** (-$22,144)
Tax Status: 501(c)(3)
Board of Directors or Trustees: Wanda Lollar.
Periodicals: *Daughters of Sarah* (magazine).
Other Information: Sarah refers to the Old Testament figure, wife of Jewish patriarch Abraham and mother of Isaac. The organization received $88,960, or 67% of revenue, from magazine subscriptions. $27,490, or 21%, from gifts and grants awarded by foundations, corporations and individuals. $8,709, or 7%, from mail-order sales of back issues. $3,910, or 3%, from advertising in *Daughters of Sarah* (the magazine only sells advertising space to promote Christian feminist literature). $3,051, or 2%, from mailing list rentals and sales. The remaining revenue came from interest on savings and temporary cash investments, dividends and interest from securities, and other miscellaneous sources.

Deer Creek Foundation
720 Olive St., Suite 1975
St. Louis, MO 63101   **Phone:**   (314) 241-3228
USA

Contact Person: Mary Stake Hawker, Director.   **Officers or Principals:** Mary Stake Hawker, Director ($127,595); Prof. Philip Kurland, Trustee ($3,500); Pamela A. Ferguson, Trustee ($3,500).
Mission or Interest: "Interested primarily in the advancement and preservation of the governance of society by rule of the majority, with protection of basic rights as provided by the Constitution and the Bill of Rights." Focus on groups that protect "the separation of church and state," abortion rights, and the environment.
Accomplishments: In 1994 the Foundation awarded $692,038 in grants. Recipients of the largest awards included: four grants totaling $85,000 for People for the American Way, three grants totaling $65,000 for the Government Accountability Project, two grants totaling $55,000 for Catholics for a Free Choice, three grants totaling $50,000 for the Center for Budget and Policy Priorities, $35,000 for the Planned Parenthood Federation of America, $30,000 for Public Employees for Environmental Responsibility, and two grants totaling $30,000 for the Center for Public Integrity.
Net Revenue: 1994 $1,342,123 **Net Expenses:** $1,031,888 **Net Assets:** $9,214,557
Tax Status: 501(c)(3)
Board of Directors or Trustees: James Kautz, Teresa Fischer, Peter Fischer, Dr. Lattie Coor.
Other Information: The Foundation received $675,125, or 50% of revenue, from gifts and grants awarded by foundations, businesses, and individuals. $336,098, or 25%, from dividends and interest from securities. $307,423, or 23%, from capital gains on the sale of securities. The remaining income came from interest on savings and temporary cash investments, and other miscellaneous sources. The Foundation held $8,710,847, or 95% of assets, in corporate stock.

Defenders of Animal Rights
14412 Old York Rd.
Phoenix, MD 21131   **Phone:**   (410) 527-1466
USA

Contact Person: James Kovic, Vice President.   **Officers or Principals:** Mary Jo Kovic, President ($44,011); James Kovic, Vice President ($41,018); Elizabeth Brooks, Secretary ($0).
Mission or Interest: Animal rights organization that provides animal rescue, shelter and care.
Accomplishments: In 1994, Defenders of Animal Rights spent $584,794 on its programs. Most of this, $446,631, was spent on care and shelter for animals. The rest, $138,163, was spent on public education about the rights of animals.
Net Revenue: 1994 $692,818 **Net Expenses:** $754,564 78%/11%/11% **Net Assets:** $1,241,733 **Citations:** 3:222
Tax Status: 501(c)(3)
Board of Directors or Trustees: Pat Hopkins, Maureen Myers, A. Hopkins, Bobbie Stadler, Eileen Rathburn.
Other Information: The organization received $609,733, or 88% of revenue, from gifts and grants awarded by foundations, businesses, and individuals. $62,651, or 9%, from program services, such as spaying and neutering, and animal adoptions. $13,020, or 2%, from interest on savings and temporary cash investments. The remaining revenue came from miscellaneous sources.

Democratic Leadership Council (DLC)
518 C St., N.E.
Washington, DC 20002   **Phone:**   (202) 546-0007   **E-Mail:** info@dlcppi.org
USA   **Fax:**   (202) 544-5002   **Web-Page:** http://www.dlcppi.org

Contact Person: Al From, President/Treasurer.   **Officers or Principals:** Al From, President/Treasurer ($225,000); Deb Smulyan, Secretary ($140,000); Sen. Joe Lieberman (D-CT), Chairman.
Mission or Interest: Democratic policy organization associated with the centrist wing of the Democratic party. Lobbies and holds debate forums on national defense, trade, the economy, and social policy. "The Democratic Leadership Council was founded in 1985 by Democrats who sought to renew our party's sense of national purpose and restore its competitiveness in presidential elections...Shaped by a succession of distinguished Democratic elected officials, including Bill Clinton and Al Gore, the DLC agenda challenged conventional wisdom on issues from national service to welfare reform and reintroducing the long-missing values of responsibility and community into the party's intellectual debate." The Progressive Policy Institute is the DLC's in-house think tank, and is not separately incorporated (for more information see the separate listing for the Progressive Policy Institute.)

Accomplishments: In 1993 the Council spent $1,652,873 on its programs.
Net Revenue: 1993 $3,431,166 (1994 expenses were up to $4,441,195) **Net Expenses:** $3,492,990 53%/44%/3%
Net Assets: $3,804,918 **Citations:** 616:37
Products or Services: Conferences and training sessions for Democratic candidates. Research and policy studies.
Tax Status: 501(c)(4)
Board of Directors or Trustees: Michael Steinhardt, Loyd Hackler, Lindy Boggs. Previous Chairmen included: then-Governor Bill Clinton, Democratic Senators Chuck Robb (VA), Sam Nunn (GA), and John Breaux (LA), and Representatives Dick Gephardt (MO), and Dave McCurdy (OK).
Periodicals: *The New Democrat* (magazine).
Other Information: Founded in 1985. Affiliated with the 501(c)(3) Progressive Foundation at the same address. The Council received $2,128,670, or 62% of revenue, from membership dues from elected officials and others. $1,214,912, or 35%, from gifts and grants awarded by foundations, businesses, and individuals. $47,423, or 1%, from interest on savings and temporary cash investments. $40,253, or 1%, from dividends and interest from securities. The remaining revenue came from publications and other miscellaneous income.

Democratic National Committee (DNC)

430 S. Capitol St., S.E.
Washington, DC 20003   **Phone:** (202) 863-8000
USA

Officers or Principals: Sen. Christopher Dodd (D-CT), General Chair; Don Fowler, National Chair.
Mission or Interest: National organization of the United States Democratic Party.

Democratic Socialists of America (DSA)

180 Varick St., 12th Floor
New York, NY 10038   **Phone:** (212) 927-8610   **E-Mail:** dsa@igc.apc.org
USA   **Web-Page:** http://www.dsausa.org/dsa

Contact Person: Michael Lighty, Director. **Officers or Principals:** Michael Lighty, Director ($37,905); Alan Charney, Director ($5,583); Christine R. Riddiough, Political Director; Prof. Cornel West, Dolores Huerta, Barbara Ehrenreich, Honorary Chairs.
Mission or Interest: Promotion of democratic socialism in the Unites States. Seeks to create a broad-based coalition of labor unions, minorities, feminists, lesbians and homosexuals, peace activists, and others.
Accomplishments: In January 1996 the DSA held public hearings in Boston on "Economic Insecurity." Panelists included Democratic congressmen Sen. John Kerry, and Reps. Barney Frank, John Oliver, Martin Meehan, J. Joseph Moakley, and John P. Kennedy II. Other speakers and panelists included Ellen Frank of the Center for Popular Economics, Massachusetts NOW, ACORN, Massachusetts AFL-CIO, and Ronnie Dugger of the National Alliance. Other DSA hearings on economic insecurity are planned. DSA is the largest socialist organization in the U.S. and a member of the Socialist International. Approximately forty Youth Section Chapters on campuses nationwide. In 1993 the organization spent $210,022 on its programs. The largest program, with expenditures of $102,781, was public education to "promoted greater public understanding of the traditions of democratic socialism in the U.S. and of the achievements of individual democratic socialists and institutions with democratic socialist traditions." $61,743 was spent on the distribution of pamphlets and newsletters. $45,498 was spent "educating the public on the benefits of the Canadian health care system."
Net Revenue: 1993 $403,403 **Net Expenses:** $417,304 50%/20%/30% **Net Assets:** $310,467
Tax Status: 501(c)(4) **Annual Report:** No. **Employees:** 7
Board of Directors or Trustees: Theresa Alt, Pat Belcon, Dorothy Benz, Jack Clark, Howard Croft, Suzanne Crowell, Virginia Franco, J. Hughes, Claire Kaplan, Jeff Lacher, Jose Laluz, Frank Llewellyn, Sherri Levine, Mark Levinson, Jo-Ann Mort, Dave Rathke, Chris Riddiough, Krista Schneider, Joe Schwartz, Ruth Spitz, Kurt Stand, Steve Tarzynski, Juanita Webster.
Periodicals: *Democratic Left* (bimonthly magazine).
Internships: Yes, paid summer internships.
Other Information: Affiliated with the 501(c)(3) Institute for Democratic Socialism at the same address. The two affiliates had combined net revenues of $484,235, net expenses of $466,192, and net assets of $239,099. The DSA received $351,475, or 87% of revenue, from gifts and grants awarded by foundations, businesses, and individuals. $14,001, or 3%, from dividends and interest from securities. $10,151, or 3%, from conference fees. $9,458, or 2%, from the sale of subscriptions. $9,075, or 2%, from the sale of advertising. $8,405, or 2%, from capital gains on the sale of assets. The remaining revenue came from mailing list rentals.

Denver - Havana Friendship / Sister Cities Project

1700 Lincoln, Suite 3901
39th Floor at One Norwest Center
Denver, CO 80203   **Phone:** (303) 861-4305
USA   **Fax:**   (303) 832-5010

Contact Person: Harry Nier. **Officers or Principals:** Harry Nier; Emily Coffey.
Mission or Interest: Working to develop a sister city project with the capitol of communist Cuba.
Accomplishments: Obtained hundreds of endorsements locally and nation-wide.

Desert Moon Periodicals

1226 A Calle De Comercio
Santa Fe, NM 87505   **Phone:** (505) 474-6311   **E-Mail:** xines@nets.com
USA   **Fax:** (505) 474-6317   **Web-Page:** http://www.xines.com

Contact Person: Joseph H. Enenbach, President.
Mission or Interest: Distributes magazines and 'zines that cover a multitude of topics. Includes: politics, culture, fashion, music, counter-culture, technology, environment, gay and lesbian issues, more. Many of the periodicals offered by groups in The Left Guide are available here.
Products or Services: Catalog of materials.
Tax Status: For profit. **Annual Report:** No. **Employees:** 15
Periodicals: *The Usual Suspects* (catalog).   **Internships:** No.

Design Industries Foundation Fighting AIDS

150 W. 26th St., Suite 602
New York, NY 10001   **Phone:** (212) 727-3100
USA

Contact Person: Rosemary Kuropat, Executive Director.   **Officers or Principals:** Rosemary Kuropat, Executive Director ($85,750); Anneliese Estrada, Creative Director ($69,835); Steven Kolb, Director ($62,017); Michael Sorrentino, Chairman; Patricia Green, Fern Mallis, Vice Chairs; Dorothy Kallins, Secretary; William Murphy, Treasurer.
Mission or Interest: Programs to educate firms and associations, and grants for organizations fighting AIDS.
Accomplishments: In the fiscal year ending June 1994, the Foundation spent $2,855,255. Of this, $1,939,906 was awarded in grants. $626,106 was spent on training and education.
Net Revenue: FY ending 6/94 $3,679,432 **Net Expenses:** $4,098,688 70%/15%/15% **Net Assets:** (-$410,990)
Citations: 77:118   **Tax Status:** 501(c)(3)
Board of Directors or Trustees: Daniel Baldinger, Phil Beuth (pres., Early Morning & Late Night Television, Capital Cities/ABC), Darwin Davis (senior V.P., The Equitable), Louis Fabrizio (advertising manager, *The New York Times*), Annie Flanders, Amy Gross (editorial director, *ELLE*), John Jay, Ayse Kenmore, William Maguire (Interiorspace Intl.), Michael Perlis (publisher, *DETAILS Magazine*), David Sheppard, George Slowik Jr. (publisher, *Out Magazine*).
Other Information: The Foundation received $3,026,393, or 82% of revenue, from gifts and grants awarded by foundations, businesses, and individuals. $417,173 net, or 11%, from special fundraising events. (The Foundation hosted 52 events, including: Art for Life, Christmas Oratio, Demand Performance, Living Proof, Boy Dance, Classic Rock with Cousin Brucie, Dykes on Tap Dance, Tom of Finland Dance, Carnival, Lesbian Avengers Dance, Homo Hoedown, Stonewall Night Dream, Playboy 40th Anniversary, She Thing, Tootsies, Tree of Hope, and others.) $225,670 net, or 7%, from the sale of inventory.

Directors Guild of America

7920 Sunset Blvd.
Los Angeles, CA 90046   **Phone:** (310) 289-2000
USA   **Fax:** (310) 289-2029

Contact Person: Glenn J. Gumpel, Executive Director.   **Officers or Principals:** Glenn J. Gumpel, Executive Director ($478,234); Alan Gordon, Executive Director ($195,523); Elliott Williams, General Counsel ($167,214); Warren Adler, Executive Secretary ($150,525); Gene Reynolds, President; Sheldon Leonard, Secretary/Treasurer.
Mission or Interest: "Provides professional representation and education for all its members in addition to promoting the craft of directing."
Accomplishments: Represents approximately 9,500 members.
Net Revenue: 1994 $11,524,320 **Net Expenses:** $8,367,909 **Net Assets:** $34,283,799
Tax Status: 501(c)(5)
Board of Directors or Trustees: Burt Bluestein, Robert Butler, Gilbert Cates, Anita Cooper-Avrick, Andrew Costikyan, Cheryl Downey, Milt Felsen, Arthur Hiller, Jeremy Kagan, John Rich, Elliot Silverstein, Herb Adelman, Bob Jeffords, Scott Berger, Barbara Roche, Peter Runfold.
Periodicals: Newsletter.
Other Information: Founded in 1959. The Guild received $10,838,304, or 86% of gross revenue, from membership dues. $774,286, or 6%, from dividends and interest from securities. $603,978, or 5%, from interest on savings and temporary cash investments. $271,562, or 2%, from program services, including workshops and events. The remaining revenue came from advertising income and other miscellaneous sources.

Disability Rights Education and Defense Fund

2212 6th St.
Berkeley, CA 94710   **Phone:** (510) 644-2555
USA

Contact Person: Linda Kilb, Executive Director.
Officers or Principals: Patrisha A. Wright, Director of Government Affairs ($59,545); Elaine Feingold, Attorney ($59,545); Arlene Mayerson, Attorney ($59,545); Mary Lou Breslin, President; Margaret Jakobson, Secretary; Jeanette Harvey, Treasurer.

Mission or Interest: "Provides research and education on the development of public policy to further the civil rights of disabled people and the independent living movement."
Accomplishments: In the fiscal year ending September 1994, the Fund spent $1,016,983 on its programs. Provided training for the public on the Americans with Disabilities Act. Operates the ADA National Support Center which monitors implementation of the Americans with Disabilities Act. Received $578,293 in court-awarded attorney's fees.
Net Revenue: FY ending 9/94 $1,855,454 **Net Expenses:** $1,351,255 75%/8%/17% **Net Assets:** $482,510
Citations: 47:140
Products or Services: Litigation, training, publications, and lobbying. Conducts lobbying through the Director of Government Affairs, Patrisha Wright.
Tax Status: 501(c)(3)
Board of Directors or Trustees: Ralph Neas (Leadership Conference on Civil Rights), Kim Conner (Senate Office of Research, CA State Senate).
Other Information: The Fund received $611,457, or 33% of revenue, from government grants. $578,293, or 31%, from court-awarded attorney's fees. $532,079, or 28%, from gifts and grants awarded by foundations, businesses, affiliates, and individuals. (These grants included $25,000 from the Rockefeller Family Fund, $20,000 from the Norman Foundation, $10,000 from the Wallace Alexander Gerbode Foundation.) $113,286, or 6%, from training fees. $22,747, or 1%, from product sales. The remaining revenue came from interest on savings and temporary cash investments, and other miscellaneous income. The fund lost $11,737 on the sale of assets other than securities.

Discount Foundation
30 Winter St., Suite 1002
Boston, MA 02108-4720   **Phone:**   (617) 426-7471
USA

Contact Person: Susan Chinn, Executive Director. **Officers or Principals:** Susan Chinn, Executive Director ($34,853); Jeffrey Zinsmeyer, President ($0); Thomas Asher, Secretary/Treasurer ($0).
Mission or Interest: Grant-making foundation focusing on low-income community organizing, homelessness, and public housing tenants' advocacy.
Accomplishments: In the fiscal year ending September 1994, the Foundation awarded $365,000 in grants. Recipients included; $40,000 for the Arkansas Institute for Social Justice, $15,000 each for the National Coalition for the Homeless, Ohio Coalition for the Homeless, Union Neighborhood Assistance Corporation, and National Community Reinvestment Coalition, and $12,000 for the Low Income Housing and Information Service.
Net Revenue: FY ending 9/94 $1,283,048 **Net Expenses:** $538,006 **Net Assets:** $6,594,897
Products or Services: Awards the annual Henry A. Fagan award, "a civic achievement award for outstanding service to poor people."
Tax Status: 501(c)(3)
Board of Directors or Trustees: Margery Tabankin, Garland Yates, Andrea Kydd.
Other Information: The Foundation received $1,060,803, or 83% of revenue, from capital gains on the sale of assets. $203,060, or 16%, from dividends and interest from securities. The remaining revenue came from interest on savings and temporary cash investments, and other miscellaneous sources.

Dissent
(see the Foundation for the Study of Independent Social Ideas)

Dollars & Sense
(see the Economic Affairs Bureau)

E. F. Schumacher Society
140 Jug End Road
Great Barrington, MA 01230   **Phone:**   (413) 528-1737   **E-Mail:** efssociety@aol.com
USA   **Fax:**   (413) 528-4472

Contact Person: Susan Witt, Executive Director.
Officers or Principals: Susan Witt, Executive Director ($26,817); Robert Swann, President ($500); Hildegarde Hannum, Vice President ($0); John McClaughry, Chairman; Gustav Peterson, Treasurer; William Schrenk, Secretary.
Mission or Interest: "To educate in the use and preservation of the natural environment, the importance of the appropriate scale in technology, and in human organizations, and the value of self-sufficient communities...Promotes the ideas inherent in the decentralist tradition and to implement them in practical programs."
Accomplishments: Developed model "micro-lending program," which pooled local citizens savings to make loans considered too small or risky by banks. Developed local currencies, and community land trust systems. In 1995 the Society spent $11,545 on its programs. In June 1996 the Society held a conference on decentralization. Diverse participants include the American Friends Service Committee, Appalachia Science in the Public Interest, Center for Living Democracy, Center for Reflection on the Second Law, Co-op America, Ethan Allen Institute, Family Research Council (conservative policy institute affiliated with Focus on the Family), Heather Foundation, Institute for American Values, Institute for Liberty and Community, International Society for Ecological Economies, Jobs and Environment Campaign, Rockford Institute (paleo-conservative institute), TRANET, and many others.
Net Revenue: 1995 $149,720 **Net Expenses:** $143,738 78%/22%/0% **Net Assets:** $43,414

Products or Services: Publications, papers, conferences, plans and models for community-level democracy. Library including over 2,000 books and unpublished papers from the personal collection of E. F. Schumacher.

Tax Status: 501(c)(3)   **Employees:** 3

Board of Directors or Trustees: Kirkpatrick Sale (author, Human Scale), David Ehrenfeld (author, The Arrogance of Humanism), Nancy Jack Todd, Joyce Scheffey.

Periodicals: *Newsletter* (quarterly).   **Internships:** Yes.

Other Information: Ernst Friedrich Schumacher (1911-1977) is best known as the author of the best-selling Small is Beautiful. He was Chief Economic Adviser to the British Coal Board from 1950 to 1970. In 1955 Schumacher traveled to Burma as an adviser. While there he developed the principles of what he called "Buddhist economics," based on the belief that "production from local resources for local needs is the most rational way of economic life." These theories led him to become an innovator in "appropriate technology: earth and user-friendly technology matched to the scale of community life." Chairman John McClaughry is the conservative/libertarian president of the Ethan Allen Institute and the Institute for Liberty and Community. He is a former Vermont State Senator and a policy advisor to President Ronald Reagan. The Society received $116,381, or 78% of revenue, from gifts and grants awarded by foundations, individuals, and businesses. (These grants included $27,632 from Ecologically Sustainable Development - a USAID funded organization, $5,000 from the Trust for Mutual Understanding, and $5,000 from the Weeden Foundation). $12,435, or 8%, from service fees. $11,744, or 8%, from membership dues. $6,976, or 5%, from the sale of literature. The remaining revenue came from speaking fees.

Earth Action

143 W. 29th St., Suite 902
New York, NY 10001
USA

Contact Person: Gayle Anne Kelley, Executive Director.

Officers or Principals: Gayle Anne Kelley, Executive Director ($14,185).

Mission or Interest: Preserving the planet, native cultures, and providing food and clothing for the needy.

Accomplishments: In 1993 Earth Action spent $135,294 on its programs. The largest program, with expenditures of $72,462, produced the film. "Circle of Women," which deals with "the daily struggles of Native American women living in the Central United States." $23,923 was spent on the World Mission, to "show respect for native people which is paramount to our survival." $15,416 was spent on Street Action, to provide food and clothing for the homeless and elderly. $11,748 was spent on Environmental Action, including lectures about preserving the planet. $11,745 was spent on Children in Action, a program that works with children in New York City schools, whereby the children collect food and clothes for the needy.

Net Revenue: 1993 $193,690 **Net Expenses:** $200,321 68%/21%/12% **Net Assets:** $12,972

Tax Status: 501(c)(3)

Board of Directors or Trustees: Deborah Ann Blakeslee, Barbara Darwell Collins, James Quincy Collins, Elliot Glenn Fread, Edwin Curtis Fry, Lisa Ann Johnson, Christie Marie McGinn, Jeffrey Steiger.

Other Information: Earth Action received $192,820, or 99.5% of revenue, from gifts and grants awarded by foundations, businesses, and individuals. The remaining revenue came from membership dues, the sale of inventory, program service fees, and other miscellaneous sources.

Earth Action Network / *E: The Environmental Magazine*

28 Knight St.
Norwalk, CT 06851   **Phone:** (203) 854-5559
USA   **Fax:**   (203) 866-0602

Contact Person: Douglas Moss, President.   **Officers or Principals:** Douglas Moss, President ($17,625); Deborah Kamlani, Secretary ($10,887); Leslie Pardue, Vice President ($0).

Mission or Interest: Publishes *E: The Environmental Magazine*. *E* "promotes respect for the environment and creates a greater public awareness of environmental problems and possible solutions to these problems."

Accomplishments: In the fiscal year ending June 1994, the Network spent $666,281 to publish and distribute *E*. The magazine has a circulation of approximately 70,000. The typical reader is female, age 25-34, has a median household income of $45,250, and has graduated from college and done some post-graduate study. *E* won the 1992 Utne Reader Award for Best Special Interest Publication, a 1993 Project Censored Citation, the 1992 Ozzie Award for Design Excellence (awarded by *Magazine Design and Production*), and other awards. Turner Broadcasting and the Eco-Channel choose stories from *E* to be featured on weekly environmental television programming. *The Washington Post* said *E* is "...bursting with good reading...much finely edited material."

Net Revenue: FY ending 6/94 $859,324 **Net Expenses:** $811,573 82%/15%/3% **Net Assets:** (-$486,533) **Citations:** 1:240

Tax Status: 501(c)(3)

Periodicals: *E: The Environmental Magazine* (bimonthly).

Other Information: The Network received $294,367, or 34% of revenue, from the sale of advertising space in *E*. $279,474, or 33%, from magazine subscriptions. $265,682, or 31%, from gifts and grants awarded by foundations, businesses, and individuals. (These grants included $100,891 from the Charles Stewart Mott Foundation, $10,000 from the Town Creek Foundation.) $10,957, or 1%, from mailing list rentals to other tax exempt organizations. The remaining revenue came from syndication fees, and interest on savings and temporary cash investments. Total revenue generated by the publication of the magazine (subscriptions, advertising, syndication and mailing lists) was $593,538. The cost of producing and distributing the magazine was $666,281. So the magazine required subsidization of $72,743. This equals a subsidization of approximately $1.04 per subscriber for the year.

Earth Communications / Radio For Peace International (RFPI)

P.O. Box 20728
Portland, OR 97220   **Phone:** (508) 252-3639   **E-Mail:** rfpicr@sol.racsa.co.cr
USA   **Fax:** (508) 255-5216

Contact Person: F. Richard Schneider, Co-Founder.
Mission or Interest: Shortwave radio broadcasting 18 hours a day, Radio For Peace International. Programing includes. "Feminist International Radio Endeavor" (FIRE), "The Far Right Radio Review" which monitors and analyzes right-wing and hate-radio broadcast on shortwave, United Nations and UNESCO reports, "This Way Out" lesbian and gay radio magazine, "Food Not Bombs" radio network, "World Goodwill Forum/Lucius Productions," "Voices of Our World" from Maryknoll Media Relations, and much more. Radio For Peace transmitters are located on the campus of the University for Peace (created by Resolution 35/55, Dec. 5, 1980, in the UN General Assembly) in Costa Rica. Programing can be picked up on various frequencies at different times of the day. Call or write for details.
Accomplishments: Approximately 35,000 listeners a day. Following the bombing of the Murrah Federal Building in Oklahoma City, numerous media organizations contacted the Far Right Radio Review. Organizations included CNN, ABC TV, CBS Radio, *The New York Times, The Chicago Tribune, The Miami Herald, The Plains Dealer, The Boston Globe, The San Francisco Examiner, The Nashville Banner, The Detroit News, The Wall Street Journal, U.S. News & World Report,* NPR, and even some news organizations from outside of the United States. Information was also requested by The National Democratic Committee and the Southern Poverty Law Center. In 1995, Feminist International Radio Endeavor won awards from the United Nations Educational, Scientific and Cultural Organization (UNESCO), and the Women's International News Gathering Service (WINGS). In 1994 Earth Communications spent $136,831 on its programs. $131,875 was spent on broadcasting, and $4,955 on other projects such as workshops and symposiums.
Net Revenue: 1994 $171,572 **Net Expenses:** $165,824 83%/17%/0% **Net Assets:** $92,161
Tax Status: 501(c)(3)
Periodicals: *VISTA* (monthly newsletter).
Other Information: Earth Communications received $90,883, or 53% of revenue, from gifts and grants awarded by foundations and individuals. (These grants included $10,000 from the Rex Foundation.) $71,258, or 42%, from air time and programming. $4,955, or 3%, from conferences. $4,263, or 2%, from membership dues. The remaining revenue came from capital gains on the sale of securities.

Earth Day 2000

116 New Montgomery St., Suite 530
San Francisco, CA 94105   **Phone:** (415) 495-5987
USA   **Fax:** (415) 543-1480

Contact Person: Caroline Harwood.
Mission or Interest: Environmental lobbying organization.
Accomplishments: Free the Planet Campaign which delivered 1.2 million signatures in support of an Environmental Bill of Rights to Congress.
Tax Status: 501(c)(4)
Board of Directors or Trustees: Paul Hawker, Joel Makower, Alice Tepper-Marlin, Alan Gravitz, Chris Desser, Jeffrey Hollender.
Internships: Yes.
Other Information: Affiliated with the 501(c)(3) Earth Day Resources.

Earth Day Resources

116 New Montgomery St., Suite 530
San Francisco, CA 94105   **Phone:** (415) 495-5987
USA   **Fax:** (415) 543-1480

Contact Person: Caroline Harwood.   **Officers or Principals:** Christine Desser, President ($0); Gina Collins, Treasurer ($0); Joan Clayburgh, Secretary ($0); Matt Wilson, Director.
Mission or Interest: "Developing educational materials for schools and the general public regarding various local and global environmental problems; coordinating events urging recycling and responsible solid waste management; promoting and assisting local Earth Day events and activities...Green consumer clearinghouse."
Accomplishments: "Settlements over green labeling laws; lead sponsor of Earth Day 1995; Free the Planet Campaign which delivered 1.2 million signatures in support of an Environmental Bill of Rights to Congress." In the fiscal year ending June 1994, the organization spent $20,055 on its programs. This included $3,121 in grant awards.
Net Revenue: FY ending 6/94 $11,381 **Net Expenses:** $21,110 **Net Assets:** $1,757
Products or Services: Earth Day curriculum guides, How to Organize an Environmental Event, fact sheets, more.
Tax Status: 501(c)(3)
Board of Directors or Trustees: Paul Hawker, Joel Makower, Alice Tepper-Marlin (Council on Economic Priorities), Alan Gravitz, Chris Desser, Jeffrey Hollender.
Internships: Yes.
Other Information: Affiliated with the 501(c)(4) Earth Day 2000. The organization received $11,381, or 100% of revenues, from gifts and grants awarded by foundations, businesses, and individuals.

Earth Day USA
P.O. Box 470
Peterborough, NH 03458   **Phone:**   (603) 924-7720
USA

Contact Person: Bruce Anderson, President.   **Officers or Principals:** Bruce Anderson, President ($34,462).
Mission or Interest: Instructs, assists, coordinates, and promotes Earth Day events.
Accomplishments: In the fiscal year ending June 1994, Earth Day USA spent $219,923 on its programs. The largest program, with expenditures of $80,780, was outreach which works with "thousands of Earth Day volunteers, other organizers, and companies to support them in their efforts in coordinating their Earth Day activities with newsletters, organizers manuals, networking, press exposure, other support material and information, sponsorship opportunities, and fund raising mechanisms." $65,294 on media relations and the creation of public service announcements. $50,765 was spent hosting an annual conference.
Net Revenue: FY ending 6/94 $396,865 **Net Expenses:** $359,444 59%/28%/13% **Net Assets:** (-$30,007)
Tax Status: 501(c)(3)
Board of Directors or Trustees: Carolyn Chase (San Diego Earth Day), Glen Gaskins (Environmental Education Concepts), Rick Katzenberg, Pam Lippe (Earth Day New York), Paul Miller, Claes Nobel (United Earth), John Quigley (Earth Services), Marie Toohey (Earth Day New Jersey).
Periodicals: *Earth Day News* (newsletter).
Other Information: Earth Day USA received $219,923, or 55% of revenue, from gifts and grants awarded by foundations, businesses, and individuals. $138,167, or 35%, from royalty and licencing fees for the use of the Official Earth Day Logo. $24,672, or 6%, from conference fees. $9,711, or 2%, from the sale of *Earth Day News*. $4,126, or 1%, from the sale of inventory. The remaining revenue came from interest on savings and temporary cash investments.

Earth First!
P.O. Box 1415
Eugene, OR 97440   **Phone:**   (741) 541-9191   **E-Mail:** earthfirst@igc.apc.org
USA   **Fax:**   (741) 541-9192

Contact Person: Kimberly Dawn, Managing Editor.
Officers or Principals: Connie Ross, Business Manager; Leslie Hemstreet, Craig Beneville, Pam Reber, Jim Flynn, Editorial Staff.
Mission or Interest: "No Compromise in defense of Mother Earth!" Radical environmentalists who are most closely associated with sabotaging lumber equipment and 'spiking' trees with a metal stake so that cutting the tree could result in the breaking of a saw blade or chain saw chain and the injury of the cutter. Earth First! claims no injury due to spiking has been linked to them, and that this is an invention of the "corporate press." Earth First! claims to carry out only non-violent protests, such as chaining themselves to trees and equipment, but has no qualms about causing the destruction of property and economic damage to logging companies and others. This practice is often referred to as "monkey wrenching", a term from the 1975 Edward Abbey novel, The Monkey Wrench Gang. Earth First! members, including founder Dave Foreman, have pled guilty to charges of destroying ski lift pylons, cutting a powerline tower, and other acts of criminal destruction. In 1990 Earth First! members Judy Bari, a former union organizer, and Darryl Cherney were injured when a pipe bomb went off in Bari's car. Initially the FBI suspected Bari and Cherney of transporting the bomb, but no charges were brought.
Accomplishments: The organization is best known for its activities to preserve forests and stop timber cutting. Earth First! has played a "critical role" in a number of environmental campaigns. "The tree sits and blockades which led to the 'spotted owl controversy;' the naming and mapping of the Headwaters Forest in the redwoods of northern California; the road building delays which held off the Forest Service until the injunction on Cove/Mallard in Idaho; Oxleas Wood in England being spared; Mt. Graham telescope project delays." Earth First! helped to make the philosophy of 'deep ecology' - a concept of the world as nature-centered rather than human-centered - a larger part of the environmental movement.
Products or Services: T-shirts, bumperstickers, hats, and "other Trinkets and Snake Oil."
Tax Status: 501(c)(4)   **Annual Report:** No.
Periodicals: *Earth First!* (eight times a year).   **Internships:** No.
Other Information: The *Earth First!* journal has been publishing since 1986. Earth First! is frequently critical of Washington, DC-based lobbying environmental organizations, including Greenpeace. These organizations are considered all talk and fundraising, with little action. Earth First! Was founded in 1980 by Dave Foreman - a lobbyist for the Wilderness Society, Howie Wolke, Bart Koehler, Ron Kezar, Mike Roselle, and Susan Morgan. Dave Foreman left the group charging them with being more interested in promoting class warfare than with preserving the wilderness. Members charged Foreman, who had supported Barry Goldwater's presidential campaign in 1964, with being "an un-repentant right-wing thug" who happened to support wilderness preservation.

Earth Island Institute (EII)
300 Broadway, Suite 28
San Francisco, CA 94133   **Phone:**   (415) 788-3666   **E-Mail:** earthisland@igc.apc.org
USA   **Fax:**   (415) 788-7324   **Web-Page:** http://www.earthisland.org/ei/

Contact Person: John Knox, Executive Director.   **Officers or Principals:** Daniel Moses, project Director ($37,303); John Knox, Executive Director ($26,732); David Phillips, Executive Director ($26,732); Carl Anthony, President; Robert Wilkinson, Vice President; Tim Rands, Secretary; Peter Winkler, Counsel; David R. Brower, Chairman. (Compensation is from 1993.)
Mission or Interest: Develops and supports "CPR" (Conservation, Preservation, and Restoration) of the environment. EII helps initiate new projects and supports existing projects through a core facility and staff. The core group helps with program development, fundraising, strategic planning, public outreach, accounting, computer and other technical skills.

Accomplishments: First magazine, *Earth Island Journal*, to be printed on tree-free paper made from kenaf. Funding for this switch to tree-free paper, that costs more than standard paper, initially came from a $10,000 grant from the True North Foundation. The *Utne Reader* called the *Journal* one of the "ten new magazines that made a difference in the past ten years." Helped indigenous people in Borneo map ancestral lands. Rehabilitating Keiko, the whale featured in the movie "Free Willy." Projects investigating environmental quality in minority communities. Their top five projects in 1994 and the amounts spent on them were: International Marine Mammal Project ($1,662,023), Urban Habitat Program ($594,653), Network Services ($315,458), Sea Turtle Restoration Project ($176,827), and Baikal Watch, to fight development of the Siberian lake ($161,455). They also fund the Ben Linder Memorial Fund for Appropriate Technology named for an American citizen killed by Contras in Nicaragua in 1987.
Net Revenue: 1994 $3,593,987 **Net Expenses:** $3,379,369 83%/7%/10% **Net Assets:** $1,020,545 **Citations:** 219:76
Products or Services: Grants and Support for various projects. Lobbying - in 1993 they spent $8,797 on grassroots lobbying.
Tax Status: 501(c)(3) **Annual Report:** Yes. **Employees:** 40
Board of Directors or Trustees: Patricia Cummings, Peter Fugazzotto, Michael Hathaway, Justin Lowe, Maria Moyer-Angus, Melissa Nelson. Advisors include: Lester Brown, Anne and Paul Ehrlich (author, The Population Bomb); Amory Lovins, Eric Utne: others.
Periodicals: *Earth Island Journal, Ocean Alert,* and *Race Poverty and the Environment.*   **Internships:** Yes.
Other Information: The Earth Island Institute was founded in 1982 by David Brower. Brower is often referred to as the "grandfather of the modern environmental movement." He built the Sierra Club from a 2,000 member organization in 1956 into a national organization 77,000 strong in 1969. He was ousted as director of the Sierra Club and went on to found not only the Earth Island Institute, but also the League of Conservation Voters and Friends of the Earth. Brower sees the planned development of society as the key to protecting the environment. The Institute received $2,700,609, or 93% of revenue, from gifts and grants awarded by foundations, businesses, and individuals. (These grants included $50,000 from the Nathan Cummings Foundation, $30,000 from the General Service Foundation, $25,000 from the Columbia Foundation, $10,000 from the Joyce Mertz-Gilmore Foundation, $4,505 from the Environmental Federation of California, $2,000 from the Compton Foundation, $1,000 from the Tides Foundation, $500 from the Animal Welfare Institute, $330 from the Compton Foundation, and $300 from the One World Fund.) $83,505, or 3%, from program service revenues. $45,398, or 2%, from royalties. The remaining income came from interest on savings and temporary cash investments, special fund-raising events, sale of inventory, advertising income, and other miscellaneous sources.

Earth Trust Foundation
20110 Rockport Way
Malibu, CA 90265   **Phone:**   (310) 456-2267
USA

Contact Person: Andrew Beath, President.   **Officers or Principals:** Andrew Beath, President/Secretary/Treasurer ($0).
Mission or Interest: Works with grassroots and 'social justice' activists. Awards grants.
Accomplishments: In 1994 the Foundation spent $382,980 on its programs.
Net Revenue: 1994 $414,050 **Net Expenses:** $408,141 94%/3%/3% **Net Assets:** $81,575
Products or Services: Grants, speakers, books and tapes.
Tax Status: 501(c)(3)
Board of Directors or Trustees: Robert Chartoff, John Zidell, Mark Gerzon.
Other Information: The Foundation received $369,827, or 89% of revenue, from gifts and grants awarded by foundations, companies and individuals. (These grants included $10,000 from the Tides Foundation.) $33,719, or 8%, from the speakers program. $5,586, or 1%, from the sale of books and tapes. The remaining revenue came from membership dues, interest on savings and temporary cash investments, and other miscellaneous sources.

EarthAction
30 Cottage St.
Amherst, MA 01002   **Phone:** (413) 549-8118   **E-Mail:** EarthAction@igc.apc.org
USA   **Fax:**   (413) 549-0544

Contact Person: Lois Barber, International Coordinator.
Officers or Principals: Nicholas Dunlop, President ($79,026); Johannah Bernstein, Regional Coordinator ($73,126); Lois Barber, International Coordinator ($67,542); Teresa McGlashan, Regional Coordinator.
Mission or Interest: "To build political will on a global level in three areas: the global environment, peace, and social justice."
Accomplishments: They work with a network of over 1,300 organizations in more than 137 countries.
Net Revenue: 1993 $648,472 ($265,694, or 41%, comes from government grants) **Net Expenses:** $568,074 53%/25%/22%
Net Assets: $64,309 **Citations:** 0:255
Products or Services: "Tool Kits" to assist grassroots activists and groups. Publications, updates.
Tax Status: 501(c)(3) **Annual Report:** No. **Employees:** 10
Board of Directors or Trustees: Rudo Chitiga (Zimbabwe), Ashish Kothari (India), Elin Enge (Norway), Raul Montenegro (Argentina), Prof. Robert Johnson (United States).
Periodicals: *Action Alerts* (8-12 times a year). **Internships:** Yes, year round.
Other Information: EarthAction was created out of the 1992 Rio Earth Summit. Affiliated with the 501(c)(4) EarthAction International at the same address. The organization has two other offices besides their Massachusetts location; Chile - Antonio Lopez de Bello 024, Providencia, Santiago, Chile, voice (56-2) 735-7559, fax (56-2) 737-2897, and the United Kingdom - 9 White Lion St., London, N1 9PD, UK, voice (44-171) 865-9009, fax (44-171) 278-0345. EarthAction received $382,344, or 59% of revenue, from gifts and grants awarded by foundations, companies and individuals. (These grants included $25,000 from the Richard and Rhoda Goldman Fund, $15,000 from the C.S. Fund, and $2,000 from the Peace Development Fund). $265,694, or 41%, from government grants. The remaining revenue came from interest on savings and temporary cash investments.

Earthkind USA

2100 L St., N.W.
Washington, DC 20037   **Phone:**   (202) 452-1100
USA

Contact Person: Jan A. Hartke, Executive Director.
Officers or Principals: John A. Hoyt, President ($0); Paul G. Irwin, Executive Vice President/Treasurer ($0); Murdaugh S. Madden, Secretary ($0); John E. Taft, Chairman; Amy Freeman Lee, Vice Chairman.
Mission or Interest: "To increase global awareness on various environmental issues. Programs include publication of educational materials, monitoring plant and animal species and participating in environmental conferences."
Accomplishments: In 1994 Earthkind spent $569,443 on its programs. This included $11,666 in grants awarded to other organizations.
Net Revenue: 1994 $737,368 **Net Expenses:** $737,368 77%/13%/9% **Net Assets:** $0 **Citations:** 0:255
Tax Status: 501(c)(3)
Board of Directors or Trustees: K. William Wiseman, Judi Friedman, Alice Garey, Virginia Lynch, Thomas Meinhardt, O.J. Ramsey, Marilyn Wilhelm.
Other Information: Earthkind is an affiliate of the Humane Society. The organization received $681,418, or 84% of revenue, from grants awarded by affiliates. $55,950, or 16%, came from grants awarded by foundations, businesses, and individuals.

Earthsave Foundation

706 Frederick St.
Santa Cruz, CA 95062   **Phone:**   (408) 423-4069
USA

Contact Person: Patricia Carney, President/Executive Director.
Officers or Principals: Patricia Carney, President/Executive Director ($26,676); Shams Kairys, Chairman ($15,780); John Robbins, Founder ($8,999); Terry Thiermann, Treasurer; Deo Robbins, Vice President.
Mission or Interest: Environmental organization that "educates through lectures, conferences, interviews and local events. Our scope is national and international and is directed to all classes and ages," although they have a special focus on high-school students.
Accomplishments: In 1993 the Foundation spent $501,073 on its programs. The largest program, with expenditures of $216,376, was general educational activities. $186,064 was spent on Youth for Environmental Sanity (YES), a program that tours twelve youths aged 17-20 accross the country giving presentations to junior and senior high-school assemblies, providing peer education on "what students can do to help stop environmental damage." $57,173 was spent on Local Action Groups, volunteer groups in twenty cities around the nation who carry out educational activities. $41,460 was spent educating parents, students, and teachers on "nutritional and environmental education," and is working to build healthier school lunch programs with pilot programs in Santa Cruz, CA and Madison, WI.
Net Revenue: 1993 $668,786 **Net Expenses:** $638,035 79%/14%/7% **Net Assets:** $114,921 **Citations:** 1:240
Products or Services: Realities factbook. Educational materials, videos, books, audio tapes, and lobbying. The Foundation spent $7,315 on lobbying, $6,965 on grassroots lobbying and $500 on the direct lobbying of legislators.
Tax Status: 501(c)(3)
Board of Directors or Trustees: David Bernstein, Gary Dunn, Donald Epstein, Arnoldo Gil-Osorio, Richard Glantz, Earle Harris, Jackie Knowles, Ian Thiermann.
Periodicals: *Connecting the Dots* (newsletter).
Other Information: Founder John Robbins is the author of Diet for a New America. The Foundation received $529,309, or 79% of revenue, from gifts and grants awarded by foundations, businesses, and individuals. $40,230, or 6%, from membership dues. $29,132, or 4%, from the YES program. $28,648 net, or 4%, from the sale of inventory. $25,945, or 4%, from educational activities. $15,142, or 2%, from the Local Action Groups.   The remaining revenue came from interest on savings and temporary cash investments.

Earthstewards Network

720 Lovell Ave., N.
Bainbridge Island, WA 98110   **Phone:**   (206) 842-7986
USA

Contact Person: Danaan Parry, Executive Director.   **Officers or Principals:** Danaan Parry, Executive Director ($22,554); William Newby, Financial Officer ($0); Robert Cleland, Vice President ($0); Lynne Cleland, Secretary.
Mission or Interest: Network promoting global peace, international cooperation, conflict resolution, and environmentalism.
Accomplishments: In the fiscal year ending September 1994, the Network spent $209,556 on its programs. These programs included: Sending 25 people to Russia for an exchange with the Culinary Institute of St. Petersburg, to create a demonstration cafe at the Goodwill Games. "Citizen Diplomacy" by sending 25 people to the West Bank, El Salvador, and Nicaragua. Workshops teaching "gender communication" skills.
Net Revenue: FY ending 9/94 $238,330 **Net Expenses:** $246,604 85%/15%/1% **Net Assets:** $21,073
Tax Status: 501(c)(3)
Board of Directors or Trustees: Susan Johnson, Larry Hulburt.
Periodicals: Newsletter.
Other Information: The Network received $174,521, or 73% of revenue, from program service fees from conferences, workshops, trips, etc. $38,670, or 16%, from gifts and grants awarded by foundations, businesses, and individuals. $21,409, or 9%, from membership dues. $3,462, or 1%, from special fund-raising events, including a rummage sale, three dances, and a raffle. The remaining revenue came from interest on savings and temporary cash investments.

Earthtrust
25 Kaneohe Bay Dr.
Kailua, HI 96734
USA

Phone: (808) 254-2866

Contact Person: Donald J. White, President.
Officers or Principals: Donald J. White, President ($81,413); Kenneth Lee Marten, Researcher ($36,084); John Lindelow, Fundraising Manager ($35,383); Robert L. Loy, Executive Director; Dr. Michael Chaffin, Program Director.
Mission or Interest: Environmental organization focusing on marine mammals and ecosystems.
Accomplishments: In 1993 the organization spent $880,505 on its programs. These included $34,300 in grants awarded to researchers.
Net Revenue: 1993 $1,168,840 **Net Expenses:** $1,061,898 83%/7%/10% **Net Assets:** $432,114 **Citations:** 9:203
Tax Status: 501(c)(3)
Board of Directors or Trustees: James Schenkel.
Other Information: Earthtrust paid an additional $2,184 in rent to its president, Donald White. The organization paid $34,635 to the firm of Myerberg and Shain, of Honolulu, HI, for organizational consulting and fundraising. Earthtrust received $1,134,647, or 97% of revenue, from gifts and grants awarded by foundations, businesses, and individuals. $14,019, or 1%, from its whale and dolphin educational presentations. The remaining revenue came from interest on savings and temporary cash investments, dividends and interest from securities, the sale of inventory, and other miscellaneous sources. The organization realized a loss of $13,348 on the sale of securities and other assets.

EcoNet
(see the Institute for Global Communications)

Economic Affairs Bureau / *Dollars & Sense*
1 Summer St.
Somerville, MA 02143
USA

Phone: (617) 628-8411   **E-Mail:** Dollars@igc.apc.org
Fax: (617) 628-2025

Contact Person: Ethan Fletcher.
Officers or Principals: Marc Breslow, Betsy Reed, Editors; Randy Divinski, Circulation; Gene Mason, Publisher.
Mission or Interest: Publishes *Dollars & Sense: What's Left in Economics*. "Progressive economics magazine written for a popular audience." Concerned with 'socially conscious' investing.
Accomplishments: In 1995 the magazine celebrated its twentieth anniversary, with commentator Barbara Ehrenreich as guest of honor. Recently named the first four Fellows; Barbara Ehrenreich, Edward Herman, former radio host Jim Hightower, and columnist and Radio Pacifica commentator and columnist Julianne Malveaux. Issues often have specific themes, such as a recent edition on the environment. The issue included articles by an economist from Greenpeace International, a new way of measuring economic growth (this new measure includes housework while discounting inequality, loss of leisure time, under-employment, pollution, loss of forests and wetlands, fossil fuel depletion, ozone depletion and global warming), an article on environmental racism, an article on pollution trading and credits by an instructor from the Institute for Social Ecology, and others.
Products or Services: Economic readers and classroom supplements, *Real World Micro*, *Real World Macro*, and *Real World Banking*. Decoding the Contract: Progressive Perspectives on Current Economic Policy Debates, an anthology of articles.
Tax Status: 501(c)(3) **Employees:** 5
Board of Directors or Trustees: Randy Albelda, Phineas Baxandall, Leslie Brokaw, Brian Burgoon, Laurie Daugherty, Amy Gluckman, John Miller.
Periodicals: *Dollars & Sense* (bimonthly magazine).
Internships: Yes, both paid and unpaid.
Other Information: "*Dollars & Sense* intends to flourish and improve itself in the years to come. The Fellows program is one ingredient, as well as concerted efforts to expand both bulk sales and circulation." In 1995 the Bureau received a $1,000 loan from Resist.

Economic Policy Institute (EPI)
1730 Rhode Island Ave., N.W., Suite 200
Washington, DC 20036
USA

Phone: (202) 775-8810
Fax: (202) 775-0819   **Web-Page:** http://epinet.org

Contact Person: Jeff Faux, President.   **Officers or Principals:** Jeff Faux, President ($86,431); Eileen Applebaum, Economist ($77,535); Cindy Sadler, Director of Development ($69,300); Nan Gibson, Director, Public Education; Lawrence Mischell, Research Director; Robert Bergland, Secretary/Treasurer, Dean Baker, Economist.
Mission or Interest: "Educating the public and policy makers about new ideas concerned with promoting public discussions of economic policies which can achieve economic opportunity for the lower class, minorities, and the poor." EPI was founded in 1986 by Barry Bluestone, Robert Kuttner, Ray Marshall, Robert Reich, Lester Thurow, and Jeff Faux.
Accomplishments: In 1994 the Institute spent $2,160,428 on its programs. Pilot project in Maine to explore an expanded role for the federal government in the development of new civilian markets for companies facing defense cuts. EPI's work has appeared in Fairness and Accuracy in Media's publications.
Net Revenue: 1994 $2,948,249 ($111,909, or 4%, from government grants) **Net Expenses:** $2,751,798 79%/17%/4%
Net Assets: $57,905 **Citations:** 617:36

Products or Services: <u>Reclaiming Prosperity: A Blueprint for Progressive Economic Reform</u> edited by Todd Schafer and Jeff Faux, <u>Robbing the Cradle? A Critical Assessment of Generational Accounting</u> by Dean Baker, False Prophets: The Selling of NAFTA by Thea Lee, and many other publications. Research, fellowships for individuals pursuing a Masters or Ph.D.
Tax Status: 501(c)(3)
Board of Directors or Trustees: Morton Bahr (Communication Workers of America), Owen Bieber (UAW), Prof. Barry Bluestone (Univ. of Massachusetts), Robert Kuttner (*Business Week*), Raymond Marshall (LBJ School of Public Affairs), Alex Mercure, Rep. Eleanor Holmes Norton (D-DC), Bernard Rapoport, Prof. Lester Thurow (MIT), Richard Trumka, Lynn Williams, Jack Sheinkman, Rosabeth Moss Kanter (Howard Univ.), John Jacob (Anheuser-Busch Co.), Michael Peevey, Ann Roell Markusen (Rutgers Univ.), Gerald McEntee (AFSME), Roger Wilkins.
Other Information: EPI economists Dean Baker and Thea Lee recently stated that they are "Struggling to keep the world safe from economists," and that "We've had a lot of disappointments in the last 10 years as progressive movements have bee set back in the U.S. and around the world. But there are still considerable grounds for hope...In places such as Haiti and Chiapas, millions of people are struggling against the logic of a world capitalist system that places profit above basic human rights and the survival of the environment. These struggles provide a basis for believing that the tide will turn and that there is a future for progressive politics, and a future period." EPI received $2,799,348, or 95% of revenue, from gifts and grants awarded by foundations, businesses, and individuals. (These grants included $25,000 from the Rosenberg Foundation, $20,000 from the Ploughshares Fund, $586 from the Henry J. Kaiser Institute. In 1993, $100,000 from the Carnegie Corporation, and in 1995, $52,797 from the Rockefeller Foundation.) $111,909, or 4%, from government grants. The remaining revenue came from the sale of publications, and interest on savings and temporary cash investments.

Ecostewards Alliance
601 Pennsylvania Ave., N.W., Suite 900
Washington, DC 20004
USA

Contact Person: Peter B. Keisey, President.
Mission or Interest: Environmental organization.
Net Revenue: 1994 less than $25,000   **Tax Status:** 501(c)(3)

Education 1st!
3400 Riverside Dr., 6th Floor
Burbank, CA 91505   **Phone:**   (818) 972-0677
USA

Contact Person: August Coppola, CEO.
Officers or Principals: David Garcia, Director ($30,000); Gloria Dobson, Secretary ($22,501); Tarin Wilson, Fundraiser ($20,769); Linda Guber, Chairman; Carole Isenberg, Vice Chairman; Annie Gilbar, Secretary; Len Jacoby, Treasurer.
Mission or Interest: "Provides educational programs, and uses the resources of the media to inform the general public about the weakness of our educational system," and contributes "to the public awareness of the importance of public education." Advocates more funding for public education.
Accomplishments: In the fiscal year ending June 1994, the organization spent $31,789 on its programs.
Net Revenue: FY ending 6/94 $212,334 **Net Expenses:** $267,151 12%/43%/45% **Net Assets:** $41,260
Tax Status: 501(c)(3)
Other Information: Education 1st! received $207,572, or 98% of revenue, from gifts and grants awarded by foundations, businesses, and individuals. (These grants included $16,000 from the Barbra Streisand Foundation. $4,502, or 2%, from program service fees. The remaining revenue came from interest on savings and temporary cash investments.

Education Law Center, PA (ELC-PA)
801 Arch St.
Philadelphia, PA 19107   **Phone:**   (215) 238-6970
USA

Contact Person: Janet F. Stotland, Co-Director.   **Officers or Principals:** Leonard Rieser, Co-Director ($74,104); Janet F. Stotland, Co-Director ($74,140); Edith Miller, Staff Attorney ($52,500).
Mission or Interest: "To represent the broad public interest by providing legal assistance to individuals and groups, including children with physical and mental disabilities and groups working on their behalf, in connection with improving the operation of Pennsylvania's public education system and other systems that affect children and youth...Through our law reform and policy work, we seek to bring about systemic reform so that all children will ultimately receive a free appropriate education in the least restrictive environment."
Accomplishments: In the fiscal year ending September 1995, the Center spent $853,667 on its programs. Fifty workshops were held, and 1,004 parents and 1,344 professionals were trained. The Center received $177,637 in court-awarded attorney's fees.
Net Revenue: FY ending 9/95 $998,869 ($438,167, or 44%, from government grants) **Net Expenses:** $933,980 91%/8%/1%
Net Assets: $617,065 **Citations:** 87:112
Tax Status: 501(c)(3)
Board of Directors or Trustees: Gilbert Paul Carrasco (Villanova Univ., School of Law), Jeff Crosby, Hon. Happy Fernandez, Dr. David Allen Frisby, Joan Friendly Goodman, Dr. Peter Kuriloff (Univ. Of PA, Graduate School of Education), Janet Lonadale, Joyce Miller, David Richman, Anita Santos, Rochelle Solomon, Suzanne Turner, Robert Vogel.

Other Information: The Law Center received $438,167, or 44% of revenue, from government grants. $338,424, or 34%, from gifts and grants awarded by foundations, businesses, and individuals. $177,637, or 18%, from court-awarded attorney's fees. $27,071, or 3%, from the sale of publications and materials. $14,588, or 1%, from interest on savings and temporary cash investments. The remaining revenue came from various miscellaneous sources.

Educational Foundation for Nuclear Science / *The Bulletin of the Atomic Scientists*

6042 S. Kimbark Ave.
Chicago, IL 60637   **Phone:**   (312) 702-2555   **E-Mail:** bullatomsci@igc.apc.org
USA   **Fax:**   (312) 702-0725

Contact Person: Nancy Myers, Executive Director.   **Officers or Principals:** Mike Moore, Editor; Linda Rothstein, Managing Editor; Leonard Rieser, Chairman; Leon Lederman, Vice Chairman; Michael McCally, Treasurer.
Mission or Interest: "Albert Einstein and his colleagues founded *The Bulletin of the Atomic Scientists* 50 years ago, on the premise that the unleashed power of the atom had changed everything except the way people think. And so, the *Bulletin* was created to do precisely that. Widely hailed as one of the world's most influential publications, it remains today the premier forum for bringing people closer to the realities of the nuclear age."
Accomplishments: 12,000 subscribers in over 60 countries. Awards won included: Investigative Reporters and Editors' "Best Investigative Story for "U.S. Coverup of Nazi Scientists," American Society of Magazine Editors' "National Magazine Award, Best Single Topic Issue" for "Chernobyl: The Emerging Story." Founded in 1947.
Tax Status: 501(c)(3)   **Annual Report:** No.   **Employees:** 10
Board of Directors or Trustees: Anne Cahn (former director, Committee for National Security), Dorinda Dallmeyer (research director, Dean Rusk Center for International and Comparative Law), Prof. Hans-Peter Dürr (Max Planck Inst.), Betsy Fader (former director, Student Pugwash), Prof. Howard Hiatt (Harvard Univ.), Dean Michael Janeway (Medill School of Journalism, Northwestern Univ.), Michael Klare (former director, National Security Project, Institute for Policy Studies), Prof. Don Lamb (Univ. of Chicago), Prof. Lawrence Lidsky (MIT), Mary Lord (Fund for Peace), Prof. Alejandro Nadal (El Colegio de Mexico), John Pike (Federation of American Scientists), Nicholas Pritzker, Prof. Martin Rees (Univ. of Cambridge), Prof. Stephen Walt (Univ. of Chicago).
Periodicals: *The Bulletin of the Atomic Scientists* (bimonthly journal).
Internships: "Visiting fellowships for foreign, early-career journalists."
Other Information: *The Bulletin of the Atomic Scientists* is perhaps best known for its "doomsday clock," a clock which has been used over the years to gauge the state of international security. The closer the hands are to midnight, the greater the danger. The closest the hands ever were was two minutes to midnight in 1953 when the United States successfully tested a hydrogen bomb. The hands were moved back "in response to the growing public understanding that nuclear weapons made war between major technical nations irrational." The hands moved up again to three minutes to midnight in 1984 as "the blunt simplicities of force threaten to displace any other form of discourse between the super powers." In 1990 the hands moved back to ten minutes to midnight, as "Democratic movements in Eastern Europe shatter the myth of monolithic communism; the Cold War ends." In 1994 the Foundation received $30,000 from the Compton Foundation.

Educational Fund to End Gun Violence

100 Maryland Ave., N.E.
Washington, DC 20002   **Phone:**   (202) 544-7214
USA

Contact Person: Joshua M. Horowitz, Executive Director.   **Officers or Principals:** Richard Meltzer, Chairman ($0); Hilary Shelton, Vice Chairman ($0); Joel Kanter, Treasurer ($0); Michael K. Beard, Secretary.
Mission or Interest: To reduce and end violence involving guns through the restriction and prohibition of gun ownership.
Accomplishments: In 1994 the Fund spent $180,173 on its programs. The largest program, with expenditures of $93,524, was public education. This includes answering reporters' and the general public's questions regarding firearms and ownership, and working with schools on curriculum and special projects. $47,043 was spent to research and produce a plan "to reduce firearm violence through the use of health care providers in the communities." $39,606 was spent on a Products Liability Clearinghouse, which "assists plaintiffs in recovering damages from firearms manufacturers." Also produces a newsletter, provides expert consulting for plaintiffs' attorneys, and maintains a library of gun publications.
Net Revenue: 1994 $214,582 **Net Expenses:** $199,061 91%/6%/3% **Net Assets:** $60,691
Products or Services: Grassroots organizing manual.
Tax Status: 501(c)(3)
Board of Directors or Trustees: Rev. James Atwood, J. Elliott Corbett, Marqerite Gilstrap, Sanford Horwitt Ph.D., Elliott Andalman MD, Peter Nachajski M.D., Linda Vasquez.
Other Information: Affiliated with the 501(c)(4) Coalition to Stop Gun Violence at the same address. The two had combined net revenues, expenses, and assets of $1,205,241, $1,660,117, and $105,419. The Fund received $138,272, or 64% of revenue, from gifts and grants awarded by foundations, businesses, and individuals. (These grants included $2,951 from their 501(c)(4) affiliate, $1,000 from the Joyce Mertz-Gilmore Foundation, and $1,000 from the Stewart R. Mott Charitable Trust.) $50,502, or 23%, from special fund-raising events including an auction and a convention. $21,078, or 10%, from attorney's fees for "helping plaintiffs' attorneys recover from gun manufacturers." $2,086, or 1%, from interest on savings and temporary cash investments. The remaining revenue came from other miscellaneous sources.

Educators for Social Responsibility (ESR)

23 Garden St.
Cambridge, MA 02138   **Phone:**   (617) 492-1764
USA

Contact Person: Lawrence Dieringer.   **Officers or Principals:** Lawrence Dieringer, Executive Director ($47,948); David Hyerle, Chairperson ($0); Rick Abrams, Treasurer ($0); Dick Mayo-Smith, Secretary.
Mission or Interest: Association of educators that develops and promotes curricula and professional development promoting peace, non-violence, and conflict resolution.
Accomplishments: In the fiscal year ending June 1994, the organization spent $672,011 on its programs. The largest program, with expenditures of $320,964, was the "Resolving Conflict Creatively" program. $165,085 was spent on program and professional development. $151,421 on publications and marketing. $34,541 on chapter and membership services.
Net Revenue: FY ending 6/94 $950,501 **Net Expenses:** $877,525 77%/18%/5% **Net Assets:** $109,695 **Citations:** 15:182
Tax Status: 501(c)(3)
Board of Directors or Trustees: Kathy Augustine (Principal, McDonough #38 Elementary School, New Orleans, LA), Shelley Berman (Superintendent of Schools, Hudson, MA), Carol Bershad, Greg Ciardi (Research for Better Teaching), Meg Gage (Ottinger Found.), Patricia Harrison (Deputy Superintendent, Rochester City School District, NY), Carol Lieber, Marion O'Malley (NC Center for Peace Education), Jan Phlegar, Richard Rowe (MA State Board of Education), Emily Young.
Periodicals: *Forum* (quarterly newsletter).
Other Information: ESR received $883,018, or 93% of revenue, from gifts and grants awarded by foundations, businesses, and individuals. (These grants included $30,000 from the Compton Foundation, $17,500 from the Peace Development Fund, $10,000 from the Town Creek Foundation, $1,000 from the Haymarket People's Fund, and $500 from the New Prospect Foundation.) $45,057, or 5%, from "Summer Institute" fees. $21,870, or 2%, from membership fees. The remaining revenue came from interest on savings and temporary cash investments.

EduComics
P.O. Box 45831
Seattle, WA 98145-0831   **Phone:**   (206) 322-6838
USA   **Fax:**   same

Contact Person: Leonard RIFAS, Ph.D.
Mission or Interest: Comic books on a variety of topics including nuclear power, corporate crime, cigarettes and the tobacco industry, and the American Revolution.
Accomplishments: Published atomic bomb-survivor-cartoonist Keiji Nakazawa's *Gen of Hiroshima* and *I Saw It*. Also produced comic books for nonprofit organizations; *Food First Comics, AIDS News, A Graphic Intro to Critical Thinking* and *Tobacco Comics*.
Tax Status: For profit. **Annual Report:** No. **Employees:** 0

El Rescate
1340 S. Bonnie Brae
Los Angeles, CA 90006   **Phone:**   (213) 387-3284
USA

Contact Person: Oscar Andrade, Executive Director.   **Officers or Principals:** Oscar Andrade, Executive Director ($15,075); Neils Frenzen, Chairman ($0); Rev. Roger Rogahn, Secretary ($0); Rich Norris, Treasurer.
Mission or Interest: Provides social services, "seeks to facilitate long-term socio-economic development of the Central American community and builds links with other minority communities," reports on human rights in El Salvador.
Accomplishments: In 1994 El Rescate spent $500,995 on its programs. The largest program, with expenditures of $355,850, was Social Services, which included meals and grocery distribution, a homeless shelter, youth programs, literacy and "survival English" classes. $90,306 was spent on human rights reporting "which was relied upon by international groups and the U.S. Congressional staff." $54,839 was spent on community economic development.
Net Revenue: 1994 $636,141 ($283,201, or 45%, from government grants) **Net Expenses:** $594,677 84%/10%/6%
Net Assets: $55,175 **Citations:** 526:40
Tax Status: 501(c)(3)
Board of Directors or Trustees: Jaime Penate, Sandra Pettit, Rev. Donald Smith, Julio Cristales, Rosana Perez, Michelle Prichard, James Werner.
Other Information: El Rescate has an El Salvador office. It is also affiliated with the 501(c)(3) El Rescate Legal Services at the same address. The two organizations had 1994 combined net revenues of $823,207, net expenses of $767,423, and net assets of $86,584. El Rescate received $339,588, or 53% of revenue, from direct and indirect public support in the form of gifts and grants awarded by foundations, businesses, affiliates, and individuals. (These grants included $6,250 from the McKay Foundation, $200 from the Liberty Hill Foundation.) $283,201, or 45%, from government grants. $5,583, or 1%, from the El Salvador office. $5,253 net, or 1%, from special fund-raising events. The remaining revenue came from interest on savings and temporary cash investments.

El Rescate Legal Services
1340 S. Bonnie Brae
Los Angeles, CA 90016   **Phone:**   (213) 387-3284
USA

Contact Person: Niels Frenzen, Chair.   **Officers or Principals:** Rev. Roger Rogahn, Secretary ($0); Rick Norris, Treasurer ($0).
Mission or Interest: Offers legal services to indigent Central Americans in the U.S.
Accomplishments: In 1994 the organization spent $121,506 on its services.
Net Revenue: 1994 $187,066 ($36,844, or 20%, from government grants) **Net Expenses:** $172,746 70%/18%/12%
Net Assets: $31,409

Tax Status: 501(c)(3)
Board of Directors or Trustees: Jaime Penate, Sandra Pettit, Rev. Donald Smith, Julio Cristales, Rosana Perez, Michelle Prichard, James Wener.
Other Information: El Rescate Legal Services is also affiliated with the 501(c)(3) El Rescate at the same address. The two organizations had 1994 combined net revenues of $823,207, net expenses of $767,423, and net assets of $86,584. The organization received $83,596, or 45%, from gifts and grants awarded by foundations, businesses, and individuals. (These grants included $20,000 from the Joyce Mertz-Gilmore Foundation.) $64,079, or 34%, from client fees. $36,844, or 20%, from government grants The remaining revenue came from interest on savings and temporary cash investments, and other miscellaneous sources.

Ending Men's Violence Network
P.O. Box 73559
Washington, DC 20056   **Phone:**   (202) 829-6703
USA

Contact Person: Rus Ervin Funk. **Officers or Principals:** John Cohen.
Mission or Interest: "To coordinate service programs throughout the U.S. and Canada focused on men working against rape, harassment, pornography, prostitution, child abuse and woman abuse."
Accomplishments: Rus Ervin Funk is a Senior Social Worker and Community Organizer for the Baltimore Sexual Abuse Treatment Center. "He was actively involved in the passage of the 1992 Civil Rights Re-Authorization Act, co-wrote the Violence Against Women Act of 1994, and was part of the team that created and passed the UN Convention for the Rights of the Child." Funk is the author of Stopping Rape: A Challenge for Men (New Society Publishers, 1992).
Products or Services: Annual meetings, annual "Brother Peace" events, networking.
Annual Report: No. **Employees:** All volunteer.

Environmental Action
6930 Carroll Ave., Suite 600
Takoma Park, MD 20912   **Phone:**   (301) 891-1100   **E-Mail:** eaf@igc.apc.org
USA   **Fax:**   (301) 891-2218   **Web-Page:** http://www.cconct.apc.org/eaf/

Contact Person: Margaret Morgan-Hubbard, President.
Officers or Principals: Barbara Ruben, Director ($24,881); Margaret Morgan Hubbard, President ($6,061).
Mission or Interest: Lobbying affiliate of the Environmental Action Foundation. The two affiliates merged together into EAF on July 1, 1994. The actions of the lobbying affiliate have been assumed by the Foundation.
Accomplishments: In the fiscal year ending September 1994 Environmental Action spent $144,595 on its activities.
Net Revenue: FY ending 9/94 $210,774 **Net Expenses:** $183,192 79%/10%/11% **Net Assets:** $1,091
Tax Status: 501(c)(4)
Other Information: The organization was affiliated with the 501(c)(3) Environmental Action Foundation, until EA was merged with EAF on July 1, 1994. Now the functions of both are carried out under the 501(c)(3) incorporation of EAF. Before the merger, the two separate organizations had combined net revenues of $801,268, net expenses of $929,640, and net assets of (-$119,108). Margaret Morgan Hubbard received compensation from both organizations totaling $51,535. Environmental Action received $119,098, or 56% of revenue, from membership dues. $75,768, or 36%, from a forgiven debt. $11,608, or 6%, from subscriptions. The remaining revenue came from the sale of publications, and other miscellaneous sources.

Environmental Action Foundation (EAF)
6930 Carroll Ave., Suite 600
Takoma Park, MD 20912   **Phone:**   (301) 891-1100   **E-Mail:** eaf@igc.apc.org
USA   **Fax:**   (301) 891-2218   **Web-Page:** http://www.cconct.apc.org/eaf/

Contact Person: Margaret Morgan-Hubbard, Executive Director. **Officers or Principals:** Margaret Morgan-Hubbard, Executive Director ($45,474); Nancy Hirsh, Secretary ($36,705); Andrew Stevenson, President ($0); James Overton, Treasurer.
Mission or Interest: Environmental organization founded in 1970 "to ensure a grassroots voice in national environmental debates...Our work is guided by the knowledge that creating environmental sustainability is inextricably linked to achieving social justice."
Accomplishments: In 1994 EAF was the first national environmental group to interject sustainable energy issues into preparations for the 1995 U.N.'s World Summit for Social Development. In a partnership with the Department of Energy, EAF staff traveled to New England and the Midwest to facilitate the inclusion of various interest groups into the federal government's energy policy making process. EAF testified at a March hearing that took a "giant step forward in ensuring that renewable energy providers are able to ship clean power to the market." In the fiscal year ending September 1994, EAF spent $156,125 on its Energy Project. $134,021 was spent on Energy Conservation projects. $74,842 on Waste and Toxic Substances project that provides public education on the community's right to know about toxic substances and legal assistance to "toxic victims."
Net Revenue: FY ending 9/94 $590,494 ($17,665, or 3%, from government grants) **Net Expenses:** $746,448 84%/6%/10%
Net Assets: (-$120,199) **Citations:** 3:222
Products or Services: Educational materials, grassroots coordination, information, testimony, and lobbying. EAF spent $1,248 on lobbying; $198 on grassroots lobbying and $1,050 on the direct lobbying of legislators. This was up from $826 the previous year, but down from $3,783 two years prior.

Tax Status: 501(c)(3) **Annual Report:** Yes. **Employees:** 14
Board of Directors or Trustees: Scott Bernstein (Center for Neighborhood Technology), Maurice Sampson (Inst. for Local Self-Reliance).
Periodicals: *Environmental Action* (quarterly magazine).
Internships: Yes, for those with skills such as researching and writing.
Other Information: Environmental Action Foundation was founded by the organizers of the original Earth Day in 1970. It was affiliated with the 501(c)(4) Environmental Action, until EA was merged with EAF on July 1, 1994. Now the functions of both are carried out under the 501(c)(3) incorporation of EAF. Before the merger, the two separate organizations had combined net revenues of $801,268, net expenses of $929,640, and net assets of (-$119,108). Margaret Morgan Hubbard received compensation from both organizations totaling $51,535. EAF prides itself on remaining grassroots. To that end they raise funds through a growing canvassing operation and maintain a mailing list valued at $140,442. The Foundation received $513,578, or 87% of revenue, from gifts and grants from foundations, businesses, affiliates and individuals. (These grants included $70,000 from the Joyce Mertz-Gilmore Foundation, $42,159 from the Environmental Federation of America, $35,000 from the Rockefeller Family Fund, $20,000 from the Beldon Fund, $15,000 from the Tides Foundation, $15,000 from the Compton Foundation, and $15,000 from the Town Creek Foundation.) $17,665, or 3%, from government grants. $15,418, or 3%, from interest on savings and temporary cash investments. $12,170, or 2%, from consulting fees. The remaining revenue came from other program services, membership dues, rental income, and miscellaneous sources.

Environmental and Energy Study Institute (EESI)

122 C St., N.W., Suite 700
Washington, DC 20001   **Phone:**   (202) 628-1400
USA

Contact Person: John Babbitt, Controller.   **Officers or Principals:** Kenneth Murphy, Executive Director ($157,632); Carol Werner, Energy Project Director ($91,145); Gareth Porter, International Project Director ($83,483); William Gray, Water Project Director; Diane Schwartz, Development Director; Michael Witt, Program Coordinator.
Mission or Interest: To address issues regarding the environment and energy.
Accomplishments: In 1994 ESSI spent $1,363,528 on its programs. The largest program, with expenditures of $316,405, was research and education regarding "Energy, Climate Change and Environmental Taxes." This program sought to explain how the tax code could be used to make energy use more efficient. It included sixteen briefings, numerous workshop meetings, six reports, and Congressional testimony. The International Environment Program, with expenditures of $281,222, provided information to policymakers and the general public regarding cooperation with other nations in environmental enforcement and trade. Other programs included water quality, environmental security (as a key component of national security), sustainable agriculture, and more.
Net Revenue: 1994 $1,618,780 ($18,111, or 1%, from government grants) **Net Expenses:** $1,617,772 84%/9%/7%
Net Assets: $108,393 **Citations:** 3:222
Products or Services: Publications, conferences, congressional testimony, and lobbying. "Earth Press" to demonstrate environmentally sound publishing practices. The Institute spent $14,514 on the direct lobbying of legislators. This was an increase of 62% over the previous year.
Tax Status: 501(c)(3)
Board of Directors or Trustees: Robert Blake (Committee on Agricultural Sustainability for Developing Countries), Lester Brown (Worldwatch Inst.), Sen. John Chafee (R-RI), Carol Dinkins, Gerald Decker, Robert Fri (Resources for the Future), Sen. James Jeffords (R-VT), C. Payne Lucas (Africare), Sen. Barbara Mikulski (D-MD), Bernice McIntyre, Richard Ottinger (Pace Univ. School of Law), Ruth Patrick (Academy of Natural Sciences), Sen. Chuck Robb (D-VA), John Seiberling (Univ. of Akron), John Sheehan (United Steel Workers of America), Victoria Tschinkel, Robert Wallace (Population Action Intl.), Donna Wise (World Resource Council).
Other Information: The Institute received $1,014,726, or 63% of revenue, from direct and indirect public support in the form of gifts and grants awarded by foundations, businesses, and individuals. (These grants included $165,000 from the Joyce Foundation, and $34,140 from the Environmental Federation of America.) $515,059, or 32%, from educational services revenue. $91,568, or 6%, from interest on savings and temporary cash investments. $18,111, or 1%, from government grants. The remaining revenue came from other miscellaneous sources. Net revenue was reduced by losses of $17,641 from investments and $16,838 from the sale of securities.

Environmental Community Action (ECO Action)

250 10th St., N.E., Suite 201
Atlanta, GA 30309   **Phone:**   (404) 873-2474
USA

Contact Person: Carol Williams, Executive Director.   **Officers or Principals:** Rebecca Kiefer, President ($0); Sandra Lark, Vice President ($0); Claude Sullivan, Secretary ($0); Cheryl Randolph, Treasurer.
Mission or Interest: Environmental organization with an emphasis on training community groups and leaders.
Accomplishments: In the shortened fiscal year running from August 1993 to June 1994, the organization spent $72,695 on its programs. The largest program, with expenditures of $47,979, was citizen training on "accessing public records, meeting facilitation, leadership development, skills workshops on group structure, media, and conflict resolution." $24,716 was spent providing the public with research and information.
Net Revenue: FY from 8/93 to 6/94 $114,806 **Net Expenses:** $82,584 88%/12%/1% **Net Assets:** $60,402
Tax Status: 501(c)(3)

Board of Directors or Trustees: Christa Frangiamore, Jimmy Johnston, Ellen Spears, Karen Watson.
Other Information: ECO Action received $114,003, or 99% of revenue, from direct support in the form of gifts and grants awarded by foundations, businesses, individuals, and affiliates. (These grants included $30,000 from the Sapelo Island Research Foundation, $20,000 from the Jessie Smith Noyes Foundation, $25,000 from the Norman Foundation, $10,000 from the Beldon Fund, $10,000 from the Turner Foundation, and $5,000 from the Tides Foundation.) $803, or 1%, from interest on savings and temporary cash investments.

Environmental Defense Fund (EDF)

257 S. Park Ave.
New York, NY 10010   **Phone:**   (212) 505-2100
USA

Contact Person: Frederic Krupp, Executive Director.   **Officers or Principals:** Frederic Krupp, Executive Director ($249,656); Marcia Aronoff, Director, Programs ($150,867); Michael Oppenheimer, Senior Scientist ($142,373); Tom Graff, Senior Attorney ($130,318); Joel Plagenz, Director, Marketing ($127,452); Adam Stern, Director of Operations ($127,981); George Montgomery, Chair; Frank Loy, Teresa Heinz, John H.T. Wilson, Vice Chairs; Freeborn G. Jewett, Jr., Treasurer; Arthur P. Cooley, Secretary.
Mission or Interest: Research, education, litigation, and other activities to benefit the environment.
Accomplishments: EDF is one of the oldest and best known of the environmental organizations. In the fiscal year ending June 1994, EDF spent $16,142 on its programs. The largest program, with expenditures of $5,530,708, was energy and air quality. This program included: Efforts to reduce "carbon dioxide and other 'greenhouse gasses' that could cause global warming." Defended state's rights to impose California's strict auto standards, including an electric car mandate; but unlike California, EDF proposed giving auto makers a choice in how to go about reducing emissions. Was instrumental in convincing the Walt Disney Company not to build a historic theme park in Virginia. $4,480,785 was spent on education, legislative action, and membership activities. Programs included: A leading role at the Cairo International Conference on Population and Development. $3,216,901 was spent on wildlife and water resources. Programs included: Building support for the Endangered Species Act with a strategy that rewards landowners who create or improve habitat for the endangered species. After the 1993 midwestern floods, EDF was asked to brief Vice President Gore on environmentally sound options for disaster relief. Focused attention on the World Bank's poor environmental record. $2,914,138 was spent on toxic chemicals and solid waste programs. This included: Winning a legal victory in the U.S. Supreme Court which ruled that ash from municipal trash incinerators must be handled as hazardous waste if it fails to meet toxicity tests designed to protect groundwater. Helped convince the EPA to deny the request to add manganese to gasoline. Co-authored California's Proposition 65. Worked with the Advertising Council of America on a series of public service adds. EDF also awarded $69,000 in grants to other organizations, mostly outside the U.S. For its litigation, the Fund received $109,665 in court-awarded attorney's fees.
Net Revenue: FY ending 9/94 $21,379,753   ($723,673, or 3%, from government grants)
Net Expenses: $20,772,644   78%/4%/18%   **Net Assets:** $6,376,477   **Citations:**   670:32
Products or Services: Publications, litigation, coalition building, and lobbying. EDF spent $256,252 on lobbying, $4,444 on grassroots lobbying and $251,808 on the direct lobbying of legislators. This was an increase of 31% over the previous year, and 140% over two years prior.
Tax Status: 501(c)(3)
Board of Directors or Trustees: Wendy Benchley, Sally Bingham, Jessica Catto, Mary Cecil, Christopher Elliman, Jon Firor, Ph.D. (Natl. Center for Atmospheric Research), Daniel Garcia (Warner Bros.), Robert Grady, Charles Hamilton, Jr., Lisa Henson (Columbia Pictures Entertainment), Norbert Hill, Jr., (American Indian Science and Engineering Soc.), Lewis Kaden, Gene Likens, Ph.D., (Institute of Ecosystem Studies), Frank Loy (German Marshall Fund of the United States), Percy Luney (NC University School of Law), Susan Manilow, Harold Mooney, Ph.D. (Stanford Univ.), Robert Musser, William Newsom, Paul Nitze (Paul Nitze School of Advanced International Studies, Johns Hopkins Univ.), David Rall, M.D., Ph.D., Lewis Ranieri, John Scanlan, David Smith, M.D., Frank Taplin Jr., W. Richard West, Jr. (Natl. Museum of the American Indian), Robert Wilson, Wren Wirth, Paul Junger Witt, Charles Wurster, Ph.D. (Marine Sciences Research Center).
Periodicals: *EDF Letter* (quarterly newsletter).
Other Information: The Fund received $18,935,748, or 86% of revenue, from direct and indirect public support in the form of gifts and grants awarded by foundations, affiliates, businesses, and indiviudals. (These grants included $800,000 over four years from the John D. and Catherine T. MacArthur Foundation, $520,000 from the Joyce Foundation, $200,000 from the Rockefeller Brothers Foundation, $200,000 from the Nathan Cummings Foundation, $187,451 from the Environmental Federation of America, $154,102 from the Environmental Federation of America, $150,000 from the Joyce Mertz-Gilmore Foundation, $50,000 from the Barbra Streisand Foundation, $38,681 from the Environmental Federation of California, $30,000 from the Philip D. Reed Foundation, $30,000 from the General Service Foundation, $30,000 from the Compton Foundation, $30,000 from the Robert Sterling Clark Foundation, $25,000 from the Cary Charitable Trust, $25,000 from the Bauman Family Foundation, $25,000 from the F. M. Kirby Foundation, $15,000 from the New-Land Foundation, $10,000 from the Wallace Genetic Foundation, $3,000 from the Haymarket People's Fund.) $835,002 net, or 4%, from special fund-raising events. $723,673, or 3%, from government grants. $217,577, or 1%, from the leasing of conservation software to utilities. $127,175, or 1%, from dividends and interest on securities. The remaining revenue came from mailing list rentals, royalties, court-awarded attorney's fees, exhibit fees, capital gains on the sale of securities, interest on savings and temporary cash investments, and other miscellaneous sources.

Environmental Federation of America

3400 International Dr., N.W., Suite 2K
Washington, DC 20008   **Phone:**   (202) 537-7100
USA   **Fax:**   (202) 537-7101

Contact Person: Kalman Stein, Executive Director.   **Officers or Principals:** Kalman Stein, Executive Director ($86,130); Patricia DeSanctis, Vice President of Business Development ($67,512); James O'Keefe, Vice President of Campaigns ($64,930); Erik Meyers, Chair; Liz Ulmer, Vice Chair; Jay Feldman, Treasurer; Elizabeth McCorkle, Secretary.

Mission or Interest: A federation of 31 environmental organizations that conducts various campaigns to promote their shared agenda. (See the Board of Directors' affiliations for member organizations.)

Accomplishments: In the fiscal year ending June 1994, the Federation spent $6,824,563 on its programs. The largest portion of that, $5,957,180, was spent on grants awarded to member organizations. The recipients of the largest grants included: $1,152,418 for the Nature Conservancy, $731,749 for the World Wildlife Fund, $712,915 for the National Wildlife Federation, $338,247 for the National Parks and Conservation Association, $336,942 for the Rails-to-Trails Conservancy, $280,013 for the Center for Marine Conservation, $211,996 for Defenders of Wildlife, and $205,302 for the Rainforest Alliance. Other projects included $483,965 to carry out campaigns on behalf of members, and $383,418 for a public education campaign through the Ad Council on "what the individual can do to help the environment."

Net Revenue: FY ending 6/94 $7,714,767   **Net Expenses:** $7,627,508   89%/5%/5%   **Net Assets:** $900,913   **Citations:**   2:231

Tax Status: 501(c)(3)

Board of Directors or Trustees: Elizabeth McCorkle (African Wildlife Found.), Bernadine Prince (American Farmland Trust), Jim Scott (American Forests), Michael Brodie (American Rivers), David Knight (Center for Marine Conservation), Barbara Schecter (Clean Water Fund), Anita Gottlieb (Defenders of Wildlife), Margaret Morgan-Hubbard (Environmental Action Found.), Paula Hayes (Environmental Defense Fund), Diane Schwartz (Environmental and Energy Study Inst.), Erik Meyers (Environmental law Inst.), Jennifer Jones (Friends of the Earth), Maryll Kleibrink (Izaak Walton League of America), Tom Exton (National Audubon Society), Jay Feldman (National Coalition Against the Misuse of Pesticides), Jessie Brinkley (National Parks and Conservation Association), John Jensen (National Wildlife Federation), Jack Murray (Natural Resources Defense Council), Michael Coda (Nature Conservancy), Rebecca Gershow (Rails-to-Trails Conservancy), Liz Ulmer (Sierra Club Legal Defense Fund), Kathryn Morelli (Trust for Public Land), Yolanda Duarte-White (Wilderness Society), Marsha Mogowski (World Resources Inst.), Tom McGuire (World Wildlife Fund), Eral Blauner, Peter Camejo (Progressive Asset Management), Richard Angle (Save the Children), Gene Karpinski (U.S. PIRG, Education Fund), Ray Foote (Scenic America), Chris Nichols (Safe Energy Communication Council), Mary MacDonald (Rainforest Alliance).

Other Information: The Federation received $7,651,182, or 99% of revenue, from direct and indirect public support in the form of gifts and grants from foundations, businesses, affiliates, and individuals. The remaining revenue came from interest on savings and temporary cash investments, royalties, and membership dues. The Federation contracted Vanguard Communications of Washington, DC, for public relations, and paid them $96,000.

Environmental Federation of California

116 New Montgomery St., Suite 800
San Francisco, CA 94105   **Phone:**   (415) 882-9330
USA

Contact Person: Nancy Snow, Executive Director.   **Officers or Principals:** Nancy Snow, Executive Director ($57,960); Ronald C. Kinkeade, Controller ($43,470); Jacquelyn W. Hedlund ($41,400); Steve Katz, President; Marilyn Morrish, First Vice President; Louie Gonzalez, Second Vice President; Sue Liskovec, Secretary; David McDonald, Treasurer.

Mission or Interest: Works with affiliated organizations to provide education and outreach on environmental issues. Awards grants.

Accomplishments: In the fiscal year ending June 1994, the Federation spent $1,688,665 on its programs; including $1,291,324 awarded in grants. The recipients of the largest grants included: $87,608 for the Greenpeace Fund, $57,372 for California Trout, $51,119 for Defenders of Wildlife, $47,056 for Sierra Club Foundation, $41,987 for TreePeople, $41,722 for Heal the Bay, $41,670 for the California Audubon Society Chapters, $41,461 for the Greenbelt Alliance, and $40,012 for Friends of the River.

Net Revenue: FY ending 6/94 $2,133,664   **Net Expenses:** $2,115,327   80%/11%/9%   **Net Assets:** $192,926   **Citations:**   0:255

Tax Status: 501(c)(3)

Board of Directors or Trustees: Jerri Brown, Tim Little, Steve Scholl-Buckwald (Pesticide Action Network), Michele DiFrancia (Coalition for Clean Air), Don Archer, Michael Bowen (CA Trout), Mark Baldwin (Sierra Club Legal Defense Fund), Megan Barton (Nature Conservancy), Tom Bowman, John Bodnar (Environmental Defense Center), David Chatfield (Greenpeace Fund), Lisa Dreier (Environmental Defense Fund), W. Russell Ellis (Vice Chancellor for Undergraduate Affairs, UC Berkeley), Kim Francis (Heal the Bay), Bob Hennessy (San Jose Conservation Corps.), Lance King (Californians Against Waste Found.), Bob Kruger (Friends of the River), Eric Makus (TreePeople), Jun Lee (Desert Tortoise Preserve Committee), Michael Mantell (Resources Agency of CA), Halli Mason (California Native Plant Society), Mary Menees (Trust for Public Land), Jerry Meral (Planning and Conservation League Found.), Tamra Peters, Hope Singsen (Natural Resources Defense Council), Lawrence Smith (Marin Conservation League), Paul Tebbel, Stan Weidert (Sierra Club Found.), Kimery Wiltshire.

Other Information: The Federation received $1,878,081, or 88% of revenue, from gifts and grants awarded by foundations, businesses, affiliates, and individuals. $230,000, or 11%, from fees paid by affiliates. $21,116, or 1%, from membership dues. The remaining revenue came from interest on savings and temporary cash investments.

Environmental Fund of Washington

1402 3rd Ave., Suite 825
Seattle, WA 98101   **Phone:**   (206) 622-9840
USA

Contact Person: Maria Denny, Executive Director.

Officers or Principals: Maria Denny, Executive Director ($28,707); Edie Jorgensen, Chair ($0); Frank Stowell, First Vice Chair ($0); Tom Thomas, Second Vice Chair; Andi Anderson, Secretary; Mark Bergeson, Treasurer.

Mission or Interest: Established to participate in charitable fund drives in the work place. Pledged funds are distributed to affiliates to preserve the environment.

Accomplishments: In 1993 the Fund distributed $263,932 in grants and allocations.

Net Revenue: 1993 $407,909 **Net Expenses:** $336,037 95%/4%/1% **Net Assets:** $127,405

Tax Status: 501(c)(3)

Board of Directors or Trustees: Bob Sieh, Carolyn Thames, Dale Crane, Dave Flotree, David Ortman, Debbie Helpert, Erin Donner, Helen Welborn, James Maxson, Jan Milligan, Jim Pissot, Karen Fant, Karen Wolf, Konrad Liegel, Leslie Nelson, Margaret Liddiard, Mike Howell, Peter Sanborn, Priscilla Stanford, Scott Kroeker, Ron Holtcamp, Stebbo Hill, Steve Grayson, Steve Whitney, Vance Harris.

Other Information: The Fund received $398,793, or 98% of revenue, from direct and indirect public support in the form of gifts and grants from foundations, companies, and individuals. $7,660, or 2%, from membership dues. The remaining revenue came from interest on savings and temporary cash investments.

Environmental Health Coalition

1717 Kettner Blvd., Suite 100
San Diego, CA 92101   **Phone:**   (619) 235-0285
USA

Contact Person: Diane Takvorian, Executive Director.   **Officers or Principals:** Diane Takvorian, Executive Director ($33,229); Beatriz Barraza-Roppé, President ($0); Michael Skames, Vice President ($0); Tony Pettina, Treasurer.

Mission or Interest: Environmental organization working to eliminate toxic pesticides and other health threats.

Accomplishments: In the fiscal year ending June 1994, the Coalition spent $303,590 on its programs. These programs included $87,570 to reduce industrial pollution and urban run-off in the San Diego Bay. $78,151 was spent providing assistance to community action campaigns. $74,193 was spent to "implement strategies for effective reduction of toxic hazards in local neighborhoods." $53,110 was spent working with local schools and government to reduce the use of pesticide applications.

Net Revenue: FY ending 6/94 $395,696 ($47,921, or 12%, from government grants) **Net Expenses:** $460,296 66%/24%/10%

Net Assets: $21,229

Products or Services: Organizing, educational activities and lobbying. The Coalition spent $14,425 on the direct lobbying of legislators. Lobbying at the national level included opposition to NAFTA, support of HR 2898 (the Richardson-Waxman Bill) which would phase out the discharge of organochlorines, and HR 1490 to amend the Endangered Species Act. At the state level, the Coalition encouraged passage of SB 422 to eliminate toxic pesticides, SB 475 requiring reductions in pesticide use, and SB 1623 to increase funding available to Regional Quality Control Boards for enforcement.

Tax Status: 501(c)(3)

Board of Directors or Trustees: Doug Ballis (Intl. Association of Iron Workers), Jim Bell (Ecological Life Systems), Scott Chatfield (101 KGB-FM), Marc Cummings (Nathan Cummings Found.), Laura Durazo (Proyecto Fronterizo de Educacion Ambiental), Ruth Heifetz (UCSD School of Medicine), Jose Lamont Jones (Science Educator, Gompers School), Richard Juarez, Sharon Kalemkiarian (USD Children's Advocacy Inst.), Lyn Lacye, Mark Mandel, Dan McKirnan (UCSD School of Medicine), Reynalso Pisafio, Jay Powell.

Other Information: The Coalition received $334,695, or 85% of revenue, from gifts and grants awarded by foundations, businesses, and individuals. (These grants included $40,000 from the Nathan Cummings Foundation, $27,500 from the New World Foundation, $25,000 from the Jessie Smith Noyes Foundation, $15,000 from the Campaign for Human Development, $10,000 from the C.S. Fund, $7,500 from the McKay Foundation, $7,500 from the Beldon Fund, $1,599 from the Environmental Federation of California.) $47,921, or 12%, from government grants. $12,102, or 3%, from membership dues. The remaining revenue came from interest on savings and temporary cash investments.

Environmental Health Watch (EHW)

4115 Bridge Ave., Suite 104
Cleveland, OH 44113   **Phone:**   (216) 961-4646
USA

Contact Person: Stuart Greenberg, Executive Director.   **Officers or Principals:** Stuart Greenberg, Executive Director ($34,062); Kathleen Fagan, M.D., M.P.H., President ($0); Chuck Soup, Vice President ($0); June Kreuzer, Secretary; Shari Weir, Treasurer.

Mission or Interest: "Founded in 1985 as an environmental health information center and clearinghouse, EHW helps individuals and community groups threatened by exposure to toxic materials their homes and neighborhoods." Focus on low-income and urban areas.

Accomplishments: EHW has a joint project with the Cleveland Health Department. This project focuses on the reduction of lead exposure through educational programs and abatement. In the fiscal year ending March 1994, EHW spent $537,303 on its projects.

Net Revenue: FY ending 3/94 $650,092 **Net Expenses:** $594,669 90%/9%/1% **Net Assets:** $72,598 **Citations:** 2:231

Products or Services: Educational activities, technical training in lead abatement and hazardous waste reduction, monitoring of industrial toxins and making that information available to community groups.

Tax Status: 501(c)(3)

Board of Directors or Trustees: Betty Long (Western Reserve Alliance for Safe Energy), Linda Post, M.D. (Dir., Residency Program, Dept. of Family Practice, MetroHealth Medical Center), Rich Schiferl, Ph.D. (Reliance Electric), Wornie Reed, Ph.D. (Dir., Urban Child Research Center, Cleveland State Univ.), Gary Reimer.

Other Information: Environmental Health Watch received $597,785, or 92% of revenue, from contract service fees from a reimbursement contract with the city of Cleveland for the lead hazard abatement project. $50,710, or 8%, from direct and indirect public support in the form of gifts and grants from foundations, companies and individuals. The remaining revenue came from reimbursement for technical assistance for a lead summit conference.

Environmental Investigation Agency

1611 Connecticut Ave., N.W., Suite 3B
Washington, DC 20009   **Phone:**   (202) 483-6621
USA

Contact Person: Allan Thornton, Director.   **Officers or Principals:** Susan Fountain, Director ($0); Jennifer Lonsdale, Director ($0); Allan Thornton, Director ($0).
Mission or Interest: Investigates instances of violations of environmental law and conducts research that promotes the protection of the environment and wildlife.
Accomplishments: In the fiscal year ending August 1994, the Agency spent $130,400 on its programs. The Cetacean Campaign conducted investigations into illegal whaling and tried to transform the International Whaling Commission into a conservation organization. The Cetacean Campaign spent $57,260. $37,033 was spent on the Elephant Campaign focusing on the benefits of the ivory ban and the problem of shrinking elephant habitats. $36,107 was spent on the Bird Campaign investigating international trade of parrots and other wild birds.
Net Revenue: FY ending 8/94 $148,160 **Net Expenses:** $168,778   77%/23%/0% **Net Assets:** (-$5,368)
Products or Services: Educational materials, research, more.
Tax Status: 501(c)(3)
Other Information: Affiliated with the Environmental Investigation Agency, Limited, of London, England. The Agency received $131,715, or 89% of revenue, from gifts and grants awarded by foundations, companies and individuals. (These grants included $55,000 from the Animal Welfare Institute.) $10,570, or 7%, from membership dues. $5,875, or 4%, from publication sales.

Environmental Law Institute

1616 P St., N.W.
Washington, DC 20036   **Phone:**   (202) 939-3841
USA

Contact Person: J. William Futrell, President.   **Officers or Principals:** J. William Futrell, President ($151,772); Erik J. Meyers, Assistant Secretary/General Counsel ($104,513); Adam Babich, Director of Publications ($102,089); Elissa Parker, Director of Research, Policy and Training ($99,871); David J. Hayes, Chairman; Turner Smith, Secretary/Treasurer; Mary J. Swan, Director of Finance; James McElfish, John Pendergrass, Swellen Keiner, Senior Attorneys.
Mission or Interest: Research and education in environmental law, policy, and management.
Accomplishments: Circulation for the *Environmental Law Reporter* was 1,000 and 2,000 for the *National Wetlands Newsletter*. In 1994 the Institute spent $4,096,922 on its programs. The largest program expenditure was $2,487,729 for research, training, and technical assistance for state and local governments, foreign officials, public law enforcement, judicial personnel, businesses, and private interests. The next largest expenditure, $962,548, for the publication and distribution of journals, monographs and treatises. $646,645 was spent on membership and outreach services, such as public forums.
Net Revenue: 1994 $5,364,915 ($2,166,693, or 40%, from government grants) **Net Expenses:** $4,984,616   82%/15%/3%
Net Assets: $1,628,719 **Citations:** 28:160
Products or Services: Publications, public forums, research, and training.
Tax Status: 501(c)(3)
Board of Directors or Trustees: Elizabeth Ingram Bauereis Ph.D. (Dir., Environmental Affairs, Baltimore Gas and Electric Co.), Michael Bean (Chair, Wildlife Program, Environmental Defense Fund), Leslie Carothers (V.P., Environment, Health & Safety, United Technologies), Brock Evans (V.P., National Issues, National Audubon Society), Edmund Frost (Senior V.P., Clean Sites), F. Henry Habicht II (Senior V.P., Safety-Kleen Corp.), Barry Hill (Dir., Office of Hearings & Appeals, U.S. Dept. of Interior), Prof. Oliver Houck (Tulane Law School), Peter Kelsey (Pres., EcoStewards Alliance), Nancy Maloley (Fellow, J.F. Kennedy School of Government, Harvard Univ.), Rep. Eleanor Holmes Norton (D-DC), Prof. Robert Percival (Univ. of Maryland School of Law), Helen Petrauskas (V.P., Environmental & Safety Engineering, Ford Motor Co.), Kathy Prosser (Commissioner, Indiana Dept. of Environmental Management), Stephen Ramsey (V.P., Corporate Environmental Programs, General Electric Co.), Michael Richardson (V.P., Environment, Health & Safety, Pfizer Inc.), Karin Sheldon (Vermont Law School), Hon. Robert Stafford (former Senator, R-VT), James Strock (Sec. for Environmental Protection, California EPA), Thomas Udall (Attorney General, State of New Mexico), many others from the legal community.
Periodicals: *Environmental Law Reporter* and *National Wetlands Newsletter*.
Other Information: The Institute received $2,166,693, or 40% of revenue from, government grants. $1,286,020, or 24%, from gifts and grants awarded by foundations, affiliates, businesses and individuals. (These grants included $48,100 from the Environmental Federation of America.) $1,138,147, or 21%, from publication subscriptions and sales. $269,523, or 5%, from membership dues. $118,886, or 2%, from royalties. $106,637, or 2%, from fees and contracts paid by government agencies. $83,101 net, or 2%, from the sale of inventory. The remaining revenue came from dividends and interest from securities, interest on savings and temporary cash investments, special events, mailing list rentals, conferences, advertising, and miscellaneous sources.

Environmental Media Services

1606 20th St., N.W.
Washington, DC 20009   **Phone:**   (202) 745-0707
USA

Contact Person: Arlie Schardt.
Mission or Interest: Informs and updates reporters and the media on environmental concerns.
Tax Status: 501(c)(3)
Other Information: Shares office space with Fenton Communications, a for-profit public relations firm that represents environmental groups. Schardt is a former press secretary to Vice President Al Gore.

Environmental Research Foundation

P.O. Box 5036
Annapolis, MD 21403   **Phone:**   (410) 263-1584   **E-Mail:** erf@igc.apc.org
USA   **Fax:**   (410) 263-8944

Contact Person: Peter Montague, Executive Director.   **Officers or Principals:** Peter Montague, Executive Director ($60,000);
Ed Begley, Jr., President ($0); Gel Stevenson, Vice President/Treasurer ($0); Katherine Montague, Secretary.
Mission or Interest: "Provides consulting services and is developing a database on environmental matters for use by community
groups...Provides technical assistance to environmental groups to strengthen democracy at the local level. We gather technical
information, translate it into laymen's terms, then disseminate it using our weekly newsletter, our database, and direct personal
assistance."
Accomplishments: In 1994 the Foundation spent $368,307 on its projects.
Net Revenue: 1994 $472,426 **Net Expenses:** $395,499 93%/4%/3% **Net Assets:** $118,860 **Citations:** 10:198
Products or Services: Technical assistance and consulting. No lobbying in 1994, but in 1993 the Foundation spent $4,000 on
lobbying.
Tax Status: 501(c)(3)
Board of Directors or Trustees: Tom Webster.
Periodicals: *Rachel's Hazardous Waste News* (weekly).
Other Information: The Foundation received $438,889, or 93% of revenue, from gifts and grants awarded by foundations,
businesses, and individuals. (These grants included $100,000 from the Florence and John Schumann Foundation, $25,000 from the
Bauman Family Foundation, $25,000 from the Jessie Smith Noyes Foundation, $25,000 from the Bullitt Foundation, $10,000 from
the Beldon Fund, $5,500 from the Ruth Mott Fund, and $5,000 from the Compton Foundation.) $30,319, or 6%, from the sale of
publications. The remaining revenue came from interest on savings and temporary cash investments.

Environmental Support Center

1825 Connecticut Ave., N.W., Suite 220
Washington, DC 20009   **Phone:**   (202) 328-7813
USA

Contact Person: James W. Abernathy, Executive Director.   **Officers or Principals:** James W. Abernathy, Executive Director
($66,023); Patrick Sweeney, President ($0); Pat Bryant, Vice President ($0); Bill Davis, Treasurer; Lois Gibbs, Secretary.
Mission or Interest: "To assist in improving the environment in the United States through enhancing the health and well being of
regional, state, and local organizations working on environmental issues."
Accomplishments: In 1994 the Center spent $447,153 on its programs. The largest program, with expenditures of $177,796, was
training and technical assistance in fund raising strategy and organizational development. $129,243 was spent promoting "workplace
solicitation," which helps state and local environmental groups maximize their benefits from existing workplace giving programs."
$104,691 was spent distributing equipment and software. $35,423 was spent on a State Environmental Leadership Conference.
Net Revenue: 1994 $543,487 **Net Expenses:** $583,856 77%/12%/11% **Net Assets:** $56,658 **Citations:** 1:240
Tax Status: 501(c)(3)
Board of Directors or Trustees: Dorreen Carey, Brownie Carson (Natural Resources Council of Maine), Bruce Hamilton (Sierra
Club), Lark Hayes (Southern Environmental Law Center), Pablo Eisenberg (Center for Community Change), Richard Moore
(Southwest Network for Environmental and Economic Justice).
Other Information: Established in 1990. The Center received $540,995, or 99.5% of revenue, from gifts and grants awarded by
foundations, businesses, and individuals. (These grants included $35,000 from the Rockefeller Family Fund, $33,000 from the Joyce
Foundation, $20,000 from the Tides Foundation, $20,000 from the James C. Penney Foundation, $20,000 from the Jessie Smith
Noyes Foundation, and $10,000 from the Beldon Fund.) The remaining revenue came from interest on savings and temporary cash
investments.

Episcopal Church Public Policy Network

815 2nd Ave.
New York, NY 10017   **Phone:**   (212) 867-8400
USA

Mission or Interest: Public policy organization of the Episcopal Church. Pursues peace and justice, equality for women,
homosexual rights, ending racism, alleviating hunger and poverty, and a healthy environment.

Episcopal Peace Fellowship (EPF)

P.O. Box 28156
Washington, DC 20038   **Phone:**   (202) 783-3380
USA   **Fax:**   (202) 393-3695

Contact Person: Mary H. Miller, executive Secretary.   **Officers or Principals:** Mary H. Miller, Executive Secretary ($24,000);
Rev. Philip C. Jacobs, Chair ($0); Rev. David O. Selzar, Secretary ($0); Christopher Pottle, Treasury.
Mission or Interest: Episcopalians committed to peace, non-violence, and renouncing, as far as possible, participation in war and
other violent activities.
Accomplishments: Approximately 1,600 members. In 1994 the Fellowship spent $32,100 on its programs.
Net Revenue: 1994 $45,161 **Net Expenses:** $43,805 **Net Assets:** $39,312

Tax Status: 501(c)(3)
Periodicals: Newsletter.
Other Information: The Fellowship received $35,456, or 78% of revenue, from gifts and grants awarded by foundations, businesses, affiliates, and individuals. $7,533, or 17%, from program service revenues. $1,035, or 2%, from investment income. The remaining revenue came from various miscellaneous sources.

EPL / Environmental Advocates

353 Hamilton St.
Albany, NY 12210   **Phone:**   (518) 462-5526
USA

Contact Person: Lee Wasserman, Director.   **Officers or Principals:** Amy M. Klein, Assistant Director ($9,900); Lee Wasserman, Director ($6,828); Jim Tripp, President ($0); Val Washington, Vice President Administration; Charlie Kruzansky, Vice President, Public Policy; Patricia Rodriguez, Treasurer/Secretary.
Mission or Interest: Lobbying organization "which educates citizens, lawmakers, legislative staff and state agencies on New York state environmental and health policy."
Accomplishments: In 1994 the Advocates spent $174,709 on its programs.
Net Revenue: 1994 $260,419 **Net Expenses:** $264,470 66%/18%/16% **Net Assets:** $21,089
Tax Status: 501(c)(4)
Board of Directors or Trustees: Steve Allinger, Linda Davidoff (Parks Council), Kevin McDonald (Group of the South Fork), Rosemary Nichols, Ellen Pratt, Jim Tripp (Environmental Defense Fund).
Other Information: The organization was previously called the Environmental Planning Lobby. The organization received $240,308, or 92% of revenue, from gifts and grants awarded by foundations, businesses, and individuals. $17,564 net, or 8%, from special fund-raising events, including a Bonnie Raitt concert, a 25th Anniversary celebration, and a cocktail reception. The remaining revenue came from interest on savings and temporary cash investments. The organization lost $693 on the sale of assets.

Equal Rights Advocates (ERA)

1663 Mission St., Suite 550
San Francisco, CA 94103   **Phone:**   (415) 621-0672
USA

Contact Person: Nancy Lee Davis, President.
Officers or Principals: Nancy Lee Davis, President ($64,652); Judith Kurtz, Staff Attorney ($53,602); Gail Kaufman, Vice President ($51,050); Suzanne Lampert, Chair, Molly Martin, Vice Chair, Jean Crosby, Secretary/Treasurer.
Mission or Interest: Promotion of women's equality through litigation, public education, and policy advocacy.
Accomplishments: In the fiscal year ending March 1995 ERA spent $810,434 on their activities. The largest program was legal advocacy, at $243,130. Next were the public education efforts at $202,608. Three other areas, advice and counseling, public policy advocacy, and coalition building each received $121,565. Among the legal activities were the following: Adarand v. Pena, submitted an amicus brief before the U.S. Supreme Court supporting federal affirmative action programs. Csutoras v. KRPQ, FM, filed an amicus brief on behalf of an appeal by a lawyer who was not awarded court-ordered attorneys' fees despite his winning a sexual harassment case. Doe v. Petaluma, represented a sixteen-year-old girl in a sexual harassment lawsuit against the Petaluma school district. They claimed that their client was sexually harassed verbally and physically by other students in junior high. Farris v. Compton, signed an amicus brief authored by the NOW Legal Defense and Education Fund which sought to extend the discovery exception to the statute of limitations so that it extends to 'repressed memories' of a crime that occurred twenty to forty years ago. Virginia Military Institute v. United States, joined in an amicus brief against the military academy challenging their policy of excluding females from the Institute. They received $60,152 in court-awarded attorneys' fees. Most of those court-awarded fees, 76%, were paid by city and county governments.
Net Revenue: FY ending 3/95 $754,292 **Net Expenses:** $1,013,447 80%/9%/11% **Net Assets:** $1,002,693
Citations: 36:149150
Products or Services: Litigation, research and education, coalition building. Lobbying - in the fiscal year ending March 1995 they spent $9,874. $1,949 on grassroots lobbying and $7,925 on the direct lobbying of legislators. This was up about 24% over the previous year.
Tax Status: 501(c)(3)
Board of Directors or Trustees: Ann Brick (ACLU, Northern California), David Drumond (Lawyers Committee for Civil Rights), Cassandra Flipper (general counsel, The Nature Company), Lillian Ladaga Galedo (Exec. Dir., Filipinos for Affirmative Action), Miriam Goodman (Pres., Quality Time Video), Irma Herrera (San Francisco La Raza Lawyers), Marjorie Holmes (Vice Pres., Human Resources, Mervyn's), Herma Hill Kay (Dean, Berkeley School of Law), Rachel Morello-Frosch, Irving Pfeffer, Elizabeth Salveson, Diane Scheiman, Deborah Schmall, Kathleen Owyang Turner.
Other Information: ERA received $602,711, or 80% of revenue, from direct and indirect public support in the form of gifts and grants from foundations, businesses, and individuals. (These grants included $30,000 from the Rockefeller Family Fund, $10,000 from the Wallace Alexander Gerbode Foundation, $500 from the Tides Foundation.) $60,152, or 8%, from court-awarded attorney's fees. $28,699 net, or 4%, from special fund-raising events. $27,718, or 4%, from dividends and interest on securities. $18,844, or 2%, from interest on savings and temporary cash investments. $16,733, or 2%, from educational program fees. ERA has received continuing support from the Ford Foundation, San Francisco Foundation, and the Rockefeller Foundation.

Esperanza Peace and Justice Center
922 San Pedro St.
San Antonio, TX 78212   **Phone:**   (210) 228-0201
USA

Mission or Interest: Multicultural organization that conducts educational activities combining issues of race, class and gender with homosexual politics and culture.
Other Information: In 1994 donors included the Astraea National Lesbian Action Foundation. In 1995 the Center received $50,000 from the Rockefeller Foundation.

Essential Information
P.O. Box 19405
Washington, DC 20036   **Phone:**   (202) 387-8030   **E-Mail:** books@essential.org
USA   **Fax:**   (202) 234-5776   **Web-Page:** http://www.essential.org

Contact Person: Cynthia Renfro, Business Manager.   **Officers or Principals:** Rob Weissman, Editor; Russell Mokhibee, President ($0); Joan Claybrook, Treasurer ($0); John Richard, Secretary ($0).
Mission or Interest: Provides information on topics neglected by the mass media. Topics include: multinational corporations and their effect on our economy and the third world, labor movements, consumer information and environmental issues. Bank Accountability Project that "investigates racial discrimination by banks and mortgage companies."
Accomplishments: In 1993 97% of their expenditures went to their programs. They spent $174,524 on publication and distribution of the *Multinational Monitor*, a weekly publication dealing with the effects of multinational corporations on social conditions. In 1990 the *Multinational Monitor* won the *Utne Reader* Alternative Press award for Best International Reporting. $502,287 spent on research and analysis. They awarded $88,050 in grants. Top recipients included $50,000 for the Time Dollar Network, $11,300 for the Alaska Public Interest Research Group, and $10,250 for the MetroDC Environmental Network.
Net Revenue: 1993 $707,576 **Net Expenses:** $700,472 97%/3%/1% **Net Assets:** (-$155,004) **Citations:** 332:55
Products or Services: Grants, publications, and research. A listing of pertinent books. "Multinationals and Development Clearinghouse" that provides individuals and organizations with information on a wide variety of topics pertaining to multinational corporations. Good Works: A Guide to careers in Social Change.
Tax Status: 501(c)(3) **Annual Report:** No. **Employees:** 30
Periodicals: *Multinational Monitor* (monthly magazine), and *Newsprints* (biweekly compilation of news, cartoons and stories from local papers nationwide).
Internships: Yes.
Other Information: Founded in 1982 by Ralph Nader. Essential Information received $575,045, or 81% of revenue, from gifts and grants awarded by foundations, companies, and individuals. (In 1994 these grants included $159,300 from the Tides Foundation, $25,000 from the Rockefeller Family Foundation and $5,000 from the Joyce Foundation.) $83,047 net, or 12%, from the sale of inventory. $47,949, or 7%, from subscriptions to *Multinational Monitor*. The remaining revenue came from interest on savings and temporary cash investments, and dividends and interest on securities.

Evangelicals for Social Action (ESA)
10 Lancaster Ave.
Wynnewood, PA 19096   **Phone:**   (215) 645-9390
USA

Contact Person: Cliff R. Benzel, Executive Vice President.
Officers or Principals: Cliff R. Benzel, Executive Vice President ($8,292); Ronald J. Sider, President ($0); Bryant Myers, Chair ($0); Gretchen Hull, Vice Chair; Herb Van Denend, Treasurer; Polly Ann Brown, Secretary.
Mission or Interest: Christian association working for social change. Focus on the rights of women and minorities, social inequality, and the environment.
Accomplishments: In the shortened fiscal year from January to September 1993, ESA spent $143,050 on its programs. These programs included $21,751 in grants and assistance for scholarships at the neighboring Eastern Baptist Theological Seminary. Scholarships are awarded for "Evangelism and Social Change," graduate research with Prof. Ronald J. Sider (author of Rich Christians in an Age of Hunger and One-Sided Christianity), and special scholarships on the environment. Social Change scholarships are named after Charles Finney, "the most famous American Evangelist of the 19th century an active abolitionist, in the crusade against slavery, and an early champion of women's rights." Environmental scholarships work with the Evangelical Environmental Network which has, among other things, opposed reforming the Endangered Species Act, calling it the "Noah's Ark of our day." "Women and minorities are especially encouraged to apply."
Net Revenue: FY running from 1/93 to 9/93 $353,544 **Net Expenses:** $225,004 64%/30%/7% **Net Assets:** $252,379
Products or Services: Scholarships, educational materials, seminars, and speakers.
Tax Status: 501(c)(3)
Board of Directors or Trustees: Polly Ann Brown, Samuel Escobar (Eastern Baptist Theological Seminary), Art Simon (Christian Children's Fund), Kathy Tuan McLean, Raleigh Washington.
Other Information: ESA received $324,656, or 92% of revenue, from gifts and grants awarded by foundations, businesses, and individuals. $24,579, or 7%, from membership dues. $2,770, or 1%, from interest on savings and temporary cash investments. The remaining revenue came from expense reimbursements.

Evangelicals for Social Action, Fresno

680 W. Shaw Ave.
Fresno, CA 93710-7704   **Phone:**   (209) 244-0105
USA

Contact Person: Allen Doswald, Executive Director.   **Officers or Principals:** Allen Doswald, Executive Director ($56,026); Paul Binion, Chairman ($0); Jim Westgate, Vice Chairman ($0); David Knowles, Secretary; Keith Brown, Treasurer.
Mission or Interest: Evangelical Christians focusing on public policy and various social problems. Public education on the poor, homeless, refugees, and the environment. Evangelicals for Social Action called the Endangered Species Act "the Noah's ark of our day," and called on the public to resist Republican efforts to alter the Act.
Accomplishments: In 1994 the Fresno Evangelicals for Social Action spent $268,307 on its programs. The largest program spent $107,323 "finding resources in neighborhood revitalization." This was the Christian Community Development project. $80,492 was spent organizing area churches to "meet the emergency needs of people due to economic conditions." $53,661 was spent locating churches to assist the homeless. $26,831 was spent developing "caring ministries to disabled persons, community leaders and refugee children."
Net Revenue: 1994 $373,104 **Net Expenses:** $350,862 76%/19%/5% **Net Assets:** $76,644
Tax Status: 501(c)(3)
Board of Directors or Trustees: Rick Arri, Steve Davidson, Linda Decker, Angelica Gonzalez, Mark Helm, Tcher Her, Bruce McAllister, Don Neufeld, Jonathan Villalobos, Paul Warkentin.
Other Information: The organization received $372,861, or 99.9% of revenue, from gifts and grants awarded by foundations, businesses, and individuals. The remaining revenue came from interest on savings and temporary cash investments.

Factsheet Five

P.O. Box 170099
San Francisco, CA 94117   **Phone:**   (415) 621-1761
USA

Contact Person: R. Seth Friedman.
Mission or Interest: Promotes free speech by reviewing independent publications of all types. Reviews and lists magazines and 'zines. Organizes shows of the various publications.
Tax Status: For profit.   **Periodicals:** *Factsheet Five* (magazine).   **Internships:** No.

Fairness and Accuracy In Reporting (FAIR)

130 W. 25th St.
New York, NY 10001   **Phone:**   (212) 633-6700
USA   **Fax:**   (212) 727-7668

Contact Person: Jeff Cohen, President.   **Officers or Principals:** Jeff Cohen, President ($35,000); Steve Revdell, Secretary ($26,900); Linda Valentino, Vice President ($0); Andy Breslau, Treasurer.
Mission or Interest: "A media watch organization engaged in correcting media bias and practices that slight public interest and minority viewpoints...analysis of biased and inaccurate news; censorship issues; racism, sexism and homophobia in the press; and the influence of corporate ownership of media outlets."
Accomplishments: FAIR sponsored the 1996 Media and Democracy Congress in San Francisco. Topics included strengthening independent journalism, grappling with new technology, and responding to threats from the Right. Other sponsors included the Center for Media Education, Pacifica, *The Progressive*, Political Research Associates, and *Utne Reader*. In the fiscal year ending June 1994, FAIR spent $686,510 on its programs. The majority, $655,816, was spent on media monitoring and the production of research and publications. $30,694 was spent to produce a weekly syndicated radio show, CounterSpin. CounterSpin aired on over 80 stations nationwide, and on shortwave's Radio For Peace International. CounterSpin is distributed via satellite and audio cassettes. FAIR's journal, *EXTRA!*, is received by over 17,000 subscribers.
Net Revenue: FY ending 6/94 $779,124 **Net Expenses:** $822,836 83%/11%/6% **Net Assets:** (-$103,054) **Citations:** 145:97
Products or Services: The Way Things Aren't: Rush Limbaugh's Reign of Error (the magazine *Extra!* devotes a section every month to contradicting and correcting radio host Rush Limbaugh's statements), other books.
Tax Status: 501(c)(3)
Periodicals: *EXTRA!* (eight times a year magazine).
Other Information: FAIR's Jeff Cohen is the author of several books, including Through the Media Looking Glass: Decoding Bias and Blather in the News (Common Courage Press, 1995). FAIR received $616,137, or 79% of revenue, from gifts and grants awarded by foundations, businesses, and individuals. (These grants included $20,000 from the Angelina Fund, $15,000 from the Barbra Streisand Foundation, $15,000 from the Bydale Foundation, $3,000 from the Tides Foundation, $2,500 from the New World Foundation, $2,000 from the Stewart R. Mott Charitable Trust.) $136,417, or 18%, from subscriptions to *EXTRA!* $21,511, or 3%, from the sale of printed matter and audio tapes. $4,272, or 1%, from radio show distribution fees. The remaining revenue came from interest on savings and temporary cash investments.

FairTest: The National Center for Fair and Open Testing

342 Broadway
Cambridge, MA 02139   **Phone:**   (617) 864-4810   **E-Mail:** FairTest@aol.com
USA   **Fax:**   (617) 497-2224

Contact Person: Carolyn Thall

Officers or Principals: Donald Neill, Assistant Director ($47,000); Bob Schaeffer, Secretary/Treasurer ($37,800); Pamela Zappardino, Executive Director; John Weiss, President; Sophia Sa, Chair.

Mission or Interest: FairTest works to "end the abuses, misuses and flaws of standardized testing; we recognize that standardized testing reinforces racial, class, gender and cultural barriers to equal opportunity, and that it damages the quality of education."

Accomplishments: FairTest spearheaded new York's "Truth in Testing" legislation. Took legal action against the National Merit Scholarship's use of the PSAT for selecting semi-finalists. Launched a campaign against the NCAA using SAT and ACT scores to grant athletic eligibility. In the fiscal year ending September 1994 they spent $328,169 to research the use of standardized testing to evaluate students and workers.

Net Revenue: FY ending 9/94 $350,909 **Net Expenses:** $361,339 91%/7%/2% **Net Assets:** $36,263

Products or Services: Studies and reports. Guides to reform, "Implementing Performance Assessments" and "Principals and Indicators for Student Assessment Systems." Information clearinghouse. Technical assistance to reformers.

Tax Status: 501(c)(3)

Board of Directors or Trustees: Ron Ellis (NAACP Legal Defense and Education Fund), Pamela George (School of Education, NC Central Univ.), Deborah Meier (Central Park East Secondary School), Susan Navarro (Dir., SW Center for Academic Excellence, Univ. of TX, El Paso), Vito Perrone (Harvard Graduate School of Education), Bill Robinson (DC School of Law), Chuck Stone, Ron Vera (Loyola Law School).

Other Information: The Center received $325,141, or 93% of revenue, from gifts and grants awarded by foundations, companies, and individuals. (These grants included $35,000 from the Rockefeller Family Fund.) $23,061, or 7%, from the distribution of research. The remaining revenue came from interest on savings and temporary cash investments.

Families USA

1334 G St., N.W., 3rd Floor
Washington, DC 20005   **Phone:** (202) 628-3030
USA   **Fax:** (202) 347-2417

Contact Person: Ronald F. Pollack, Executive Director. **Officers or Principals:** Ronald F. Pollack, Executive Director ($11,791); Barbara Campbell, Counsel ($5,843); David L. Engel, Secretary ($118); Philippe Villers, President.

Mission or Interest: Public policy lobbying organization that focuses on health care.

Accomplishments: In 1994 the organization spent $279,486 on its programs. These included $263,473 on public information and lobbying efforts. Efforts included a grant of $100,000 for the Health Security Express, the bus trip accross the country promoting the Clinton's health care plan. $16,013 was spent on a grassroots lobbying network comprised of approximately 10,000 persons "interested in health care, long term care, and economic issues affecting America's families." Families USA started the year with a deficit of $4,246,004. Some of the deficit was incurred during the previous year when Families USA was one of the most prominent and ardent supporters of the Clinton health care plan, spending $792,796 to promote these proposed reforms.

Net Revenue: 1994 $532,074 **Net Expenses:** $349,057 80%/8%/12% **Net Assets:** (-$4,062,987) **Citations:** 209:79

Tax Status: 501(c)(4)

Board of Directors or Trustees: Dr. Robert Crittenden (Health Policy Analysis, Washington School of Medicine), Dr. Arthur Flemming, Douglas Fraser, Robert Kuttner (*American Prospect*, syndicated columnist), Lance Lindblom, Velvet Miller, Katherine Villers, Esther Peterson.

Other Information: Affiliated with the 501(c)(3) Families USA Foundation at the same address. Ronald Pollack is the executive director of both, and in 1994 was compensated with a combined $115,088 from the two organizations. The organization had, in the past, received significant funding from a personal loan from president Philippe Villers. At the start of 1994, Families USA owed $4,350,375 on the loan, and at the end of the year, owed $4,071,452. The organization received $325,577 net, or 66% of revenue from the sale of assets, all of it from the sale of the organization's mailing list. $175,306, or 33%, from gifts and grants awarded by foundations, businesses, and individuals. $2,819, or 1%, from interest on savings and temporary cash investment. The remaining revenue came from mailing list rentals.

Families USA Foundation

1334 G St., N.W.
Washington, DC 20005   **Phone:** (202) 628-3030
USA   **Fax:** (202) 347-2417

Contact Person: Ronald F. Pollack, Vice President. **Officers or Principals:** Ronald F. Pollack, Vice President ($89,512); Phyllis Torda, Director of Health and Social Policy ($65,874); Margaret Ross, Administrator ($60,862); Philippe Villers, President; Katherine S. Villers, Assistant Treasurer; David L. Engel, Clerk.

Mission or Interest: Foundation that engages in direct charitable activities, as well as awarding grants to other organizations. Primary focus is on health care. The Foundation was an ardent supporter of the Clinton health care plan.

Accomplishments: In 1993 the Foundation spent $2,271,163 on direct charitable activities. These activities included $1,966,222 spent on public education about health care reform. $139,060 was spent providing training and assistance to other organizations around the country. Other programs were devoted to increasing awareness about Supplemental Security Income benefits in Massachusetts, and a project to assess the future health care needs of Boston's population. The Foundation awarded $82,192 in grants. Recipients included: four grants totaling $27,500 for Health Care for All, $20,000 for Massachusetts Senior Action Council, and $10,792 for the Franklin County Home Care Corporation to continue production and distribution of "Seniorgrams," radio public service announcements on aging and other public policy issues. Other recipients included the Northeast Citizen Action Research Center, Massachusetts Tenants Resource Center, and the Maine People's Resource Center.

Net Revenue: 1993 $2,994,751 **Net Expenses:** $4,341,048 **Net Assets:** $15,475,929 **Citations:** 209:79

Tax Status: 501(c)(3)

Periodicals: *SeniorWatch*.
Other Information: Formerly called the Villers Foundation. Affiliated with the 501(c)(4) Families USA. The Foundation received $1,590,717, or 53% of revenue, from gifts and grants awarded by foundations, businesses, and individuals. (These grants included $65,000 from the labor-backed Committee for National Health Insurance. In 1994 these included $75,000 from the Tides Foundation.) $753,082, or 25%, from capital gains on the sale of securities. $352,813, or 12%, from rental income. $241,014, or 8%, from dividends and interest from securities. The remaining income came from interest on savings and other temporary cash investments, sale of publications, royalties, and contract income. Between July 1993 and June 1994, the Families USA Foundation received $250,000 from the U.S. Department of Health and Human Services.

Farm Animals Reform Movement (FARM)

10101 Ashburton Lane
Bethesda, MD 20817   **Phone:**   (301) 530-1737   **E-Mail:** farm@gnn.com
USA   **Fax:**   (301) 530-5747   **Web-Page:** http://members.gnn.com/farm

Contact Person: Beth Fiteni.   **Officers or Principals:** Alex Hershaft, President ($0); Melinda Marks, Vice President ($0); Michael Klaper ($0); Scott Williams, Executive Director.
Mission or Interest: Animal rights, environmentalism, and vegetarianism. "To expose and stop animal abuse and other negative impacts of intensive animal agriculture."
Accomplishments: Provides national coordination, guidance, media liaison, and handouts for the "Great American Meatout," a national day of meatless eating. Other events include World Farm Animals Day, and National Veal Ban Action. Consumers for Healthy Options in Children's Education, a program advocating meatless meals in schools. In 1994 the organization spent $103,200 on its programs.
Net Revenue: 1994 $120,861 **Net Expenses:** $119,764 86%/6%/8% **Net Assets:** $7,163
Tax Status: 501(c)(3) **Annual Report:** Yes. **Employees:** 3
Periodicals: *The FARM Report* (quarterly newsletter).
Internships: Yes, positions available for January - March, and September - October.
Other Information: Previously called the Vegetarian Information Service (1976-1981). FARM received $121,666, or 100% of gross revenue, from gifts and grants awarded by foundations, businesses, and individuals. FARM lost $805 on the sale of inventory (videos, books, t-shirts, etc.).

Farm Labor Organizing Committee

507 S. St. Clair
Toledo, OH 43602   **Phone:**   (419) 243-3456
USA

Contact Person: Baldemar Velasquez, President.   **Officers or Principals:** Baldemar Velasquez, President ($38,100); Ricky Velasquez, Secretary/Treasurer ($28,500); Fernando Cuevas, Vice President ($0).
Mission or Interest: "Labor organizing among migrant farmworkers and resident seasonal workers...possible collective solutions via labor organizing."
Accomplishments: In 1994 the Farm Labor Organizing Committee spent $203,943 on its programs.
Net Revenue: 1994 $321,290 **Net Expenses:** $254,064 80%/15%/5% **Net Assets:** $423,295
Products or Services: Labor union organizing and leadership training.
Tax Status: 501(c)(5)
Board of Directors or Trustees: Fernando Cuevas, Jr., Berna Romero, Juan Rizo, German De La Cruz.
Other Information: The Farm Labor Organizing Committee and President Baldemar Velasquez have been strong supporters of the building of a new labor party in the U.S. Velasquez says that the unions' unconditional support of the Democratic Party has hurt them. Commenting on the AFL-CIO's newly elected president, Velasquez said "One thing Sweeney has to do if he's going to modernize the labor movement and get past the racism, the xenophobia, the provincialism of American labor - he needs to make an all out effort to really internationalize the labor movement." Velasquez believes U.S. unions ought to build ties with Mexican labor unions. Affiliated with the 501(c)(3) Farm Labor Research Project. The Committee pays union dues to the AFL-CIO; $6,332 in 1994. The Committee received $137,804, or 43% of revenue, from health, education, and leadership project services. $93,887, or 29%, from membership dues. $58,275, or 18%, from gifts and grants awarded by foundations, companies, and individuals. $12,965, or 4%, from fees for camp representatives who assist farmworkers in contract issues and personal problems at migrant camps. $9,036, or 3%, from interest on savings and temporary cash investments. The remaining revenue came from dividends and interest from securities, special fund-raising events, and other miscellaneous sources,

Farm Labor Research Project (FLRP)

P.O. Box 550
Toledo, OH 43697   **Phone:**   (419) 243-3456
USA

Contact Person: Baldemar Velasquez, President.
Officers or Principals: Baldemar Velasquez, President ($0); Sara Rios, Secretary/Treasurer ($0).

Mission or Interest: Charitable, educational, and scientific activities for the benefit of migrant and former farmworkers in Northwestern Ohio. Provides charitable services including "emergency food, clothing and shelter, as well as health care, legal services, and social services which address the root cause of the recipient's poverty-related problem." Helps migrant farm workers apply for and receive welfare services.

Accomplishments: In 1994 the Project spent $478,752 on its programs. Provided research, technical assistance, and leadership development to "90,000 farmworkers and their organizations."

Net Revenue: 1994 $576,339 **Net Expenses:** $625,472 77%/10%/13% **Net Assets:** $141,490 **Citations:** 0:255

Products or Services: Social services, educational programs, leadership development, monitoring of pesticides and possible effects on laborers.

Tax Status: 501(c)(3)

Board of Directors or Trustees: Kenneth Barger, Mike Ferner, Ernesto Reza, Antero Rodriguez, Olga Villa-Parra.

Other Information: FLRP is affiliated with the 501(c)(5) Farm Labor Organizing Committee. The Project received $518,918, or 90% of revenue, from gifts and grants awarded by foundations, companies, and individuals. (These grants included $70,000 from the Campaign for Human Development, $20,000 from the New World Foundation.) $23,407, or 4%, from the educational and training projects. $22,681, or 4%, from the sale of inventory. The remaining revenue came from interest on savings and temporary cash investments, sale of assets, dividends and interest from securities.

Federally Employed Women
1400 Eye St., N.W., Suite 425
Washington, DC 20005   **Phone:**   (202) 898-0994
USA

Contact Person: Karen Scott, Executive Director.

Officers or Principals: Lunn Epherdt, Legislative Director ($42,354); Karen Scott, Executive Director ($38,758).

Mission or Interest: Lobbies to "end sex discrimination in the federal government; to increase job opportunities for women in the federal government and to further the use of the potential of women who work within the federal government."

Accomplishments: In the fiscal year ending June 1993, Federally Employed Women spent $290,524 on its programs.

Net Revenue: FY ending 6/93 $449,426 **Net Expenses:** $463,881 63%/37%/0% **Net Assets:** $461,455

Products or Services: Lobbying, publications, videos, training programs, legislative breakfast, more.

Tax Status: 501(c)(4)

Board of Directors or Trustees: Mahealani Tolbert, Randy Cross, Dorothy Renteria, Dolores Tiburcio, Beatrice Bolds, Dorothy Nelms, Marie Argana, Mary Holzer, Yvonne Duncan, Eleanor Friendenberg, Audrey Phillips, Judith Hartwell, Patricia Wolfe.

Other Information: Affiliated with the 501(c)(3) Federally Employed Women's Legal and Education Fund at the same address. The organization received $296,092, or 66% of revenue from its National Training Program. $98,390, or 22%, from membership dues. $24,707, or 5%, from a Legislative Breakfast. $10,841, or 2%, from interest on savings and temporary cash investments. The remaining revenue came from miscellaneous sources.

Federation for Industrial Retention and Renewal (FIRR)
3411 W. Diversey Ave., Suite 10
Chicago, IL 60647   **Phone:**   (312) 278-7676
USA

Contact Person: Jimm Benn.

Mission or Interest: Network of community organizations. Focus on local development and community reinvestment. Urban economic planning with a focus on creating jobs that pay 'a living wage.'

Accomplishments: Thirty-three member organizations. Have devloped plans for Cleveland, OH, Birmingham, AL, and Charleston, SC.

Federation of American Scientists (FAS)
307 Massachusetts Ave., N.E.
Washington, DC 20002   **Phone:**   (202) 546-3300   **E-Mail:** fas@fas.org
USA   **Fax:**   (202) 675-1010   **Web-Page:** http://www.fas.org/pub/gen/fas/

Contact Person: Jeremy J. Stone, President. **Officers or Principals:** Jeremy J. Stone, President ($6,600); Carl Kaysen, Vice Chairman; Ann Druyan, Secretary; Charles C. Price, Treasurer; Robert M. Solow, Chairman.

Mission or Interest: FAS was founded in 1945 by members of the Manhattan Project. Originally founded to deal with issues relating to nuclear weaponry, they have expanded to cover other issues facing science and scientists. Their early slogan regarding nuclear weapons was "No secret, no defense and international control." That is, the secret of the atomic bomb's operation should not be kept, that nations should not prepare to defend against it, and international controls were the only hope for preventing nuclear war.

Accomplishments: Credited with the defeat of the proposal to build the B-1 Bomber in 1976. Played a major role in the defeat of the Strategic Defense Initiative (Star Wars). Played a key role in assisting Soviet dissident scientist Andrei Sakharov secure his freedom. More recently they have lobbied for an energy policy and worked for animal rights. Had a major impact on scaling back the B-2 Bomber program.

Net Revenue: FY ending 6/94 $86,956 **Net Expenses:** $83,796 51%/30%/19% **Net Assets:** $42,372

Products or Services: Lobbying, research. They present an annual Public Service Award; 1995's winner was the Worldwatch Institute's Lester Brown.

Tax Status: 501(c)(4) **Annual Report:** No. **Employees:** 12
Board of Directors or Trustees: Their Board of Sponsors includes Nobel Laureates; Philip Anderson, Christian Anfinsen, Kenneth Arrow, David Baltimore, Hans Bethe, Konrad Bloch, Norman Borlaug, Owen Chamberlain, Leon Cooper, Andre Cournand, Renato Dulbecco, Val Fitch, Walter Gilbert, Donald Glaser, Sheldon, Glashow, Alfred Hershey, Robert Holley, H. Gobind Khorana, Arthur Kornberg, Polykarp Kusch, Willis Lamb, Jr., Wassily Leontief, William Lipscomb, S.E. Luria, Daniel Nathans, Marshall Nirenberg, Severo Ochoa, Arno Penzias, Edward Purcell, Burton Richter, J. Robert Scrieffer, Julian Schwinger, Glenn Seaborg, Herbert Simon, Henry Taube, Howard Temin, James Tobin, Charles Townes, and George Wald.
Periodicals: *Public Interest Report* (bimonthly newsletter).
Internships: No.
Other Information: Affiliated with the 501(c)(3) Federation of American Scientists Fund at the same address. Jeremy Stone served as president of both affiliates and received compensation from both. The Federation received $85,560, or 98% of revenue, from membership dues. The remaining revenue came from interest on savings and temporary cash investments.

Federation of American Scientists Fund

307 Massachusetts Ave., N.E.
Washington, DC 20002   **Phone:** (202) 546-3300   **E-Mail:** fas@fas.org
USA   **Fax:**   (202) 675-1010   **Web-Page:** http://www.fas.org/pub/gen/fas/

Contact Person: Jeremy J. Stone, President. **Officers or Principals:** Jeremy J. Stone, President ($94,534); John Pike, Associate Director ($93,006); George Rathjens, Chairman ($0).
Mission or Interest: FAS was founded in 1945 by members of the Manhattan Project. Membership includes scientists pursuing peace through disarmament and regulation.
Accomplishments: In the fiscal year ending June 1995, the Fund spent $628,608 on its programs. The largest program, with expenditures of $272,329, was the Space Policy Project, "an educational project designed to alert the media and others to technical issues of the Strategic Defense Initiative and other space policy." $219,976 was spent on arms sales and secrecy in government programs. $72,379 for chemical and biological warfare studies. $45,000 on the Zero Ballistic project "to organize a worldwide regime banning ballistic missiles for offensive purposes."
Net Revenue: FY ending 6/95 $546,256 **Net Expenses:** $801,844 78%/16%/6% **Net Assets:** $2,063,273 **Citations:** 0:255
Tax Status: 501(c)(3)
Board of Directors or Trustees: Rosalyn Schwartz, Martin Stone, Moshe Alafi, Martin Thaler, William Higinbotham, Alan Thorndike, Robert Weinberg (Whitehead Inst.), Proctor Houghton (Houghton Chemical Co.), Ann Druyan, Mark Kleiman, Richard Muller, William Revelle, Raymond Sczudlo.
Other Information: Affiliated with the 501(c)(4) Federation of American Scientists at the same address. Jeremy Stone serves as president of both and is compensated by both. The Fund received $444,942, or 81% of revenue, from gifts and grants awarded by foundations, businesses, and individuals. (These grants included $68,640 from the Rockefeller Foundation, $30,000 from the Rockefeller Family Fund, $20,000 from the Ploughshares Fund, $20,000 from the New-Land Foundation, $15,000 from the Deer Creek Foundation, $15,000 from the Compton Foundation, $10,000 from the C.S. Fund, $2,000 from the Stewart R. Mott Charitable Trust.) $92,014, or 17%, from interest on savings and temporary cash investments. $8,281 net, or 2%, from rental income. The remaining revenue came from capital gains on the sale of securities and other miscellaneous sources.

Fellowship of Reconciliation (FOR)

P.O. Box 271
Nyack, NY 10960   **Phone:** (914) 358-4601   **E-Mail:** fornatl@igc.apc.org
USA   **Fax:**   (914) 358-4924

Contact Person: Jo Becker, Executive Director.
Officers or Principals: Doug Hostetter, Interfaith Director ($40,319); David Schilling, Disarmament Coordinator ($36,630); Richard Deats, Communications Director ($36,102); James Lawson, Chair; Lou Ann Gaunson, Vice Chair.
Mission or Interest: "Founded in 1914, the Fellowship of Reconciliation is an international, spiritually-based movement composed of women and men committed to active nonviolence as a means of personal, social and political change. While it has always been vigorous in its opposition to war, the Fellowship has insisted equally that this effort must be based on a commitment to achieving a just and peaceful world community with full dignity and freedom for every human being."
Accomplishments: Chapters and affiliates in over 40 countries. Helped organize the National Civil Liberties Bureau, now the ACLU, in 1916. Sent a peace delegation to meet Sandino in Nicaragua in the 1920's. Worked with the labor movement in the 1930's. Worked with conscientious objectors and encouraged nonviolent resistance to World War II. Worked with Martin Luther King Jr. during the Montgomery bus boycott. Raised money for medical aid for both sides during the Vietnam War. Recent campaigns opposed the Gulf War, helped victims of the war in former Yugoslavia. "Stop the Killing, Start the Healing" campaign that "focuses on the causes of violence in local communities, linking analyses of militarism, racism, economic injustice, gun violence and other issues with faith-based nonviolent responses and strategies. The initial stage of this work began as a pilot project in Louisville, KY, where FOR has worked to build a city-wide campaign to eliminate handgun violence while creating a climate for public health and safety." In the fiscal year ending June 1994, the Fellowship spent $851,584 on its programs.
Net Revenue: FY ending 6/94 $1,381,532 **Net Expenses:** $1,356,621 63%/22%/15% **Net Assets:** $1,804,485
Citations: 84:113
Tax Status: 501(c)(3) **Annual Report:** Yes. **Employees:** 22
Board of Directors or Trustees: Glen Anderson, William Anderson, Lillian Baxter, Nadjla Birkland, Bonnie Block, Katy Gray Brown, Dorothy Cotton, Arun Gandhi, Paula Green, Nisar Hai, Ann Hardt, Tarek El Heneidy, Robert Holmes, Edythe Jones, Ron Krabill, Stefan Merken, Cecil Prescod.

Periodicals: *Fellowship* (bimonthly magazine), *Panama Update* (quarterly newsletter).
Internships: Yes. FOR hosts three full-time, one year, internships. Room, stipend, and health insurance provided.
Other Information: "The FOR began in the earliest days of World War I, when a German Lutheran and a British Quaker pledged to find a way of working for peace even while their countries were at war." The Fellowship received $979,485, or 71% of total revenue, from gifts and grants awarded by foundations, businesses, affiliates, and individuals. (These grants included $1,250 from the Vanguard Public Foundation, $1,000 from the Joyce Mertz-Gilmore Foundation.) $214,687, or 16%, from the sales and subscriptions of Fellowship publications. $91,530, or 7%, from annuity income. $80,860, or 6%, from interest on savings and temporary cash investments. $16,998, or 1%, from dividends and interest from securities. The remaining revenue came from royalties. The Fellowship lost $2,199 on the sale of securities.

Feminist Majority Foundation

8105 W. Third St., Suite 1
Los Angeles, CA 90048   **Phone:**   (213) 651-0495
USA   **Fax:**   (213) 653-2689   **Web-Page:** http://www.feminist.org

Contact Person: Susan Gilligan, Manager.
Officers or Principals: Eleanor Smeal, President ($83,637); Katherine Spillar, Secretary ($65,425); Charles Smeal, Mail Manager ($64,661); Toni Carabillo, Vice President; Peg Yorkin, Chair; Ann Tansey, Treasurer.
Mission or Interest: "The Feminist Majority, a feminist think tank, develops creative long-term strategies and permanent solutions for the pervasive social, political, and economic obstacles facing women." Supports: The Equal Rights Amendment, the expansion of affirmative action, abortion rights, lesbian and gay rights, economic justice, recognition of homemakers' work in the Social Security System, elimination of poverty, elimination of violence, and more.
Accomplishments: The Feminist Majority Foundation sent a ten person delegation to the Fourth World Conference in Beijing, China. In 1994 the Foundation spent $1,682,149 on its programs. The largest program, with expenditures of $640,468, was the abortion clinic access program. $583,395 was spent on research and education. $211,250 was spent on leadership training. $118,792 was spent on reproductive rights. Other programs included "Women Empowerment," violence against women, and equality education and research.
Net Revenue: 1994 $2,612,085 **Net Expenses:** $2,241,233 75%/14%/11% **Net Assets:** $4,243,115 **Citations:** 149:94
Products or Services: Research and education. Policy advocacy. Speaking engagements. Lobbying - in 1994 they spent $15,000 on grassroots lobbying. This was down 65% from the previous year, and down 91% from two years prior.
Tax Status: 501(c)(3)
Board of Directors or Trustees: Dolores Huerta, Dorothy Jonas, Judith Meuli, Rae Wyman.
Internships: Yes, many openings.
Other Information: The Foundation is affiliated with the 501(c)(4) lobbying Fund For the Feminist Majority at the same address. The Foundation transferred $102,432 to this affiliate in 1994. In 1993 the two affiliates had combined net revenues of $2,118,649, net expenses of $1,998,695, and net assets of $3,758,635. Eleanor Smeal served as president of both and was paid a combined $94,946. Katherine Spillar received a combined $70,213. The Foundation also has a Virginia office near the District of Columbia: 1600 Wilson Blvd., Suite 801, Arlington, VA 22209, (703) 522-2214, fax (703) 522-2219. Eleanor Smeal is a former president of the National Organization for Women. In 1993 the highest paid employee of the Feminist Majority Foundation was a male, Charles Smeal, who held the position of Mail Manager. The Foundation received $2,270,907, or 87% of revenue, from gifts and grants awarded by foundations, businesses, and individuals. (These grants included $25,000 from the General Services Foundation, and $25,000 from the Jessie Smith Noyes Foundation, $20,000 from the Robert Sterling Clark Foundation.) $264,063, or 10%, from dividends and interest from securities. $62,165 net, or 2%, from special fund-raising events. The remaining revenue came from mailing list rentals, and interest on savings and temporary cash investments. In 1994 the Foundation's net revenue increased 93% over the previous year. Net expenses increased 18%, and net assets increased 8%.

Feminist Press

311 E. 94th St.
New York, NY 10128   **Phone:**   (212) 360-5790
USA   **Fax:**   (212) 348-1241

Contact Person: Susan Cozzi, Associate Director.   **Officers or Principals:** Susannah Driver, Associate Director ($41,200); Susan Cozzi, Associate Director ($38,875); Florence Howe, Director ($4,500); Helene Goldfarb, Chair; Nida E. Thomas, Vice Chair; Margaret M. Smyth, Treasurer; Sue Rosenberg Zalk, Secretary.
Mission or Interest: "Publishing and distributing publications aimed toward changing male and female stereotypes...Development of non sexist texts with a focus on women...Dissemination of information relating to the changing images about women to the general public by means of consultations and lectures."
Accomplishments: In 1994 the Feminist Press spent $878,182 on its programs. The Press received a grant from the Population Council for the production of a book.
Net Revenue: 1994 $1,195,293 ($9,120, or 1%, from government grants) **Net Expenses:** $1,005,058 87%/9%/4%
Net Assets: $194,438 **Citations:** 40:144
Tax Status: 501(c)(3)
Board of Directors or Trustees: Alida Brill, William Burgess III, Kay Ann Cassell (New York Public Library), Mariam Chamberlain, Mary Cunnane (V.P. & Senior Editor, W.W. Norton & Co.), Allan Ecker, Frances Farenthold, Liza Fiol-Matta, Marilyn French, Florence Howe, Iva Kaufman, Frances Horowitz, Shirley Strum Kenny (Pres., SUNY Stony Brook), Joanne Markell, Shirley Mow (Westchester Education Coalition), Margarita Rosa (Commissioner, State of New York, Division of Human Rights), Barbara Smith, M. Jane Stanicki, Caroline Urvater. Honorary board members include Johnetta Cole (Pres., Spelman College), Paul Leclerc (Pres., New York Public Library), Genevieve Vaughn (Found. for a Compassionate Society).

Other Information: The Feminist Press received 0% interest loans from several sources. City University of New York, with whom the Press is affiliated, made a loan of $32,887; at the end of 1994, a balance of $30,887 was outstanding. Chemical Bank made a 0% interest loan of $46,000; at the end of 1994 a balance of $45,391 was outstanding. The Feminist Press received $620,066, or 52% of revenues, from the sale of publications and educational material. $533,491, or 47%, from gifts and grants awarded by foundations, businesses, and individuals. (These awards included a grant from the Population Council for production of a book. In 1995, the Press received $8,000 from the Rockefeller Foundation.) $17,138, or 1%, from royalties and permissions. $9,364, or 1%, from mailing list rentals. $9,120, or 1%, from government grants. The remaining revenue came from interest on savings and temporary cash investments, and insurance money received from the robbery of equipment.

Feminist Studies

c/o Women's Studies Program
University of Maryland
College Park, MD 20742
USA

Contact Person: Lynne Bolles, President.
Officers or Principals: Deborah Rosenfelt, Director ($0); Claire G. Moses, Director ($0).
Mission or Interest: An academic journal of feminist ideas and scholarship.
Accomplishments: *Feminist Studies* has a circulation of about 7,000. In 1994, $122,421 was spent on publishing and distributing *Feminist Studies*.
Net Revenue: 1994 $123,345 **Net Expenses:** $122,421 100%/0%/0% **Net Assets:** $96,456
Tax Status: 501(c)(3)
Periodicals: *Feminist Studies* (three times a year academic journal).
Other Information: First published in 1972. The journal received $98,355, or 75% of gross revenue, from sales and subscriptions. $11,266, or 9%, from dividends and interest from securities. $7,060, or 6%, from the sale of advertising. The remaining revenue came from interest on savings and temporary cash investments, and other miscellaneous sources. The journal lost $7,516 on the sale of securities.

Feminist Women's Health Center (FWHC)

106 East E St.
Yakima, WA 98901   **Phone:**   (509) 575-6422
USA   **Fax:**   (509) 575-0477

Contact Person: Beverly Whipple, President.
Officers or Principals: Jude Hanzo, Secretary ($0); Shauna Heckert, Treasurer ($0); Dido Hasper, Director ($0).
Mission or Interest: Support and provide abortion procedures, contraception and reproductive health exams. "We have a vision of a world where all women freely make their own decisions regarding their bodies, reproduction and sexuality - a world where all women can fulfill their own unique potential and live healthy, whole lives."
Accomplishments: In 1986 they brought suite against anti-abortion groups charging them with violating RICO (racketeering) statutes and conspiring to commit unlawful acts with the intent to close the clinics. Volunteer attorneys associated with the Center for Constitutional Rights in New York filed the lawsuit. FWHC was awarded approximately $250,000, but the decision was overturned on appeal. One of the 9th Circuit Appeal Judges had been a board member of the National Right to Life, and so the 9th Circuit Court has agreed to re-hear the case. President Beverly Whipple attended Non-Governmental Organization Forum which paralleled the U.N. Fourth World Conference on Women in Beijing.
Net Revenue: 1994 $51,780 **Net Expenses:** $52,749 89%/11%/0% **Net Assets:** $11,497
Products or Services: Operates two clinics. "Provided abortion services for 15 years." Trains physicians in abortion procedures. Promotes women's health issues. Other activist and educational activities.
Tax Status: 501(c)(3) **Annual Report:** No. **Employees:** All volunteer.
Periodicals: *Voice for Choice* (quarterly newsletter).
Internships: Yes.
Other Information: The Center received $37,999, or 73% of revenue, from membership dues. $13,768, or 27%, from gifts and grants awarded by foundations, companies, and individuals.

Feminist Writers Guild

c/o Outrider Press
1004 E. Steger Rd.
Crete, IL 60417
USA

Contact Person: Whitney Scott, President.
Officers or Principals: Patricia Herczfeld, Treasurer ($0); Karen Darr, Secretary/Editor ($0); Jennifer Hinton, Publicity ($0).
Mission or Interest: Publishes a newsletter for members containing information on publishing, manuscript requests, and book reviews. Sponsors readings by members and other writers.
Accomplishments: In the fiscal year ending June 1994, the Guild spent $1,550 on its programs.
Net Revenue: FY ending 6/94 $2,933 **Net Expenses:** $1,1687 92%/8%/0% **Net Assets:** $2,063
Tax Status: 501(c)(3)

Periodicals: Newsletter.
Other Information: The Guild received $2,285, or 78% of revenue, from membership dues. $375, or 13%, from service revenues, such as open microphone readings. The remaining revenue came from gifts from members, and interest on savings and other temporary cash investments.

Fenton Communications

1606 20th St., N.W.
Washington, DC 20009   **Phone:** (202) 745-0707   **E-Mail:** fenton@fenton.com
USA   **Fax:** (202) 332-1915

Contact Person: Tessa Woollatt.   **Officers or Principals:** David Fenton, President
Mission or Interest: Public relations firm that has worked on behalf of various leftists causes. "To use the mass media as a tool for social change." Their motto, "If you don't like the news, go out and make your own."
Accomplishments: Fenton Communications represented various Marxist governments, including Angola's MPLA regime, Grenada's Maurice Bishop, the Nicaraguan Sandinistas, and communist guerillas such as the Salvadoran FMLN. (David Fenton maintains, "I'm not a Marxist, I'm a Democrat!") Fenton represented American lawyer Jennifer Harbury, whose hunger strike (which was featured on CBS's 60 Minutes) called attention to her search for the killers of her Guatemalan guerilla husband, Efrain Bamaca. (The Guatemalan military officer who executed Bamaca was found to have been a CIA-paid informant.) Fenton did publicity work for the Christic Institute's lawsuit alleging that a secret team of U.S. Government officials was engaged in drug-running and assassinations. More recently, Fenton Communications has turned to representing environmental organizations and campaigns. Fenton launched the anti-Alar (a chemical used to increase the shelf-life of apples) campaign by promoting the Natural Resources Defense Council's (NRDC) report "Intolerable Risk: Pesticides in Our Children's Food." Fenton helped set up a coalition to follow up on the anti-Alar campaign, Mothers and Others Against Pesticides, headed by actress Meryl Streep. Fenton told the leftist journal *Propaganda Review*, "We also designed (the campaign) so that revenue would flow back to NRDC from the public and we sold this book about pesticides through a 900-number and the Donahue show, and to date, there has been $700,000 in net revenues from it." Fenton has worked on a campaign linking Wise Use and property-rights activists to the militia movement, and to violence and threats against environmentalists and government employees. For this campaign Fenton relied on the group Public Employees for Environmental Responsibility, and journalist David Helvarg, whose book The War on the Greens (Sierra Club, 1994) and articles in *The Nation* were perhaps the most prominent examples. Most recently, Fenton has been promoting the book, Our Stolen Future by World Wildlife Fund scientist Theo Colburne, John Peterson Myers of the W. Alton Jones Foundation and Diane Dumanoski of the *Boston Globe*. The thesis of the book and campaign is that man-made chemicals are lowering testosterone levels and threatening "our fertility, intelligence, and survival."
Products or Services: Public relations services.
Tax Status: For profit. **Annual Report:** No. **Employees:** 2
Board of Directors or Trustees: Robert Zevin, David Lubell.
Periodicals: *Fenton Communique* (newsletter).
Other Information: Fenton started his career as a photographer for the anti-Vietnam War, pro-Vietcong News service, Liberation news Service. He later became public relations director for *Rolling Stone*. Fenton Communications is located at the same address and shares staff with the nonprofit Environmental Media Services, headed by Al Gore's former press secretary, Arlie Schardt. The firm has a New York office: 2 Horatio St., Suite 8P, New York, NY 10014, (212) 989-3337.

Fifth Estate Newspaper

4632 Second Ave.
Detroit, MI 48201   **Phone:** (313) 831-6800
USA

Contact Person: E.B. Maple.
Mission or Interest: Leftist anarchy and radical, anti-technology environmentalism.
Accomplishments: The University of Michigan's Labadie Collection lists the Fifth Estate as "the longest running English language anarchist newspaper in American history." It celebrated its 30th anniversary in November, 1995. "Best known for linking the anarchist vision of a stateless, decentralized, communal economy with a critique of modern technology which it pronounces as a principle element of domination."
Tax Status: Un-owned and unregistered, as a matter of principle. **Annual Report:** No. **Employees:** About 20 volunteers.
Periodicals: *Fifth Estate* (quarterly newspaper).

Filipinos for Affirmative Action

310 8th St., Suite 308
Oakland, CA 94607   **Phone:** (510) 465-9876
USA

Contact Person: Lillian Galedo, Executive Director.   **Officers or Principals:** Lillian Galedo, Executive Director ($43,943); Donnalynn Rubiano, President ($0); Edwin Batongbacal, Vice President ($0); Steve Dorado, Secretary, Floreida Quiaoit, Treasurer.
Mission or Interest: Provides social services for immigrants, youths, and others in the Filipino community.
Accomplishments: In 1993 the organization spent $487,333 on its programs. The largest was AIDS, tobacco and substance abuse prevention programs, costing $275,110. Immigration and employment counseling, including referrals, advocacy, and community education, cost $138,539. Youth services, including tutorial services, career counseling, and small "group rap sessions," cost $73,684.

Net Revenue: 1993 $562,490 ($386,784, or 69%, from government grants) **Net Expenses:** $562,432   87%/13%/0%
Net Assets: $51,825
Products or Services. Social services.
Tax Status: 501(c)(3)
Board of Directors or Trustees: Helen Toribo, Geline Avila, Antonio Edayan, Don Rodis, Priscilla Enriquez.
Other Information: Filipinos for Affirmative Action received $386,784, or 69% of revenue, from government grants. $148,096, or 26%, from direct and indirect public support in the form of gifts and grants from foundations, companies and individuals. $16,388, or 3%, from client fees and form fees. $10, 072 net, or 2%, from special events. The remaining revenue came from interest on savings and temporary cash investments, and other miscellaneous sources.

Film Arts Foundation
346 9th St., 2nd Floor
San Francisco, CA 94103   **Phone:**   (415) 552-8760
USA

Contact Person: Jack Walsh, President.
Officers or Principals: Janet Cole, Vice President ($0); Omar Khan, Secretary ($0); Cleo Protopapas, Treasurer ($0).
Mission or Interest: Assists independent film makers with financial and technical support. Assists in the productions of documentaries with strong political content.
Accomplishments: "No Mas!" "My Home, My Prison" video projects. "Bound By the Wind" documentary film on the effects of nuclear weapons testing and the international campaign for a Comprehensive Test Ban. Documentary on 'socially responsible' investment. In 1994 the Foundation spent $325,958 on its projects. The largest project, with expenditures of $162,033, was a series of seminars and exhibitions on film making techniques and financing. $95,824 was spent producing a newsletter sent to 3,000 members. $46,039 was spent on an editing facility used by members at subsidized rates. Other projects included meetings on grant-seeking and fund solicitation information.
Net Revenue: 1994 $637,788 ($78,099, or 12%, from government grants) **Net Expenses:** $620,776   53%/41%/6%
Net Assets: $549,591 **Citations:** 18:176
Tax Status: 501(c)(3)
Periodicals: Newsletter.
Other Information: In 1994 the Foundation received $115,638, or 18% of total revenue, from gifts and grants awarded by foundations, businesses, and individuals. (These grants included $25,000 from the Wallace Alexander Gerbode Foundation, $5,000 from the Ploughshares Fund, $5,000 from the Vanguard Public Foundation, and $1,000 from the Compton Foundation). $108,188, or 17%, from membership dues. $105,775, or 16%, from seminar income. $78,766, or 12%, from facility-use fees. $78,099, or 12%, from government grants. $55,661, or 9%, from grant fees. $51,712, or 8%, from festival and special project fees. $40,000, or 6%, from the grants program. $34,407, or 5%, from advertising and mailing list rentals. The remaining revenue came from dividends and interest from securities, exhibition income, and other miscellaneous sources. The Foundation lost $7,549 on the sale of securities.

First Amendment Coalition of Texas
1104 West Ave., Suite 101
Austin, TX 78701   **Phone:**   (512) 478-9132
USA

Contact Person: Sylvia Fenstermacher.
Officers or Principals: Douglas Richards, Vice President ($0); Paul Rednitz, Secretary ($0); Chuck Carlock, Director ($0).
Mission or Interest: Coalition of organizations supporting the first amendment.
Accomplishments: In 1994 the Coalition spent $127,357 on its programs. $126,681 of this went toward lobbying.
Net Revenue: 1994 $127,074 **Net Expenses:** $131,227 97%/3%/0% **Net Assets:** $1,253
Tax Status: 501(c)(6)
Other Information: The Coalition received $127,074, or 100% of revenue, from membership dues.

First Amendment Congress
2301 S. Gaylord
Denver, CO 80208   **Phone:** (303) 871-4430   **E-Mail:** jlucas@du.edu
USA   **Fax:**   (303) 871-4585

Contact Person: Julie M. Lucas, Executive Director.   **Officers or Principals:** Jean Otto, President ($0); Louis E. Ingelhart, Vice President ($0); Richard Kleeman, Secretary/Treasurer ($0).
Mission or Interest: A national coalition of media and communications organizations. "To promote an understanding of First Amendment rights and citizen responsibilities to the general public.." "Under the First Amendment to the U.S. Constitution, which has protected our freedom to write and speak for more than 200 years, censorship is narrowly interpreted by some to mean only governmental interference with free speech," however, explains secretary/treasurer Richard Kleeman, "...Some (censorship) is economic: that is, censorship by pricing the less affluent information seekers out of the market...In the 104th Congress we have seen determined efforts made to censor the outspoken speech of activist groups by slashing or eliminating their federal funding, e.g., the National Endowment for the Arts, the National Endowment for the Humanities, the Corporation for Public Broadcasting and its beneficiaries in TV and radio, and the Legal Services Corporation, all of them targets of congressional wolves in budget-balancers' clothing." The First Amendment Congress opposes all forms of censorship.

Accomplishments: In 1994 the Congress spent $45,986 on its programs. The largest program, with expenditures of $18,195, was the production and dissemination of the *First Amendment Congress Newsletter* to over 5,300 subscribers. $8,057 was spent training regional representatives in implementing educational activities. $7,161 providing research awareness on topics regarding the separation of church and state. $6,339 developing K-12 curriculum materials. $3,812 spent on Colorado teacher training workshop for over 350 educators. $2,422 for local education efforts. The Congress is sponsoring the "Colorado Religious Freedom Project" in cooperation with the ACLU of Colorado. Various programs and an upcoming 1997 conference on censorship and electronic communications.

Net Revenue: 1994 $65,179 **Net Expenses:** $80,775 57%/36%/8% **Net Assets:** $47,248

Products or Services: K-12 curriculum materials, "Education for Freedom," which includes video tape and course manuals. Other publications and pamphlets.

Tax Status: 501(c)(3) **Annual Report:** Yes. **Employees:** 2

Board of Directors or Trustees: Affiliations represent member organizations. Jean Otto (American Society of Newspaper Editors), Louis Ingelhart (College Media Advisors), Richard Kleeman (Association of American Publishers), Lou Boccardi (Associated Press), Lawrence Beaupre (Associated Press Managing Editors), Daniel Jaffe (Association of National Advertisers), Judith Krug (American Library Association), Steve Bookshester (National Association of Broadcasters), Paul Schatt (National Conference of Editorial Writers), Marsha Shuler (National Federation of Press Women), Diane Everson (National Newspaper Association), Robert Healy (Newspaper Association of America), David Eisen (Newspaper Guild), Patrick Jackson (Public Relations Society of America), David Bartlett (Radio-Television News Directors Association), Jane Kirtley (Reporters Committee for Freedom of the Press), Lucy Dalglish (Society of Professional Journalists), Robert Kieckhefer (United Press International), Mike Wirth (School of Communications, Univ. of Denver), Sue Hale (Women in Communications).

Periodicals: *First Amendment Congress Newsletter* (quarterly newsletter).

Internships: Yes, for communications, political science, and law students.

Other Information: The Congress is affiliated with the University of Denver. The Congress received $60,400, or 84% of gross revenue, from gifts and grants awarded by foundations, businesses, and individuals. $7,750, or 11%, from membership dues. $1,583, or 2%, from interest on savings and temporary cash investments. The remaining revenue came from other miscellaneous sources. The Congress lost $6,630 on the sale of securities and other assets.

First Amendment Foundation

1313 W. 8th St., Suite 313
Los Angeles, CA 90017   **Phone:** (213) 484-6661
USA

Contact Person: Chauncey A. Alexander, President.

Officers or Principals: Walter M. Kearns, M.D., Treasurer ($0); Carole Goldberg-Ambrose, Secretary ($0).

Mission or Interest: Educational work on behalf of civil liberties and free speech.

Accomplishments: In 1994 the Foundation spent $8,714 on its programs. $5,040 was spent producing and distributing pamphlets. $3,674 was spent giving lectures to high school and middle school teachers and students.

Net Revenue: 1994 $45,746 **Net Expenses:** $36,879 **Net Assets:** $25,190

Tax Status: 501(c)(4)

Other Information: The Foundation received $45,746, or 100% of revenue, from gifts and grants awarded by foundations, businesses, and individuals. (These grants included $3,000 from the Peace Development Fund.)

Florence and John Schumann Foundation

33 Park St.
Montclair, NJ 07042   **Phone:** (201) 783-6660
USA

Contact Person: Patricia McCarthy, Vice President. **Officers or Principals:** William D. Moyers, President ($143,795); Patricia McCarthy, Vice President ($110,479); John D. Moyers, Executive Director ($68,721); David S. Bate, Secretary/Treasurer; Howard D. Brundage, Vice President Finance; Robert Schumann, Chairman.

Mission or Interest: Grant-making foundation with awards in four main areas; effective governance, the environment, international relations, and the media.

Accomplishments: In 1994 the Foundation awarded $2,935,800 in grants. Recipients of the largest grants included: $1,000,000 for the Center for Public Integrity, $660,000 for the Center for Responsive Politics, $400,000 for the Public Media Center, $200,000 each for the Center for Governmental Studies and the Center for Teaching Peace, $160,000 for the Northeast Citizen Action Resource Center, $150,000 each for the Institute for Agriculture and Trade Policy and the Center for International Environmental Law, and $100,000 each for the Government Accountability Project and the Western States Center.

Net Revenue: 1994 $4,171,050 **Net Expenses:** $3,762,993 **Net Assets:** $71,251,114

Tax Status: 501(c)(3)

Board of Directors or Trustees: Edwin Etherington, Caroline Mark, John Whitehead, W. Ford Schumann.

Other Information: The Foundation received $3,697,507, or 89% of revenue, from dividends and interest from securities. $442,860, or 11% from capital gains on the sale of securities. The remaining revenue came from income from partnerships and rental income. The Foundation held $70,904,843, or 99.5% of assets, in U.S. and state government obligations.

Focus Project

1742 Connecticut Ave., N.W.
Washington, DC 20009   **Phone:** (202) 234-8494   **E-Mail:** rtk.net
USA   **Fax:**   (202) 234-8584

Contact Person: Gary Bass, Executive Director.
Accomplishments: Created OMB Watch (Office of Management and Budget Watch), a project which monitors the government and improves accountability. Created the Right to Know Computer Network (RTK NET).
Tax Status: 501(c)(3)
Other Information: Founded in 1983. In 1994 the Project received grants of $105,000 from the Bauman Family Foundation, $25,000 from the Jessie Smith Noyes Foundation, $20,000 from the J. Roderick MacArthur Foundation, $5,000 from the New World Foundation.

Food Research and Action Center (FRAC)
1875 Connecticut Ave., N.W., Suite 540
Washington, DC 20009   **Phone:** (202) 986-2200
USA

Contact Person: Robert J. Fersh, President.
Officers or Principals: Robert J. Fersh, President ($110,719); Edward Cooney, Deputy Director ($88,686); Bessie Wash, Vice President, Operations ($58,569); Carol Tucker Foreman, Chair; Matthew Melmed, Vice Chair.
Mission or Interest: "Assistance to persons and groups participating in federal, state and other governmental food and nutrition programs and to those experiencing nutritional problems, by means of legal and legislative representation, information, referral and counseling services. FRAC also conducts research and studies in the field of nutrition and disseminates information to governmental officials, interested parties and the general public."
Accomplishments: In 1994 FRAC spent $1,517,719 on its programs. The largest program, with expenditures of $508,329, was public policy development which included "analysis of proposed or pending public policy changes affecting low income Americans. Assisted local groups in developing strategies to expand the school breakfast and other child nutrition programs." $250,167 was spent on nutrition research "providing data and technical assistance on the nutritional status of low income Americans to other organizations, the public and local, state and federal government agencies." $201,080 on coalition building "to alleviate hunger and poverty." $202,275 on public education. Legal assistance was provided. FRAC assisted in the law suit of Graeser v. Espy; a suit challenging "the failure of the Department of Agriculture to promulgate regulations implementing a Congressional mandate to simplify food stamp procedures for elderly and disabled applicants and recipients." FRAC awarded grants of $5,000 to both the Washington Food Policy Action Center and California Food Policy Advocates.
Net Revenue: 1994 $1,878,133 ($6,950, or less than 1%, from government grants) **Net Expenses:** $1,956,612 78%/12%/10%
Net Assets: $115,830 **Citations:** 57:134
Products or Services: Research, publications, coalition building, and lobbying. FRAC spent $118,761 on lobbying, $41,502 on grassroots lobbying and $77,259 on the direct lobbying of legislators. The amount spent on lobbying has steadily risen over the past few years; 1994's expenditures increased 21% over 1993, 43% over 1992, and 183% over 1991.
Tax Status: 501(c)(3)
Board of Directors or Trustees: Willie Baker (Intl. V.P., United Food and Commercial Workers International Union), Thomas Downey, Martha Echols, David Greenberg (Philip Morris Companies), Timothy Hammonds (Food Marketing Inst.), Helen Hershkoff (Assoc. Legal Dir., ACLU), Charles Hughes (AFSCME), Clinton Lyons (National Legal Aid and Defender Assoc.), Daniel Marcus, Marshall Matz, C. Manly Molpus (Grocery Manufacturers of America), John Polk, Ronald Pollack (Families U.S.A. Found.), Diann Rust-Tierney (Capital Punishment Project, ACLU), Gerald Sanders (AL Coalition Against Hunger), Judah Sommer (Goldman, Sachs & Co.), Marion Standish (CA Food Policy Advocates), Johnny Thompson, Judith Whittlesey.
Periodicals: *Foodlines* (monthly newsletter).
Other Information: The Center received $1,891,654, or 98% of gross revenue, from direct and indirect public support in the form of gifts and grants awarded by foundations, businesses, affiliates and individuals. (These grants included $70,000 from the Nathan Cummings Foundation, $30,000 from the Ruth Mott Fund, $20,000 from the James C. Penney Foundation, $5,000 from the New Prospect Foundation, and $750 from the Haymarket People's Fund.) $10,596, or 1%, from the sale of publications. The remaining revenue came from interest on savings and temporary cash investments, conference registration fees, and honoraria. FRAC lost $45,795 on its annual Dinner for the Campaign to End Childhood Hunger. This loss does not include the gifts awarded during this dinner, these are counted under direct public support.

Ford Foundation
320 E. 43rd St.
New York, NY 10017   **Phone:** (212) 573-5000
USA   **Fax:**   (212) 599-4584

Contact Person: Barron M. Tenny, Vice President.   **Officers or Principals:** Susan Vail Berresford, President; Henry Brewer Schacht, Chairman; Nancy P. Feller, Associate General Counsel; Nicholas M. Gabriel, Treasurer; Linda B. Strumpf, Vice President.
Mission or Interest: "To advance the public well-being by identifying and contributing to the solution of problems of national and international importance." Awards grants in the following areas - urban and rural poverty policy development, education and culture, civil rights/social justice, public policy and government, and international affairs.
Accomplishments: In the fiscal year ending September 1993 the Foundation awarded $262,938,000 in grants. The recipients of the largest grants included (these grants were often disbursed over several years, not in one lump sum): $7,000,000 over five years for the Urban Institute, $1,300,000 over two years for the Mexican American Legal Defense and Educational Fund, $1,200,000 over two years for the Native American Rights Fund, $1,000,000 over two years for National Public Radio, $950,000 for the International Food Policy Research Institute, $750,000 over two years for the Pratt Institute, $550,000 over two years for the National Council for Research on Women ("for research and training programs on gender awareness"), $340,000 for the National Puerto Rican Coalition, $300,000 each for the Latino Institute, Ecotrust, Development Alternatives with Women for a New Era, and World Wildlife Fund, $275,000 each for the Mexican American Unity Council, and National Black Women's Health Project, and $250,000 for the Institute for Women's Policy Research, Advocacy Institute, and the Government of Vietnam (for research and training in international affairs).

Net Assets: FY ending 9/93 $6,938,849,000
Tax Status: 501(c)(3)   **Annual Report:** Yes.
Board of Directors or Trustees: Robert Coles (Harvard Univ., Health Services), Frances Daly Fergusson (Pres., Vassar College), Kathryn Scott Fuller (World Wildlife Fund), Robert Haas (Chair/CEO, Levi Strauss Assoc.), Christopher Anthony Hogg, Vernon Eulion Jordan, Jr., David Todd Kearns, Wilma Pearl Mankiller (National Congress of American Indians), Luis Guerrero Nogales (Stanford Univ., Center for Public Service), Olusegun Obasanjo, Dorothy Sattes Ridings (Publisher, *Bradenton Herald*), Monkombu Swaiminathan, Ratan Naval Tata.
Other Information: Established in 1936 by Henry Ford, founder of Ford Motor Company, and his son Edsel Ford. The Foundation originally concentrated on charitable activities in Michigan. The Foundation no longer has any ties to the Ford family or company.

Foreign Policy
(see the Carnegie Endowment for International Peace)

Forest Ecosystem Rescue Network (FERN)
P.O. Box 672
Dahlonega, GA 30533-0672
USA

Contact Person: Dan Hemenway.
Mission or Interest: Preserve and restore forests by collecting seeds and raising saplings of dwindling species, and in some cases breeding saplings for pollution resistance. Special focus on temperate forest species.
Accomplishments: Established a "Tree Bank" genetic reserve in New Zealand.
Tax Status: Unincorporated. **Annual Report:** No. **Employees:** All volunteer.
Periodicals: *Robin* (monthly newsletter).

Forgotten Families of the Cold War
P.O. Box 2745
Bangor, ME 04402   **Phone:** (207) 989-3021
USA   **Fax:** same

Contact Person: Sherry Sullivan.
Mission or Interest: Uses the Freedom of Information Act to "search for men and women missing during the Cold War era" as a result of "CIA involvement."
Accomplishments: "Completed investigations, conducted Freedom of Information Act suits through the court systems."
Tax Status: 501(c)(3) **Annual Report:** No. **Employees:** All volunteer.
Other Information: Small, but working to network with like-minded organizations to "combat the isolation of operating from Maine."

Foundation for a Peaceful Environment Among Communities Everywhere (Foundation for PEACE)
P.O. Box 1238
Garner, NC 27529   **Phone:** (919) 773-0924   **E-Mail:** JLRoush@aol.com
USA

Contact Person: James L. Roush, President.
Mission or Interest: "To promote community and international peace; to foster the use of conflict resolution techniques in family and community affairs, in international development, and in political processes within and between nations."
Accomplishments: "Publishing an international magazine since 1985; supporting locally the Great Decisions program of the Foreign Policy Program; and organizing and/or participating in workshops/seminars on peacemaking and conflict resolution/prevention."
Tax Status: 501(c)(3) **Annual Report:** No. **Employees:** All volunteer.
Board of Directors or Trustees: Dr. Alan Geyer (Center for Theology and Public Policy), Dr. David Krieger (Nuclear Age Peace Found.), Ambassador John McDonald Jr. (Inst. for Multi-Track Diplomacy), Dr. Richard Rubenstein (Inst. for Conflict Analysis and Resolution, George Mason Univ.).
Periodicals: *PEACE in Action* (annual journal).   **Internships:** No.
Other Information: "Our publication is distributed world-wide (including to all governments and a number of Non-Governmental Organizations), the United Nations and U.N. missions, the U.S. government and Congress, various policy-making organizations, the media, and about 500 individual supporters and subscribers."

Foundation for Global Community
222 High St.
Palo Alto, CA 94301   **Phone:** (415) 328-7756
USA

Contact Person: Joseph Kresse, President.
Officers or Principals: Neil Lancefield, Chief Financial Officer ($73,000); Richard Rathbun, Secretary ($34,634).
Mission or Interest: "Educates humanity that the earth and all its life, although diverse, are interdependent and interconnected, and that the well-being of each individual is inextricably linked to the well-being of the whole. Foundation for Global Community is dedicated to living in concert with the planet and with each other, and to contributing to the continuity of life and a world beyond war."

Accomplishments: In the fiscal year ending June 1994, the Foundation spent $758,606 on its programs.
Net Revenue: FY ending 6/94 $791,932 **Net Expenses:** $960,886 79%/15%/6% **Net Assets:** $5,891,942 **Citations:** 7:209
Tax Status: 501(c)(3)
Board of Directors or Trustees: Kern Beare, Phil Brown, Karen Harwell, Holly Taylor, Ellen Bishop, Don Fitton, Tony Lee, Lenore Ray, Alice Fenton, Elleen Rinde.
Other Information: Before 1992, the Foundation for Global Community was called "Beyond War." Beyond War had an affiliate, "The Creative Initiative Foundation," with whom it merged, assuming the corporate identity and taxpayer status of The Creative Initiative Foundation. The resulting organization took the name Foundation for Global Community. The Foundation received $337,947, or 43% of revenue, from gifts and grants awarded by foundations, businesses, and individuals. (These grants included $5,000 from the Compton Foundation.) $171,762 net, or 22%, from rental income. $144,164, or 18%, from seminar and course fees. $71,465, or 9%, from interest and dividends from securities. $35,000, or 4%, from interest on savings and temporary cash investments. The remaining revenue came from the sale of assets and inventory, special fund-raising events, royalties, and other miscellaneous sources.

Foundation for Independent Video and Film

625 Broadway, 9th Floor
New York, NY 10012   **Phone:** (212) 473-3400
USA

Contact Person: Ruby Lerner, Executive Director. **Officers or Principals:** Ruby Lerner, Executive Director ($42,000); Laura Davis, Ad Manager ($38,158); Patricia Thompson, Editor ($33,000); Debra Zimmerman, Chairperson; Robert Richter, President; Loni Ding, Vice President; Jim Klein, Treasurer; Bart Weiss, Secretary.
Mission or Interest: Supports independent video and film makers. "Offers practical information on various aspects of the production process and provides a forum for film, video and social issues concerning the independent community."
Accomplishments: In the fiscal year ending June 1994, the Foundation spent $466,841 on its programs.
Net Revenue: FY ending 6/94 $730,704 ($142,650, or 20%, from government grants) **Net Expenses:** $701,505 67%/30%/3%
Net Assets: $84,875 **Citations:** 1:240
Products or Services: "Festival Bureau" that provides information on film and video festivals.
Tax Status: 501(c)(3)
Board of Directors or Trustees: Joan Braderman, Dee Davis, Barbara Hammer, Dai-Sil Kim-Gibson, Bienvenida Matias, Robb Moss, Helen De Michiel, Johnathan Berman, Eugene Aleinikoff, James Schamus, Norman Wang.
Periodicals: *The Independent* (ten times a year magazine).
Other Information: Affiliated with the 501(c)(6) Association for Independent Video and Filmmakers. The Foundation received $192,563, or 26% of revenue, from subscriptions, royalties and advertising associated with *The Independent*. $189,500, or 26%, from support provided by the Association for Independent Video and Filmmakers. $142,650, or 20%, from government grants. $123,316, or 17%, from gifts and grants awarded by foundations, businesses, and individuals. (In 1995 the Foundation received $60,000 from the Rockefeller Foundation.) $41,614, or 6%, from the sale of books. $31,438, or 4%, from rental income. The remaining income came from seminars, the Festival Bureau, interest on savings and temporary cash investments, and other miscellaneous sources.

Foundation for Middle East Peace

555 13th St., N.W., Suite 800
Washington, DC 20004   **Phone:** (202) 637-6558
USA

Contact Person: Geoff Aronson, Editor. **Officers or Principals:** Geoff Aronson, Editor ($45,772); Jean C. Newsom, Executive Director ($26,000); Ambassador Lucius D. Battle, President ($4,000); Peter M. Castleman, Vice President/Treasurer; Joan Birdzell, Secretary; Calvin H. Cobb, Jr., Vice President; Stephen Hartwell, Treasurer.
Mission or Interest: Foundation that publishes a bimonthly report and awards grants to individuals and organizations supporting Middle East peace.
Accomplishments: In the fiscal year ending September 1994, the Foundation spent $340,752 to produce and disseminate its *Report on Israeli Settlement in the Occupied Territories*, sent to approximately 2,000 subscribers, including media, advocacy organizations, and individuals. The Foundation awarded $69,350 in grants to individuals and organizations in the United States and abroad. U.S. organizations that received grants were: $11,000 for American Near East Refugee Aid, $6,000 for Americans for Peace Now, $1,250 for the Pax World Foundation, $500 for the Middle East Institute, and $100 for the Coalition for Hebron Relief. Individuals affiliated with U.S. organizations who received grants were: $5,000 for both Sari Nusseibeh (Woodrow Wilson Center) and Gail Pressberg (Americans for Peace Now).
Net Revenue: FY ending 9/94 $367,787 **Net Expenses:** $355,565 **Net Assets:** $5,846,327
Tax Status: 501(c)(3)
Board of Directors or Trustees: Richard Marsh, Frank Reifsnyder, James Cromwell.
Periodicals: *Report on Israeli Settlement in the Occupied Territories* (bimonthly report).
Other Information: The Foundation received $209,983, or 54% of gross revenue, from dividends and interest from securities. $109,094, or 28%, from capital gains on the sale of securities. $34,627, or 9%, from gifts awarded by individuals. $32,397, or 8%, from interest on savings and temporary cash investments. The Foundation incurred a loss of $18,314 on an investment partnership.

Foundation for National Progress / *Mother Jones*

731 Market St.
San Francisco, CA 94103   **Phone:** (415) 665-6637
USA   **Fax:** (415) 665-6696   **Web-Page:** http://www.mojones.com/

Contact Person: Richard Reynolds, Communications Director.   **Officers or Principals:** Jeffrey Klein, President/Editor ($87,000); John (Jay) Harris, III, Vice President/Publisher ($78,500); Dynnel B. Lohr, National Affairs ($58,000); John Simmons, Chair.
Mission or Interest: Publishes *Mother Jones*, a bimonthly magazine specializing in investigative reporting. Established in 1976. *Inside Media* describes *Mother Jones*; "Has its roots in Sixties idealism and activism, but has successfully toned down its strident leftist inclinations. Baby boomers of the Sixties are still interested in politics, but now they are old enough to have the cash and credibility to make a difference within the confines of a corporate world. *Mother Jones* addresses that desire to make a difference."
Accomplishments: Average paid circulation per issue is 120,000 copies. The American Journalism Review awarded them with the "Best Magazine for Investigative Journalism" in 1995. *Mother Jones* published a story on House Speaker Newt Gingrich in 1984, exposing his marital and personal problems. This story came back into the news again following Gingrich's ascension to House Speaker and *Mother Jones* was cited in *The Boston Globe, Newsweek, Knight-Ridder News Service, The New York Times, New York Daily News, Los Angeles Times, New York Magazine, The New Yorker*, and others. In 1993 the majority of *Mother Jones* readers were female, 96% of the readers had college degrees, and a median income of $63,600. In 1994 the Foundation spent $2,464,770 to research, publish, and distribute *Mother Jones*. Regular contributors include award-winning columnist Molly Ivins and comedienne Paula Poundstone.
Net Revenue: 1994 $3,550,201   **Net Expenses:** $3,568,118   72%/19%/9%   **Net Assets:** (-$1,785,344)   **Citations:** 618:34
Products or Services: Publishes *Mother Jones*. Photography fund with a particular interest in photographing indigenous people.
Tax Status: 501(c)(3)
Board of Directors or Trustees: Harriet Barlow, Marjorie Craig Benton, Jane Butcher, Dr. Price Cobbs, Christina Desser, Rob Glaser, Adam Hochschild, Rob McKay, Al Meyerhoff, Beverly Brazier Noun, Anita Roddick, Rabbi John Rosove, Jeri Smith-Fornara, Rose Styron.
Periodicals: *Mother Jones* (bimonthly magazine).
Other Information: *Mother Jones* is named after the 19th century reformer and self-professed hellraiser, Mary Harris, better known as Mother Jones. Founding editor Jeffrey Klein returned to the magazine in 1992 after nine years as editor of Knight-Ridder's *San Jose Mercury News' West* magazine. Publisher Jay Harris came to the magazine in 1991 after nine years with Newsweek International, where he was general manager of its Pacific edition. The Foundation received $2,068,956, or 58% of revenue, from gifts and grants awarded by foundations, companies, and individuals. (These grants included $25,000 from the Winston Foundation for World Peace, $20,000 from the Rockefeller Brothers Fund, and $5,000 from the Ploughshares Fund.) $1,059,393, or 30%, from program services, including subscriptions to *Mother Jones* and membership fees. $341,087, or 10%, from advertising in *Mother Jones*. $102,216, or 3%, from mailing list rentals. The remaining revenue came from interest on savings or temporary cash investments. Revenues were slightly decreased by the loss of $22,543 on the sale of assets other than inventory. The cost of publishing, printing and distributing Mother Jones was $2,464,770, while the revenue it provided (subscriptions, advertising, mailing list rentals) was $1,502,696; so in 1994 *Mother Jones* operated at a deficit of $962,074 that required subsidization.

Foundation for the Study of Independent Social Ideas / *Dissent*

521 5th Ave.
New York, NY 10175   **Phone:**   (212) 595-3084
USA

Contact Person: Michael Walzer, President.
Officers or Principals: Simone Plastrik, Treasurer ($13,913); Mitchell Cohen, Secretary ($0).
Mission or Interest: Research and discussion of social problems. Publishes *Dissent*, an academic journal of democratic socialism.
Accomplishments: The *Utne Reader* said of *Dissent*, "Politics, economics, and culture come together in every article, giving the entire publication a balance most political journals lack." Paid circulation is approximately 11,000. In 1994 the Foundation spent $152,959 on its programs.
Net Revenue: 1994 $249,374   **Net Expenses:** $208,464   73%/22%/5%   **Net Assets:** $650,406
Tax Status: 501(c)(3)
Board of Directors or Trustees: The Editorial Board includes: Paul Berman, Jeff Faux, Cynthia Fuchs Epstein, Todd Gitlin, Robert Heilbroner, Harold Meyerson (editor, *L.A. Weekly*), Martin Peretz, Ronald Radosh, Bernard Rosenberg, Prof. Cornel West (Harvard Univ.), and others.
Periodicals: *Dissent* (quarterly journal).
Other Information: The Foundation received $125,142, or 50% of revenue, from the sale of subscriptions. $80,059, or 32%, from gifts and grants awarded by foundations, businesses, and individuals. (These grants included $4,200 from the Joyce Mertz-Gilmore Foundation. In 1995, $45,000 from the Rockefeller Foundation.) $40,493, or 16%, from dividends and interest from securities. $2,779, or 1%, from advertising sales. The remaining revenue came from mailing list rentals. The publication and distribution of Dissent cost $152,959, and the sale of subscriptions, individual copies, advertising and mailing list rentals brought in revenues of $128,825. The journal required subsidization of $24,134, or approximately $2.20 per subscriber per year.

Foundation for the Study of Individual and World Peace

2101 Wilshire Blvd., Suite 201
Santa Monica, CA 90403   **Phone:**   (310) 828-0535
USA

Contact Person: Katherine B. Hall, Vice President.   **Officers or Principals:** Jack Espey, Ranch Manager ($36,720); John-Roger Hinkins, President ($0); Phil Danza, Treasurer ($0); John Forrister, Secretary.
Mission or Interest: Operation of a retreat center in Santa Barbara which hosts retreats, seminars, and workshops to work for world and individual peace.
Accomplishments: In the fiscal year ending June 1994 the Foundation spent $1,011,518 on its programs.
Net Revenue: FY ending 6/94 $947,405   **Net Expenses:** $1,231,259   82%/2%/16%   **Net Assets:** $1,554,415   **Citations:** 0:255

Products or Services: Lectures, seminars, workshops, and audio tapes.
Tax Status: 501(c)(3)
Other Information: The Foundation received $876,354, or 92% of revenue, from gifts and grants awarded by foundations, businesses, and individuals. $61,300, or 6%, from workshop fees. $9,751, or 2%, from interest on savings and temporary cash investments.

Foundation on Economic Trends

1660 L St., N.W., Suite 216
Washington, DC 20036   **Phone:**   (202) 466-2823
USA

Contact Person: Jeremy Rifkin, President.
Mission or Interest: Focuses on trends and changes in society, culture, the economy and the environment that result from technological change. Monitors biotechnology and other new technologies.
Accomplishments: "Beyond Beef" campaign. Jeremy Rifkin is the author of numerous books, including Entropy: Into the Greenhouse World, and The End of Work: The Decline of the Global Labor Force and the Dawn of the Post-Market Era (Putnam, 1995). An example of Rifkin's ideas: "The computer introduces an entirely new time frame and with it a new vision of the future. The clock measures time in relationship to human perceptibility. It is possible to experience an hour, a minute, a second, even a tenth of a second. With computers, however, the nanosecond (a billionth of a second) is the primary measurement of time...This marks a radical turning point in the way humans relate to time...this new concept of time will pose a variety of problems...This new computer time represents the complete separation of time from human experience and the rhythms of nature."
Tax Status: 501(c)(3)
Other Information: In 1994 the Foundation received $50,000 from the C.S. Fund, $20,000 from the Bydale Foundation.

Fourth World Movement

7600 Willow Hill Dr.
Landover, MD 20785   **Phone:**   (301) 336-9489   **E-Mail:** 4thworld@his.com
USA   **Fax:**   (301) 336-0092

Contact Person: Hyacinth Egner, Internship Coordinator.   **Officers or Principals:** Dr. Charles Courtney, President; Susan Devins, Vice President: Jane Dewey, Secretary; Carl Egner, Treasurer.
Mission or Interest: "International organization working to build a partnership between those living in poverty and the rest of society. Activities range from direct programs with very poor families (street libraries, People's Universities, skills training, etc.) to research and representation at the United Nations and other official bodies."
Accomplishments: Survival since 1964 on a 'shoe-string' budget. The Movement has Non-Governmental Organizational status (NGO) with consultative "Status 1" with UNESCO, ECOSOC, UNICEF, ILO and the Council of Europe.
Products or Services: Research, publications, and representation before international bodies.
Tax Status: 501(c)(3) **Annual Report:** Yes. **Employees:** 13
Board of Directors or Trustees: Moya Amateau, Dr. Charles Courtney (Drew Univ.), Denis Cretinon, Daniel Kronenfeld, Sr. Fara Impastato, OP (Loyola Univ.), William Irelan, Charles Sleeth, Eugen Brand. Advisory Committee includes: Associate Dean Bertram Beck (Fordham Univ.), Most Rev. Alvaro Corrada (Catholic Regional Bishop, Archdiocese of Washington, DC), Prof. Emerita Dorothy Hewes (San Diego State Univ.), Rev. Michael Kendall (Episcopal Archdeacon of NYC), Mrs. Robert F. Kennedy, Jonathan Kozol (author, Savage Inequalities), Prof. S. M. Miller (Boston Univ.), Most Rev. Paul Moore, Jr. (Former Episcopal Bishop of New York), Hon. Edward Sullivan (State Assemblyman, New York), Prof. Harold Weissman (Hunter College), Prof. William Julius Wilson (Univ. of Chicago), Elie Wiesel (Nobel Peace Prize laureate).
Periodicals: *Fourth World Journal* (bimonthly newsletter), *Tapori* (monthly newsletter for children), and *Letter to Friends Around the World* (quarterly newsletter).
Internships: Yes. Three-month internships to study poverty issues and work directly with impoverished children and their families. Housing is provided. Following the internship, interns have the opportunity to join the Fourth World Movement Volunteer Corps and serve around the world. Volunteer Corps offers a trainee stipend during the first year, and opportunities for a higher paid stipend thereafter.
Other Information: A division of the International Movement ATD Fourth World. Established first in France in 1957, then in the U.S. in 1964 by Fr. Joseph Wresinski (1914-1988). Fr. Wresinski believed that "To eliminate poverty is not just a question of distributing money, nor of planning programs from offices; neither is it a matter of waving banners or shouting slogans. To eliminate poverty requires an encounter with men and women living in poverty, seeking them out wherever they are, not in order to teach them, but to learn from who they are and what they expect from us."

Free Trade Union Institute

1101 14th St., N.W., Suite 300
Washington, DC 20005   **Phone:**   (202) 842-0322
USA

Contact Person: Paul J. Somogyi, Executive Director
Officers or Principals: Paul J. Somogyi, Executive Director ($125,854); Lane Kirkland, President ($0); Thomas Donahue, Secretary/Treasurer ($0).

Mission or Interest: To promote organized labor worldwide.
Accomplishments: In 1993 the Institute spent $10,931,795 on its programs. All of this was spent on grants that; brought international visitors to the U.S. to "observe, interact, and consult with specialists on labor issues," and promoted "freedom of association, collective bargaining, and other democratic processes abroad." The main focus was on former Soviet-bloc countries.
Net Revenue: 1993 $12,611,154 ($12,580,563, or 99.8%, from government grants) **Net Expenses:** $12,638,422 86%/14%/0%
Net Assets: (-$30,422) **Citations:** 1:240
Products or Services: Grants.
Tax Status: 501(c)(3)
Other Information: The Institute received $12,580,563, or 99.8% of revenue, federal government grants. The remaining revenue came from a program contribution from the AFL-CIO, with whom they are affiliated.

Freedom of Expression Foundation

416 New Jersey Ave., S.E.
Washington, DC 20003
USA

Contact Person: Craig Smith, President. **Officers or Principals:** Craig Smith, President ($15,501); David Barrows, Chairman ($0); John R. Faust, Vice Chairman/Secretary ($0); Cathy Wagner Cormack, Treasurer.
Mission or Interest: "Promotion of the freedom of speech in electronic media via the use of research study, books, articles, lectures, discussion groups, and other educational programs."
Net Revenue: FY ending 6/94 $19,919 **Net Expenses:** $54,466 **Net Assets:** $212,654
Tax Status: 501(c)(6)
Other Information: The Foundation received $15,383, or 77% of revenue, from dividends and interest from securities. $4,500, or 23%, from gifts and grants awarded by foundations, businesses, and individuals. The remaining revenue came from interest on savings and temporary cash investments.

Freedom to Read Foundation

50 E. Huron St.
Chicago, IL 60611   **Phone:**   (312) 944-6780
USA

Contact Person: Judith F. Krug, Executive Director.
Mission or Interest: Promotes and protects freedom of speech and freedom of the press. Supports legal access for libraries and the public to any creative work. Opposed to censorship and book banning in libraries and schools. Supplies legal counsel and support to librarians and libraries who face censorship challenges.
Accomplishments: In the fiscal year ending August 1994, the Foundation spent $79,162 on its programs. $17,500 was awarded in grants to organizations promoting intellectual freedom, and to individuals "whose freedoms have been violated."
Net Revenue: FY ending 8/94 $93,853 **Net Expenses:** $96,231 82%/18%/0% **Net Assets:** $221,803
Tax Status: 501(c)(3)
Periodicals: *Freedom to Read Foundation News* (quarterly journal).
Other Information: Founded in 1969. Affiliated with the American Library Association at the same address. The Foundation received $82,702, or 79% of gross revenue, from membership dues. $12,571, or 12%, from gifts and grants awarded by foundations, businesses, and individuals. $7,707, or 7%, from dividends and interest from securities. $2,185, or 2%, from the sale of materials. The remaining revenue came from interest on savings and temporary cash investments. The Foundation lost $11,472 on the sale of securities.

Friends Committee on Legislation of California (FCL)

926 J St., Suite 707
Sacramento, CA 95814   **Phone:**   (916) 443-3734
USA

Contact Person: Bob Maynard, Clerk.
Officers or Principals: Henry Helson, Treasurer ($0); Anne Friend, Recording Clerk ($0); James Robertson, Finance Clerk.
Mission or Interest: Lobbies the California Legislature "in accordance with the faith and practices of the Religious Society of Friends (Quakers) and the policies and by-laws of the organization, mostly in the areas of criminal justice, peace, and the death penalty." Other policies included welfare reform and immigration.
Accomplishments: In 1994 the Committee spent $75,084 on its lobbying.
Net Revenue: 1994 $137,917 **Net Expenses:** $167,656 45%/32%/23% **Net Assets:** $89,691
Tax Status: 501(c)(4)
Other Information: Affiliated with the 501(c)(4) Friends Committee on National Legislation in Washington, DC, and the 501(c)(3) FCL Education Fund. The Committee received $117,797, or 85% of revenue, from gifts and grants awarded by foundations, businesses, and individuals. $8,000, or 6%, from contract services provided for the FCL Education Fund. $7,475 net, or 5%, from special fund-raising events. $3,018, or 2%, from dividends and interest from securities. $1,627, or 1%, from interest on savings and temporary cash investments.

Friends Committee on National Legislation (FCNL)

245 Second St., N.E.
Washington, DC 20002-5795   **Phone:**   (202) 547-6000   **E-Mail:** fcnl@igc.apc.org
USA   **Fax:**   (202) 547-6019

Contact Person: Barbara Ginsburg.
Officers or Principals: Earl J. Volk, Executive Director ($37,698); Victor Kaufman, Treasurer; Susan Rose, Assistant Treasurer.
Mission or Interest: "Since 1943, FCNL has worked toward a non-military world order so firmly based on justice and voluntary cooperation that there would be no place for war. FCNL has brought the concerns, experience and testimonies of the Religious Society of Friends (Quakers) to the attention of policy makers in the Nation's capitol."
Accomplishments: In 1994 the Committee spent $426,731 on lobbying congress. Their advocacy covers a wide range of issues: peace among nations, opposition to militarism and the proliferation of weapons, civil rights, sustainable development and other environmental concerns, increased public housing, health care, and more.
Net Revenue: 1994 $640,708 **Net Expenses:** $592,241 72%/19%/9% **Net Assets:** $363,164 **Citations:** 6:213
Products or Services: Lobbying and educational activities.
Tax Status: 501(c)(4) **Annual Report:** Yes. **Employees:** 15
Board of Directors or Trustees: Arthur Meyer Boyd, Jonathan Brown, Binford Farlow, Susie Fetter, Jonathan Fisch, Jeanne Herrick-Stare, Mark Hulbert, Nils Pearson, Don Reeves, Marietta Wright, Robert Schultz.
Periodicals: *FCNL Washington Newsletter*, and *The Indian Report*.
Internships: Yes. Interns work for eleven months. Each intern is part of a legislative working team headed by a professional lobbyist. Interns are expected to have a college degree.
Other Information: "FCNL was founded in 1943 largely to seek support for the rights of conscientious objectors during World War II, and out of a deep concern over the pervasive influence of military policy on American life." They are affiliated with the FCNL Education Fund at the same address. The Committee received $581,998, or 91% of revenue, from gifts and grants awarded by foundations, companies and individuals. (These grants included $15,000 from the Peace Development Fund.) $31,887, or 5%, from conference registration fees. $21,615 net, or 3%, from rental income. $4,686, or 1%, from the sale of literature. The remaining revenue came from interest on savings and temporary cash investments.

Friends for Jamaica

P.O. Box 20392
New York, NY 10025
USA

Contact Person: Rod Neyist.
Mission or Interest: "Promoting workers' struggles in the Caribbean." Political, economic and social analysis.
Accomplishments: Published the *Caribbean Newsletter* since 1980 on a shoe-string budget.
Periodicals: *Caribbean Newsletter* (quarterly).

Friends of the Earth

1025 Vermont Ave., N.W., 3rd Floor
Washington, DC 20005   **Phone:**   (202) 544-2600
USA

Contact Person: Jane Perkins, President.
Officers or Principals: Jane Perkins, President ($81,392); Brent Blackwelder, Vice President of Policy and Programs ($77,276); James Barns, Director of International Development ($62,353); Jennifer Jones, Director of Development; Janet Welsh Brown, Chair; Alan Gussow, Secretary; James Thompson, Assistant Treasurer; Lyndee Wells, Vice Chair; David Zwick, Treasurer.
Mission or Interest: Environmental organization with active members in over 30 nations worldwide. Works to "Shift patterns of multilateral development bank lending toward sustainable development policies...Works to protect tropical forests, the ozone, land rights of indigenous cultures...Focuses on empowering citizens to improve policies affecting groundwater, drinking water and chemical safety...Promotes fiscal reform to protect the environment through better federal spending, green taxes and jobs creation in green industries, and sustainable trade policies."
Accomplishments: In the fiscal year ending June 1994, the organization spent $2,058,786 on its programs. $992,032 was spent on domestic programs, and $594,766 was spent on international programs. $171,755 supported outreach to the media, teachers, students, and the general public. $300,233 was used for membership services. Friends of the Earth awarded $105,185 in grants to individuals and organizations. Recipients of the largest grants included: $20,000 each for the firm of Greer, Margolis, Mitchess & Burns (to raise awareness regarding the General Agreement on Tariffs and Trade) and the Institute of Agriculture, $10,400 for the Citizens Fund, $8,000 for Clean Water Action, $5,000 for the Sierra Club, and $4,700 for the Greenpeace Fund.
Net Revenue: FY ending 6/94 $2,710,837 **Net Expenses:** $2,642,224 78%/10%/12% **Net Assets:** (-$52,146)
Citations: 1,060:22
Products or Services: Publications, grants, research, local grassroots organizing, and lobbying. Friends of the Earth spent $34,878 on the direct lobbying of legislators. This was up 44% over the previous year, but down 31% from $50,235 three years prior.
Tax Status: 501(c)(3)
Board of Directors or Trustees: Darryl Alexander, Robert Banks, Jayni Chase, Harriet Crosby, Clarence Ditlow (Center for Highway and Automotive Safety), Marion Edey, Paul Hawken, Michael Herz, Marion Hunt-Badiner, Alvin Josephy, Linda Heller Kamm, Kai Lee, Janet Maughan, Helen Mills, Josephine Murray, Avis Ogilvy-Moore, Anthony Robbins, Ocean Robbins, Ron Judd.

Periodicals: *Environmental Update* (monthly newsletter), *Ocean Magazine*, and *Man Not Apart* (magazine).
Other Information: Friends of the Earth is affiliated with the 501(c)(4) Friends of the Earth Action, whose gross receipts were less than $25,000 during this fiscal year, at the same address. The 501(c)(4) Action organization reimbursed the 501(c)(3) Friend of the Earth with net $6,713 for expenses. Friends of the Earth used the O'Brien McConnell Company, of Washington DC, for fundraising and paid the Company $39,900. Friends of the Earth received $2,583,303, or 95% of revenue, from gifts and grants awarded by foundations, businesses, and individuals. (These grants included $260,100 from the Tides Foundation, $200,000 from the Charles Stewart Mott Foundation, $79,320 from the Environmental Federation of America, $30,000 from the Bullitt Foundation, $1,733 from the Environmental Federation of California, and $1,000 from the Compton Foundation.) $50,080, or 2%, from government grants. $47,348, or 2%, from royalties. The remaining revenue came from publication and merchandise sales, honoraria, interest on savings and temporary cash investments, and other miscellaneous sources.

Friends of the Third World

611 W. Wayne St.
Fort Wayne, IN 46802   **Phone:**   (219) 422-6821   **E-Mail:** fotw@igc.apc.org
USA   **Fax:**   (219) 422-1650

Contact Person: James F. Goetsch.   **Officers or Principals:** Marion R. Waltz, John R. Howell, Charles Haddox.
Mission or Interest: "To provide an example of an alternative system of trade working cooperatively in the market place with low income persons and groups and to educate the general public about ways to alleviate the poverty cycle and hunger." Advocates local agriculture, co-op food distribution, and food banks. The organization buys products, such as coffee from Nicaragua, that is grown by "cooperatives of low-income farmers or through nonprofit alternative channels," and sells them to members.
Accomplishments: "Founded the International Federation for Alternative Trade (IFAT) and North American Fair Trade Federation. Actively works in partnership with cooperatives in 35 countries. Operates eight volunteer-run retail 'Third World Shoppes.' Markets to 600 nonprofit community groups."
Products or Services: Catalog of food products.
Tax Status: 501(c)(3) **Annual Report:** No. **Employees:** 7 part-time employees in three locations.
Board of Directors or Trustees: Jim Goetsch, Marian Waltz, John Howell, Charles Haddox, Susan Fenwick, Pauline Mcnaney, Angelo Tomedi, Carol Schrantz, Diane Chavez, Ruth Shunick.
Periodicals: *Alternative Trading News* (quarterly newsletter).   **Internships:** Yes.
Other Information: Began as the Young World Development in 1972.

Friends of the United Nations

87 School St.
Hatfield, MA 01038   **Phone:**   (413) 247-9301
USA

Contact Person: Christine Austin, President.   **Officers or Principals:** Irving Sernoff, Treasurer ($0).
Mission or Interest: Promoting the United Nations in the United States. Educates the public about the U.N.'s programs and functions.
Accomplishments: In 1993 the organization spent $68,721 on its programs.
Net Revenue: 1993 $111,326 **Net Expenses:** $113,973 60%/34%/6% **Net Assets:** (-$904)
Tax Status: 501(c)(3)

Fund For the Feminist Majority

8105 W. Third St., Suite 1
Los Angeles, CA 90048   **Phone:**   (213) 651-0495
USA   **Fax:**   (213) 653-2689   **Web-Page:** http://www.feminist.org

Contact Person: Susan Gilligan, Manager.   **Officers or Principals:** Eleanor Smeal, President ($39,098); Katherine Spillar, Director ($21,052); Toni Carabillo, Vice President ($0); Judith Meuli, Secretary; Rae Wyman, Treasurer; Peg Yorkin, Chair.
Mission or Interest: Lobbying affiliate of the Feminist Majority Foundation.
Accomplishments: In 1996 the Fund sponsored the "Feminist Expo '96 for Women's Empowerment." More than 299 organizations co-sponsored the Expo. Speakers included Barbara Ehrenreich, Sen. Carol Moseley-Braun (D-IL), Gloria Steinem, Julianne Malveaux, Bella Abzug, Rep. Eleanor Holmes-Norton (D-DC), and others. A session on "Developing a Feminist Budget" focused on economics and included columnist Julianne Malveaux. Malveaux stated that if you divided up the assets of the federal government, there would be no poor people and that "genuflecting at the altar of a balanced budget is a sick religion." Rutgers economist Marlene Kim stated "We as feminists need to fall in love with taxes." Another session was devoted to "Eliminating Poverty: Reframing the Debate", where a panelist from the Welfare Warriors stated "Welfare reform provides cheap, forced labor for corporations unwilling to pay family supporting wages that fathers demand." Other sessions focused on electoral politics, women and sports, and more. There was no planned session, however, focusing exclusively on lesbians' issues, so participants formed an impromptu "Dyke Caucus" to demand that these issues be discussed publicly. The conference was broadcast on C-Span. In 1993 the Fund spent $411,451 on its programs. The largest program, with expenditures of $262,877, was communications through the production and distribution of a newsletter. $119,455 was spent on the "Feminization of Power Project" which encourages women to participate in the political process, and promotes women in leadership positions in government, business, law, and universities. $29,119 was spent on public education about feminist issues such as abortion rights.

Net Revenue: 1993 $768,622 **Net Expenses:** $648,668 63%/19%/17% **Net Assets:** (-$186,628) **Citations:** 24:168
Tax Status: 501(c)(4)
Board of Directors or Trustees: Dolores Huerta, Dorothy Jonas, Karen Sergi.
Periodicals: *Feminist Majority Report* (quarterly newsletter).
Other Information: The Foundation is affiliated with the 501(c)(3) Feminist Majority Foundation at the same address. In 1993 the two affiliates had combined net revenues of $2,118,649, net expenses of $1,998,695, and net assets of $3,758,635. Eleanor Smeal served as president of both and was paid a combined $94,946. Katherine Spillar received a combined $70,213. The Fund received $709,875, or 92% of revenue, from gifts and grants awarded by foundations, businesses, and individuals. $57,759, or 8%, from mailing list rentals. The remaining revenue came from speaking fees and interest on savings and temporary cash investments.

Fund for a Free South Africa
729 Boylston St.
Boston, MA 02116   **Phone:**   (617) 267-8333
USA

Contact Person: Themba Vilakazi, Executive Director.   **Officers or Principals:** Themba Vilakazi, Executive Director ($31,200); Mokubung Nkomo, Chairperson ($0); Glaudine Mtshali, Vice Chair ($0); Geoffrey Norman, Secretary.
Mission or Interest: "Advancement of basic human rights and democracy in South Africa by making grants and technical assistance."
Accomplishments: In the fiscal year ending June 1994, the Fund spent $603,412 on its programs. This included $314,134 in grants.
Net Revenue: FY ending 6/94 $693,040 **Net Expenses:** $714,288 84%/5%/11% **Net Assets:** $126,299 **Citations:** 0:255
Tax Status: 501(c)(3)
Board of Directors or Trustees: Beate Klein Becker, Joyce Williams-Mitchell, Janet Axelrod, Margaret Burnham, Toby D'Oench, Ben Magubane.
Other Information: The Fund received $674,464, or 97% of revenue, from gifts and grants received from foundations, businesses, and individuals. (These grants included $74,548 from the Vanguard Public Foundation, $20,000 from the Tides Foundation, $19,900 from the Haymarket People's Fund, $6,000 from the North Star Fund, $2,500 from the Bydale Foundation, and $500 from the Peace Development Fund.) $6,680, or 1%, from workshop fees. $6,360, or 1%, from rental income. The remaining revenue came from interest on savings and temporary cash investments.

Fund for an OPEN Society
311 S. Juniper St., Suite 400
Philadelphia, PA 19107   **Phone:**   (215) 735-6915   **E-Mail:** 102400.733@compuserve.com
USA   **Fax:**   (215) 735-2507

Contact Person: Don DeMarco, Executive Director. **Officers or Principals:** Don DeMarco, Executive Director ($47,527); Morris Milgram, President ($11,093); James Farmer, Chair; Marvin Wahman, Treasurer; Charles Mason, Jr., Secretary.
Mission or Interest: To provide subsidized mortgages to qualified families "whose introduction into a neighborhood will, in the organization's opinion, foster housing integration." Through this they hope to promote and sustain housing integration.
Accomplishments: Their National Committee includes: Rep. Barney Frank (D-MA), Betty Friedan, Hon. William H. Gray, III, Lane Kirkland (AFL-CIO), Franco Modigliani (Nobel Laureate, Economics), Vice President Walter Mondale (1977-1981), Hon. Andrew Young (former mayor of Atlanta and Pres. Carter's Amabassador to the U.N.), and many others.
Net Revenue: FY ending 5/94 $504,176 **Net Expenses:** $376,456 67%/20%/13% **Net Assets:** $539,965
Products or Services: Offers "financially advantageous" mortgage loans to qualified families.
Tax Status: 501(c)(3) **Annual Report:** No. **Employees:** 2 full time, 4 part time.
Board of Directors or Trustees: Hugh Schwartzberg, Roland Baker, Cherie Gaines, Joseph Hairston, Sister Patricia Marshall, Kenneth Gray, Rufus Sylvester Lynch, Jay Mazur, Martin Peretz, Anne Rudin, Matthew Watson, Mildred Wurf, Charles Wyzanski.
Internships: Yes, "requires analytical skills, computer facility, and understanding of the law of supply and demand."
Other Information: The Fund received $321,184, or 64% of revenue, from gifts and grants awarded by foundations, businesses and individuals. (These grants included $500 from the Haymarket People's Fund, and $500 from the Compton Foundation.) $150,544, or 30%, from mortgage interest received. The remaining revenue came from interest on savings and temporary cash investments.

Fund for Animals
200 W. 57th St., Suite 508
New York, NY 10019   **Phone:**   (212) 246-2096
USA

Contact Person: Cleveland Amory, President. **Officers or Principals:** Heidi Prescott, Executive Director ($0); Marian Probst, Secretary ($0); Michael Killian, Vice President ($0).
Mission or Interest: "The alleviation of fear, the prevention of pain and the relief of suffering of animals everywhere and to foster human conduct toward animals and encourage and support the cooperation among all persons interested in human activities." Animal rights and opposition to sport hunting.
Accomplishments: In 1994 the Fund spent $1,990,363 on its programs. The largest program, with expenditures of $1,148,442, was the operation of a ranch in Texas for abused and rescued animals. $727,595 was spent on educating the public about animal rights and welfare.

Net Revenue: 1994 $4,164,626 **Net Expenses:** $2,789,639 71%/13%/16% **Net Assets:** $11,290,059 **Citations:** 442:44
Products or Services: Education, animal care, and lobbying. The Fund spent $114,326 on lobbying, $58,814 on grassroots lobbying and $55,512 on the direct lobbying of legislators. This was down 40% from the year before.
Tax Status: 501(c)(3)
Board of Directors or Trustees: James Corrigan, Mrs. Enrico Donati, Prof. Priscilla Cohn, Mrs. Edward Ney (wife of a former Ambassador to Canada), Kathryn Walker (actress), Mrs. Amory Winthrop (Winley Foundation for Animals).
Other Information: Although the officers received no compensation, the fund spent $504,315 on payroll. No employee was paid over $50,000. The Fund received $3,870,790, or 88% of gross revenue, from gifts and grants awarded by foundations, businesses, and individuals. $514,532, or 12%, from dividends and interest from securities. The remaining revenue came from interest on savings and temporary cash investments. The Fund lost $250,859 on the sale of securities.

Fund for Equal Justice

32000 Northwestern Highway, Suite 275
Farmington Hills, MI 48334   **Phone:**   (810) 851-9444
USA

Contact Person: Richard Edgar, Treasurer.   **Officers or Principals:** Sheldon J. Stark, Chairman ($0); Donald Loria, Vice Chairman ($0); James R. Neuhard, Secretary ($0); Richard S. Edgar, Treasurer.
Mission or Interest: To provide assistance to "persons denied equal justice" because of race, income, gender, sexual orientation, or other reasons.
Accomplishments: In 1994 the Fund awarded $72,449 in grants. The recipients of these grants were; $45,394 for the ACLU Fund of Michigan, $13,635 for the National Lawyers Guild, $7,500 for Michigan Legal Services, and $5,920 for the Sugar Law Center.
Net Revenue: 1994 $61,783 **Net Expenses:** $72,863 **Net Assets:** $2,187
Products or Services: Fund-raising activities to provide money for grants.
Tax Status: 501(c)(3)
Other Information: The Fund received $61,429, or 99% of revenues, from gifts and grants awarded by foundations, companies and individuals. The remaining revenue came from investment income.

Fund for Peace

1511 K St., N.W., Suite 643
Washington, DC 20005   **Phone:**   (202) 783-4767
USA

Contact Person: Stephen R. Paschke, Associate Director.   **Officers or Principals:** Nina K. Solarz, Executive Director ($92,813); Donald P. Morrissey, Chief Financial Officer ($72,000); Stephen R. Paschke, Associate Director ($71,500); Thomas S. Blanton, Mary Lord, Project Directors; James R. Compton, Chair; Harry W. Earle, Treasurer; Barbara M. Cox, Secretary.
Mission or Interest: Research and education on topics relating to world peace, human rights and national security.
Accomplishments: In 1993 the Fund spent $2,837,691 on its programs. These programs included the National Security Archive, with expenditures of $1,027,349, that "collects, indexes, and distributes documentary materials on foreign policy topics for use by scholars, journalists, and other researchers." $702,873 was spent on the Institute for the Study of World Politics which "supports research, by awarding doctoral dissertation fellowships in annual open competition...on topics in arms control, international economic and social issues, human rights, and environmental concerns." $347,588 was spent on the Center for National Security Studies, which "carries out research and public education on the relationship between measures essential for the protection of the rights of individual citizens." These programs included $868,275 in grants to fellows at various universities.
Net Revenue: 1993 $2,554,925 **Net Expenses:** $3,000,656 95%/4%/1% **Net Assets:** $1,460,017 **Citations:** 83:115
Products or Services: Research, archives, fellowships, and lobbying. In 1993 the Fund spent $10,131 directly lobbying legislators. This was up 18% over the previous year, but down 86% from $74,843 in 1991.
Tax Status: 501(c)(3)
Board of Directors or Trustees: Avery Brooke, Dick Clark, Beatrice Duggan, Edward Fogel, Gerald Freund, Stanley Heginbotham, Russell Hemenway, Betty Lall, Alice Rush Levy, Franklin Long (Univ. of Calif.), Blanche Blank, Francis Deng, Donald Fraser, Doris Greenough, Samuel Heins, Peggy Korn, Tilden LeMelle, Gerald Levy, David Morey, Stewart Mott, David Phillips, Maurine Rothschild, Gregory Robeson Smith, Paul Warnke, W. Howard Wriggins, Richard Nolte, Judith Reppy (Cornell Univ.), Erwin Salk, F. Champion Ward, Myron Weiner (MIT).
Periodicals: *Access* (journal).
Other Information: The Center for Defense Information was originally a project of the Fund for Peace. The Fund received $2,554,925, or 84% of revenue, from gifts and grants awarded by foundations, businesses, and individuals. (These grants included $582,770 from the Compton Foundation, $300,000 over two years from the John D. and Catherine T. MacArthur Foundation, $40,000 from the John Merck Fund, $15,000 from the C.S. Fund, $10,000 from the Barbra Streisand Foundation, and $10,000 from the Deer Creek Foundation, and $2,000 from the New World Foundation.) $267,963, or 10%, from subscriptions and royalties from publications. $69,664, or 2%, from capital gains on the sale of securities. $53,440, or 2%, from interest on savings and temporary cash investments. $48,609, or 2%, from dividends and interest from securities. The remaining revenue came from an unrealized gain on securities held.

Fund for Popular Education

1500 Massachusetts Ave., N.W., Suite 241
Washington, DC 20005   **Phone:**   (202) 223-6474
USA

Contact Person: F. Michael Willis, President.   **Officers or Principals:** Karen Brandow, Vice President ($0).
Mission or Interest: Grant-making fund that awards money to organizations focusing on Guatemala.
Accomplishments: In 1994 the Fund awarded $152,901 in grants. The recipients were: $116,850 for Center for Human Rights Legal Action, $32,878 for the Network in Solidarity with the People of Guatemala, $2,850 for the Guatemala News and Information Bureau, and $323 for the Guatemala Solidarity Committee.
Net Revenue: 1994 $152,462 **Net Expenses:** $153,001 99%/1%/0% **Net Assets:** $947
Tax Status: 501(c)(3)
Other Information: The Fund received $152,353, or 99.9% of revenue, from gifts and grants awarded by foundations, businesses, and individuals. (These grants included $1,000 from the Vanguard Public Foundation, and $235 from the Ruth Mott Fund.) The remaining revenue came from interest on savings and temporary cash investments.

Fund for Southern Communities
547 Ponce de Leon Ave., Suite 100
Atlanta, GA 30308   **Phone:** (404) 876-4147   **E-Mail:** fsc@igc.apc.org
USA   **Fax:** (404) 876-3453

Contact Person: Joan Garner, Executive Director.   **Officers or Principals:** Joan Garner, Executive Director ($31,138).
Mission or Interest: Provides grants, technical assistance, and educational services to support grassroots nonprofit organizations in the South.
Accomplishments: In the fiscal year ending June 1994, the Fund spent $376,794 on its programs. $290,713 of this went for grants to various organizations.
Net Revenue: FY ending 6/94 $526,942 **Net Expenses:** $500,504 75%/13%/11% **Net Assets:** $344,181
Citations: 4:217 **Tax Status:** 501(c)(3)
Other Information: The Fund received $443,783, or 84% of revenue, from gifts and grants awarded by foundations, businesses, and individuals. (These grants included $25,000 from the Joyce Mertz-Gilmore Foundation, $8,000 from the Vanguard Public Foundation, $5,000 from the New World Foundation, $2,000 from the Haymarket People's Fund.) $45,768, or 9%, from special fund-raising events. $19,857, or 4%, from interest on savings and temporary cash investments. $17,534, or 3%, from administrative fees charged to cover the cost of processing grants.

Fund for the Center for Community Change
1000 Wisconsin Ave., N.W.
Washington, DC 20007   **Phone:** (202) 342-0519
USA   **Fax:** (202) 342-1132

Contact Person: Pablo Eisenberg, President.   **Mission or Interest:** Endowment for the Center for Community Change.
Accomplishments: In the fiscal year ending September 1994 the Fund awarded $425,000 to the Center for Community Change.
Net Revenue: FY ending 9/94 $1,093,472 **Net Expenses:** $468,297 91%/9%/0% **Net Assets:** $6,706,235
Tax Status: 501(c)(3)
Board of Directors or Trustees: Edwin Booth, Ronald Grzywinski, Ann Partlow, Rebecca Doggett (Auditor General, State Dept. of Education, NJ), Mitchell Johnson (Senior V.P., Corporate Finance, Sallie Mae), Benson Roberts.
Other Information: Affiliated with the 501(c)(3) Center for Community Change at the same address. The Fund received $719,295, or 66% of revenue, from dividends and interest from securities. $364,624, or 33% of revenue, from capital gains on the sale of securities. $9,553, or 1%, from interest on savings and temporary cash investments.

Funding Exchange
666 Broadway, 5th Floor
New York, NY 10012   **Phone:** (212) 529-5300 **E-Mail:** FEXEXC@AOL.COM
USA   **Fax:** (212) 982-9272

Contact Person: Cassandra Perkins, Office Manager.
Officers or Principals: Cecilia Rodriguez, Executive Director ($69,279); Ronald Hanft, Administrative Director ($48,198); Steve Fahrer, Resource Director ($48,098); Raymond Santiago, Officer; Charles Hey Maestre, Chair; Jerome Scott, Vice Chair; Esther Nieves, Secretary; Julia Classen, Treasurer; Judy Hatcher, Grant Director; Michael Roger, Development Director.
Mission or Interest: Philanthropy that gives to community and grassroots organizations through a network of member funds. These members are: Appalachian Community Fund (Knoxville, TN), Bread & Roses Community Fund (Philadelphia, PA), Chinook Fund (Denver, CO), Crossroads Fund (Chicago, IL), Fund for Southern Communities (Atlanta, GA), Haymarket People's Fund (Boston, MA), Headwaters Fund (Minneapolis, MN), Liberty Hill Foundation (Santa Monica, CA), McKenzie River Gathering Foundation(Portland & Eugene, OR), North Star Fund (New York, NY), Vanguard Public Foundation (San Francisco, CA), Wisconsin Community Fund (Madison, WI), associate fund The People's Fund (Honolulu, HI), and affiliate fund the Three Rivers Community Fund (Pittsburgh, PA). The Funding Exchange awards grants in certain areas; International grantmaking "to countries in which there are viable struggles against the anti-democratic effects of either U.S. corporate and government policies and/or policies of international lending institutions." The Saguaro Fund for "funding organizing in communities of color, where resources are scarce and survival difficult." The OUT Fund for Lesbian and Gay Liberation "to support radical organizing projects working to build community among lesbians, gay men, bisexuals and transgender people." The Paul Robeson Fund for Independent Media "to support independent social issue film, video and radio production...Projects addressing AIDS and other health issues; censorship and the 'culture wars;' homophobia, heterosexism and other sexual politics; international issues; racial and gender justice; reproductive rights; homelessness, welfare reform and other economic justice issues; environmental justice; militarism and violence; and corporate and government accountability." The Ignacio Martin-Baro Fund for Mental Health and Human Rights. Other programs are donor advised, activist advised, and emergency funding.

Accomplishments: In the fiscal year ending June 1994, the Fund spent $4,126,009 on its programs. This included $3,360,903 in grants. The Fund also makes loans through its Florian Loan Program. Recipients of loans or notes payable and the value of that loan at the end of the fiscal year include: $1,000,000 for the National Association of Community Development, $203,150 for the North Star Fund, $150,000 for the Ecumenical Development Corp., $50,000 for the Delaware Valley Community Reinvestment Fund, $40,000 for the Tides Foundation, $20,000 for the Interreligious Foundation, and $15,000 for the Institute for Community Economics.

Net Revenue: FY ending 6/94 $6,454,915 ($23,000, or less than 1%, from government grants)

Net Expenses: $4,764,205 87%/11%/2% **Net Assets:** $19,213,047

Products or Services: Grants, loans, coordination of resources, technical support, and lobbying. The Fund spent $6,413 on lobbying at the grassroots level. This was down 46% from the year before, and down 86% from the $44,790 that was spent on lobbying two years prior.

Tax Status: 501(c)(3)

Board of Directors or Trustees: Sylvia Castillo, Helen Cohen, Hari Dillon (Vanguard Public Found.), Joan Garner (Fund for Southern Communities), Nancy Hilsbos, Cliff Jones (TACS), Gary Kalman, Pat Maher (Haymarket People's Fund), Jose Morin (North Star Fund), Ralph Navarro, Shad Reinstein, Mike Roque (Chinook Fund), Faith Smith (NAES College).

Other Information: The Funding Exchange is located at the same address as the Common Giving Fund and North Star Fund. During the fiscal year ending April 1995, the Funding Exchange managed the Common Giving Fund, and was paid $50,000. The Fund received $4,924,132, or 76% of revenue, from direct and indirect public support in the form of gifts and grants awarded by foundations, affiliates, corporations and individuals. (These grants included $37,000 from the Aaron and Martha Schecter Foundation, $27,870 from the Vanguard Public Foundation, $26,307 from the Haymarket People's Fund, $5,900 from The People's Fund, $5,000 from the Jessie Smith Noyes Foundation, $1,130 from the People's Fund, and $1,000 from the New World Foundation.) $920,167, or 14%, from dividends and interest from securities. $439,427, or 7%, from capital gains on the sale of securities. $50,000, or 1%, from administrative services provided to other nonprofit organizations. $49,448, or 1%, from interest on savings and temporary cash investments. The remaining revenue came from conference fees, government grants, publication sales, and other miscellaneous sources. At the end of the fiscal year most of the assets, 78%, were held in securities, including corporate securities, mutual funds, and government securities. 10% were in savings and temporary cash investments, 8% were held in loans and notes payable, and 3% were held in buildings, land and equipment.

Fur-Bearer Defenders

P.O. Box 188950
Sacramento, CA 95818   **Phone:** (415) 945-9309   **E-Mail:** Furbearers@igc.apc.org
USA   **Fax:**   (415) 945-0929

Contact Person: Camilla Fox, Executive Director.   **Officers or Principals:** Bunty Clements, President ($0); Terri Barnato, Vice President ($0); George Clements, Secretary/Treasurer ($0).

Mission or Interest: To stop the trapping of fur-bearing animals and protect wildlife in the United States.

Accomplishments: Helped various grassroots organizations ban trapping at the state and local level. Have produced two videos on the subject, "Time to Care" narrated by actress Loretta Swit, and "America's Shame" narrated by actress Kim Bassinger.

Net Revenue: 1994 $161,979 **Net Expenses:** $198,833 71%/9%/20% **Net Assets:** $8,760

Products or Services: Brochures, videos, posters, mail and media campaigns.

Tax Status: 501(c)(3) **Annual Report:** Yes. **Employees:** 1

Periodicals: *The Fur-Bearer Defenders* (quarterly newsletter).

Internships: Yes.

Other Information: *The Fur-Bearer Defenders* refutes the notion that fur is making a fashion comeback. They charge that the rising prices for pelts is because "With consumer demand low, the supply of pelts is low which means prices-per-pelt are high." The organization received $161,786, or 99.8% of revenue, from gifts and grants awarded by foundations, companies and individuals. The remaining revenue came from interest on savings and temporary cash investments.

Gay and Lesbian Alliance Against Defamation, Los Angeles (GLAAD)

8455 Beverly Blvd., Suite 305
Los Angeles, CA 90048   **Phone:** (213) 658-6775
USA   **Fax:**   (213) 658-6776

Contact Person: Lee Werbel, Executive Director.   **Officers or Principals:** Lee Werbel, Executive Director ($46,667); Nancy Perez, Office Manager; Loren R. Javier, Development Assistant.

Mission or Interest: Media watch-dog organization fighting the defamation of lesbians and gays.

Accomplishments: GLAAD's monthly newsletter has a circulation of over 5,000. Sponsored Out on the Screen's "Outfest," a festival of homosexual films. Working on the "Textbook Equity and Accuracy Campaign" to insure that homosexuals are included and presented positively in textbooks used in California schools. In 1994 the Alliance spent $138,450 on its programs. The largest program, with expenditures of $83,999, was the publication and distribution of a monthly newsletter. $27,232 was spent on outreach efforts that "provide information for speakers, arrange and coordinate speaking functions, train and educate speakers on gay and lesbian rights." $8,304 was spent on a hotline "to get reports on positive and negative images of gays and lesbians in the media." $1,447 was spent on meetings and conventions.

Net Revenue: 1994 $399,135 **Net Expenses:** $332,192 42%/30%/28% **Net Assets:** $107,496

Tax Status: 501(c)(3)

Board of Directors or Trustees: Lynn Ballen, Stephanie Farrington-Domingue, Will Halm, Nazila Hedayat, Garrett Hicks, Jody Hoenninger, Richard Jennings, Michael Keegan, Myra Riddell, Carmichael Smith-Low, Steven Solomon, Tracey Stern, Angela West.
Periodicals: Monthly newsletter.
Other Information: The Alliance received $192,468 net, or 48% of revenue, from special fund-raising events. $145,122, or 36%, from gifts and grants awarded by foundations, businesses, and individuals. (These grants included $4,000 from the Vanguard Public Foundation, $3,098 from Progressive Way, $2,000 from Gay Men's Health Crisis.) $42,472, or 11%, from membership dues. $16,815, or 4%, from newsletter sales and subscriptions. The remaining revenue came from interest on savings and temporary cash investments, and the sale of inventory.

Gay and Lesbian Community Action

310 E. 38th St., Suite 204
Minneapolis, MN 55409   **Phone:**   (612) 822-0127
USA

Contact Person: Ann M. DeGroot, Executive Director.
Officers or Principals: Ann M. DeGroot, Executive Director ($41,752); Doug Federhart, Program Director ($33,752); Thomas L. Hoch, Chair ($0); Sherry Angus, Vice Chair; Christopher Webb, Secretary; Jon Gossett, Treasurer.
Mission or Interest: "Providing effective, professional, low-cost, gay/lesbian identified direct services to assist in relieving the impact of the stress of homophobia."
Accomplishments: In 1993 the organization spent $336,701 on its services. The largest program, with expenditures of $259,118, was support and advocacy services. $44,915 was spent on technical assistance for organizations and activists "for the purpose of strengthening community planning and project efforts." $32,668 for "system change" for "reducing the impact of discriminatory political, social and economic barriers on the gay and lesbian community."
Net Revenue: 1993 $369,640 ($134,582, or 36%, from government grants) **Net Expenses:** $422,464 80%/15%/6%
Net Assets: (-$57,482)
Products or Services: Technical assistance and consulting, and lobbying, the organization spent $18,680 on lobbying, $14,010 on grassroots lobbying and $4,670 on the direct lobbying of legislators. This was a 592% increase over the previous year.
Tax Status: 501(c)(3)
Board of Directors or Trustees: Anita Bellant (Metropolitan Airports Commission), Marjorie Cowmeadow (Assoc. Dean of General College, Univ. of MN), Ginger Ehrman, Artemis Giem, Kathy Hagen (Investigator, MN Dept. of Human Rights), Robert Jansen (owner, The Main Club), Paul Kaminski, Gil Kiekenapp, Gary Lingen (Univ. of MN Hospital), Timothy Lupton, Elise Matthesen (MN Public Radio), Lynn Pierce, Chris Riesdorf (MN Dept. of Human Services), Ashley Ann Rukes (coordinator Gay/Lesbian Pride Parade), Patrick Troska (coordinator, Catholic Youth Services).
Other Information: Gay and Lesbian Community Action received $146,728, or 40% of revenue, from direct and indirect public support in the form of gifts and grants awarded by foundations, businesses, and individuals. $134,582, or 36%, from government grants. $78,196 net, or 21%, from special fund-raising events. $9,915, or 3%, from service fees for consulting and technical assistance. The remaining revenue came from interest on savings and temporary cash investments, and other miscellaneous sources.

Gay and Lesbian Media Coalition

8455 Beverly Blvd., Suite 309
Los Angeles, CA 90048
USA

Other Information: In the fiscal year ending June 1994 the Coalition received $1,600 from the Ms. Foundation for Women. Other donors included the Astraea National Lesbian Action Foundation.

Gay and Lesbian Parents Coalition International (GLPCI)

P.O. Box 50360
Washington, DC 20091   **Phone:**   (202) 583-8029   **E-Mail:** GLPCINat@ix.netcom.com
USA   **Fax:**   (201) 783-6204 (New Jersey)

Contact Person: Tim Fisher, Executive Director.   **Officers or Principals:** Patricia K. Ban, Ph.D., Treasurer
Mission or Interest: "Provide advocacy, education and support for gay and lesbian persons in child-rearing roles and their families - in all their diversity - worldwide."
Accomplishments: "Explosive growth and unprecedented visibility since 1992 'Family Values' theme entered political debate." Over 100 local chapters in 8 countries. Programs such as COLAGE - Children of Lesbians and Gays Everywhere.
Net Revenue: FY ending 4/93 less than $25,000
Tax Status: 501(c)(3) **Annual Report:** No, **Employees:** 2
Periodicals: *NETWORK.*   **Internships:** Yes.

Gay Community News (GCN)

29 Stanhope St.
Boston, MA 02116   **Phone:**   (617) 262-6969
USA

Mission or Interest: National newspaper focusing on homosexual life and politics.
Periodicals: *Gay Community News.*

Gay Men's Health Crisis (GMHC)

129 W. 20th St.
New York, NY 10011   **Phone:**   (212) 337-1950
USA

Contact Person: Louis Bradbury, President.   **Officers or Principals:** John J. Richardson, Executive Director, ($138,308); Mark Robinson, Chief Financial Officer ($104,216); Addie Guttag, Deputy Executive Director for Development ($95,000); Louis Bradbury, President; Todd Yancey, M.D., Vice President; Randy Wojcak, Secretary; David Hollander, Treasurer.
Mission or Interest: Provides clinical and social services for gay men with AIDS. Promotes public policy and lobbies on behalf of increased public funding for HIV/AIDS research and social services.
Accomplishments: In the fiscal year ending June 1994, the organization spent $16,623,991 on its programs. The largest program, with expenditures of $9,675,997, was clinical services. This included "crisis intervention and counseling, direct financial aid, recreational activities, welfare and legal counseling, buddy and home attendant services." Also assists clients in obtaining public welfare benefits from Social Security Disability, Income Support, Medicaid, and others. $3,521,630 was spent on public information and education, including a telephone hotline, public forums, a newsletter, handbooks, and other resources. $3,426,364 was spent on policy development, "GMHC actively supports fair and effective public policies and practices concerning HIV infection." Awarded $519,780 in grants to other organizations. Recipients of the largest grants were: $290,000 for Community Funds, $200,000 for the AIDS Action Council, $6,000 for the New York AIDS Coalition, $5,000 for the AIDS Action Foundation, $5,000 for the San Francisco AIDS Project. Other recipients included; the Black Leadership Commission on AIDS, Gay and Lesbian Alliance Against Defamation, Campaign for Health Security, WPA-HIV Law Project, New York Jobs With Justice, Institute for Human Identity, and others.
Net Revenue: FY ending 6/94 $22,804,301 ($3,714,764, or 16%, from government grants)
Net Expenses: $23,828,768 70%/7%/23% **Net Assets:** $13,482,440 **Citations:** 252:65
Products or Services: Social services, clinical services, educational materials, and lobbying. GMHC spent $389,120 on lobbying, $27,910 on grassroots lobbying and $361,210 on the direct lobbying of legislators. This was a decrease of 26% from the previous year.
Tax Status: 501(c)(3)
Board of Directors or Trustees: Bernard Bihari, M.D., Esther Chachkes, Dennis deLeon, Suzanne DuBose, Gretchen Dykstra, Jose Ramon Fernandez-Pena, Ethan Geto, Jerome Goldsmith, Ed.D., Darrell Greene, Ph.D., Howard Grossman, M.D., Tonya Hall, Marjorie Hill, Ph.D., Richard Jasper, Rabbi Sharon Kleinbaum, Michael mast, Hal Moskowitz, Kenneth Ong, M.D., M.P.H., Michael Palm, James Pepper, Samuel Phillips, Lourdes Quinones, R.N., Michael Recanati, Doug Robinson, Michele Russell, Jeff Soref, Joan Tisch, Robert Woolley.
Periodicals: Newsletter.
Other Information: Affiliated with the 501(c)(4) Gay Men's Health Crisis Action at the same address. GMHC received $17,014,048, or 75% of revenue, from gifts and grants awarded by foundations, affiliates, businesses, and individuals. (These grants included $20,000 from the Henry J. Kaiser Foundation.) $3,714,764, or 16%, from government grants. $1,476,796 net, or 6%, from special fund raising events including a Barbra Streisand Concert, an art auction, a radio-thon, a "Morning Party," and other events. $246,948, or 1%, from the sale of publications. $180,666, or 1%, from rental income. The remaining revenue came from fees reimbursed by New York State Medicare, interest on savings and other temporary cash investments, and other miscellaneous sources.

Gayshine Press

P.O. Box 410690
San Francisco, CA 94141   **Phone:**   (510) 820-9321
USA

Contact Person: Winston Leyland, President.   **Officers or Principals:** Winston Leyland, President ($15,562); Charles Shively, Secretary ($0); Richard Yaxley, Treasurer ($0).
Mission or Interest: Publication of books and materials of special interest to lesbians and gays. "Publication and sale of artistic and educational merit poetry, fiction, and anthologies."
Accomplishments: In 1994 the Press spent $21,353 on its programs and publications.
Net Revenue: 1994 $13,687 **Net Expenses:** $28,497 75%/21%/4% **Net Assets:** $140,877
Tax Status: 501(c)(3)
Other Information: The Press received $13,687 net, or 100% of revenue, from the sale of publications. The Press had $82,411 in gross sales.

General Service Foundation

411 E. Main St., Suite 205
Aspen, CO 81611   **Phone:**   (970) 920-6834   **E-Mail:** gsf@rof.net
USA   **Fax:**   (970) 920-4578

Contact Person: Lani Shaw.   **Officers or Principals:** Robert W. Musser, President ($0); Marcie J. Musser, Vice President/Treasurer ($0); Mary L. Estrin, Vice President ($0).
Mission or Interest: Grant-making foundation with awards in the areas of "international peace, population, and resources." The Foundation was created and endowed in 1946 by Clifton R. Musser (1869-1956) and his wife, Margaret Kulp Musser (1875-1967).

Accomplishments: In 1994 the Foundation awarded $1,909,040 in grants. The recipients of the largest grants included; four grants totaling $77,500 for the Tides Foundation, three grants totaling $75,000 for the Washington Office on Latin America, two grants totaling $55,000 for the Columbia University School of Public Health, two grants totaling $40,000 for the American Association for the Advancement of Science, $40,000 for the Center for Reproductive Law and Policy, $35,000 each for the Alan Guttmacher Institute and Planned Parenthood Federation of America, three grants totaling $31,290 for the Center for International Policy, $30,000 each for the Lawyers Committee for Human Rights, Earth Island Institute, Indian Law Resource Center, Native American Rights Fund, Environmental Defense Fund, Washington Law School Foundation, and International Women's Health Coalition.
Net Revenue: 1994 $2,925,512 **Net Expenses:** $2,383,186 **Net Assets:** $35,395,062
Tax Status: 501(c)(3) **Annual Report:** Yes. **Employees:** 2
Board of Directors or Trustees: Robin Halby, Robert Estrin, Gary Hartshorn, Heidi Lloyd, Christine Cassel, M.D., Elizabeth Musser, Terry Karl.
Other Information: The Foundation received $2,349,725, or 80% of revenue, from capital gains on the sale of securities. $338,975, or 12%, from interest on savings and temporary cash investments. $186,075, or 6%, from dividends and interest from securities. The remaining revenue came from other investment income. The Foundation held $17,331,170, or 49% of assets, in corporate stocks. $17,253,419, or 49%, in off-shore corporations and mutual funds.

Georgians for Choice

P.O. Box 8551
Atlanta, GA 30306   **Phone:**   (404) 607-7959
USA   **Fax:**   (404) 875-0169

Contact Person: Tina Trent, Executive Director.
Mission or Interest: Coalition of 45 organizations serving as "a unified voice for reproductive freedom."
Products or Services: Candidate report cards, coalition building, lobbying.
Tax Status: 501(c)(3)
Other Information: Founded in 1986. In 1994 the organization received $10,000 from the Ms. Foundation for Women, $7,000 from the Jessie Smith Noyes Foundation.

Global 2000

One Copenhill
Atlanta, GA 30307   **Phone:**   (404) 872-3848
USA

Contact Person: Craig Withers, Associate Director of Operations.
Officers or Principals: Dr. Donald Hopkins, Senior Health Consultant ($150,677); Andrew W. Agle, Operations Director ($105,014); Michael Street, Resident Advisor ($89,689); President Jimmy Carter, Chairman; Charles H. Kirbo, Treasurer; William H. Foege, Secretary; John B. Hardman, Associate Executive Director; Rosalynn Carter, Trustee.
Mission or Interest: "Global 2000 draws its inspiration from The Global 2000 Report to the President commissioned by former U.S. President Jimmy Carter during his administration. Projecting trends in population growth and environmental degradation into the 21st century, that report depicts a spiral of poverty, disease, hunger, and social injustice in rural areas of developing countries that could seriously threaten economic stability and world peace. Global 2000's goal is to encourage sustainable development and equitable and responsible use of resources by promoting food self-reliance, improving health and the environment and encouraging sound population policies.
Accomplishments: "Increased maize production in Ghana by 40% and wheat production in Sudan by over 200%. Helped train more than 9,000 special education teachers in China. 'Graduated' more than 200,000 village farmers in Africa from test plot technology transfer programs in basic food crops. Cosponsored a symposium: 'Forests and the Environment: A U.S. Response to the Rio Earth Summit,' which increased public awareness and advanced policy dialogue about appropriate U.S. notes on forest issues in the post-Rio era." In the fiscal year ending August 1994, Global 2000 awarded $4,827,958 in grants to carry out its projects.
Net Revenue: FY ending 8/94 $6,986,023 **Net Expenses:** $7,129,091 **Net Assets:** $2,123,109
Tax Status: 501(c)(3)
Other Information: Global 2000 is at the same address as its affiliate, the Carter Center, which they paid $280,014 for management services. Global 2000 received $6,950,021, or 99% of revenue, from gifts and grants awarded by foundations, businesses, and individuals. $36,002, or 1%, from interest on savings and temporary cash investments.

Global Committee of Parliamentarians on Population and Development

336 E. 45th St., 10th Floor
New York, NY 10017   **Phone:**   (212) 953-7947
USA   **Fax:**   (212) 557-2061

Contact Person: Akio Matsumura, Executive Director
Mission or Interest: "Planning and coordinating of seminars, projects, and conferences for present and former parliamentary leaders."
Accomplishments: In 1994 the Committee spent $60,538 on its programs. The largest expense, $39,425, or 65% of the program budget, went for travel. Consultants was the next highest expense.
Net Revenue: 1994 $50,987 **Net Expenses:** $102,054 59%/41%/0% **Net Assets:** (-$359,234)
Tax Status: 501(c)(3)

Other Information: The Committee received $50,987, or 100% of revenue, from gifts and grants awarded by foundations, businesses, and individuals. The Committee ran a deficit of $51,067 in 1994, added to a deficit of $308,166 from previous years. The liabilities owed by the Committee consisted of mortgages and notes payable, $200,000, and loans payable to officers and directors, $185,000.

Global Education Associates

4 /5 Riverside Dr., Suite 456
New York, NY 10115   **Phone:**   (212) 870-3290
USA

Contact Person: Gerald Mische, President.
Officers or Principals: Douglas Roche, Chairperson ($0); Harriett Zullo, Secretary ($0); Michael Feeley, Treasurer ($0).
Mission or Interest: "To catalyze a transnational, multi-issue movement for world order based on values of peace, social justice, ecological balance, and participation in decision making."
Accomplishments: In the fiscal year ending June 1994, the Associates spent $161,892 on their programs.
Net Revenue: FY ending 6/94 $236,739 **Net Expenses:** $229,569 71%/24%/6% **Net Assets:** (-$18,350)
Tax Status: 501(c)(3)
Board of Directors or Trustees: Rosalle Bertell (Intl. Inst. of Concern for Public Health), Jane Bodine, S.P. (Sisters of Providence), Dr. Noel Brown (UN Environment Programme Liaison Office), Sjef Donders (Washington Theological Union), Edmund Kleissler, Rev. Paul Lauby, James Lippke (Employment and World Order Task Force, Project Global 2000), Peter Mann (World Hunger Awards), Miriam Therese MacGillis, O.P., Dr. Saul Mendlovitz (World Order Models Project), Dr. Patricia Mische, Dr. Betty Reardon (Dir. of Peace Studies, Columbia Univ.), Dr. Abdul Aziz Said (American Univ.), Rev. Donald Shriver, Jr. (Union Theological Seminary), Dr. Jennifer Simons (Simons Foundation).
Periodicals: *Breakthrough* (magazine).
Other Information: The Associates received $157,586, or 67% of revenue, from gifts and grants awarded by foundations, businesses, and individuals. (These grants included awards from the UN Institute, UNICEF, and the World Federalist Association.) $61,510, or 26%, from membership dues. The remaining revenue came from the sale of inventory and other miscellaneous sources.

Global Environment Project Institute (GEPI)

411 E. 6th St., 2nd Floor
Ketchum, ID 83340   **Phone:**   (208) 726-3025
USA   **Fax:**   (208) 726-4068

Contact Person: Michelle Richer, Grants Coordinator.   **Officers or Principals:** J. Christopher Hormel, Executive Director; Angela Ocone, Vice President; Thomas Hormel, Rampa Hormel, Chairs; Michelle Richer, Secretary.
Mission or Interest: "GEPI promotes the conservation of biodiversity and sustainability of life on earth. GEPI selects projects or actions that, in a highly leveraged manner, will affect life on this planet for generations to come." Awards grants to other environmental organizations.
Accomplishments: Previous programs include Globescope Idaho, a five day international conference on sustainable development held in Idaho in 1987; co-sponsored by the Global Tomorrow Coalition and the United Nations Environment Programme. E2, Environment and Education, which develops a curriculum for middle and high-school students that helps them evaluate the environmental impact of resource use in their schools. E2 is now a project of the Tides Foundation. The Sawtooth Community Garden Project which was created in 1994 to produce models of sustainable building and gardening practices. Recipients of grants in 1995 included: $50,000 for Green Seal, $35,000 for the East Africa Environmental Network, $30,000 for the Idaho Conservation League, $15,000 Oregon Natural Resources Council, $10,000 each for the Naropa Institute, USPIRG Education Fund, Foundation on Economic Trends, Save America's Forests, and Conservation International.
Tax Status: 501(c)(3) **Annual Report:** Yes. **Employees:** 4   **Internships:** No.
Board of Directors or Trustees: Diane Ives, LuAnne Finch Hormel.

Global Exchange

2017 Mission St., Suite 303
San Francisco, CA 94110   **Phone:**   (415) 255-7296
USA

Contact Person: Kevin Danaher, Secretary.
Officers or Principals: Kevin Danaher, Secretary ($19,919); Jennifer Carino, Staff Representative ($18,000); Steve McKay, Staff Representatives ($18,000); Walter Turner, President; Carol Wagner, Vice President; Maya Miller, Treasurer.
Mission or Interest: Hosts "Reality Tours" to developing countries so that North Americans can see firsthand the problems and issues facing these countries. Encourages tourists to report back to church and community organizations on the needs of these countries. Also works directly with third world grassroots organizations.
Accomplishments: In 1993 the Exchange spent $509,476 on its programs. The largest of these programs, with expenditures of $168,252, was the "Alternative Trade" program and "Third World Craft Stores (that) use arts and crafts and cultural events to educate the public and raise funds for small charitable grants to groups working to alleviate poverty in the developing world." $128,011 was spent on the Campaign/Partnerships with grassroots third world organizations. These partnership programs included $42,203 in grants. $106,588 was spent on the "Reality Tours" program, which hosted approximately 400-500 tourists. Other programs included public education and $19,019 in grants for other organizations seeking to help the developing world.

Net Revenue: 1993 $638,133 **Net Expenses:** $625,510 81%/1%/16% **Net Assets:** $403,256 **Citations:** 247:67
Products or Services: Grants, tours, partnerships, educational materials, and lobbying. The Exchange spent $6,168 on lobbying, $4,614 on grassroots lobbying and $1,554 on the direct lobbying of legislators.
Tax Status: 501(c)(3)
Board of Directors or Trustees: John Harrington, Max Blanchet, David Cone, Rick Tejada-Flores, Judy Wicks.
Other Information: The Global Exchange received $316,430, or 50% of revenue, from gifts and grants awarded by foundations, businesses, and individuals. (These grants included $20,000 from the J. Roderick MacArthur Foundation, $3,500 from the South Coast Foundation, $2,500 from the Peace Development Fund, and $1,000 from the Jessie Smith Noyes Foundation.) $174,171 net, or 27%, from the sale of inventory from the Alternative Trade program. $96,675, or 15%, from tour fees. $30,021 net, or 5%, from special fund-raising events, including "Reggae in the Park." $10,267, or 2%, from non-tour service fees. $7,472, or 1%, from interest on savings and temporary cash investments. The remaining revenue came from dividends and interest from securities; the Exchange held $165,049 in assets in the Pax World Fund and Progressive Asset Management.

Global Fund for Women
2480 Sand Hill Rd., Suite 100
Menlo Park, CA 94025   **Phone:** (415) 854-0420
USA

Contact Person: Anne Firth Murray, President.
Mission or Interest: Provides funds for domestic and foreign groups committed to "women's well-being and their full participation in society." Works on abortion rights and environmental issues.
Tax Status: 501(c)(3)
Other Information: In 1994 the Fund received $40,000 from the Jessie Smith Noyes Foundation, $32,000 from the General Service Foundation, $30,000 from the Compton Foundation, $6,000 from the Vanguard Public Foundation, $600 from the Tides Foundation, and $500 from the Stewart R. Mott Charitable Trust. In 1993 the Global Fund for Women received $750,000 over three years from the John D. and Catherine T. MacArthur Foundation, and $50,000 from the John Merck Fund.

Global Options
P.O. Box 40601
San Francisco, CA 94140   **Phone:** (415) 550-1703
USA

Contact Person: Cecilia O'Leary, President.
Officers or Principals: Nancy Cook, Vice President ($0); Nancy Stein, Secretary/Treasurer ($0).
Mission or Interest: Educational materials and seminars on "social justice issues."
Accomplishments: In 1994 the organization spent $13,255 on its programs. Topics of publications included Women and Welfare Reform, Japan Enters the 21st Century, Crime and Justice in the Clinton Era, and Justice and the World System. About 2,000 copies of each publication was distributed.
Net Revenue: 1994 $42,448 **Net Expenses:** $15,686 **Net Assets:** $133,843
Products or Services: Publications and seminars.   **Tax Status:** 501(c)(3)
Board of Directors or Trustees: Barbara Bishop, Pat Brown, Suzie Dod, Bill Felice, Jon Frappier, Susanne Jonas, Beth Harding, June Kress, Janis Lewin, Elizabeth Martinez, Ed McCaughan, Patti McSherry, Tony Platt, Mark Rabine, Gerda Ray, Richard Schauffler, Greg Shank.
Periodicals: *Social Justice* (quarterly journal).
Other Information: Global Options received $35,314, or 83% of revenue, from the sale of inventory. $5,553, or 13%, from royalties. $1,090, or 2%, from gifts and grants awarded by foundations and individuals. The remaining revenue came from interest on savings and temporary cash investments.

Government Accountability Project (GAP)
810 1st St., N.E., Suite 630
Washington, DC 20002   **Phone:** (202) 408-0034
USA

Contact Person: Louis Clark, Executive Director.
Mission or Interest: Protects the rights and litigates on behalf of corporate and government 'whistle blowers' who expose waste and mismanagement, especially in the nuclear weapons production industry.
Accomplishments: Recently supported U.S. Forest Service 'whistle blowers' and their efforts to reform management of national forests bordering the Chattanooga River. In 1994 the Project spent $575,006 on its programs. This included litigation on behalf of clients whose rights were violated after their 'whistle blowing'. Trained over 50 student interns. Received $106,354 in court-awarded attorneys fees for its litigation.
Net Revenue: 1994 $565,573 **Net Expenses:** $678,794 85%/11%/4% **Net Assets:** (-$39,479) **Citations:** 82:116
Tax Status: 501(c)(3)
Periodicals: *Bridging the Gap* (quarterly newsletter).   **Internships:** Yes.
Other Information: Founded in 1977. In 1994 the Project received $433,957, or 77% of revenue, from gifts and grants awarded by foundations, businesses, and individuals. (These grants included $100,000 from the Florence and John Schumann Foundation, $65,000 from the Deer Creek Foundation, $40,000 from the Bauman Family Foundation, $35,000 from the Bullitt Foundation, $30,000 from the C.S. Fund, $30,000 from the Rockefeller Family Fund, $30,000 from the Ploughshares Fund, $10,000 from the Compton Foundation, $5,000 from the Tides Foundation, $5,000 from the Angelina Fund, and $1,000 from the Haymarket People's Fund.) $106,354, or 19%, from court-awarded attorneys fees. $15,141, or 3%, from litigation fees reimbursed by clients. The remaining revenue came from rental income, and the sale of merchandise.

Grassroots International

48 Grove St., Suite 103
Somerville, MA 02144   **Phone:** (617) 628-1664   **E-Mail:** grassroots@igc.apc.org
USA   **Fax:**   (617) 628-4737

Contact Person: Dan Connell, Executive Director.
Mission or Interest: Third world peace and justice. "We focus on strategically important areas where national movements are challenging economic and social inequalities and regressive political systems."
Tax Status: 501(c)(3)
Other Information: In 1994 Grassroots international received $53,111 from the Tides Foundation, $20,000 from the General Service Foundation, and $1,000 from the One World Fund.

Grassroots Leadership

P.O. Box 36006
Charlotte, NC 28236   **Phone:** (704) 332-3090
USA

Contact Person: Simon Kahn, Director. **Officers or Principals:** Simon "Si" Kahn, Director ($42,886); Cathy Howell, Director ($35,739); Kamau Marcharia, Director ($34,698); Joe Szakos, Treasurer; Leslie Hill, Secretary.
Mission or Interest: Grassroots organizing and coalition building in the south. "To help community organizations with issues of race, gender, and class in ways that build on the strengths of their differences." Grassroots Leadership works with "all major southern movements and organizations, including civil rights, women, labor, lesbian and gay, environment, peace and religious action."
Accomplishments: In 1994 Grassroots Leadership spent $379,540 on its programs. The largest program, grassroots organizing, had expenditures of $138,026. $102,418 was spent on "Barriers and Bridges" to help community organizations with diverse constituencies work together. The other two programs were the "Framework Expansion Project" to learn what works in southern community organizing, and "Rural Black Leadership" to help build new organizations.
Net Revenue: 1994 $500,561 **Net Expenses:** $438,162 87%/0%/13% **Net Assets:** $5,067
Tax Status: 501(c)(3)
Board of Directors or Trustees: Dave Bortz, James Ghee, James Andrews, John McCutcheon, Jerann King, Rose Sackey-Milligan, Alfreda Barringer, Margaret Chambers, Charles Barrson, Cora Tucker, Joanne Deplaine, James Williams, Meredith Emmett, Chandra Mohanty, Karimah Nonyamenko, Mitty Owens, June Rostan, Naomi Swinton.
Other Information: The organization received $337,351, or 67% of income, from gifts and grants awarded by foundations, companies, and individuals. (These grants included $26,600 from the Jessie Smith Noyes Foundation, $25,000 from the Campaign for Human Development, $20,000 from the New World Foundation, $5,000 from the Bydale Foundation, $4,587 from the Peace Development Fund, and $2,500 from the Tides Foundation.) $155,671, or 31%, from contracts with various other nonprofits for leadership and organizing assistance. The remaining revenue came from interest on savings and temporary cash investments, royalties, and the sale of inventory.

Gray Panthers Project Fund

2025 Pennsylvania Ave., N.W., Suite 821
Washington, DC 20006   **Phone:** (202) 466-3132
USA

Contact Person: Dixie Horning.   **Officers or Principals:** Jules Sugarman, Executive Director ($14,400); Charlotte Flynn, National Chair; Arthur Pappis, National Vice Chair.
Mission or Interest: Research and education on public policy with a focus on seniors. "A national organization of inter-generational activists dedicated to social change. Issues include: health care, housing, jobs, environment, and peace." Priorities are 1) A nationally-administered health care program, 2) Federally subsidized housing, 3) Reduced military spending, 4) A clean environment, 5) "Economic and Social Justice," and 6) The elimination of ageism, sexism, and racism.
Accomplishments: Approximately 30,000 members. In 1993 the Fund spent $238,042 on its projects. Provided testimony at congressional hearings, entered comments for the record during legislation consideration, organized rallies, hosted Age and Youth Summit.
Net Revenue: 1993 $274,178 **Net Expenses:** $328,499 72%/12%/16% **Net Assets:** $1,021,547
Tax Status: 501(c)(3) **Annual Report:** Yes. **Employees:** 6
Board of Directors or Trustees: Abe Bloom, Selma Bonham, Cliff Carlstedt, Susan Eklund, Anna Elwood, Ruth Inabu Fox, Bill Gordon, Sigrid Hawkes, Flora Hommel, Violet Jacobson, Sylvia Kleinman, Maggie Kuhn, Henrietta Phillips, Irvin Rautenberg, Varya Simpson.
Periodicals: *Network* (newsletter).
Internships: Yes, working on media projects, legislative activities, and "social justice" issues.
Other Information: Founded in 1970. The organization was originally named the Consultation of Older and Younger Adults. While protesting the war in Vietnam, a television reporter referred to them as the "Gray Panthers," a comparison to the Black Panthers, and the name stuck. The Fund received $184,016, or 67% of revenue, from direct and indirect public support in the form of gifts and grants awarded by foundations, businesses, affiliates, and individuals. $58,177, or 21%, from interest on savings and temporary cash investments. $20,000, or 7%, from management fees. $8,078, or 3%, from royalties. The remaining revenue came from the sale of publications, rental income, and convention fees.

Greater Ecosystem Alliance

P.O. Box 2813
Bellingham, WA 98227   **Phone:**   (206) 671-9950
USA   **Fax:**   (206) 271-8429

Contact Person: Deb Ferber, President.
Officers or Principals: Joe Scott, Vice President ($0); Tom Campion, Treasurer ($0); George Draffan, Secretary ($0).
Mission or Interest: Protecting the environment and biodiversity in the Pacific Northwest.
Accomplishments: In 1994 the organization spent $225,690 on its programs. The largest program, with expenditures of $55,547 was an effort to educate the public about biodiversity. Other programs focused on the protection of grizzly bear populations and ecosystem management.
Net Revenue: 1994 $300,519 **Net Expenses:** $277,495 81%/19%/0% **Net Assets:** $74,290
Products or Services: Research and educational materials, posters, videos, publications, and lobbying. The Alliance spent $908 on the direct lobbying of legislators, up 62% over the previous year.
Tax Status: 501(c)(3)
Periodicals: *Northwest Conservation* (newsletter).
Other Information: The Alliance received $228,778, or 76% of revenue, from program service fees. $32,891, or 11%, from a grant from the Bullitt Foundation. $23,652, or 8%, from membership dues. $10,766 net, or 4%, from the sale of inventory. $3,407 net, or 1%, from special fund-raising events. The remaining income came from interest on savings and temporary cash investments.

Greenbelt Alliance

116 New Montgomery St., Suite 640
San Francisco, CA 94105   **Phone:** (415) 543-4291   **E-Mail:** greenbelt@igc.apc.org
USA   **Fax:**   (415) 543-1093   **Web-Page:** http://www.greenbelt.org/gba

Contact Person: Jim Sayer .
Officers or Principals: Larry Orman, Executive Director ($51,800); Dee Swanhuyser, Field Representative ($6,140); Bud Johns, President ($0); F. Jerome Tone, Secretary/Treasurer; Andrew Butler, Zach Cowan, Dick Catalano, Vice President.
Mission or Interest: Works to stop growth and protect undeveloped lands in the "Greenbelt" of the Bay Area in California through grassroots and educational efforts.
Accomplishments: In 1994 the organization spent $567,221 on its programs. The largest program, with expenditures of $246,080, was the Policy Program "to secure protection of Greenbelt lands currently at high risk of development, and expand the number of cities with urban growth boundaries." $175,892 was spent on educational materials, including maps and outings. $65,907 for the Greenspace project "to define natural land resources in urban areas as greenspace systems, demonstrate their important role in urban areas across the country, and support these systems." Other programs included membership services and representation at the Bay Area Environmental Educational Resource Fair.
Net Revenue: 1994 $834,401 ($28,727, or 3%, from government grants) **Net Expenses:** $762,025 74%/11%/15%
Net Assets: $210,849
Products or Services: Maps, brochures, grassroots organizing, nature outings, and lobbying. The organization spent $13,615 on its lobbying, $7,721 on grassroots lobbying and $5,894 on the direct lobbying of legislators. Lobbying activities centered mostly around local land-use issues, but the organization also lobbied against redefining wetlands and against private property 'takings' protection.
Tax Status: 501(c)(3) **Annual Report:** Yes. **Employees:** 14
Board of Directors or Trustees: George Ellman, Dr. John Erskine, John Fioretta, John-Scott Forester, Lester Gee, Robert Hawn, Robert Johnson, Rami Kahlon, T.J. Kent, Jr., Ted Lempert, Trish Mulvey, Maeve Mitchell, Bonnie Mitsui, Andrew Nash, Paul Okamoto, Audrey Penn Rodgers, Cindy Rubin, Ellen Straus, Laney Thornton, Barbara Winiarski, Renate Woodbury, Gary Zimmerman.
Internships: Yes.
Other Information: Formerly called People for Open Space. The organization received $700,689, or 84% of revenue, from direct and indirect public support in the form of gifts and grants awarded by foundations, businesses, affiliates, and individuals. (These grants included $41,461 from the Environmental Federation of California, $30,000 from the Columbia Foundation, $15,000 from the Wallace Alexander Gerbode Foundation, $10,000 from the Compton Foundation.) $93,518, or 11%, from membership dues. $28,727, or 3%, from government grants. $7,900, or 1%, from educational services. The remaining revenue came from interest on savings and temporary cash investments, and the sale of inventory.

Greenpeace

1436 U St., N.W.
Washington, DC 20009   **Phone:** (202) 462-1177
USA   **Fax:**   (202) 462-4507

Contact Person: Marcy Hirschfield. **Officers or Principals:** Barbara Dudley, Executive Director ($65,000); Jairo Rios, Treasurer ($63,000); Gasby Greely, Director of Communications ($61,000); Carol Booker, Legal Council ($61,000); Peg Stevenson, Chairman; Andre Carothers, Vice Chairman/Secretary.
Mission or Interest: Lobbying affiliate of Greenpeace. "To promote and advocate the protection and preservation of the environment through lobbying, education and advocacy efforts."

Accomplishments: In 1994 Greenpeace spent $17,261,446 on its efforts. These included: $5,232,699 on the Nuclear, Atmosphere and Energy Campaign, that "works toward a goal of elimination of all nuclear weapons...works to decrease our reliance on fossil fuels and nuclear power." $4,349,332 on the Toxics Campaign that "continued its work on behalf of a phase-out of industrial uses of chlorine and a future of environmental justice...A major focus was pressuring Time, Inc. to keep its promise to purchase paper bleached without chlorine and chlorine compounds for its publications." $2,907,405 on The Ocean Ecology Campaign that "advocated an end to fishing practices that have negative impacts on fish stocks, marine mammals and marine ecosystems...also successful in helping achieve a whale sanctuary in the Southern Ocean near Antarctica." $1,428,623 on media relations. $708,804 on the Action Resources Department, which maintains Greenpeace's boats, building equipment, and other supplies. Other programs included the production of merchandise. Awarded $46,792 in grants to other organizations. The largest grants were $18,679 for the Tides Foundation to fund the Women's Health and the Environment Project, and $9,330 for the UCLA Foundation to fund an alternative fuel vehicle study.
Net Revenue: 1994 $26,560,606 **Net Expenses:** $28,369,083 61%/6%/33% **Net Assets:** (-$7,504,852) **Citations:** 4,675:6
Tax Status: 501(c)(4)
Board of Directors or Trustees: Tani Adams, Jeanne Gauna, Ken Geiser, Winona LaDuke (Indigenous Women's Network).
Periodicals: *Greenpeace Action* (bimonthly magazine).
Other Information: Greenpeace is affiliated with the 501(c)(3) Greenpeace Fund and 501(c)(3) Greenpeace International at the same address. The organization received $24,948,028, or 94% of revenue, from direct and indirect public support in the form of gifts and grants awarded by foundations, businesses, affiliates, and individuals. (These grants included $2,500 from the Bydale Foundation, $1,000 from the Haymarket People's Fund, $500 from the Aaron and Martha Schecter Private Foundation, and $250 from the Vanguard Public Foundation.) $879,404, or 3%, from merchandise sales. $389,066, or 1%, from mailing list rentals. $260,827, or 1%, from royalties. The remaining revenue came from interest on savings and other temporary cash investments, and other miscellaneous sources.

Greenpeace Fund
1436 U St., N.W.
Washington, DC 20009   **Phone:** (202) 462-1177
USA

Contact Person: Martha Diaz-Oritz, Assistant Secretary. **Officers or Principals:** Barbara Dudley, Executive Director ($0); Venola Johnson, Deputy Director ($0); Jairo Rios, Treasurer ($0); Christina Davis Assistant Treasurer; Carol Booker, Legal Counsel.
Mission or Interest: Research and education arm of Greenpeace. Awards grants and publishes a newsletter.
Accomplishments: In 1993 the Fund spent $11,597,666 on its programs. $11,488,479 in grants were awarded, $7,000,000 to Greenpeace International, and $4,488,479 to Greenpeace. $109,187 was spent producing and distributing a newsletter.
Net Revenue: 1993 $8,386,505 **Net Expenses:** $13,431,626 86%/4%/10% **Net Assets:** $18,902,832 **Citations:** 4,675:6
Tax Status: 501(c)(3)
Board of Directors or Trustees: David Chatfield, Tani Adams, Naomi Roht-Arriaza, William Keller, Sarah Jane Knoy, Adrienne Puches, Christina Davis.
Periodicals: *Greenpeace Magazine* (bimonthly).
Other Information: Affiliated with the 501(c)(3) Greenpeace International and the 501(c)(4) Greenpeace at the same address. The Fund received $7,693,191, or 92% of revenue, from gifts and grants awarded by foundations, affiliates, businesses, and individuals. (These grants included $87,608 from the Environmental Federation of California, $10,000 from the Town Creek Foundation, $4,700 from Friends of the Earth, and $500 from the Haymarket People's Fund.) $293,422, or 3%, from dividends and interest from securities. $246,092, or 3%, from interest on savings and temporary cash investments. $103,692, or 1%, from capital gains on the sale of securities. The remaining revenue came from mailing list rentals and royalties.

Greenpeace International
1436 U St., N.W.
Washington, DC 20009   **Phone:** (202) 462-1177
USA

Contact Person: Cliff Curtis, Coordinator.
Officers or Principals: Tani Adams, Regional Coordinator ($69,514); Cliff Curtis, Coordinator ($68,630); Marcie Mersky, Assistant to the Coordinator ($33,594); Douglas A. Faulkner, President; Josselien Janssens, Secretary.
Mission or Interest: Provides funding for Greenpeace's international affiliates.
Accomplishments: In 1993 Greenpeace International spent $6,933,057 on its programs. Funded projects included; $1,275,604 for the Latin America Project to establish programs and self-sufficiency, $725,335 for the Ocean Ecology Campaign to protect marine ecosystems, $703,000 for the Chlorine Campaign to end the release of organo-chlorines and phase out the chlorine industry, $689,204 for the Toxic Trade Campaign, $574,232 for the Nuclear Campaign to phase out commercial nuclear power, $415,915 for the Global Warming Campaign, $383,000 for the Pacific Campaign to protect Pacific Ocean ecosystems, $375,000 for the Communications Division to give media support and advice, $314,000 for the Economics Unit to give strategic advice to campaigns on economic development and its implications, and $311,944 for the Disarmament Campaign to rid the world of nuclear weapons and nuclear technology. Other funded campaigns included the Forest Campaign, the Ozone Campaign, Mediterranean Campaign, Marine Services, Political Unit to provide campaigners "with a clear international perspective of relevant political developments, constraints and opportunities," the Action Team to provide support for the international organizations, the Development Division, and the Science Unit to "ensure the credibility of (the) scientific output of Greenpeace. Project funding was divided up between Greenpeace organizations in Argentina, Austria, Belgium, Brazil, Canada, Chile, United Kingdom, Czech Republic, Denmark, Guatemala, Japan, Netherlands, and Mexico.

Net Revenue: 1993 $7,110,092 **Net Expenses:** $7,034,939 99%/1%/1% **Net Assets:** $32,190 **Citations:** 288:59
Tax Status: 501(c)(3)
Board of Directors or Trustees: David McTaggart, Dick Dillman.
Other Information: Affiliated with the 501(c)(3) Greenpeace Fund and the 501(c)(4) Greenpeace, all at the same address. Greenpeace International received $7,000,000, or 98% of revenue, from Greenpeace Fund. $47,257, or 1% from interest on savings and temporary cash investments. $44,664, or 1%, from royalties. The remaining revenue came from gifts and grants awarded by foundations, businesses, and individuals.

Greens/Green Party USA
P.O. Box 100
Blodgett Mills, NY 13738   **Phone:** (607) 756-4211   **E-Mail:** gpusa@igc.apc.org
USA   **Fax:**   (607) 758-5417   **Web-Page:** http://www.greens.org/

Contact Person: Betty K. Wood, Clearinghouse Coordinator.
Mission or Interest: A political party united in their opposition to industrial society and support of a "Green ecology." "Green ecology moves beyond environmentalism by understanding the common roots of the abuse of nature and the abuse of people. Whatever we do to the web of life, we do to ourselves...Greens want to replace the worldwide system of poverty and injustice with a world free of all oppression based on class, gender, race, citizenship, age, or sexual orientation."
Accomplishments: Following an unopposed primary race in California, activist Ralph Nader won the right to campaign for President of the U.S. on the Green Party ticket. The Green Party USA is a descendent of the German Green Party. In 1984 American activists inspired by the German's success created the Green Committees of Correspondence network, which grew at the local level and evolved into the Greens. They currently have 54 elected officials holding public office "from Hawaii to New England." They have ballot status in six states. In 1994 Roberto Mondragon ran for Governor of New Mexico as a Green and won 47,080 votes, about 10% of the total. In that election Republican Gary Johnson won over incumbent Democrat Bruce King by 42,257 votes. *Green Politics* has a circulation of approximately 10,000.
Products or Services: Political campaigns, local activism, books and pamphlets.
Tax Status: Political party.
Periodicals: *Green Politics* (quarterly newsletter) and *Synthesis/Regeneration* (quarterly magazine).

Groundwork for a Just World
11224 Kercheval
Detroit, MI 48214   **Phone:** (313) 822-2055   **E-Mail:** gdwk@aol.com
USA   **Fax:**   (313) 822-5197

Contact Person: Margaret Weber.
Officers or Principals: Paula Cathcart, President ($0); Cecilia Marie Zondlo, Secretary/Treasurer ($0).
Mission or Interest: An organization of religious, primarily Catholic, activists working for "systemic change in five issue areas: Economic Justice, Eco-Justice, Peace, Racial Justice, Women's Justice."
Accomplishments: "Twenty years of witness, action and education." A member of Groundwork attended the UN Fourth Conference on Women in Beijing, China.
Net Revenue: FY ending 6/94 $137,306 **Net Expenses:** $121,646 81%/18%/1% **Net Assets:** $40,576
Products or Services: Conferences, books, publications and "public acts of prophetic witness." Lobbying. Although their 1994 tax returns indicate that they did not engage in lobbying during that year, their pamphlets and publications in 1995 make references to contacting and attempting to influence legislators. Biennial "Political Action Guide."
Tax Status: 501(c)(3) **Employees:** 4
Periodicals: *Groundwork* (7-8 issues a year).   **Internships:** No.
Other Information: The organization received $93,990, or 68% of revenue, from membership dues. $22,962, or 17%, from program services, including a conference on violence against women, and education and articles on corporate social responsibility. $16,237, or 12%, from gifts and grants awarded by foundations, companies and individuals. The remaining revenue came from interest on savings and temporary cash investments, and net income from special events honoring community leaders.

Guatemala Information Documentation
918 S. George Mason Dr.
Arlington, VA 22204   **Phone:** (703) 920-9118
USA

Contact Person: Frank LaRue, President.
Officers or Principals: Maria LaRue, Secretary/Treasurer ($0); Juan Quinzo, Director ($0).
Mission or Interest: Educational research and speeches regarding human rights in Guatemala.
Accomplishments: In 1994 the organization spent $1,632 on its programs.
Net Revenue: 1994 $2,888 **Net Expenses:** $2,821 **Net Assets:** $67
Tax Status: 501(c)(3)
Other Information: The organization received $2,888, or 100% of its revenues, from gifts and grants awarded by foundations and individuals.

Guatemala Partners

945 G St., N.W., Suite 201
Washington, DC 20001   **Phone:**   (202) 783-1123
USA

Contact Person: Anne Ewing, President.
Officers or Principals: Shawn Roberts, Vice President ($0); Kathy Wright, Secretary/Treasurer ($0).
Mission or Interest: Supports "Guatemalan Indians in their struggle for survival" through development projects in Guatemala and educational outreach in the U.S.
Accomplishments: In the fiscal year ending June 1994, the Partners spent $97,345 on their programs. These included grants of $42,700 for development projects.
Net Revenue: FY ending 6/94 $171,152 **Net Expenses:** $156,634 62%/16%/22% **Net Assets:** $34,273
Tax Status: 501(c)(3)
Board of Directors or Trustees: Barbara Harrington, David Funkhouser, Ann Gallagher, Portia Jones, Brinton Lykes, Alex Morisey.
Other Information: The Partners received $170,111, or 99% of revenue, from gifts and grants awarded by foundations, businesses, and individuals. $1,041, or 1%, from interest on savings and temporary cash investments.

Guild Sugar Law Center

2915 Cadillac Towers
Detroit, MI 48226   **Phone:**   (313) 962-6540
USA

Contact Person: Kary Moss.
Mission or Interest: Litigation project of the National Lawyers Guild. Litigation focuses on plant closings, lay-offs, labor organizing, civil rights, and 'institutional racism.'

Handgun Control, Inc. (HCI)

1225 I St., N.W., Suite 1100
Washington, DC 20005   **Phone:**   (202) 898-0792
USA

Contact Person: Richard Aborn, President. **Officers or Principals:** Sarah Brady, Chairman ($122,768); Richard Aborn, President ($78,776); Mark Ingram, Treasurer ($21,960); Lois Hess, Secretary.
Mission or Interest: Lobbies to restrict and outlaw the ownership of guns and ammunition with an emphasis on handguns.
Accomplishments: Successfully pushed for the victorious "Brady Bill" which imposed a national five-day waiting period on the purchase of handguns. The law is named after chairman Sarah Brady's husband, James Brady, who was wounded during an attempt to assassinate President Reagan in 1981. Supported the 1994 Crime Bill which contained a provision outlawing the sale of certain semi-automatic guns in their then-current configuration, and limiting the number of bullets a gun's magazine could hold. In 1994 HCI spent $4,013,367 on its programs. The largest program, with expenditures of $2,172,874, was lobbying for "the formulation and adoption of reasonable and practical measures for the control of guns." $986,641 for membership services. $834,104 on public and media relations. $19,748 paid for administrative and fundraising costs for the Voter Education Fund, a political action committee.
Net Revenue: 1994 $6,285,196 **Net Expenses:** $6,109,871 66%/6%/28% **Net Assets:** $1,231,903 **Citations:** 747:29
Tax Status: 501(c)(4)
Board of Directors or Trustees: Frank Hartmann, John Hechinger, Kevin Chavous, Larry Lowenstein, Dick Parise, Nancy Schenke, Stan Foster, Mary Lewis Grow, Joe Casey, M.D., Jerry TerHorst, Alice Darnell Lattal, John Phillips.
Other Information: Affiliated with the 501(c)(3) Center to Prevent Handgun Violence at the same address. The two affiliates had combined net revenues of $9,080,816, net expenses of $8,520,139, and net assets of $3,079,176. Richard Aborn served as president of both and received combined compensation of $122,768. HCI received $6,042,366, or 96% of revenue, from gifts and grants awarded by foundations, businesses, and individuals. (In 1995 these grants included $19,832 from the Tides Foundation.) $210,526, or 3%, from mailing list rentals. The remaining revenue came from dividends and interest from securities, interest on savings and temporary cash investments, and other miscellaneous sources.

Haymarket People's Fund

42 Seaverns Ave.
Jamaica Plain, MA 02130   **Phone:**   (617) 522-7676   **E-Mail:** haymarket@igc.apc.org
USA   **Fax:**   (617) 522-9580

Contact Person: Patricia Maher, Executive Director. **Officers or Principals:** Patricia Maher, Executive Director ($48,883); Pamela Rogers, Special Projects Coordinator ($44,459); Hillary Smith, Development Coordinator ($42,396); Nury Marquez, President; Lynne Brandon, Treasurer; Tommie Harris Grants Coordinator; Pamela Flood, Office Coordinator.
Mission or Interest: Awards grants primarily to small grassroots organizations and provides technical assistance to these organizations.

Accomplishments: In the fiscal year ending June 1994 the Fund spent $1,239,942 on its programs, including $922,627 in grant awards. Recipients of the largest grants included; five grants totaling $26,307 for the Funding Exchange, four grants totaling $24,200 for the Ms. Foundation for Women, two grants totaling $21,000 for the American Friends Service Committee, two grants totaling $20,500 for Bikes Not Bombs, $20,000 each for the Commonwealth Education Project, Dorchester Women's Committee, Progresso Latino, Immigrant Workers Resource Center, Project FREE, Women's Alliance, and Worker-Ownership Resource Center, nine grants totaling $19,900 for the Fund for a Free South Africa, $15,000 for Kitchen Table: Women of Color Press, $14,000 for the Peace Development Center, $13,000 for the Men's Resource Connection, six grants totaling $12,050 for the Boston Women's Fund, $11,350 for the AIDS Action Committee, and five grants totaling $10,300 for Oxfam America.
Net Revenue: FY ending 6/94 $1,219,125 **Net Expenses:** $1,430,826 87%/10%/4% **Net Assets:** $1,169,319
Products or Services: Grants and technical assistance.   **Tax Status:** 501(c)(3)
Board of Directors or Trustees: Charlie Bernstein, Lynne Brandon, Deahdra Butler-Henderson, Robin Cappuccino, Carol Chichetto, Luz Gonzales, Angel Nieto Romero, Susan Ostrander, Terri Reid, Elaine Reily, Rosemary Santos.
Other Information: The Haymarket People's Fund is a member of the Funding Exchange. The Fund received $1,219,125, or 84% of revenue, from gifts and grants awarded by foundations, businesses, affiliates and individuals. (These grants included $9,000 from the Aaron and Martha Schecter Foundation.) $119,965, or 8%, from interest on savings and temporary cash investments. $83,334 net, or 6%, from capital gains on the sale of securities. $26,643 net, or 2%, from rental property. The remaining revenue was from program service fees.

Headwaters Fund
122 W. Franklin Ave., Suite 518
Minneapolis, MN 55404   **Phone:** (612) 879-0602   **E-Mail:** justfund@aol.com
USA   **Fax:**   (612) 879-0613

Contact Person: Sandy Jones, Administrative Assistant.
Officers or Principals: Steven Newcom, Executive Director ($48,450); Jay Palmer, Program Associate; Linda Bjodre, Development Associate; Ron McKinley, Lucy Rogers, Co-Chairs; Becky Glass, Secretary; Julia Classen, Treasurer.
Mission or Interest: Headwaters supports leftist/progressive nonprofit organizations in the Minneapolis/St. Paul area. "Funding is designed to promote a more just and equitable society." They specifically target small, grassroots organizations for funding.
Accomplishments: In the fiscal year ending June 1994 they distributed $189,427 in grants. In June of 1995 they held a conference entitled "Allies for Justice: Organizing for Diversity and Democracy." The purpose of the conference was to organize "constituencies negatively affected by the Radical Right." Participants included Jean Hardisty of Political Research Associates, as well as numerous local organizations. Attendees included members of organizations as diverse as the Gay and Lesbian Action Council, Planned Parenthood, Catholic Charities, Sierra Club, and many others.
Net Revenue: FY ending 6/94 $287,260 **Net Expenses:** $435,696 66%/8%/26% **Net Assets:** $94,109
Products or Services: Grants and technical support for grassroots organizations.
Tax Status: 501(c)(3) **Annual Report:** Yes. **Employees:** 4
Board of Directors or Trustees: Don Poll (The Poll Group), Elsa Batica, Catherine Reid, Gary Kelsey, John Schultz (Ethical Investments), Alice Lynch (BIHA Women in Action), Laura Tiffany, Alida Messinger, Angelita Velasco, Rick Cardenas.
Internships: No.
Other Information: The Headwaters Fund is affiliated with the Funding Exchange. The Fund received $455,888, or 99.5% of revenue from gifts and grants awarded by foundations, affiliates, companies and individuals. The remaining revenue came from interest on savings and temporary cash investments and other miscellaneous sources.

Health Care for All
30 Winter St.
Boston, MA 02108   **Phone:** (617) 350-7279
USA

Contact Person: Robert Restuccia.
Mission or Interest: "Representing the major constituencies disenfranchised from the health care system. We are campaigning for universal access to health care and passage of universal health care."
Accomplishments: In the fiscal year ending June 1995 Health Care for All spent $403,368 on its programs. In 1995 the organization celebrated its tenth anniversary.
Net Revenue: FY ending 6/95 $515,410 **Net Expenses:** $457,022 88%/9%/2% **Net Assets:** $137,750
Products or Services: Health care guides, lobbying. The organization spent $3,178 on lobbying.
Tax Status: 501(c)(3)
Other Information: Health Care for All received $333,795, or 65% of revenue, from gifts and grants awarded by foundations, businesses, and individuals. $102,242, or 20%, from fees reimbursed by other nonprofit organizations for programs developed by Health Care for All. $48,297 net, or 9%, from special fund raising events celebrating their tenth anniversary. $25,476, or 5%, from membership dues. The remaining revenue came from expense reimbursements, interest on savings and temporary cash investments, sale of health care guides, and honoraria.

Health Security Action Council
1757 N St., N.W.
Washington, DC 20036   **Phone:** (202) 223-9685
USA

Contact Person: Douglas A. Glasser, President.

Officers or Principals: Douglas A. Fraser, Chairman ($0); Thomas R. Donahue, Vice Chair ($0).
Mission or Interest: Lobbying affiliate of the labor-backed Committee for National Health Insurance.
Accomplishments: In the fiscal year ending April 1994, the Council spent $100,000 on its programs.
Net Revenue: FY ending 4/94 $99,651 ($85,000, or 85%, from government grants) **Net Expenses:** $189,325 53%/47%/0%
Net Assets: $213,206
Tax Status: 501(c)(4)
Board of Directors or Trustees: Owen Bieber (UAW)
Other Information: Affiliated with the 501(c)(3) Committee for National Health Insurance at the same address. The two affiliates had combined net revenues of $129,182, net expenses of $339,784, and net assets of $760,555. The Council received $85,000, or 85% of revenue, from government grants. $144,482, or 15%, from interest on savings and temporary cash investments. The remaining revenue came from reimbursed expenses.

Henry J. Kaiser Family Foundation
2400 Sand Hill Road
Menlo Park, CA 94025   **Phone:**   (415) 854-9400
USA

Contact Person: Janice Eldred, Program Director.   **Officers or Principals:** Drew E. Altman, President ($322,728); Mark D. Smith, Executive Vice President ($221,397); Bruce W. Madding, Vice President ($207,136); Dennis F. Beatrice, Vice President ($176,191); David M. James, Vice President ($165,678); Michael Sinclair, Vice President ($159,767); Janice Eldred, Program Director ($116,688); Diane Rowland, Vice President ($101,696).
Mission or Interest: Grant-making foundation that "directs the major share of its resources to programs in health and medicine, viewing these fields in their broadest terms."
Accomplishments: The Kaiser Family Foundation figures prominently in the Clinton Administration's health care efforts. Bruce Vladeck, the Administrator of the Health Care Financing Administration (HCFA, the agency that oversees the Medicare and Medicaid programs), and Brian Biles, another official at the HCFA, serve on the Family Foundation's Board. In addition to its grants, the Foundation carried out some direct educational activities. In 1994, $446,327 was spent on the Kaiser Commission on the Future of Medicaid. $379,936 was spent on Kaiser Media Fellowships for print and broadcast reporters in health. $241,996 was spent on public education about health care reform. $141,403 on other public education. The Foundation awarded $16,755,603 in grants. Some of the recipients included: $1,300,000 for the Population Council, $590,000 for the Urban Institute, $412,500 for the League of Women Voters Education Fund, $405,000 for National Public Radio, $296,250 for the National Progressive Primary Health Care Network, $253,228 for the Alan Guttmacher Institute, $241,544 for the Robert Wood Johnson Foundation, $106,667 for Population Services International, $101,814 for the Children's Defense Fund, $86,211 to host a debate on the proposed (and later defeated) California Single Payer Plan, $80,510 for the Center on Budget and Policy Priorities, $50,505 for the League of Women Voters, $50,000 for the Women's Environment and Development Organization, and $50,000 for the Center for Reproductive Law and Policy.
Net Revenue: 1994 $31,887,319 **Net Expenses:** $30,452,819 **Net Assets:** $421,315,212
Products or Services: Awards the "Mandela Award for Health and Human Rights."
Tax Status: 501(c)(3)
Board of Directors or Trustees: James Mongan, Richard Cooley, Daniel Evans, Kim Kaiser, Philip Lee, June Osborn M.D., Richard Ravitch, William Richardson, Carlyn Kaiser Stark, George Strait, Bruce Vladeck, Faye Wattleton, Marta Tienda, Michael Sovern, Henry Kaiser III.
Other Information: The Foundation received $13,330,444, or 42% of revenue, from capital gains on the sale of securities. $12,328,179, or 39%, from dividends and interest from securities. $4,800,152, or 15%, from rental income. $1,428,544, or 4%, from interest on savings and temporary cash investments. The Foundation held $304,417,100, or 72% of assets, in corporate stock and investment partnerships.

Heresies Collective / *Heresies*
P.O. Box 1306
New York, NY 10013   **Phone:**   (212) 227-2108
USA

Contact Person: Avis Lang, Secretary.   **Officers or Principals:** Avis Lang, Secretary ($1,152); Sara Pasti, President ($0); Verita Nerec, Vice President ($0); Barbara Duarte Esquinade, Treasurer.
Mission or Interest: Publishes *Heresies: A Feminist Publication on Art and Politics*.
Accomplishments: In the fiscal year ending April 1994, the Collective spent $32,373 to publish and distribute *Heresies*.
Net Revenue: FY ending 4/94 $19,794 ($5,000, or 25%, from government grants) **Net Expenses:** $36,132 90%/10%/0%
Net Assets: (-$5,245)
Tax Status: 501(c)(3)
Periodicals: *Heresies: A Feminist Publication on Art and Politics* (biannual journal).
Other Information: The Collective received $14,147, or 72% of revenue, from the sale of books, booklets, and journal subscriptions. $5,000, or 25%, from government grants. $538, or 3%, from gifts and grants awarded by foundations and individuals. The remaining revenue came from dividends and interest from securities.

Hetrick-Martin Institute (HMI)
2 Astor Place
New York, NY 10003   **Phone:**   (212) 674-2400
USA   **Fax:**   (212) 674-8650

Contact Person: Frances Kunreuther, Executive Director

Officers or Principals: Frances Kunreuther, Executive Director ($77,930); Dennis Luczak, Director of Development ($57,663); Stephen Lisner, Controller ($56,375); Andrew Humm, National Outreach; Jed Mattes, President; Thomas G. Veeder, Secretary/Treasurer; Clyde Jones, Vice President.

Mission or Interest: "A nonprofit social service, education and advocacy organization dedicated to meeting the diverse needs of lesbian, gay and bisexual youth of all social and ethnic backgrounds and to educating society about their unique issues." The Institute offers six programs: 1) An after-school drop in center which provides social and educational opportunities, 2) Individual and family counseling, 3) Project First Step that reaches out to homeless homosexual youths, 4) The Harvey Milk School - a high school established in 1985 by the New York Board of Education as the first alternative high school for homosexuals, 5) Training and resources for guidance counselors, social workers, and teachers, 6) National Advocacy Coalition on Youth and Sexual Orientation that works to "effect systemic change throughout the country. The Institute makes use of "peer trainers" who direct classroom sessions designed to teach acceptance of homosexuals among heterosexual teens.

Accomplishments: In the fiscal year ending June 1994, the Institute spent $2,130,109 on its programs.

Net Revenue: FY ending 6/94 $2,871,480 ($1,593,708, or 56%, from government sources)

Net Expenses: $2,556,840 83%/9%/8% **Net Assets:** $1,231,029 **Citations:** 9:202

Products or Services: Social services, educational programs, "Tales From the Closet" comic books, and numerous "FACTFILE" fact sheets. The fact sheets include controversial facts based on the disputed research of Alfred Kinsey.

Tax Status: 501(c)(3)

Board of Directors or Trustees: Dennis Anderson, M.D., Janet Cyril (LaGuardia Community College), Prof. Arnold Grossman (Dept. of Health Studies, NYU), Annette Hernandez, Ph.D. (South Bronx Mental Health Center), Bill Hibsher, Joyce Hunter, MSW (HIV Venter for Clinical and Behavioral Studies), Richard Isay, M.D., Craig Logan Jackson, Charles Kaiser, Zachary Knight, Peggy Northrog (Health and Politics editor, *Vogue*), Renny Reynolds, Raymond Rodriguez, Barbara Turk, Cindy Tzerman.

Other Information: The Institute was founded in 1979 by Emery S. Hetrick and A. Damien Martin. Hetrick and Martin's research on the problems of homosexual youth has been published in the *Journal of Homosexuality*. The Institute received $1,593,708, or 56% of revenue, from government grants. $1,232,223, or 43%, from gifts and grants awarded by foundations, businesses, and individuals. (These grants included $335,000 from the Joyce Mertz-Gilmore Foundation, $4,991 from the American Foundation for AIDS Research.) The remaining revenue came from honoraria and comic book sales, and interest on savings and temporary cash investments.

Highlander Research and Education Center

1959 Highlander Way
New Market, TN 37820
USA

Phone: (423) 933-3443   **E-Mail:** hrec@igc.apc.org
Fax: (423) 933-3424

Contact Person: Jim Sessions, Director.   **Officers or Principals:** Jim Sessions, Director ($34,999).

Mission or Interest: Adult education and leadership training for activists in Appalachia and the South. Programs include the Community Environmental Justice Program, Economic Education Program, Culture and Diversity Initiative, Global Education Project, and others.

Accomplishments: Operating for almost 60 years. In the fiscal year ending August 1994 they spent $105,968 on their Environmental Health Program, including their "Stop the Poisoning Schools."

Net Revenue: FY ending 8/94 $814,516 **Net Expenses:** $879,106 77%/13%/0% **Net Assets:** $2,059,000 **Citations:** 6:210

Products or Services: Grassroots leadership training and networking. Educational programs on diversity, economic justice, the environment and more. Grants.

Tax Status: 501(c)(3)

Other Information: Highlander's programs are labor and travel intensive as they require educators to travel throughout the South and Appalachia. Highlander's biggest expense was salaries at $387,263, or 44% of their total budget. Add other compensation, travel expenses, and consultants' fees and expenses, and it comes to $551,319, or 63% of the budget. The Center received $363,183, or 45% of revenue, from gifts and grants awarded by foundations, companies, and individuals. (These grants included $25,000 from the Jessie Smith Noyes Foundation, $20,000 from the New World Foundation, $8,100 from the Tides Foundation, $1,000 from the Haymarket People's Fund and $500 from the Peace Development Fund. In 1995, $41,200 from the Rockefeller Foundation.) $343,498, or 42%, from grants awarded for specific program use. $73,071, or 9%, from dividends and interest from securities. $42,246, or 5%, from the sale of books. $36,414, or 4%, from workshop fees. $22,722, or 3%, from interest on savings and temporary cash investments. $21,250, or 3%, from royalties. These revenues were offset by a large loss, $87,871, from the depreciation of endowment fund securities.

Historians of American Communism

P.O. Box 1216
Washington, CT 06793
USA

Contact Person: Dan Leab, Secretary.   **Officers or Principals:** Harvey Klehr, President ($0); John Haynes, Editor ($0).

Mission or Interest: History of American communism and anti-communism. Clearinghouse for scholars, researchers, and other "serious students of history."

Accomplishments: The *Newsletter of the Historians of American Communism* notifies scholars of on-going research and provides contact information. Publishes calls for papers. Posts archival notices and the release of classified government documents.

Net Revenue: 1994 $1,135 **Net Expenses:** $989 **Net Assets:** $796

Tax Status: 501(c)(3) **Annual Report:** No. **Employees:** 0

Periodicals: *Newsletter of the Historians of American Communism* (quarterly).

Internships: No.

Hollywood Policy Center Foundation (HPC)

3679 Motor Ave., Suite 300
Los Angeles, CA 90334   **Phone:**   (310) 287-2803
USA   **Fax:**   (310) 287-2815

Contact Person: Lara Bergthold, Executive Director.
Officers or Principals: Kathy Garmezy, former Executive Director ($84,577).
Mission or Interest: "Created to serve as a unique bridge between the entertainment industry and policy advocates by bringing the talent, commitment, and skills of our community together with grassroots organizers and activist organizations...The HPC's broad agenda includes a commitment to freedom of choice, freedom of expression, international human rights, civil rights and liberties, Native American religious freedom, gay rights, citizen participation in democracy, equality, peace and the rights of children...With an eye to the delicate relationship between public opinion and the media, much of HPC's work is directed toward using our industry's media expertise and visibility to help add eloquence and understanding to the public perception of those issues."
Accomplishments: In 1994 the HPC spent $574,316 on its projects.
Net Revenue: 1994 $937,331 ($49,600, or 5%, from government grants) **Net Expenses:** $881,175 65%/12%/22%
Net Assets: $86,771 **Citations:** 2:231
Products or Services: Activism, and lobbying. The HPC spent $7,097 on grassroots lobbying. This was a 16% increase over the previous year.
Tax Status: 501(c)(3)
Board of Directors or Trustees: June Baldwin (Quincy Jones Entertainment), Julie Bergman (Producer, Caravan Pictures), Marilyn Bergman (Academy Award winning songwriter), Bob Burkett (Yucaipa Co.), Sean Daniel (Producer, Alphaville), Mike Farrell (actor), Jane Fonda (actor), Danny Goldberg (CEO, Warner Bros. Records), Joshua Grode, Susan Grode, Susan Harbert (Mainstreet Communications), Rosilyn Heller (Producer, Dresden Drive Productions), Richard Masur (actor), Diana Meehan (President, Vu Productions), Jerry Moss (Chair, Rondor Music Intl.), Eileen Norton, Jimmie Ritchie, Michael Ritchie, Stanley Sheinbaum (Publisher, *New Perspectives Quarterly*), Diane Meyer Simon (ECO Partners/Educators), Barbra Streisand (Barbra Streisand Foundation), Rosalie Swedlin (President, Longview Entertainment), Anthea Sylbert (President, The Hawn-Sylbert Movie Co.), Margery Tabankin, Paula Weinstein (Producer, Spring Creek Productions), Stacey Winkler, Alfred Woodard (actor), Hiro Yamagata.
Other Information: The HPC received $887,731, or 95% of revenue, from gifts and grants awarded by foundations, businesses, and individuals. (These grants included $75,000 from the Esprit de Corp Foundation, and $50,000 from the Barbra Streisand Foundation.) $49,600, or 5%, from government grants.

Honor Our Neighbors Origins and Rights (HONOR)

2647 N. Stowell Ave.
Milwaukee, WI 53211   **Phone:**   (414) 963-1324   **E-Mail:** mthee@earth.execpc.com
USA   **Fax:**   (414) 963-0137

Contact Person: Mike Thee.   **Officers or Principals:** Sharon Metz, Executive Director ($6,000); Larry Balber, First Vice President ($0); Father James Dolan, Second Vice President ($0), Sister Patricia Marshall, Secretary, Dianne Wyss, Treasurer.
Mission or Interest: "HONOR is an ecumenical and secular human rights coalition that focuses on American Indian issues. Members, Indian and non-Indian, stand together as allies, seeking justice on critical concerns facing Indigenous peoples today...We are continually involved in the fight against the use of Indian logos, mascots, and nicknames by athletic teams."
Accomplishments: Facilitated the return of 32 acres of land to the Oneida tribe. Generated support to stop the removal of burial sites in Paso Robles, CA, for the Chumash and Salinan tribes.
Net Revenue: 1994 $111,391 **Net Expenses:** $115,832 63%/27%/10% **Net Assets:** $12,632
Products or Services: Books, brochures, videos and handbooks.
Tax Status: 501(c)(3) **Annual Report:** Yes. **Employees:** 5
Board of Directors or Trustees: Margaret Cameron, Ed Gray, Shannon Martin (Potawatomi-Ojibwe), Ramona (Klamath), Jeff Smith (Makah), Don Wedll, Dianne Wyss.
Periodicals: *The Digest* (seven times a year newsletter).
Internships: Yes, they have hosted 16 interns over the last four summers. Interns usually stay and work on a reservation.
Other Information: HONOR's advisors include: Dr. Owanah Anderson (Episcopal Native American Ministries), Ray Apodaca (Pueblo Ysleta del Sur), Joe DeLaCruz (former Chairman, Quinault Nation), Bill Frank (Northwest Indian Fisheries Commission), Reverend Marlene Whiterabbit Helgemo (All Nations Indian Church), Ivan Makil (Salt River Pima Maricopa Indian Community), Elmer Manatowa (Principal Chief, Sac and Fox Nation), Lloyd Powless (Oneida Nation), Lorenda Sanchez (California Indian Manpower Consortium), Harold Tarbell (Mohawk). Honor received $65,584, or 59% of revenue, from direct and indirect public support in the form of gifts and grants awarded by foundations, companies, and individuals. (These grants included $5,000 from the Wisconsin Community Fund, and $4,500 from the Peace Development Fund.) $30,864, or 28%, from program services. The remaining revenue came from interest on savings and temporary cash investments and other miscellaneous sources.

Hotel Employees and Restaurant Employees International Union (HERE)

1219 26th St., N.W.
Washington, DC 20007   **Phone:**   (202) 393-4373
USA   **Fax:**   (202) 333-0468

Contact Person: Edward T. Hanley, President.
Officers or Principals: Edward T. Hanley, President ($265,838); Herman Leavitt, Secretary/Treasurer ($224,833); John O'Gara, Vice President ($191,108); Thomas Hanley, Director of Organizing ($191,108); John W. Wilhelm, Vice President ($117,750).

Mission or Interest: Union representing approximately 370,000 members. "To organize all workers for the economic, moral and social advancement of their conditions and status." Affiliated with the AFL-CIO.
Accomplishments: In the fiscal year ending April 1995, the Union awarded $1,077,380 in grants. The largest grant, $1,032,070 went to an affiliate for local political activities. Other awards went for the Edward T. Hanley Scholarships, including $22,965 for the Culinary Institute of America, and $20,000 for the St. Joseph Seminary. The Union paid $1,177,297 to the AFL-CIO, and another $483,303 to other unions, including other AFL-CIO affiliates.
Net Revenue: FY ending 4/95 $27,555,797 **Net Expenses:** $26,334,130 **Net Assets:** $21,279,083
Tax Status: 501(c)(5)
Board of Directors or Trustees: John Kenneally, Val Connolly, Florence Farr, Vincent Gallo III, Wolfgang Hummer, Ted Hansen, Valentin Hernandez, Candace Landers, Timothy Luebbert, Terry Maloney, Joseph Massimino, Gerald McHugh, Vito Pitta, Howard Richardson, Ronald Richardson, Frank Riggio, Anthony Rutledge, Herbert Schiffman, Anthony Scimeca, Joseph Spano, James Stamos, Henry Tamarin, Harvey Totzke, Nick Worhaug.
Periodicals: *Catering Industry Employee* (monthly newsletter).
Other Information: Founded in 1891. The Union received $26,634,020, or 96% of gross revenue, from membership dues. $635,413, or 2%, from interest on savings and temporary cash investments. $175,454, or 1%, from dividends and interest from securities. $170,853, or 1%, from reimbursements for administrative expenses. The remaining revenue came from the sale of supplies and other miscellaneous sources. The Union lost $46,542 on rental properties and $21,346 on the sale of computer hardware.

Human Ecology Action League (HEAL)

P.O. Box 49126
Atlanta, GA 30359   **Phone:**   (404) 248-1898
USA

Contact Person: Lydia Jones, Treasurer.   **Officers or Principals:** Muriel A. Dando, President ($0); Kenneth L. Dominy, Vice President ($0); Kenneth V. King, Secretary ($0).
Mission or Interest: Educational activities regarding chemicals and toxins in the environment. Specifically concerned with "multiple chemical sensitivity," the belief that man-made chemicals in the environment produce a severe, even deadly reaction in certain sensitive individuals.
Accomplishments: *The Human Ecologist* magazine is distributed to over 3,500 members.
Net Revenue: 1994 $124,150 **Net Expenses:** $115,782 84%/11%/5% **Net Assets:** (-$35,248)
Tax Status: 501(c)(3)
Board of Directors or Trustees: Ty Bridges, J.D., Virginia Carlson, Beatrice Trum Hunter, Madeline Rivera.
Periodicals: *The Human Ecologist* (quarterly magazine).
Other Information: The League received $61,462, or 49% of revenue, from membership dues. $34,043, or 27%, from sales and subscriptions of *The Human Ecologist*. $28,208, or 23%, from gifts and grants awarded by foundations, businesses, and individuals. The remaining revenue came from interest on savings and temporary cash investments.

Human Rights Campaign Fund

1101 14th St., N.W., Suite 200
Washington, DC 20005   **Phone:**   (202) 628-4160
USA

Contact Person: David Simmons, Secretary.   **Officers or Principals:** Timothy McFeeley, President ($88,574); Cathy Nelson, Vice President ($57,783); Mark Cellucci, Treasurer ($41,611).
Mission or Interest: Lobbying on behalf of lesbian and gay rights.
Accomplishments: Sponsored "Outfest," a 1995 festival of gay and lesbian films hosted by the organization "Out on the Screen." In the fiscal year ending March 1994, the Fund spent $3,187,446 on its programs. The largest program, with expenditures of $1,090,285, was membership services, including "Speak-Out, a program to send mailgrams to legislators on behalf of members...Advocacy of health issues such as HIV disease and women's health." $1,063,081 was spent on "a staff of legislative professionals who inform the U.S. Congress and the Executive branch on positions of the gay and lesbian community." $699,480 was spent on a Political Action Committee that donates money and staff to candidates for federal office. $334,600 was spent on communications, including a newsletter and press conferences.
Net Revenue: FY ending 3/94 $5,466,250 **Net Expenses:** $5,047,908 63%/9%/28% **Net Assets:** $454,024
Citations: 251:66
Tax Status: 501(c)(4)
Board of Directors or Trustees: Diane Abbitt, Terry Bean, Linda Blackmore, Richard Colberg, Curt Decker, Todd Dickinson, Joe Tom Easley, Julia Fitz-Randolph, Vincent Friia, Stephen Glassman, Toni Grabler, Nancy Hamilton, Fred Hochberg, Lory Masters, Don McCleary, Sue Messenger, Glenda Rider, Avi Rome, Hilary Rosen, Worth Ross, Eli Saleeby, Steven Shellabarger, Lisa Sherman, Lena Thompson, Mary Kay Wright.
Periodicals: Newsletter.
Other Information: Affiliated with the 501(c)(3) Human Rights Campaign Fund Foundation. The Fund received $4,630,608, or 85% of revenue, from direct and indirect public sources in the form of gifts and grants awarded by foundations, businesses, affiliates, and individuals. $793,882, or 15%, from fees collected for Speak-Out mailgrams. The remaining revenue came from the sale of inventory, and interest on savings and temporary cash investments.

Human Rights Watch (HRW)

485 Fifth Ave.
New York, NY 10017   **Phone:** (212) 972-8400   **E-Mail:** hrwatch@hrw.org
USA   **Fax:**   (212) 972-0905

Contact Person: Gara Lamarche, Associate Director.
Officers or Principals: Kenneth Roth, Executive Director ($114,125), Juan Mendez, Director, Americas ($87,210); Sidney R. Jones, Director, Asia ($82,500), Robert Bernstein, Chairman; Adrian Dewind, Vice Chairman; Bruce Rabb, Secretary; Holly Burkhalter, Director, Washington Office; Abdullahi An-Na'Im, Director, Middle East.
Mission or Interest: Monitors and promotes human rights worldwide. They work with numerous other organizations to research and track possible human rights abuses. HRW has several special projects: the Arms Project, Children's Rights Project, the Free Expression Project, and the Women's Rights Project.
Accomplishments: "Helped to expand parameters of human rights concerns to include, for example, women's rights and conditions for ordinary prisoners. Pioneer in the use of aid and trade as leverage against abusive governments." In 1994 they spent $2,930,057 on general promotion and monitoring. For special programs emphasizing the Caribbean and the Americas they spent $1,013,200. Africa programs, $1,098,886. Asia, $1,210,368. Middle East, $1,143,548.
Net Revenue: 1994 $9,877,277 **Net Expenses:** $9,170,594 81%/2%/17% **Net Assets:** $12,034,605 **Citations:** 1,725:17
Products or Services: Various grants to other human rights organizations and affiliates totaling $2,547,774. Lobbying - they spent $8,740 for the direct lobbying of legislators; more than double the $3,609 they spent the previous year. Numerous publications.
Tax Status: 501(c)(3) **Annual Report:** Yes. **Employees:** 106
Board of Directors or Trustees: Roland Agrant, Lisa Anderson, Peter Bell, Alice Brown, William Carmichael, Dorothy Cullman, Irene Diamond, Edith Everett, Jonathan Fanton, Jack Greenberg, Alice Henkin, Harold Honju Koh, Jeh Johnson, Stephen Kass, Marina Kaufman, Alexander MacGregor, Josh Mailman, Andrew Nathan, Jane Olson, Peter Osnos, Kathleen Peratis, Bruce Rabb, Orville Schell, Sid Sheinberg, Gary Sick, Malcolm Smith, Nahid Toubia, Maureen White, Rosalind Whitehead.
Internships: Four one-year post-graduate fellowships.
Other Information: The organization received $8,918,122, or 90% of revenue, from gifts and grants awarded by foundations, companies and individuals. (These grants included $600,000 from the Joyce Mertz-Gilmore Foundation, $100,000 over two years from the Carnegie Corporation, $5,000 from the New-Land Foundation, $1,000 from the Aaron and Martha Schecter Private Foundation, and $500 from the New Prospect Foundation. In 1995, $500,000 from the Rockefeller Foundation.) $403,198 net, or 4%, from investment income from four funds, the Quantum Fund, Paloma Partners, Acorn Partners, and GNMA. Other investments in securities provided a net gain of $396,952, or 4%. $246,425, or 2%, from the sale of publications. $61,716, or 1%, from "subtenant revenue." The remaining revenue came from interest on savings and temporary cash investments. Revenue was partially offset by a net loss of $159,414 on the sale of assets other than inventory. In 1993 the organization received $1,500,000 over three years from the John D. and Catherine T. MacArthur Foundation, $370,000 from the Rockefeller Foundation.

Human SERVE

622 W. 113 St., Suite 410
New York, NY 10025   **Phone:** (212) 854-4053
USA   **Fax:**   (212) 854-8727

Contact Person: Richard A. Cloward, Executive Director.
Officers or Principals: Juan Carlaggna, President; Frances Fox Piven, Secretary; Jo-Anne Chasnow, Louise Altman, Associate Directors; David Plotkin, State Programs Director; Rebekah Evenson, Program Associate; Deborah Karpatkin, General Counsel.
Mission or Interest: Assists state and local governments in implementing the 'Motor Voter' registration act that allows citizens to register to vote at numerous government agencies. The 1993 National Voter Registration Act permitted people to register to vote when they renew their drivers' license, or when they apply for Food Stamps, AFDC, Medicaid, WIC, or services for the disabled.
Accomplishments: In 1994 Human SERVE won the Jim Waltermire Voter Participation Award of the National Association of Secretaries of State. Operates a project called "Enfranchise America" that encourages private sector social agencies, such as day care and family planning agencies, to establish voter registration services. Human SERVE has also been monitoring the effects of the new legislation on voter registration. Human SERVE revealed that 11 million new voters have signed up under the new law. To the surprise of many, Human SERVE monitoring has shown that these new voter registrations have benefitted the Republican Party more than the Democrats in terms of numbers of registered voters, especially in the South.
Tax Status: 501(c)(3)
Board of Directors or Trustees: Roger Alcaiv, Margaret Carev, Linda Davidoff, Jessie Deer-in-Water, Hazel Dukes, Juan Figueroa, Jim Hightower, Stanley Hill, Jacqueline Jackson, Michelle Kourouma, Paul Anders Ogren, Cheryl Patterson Artis, Jan Pierce, Anthony Robbins, Baldomar Velasquez, George Wallerstein, Juanita White.
Other Information: In 1994 the Campaign received $50,000 from the Joyce Foundation, $20,000 from the Rockefeller Family Foundation.

Humane Farming Action Fund

1550 California St., Suite 6
San Francisco, CA 94109   **Phone:** (415) 485-1495
USA

Contact Person: Bradley Miller, Executive Director.
Officers or Principals: Cynthia Kaufman, Vice President/Treasurer ($0); Bonnie Miller, Secretary ($0).
Mission or Interest: Lobbying affiliate of the Humane Farming Association.

Accomplishments: In 1993 the Fund spent $66,858 on its programs.
Net Revenue: 1993 $68,082 **Net Expenses:** $66,858 93%/7%/0% **Net Assets:** $265,308 **Citations:** 0;255
Tax Status: 501(c)(4)
Board of Directors or Trustees: Nina Hagen, Vanja Palmers.
Other Information: Affiliated with the 501(c)(3) Humane Farming Association. The Action Fund received $64,033, or 94% of revenue, from gifts and grants awarded by foundations, businesses, and individuals. $4,049, or 6%, from interest on savings and temporary cash investments.

Humane Farming Association
1550 California St., Suite 6
San Francisco, CA 94109   **Phone:**   (415) 485-1495
USA

Contact Person: Bradley Miller, President.   **Officers or Principals:** Bradley Miller, President ($29,000); Bonnie Miller, Secretary/Treasurer ($29,000); Cynthia Kaufman, Vice President ($0).
Mission or Interest: Research and educational activities to expose and prevent cruelty to farm animals. Cares for abused farm animals.
Accomplishments: In 1994 the Association spent $890,053 on its programs. These programs included "anti-cruelty investigations, consumer awareness ads, video documentaries, educational materials, public service announcements, speakers bureau, agricultural consultation, clearinghouse on farm animal and food safety issues, and operation of farm animal refuge and emergency care center." Also awarded $3,020 in grants to other organizations, $1,400 for Action for Animals, and $1,000 for Animal Agenda.
Net Revenue: 1994 $1,001,638 **Net Expenses:** $971,015 92%/4%/4% **Net Assets:** $1,553,457
Products or Services: Numerous educational materials and activities, animal care, and lobbying. In 1994 the Association spent $1,684. In 1993 it did not lobby, but in 1992 the Association spent $90,000 on lobbying.
Tax Status: 501(c)(3)
Board of Directors or Trustees: Vanja Palmers.
Other Information: Affiliated with the 501(c)(4) Humane Farming Action Fund. The Association received $929,485, or 93% of revenue, from gifts and grants awarded by foundations, businesses, and individuals. (These grants included $5,000 from the Rex Foundation.) $43,166, or 4%, from interest on savings and temporary cash investments. $21,140, or 2%, from reimbursed expenses from its 501(c)(4) affiliate. $5,829, or 1%, from dividends and interest from securities. The remaining income came from special fund-raising events.

Idaho Rural Council (IRC)
110 West 31st St., Suite 200
Boise, ID 83701   **Phone:**   (208) 344-6184   **E-Mail:** irc@execu.net
USA   **Fax:**   (208) 344-6382

Contact Person: Roger L. Hoffmann, Staff Director.   **Officers or Principals:** Becky Ihli, Director ($17,000); Mabel Dobbs, President ($0); Diane Hollen, Treasurer ($0); Rob Hansing, Secretary.
Mission or Interest: "Committed to preserving the economic well-being of Idaho's family farms and rural communities; to build a more sustainable society which will guarantee positive economic and social choices for present and future generations; to achieving good stewardship of humanity, land, air and water." Promotes "sustainable agriculture, fighting against corporate concentration in the food system, careful stewardship of natural resources."
Accomplishments: Successfully defeated a proposed out-of-state landfill. IRC's sustainable agriculture project has brought together five different groups of farmers and community members. IRC is "the only organization in Idaho working on declining cattle prices and their relationship to a shared monopoly in meat packing." In 1994 IRC spent $50,100 on its programs.
Net Revenue: 1994 $83,762 **Net Expenses:** $88,457 **Net Assets:** $22,618
Products or Services: Publications, organization, and lobbying. In 1994 IRC spent $2,209 on lobbying.
Tax Status: 501(c)(3) **Annual Report:** Yes. **Employees:** 5
Board of Directors or Trustees: Susan Duncan Burley, Gary Thomas, Emmett Jones, Nathan Jones, King Hill.
Periodicals: *The cIRCular* (quarterly newsletter).
Internships: Yes, legislative internships from December through April and year-round Sustainable Agriculture and Community Organizing internships.
Other Information: The Council was founded in 1986, and is one of the few organizations with roots in the family farm movement still around today. IRC received $81,990, or 98% of revenue, from gifts and grants awarded by foundations, companies, and individuals. (These grants included $30,000 from the Campaign for Human Development, $20,000 from the Jessie Smith Noyes Foundation, and $5,700 from the Peace Development Fund.) $1,180, or 1%, from membership dues. The remaining revenue came from investment income.

Idaho Women's Network (IWN)
817 W. Franklin St.
Boise, ID 83702   **Phone:**   (208) 344-5738
USA   **Fax:**   same

Contact Person: Wendy Jordan, Assistant Director.
Officers or Principals: Janine Smith, President ($0); Susan Bruns-Rowe, Secretary ($0); Katie Kempton, Vice President ($0).

Mission or Interest: Lobbying network that is "a coalition of 33 organizations and hundreds of individual members working together to improve the quality of opportunity in the lives of Idaho women and their families." Member organizations included: Planned Parenthood, National Association of Social Workers, Idaho Nurses Association, Women's Health Care, North Idaho Pro-Choice Network, and local chapters of the YWCA and other organizations.

Accomplishments: In 1995 the Network expressed its displeasure with the Idaho Legislature, stating that it "expressed its potent conservative philosophy with impressive -- some might say depressing -- results. *Big Business won big gains, while education, environmental programs, working people, families and children lost financial and philosophical support.*" Legislative activity that IWN was involved with included the following: Supported giving subpoena power to the Human Rights Commission. Supported giving peace officers the power to make an arrest at the scene of a domestic violence dispute without having witnessed the crime. Opposed allowing a person investigated for child abuse to recover attorney fees, witness fees, and expenses if it was found that abuse did not occur. Opposed exempting ministers from requirements to report child abuse, this included abuse discovered in confession. Opposed requiring videotaping of all investigations of alleged sexual abuse, and allowing the alleged offender or representative to be present during the interview. Opposed the reducing of staff requirements at child care centers. In 1994 the IWN spent $89,737 on its programs. The largest program, with expenditures of $88,626, was general activities, which included a campaign skills workshop for 25 women to run for elective office, the issuing of legislative reports, produced a bimonthly newsletter sent to over 400 individuals. "Healthy Mothers, Daughters and Grandmothers" campaign to "promote and protect the health care needs of Idaho women, more. $65,505 for the "Idea Idaho Project," a series of projects supporting abortion rights.

Net Revenue: 1994 $127,168 **Net Expenses:** $128,508 70%/22%/9% **Net Assets:** $7,691

Tax Status: 501(c)(4)

Board of Directors or Trustees: Corrine Lyle, Stephanie Witt.

Periodicals: *Legislative Report.*

Other Information: The Fund is affiliated with the 501(c)(3) Idaho Women's Network Research and Education Fund at the same address. The two affiliates had combined net revenues of $183,506, net expenses of $223,921, and net assets of $3,567. The Network received $116,739, or 90% of total revenue, in gifts and grants awarded by foundations, businesses, and individuals. (These included $15,000 from the Tides Foundation, $12,500 from the Ms. Foundation for Women.) $10,465, or 8%, from membership dues. $2,039, or 2%, from board meeting fees. The Network lost $2,075 on special fund-raising events, including campaign training, a convention, a Women's Policy Conference, and other events.

Idaho Women's Network Research and Education Fund

817 West Franklin
Boise, ID 83701   **Phone:** (208) 344-5738
USA   **Fax:** same

Contact Person: Jaimie R. Moss, President.

Officers or Principals: Jaimie R. Moss, President ($0); Barbara Beehner Kane, Secretary ($0); Pam Kane, Treasurer ($0).

Mission or Interest: Research and education organization focusing on abortion rights, women in poverty, gender equity, child care and domestic violence.

Accomplishments: Newsletter reaches over 400 members and 25 organizational members including the Idaho Nurse's Association, American Association of University Women, National Association of Social Workers, and the Idaho Trial Lawyer's Association. Hosted a workshop featuring keynote speaker Bella Abzug. In 1994 the Fund spent $95,248 on its programs.

Net Revenue: 1994 $56,338 **Net Expenses:** $95,413 **Net Assets:** (-$4,224)

Products or Services: Legislative reports, conferences, workshops, pro-choice voter identification research, training for female candidates for elective office, more.

Tax Status: 501(c)(3)

Board of Directors or Trustees: Katie Kempton, Susan Graham.

Periodicals: Newsletter.   **Internships:** Yes.

Other Information: The Fund is affiliated with the 501(c)(4) Idaho Women's Network at the same address. The two affiliates had combined net revenues of $183,506, net expenses of $223,921, and net assets of $3,567. The Fund received $55,904, or 99% of revenue, from gifts and grants awarded by foundations, companies, and individuals. (These grants included $12,500 from the Ms. Foundation, $8,000 from the Abelard Foundation, and $4,700 from the Peace Development Fund.) The remaining revenue came from investment income.

Illinois Peace Action Education Fund

202 S. State St., Suite 1500
Chicago, IL 60604   **Phone:** (312) 939-3316
USA

Contact Person: Elliott Zashin, President.

Officers or Principals: Sandra Berliant, Vice President ($0); Gloria Smith, Secretary/Treasurer ($0); Lucy Ascoli, Director ($0).

Mission or Interest: Research and education on "peace issues" such as the arms race, nuclear proliferation, and the international arms trade.

Accomplishments: In the fiscal year ending June 1994, the Fund spent $17,989 on its programs, including $14,656 in grants to its 501(c)(4) affiliate.

Net Revenue: FY ending 6/94 $23,261 **Net Expenses:** $21,897 **Net Assets:** $1,725

Products or Services: Speakers, newsletter, publications, and public forums.

Tax Status: 501(c)(3)

Periodicals: Newsletter.

Other Information: Affiliated with the 501(c)(4) Illinois Peace Action at the same address. The Fund received $23,261, or 100% of revenue, from gifts and grants awarded by foundations, companies, and individuals.

Immigration and Refugee Services of America (IRSA)

1717 Massachusetts Ave., N.W., Suite 701
Washington, DC 20036   **Phone:**   (202) 797-2105   **E-Mail:** irsa@irsa-uscr.org
USA   **Fax:**   (202) 797-2363

Contact Person: Alison Seiler.   **Officers or Principals:** Roger P. Winter, Executive Director ($109,161); Christine P. Gaffney, Assistant Secretary ($92,490); James T. McElroy, Comptroller ($64,935); Edward B. Marks, Chairperson; Harriet C. Greenfield, President; Lawrence M. Rosenthal, Vice President; Muzzafar Chishti, Treasurer; Wayne Dale Collins, Secretary.
Mission or Interest: "In the forefront of defending immigrants and refugees and the contributions they bring to this country of opportunity and haven." IRSA provides services to immigrants and refugees such as citizenship counseling, resettlement and placement services. They also advocate policy on behalf of immigrants and refugees. "Around us, the people we exist to serve - immigrants and refugees - are in turmoil, confronted with a level of 'Know Nothing' hostility unseen for decades."
Accomplishments: In the fiscal year ending September 1995, IRSA rose to number two nationally among resettlement agencies in refugee employment, rose to second place in the State Department's resettlement agency scorecard, and received a rating of "commendable" from the State Department in their monitoring of resettlement through partner agencies. Through a grant from the Ford Foundation they were able to host mass processing of naturalization applications to meet the increased demand for U.S. Citizenship. IRSA staff worked with Senator Edward Kennedy's (D-MA) staff to clarify language in welfare reform legislation that affected refugee job training funds. In the fiscal year ending September 1994, they spent $7,799,986 on their programs.
Net Revenue: FY ending 9/94 $8,509,062 ($6,752,913, or 79%, from government grants) **Net Expenses:** $8,898,678
88%/10%/2% **Net Assets:** $615,968 **Citations:** 0:255
Products or Services: Programs to aid immigrants and refugees. Minority Fellowship Project to "open doors of opportunity to people of color interested in working on behalf of immigrants and refugees." English-as-a-Second Language (ESL) classes. These ESL classes work with youth volunteers who tutor after school and learn "cultural sensitivity skills." Lobbying.
Tax Status: 501(c)(3) **Annual Report:** Yes.
Board of Directors or Trustees: Thomas Belote, Hinke Boot, Matthew Giuffrida, Berjoohy Haigazian, Phillip Hawkes, Wade Henderson, Elizabeth Hubbard, Hubert Jones, Nina Köprülü, Joel Montague, Jim Moody, Lily O'Boyle, Myra Oliver, Nancy Präger-Kamel, Zeyba Rahman, Sichan Siv, Leaford Williams, Raul Yzaguirre.
Other Information: IRSA is the country's oldest and largest network of nonprofits serving "the foreign-born and non-English speakers, especially immigrants, refugees, and their descendants." The national agency that IRSA is directly descended from began in 1917. The Services received $6,752,913, or 79%, of revenue from government grants. $1,044,733, or 12%, from grants awarded by foundations, companies and individuals. (These grants included $50,000 from the Joyce Mertz-Gilmore Foundation.) $533,884, or 6%, came from the collection of fees owed by refugees for air fare to the U.S. $104,665, or 1%, came from membership dues. The remaining revenue came from publications, interest on savings and cash investments, and dividends and interest from securities.

In Defense of Animals (IDA)

131 Camino Alto, Suite E
Mill Valley, CA 94941   **Phone:**   (415) 388-9641
USA   **Fax:**   (415) 388-0388

Contact Person: Elliot M. Katz, DVM, President.   **Officers or Principals:** Elliot M. Katz, DVM, President ($41,500); Suzanne Roy, Administrative Assistant ($34,050); Betsy Swart, Treasurer ($0); Ronny Berinstein, Secretary.
Mission or Interest: "Protecting the rights, welfare and habitat of animals."
Accomplishments: Leading the boycott against Proctor & Gamble because of the company's animal testing. Helped end crack-smoking experiments performed on monkeys at NYU. National coordinator of "World Laboratory Animal Liberation Week." Protested President Clinton's duck hunting trip. In 1993 IDA spent $772,315 on its programs.
Net Revenue: 1993 $1,018,942 **Net Expenses:** $996,906 77%/11%/12% **Net Assets:** $241,077 **Citations:** 123:106
Products or Services: Protests, publications, conferences, and lobbying. In 1993 IDA spent $26,975 on the direct lobbying of legislators.
Tax Status: 501(c)(3) **Annual Report:** Yes. **Employees:** 17
Periodicals: *In Defense of Animals* (quarterly magazine).   **Internships:** Yes.
Other Information: IDA was previously located in San Rafael. The organization received $982,735, or 96% of revenue, from gifts and grants awarded by foundations, companies and individuals. (These grants included $800 from People for the Ethical Treatment of Animals.) $21,648, or 2%, from mailing list rentals. $8,476, or 1%, from royalties. The remaining revenue came from interest on savings and temporary cash investments, and special fund-raising events.

In These Times

(see Institute for Public Affairs)

Income Rights Project (IRP)

333 Valencia St., Suite 450
San Francisco, CA 94103
USA

Contact Person: Karen Bishop, President.   **Officers or Principals:** Karen Bishop, President ($0); Esther Chavez, William Goring, Secretaries ($0); Cooley Windsor, Treasurer.

Mission or Interest: Brings together low-income families to identify their needs. Provides information regarding their rights to income support programs. Helps them receive welfare funds, including AFDC, food stamps, Medi-Cal, and others. Provides "homelessness prevention, counseling, education, training and child care referrals."
Accomplishments: In 1994 the Project spent $112,427 on its projects, helpding over 100 families.
Net Revenue: 1994 $93,042 **Net Expenses:** $124,918 **Net Assets:** (-$14,262)
Tax Status: 501(c)(3)
Board of Directors or Trustees: Steve Phillips, Millard Larkin II, Shanna Pitts, James Bell, Carmen Castillo.
Other Information: The Project received $54,500, or 58% of revenue, from program service revenues. $38,541, or 42%, from gifts and grants awarded by foundations, businesses, and individuals. (These grants included $12,500 from the Rosenberg Foundation.)

Independent Publications
P.O. Box 102
Ridgefield, NJ 07657   **Phone:** (201) 943-7299
USA

Contact Person: Carl Shapiro, Publisher.
Mission or Interest: Books, essays, reprints and materials on American history and political philosophy. Covers a wide range of viewpoints, including libertarian, but mostly publications supporting atheism.
Accomplishments: Commendations from the National Flag Foundation and other national groups for their patriotic material.
Products or Services: Publications, prints, video cassettes and other materials.
Tax Status: For profit.

Indigenous Women's Network
P.O. Box 174
Lake Elmo, MN 55042   **Phone:** (612) 777-3629
USA

Contact Person: Lea Foushee, President.
Officers or Principals: Lea Foushee, President ($6,900); Winona LaDuke ($0); Ingrid Wasinawatok, Chair ($0).
Mission or Interest: Organization devoted to educating "the larger society about our culture and social conditions; and to demonstrate what we, as Native Women, are doing to protect our families, ourselves, and our Mother Earth from racism, pollution, and other social ills." Publish *Indigenous Women* magazine.
Accomplishments: In 1995 Winona LaDuke toured with the rock band Indigo Girls, and made nightly speeches. In the fiscal year ending June 1994, the Network spent $35,347 on its programs. $18,200 was spent to produce and distribute *Indigenous Women* magazine, which has a circulation of about 4,000 subscribers. $13,685 was spent to host a "Sustainable Communities Gathering." The gathering developed strategies to "restore our culture, ecological, political and spiritual foundations...provide tangible examples of community projects such as alternative energy, housing, language, and economic self-sufficiency initiatives...provided a forum for journalists and other publicists to gain access to the information needed to educate the world community about the issues facing Native women." Other projects included the "Honor the Earth Campaign" and an educational forum for women from various reservations.
Net Revenue: FY ending 6/94 $71,738 **Net Expenses:** $41,548 85%/12%/3% **Net Assets:** $81,667
Tax Status: 501(c)(3)
Board of Directors or Trustees: Nilak Butler, Mililani Trask, Agnes Williams, Marsha Gomez, Arlene Logan, Dorothy Davids, Kimberly Craven, Lisa Bellanger, Priscilla Settee.
Periodicals: *Indigenous Women* (biannual).
Other Information: The Network received $66,420, or 93% of revenue, from gifts and grants awarded by foundations and individuals. (These grants included $10,000 from the Tides Foundation, $6,500 from the Jessie Smith Noyes Foundation, and $3,000 from the Ruth Mott Fund.) $4,782, or 7%, from subscriptions to *Indigenous Women*. The remaining revenue came from interest on savings and temporary cash investments.

Indochina Project
2001 S St., N.W., Suite 740
Washington, DC 20009
USA

Mission or Interest: Third world peace and justice, with a particular focus on the U.S.'s foreign policy regarding southeast Asia.
Accomplishments: In 1994 the Project only spent money to maintain operations, it did not conduct any programs.
Net Revenue: 1994 $446 **Net Expenses:** $937 0%/100%/0% **Net Assets:** $60
Tax Status: 501(c)(3)
Periodicals: *Indochina Issues* (ten times a year newsletter), historically published by the Project, although none were published in 1994.
Other Information: The Project received $446, or 100% of revenue, from gifts and grants awarded by foundations and individuals.

Industrial Areas Foundation
36 New Hyde Park Rd.
Franklin Square, NY 11010   **Phone:** (516) 354-1076
USA

Contact Person: Arnold Graf, Supervisor.   **Officers or Principals:** Edward T. Chambers, Executive Director ($159,000); Ernesto Cortes, Jr., Supervisor ($111,000); Larry McNeil, Supervisor ($104,783); Arnold Graf, Supervisor ($104,333); Michael Gecan, Supervisor ($102,000); Marvin D. Worth, President; D. Barry Menuez, Vice President; Msgr. John J. Egan, Treasurer.
Mission or Interest: Foundation that conducts seminars and conventions to promote community and labor organizing in industrialized areas. Conducts seminars for various organizations for a fee. Works with the religious community. The Foundation was founded by Saul Alinsky. Alinsky was a pioneer in community organizing. Starting in the Chicago area, he brought together immigrants, the religious community, unions, communists and other radicals into coalitions. Alinsky was the author of Rules for Radicals, a collection of stories, anecdotes, and useful information from his career as an organizer.
Accomplishments: In the fiscal year ending September 1994 the Foundation spent $1,147,461 on its programs.
Net Revenue: FY ending 9/94 $1,559,927   **Net Expenses:** $1,400,906   82%/18%/0%   **Net Assets:** $1,226,741
Citations: 156:93
Tax Status: 501(c)(3)
Board of Directors or Trustees: Bishop John Adams, Rt. Rev. Hays Rockwell, Patrick Flores (Archdiocese of San Antonio), Dr. Jean Elshtain.
Other Information: The Foundation received $1,517,319, or 97% of revenue, from fees paid by other nonprofit organizations for seminars and conferences. (e.g. In 1994 the Texas Interfaith Education Fund received a grant of $799,000 from the Florence and John Schumann Foundation to hire the services of the Industrial Areas Foundation.) $25,678, or 2%, from interest on savings and temporary cash investments. $16,930, or 1%, from gifts and grants awarded by foundations, businesses, and individuals. (The Foundation has received extensive support from the Campaign for Human Development, $5 million between 1991-1993.)

Industrial Workers of the World (IWW)

1095 Market St.
San Francisco, CA 94103   **Phone:**   (415) 863-9627
USA

Contact Person: Robert Rush, General Secretary.   **Officers or Principals:** Bill Meyers ($4,760); Harry Siitonen ($0).
Mission or Interest: Also known as the "Wobblies," Industrial Workers of the World is a union dating back to the start of the century, founded in 1905. The Workers advocate a single industrial union. The Wobblies were taken very seriously for their radical activities in the early 1900's. They were often beaten and shot at. Distinctly Marxist, they fight for the end of the wage system, and for "the establishment of a cooperative commonwealth to replace exploitation of the planet and its people." Today they are small in number, approximately 5,000 members.
Net Revenue: FY ending 6/94 $41,747   **Net Expenses:** $90,217   **Net Assets:** $135,081
Products or Services: Little Red Songbook, monographs, publications, books, records, posters, annual conference.
Tax Status: 501(c)(5)
Board of Directors or Trustees: Ingrid Kock, Marc Janowitz, Stan Anderson, Mike Ballard, Franklin Devore, Jeff Ditz, Lenny Flank, Mike D'Amore, Fred Chase, John Friesen, Fred Lee, Ray Elbourne.
Periodicals: Industrial Worker (monthly newsletter).
Other Information: The IWW received $26,180, or 63% of revenue, from membership dues. $8,523, or 20%, from program service fees. $3,410, or 8%, from investment income. $2,234 net, or 5%, from the sale of inventory. $1,398, or 3%, from gifts and grants awarded by foundations and individuals.

INFORM

120 Wall St., 16th Floor
New York, NY 10005   **Phone:**   (212) 631-2400   **E-Mail:** Inform@igc.apc.org
USA   **Fax:**   (212) 631-2412

Contact Person: Joanna Underwood, President.   **Officers or Principals:** Charles A. Moran, Chairman; Joanna Underwood, President; Christopher J. Daggett, Vice Chair; C. Howard Hardesty, Jr., Director Emeritus; KiKu Hoagland Hanes, Vice Chair.
Mission or Interest: Monitors the environment, focusing on toxic waste and solid waste management, and proposes solutions for industry.
Accomplishments: Published more than 60 studies and hundreds of articles. "INFORM's research on industry's potential to reduce emissions of toxic wastes through source reduction (preventing the creation of wastes in the first place), starting in 1986 with Cutting Chemical Wastes, was instrumental in shaping the first federal legislation on waste prevention. It also helped spur the creation of EPA's Toxics Release Inventory...Drive for Clean Air, released in mid-1989, played a significant role in turning the tide of political and regulatory interest toward natural gas (for automobiles)." John Adams, executive director of the Natural Resources Defense Council, said of INFORM, "For nearly twenty years, their cutting-edge field research and expert reports have provided accessible technical information to policy-makers and environmental advocates pursuing policy reforms. In particular, INFORM's work on alternative vehicle fuels has greatly influenced the shaping of the national debate."
Tax Status: 501(c)(3)
Board of Directors or Trustees: Victor Alicea, Ph.D. (Pres., Boricua College), Paul Brooke (Managing Director, Morgan Stanley & Co.), Christopher Daggett (Managing Director, William E. Simon & Sons), William Graves (former editor, National Geographic Magazine), Martin Krasney (Pres., Coalition for the Presidio Pacific Center), Stephen Land, Philip Landrigan, M.D. (Chair, Dept. of Community Medicine, Mount Sanai Medical Center), Kenneth Mountcastle, Jr. (Senior V.P., Dean Witter Reynolds), Margaret Murphy, Olivia Nordberg (Alan Guttmacher Inst.), Carol Noyes, S. Bruce Smart, Jr., (former Undersecretary of Commerce for Intl. Trade), Grant Thompson, Hon. Howard Wolpe (former Rep., D-MI).

Periodicals: *INFORM* Reports (quarterly newsletter).
Other Information: Founded in 1974. In 1994 INFORM received $60,000 from the Joyce Foundation, $40,000 from the Nathan Cummings Foundation, $30,000 from the Robert Sterling Clark Foundation, $30,000 from the Joyce Mertz-Gilmore Foundation, $20,000 from the Compton Foundation, and $5,841 from the Environmental Federation of America.

Institute for Consumer Responsibility (ICR)

3618 Wallingford Ave., N.
Seattle, WA 98103   **Phone:** (206) 632-5230
USA   **Fax:** (206) 523-0421   **Web-Page:** http:\\\\www.Seattle.cafe.com\boycott

Contact Person: Todd Putnam, President.   **Officers or Principals:** Todd Putnam, President; Katrina Moore, Vice President.
Mission or Interest: "To educate consumers about their power to influence corporate policies and practices in accordance with their own values and principles." The guiding principle is, "Every time we spend money, we are voting with our dollars." To this end they advocate boycotts of products, companies, and even the products of certain countries.
Accomplishments: Published the discontinued *National Boycott News* for ten years. Featured on the "Today Show" and a front page article in *The Wall Street Journal*.
Products or Services: Pamphlets, boycott lists, and other information.
Tax Status: 501(c)(3) **Annual Report:** No. **Employees:** All volunteer.
Internships: Yes. Interns perform research, write grant requests, do office work and more.
Other Information: *National Boycott News* was absorbed by *Boycott Quarterly* in 1994. "Many liberal/left groups hate our message since we target consumers rather than corporations or government...We feel corporate responsibility is impossible without consumer responsibility and that government regulation is largely ineffective and undermines individual responsibility."

Institute for Defense and Disarmament Studies

675 Massachusetts Ave.
Cambridge, MA 02139   **Phone:** (617) 354-4337
USA   **Fax:** (617) 354-1450

Contact Person: Randall Forsberg, Executive Director.   **Officers or Principals:** Randall Forsberg, Executive Director ($61,065); Hayward Alker, Jr., President ($0); Dr. Judith Reppy, Chair ($0); George Sommaripa, Treasurer; Laura Reed, Secretary; Ann Hallan Lakhdhir, United Nations Non-Governmental Organization Representative.
Mission or Interest: Seeks the demilitarization of world affairs, the end of nuclear weapons, and world peace.
Accomplishments: In 1994 the Institute spent $387,758 on its programs. The largest program, with expenditures of $258,796, was "research, writing and public outreach on reducing arms industries and arms exports." $104,292 was spent producing and distributing the *Arms Control Reporter*. $14,724 was spent on research and education to reduce U.S. military spending. $9,946 was spent on research and education for the "principles of multilateral peacekeeping." The Institute made a $27,000 contribution to the Center for Geopolitical and Military Forecasts.
Net Revenue: 1994 $548,530 **Net Expenses:** $495,058 78%/22%/1% **Net Assets:** $44,341 **Citations:** 6:210
Tax Status: 501(c)(3)
Board of Directors or Trustees: Hayward Alkers, Jr. (MIT), Dr. Philip Morrison (MIT), Jane Sharp (Centre for Defense Studies), Dr. Lynn Eden (Stanford Univ.), Amb. Jonathan Dean (Union of Concerned Scientists), Natalie Goldring (British American Security Information Council), Robert Legvold (Harriman Inst., Columbia Univ.).
Periodicals: *Arms Control Reporter* (monthly report).
Other Information: The Institute received $396,936, or 72% of revenue, from gifts and grants awarded by foundations, businesses, and individuals. (These grants included $40,000 from the Joyce Mertz-Gilmore Foundation, $15,000 from the New-Land Foundation.) $143,108, or 26%, from *Arms Control Reporter* subscriptions. $4,935, or 1%, from honoraria. The remaining revenue came from the sale of literature and royalties, and interest on savings and temporary cash investments.

Institute for Democratic Socialism

180 Varick St., 12th Floor
New York, NY 10038   **Phone:** (212) 927-8610
USA

Contact Person: Michael Lighty, Director.   **Officers or Principals:** Michael Lighty, Director ($0); Alan Charney, Director ($0).
Mission or Interest: Research and education promoting democratic socialism.
Accomplishments: In 1993 the Institute spent $39,538 on its programs. The largest program, with expenditures of $25,806, was the Youth Section, "a program to educate college students and young adults to acquaint them with the principles and history of democratic socialism." $10,040 was spent on public education. $3,692 was spent promoting the "benefits of the Canadian health care system."
Net Revenue: 1993 $80,832 **Net Expenses:** $48,888 **Net Assets:** (-$71,368)
Tax Status: 501(c)(3)
Board of Directors or Trustees: Theresa Alt, Pat Belcon, Dorothy Benz, Jack Clark, Howard Croft, Suzanne Crowell, Virginia Franco, J. Hughes, Claire Kaplan, Jeff Lacher, Jose Laluz, Frank Llewellyn, Sherri Levine, Mark Levinson, Jo-Ann Mort, Dave Rathke, Chris Riddiough, Krista Schneider, Joe Schwartz, Ruth Spitz, Kurt Stand, Steve Tarzynski, Juanita Webster.
Other Information: Affiliated with the 501(c)(4) Democratic Socialists of America at the same address. The two affiliates had combined net revenues of $484,235, net expenses of $466,192, and net assets of $239,099. The Institute received $55,633, or 69% of revenue, from gifts and grants awarded by foundations, businesses, and individuals. (These grants included $1,500 from the North Star Fund, $1,000 from the Aaron and Martha Schecter Private Foundation.) $19,102, or 24%, from fund-raising appeals. $3,239 net, or 4%, from the sale of inventory. $2,827, or 3%, from program services. The remaining revenue came from investment income.

Institute for Economic Democracy
P.O. Box 303
Cambria, CA 93428   **Phone:** (805) 927-1873   **E-Mail:** jwsmith@slonet.org
USA   **Fax:**   same   **Web-Page:** http://www.slonet.org/~jwsmith/

Contact Person: Ralph Hansen, Executive Director.
Mission or Interest: Research and educational foundation devoted to the idea that underdeveloped countries can be raised to a higher standard of living through the redistribution of capitaland elimination of free trade.
Accomplishments: World's Wasted Wealth was called "in the spirit of Stuart Chase's The Economy of Abundance (1934), Thorstein Veblen's The Vested Interests (1919), and Seymour Melman's Profits Without Production (1938), this book provides a comprehensive examination of waste in specific industries of the economy and how current property rights contribute to this waste. This is a controversial book that brings together a vast amount of information and analysis" by P.M. Titus, emeritus, Kenyon College, in *Choice*. Francis Moore Lappe, author of Diet for a Small Planet, said, "I believe that it will be an extremely valuable contribution."
Products or Services: World's Wasted Wealth 2, book by J.W. Smith.

Institute for Environmental Education
18554 Haskins Rd.
Chagrin Falls, OH 44023-1823   **Phone:** (216) 543-7303
USA   **Fax:**   (216) 543-7160

Contact Person: Joseph H. Chadbourne, President.   **Officers or Principals:** Mary Chadbourne, Vice President ($8,190); Joseph H. Chadbourne, President ($2,211); Joan Holmes, Chairman ($0).
Mission or Interest: Environmental education for primary and secondary school teachers.
Accomplishments: In 1993 the Institute spent $251,243 on its programs.
Net Revenue: 1993 $238,744 **Net Expenses:** $259,405 97%/3%/0% **Net Assets:** $677
Tax Status: 501(c)(3)
Board of Directors or Trustees: Dr. Harry Bury (Baldwin-Wallace College), Ron Yarian.
Other Information: The Institute received $202,144, or 85% of revenue, from direct and indirect public support in the form of gifts and grants awarded by foundations, businesses, and individuals. $16,035, or 7%, from the sale of publications. $15,204, or 6%, from consulting services. The remaining revenue came from teacher's fees, interest on savings and temporary cash investment, and other miscellaneous sources.

Institute for First Amendment Studies
P.O. Box 589
Great Barrington, MA 01230
USA

Contact Person: Barbara Simon, President/Treasurer.
Officers or Principals: Charles R. Porteous, Secretary ($3,000); Barbara Simon, President/Treasurer ($1,000).
Mission or Interest: "Research and development of information regarding social and political issues affecting human rights."
Accomplishments: In the fiscal year ending September 1994, the Institute spent $87,202 on its programs.
Net Revenue: FY ending 9/94 $178,139 **Net Expenses:** $105,668 83%/17%/0% **Net Assets:** $161,079
Tax Status: 501(c)(3)
Other Information: The Institute received $157,629, or 88% of revenue, from gifts and grants awarded by foundations, businesses, and individuals. (These grants included $12,500 from the Robert Sterling Clark Foundation, $500 from the Aaron and Martha Schecter Private Foundation.) $10,534 net, or 6%, from the sale of inventory. $7,025, or 4%, from honoraria. The remaining revenue came from interest on savings and temporary cash investments, and other miscellaneous sources.

Institute for Global Communications (IGC)
Presidio Building 1012, First Floor
P.O. Box 29904
San Francisco, CA 94129-0904   **Phone:** (415) 561-6100   **E-Mail:** outreach@igc.apc
USA   **Fax:**   (415) 561-6101   **Web-Page:** http://www.igc.org/

Mission or Interest: A project of the Tides Foundation. The Institute for Global Communications is an on-line computer service catering to the leftist advocacy and policy community. Computer E-Mail addresses and web pages with the letters "igc" in their address work through this service. The IGC is home to several networks, including PeaceNet, EcoNet, ConflictNet, LaborNet, and WomensNet. These networks all offer studies, legislative updates, and lobbying efforts for their respective causes. IGC is the U.S. member of the Association for Progressive Communications, the "apc" in computer addresses. The APC links up more than 40,000 organizations and individuals in over 133 countries worldwide. APC is dedicated to serving the "Non-Governmental Organization (NGO) community, citizen activists, UN agencies, and others who work with NGOs." IGC works on a subscription basis.
Accomplishments: IGC has over 6,000 subscribers in the U.S.
Net Revenue: (see the Tides Foundation for financial information)
Products or Services: Computer network services, including assistance in developing web sites, consultation, training, and faxing over the internet.
Other Information: The IGC is also associated with HandsNet, another organization linking advocacy organizations on the internet. HandsNet received a $200,000 grant from the U.S. Commerce Department's new National Telecommunications and Information Administration. (For more information see the Tides Foundation).

Institute for Labor and Mental Health / *Tikkun*

5100 Leona St.
Oakland, CA 94619   **Phone:**   (510) 482-0788   **E-Mail:** tikkun@panix.com
USA

Contact Person: Michael Lerner, Director.   **Officers or Principals:** Richard Epstein, Director ($68,550); Michael Lerner, Director ($45,000); Alice Chasan, Executive Editor ($40,000).
Mission or Interest: Publishes the Jewish-Left magazine, *Tikkun*. *Tikkun* is a "progressive Jewish critique of politics, culture and society," that was "created as an alternative to the voices of Jewish conservatism," especially to counter *Commentary*. Tikkun means "to heal, repair and transform the world." The Institute also provides counseling and services for stress-related problems.
Accomplishments: *Tikkun* has a circulation of about 40,000. *Newsweek* said about *Tikkun*, "Now Jewish liberals have an alternative voice to turn to." *The Los Angeles Times* said, "(*Tikkun* is) reinventing liberal thinking, creating a new frame of reference to make sense of a new world." In the fiscal year ending March 1994, the Institute spent $402,831 on its programs. *Tikkun*'s readers are "well educated...affluent...predominantly bicoastal, urban, and Jewish, although 25% of its readers are non-Jews." Publishing *Tikkun* was profitable and in the fiscal year ending March 1994, did not require subsidization. The Institute spent $384,439 producing and distributing *Tikkun*, and received $385,220 from the sale of the magazine.
Net Revenue: FY ending 3/94 $745,319 **Net Expenses:** $746,332 54%/46%/0% **Net Assets:** $678,181 **Citations:** 3:222
Products or Services: Magazine, counseling, conferences.
Tax Status: 501(c)(3)
Board of Directors or Trustees: The Editorial Board includes: Laura Geller (Americans for Peace Now), Todd Gitlin (Campaign for Peace and Democracy), Robert Heilbroner, Judith Plaskow, Letty Cottin Pogrebin (Americans for Peace Now), Chaim Seidler-Feller (Americans for Peace Now), Stanley Sheinbaum (Barbra Streisand Found.), and many others.
Other Information: Director Michael Lerner is a psychotherapist and author of <u>Jewish Renewal</u> (Grosset Putnam, 1994), a book that was hailed as "one of the most important Jewish books of our times" by Rabbi Michael Paley. Lerner has been a guest at the White House and a primary influence on Hillary Rodham Clinton's "Politics of Meaning" efforts. Lerner has, over the years, been urging a "progressive politics of meaning" that would "include the creation of a progressive pro-families coalition and local family-support networks designed not only to help people engage in mutual self-help, but also to understand the crisis of love and caring as rooted in the psychodynamics of selfishness and materialism fostered by the competitive market society." In the 1970's Lerner was a radical who advocated a Marxist revolution in the United States. In his book, <u>The New Socialist Revolution</u> (Delacorte Press, 1973), Lerner advocated an overthrowing of "the ruling class." "It is quite true that eventually we must resort to armed struggle and self-defensive violence, because it will be the only way to act in solidarity with our brothers and sisters around the world and to create a new American society. But this violence will be accompanied by great sadness. The revolutionary hates violence and hates to see innocent people killed." But he justified this as necessary self defense. "The pleasant gentleman on the Long Island Railroad reading his *Wall Street Journal* or the quiet technician working in Palo Alto or on Route 128 in Massachusetts, the Wall Street banker or assistant secretary of state or agriculture or defense, the professor of political science who runs the institute on Latin America or the liberal senator - all participate daily in making decisions that sustain the daily violence upon which this system rests. If it was right to try Eichmann and other officials of the Nazi regime for crimes against humanity, even though they did not personally kill anyone, then surely the violent men who surround us, with their gentle manners and sweet smiles and well-manicured lawns and all the rest of the petty concealments that hide a life of 'honorable' crime, they should be tried for their crimes by the people of the world." *Tikkun*'s editorial office is located at: 251 W. 100th St., 5th Floor, New York, NY 10025, (212) 864-4110, fax (212) 864-4137. The Institute received $276,968, or 37% of revenue, from counseling fees. $269,372, or 36%, from gifts and grants awarded by foundations, businesses, and individuals. (These grants included $5,000 from the Barbra Streisand Foundation, and $3,000 from the Naomi and Nehemiah Cohen Foundation.) $52,185, or 7%, from conference fees. $38,829, or 5%, from capital gains on the sale of securities. $37,566, or 5%, from dividends and interest from securities. $28,769, or 4%, from honoraria from speeches given by Lerner. $24,978, or 3%, from advertising revenue. $10,596, or 1%, from the sale of literature and videos. The remaining revenue came from rental income, interest on savings and temporary cash investments, net revenue from the sale of *Tikkun*, and special fund-raising events.

Institute for Peace and International Security (IPIS)

237 Brattle St.
Cambridge, MA 02138   **Phone:**   (617) 547-3338
USA

Contact Person: Paul Walker, Director.   **Officers or Principals:** Everett Mendelson, Director ($0).
Mission or Interest: Concerned with peace in the Middle East in the post-Gulf War period. "Effort to educate faculty and students on campuses regarding military research."
Accomplishments: In 1993 the Institute spent $15,305 on its programs.
Net Revenue: 1993 $18,391 **Net Expenses:** $17,712 **Net Assets:** $3,239
Tax Status: 501(c)(3)
Other Information: The Institute received $18,287, or 99.4% of revenue, from gifts and grants awarded by foundations, businesses, and individuals. The remaining revenue came investment income.

Institute for Policy Studies (IPS)

1601 Connecticut Ave., N.W.
Washington, DC 20009   **Phone:**   (202) 234-9382   **E-Mail:** tessmer@igc.apc.org
USA   **Fax:**   (202) 387-7915

Contact Person: Melissa Tessmer.   **Officers or Principals:** Marc Raskin, Senior Fellow ($83,831); Richard Barnet, Senior Fellow ($75,846); Saul Landau, Senior Fellow ($67,981); Michael Shuman, Executive Director; John Cavanagh, Secretary; Robert Borosage, Senior Fellow; Christopher Jenks, Chair.

Mission or Interest: Formed in 1963, the Institute for Policy Studies has been a leading organization linking academics and activists on the Left. "(Marxist journalist) I.F. Stone once said that the Heritage Foundation is for right-wingers, the American Enterprise Institute for the Fortune 500, Brookings Institution for the Establishment - and IPS is for the rest of us."

Accomplishments: IPS fellows edited "The Vietnam Reader," which was used during 'teach-ins' accross the country in the 1960's. In 1968 IPS was illegally investigated and spied upon by the FBI, resulting in a lawsuit settled in the Institute's favor. In 1974 Fellow Saul Landau directed a CBS report, "Castro, Cuba, and the USA" with Dan Rather. In 1992 Richard Barnet became a regular commentator on National Public Radio. Many IPS fellows have gone on to form other major projects and publications of the Left, including; The Center for Black Education, *Quest*, *Off Our Backs*, Government Accountability Project, *Mother Jones*, Progressive Alliance, Progressive Urban Planners Network, Free South Africa Network, and Alliance for Responsible Trade. Currently IPS has about 2,000 dues-paying members, and distributes its newsletter to about 6,000. IPS Fellows and their work routinely appear in *The Nation*, *Mother Jones*, *In These Times*, *The Progressive*, The MacNeil-Lehrer News Hour, NPR's "Marketplace," *The New York Times*, *Washington Post*, *Los Angeles Times*, *Foreign Policy*, *Harpers*, *New Yorker*, *World Policy Journal*, *Diplomatic History*, *Technology Review*, and *Rolling Stone*.

Net Revenue: FY ending 6/94 $1,467,249 **Net Expenses:** $1,559,243 72%/25%/3% **Net Assets:** $89,065 **Citations:** 349:52

Products or Services: Books, studies, commentary, organization, conferences, more. They recently began their activist training program, SALSA - Social Action and Leadership School for Activists.

Tax Status: 501(c)(3) **Annual Report:** No. **Employees:** 20

Board of Directors or Trustees: Arthur Carter (Publisher, *The Nation*), Adrian De Wind, Frances Farenthold, Hal Harvey (Energy Foundation), Katrina vanden Heuvel (Assoc. Editor, *The Nation*), David Horowitz, Prof. E. Ethelbert Miller (Howard Univ.), Marcus Raskin, Emily Rose, Lewis Steel.

Internships: Yes.

Other Information: Financially, 1993 was a big year for IPS, receiving a three-year, $650,000 grant from the MacArthur Foundation and bequest promises of $1.4 million. Their prospects for influence dimmed somewhat, however, in 1994. On the occasion of their 30th anniversary in 1993 they predicted "with the Cold War over and Democrats in power in the White House and Congress, Americans now have unprecedented opportunities to enact progressive ideas into law and policy." Rep. George Miller (D-CA) predicted "The '80s belonged to The Heritage Foundation and the American Enterprise Institute. The '90s belong to IPS." The Institute received $1,350,009, or 92% of revenue, from grants awarded by foundations, companies and individuals. (These grants included $650,000 over three years from the John D. and Catherine T. MacArthur Foundation, $40,000 from the New-Land Foundation, $25,000 from the General Services Foundation, $5,000 from the Winston Foundation for World Peace, $1,250 from the Stewart R. Mott Charitable Trust, $1,000 from the Hunt Alternatives Fund, and $250 from the Compton Foundation.) $90,158, or 6%, from program revenues. $10,524 net, or 1%, from the sale of assets other than inventory. The remaining revenue came from interest on savings and temporary cash investments, dividends and interest from securities, and other miscellaneous sources.

Institute for Public Affairs / *In These Times*

2040 N. Milwaukee Ave.
Chicago, IL 60647   **Phone:** (312) 772-0100   **E-Mail:** itt@igc.apc.org
USA   **Fax:**   (312) 772-4180

Contact Person: James Weinstein, Editor/Publisher.   **Officers or Principals:** Jake Blankenship, Circulation; Chris Lehmann, Managing Editor; Joel Bleifuss, David Moberg, Salim Muwakkil, Senior Editors.

Mission or Interest: Publishes *In These Times*, a democratic socialist weekly that covers "politics, culture, educating the Left." The editors recommend a reinvigoration of the American economy through, "first, a steady reduction in the hours of work - say, to 30 hours a week - with no reduction in pay. Second, a massive program of infrastructure building and rebuilding." Then in the long term, "employ millions of people in labor-intensive work such as education, health care and culture."

Accomplishments: Twenty years of publication. In 1996 *In These Times* co-sponsored the Media and Democracy Congress. Topics included electronic and the 'new' media, reviving the Left and improving its ability to influence the mainstream, and examining race, class and gender in media. Speakers included Jim Hightower, Ben Bagdikian, Susan Faludi, and Barbara Ehrenreich. Other sponsors included the Center for Media Education, Fairness and Accuracy in Media, Pacifica Foundation, *The Progressive*, Political Research Associates, and the *Utne Reader*. Circulation is approximately 120,000. In 1993 the Institute spent $718,684 on its programs.

Net Revenue: 1993 $1,006,518 **Net Expenses:** $913,945 79%/15%/7% **Net Assets:** (-$349,001) **Citations:** 260:62

Tax Status: 501(c)(3)

Other Information: In 1993 the Institute received $574,967, or 57% of revenue, from gifts and grants awarded by foundations, businesses, and individuals. (These grants included $5,000 from the Peace Development Fund.) $428,386, or 43%, from program services including magazine subscriptions and advertising. The remaining revenue came from various miscellaneous sources. The publication of *In These Times* cost $718,684, and brought in revenues of $428,386, requiring $290,298 in subsidization; or approximately $2.40 per year per subscriber/newsstand purchaser.

Institute for Social and Cultural Communications / *Z Magazine*

18 Millfield St.
Woods Hole, MA 02543   **Phone:** (508) 548-9063   **E-Mail:** Lydia_Sargent@lbbs.org
USA   **Fax:**   (508) 457-0626   **Web-Page:** http://www.lbbs.org

Contact Person: Lydia Sargent, Editor. **Officers or Principals:** Michael Albert, Publisher; Eric Sargent, Managing Editor.

Mission or Interest: Publishes *Z Magazine*, "an independent magazine of critical thinking on political, cultural, social, and economic life in the U.S. It sees the racial, gender, class, and political dimensions of personal life as fundamental to understanding and improving contemporary circumstances; and it aims to assist activist efforts for a better future." Also hosts the "Z Media Institute", or ZMI, which offers courses in "radical theory, foreign policy, ecology, radical strategy, history of racism, legacy of slavery, feminist theory, political economy, economic theory, queer theory, third parties," and how to apply these to media analysis, organizing, and publishing.

Accomplishments: Publishing since 1988. Circulation is approximately 21,700. Regularly features Prof. Noam Chomsky's analyses.

Net Revenue: 1994 est. $420,000 **Tax Status:** 501(c)(3)

Periodicals: *Z Magazine* (monthly).

Institute for Social and Economic Studies / *CrossRoads*

P.O. Box 2809
Oakland, CA 94609 **Phone:** (510) 843-7495 **E-Mail:** crossroads@agc.apc.org
USA **Fax:** (510) 843-5877

Contact Person: Sushawn Robb, Executive Director.

Officers or Principals: Sushawn Robb, Executive Director ($17,257); Jude Thilman, President ($0); Frances Beal, Secretary ($0); Felix Huerta, Treasurer ($0); Kim Benita Furumoto, Managing Editor; James Vann, Executive Committee.

Mission or Interest: "Developing dialogue among diverse progressive and left individuals and organizations to help rebuild an effective left in American politics."

Accomplishments: Publishing a monthly magazine, *CrossRoads*, since 1990 on a very small budget. In 1994 they spent $57,131 to produce and distribute *CrossRoads*. Also in 1994 they spent $16,541 on their annual four-day seminar.

Net Revenue: 1994 $92,145 **Net Expenses:** $99,186 **Net Assets:** $1,035

Products or Services: Publications and conferences. Audio and video tapes available of a roundtable session on campaign strategies (with KPFA-FM radio).

Tax Status: 501(c)(3) **Annual Report:** No. **Employees:** 2

Board of Directors or Trustees: Joe Berry, Linda Burnham (Women of Color Resource Center), Peter Camejo (Progressive Assets Management), Max Elbaum, Jan Gilbrecht, Roma Gay (Bay Area Homeless Project), Lisa Hoyos (Legislative Aid to Tom Hayden), Felix Huerta (AFSCME), Tahan Jones, Guiliana Milanese (California Nurses Assoc.), Michael Myerson, Gary Phillips (Multi-Cultural Collaborative), Carl Pinkston (Freedom Road Socialist Organization), Jeremy Raw (Committee of Correspondence), Teresa Sanchez (Mexican Rights Project), Ellie Schitzer, Barry Shepard (Solidarity), Jude Thilman (KPFA-FM radio), John Trinkl, James Vann (National Committee for Independent Politics), Michael Wyman (Committee in Solidarity with the People of El Salvador), Ethan Young (Monthly Review Press).

Periodicals: *CrossRoads* (monthly).

Internships: Yes. Editorial interns, art interns and business interns to help produce *CrossRoads*.

Other Information: The Institute received $44,668, or 48% of revenue, from gifts and grants awarded by foundations, businesses and individuals. (These grants included $23,200 from the South Coast Foundation.) $13,645, or 17%, from program services, including the sale of *Crossroads*. $2,692 net, or 3%, from special fund-raising events, including a poetry reading and an art sale. The remaining revenue comes from investment income and other miscellaneous sources.

Institute for Social Justice

739 8th St., S.E.
Washington, DC 20003 **Phone:** (202) 547-9292
USA

Mission or Interest: Research and education affiliate of ACORN.

Products or Services: Two-week training programs. **Tax Status:** 501(c)(3)

Other Information: Called the Arkansas Institute for Social Justice until 1978. In 1994 it received $10,000 from the Bydale Foundation.

Institute for Southern Studies (ISS)

P.O. Box 531
Durham, NC 27702 **Phone:** (919) 419-8311 **E-Mail:** pmacdowell@igc.apc.org
USA **Fax:** (919) 419-8315

Contact Person: Sharon Ugochukwu. **Officers or Principals:** Isaiah Madison, Executive Director.

Mission or Interest: Research, analysis, and dissemination on topics such as community economic development, environmental and occupational health, economic rights, political accountability, campaign finance, and constitutional issues. Publishes *Southern Exposure*. Encourages investigative journalism.

Accomplishments: In 1994 the Institute spent $612,765 on its programs. These included grants of $119,994 to the Research Consortium on the Southside Textile Strike of 1934 to produce a film, and $1,500 to the North Carolina Rural Health Coalition.

Net Revenue: 1994 $709,874 **Net Expenses:** $728,047 84%/8%/7% **Net Assets:** $207,157 **Citations:** 36:149

Products or Services: Southern Journalism Awards. Research, writings, consultations, film and video production, workshops, conferences, and lobbying. The Institute spent $7,687 on lobbying; $3,967 on grassroots lobbying and $3,720 on the direct lobbying of legislators. This was an 85% increase over the previous year.

Tax Status: 501(c)(3)

Periodicals: *Southern Exposure* (quarterly journal).
Other Information: The Institute received $606,864, or 85%, from gifts and grants awarded by foundations, businesses, and individuals. (These grants included $35,000 from the Florence and John Schumann Foundation, $20,000 from the Jessie Smith Noyes Foundation, $15,000 from the Ruth Mott Fund, $5,000 from the Bydale Foundation.) $66,270, or 9%, from the sale of publications. $22,312, or 3%, from membership dues. The remaining revenue came from rent and copy fees from other nonprofits, dividends and interest from securities, interest on savings and temporary cash investments, entry fees for journalism awards, research contracts, and other miscellaneous sources.

Institute for the Study of the Religious Right (ISRR)

P.O. Box 26656
Los Angeles, CA 90026   **Phone:**   (213) 243-7598
USA   **Fax:**   (213) 653-1737

Contact Person: Julie Schollenberger, President.
Mission or Interest: "Formed to research and disseminate information about the activities of the Religious Right throughout the United States...The term 'Religious Right' refers to any individual or organization that seeks to impose their oppressive, religiously based ideology on mainstream political, social, and religious thought and institutions."
Tax Status: 501(c)(3)
Other Information: In 1993-94 the Institute received $4,000 from the Liberty Hill Foundation. In 1995, $1,000 from Resist.

Institute for Women, Law and Development

1350 Connecticut Ave., N.W., Suite 407
Washington, DC 20036   **Phone:**   (202) 463-7477   **E-Mail:** iwld@igc.apc.org
USA   **Fax:**   (202) 463-9480

Contact Person: Seema Kumar.   **Officers or Principals:** Margaret Schuler, Executive Director ($27,500); Florence Butegwa, Chair ($0); Sakuntala Rajasingham, Secretary ($0); Akua Kuenyehia (Ghana), Shireen Huq (Bangladesh), Gladys Acosta (Columbia), Roberta Clark (Trinidad & Tobago), Irina Mouleshkova (Bulgaria), Judy Lyons Wolf, Vice Chairs.
Mission or Interest: Defense and promotion of women's rights through litigation and the law. "Changing negative social attitudes toward women and articulating new and empowering forms of behavior." Seeks to influence policy at the national and international level.
Accomplishments: The organization has Non-Governmental Organization consultative status with the Economic and Social Council of the United Nations. In the abbreviated period between July 1994 and December 1994 the Institute spent $278,493 on its programs. The largest program, with expenditures of $243,353, was the "Women's Campaign" to change societal attitudes toward women. Other programs sought to; clarify issues and strategies "relevant to the defense and promotion of women's rights," train activists, and research women and Islamic family law in the Sudan.
Net Revenue: FY from 7/94 to 12/94 $373,121 **Net Expenses:** $333,107 84%/15%/2% **Net Assets:** $24,338
Products or Services: "Five books on legal literacy and empowerment through the law."
Tax Status: 501(c)(3)
Other Information: The Institute received $341,356, or 91% of revenue, from gifts and grants awarded by foundations, businesses, and individuals. (These grants included $1,000 from the Stewart R. Mott Charitable Trust.) The remaining income came from interest on savings and temporary cash investments, conference registration fees, and other miscellaneous sources. In the previous complete fiscal year, covering July 1, 1993 to June 30 1994, revenue was $316,214 with $348,676 in expenses, and (-$15,676) in assets. Margaret Schuler was compensated with $56,527, and a research associate, Asthma Abdel Halim was compensated with $35,000.

Institute for Women's Policy Research (IWPR)

1400 20th St., N.W., Suite 104
Washington, DC 20036   **Phone:**   (202) 785-5100
USA   **Fax:**   (202) 833-4362   **Web-Page:** http://www.iwpr.org

Contact Person: Heidi Hartmann, President.   **Officers or Principals:** Heidi Hartmann, President ($79,899); Roberta Spalter-Roth, Vice President ($39,698); Young-Hee Yoon, Senior Researcher ($39,698).
Mission or Interest: Research organization that focuses on issues of particular interest to women. "Unlike most other research institutes, IWPR's work places women's experience at the center of each analysis. All our research addresses issues of race, ethnicity, and class and specifically promotes policies that help low-income women achieve self-sufficiency and autonomy." IWPR specializes in the use of quantitative data and original research, then works in partnership with women's advocacy groups to respond to the policy implications of the research.
Accomplishments: IWPR staff have appeared on the MacNeil / Lehrer NewsHour, C-Span, NPR, BBC, ABC's Good Morning America, and the CBS Evening News. Featured in articles in the *New York Times*, *Wall street Journal*, *Washington Post*, *Chicago Tribune*, and *Business Week*. President Heidi Hartmann recently won a MacArthur Foundation Fellowship. In the fiscal year ending September 1994, the Institute spent $673,153 on its programs.

Net Revenue: FY ending 9/94 $713,952 **Net Expenses:** $705,396 95%/2%/2% **Net Assets:** (-$54,057) **Citations:** 36:149
Products or Services: Congressional testimony, conferences, lectures, brown-bag lunch series, media events, more. Recent reports include: Welfare that Works, Microenterprise and Women, Women's Access to Health Insurance, The Impact of the Glass Ceiling and Structural Change on Minorities and Women.
Tax Status: 501(c)(3) **Annual Report:** No. **Employees:** 16
Internships: Yes, administrative and research positions.
Other Information: Founded in 1987. The Institute received $414,649, or 58% of revenue, from its research program. $207,405, or 29%, from gifts and grants awarded by foundations, companies, and individuals. (These grants included $250,000 over two years from the Ford Foundation, $20,000 from the Rockefeller Family Fund, $20,000 from the Ms. Foundation for Women, $5,000 from the Angelina Fund.) $77,911, or 11%, from fees and contracts from government agencies. $4,944, or 1%, from the sale of publications. The remaining revenue came from interest on savings and temporary cash investments, and other miscellaneous sources.

Institute on Women and Technology

P.O. Box 9338
North Amherst, MA 01059   **Phone:** (413) 367-9725
USA

Contact Person: H. Patricia Hynes, Director.
Mission or Interest: Development of educational materials "for activists seeking to bring a women's health and reproductive rights perspective to population policy formation."
Products or Services: Taking Population Out of the Equation, booklet.
Tax Status: 501(c)(3)
Other Information: In 1994 the Institute received $3,785 from the Jessie Smith Noyes Foundation.

Interfaith Center on Corporate Responsibility (ICCR)

475 Riverside Dr., Suite 566
New York, NY 10115   **Phone:** (212) 870-2293
USA

Contact Person: Timothy H. Smith, Executive Director.   **Officers or Principals:** Sr. Toni Harris, O.P., Chairperson; Rev. J. Andy Smith, III, Vice Chairperson; Sr. Susan Mika, O.S.B., Treasurer; Diane Bratcher, Editor.
Mission or Interest: Coalition of nearly 275 Protestant, Jewish and Roman Catholic institutional investors who use pension fund investments to force changes in corporate practices. Concerned with the environment, military weapons production, equal employment, tobacco production, third-world development, foreign policy and other issues. The ICCR helps stockholders prepare shareholder proxy resolutions to be voted on at shareholder meetings.
Accomplishments: Forced many companies to divest in South Africa during the apartheid regime. Helped convince Kimberly-Clark to spin-off its tobacco business. Helped persuade railway company CSX to release data on equal opportunity employment and programs. "New York City Comptroller Alan Hevesi, Calvert Group and twenty-seven other institutional investors, working through ICCR, formally petitioned the SEC. They asked the SEC to change its current interpretation of proxy rules and again advise companies not to omit shareholder resolutions on employment issues from company proxy statements."
Net Revenue: 1994 $830,362 **Net Expenses:** $811,403 **Net Assets:** $122,972
Products or Services: Guides to socially conscious investing, proxy resolutions, and consumer purchases.
Tax Status: 501(c)(3) **Annual Report:** Yes. **Employees:** "As of June 30, 1995, ICCR staff included eleven persons - eight women (three of whom are racial or ethnic minorities) and three men (one of whom is a Native American)."
Periodicals: Corporate Examiner (ten times a year newspaper).
Other Information: Founded in 1971 when the Episcopal Church submitted a shareholder resolution calling on General Motors to divest from South Africa. In 1994 the Center received $10,000 from the Bauman Family Foundation, $5,000 from the Jessie Smith Noyes Foundation, $5,000 from the New World Foundation, and $250 from the Vanguard Public Foundation.

Interfaith Hunger Appeal

475 Riverside Drive, Suite 1630
New York, NY 10115
USA

Contact Person: Donald M. Robinson, President.
Officers or Principals: Donald M. Robinson, President ($0); Kenneth Hackett, First Vice President ($0); Lonnie Turnipseed, Second Vice President ($0); Kathryn Wolford, Treasurer; William J. O'Shea, Secretary.
Mission or Interest: Hunger relief organization that distributes grant money equally to four other religious relief organizations; Catholic Relief Services, Church World Services, Lutheran World Relief, and the American Jewish Joint Distribution Committee. Also performs public education activities.
Accomplishments: In 1994 the organization spent $495,099 on its programs. $270,000 was split four ways and given as grants to the four member organizations. $225,099 was spent on public education.
Net Revenue: 1994 $665,437 ($41,159, or 6%, from government grants) **Net Expenses:** $655,595 76%/12%/12%
Net Assets: $126,454 **Citations:** 0:255

Tax Status: 501(c)(3)
Board of Directors or Trustees: Rev. Alfred Bartholomew, Carol Capps (Lutheran World Relief), Tom Dart (Catholic Relief Services), Walter Jensen (Lutheran World Relief), Patrick Johns (Catholic Relief Services), Rev. Monsignor Andrew Landi, Mel Lehman (Church World Service), Marie Meyer, Lowell Scher (American Jewish Joint Distribution Committee), Michael Schneider (American Jewish Joint Distribution Committee), Herbert Singer, Henry Taub, Anna Belle Thiemann (Lutheran World Relief), Loretta Whalen (Church World Service), Rev. Donald Wilson (Presbyterian Church).
Other Information: The Appeal received $620,000, or 93% of revenue, from direct and indirect public support in the form of gifts and grants awarded by foundations, businesses, and individuals. (These grants included $500 from the Vanguard Public Foundation.) $41,159, or 6%, from government grants. $3,988, or 1%, from interest on savings and temporary cash investments.

Interhemispheric Resource Center
P.O. Box 4506
Albuquerque, NM 87196   **Phone:** (505) 842-8288   **E-Mail:** resourcectr@igc.apc.org
USA   **Fax:** (505) 246-1601

Contact Person: Kim L. Avender.
Officers or Principals: Debra Preusch, Executive Director; Tom Barry, Senior Analyst; Beth Wood, Director.
Mission or Interest: "Research and policy institute dedicated to providing information and analysis that will assist activists and policymakers in the areas of U.S. foreign policy, environmental and economic justice, fair trade, and sustainable development...Working to make the United States a responsible member of the world community."
Accomplishments: Worked with other organizations, including Friends of the Earth, Bank Information Center, Institute for Policy Studies, Washington Office on Latin America, Border Ecology Project, National Council of Churches, Fellowship of Reconciliation, Latin American Working Group, Bread for the World, and several organizations in Latin America.. Co-published A Citizen's Guide to NAFTA's Environmental Commission with Friends of the Earth. Zapata's Revenge: Free Trade and the Farm Crisis in Mexico (South End Press). Many other publications. In 1994 the Institute spent $202,320 on its programs.
Net Revenue: 1994 $249,346 **Net Expenses:** $269,761 75%/22%/3%
Tax Status: 501(c)(3) **Annual Report:** Yes. **Employees:** 5 full-time, 5 part-time.
Board of Directors or Trustees: Rosa Della Caudillo, John Cavanagh (Institute for Policy Studies), Prof. Noam Chomsky (MIT), Phil Dahl-Bredine, Kathy Engel (Riptide Communications), Don Hancock (Southwest Research and Information Center), Carlos Heredia, Luis Hernandez, Patricia Hynds (Maryknoll Lay Missioner), Claudia Issac, Antonio Lujan (Diocese of Las Cruces), Mary MacArthur (Diversity Project), Jennifer Manriquez, Carmen Alicia Nebot (United Church of Christ), Debra Preusch, Margaret Randall, Michael Ratner (Center for Constitutional Rights), Primitivo Rodriguez (American Friends Service Committee), Frank Sanchez (New Mexico Community Development Assoc.), Moises Sandoval, Beth Wood.
Periodicals: BorderLines (monthly newsletter), Resource Center Bulletin (quarterly bulletin), Democracy Backgrounder (bimonthly newsletter).
Internships: Yes. One paid internship "for a person of color," other internships for college credit.
Other Information: In 1994 the Institute received $157,088, or 63% of revenue, from gifts and grants awarded by foundations, businesses, and individuals. ($9,900 from individuals.) $84,777, or 34%, from the sale of publications and royalties. The remaining revenue came from various miscellaneous sources.

International Association of Machinists and Aerospace Workers (IAM)
9000 Machinists Place
Upper Marlboro, MD 20772   **Phone:** (301) 967-4500
USA   **Fax:** (301) 967-4588

Contact Person: George J. Kourpias, President
Mission or Interest: Union representing machinists and those in the aerospace industry. Member of the AFL-CIO.
Accomplishments: Approximately 800,000 members.
Tax Status: 501(c)(5)
Periodicals: The Machinist (monthly newsletter).
Other Information: Founded in 1888. In the year between July 1993 and June 1994 the Association received $1,770,000 in funding from the federal government.

International Black Women's Congress
P.O. Box 4250
Newark, NJ 07112   **Phone:** (201) 926-0570
USA

Contact Person: Dr. La Francis Rodgers-Rose, President.
Officers or Principals: Dr. La Francis Rodgers-Rose, President ($20,000); Mattie J. Holloway, Secretary; Elaine H. Robinson, Treasurer; Sharon Brown Bailey, Membership Director; Willa M. Hemmons, Ph.D., Public Relations; Sandra Y. Lewis, Ph.D., Program Director; Frederica K. Gray, International Development Director; Diane P. Reeder, Speakers Bureau.
Mission or Interest: Various educational programs focusing on the issues of black women.
Accomplishments: In 1994 the Congress spent $193,762 on its programs. The largest program, with expenditures of $51,920, was a series of events held during the year to encourage networking among black women. Next was the Genesis Project, with expenditures of $49,058, a weekly program designed to teach history and positive social development to black girls between the ages of 11 and 18. The annual Tour to Africa, with 15 participants, cost $47,029, or $3,135 per person. $45,755 was spent on conferences where speakers discussed issues facing black women, including "health and self esteem." These conferences were attended by approximately 200 participants, for a cost per person of about $230.

Net Revenue: 1994 $200,135 ($72,110, or 36%, from government grants) **Net Expenses:** $204,167 95%/4%/1%
Net Assets: $2,685
Products or Services: Conferences, tours, and other educational projects.   **Tax Status:** 501(c)(3)
Board of Directors or Trustees: Delores Alridge, Ph.D., Lauvenia Alston, Joseph Balfour-Senchire, Ph.D. (Ghana), Dorothy Brunson, Elwood Clough, Tandi Lutuli Gcabaske (South Africa), Sally Malone Hawkins, Ph.D., Ella Gates-Mahmoud, Uzo Osili, Cynthia Pullen, Cynthia Rodgers, Essie Manuel Rutledge, Ph.D., Sokhna Thiam (Senegal), Margaret Walker, Ph.D.
Other Information: The Congress received $72,110, or 36% of revenue, from government grants. $62,939, or 31%, from direct and indirect public support in the form of gifts and grants from foundations, businesses, affiliates, and individuals. $48,769, or 24%, from the tours. $16,315, or 8%, from conference fees.

International Brotherhood of Electrical Workers (IBEW)

1125 15th St., N.W.
Washington, DC 20005   **Phone:** (202) 833-7000
USA   **Fax:**   (202) 467-6316

Contact Person: J. J. Barry, International President.
Officers or Principals: J. J. Barry, International President ($176,883); John F. Moore, International Secretary ($156,251); J. Conway, R. Edwards, P. Loughran, C. Lansden, S. McCann, E. Hill, N.D. Schwitalla, O. Tate, J. Walters, P. Witte, International Vice Presidents (all received $109,079); T. Van Arsdale, International Treasurer.
Mission or Interest: "To organize all workers for the moral, economic and social advancement and their condition and status." Affiliated with the AFL-CIO.
Accomplishments: Represents approximately one million workers.
Net Revenue: FY ending 6/94 $83,613,163 **Net Expenses:** $69,080,701 **Net Assets:** $160,591,747
Tax Status: 501(c)(5)
Board of Directors or Trustees: R. Acton, W. Blackstock, Sr., C. Bowden, F. Carroll, Jr., A. Head, J. McAvoy, J. McCafferty, L. Querry, T. Sweeney.
Periodicals: *IBEW Journal* (monthly newsletter).
Other Information: The Brotherhood paid $5,085,949 to affiliates, including $3,331,611 to the AFL-CIO. The Brotherhood received $68,510,340, or 82% of revenue, from membership dues. $10,283,349, or 12%, from dividends and interest from securities. $4,591,000, or 4%, from reimbursed administrative expenses from affiliated organizations. The remaining revenue came from investment income, sale of inventory, interest on savings and other temporary cash investments, and other miscellaneous sources. Net revenue was reduced by a loss of $694,361 on the sale of securities.

International Brotherhood of Teamsters (IBT)

25 Louisiana Ave., N.W.
Washington, DC 20001   **Phone:** (202) 624-6800
USA

Contact Person: Ron Carey, President.
Mission or Interest: Union representing truck drivers and transportation workers.
Accomplishments: Approximately 1,600,000 members.
Net Revenue: 1993 est. $1,400,000 **Tax Status:** 501(c)(5)
Periodicals: *The New Teamster* (eight times a year).
Other Information: Founded in 1903. In the year between July 1993 and June 1994, the Teamsters received $3,542,000 in funding from the federal government. The included; $1.7 million grant from Health and Human Services for worker training related to the Superfund program, and a similar amount from Housing and Urban Development for Section 8 Housing Rehabilitation.

International Center for Research on Women (ICRW)

1717 Massachusetts Ave., N.W., Suite 302
Washington, DC 20036   **Phone:** (202) 797-0007
USA   **Fax:**   (202) 797-0020

Contact Person: Jill Merrick, Director of Communications.   **Officers or Principals:** Mayra Buvinic, President ($105,962); Margarette A. Lycette, Vice President ($77,134); Michael Paolisso, Director of Research ($62,801); Nancy Birdsall, Chair.
Mission or Interest: Research institute that focuses on women and girls in developing countries. Areas of research include socio-economic status, population concerns, women's health, the environment, women and HIV, and the rights of women.
Accomplishments: In the fiscal year ending September 1994, the Center spent $1,568,644 on its programs. The largest program, with expenditures of $457,040, was a series of studies "to identify ways to reduce women's risk of HIV infection in developing countries." Fifteen projects were under this program, six in Africa, five in Asia and the Pacific Rim, and four in Latin America and the Caribbean. $210,285 in grants were distributed through this program. $417,533 was spent to "guide formulation of policies and programs that improve the nutritional status of adolescent girls in developing countries." Other programs strengthened ICRW's research programs and links with other countries, and worked on ways to strengthen the links between researchers and service providers.
Net Revenue: FY ending 9/94 $2,192,103 ($1,225,248, or 56%, from government grants)
Net Expenses: $2,159,326 73%/27%/0% **Net Assets:** $175,381 **Citations:** 11:195

Tax Status: 501(c)(3)
Board of Directors or Trustees: Ann Crittenden, Elaine Dinn (Senior V.P., Chase Manhattan Bank), Kay Davies (Legislative Dir., Office of Sen. Pete Domenici, R-NM), Neva Doodwin, Peter Hakim (Pres., Inter-American Dialogue), Charles William Maynes (Editor, *Foreign Policy*), Moises Naim (Senior Assoc., Carnegie Endowment for Int'l Peace), Eileen Kennedy (Int'l Food Policy Research Inst.), Juliette Clagett McLennan, Mary Okelo, A. Wayne Patterson (Caribbean Food and Nutrition Inst.), Elise Smith (African Women Leaders Program), George Zeidenstein (Harvard Center for Population and Development Studies), John Sewell (Pres., Overseas Development Council), Sarah Tinsley.
Other Information: The Center received $1,225,248, or 56% of revenue, from government grants. $909,710, or 41%, from gifts and grants awarded by foundations, businesses, and individuals. (These grants included $6,000 from the Stewart R. Mott Charitable Trust. In 1995, $151,000 from the Rockefeller Foundation.) $28,830, or 1%, from dividends and interest from securities. $15,914, or 1%, from an insurance claim. The remaining revenue came from honoraria, rental income, sale of assets, and the sale of reprints.

International Center for the Solution of Environmental Problems (ICSEP)

535 Lovett
Houston, TX 77006   **Phone:** (713) 527-8711
USA

Contact Person: Dr. Joseph L. Goldman, Technical Director. **Officers or Principals:** Dr. Joseph L. Goldman, Technical Director ($109,352); Daniel J. Blaxsom, President ($0); Joseph T. Blaxsom, Director ($0).
Mission or Interest: Research and computer mathematical modeling to generate data and projections on environmental problems, disseminate technical results, and offer solutions.
Accomplishments: In the fiscal year ending June 1994, the Center spent $208,387 on its programs. The largest program, with expenditures of $123,127, was mathematical modeling. $77,375 to conduct research on environmental problems. $7,885 to disseminate the results of the research.
Net Revenue: FY ending 6/94 $120,362 **Net Expenses:** $290,269 72%/28%/0% **Net Assets:** $130,320
Tax Status: 501(c)(3)
Board of Directors or Trustees: N. Dexaun Boudreaux, John Spaulding, Peg Morrison John, Robert Maurice, R.M. Tooley, Mary Yturria.
Other Information: The Center received $93,818, or 78% of revenue, from contract services provided. $11,621, or 10%, from capital gains on the sale of securities. $7,974, or 7%, from dividends and interest from securities. $5,750, or 5%, from gifts and grants awarded by foundations, businesses, and individuals. The remaining revenue came from other miscellaneous sources. During the fiscal year the Center sold off various Merrill Lynch stock and bond funds. At the end of the year, the securities held were in more 'socially aware' funds. All securities held were in the New Alternatives Fund, Pax World Fund, Crescent Fund, and SBA Bonds.

International Chemical Workers Union (ICWU)

1655 W. Market St.
Akron, OH 44313   **Phone:** (216) 867-2444
USA   **Fax:**   (216) 867-0544

Contact Person: Frank D. Martino, President
Mission or Interest: Union representing workers in the chemical industry. Member of the AFL-CIO.
Accomplishments: Approximately 65,000 members.
Net Revenue: 1993 est. $35,000 **Tax Status:** 501(c)(5)
Periodicals: *Chemical Worker* (monthly newsletter).
Other Information: In the year between July 1993 and June 1994, the Union received $3,319,000 from the U.S. Department of Health and Human Services' Superfund Worker Training program.

International Foundation for Ethical Research

53 W. Jackson Blvd., Suite 1552
Chicago, IL 60604   **Phone:** (312) 427-6065
USA

Contact Person: Mary Margaret Cunniff, President.
Officers or Principals: Thomas Moore, Vice President/Secretary ($0); Linda Petty, Treasurer ($0).
Mission or Interest: To increase public awareness about alternatives to using animals in medical research.
Accomplishments: In 1994 the Foundation spent $73,284 on its programs. This included $48,118 in grants to other organizations.
Net Revenue: 1994 $104,909 **Net Expenses:** $106,924 69%/31%/1% **Net Assets:** $65,672
Tax Status: 501(c)(3)
Board of Directors or Trustees: Ann McGivern.
Other Information: Affiliated with the 501(c)(3) National Anti-Vivisection Society at the same address. The Foundation received $103,561, or 99% of revenue, from direct and indirect public support in the form of gifts and grants awarded by foundations, affiliates, businesses, and individuals. (These grants included $100,000 from the National Anti-Vivisection Society). $1,348, or 1%, from dividends and interest from securities.

International Gay and Lesbian Human Rights Commission

1360 Mission St., Suite 200
San Francisco, CA 94103   **Phone:**   (415) 255-8680
USA   **Fax:**   (415) 255-8662

Contact Person: Julie Dorf, Executive Director.
Officers or Principals: Julie Dorf, Executive Director ($23,333); Russ Gage, Program Director ($13,440)
Mission or Interest: Research and documentation of human rights abuses committed against homosexuals and people with AIDS.
Accomplishments: In 1995 Executive Director Julie Dorf attended the Fourth World Conference on Women in Beijing. In the fiscal year ending September 1993, the Commission spent $120,925 on its projects. The largest program, with expenditures of $52,456, was the Emergency Response Network and other quickly mobilized educational activities. $34,971 was spent on research and documentation. $27,988 was spent on a mission to the former Soviet Union with Congressman Barney Frank (D-MA) to visit Russian homosexual activists, Amnesty International, and governmental bodies. $5,510 was awarded in grants to other organizations.
Net Revenue: FY ending 9/93 $148,157   **Net Expenses:** $147,403 82%/8%/10%   **Net Assets:** $4,041
Tax Status: 501(c)(3)
Board of Directors or Trustees: Laurie Coburn, Joe Collins, Charlie Fernandez, Tinku Ishtiaq, Cary Alan Johnson (Amnesty International), Paul O'Dwyer, Augustus Nasmith, Jeff O'Malley, Ann Rosenfield, Michael Shriver.
Other Information: The Commission received $116,650, or 79% of revenue, from gifts and grants awarded by foundations, businesses, and individuals. (These included $25,000 from the Joyce Mertz-Gilmore Foundation, and $1,000 from the Vanguard Public Foundation.) $28,842, or 19%, from fees collected for the Russian mission. $2,464, or 2%, from fees for documentation services. The remaining revenue came from interest on savings and temporary cash investments.

International Ladies' Garment Workers' Union (ILGWU)

1710 Broadway
New York, NY 10019   **Phone:**   (212) 265-7000
USA

Contact Person: Jay Mazur, President.   **Officers or Principals:** Sidney Gerstein, Manager ($67,983); Joseph Fisher, Manager ($65,136); Anthony Sciuto, Manager ($64,546).
Mission or Interest: Union representing approximately 150,000 members. Member of the AFL-CIO.
Net Revenue: 1994 $32,292,828   **Net Expenses:** $37,792,137   **Net Assets:** $49,307,095
Tax Status: 501(c)(5)
Periodicals: *Justice* (eight times a year newsletter).
Other Information: ILGWU recently merged with the Amalgamated Clothing and Textile Workers Union to form the Union of Needle Trades, Industrial and Textile Employees (UNITE). The Union received $19,184,126, or 59% of revenue, from membership dues. $6,878,047, or 21%, from administrative fees for managing benefit funds. $2,746,899, or 9%, from affiliated organizations for administrative support. $2,284,714, or 7%, from dividends and interest from securities. $811,274, or 3%, from rental income. The remaining revenue came from damages paid by employers for contract violations, the sale of union labels, interest on savings and temporary cash investments, and other miscellaneous sources.

International League for Human Rights

432 Park Ave., S., Suite 1103
New York, NY 10016   **Phone:**   (212) 684-1221
USA

Contact Person: Felice Gaer, Executive Director.   **Officers or Principals:** Felice Gaer, Executive Director ($32,897); Leo Nevas, President ($0); Dorothy Hibbert, Secretary ($0); Richard Maass, Treasurer; Jerome Shestack, Chairman.
Mission or Interest: Supports public interest in and adherence to international human rights. "When we receive complaints alleging violations of international human rights around the world, we investigate them. This may consist of commissioning researchers, appointing observers, or preparing and/or publishing educational reports, or discussing and/or submitting these reports or other information to relevant authorities to inform them about the situation." Supports the strengthening of human rights through the United Nations.
Net Revenue: 1990 $203,287   **Net Expenses:** $202,952 71%/15%/14%   **Net Assets:** $19,166
Tax Status: 501(c)(3)
Other Information: The League received $192,868, or 95% of revenue, from gifts and grants awarded by foundations, businesses, and individuals. $8,225, or 5%, from the cancellation of a lease on office equipment. $1,257, or 1%, from the sale of publications. (In 1993 the League received $1,000 from the Barbra Streisand Foundation.)

International Longshoremen's and Warehousemen's Union (ILWU)

1188 Franklin St.
San Francisco, CA 94109   **Phone:**   (415) 775-0533
USA

Contact Person: David Arian, President.
Officers or Principals: Brian McWilliams, President ($75,072); Thomas Trask, Vice President, Hawaii ($63,034); David Arian, President ($54,495); Leon Harris, Joe Ibarra, Secretaries/Treasurers; Richard Austin, Vice President.
Mission or Interest: "To organize unorganized workers into the union."

Accomplishments: Approximately 50,000 members, five area offices, and 62 area locals.
Net Revenue: 1994 $2,853,800 **Net Expenses:** $3,114,826 **Net Assets:** $256,366
Tax Status: 501(c)(5)
Periodicals: *Dispatcher* (monthly newsletter, special edition for Hawaiian members).
Other Information: A member of the AFL-CIO. The ILWU paid the AFL-CIO $185,336 in dues. The Union received $2,818,665, or 98% of gross revenue, from membership dues. $28,625, or 1%, from newsletter subscriptions. The remaining revenue came from interest on savings and temporary cash investments, dividends and interest from securities, and other miscellaneous sources. The Union lost $11,033 on the sale of securities.

International Physicians for the Prevention of Nuclear War (IPPNW)
126 Rogers St.
Cambridge, MA 02142   **Phone:**   (617) 868-5050   **E-Mail:** lforrow@igc.apc.org
USA   **Fax:**   (617) 868-2460

Contact Person: Lynn Martin, Public Affairs.   **Officers or Principals:** Barry Levy, Executive Director ($114,004); Linda Irven, Director of Finance ($58,573); Bastiaan Bruijne, Program Manager ($57,890); Lachlan Forrow, M.D., CEO.
Mission or Interest: "To focus international attention on the medical and environmental consequences of nuclear war."
Accomplishments: In the fiscal year ending June 1994 the IPPNW spent $1,082,140 on its programs.
Net Revenue: FY ending 6/94 $1,209,327 **Net Expenses:** $1,795,480 60%/26%/14% **Net Assets:** $987,047
Citations: 67:126   **Tax Status:** 501(c)(3)
Board of Directors or Trustees: Hikmat Ajjuri, M.D. (U.K.), Aurora Bilbao, M.D. (Spain), Fred Bukachi, M.D. (Kenya), Prof. Ulrich Gottstein, M.D. (Germany), Jans Fromow Guerra (Mexico), Kurt Hanevik (Norway), Ira Helfand, M.D. (U.S.A.), Ann Marie Janson, M.D. (Sweden), Antonio Jarquin, M.D. (Nicaragua), Ernesto Kahan, M.D. (Israel), Wout J. Klein Haneveld, M.D. (The Netherlands), Acad. Sergei Kolesnikov (Russia), M.A. Majed, M.D. (Bangladesh).
Periodicals: *IPPNW Report* (newsletter).
Other Information: Founded in 1980. The IPPNW received $1,068,319, or 88% of revenue, from gifts and grants awarded by foundations, businesses, and individuals. (In 1995 the organization received $18,100 from the Rockefeller Foundation.) $55,017, or 5%, from the sale of assets. $44,803, or 4%, from interest on savings and temporary cash investments. $30,155, or 2%, from other investment income. The remaining revenue came from other miscellaneous sources.

International Publishers Co.
239 West 23rd St., Fifth Floor
New York, NY 10011   **Phone:**   (212) 366-9816
USA   **Fax:**   (212) 366-9820

Contact Person: Betty Smith, President.
Mission or Interest: Publishes "The Marxist Classics," books on labor, black studies, biography, philosophy, occasional literary criticism, and fiction.
Accomplishments: Continuously publishing since 1924. About 200 titles in print. Publishers of the 50-volume set, Collected Works of Karl Marx and Frederick Engels.
Tax Status: For profit. **Annual Report:** No. **Employees:** 4

International Rivers Network
1847 Berkeley Way
Berkeley, CA 94703   **Phone:**   (510) 848-1008   **E-Mail:** irn@igc.apc.org
USA

Mission or Interest: Third World development with an emphasis on eliminating the influence of the World Bank and International Monetary Fund. Publishes *Bank Check*.
Accomplishments: Operates the "50 Years is Enough" project that seeks the reformation of the World Bank (see separate listing).
Periodicals: *Bank Check* (quarterly newsletter).

International Society for Animal Rights (ISAR)
421 S. State St.
Clarks Summit, PA 18411   **Phone:**   (717) 586-2200   **E-Mail:** isar@aol.com
USA   **Fax:**   (717) 586-9580

Contact Person: Anthony McHugh, Administrator.   **Officers or Principals:** Helen E. Jones, President ($73,350); Susan Altieri, Secretary/Treasurer ($27,667); Rev. Alvin Van Pelt Hart, Vice President ($0).
Mission or Interest: To expose and prevent the exploitation and abuse of animals. They seek to establish animal rights as a recognized philosophy and goal rather than promoting humane treatment, which they feel is too limited.
Accomplishments: A Harvard University Office of Government and Community Affairs study of the animal rights movement in 1982 found that "abolitionists, such as the Society for Animal Rights...constitute a minority within the movement. They are however the most diligent, tactical and clear thinking. They use the law, publications and education to work for their ultimate goal - abolishing vivisection, hunting, and other 'animal abuse.' The Society for Animal Rights is probably the most 'hard core' of all anti-vivisection groups. Its approach is low key and professional, but its goals would be considered extreme by many." ISAR uses this quote in their promotional materials and adds, "Striving to end injustice has often been considered extreme." ISAR requested that members clip classified ads that offered animals for sale. They then turned these ads over to the IRS Investigations Division suggesting that the IRS check to see if these people had reported the sale of these animals as income. Led the fight against the Alaskan Iditarod dog race.

Net Revenue: 1994 $374,942 **Net Expenses:** $398,808 80%/18%/3% **Net Assets:** $433,941
Products or Services: Homeless Animals Day and other candlelight vigils. Brochures, monographs, and other publications. Peach Awards for people who rescue animals. Lemon Awards for ads that depict animals in demeaning ways.
Tax Status: 501(c)(3) **Annual Report:** Yes. **Employees:** 6 full time, 4 part time.
Board of Directors or Trustees: Erika Holzer, Esq., Prof. Henry Mark Holzer, Carol Michael-Wade.
Periodicals: *ISAR Report* (quarterly newsletter).
Other Information: ISAR was incorporated in 1959 and they were the first organization to include "Animal Rights" in their name. The Society received $292,489, or 78% of revenue, from gifts and grants awarded by foundations, businesses, and individuals. $64,560, or 17%, from membership dues. $5,768, or 2%, from interest on savings and temporary cash investments. $5,131, or 1%, from dividends and interest on savings and temporary cash investments. The remaining revenue came from rental income, royalties, the sale of assets, and other miscellaneous sources.

International Union of Bricklayers and Allied Craftsmen

815 15th St., N.W.
Washington, DC 20005   **Phone:**   (202) 783-3788
USA

Contact Person: John T. Joyce, President.   **Officers or Principals:** John T. Joyce, President ($166,958); L. Gerald Carlisle, Secretary/Treasurer ($154,582); John J. Flynn, Executive Vice President ($142,206); Thomas J. Uzzalino, Executive Vice President ($142,206); Frank Stupar, Executive Vice President ($139,128).
Mission or Interest: "To organize all workers for the economic, moral and social advancement of their conditions and status." Affiliated with the AFL-CIO.
Accomplishments: The Union represents approximately 106,000 members. It awarded $305,911 in grants and scholarships.
Net Revenue: 1994 $23,930,132 ($1,188,022, or 5%, from government grants) **Net Expenses:** $20,797,145
Net Assets: $12,297,111
Tax Status: 501(c)(5)
Periodicals: *Chalkline* (monthly newsletter).
Other Information: The Union paid $947,440 in per capita dues to the AFL-CIO. The Union received $19,882,622, or 83% of revenue, from membership dues. $2,652,352, or 11%, from reimbursements for training and educational services. $1,188,022, or 5%, from government grants. The remaining revenue came from rental income, interest on savings and temporary cash investments, the sale of inventory, dividends and interest from securities, and other miscellaneous income.

International Union of Operating Engineers (IUOE)

1125 17th St., N.W.
Washington, DC 20036   **Phone:**   (202) 429-9100
USA   **Fax:**   (202) 429-0316

Contact Person: Frank Hanley, President.   **Officers or Principals:** Frank Hanley, President ($210,512); N. Budd Coutts, Secretary/Treasurer ($152,812); Vincent J. Giblin, Vice President ($64,414).
Mission or Interest: Union representing approximately 360,000 members. "To organize all workers for the economic moral and social advancement of their condition." Affiliated with the AFL-CIO.
Accomplishments: In 1994 the Union received $427,896 in voluntary political contributions from members, and made $441,225 in political contributions. The Union paid $133,060 in strike benefits to local unions, and $1,467,800 in payments to the AFL-CIO.
Net Revenue: 1994 $39,242,112 ($5,472,016, or 14%, from government grants) **Net Expenses:** $28,197,683
Net Assets: $104,319,332
Tax Status: 501(c)(5)
Board of Directors or Trustees: Gerald Ellis, James DeJuliis, Gary Kroeker, Jan Pelroy, James Gardner.
Periodicals: *International Operating Engineer* (bimonthly newsletter).
Other Information: The Union received $26,071,782, or 66% of revenue, from membership dues. $6,215,816, or 16%, from dividends and interest from securities. $5,472,016, or 14%, from government grants. (These included $2,532,000 from the U.S. Department of Health and Human Services' Superfund Worker Training Program.) $469,302, or 1%, from rental income. $461,772, or 1%, from interest on savings and temporary cash investments. $427,896, or 1%, from voluntary political contributions. The remaining revenue came from the sale of inventory, program service fees, and other miscellaneous sources.

International Union, United Automobile, Aerospace and Agricultural Implement Workers of America (UAW)

8000 E. Jefferson
Detroit, MI 48214   **Phone:**   (313) 926-5000
USA   **Fax:**   (313) 823-6016

Officers or Principals: Stephe Yokich, President.
Mission or Interest: Union representing approximately 1,300,000 members. Affiliated with the AFL-CIO.
Tax Status: 501(c)(5)
Periodicals: *Ammo* (monthly magazine), *Skill* (quarterly newsletter), and *Solidarity* (ten times a year newsletter).
Other Information: The UAW, Steelworkers, and Machinists have agreed to merge before the year 2000 to form the largest union within the AFL-CIO. In the year between July 1993 and June 1994, the UAW received $671,000 from the U.S. Department of Health and Human Services' Superfund Worker Training program.

International Women's Health Coalition

24 E. 21st St., 5th Floor
New York, NY 10010   **Phone:**   (212) 979-8500
USA

Contact Person: Susan Wood, Senior Program Officer.   **Mission or Interest:** Working to bridge the gap between feminist health advocates and mainstream national and international groups. Works in Latin America.
Tax Status: 501(c)(3)
Other Information: In 1994 the Coalition received $35,000 from the Compton Foundation, $30,000 from the General Service Foundation, and $25,000 from the Jessie Smith Noyes Foundation.

International Women's Tribune Centre (IWTC)

777 United Nations Plaza
New York, NY 10017   **Phone:**   (212) 687-8633
USA

Contact Person: Anne Walker, Executive Director.
Officers or Principals: Anne Walker, Executive Director ($61,303); Vickie Semler, Associate Director ($54,148); Alice Quinn, Finance Coordinator ($50,904); Cecilia Lotse, President; Elizabeth Calvin, Treasurer; Pamela Fraser-Abder, Secretary.
Mission or Interest: "To facilitate the exchange of skills, experiences and ideas among groups working to promote the more active and equitable role of women in a development process which is participatory and inclusive of all people. This process is regarded as a prerequisite to sustainable development and essential to the emergence of a more humane and just society in which women and men participate equally."
Accomplishments: In the fiscal year ending September 1995, the Centre spent $1,056,211 on its programs. The largest program, with expenditures of $373,829, was planning, participation, networking, and follow-up activities associated with the United Nation's Fourth World Conference in Beijing and the Non-Governmental Organizations forum held in conjunction. (The previous year the Centre spent $134,331 planning for the event.) $288,982 was spent on "Women, Ink.", "a new initiative to market and distribute women and development resource materials worldwide." $257,477 was spent on communication support, "linking together individuals and groups working on similar issues; compiling directories of organizations by region and/or issues; preparing specialized bibliographies around the specific subject areas; and, maintaining a project oriented resource centre with an emphasis on training manuals, audio-visuals case studies and an extensive collection of women and development periodicals." Other programs included technical assistance and training.
Net Revenue: FY ending 9/95 $1,394,028 ($867,677, or 62%, from government grants)
Net Expenses: $1,207,220 87%/11%/2% **Net Assets:** $634,650 **Citations:** 1:240
Tax Status: 501(c)(3)
Board of Directors or Trustees: Sushma Kapoor (UNIFEM), Bonnie Kettel (Environmental Studies, York University, Canada), Barbara McLean (Presbyterian Church, Canada), Shirley Malcolm (American Association for the Advancement of Science), Hilda Paqui (Uganda), Mallika Vajrathon (Principal Adviser to the Secretary General, U.N. Fourth World Conference on Women).
Periodicals: *Tribune* (quarterly journal).
Other Information: The Centre received $867,677, or 62% of revenue, from government grants. (These grants were; $365,408 from the Swedish Ministry of Foreign Affairs, $203,972 from the Swedish International Development Authority, $96,603 from the Finland Ministry of Foreign Affairs, $65,486 from the Canadian International Development Agency, $51,350 from the Denmark Ministry of Foreign Affairs, $47,708 from the Royal Norwegian Ministry of Foreign Affairs, and $27,150 from the U.S. Agency for International Development.) $355,730, or 26%, from gifts and grants awarded by foundations, businesses, and individuals. (These included $229,433 from UNIFEM, $50,000 from the Ford Foundation, $30,000 from the United Methodist Church, $25,000 from the Shaler Adams Foundation, $14,247 from the World association for Christian Communications, $3,500 from the Joslow Foundation, and $2,000 from the Stanley Foundation.) $141,172 net, or 10%, from the sale of inventory. $26,359, or 2%, from program services, including fees for the advocacy facility. The remaining revenue came from interest on savings and temporary cash investments.

Irish National Caucus Foundation

413 E. Capitol St., S.E.
Washington, DC 20003   **Phone:**   (202) 544-0568
USA   **Fax:**   (202) 543-2491

Contact Person: Sean McManus, President.
Officers or Principals: Sean McManus, President ($27,128); James McDonald, Director ($0); Daniel Sheehy, Director ($0).
Mission or Interest: "To inform Irish Americans on issues affecting Ireland and its citizens and their efforts to gain peace." Seeks a lasting peace in Ireland, without English governance. Generally supportive of the Irish Republican Army (IRA).
Accomplishments: Approximately 200,000 members. Initiated the "MacBride Principles" for U.S. businesses operating in Northern Ireland. In the fiscal year ending June 1994 the Foundation spent $75,559 on its programs.
Net Revenue: FY ending 6/94 $147,243 **Net Expenses:** $143,627 53%/28%/19% **Net Assets:** (-$104,299)
Tax Status: 501(c)(3)
Periodicals: *Irish Lobby* (newsletter).
Other Information: Founded in 1974. Affiliated with the 501(c)(4) lobbying Irish National Caucus at the same address. The Foundation received $147,243, or 100% of revenue, from gifts and grants awarded by foundations, businesses, and individuals.

J. Roderick MacArthur Foundation

9333 N. Milwaukee Ave.
Niles, IL 60714   **Phone:**   (708) 966-0143
USA

Contact Person: Marylou Bane, Assistant Treasurer.   **Officers or Principals:** Locke E. Bowman, Legal Director ($90,410); Kathleen M. Banar, Attorney ($65,223); Marylou Bane, Assistant Treasurer ($39,108); Gregoire MacArthur, Chairman; Solange D. MacArthur, Vice Chair; James D. Liggett, President; John R. MacArthur, Secretary/Treasurer.
Mission or Interest: Grant-making philanthropy that focuses on civil rights and freedom of the press issues. Also conducts legal services through its MacArthur Justice Center "that fights for human rights and social justice through litigation."
Accomplishments: In the abbreviated fiscal year running from February 1994 to December 1994, the Foundation spent $341,181 on its Justice Center located at the University of Chicago Law School. The Justice Center provides free representation to "indigent defendants facing execution or lengthy incarceration, and in cases involving constitutional or significant issues in the field of criminal justice." $194,400 was spent on the Death Penalty Information Center, that provides "information about capital punishment to the media, so as to better inform public opinion." $487,775 was awarded in grants. The recipients included: $300,000 for Article 19 (an English group focusing on freedom of expression), $90,000 for Rutgers' Walt Whitman Center for Culture and Politics, $27,775 for the Committee to Protect Journalists, and $20,000 each for the Center for Media Education, and the Harper's Magazine Foundation for "a journalistic investigation on the occupation of Haiti by the U.S. Military."
Net Revenue: FY from 2/94 through 12/94 $1,326,285 **Net Expenses:** $1,342,226 **Net Assets:** $31,297,308
Tax Status: 501(c)(3)
Other Information: The Foundation received $752,463, or 54% of total revenue, from dividends and interest from securities. $518,500, or 37%, from gifts and grants awarded by foundations, businesses, and individuals. $86,512, or 6%, from interest on savings and temporary cash investments. The remaining revenue came from other miscellaneous sources. The Foundation lost $56,632 on the sale of securities. The Foundation held $16,448,921, or 53% of assets, in corporate stock. $10,901,482, or 35%, in government obligations.

James C. Penney Foundation

1633 Broadway, 39th Floor
New York, NY 10019   **Phone:**   (212) 830-7490
USA

Mission or Interest: A family foundation established by James Cash Penney and Caroline Autenrieth Penney. Penney was the founder of J.C. Penney department stores. The Foundation, however, is not affiliated with the J.C. Penney Company. The Foundation awards grants based on: "Empowering politically and economically disenfranchised people to become more self-reliant and effective in their lives and their communities...Supporting innovative efforts to address the underlying causes of problems in our society...Influencing public opinion and policy to promote a more just, equitable, and sustainable society...Understanding and promoting respect for an increasingly racially and culturally diverse society."
Accomplishments: In 1994 the Foundation awarded $702,249 in grants. Recipients of the largest grants included: $50,000 each for the Tides Foundation, Penn Center (Sea Island Preservation Project), the Sundra Foundation, East Bay Community Foundation, $25,000 for the Tri-County Youth Services Consortium, and $20,000 each for the Child Care Action Campaign, Coalition for Immigrant and Refugee Rights and Services, Community Farm Alliance, Conservancy, Conservation Law Foundation, Enterprise Foundation, Environmental Careers Organization, Environmental Support Center, Food Research Action Center, Natural Resources Council of Maine, Natural Resources Defense Council, and the Smithsonian Environmental Research Center.
Net Revenue: 1994 $467,839 **Net Expenses:** $936,525 **Net Assets:** $14,556,179
Tax Status: 501(c)(3)
Other Information: The Foundation is a member of the Council on Foundations, New York Regional Association of Grant Makers, Environmental Grant Makers Association, Communitarian Network, Neighborhood Funders Group, and Northern California Grant Makers. The Foundation received $446,753, or 95% of revenue, from dividends and interest from securities. $20,403, or 4%, from capital gains on the sale of securities. The remaining revenue came from interest on savings and temporary cash investments. The Foundation held $10,370,850, or 71% of assets, in corporate stock. $3,099,359, or 21%, in corporate bonds.

Jane Addams Peace Association

777 United Nations Plaza
New York, NY 10017   **Phone:**   (212) 682-8830
USA

Contact Person: Ruth Chalmers, Executive Director.   **Officers or Principals:** Andrea Spencer-Linzie ($22,000), Ruth Chalmers ($21,252), Executive Directors; Dolores Taller, President ($0); Yvonne Logan, First Vice President; Judith Botwin, Second Vice President; Margaret Fisher, Secretary; Sylvia Lundt, Treasurer.
Mission or Interest: Promotes world peace and conflict resolution. Also works against racism, sexism, and militarism.
Accomplishments: In 1994 the Association spent $227,983 on its programs. The largest program, with expenditures of $122,276, was national education on subjects pertaining to its mission. $80,852 was spent on international programs, including educational materials, interns, and conferences. $24,855 was spent on grassroots activities. All three programs included grants made to the Women's International League for Peace and Freedom, a 501(c)(4) affiliate at the same address. Although 501(c)(4), the Association maintains that enough of the League's activities are educational, 26% of expenses, and so qualify for grants.
Net Revenue: 1994 $477,341 **Net Expenses:** $276,205 83%/10%/7% **Net Assets:** $276,205

Products or Services: Publications, conferences, workshops, "Peace Camps," more.
Tax Status: 501(c)(3)
Board of Directors or Trustees: Ione Biggs, Doris Bolef, Betty Burkes, Minnie Hoch, Anne Ivey, Terry Galpin-Plattner, Margaret Shapiro.
Internships: Yes.
Other Information: Affiliated with the 501(c)(4) Women's International League for Peace and Freedom. The Association is named after an American social worker and peace activist who lived from 1860-1935. The Association received $496,095 from gifts and grants awarded by foundations, companies and individuals. (These grants included $10,300 from the Women's International League for Peace and Freedom.) $17,850 from dividends and interest on securities, $4,240 from interest on savings and temporary cash investments, and $1,699 from the sale of literature. These revenues were offset by the net losses from rental properties, $10,572, and the sale of securities and other assets, $31,971.

Japanese American Citizens League
926 E. 8th Ave.
Spokane, WA 99202   **Phone:**   (509) 489-8940
USA

Contact Person: Susie Uyeno, Treasurer.
Officers or Principals: Doug Heyamoto, President ($0); Tina Weinberger, Secretary ($0).
Mission or Interest: Promotes civil rights, community awareness, and responsible treatment for Japanese-American citizens.
Accomplishments: Instrumental in seeking reparations for Japanese Americans interred during World War II. In 1994 the League spent $23,024 on its programs. The largest program, with expenditures of $13,058, was the defense fund to promote civil rights. $7,466 was spent on community services to promote cultural identity. $2,500 was spent on grants and scholarships.
Net Revenue: 1994 $28,471 **Net Expenses:** $26,186 88%/9%/3% **Net Assets:** $186,860
Tax Status: 501(c)(3)
Other Information: The League received $12,526, or 39% of total revenue, from gifts and grants awarded by foundations, businesses, and individuals. $10,548, or 33%, from dividends and securities. $8,430 net, or 26%, from special fund raising events. The remaining revenue came from interest on savings and temporary cash investments. The League lost $3,294 on the sale of securities.

Jessie Smith Noyes Foundation
6 E. 39th St., 12th Floor
New York, NY 10016   **Phone:**   (212) 684-6577   **E-Mail:** noyes@igc.org
USA   **Fax:**   (212) 689-6549

Contact Person: Stephen Viederman, President.   **Officers or Principals:** Stephen Viederman, President ($146,954); Edward B. Tasch, Treasurer ($78,750); Victor Deluca, Program Officer ($73,643); Joan Gussow, Chair.
Mission or Interest: Grant-making foundation that funds organizations focusing on abortion rights, the environment, and population.
Accomplishments: In 1994 the Foundation awarded $3,283,285 in grants. Recipients of the largest grants included: $40,000 for the Religious Coalition for Reproductive Choice, $35,000 each for the Hampshire College Civil Liberties and Public Policy Program (abortion rights), the National Women's Law Center, Women's USA Fund, and the Labor/Community Strategy Center, $30,000 each for the Citizens Clearinghouse for Hazardous Waste, the National Sustainable Agriculture Coordinating Council, ACLU (Reproductive Freedom Project), Center for Reproductive Law and Policy, Ms. Foundation for Women, National Abortion Federation, National Family Planning and Reproductive Health Association, National Latina Health Organization, Women Judges' Fund for Justice, and Women's Legal Defense Fund.
Net Revenue: 1994 $3,228,538 **Net Expenses:** $4,513,601 **Net Assets:** $56,249,213
Tax Status: 501(c)(3)
Board of Directors or Trustees: Dorothy Anderson, Catherine Bedell, Rosemary Bray, Donna Chavis, Donald Collat, Nicholas Jacangelo, Dorothy Muma, Edith Noyes Muma, David Orr, Chad Raphael, Elsa Rios, Ann Wiener.
Other Information: The Foundation received $2,598,432, or 74% of gross revenue, from dividends and interest from securities. $732,488, or 21%, from capital gains on the sale of securities. $154,694, or 4%, from interest on savings and temporary cash investments. $21,000, or 1%, from gifts. The remaining revenue came from rental income. The Foundation lost $282,086 on other investments. The Foundations assets were held primarily in corporate stock, $21,701,025 or 39% of total assets, $15,967,468 or 28%, in government securities. $11,472,160, or 20%, from corporate bonds.

Jewish Fund for Justice
35 W. 44th St.
New York, NY 10036   **Phone:**   (212) 213-2113
USA

Contact Person: Amy Willis, Director of Operations.   **Officers or Principals:** Marlene Provizer, Executive Director ($80,276); Beth Edelson, Director of Development ($63,654); Jeannie Appleman, Program Officer ($42,500).
Mission or Interest: "To educate the Jewish community about poverty and its consequences, and to emphasize the Jewish community's stake in promoting a socially and economically just society."
Accomplishments: In the fiscal year ending June 1995, the Fund spent $745,506 on its programs and awarded $482,000 in grants to 65 groups combating poverty in 25 states and the District of Columbia. Provides technical and fund-raising assistance to grantees. "Synagogue Challenge Program" that matches funds raised by synagogues for local 'social justice' projects.

Net Revenue: FY ending 6/95 $1,004,454 **Net Expenses:** $957,920 78%/6%/16% **Net Assets:** $522,434
Citations: 1:240
Tax Status: 501(c)(3)   **Periodicals:** Semi-annual newsletter.
Other Information: The Fund received $927,545, or 92% of revenue, from gifts and grants awarded by foundations, businesses, affiliates, and individuals. (These grants included $1,000 from the Hauser Foundation.) $57,500, or 6%, from the sale of a Lichtenstein lithograph. $16,679, or 2%, from interest on savings and temporary cash investments. The remaining revenue came from other miscellaneous sources.

Jewish Peace Lobby
8604 2nd Ave., Suite 317
Silver Spring, MD 20910   **Phone:** (301) 589-8764
USA

Contact Person: Jerome Segal, President.
Officers or Principals: Jerome Segal, President ($26,000); Naomi Nim, Vice President ($0); Amy Weinberg, Treasurer ($0).
Mission or Interest: Jewish organization advocating peace in the Middle East with Israel's right to secure borders and Palestine's right to self-determination and statehood. Actively lobbied congress to pursue these goals.
Accomplishments: In 1994 the Lobby spent $53,266 on its programs. The largest program, with expenditures of $19,850, was the "Rabbi's Petition on Israeli-Palestinian Cooperation" which collected 800 signatures and was sent to President Clinton.
Net Revenue: 1994 $140,256 **Net Expenses:** $126,190 42%/26%/32% **Net Assets:** $13,086
Tax Status: 501(c)(4)
Other Information: The Lobby received $118,190, or 84% of revenue, from membership dues. $21,390, or 15%, from gifts and grants awarded by foundations, businesses, and individuals. The remaining revenue came from interest on savings and temporary cash investments, and a tax refund.

Jobs With Peace, Milwuakee
750 North 18th St.
Milwaukee, WI 53233   **Phone:** (414) 933-6010
USA

Contact Person: Ann Wilson, President.   **Officers or Principals:** Ann Wilson, President ($0).
Mission or Interest: Public education and training on issues regarding employment and defense. Opposed to high military spending and working to convert defense industry jobs into peace-time jobs.
Accomplishments: In 1993 the organization spent $18,788 on their programs.
Net Revenue: 1993 $30,347 **Net Expenses:** $26,532 71%/29%/0% **Net Assets:** $7,917
Tax Status: 501(c)(3)
Board of Directors or Trustees: Nathan Conyers, Peter Earle, Mark Foreman, Kathleen Hart, Gycell Humphrey, Zachary Johnson, Joseph Jones, Roger Quindel, Ann Rovito, Dan Ulrich, Bruce Ware, Steve Watrous, Dorothy Woods, Ellen Zimmermann.
Other Information: The organization received $13,802, or 45% of revenue, from direct and indirect public support such as grants from individuals, foundations and affiliates. (These grants included $1,000 from the Haymarket People's Fund.) $25,251, or 83%, from "miscellaneous" sources. $5,830, or 20%, from membership dues. These revenues were offset by a net loss of $14,574, or 48%, of revenue, from a bingo game that was intended to raise funds.

Jobs With Peace Educational Fund
38 Chauncey St., Suite 812
Boston, MA 02111   **Phone:** (617) 338-5783
USA

Contact Person: Larry Locke, Chair.   **Officers or Principals:** Ann Wilson, Executive Director ($34,500); Roger Newell, Secretary ($0); Bruce Parry, Treasurer ($0); Barbara Smith, Vice Chair.
Mission or Interest: Research and analysis on the effects of federal budget and tax policies, particularly as they apply to defense spending. Provides technical assistance to other organizations. Advocates the redirection of resources to social programs. Uses grassroots methods to place referendums on state and local ballots calling for a redirection of resources.
Accomplishments: Approximately 16,000 members. Chapters in nine cities nationwide. Former Massachusetts Governor and Presidential candidate Michael Dukakis was once on the Jobs With Peace Advisory Board. In 1992 the Fund spent $376,462 on its programs. Promoted the "Build Homes not Bombs" program that works with housing activists and public housing tenants.
Net Revenue: 1992 $520,450 **Net Expenses:** $526,277 72%/10%/18% **Net Assets:** $3,447
Products or Services: High school curriculum program "Books not Bombs."
Tax Status: 501(c)(3) **Employees:** 7
Board of Directors or Trustees: Cecilia Nnadozie, Greg Ward.
Periodicals: *Jobs With Peace Campaign Report* (biannual).
Other Information: The Fund received $518,900, or 99.7% of revenue, from gifts and grants awarded by foundations, businesses, and individuals. The remaining revenue came from the sale of publications.

John D. and Catherine T. MacArthur Foundation

140 S. Dearborn St., Suite 1100
Chicago, IL 60603   **Phone:** (312) 726-8000   **E-Mail:** 4answers%macfdn@mcimail.com
USA   **Fax:** (312) 917-0330

Contact Person: Woodward A. Wickham, Vice President, Public Affairs.   **Officers or Principals:** Adele Smith Simmons, President; Elizabeth J. McCormick, Chair; Philip M. Grace, Treasurer; Nancy Best Ewing, Secretary; Victor Rabinowitch, Senior Vice President; John Hurkey, Associate Vice President; Carmen Barroso, Director, Population Program; Kennette Benedict, Director, Peace and International Cooperation; Ray Boyer, Director, Communications; Richard J. Kaplan, Director, Grants Management; William F. Lowry, Director, Human Resources; Dan M. Martin, Director, World Environment and Resources; Rebecca Riley, Director, Health; Camille E. Seamans, Director, Human Resources; Peter Gerber, Director, Education.
Mission or Interest: Grant-making foundation that focuses on General Programs "which undertake special initiatives and supports projects that promote diversity in the media", Health Programs, MacArthur Fellows programs (Genius Grants) "which awards fellowships to exceptionally creative individuals, regardless of field of endeavor", Programs on Peace and International Cooperation, Population Programs "which address complex issues related to population, reproductive rights, and women's reproductive health", and the World Environment and Resources Program.
Accomplishments: In 1993 the Foundation awarded $151,164,925 in grants. Approximately 24% went to environmental groups, and 21% to international programs. Some of the recipients of the largest grants included (these grants were usually disbursed over several years, and not in one lump-sum payment): $13,500,000 for the Energy Foundation, $1,500,000 for Human Rights Watch, $1,300,000 for the Institute for East-West Studies, $1,000,000 for National Public Radio, $900,000 for the Population Council, $800,000 for the Environmental Defense Council, $750,000 each for the Carter Center, and the Global Fund for Women, $650,000 for the Institute for Policy Studies, $600,000 for the Synergos Institute, $525,000 each for Catholics for a Free Choice, and the Women's Self-Employment Project, $500,000 each for the Center for Investigative Reporting, Ms. Foundation for Women, NAACP Legal Defense and Educational Fund, the New Press, and the Peace Development Fund, $450,000 for the Lawyers Committee for Human Rights, $325,000 for Student Pugwash, and $300,000 each for the ACLU, Women's Environment and Development Organization, the Center for National Security Studies, Center for Population Options, and the Physicians for Human Rights.
Net Assets: $3,098,244,000
Tax Status: 501(c)(3)   **Annual Report:** Yes.
Board of Directors or Trustees: John Edward Corbally, Robert Ewing (Retirement Research Found.), William Foege M.D., James Merle Furman (National Task Force on Higher Education and the Public Interest), Alan Montgomery Hallene, Ralph Hamilton, Paul Harvey (radio commentator), John Paul Holdren (Lawrence Livermore Labs), Shirley Mount Hufstedler (Carnegie Endowment for Intl. Peace), Margaret Ellerbe Mahoney (Alliance Aging Research), George Ranney Jr., Dr. Jonas Edward Salk, Dale Smith, Thomas Theobald.
Other Information: The Foundation was endowed by John D. MacArthur, who died in 1978. MacArthur made his fortune through insurance and real estate.

John Merck Fund

11 Beacon St., Suite 1230
Boston, MA 02108   **Phone:** (617) 723-2932
USA   **Fax:** (617) 523-6029

Contact Person: Ruth Hennig, Administrator.
Officers or Principals: Francis Whiting Hatch, Jr., Chairman; Huyler C. Held, Treasurer.
Mission or Interest: Philanthropy awarding grants for environmental, abortion rights, human rights, and population control organizations.
Accomplishments: In 1993 the Fund awarded $5,408,296 in grants. Recipients included; $166,000 for the National Women's Law Center, $120,000 for the Carnegie Institution of Washington, $100,000 each for the Center for Reproductive Law and Policy, and Lawyers Committee for Human Rights, $90,000 for the National Black Women's Health Project, $75,000 each for the Conservation Law Foundation, Planned Parenthood Federation, and the Population Council, $65,000 for the Human Rights Watch, $60,000 each for the National Abortion and Reproductive Rights Action League, National Council of Negro Women, Physicians for Human Rights, and the Sierra Club, $50,000 each for the Foundation for International Environmental Law and Development, Advocates for Youth, Centre for Development and Population Activities, Global Fund for Women, International Institute for Energy Conservation, and Tides Foundation, $45,000 for the NOW Legal Defense and Education Fund, and $40,000 for the Fund for Peace.
Net Assets: 1993 $106,711,950
Board of Directors or Trustees: Serena Merck Hatch, Robert Pennoyer (Council on Foreign Relations).
Other Information: Established in 1970.

Journal of Women's History

c/o Department of History, Ballantine Hall
Indiana University
Bloomington, IN 47405
USA

Contact Person: Christie Farnham Pope, President.
Officers or Principals: Christie Farnham Pope, President/Editor ($0); Joan Hoff, Vice President/Editor ($0).
Mission or Interest: Scholarly journal of women's history with a feminist emphasis.

Accomplishments: Spent $29,114 in 1993 to publish and distribute the journal.
Net Revenue: 1993 $34,277 **Net Expenses:** $30,134 97%/3%/0% **Net Assets:** $9,257
Tax Status: 501(c)(3)
Periodicals: *Journal of Women's History.*
Other Information: The Journal received $27,500, or 80% of revenue, from direct and indirect public support in the form of gifts and grants awarded by foundations, companies, and individuals. $6,599, or 19%, from subscriptions. The remaining revenue came from interest on savings and temporary cash investments.

Joyce Foundation
135 S. LaSalle St., Suite 4010
Chicago, IL 60603   **Phone:**   (312) 782-2464
USA

Contact Person: Linda K. Schelinski, Vice President.
Officers or Principals: Deborah Leff, President ($201,000); Joel D. Getzendanner, Vice President/Secretary ($95,832); Linda K. Schelinski, Vice President/Treasurer ($84,408); John T. Anderson, Chairman; Richard K. Donahue, Vice Chairman.
Mission or Interest: Grant-making foundation that focuses on culture, environment and conservation, gun control, education, and economic development.
Accomplishments: In 1994 the Foundation awarded $19,947,493 in grants. Conservation and environmental programs received the most, $5,613,701, followed by $5,341,205 for education, $3,247,876 for economic development, $1,243,043 for gun violence and control, $896,135 for culture, $839,308 for election and campaign reform, then various special projects. The recipients of the largest grants included: four grants totaling $520,000 for the Environmental Defense Fund, three grants totaling $360,023 for Johns Hopkins University (Center for Gun Policy and Research), three grants totaling $324,445 for the Natural Resources Defense Council, two grants totaling $295,000 for the Union of Concerned Scientists, two grants totaling $250,000 for the Environmental Law and Policy Center of the Midwest, two grants totaling $233,941 for Citizens for a Better Environment, two grants totaling $221,875 for Council for Adult and Experiential Learning, two grants totaling $200,000 for the Sierra Club Foundation, $175,000 for the American Federation of Teachers-Chicago Teachers Union, two grants totaling $170,310 for the Center for Rural Affairs, three grants totaling $165,000 for the Environmental and Energy Study Institute, three grants totaling $157,000 for the World Wildlife Fund, $150,000 for the World Resources Institute, Harvard University (Harvard Project on Guns, Violence and Public Health), and League of Women Voters Education Fund, two grants totaling $149,000 for Business and Professional People for the Public Interest, two grants totaling $135,000, and two grants totaling $112,600 for the Alliance to Save Energy. The Foundation also awarded some grants to individuals, such as $124,000 to Sonia Jarvis (Dir., Center for Public Integrity), to "analyze the interplay between race, politics and the media over the last thirty years and to develop ways to communicate that period's most important lessons in order to strengthen ongoing efforts to improve race relations."
Net Revenue: 1994 $65,351,129 **Net Expenses:** $24,115,891 **Net Assets:** $458,397,350
Tax Status: 501(c)(3)
Board of Directors or Trustees: Cushman Bissell Jr., Robert Bottoms (DePauw Univ.), Lewis Butler (California Tomorrow), Carin Clauss (Univ. of WI Law School), Charles Daly (John F. Kennedy Library Found.), Roger Fross, Carlton Guthrie, Marlon Hall, Barack Obama, Paula Wolff (Governors State Univ.).
Other Information: The Foundation received $47,204,161, or 72% of revenue, from capital gains on the sale of assets. $11,845,773, or 18%, from dividends and interest from securities. $4,807,850, or 7%, from various investment partnerships. $1,489,267, or 3%, from interest on savings and temporary cash investments. The Foundation held $259,502,692, or 57% of assets, in corporate stock. $87,384,487, or 19%, in investment partnerships. $43,563,251, or 10%, in corporate bonds.

Joyce Mertz-Gilmore Foundation
218 E. 18th St.
New York, NY 10003   **Phone:**   (212) 475-1137
USA

Contact Person: Robert J. Crane, Vice President of Programs.   **Officers or Principals:** Larry E. Condon, President ($144,000); Robert J. Crane, Vice President ($130,161); Jacqueline Novogratz, Special Projects ($70,750); Charles Bloomstein, Treasurer; Elizabeth B. Gilmore, Secretary; William B. O'Connor, Assistant Secretary.
Mission or Interest: Foundation awarding grants to support culture, the environment, human rights, peace and world security, and civil liberties.
Accomplishments: In 1994 the Foundation awarded $44,901,006 in grants. The recipients of the largest grants included: four grants totaling $605,000 for the Lawyers Committee for Human Rights, three grants totaling $600,000 for Human Rights Watch, three grants totaling $500,000 for the National Center for Lesbian Rights, two grants totaling $485,000 for the Indian Law Resource Center, two grants totaling $460,000 for the Washington Office on Latin America, eight grants totaling $425,500 for the Tides Foundation, six grants totaling $400,000 for the Solar Electric Light Fund, two grants totaling $350,000 each for the Natural Resources Defense Council and Physicians for Human Rights, three grants totaling $335,000 for the Hetrick-Martin Institute, four grants totaling $327,100 for Gay and Lesbian Alliance Against Defamation, $275,000 for the Hopi Foundation, three grants totaling $267,000 for the Astraea Foundation, four grants totaling $260,000 for the ACLU Foundation, two grants totaling $220,000 for the National Gay and Lesbian Task Force, two grants totaling $170,000 for the Union of Concerned Scientists, three grants totaling $160,000 for the International Energy Initiative, $150,000 for the Environmental Defense Fund, $130,000 for the American Association of Blacks in Energy, $100,000 each for the Community Resource Exchange, Conservation Law Foundation and the AIDS Action Foundation.

Net Revenue: 1994 $26,036,872 **Net Expenses:** $24,771,578 **Net Assets:** $63,947,121
Tax Status: 501(c)(3)
Board of Directors or Trustees: Harlan Cleveland (Humphrey Inst. of Public Affairs, Univ. of MN), Hal Harvey (Energy Found.), Denise Nix Thompson (Chemical Community Development), Patricia Ramsey, Franklin Wallin.
Other Information: The Foundation received $21,650,000, or 83% of revenues, from gifts and grants awarded by foundations, businesses, and individuals. $1,706,054, or 7%, from dividends and interest from securities. $1,703,006, or 7%, from capital gains on the sale of securities. The remaining income came from interest on savings and temporary cash investments and rental income. The Foundation held $49,297,461, or 77% of assets, in corporate stocks. $4,487,853, or 7%, in U.S. and state government obligations. $4,059,138, or 6%, in corporate bonds.

Judge David L. Bazelon Center for Mental Health Law

1101 15th St., N.W., Suite 1212
Washington, DC 20005-5002   **Phone:**   (202) 467-5730   **E-Mail:** hn1660@handsnet.org
USA   **Fax:**   (202) 223-0409

Contact Person: Ms. Lee Anderson Carty, Director of Communications.   **Officers or Principals:** Leonard S. Rubenstein, President ($99,553); Lee Anderson Carty, Secretary/Director of Communications ($82,553); Ira Burnim, Legal Director ($78,386); Robert A. Burt, Chairman; Joseph Manes, Christine Koyanagi, Co-Directors of Government Affairs.
Mission or Interest: "The pre-eminent national legal advocate for children and adults with mental disabilities. It has successfully challenged the barriers that face children and adults with mental illness or developmental disabilities, opening up public schools, workplaces, housing and other opportunities for community life...In addition to pursuing test-case litigation and federal policy reform, provides training and technical assistance to legal services offices, protection and advocacy agencies, state ombudsman programs and other advocates for low income individuals and families."
Accomplishments: In the fiscal year ending September 1994, the Center spent $2,413,257 on its programs. The largest program, with expenditures of $1,054,029, was general services, which included public policy analysis, and litigation. Litigation included Clark v. Virginia Board of Examiners which challenged the practice of the state bar asking applicants questions about any counseling received in the last five years, and Taylor v. INS which "addresses employers' responsibility to assure reasonable accommodations" in the case where a supervisor was fired after requesting a less stressful position, "an accommodation often requested by people with depression." The Center was joined in litigation by several affiliates of the ACLU, various Legal Aid Societies, Texas Rural Legal Aid, and the Southern Poverty Law Center. The Center received $238,397 in court-awarded attorneys' fees. $326,092 was spent on the SSI Kids Program, a program to ensure that eligible children receive Supplemental Security Income. "The numbers document our success. In 1991, when the Social Security Administration reported 438,853 child SSI recipients, we estimated that a million children should be eligible. By December 1993, the SSI disability rolls included 720,000 children." The Children's SSI Campaign involved school officials discussing benefits at PTA meetings, and writing articles for parent newsletters. State child welfare agencies made applications available in foster care. Preschool social workers referred potentially eligible children and helped families with the application process. $282,388 was spent on the Childrens' Program which focused on the "problems in state foster care and child mental health systems that lead to children being denied services they needed." Other programs sought to protect the rights of institutionalized elders and children, monitor compliance with the Americans with Disabilities Act and various court decisions, provide technical assistance on legal representation, promote housing programs, and other activities.
Net Revenue: FY ending 9/94 $2,844,034   ($400,112, or 14%, from government grants)   **Net Expenses:** $2,691,438 90%/2%/8% **Net Assets:** $1,663,754 **Citations:** 1:240
Products or Services: Numerous publications, litigation and lobbying. The center spent $140,324 on lobbying, $58,391 on grassroots lobbying and $81,933 on the direct lobbying of legislators. Much of this lobbying revolved around the Clinton administration's health care plan. The Center advocated the full inclusion of mental health care and addiction treatment. Joe Manes and Chris Koyanagi drafted a set of recommendations sent to the White House Task Force on Health Care. The two worked with Tipper Gore, who led the Task Force's mental health work group.
Tax Status: 501(c)(3) **Annual Report:** Yes. **Employees:** 25
Board of Directors or Trustees: Miriam Bazelon Knox, Eileen Bazelon, M.D., James Clements, M.D., Mary Jane England, M.D. (Washington Business Group on Health), Kenneth Fienberg, Howard Goldman, M.D., Susan Halpern (Access Development Fund), Brent Henry, Emily Hoffman (Policy Research, Inc.), C. Lyonel Jones (Legal Aid Society of Cleveland), Prof. Martha Minow (Harvard Law School), Prof. Stephen Morse (Univ. of PA, School of Law), Carlos Perez, John Pickering, David Rothman, Ph.D. (Columbia Univ.), Louise Sagalyn, Jose Santiago, M.D., Prof. Rud Turnbull (Univ. of KS).
Other Information: In 1954, Judge David L. Bazelon, as an appeals court judge, decided the case that for many years set the standard for the insanity defense. His ruling in Durham v. United States said that a defendant is not criminally responsible if his crime was the "product of mental disease or defect." In 1972 another appeals court restricted the standard. The Center was founded in 1972, and was called the Mental Health Law Project until 1993. The Center received $2,157,656, or 76% of revenue, from direct and indirect public support in the form of gifts and grants from foundations, businesses, affiliates, and individuals. $400,112, or 14%, from government grants. These government grants were awarded by Housing and Urban Development, Administration for Aging, Center for Mental Health Services, Substance Abuse and Mental Health Services Agency, and the Department of Justice. $238,397, or 8%, from court-awarded attorneys' fees. $81,741, or 3%, from dividends and interest from securities. The remaining revenue came from interest on savings and investments, honoraria, publication sales, and other miscellaneous sources. Net revenue was reduced by net losses of $28,009 on the sale of securities, and $54,114 from the "Festival to Celebrate the Future of Children."

Juvenile Law Center

801 Arch St., 6th Floor
Philadelphia, PA 19107   **Phone:**   (215) 625-0551
USA

Contact Person: Robert Schwartz, Director.   **Officers or Principals:** Robert Schwartz, Director ($71,150); Emily Buss, Attorney ($52,365); Eleanor Bush, Attorney ($45,000); Joann Viola, Office Manager; Carl Oxholm, III, President; Charisse R. Lillie, Vice President; Anna M. Durbin, Secretary; Dr. Ione Vargus, Treasurer.

Mission or Interest: "Provides legal services, law reform litigation, and community education on issues relating to children and the law."

Accomplishments: Litigation involvement included: <u>Coleman v. Stanziani</u>, which challenged the Pennsylvania system of "detaining allegedly delinquent juveniles in secure detention centers. The litigation has resulted in the decrease in the number of unnecessary detentions." <u>T.M. v. City of Philadelphia</u>, "seeking enforcement of the right to counsel for all children alleged to be dependent (abused or neglected, truant or ungovernable) and whose cases have taken place in Philadelphia Family Court." <u>Scott v. Snider</u> challenging "the state's provision of health care to poor children." Other class action suites challenging the governments provision of adequate social services. For its litigation the Center received $43,092 in court-awarded attorney's fees from state and local governments. In the fiscal year ending August 1994, the Center spent $482,993 on its programs. The largest program, with expenditures of $109,993, was general representation of children in Philadelphia family court dependency cases. $30,000 was spent on community education and outreach. The Center awarded grants to other foundations, including: Two grants totaling $99,000 for the Annie E. Casey Foundation , $66,000 for the Edna McConnell Clark Foundation for a "family preservation project aimed at reducing unnecessary removal of children from families in Pennsylvania dependency cases," $50,000 for the Developmental Disabilities Planning Council, $45,000 for the Public Welfare Foundation, and others.

Net Revenue: FY ending 8/94 $553,010   **Net Expenses:** $630,775   77%/19%/4%   **Net Assets:** (-$40,221)

Citations: 33:155   **Tax Status:** 501(c)(3)

Board of Directors or Trustees: Stewart Cades, Jane Dustan, Carol Fuchs, Prof. Frank Furstenberg (Univ. of PA), Lani Guinier (Univ. of PA, School of Law), Germaine Ingram (CHOICE), Kathryn Jordan, Stuart Kline, Jane Knitzer Ed.D., Juan Laureda, Marsha Levick (former Legal Director, NOW Legal Defense Fund), Pamela Grace Model (Ms. Foundation for Women), Joe Quinlan (television consultant to Time, Inc.), Daniel Segal (ACLU and Women's Law Project), Geraldine Segal Ph.D. (author, <u>Blacks in the Law</u>), Ronald Sharp Ed.D. (Penn State Univ.), Mark Soler (Youth Law Center), Eileen Tyrala M.D., Juan Williams (author, <u>Eyes on the Prize</u>).

Other Information: The Center received $543,033, or 98% of revenue, from direct and indirect public support in the form of gifts and grants awarded by foundations, affiliates, businesses, and individuals. $7,437, or 1%, from program service revenues. The remaining revenue came from interest on savings and temporary cash investments.

Kentucky Coalition

P.O. Box 1450
London, KY 40743
USA

Contact Person: Jerry Harlot.   **Officers or Principals:** Ray Tucker, Jr., Chairman ($0); Carol Wright, Vice Chairman ($0); Debra Cornett, Secretary/Treasurer ($0).

Mission or Interest: Grassroots organizing and litigation on behalf of environmental issues.

Accomplishments: In 1994 the Coalition spent $267,965 on its programs. The largest program, with expenditures of $90,672, was the Environmental Rights Project which provided technical and organizational support to groups addressing waste disposal issues. $68,004 was spent on the Leadership Development project that provided skill training. $19,721 was spent on litigation issues through the Kentucky Citizens Law Center. Other programs supported general research and education programs.

Net Revenue: 1994 $267,965   **Net Expenses:** $254,124   89%/10%/1%   **Net Assets:** $621,873

Tax Status: 501(c)(3)

Other Information: Affiliated with the 501(c)(4) Kentuckians for the Commonwealth at the same address. The Coalition received $224,599, or 82% of total revenue, from gifts and grants awarded by foundations, businesses, and individuals. (These grants included $30,000 from the W. Alton Jones Foundation, $25,000 from the Public Welfare Foundation, $25,000 from the Schumann Foundation, $20,000 from the Angelina Fund, $20,000 from the Needmor Fund, $20,000 from the Jessie Smith Noyes Foundation, $10,000 from the Norman Foundation, $10,000 from the Beldon Fund, and $10,000 from the George W. Norton Foundation.) $26,174, or 10%, from dividends and interest from securities. $13,207, or 5%, from reimbursements from other organizations. $4,800 or 2%, from rental reimbursements. $3,583, or 1%, from interest on savings and temporary cash investments. The remaining revenue came from rental income. The Coalition lost $4,409 on the sale of securities and other assets.

Kids For A Clean Environment (Kids FACE)

P.O. Box 158254	
Nashville, TN 37215	**Phone:** (615) 331-7381
USA	**Fax:** (615) 333-9879

Contact Person: Trish Poe.

Officers or Principals: Trish Poe, Executive Director ($21,000); Melissa Poe, CEO; Michelle Scott, Director of Youth Services.

Mission or Interest: "An environmental organization created *by* a child and *for* children." Creates community projects for children's participation.

Accomplishments: Kids FACE was founded when nine year-old Melissa Poe saw an episode of "Highway to Heaven" which convinced her of the dangers of environmental degradation. She wrote a letter to the president which said (original spelling retained), "Dear Mr. President: Please will you do something about pollution. I want to live till I am a hundred years old. I am nine years old write now. My name is Melissa Poe. You ans some other people could put up signs saying: PLEASE HELP STOP POLLTOIN IT IS KILLING THE WORLD! Please help stop pollution Mr. president. Please if you ecnor (ignore) this letter we will all die of pollutoin and the ozone layer." Distributed seedling trees. Produces a newsletter that is distributed by Wal-Mart. Produced a Public Service Announcement with a toll-free number that generated 122,636 calls in a month. Produced the "Kid's Earth Flag", a giant (100' x 200') banner comprised of 20,000 individual 12" x 12" squares received from children around the world, and one from Vice President Al Gore. The flag is displayed in cities across the country. In 1994 Kids FACE spent $148,459 on its programs.

Net Revenue: 1994 $157,467 **Net Expenses:** $164,602 90%/10%/0% **Net Assets:** $17,239 **Tax Status:** 501(c)(3) **Annual Report:** No. **Employees:** 2

Periodicals: *Kids FACE Illustrated* (bimonthly tabloid) in full color.
Internships: No.
Other Information: Kids FACE has a toll-free number, (800) 952-3223.

Kitchen Table: Women of Color Press
P.O. Box 40-4920
Brooklyn, NY 11240   **Phone:**   (718) 935-1082
USA   **Fax:**   (718) 935-1107

Contact Person: Andrea Lockett, Publisher.
Mission or Interest: "Kitchen Table: Women of Color Press is the only U.S. publishing company run autonomously by women of color and publishing the work of women of color of all races/ethnicities, national origins, classes, and sexual orientations."
Accomplishments: "Kitchen Table, which has always operated on a shoestring budget, will be fifteen years old in 1996. We have fifteen award-winning titles, which have been largely responsible for changing the face of women's studies, ethnic studies, lesbian and gay, and multicultural curricula. This Bridge Called my Back: Writings by Radical Women of Color is an all-time bestseller for a small press publication, with more than 100,000 copies in print."
Products or Services: Numerous titles, including fiction, poetry, and nonfiction. Also sells posters, post-cards, and t-shirts.
Tax Status: 501(c)(4) **Annual Report:** No. **Employees:** 2
Board of Directors or Trustees: Asst. Prof. Cathy Cohen (African and African American Studies, Yale Univ.), Franciene Forte (Bantam Books), Joo-Hyun Kang (Women's Environmental and Development Organization).
Other Information: Affiliated with the Union Institute Center for Women in Washington, DC. "In addition to publishing our own books, we also distribute the books of other small press publishers. We are a political activist organization as well as a literary and cultural institution." In 1994 the Press received $15,000 from the Haymarket People's Fund. Other donors included the Astraea National Lesbian Action Foundation

La Raza Centro Legal
474 Valencia St., Suite 295
San Francisco, CA 94103   **Phone:**   (415) 826-5506
USA

Contact Person: Victor Marquez, Executive Director.
Officers or Principals: Victor Marquez, Executive Director ($47,917); Maria Pineda-Kamariotis, Director ($31,940); Robert Retana, President ($0); Sal Torres, Secretary; Linda Lopez Chavez, Vice President; Pedro Rodriguez, Treasurer.
Mission or Interest: Provides legal services in the area of immigration and employment discrimination on behalf of Hispanics.
Accomplishments: In the fiscal year ending June 1994, the organization spent $492,171 on its programs. The largest program, with expenditures of $179,340, was litigation and education in the area of employment discrimination. $80,102 was spent on immigration services. $46,879 was spent on housing discrimination programs. Other programs included *pro bono* projects, and lawyer referral services.
Net Revenue: FY ending 6/94 $573,538 ($260,479, or 45%, from government grants) **Net Expenses:** $555,100 89%/9%/2%
Net Assets: $66,988 **Citations:** 10:198
Tax Status: 501(c)(3)
Board of Directors or Trustees: Katherine Salazar-Poss, Collin Petheram (Pacific Bell), Mary Lu Christie (Pacific Bell Legal Dept.), Rosa Mar (Levi Strauss), Yvonne Gonzalez Rogers, Fernando Padilla (Hewlett-Packard), Luis Garcia, Brian Cabrera, Alice Amador McTighe, Miguel Marquez.
Other Information: The organization received $238,070, or 41% of revenue, from direct and indirect public support in the form of gifts and grants awarded by foundations, affiliates, businesses, and individuals. (These grants included $400 from the Vanguard Public Foundation. In 1995 La Raza received $20,000 from the Tides Foundation.) $260,479, or 45%, from government grants. $59,283 net, or 10%, from special fund-raising events. $13,875, or 2%, from fees for services. The remaining revenue came from referral fees, interest on savings and temporary cash investments, and other miscellaneous fees.

Labor / Community Strategy Center
3780 Wilshire Blvd.
Los Angeles, CA 90010   **Phone:**   (213) 387-2800
USA

Contact Person: Eric Mann, Executive Director. **Officers or Principals:** Eric Mann, Executive Director ($60,276); Chris Mathis, Organizer ($36,000); Marta Duran, Program Director ($33,666); Kate Kinkade, Chair.
Mission or Interest: "Community and labor education on the social and economic needs of the Los Angeles area. It includes review of the hazards of the workplace, public health and educational work in low income and minority communities. It integrates the environment with the community, around the specific issue of a healthy workplace and a healthy family environment."
Accomplishments: In 1993 the Center spent $345,403 on programs. Hosted fundraisers that "provide an arena for consciousness-raising." They awarded $6,619 in grants. Recipients include $5,000 for the National Chicana/Chicano Empowerment Network, $564 for the Sundry Community Educational Organizations, $100 for the Office of the Americas and smaller grants for *Christianity and Crisis*, *Cultural Liberation*, and KPFK radio.

Net Revenue: 1993 $539,872 **Net Expenses:** $575,299 60%/25%/15% **Net Assets:** $279,454 **Citations:** 10:198
Products or Services: Educational materials, grants, books, and forums.
Tax Status: 501(c)(3)
Board of Directors or Trustees: Patrick Ramsey, Rodolfo Acuna, Jorge Garcia, Cynthia Hamilton, Mark Masaoka.
Other Information: The Center received substantial support from the Schuman Foundation, the Wallis Trust, the Ottinger Foundation, the Gilmore Foundation, and the Noyes Foundation. The Center received $516,549, or 96% of revenue, from these and other foundations, companies and individuals. (These grants included $30,000 from the Jessie Smith Noyes Foundation, $15,000 from the Norman Foundation, $15,000 from the Ruth Mott Fund and $9,000 from the McKay Foundation. In 1994-95 the Center recieved $75,000 from the Bauman Family Foundation, and $5,000 from the Tides Foundation.) $10,231, or 2%, came from fund-raising events. $6,956 net, or 1%, came from the sale of inventory. The remaining revenue came from interest on savings and temporary cash investments.

Labor Council for Latin American Advancement

815 16th St., N.W.
Washington, DC 20006   **Phone:** (202) 347-4223
USA   **Fax:**   (202) 347-5095

Contact Person: Carmen Perez, Office Manager.
Officers or Principals: Alfredo C. Montoya, President ($53,087); Carmen Perez, Office Manager ($39,167).
Mission or Interest: "To promote the participation of workers of Latin American descent in the trade union movement and the political process." The Council performs voter education and get-out-the-vote activities.
Accomplishments: In 1994 the Council spent $467,126 on its activities. These included $143,955 in grants for local get-out-the-vote projects, primarily in major cities and the Southwest. The Council spent $9,163 on NAFTA-related informational activities.
Net Revenue: 1994 $587,360 **Net Expenses:** $572,821 82%/18%/0% **Net Assets:** $59,193 **Citations:** 16:180
Tax Status: 501(c)(3)
Board of Directors or Trustees: Linda Chavez-Thompson (AFSCME), Ricardo Icaza, Ralph Jimenez, Rudy Mendoza, Chano Merino (AFL-CIO), Tony Padilla (Transportation/Communications Union), Maria Portalatin (American Federation of Teachers), Eva Savala (UAW), Damaso Seda (Transport Workers Union), and many others from the organized labor community.
Other Information: The Council is an affiliate of the AFL-CIO, and headquarter space is provided rent-free by the United Steel Workers of America. The Council received $468,860, or 80% of revenue, from gifts and grants from affiliates. $92,100, or 16%, from convention participants. $25,160, or 4%, from membership dues. The remaining income came from interest on savings and temporary cash investments.

Labor Education and Research Project

7435 Michigan Ave.
Detroit, MI 48210   **Phone:** (313) 842-6262
USA

Contact Person: Kimberly Moody, President.
Officers or Principals: Elissa Karg, Vice President ($0); Mary Hollens, Secretary ($0); Wendy Thompson, Treasurer ($0).
Mission or Interest: Research and publication on issues bringing organized labor together, working to "put the movement back into the labor movement."
Accomplishments: In the fiscal year ending January 1994 the Project spent $261,490 on its programs. The largest program, with expenditures of $196,353, was the publication of *Labor Notes*, a monthly newsletter sent to over 10,000 subscribers. $54,513 was spent on a conference attended by 1,000 on labor and workplace issues. The project awarded a grant of $3,000 to the Black Rank and File Exchange.
Net Revenue: FY ending 1/94 $312,328 **Net Expenses:** $333,289 78%/12%/9% **Net Assets:** $50,628
Tax Status: 501(c)(3)
Board of Directors or Trustees: Selwyn Roger, Angaza Laughinghouse.
Periodicals: *Labor Notes* (monthly newsletter).
Other Information: The Project received $97,858, or 31% of revenue, from gifts and grants awarded by foundations, businesses, and individuals. (These grants included $25,000 from the Angelina Fund.) $85,508, or 27%, from newsletter subscriptions. $67,833, or 22%, from conference and workshop fees. $56,829, or 18%, from book sales. $2,731, or 1%, from honoraria. The remaining revenue came from dividends and interest from securities.

Labor Institute

853 Broadway
New York, NY 10003   **Phone:** (212) 674-3322
USA

Contact Person: Howard Saunders, Media Director.   **Officers or Principals:** Howard Saunders, Media Director ($57,612); Leslie J. Leopold, Director ($56,235); Cydney Pullman, Treasurer ($50,689).
Mission or Interest: "Lecture courses and audio visual displays concerning economics and other topics related to working people." Provides these services for "working adults in a wide variety of community and church groups, educational organizations and labor organizations on topics that are important to their jobs."

Accomplishments: In 1994 the Institute spent $601,596 on its programs.
Net Revenue: 1994 $731,770 ($634,253, or 87%, from government sources)   **Net Expenses:** $757,090   79%/21%/0%
Net Assets: $559,353
Tax Status: 501(c)(3)
Board of Directors or Trustees: Phyllis Atwater, Philip Frazer, Michael Merrill, Juliet Schor.
Other Information: Affiliated with the Public Health Institute at the same address. In 1994 the Institute received $634,253, or 87% of revenue, from government grants. (These grants included $494,573 from the National Institute for Environmental Health Services, and $137,410 from the Department of Labor.) $32,283, or 4%, from educational services and the sale of publications. $30,082, or 4%, from gifts and grants awarded by foundations, businesses, and individuals. $17,297, or 2%, from dividends and interest from securities. $15,324, or 2%, from interest on savings and temporary cash investments. The remaining revenue came from capital gains on the sale of securities.

Labor Institute of Public Affairs

815 16th St., N.W.
Washington, DC 20006   **Phone:**   (202) 637-5334
USA

Contact Person: Richard S. Foster, Assistant Director.   **Officers or Principals:** William H. Wagner, Executive Director ($97,093); Richard S. Foster, Assistant Director ($89,095); Lane Kirkland, President/Chairman ($0); Thomas R. Donahue, Secretary.
Mission or Interest: Affiliated with the AFL-CIO, the Institute produces and distributes materials that promote the labor movement.
Accomplishments: In 1994 the Institute spent $819,689 on its programs. These programs included media campaigns such as: the "Union Yes" campaign, education about NAFTA, health care reform promotion, Labor Day activities, the "Striker Replacement" bill, labor law reform, public service announcements, and other programs.
Net Revenue: 1994 $2,674,037   **Net Expenses:** $2,695,804   **Net Assets:** $7,906
Tax Status: 501(c)(5)
Other Information: The Institute received $2,552,325, or 95%, from the AFL-CIO. $119,241, or 4%, from the sale of materials and reimbursements for programs provided. The remaining revenue came from other miscellaneous sources.

Labor Research Association

145 W. 28th St.
New York, NY 10001   **Phone:**   (212) 714-1677
USA

Contact Person: Greg Tarpinian, Director.
Officers or Principals: Greg Tarpinian, Director ($70,200); Jeannine Rudolph, Research Director ($50,521).
Mission or Interest: Research and educational programs to benefit labor unions.
Accomplishments: In 1994 the Association spent $922,952 on its programs. The largest program, with expenditures of $856,127, was consulting services for unions to provide them with "economic and strategic analysis to help them prepare for contract negotiations and organizing campaigns." Other programs produced publications and gave awards.
Net Revenue: 1994 $1,044,074   **Net Expenses:** $1,097,180   84%/2%/14%   **Net Assets:** $148,342   **Citations:** 36:152
Products or Services: Consulting and publications. Annual yearbook of reference information relevant to labor unions. Presents the annual Ernest Demaio Awards for rank and file trade union activism.
Tax Status: 501(c)(3)
Periodicals: *Economic Notes* (monthly newsletter), and *Trade Union Advisor* (biweekly newsletter).
Other Information: The Association received $819,135, or 78% of revenue, from consulting fees. $104,508, or 10%, from a fund-raising dinner. $94,281, or 9%, from subscription income. $11,861, or 1%, from the sale of the yearbook. The remaining revenue came from an awards dinner, gifts and grants, and interest on savings and temporary cash investments.

Labor Zionist Institute

25900 Greenfield, Suite 205-B
Oak Park, MI 48237   **Phone:**   (810) 967-3170
USA

Contact Person: Helen Naimark, President.   **Officers or Principals:** Jeffrey Ram, Vice President ($0); Evelyn Noveck, Second Vice President ($0); Esther Klein, Secretary ($0); David Silberg, Treasurer.
Mission or Interest: "Support of Israeli and Zionist labor and Jewish cultural organizations."
Accomplishments: In 1994 the Institute spent $41,557 on its programs. This included $12,833 in grants to the "Haonim Camp Tavor" in Michigan, and the "Machanah Bonim B'Israel."
Net Revenue: 1994 $12,202   **Net Expenses:** $41,557   100%/0%/0%   **Net Assets:** $393,028
Tax Status: 501(c)(3)
Board of Directors or Trustees: Alex Blumenberg, Henry Faigin, Sonia Glaser, Dena Greenberg, Norman Naimark, Bernard Schiff, Belle Glenner Schwartz, Judy Silberg Loebl, Sarah Schiff, Ethel Silberg, Arthur Slabosky.
Other Information: The Institute received $20,838 from interest on savings and temporary cash investments. $4,227 from dividends and interest from securities. The remaining revenue came from gifts from individuals. Net revenue was offset by a loss of $12,882 on the sale of securities.

Labor Zionist Letters

275 7th Ave.
New York, NY 10001   **Phone:**   (212) 229-2280
USA

Contact Person: Ruby Vogelfanger, President.
Mission or Interest: Publication regarding labor unionism and Zionism.
Net Revenue: FY ending 9/94 $93,969 **Net Expenses:** $105,525 **Net Assets:** (-$25,546)
Tax Status: 501(c)(3)
Board of Directors or Trustees: *Labor Zionist Letters.*
Other Information: The organization received $63,484, or 68% of revenue, from gifts or grants awarded by foundations, businesses, and individuals. $30,485, or 32%, from program service revenues.

Laborers' International Union of North America (LIUNA)

905 16th St., N.W.
Washington, DC 20006   **Phone:**   (202) 737-8320
USA   **Fax:**   (202) 737-2754

Contact Person: Arthur Coia, President.   **Officers or Principals:** Mason M. Warren, First Vice President ($262,385); Samuel J. Caivano, Fourth Vice President ($247,939); Arthur Coia, President ($205,112); Enrico H. Mancinelli, Fifth Vice President ($201,535); Robert J. Connerton, General Counsel ($182,621); Rollin P. Vinall, Secretary/Treasurer ($180,210); James J. Norwood, Secretary/Treasurer ($167,990); George R. Gudger, Eighth Vice President ($149,825); Charles D. Barnes, Sixth Vice President ($149,286); Victor N. Morden, Regional Manager ($147,806); Jack S. Wilkinson, Seventh Vice President ($146,564); John T. Curran, Director ($145,686); Carl E. Booker, Assistant to the President ($145,652); Nello Scipioni, Subregional Manager ($144,840); Howard I. Henson, Regional Manager ($144,083); Charles R. Ager, Financial Consultant ($137,478); Joseph S. Mancinelli, Regional Manager ($136,379); John Serpico, Second Vice President ($132,499); Armand Eric Sabitoni, Tenth Vice President ($118,324); Thomas W. Needham, Comptroller ($114,000); Terrence Matthew Healy, Regional Manager ($111,172); Joseph Mazza, Assistant Organizing Director ($110,799); Joseph J. Licastro, Regional ($110,523); Peter J. Fosco, Regional Manager ($109,643); Edward B. Thornton, International Representative ($102,912).
Mission or Interest: Union of construction workers, brick haulers, asbestos removers, and mail carriers. Member of the AFL-CIO.
Accomplishments: LIUNA lent $100,000 to President Clinton's inaugural committee in 1993. In the 1994 elections, LIUNA gave $1.1 million to Democrats. LIUNA president, Arthur Coia, attended a White House dinner and Oval Office meeting, and was given a golf club by President Clinton. LIUNA had previously retained Harold Ickes, now Deputy White House chief of staff, for legal services. Hillary Rodham Clinton addressed the Union's conference in Florida. LIUNA has approximately 770,000 members. In 1994 the Union spent $44,037,459 on its programs. This included $699,728 spent on organizing, and $150,000 spent on the Laborers' Political League Education Account. The Union also supports a political action committee.
Net Revenue: 1994 $46,231,720 **Net Expenses:** $45,521,603 **Net Assets:** $155,226,058
Tax Status: 501(c)(5)
Periodicals: *The Laborer* (bimonthly newsletter).
Other Information: LIUNA and Arthur Coia have been the subject of a three-year U.S. Justice Department investigation into ties with organized crime, according to the July 24, 1996 *Wall Street Journal.* The draft civil racketeering complaint filed by the Justice Department said Coia "associated with, and has been controlled and influenced by, organized crime figures." Former LIUNA official Ron Fino said that "during my nearly 24 years in the Laborers' Union, I learned that the union was run by and for the benefit of the mob, its members, and its associates." LIUNA reached a consent decree with the Justice Department. Some union officials were forced out, and Coia pledged to reform the Union. *Reader's Digest* has published a story on the Union and its legal troubles. The Union received $33,558,964, or 73% of total revenue, from membership dues. $10,784,460, or 23%, from dividends and interest from securities. $1,241,710, or 3%, from "miscellaneous sources." $522,731, or 1%, from interest on savings and temporary cash investments. The remaining revenue came from capital gains on the sale of securities, and the sale of supplies. In addition to its headquarters, the Union owns a condominium in Washington, DC that originally cost $223,601.

LaborNet

(see the Institute for Global Communications)

Ladyslipper

3205 Hillsborough Rd.
Durham, NC 27705   **Phone:**   (919) 383-8773   **E-Mail:** Ladyslip@nando.net
USA   **Fax:**   (919) 383-3525

Contact Person: Laurie Fuchs, President.   **Officers or Principals:** Laurie Fuchs, President ($39,833); Karen Miller, Treasurer ($23,225); Mandy Carter, Vice President ($0); Donna Giles, Secretary.
Mission or Interest: "To educate the public about the accomplishments of women musicians; to expand the scope and availability of recordings by women."
Accomplishments: "We publish the worlds most comprehensive catalog of music by women." In 1994 Ladyslipper spent $1,699,799 on its programs. The largest program, with expenditures of $1,487,875, was the production and distribution of their catalog. They state that 450,000 were distributed. $154,977 was spent to provide schools, libraries and individuals with materials that demonstrate the achievements of female artists and musicians. $45,363 was spent to produce records on the Ladyslipper label. $11,584 was spent to distribute materials and information at music festivals and cultural events.

Net Revenue: FY ending 1/95 $2,000,453 **Net Expenses:** $1,840,220 92%/8%/0% **Net Assets:** $989,294 **Citations:** 23:169
Products or Services: Catalog of "non-sexist / non-racist recordings by women in order to expand knowledge about and accessibility of those works." Catalog lists over 1,500 annotated titles by women, plus "non-sexist music for children and non-sexist music by men, videos, songbooks, and music related books.
Tax Status: 501(c)(3)
Board of Directors or Trustees: Joanne Abel.
Other Information: Ladyslipper received $1,947,845, or 97% of revenue, from the sale of educational materials. $29,556, or 1%, from mailing list rentals. The remaining revenue came from gifts and grants, interest on savings and temporary cash investments, and other miscellaneous sources.

Lambda Legal Defense and Education Fund

666 Broadway, 12th Floor
New York, NY 10012   **Phone:** (212) 995-8585
USA   **Fax:**   (212) 995-2306

Contact Person: William A. Peters, Development Director. **Officers or Principals:** Kevin M. Cathcart, Executive Director ($99,040); William Peters, Development Director ($63,543); Beatrice Dohrn, Legal Director ($62,830); Noemi Masliah, Barry C. Skovgaard, Co-Chairs; Wayne S. Braveman, Secretary; Frances J. Goldstein, Treasurer; J. Fong, Director, West Coast Region.
Mission or Interest: National organization "committed to achieving full recognition of the civil rights of lesbians, gay men, and people with HIV/AIDS, through impact litigation, education, and public policy work."
Accomplishments: They send their newsletter to about 12,000 Lambda members. Their legal department receives about 100-120 calls per week from attorneys and other individuals seeking assistance. Lambda has won several lawsuits that were chosen to have maximum impact on future cases and legislation. At any given time they have a docket of approximately 60 cases. Their legal cases generate revenues in the form of attorney's fees. In the fiscal year ending October 1994 they received $193,444, or 8.8% of their revenue, from legal fees. Playing a crucial part in the fight to allow openly gay individuals to serve in the military.
Net Revenue: FY ending 10/94 $2,198,549 **Net Expenses:** $1,893,139 73%/14%/14% **Net Assets:** $884,887
Citations: 240:69
Products or Services: Litigation, workshops, conferences, publications and other informational materials. Publishes an attorney's guide to AIDS laws.
Tax Status: 501(c)(3) **Annual Report:** Yes. **Employees:** 30
Board of Directors or Trustees: Barbara Bailey, Nan Bailey, Michael Bauer, Alvin Baum, Jr., Michael Becker, Daniel Bowers, M.D., Shedrick Davis, III, Stephen Davis, Douglas Jones, Jill Kasofsky, Monica Lord, Sandra Lowe, Edwin McAmis, Theresa McPherson, Robert Ollis, Jr., Lynn Palma, Miriam Pickus, Jennifer Pizer, Gale Richards, Judith Schaeffer, Jayne Sherman, Ruth Spencer, Charles Spiegel, Jay Swanson, Lee Taft.
Periodicals: *Lambda Update* (three times a year).
Internships: Yes, law students.
Other Information: They have three offices, New York, Chicago and Los Angeles. The Fund received $2,107,777, or 90% of total revenue, from gifts and grants awarded by foundations, companies, and individuals. (These grants included $50,660 from the Joyce Mertz-Gilmore Foundation.) $193,444, or 8%, from attorney's fees. The remaining revenue came from interest on savings and temporary investments, and other miscellaneous sources. Revenue was partially offset by losses from special events including the Lambda Liberty Awards, the Fire Island cocktail reception, a cocktail party and "dinner passion," and a cocktail reception and theater, totaling $132,522. This loss does not include the $530,595 in gifts and grants that weere made at these events.

Lavender Families Resource Network

P.O. Box 21567
Seattle, WA 98111   **Phone:** (206) 325-2643
USA

Contact Person: Jenny Sayward, Executive Director.
Mission or Interest: "Supports lesbians, gay men, and bisexuals in their efforts to parent children, including adoption, insemination, and custody issues."
Products or Services: Series of pamphlets on various topics.
Tax Status: 501(c)(3) **Annual Report:** Yes. **Employees:** No paid employees.
Periodicals: *Mom's Apple Pie* (quarterly newsletter).
Internships: Yes, unpaid. Interns do research, grant writing, coalition building, and client support. Undergraduate social science and humanities majors, and law students wanted.
Other Information: From 1974 until 1994 the network was called the Lesbian Mothers' National Defense Fund.

Lawyers Alliance for World Security

1601 Connecticut Ave., N.W., Suite 600
Washington, DC 20009   **Phone:** (202) 745-2540
USA

Contact Person: John Parachini, Executive Director. **Officers or Principals:** John Parachini, Executive Director ($43,130); Ralph Earle, Chairman ($10,767); Shirley M. Hufstedler, Vice Chair ($0); Mark P. Schlefer, President; Leonard M. Marks, Vice President; Frederick C. Williams, Treasurer; David A. Koplow, Clerk.

Mission or Interest: "To provide a forum for the analysis and exchange of serious and responsible ideas concerning the threat of nuclear war, advancing non-proliferation and enhancing movement towards the rule of law in the former Soviet Union."
Accomplishments: In 1994 the Alliance spent $358,405 on its programs.
Net Revenue: 1994 $412,858 **Net Expenses:** $400,629 89%/6%/4% **Net Assets:** $20,958
Tax Status: 501(c)(3)
Board of Directors or Trustees: George Adams Jr., Edward Aguilar, Howard Aibel, Daniel Arbess, Donna Baker, Victor Bass, George Bunn, David Clinard, William Colby, Frederick Conover II, Ellen Craig, Adrian DeWind, George Denney, John Douglas, J. Stephen Dycus, Harold Field Jr., Philip Fleming, John French, J. Edward Fowler, Peter Gamer, Jonathan Granoff, Michael Greco, Barry Kellman, Gaylen Kemp, Lawrence Korb, Scott Lassar, Hans Loeser, Alexander Papachristou, Michael Parker, Penny Parker, Martin Payson, Stanley Resor, John Rhinelander, David Rideout, Donald Rivkin, Thomas Robertson, Wm. Warfield Ross, Lowell Sachnoff, Anthony Sager, Alice Slater, McNeill Smith, Suzanne Spaulding, Edward Strohbehn, Edward Tanzman, Louise Walker, Sheryl Walter, Allan Weiss.
Other Information: Formerly the Lawyers Alliance for Nuclear Arms Control. Affiliated with the Committee for National Security. The Alliance received $371,838, or 90% of revenue, from gifts and grants awarded by foundations, businesses, and individuals. $25,225, or 6%, from membership dues. $3,395, or 1%, from interest on savings and temporary cash investments. The remaining revenue came from various miscellaneous sources.

Lawyers Committee for Human Rights

330 7th Ave.
New York, NY 10001   **Phone:** (212) 629-6170
USA

Contact Person: Michael Posner, Executive Director.   **Officers or Principals:** Michael Posner, Executive Director ($98,431); Arthur Helton, Director of Refugee Programs ($71,285); Julie Brown, Development Director ($60,692); Sandra Cole, Director of Finance and Administration; Patricia Armstrong, World Bank Coordinator; Joseph Eldridge, Director of Washington Office.
Mission or Interest: Promotes human rights and refugee rights worldwide. "Serves as a legal resource center to indigent and low income refugees in New York city, particularly those who are incarcerated pending a determination of their claim." Monitors U.S. foreign aid to countries with a pattern of human rights violations.
Accomplishments: In the fiscal year ending May 1994, the Committee spent $1,761,251 on its programs. The program helping indigent refugees in New York assisted more than 400 cases.
Net Revenue: FY ending 5/94 $2,722,339 **Net Expenses:** $2,682,244 66%/19%/15% **Net Assets:** (-$399,926)
Citations: 23:169   **Tax Status:** 501(c)(3)
Board of Directors or Trustees: M. Bernard Aidinoff, Susan Berkwitt-Malefakis, Robert Bernstein (John Wiley & Sons), Tom Bernstein, Charles Breyer, Alice Brown (NAACP Legal Defense & Education Fund), Haywood Burns (CUNY Law School), Kerry Kennedy Cuomo (RFK Memorial Center for Human Rights), Michael Davis, Adrian DeWind, Norman Dorsen (NY Univ., School of Law), Fr. Robert Drinan (Georgetown Law Center), A. Whitney Ellsworth, Kenneth Feinberg, John Finley, Marvin Frankel, Stephen Friedman, R. Scott Greathead, Deborah Greenberg (Columbia Univ., School of Law), Robert Joffe, Robert Juceam, Lewis Kaden, Rhoda Karpatkin (Consumers Union), Prof. Harold Hongju Koh (Yale Law School), Nancy Kuhn, Philip Lacovara, Jo Backer Laird, R. Todd Lang, Charles Lister, Stanley Mailman, Charles Mathias, Bruce Rabb, Benito Romano, Barbara Schatz (Columbia Univ., School of Law), Steven Shapiro (ACLU), Jerome Shestack, James Silkenat, Warren Stern, Rose Styron, Jay Topkis, George Vradenburg, III (Fox), Sigourney Weaver, Ruth Wedgwood (Yale Law School), Lois Whitman, William Zabel, Selig Zises.
Periodicals: *Newsbriefs* (quarterly newsletter).
Other Information: The Committee received $2,713,862, or 99.7% of revenue, from gifts and grants awarded by foundations, businesses, and individuals. (These grants included $605,000 from the Joyce Mertz-Gilmore Foundation, $450,000 over three years from the John D. and Catherine T. MacArthur Foundation, $100,000 from the John Merck Fund, $100,000 over two years from the Carnegie Corporation, $30,000 from the General Services Foundation, $15,000 from the Winston Foundation.) The remaining revenue came from interest on savings and other temporary cash investments.

Lawyers' Committee for Civil Rights Under Law

1450 G St., N.W., Suite 400
Washington, DC 20005   **Phone:** (202) 662-8600
USA   **Fax:**   (202) 783-0857

Contact Person: Barbara R. Arnwine, Executive Director.   **Officers or Principals:** Barbara R. Arnwine, Executive Director ($151,673); Richard Seymour, Project Director ($107,001); Thomas Henderson, Deputy Director, Litigation ($106,454); Michael Cooper, Herbert J. Hansell, Co-Chairs; Prof. Eleanor Fox, Secretary; Myles V. Lynk, Treasurer; Jerome Libin, Counsel.
Mission or Interest: "Promotion of better public understanding of civil rights and the related judicial processes, also provides legal services without cost to class action litigants in employment discrimination matters."
Accomplishments: In 1994 the Committee spent $2,886,999 on its programs. The Committee received $1,093,909 in court-awarded attorney's fees from its litigation.
Net Revenue: 1994 $3,803,802 **Net Expenses:** $3,831,575 75%/21%/3% **Net Assets:** $3,728,481 **Citations:** 277:60
Products or Services: Litigation, public education, and lobbying. The Committee spent $34,397 on lobbying, $6,159 on grassroots lobbying and $28,238 on the direct lobbying of legislators. The amount spent on lobbying has decreased steadily in recent years, down 4% from the year before, 23% from 1992, and down 66% from $101,879 in 1991.

Tax Status: 501(c)(3)
Board of Directors or Trustees: Julius Chambers (Chancellor, NC Central Univ.), Hon. William Coleman Jr., Peter Connell (Senior Counsel, Aetna Life and Casualty), Prof. Owen Fiss (Yale Law School), Prof. Eleanor Fox (New York Univ. Law School), Ira Heyman (Secretary of the Smithsonian), Hon. Nicholas Katzenbach (former U.S. Attorney General, 1964-67), Dean Maximilian Kempner (VT Law School), Dean William Robinson (DC School of Law), Hon. Harold Tyler Jr., Roger Wilkins (George Mason Univ.), and many others from the legal community.
Periodicals: Newsletter.
Other Information: The Committee received $1,759,156, or 46% of revenue, from gifts and grants awarded by foundations, businesses, and individuals. (These grants included $80,000 from the Joyce Foundation.) $1,093,909, or 29%, from court-awarded attorney's fees. $748,441, or 20%, from government grants. $181,839, or 5%, from dividends and interest from securities. The remaining revenue came from interest on savings and temporary cash investments, and other miscellaneous sources.

Leadership Conference Education Fund
1629 K St., N.W., Suite 1010
Washington, DC 20006   **Phone:**   (202) 466-3434
USA

Contact Person: Karen McGill Arrington, Deputy Director.
Officers or Principals: Karen McGill Arrington, Deputy Director ($67,406); Ralph G. Neas, Executive Director ($21,224); William Taylor, Vice President ($9,000); Arnold Aronson, President; William L. Robinson, Secretary; Patricia A. Wright, Treasurer.
Mission or Interest: Educates the public about civil rights and monitors the civil rights activities of the federal government.
Accomplishments: In 1994 the Fund spent $244,217 on its programs. The largest program, with expenditures of $98,538, was monitoring the civil rights activities of the federal government. $87,106 was spent on public education, including public service announcements. $49,981 was spent on a "Housing Mobility Conference to bring together policy makers, academicians, and housing advocates to discuss housing mobility programs across the nation." $8,592 was spent on a roundtable to discuss urban poverty and examine strategies to address this issue.
Net Revenue: 1994 $472,634 **Net Expenses:** $282,654 86%/11%/2% **Net Assets:** $489,047 **Citations:** 129:104
Tax Status: 501(c)(3)
Board of Directors or Trustees: Barbara Arnwine, Mary Frances Berry, Muriel Morisey Spence, Caroline Osolinik, Kenneth Young, Ricardo Fernandez.
Periodicals: *Civil Rights Monitor.*
Other Information: Affiliated with the 501(c)(4) Leadership Conference on Civil Rights. Ralph Neas is the executive director of both and received combined compensation of $125,918. The two affiliates had combined net revenues of $765,363, net expenses of $588,140, and net assets of $715,013. The Fund received $454,990, or 96% of revenue, from gifts and grants awarded by foundations, businesses, and individuals. $9,955, or 2%, from subscriptions. $6,109, or 1%, from interest on savings and temporary cash investments. The remaining revenue came from miscellaneous sources.

Leadership Conference on Civil Rights (LCCR)
1629 K St., N.W., Suite 1010
Washington, DC 20006   **Phone:**   (202) 466-3311
USA

Contact Person: Ralph G. Neas, Executive Director.   **Officers or Principals:** Ralph G. Neas, Executive Director ($104,693); Arnold Aronson, Founder ($0); Gerald W. McEntee, Treasurer ($0); June O'Grady, Legislative Chair; Dorothy I. Height, Chairperson; William Taylor, Antonia Hernandez, Judith L. Lichtman, Vice Chairpersons.
Mission or Interest: "Seeks to advance civil rights for all Americans through government action at the national level...Helps coordinate the lobbying activities of 185 national organizations on national civil rights legislation."
Accomplishments: In 1994 the Conference spent $218,078 on its programs. These included "Justice for Wards Cove Workers Act, D.C. Statehood, The Gay and Lesbian Civil Rights Bill, Employment Non-Discrimination Act, Civil Rights Amendments to Chapter one of the Elementary and Secondary Education Act, Danforth Amendment to the ESEA, Civil Rights Amendments to Health Care Reform Legislation, nominations to the EEOC, and the Deval Patrick nomination."
Net Revenue: 1994 $292,729 **Net Expenses:** $305,486 71%/21%/8% **Net Assets:** $225,966 **Citations:** 129:104
Tax Status: 501(c)(4)
Board of Directors or Trustees: Barbara Arnwine, Owen Bieber (UAW), Kenyon Burks, Becky Cain, Maria Gaston, Keith Geiger, Eugene Glover, Marcia Greenberger, Lealle Harris, Patricia Ireland (NOW), Hugh Price, Elaine Jones, Laura Murphy Lee, Joseph Lowry, Leon Lynch, Karen Narasaki, David Saperstein, Jackie Defazio, Richard Womack, Harriet Woods, Patricia Wright, Paul Yzaguirre, Charles Kamasaki, Daniel Zingale (Human Rights Campaign).
Other Information: Affiliated with the 501(c)(3) Leadership Conference Education Fund. Ralph Neas is the executive director of both and received combined compensation of $125,918. The two affiliates had combined net revenues of $765,363, net expenses of $588,140, and net assets of $715,013. The Conference received $141,210, or 48% of revenue, from membership dues. $122,141 net, or 42%, from special fund-raising events. $23,465, or 8%, from gifts and grants awarded by foundations, businesses, and individuals. The remaining income came from interest on savings and temporary cash investments, and other miscellaneous sources.

League of Conservation Voters (LCV)
1707 L St., N.W., Suite 550
Washington, DC 20036   **Phone:**   (202) 785-8683   **E-Mail:** publications@lcv.com
USA   **Fax:**   (202) 835-0491   **Web-Page:** http://www.econet.org

Contact Person: Sarah Anderson, Research Director.

Officers or Principals: James Maddy, President ($153,369); Elaine Lynch Jones, Vice President; Frank Loy, Chair; Deborah Tuck, Vice Chair.

Mission or Interest: Lobbying on behalf of environmental legislation and supporting environmentalists legislators. "LCV is the 25 year old, bipartisan political action arm of the U.S. environmental movement. LCV helps elect members of Congress who will vote for the Earth; and produces the *National Environment Scorecard* to hold them accountable."

Accomplishments: LCV played a large role in the 1994 elections. Among its many accomplishments: Passed the $1 million mark in campaign contributions, making it one of the top 25 PACs. 63% of the candidates LCV endorsed won their races. Introduced the Campaign Fellowship program which "placed 16 trained staff persons on key Congressional campaigns. The Fellows assumed significant positions managing volunteers, coordinating the candidate's events, and running field operations...The Fellows' salaries were paid for by LCV in lieu of cash contributions to the candidates." Started a national network called EarthList, modeled after EMILY's List, which recruits members to 'bundle' together campaign contributions. This 'bundling' of many checks together clearly shows the candidates where the money is coming from, and allows contributors bundled together to give more than the law allows a single organization to give to a candidate. LCV has published the National Environmental Scorecard since 1970. This Scorecard rates members' voting records on environmental issues. The Scorecard is available through e-mail at "scorecard@econet.apc.org, and through the World Wide Web page. "LCV successfully implemented an aggressive press strategy that has positioned the organization as one of the first environmental sources reporters call. *The New York Times, Los Angeles Times, Time Magazine*, ABC, NPR, and many other news organizations routinely check with us for background information." Actor Robert Redford has done many radio ads for political candidates at the request of LCV. In 1993 LCV spent $1,506,192 on its programs.

Net Revenue: 1993 $2,488,902 **Net Expenses:** $2,110,352 71%/6%/22% **Net Assets:** $150,181 **Citations:** 542:39

Products or Services: Lobbying, National Environmental Scorecard, campaign contributions and assistance, more.

Tax Status: 501(c)(4)

Board of Directors or Trustees: Richard Ayres, Brent Blackwelder, Tom Brokaw, Bunyon Bryant, Syd Butler, Ruth Caplan, Charles Clusen, John Deardourff, Brock Evans, Christopher Hormel, John Hunting, Paul Pritchard, William Roberts, Claudine Schneider, Maitland Sharpe, Deborah Tuck, John Watts, Darryl Banks, Nancy Green, Jay Harris, Teddy Rosevelt, Debbie Sease.

Periodicals: *National Environmental Scorecard* (annual).

Other Information: Affiliated with the League of Conservation Voters Education Fund at the same address. The two organizations had 1993 combined net revenues, expenses, and assets of $2,702,354, $2,395,283, and $175,530. The League of Conservation Voters received $2,484,560, or 99.8% of revenue, from gifts and grants awarded by foundations, businesses, and individuals. (These grants included $15,000 from the Wallace Genetic Foundation.) The remaining revenue came from interest on savings and temporary cash investments.

League of Conservation Voters Education Fund

1707 L St., N.W., Suite 550
Washington, DC 20036   **Phone:** (202) 785-8683   **E-Mail:** publications@lcv.com
USA   **Fax:** (202) 835-0491   **Web-Page:** http://www.econet.org

Officers or Principals: Roger Stephenson, President ($60,000).

Mission or Interest: Research and education affiliate of the League of Conservation Voters.

Accomplishments: In the fiscal year ending June 1994, they spent $68,970 on their publication, *Greenwire*. Greenwire encapsulates environmental news and is distributed to opinion leaders outside Washington, DC. Spent $60,001 on a project investigating the 'Wise Use' movement.

Net Revenue: FY ending 6/94 $213,452 **Net Expenses:** $284,931 67%/25%/8% **Net Assets:** $25,349

Citations: 542:38

Products or Services: Research, publications, seminars, activist training and more.

Tax Status: 501(c)(3)

Board of Directors or Trustees: Susan Tharesen, David Shiah, Michael Oppenheimer.

Periodicals: *Greenwire*.

Other Information: The Fund is affiliated with the 501(c)(4) League of Conservation Voters. The two organizations had 1993 combined net revenues, expenses, and assets of $2,702,354, $2,395,283, and $175,530. The Fund received $213,225, or 100% of its revenue from grants awarded by foundations, companies and individuals. (These grants included $15,000 from the Bullitt Foundation, $15,000 from the American Conservation Association, $10,000 from the New-Land Foundation, $7,500 from the Beldon Fund, $1,000 from the Stewart R. Mott Charitable Trust.)

League of Women Voters

1730 M St., N.W.
Washington, DC 20036   **Phone:** (202) 429-1965
USA   **Fax:** (202) 429-0854

Contact Person: Judith A. Conover, Executive Director.

Officers or Principals: Gracia Hillman. Former Executive Director ($90,062); Becky Cain, President ($0); Diane Sheridan, First Vice President ($0); Peggy Lucas, Second Vice President; Robin Seaborn, Secretary/Treasurer.

Mission or Interest: "To encourage the active and informed participation of citizens in government and to increase understanding of major public policy issues...To secure public policies that promote League goals reached through member participation and agreement." Membership is open to men and women. The League has taken positions that support gun control, abortion rights, U.S. participation in the United Nations, environmental legislation, "social and economic justice," and a federal health care program that includes universal coverage and price controls. Recently the League encouraged its members to reject the Balanced Budget Amendment on the basis that, "what it will really do is prohibit Congress from creating new programs."

Accomplishments: More than 90,000 members. Worked on a book about New York state government with the Council on International Public Affairs. In the fiscal year ending June 1994, the League spent $1,777,370 on its programs. The largest program, with expenditures of $620,691, was communications, which "prepares and disseminates material and publications which promote political responsibility and address select issues." $497,880 was spent on membership service, including improving the internal workings of the national office and relations with state and local programs. $334,890 was spent on national programs that "promotes political responsibility through informed and active participation of citizens in government and to act on select issues." Other programs were devoted to the League's annual convention and council. The League awarded $200,000 to its 501(c)(3) research and education affiliate.
Net Revenue: FY ending 6/94 $2,953,502 **Net Expenses:** $1,777,370 63%/21%/16% **Net Assets:** $1,137,834
Citations: 4,545:7
Tax Status: 501(c)(4)
Board of Directors or Trustees: Pat Brady, Jane Garbacz, Marilyn Brill, Bobbie Hill, Beverly McKinnell, Nancy Pearson, Carole Wagner Vallianos, Kathleen Weisenberg.
Periodicals: *The National Voter* (quarterly magazine).
Other Information: Founded in 1920 by suffragettes. Executive director Gracia Hillman also sits on the board of the Center for Community Change. Affiliated with the 501(c)(3) League of Women Voters Education Fund at the same address. The two affiliates had combined net revenues of $6,255,810, net expenses of $6,102,595, and net assets of $1,674,271. The League received $1,692,194, or 57% of revenue, from membership dues. $751,162, or 25%, from gifts and grants awarded by foundations, businesses, and individuals. (These grants included $150,000 from the Joyce Foundation, $50,505 from the Henry J. Kaiser Family Foundation.) $222,651, or 8%, from council and convention fees. $127,603, or 4%, from mailing list rentals. $76,186, or 3%, from the sale of publications. $33,367, or 1%, from sublease income. The remaining revenue came from dividends and interest from securities, other investment income, interest on savings and temporary cash investments, and other miscellaneous sources.

League of Women Voters Education Fund (LWVEF)
1730 M St., N.W.
Washington, DC 20036   **Phone:** (202) 429-1965   **E-Mail:** 75352.2614@compuserve.com
USA   **Fax:**   (202) 429-0854

Contact Person: Sherry Rockey, Senior Manager.   **Officers or Principals:** Sherry Rockey, Senior Manager ($50,451); Marlene Cohn, Senior Manager ($48,007); Elizabeth Kraft, Project Manager ($37,406); Becky Cain, President; Diane Sheridan, First Vice President; Peggy Lucas, Second Vice President; Robin Seaborn, Secretary/Treasurer.
Mission or Interest: Research and education affiliate of the League of Women Voters.
Accomplishments: In the fiscal year ending June 1994, the Fund spent $2,034,993 on its programs. The largest program, with expenditures of $1,342,683, was general National Office projects "conducted for educational, social, and economic purposes." $510,370 was spent on research and citizen education services "devoted to informing the public about League ecological, social, and economic issues." $181,940 was spent on state and local projects.
Net Revenue: FY ending 6/94 $3,302,308 ($629,720, or 19%, from government grants)
Net Expenses: $3,285,250 62%/15%/24% **Net Assets:** $536,437 **Citations:** 4,545:7
Tax Status: 501(c)(3)
Board of Directors or Trustees: Pat Brady, Jane Garbacz, Marilyn Brill, Bobbie Hill, Beverly McKinnell, Nancy Pearson, Carole Wagner Vallianos, Kathleen Weisenberg, Garcia Hillman.
Periodicals: *Report from the Hill* (newsletter).
Other Information: Founded in 1957. Affiliated with the 501(c)(4) League of Women Voters of the United States. The two affiliates had combined net revenues of $6,255,810, net expenses of $6,102,595, and net assets of $1,674,271. The Fund received $2,241,520, or 68% of revenue, from gifts and grants awarded by foundations, businesses, affiliates, and individuals. (These grants included $412,500 from the Henry J. Kaiser Family Foundation, $200,000 from the 501(c)(4) League of Women Voters, $75,000 from the Carnegie Corporation, and $200 from the Compton Foundation.) $629,720, or 19%, from government grants. $274,253, or 8%, from an insurance recovery. $62,708, or 2%, from the sale of publications. $54,818, or 2%, from dividends and interest from securities. The remaining revenue came from membership dues, capital gains on the sale of securities, and other miscellaneous sources.

Left Curve
P.O. Box 472
Oakland, CA 94604   **Phone:** (510) 763-7193
USA

Contact Person: Csaba Polony. **Officers or Principals:** Csaba Polony, Editor/Publisher; Jack Hirschman, Associate Editor.
Mission or Interest: Publish *Left Curve*, "an artist-produced open critical, journal that addresses the problem(s) of cultural forms, emerging from the crisis of modernity, that strive to be independent from the control of dominant institutions, and free from the shackles of instrumental rationality. Our orientation is premised on the recognition of the destructiveness of commodity (capitalist) systems to all life, and the need to build a non-comodified culture that could potentially create a more harmoneous (sic) relationship among people, and between the human and natural world."
Accomplishments: *Left Curve* has been published since 1974, with the exception of 1979-1982. *Left Curve* has been used in classroom instruction at Georgetown University, the University of Connecticut, and probably others, the publishers believe.

Tax Status: For profit. (Although never profitable.) **Annual Report:** No. **Employees:** 2-3 volunteers.
Periodicals: *Left Curve* (irregularly published journal).
Internships: No.

Legal Action Center for the Homeless
27 West 24th St., Suite 600
New York, NY 10010
USA

Contact Person: Douglas H. Lasdon, Executive Director.   **Officers or Principals:** Douglas H. Lasdon, Executive Director ($68,953); Patrick Horvath ($53,820); Alisa Del Tufo ($41,250); David Tobias, Chairman; Jeffery D. Haroldson, Secretary.
Mission or Interest: Advising the homeless of their rights and defending them in court.
Accomplishments: In the fiscal year ending June 1994 the Center spent $435,132 on its programs.
Net Revenue: FY ending 6/94 $678,463 ($72,000, or 11%, from government grants) **Net Expenses:** $526,528   83%/14%/4%
Net Assets: $778,271 **Citations:** 0:255
Products or Services: Litigation.   **Tax Status:** 501(c)(3)
Board of Directors or Trustees: Father David Kirk, Richard Stengal (*Time Magazine*), Prof. Sue Halpern (Bryn Mawr), Anne Davidson, Michael Barasch, Alberta Fuentes, Haywood Burns (Dean, CUNY Law School), Mitchell Lowenthal, Stephen Loffredo (CUNY Law School), Ellen Baxter, Helen Hershkoff (ACLU), Arnold Peinado, III.
Other Information: The Legal Action Center received $570,313, or 84% of revenue, from gifts and grants awarded by foundations, companies, and individuals. (These grants included $22,500 from the Robert Sterling Clark Foundation.) $72,000, or 11%, from government grants. $36,150, or 5%, from interest on savings and temporary cash investment.

Legal Aid Society of San Francisco
1663 Mission St., Suite 400
San Francisco, CA 94103   **Phone:**   (415) 864-8848
USA

Contact Person: Joan Graff, Executive Director.   **Officers or Principals:** Joan Graff, Executive Director ($83,000); William C. McNeill, III, Senior Staff Attorney ($75,350); Patricia Shiu, Senior Staff Attorney ($62,700).
Mission or Interest: Provides legal services for the indigent. Focus on employment law and workers' rights.
Accomplishments: In the fiscal year ending June 1995, the Society spent $956,435 on its programs. $829,600 was spent on "free legal services for employment related problems of working and unemployed poor persons." This took 6,253 attorney hours, and affected a reported 450,000 clients. $126,835 was spent on "Workers' Rights Clinics" that provided "information and referral for employment related and general legal aid for the indigent.' This served a reported 1,799 clients. The Society spent $54,982 on litigation, and received $336,960 in court-awarded attorney's fees and $384,348 from a court-awarded class action settlement.
Net Revenue: FY ending 6/95 $1,656,712 **Net Expenses:** $1,242,992 77%/16%/8% **Net Assets:** $1,235,407
Citations: 6:210
Products or Services: Litigation, law library, workshops, and lobbying. The Society spent $3,529 on the direct lobbying of legislators. The Society's staff attorneys contacted California state legislators, urging the passage of "civil rights legislation regarding the protection of employment rights of indigent persons, and commented on the California Family Rights Act regulation modifications."
Tax Status: 501(c)(3)
Board of Directors or Trustees: Robert Erickson (Senior V.P., Government Relations, Kaiser Foundation Health Plan), Hon. Joseph Grodin (Hastings College of the Law), Gary Hernandez (Dept. of Insurance), Harvey Hinman (V.P./General Counsel, Chevron Corp.), Richard Odgers (General Counsel, Pacific Telesis Group), James Roethe (Senior V.P., Dir. of Litigation, Bank of America), Guy Rounsaville Jr. (Exec. V.P./Chief Counsel, Wells Fargo Bank), and many others from the legal community.
Other Information: The Society received $892,609, or 54% of revenue, from direct and indirect public support in the form of gifts and grants awarded by foundations, businesses, affiliates, and individuals. $384,348, or 23%, from a court-awarded class action settlement. $336,960, or 20%, from court-awarded attorney's fees. $21,020, or 1%, from dividends and interest from securities. $17,111, or 1%, from interest on savings and temporary cash investments. The remaining revenue came from honoraria, and from an annual lunch honoring officers and board members.

Legal Environmental Assistance Foundation (LEAF)
1115 N. Gadsden St.
Tallahassee, FL 32303   **Phone:**   (904) 681-2591   **E-Mail:** leaf@igc.apc.org
USA   **Fax:**   (904) 224-1275

Contact Person: Cynthia Valencic, Vice President.   **Officers or Principals:** B. Suzi Ruhl, President ($57,377); David Ludder, Vice President ($56,947); Cynthia Valencic, Vice President ($32,229); John Galvin, Chair; Pat Walker, Vice Chair; Larry Thompson, Vice Chair; Robert Kuehn, Secretary; Richard Bronson, Treasurer.
Mission or Interest: Litigation on behalf of environmental causes. "LEAF helps people protect their water, air, land and community from pollution. We work in Alabama, Florida and Georgia. We fix governmental systems which perpetuate degradation of communities and the health of the most vulnerable members of those communities. We build the capacity of communities to bridge the fault lines of race and class and to invest in solutions that will protect environmental and human health for the long term."
Accomplishments: Helped stop a biomedical waste incinerator in "Rural, low-income, majority African-American Quitman County, GA (the first county in the nation to have an ordinance requiring baseline and ongoing epidemiological health assessments by polluting facilities wishing to locate in the community)." Stopped other incinerators and landfills. "A weak dioxin standard was successfully defeated in Florida...Florida passed an Environmental Justice and Equity law (model legislation developed by LEAF) and now has an Environmental Justice and Equity Commission, of which LEAF is a member...Legislators in Georgia introduced an Environmental Justice bill modeled after Florida's...Citizens in Alabama have the right to challenge agency permits without fear of being held responsible for attorneys' fees and costs." In 1994 LEAF spent $489,238 on its programs.

Net Revenue: 1994 $728,207 **Net Expenses:** $511,529 96%/0%/4% **Net Assets:** $738,674 **Citations:** 17:179
Products or Services: Legal and technical services, and lobbying. LEAF spent $165 on lobbying.
Tax Status: 501(c)(3) **Annual Report:** Yes. **Employees:** 10
Board of Directors or Trustees: Col. Richard Bronson (USA, ret.), Joy Towles Cummings, James Hargrett (Florida State Senate-Tampa Bay area), Jefferson Holt (manager of rock band R.E.M.), Assoc. Prof. Robert Kuehn (Tulane Univ. Law School), Ted Mankin (concert promoter), Dean Richard Ottinger (Pace Univ. Law School), Thomas Pelham, Assoc. Prof. Jeffrey Roseman (Univ. of AL, Birmingham, School of Public Health), Pam Shelton, Rep. Doug Teper (Georgia State House). Rep. John Lewis (D-GA) is an honorary member.
Periodicals: *LEAF Briefs* (quarterly newsletter).
Internships: Yes, unpaid internships for law students during the summer.
Other Information: LEAF received $711,501, or 98% of revenue, from direct and indirect public support in the form of gifts and grants awarded by foundations, businesses, affiliates, and individuals. (These grants included $50,000 from the Joyce Mertz-Gilmore Foundation.) $16,706, or 2%, from interest on savings and temporary cash investments.

Legal Services Corporation
750 1st St., 11th Floor
Washington, DC 20002   **Phone:**   (202) 336-8800
USA   **Fax:**   (202) 336-8959

Contact Person: Alexander Forger, President.
Officers or Principals: David L. Richardson, Treasurer ($96,543); Edouard Quatrevaux, Inspector General ($90,950); Victor Fortuno, General Counsel ($90,907); Alexander Forger, President; Martha Bermark, Vice President; Patricia D. Batie, Secretary.
Mission or Interest: Established in 1974 to provide legal counsel to those who cannot afford it. "Provides financial support to independent organizations that provide legal assistance in non-criminal matters." Much of the work done by the funded organizations focuses on the rights of welfare recipients and the compliance with civil rights laws. Created and funded by the U.S. federal government.
Accomplishments: In the fiscal year ending September 1994, the Corporation awarded $389,922,348 to legal advocacy organizations. Funded organizations focused on; legal advocacy training, legal research, migrant workers' rights, immigrants' rights, consumers' rights, housing rights, and Native Americans' rights. The Corporation spent $19,769 on advertising, $11,349 on employee lectures, and $81,778 on recruiting fees.
Net Revenue: FY ending 9/94 $403,103,816 ($402,294,259, or 99.8%, from government grants)
Net Expenses: $399,856,787 98%/2%/0% **Net Assets:** $1.084,956 **Citations:** 311:56
Products or Services: Financial support for legal advocacy groups.
Tax Status: 501(c)(3)
Board of Directors or Trustees: Hulett Askew, LaVeeda Morgan Battle, John Broderick Jr., John Brooks, Douglas Eakeley, Edna Fairbanks-Williams, F. William McCalpin, Maria Luisa Mercado, Nancy Hardin Rogers, Thomas Smegal Jr.
Other Information: The Corporation hired the San Francisco firm of Cotton & Company, the Boston firm of Isaacson, Miller, Inc., the DC firm of Lictman, Trister, et al, and the Baltimore firm of Shapiro & Olander for consulting. They were paid $104,613, $56,425, $46,453, and $36,589 respectively. The Corporation received $402,294,259, or 99.8% of total revenue, from government grants. The remaining revenue came from interest on savings and temporary cash investments, rental income, litigation awards, and other miscellaneous sources. The Corporation held $68,524,592, or 98.5% of total assets, in cash and savings and temporary cash investments.

Leonard Peltier Defense Committee
P.O. Box 583
Lawrence, KS 66044   **Phone:**   (913) 842-5774   **E-Mail:** lpdc@idir.net
USA   **Fax:**   (913) 842-5796   **Web-Page:** http://www.unicom.net/peltier/index/html

Mission or Interest: Committee dedicated to the release of Leonard Peltier, an American Indian activist convicted of killing two FBI agents at Okalala. The Committee and others believe that he was wrongly convicted, and that new evidence proves his innocence.

Lesbian and Gay Immigration Rights Task Force (LGRITF)
P.O. Box 7741
New York, NY 10016   **Phone:**   (212) 802-7264
USA

Mission or Interest: Challenges the immigration law that discriminates against homosexuals.

Lesbian and Gay Public Awareness Project
P.O. Box 60881
Phoenix, AZ 85082
USA

Contact Person: Peter Crozier, President. **Officers or Principals:** Chris Yalda, Facilitator ($0); Tony Fernandez-Vinas, Secretary ($0); Catherine Cooker, Statutory Agent ($0); Bruce Bouldin, Treasurer.

Mission or Interest: Promotion and education about homosexuality.
Accomplishments: In the fiscal year ending June 1995, the Project spent $9,670 on its programs. The largest program, with expenditures of $2,681, was events and activities in conjunction with National Coming Out Day. $1,500 was spent on a Martin Luther King Breakfast "to increase awareness with other Arizona minority organizations." $1,269 to produce and distribute a quarterly newsletter. $968 to produce a "Homophobia Brochure," "describing the effects of Homophobia." Other programs included a Speaker's Bureau, gay pride festival, Hispanic outreach efforts, a radio show, Adopt-A-Highway participation, and more.
Net Revenue: FY ending 6/95 $24,858 **Net Expenses:** $15,234 63%/33%/4% **Net Assets:** $12,028
Tax Status: 501(c)(3)
Periodicals: Quarterly newsletter.
Other Information: The Project received 100% of its funding from gifts and grants awarded by foundations, businesses, and individuals. All of its assets were held in non-interest bearing cash.

Lesbian Herstory Educational Foundation
P.O. Box 1258
New York, NY 10116   **Phone:** (212) 874-7232
USA

Contact Person: Deborah Edel, Treasurer.
Officers or Principals: Joan Nestle, Secretary ($0); Judith Schwartz, Records Manager ($0).
Mission or Interest: "Resource and information service for all aspects of lesbian culture. Provide print information and public speakers to community at large."
Accomplishments: In 1994 the Foundation spent $39,602 on its programs.
Net Revenue: 1994 $59,482 **Net Expenses:** $39,602 57%/40%/3% **Net Assets:** $338,033
Tax Status: 501(c)(3)
Other Information: The Foundation received $59,482, or 95% of revenue, from gifts and grants awarded by foundations, businesses, and individuals. (The Foundation has historically received grant funding from the Ms. Foundation.) $1,474, or 2%, from interest on savings and temporary cash investments. $1,148, or 2%, from honoraria. The remaining revenue came from the sale of inventory.

Letters for Animals
P.O. Box 7-EA
La Plume, PA 18440   **Phone:** (717) 945-5312   **E-Mail:** LMANHEIM@aol.com
USA   **Fax:**   (717) 945-3471

Contact Person: Lynn Manheim.
Mission or Interest: Advocates animal rights by organizing letter writing campaigns to newspapers, public officials, and corporations.
Accomplishments: Many successful campaigns. A "Letters for Animals" column is now carried in Pennsylvania newsweekly.
Products or Services: Various letters that are sent out to subscribers who sign and send them.
Tax Status: For profit (but may become 501(c)(3) in the future). **Employees:** 1

Liberal Opinion Week
P.O. Box 468
Vinton, IA 52349   **Phone:** (800) 338-9335
USA   **Fax:**   (319) 472-4811

Mission or Interest: Weekly collection of columnists from the left. Featured columnists include Molly Ivins, Mary McGrory, Richard Cohen, Jesse Jackson, Calvin Trillin, Deb Price, Linda Ellerbee, David Broder, Ralph Nader, Nat Hentoff, Clarence Page, Ellen Goodman, Anna Quindlen, Mark Shields, Alexander Cockburn, and others.
Tax Status: For profit.

Liberal Religious Charitable Society
61 Thicket St.
Weymouth, MA 02190   **Phone:** (617) 337-7566
USA

Contact Person: William N. Holway, President.
Officers or Principals: Dr. Robert Adelman, Vice President ($0); William A. Donovan, Treasurer/Clerk ($0).
Mission or Interest: Grant-making foundation "To promote and provide religious, educational and charitable programs, particularly those associated with the Unitarian Universalist Association."
Accomplishments: In 1994 the Society awarded $239,500 in grants.
Net Revenue: 1994 $239,500 **Net Expenses:** $290,073 87%/13%/0% **Net Assets:** $6,218,141
Tax Status: 501(c)(3)
Board of Directors or Trustees: Dr. Charles Davidson, Juliet Underwood, Robert Senghas.
Other Information: Affiliated with the Unitarian Universalist Association. The Society received $430,104 net, or 72% of revenue, from capital gains on the sale of securities. $141,287, or 24%, from dividends and interest from securities. $22,728, or 4%, from interest on savings and temporary cash investments.

Liberty Hill Foundation

1316 Third St. Promenade, Suite B-4
Santa Monica, CA 90401-1325   **Phone:**   (310) 458-1450
USA   **Fax:**   (310) 451-4283

Contact Person: Michele Prichard, Secretary.   **Officers or Principals:** Michele Prichard, Secretary ($46,038); Margarita Ramirez, Vice President ($19,329); Paula Litt, Treasurer ($0).
Mission or Interest: "Liberty Hill Foundation awards grants to organizations which advocate progressive social change. We support groups which organize people to address fundamental problems affecting their lives, and which educate the community about social and economic conditions... Grants range from $500 to a maximum of $8,000."
Accomplishments: In the fiscal year ending June 1994, the Foundation awarded $538,453 in grants. Recipients included; four grants totaling $47,500 for the Black Awareness Community Development Organization, two grants totaling $25,000 for the Korean Immigrant Workers Advocates, two grants totaling $22,500 for Citizens for a Better Environment , two grants totaling $20,500 for the St. Joseph Center, $20,000 for the Latino Unity Forum, and three grants totaling $18,500 for the Al Wooten Jr. Heritage Center.
Net Revenue: FY ending 6/94 $586,454 **Net Expenses:** $722,619 83%/11%/6% **Net Assets:** $1,265,474
Products or Services: Grants, technical assistance, and lobbying. In the fiscal year ending June 1994 the Foundation spent $1,346 on grassroots lobbying. This was down 57% from the previous year and down 90% from $13,445 two years prior.
Tax Status: 501(c)(3)
Board of Directors or Trustees: Leo Baefsky, Miven Booth, Sylvia Castillo, Barbara Cohn, Alan Gleitsman (ACLU of Southern CA), Win McCormack, Wally Marks, Paul Moore, Sarah Pillsbury, Moe Stavnezer, Gary Stewart (Rhino Records), Angel Zapata, Lori Zimmerman.
Periodicals: Newsletter.
Other Information: The Foundation is a member of the Funding Exchange. The Foundation received $538,579, or 92% of revenue, from gifts and grants awarded by foundations, businesses, and individuals. (These grants included $12,500 from the McKay Foundation.) $84, 274, or 14%, from interest on savings and temporary cash investments. Revenues were partially offset by a loss of $16,153 on the sale of securities, and a loss of $25,395 from the "Upton Sinclair Dinner."

Light Party, The

20 Sunnyside Ave., Suite A-156
Mill Valley, CA 94941   **Phone:**   (415) 381-2357   **E-Mail:** 75127,1231@compuserve.com
USA   **Fax:**   (415) 381-2645

Contact Person: Da Vid.
Mission or Interest: Political party devoted to "Health, Peace, and Freedom for All." Platform calls for a Canadian-style single-payer health program, the dissolution of the IRS and all personal and corporate income taxes be replaced with a 10%-12% national sales tax, demilitarization, an economy run on solar power, hydrogen power and other 'sustainable' power sources. They also propose a global television network which features continuous programming that "inspires, delights, heals, and enlightens."
Accomplishments: Da Vid (a.k.a. Raphael Ornstein, M.D.) has run for president as a write-in candidate on the predecessors of the Light Party ticket, the Yes Party and the Human Ecology Party.
Tax Status: 501(c)(3)
Other Information: They plan to transform Alcatraz Island into a "Global Peace Center."

LightHawk

P.O. Box 8163
Santa Fe, NM 87504
USA

Mission or Interest: Anti-lumber environmental organization. Makes use of flights to provide tours and mapping of forests in the Pacific Northwest.
Accomplishments: Introduced a new technology called "multispectral imaging," that can map land cover and land use, survey wildlife and access the environment.
Other Information: LightHawk provided footage for an NBC news story on Clearwater National Forest in Idaho showing dead fish and clear-cut forests. The footage was revealed to have come from another location, and NBC publicly apologized. In 1994 LightHawk received $150,000 from the Pew Caritable Trusts, $50,000 from the Bullitt Foundation, $30,000 from the Tides Foundation, $500 the Jessie Smith Noyes Foundation, and $500 from the Haymarket People's Fund.

Lilith Publications / *Lilith*

250 W. 57th St., Suite 2432
New York, NY 10107   **Phone:**   (212) 757-0818   **E-Mail:** lilithmag@aol.com
USA   **Fax:**   (212) 757-5705

Contact Person: Naomi Danis.
Officers or Principals: Susan Weidman Schneider, President ($63,600).
Mission or Interest: Publication of *Lilith*, a magazine of Jewish feminism.
Accomplishments: Circulation of approximately 1,200 subscribers. Maintains a talent bank and resource center. In 1994 the publishers spent $278,502 on its programs. $253,726 was spent producing and distributing *Lilith*.
Net Revenue: 1994 $292,189 **Net Expenses:** $307,069 91%/6%/3% **Net Assets:** (-$91,416)

Tax Status: 501(c)(3) **Employees:** 6
Periodicals: *Lilith* (quarterly magazine).
Internships: Yes. Part-time internships for students that pay a "small" stipend.
Other Information: In 1994 the publisher received $180,870, or 62% of revenue, from gifts and grants awarded by foundations, businesses, and individuals. $101,394, or 35%, from subscriptions and newsstand sales. $9,910, or 3%, from the sale of advertising.

Live Oak Fund for Change
702 Buckingham Circle
Austin, TX 78704
USA

Contact Person: Kate Fitzgerald, Executive Director.   **Officers or Principals:** Kate Fitzgerald, Executive Director ($3,300).
Mission or Interest: Grant-making organization supporting social change organizations.
Accomplishments: In the fiscal year ending June 1993, the Fund awarded $3,135. This was substantially less than previous years due to a decrease in revenues.
Net Revenue: FY ending 6/93 $31,369 **Net Expenses:** $28,238 **Net Assets:** $14,159
Tax Status: 501(c)(3)
Board of Directors or Trustees: Susan DeMarco, Carol Rodriguez, Frank Cook, Wendy Watriss, S. Meacham, G. Shartle, L. Miller.
Other Information: The Fund received $31,911, or 98% of gross revenue, from gifts and grants awarded by foundations, businesses, and individuals. The remaining revenue came from investment income and other miscellaneous sources. The Fund lost $1,260 on the sale of assets.

Louisiana Environmental Action Network (LEAN)
555 St. Tammany St.
Baton Rouge, LA 70806   **Phone:** (504) 928-1315
USA

Contact Person: Marylee Orr, Executive Director.
Officers or Principals: Marylee Orr, Executive Director ($28,708); Lorena Pespisil ($0); Jerry Speil ($0); Florence Robinson.
Mission or Interest: "Support environmental groups with an emphasis on low income and minority groups."
Accomplishments: In 1994 the Network spent $197,192 on its programs. This included $13,859 in grants awarded to other organizations.
Net Revenue: 1994 $267,881 **Net Expenses:** $260,235 76%/24%/0% **Net Assets:** $62,667
Products or Services: Grants and other assistance, lobbying. The Network spent $5,000 on lobbying.
Tax Status: 501(c)(3)
Other Information: The Network received $223,000, or 83% of revenue, from gifts and grants awarded by foundations, businesses, and individuals. (These grants included $50,000 from the Florence and John Schumann Foundation, $25,000 from the Jessie Smith Noyes Foundation, $15,000 from the Ruth Mott Fund, $10,000 from the Beldon Fund, $7,500 from the New World Foundation.) $44,881, or 17%, from membership dues.

Lucius and Eva Eastman Fund
5926 Fiddletown Place
San Jose, CA 95120
USA

Contact Person: Lucius R. Eastman, Jr., President.
Mission or Interest: Grant-making philanthropy focusing on feminism and the arts.
Accomplishments: In 1993 the Fund awarded $61,790 in grants. The recipients of the largest grants included: four grants totaling $6,690 for the Film Arts Foundation, $3,500 for the Iris Feminist Collective, $2,500 each for the Napa Valley Arts Council, Theater for New County Foundation, Media Alliance, and Women Making Movies. Other recipients included: the National Center for Women and Family Law, Center for Community Change, Cheer for Vietnam, Data Center, Media Network, and the Institute for Social and Economic Studies.
Net Revenue: 1993 $850,229 **Net Expenses:** $97,014 **Net Assets:** $1,960,416
Tax Status: 501(c)(3)
Other Information: The Fund received $700,000, or 82% of revenue, from gifts and grants awarded by foundations, businesses, and individuals. $90,866, or 11%, from dividends and interest from securities. $59,363, or 7%, from capital gains on the sale of securities. The Fund held $1,116,455, or 57% of assets, in corporate stocks and bonds. $489,645, or 25%, in cash, and $354,315, or 18% in government obligations.

Lucius Trust and Arcane School
120 Wall St., 24th Floor
New York, NY 10005   **Phone:** (212) 292-0707
USA   **Fax:**   (212) 292-0808

Contact Person: Ida Urso. **Officers or Principals:** Josette Allan, Secretary/Treasurer ($16,968); Sarah McKechnie, President ($14,400); Dave McKechnie, Vice President ($14,400).
Mission or Interest: Promotes world peace based on the ideas of Alice A. Bailey. "They promote the education of the human mind towards recognition and practice of the spiritual principles and values upon which a stable and interdependent world society may be based."
Accomplishments: The Lucius Trust is on the Roster of the United Nations Economic and Social Council and is represented at regular briefing sessions at the UN in New York and Geneva. They have offices in London and Geneva. In 1994 they spent $85,791 on their Arcane School, an adult education program conducted through correspondence courses. Course materials are provided free-of-charge. They spent $52,260 on their World Goodwill program. $43,666 was spent on their Triangle service that joins individuals through the power of thought and prayer.
Net Revenue: 1994 $358,578 **Net Expenses:** $370,148 64%/36%/0% **Net Assets:** $238,573
Products or Services: Publishes the works of Alice Bailey. Courses, a lending library and other services.
Tax Status: 501(c)(3) **Annual Report:** Yes. **Employees:** 3
Board of Directors or Trustees: Mary Bailey, J.J.G. Bourne, Winifred Brewin, Perry Coles, Janet Nation, S.I.W. Nation, Peter Peuler.
Periodicals: *World Goodwill Newsletter* (quarterly).
Internships: No.
Other Information: The Arcane School was founded in 1923, World Goodwill in 1932, and Triangles in 1937. "A new and better way of life for all people everywhere in the world can become a reality in our time. Practical techniques in operation today can be learned and applied to the fulfilment of the divine plan for humanity." The Trust received $177,664, or 50% of revenue, from grants awarded by foundations, companies and individuals. $172,171, or 48%, from program service revenues. $7,214, or 2%, from interest on savings and temporary cash investments.

Lumpen Media Group \ *Lumpen Times*

2558 W. Armitage Ave.
Chicago, IL 60647   **Phone:** (312) 227-2072   **E-Mail:** lumptime@mcs.com
USA   **Fax:** same

Contact Person: Chris Molnar, Co-Publisher.
Officers or Principals: Ed Marszewski, Co-Publisher; Leslie Stella, Managing Editor.
Mission or Interest: Publishes the *Lumpen Times* "to dig up the dirt in mainstream discourse, exposing and resisting the degradation in our mental and physical environment."
Accomplishments: "Chosen one of the top ten 'zines in the country by *Factsheet 5*. Challenged and defeated the *Chicago Reader*, the local weekly, on community rights. Have been publishing for four solid years with no start-up money. A truly independent cultural/political magazine with a circulation of 20,000."
Tax Status: For profit. **Annual Report:** No. **Employees:** 12
Periodicals: *Lumpen Times*.
Internships: Yes. Interns perform clerical duties, editing, layout and design, research, fact-checking, and writing.

Lunatic Fringe

P.O. Box 7652
Santa Cruz, CA 95061   **Phone:** (408) 425-6526
USA

Contact Person: Morgan Firestar, Publisher.
Mission or Interest: Newsletter, or 'zine, revealing psychiatric abuses and how to stop them. Also supports increases in welfare. Newsletter contains songs, poems, and calls for revolutionary anarchy.
Accomplishments: Published on a shoe-string budget. Now has a weekly radio show on Free Radio Santa Cruz.
Products or Services: Newsletter, radio show, tapes of programs.
Periodicals: *Lunatic Fringe* (newsletter).
Other Information: Copies are free to "psychiatric inmates" and prisoners. As a youth, Firestar was held against his will in a psychiatric treatment facility.

Macrocosm USA

P.O. Box 185
Cambria, CA 93428   **Phone:** (805) 927-8030   **E-Mail:** brockway@macronet.org
USA   **Web-Page:** http://www.macronet.org/macronet/

Contact Person: Sandi Brockway.
Mission or Interest: "Promoting environmental education, progressive politics, peace and justice." Produces "an environmental, political, and social solutions handbook with directories" called Macrocosm USA: Possibilities for a New Progressive Era. Also maintains a computer bulletin board, MacroNET, which contains continually updated information on progressive organizations.
Accomplishments: Vice President Al Gore said, "There are many crucial challenges that await us in the next few years...I need your help now as we work to build a better future for all Americans. I appreciate your expression of support and generosity. Thank you for Macrocosm." The *Utne Reader* said, "There is no guide to the social change movements comparable to this: It seems destined to become indispensable."

Products or Services: Directory/handbook, computer network.
Tax Status: 501(c)(3) **Employees:** All volunteer.
Internships: Yes, provides room and board, and computer training.

MADRE

121 W. 27th St., Suite 301
New York, NY 10001   **Phone:** (212) 627-0444
USA

Contact Person: Sarah Santana, Executive Director.
Mission or Interest: Feminism and peace and justice in the third world.
Tax Status: 501(c)(3)
Other Information: In 1993 Madre received $3,000 from the Peace Development Fund. In 1994 it received $5,000 from the New-Land Foundation, $1,000 from the Peace Development Fund, $750 from the Haymarket People's Fund, $500 from the Stewart R. Mott Charitable Trust, $500 from the Bread and Roses Community Fund, and $250 from the Vanguard Public Foundation.

Maine Peace Fund

P.O. Box 3842
Portland, ME 04104   **Phone:** (207) 772-0680
USA

Contact Person: David Hart.
Officers or Principals: Andrew Tonks, Chair ($0); Chris Davis, Treasurer ($0); Jeanne Davis, Secretary ($0).
Mission or Interest: "General research and education activities to promote peace and global security."
Accomplishments: In 1994 the Fund spent $99,176 on its activities.
Net Revenue: 1994 $144,074 **Net Expenses:** $160,448 62%/26%/12% **Net Assets:** $5,923
Tax Status: 501(c)(3)
Board of Directors or Trustees: Judy Feinstein, Kathy Greason, Susie Schweppe.
Other Information: The Fund received $143,459, or 99.5% of revenue, from gifts and grants awarded by foundations, businesses, and individuals. (These grants included $25,000 from the Joyce Mertz-Gilmore Foundation, $20,000 from the Peace Development Fund, and $15,000 from the Ploughshares Fund.) The remaining revenue came from membership dues and interest on savings and temporary cash investments.

Maine People's Alliance

65 W. Commercial St.
Portland, ME 04101   **Phone:** (207) 781-3853
USA

Contact Person: Art Shea, Co-Chair.   **Officers or Principals:** Mark Donnelly, Co-Chair; Jeannie Guisinger, Secretary.
Mission or Interest: Public policy and advocacy and education in Maine.
Accomplishments: In 1994 the Alliance spent $210,927 on its programs. The largest program, with expenditures of $119,813, was door-to-door canvassing which served to distribute information, recruit new members, and solicit funds. $66,271 was spent on state-wide and community organizing. $24,769 for telephone canvassing. The Alliance has a political action committee that was mostly inactive in 1994, spending only $74. The Alliance performed organizing work in Maine for Citizens for Affordable Health Care.
Net Revenue: 1994 $263,607 **Net Expenses:** $259,808 81%/11%/8% **Net Assets:** $3,643
Tax Status: 501(c)(4)
Other Information: Affiliated with the 501(c)(3) Maine People's Resource Center at the same address. The two affiliates had combined net revenues of $485,577, net expenses of $505,808, and net assets of $7,624. In 1994 the Alliance received $209,328, or 79% of revenue, from gifts and grants awarded by foundations, affiliates, businesses, and individuals. (These grants included $65,300 from the affiliated Maine People's Resource Center.) $44,251, or 17%, from reimbursed expenses from the Maine People's Resource Center for canvassing services. $7,786, or 3%, from reimbursed expenses from the Citizens for Affordable Health Care for organizing activities. The remaining revenue came from advertising and interest on savings and temporary cash investments.

Maine People's Resource Center

65 W. Commercial St.
Portland, ME 04101   **Phone:** (207) 781-3853
USA

Contact Person: Jack Comart, President.   **Officers or Principals:** Matt Howe, Secretary ($0); Joe Ditro, Treasurer ($0).
Mission or Interest: Research and education on public policy in Maine.
Accomplishments: In 1994 the Center spent $213,496 on its programs. The largest program, with expenditures of $165,996, was public education through door-to-door canvassing, conferences, publications, community organizing, leadership training and technical assistance. This included a grant of $65,300 to its lobbying affiliate, the Maine People's Alliance, although the Center claims these funds were not used for lobbying. $47,500 was spent on a research project to study "the impact of state budget decisions on the lives of Maine citizens, including lower income citizens." The project resulted in a published report.

Net Revenue: 1994 $221,970 **Net Expenses:** $246,000 87%/9%/4% **Net Assets:** $3,981
Tax Status: 501(c)(3)
Other Information: Affiliated with the 501(c)(4) Maine People's Alliance at the same address. The two affiliates had combined net revenues of $485,577, net expenses of $505,808, and net assets of $7,624. In 1994 the Center received $219,497, or 99% of revenue, from gifts and grants awarded by foundations, businesses, and individuals. (These grants included $40,000 from the Public Welfare Foundation, $35,000 from the Jesse B. Cox Charitable Trust, $18,750 from the Campaign for Human Development, and $7,000 from the Maine Trial Lawyers.) The remaining revenue came from the sale of inventory, interest on savings and temporary cash investments, and other miscellaneous sources.

Management Assistance Group (MAG)

1555 Connecticut Ave., N.W., 3rd Floor
Washington, DC 20036   **Phone:**   (202) 659-1963
USA   **Fax:**   (202) 659-3105

Contact Person: Susan Gross, Executive Director.
Officers or Principals: Susan Gross, Executive Director ($90,169); Karl Mathiasen, III, Assistant Treasurer ($79,551); Kathryn Waller, Chairman ($0); Julia Scott, Vice Chairman; Nancy Franco, Steve Plumer, Senior Counselors.
Mission or Interest: Works with social change nonprofits to increase their capabilities by improving internal structure, leadership, planning, management capabilities, and fund-raising skills.
Accomplishments: Over the past 15 years, MAG has worked with over 700 organizations. These organizations included: AIDS Action Council, Alliance for Justice, various ACLU affiliates, Bazelon Center for Mental Health Law, Center for Community Change, Center on Budget and Policy Priorities, Children's Defense Fund, Council on Economic Priorities, Economic Policy Institute, FairTest, Friends of the Earth, Gay and Lesbian Alliance Against Defamation, Global Fund for Women, Government Accountability Project, NAACP Legal Defense and Educational Fund, National Abortion and Reproductive Rights Action League, National Council of La Raza, Natural Resources Defense Council, People for the American Way, Physicians for Social Responsibility, Religious Coalition for Reproductive Rights, Sierra Club, Zero Population Growth, and others. In the fiscal year ending September 1995, the Group spent $416,862 on its programs. The Group assisted 75-80 organizations that year.
Net Revenue: FY ending 9/95 $623,369 **Net Expenses:** $588,574 71%/21%/8% **Net Assets:** $247,794
Citations: 3:222
Products or Services: Numerous publications. **Tax Status:** 501(c)(3)
Board of Directors or Trustees: Bill Bondurant, Isabel Carter Stewart (Girls Inc.), Mark Rosenman (Union Inst.), Whitney Hatch (Regulatory Affairs, GTE Corp.), Paul Kawata (Minority AIDS Council).
Other Information: The Group received $386,193, or 62% of revenue, from fees for service from nonprofit organizations. $220,582, or 35%, from gifts and grants awarded by foundations, businesses, and individuals. (These grants included $50,000 from the Joyce Mertz-Gilmore Foundation, $10,000 from the Jessie Smith Noyes Foundation.) $11,500, or 2%, from sublease income. $5,094, or 1%, from interest on savings and temporary cash investments.

Maoist Internationalist Movement (MIM)

P.O. Box 3576
Ann Arbor, MI 48106   **E-Mail:** mim@nyxfer.blythe.org
USA

Mission or Interest: "A revolutionary communist party that upholds Marxism-Leninism-Maoism. MIM is an internationalist organization that works from the vantage point of the Third World proletariat; thus its members are not Amerikans, but world citizens...MIM struggles to end the oppression of all groups over other groups; classes, genders, nations. MIM knows this is only possible by building public opinion to seize power through armed struggle...MIM upholds the Chinese Cultural Revolution as the farthest advance of communism in human history." MIM works primarily through its monthly tabloid, *MIM Notes*. *MIM Notes* articles are signed by authors who only identify themselves as "MC" (for Maoist Comrade) followed by a number; e.g. MC7.
Periodicals: *MIM Notes* (monthly tabloid), and *Maoist Sojourner* (monthly), a publication for "Third World Maoist exiles."
Other Information: Also maintains a Los Angeles office; P.O. Box 29670, Los Angeles, CA 90029.

Martin Luther King, Jr., Center for Nonviolent Social Change

449 Auburn Ave., N.E.
Atlanta, GA 30312   **Phone:**   (404) 524-1956
USA

Contact Person: Ronald L. Guincy, Executive Director.
Officers or Principals: Ronald L. Quincy, Executive Director ($186,719); Coretta Scott King, CEO ($114,922); Johnny J. Mack, Financial Director ($71,796); Christin King Farris, Treasurer; Marvin Goldstein, Vice Chair; John W. Cox, Secretary.
Mission or Interest: Promotion of social change through the methods and philosophies advocated by Martin Luther King, Jr.
Accomplishments: In the fiscal year ending June 1994, the Center spent $4,277,386 on its programs.
Net Revenue: FY ending 6/94 $4,915,087 ($2,235,335, or 45%, from government grants)
Net Expenses: $5,517,724 78%/21%/1% **Net Assets:** $8,206,884 **Citations:** 137:99
Products or Services: Research, education, training, and community services. Although the Center did not do any lobbying during 1994, it has in the past. In the fiscal year ending June 1992 the Center spent $70,280 on lobbying.
Tax Status: 501(c)(3)

Other Information: The Center received $2,235,335, or 45% of revenue, from the government. $1,289,080, or 26%, came from program service fees, including the sale of materials on the life and work of Martin Luther King, Jr., fees for training programs, and tour fees. $1,045,038, or 21%, from grants awarded by foundations, companies and individuals. $111,094 net, or 2% from fund-raising events. The remaining revenue came from net interest, rents, dividends, and profits from the sale of inventory.

Massachusetts Senior Action Council

186 Lincoln St.
Boston, MA 02111   **Phone:**   (617) 350-6722
USA

Contact Person: Geoffrey Wilkinson, Executive Director.
Officers or Principals: Geoffrey Wilkinson, Executive Director ($37,376); Madeline Therrien, President ($0); Oscar Farmer, Vice President ($0); Ida Abreu, Secretary; Inez Edmead, Treasurer; Manny Weiner, Legislative Director.
Mission or Interest: Organizes and educates senior citizens "in such areas as health care, housing, and public benefits."
Accomplishments: In the fiscal year ending March 1995 the Council spent $250,723 on its programs.
Net Revenue: FY ending 3/95 $320,936 **Net Expenses:** $298,798 84%/7%/9% **Net Assets:** $60,408
Products or Services: Organizing, educational materials, and lobbying. The Council spent $5,966 on its lobbying efforts.
Tax Status: 501(c)(3)
Board of Directors or Trustees: Freda Mulkern, Della Webb, Jeanne Patterson, William Heatherman, Angie Medeiros, Edith Quintin, Jean Wilbur, Joe Quinn, Bea Cevasco, Irene Kamila, Betty Ormon, Steve Rosner (AFSME).
Periodicals: Newsletter.
Other Information: The Council received $292,290, or 91% of revenue, from gifts and grants awarded by foundations, businesses, and individuals. (These grants included $50,000 from the J. Cox Foundation, $35,000 from the Boston Foundation, $30,000 from the Campaign for Human Development, $20,000 from the Hyams Foundation, $15,000 from the Island Foundation, $12,838 from Community Works, $12,000 from the Grimes-King Foundation, $10,000 from the Needmor Trust, and $7,500 from the Stearns Foundation.) $13,897, or 4%, from membership dues. $13,472, or 4%, from special fund-raising events. The remaining revenue came from interest on savings and temporary cash investments.

McKay Foundation

383 Rhode Island St.
San Francisco, CA 94103   **Phone:**   (415) 554-0166
USA

Contact Person: Robert McKay, Executive Director.
Officers or Principals: Robert L. McKay, Chairman ($0); John P, McKay, Vice President ($0); Elaine McKay, Secretary ($0).
Mission or Interest: Grant-making foundation that gives to progressive groups, mostly in California.
Accomplishments: In 1993 the Foundation awarded $282,350 in grants. Top recipients included; $24,500 for the California Rural Legal Assistance Foundation, $17,000 for the Center for Community Advocacy, $15,000 each for the East Bay Community Foundation, Encampment for Citizenship, Hollywood Urban Project, Bay Area Black Women's Health Project, Center for Third World Organizing, Coalition for Immigrant and Refugee Rights, $12,500 for the Liberty Hill Foundation, $12,000 for the San Francisco Organizing Project, and $10,000 for the Center for Community Change.
Net Revenue: 1993 $1,307,926 **Net Expenses:** $313,497 **Net Assets:** $1,509,375
Tax Status: 501(c)(3)
Other Information: The Foundation received $1,289,375, or 99% of revenue, from gifts and grants awarded by foundations, corporations and individuals. $7,842, or 1%, from the sale of assets. The remaining revenue came from interest on savings and temporary cash investments and interest and dividends from securities. Most of the assets, 76%, were held in Pepsico stock.

McKenzie River Gathering Foundation (MRG)

3558 S.E. Hawthorne Blvd.
Portland, OR 97214   **Phone:**   (503) 233-0271   **E-Mail:** mrgf@aol.com
USA   **Fax:**   (503) 233-0452

Contact Person: Madeline Moore. **Officers or Principals:** Linda Reymers, Co-Director ($36,520); Tarso Ramos, Chair; Teresa Enrico, Vice Chair; Foncy Prescott, Secretary. (Salaries are from the fiscal year ending 6/94)
Mission or Interest: Philanthropy supporting progressive, multi-issue, social change projects in Oregon. Focus on grassroots activist organizations.
Accomplishments: In the fiscal year ending June 1995 they awarded $358,776 in grants. Top recipients included; $10,000 for the FarmWorker Housing Development Corporation and Proyecto (organizing and advocacy in the Latino community), $8,000 each for the Clergy and Laity Concerned of Lane County and the Hotel Workers Organizing Committee, $6,750 for the Willamette Valley Law Project, $6,500 for the Theater Adelante/Theatro Nuestro (a Latino youth play which addresses the anti-immigration movement), $5,760 for the Umpqua Watersheds (environmental organization), and $5,000 each for the Rural Organizing Project, Sacred Earth Coalition, and the Tygh of Tlxni Cultural Conservancy. MRG recently completed its Endowment Campaign to raise $1,000,000. Their goal was to raise the funds by December 1995, but they reached it ahead of schedule in June of that year.

Net Revenue: FY ending 6/95 $982,573 **Net Expenses:** $547,535 77%/16%/6% **Net Assets:** $1,296,960
Products or Services: Grants and other support. Conferences and seminars, such as their "Socially Responsible Investing" seminar and their "Inherited Wealth Conferences." The Inherited Wealth Conferences "offer a safe place for progressive women and men with wealth to come together and explore personal, technical and political issues specific to their situation."
Tax Status: 501(c)(3) **Annual Report:** Yes. **Employees:** 3
Board of Directors or Trustees: Jan Fenton, Glenn Harris, Gillian Leichtling, John Lunsford, Trevor Monteith, Cecil Prescod, Guadalupe Quinn, Kelley Weigel, Marcy Westerling.
Internships: No.
Other Information: They also have an office in Eugene: 454 Willamette, Eugene, OR 97401, voice (541) 485-2790, fax (541) 485-7604, e-mail mrfg@efn.org, contact Linda Reymers. The McKenzie River Gathering Foundation is a member of the Funding Exchange Network. The Foundation received $922,743, or 94% of revenue, from gifts and grants awarded by foundations, companies, affiliates and individuals. (These grants included $2,000 from the Vanguard Public Foundation.) $41,664, or 4%, from interest and dividends from securities. $5,219, or 1%, from special events and conferences. The remaining revenue came from administrative fees, loan loss adjustments, and other miscellaneous sources.

Media Alliance
814 Mission St., Suite 205
San Francisco, CA 94103   **Phone:** (415) 546-6334   **E-Mail:** ma@igc.org
USA   **Fax:**   (415) 546-6218

Contact Person: Ann Wrixon, Executive Director.   **Officers or Principals:** Ann Wrixon, Executive Director ($37,520); Linda Jue, President ($0); Rich Yurman, Secretary ($0); Jeff Savage, Treasurer.
Mission or Interest: "Support freedom of the press and increased diversity of perspectives in the media." Promotes investigative journalism, especially investigation of governmental activities and foreign policy. Offers classes for journalists and others on such subjects as documenting and exposing sexism and racism in the media, and becoming effective spokespeople for advocacy organizations. Publishes information about "microradio" stations (stations operating with out FCC license).
Accomplishments: In 1994 the Alliance spent $373,897 on its programs. These programs included classes, computer services, seminars, and other programs to provide journalists with new skills, to teach community organizations media relation skills. Offers membership services to freelance media professionals, including access to health benefits and a credit union. Analysis of propaganda.
Net Revenue: 1994 $445,327 **Net Expenses:** $460,870 81%/19%/1% **Net Assets:** $35,936
Products or Services: Grants, scholarships, "MACMAG" media relations training manual and "JobFile" job postings.
Tax Status: 501(c)(3)
Periodicals: *MediaFile* (bimonthly newspaper) of media critiques.
Other Information: The Alliance received $295,912, or 66% of revenue, from program service fees. $111,796, or 25%, from membership dues. $19,220, or 4%, from gifts and grants awarded by foundations, businesses, and individuals. $7,285 net, or 2%, from the sale of inventory. The remaining revenue came from dividends and interest from securities, interest on savings and temporary cash investments, and other miscellaneous sources.

Media Coalition
1221 Avenue of the Americas, 24th Floor
New York, NY 10020   **Phone:** (212) 768-6770
USA

Contact Person: Christopher Finan, Executive Director.   **Officers or Principals:** Christopher Finan, Executive Director ($77,458); Oren Teicher, Chairman ($0); John Harrington, Treasurer ($0).
Mission or Interest: "Defends the First Amendment right to produce and sell books, magazines and video tapes; and the American Public's right to have the broadest range of opinion and entertainment." A coalition of associations formed following the 1973 Supreme Court decision on obscenity. Monitors anti-obscenity legislation and organizes locally to defeat it. Prepares legal briefs. Provides educational efforts on the dangers of censorship. Members include the American Booksellers Association, Association of American Publishers, Council for Periodical Distribution Associations, International Periodical Distributors Association, Motion Picture Association of America, National Association of College Stores, and the Periodical and Book Association of America.
Accomplishments: In 1994 the Coalition spent $307,418 on its programs. The Coalition received $67,633 in a litigation settlement.
Net Revenue: 1994 $427,126 **Net Expenses:** $336,408 91%/9%/0% **Net Assets:** $106,397
Tax Status: 501(c)(6)
Other Information: The Coalition received $358,710, or 84% of revenue, from membership dues. $67,633, or 16%, from a litigation settlement. The remaining revenue came from interest on savings and other temporary cash investments.

Media Watch
P.O. Box 618
Santa Cruz, CA 95061-0618   **Phone:** (408) 423-6355   **E-Mail:** mediawok@aol.com
USA   **Fax:**   same

Contact Person: Ann Simton, Director. **Officers or Principals:** Laura Kuhn and Ann Simonton, Editors.
Mission or Interest: "Challenging sexism and violence in the media through education and action."

Accomplishments: The work of Media Watch, and their linking of violent images in the media with violence against women, have been included in stories in *The New York Times, Life, London Observer, Ms., Mother Jones, Sports Illustrated*, Germany's *Stern*, MTV, the Phil Donahue Show, and Larry King Live. Media Watch has gained attention over the years for their protests of the Miss America Pageant and other beauty pageants.

Products or Services: Publications, videos, posters and other educational materials linking media images with violence against women.

Tax Status: 509(a)(2) **Annual Report:** No. **Employees:** All volunteer.

Board of Directors or Trustees: Jill Ginghofer (Women Crisis Support), Ardena Shankar (Prejudice Reduction Workshops), Dr. Diana E.H. Russell (author).

Periodicals: *Action Agenda* (quarterly news journal).

Other Information: "Media Watch does not believe that the existence of shelters and rape crisis lines alone will end rape. The answer lies in massive re-education concerning the ways our culture teaches that rape, violence and the dehumanization of women are acceptable and even glamorous."

Meiklejohn Civil Liberties Institute

1715 Francisco St.
Berkeley, CA 94703   **Phone:**   (510) 848-0599
USA

Contact Person: Anne Fagan Ginger, Executive Director.   **Officers or Principals:** Ying Lee, President ($0); Zipporah Collins, Vice President ($0); Anne Fagan Ginger, Executive Director ($0); Seth Chazin, Secretary.

Mission or Interest: Edits and publishes anthologies on civil liberties and human rights. Training law students to do legal research and writing. The Meiklejohn Civil Liberties Institute was a pioneer in the prisoners' rights movement in the 1960's.

Accomplishments: Ann Fagan Ginger participated in the 1995 United Nations first-ever review of human rights in the United States as a non-governmental organization representative. The review found the U.S. lacking, citing prisoners' treatment, the death penalty, and Native Americans' rights among others, and the U.S. delegation agreed to file a report by 1998. Executive director Ginger stated, "We in the progressive community have two-and-a-half years in which to study civil and human rights and make an honest report...I think the United States is actually going to have to change...The same thing we're trying to do to China, to shame them in their human-rights field, will happen to us." In 1994 the Institute spent $20,578 on its projects. Approximately 420 publications were sold, and two law students were trained.

Net Revenue: 1994 $62,016 **Net Expenses:** $49,316 **Net Assets:** (-$25,455)

Products or Services: Publications, conferences, law student training.

Tax Status: 501(c)(3)

Board of Directors or Trustees: Anne Braden, Ignacio De La Fuente, Aileen Hernandez, Troy Duster (Dept. of Sociology, UC Berkeley), Abby Ginzberg, Seigfried Newman, Ying Lee (Office of Rep. Ron Dellums, D-CA), Prof. Frank Newman (School of Law, UC Berkeley), Seymour Kramer, Prof. Jim Syfers (San Francisco State Univ.), Collen Rohan, Anne Wagley.

Other Information: The Institute received $55,913, or 90% of revenue, from gifts and grants awarded by foundations, companies, and individuals. $4,226, or 7%, came from the sale of inventory. The remaining revenue came from royalties, conference fees, and other miscellaneous sources.

Merck Family Fund

6930 Carroll Ave., Suite 500
Takoma Park, MD 20912   **Phone:**   (301) 270-2970   **E-Mail:** merck@igc.apc.org
USA   **Fax:**   (301) 270-2973

Contact Person: Betsy Taylor, Executive Director.

Officers or Principals: Patience Chamberlain, President; Francis W. Hatch, III, Vice President; William M. Merck, Treasurer; Anne Merck-Abeles, Secretary.

Mission or Interest: Philanthropy dedicated to "protecting the natural environment and addressing the root causes of problems faced by socially and economically disadvantaged people."

Accomplishments: In 1993 the Fund awarded $1,255,500 in grants. Recipients included: $60,000 for the Tides Foundation, $50,000 each for the New York Women's Foundation, and Southern Environmental Law Center, $40,000 each for the Mineral Policy Center, and Trust for Public Land, $35,000 for the Government Accountability Project, $30,000 for the Wilderness Society, $25,000 each for the Women's Initiative for Self Employment, and the Women's Self-Employment Project, $20,000 for the Natural Resources Defense Council, and $10,000 for the Sierra Club Foundation.

Net Assets: 1993 $26,665,379

Products or Services: "Yearning for Balance: Views of Americans on Consumption, Materialism & the Environment," other reports.

Tax Status: 501(c)(3)

Board of Directors or Trustees: Sharman Altshuler, Katherine Arthaud, Olivia Farr, George W. M. Hatch, Serena Merck Hatch, Albert Merck, Jr., Antony Merck, George Merck, Josephine Merck, Dinah Vischer, Serena Whitridge.

Methodist Federation for Social Action / Methodist Federation Fund

76 Clinton Ave.
Staten Island, NY 10301   **Phone:**   (718) 273-6372
USA

Contact Person: George D. McClain, Executive Director.   **Officers or Principals:** Rev. George D. McClain, Executive Director ($36,678); Dan Lerch-Walters, Mary Ann Haxton, Co-Presidents ($0); Larry Medsker, Treasurer.
Mission or Interest: To work within the church and society to promote a deeper sense of social obligation. Works for peace, non-discrimination and civil liberties, and assistance for the needy.
Accomplishments: In 1994 the Federation spent $106,404 on programs. $42,562 was spent on educational and inspirational meetings, conferences and seminars attended by about 3,500 people. $26,601 was spent publishing and distributing newsletters and study materials; the newsletter has a circulation of 2,500 subscribers. $21,281 for the presentation of information and analysis on social issues before various church judicatories. The Federation also awarded $6,175 in grants. The twenty grants, averaging $335, went to Catholic Peace Ministry, Witness for Peace, American Civil Liberties Union, American Friends Service Committee, Amnesty International, Greenpeace, NAACP, Southern Poverty Law Center, United Farm Workers, and others.
Net Revenue: 1994 $160,395 **Net Expenses:** $149,360 71%/19%/10% **Net Assets:** $87,640
Products or Services: Publications, presentations, conferences, networking, more.
Tax Status: 501(c)(3)
Periodicals: Newsletter.
Other Information: The Federation received $91,157, or 57% of revenue, from gifts and grants awarded by foundations, companies, and individuals. $53,525, or 33%, from membership dues. $17,867, or 11%, from program services. The remaining income came from interest on savings and temporary cash investments. These revenues were partially offset by a loss of $3,665 on the sale of inventory.

Mexican American Legal Defense and Education Fund (MALDEF)

634 S. Spring St., 11th Floor
Los Angeles, CA 90014   **Phone:**   (213) 629-2512
USA   **Fax:**   (213) 629-1916

Contact Person: Antonia Hernandez, President.
Officers or Principals: Antonia Hernandez, President/General Counsel ($115,000); E. Richard Larson, Vice President, Litigation ($88,200); Luis Wilmot, Regional Counsel ($84,776); Albert H. Kauffman, Senior Litigation Attorney; Barbara L. Harvey, Vice President, Finance; Elba Bautista-Smith, Vice President, Development; Alicia Chacon, Chair; Tom Reston, First Vice Chair; Maria Luisa Mercado, Second Vice Chair; Joseph Stern, Third Vice Chair; Edward L. Lujan, Secretary/Treasurer.
Mission or Interest: "Protects the civil rights of Hispanics nationwide by undertaking class action litigation in education, employment, voting rights, immigration and English language rights." Conducts policy research and public education.
Accomplishments: In the fiscal year ending April 1994, MALDEF spent $4,588,245 on its programs. The largest program, with expenditures of $3,174,867, was litigation activities. Direct litigation expenses were $318,440, and the Fund received $385,709 in court-awarded attorneys' fees. Of these fees, at least $79,003 was paid by governments at various levels, and ultimately by taxpayers. $1,018,419 was spent on community education and services, such as leadership training and scholarships for Hispanic law students. The rest went for public policy research.
Net Revenue: FY ending 4/94 $4,392,434 **Net Expenses:** $5,041,740 91%/7%/2% **Net Assets:** $2,999,824
Citations: 132:102
Products or Services: Litigation, education, scholarships, law library, and lobbying. MALDEF spent $46,815 on lobbying; $22,104 on grassroots lobbying, and $24,711 on the direct lobbying of legislators. This was an increase of 41% from the previous year.
Tax Status: 501(c)(3)
Board of Directors or Trustees: Barbara Aldave (Dean, St. Mary's Univ., School of Law), Fred William Alvarez, Mario Antoci (Chair/CEO, American Savings Bank), Joseph Barish, Javier Aguirre, Gregory Craig, James Johnson (Chair/CEO, Fannie Mae), Luis Nogales (Chair/CEO, Embarcadero Media), Vilma Martinez, Daniel Ortega Jr., Joaquin Pelaez (V.P., Technology & Quality, Taco Bell), Gloria Molina (Supervisor, Los Angeles County), Drucilla Stender Ramey (Exec. Dir./General Counsel, Bar Association of San Francisco), Jesus Rangel (V.P., Corporate Relations, Anheuser-Busch Co.), Marcia Silverman.
Other Information: Affiliated with the MALDEF Property Management Corp. The Fund has regional offices in Chicago, San Francisco, San Antonio, and Washington DC. The Fund received $3,020,955, or 69% of revenue, from gifts and grants awarded by foundations, businesses, and individuals. (These grants included $1,300,000 over two years from the Ford Foundation, $112,500 from the Rosenberg Foundation, $75,000 from the Joyce Foundation, $30,000 from the Joyce Mertz-Gilmore Foundation, and $100 from the Ruth Mott Fund.) $520,004, or 12%, from special fund-raising events, including dinners in San Francisco, Los Angeles, Chicago and San Antonio, and a concert in Los Angeles. $385,709, or 9%, from court-awarded attorneys' fees. $192,358, or 6%, from capital gains on the sale of securities. $159,983, or 4%, from dividends and interest from securities. The remaining revenue came from interest on savings and temporary cash investments, and other miscellaneous sources.

Mexican American Women's National Association (MANA)

1725 K St., N.W., Suite 501
Washington, DC 20006   **Phone:**   (202) 833-0060
USA

Mission or Interest: "Providing a voice for Latina's in the nation's capital."
Accomplishments: In 1994 the Association spent $99,749 on its programs. These included $40,660 in scholarships for Hispanic students. Scholarships are evaluated based on the following criteria: 1) Commitment to Hispanic women's progress and development. 2) Contribution to local/national community and/or issues. 3) Personal qualities and strengths. 4) Demonstration of overcoming unique obstacles in obtaining education. 5) Academic achievement. 6) Financial need. 7) Letter of recommendation. MANA also hosted a 20th anniversary conference and hosted luncheons to honor Hispanic women who are leaders in their respective fields.

Net Revenue: 1994 $111,467 **Net Expenses:** $119,931 83%/17%/0% **Net Assets:** $40,628
Tax Status: 501(c)(3) **Employees:** All unpaid.
Periodicals: Quarterly newsletter.
Other Information: The Association received $74,434, or 67% of revenue, from gifts and grants awarded by foundations, businesses, and individuals. $31,223, or 28%, from membership dues. $3,110 net, or 3%, from special fund-raising events. $2,430, or 2%, from interest on savings and temporary cash investments. The remaining revenue came from miscellaneous sources.

Middle East Children's Alliance (MECA)

905 Parker St.
Berkeley, CA 94710   **Phone:** (510) 548-0542
USA   **Fax:** (510) 548-0543

Contact Person: Barbara Lubin. **Officers or Principals:** Barbara Lubin, Executive Director ($39,600); Eugene "Gus" Newport, President ($0); Howard Levine, Editor.
Mission or Interest: "Working for Peace in the Middle East" by providing financial aid to groups in the Middle East and the U.S. who are working towards that goal. To achieve peace in the Israeli-Palestinian conflict MECA calls for: A) the disarming of settlers, B) dismantling the settlements, C) bringing in United Nations peacekeepers to replace the Israeli army while Palestinians make the transition to self-rule, D) negotiations between them must be headed towards a Palestinian state.
Accomplishments: They have delivered "over $5 million of food and medicine to children in The West Bank, Gaza, Lebanon and Iraq." They are providing technical assistance to the Palestinian community to design and build three parks in Nablus, Al-Bireh and Gaza. In the fiscal year ending June 1994 they awarded $1,328,325 in grants. The largest was $1,294,000 for UNICEF to provide medicine for refugee camps in Lebanon. MECA fundraisers have featured Prof. Noam Chomsky and folk singer Pete Seeger, who are both on MECA's Advisory Board.
Net Revenue: FY ending 6/94 $1,442,234 **Net Expenses:** $1,451,754 91%/9%/0% **Net Assets:** (-$719)
Citations: 0:255
Products or Services: Grants and educational activities. MECA owns a graphics company, Alliance Graphics, that produces silk-screened items.
Tax Status: 501(c)(3) **Employees:** 8
Board of Directors or Trustees: Fuad Mogannam, Susan Nelson, Fr. William O'Donnell, Robie Osman. Their Advisory Board includes: Maya Angelou (poet), Ed Asner (actor), Dr. Fathi Arafat, Rabbi Leonard Beerman, Prof. Noam Chomsky (MIT), Ramsey Clark (former Attorney General, 1967-69), Rep. John Conyers (D-MI), Rep. Ronald Dellums (D-CA), Casey Kasem (radio host), Pete Seeger (folk singer), Alice Walker (author), Rep. Maxine Waters (D-CA).
Periodicals: *Middle East Children's Alliance News* (quarterly newsletter).
Other Information: Although the Alliance's tax returns state that during the fiscal year ending June 1994 it incurred no fundraising expenses, a newsletter during that period announces two fundraisers, a lecture featuring Noam Chomsky and a benefit concert featuring Pete Seeger and Richie Havens. A written request for clarification on this discrepancy did not receive a response. The Alliance received $1,440,672, or 99.9% of revenue from gifts and grants awarded by foundations, companies, affiliates and individuals. The remaining income came from interest on savings and temporary cash investments, and other miscellaneous sources.

Middle East Policy Council

1730 M St., N.W., Suite 512
Washington, DC 20036   **Phone:** (202) 296-6707
USA

Contact Person: Anne Joyce, Vice President. **Officers or Principals:** Sen. George McGovern, President ($117,208); Anne Joyce, Vice President ($64,250); Richard Wilson ($61,750).
Mission or Interest: "Produce publications and organize conferences which educate members and the general public about recent developments affecting American-Arab relations."
Accomplishments: In 1994 the Council spent $719,480 on its programs. The largest program, with expenditures of $376,269, was the publication of a quarterly journal. $226,444 was spent on conferences and seminars to sponsor "scholarly discussion of contemporary events relevant to the United States and Arab world." Other programs published books and reports and provided speakers.
Net Revenue: 1994 $782,974 **Net Expenses:** $892,194 81%/10%/9% **Net Assets:** $202,208 **Citations:** 27:164
Tax Status: 501(c)(3)
Board of Directors or Trustees: Marge Benton, Lt. Gen. Charles Brown, Talat Othman, Dr. Fouad Rihani, Hon. Frank Carlucci (Secretary of Def., 1987-1988), K.V.R. Dey, Witold Sulimirski, Dr. Jack Wilkinson, Naheeb Halaby, Dr. Dale Nitzschke, Pierre Salinger.
Periodicals: Quarterly journal.
Other Information: The Council received $704,629, or 90% of revenue, from gifts and grants awarded by foundations, businesses, and individuals. $55,468, or 7%, from journal subscriptions. $18,244, or 2%, from conference fees. $4,633, or 1%, from interest on savings and temporary cash investments.

Middle East Research and Information Project (MERIP)

1500 Massachusetts Ave., N.W., Suite 119
Washington, DC 20005   **Phone:**   (202) 223-3677   **E-Mail:** merip@igc.apc.org
USA   **Fax:**   (202) 223-3607

Contact Person: Geoff Hartman.   **Officers or Principals:** Peggy Hutchison, Publisher ($29,899); John Viste, Chairman ($0); Dan Connell, Vice Chairman ($0); David Cartright, Treasurer.
Mission or Interest: Public education on the politics and economics of the Middle East. Publish *Middle East Report*, an award-winning magazine.
Accomplishments: Their expertise has been sought out by news organizations including C-Span, ABC Prime Time Live, National Public Radio, CNN, 60 Minutes, the Canadian Broadcasting Co., The MacNeil Lehrer NewsHour, *Time, Newsweek, The Village Voice,* and *The Nation.*
Net Revenue: 1994 $304,281 **Net Expenses:** $275,688 78%/9%/13% **Net Assets:** $150,263
The Project received $150,757, or 50% of revenue, from gifts and grants awarded by foundations, companies, and individuals. (These grants included $20,000 from the Ruth Mott Fund.) $139,024, or 46%, from the sale of Middle East Report and other publications. $11,344, or 4%, from speaking engagements. The remaining revenue came from dividends and interest from securities.
Products or Services: Educational activities, responding to requests for information from students, organizations, and professors. In 1994 their entire program budget, $215,745, was spent on producing and distributing *Middle East Report.*
Tax Status: 501(c)(3) **Annual Report:** No. **Employees:** 4
Board of Directors or Trustees: Hady Amr, Dale Bishop, Judith Chomsky, Dan Connell, David Cortight, Nina Dodge, Rhonda Hanson, Donna Nevel, David Nygaard, Doreen Tilghman, Andrew Whitley.
Periodicals: *Middle East Report* (bimonthly magazine).
Internships: Yes, to help with publications, promotion and outreach, administration, and general office activities.

Middle Passage Foundation

1880 E. Century Park, Suite 900
Los Angeles, CA 90067   **Phone:**   (310) 553-1707
USA

Contact Person: Tracy Chapman, President.   **Officers or Principals:** Margaret Green, Vice President ($0); Lee Phillips, Secretary ($0); Marshall Gelfand, Chief Financial Officer ($0).
Mission or Interest: Grant-making philanthropy that includes, among other areas of interest, awards for civil rights and human rights.
Accomplishments: In 1994 the Foundation awarded $100,000 in grants. Recipients included: $7,500 for Amnesty International and $10,000 for the ACLU Foundation.
Net Revenue: 1994 $100,533 **Net Expenses:** $100,452 **Net Assets:** $17,910
Tax Status: 501(c)(3)
Other Information: The Foundation received $100,000, or 99.5% of revenue, from gifts and grants awarded by foundations, businesses, and individuals. The remaining revenue came from interest on savings and temporary cash investments. The Foundation held all of its assets in cash.

Midwest Center for Labor Research

3411 W. Diversey, Room 10
Chicago, IL 60647   **Phone:**   (312) 278-5418
USA

Contact Person: Daniel Swinney, Executive Director.
Officers or Principals: Daniel Swinney, Executive Director ($46,802); Xiochang Jin, Assistant Research Director ($33,881); Jacquelyne Johnson, Operations ($32,160); Bishop Jesse DeWitt, President; David Smathers, Fundraiser.
Mission or Interest: Research, consulting, and economic development projects regarding industrial problems, grassroots labor organizing, community organizations, local government, and churches.
Accomplishments: In the fiscal year ending June 1994, the Center spent $473,723 on its programs. The largest program, with expenditures of $174,956, focused on creating and retaining union jobs within the Chicago metropolitan area. $146,641 was spent providing research and consultations with community and labor organizations. $98,313 was spent publishing and distributing periodicals. $32,176 was spent providing labor-organizing training.
Net Revenue: FY ending 6/94 $587,807 ($28,218, or 5%, from government grants) **Net Expenses:** $655,000 72%/16%/12%
Net Assets: (-$61,054) **Citations:** 14:186
Tax Status: 501(c)(3)
Board of Directors or Trustees: Thomas Joyce (8th Day Center for Justice), Esther Lopez, Harvey Lyon, Roberto Maldonado, Jack Metzger, Ray Pasnick, Sam Rosenberg, Kathy Tholin (Woodstock Inst.).
Periodicals: *Labor Research Review* (biannual).
Other Information: The Center received $399,592, or 68% of revenue, from gifts and grants awarded by foundations, corporations and individuals. (These grants included $100,000 from the Joyce Foundation, $30,000 from the Woods Charitable Fund, and $15,000 from the Wieboldt Foundation. In 1995, $225,000 from the Rockefeller Foundation.) $100,257, or 17%, from fees for research and consultation. $68,088, or 12%, from subscriptions and sales of publications. $28,218, or 5%, from government contracts. The remaining revenue came from interest on savings and temporary cash investments, and other miscellaneous sources. Revenue was reduced by a loss of $8,777 on a subsidiary investment.

Military Toxics Project

P.O. Box 8246
Norway, ME 04268
USA

Contact Person: Cathy Hinds, Director.
Mission or Interest: Document the environmental degradation caused by the nation's military establishment.
Tax Status: 501(c)(3)
Other Information: Originally a project of the Tide Foundation's National Toxics Campaign Fund. In 1994 the Project received $30,000 from the Rockefeller Family Fund, $26,000 from the Jessie Smith Noyes Foundation, $6,000 from the Peace Development Fund.

Mind Matters Review

2040 Polk St., Box 234
San Francisco, CA 94109   **E-Mail:** WPPL42A@Prodigy.com
USA

Contact Person: Carrie Drake, Editor.
Officers or Principals: Bunny Williams, Assistant Editor; David Castleman, Book Review Editor; Lorraine Donfor, Poetry Editor.
Mission or Interest: Publish *Mind Matters Review* and the *Omega Project Newsletter*. "Our goals are strictly long-term goals of developing a technique for teaching a language that narrows the gap between perception of reality through groupthink and actual physical reality in economics and individual consciousness in order to eliminate waste of natural and human resources."
Accomplishments: Published since 1988 with a voluntary staff of five. "Covered issues of separation of church and state, treatment of sex offenders, conspiracy theories involving secret societies, and government intelligence agencies. MMR is one of the few publications from a leftist perspective in economics that is critical of the political correctness that has come to dominate the left, particularly the political correctness of identity politics. MMR examines the common ground of both the left and right in sexual mysticism and metaphysics."
Tax Status: "We maintain complete independence of commercial and government favor." **Annual Report:** No. **Employees:** 5
Board of Directors or Trustees: Rod Farmer, Vance Lear, David Thompson.
Periodicals: *Mind Matters Review* (annual journal), *Omega Project Newsletter* (bimonthly newsletter).

Mineral Policy Center

1612 K St., N.W., Suite 808
Washington, DC 20006   **Phone:**   (202) 887-1872
USA

Contact Person: Philip M. Hocker, President
Mission or Interest: Addresses the environmental impact of hard rock mining in the U.S. Activities include research, litigation, advocacy and technical assistance.
Tax Status: 501(c)(3)
Other Information: Founded in 1988. In 1994 the Center received $95,000 from the Pew Charitable Trusts, $50,000 from the Ruth Mott Fund, $35,000 from the Rockefeller Family Fund, $22,000 from the Tides Foundation, $20,000 from the General Service Foundation, $20,000 from the New-Land Foundation, $15,000 from the Jessie Smith Noyes Foundation, $14,000 from the American Conservation Association, $10,000 from the Deer Creek Foundation, and $9,600 from the Bullitt Foundation.

Minnesota Alliance for Progressive Action (MAPA)

1821 University Ave., Suite 307-S
St. Paul, MN 55104   **Phone:**   (612) 641-4050
USA

Contact Person: Alexa Bradley.
Mission or Interest: Community coalition of labor and grassroots activists.
Accomplishments: Produced a study that detailed Minnesota's corporate welfare programs.

Minnesota Civil Liberties Union Foundation

1021 W. Broadway
Minneapolis, MN 55411   **Phone:**   (612) 522-2824
USA

Contact Person: Mike Moore, Executive Director.
Mission or Interest: "To provide legal defense for those persons who cannot afford to pay for this type of service and to educate the public regarding the rights of free speech, press, assemblage and other human rights and liberties secured by the Constitution."
Accomplishments: In 1994 the Foundation spent $63,649 on its programs. $60,559 for legal services and $3,090 for educational programs.
Net Revenue: 1994 $84,076 **Net Expenses:** $111,455 57%/25%/18% **Net Assets:** $391,070

Tax Status: 501(c)(3)

Other Information: The Foundation is affiliated with the 501(c)(3) Minnesota Civil Liberties Union. The Foundation received $27,954 net, or 33% of revenue, from special fund-raising events. $25,909, or 31%, from interest on savings and temporary cash investments. $12,555, or 15%, from gifts and grants awarded by foundations, businesses, and individuals. $8,398, or 10%, from membership dues. $7,200 net, or 9%, from rental income. $2,000, or 2%, from legal fees.

Minnesota Coalition for the Homeless

122 W. Franklin, Suite 520
Minneapolis, MN 55404   **Phone:**   (612) 870-7073
USA

Contact Person: Rick Podvin, President. **Officers or Principals:** Alberta Carroll, Director ($12,689); Ed Murphy, Secretary ($0); Christine Jax, Treasurer ($0); Bobbi Butler, Betty Christensen, Sue Watlov Phillips, Tom Reynolds, Regional Vice Presidents.
Mission or Interest: "The Minnesota Coalition for the Homeless seeks to have everyone take responsibility for ending homelessness...The Coalition informs the public about homelessness, its causes, and ways each person can help end homelessness...has over eleven years of experience and legislative successes in working with advocates, providers, agencies, lawmakers, and the public to prevent homelessness. Its Board reflects diversity in the areas of the state, minority groups, and homelessness issues represented...The Coalition's Board always includes members who have been homeless themselves."
Accomplishments: In 1994 the Coalition spent $144,409 on its programs. The largest program, with expenditures of $112,709, was education. Educational activities included a conference co-sponsored with the National Coalition for the Homeless, attended by 832 people. Other educational programs included publication of a newsletter, networking with other organizations, and promoting Hunger and Homelessness Awareness week, and the Homeless Memorial Day which "remembered homeless people who died in Minnesota in 1994." $25,000 was spent on technical assistance which included referrals for social services, assisting government agencies in planning, and getting homeless and formerly homeless people involved in solutions to homelessness. Other programs included research and legislative activities. In 1994 the Coalition worked for legislation that resulted in "bonding authority for $1.5 million for publicly-owned transitional housing and an additional $1 million in bonding authority for shelters and transitional housing for battered women and other crime victims."
Net Revenue: 1994 $160,097 ($36,569, or 23%, from government grants) **Net Expenses:** $153,281   94%/4%/2%
Net Assets: $8,570
Products or Services: Technical assistance, research, publications, networking, and lobbying. The Coalition spent $2,302 on the direct lobbying of public officials.
Tax Status: 501(c)(3)
Board of Directors or Trustees: Shirley Anderson (Western Community Action Program), Carol Banister (East Metro Woman's Council), Therese Cain (Cabrini House), Rita Dow, Becky Fink, A.G. Huot (St. Cloud Area Housing Coalition), Pat Leary (MN Dept. of Economic Security), Sharon Novell, Susan Philliops (LSS Homeless Youth Program), Carla Solem, Margaret Steiner (Northfield Action Center), Barbara Stone, Lawrence Winans (Mankato Coalition for Affordable Housing).
Periodicals: Newsletter.
Other Information: The Coalition received $72,423, or 45% of revenue, from conference fees. $51,105, or 32%, from gifts and grants awarded by foundations, businesses, and individuals. $36,569, or 23%, from government grants.

Minnesota Jobs With Peace Campaign

122 West Franklin Ave., Suite 302
Minneapolis, MN 55404
USA

Contact Person: Janet Groat, Executive Director.   **Officers or Principals:** Janet Groat, Executive Director ($27,206).
Mission or Interest: Works with community residents, environmentalists, and labor activists to convert military sites and industries into peaceful, civilian projects. Also works to switch federal budget priorities from defense spending to social services.
Accomplishments: In 1993 the Campaign spent $47,191 on its programs.
Net Revenue: 1993 $46,796 **Net Expenses:** $54,253   87%/7%/6%   **Net Assets:** (-$4,716)
Tax Status: 501(c)(4)
Board of Directors or Trustees: State Rep. Karen Clark, Claudette Munson, Mike Goldman, Ted Lanpher, Richard Bolan (Humphrey Inst. of Public Affairs), Alexa Bradley, Martha Roth, Paul Mandell, Richard Breen.
Other Information: The Campaign received $46,688, or 99.7% of revenue, from gifts and grants received by foundations, businesses, and individuals. (These grants included $13,690 from the Minnesota CALC Foundation, and $12,500 from the Peace Development Fund.) The remaining revenue came from the interest on savings and temporary cash investments.

Modern Language Association of America (MLA)

10 Astor Place
New York, NY 10003   **Phone:**   (212) 475-9500
USA

Contact Person: Claudine A. Gilchriest, Assistant to the Executive Director. **Officers or Principals:** Phyllis Franklin, Executive Director ($168,400); Regina Vorbeck, Associate Executive Director ($106,270); Judy Goulding, Managing Editor ($101,490); Patricia M. Spacks, President; Sander L. Gilman, First Vice President; Sandra M. Gilbert, Second Vice President.

Mission or Interest: "The MLA works to improve English and foreign language programs in college and universities." The MLA has also been at the forefront of promoting diversity and multi-culturalism in higher education.

Accomplishments: In the fiscal year ending August 1994, the MLA spent $5,701,671 on its programs. The largest program, with expenditures of $3,487,233, was publication of a number of journals and reference works. $749,898 was spent on the annual meeting which attracted 8,901 registrants. $682,246 was spent on membership services for its approximately 32,000 members. $646,186 for surveys, including a survey of job placements. Other projects included various curriculum development and research.

Net Revenue: FY ending 8/94 $8,525,008 **Net Expenses:** $8,175,612 70%/30%/0% **Net Assets:** $3,065,466

Citations: 157:92

Products or Services: MLA International Bibliography, MLA Handbook for Writers of Research Papers, "Approaches to Teaching World Literature" series, several professional awards, lobbying and more. The MLA spent $28,343 on lobbying. $343 was spent on mailings to U.S. Senators regarding the separation of the copyright office from the Library of Congress. $28,000 was spent on grants to the National Council for Languages and International Studies, and the National Humanities Alliance for lobbying activities.

Tax Status: 501(c)(3)

Board of Directors or Trustees: Martha Banta, Peter Brooks, Sara Castro-Klaren, Gerald Graff, Stephen Greenblatt, Marianne Hirsch, Michael Holquist, Linda Hutcheon, Susan Kirkpatrick, Claire Kramsch, Andrea Lunsford, Nellie McKay, Sylvia Molloy, Susan Noakes, Naomi Schor, Susan Suleiman, Nancy Walker, Jack Zipes.

Periodicals: *PMLA* (scholarly journal).

Other Information: The MLA received $3,221,799 net, or 38% of revenue, from the sale of inventory. $1,884,596, or 22%, from publication subscriptions. $1,541,275, or 18%, from membership dues. $870,708, or 10%, from annual meeting registrations. $350,189, or 4%, from advertising revenues. $224,868, or 3%, from miscellaneous program services. $139,840, or 2%, from computer service fees. $105,653, or 1%, from contracts and grants, including grants from the U.S. Dept. of Education, National Endowment for the Humanities, and the American Council of Learned Societies. $79,608, or 1%, from dividends and interest from securities. $52,278, or 1%, from gifts and grants awarded by foundations, businesses, and individuals. The remaining revenue came from interest on savings and temporary cash investments, and royalties.

Montana Alliance for Progressive Policy (MAPP)

P.O. Box 961
324 Fuller
Helena, MT 59624   **Phone:**   (406) 443-7283
USA

Contact Person: Jeffrey Fox, Executive Director.

Mission or Interest: An educational coalition of statewide organizations representing the poor, seniors, Native Americans, organized labor, education, environmentalists, and feminists. Counters the 'Wise Use' movement in Montana.

Tax Status: 501(c)(3)

Other Information: In 1994 the Alliance received $20,000 from the Jessie Smith Noyes Foundation.

Montana People's Action

208 E. Main St.
Missoula, MT 59802   **Phone:**   (406) 728-5297
USA   **Fax:**   same

Contact Person: Jim Fleischman.

Mission or Interest: "Membership organization of low-income Montana families who use the strength of their numbers and direct action to achieve social and economic justice."

Accomplishments: "1) Forced Montana's largest banks to reinvest over $40 million in state's poorest neighborhoods. 2) Passed legislation to protect the rights of low-income families in mobile home courts. 3) Other victories on housing, health care and neighborhood issues."

Tax Status: 501(c)(3) **Annual Report:** No. **Employees:** 8

Periodicals: *Action Line* (periodic newsletter).

Internships: Yes, through colleges and universities. Three-month paid community organizing internships.

Other Information: Affiliated with the Montana-Community-Labor Alliance and the Northwest Federation of Community Organizations. Chapters in Missoula, Bozeman, Billings and Great Falls, Montana's four largest cities. In 1994 the organization received $24,000 from the Campaign for Human Development, $5,000 from the Peace Development Fund, $2,500 from the Ms. Foundation for Women.

Montanans for Choice

P.O. Box 279
Helena, MT 59624
USA

Other Information: In the fiscal year ending June 1994, the organization received $10,000 from the Ms. Foundation for Women.

Monthly Review Foundation / *Monthly Review*
122 W. 27th St., 10th Floor
New York, NY 10001   **Phone:** (212) 691-2555   **E-Mail:** mreview@igc.apc.org
USA   **Fax:**   (212) 727-3676

Contact Person: Paul M. Sweezy, President.   **Officers or Principals:** Susan Lowes, Director ($48,542); Paul M. Sweezy, President ($28,600); Harry Magdoff, Secretary ($5,200).
Mission or Interest: Publishes books and the *Monthly Review*, a scholarly journal of Marxist thought and criticism.
Accomplishments: In 1994 the Foundation spent $823,684 on its programs.
Net Revenue: 1994 $882,765 **Net Expenses:** $1,042,442 79%/21%/1% **Net Assets:** $4,755 **Citations:** 0:255
Products or Services: Socialist Register 1996, Let Them Eat Ketchup: The Politics of Poverty and Inequality by Sheila Collins, Under Attack, Fighting Back: Women & Welfare in the U.S., by Mimi Abramovitz, other publications.
Tax Status: 501(c)(3)
Periodicals: *Monthly Review* (monthly journal).
Other Information: *Monthly Review* secretary/editor Harry Magdoff had worked on the War Production Board during World War II and later for the Senate Labor and Public Welfare Committee, until a confessed Soviet spy named him as a fellow spy, a charge Magdoff denied. He pleaded the Fifth and was never indicted. Recently the U.S. government has released the "Venona Intercepts," deciphered cables from Soviet intelligence officers and their superiors in Moscow which were kept secret to prevent the Soviets from knowing how well the United States had deciphered their codes. The Venona files show clearly that Magdoff spied for the Soviet Union. The Foundation received $511,888, or 58% of revenue, from the sale of books. $199,562, or 23%, from gifts and grants awarded by foundations, businesses, and individuals. $150,815, or 17%, from the sale of magazines. $13,210, or 1%, from dividends and interest from securities. The remaining revenue came from other miscellaneous sources.

Mothers and Others for a Livable Planet
40 W. 20th St., 9th Floor
New York, NY 10011   **Phone:** (212) 242-0010
USA

Contact Person: Kate Roth, President.   **Officers or Principals:** Kate Roth, President ($60,375); Cynthia Cole, Treasurer ($36,424); Betsy Lydon, Secretary ($35,547); Wendy Gordon, Chairperson.
Mission or Interest: Education on environmental and safety issues. Advocates 'green' consumerism, providing households with "information about consumer choices that are safe and sustainable."
Accomplishments: In 1994 the organization spent $402,288 on its programs. The largest program, with expenditures of $282,334, was the Shopper's Campaign for Better Food Choices. This campaign "is working to increase consumer demand for access to safe, affordable and sustainably produced foods." $60,783 was spent for public education for members and the general public. $43,060 for a newsletter sent to 25,000 households. $16,111 for the "Healthy Schools" program to "address environmental health problems common to many schools."
Net Revenue: 1994 $427,569 **Net Expenses:** $540,456 74%/15%/8% **Net Assets:** (-$8,916)
Products or Services: The Green Shoppers' Survival Kit, other publications. The organization did not engage in lobbying in 1994, but in 1993 it spent $4,755 on lobbying.
Tax Status: 501(c)(3)
Board of Directors or Trustees: Andi Bernstein, Meryl Gummer, Lynette Massey Jaffe, Harvey Karp, M.D., Fred Kirschenmann, Diane Maceachern, Lawrie Mott, Anne Rosenzweig, Deborah Schimberg, Jane Stewart, Roberta Willis.
Periodicals: *Green Guide for Everyday Life* (eighteen times a year newsletter).
Other Information: Mothers and Others received $391,088, or 91% of revenue, from gifts and grants awarded by foundations, businesses, and individuals. (These grants included $25,000 from the Columbia Foundation, $25,000 from the Rockefeller Family Fund, $20,000 from the Jessie Smith Noyes Foundation.) $27,873, or 7%, from membership dues. The remaining revenue came from book royalties, the sale of inventory, dividends and interest from securities, and other miscellaneous sources.

Ms.
230 Park Ave.
New York, NY 10169   **E-Mail:** ms@echonyc.com
USA

Contact Person: Marcia Ann Gillespie, Editor in Chief.
Officers or Principals: Ruth A. Bower, Executive Vice President and Publisher; Barbara Findlen, Executive Editor; Gloria Jacobs, Editor; Gloria Steinem, Founding and Consulting Editor.
Mission or Interest: Leading magazine of feminism.
Accomplishments: Features leading feminist writers such as Susan Faludi.
Tax Status: For profit.
Board of Directors or Trustees: Advisers include: Evelyn Accad, Marjorie Agosin, Paula Gunn Allen, Kathleen Berry, Blanche Wiessen Cook, Carol Gilligan, bell hooks, Karla Jay, Ynestra King, Tatyana Mamonova, Margaret Chant Papandreou, Hikka Pietila, Nawal El Saadawi, Peggy Sanday, Alice Schwarzer, Zenebeworke Tadesse, Kazuko Watanabe.
Periodicals: *Ms.* (bimonthly magazine).

Internships: Yes.
Other Information: Published by Lang Communications. Initially, *Ms.* tried to publish for a larger audience and support itself with advertising revenue. Most popular women's magazines accept large advertising accounts from the cosmetics and tobacco industries, who put pressure on the magazine to stifle any criticism of their industries. *Ms.* found itself in the position of accepting advertising for lifestyles that conflicted with its feminism, and advertisers tending to shy away from the feminism advocated by *Ms. Ms.* eventually went with an advertisement-free design, and with its higher price, caters to a more select readership. Subscriptions to *Ms.* are subsidized for university womens' studies departments by the Ms. Foundation for Education and Communication.

Ms. Foundation for Education and Communication

115 E. 72nd St.
New York, NY 10021   **Phone:**   (212) 794-4800
USA

Contact Person: Patricia T. Carbine, President.   **Officers or Principals:** Patricia T. Carbine, President ($20,000); Gloria Steinem, Chairman ($0); Ruth Bower, Vice President ($0); Letty Pogrebin, Treasurer; Suzanne Levine, Secretary.
Mission or Interest: The purchase and distribution of feminist publications and grants for female authors, artists, photographers and business women.
Accomplishments: In the fiscal year ending June 1995 the Foundation spent $397,838 on its programs. The largest program, with expenditures of $301,150, was the purchase and placement of *Ms.* magazine in "Women's Studies departments in colleges and universities throughout the U.S." Other projects included the "International Feminist Networking Project" and $44,000 in grants. These grants were for the publication and distribution of various feminist publications, such as the teaching guide "Gender-Based Bullying and Teasing in Grades K-5."
Net Revenue: FY ending June 6/95 $350,419 **Net Expenses:** $454,762 87%/13%/0% **Net Assets:** $356,547
Tax Status: 501(c)(3)
Other Information: The Foundation received $311,650, or 87% of total revenue, from gifts and grants awarded by foundations, businesses, and individuals. (In the fiscal year ending June 1994, these grants included $65,000 from the affiliated Ms. Foundation for Women.) $27,317, or 8%, from dividends and interest from securities. $13,910, or 4%, from "recovery of unrealized loss on securities." $3,697, or 1%, from royalties. The Foundation lost $6,155 on the sale of securities.

Ms. Foundation for Women

120 Wall St., 33rd Floor
New York, NY 10005   **Phone:**   (212) 742-2300   **E-Mail:** MSFDN@INTERPORT.NET
USA   **Fax:**   (212) 742-1653

Contact Person: Marie C. Wilson, President.
Officers or Principals: Marie C. Wilson, President / Executive Director ($102,249); Idelisse Malave, Deputy Director ($73,182); Sara Gould, Program Director ($58,734); Tani Takagi, Program Director; Robin Rosenbluth, Development Director; Kristen Golden, Development Director; Bette Yee, Chief Financial Officer; Gail Maynor, Director of "Take Our Daughters to Work Day."
Mission or Interest: Grant making and training of grassroots organizations to promote; abortion rights, programs for women in the workforce, lesbian's rights, programs for minority women, affirmative action, and other feminist and leftist ideals and goals.
Accomplishments: "Take Our Daughters To Work Day" is a project of the Ms. Foundation created to "resolve problems facing adolescent girls so that they can grow up with confidence, in good health and with trust in the promise of education." In the fiscal year ending June 1994 they spent $714,121 on this program. During the same period they awarded $1,205,700 in grants to other organizations. The recipients of the largest grants were: $65,000 for the Ms. Foundation for Education and Communication, $50,000 for the National Center for the Early Childhood Work Force, $30,000 for Wider Opportunities for Women, $25,000 each for the Women Employed Institute, Tides Foundation (c/o Joyce Mertz-Gilmore Foundation/National Lesbian and Gay Funding Partnership), NOW Legal Defense and Education Fund, National Committee on Pay Equity, Ama Doo Alchini Bighan, and Ackerman Institute for Family Therapy, $21,000 for the Astrea National Lesbian Action Foundation, $20,000 each for the Center for Women Policy Studies and the Institute for Women's Policy Research. Next to their grant making, the second largest program was the "Reproductive Rights Project" spending $483,578. $453,197 was spent on "Economic Development and Technical Assistance" to grassroots organizations. Other projects included "Collaborative Projects" to benefit "low income women and women of color," $184,449, and "Public Education and Policy," $152,232.
Net Revenue: FY ending 6/94 $9,084,606 **Net Expenses:** $4,257,425 72%/13%/15% **Net Assets:** $9,317,850
Citations: 238:71
Products or Services: Grants for other nonprofit organizations and grassroots organizations. "Take Our Daughters to Work Organizers' Kit." The Ms. Foundation also engages in lobbying. In 1994 they spent $52,931 directly lobbying legislative bodies.
Tax Status: 501(c)(3) **Annual Report:** Yes. **Employees:** 24
Board of Directors or Trustees: Rebecca Adamson (Founder/Pres., First Nations Financial Project), Charlotte Bunch (Dir., Center for Global Issues and Women's Leadership), Sophia Collier (Co-Owner, Working Management Co.), Connie Evans (Exec. Dir., Women's Self-Employment Project), Susan Grode (Co-Founder, Hollywood Women's Political Committee), Caroline Hirsch (Caroline's Comedy Cafe), Carol Jenkins (anchor & correspondent, News 4, New York), Kristina Kiehl (founder, Voters for Choice), Pamela Grace Model (Leo Model Found.), Prof. Marysa Navarro (Dartmouth College), Jessye Norman (opera performer), Wendy Puricfoy (Pres., Public Education Fund Network), Marilyn Rousso (Dir., Disabilities Unlimited Psychotherapy & Consulting Services), Peggy Kyoko Saika (Asian Pacific Environmental Network). The founding directors are; Patricia Carbine, Letty Pogrebin, Marlo Thomas (actress and producer), and Gloria Steinem (best-selling writer).

Internships: Yes. Internships available in development, grants, and communication.

Other Information: The Foundation is affiliated with the Free To Be Foundation and the Ms. Foundation for Education and Communication. The Foundation received $8,521,815, or 94% of revenue, from gifts and grants awarded by foundations, businesses, and affiliates. (These grants included $500,000 over three years from the John D. and Catherine T. MacArthur Foundation, $60,000 from the Robert Sterling Clark Foundation, $50,000 from the Edna McConnell Clark Foundation, $30,000 from the Jessie Smith Noyes Foundation, $25,000 from the Compton Foundation, $24,200 from the Haymarket People's Fund, $20,000 from the Rockefeller Family Fund, $20,000 from the General Service Foundation, $10,000 from the Stewart R. Mott Charitable Trust, $10,000 from the Wallace Alexander Gerbode Foundation, and $1,000 from the Vanguard Public Foundation.) $197,020, or 2%, from the sale of publications and other items. $182,551, or 2%, from dividends and interest from securities. $87,245, or 1%, from membership dues. The remaining revenue came from interest on savings and temporary cash investments, capital gains on the sale of securities, special fund-raising events, mailing list rentals, and other miscellaneous sources.

Mujeres Project
418 Villita, Bldg. 246
HemisFair Park
San Antonio, TX 78205   **Phone:**   (210) 222-9417
USA

Contact Person: Olga Morales Aguirre, Executive Director.
Mission or Interest: Abortion rights and reproductive health organization by and for Latina women.
Tax Status: 501(c)(3)
Other Information: In 1994 the Project received $25,000 from the Jessie Smith Noyes Foundation, and $1,000 from the Haymarket People's Fund.

NAMES Project Foundation
310 Townsend St., Suite 310
San Francisco, CA 94107   **Phone:**   (415) 882-5500   **E-Mail:** info@aidsquilt.org
USA   **Fax:**   (415) 882-6200

Officers or Principals: Anthony Turney, Executive Director; Michael Berg, President; Carolyn Reidy, Vice President; Richard Hutson, Treasurer; Michael Simmons, Assistant Treasurer; Rebecca LePere, Secretary; Cleve Jones and Mike Smith, Founders.
Mission or Interest: The NAMES Project sponsors the AIDS Quilt, a quilt comprised of over 28,135 panels bearing the names of those who have died from AIDS-related illness. The entire quilt covers about 19 acres and it tours the country in sections to "help bring an end to the AIDS epidemic." The goal of displaying the quilt is to: "provide a creative means for remembrance and healing - illustrate the enormity of the AIDS epidemic - increase public awareness of AIDS - assist with HIV prevention education - raise funds for community-based AIDS service organizations."
Accomplishments: The AIDS quilt is "the most visible symbol of the AIDS epidemic and the largest community arts project in the world." In 1994 the NAMES Project and its 38 chapters put on over 1,600 displays, visited by almost 1.2 million people. The Project contributed $131,477 in grants to AIDS service organizations and $320,015 for volunteer programs and public affairs.
Net Revenue: 1994 $2,615,622 **Net Expenses:** $2,615,058 67%/14%/19% **Net Assets:** $955,488 **Citations:** 54:137
Products or Services: They have special materials for educators: a lesson guide, videos and brochures for students to accompany sections of the quilt.
Tax Status: 501(c)(3) **Annual Report:** Yes. **Employees:** 37
Board of Directors or Trustees: Michael Barrett (Campaign Treasurer for Senator Diane Feinstein, D-CA), Nancy Blanford (AIDS Treatment Data Network), Mindi Canner; Trish Drew (past co-chair), James Goodfellow, James Hicks, Charles Jackson (Project Dir., American Cancer Society, TN), Dr. Jonathan Mann (Harvard School of Public Health), Marienne McClure (V.P., Paine Webber), Lee Nordlund, Dr. Margaret Poscher (Univ. of CA, San Francisco), Margaret Robson, Julia Sawabini (Univ. of PA Press), Claude Schnier, M.P.H., Kathleen Swift, Charles Thompson, IV, Jeanne White (mother of Ryan White, Pres. of The Ryan White Found.), Geoffrey Woolley.
Periodicals: *On Display* (quarterly newsletter). **Internships:** Yes.
Other Information: The AIDS Quilt will be displayed in its entirety in Washington, DC in October 1996, "just weeks before the presidential election." Fundraising for the display was led by television producer Norman Lear, who donated $25,000, and a $20,000 grant from the National Endowment for the Arts. The quilt was begun in 1987 when gay rights activist Cleve Jones spray painted the name of his deceased friend, Marvin Feldman, on a piece of fabric. "Grief over his friend's death; a desire for him to be remembered as a person, not a statistic; and rage at the lack of government response to AIDS, all sparked Cleve's idea." The Project received $1,090,338, or 42% of revenue, from individual contributors. $805,198 net, or 31%, from the sale of merchandise. $362,688, or 14%, from display income. $184,772, or 7%, from foundations, corporations and government grants. The remaining income came from donated goods, events, and other miscellaneous sources.

Nathan Cummings Foundation
1926 Broadway, Suite 600
New York, NY 10023   **Phone:**   (212) 787-7300
USA   **Fax:**   (212) 787-7377

Contact Person: Charles R. Halpern, President.   **Officers or Principals:** Ruth Cummings Sorensen, Chairman; James K. Cummings, Vice Chairman; Diane Cummings, Secretary; Ellen S. Lazarus, Chief Financial Officer; Robert N. Mayer, Treasurer.

Mission or Interest: Grant-making foundation focusing on the environment.
Accomplishments: In 1994 the Foundation awarded over $10 million in grants. Recipients included; three grants totaling $310,000 for the Tides Foundation, $200,000 for the Environmental Defense Fund, $130,000 for the Sierra Club Foundation, $100,000 each for the Center for Neighborhood Technology, World Resources Institute, and National Campaign for Freedom of Expression, $76,218 for the Center on Budget and Policy Priorities, $75,000 for the Natural Resources Defense Council, $70,000 for the Food Research and Action Center, $50,000 each for the Earth Island Institute, Environmental Law and Policy Center of the Midwest, National Center for Economic Alternatives, Physicians for Social Responsibility, and Americans for Peace Now, $45,000 each for Project Nishma, and the Jewish Fund for Justice, $40,000 each for the Environmental Health Coalition, INFORM, Southwest Community Resources, Public Health Institute, and Public Voice for Food and Health Policy, $38,175 for the Planned Parenthood Federation of America, and $35,000 each for the Safe Energy Communication Council, Environmental Health Network, and Worldwatch Institute.
Net Assets: 1992 $279,708,793
Tax Status: 501(c)(3) **Annual Report:** Yes.
Board of Directors or Trustees: Marc Cummings, Michael Cummings, Reynold Levy, Bevis Longstreth (Rockefeller Family Fund), Beatrice Cummings Mayer.
Other Information: The Foundation was established in 1949 by Nathan Cummings and was a major beneficiary of his estate following his death in 1985. Cummings' wealth came from Consolidated Foods, the predecessor of the Sara Lee Corp., and investments in General Dynamics.

Nation Company, The / *The Nation*

72 5th Ave.
New York, NY 10011   **Phone:**   (212) 242-8400
USA   **Fax:**   (212) 675-3499

Contact Person: Victor Navasky, Publisher.
Officers or Principals: Victor Navasky, Publisher/Editorial Director; Katrina vanden Heuvel, Editor; Richard Lingeman, Editor.
Mission or Interest: Publishes *The Nation*, the longest running weekly in America. *The Nation* is a stronghold of unabashed and unreconstructed leftism and prides itself on its "spirit of dissent."
Accomplishments: As of December 1994 *The Nation* had a paid circulation of 82,788, down from about 95,000 in 1991. The average reader is male, has a graduate degree and a mean income of $65,800. The first issue was published on July 6, 1865. Featured columnists include Alexander Cockburn and Christopher Hitchens. Contributors include Molly Ivins, Toni Morrison, Calvin Trillin, Gore Vidal and others. Fifteen percent of their readers are "Nation Associates" who lend financial support and receive a special newsletter.
Products or Services: *NationAlerts*, monthly bulletins on timely issues.
Tax Status: For profit.
Periodicals: *The Nation* (weekly magazine), *NationAlerts* (monthly bulletins).

Nation Institute, The

72 5th Ave.
New York, NY 10011   **Phone:**   (212) 463-9270
USA   **Fax:**   (212) 463-9712

Contact Person: Sandy Wood, Assistant Director.
Officers or Principals: Peter Meyer, Executive Director ($47,669); Dean Haywood Burns, President ($0); Stephen Gillers, Vice President ($0); Catherine Stimpson, Treasurer; Victor Navasky, Executive Director.
Mission or Interest: "Committed to the creation of a just society and an informed public." Supports research and internships for *The Nation* magazine.
Accomplishments: The Institute has held journalism conferences in the Netherlands, England, and Russia. Sponsored award-winning investigative articles published world-wide.
Net Revenue: 1993 $106,624 **Net Expenses:** $199,108 **Net Assets:** $70,317
Products or Services: Offer internships to work on *The Nation*. "Robert Wasur Civil Liberties Fellowship" for young attorneys. In 1993 they spent $30,337 on these internships. Operate "Supreme Court Watch" and publish *Docket Report*, which has a circulation of about 15,000. This project cost $16,744. Also in 1993 they spent $40,202 on polling research. Host public events. They present the I.F. Stone Award for "excellence in student journalism." The late I.F. Stone, a self-described "Jeffersonian Marxist," was the Washington editor of *The Nation*, and publisher of the investigative *I.F. Stone's Weekly*. The prize is $1,000 and publication of the winning article.
Tax Status: 501(c)(3) **Employees:** 2 full time, 2 part time.
Board of Directors or Trustees: Alice Arlen (documentary film-maker), Arthur Carter (publisher, The New York Observer, Litchfield County Times), Howard Dodson (Dir., Schomberg Center for Research and Black Culture), Rhoda Dreyfus (Chair, Albermarle County Democratic Party), Prof. Stephen Gillers (New York Univ.), Danny Goldberg (Chair, ACLU Found. of S. Calf.), Steven Haft (film producer), Christie Hefner (CEO, Playboy Enterprises), Prof. Leonard Marsak (Univ. of CA), Tim Robbins (actor, director), Prof. Martin Sherwin (Tufts Univ.), Catharine Stimpson (Dir., Fellows Program, John D. And Catherine T. MacArthur Found.), Rose Styron (Co-Chair, PEN Freedom to Write Committee), Katrina vanden Heuvel (editor, The Nation).
Periodicals: *Docket Report*.
Internships: Yes, for college students interested in journalism.
Other Information: The Institute received $97,938, or 92% of revenue, from gifts and grants awarded by foundations, companies and individuals. (These grants included $15,000 from the Clara Miller Foundation, $10,000 from the J.M. Kaplin Fund, and $1,500 from the New World Foundation.) $5,551 net, or 5%, from the sale of tapes. $2,423, or 2%, from dividends and interest from securities. The remaining revenue came from interest on savings and temporary cash investments.

National Abortion Federation (NAF)
1436 U St. N.W. Suite 103
Washington, DC 20009   **Phone:**   (202) 667-5881
USA

Contact Person: Sylvia Stengle, Executive Director.   **Officers or Principals:** Sylvia Stengle, Executive Director ($82,958); Mary Catherine Arndorfer, Training and Education Director ($56,946); Patricia K. Anderson ($54,792); Lynne Randall, President; Suzanne T. Poppema, M.D., Vice President; Anita Wilson, Secretary; Joan Coombs, Treasurer.
Mission or Interest: Working to ensure that there is a sufficient number of abortion practitioners, and that abortion services are more widely available. Formed Medical Students for Choice.
Accomplishments: In 1994 the Federation spent $750,970 on its programs. Training and education of physicians and their staff in abortion procedures was the largest program, with expenditures of $246,142. Regional seminars for the presentation of new developments, $211,998. $201,942 was spent on government relations and on informing abortionists and other members about legislative developments. The "Access Initiative," with expenditures of $90,888, works to insure that abortion procedures are available universally.
Net Revenue: 1994 $1,068,689 **Net Expenses:** $1,032,595 73%/22%/6% **Net Assets:** (-$46,691) **Citations:** 184:86
Products or Services: Seminars, publications, and other forums to educate members. NAF provides members with discounted medical supplies bought through group purchasing of large quantities.
Tax Status: 501(c)(3)
Board of Directors or Trustees: Rachel Atkins, Betsy Aubrey, RN, Severa Austin, Curtis Boyd, M.D., Marilynn Buckham, Maria Corsillo, Bruce Ferguson, M.D., Stanley Henshaw, Ph.D., Carole Joffe, Ph.D., H. C. Jones Jr., M.D., Gary Prohaska, M.D., Jeri Rasmussen, Marcy Wilder, Jule Hallerdin, CNM, NP.
Other Information: NAF received $436,455, or 41% of revenue, from gifts and grants awarded by foundations, companies and individuals. (These grants included $60,000 from the Robert Sterling Clark Foundation, $40,000 from the Jessie Smith Noyes Foundation, and $25,000 from the General Service Foundation.) $342,969, or 32%, from membership dues. $204, 003, or 19%, from meeting revenue and registration fees. $49,745, or 5%, from group purchasing activities. The remaining revenue came from publications, interest on savings and temporary cash investments, and miscellaneous sources.

National Abortion and Reproductive Rights Action League (NARAL)
1156 15th St., N.W.
Washington, DC 20005   **Phone:**   (202) 973-3000
USA

Contact Person: Kate Michelman, President.
Officers or Principals: Kate Michelman, President ($80,832); Melonease Shaw, Chair ($0); Del. Kenneth C. Montague, Jr., Treasurer ($0); Melinda S. Rider, Assistant Treasurer; Barbara Silby, Vice Chair; Hannah Rosenthal, Secretary.
Mission or Interest: Lobbing affiliate of NARAL. Supports abortion rights.
Accomplishments: In the fiscal year ending March 1995, the League spent $2,667,461 on its programs. The largest program, with expenditures of $973,475, was Public Education and Membership Development. $738,781 was spent on lobbying efforts and political matters. $478,040 was spent on supporting thirty-four national affiliates. This included $72,355 in grants to some of these affiliates. $299,330 was spent on communications, for "use of the media to educate the public concerning reproductive rights."
Net Revenue: FY ending 3/95 $4,402,311 **Net Expenses:** $4,583,632 58%/10%/32% **Net Assets:** $608,696
Citations: 705:31
Tax Status: 501(c)(4)
Board of Directors or Trustees: Kathryn Berenson, Nancy Chen, Selina Espinoza, Bobbie Fueri, Richard Gross, Allynnore Jen, Judith Black Feather, Diane Dillingham, M. Patricia Fernandez-Kelly (Johns Hopkins Univ. Inst. for Policy Studies), Sharon Gary-Smith, Edward Howard, Susan McLane, Lawrence Ottinger, Paul Smith, Mary-Jane Wagle, Stanley Yake, Mary Lou Reed, Nancy Schwartz Sternoff, Janet Wentz.
Other Information: Affiliated with the 501(c)(3) National Abortion and Reproductive Rights Action League Foundation at the same address, as well as thirty-four national affiliates. Kate Michelman served as president of both national affiliates, and received combined compensation of $121,444. NARAL is also the majority owner, 79%, of a for-profit mailing list company, Choice Contributors at the same address. NARAL received $2,250,558, or 51% of revenue, from gifts and grants awarded by foundations, businesses, and individuals. (These grants included $80,000 from the Robert Sterling Clark Foundation, $1,614 from the Henry J. Kaiser Family Foundation.) $1,940,035, or 44%, from membership dues. $188,515, or 4%, from reimbursed expenses for lobbying services done under contract for another organization. The remaining revenue came from interest on savings and temporary cash investments, and other miscellaneous sources.

National Abortion and Reproductive Rights Action League Foundation (NARAL)
1156 15th St., N.W.
Washington, DC 20005   **Phone:**   (202) 973-3000
USA

Contact Person: Kate Michelman, President.   **Officers or Principals:** Kate Michelman, President ($44,095); Alma T. Young, Chair ($0); Macena W. Love, Secretary/Treasurer ($0).
Mission or Interest: Supports abortion rights through research, legal action, legislative action, and working with affiliates.

Accomplishments: Campaigned for the "Freedom of Choice Act." In the fiscal year ending March 1994, the Foundation spent $1,130,752 on its programs. The largest program, with expenditures of $503,362, was the work it does with its thirty-four affiliates. This included $46,229 in grants to affiliates. The next program, with expenditures of $301,341, was the Research and Special Projects program. This included "legal coalition work, reproductive rights research, analyzing legislation, drafting testimony, and general legal research." $183,665 was spent on communications, "use of the media to educate the public concerning reproductive rights." The rest was spent on lobbying.
Net Revenue: FY ending 3/94 $1,749,126 **Net Expenses:** $1,541,398 73%/14%/12% **Net Assets:** $188,414
Citations: 705:31
Products or Services: Legal action, publications, coalition building, and lobbying. The Foundation spent $142,384 on the direct lobbying of legislators. This was 5% more than the previous year, but down 46% from $264,280 two years prior.
Tax Status: 501(c)(3)
Board of Directors or Trustees: Irene Crowe, Helen Milliken, Dottie Lamm, Carol Pencke, Stanley Yake, Lois Wyse.
Other Information: The Foundation is affiliated with the 501(c)(4) National Abortion and Reproductive Rights Action League, as well as numerous state and local affiliates. NARAL president, Kate Michelman, recieved combined compensation from both affiliates totaling $121,462. The Foundation transferred $986,673 to the 501(c)(4) organization for reimbursement of expenses. The Foundation hired Greer, Margolis, Mitchell & Associates of Washington, DC, for advertising. The Associates were paid $71,942. The Foundation received $1,654,156, or 95% of revenue, from gifts and grants awarded by foundations, businesses, and individuals. (These grants included $100,000 from the Richard and Rhoda Goldman Fund, $60,000 from the John Merck Fund, $12,500 from the Bydale Foundation, $10,000 from the New Prospect Foundation, $5,000 from the Compton Foundation, $5,000 from the New-Land Foundation, $500 from the Stewart R. Mott Charitable Trust.) $111,291, or 6%, from dividends and interest from securities. The remaining revenue came from interest on savings and temporary cash investments. Net revenue was partially offset by a loss of $18,645 from a "Power Breakfast" special fund-raising event.

National Abortion and Reproductive Rights Action League, Connecticut (NARAL)

135 Broad St.
Hartford, CT 06105   **Phone:** (860) 974-6565   **E-Mail:** ctnaral@aol.com
USA   **Fax:**   (860) 543-8919

Contact Person: Laurel Tiesinga, Executive Director. **Officers or Principals:** Elaine Werner, President; Ofelia Figueriredo, Vice President; Valerie Raggio, Secretary; Sue Stanley, Treasurer; Judy Blei, Lobbyist.
Mission or Interest: Connecticut affiliate of the national NARAL. Lobbies to support abortion rights with an emphasis on Connecticut. "To develop and sustain a constituency that uses the political process to guarantee every woman the right to make personal decisions regarding the full range of reproductive choices."
Accomplishments: Only statewide grassroots abortion rights organization in Connecticut. Hosts house parties to raise money and disseminate information. Executive director Tiesinga was named "Outstanding Affiliate Director" for 1995 by the national NARAL. Lobbyist Judy Blei and executive director Tiesinga attended the United Nations' Fourth World Conference on Women in Beijing, China, where they ran a workshop.
Products or Services: Voters' Guide, and Abortion Resource Guide.
Tax Status: 501(c)(4) **Annual Report:** No. **Employees:** 1 full time, 2 part time.
Board of Directors or Trustees: Norma Arcsti, Gail Crook, Myrna Figueroa, Carol Lacoss, Beverly Newell, Susan Place, Andrea Turi-Lawas, Linda Bayer, Carmen Diaz, Evelyn Gonzalez, Elsa Monteiro, Natasha Pierre, Roxanne Roth-Davis, Jill Wood.
Periodicals: *Choice Words* (quarterly newsletter).
Internships: Yes.
Other Information: Affiliated with the CT NARAL PAC that gives money to Connecticut candidates for public office who support abortion rights.

National Abortion and Reproductive Rights Action League, New Hampshire (NARAL)

18 Low Ave.
Concord, NH 03301   **Phone:** (603) 228-1224
USA

Contact Person: Margaret A. Dobbie, Executive Director. **Officers or Principals:** Margaret A. Dobbie, Executive Director; Candace White, Chair ($0); Judith Tausch, Vice Chair ($0); Betty Shapiro, Secretary ($0); Sandra Smith, Treasurer.
Mission or Interest: Supports abortion rights, focusing on New Hampshire.
Accomplishments: They claim 3,000 members. In the fiscal year ending March 1994 the League spent $70,086 on its programs. The largest program was grassroots organizing to influence state legislators; this includes meetings, mailings, phone calls, and activist training. $20,401 was spent informing members about legislators' positions on abortion and to send fact sheets about abortion-related matters to legislators. $16,578 was spent to produce a newsletter and other publications.
Net Revenue: FY ending 3/94 $100,179 **Net Expenses:** $101,038 69%/16%/14% **Net Assets:** $15,205
Products or Services: Brochures, publications, lobbying.
Tax Status: 501(c)(4)
Board of Directors or Trustees: Marilyn Andrews, Michelle Wagner Bryan, Paula Chessin, Andrea Goldberg, Bonnie Groves, Carolyn Jones, Fran Potter, Barbara Tsairis, Susan Sard White.
Periodicals: Newsletter.
Other Information: The League received $98,165, or 98% of revenue, from gifts and grants awarded by foundations, companies and individuals. (These grants included $3,623 from the national NARAL Foundation.) $1,500 net, or 1%, from fund-raising events, including a chocolate-tasting reception, craft raffle and an anniversary reception for Roe v. Wade. The remaining revenue came from interest on savings and temporary cash investments, and net income from the sale of inventory.

National Abortion and Reproductive Rights Action League, North Carolina (NARAL)

P.O. Box 908
Durham, NC 27702   **Phone:** (919) 687-4959
USA   **Fax:**   (919) 682-4629

Contact Person: Beth Ising, Executive Director.   **Officers or Principals:** Jane Preyer, Chair ($0); Anne Lacey, Vice Chair ($0).
Mission or Interest: Support for abortion rights in North Carolina.
Accomplishments: In 1994 the League spent $106,114 on its programs.
Net Revenue: 1994 $104,514 **Net Expenses:** $117,355 90%/5%/4% **Net Assets:** $14,701
Products or Services: House meetings, publications, booths and educational information at public gatherings.
Tax Status: 501(c)(4)
Board of Directors or Trustees: Ellen Coffey, Cheryl Amana, Susan Austin, Rani Biswas, Jamie Combs, Gretchen Cooley, Sarabeth George, Gita Gulati, Betty Gunz, Robert Hawkins, Jessica Kasinoff, Barbara McPherson, Pearl Shelby, Bill Wilson.
Periodicals: Newsletter.
Other Information: The League received $72,034, or 69% of revenue, from gifts and grants awarded by foundations, companies, and individuals. $24,510 net, or 23%, from fund-raising events including a "phonathon," "Spring Swing," and the sale of t-shirts. $6,388, or 6%, from membership fees. The remaining revenue came from training fees and events, interest on savings and temporary cash investments, and other miscellaneous sources.

National Abortion and Reproductive Rights Action League, Ohio (NARAL)

760 E. Broad St.
Columbus, OH 43205   **Phone:**   (614) 267-7006
USA

Contact Person: Mindy Hedges, President.   **Officers or Principals:** Mindy Hedges, President ($0); Doug Rammel, Vice President ($0); Zina Vernon, Secretary ($0); Dr. Robert Bliss, Treasurer.
Mission or Interest: Lobbies to "keep abortion safe and legal."
Accomplishments: In 1994 the League spent $169,227 on its programs. $113,382 was spent on public education and outreach, and $55,844 was spent to train activists.
Net Revenue: 1994 $228,695 **Net Expenses:** $235,749 72%/13%/16% **Net Assets:** $408
Products or Services: Publications, special events, petition drives, lobbying. **Tax Status:** 501(c)(4)
Board of Directors or Trustees: Patricia Camp, Annetta Marion, Sarah Lynn, Roberta Geidner-Antoniotti, Chris Celeste.
Periodicals: Newsletter.
Other Information: Affiliated with the 501(c)(3) National Abortion and Reproductive Rights Action League of Ohio Education Foundation. The two affiliates combined to spend $312,883 in 1994. The League received $228,556, or 99.9%, of revenue from foundations, affiliates, companies and individuals - including $76,060 from the Education Foundation for the use of facilities. The remaining revenue came from interest on savings and temporary cash investments.

National Abortion and Reproductive Rights Action League, Ohio Education Foundation (NARAL)

760 E. Broad St.
Columbus, OH 43205   **Phone:**   (614) 267-7006
USA

Contact Person: Rita M. Atlagovich, President.
Officers or Principals: Rita M. Atlagovich, President ($0); Lana Covel, Treasurer ($0).
Mission or Interest: Educational foundation working to "keep abortion safe and legal."
Accomplishments: In 1994 the Foundation spent $65,709 on its programs.
Net Revenue: 1994 $71,201 **Net Expenses:** $77,134 85%/10%/5% **Net Assets:** $3,043
Products or Services: Educational materials and activist training.
Tax Status: 501(c)(3)
Board of Directors or Trustees: Roberta Geidner-Antoniotti, Janyce Katz, Stan Goodman.
Other Information: Affiliated with the 501(c)(4) National Abortion and Reproductive Rights Action League of Ohio at the same address. The two had combined expenditures of $312,883 in 1994. The Foundation received $70,519, or 99% of revenue, from gifts and grants awarded by foundations, companies and individuals. The remaining revenue came from the interest on savings or cash investments.

National AIDS Fund

1400 I St., N.W., Suite 1220
Washington, DC 20005
USA

Mission or Interest: Prevention of AIDS/HIV transmission. Programs that focus on adolescents.
Other Information: In 1994 the Fund was awarded $136,774 by the Henry J. Kaiser Family Foundation, but it had not been paid by the end of the year.

National Air Traffic Controllers Association (NATCA)

1150 17th St., N.W., Suite 701
Washington, DC 20036   **Phone:** (202) 223-2900
USA

Contact Person: Barry Krasner, President.   **Officers or Principals:** Barry Krasner, President ($148,850); Joseph Bellino, Executive Vice President ($140,633); Michael McNally, Executive Vice President ($42,355).
Mission or Interest: Union representing approximately 12,500 air traffic controllers. Negotiates on their behalf with the Federal Aviation Administration. Member of the AFL-CIO.
Net Revenue: 1994 $8,030,576 **Net Expenses:** $7,792,480 **Net Assets:** $1,226,501
Tax Status: 501(c)(5)
Board of Directors or Trustees: Owen Bridgeman, James Ferguson, Joseph Fruscella, Karl Grundmann, Tim Haines, Craig Lasker, Edward Mullin, Richard Phillips, Jim Poole, Mike Putzier, Sam Rich, James Schwitz, Jerry Whitaker.
Periodicals: Monthly newsletter.
Other Information: The Association received $7,920,351, or 99% of revenue, from membership dues. The remaining revenue came from convention fees, interest on savings and temporary cash investments, sales of promotional items, and other miscellaneous sources.

National Alliance to End Homelessness

1518 K St., N.W., Suite 206
Washington, DC 20006   **Phone:** (202) 638-1526
USA

Contact Person: Kirk Gibson, Director of Operations.   **Officers or Principals:** Thomas Kenyon, President ($101,895); Nan Rowan, Vice President, Policy ($51,775); Michael Mayer, Director of Programs ($42,886); Jill Rathbun, Director of Policy; Susan G. Baker, Anthony S. Harrington, Co-Chairmen; Thomas Ludlow Ashley, Treasurer; Elizabeth Boyle Roberts.
Mission or Interest: Research, education, coalition building, and policy advocacy to solve the problem of homelessness.
Accomplishments: The Alliance held its fourth annual conference in 1996, "Building Our Future: Organizing to End Homelessness in a New Era." In the fiscal year ending June 1994 the Alliance spent $808,735 on its programs. The largest program, costing $371,806, was devoted to research and education, "the Alliance educates public officials, the private sector and the public about the issues of homelessness and its solutions." Next largest, $185,797, was spent on conferences, seminars and workshops. Membership services, information and technical assistance to members, cost $130,815, and $120,317 was spent on public policy advocacy at the federal, state and local levels.
Net Revenue: FY ending 6/94 $740,402 **Net Expenses:** $971,411 83%/13%/4% **Net Assets:** $40,756
Citations: 19:173
Products or Services: Research, publications, conferences, more.   **Tax Status:** 501(c)(3)
Board of Directors or Trustees: Susan Davis, Prof. J. Raymond DePaulo, Jr. (Dir., Affective Disorders Clinic, Johns Hopkins Hospital), Barbara Easterling (Communications Workers of America, AFL-CIO), Anthony Harrington, James Johnson (Chair., Fannie Mae), Arman Simone (Peace, Love and Joy Farm), Robert Strauss, Bob Vila, Robert Villency, Dionne Warwick, Howard Williams, III, Geoffrey Worden, H.J. Young, Ralph Da Costa Nunez, Ph.D. (CEO, Homes for the Homeless), Gary Parsons (Exec., V.P., MCI Communications), D. Eric Pogue, James Dennis Rash (Pres., NationsBank Community Development Corp.), John Roe (V.P., First Boston Corp.).
Other Information: The Alliance received $622,395, or 84% of revenue from grants awarded by foundations, companies and individuals. $72,090, or 10% came from conference registration fees. $39,175, or 5%, from membership dues. The remaining revenue came from interest on savings and temporary cash investments, and other fund-raising programs.

National Anti-Vivisection Society

53 W. Jackson Blvd., Suite 1552
Chicago, IL 60604   **Phone:** (312) 427-6065
USA

Contact Person: Mary Margaret Cunniff, Executive Director.
Officers or Principals: Mary Margaret Cunniff, Executive Director ($105,250); Donald J. Barnes, Director of Education ($63,300); Thomas F. Joyce, Secretary ($52,000); Helen Miller, President; Peter McGovern, Vice President; Benjamin S. Daniel, Treasurer.
Mission or Interest: Animal rights organization. "To initiate, sponsor and contribute to educational programs to acquaint the public to the evils of vivisection. To teach associations, societies, and individuals methods of combating vivisection through preparation of literature, lecture programs and holding classes for such teachings."
Accomplishments: In the fiscal year ending June 1994 the Society spent $1,157,931 on its programs. This included $106,818 in grants to individuals and organizations. The largest grant, $100,000, went to the affiliated International Foundation for Ethical Research. Other recipients included: $2,000 for the National Alliance, $500 each for the International Primate Protection League, and Summit for the Animals, and $200 for the Physicians Committee for Responsible Medicine.
Net Revenue: FY ending 6/94 $1,697,612 **Net Expenses:** $1,684,288 69%/20%/11% **Net Assets:** $3,861,947
Citations: 18:176
Tax Status: 501(c)(3)

Board of Directors or Trustees: Robert Mahoney, Patrick Beattie, John Hughes, Peter O'Donovan.
Other Information: The Society hired attorney Kenneth Cunniff; he was paid $66,778. The Society is affiliated with the 501(c)(3) International Foundation for Ethical Research. The Society received $1,494,766, or 88% of revenue, from gifts and grants awarded by foundations, businesses, and individuals. $78,020, or 5%, from membership dues. $32,158, or 2%, from interest on savings and temporary cash investments. $28,760, or 2%, from dividends and interest from securities. $26,338, or 2%, from the sale of inventory. $19,308 net, or 1%, from capital gains on the sale of securities. The remaining revenue came from miscellaneous sources.

National Association for the Advancement of Colored People (NAACP)

4805 Mt. Hope Dr.
Baltimore, MD 21215   **Phone:**   (410) 358-8900
USA   **Fax:**   (410) 486-9257   **Web-Page:** http://www.naacp.org

Contact Person: Kweisi Mfume, President.   **Officers or Principals:** Benjamin Chavis, Ex-Executive Director ($142,308); Wade Henderson, Washington Bureau Director ($68,653); William Penn, Branch and Field Services ($60,219); Julian Bond, National Leadership Chairman; Don Rojas, Communications Director; Lorena Wallace, Comptroller; Kumar Nichani, Director of Personnel; Leroy Mobley, Director of Prison Program; Earl Shinhoster, Field Secretary.
Mission or Interest: Civil rights organization for the advancement of African-Americans.
Accomplishments: 2,200 branches in the U.S., Europe and Japan. In 1909, on the centennial of Abraham Lincoln's birthday, prominent civic leaders of every major race, religion, and ethnicity signed "The Call", a declaration of the need to eliminate racial discrimination and full citizenship. The creation of this declaration led to the founding of the NAACP. In 1993 the NAACP spent $8,661,783 on its programs.
Net Revenue: 1993 $9,573,088 **Net Expenses:** $10,213,795 85%/13%/2% **Net Assets:** $6,234,629 **Citations:** 4,695:5
Products or Services: Annual Pathway to Excellence Awards. 1995 recipients included Marian Wright Edelman (Children's Defense Fund), Dr. Johnetta Cole (Spellman College), Hillary Rodham Clinton, Ella Fitzgerald, and Katherine Graham (former chair, *Washington Post*).
Tax Status: 501(c)(3)
Board of Directors or Trustees: Sixty-four member board.
Periodicals: *The Crisis: The Most Progressive Voice of Black America* (monthly magazine).
Other Information: President Kweisi Mfume, whose self-selected name means 'conquering son of kings,' was previously a Democrat Representative to the U.S. House of Representatives from Maryland. There he served as the head of the Congressional Black Caucus. He was re-elected in 1994, winning over 80% of the votes in his district, but chose to retire in 1996 to head the NAACP. Mfume's inauguration was held at the Great Hall of the U.S. Department of Justice. The NAACP owns the for-profit Crisis Publishing Company, which produces and distributes the membership magazine, *The Crisis*. The Association received $5,425,670, or 57% of revenue, from gifts and grants awarded by foundations, businesses, affiliates, and individuals. (These grants included $250,000 from the Carnegie Corporation. In 1994 these included $1,500 from the Crestar Foundation.) $3,763,710, or 39%, from membership dues. $348,170, or 4%, from net rental income. The remaining income came from interest on savings and temporary cash investments.

National Association for the Advancement of Colored People Legal Defense Fund (NAACP)

99 Hudson St., 16th Floor
New York, NY 10013   **Phone:**   (212) 219-1900
USA   **Fax:**   (212) 226-7592

Contact Person: Elaine R. Jones, Director.
Officers or Principals: Elaine R. Jones, Director/Counsel ($151,181); Peter Wilderotter, Director of Development ($110,000); Clyde Murphy, Assistant Counsel ($107,792); Charles S. Ralston, Assistant Counsel ($100,744); William T. Coleman, Jr., Chairman; Robert H. Preiskel, President; Barrington D. Parker Jr., Vice President; James M. Nabrit, III, Secretary; Eleanor S. Applewhaite, Treasurer; Norman J. Chachkin, Managing Attorney; Theodore M. Shaw, Associate Director/Counsel.
Mission or Interest: Uses litigation to advance a civil rights agenda. "Works with roughly 150 cooperating attorneys in local communities around the country. These attorneys work on 600 cases...They work under our direction and supervision in cases which we agree to work together. Our office will in most cases pay for costs of the litigation and we and the cooperating attorneys attempt to recover fees and costs at the conclusion of cases in which we prevail."
Accomplishments: In 1993 the Fund spent $6,497,315 on its programs. The largest program, with expenditures of $5,198,503, was legal assistance. On this legal action, the Fund spent $308,756 on cooperating attorneys fees, travel expenses, expert witnesses, and court costs. The Fund received $4,119,408 in court-awarded attorneys fees. $779,764 was spent on the Herbert Lehman education program that provided $458,700 for 302 scholarships for undergraduate and law students. $286,645 was spent on disseminating information to the public. $232,403 was spent on conducting surveys, studies, workshops, and conferences.
Net Revenue: 1993 $11,632,585 **Net Expenses:** $8,763,204 74%/4%/22% **Net Assets:** $19,774,515 **Citations:** 1:240
Products or Services: Litigation, scholarships, and lobbying. In 1993 the Fund spent $27,811 on lobbying, $9,730 on grassroots lobbying and $18,081 on the direct lobbying of legislators. This was an increase of 59% over the previous year, but down 69% from $88,515 two years prior.
Tax Status: 501(c)(3)

Board of Directors or Trustees: Mrs. Billye Suber Aaron, Prof. Anthony Amsterdam (NYU School of Law), Clarence Avant (Chair, Motown Record Co.), Dean John Baker (Albany Law School), Dr. Mary Frances Berry, Mrs. Anita Lyons Bond, Hon. Allen Broussard, William Brown, III, Yvonne Brathwaite Burke (Los Angeles County Board of Supervisors), Dr. I.H. Clayborn (Sovereign Grand Commander, Ancient and Accepted Scottish Right of Freemasonry), Talbot Cross (Pres., FL State Univ.), Dr. Anthony Downs (Brookings Inst.), Robert Drinan, S.J. (Georgetown Univ. Law School), Prof. Kenneth Edelin, M.D. (Obstetrics and Gynecology, Boston Univ. School of Medicine), Marian Wright Edelman (Childrens Defense Fund), Toni Fay (V.P., Community Relations, Time Warner), Prof. David Feller (Univ. of CA, School of Law), Hon. Marvin Frankel, Ronald Gault (Managing Dir., J.P. Morgan Securities), Prof. Jack Greenberg (Columbia Univ. School of Law), Prof. Charles Hamilton (Columbia Univ.), Patricia Irvin (Deputy Asst. Secretary of Defense for Humanitarian and Refugee Affairs), Anna Faith Jones (Pres., Boston Foundation), Quincy Jones (Quincy Jones Productions), Dr. John Maguire (Pres., Claremont Univ. Center and Graduate School), Right Rev. Paul Moore, Jr., Deval Patrick, Hon. Charles Renfrew, Jacob Sheinkman (Pres., Amalgamated Clothing and Textile Workers Union), Wayman Smith, III (V.P., Corporate Affairs, Anheuser-Busch), Michael Sovern (Pres. Emeritus, Columbia Univ. Law School), Prof. Chuck Stone (Journalism, Univ. of NC, Chapel Hill), Prof. James Vorenberg (Harvard Law School), Dr. George Wallerstein (Univ. of WA), M. Moran Weston, Ph.D. (Pres., Natl. Association for Affordable Housing), Prof. Roger Wilkins (George Mason Univ.), Hon. Andrew Young (former mayor of Atlanta and ambassador to the U.N. for the Carter administration), and many members of the legal community.

Other Information: Affiliated with the Earl Warren Legal Training Program. The Legal Defense Fund is not affiliated with the NAACP. The Fund was founded by the NAACP, but has had a separate board, program, staff, and officers for over thirty years. The Fund hired the Falls Church, VA, firm of Public Interest Data for mailing list maintenance, and paid them $49,800. Three New York city firms, Sanky Perlowin & Associates, McKinney & McDowell, Neuberger & Berman, and the Los Angeles firm of Charlotte Dobb & Co. were hired as consultants. The firms were paid $98,250, $66,984, $59,798, and $48,000 respectively. The Fund received $6,062,211, or 52% of revenue, from gifts and grants awarded by foundations, businesses, and individuals. (These grants included $555,000 over three years from the Carnegie Corporation, $5,000 from the Norman Lear Foundation, $1,000 from the Barbra Streisand Foundation, and $500 from the Aaron and Martha Schecter Private Foundation. In 1994 these grants included $500,000 over two years from the John D. and Catherine T. MacArthur Foundation, $45,000 from the New-Land Foundation, $10,000 from the Joyce Foundation, $2,200 from the Haymarket People's Fund, and $250 from the Ruth Mott Fund. In 1995, $60,000 from the Rockefeller Foundation.) $4,119,408, or 35%, from court-awarded attorneys fees. $545,604, or 5%, from dividends and interest from securities. $534,572, or 5%, from capital gains on the sale of securities. $370,790 net, or 3%, from special fund raising events. The Fund held $7,375,942, or 37% of its assets, in corporate stocks and bonds. $5,356,076, or 27%, in U.S. Government obligations.

National Association for the Advancement of Colored People, California (NAACP)

595 Lincoln Ave.
Pasadena, CA 91103   **Phone:**   (818) 793-1293
USA

Contact Person: Joseph Broussard.
Mission or Interest: California branch of the national organization. Works to "eliminate racial discrimination and segregation from all aspects of public life...to secure legislation banning discrimination and segregation...to secure equal job opportunities based upon individual merit without regard to race, religion or national origin...to end mob violence and police brutality."
Accomplishments: The organization investigates various claims of discriminatory activity in California. In the five years prior to 1993 they had investigated over a thousand cases.
Net Revenue: 1993 $53,103 **Net Expenses:** $45,131 **Net Assets:** $21,825
Products or Services: Annual Ruby McKnight Williams Award Banquet. Black history library.
Tax Status: 501(c)(3)
Other Information: The Association received $30,111 net, or 57% of revenue, from special fund-raising events. $11,675, or 22%, from gifts and grants awarded by foundations, businesses, and individuals. $11,152, or 21%, from membership dues. The remaining revenue came from investment income.

National Association for the Advancement of Colored People, Memphis Branch

588 Vance Ave.
Memphis, TN 38126   **Phone:**   (901) 521-1343
USA

Contact Person: Maxine Smith, Executive Secretary. **Officers or Principals:** Maxine Smith, Executive Secretary ($155,450).
Mission or Interest: To further develop civil rights for blacks in the state of Tennessee.
Accomplishments: In 1994 the Association spent $262,823 on its programs.
Net Revenue: 1994 $356,089 **Net Expenses:** $356,786 74%/8%/18% **Net Assets:** $358,527
Products or Services: Lobbying, special events, support for the national NAACP.
Tax Status: 501(c)(4)
Other Information: The Association received $216,163, or 61% of revenue, from gifts and grants awarded by foundations, companies and individuals. $79,267 net, or 22%, from special fund-raising events. $53,084, or 15%, from membership dues. The remaining revenue came from interest on savings and temporary cash investments, and other miscellaneous sources.

National Association of Black Social Workers (NABSW)

8436 W. McNichols
Detroit, MI 48221   Phone: (313) 995-1496
USA

Contact Person: Dr. Howard V. Brabson, Administrative Consultant.
Officers or Principals: Leonard G. Dunston, President ($0); Larva J. Anderson, Vice President ($0); Dorothy Newell, Recording Secretary ($0); Gwendolyn W. Darty, Corresponding Secretary; Judith Jackson, Treasurer.
Mission or Interest: "To improve the knowledge and skills of members and to increase their participation in their community activities as professional social workers...To inform members and the general public of the organization's goals and programs...of professional knowledge and programs being developed that improve social welfare in the various communities...of social welfare policies and services being developed and utilized in various countries...of the needs of African American families living in low socio-economic areas."
Accomplishments: Approximately 2,400 members. In 1994 the Association spent $285,927 on its programs. The largest program, with expenditures of $137,605, was an International Conference for 120 members and non-members. $105,872 was spent on a National Annual Conference. Other programs included the publication of a journal and newsletter. The Association awarded $5,000 in grants to local chapters and $13,450 in grants and scholarships for 13 social work students.
Net Revenue: 1994 $435,805 **Net Expenses:** $325,402 88%/7%/6% **Net Assets:** $286,342
Products or Services: Conferences, journals, working papers, professional services, and lobbying. The Association spent $915 lobbying congress on welfare reform, and addressing the issue at the National Conference.
Tax Status: 501(c)(3)
Board of Directors or Trustees: Dr. Magalene Hester, Terry Solomon, Gerald Smith.
Periodicals: *Black Caucus Journal* (quarterly scholarly journal), and a quarterly newsletter.
Other Information: The association received $200,947, or 46% from the National Annual Conference fees. $158,154, or 36%, from the International Conference fees. $52,132, or 12%, from membership dues. $19,262, or 4%, from direct and indirect public support in the form of gifts and grants awarded by foundations, affiliates, businesses, and individuals. The remaining revenue came from the subscriptions and sales of periodicals and publications, and interest on savings and temporary cash investments.

National Association of Community Action Agencies (NACAA)

1875 Connecticut Ave., Suite 416
Washington, DC 20009   **Phone:**   (202) 265-7546
USA   **Fax:**   (202) 265-8850

Contact Person: Edward L. Block, Executive Director.   **Officers or Principals:** Edward L. Block, Executive Director ($90,090); John Adams, Director of Education ($56,700); Avril Weisman, Director of Membership ($49,160).
Mission or Interest: "NACAA was established to provide continuous education and information for community action Agency members." Helps member organizations deliver social services more efficiently.
Accomplishments: In 1994 the NACAA spent $136,223 on its programs. All of this was distributed in grants providing training and assistance to community action agencies nationwide.
Net Revenue: 1994 $858,918 ($136,026, or 16%, from government grants) **Net Expenses:** $951,386 14%/86%/0%
Net Assets: $71,146 **Citations:** 50:139
Tax Status: 501(c)(3)
Other Information: The NACAA received $406,175, or 47% of revenue, from fees for educational services. $241,571, or 28%, from membership dues. $136,026, or 16%, from government grants. $55,117, or 6%, from contributions received at an annual conference. $8,152, or 1%, from interest on savings and temporary cash investments. The remaining revenue came from other miscellaneous sources.

National Association of Government Employees

159 Burgin Parkway
Quincy, MA 02169   **Phone:**   (617) 376-0220
USA

Contact Person: David Bernard, Vice President.
Officers or Principals: Kenneth Lyons, President ($98,226); Joseph L. DeLorey, Treasurer ($69,052); Harry Breen, Vice President ($63,077); Sam Alvarado, Susanne Pooler, Thomas Turco, Charles Warren, Ed Reilly, Vice Presidents.
Mission or Interest: Union representing approximately 195,000 civilian federal employees. Members in military agencies, Internal Revenue Service, Post Office, General Services Administration, Federal Aviation Administration, Veterans Administration, and other agencies.
Accomplishments: In the fiscal year ending August 1994, the union spent $3,401,230 on its activities.
Net Revenue: FY ending 8/94 $12,053,198 **Net Expenses:** $11,386,369 30%/70%/0% **Net Assets:** $6,203,893
Tax Status: 501(c)(5)
Periodicals: *The Fednews* (bimonthly newsletter).
Other Information: Affiliated with the Service Employees International Union. The union received $11,743,388, or 97% of revenue, from membership dues. $227,113, or 2%, from rental income. The remaining revenue came from interest on savings and temporary cash investments.

National Association of Letter Carriers of the USA

100 Indiana Ave., N.W.
Washington, DC 20001   **Phone:**   (202) 393-4695
USA   **Fax:**   (202) 737-1540

Contact Person: Vincent Sombrotto, President.
Mission or Interest: Union representing postal workers. Member of the AFL-CIO.
Accomplishments: Approximately 315,000 members. Hosted a Congressional breakfast to meet with leaders of Congress and talk about job-related issues.
Tax Status: 501(c)(5)
Periodicals: *NALC Activist* (quarterly newsletter), *Postal Record* (monthly newsletter).
Other Information: Founded in 1889.

National Campaign for a Peace Tax Fund

2121 Decatur Place, N.W.
Washington, DC 20008   **Phone:**   (202) 483-3751   **E-Mail:** peacetaxfund@igc.apc.org
USA   **Fax:**   (202) 986-0667

Contact Person: Carrie Mook Bridgeman, Administrative Assistant.
Officers or Principals: Marian Franz, Executive Director; Eirik Frederick Harteis, Director of Development and Outreach.
Mission or Interest: "To work for the enactment of legislation enabling taxpayers who are conscientious objectors to participation in war in any form to have their tax dollars spent for non-military purposes only."
Accomplishments: "A House Ways and Means subcommittee held a hearing on the U.S. Peace Tax Fund Bill in 1992. We also submitted written testimony to a hearing of the full Ways and Means Committee on various tax measures in 1995. The U.S. Peace Tax Fund Bill is endorsed by national civil liberties groups. It is a cry for freedom of conscience."
Products or Services: "Compelled by Conscience," video.
Tax Status: 501(c)(4) **Employees:** 4
Periodicals: *National Campaign for a Peace Tax Fund Newsletter.* **Internships:** No.

National Campaign for Freedom of Expression (NCFE)

1402 3rd Ave., Suite 421
Seattle, WA 98101   **Phone:**   (206) 340-9301   **E-Mail:** sbj@tmn.com
USA   **Fax:**   (206) 340-4303

Contact Person: Steve Johnson, Office Manager.   **Officers or Principals:** David Mendoza, Executive Director ($48,150).
Mission or Interest: Promotes freedom of expression for the arts.
Accomplishments: In the fiscal year ending June 1994, the Campaign spent $164,635 on its programs. The largest program, with expenditures of $77,424, was education and information, which included the production and distribution of publications, videos, and other products. $37,850 was spent on grassroots organizing. $28,672 was spent on media projects that "provide media support to artists and organizations whose freedom of expression is under attack, includes ongoing education of the media on freedom of expression issues." $16,814 was spent on advocacy, "working more directly with politicians and encouraging our members to work with their representatives on promoting freedom of expression." $3,873 was spent providing legal advice to "artists and art organizations whose freedom of expression are under attack."
Net Revenue: FY ending 6/94 $89,555 **Net Expenses:** $208,409 79%/12%/9% **Net Assets:** (-$55,274)
Products or Services: Publications, videos, t-shirts, and lobbying. The campaign spent $7,986 on lobbying.
Tax Status: 501(c)(3)
Board of Directors or Trustees: David Acosta, Ted Berger (NY Foundation for the Arts), Richard Bolton, Jan Brooks, Cee Scott Brown (Art Matters), Helen Brunner, Mary Dorman, Jim Dozier, Mary Jane Edwards, Kahil El' zabar, Julian Low, Charlotte Murphy, Mary Ann Peters, Patrick Scott, Ella King Torrey.
Periodicals: Newsletter.
Other Information: The Campaign also has a Washington, DC office: 918 F St., N.W., Suite 609, Washington, DC 20004, (202) 393-2787, fax (202) 347-7376, jwood@tmn.com. The Campaign received $88,888, or 99% of revenue, from gifts and grants awarded by foundations, businesses, and individuals. (These grants included $100,000 over five years from the Nathan Cummings Foundation, and $10,000 from the Joyce Mertz-Gilmore Foundation.) The remaining revenue came from the sale of t-shirts and videos, and interest on savings and temporary cash investments.

National Catholic Reporter Publishing Co. / *National Catholic Reporter* (NCR)

115 E. Armour Blvd.
Kansas City, MO 64111   **Phone:**   (816) 531-0538
USA   **Fax:**   (816) 968-2268

Contact Person: William L. McSweeney, Publisher.   **Officers or Principals:** William L. McSweeney, Publisher/President ($107,488); Thomas C. Fox, Editor, NCR ($98,184); Robert Heyer, Director, Sheed & Ward ($76,216); Arthur J. Jones, Editor-at-Large; Sr. Joan Chittister, OSB, Treasurer; Dr. Ann Weilk, Secretary.

Mission or Interest: Publishes the *National Catholic Reporter*, a national newspaper of leftist Catholicism. "A strong independent voice meeting the urgent need for solid reporting on the religious dimension of the news." Also publishes books and other publications.

Accomplishments: Readership of approximately 100,000. In 1996 NRC staff writer Leslie Wirpsa won the first Eileen Egan Journalism Award. (Eileen Egan is the founder of the peace group Pax Chrsti USA.) The award is given by Catholic Relief Services for Catholic newspapers that encourage "the people of the United States to fulfill their moral responsibilities in alleviating human suffering, removing its causes and promoting social justice in developing countries." In the past, NCR won the Catholic Press Association's award for General Excellence. The average NCR reader has a graduate degree, is female, has an annual income between $20,000-$75,000, and lives in the Midwest or East Coast. In the fiscal year ending June 1994, the Publishing Co. spent $3,697,570 on its programs. NCR was the largest program, with expenditures of $1,765,390. $870,503 was spent on other publications, *Enneagram Educator, Praying,* and other newsletters. $602,198 was spent on Sheed & Ward publishers, producers of books, video cassettes on subjects from "popular spirituality to liberation theology, women's issues, religious education and bible study." $459,479 was spent on Credence Cassettes, audio and video cassettes.

Net Revenue: FY ending 6/94 $5,016,723 **Net Expenses:** $4,929,258 75%/25%/.0% **Net Assets:** (-$297,773)
Citations: 167:90
Tax Status: 501(c)(3)
Board of Directors or Trustees: Rev. Joseph Appleyard, SJ (Boston College), Maria Berriozabal, Ken Briggs, John Caron, Dr. William D'Antonio, Rev. Howard Gray, SJ (Univ. of Detroit), Rose Lucey (Third Life Center), John McMeel (Universal Press Syndicate), Brother Cyprian Rowe (St. Peter Claver Rectory), Sister Mary Thibodeaux (SBS Center for Evangelization), Msgr. John Egan (DePaul Univ.).
Periodicals: *National Catholic Reporter* (weekly newspaper), *Praying* (bimonthly magazine), *Enneagram Educator* (quarterly newsletter).
Other Information: The Publishing Company received $3,941,573, or 79% of revenue, from the sale of publications and other inventory. $760,249, or 15%, from advertising. $233,638, or 5%, from mailing list rentals. The remaining revenue came from interest on savings and temporary cash investments, royalties, the sale of assets, and other miscellaneous sources.

National Center for Economic Alternatives
2317 Ashmead Place, N.W.
Washington, DC 20009
USA

Mission or Interest: Research on the systemic problems of democracy, equality and ecology.
Tax Status: 501(c)(3)
Other Information: In 1994 the Center received $75,000 from the Bauman Family Foundation, and $50,000 from the Nathan Cummings Foundation.

National Center for Lesbian Rights (NCLR)
870 Market St.
San Francisco, CA 94102   **Phone:** (415) 392-6257
USA   **Fax:**   (415) 392-8442

Contact Person: Elizabeth Hendrickson, Executive Director.
Officers or Principals: Elizabeth Hendrickson, Executive Director ($50,531).
Mission or Interest: "Performs and delivers legal and educational services to the lesbian and gay community." Works to change the law in the areas of civil rights, employment, housing, immigration, benefits for same sex partners, child custody, donor insemination, adoption, and foster parenting.
Accomplishments: In 1994 the Center spent $491,040 on its programs. These programs included "expanding legal services to lesbians of color."
Net Revenue: 1994 $601,596 **Net Expenses:** $592,143 83%/7%/10% **Net Assets:** $12,655 **Citations:** 68:124
Tax Status: 501(c)(3)
Board of Directors or Trustees: Abby Abinanti, Sally Elkington, Pam Haskins, Assoc. Prof. Cheri Pies (San Jose State Univ.), Alix Sabin, Maryann Simpson (Progressive Asset Management), Leonie Walker, Shannan Wilbur (Youth Law Center).
Periodicals: Newsletter.
Other Information: The Center received $530,136, or 88% of revenue, from direct and indirect public support in the form of gifts and grants awarded by foundations, affiliates, businesses, and individuals. (These grants included $500,000 from the Joyce Mertz-Gilmore Foundation, $10,000 from the Tides Foundation, $5,000 from the Vanguard Public Foundation, and $500 from the Compton Foundation. Other donors included the Astraea National Lesbian Action Foundation.) $36,271, or 6%, from membership dues. $12,040, or 2%, from newsletter subscriptions. $9,978, or 2%, from the sale of publications. $7,071 net, or 1%, from special fund-raising events, namely an annual luncheon. The remaining revenue came from interest on savings and temporary cash investments, and other miscellaneous sources.

National Center for Youth Law
114 Sansome St., Suite 900
San Francisco, CA 94104-3820   **Phone:** (415) 543-3307
USA   **Fax:**   (415) 956-9024

Contact Person: Carol Babichuk, Administrator.   **Officers or Principals:** John F. O'Toole, Director ($92,389); David Lambert, Attorney ($80,493); Alice Bussiere, Attorney ($72,243); Terrence Lee Hancock, President; Ellenor Rios, Vice President; John D. MacIntosh, Treasurer; Christopher Wu, Secretary.

Mission or Interest: "Uses the law to protect children from the harms caused by poverty, and to improve the lives of children living in poverty." Uses litigation to guarantee and increase social services and welfare spending.

Accomplishments: In 1994 the Center spent $1,252,277 on its programs. The Center received $472,213 in court-awarded attorney's fees from two cases; Angela R. v. Tucker, a class action brought against the state of Arkansas for violations of federal and state law in the foster care system, and Barajas v. Coye, a class action brought against the state of California for failing to cover "dental sealants in the Medi Cal program." Both awards were paid by the states' taxpayers. Other cases included; challenging California's welfare offices for closing during regular business days, challenging the California practice that "requires that abandoned and orphaned children living with non-legally responsible relatives be combined into one AFDC assistance unit with the relatives' own children" and thereby reducing benefits, challenging the Immigration and Naturalization Service's practice that denies the release of children taken into custody to anyone other than a parent or legal guardian, and challenging the use of pepper spray in delinquent youth facilities in Washington state.

Net Revenue: 1994 $1,577,730 (See Other Information for government support) **Net Expenses:** $1,554,266 81%/13%/6%

Net Assets: $96,518 **Citations:** 91:110

Tax Status: 501(c)(3)

Board of Directors or Trustees: Gina Baker, Alexander Brainerd, Sheila Collier, Mary Downey, Lyn Duff, Arturo Gonzalez, Eileen Hirsch (WI, State Public Defender), Arthur Houle, Danae Jackson, Mary McCutcheon, Carl Robinson, James Weill (Children's Defense Fund).

Periodicals: *Youth Law News* (six times a year newsletter).

Other Information: The Center received $1,044,232, or 66% of revenue, from direct and indirect public support from foundations, businesses, affiliates, and individuals. (These grants included $804,559 from the federally-funded Legal Services Corporation.) $472,213, or 30%, from court-awarded attorney's fees. $61,285, or 4%, from dividends and interest from securities. Through the Legal Services Corporation and court-awarded attorney's fees, the Center received approximately $1,276,772, or 81% of revenue, from government, and ultimately taxpayers', sources.

National Center on Education and the Economy (NCEE)

700 11th St., N.W., Suite 750
Washington, DC 20001   **Phone:** (202) 783-3668
USA

Mission or Interest: Research and educational organization focusing on the social benefits of education.

Accomplishments: Former Board members included Hillary Rodham Clinton, former Governor Mario Cuomo (D-NY), and Ira Magaziner, the "health czar" of Hillary Rodham Clinton's Health Care Task Force. Produced many studies on education and the skill needs of businesses.

Products or Services: To Secure Our Future: The Federal Role in Education.

Tax Status: 501(c)(3)

Periodicals: *The Alliance* (monthly newsletter).

Other Information: In 1995 the *Wall Street Journal* reported that the New York State Attorney General, Dennis Vacco (Republican), was investigating over $100,000 that was paid to Hillary Rodham Clinton during her tenure on the Board. Although uncompensated as a Board member, she was paid to direct some programs. The Center was formerly located in Rochester, NY.

National Clearinghouse on Marital and Date Rape

2325 Oak St.
Berkeley, CA 94708   **Phone:** (510) 524-1582
USA

Contact Person: Laura X, Director.   **Officers or Principals:** Traci Eckels, Vice President; Sonia Cavazos, Treasurer.

Mission or Interest: "To make intimate relationships truly egalitarian...To educate through an organization of consultants, researchers, speakers and resources for legal and medical advocates, writers, the media, student and community members concerned with marital and date rape."

Accomplishments: "Our director has been working to educate people about preventing marital and date rape since 1975. Co-produced world's first conference on marital rape in St. Louis, and the second in Des Moines. Consultants to articles for *Ms.* and *Seventeen* magazines. Worked to make date and marital rape a crime in all fifty states."

Products or Services: "State Law Chart, Law and Prosecution Statistic, The Date Rape Packet," more.

Tax Status: 501(c)(3) **Employees:** All volunteer.

Other Information: "We are an organization of researchers with over 20 years of compiled information on women's issues, specifically marital and date rape. We are also dedicated to ending rape through education and offer speaking events and seminars for this purpose." Previously called the Women's History Research Library.

National Coalition Against Censorship (NCAC)

275 Seventh Ave.
New York, NY 10001   **Phone:** (212) 807-6222   **E-Mail:** ncac@netcom.com
USA   **Fax:**   (212) 807-6245

Contact Person: Leanne Katz.   **Officers or Principals:** Leanne Katz, Executive Director ($64,243); Jeremiah S. Gutman, Jo List Levinson, Co-Chairs ($0); John Sucke, Secretary/Treasurer.

Mission or Interest: Opposition to censorship. "Freedom of communication is the indispensable condition of a healthy democracy...Some of the Coalition's participating organizations reject barriers for all adults, so long as their individual right of choice is not infringed. All of us are united in the conviction that censorship of what we see and hear and read constitutes an unacceptable dictatorship over our minds and a dangerous opening to religious, political, artistic, and intellectual repression." The Coalition is made up of participating organizations, including educational organizations like the American Associations of University Professors and Women, civil libertarian groups such as the ACLU, entertainment organizations such as the Screen Actors Guild, religious groups like Unitarian Universalist Association, and others with varied interests such as the Lambda Legal Defense and Education Fund and Planned Parenthood Federation of America. In all, forty-six organizations participate.

Accomplishments: In 1994 they spent $155,109 on grassroots programs that help those who are fighting the removal of books from schools, and other local activities. $103,663 was spent on their Women's Project which opposes censorship of pornography. $124,915 was spent on other general, information and educational activities.

Net Revenue: 1994 $449,816 **Net Expenses:** $469,934 82%/10%/9% **Net Assets:** (-$32,736)

Products or Services: Assists community groups, holds meetings and conferences, monitors legislation, prepares articles and editorials, more.

Tax Status: 501(c)(3) **Annual Report:** Yes. **Employees:** 6

Board of Directors or Trustees: Catherine Christian, Esq., Earl Jones (National Education Assoc.), Gara LaMarche (Exec. Dir., Fund for Free Expression), Gail Markels (Interactive Digital Software Assoc.), Samuel Rabinove (American Jewish Com.), Alan Reitman (ACLU), Albert Robbins (New York Law Publishing Co.), Nanette Roberts (United Church of Christ), Prof. Nadine Strossen (New York Law School), Prof. Leonore Tiefer (Montefiore Medical Center), Roz Udow (Chair, Nassau Community College), Cleo Wilson (Exec. Dir., Playboy Found.), Robert Wise.

Periodicals: *Censorship News* (five times a year), *Books on Trial* (occasional).

Internships: No.

Other Information: Founded in 1974. The Coalition received $286,123, or 64% of revenue from gifts and grants awarded by foundations, companies and individuals. (These grants included $20,000 from the J. Roderick MacArthur Foundation.) $155,109, or 34%, from program services. The remaining revenue came from interest on savings and temporary cash investments, and miscellaneous sources.

National Coalition Against Domestic Violence (NCADV)

P.O. Box 18749
Denver, CO 80218-0749   **Phone:**   (303) 839-1852
USA   **Fax:**   (303) 831-9251

Officers or Principals: Kay Mixon, Chair ($0); Naomi Tucker, Secretary ($0); Barbara A. Blunt, Treasurer ($0).

Mission or Interest: "NCADV is dedicated to the empowerment of battered women and their children and, therefore, is committed to the elimination of personal and societal violence in the lives of women and their children...(Battering) is a pattern of behavior with the effect of establishing power and control over another person through fear and intimidation, often including the threat or use of violence...Not all battering is physical. Battering includes emotional abuse, economic abuse, sexual abuse, using children, threats, using male privilege, intimidation, isolation, and a variety of other behaviors used to maintain fear, intimidation and power...Battering escalates. It often begins with behaviors like threats, name calling, violence in her presence, and/or damage to objects or pets. It may escalate to restraining, pushing, slapping, pinching. The battering may include punching, kicking, biting, sexual assault, tripping, throwing. Finally, it may become life-threatening."

Accomplishments: NCADV was invited to the White House on March 10, 1994 for a meeting with Attorney General Janet Reno to reassure them and other nonprofits that the administration intended to fully fund provisions of the 1994 Crime bill aimed at domestic violence. NCADV was also invited when President Clinton appointed a Director for the new Office on Violence Against Women in the Department of Justice. NCADV has joined with Handgun Control, Inc., to support gun-control laws. In 1994 they published the National Directory of Domestic Violence Programs which was disseminated to over 1,000 individuals and organizations. Their Public Policy Line responded to approximately 800 inquiries. They attended the United Nations Fourth World Conference on Women in Beijing.

Net Revenue: 1994 $384,307 **Net Expenses:** $363,670 90%/6%/4% **Net Assets:** $94,092

Products or Services: Teen Dating Violence Resource Project. In conjunction with the Ms. Foundation they launched the "Remember My Name" project - a national registry to document women and children killed by domestic abuse. Many other projects, conferences, information and referral services. Lobbying, in 1994 they spent $16,063 on the direct lobbying of legislators and government officials.

Tax Status: 501(c)(3) **Annual Report:** Yes. **Employees:** 9

Board of Directors or Trustees: Gayla Kidd, Candice Slaughter, Diane Olvedo Munoz, Joan Dauphine, Mikki Patterson, Karlene John, Diane Purvin, Pam Willhoite, Joan Zorza, Yolanda Vierra Allen, Rita Smith-Staff.

Periodicals: *Update* (bimonthly magazine), and *Voice* (quarterly magazine). **Internships:** Yes.

Other Information: They recently moved their headquarters to Denver, CO, from Washington, DC. They maintain a public policy office in the District of Columbia. The Coalition received $192,145, or 50% of revenue, from program fees such as conference registration. $98,179, or 26%, from direct and indirect public support from foundations, companies, affiliates and individuals. (These grants included $10,000 from the Ms. Foundation.) $91,133, or 24%, from membership dues. The remaining revenue came from interest on savings and temporary cash investments.

National Coalition Against the Misuse of Pesticides

701 E St., S.E., Suite 200
Washington, DC 20003 **Phone:** (202) 543-5450
USA

Contact Person: Jay Feldman, Executive Director.
Officers or Principals: Jay Feldman, Executive Director ($58,044); Sarah Sullivan, Operations Director ($36,200); Liza Prior, President ($0); Allen Spalt, Vice President; Joan Clayburgh, Secretary; David Hahn-Baker, Treasurer.
Mission or Interest: Education and advocacy concerning the environmental and health implications of pesticide use. Provides information on alternatives to pesticide use.
Accomplishments: In 1994 the Coalition spent $253,291 on its programs. The largest program, with expenditures of $220,779, was disseminating information to the public and media. $12,743 for organizing and hosting an annual conference "where the membership, public and advocates are educated concerning pesticide law, information, protection and alternatives." $8,167 for projects related to pesticide-use reform. The Coalition awarded $1,550 in grants to organizations concerned with "pesticide and chemical protection."
Net Revenue: 1994 $279,398 **Net Expenses:** $304,958 83%/13%/4% **Net Assets:** $86,029
Products or Services: Publications, forums, and lobbying. The Coalition spent $152 on the direct lobbying of legislators.
Tax Status: 501(c)(3)
Board of Directors or Trustees: Nancy & Jim Chuda (Collete Chuda Environmental Fund), Norma Grier (Northwest Coalition for Alternatives to Pesticides), Liza Prior Lucy, Terry Shistar (Sierra Club, KS), Sharon Taylor (Pesticide Use Reduction Advocacy), David Hahn-Baker, Berna Romero (Farm Labor Organizing Committee), Ron Simon, Daniel Wartenberg, Ph.D. (Robert Wood Johnson Medical School), Erik Jansson (Dept. of the Planet Earth), Warren Schultz, Allen Spalt (PEST Education Project), Grace Ziem, M.D.
Periodicals: *Pesticides and You* (five times a year newsletter).
Other Information: The Coalition received $238,204, or 85% of revenue, from gifts and grants awarded by foundations, businesses, and individuals. (These grants included $25,000 from the Jessie Smith Noyes Foundation, $21,762 from the Environmental Federation of America.) $13,441, or 5%, from the sale of publications. $8,397, or 3%, from membership dues. $4,309, or 2%, from conference fees. $2,087, or 1%, from interest on savings and temporary cash investments. The remaining revenue came from other miscellaneous sources.

National Coalition Against Sexual Assault (NCASA)

912 N. 2nd St.
Harrisburg, PA 17102
USA

Contact Person: Kata Issari, President.
Officers or Principals: Denise Snyder, Vice President ($0); Anne Blackwell, Secretary ($0); Cecilia McKenzie, Treasurer ($0).
Mission or Interest: Produces newsletters and educational information from a feminist perspective on the issues of sexual assault and victims of sexual assault.
Accomplishments: In the fiscal year ending September 1994, the Coalition spent $18,254 on its programs.
Net Revenue: FY ending 9/94 $43,179 **Net Expenses:** $25,188 72%/18%/10% **Net Assets:** 443,478
Tax Status: 501(c)(3)
Board of Directors or Trustees: Cassandra Thomas, Marybeth Carter, Beverly Harris Elliot, Andria Delise-Heath, Pam Von Kleist, Hameedah Carr, Judy Benitez, Stephanie Townsend, Nancy Tartt, Nicole Hall, Karen Crowley-Buckholtz.
Other Information: The Coalition received $34,550, or 80% of revenue, from membership dues. $3,532, or 8%, from conference income. $2,127, or 5%, from special fund-raising events. $1,698, or 4%, from gifts and grants awarded by foundations and individuals. The remaining revenue came from interest on savings and temporary cash investments, and other miscellaneous sources.

National Coalition for Sex Equity in Education

One Redwood Drive
Clinton, NJ 08809 **Phone:** (908) 735-5045
USA

Contact Person: Theodora Martin, Business Manager. **Officers or Principals:** Theodora Martin, Business Manager ($5,000); Bonnie Eisenberg, Editor ($3,200); Ed Litte, Chair ($0); Linda Andrade Wheeler, Vice Chair; Miguel Valenciano, Secretary.
Mission or Interest: Educational activities to heighten educators' awareness of gender-equity issues in education.
Accomplishments: Approximately 500 members. In 1994 the Coalition spent $48,162 on its programs. The largest program, with expenditures of $39,356, was a conference attended by 308 educators. $6,977 was spent to produce and distribute a newsletter, and $1,829 was spent to publish and distribute a membership directory. The Coalition awarded a grant of $1,000 to the National Women's History Project.
Net Revenue: 1994 $79,491 **Net Expenses:** $67,223 **Net Assets:** $49,773
Products or Services: Conferences, publications.
Tax Status: 501(c)(3)
Board of Directors or Trustees: Eleanor Bates, Marta Cruz-Janzen, Pat Callbeck Harper, Jo Sanders, Patricia Stewart, Naomi Stockdale, Peggy Weeks.
Periodicals: Newsletter.

Other Information: The Coalition received $61,111, or 77% of revenue, from program service fees. $14,318, or 18%, from membership dues. $3,000, or 4%, from gifts and grants awarded by foundations and individuals. The remaining revenue came from investment income.

National Coalition for the Homeless
1612 K St., N.W., Suite 1004
Washington, DC 20006   **Phone:**   (202) 775-1322
USA

Contact Person: Fred Karnas, Executive Director.
Officers or Principals: Fred Karnas, Executive Director ($49,000); Michael Stoops, Director of Field Organizing ($30,489).
Mission or Interest: Education, advocacy, and organization to expand existing programs and create new programs that assist homeless persons.
Accomplishments: In the fiscal year ending June 1994, the Coalition spent $378,017 on its programs. The largest program was Public Education, with expenditures of $237,188. This program provided research and information collected from the Coalition's own library, and from other groups and individuals around the country. This program also included a grant of $10,000 for the Task Force for the Homeless in Atlanta, GA. The second largest program, $87,207, was Policy Advocacy to educate policy makers and encourage them to provide more social services for the homeless. Field Organizing brought together local groups and individuals and provided them with technical assistance and training in social services and advocacy.
Net Revenue: FY ending 6/94 $775,217 **Net Expenses:** $765,187 49%/9%/42% **Net Assets:** $64,490
Citations: 71:121
Products or Services: Research, publications, advocacy, training, networking and lobbying. During the fiscal year the Coalition spent $9,275 on lobbying; $6,259 on grassroots lobbying, and $3,016 on the direct lobbying of legislators.
Tax Status: 501(c)(3)
Board of Directors or Trustees: Deborah Austin (Natl. Low Income Housing Coalition), Barbara Lee Bennett (Alaska Coalition for the Homeless), Lucille Bonvouloir (Vermont Coalition for the Homeless), Christine Byrd (Oklahoma Coalition for the Homeless), Diane Doherty (Children's Safety Network), John Donahue (Chicago Coalition for the Homeless), Bill Faith (Ohio Coalition for the Homeless), Bill Friskics-Warren (Nashville Coalition for the Homeless), Anita Beaty (Task Force for the Homeless), Paul Boden (Coalition on Homelessness), Sue Capers (Virginia Coalition for the Homeless), Martha Dilts (WA State Coalition for the Homeless), Donald Gaen (Maine Coalition for the Homeless), many others.
Periodicals: Newsletter.
Other Information: The Coalition received $744,377, or 96% of revenue, from direct and indirect public support in the form of gifts and grants from foundations, companies, affiliates and individuals. (These grants included $15,000 from the Discount Foundation.) $7,519, or 1%, from speaking fees and honoraria. $6,431, or 1%, from the sale of publications. The remaining revenue came from interest on savings and temporary cash investments, net sale of items, and other miscellaneous sources.

National Coalition of 100 Black Women
38 W. 32nd St., Suite 1610
New York, NY 10001   **Phone:**   (212) 947-2196
USA   **Fax:**   (212) 947-2477

Contact Person: Barbara Mills.
Officers or Principals: Shirley L. Poole, Executive Director; Jewell Jackson McCabe, Chair; Hattie Dorsey, President.
Mission or Interest: A fifty-six chapter membership organization that advocates on behalf of the concerns of black women.
Accomplishments: At the 7th Biennial Conference, sessions were devoted to "Building on Our Commonality with Black South Africa," "Affirmative Action and Political Education and Action," "Information Superhighway: National and International Implications," "Welfare and Social Reform." Also, the Coalition drafted a statement calling on Congress and the President to continue at the current levels or increase foreign aid to Africa, the Caribbean and Latin America. Since its inception the Coalition has: Secured $550,000 for a role-modeling program for pregnant teenagers. Generated $750,000 for a "Career Exploration Program" that includes internships. Launched a nation-wide abortion rights education program. Supported President Clinton's nomination of Dr. Henry Foster for U.S. Surgeon General. Formed the Shabazz Support and Defense Fund to help the daughter of Malcolm X's widow, who was charged with plotting to kill Nation of Islam Leader Louis Farrakhan (the charges were later dropped).
Products or Services: Awards the annual Candace Awards that recognizes black women who have achieved national recognition.
Tax Status: 501(c)(3) **Annual Report:** No. **Employees:** 3
Board of Directors or Trustees: Teta Banks, Ph.D., Margaret Barron, Marva Smith Battle-Bey, Verna Bennett, Betty Brown Bibbins, M.D., Patricia Allen Cole, RPC CPM, Barbara Debaptiste, Thelma Eaton, Ph.D., Beverly Guy-Sheftal, Ph.D., Leah Creque Harris, Ph.D., Janet Haynes, Carolyn Golden Hebsgaard, Susan Short Jones, Lydia Mallett, Ph.D., Yvonne Moore, Paula Parker-Sawyers, Lennell Terrell, Carolyn Odom Steele.
Periodicals: *Statement* (quarterly newsletter).
Other Information: In 1994 the Coalition received $500 from the Crestar Foundation.

National Coalition of Education Activists
P.O. Box 679
Rhinebeck, NY 12572   **Phone:**   (914) 876-4580
USA

Contact Person: Deborah Duke, Executive Director.   **Officers or Principals:** Deborah Duke, Executive Director ($25,227).
Accomplishments: In 1994 the Coalition spent $93,218 on its programs.
Net Revenue: 1994 $117,747 **Net Expenses:** $103,233 90%/10%/0% **Net Assets:** $28,434
Tax Status: 501(c)(3)
Other Information: The Coalition received $85,974, or 73% of revenue, from gifts and grants awarded by foundations, businesses, and individuals. (These grants included $25,000 from the New World Foundation, $8,550 from the Vanguard Public Foundation, and $5,000 from the Angelina Fund.) $25,016, or 21%, from an annual conference. $3,535, or 3%, from membership dues. The remaining revenue came from interest on savings and other temporary cash investments, and other miscellaneous sources.

National Coalition to Abolish the Death Penalty (NCADP)
918 F St., N.W., Suite 601
Washington, DC 20004   **Phone:** (202) 347-2411   **E-Mail:** abolition@apc.igc.org
USA   **Fax:**   (202) 347-2510

Contact Person: Bill Breedlove.   **Officers or Principals:** Steven Hawkins, Executive Director; Leigh A. Dingerson, former Executive Director ($28,682); Marshall Dayan, Chairperson ($0); Hugo Adam Bedau, Linda Thurston, Pat Clark, Vice Chairperson ($0); Kathy Lancaster, Secretary; Beth Ansheles, Treasurer.
Mission or Interest: Working to abolish the death penalty. "Mobilizes and supports people and institutions that share the unconditional rejection of the state's use of homicide as an instrument of social policy."
Accomplishments: Nearly 10,000 members. In 1994 NCADP spent $200,834 on programs. The largest program, costing $86,794, was the effort to strengthen coalitions at the state level. The next largest program, $40,104, was the Information Clearinghouse that develops and distributes information to the general public. The Brennan Project, named after the late Justice Brennan who sat on the bench from 1956-1990, was "created to fulfill the vision of Justice Brennan in speeding the day when the death penalty in the U.S. will be universally seen as a violation of the 8th and 14th amendments to the U.S. Constitution." $10,343 was spent on political and legislative activities. They spent $4,007 lobbying against the inclusion of expanded death penalty sentences in the 1994 Omnibus Crime Bill. They also held their annual conference that cost $30,060.
Net Revenue: 1994 $274,067 **Net Expenses:** $285,845 70%/19%/11% **Net Assets:** (-$9,302)
Products or Services: Produces and disseminates educational materials. Lobbying and legislative activities.
Tax Status: 501(c)(3) **Annual Report:** Yes. **Employees:** 8
Board of Directors or Trustees: Adjoa Aiyetoro (Natl. Conference of Black Lawyers), Jefari Allen, Inelle Bagwell, Bill Geimer (Washington and Lee Univ.), Jay Jacobson (ACLU, TX), Keith Jennings, Michael Johns, Greg Johnson (Harvard Univ.), Brenda Lewis (AL State Univ.), Steve Pohlmeyer, Joe Riener, Henry Scwarzschild, Hilary Shelton (United Methodist Church), Reynold Thomas.
Periodicals: *Lifelines* (newsletter).   **Internships:** Yes.
Other Information: Members of the Coalition include: American Baptist Churches, ACLU, American Friends Service Committee, Amnesty International, Center for Constitutional Rights, Episcopal Church, Feminists for Life, Friends Committee on National Legislation, Human Rights Watch, Jewish Peace Fellowship, Martin Luther King Jr. Center for Nonviolent Social Change, NAACP, National Bar Association, National Conference of Black Lawyers, National Lawyers Guild, National Urban League, Pax Christi, Presbyterian Church USA, Southern Christian Leadership Conference, Southern Poverty Law Center, U.S. Catholic Conference, Unitarian Universalist Service Committee, War Resistor's League, more. The Coalition received $225,776, or 82%, from grants awarded by foundations, companies and individuals. $24,600, or 9%, from membership dues. $12,324, or 4%, from program service revenues. $6,177 net, or 2%, came from the sale of inventory. The remaining revenue came from interest on savings and temporary cash investments, and reimbursed travel expenses.

National Commission for Economic Conversion and Disarmament
1828 Jefferson Place, N.W.
Washington, DC 20036   **Phone:** (202) 728-0815
USA   **Fax:**   (202) 728-0826

Other Information: In 1993 the Commission received $98,045 from the Center for Peace Development, $10,000 from the Town Creek Foundation. 1993/94, $30,000 from the Ploughshares Fund. 1994, $60,000 from the Peace Development Fund, $30,000 from the Joyce Mertz-Gilmore Foundation, $1,000 from the New Prospect Foundation.

National Committee for Responsive Philanthropy (NCRP)
2001 S St., N.W., Suite 620
Washington, DC 20009   **Phone:** (202) 342-0519
USA

Contact Person: Robert O. Bothwell, Executive Director.   **Officers or Principals:** Robert O. Bothwell, Executive Director ($83,508); Steven Paprocki, Research Director ($52,492); Gloria Derobles, Associate Director ($48,117); Sally Covington, Project Director; John Echohawk, Pablo Eisenberg, Raul Yzaguirre, Co-Chairs.
Mission or Interest: To develop alternative avenues for employee contribution programs in addition to the United Way. Assists in the development of "alternative funds for women, minorities, social action and environmental action."
Accomplishments: In the fiscal year ending September 1994, the Committee spent $611,017 on its projects. The largest project, with expenditures of $248,109, was the Workplace Fundraising Project which assisted in the development of social change funds. $152,368 was spent on the Corporate Minorities Study which investigated the top 200 corporations' charitable giving to minority organizations. $123,548 was spent on the Community Foundation Project, which "evaluate(s) community foundations' responsiveness to the disadvantaged, educates the public and foundation world about the results, encourages reform of local community foundations." $86,992 was spent on public education.

Net Revenue: FY ending 9/94 $831,660 **Net Expenses:** $788,288 78%/9%/13% **Net Assets:** $87,858
Citations: 30:156
Tax Status: 501(c)(3)
Board of Directors or Trustees: John Echohawk (Native American Rights Fund), Pablo Eisenberg (Center for Community Change), Raul Yzaguirre (Natl. Council of La Raza), James Abernathy (Environmental Support Center), Rebecca Adamson (First Nations Development Inst.), Jean Anderson (Cooperating Fund Drive), Barbara Bode (Council of Better Business Bureaus), William Bondurant (Mary Reynolds Babcock Foundation), Steve Brobeck (Consumer Federation of America), Paul Castro (United Latino Fund), Margaret Fung (Asian American Legal Defense and Education Fund), Margaret Gales (Girls, Inc.), Herb Chao Gunther (Public Media Center), Andy Hernandez (Southwest Voter Registration Education Project), Anna Faith Jones (The Boston Foundation), Steve Kest (ACORN), A. Gay Kingman, Moises Loza (Housing Assistance Council), Richard Male (Community Resource Center), William Merritt (National Black United Fund), Carol Mollner (National Network of Women's Funds), Louis Nunez (National Puerto Rican Coalition), Maggie Kuhn (Gray Panthers), Peter Goldberg (Prudential Foundation), Nan Steketee (Center for Responsible Funding), Dagmar Thorpe, Greg Truog (Community Shares of CO), Deborah Tuck (Ruth Mott Fund), Rev. C.T. Vivian (Center for Democratic Renewal), Lynn Yeakel (Womens Way USA).
Periodicals: *Responsive Philanthropy* (quarterly newsletter).
Other Information: Co-Chair Pablo Eisenberg is also the president of the Center for Community Change (CCC). CCC provides bookkeeping services to NCRP at no charge and acts a fiscal agent, depositing receipts and disbursing payments. The Committee received $747,622, or 90% of revenue, from gifts and grants awarded by foundations, businesses, and individuals. (These grants included $30,000 from the Joyce Mertz-Gilmore Foundation, $10,000 from the Joyce Foundation, $5,000 from the Wallace Alexander Gerbode Foundation, $3,000 from the Jessie Smith Noyes Foundation, $2,500 from the Rosenberg Foundation, $1,000 from the Stewart R. Mott Charitable Trust, and $1,000 from the New Prospect Foundation. In 1993, $721,720 from the Center for Community Change.) $31,102, or 4%, from the sale of publications. $29,374, or 4%, from membership dues. $16,662, or 2%, from conference fees. The remaining revenue came from other miscellaneous sources.

National Committee on Pay Equity

1126 16th St., N.W.
Washington, DC 20036   **Phone:**   (202) 331-7343
USA

Contact Person: Susan Bianchi-Sand, Executive Director.
Officers or Principals: Susan Bianchi-Sand, Executive Director ($52,643); Norman Hill, President ($0).
Mission or Interest: "To examine and educate the general public about the historical, legal and economic basis of the inequities in any pay between women and men, minorities and whites, in the United States."
Accomplishments: In 1994 the Committee spent $214,470 on its programs. $87,636 was spent on educational activities such as a speakers' bureau, speeches, workshops and publications. $49,068 on an information clearinghouse. $45,176 was spent on coalition development. $32,590 for advocacy which included monitoring the Equal Opportunity Commission, the U.S. Commission on Civil Rights, and the Justice Department's enforcement of wage discrimination laws. They also created strategies with other advocacy organizations for the passage of pay equity legislation, and prepared amicus briefs for litigation.
Net Revenue: 1994 $232,244 **Net Expenses:** $242,648 88%/4%/7% **Net Assets:** $67,653
Products or Services: Research, education, litigation, publications, conferences, more.
Tax Status: 501(c)(3)
Board of Directors or Trustees: Carolyn Kazdin (amalgamated Clothing & Textile Workers Union), Elizabeth Martinez (American Library Association), Cheryl Peterson (American Nurses Association), Martha Burk, Ph.D., (Center for the Advancement of Public Policy), Anna Padia (Coalition of Labor Union Women), Catherine Collette (AFSCME), Michele Leber (American Library Association), Margaret Myers (American Library Association), Audrey Tayse Haynes (Business & Professional Women), Will Duncan (Coalition of Black Trade Unionists), Ann Smith (Episcopal Church Center).
Other Information: The Committee received $158,376, or 68% of revenue, from grants awarded by foundations, companies and individuals. (These grants included $30,000 from the Rockefeller Family Fund, $25,000 from the Ms. Foundation). $66,655, or 29%, came from membership dues. $3,901, or 2%, came from program service fees, and the remaining revenue came from interest on savings and temporary cash investments.

National Committee to Reopen the Rosenberg Case

113 University Place, 8th Floor
New York, NY 10003   **Phone:**   (212) 228-4500
USA

Contact Person: Aaron Katz, Director.
Mission or Interest: Dedicated to reopening the case of Julius and Ethel Rosenberg, American scientists convicted and executed for conspiring to spy on the United States for the Soviet Union. The two were tried and found guilty of "conspiring to commit espionage." At their sentencing the presiding judge, Irving R. Kaufman, stated they were to be put to death for "putting the A-bomb into the hands of the Russians...and who knows but that millions more will pay the price of your treason." The Committee believes that the trial was wrongly conducted: That the jury systematically excluded Jews, opponents of capital punishment, as well as members of leftist organizations. The judge sentenced them to death for "stealing and transmitting" the secrets of the atomic bomb, but no such charge was made during the trial. The Committee disputes the recently released 'Venona Intercepts,' decoded communications between Soviet agents and their controllers, that "show without a doubt that the Rosenbergs spied for the Soviet Union against the United States." The Committee states that the Venona Intercepts do not excuse an improper trial, and that there "are serious doubts about the authenticity of the Intercepts."

National Conference of Puerto Rican Women

5 Thomas Circle
Washington, DC 20005
USA

Contact Person: Edna Laverdi, President.   **Officers or Principals:** Terersa Mendez, First Vice President ($0); Maria Laracuente, Second Vice President ($0); Lydia Sosa, Treasurer ($0); Milagros McGuire, Secretary.
Mission or Interest: Public awareness and education of the public concerns of Puerto Rican women.
Net Revenue: 1994 $20,337 **Net Expenses:** $13,364 **Net Assets:** $10,918
Tax Status: 501(c)(3)
Other Information: The Conference received $16,940 net, or 83% of revenue, from special fund-raising events. $2,752, or 13%, from membership dues. The remaining revenue came from program service fees.

National Congress of American Indians (NCAI)

2010 Massachusetts Ave., N.W.
Washington, DC 20036   **Phone:** (202) 466-7767
USA

Contact Person: JoAnn Chase, Executive Director.   **Officers or Principals:** JoAnn Chase, Executive Director ($29,041); Gaiashkibos, President ($0); Susan Masten, First Vice President ($0); S. Dianne Kelly, Secretary; Mary Ann Antone, Treasurer.
Mission or Interest: Lobbying affiliate of the National Congress of American Indians Fund.
Accomplishments: In 1994 NCAI spent $158,737 on its programs, down 3% from the previous year. Programs included an annual convention and an Executive Council Meeting.
Net Revenue: 1994 $477,473 **Net Expenses:** $250,718 63%/37%/0% **Net Assets:** $514,753
Tax Status: 501(c)(4)
Board of Directors or Trustees: Terry Fiddler (Cheyenne River Sioux Tribe), Raymond Apodaca (Yselta Del Sur Pueblo), Elmer Manatawa (Sac and Fox), Earl Old Person (Blackfeet Nation), Edward Thomas (Tlingit-Haida), James Crawford (Forest County Potawatomi), Donald Giles (Peoria), J. Conrad Seneca (Seneca Nation), Bruce Wynne (Spokane Tribe), A. Bruce Jones (Lumbee Tribe).
Other Information: Affiliated with the 501(c)(3) National Congress of American Indians Fund at the same address. In 1993 the two affiliates had combined net revenues of $1,049,908, net expenses of $815,309, and net assets of $147,613. Rachel Joseph served as executive director of both organizations, and received $73,096 in combined compensation. NCAI received $356,803, or 75% of revenue, from registration and banquet fees. $25,308, or 5%, from gifts and grants awarded by foundations, businesses, and individuals. $95,362, or 20%, from membership dues. Revenue was down 13% in 1994, from $549,842. This was due to decreased gifts and grants, down 76% from $107,026 in 1993.

National Congress of American Indians Fund (NCAI Fund)

2010 Massachusetts Ave., N.W.
Washington, DC 20036   **Phone:** (202) 466-7767
USA

Contact Person: Rachel Joseph, Executive Director.
Officers or Principals: Rachel Joseph, Executive Director ($36,548); Robert Holden, Project Director ($37,745); Gaiashkibos, President ($0); Joseph T. Goombi, Vice President; S. Dianne Kelly, Secretary; W. Ron Allen, Treasurer.
Mission or Interest: Projects to benefit the welfare of native Americans.
Accomplishments: In 1993 the Fund spent $310,593 on its projects. These included; $275,956 (all paid with a grant from the Department of Energy) for the Nuclear Waste Project which assisted the Department of Energy in providing information "for tribal councils in the United States for implementation of the Nuclear Waste Policy Act." $15,670 (paid for with a grant from Health and Human Services) for a project to gather information from Indian tribes "as to what they need for AIDS treatment in policy." Other projects included gathering information for community-based programs and services, and the dissemination of information about legislation regarding veterans.
Net Revenue: 1993 $500,066 ($294,923, or 59%, from government grants) **Net Expenses:** $420,424 74%/26%/0%
Net Assets: (-$140,383) **Citations:** 140:98
Tax Status: 501(c)(3)
Board of Directors or Trustees: Terry Fiddler (Cheyenne River Sioux Tribe), Raymond Apodaca (Yselta Del Sur Pueblo), Elmer Manatawa (Sac and Fox), Earl Old Person (Blackfeet Nation), Edward Thomas (Tlingit-Haida), James Crawford (Forest County Potawatomi), Donald Giles (Peoria), J. Conrad Seneca (Seneca Nation), Bruce Wynne (Spokane Tribe), Susan Masten (Yurok Tribe), A. Bruce Jones (Lumbee Tribe).
Other Information: Affiliated with the 501(c)(4) National Congress of American Indians (NCAI). The two affiliates had combined

net revenues of $1,049,908, net expenses of $815,309, and net assets of $147,613. Rachel Joseph served as executive director of both organizations, and received combined compensation of $73,096. The Fund received $294,923, or 59% of revenue, from government grants, $275,956 from the U.S. Department of Energy and $18,967 from the U.S. Department of Health and Human Services. $186,967, or 37%, from a loan from the 501(c)(4) NCAI. $18,176, or 4%, from gifts and grants awarded by foundations, businesses, and individuals.

National Council for Research on Women (NCRW)

530 Broadway, 10th Floor
New York, NY 10012   **Phone:**   (212) 274-0730
USA

Contact Person: Mary Ellen Capek, Executive Director.   **Officers or Principals:** Mary Ellen Capek, Executive Director ($60,135); Patricia King, Chairperson ($0); Miriam K. Chamberlain, Founding President.
Mission or Interest: Feminist organization that serves as a clearinghouse for research information and conducts original research. Awards grants to women for travel and speaking engagements. International in focus.
Accomplishments: In the fiscal year ending September 1994 the Council spent $441,359 on its programs. The largest program, with expenditures of $183,015, was its coalition and network building activities, including several conferences, seminars, and information exchanges. $92,270 was spent publishing the NCRW's research. $56,816 was spent on a "program that develops a procedure and system of effective response to emerging issues of special importance to women." $29,524 was spent on grants for travel and speaking fees. This included $5,318 for Barbara Enrenreich to "lecture Indian women on U.S. culture."
Net Revenue: FY ending 9/94 $583,281 **Net Expenses:** $626,533 **Net Assets:** $498,864 **Citations:** 19:173
Products or Services: "Affirmative Action: Beyond the Glass Ceiling and the Sticky Floor" and other studies.
Tax Status: 501(c)(3)
Board of Directors or Trustees: Ruth Mandel, Donna Shavhk, Helen Astin, Susan Bailey, Betty Dooley, Sara Evans, Carol Hollenshead, Janet Sibley Hyde, Deborah Rhode, Leslie Wolfe.
Periodicals: *Women's Research Network News* (quarterly newsletter), *Issues Quarterly* (quarterly journal).
Other Information: The Council received $419,343, or 72% of revenue, from gifts and grants awarded by foundations, businesses, and individuals. (These grants included $25,000 from the Joyce Mertz-Gilmore Foundation.) $117,544 net, or 20%, from the sale of publications. $18,222, or 3%, from membership dues. $14,768, or 3%, from grant administration fees. $13,404, or 2%, from interest on savings and temporary cash investments.

National Council of La Raza (NCLR)

1111 19th St., N.W., Suite 1000
Washington, DC 20036   **Phone:**   (202) 785-1670
USA   **Fax:**   (202) 289-8173

Contact Person: Raul Yzaguirre, President.   **Officers or Principals:** Raul Yzaguirre, President ($143,500); Emily Gantz McKay, former Senior Vice President ($81,959); Charles Kamanski, Senior Vice President ($72,964); Norma Lopez, Senior Vice President; Dr. Audrey R. Alvarado, Chairperson; Irma Flores Gonzales, First Vice Chair; Amos Atencio, 2nd Vice Chair; John Huerta, Secretary/Treasurer; Christopher Lipsett, Legal Counsel.
Mission or Interest: Educational resource and lobbying organization advocating rights for the Hispanic population.
Accomplishments: In the fiscal year ending September 1994 the Council spent $5,689,516 on its programs. The Council awarded $683,234 in grants and contributions to community organizations.
Net Revenue: FY ending 9/94 $7,267,968 ($1,590,674, or 22%, from government sources)
Net Expenses: $7,262,121 78%/18%/4% **Net Assets:** $122,088 **Citations:** 564:38
Products or Services: Grassroots organizing, educational activities, and lobbying. The Council spent $84,719 on the direct lobbying of legislators. This was a 48% increase over the previous year.
Tax Status: 501(c)(3)
Board of Directors or Trustees: Patricia Asip (Manager of Multi-Cultural Affairs, J.C. Penney Co.), Hon. Rita DiMartino (Dir., Federal Gov. Affairs, AT&T), Dr. Herminio Martinez (Assoc. Provost, Baruch College, CUNY), Mari Carmen Aponte, Hon. Ed Avila (Los Angeles Board of Public Works), Mateo Camarillo, Hon. Fernando Ferrer (Bronx Borough President); Humberto Fuentes (Idaho Migrant Council), Dr. Catalina Garcia (TX State Board of Medical Examiners), Mary Gonzalez Koenig (Office of Employment and Training, Chicago), Dr. Pedro Jose Greer Jr., Linda Griego, Helen Hernandez, Hon. Guillermo Linares (Councilman, NYC), Arabella Martinez (CEO, Spanish Speaking Unity Council), Ramon Murguia, Ella Ochoa, Daniel Ortega, Jr., Hon. Angel Luis Oritz (City Councilman, Philadelphia), A.R. Sanchez, Jr., Deborah Szekely, Maria Elena Torralva-Alonso (Director of Diversity, Hearst Newspaper Group), Arturro Torres, Hon. Carlos Truan (State Senator, TX), Charles Vela, Hon. Mary Rose Wilcox (Maricopa County Board of Supervisors).
Periodicals: *Agenda* (bimonthly).
Other Information: The Council received $5,083,441, or 70% of revenue, from gifts and grants awarded by foundations, businesses, and individuals. (These grants included $228,603 from the Charles Stewart Mott Foundation, $30,000 from the Joyce Mertz-Gilmore Foundation, $12,000 from the Center on Budget and Policy Priorities. In 1995, $631,250 from the Rockefeller Foundation.) $1,590,674, or 22%, from government grants. $508,431, or 7%, from special fund-raising events. $52,589, or 1%, from interest on savings and temporary cash investments. The remaining revenue came from the sale of publications, and other miscellaneous sources.

National Council of Negro Women

1001 G St., N.W., Suite 800
Washington, DC 20001   **Phone:**   (202) 628-0015
USA

Contact Person: Eleanor Hinton-Hoytt, Director of Programs.
Officers or Principals: Brenda Girton, Assistant Executive Officer ($80,000); Dr. Addison Richard ($78,000); Dorothy Height, President ($75,000); Willie B. Kennedy, Bobbie W. Moorehead, Denise Glaude, Toni Fay, Vice Presidents; Juetta Coleman, Secretary; Mary Burciaga, Assistant Treasurer; Dovey Roundtree, General Counsel; Peola McCaskill, Parliamentarian.
Mission or Interest: Programs to meet the needs of black women in the U.S. and Africa.
Accomplishments: Provided training and services to meet the special needs of black women. In the fiscal year ending September 1994, the Council spent $6,746,786 on its programs. The largest program, with expenditures of $3,464,953, included efforts "designed to improve the social and economic status of women and their families in Africa by providing technical assistance and training to improve the capacity of community-based organizations." $1,321,174 was spent on Black Family Reunion, a program to call attention to the historic strengths of the black family. Other programs provided job training, mentoring, HIV and sexually transmitted disease prevention, programs for elderly women, abortion rights advocacy and more.
Net Revenue: FY ending 9/94 $10,058,723 ($3,892,706, or 39%, from government grants)
Net Expenses: $6,746,786 85%/11%/4% **Net Assets:** $7,906,236 **Citations:** 413:47
Tax Status: 501(c)(3)
Board of Directors or Trustees: Camille Cosby, Juanita Leonard Nixon, Thelma Johnson, Jacquelyn Parker, Grace Phillips, Dr. Vanessa Weaver, Edna Henry Rivers.
Other Information: The Council is a partner in the Religious Coalition for Reproductive Choice Education Fund's "Women of Color Partnership." Eleanor Hinton-Hoytt is also a director of the Coalition to Stop Gun Violence, and Dorothy Height is on the board of the Children's Defense Fund and TransAfrica. The Council received $3,892,706, or 39% of revenue, from government grants. $3,311,251, or 33%, from gifts and grants awarded by foundations, businesses, individuals, affiliates, and individuals. (These grants included $60,000 from the John Merck Fund, and $25,000 from the Jessie Smith Noyes Foundation.) $1,130,134, or 11%, from fees collected for the Black Family Reunion program. $587,216, or 6%, from membership dues. $519,826, or 5%, from the sale of assets. $336,153, or 3%, from fees from a biennial convention. The remaining revenue came from various other program fees.

National Council of Negro Women, New Orleans

1508 Carondelet St.
New Orleans, LA 70130
USA

Contact Person: Emma Bromon, Executive Director.   **Officers or Principals:** Emma Bromon, Executive Director ($50,620).
Mission or Interest: Provides social services and educational activities for black women.
Accomplishments: In 1993 the Council spent $564,780 on its programs. The largest program, with expenditures of $179,162, provided services for teenage mothers. $162,851 was spent on job placement and referrals. $107,619 for AIDS/HIV education. Other programs focused on preventing teen pregnancy and vocational preparation.
Net Revenue: 1993 $788,297 ($515,303, or 65%, from government grants) **Net Expenses:** $768,695 73%/27%/0% **Net Assets:** $131,115
Tax Status: 501(c)(3)
Other Information: The Council received $515,303, or 65% of revenue, from government grants. $272,994, or 35%, from gifts and grants awarded by foundations and affiliates.

National Council of Senior Citizens (NCSC)

1331 F St., N.W.
Washington, DC 20004   **Phone:**   (202) 347-8800
USA   **Fax:**   (202) 624-9595

Officers or Principals: Eugene Glover, President; Dr. Mary C. Mulvey, Vice President; John E. Turner, Secretary/Treasurer.
Mission or Interest: Lobbying organization representing retired member of the United Autoworkers Union, United Steelworkers, and other members of the AFL-CIO. Lobbies on the behalf of senior citizens and for increased social welfare programs for seniors and others. A nationally-administered health care program is currently one of its top agenda items.
Accomplishments: NCSC was a driving force behind Medicare, Social Security cost-of-living adjustments, the conversion of welfare programs for the elderly and disabled into the Supplemental Security Income program, Medicaid, and the expansion of food stamps. At the time of the Medicare amendments to Social Security, the AARP was not a lobbying force, and the NCSC was the strongest lobby for seniors. NCSC staff are unionized and are members of the Professional Employees International Union. NCSC administers jobs and job training programs for seniors funded by the Department of Labor and the Environmental Protection Agency. Approximately 300,000 members.
Net Revenue: FY ending 6/95 $74,696,957 ($69,994,065, or 94%, from government grants)
Net Expenses: $74,403,138 98%/2%/0% **Net Assets:** $4,303,675 **Citations:** NA
Products or Services: Congressional Voting Record, supplemental health insurance, low-cost pharmaceuticals.
Tax Status: 501(c)(4)
Periodicals: Senior Citizen News (monthly newsletter).
Other Information: Founded in 1961. In the year between July 1993 and June 1994, the NCSC received government funding of $61,000,000 from the Department of Labor's Employment and Training Administration, and $165,000 from the EPA's Senior Environmental Employment Training Program.

National Council of the Churches of Christ (NCCC)

475 Riverside Dr., Suite 572
New York, NY 10115   **Phone:**   (212) 870-2385
USA   **Fax:**   (212) 870-3220

Contact Person: Jean Sindab, Program Director.   **Officers or Principals:** Rodney Page, Deputy General Secretary.
Mission or Interest: An ecumenical organization developing programs to train, establish networks, and collect resources to engage the American religious community in the pursuit of peace and justice.
Accomplishments: The Council, along with the Center for Democratic Renewal, was at the forefront of the black church burnings controversy in the summer of 1996. The Council researched the church fires and hosted two press conferences to call attention to its findings. The Council then created a fund to rebuild the burned churches and to fund programs on "racial justice...economic justice...interlocking oppressions from gender to homophobia." As of August 1996, the fund had collected $8.9 million, although many donors were reportedly unaware that the fund would go toward programs other than rebuilding the churches. (For more information on the church burnings, see the Center for Democratic Renewal.) The Council is well known for its foreign policy activities. During the 1980's the Council consistently supported communist revolutionaries in the Caribbean, Latin America, and Africa and fought any U.S. policy that opposed these forces. Worked with the Hawaii Ecumenical Coalition on issues involved with Hawaiian sovereignty.
Net Revenue: 1994 est. $55,000,000 **Citations:** 1,217:19
Tax Status: 501(c)(3)
Other Information: The Council also has a Washington, DC office; 110 Maryland Ave., N.E., Washington, DC 20002. In 1994 the Council received $26,000 from the General Service Foundation, $15,000 from the Jessie Smith Noyes Foundation, $5,000 from the New World Foundation. In 1993 the Council received $905 from the Alexander Gerbode Foundation, and in 1995, $49,510 from the Rockefeller Foundation.

National Council of Women of the United States

777 United Nations Plaza
New York, NY 10017   **Phone:**   (212) 697-1278
USA

Contact Person: Iryna Kurowyckyj, President.   **Officers or Principals:** Vera Rivers, Pamela Moffat, Blythe Foot-Finke, Vice Presidents ($0); Emma Broisman, Secretary; Mary Tomorug, Treasurer.
Mission or Interest: Feminist organization that holds seminars to develop "leadership qualities in women" and honors corporations "in the area of advancement of women in business."
Accomplishments: In 1994 the Council spent $24,878 on its programs.
Net Revenue: 1994 $66,349 **Net Expenses:** $63,408 31%/69%/0% **Net Assets:** $45,135
Tax Status: 501(c)(3)
Other Information: The Council received $26,713, or 40% of revenue, from gifts and grants awarded by foundations, businesses, and individuals. $24,650, or 37%, from "fees for honoring corporations for outstanding achievement in supporting women." $8,559, or 13%, from seminar fees. $6,035, or 9%, from membership fees. The remaining revenue came from dividends and interest from securities.

National Education Association (NEA)

1201 16th St., N.W.
Washington, DC 20036   **Phone:**   (202) 833-4000
USA   **Fax:**   (202) 822-7974

Contact Person: Don Cameron, Executive Director.   **Officers or Principals:** Keith Geiger, President ($172,026); Robert Chase, Vice President ($151,226); Marilyn Monahan, Treasurer ($151,226). (These three officers had large expense accounts as well, receiving an additional $77,796, $66,687, and $62,249 respectively.)
Mission or Interest: Union representing teachers and the education establishment. Represents more than 2 million members. Conducts operations through a number of Committees, including: Civil Rights, Human Relations, Legislation, Minority Affairs, National Public Relations, Peace and International Relations, Political Action, and Women's Concerns.
Accomplishments: In 1996 the NEA passed a resolution calling for a "Lesbian and Gay History Month" celebration in public schools. The resolution was dropped after negative reaction from the membership.
Net Revenue: FY ending 8/95 $184,473,367 **Net Expenses:** $181,588,288 **Net Assets:** $40,201,930
Tax Status: 501(c)(5)
Periodicals: *NEA Today* (eight times a year).
Other Information: The NEA received $181,457,881, or 98% of revenue, from membership dues. $2,189,942, or 1%, from advertising revenue. The remaining revenue came from interest on savings and temporary cash invetsments, and royalties. In the year between July 1993 and June 1994 the Association received $385,000 in funding from the federal government. Most of this came from Health and Human Services for AIDS-related projects. The NEA owns 100% of a for-profit business, the Member Benefits Corporation. The Corporation had revenues of $29,626,394 and assets valued at $8,424,248.

National Emergency Civil Liberties Foundation

175 Fifth Ave., 8th Floor
New York, NY 10010   **Phone:**   (212) 673-2040
USA   **Fax:**   (212) 460-8359

Contact Person: Edith Tiger, Coordinator.   **Officers or Principals:** Edith Tiger, Coordinator ($18,000).
Mission or Interest: Provides legal help for those whose civil rights have been violated. Hosts seminars and lectures on civil, constitutional and human rights.
Accomplishments: In 1994 the Foundation spent $78,502 on its programs. $50,000 of that was spent on legal fees paid to the firm of Rabinowitz, Boudin, Standard, Krinsky & Lieberman for representation in civil liberties matters.
Net Revenue: 1994 $96,220 **Net Expenses:** $112,649 70%/30%/0% **Net Assets:** $62,541
Tax Status: 501(c)(3)
Periodicals: *Rights* (bimonthly magazine), and *Bill of Rights Journal* (annual journal).
Other Information: Founded in 1951 and originally called the Emergency Committee for Civil Liberties. The Committee was originally a defender of communists and 'fellow travelers.' In 1954 Norman Thomas, a leading figure in the ACLU, said "persons now leading the Emergency Committee have condoned, if they have not actually defended, Communist crimes against liberty, which crimes are inherent in the doctrine and practice of a conspiratorial movement seeking universal power over the bodies, minds, and souls of men. These men and women work under a double standard...civil liberties cannot effectively be defended by Americans who through the years have condoned its absolute denial in the Soviet Union." The Foundation received $94,584, or 98% of revenue, from gifts and grants awarded by foundations, businesses, and individuals. (These grants included $400 from the Stewart R. Mott Charitable Trust.) $1,636, or 2%, from interest on savings and temporary cash investments.

National Employment Lawyers Association (NELA)

600 Harrison St., Suite 535
San Francisco, CA 94107   **Phone:**   (415) 227-4655   **E-Mail:** nelahq@igc.apc.org
USA   **Fax:**   (415) 495-7465

Contact Person: Terisa Chaw, Executive Director. **Officers or Principals:** Terisa E. Chaw, Executive Director ($55,000); Janice Goodman, Vice President ($0); Barry D. Roseman, Vice President ($0); Mary Anne Sedey, President; Paul H. Tobias, Founder.
Mission or Interest: "NELA is the only professional organization in the United States whose membership is exclusively limited to lawyers who represent workers in cases involving employment discrimination, wrongful termination, employee benefits and other employment-related matters."
Accomplishments: Membership of over 2,600.
Net Revenue: 1994 $468,189 **Net Expenses:** $506,122 **Net Assets:** $106,200 **Citations:** 20:172
Products or Services: "Brief Bank," Member Service Guide and National Directory, Expert Witness Bank, "NELANet" electronic bulletin board. Audio and videotape "Sexual Harassment Litigation for the Plaintiff Employment Lawyer" manual. Annual conference.
Tax Status: 501(c)(6)
Board of Directors or Trustees: Carla Barboza, Robert Belton, Joseph Garrison, Frederick Gittes, Janice Goodman, Margaret Harris, Douglas Hedin, Janet Hill, Janette Johnson, Ellen Messing, Mark O'Melveny, L. Steven Platt, Joseph Posner, Barry Roseman, Nancy Erika Smith, William Smith, Cathy Ventrell-Monsees, Claudia Withers, Brad Yamauchi.
Periodicals: *Employee Advocate Newsletter and Supplement* (quarterly newsletter).
Other Information: NELA received $215,903, or 46% of revenue, from membership dues. $187,126, or 40%, from seminar fees. $63,037, or 13%, from book sales. The remaining revenue came from interest on savings and temporary cash investments, and other miscellaneous sources.

National Environmental Law Center (NELC)

29 Temple Place
Boston, MA 02111   **Phone:**   (617) 422-0880
USA   **Fax:**   (617) 422-0881

Contact Person: David Nicholas, Program Staff.
Officers or Principals: Charles Caldart, Program Director ($38,134); Andrew Bushbaum, Program Staff ($37,695); Hillel Gray, Program Staff ($35,205); Kenneth Ward, President; Marjorie Alt, Vice President/Treasurer; Richard Hannigan, Secretary.
Mission or Interest: Litigation and policy advocacy institute that works mostly at the state level. NELC was founded in 1990 by the Public Interest Research Groups (PIRGs), a nationwide network of consumer and environmental advocacy organizations.
Accomplishments: NELC was named an EPA Pollution Prevention Award finalist. The Center claims 50,000 citizen contributors. In the fiscal year ending June 1994, NELC spent $598,264 on its programs. The Center's largest program was its Litigation Project, spending $281,243. The Litigation Project brings law suits against companies that violate the Clean Water Act. When settled, the defendant company usually has to pay clean-up costs, a penalty to the local, state, or federal government, and fees to the National Environmental Law Center. NELC has won settlements against General Electric, Kraft General Foods, General Electric Aircraft Division, the Kelco Division of Merck & Co., Shell Oil Co., and many other, smaller companies. During the fiscal year NELC received $165,015 in court-awarded fees. The next largest project, at $183,033, was the Citizen Outreach and Membership Services program. The Public Policy Program develops policies, model legislation, public education and more.
Net Revenue: FY ending 6/94 $654,045 ($47,548, or 7%, from government grants) **Net Expenses:** $685,565 87%/3%/10%
Net Assets: $95,421 **Citations:** 0:255
Products or Services: Litigation, publications, expert testimony, model laws, more.
Tax Status: 501(c)(3)
Periodicals: Quarterly newsletter.

Other Information: NELC has additional litigation staff in Ann Arbor, MI, and policy staff in Sacramento, CA. Formerly called the National Environmental Policy and Law Center. The Center received $436,165, or 67% of revenue from gifts and grants awarded by foundations, companies, and individuals. (These grants included $60,000 from the Joyce Foundation, and $10,000 from the Town Creek Foundation.) $165,015, or 25%, from court-awarded legal fees. $47,548, or 7%, from government grants. $5,317, or 1%, from interest on savings and temporary cash investments.

National Family Planning and Reproductive Health Association (NFPRHA)
122 C St., N.W., Suite 380
Washington, DC 20001   **Phone:**   (202) 628-3535
USA   **Fax:**   (202) 737-2690

Contact Person: Shauna Walden, Director of Membership Services.   **Officers or Principals:** Judith DeSarno, President/CEO ($90,603); Megan Jackson, Director of Finance ($51,327); Deborah L. Horan, Director of Government Relations ($50,242); Joan Henneberry, Chairperson; Betsye Render, Vice Chairperson; Jill June, Treasurer.
Mission or Interest: Promotes birth control and abortion rights. Research and education on public policy surrounding these issues. Represents the nearly 4,000 clinics that receive federal funds for family planning through the Title X program.
Accomplishments: In the fiscal year ending June 1994, the Association spent $535,221 on its programs. The largest program, with expenditures of $248,996, was policy analysis. $129,445 was spent providing member services such as "technical assistance, policy analysis, information and professional development opportunities which improve their ability to deliver quality reproductive care." $96,341 for an annual meeting. Other programs include publications and a telephone report line.
Net Revenue: FY ending 6/94 $683,398 **Net Expenses:** $708,753 76%/15%/9% **Net Assets:** $116,641 **Citations:** 9:202
Tax Status: 501(c)(3)
Board of Directors or Trustees: Norma Alvarez (TX State Dept. of Health), Libby Antarsh (Assoc. of Voluntary Surgical Contraception), Karen Cody Carlson (East Central IL Planned Parenthood), Sylvia Clark (Rocky Mountain Planned Parenthood), Mary Cooper (Family Planning Services of Onondaga County, NY), Lynn Cooper Breckenmaker (Family Health Council of Central PA), Karen Gluck (Greater Dallas Family Planning Program), Shirley Gordon (Family Planning Advocates of NY), Cindy Groff (Family Services), Riley Hall (Basic Health Management), George Hill (Family Planning Assoc. of ME), Lisa Kaeser (Alan Guttmacher Inst.), Sima Michaels (Los Angeles Regional Family Planning Council), April Pace, Irene Pinela-Piaseck (CO Dept. of Health), Peggy Romberg (TX Family Planning Assoc.), Kevin Vaughan (Philadelphia Commission on Human Relations).
Periodicals: *NFPRHA News.*
Other Information: The Association received $554,326, or 81% of revenue, from gifts and grants awarded by foundations, businesses, and individuals. (These grants included $55,000 from the Robert Sterling Clark Foundation, $30,000 from the Jessie Smith Noyes Foundation.) $96,358, or 14%, from the annual meeting. $4,352, or 1%, from interest on savings and temporary cash investments. $4,250, or 1%, from mailing list rentals. The remaining revenue came from advertising, the sale of publications, and other miscellaneous sources.

National Federation of Independent Unions (NFIU)
1166 S. 11th St.
Philadelphia, PA 19147   **Phone:**   (215) 336-3300
USA

Contact Person: Francis J. Chiappardi, President.
Officers or Principals: Francis J. Chiappardi, President ($15,600); Alonzo Wheeler, Secretary Treasurer ($0); James Radosevich, Paul J. Diana, Donald E. Rothrock, Michael Roeder, Maxon Powell, Vice Presidents ($0).
Mission or Interest: Labor organizing and membership services.
Net Revenue: 1994 $39,152 **Net Expenses:** $39,164 **Net Assets:** $5,390
Tax Status: 501(c)(5)
Other Information: The Federation received $33,748, or 86% of revenue, from membership dues. $5,290, or 13%, from registration fees. The remaining revenue came from interest on savings and temporary cash investments.

National Federation of Societies for Clinical Social Work
239 N. Highland St.
Arlington, VA 22201   **Phone:**   (703) 522-5866
USA   **Fax:**   (703) 522-9441

Contact Person: Chad Breckenridge, President.   **Officers or Principals:** Jaclyn Miller, Ph.D., Treasurer ($0).
Mission or Interest: Represent those in the profession of psychoanalysis. Programs include education and professional development, as well as litigation and lobbying to advance clinical social work.
Accomplishments: In the fiscal year ending June 1994 the Federation spent $45,834 on its lobbying/advocacy and political expenditures.
Net Revenue: FY ending 6/94 $222,170 **Net Expenses:** $220,994 **Net Assets:** $121,809
Tax Status: 501(c)(6)
Periodicals: Newsletter.
Other Information: The Federation received $185,875, or 84% of revenue, from membership dues. $11,569, or 5%, from gifts and grants awarded by foundations, businesses, and individuals. $8,784, or 4%, from the sale of publications. $8,004, or 4%, from dividends and interest from securities. $3,256, or 1%, from capital gains on the sale of securities. The remaining revenue came from interest on savings and temporary cash investments, and other miscellaneous sources.

National Gay and Lesbian Task Force

2320 17th St., N.W.
Washington, DC 20009   **Phone:**   (202) 332-6483
USA

Contact Person: Melinda Parm, Executive Director.   **Officers or Principals:** P.J. Radecic, Former Executive Director ($8,668).
Mission or Interest: Lobbying organization "working at the federal level to influence government decisions on issues such as health care policy and civil rights; safeguarding gay and lesbian interests with unions, corporations, professional, religious, and political organizations." Monitors hate crimes.
Accomplishments: In 1994 the Task Force spent $149,090 on its programs.
Net Revenue: 1994 $336,329 **Net Expenses:** $290,087 57%/16%/32% **Net Assets:** $447,506 **Citations:** 3:227
Products or Services: "Fight the Right Action Kit", and other publications.
Tax Status: 501(c)(4)
Other Information: Affiliated with the 501(c)(3) National Gay and Lesbian Task Force Policy Institute at the same address. The two affiliates had combined net revenues of $2,752,040, net expenses of $2,640,829, and net assets of $442,282. The Task Force received 100% of its revenues from gifts and grants awarded by foundations, businesses, and individuals. (These grants included $220,000 from the Joyce Mertz-Gilmore Foundation, and $5,000 from the Haymarket People's Fund.)

National Gay and Lesbian Task Force Policy Institute

2320 17th St., N.W.
Washington, DC 20009   **Phone:**   (202) 332-6483
USA

Contact Person: Melinda Parm, Executive Director.
Mission or Interest: "Working with grassroots organizations to combat anti-gay violence, discriminatory policies, homophobia, and AIDS."
Accomplishments: In 1994 the Policy Institute spent $1,756,658 on its programs. The largest program, with expenditures of $1,432,033, was political organizing. $323,867 was spent "working with reporters, producers, and editors in gay and mainstream media to battle prejudice and assure fair and informed coverage of gay and lesbian lives; offering media training and consultation to local activists."
Net Revenue: 1994 $2,415,711 **Net Expenses:** $2,350,742 75%/19%/6% **Net Assets:** (-$5,224) **Citations:** 3:225
Tax Status: 501(c)(3)
Other Information: Affiliated with the 501(c)(4) National Gay and Lesbian Task Force at the same address. The two affiliates had combined net revenues of $2,752,040, net expenses of $2,640,829, and net assets of $442,282. The Policy Institute received $2,290,573, or 95% of revenue, from gifts and grants awarded by foundations, businesses, and individuals. (These grants included $2,500 from the Tides Foundation, $250 from the Stewart R. Mott Charitable Trust.) $88,666, or 4%, from conference fees. $13,059, or 1%, from honoraria. The remaining revenue came from mailing list rentals, advertising in conference programs, interest on savings and temporary cash investments, and other miscellaneous sources.

National Health Care for the Homeless Council

P.O. Box 68019
Nashville, TN 37206   **Phone:**   (615) 226-2292
USA   **Fax:**   (615) 226-1656

Contact Person: Polly Bullock, Administrative Assistant.   **Officers or Principals:** John Lozier, Executive Director ($0); Wayne Anderson, Associate Director ($0); Karen McGee, President ($0); Ernesto Gomez, Vice President; Barbara Conanan, Treasurer.
Mission or Interest: To provide support, coordination and coalition building. To provide services and influence public policy relating to the needs of the homeless, particularly health care.
Accomplishments: In 1994 the Council spent $387,443 on its programs. These included analysis of the Clinton Health Care Plan. Various symposiums and meetings. This also included $59,287 in grants awarded to Health Care for the Homeless of Seattle, $57,287, and the Metro Health Department of Nashville, $2,000.
Net Revenue: 1994 $461,292 ($82,591, or 18%, from government fees and contracts) **Net Expenses:** $402,506 96%/3%/1%
Net Assets: $182,344
Products or Services: Membership meetings, networking, policy analysis and advocacy, research papers, conferences, and lobbying. The Council spent $7,717 on lobbying.
Tax Status: 501(c)(3)
Board of Directors or Trustees: Alice Fletcher, Elaine Fox, Jacquelyn Gaines, Mary Ann Gleason, Luz-Mary Harris, Terisa James, Mandy Johnson, Frank Jordan, Vincent Keane, Anne Lesser, William Mabee, John McKinney, Ken McKnight, Susan Neibacher, Charlotte Nelson, James O'Connell, M.D., Bonnie Olson, Scott Orman, Heidi Romans, Marjorie Sa'adah, Judy Wellepp.
Periodicals: Bimonthly newsletter.
Other Information: The Council paid the Council of Community Services, Nashville, TN, for personnel. The Council received $310,000, or 67% of revenue, from Comic Relief. $82,591, or 18%, from government fees and contracts. $50,050, or 11%, from membership dues. The remaining revenue came from interest on savings and temporary cash investments.

National Hook-Up of Black Women

5117 S. University Ave.
Chicago, IL 60615
USA

Phone: (312) 291-2113
Fax: (312) 413-1993

Contact Person: Wynetta Frazier, Ph.D., National President.
Officers or Principals: Bertha Thomas, Vice President; Annette Stewart, Secretary.
Mission or Interest: "To provide a communication network for Black women that will help meet their needs through referrals and direct services...A collective voice for Women's issues and concerns...Open to all Black women who are concerned about and committed to equality and social justice."
Accomplishments: Four community forums annually in eleven major cities.
Products or Services: $25,000 per year annual scholarship program.
Tax Status: 501(c)(3) **Annual Report:** Yes. **Employees:** All volunteer.
Periodicals: *Hook-Up News and Views.*   **Internships:** No.
Other Information: Founded by Anita Young Boswell in 1973 during the fourth Congressional Black Caucus Legislative Weekend.

National Independent Politics Summit

P.O. Box 170610
Brooklyn, NY 11217
USA

Phone: (718) 643-9603   **E-Mail:** tglick@igc.apc.org
Fax: (718) 643-8265

Contact Person: Ted Glick, Coordinator.
Mission or Interest: "To unite progressive third-party organizations and other progressive organizations to build a unified third party movement."
Accomplishments: Convened a national summit in August 1995 attended by representatives of more than 100 organizations from 25 states. Established an ongoing network.
Employees: 2
Periodicals: *Independent Political Action Bulletin.*   **Internships:** No.
Other Information: In 1995 the Summit received $1,000 from Resist.

National Institute for Women of Color

429 N St., S.W., Suite 805
Washington, DC 20024-3713
USA

Contact Person: Veronica Collazo, Chair.   **Officers or Principals:** Cheryl A. Sloan, Treasurer ($0).
Mission or Interest: Research and education on the status of women of color.
Accomplishments: In 1992 the Institute spent $3,709 completing a project of data collection and analysis on the status of women of color.
Net Revenue: 1992 $13,291 **Net Expenses:** $14,223 **Net Assets:** $3,298
Tax Status: 501(c)(3)
Board of Directors or Trustees: Marguerite Gee, Caroline Chang (Office for Civil Rights, U.S. Dept. of Health and Human Services), June Inuzuka, Patricia Gill Turner (Presbyterian Church, USA, Women's Ministry Unit), Eddie Mae Sloan, Virginia Apodaca (Office for Civil Rights, U.S. Dept. of Health and Human Services), Clotilde Molina, Sabrae Yulone Jenkins, Deanna Martinez, Thelma Stiffarm, Alice Lynch, Sharon Parker.
Periodicals: *NIWC Network News* (newsletter).
Other Information: The Institute received $12,157, or 92% of revenue, from gifts and grants awarded by foundations, businesses, and individuals. The remaining revenue came from program services, investment income, and other miscellaneous sources.

National Labor Committee Education Fund in Support of Worker and Human Rights in Central America (NLC)

275 7th Ave.
New York, NY 10001
USA

Phone: (212) 242-3002
Fax: (212) 242-3821

Contact Person: David Cook.
Officers or Principals: Charles Kernaghan, Executive Director; Owen Bieber, George J. Kourpias, Jack Sheinkman, Co-Chairs.
Mission or Interest: Represents 23 national unions. Works to eliminate low-paying sweatshops in Latin America and the Caribbean. Promotes human rights and organized labor.
Accomplishments: Has called attention to sweatshops by linking them to high-profile celebrities whose clothing lines or signature apparel is produced in these sweatshops. Exposed the role television celebrity Kathy Lee Gifford played in using sweatshop labor, and turning her into a spokesperson against such production methods. Called attention to the U.S. government's assisting factories to relocate in low-wage countries. Conducted a U.S. tour of 'maguila' workers to travel to twenty cities and tell of working conditions in their home country. Persuaded The GAP to allow independent human rights inspectors to investigate its' contractor plants. Called attention to the Walt Disney Co.'s production of clothing in Haiti at "starving wages."

Net Revenue: 1994   est. $250,000
Products or Services: Reports such as "Free Trade's Hidden Secrets: Why We Are Losing Our Shirts," "The U.S. in Haiti: How to Get Rich on 11¢ an Hour," and "Paying to Lose Our Jobs." Videos, "Zoned for Slavery," and "Mickey Mouse in Haiti."
Tax Status: 501(c)(3)   **Annual Report:** No.   **Employees:** 3 full-time, 3 part-time.
Board of Directors or Trustees: David Arian (Intl. Longshoremen's and Warehousemen's Union), Morton Bahr (Communications Workers of America), William Bywater (Intl. Union of Electric, Electrical, Technical, Salaried & Machine Workers), Ron Carey (Intl. Brotherhood of Teamsters), Charles Dale (Newspaper Guild), Mac Fleming (Brotherhood of Maintenance of Way Employees), Keith Geiger (National Education Association), John Hovis Jr. (United Electrical, Radio and Machine Workers of America), Frank Hurt (Bakery, Confectionery and Tobacco Workers Intl. Union), Jay Mazur (Intl. Ladies Garment Workers Union), Gerald McEntee (AFSCME), Henry Nicholas (National Hospital and Health Care Employees), James Norton (Graphic Communications Intl. Union), Arturo Rodriguez (United Farm Workers of America), Vincent Sombrotto (National Association of Letter Carriers), John Sturdivant (American Federation of Government Employees), John Sweeney (AFL-CIO), Robert Wages (Oil, Chemical and Atomic Workers Intl. Union), William Wynn (United Food and Commercial Workers Intl. Union).
Internships: Yes.

National Law Center on Homelessness and Poverty

918 F St., N.W., Suite 412
Washington, DC 20004   **Phone:**   (202) 638-2535
USA

Contact Person: Maria Foscarinis, Executive Director.
Officers or Principals: Maria Foscarinis, Executive Director ($34,438); Glenn Manishin, Chair ($0); Ellen Bassuk, M.D., President ($0); Jim Sheibel, Vice President; Susan Bennett, Secretary; William Tyndall, Treasurer.
Mission or Interest: "To monitor compliance with the statutory programs benefitting the poor and homeless; to institute litigation when necessary in defense of the rights of the poor and the homeless; to educate the public on poverty and homelessness; and to promote the expansion and enforcement of programs to aid the very poor and the homeless."
Accomplishments: In 1994 the Center spent $137,798 on its programs. The largest program, public education, cost $51,790 and responded to over 6,000 requests for information and produced two reports; "To Protect and Defend" which recommends changes to a federal program that makes unused federal property available for housing the homeless, and "No Homeless People Allowed" which examines laws restricting the actions of homeless people in 49 U.S. cities. Policy advocacy, that cost $39,094, collaborated with dozens of national and local groups to promote policy. $24,703 was spent on litigation, and $22,211 was spent monitoring compliance with federal laws.
Net Revenue: 1994 $178,661 **Net Expenses:** $153,924 90%/4%/7% **Net Assets:** $63,579
Products or Services: "No Room for the Inn: A Report on Local Opposition to Housing & Social Services Facilities for Homeless People in 36 U.S. Cities," other publications, litigation, and lobbying. In 1994 the Center spent $4,501 on lobbying. $2,250 on mailings to the public and legislators, and $2,251 on the direct lobbying of legislators.
Tax Status: 501(c)(3)
Board of Directors or Trustees: Al Cacozza, C.K. Casteel, Jr. (MCI Communications), Craig Champ (Keys of Hope), Alfred Chiplin (National Senior Citizens Law Center), Stan Herr (Univ. of Maryland Law School), Susan Hoffman, Kim Hopper (Nathan S. Kline Inst.), Jonathan Kozol (author), Elliot Liebow, Pam Malester, Susanne Sinclair-Smith (Local Initiatives Support Corp.), James Stockdill, Prof. James Wright (Tulane Univ.).
Periodicals: *In Just Times* (newsletter).
Other Information: By the Law Center's count, there are 2 million homeless Americans, and 450,000 of them are children. The Center received $173,333, or 97% of revenue, from grants awarded by foundations, companies and individuals. (These grants included $20,000 from the J. Roderick MacArthur Foundation, $15,000 from the Deer Creek Foundation.) $4,180, or 2% came from the sale of *In Just Times* and other literature. The remaining $1,148 came from interest on savings and temporary cash investments.

National Lawyers Guild Foundation

55 Avenue of the Americas
New York, NY 10013   **Phone:**   (212) 966-5000
USA

Contact Person: Rick Best, Director.   **Officers or Principals:** Dean Haywood Burns, President ($0); Peter Erlinder, Vice President ($0); Cathy Connealy, Secretary/Treasurer ($0).
Mission or Interest: Provides legal support for various leftist causes and crusaders.
Accomplishments: In 1993 the Foundation spent $294,764 on its programs. Most of this, $277,145, was awarded in grants to "provide training and resources to members of the legal community and general public on the law and current legal developments."
Net Revenue: $302,458 97%/3%/0% **Net Expenses:** $207,264
Tax Status: 1993 $275,642
Board of Directors or Trustees: Rick Best, Peter Franck, Barbara Dudley, Victor Rabinowitz, Ellen Capnick, Dale Wiehoff, Julie Hurwitz, Kent Lebsock, Pete Waack.
Other Information: Affiliated with the National Lawyers Guild at the same address. The Foundation received $270,382, or 98% of revenue, from gifts and grants awarded by foundations and individuals. (In 1994 these grants included $15,000 from the C.S. Fund.) $2,580, or 1%, from administrative fees. $2,492, or 1%, from interest on savings and temporary cash investments. The remaining revenue came from dividends and interest from securities.

National Lead Information Center

1019 19th St., N.W., Suite 401
Washington, DC 20036   **Phone:** (202) 833-1071
USA

Mission or Interest: Provides research and education on the public health consequences of exposure to lead, especially its effects on children.
Periodicals: *Lead Inform* (quarterly newsletter).

National Leadership Coalition for Health Care Reform

555 13th St.
Washington, DC 20004   **Phone:** (202) 637-6830
USA

Contact Person: Henry E. Simmons, President.   **Officers or Principals:** Henry E. Simmons, President ($166,072); Margaret Rhoades, Executive Director ($92,250); Martin Dunleavy ($57,871); Hon. Robert D. Ray, Hon. Paul G. Rogers, Co-Chairs.
Mission or Interest: Bipartisan commission of Democrats and moderate Republicans that makes recommendations and develops plans for health care reform. The Coalition's recommendations are set forth in "Excellent Health Care for All Americans at a Reasonable Cost." The Coalition calls for; 1) Guaranteed universal coverage funded by employers and a payroll tax. 2) Cost controls that set a cap on the nation's total health care spending, to eventually be held to the rate of GNP growth (with no accommodations mentioned for increases due to aging of the general population). These caps would be set by a new National Health Review Board and approved by Congress. 3) The setting of rates by the Review Board for all medical procedures. 4) National guidelines to protect against "frivolous" malpractice lawsuits. 5) Standardization of all billing, benefit packages, and uniform rates for services.
Accomplishments: In the fiscal year ending June 1994, the Coalition spent $875,842 on its programs.
Net Revenue: FY ending 6/94 $753,016 **Net Expenses:** $1,094,817 80%/20%/0% **Net Assets:** (-$121,097)
Citations: 1:240
Products or Services: Research, reports, advocacy and lobbying. The Coalition spent $7,875 lobbying legislators and government officials.
Tax Status: 501(c)(3)
Board of Directors or Trustees: Presidents Jimmy Carter and Gerald Ford served as Honorary Co-Chairs. Frank Carlucci (National Security Advisor, 1986-87), William Ketchum, Robert Ray, Paul Rogers, John Sweeney (AFL-CIO).
Other Information: The Coalition employed Mark Goldberg and Par Associates of Whitehall, OH, as consultants, paying them $94,250 and $33,500 respectively. The Coalition received $753,016, or 99.6% of revenue, from gifts and grants awarded by foundations, businesses, and individuals. The remaining revenue came from interest on savings and temporary cash investments and the sale of reports.

National Low Income Housing Coalition

1012 14th St., N.W., Suite 1200
Washington, DC 20005   **Phone:** (202) 662-1530
USA

Contact Person: Kate Crawford, Associate Director.
Mission or Interest: Lobbying coalition that seeks increased funding for housing programs that provide low-cost housing, in a good environment, with safe neighborhoods, and freedom of housing choice, for low-income residents.
Accomplishments: Held conferences at various cities in 1996 to explain new budget and policy legislation.
Products or Services: 1996 Advocates Resource Book, Housing America's Future: Children At Risk, other publications.
Tax Status: 501(c)(4)
Other Information: Affiliated with the 501(c)(3) Low Income Housing and Information Service at the same address.

National Network of Abortion Funds (NNAF)

c/o CLPP, Hampshire College
Amherst, MA 01002   **Phone:** (413) 582-5645   **E-Mail:** mjmSS@hamp.hampshire.edu
USA   **Fax:**   (413) 582-5620

Contact Person: M. J. Maccardini, Program Coordinator.
Officers or Principals: Marlene Gerber Fried, President; Shawn Towey, Vice President.
Mission or Interest: "We believe that: The right to choose abortion is meaningless without access to abortion services. All restrictions on abortion access and funding are discriminatory because they especially burden poor women, young women, women of color and rural women. It is the responsibility of government to fund abortions, either through Medicaid or within a universal, national health care plan. We must act now to support women who want abortions and cannot afford them." NNAF works with thirty-five abortion funds nationwide, assisting in the provision of abortions, and in building coalitions to protect and expand access to abortion procedures. NNAF also has a task force linking anti-abortion activities to violence against women. The Network also opposes welfare reform as advocated by the 104th Congress and president Clinton.
Accomplishments: "Through direct grants or loans, NNAF member funds annually assist more than 6,000 women who would not have been able to obtain safe, legal abortions with their own resources."

Products or Services: <u>Legal But Out of Reach</u> booklet, pamphlets.
Tax Status: 501(c)(3) **Employees:** 1
Periodicals: *NNAF News* (monthly newsletter). **Internships:** No.
Other Information: In 1994 the Network received $10,000 from the Ms. Foundation for Women. Other supporters included the Haymarket People's Fund, Resist, Jessie Smith Noyes Foundation, Threshold Foundation, Naomi and Nehemiah Cohen Foundation.

National Network of Grantmakers

1717 Kettner Blvd., Suite 100
San Diego, CA 92101   **Phone:**   (619) 231-1348
USA

Contact Person: Terry Odendahl, Executive Director.
Mission or Interest: A network of progressive grantmakers.
Other Information: In 1994 the Network received $1,000 from the Wieboldt Foundation.

National Network on Cuba

198 Broadway, Suite 800
New York, NY 10098   **Phone:**   (212) 227-3422
USA

Mission or Interest: A coalition of 70 local and national groups calling for the end on the U.S. economic blockade of Cuba and the normalization of relations.
Accomplishments: In 1995 the Network organized rallies in Atlanta, Chicago, San Francisco, and New York City to "demand that the U.S. government end its economic blockade, lift the travel ban, normalize relations with Cuba and respect Cuba's self-determination."

National Organization for the Reform of Marijuana Laws (NORML)

1001 Connecticut Ave., N.W., Suite 1010
Washington, DC 20036   **Phone:**   (202) 483-5500
USA

Contact Person: Richard C. Cowan, Executive Director.   **Officers or Principals:** Richard C. Cowan, Executive Director ($37,538); Al Byrne, Secretary ($0); Jim Turney, Treasurer ($0); Dan Viets, Vice President.
Mission or Interest: Advocates the reform and removal of laws prohibiting the use of marijuana for enjoyment and medicinal purposes.
Accomplishments: NORML has received support from all areas of the political spectrum. In 1993 the Organization spent $207,744 on its programs. $58,069 on public education programs. $38,713 on conferences and seminars. $25,809 on professional consulting for members of the media, health care officials and others. $6,452 on legal referrals and litigation.
Net Revenue: 1993 $323,184 **Net Expenses:** $312,851 66%/20%/14% **Net Assets:** $39,263
Products or Services: Educational materials, consulting, conferences, t-shirts bumper stickers, and lobbying. In 1993 the Organization spent $15,723 on lobbying, $9,748 on grassroots lobbying and $5,975 on the direct lobbying of legislators.
Tax Status: 501(c)(3)
Board of Directors or Trustees: Susan Anderson, David Busch, A. Wayne Davis, Steve Dillon, Gatewood Galbraith, Dale Gieringer, Neil Jacobs, Norman Elliot Kent, Jeanne Lang, Mary Lynn Mathre, Marvin Miller.
Other Information: The Organization received $119,002, or 37% of revenue, from membership dues. $101,672, or 31%, from gifts and grants awarded by foundations and individuals. $99,713, or 31%, from program services. The remaining revenue came from the net sale of inventory other than assets.

National Organization for Women (NOW)

1000 16th St., N.W., Suite 700
Washington, DC 20036   **Phone:**   (202) 331-0066   **E-Mail:** now@now.org
USA   **Fax:**   (202) 785-8576   **Web-Page:** http://now.org/now/hopme.html

Contact Person: Patricia Ireland, President.
Officers or Principals: Patricia Ireland, President ($127,679); Kim Gandy, Executive Vice President ($104,680); Rosemary Dempsey, Vice President ($104,680); Karen Johnson, National Secretary ($102,021); Eleanor Smeal, Chair.
Mission or Interest: Lobbying organization promoting feminism and feminist issues. "To take action to bring women into full participation in the mainstream of American society now, exercising all the privileges and responsibilities thereof in truly equal partnership with men."
Accomplishments: "NOW is the largest feminist organization in the United States." In 1996 NOW took the lead in preserving affirmative action and other programs in its "Fight the Right" campaign. The California Civil Rights Initiative, which would eliminate all preferential hiring and contracts in California state government and admissions in the state universities, has been the primary target of the Fight the Right effort. In 1994 NOW spent $3,819,137 on its programs. This included $1,005,264 in grants to state, region and local chapters.
Net Revenue: 1994 $5,655,966 **Net Expenses:** $5,383,801 71%/23%/6% **Net Assets:** (-$802,450) **Citations:** 2,213:13

Tax Status: 501(c)(4) **Employees:** 31
Board of Directors or Trustees: Kathy Austin, Linda Berg, Carencay Bowen, Tammy Bruce, Don Cannon, Phyllis Carlson-Riehm, Jeanne Clark, Kathy Conroy, Ellen Convisser, Barbara Cox, Beth Edmonds, Claudia Ellquist, Laurene Facey-Muench, Minerva Glidden, Karen Godshall, Cindy Guerra, Colleen Kelly Johnston, John Katz, Patricia Lassiter, Ruth Laws, Pat Murphy, Efia Nwangaza, Jan Osborn, Alice Patton, Claire Peirce, Clarice Pollock, Irene Secada, Virginia Stallworth, David Stewart, Elizabeth Toledo, Harriet Trudell, Erima Vaughn, Marion Wagner, Jeanne Walton, Marty Whitehead, E. Faye Williams, Kathy Wilson, Judy Knee.
Periodicals: *National NOW Times.*
Internships: Yes, unpaid internships in political action, government relations, individual issues marketing, communications and more.
Other Information: Affiliated with the NOW Political Action Committee and the 501(c)(3) National Organization for Women Foundation at the same address. In 1993 the two affiliates had combined revenues, expenses, and net assets of $7,096,844, $7,014,759, and -$972,407. NOW received $3,853,500, or 68% of revenue, from membership dues. $1,270,806, or 22%, from gifts and grants awarded by foundations, businesses, and individuals. $217,953, or 4%, from the sale of promotional and educational material. $183,231, or 3%, from mailing list rentals. The remaining revenue came from conferences, special events, advertising, royalties and commissions, and other miscellaneous sources.

National Organization for Women Foundation (NOW)

1000 16th St., N.W., Suite 700
Washington, DC 20036   **Phone:** (202) 331-0066   **E-Mail:** now@now.org
USA   **Fax:**   (202) 785-8576   **Web-Page:** http://now.org/now/home.html

Contact Person: Patricia Ireland, President.   **Officers or Principals:** Patricia Ireland, President ($0); Kim Gandy, Executive Vice President ($0); Rosemary Dempsey, Vice President ($0); Eleanor Smeal, Chair.
Mission or Interest: Research and education affiliate of the National Organization for Women.
Accomplishments: In 1993 the Foundation spent $144,867 on its programs. The largest program, with expenditures of $50,327, was "Global Feminism" that "focus(ed) on enlightening education and raising the conscientiousness of society." $48,511 was spent on diversity training. $24,601 was spent on leadership training targeting young women. $19,726 was spent on "Economic Purity - providing a framework for independence and self-sustenance for women in modern society."
Net Revenue: 1993 $220,695 **Net Expenses:** $155,113 93%/4%/3% **Net Assets:** $102,208 **Citations:** 2,213:13
Tax Status: 501(c)(3)
Board of Directors or Trustees: Kathy Austin, Linda Berg, Carencay Bowen, Tammy Bruce, Don Cannon, Phyllis Carlson-Riehm, Jeanne Clark, Kathy Conroy, Ellen Convisser, Barbara Cox, Beth Edmonds, Claudia Ellquist, Laurene Facey-Muench, Minerva Glidden, Karen Godshall, Cindy Guerra, Colleen Kelly Johnston, John Katz, Patricia Lassiter, Ruth Laws, Pat Murphy, Efia Nwangaza, Jan Osborn, Alice Patton, Claire Peirce, Clarice Pollock, Irene Secada, Virginia Stallworth, David Stewart, Elizabeth Toledo, Harriet Trudell, Erima Vaughn, Marion Wagner, Jeanne Walton, Marty Whitehead, E. Faye Williams, Kathy Wilson, Judy Knee.
Other Information: Affiliated with the NOW Political Action Committee and the 501(c)(4) National Organization for Women at the same address. In 1993 the two affiliates had combined revenues, expenses, and net assets of $7,096,844, $7,014,759, and -$972,407. The Foundation received $109,355, or 50% of revenue, from gifts and grants awarded by foundations, businesses, and individuals. $88,974, or 40%, from a "nationwide campaign to assist implementation of education programs involving current women's issues." $20,779 net, or 9%, from capital gains on the sale of securities. The remaining revenue came from interest on savings and temporary cash investments, and dividends and interest from securities.

National Organization for Women Legal Defense and Education Fund (NOW)

99 Hudson St.
New York, NY 10013   **Phone:** (212) 925-6635
USA   **Fax:**   (212) 226-1066

Contact Person: Kathryn Rodgers, Executive Director.   **Officers or Principals:** Kathryn J. Rodgers, Executive Director ($135,164); Deborah Ellis, Legal Director ($79,843); Lynn Hecht Schafran, Director ($68,752); Barbara M. Cox, President; Catherine Samuels, General Counsel; Myra H. Strober, Secretary; Rosalie J. Wolf, Treasurer.
Mission or Interest: Feminist organization that uses litigation and educational efforts to achieve its goals.
Accomplishments: In 1995 the Fund spent $1,924,934 on its programs. The largest program, with expenditures of $1,010,830, was legal research and litigation. Most of the litigation was related to abortion rights; other cases involved employment rights, lesbians' rights, "economic justice," sexual harassment, violence against women, military exclusion, and child custody. The Fund received $145,097 in court awarded-attorney's fees. $584,516 was spent on public information and education. Other programs focused on public policy and coalition building.
Net Revenue: 1995 $2,886,186 **Net Expenses:** $2,834,177 68%/10%/22% **Net Assets:** $1,860,531 **Citations:** 14:185
Products or Services: Litigation and lobbying. In 1995 the Fund spent $112,015 on lobbying; $52,979 on grassroots lobbying, and $59,036 on the direct lobbying of legislators.
Tax Status: 501(c)(3)
Board of Directors or Trustees: Simon Chazen, Rosemary Dempsey, Mary Maples Dunn (Dir., Schlesinger Library), Sara Engelhardt (The Foundation center), Lani Guinier (Univ. of PA Law School), Anne Harper (Atlanta Board of Education), Patricia

Ireland, Ralph Knowles, Jr., Stephen Oleskey, Alice Richmond, Minna Schrag, Lisa Specht, Isabel Carter Stewart (Exec. Dir., Girls Inc.), Catherine R. Stimpson (Fellows Program, John D. and Catherine C. MacArthur Foundation), Patricia Williams (Columbia Univ. Law School), Rosalie Wolf (Rockefeller Foundation), Adele Yellin, Nancy Hoffmeier Zamora.

Other Information: Affiliated with the 501(c)(4) National Organization for Women at the same address. The Fund contracted the New York city firm of Projects Plus, Inc., for special events. The firm was paid $98,589. The Fund received loans of $235,119 and $126,400 from the Ford Foundation and New York Job Development Authority respectively. At the end of the year the outstanding balances were $30,318 and $49,741. The Fund received $2,280,214, or 79% of revenue, from gifts and grants awarded by foundations, businesses, and individuals. (In 1994 these grants included $25,000 from the Rockefeller Family Fund, $25,000 from the Ms. Foundation for Women, $25,000 from the Robert Sterling Clark Foundation, $25,000 from the Jessie Smith Noyes Foundation, $5,000 from the Angelina Fund, $500 from the Stewart R. Mott Charitable Trust, and $500 from the New Prospect Foundation. In 1993 it received $20,000 from the Norman Foundation, and $10,000 from the Wallace Alexander Gerbode Foundation.) $386,500, or 13%, from special fund-raising events. $145,097, or 5%, from court-awarded attorney's fees. $41,425, or 1%, from interest on savings and other temporary cash investments. The remaining revenue came from rental income, literature sales, honoraria, and other miscellaneous sources.

National Organization for Women, Boston (NOW)

971 Commonwealth Ave., Suite 20
Boston, MA 02215
USA

Phone: (617) 782-1056
Fax: (617) 782-4127

Contact Person: Ellen Zeller, President.
Officers or Principals: Judy Bornstein, Sara Borden, Co-Vice Presidents for Fundraising ($0); Beth Arnold, Vice President, Action ($0); Lynn Harris, Vice President, Public Relations; Toni Troop, Ember Deitz, Co-Treasurers.
Mission or Interest: Boston affiliate of the National Organization for Women.
Accomplishments: In 1993 the Organization spent $46,292 on its programs. The largest program, with expenditures of $39,819, was Lesbian Rights. This included transporting thousands to the "National Mobilization" on April 25 1993, to demonstrate on behalf of lesbian, gay, and bisexual rights. Other programs included the Violence Against Women, Racial and Ethnic Diversity, and Reproductive Rights Task Forces.
Net Revenue: 1993 $108,370 **Net Expenses:** $120,192 39%/47%/14% **Net Assets:** $17,758
Products or Services: Lobbying and organization.
Tax Status: 501(c)(4)
Periodicals: Newsletter.
Other Information: The Organization received $61,230, or 57% of revenue, from money collected during the National Mobilization. $21,759, or 20%, from membership dues. $12,600, or 12%, from special fund-raising events. $7,280, or 7%, from "Outreach" tables set up at various locations and events. $3,383, or 3%, from reimbursements for expenses. $1,612, or 1%, from gifts collected through phone solicitations. The remaining revenue came from interest on savings and temporary cash investments, and newsletter sales.

National Organization for Women, Chicago (NOW)

53 W. Jackson
Chicago, IL 60604
USA

Contact Person: Suzanne Purrington, Executive Director.
Officers or Principals: Shirleen Kajiwara, President ($0); Lisa Kuklinski, Secretary ($0); Angela West Bank, Treasurer ($0).
Mission or Interest: Chicago chapter of the National Organization for Women.
Accomplishments: In 1993 the Organization spent $57,023 on its programs. The largest program, with expenditures of $23,950, was to "increase awareness and participation in current legislation." $15,966 was spent to "educate the public about issues concerning women." $17,107 was spent on referrals, and membership and public service.
Net Revenue: 1993 $96,043 **Net Expenses:** $135,251 42%/58%/0% **Net Assets:** (-$68,929)
Tax Status: 501(c)(4)
Board of Directors or Trustees: Rocio Cordoba, Lisa Diamond, Lorna Brett Glickman, Anne Manly, Smudge Perry, Kim Rutherford, Trudy Seabrook-McLaurine.
Other Information: The Organization received $48,038 net, or 50% of revenue, from special fund-raising events. $40,816, or 43%, from gifts and grants awarded by foundations, businesses, and individuals. $7,124, or 7%, from membership dues. The remaining revenue came from interest on savings and temporary cash investments.

National Organization for Women, Connecticut (NOW)

21 Sunset Beach Rd.
Branford, CT 06405
USA

Contact Person: Theresa Weiner, President.   **Officers or Principals:** Sharon McClure, Vice President ($0); Marguerite Boslaugh, Secretary ($0); Alice L. Lambert, Treasurer ($0).

Mission or Interest: Connecticut affiliate of the National Organization for Women. Lobbying, legislative monitoring, public awareness and education.

Accomplishments: In 1994 the Organization spent $26,806 on its activities.

Net Revenue: 1994 $39,924 **Net Expenses:** $45,590 **Net Assets:** $13,663

Tax Status: 501(c)(4)

Other Information: The Organization received $20,118, or 50% of revenue, from membership dues. $15,294, or 38%, from gifts and grants awarded by foundations, affiliates, businesses, and individuals. $4,292, or 11%, from special fund-raising events, including a dinner, movie, and auction. The remaining revenue came from investment income.

National Organization for Women, Minnesota (NOW)

550 Rice St., Suite 106A
St. Paul, MN 55103   **Phone:**   (612) 631-8319
USA

Contact Person: Barbara Born, Treasurer. **Officers or Principals:** Barbara Born, Treasurer ($0); Betty Ann Burch, Vice President ($0); Laurel Parrott, President; Jacqueline McMillan, Secretary; Marilyn Rushenberg, Legislative Coordinator.

Mission or Interest: Minnesota affiliate of NOW. Lobbies on behalf of feminist goals. "Taking action to bring women into full participation in the mainstream of American society NOW, exercising all the priveleges and responsibilities thereof in truly equal partnership with men."

Accomplishments: Approximately 4,800 members. In 1993 the Organization spent $51,441 on its programs. The largest expenditure, $22,926, was for lobbying at the state level. $21,000 of that paid a professional lobbyist. Spent $8,868 on producing and distributing a newsletter. $4,243 was contributed to the Minnesota NOW PAC.

Net Revenue: 1993 $50,326 **Net Expenses:** $65,825 78%/20%/2% **Net Assets:** $3,154

Products or Services: Publications, legislative monitoring, lobbying.

Tax Status: 501(c)(4) **Annual Report:** No. **Employees:** 3

Periodicals: *Minnesota NOW Times* (quarterly newsletter).

Internships: Yes.

Other Information: Founded in 1971. The Organization received $31,030 net, or 62% of revenue, from special fund-raising activities, including mail and telephone solicitation of members and non-members. $18,052, or 36%, from membership dues, including a portion of membership fees paid to National NOW. The remaining revenue came from gifts and grants, interest on savings and temporary cash investments, and net sales of inventory.

National Organization for Women, Nassau (NOW)

148 Greenwhich St.
Hempstead, NY 11550
USA

Contact Person: Gloria Freund, Executive Director.

Officers or Principals: Christina Davis, President ($0); June Leihton, Secretary ($0); Madge Heron, Treasurer ($0).

Mission or Interest: Nassau affiliate of the national NOW. Works through committees, including a Women of Color Task Force, Lesbian Rights Task Force, and Violence Against Women Task Force.

Accomplishments: In 1994 the Organization spent $12,626 on its programs. The largest program, with expenditures of $6,093, was the work done in various committees. $4,403 was spent producing and mailing a newsletter. $2,130 in dues was paid to the national organization.

Net Revenue: 1994 $28,251 **Net Expenses:** $26,033 **Net Assets:** $16,642

Tax Status: 501(c)(4)

Periodicals: Newsletter.

Other Information: The Organization received $12,818, or 45% of revenue, from program services. $11,827, or 42%, from membership dues. $3,176 net, or 11%, from special fund-raising events, including an awards dinner and a "Black and White Gala." The remaining revenue came from investment income.

National Organization for Women, New Jersey

114 W. State St.
Trenton, NJ 08608   **Phone:**   (609) 393-0156
USA

Contact Person: Myra Terry, President.

Officers or Principals: Myra Terry, President ($27,000); Mariann Mann, Vice President, Finance ($5,220).

Mission or Interest: Promotes feminist issues, including; abortion rights, racism, health care, the Equal Rights Amendment, lesbians' rights, violence against women, and divorce reform.

Accomplishments: In 1994 the Organization spent $77,079 on its programs to influence public policy. $72,560 on public education and $4,519 on the publication and distribution of a newsletter.

Net Revenue: 1994 $114,488 **Net Expenses:** $105,317 73%/13%/11% **Net Assets:** $7,248

Products or Services: Lobbying, publications, conferences, speakers, t-shirts, bumper stickers and other paraphernalia.

Tax Status: 501(c)(4)
Board of Directors or Trustees: Bear Atwood, Denise Beckman, Joane Parks.
Periodicals: Newsletter.
Other Information: Affiliated with the 501(c)(3) National Organization for Women of New Jersey Foundation at the same address. The two affiliates had combined net revenues of $115,636, net expenditures of $105,705, and assets of $8,202. The Organization received $40,220, or 35% of revenue, from membership dues. $32,326, or 28%, from special fund-raising events, including a raffle, walk-a-thon, "Pig Award," and a party for the president, Myra Terry. $30,787, or 27%, from gifts and grants awarded by foundations, companies, affiliates and individuals. $10,836, or 9%, from program services, including conferences and the president's speaking fees. The remaining revenue came from miscellaneous sources.

National Organization for Women, New Jersey Foundation (NOW)

114 W. State St.
Trenton, NJ 08608-1102   **Phone:**   (609) 393-0156
USA

Contact Person: Jennifer Gano, Administrative Assistant.
Officers or Principals: Mariann Mann, Treasurer ($0); Myra Terry, President ($0).
Mission or Interest: Research and education affiliate of the National Organization for Women of New Jersey.
Accomplishments: In 1994 the Organization spent $194 on its activity. This was a telephone referral service available to the public, public policy organizations, government agencies, and attorneys who can help with issues affecting women. "Over 400 people served per month." Hosted a tribute dinner to raise funds. The dinner honored prominent New Jersey women; 75 people attended.
Net Revenue: 1994 $1,148 **Net Expenses:** $194 **Net Assets:** $954
Tax Status: 501(c)(3)
Other Information: Affiliated with the 501(c)(4) National Organization for Women of New Jersey. The two affiliates had combined net revenues of $115,636, net expenditures of $105,705, and assets of $8,202. The Foundation received all of its revenue from the fund-raising tribute dinner.

National Organization for Women, Virginia (NOW)

P.O. Box 25831
Richmond, VA 23260   **Phone:**   (804) 786-8218
USA

Contact Person: Denise Lee, State Coordinator.   **Officers or Principals:** Phyllis Stevens, Assistant State Coordinator ($0); Alida Wadley, Recording Secretary ($0); Alia Khan, Amy Peloff, Legislative Coordinators ($0); Lynn Bradford, Financial Coordinator; Jere Gibber, Media Coordinator; Kelly Anderson, Fundraising Coordinator.
Mission or Interest: Virginia lobbying affiliate of the National Organization for Women. "Promoted awareness and action on violence against women, women and poverty, and the religious right's war on women."
Accomplishments: Approximately 5,000 members. In 1994 the Organization spent $14,558 on its programs.
Net Revenue: 1994 $46,495 **Net Expenses:** $41,600 **Net Assets:** $50,928
Tax Status: 501(c)(4)
Periodicals: Newsletter.
Other Information: The Organization received $24,854, or 53% of revenue, from gifts and grants awarded by foundations, businesses, and individuals. $17,984, or 38%, from membership dues. $1,137, or 2%, from investment income. $993, or 1%, from a reimbursement. $635, or 1%, from a state conference. $635, or 1%, from a legislative forum. The remaining revenue came from a rent deposit, and the sale of a manual.

National Organization of Industrial Trade Unions (NOITU)

148-06 Hillside Ave.
Jamaica, NY 11435   **Phone:**   (718) 291-3434
USA   **Fax:**   (718) 526-2920

Contact Person: Sam Kerr, President.   **Officers or Principals:** Sam Kerr, President ($74,615); Daniel Lasky, President Emeritus ($40,200); Gerard Jones, National Vice President ($31,957); Phillip Seigel, Secretary/Treasurer.
Mission or Interest: "Improve wages and working conditions of union members."
Accomplishments: Approximately 4,630 members.
Net Revenue: FY ending 3/95 $1,080,412 **Net Expenses:** $1,010,484 **Net Assets:** $2,772,566
Products or Services: Louis Lasky Scholarship Fund.
Tax Status: 501(c)(5)
Periodicals: *Unioncraft* (quarterly journal).
Other Information: In the fiscal year ending March 1995 the Organization received $785,470, or 73% of revenue, from membership dues. $174,902, or 16%, from "per capita" revenues. $99,598, or 9%, from dividends and interest from securities. $11,784, or 1%, from reimbursed expenses. The remaining revenue came from interest on savings and temporary cash investments.

National Parks and Conservation Association

1776 Massachusetts Ave., N.W., Suite 200
Washington, DC 20036   **Phone:**   (202) 223-6722
USA

Contact Person: Paul C. Pritchard, President.   **Officers or Principals:** Paul C. Pritchard, President ($242,521); Carol Aten, Senior Vice President ($86,285); William Chandler, Director, Conservation ($86,249); Gordon Beaham, Chair; Nancy Lampton, James MacFarland, William Resor, Vice Chairs; William Leedy, Secretary; Edward Roberts, Treasurer.
Mission or Interest: Environmental and conservation organization that focuses on the National Park system and lobbies to protect it against environmental threats, development, over use, and sell-offs. Also advocates and lobbies for expansion of the Park system.
Accomplishments: In the fiscal year ending June 1994, the Association spent $12,728,388 on its programs. The largest program, with expenditures of $7,153,501, was public education. $3,692,414 was spent on membership services. $1,342,483 was spent on park preservation and expansion. Other activities included grassroots activities and science and research.
Net Revenue: FY ending 6/94 $17,595,960   **Net Expenses:** $17,165,324   74%/3%/6%   **Net Assets:** $3,187,577
Citations: 428:45
Products or Services: Public education and lobbying. In the fiscal year ending June 1994 the Association spent $190,684 on lobbying, $100,758 on grassroots lobbying and $89,926 on the direct lobbying of legislators. This was an increase of 19% over the previous year, 51% over two years prior, and 244% over three years prior.
Tax Status: 501(c)(3)
Board of Directors or Trustees: Aubra Hayes Anthony, Jr., Victor Ashe, Mrs. Edward Blackburn, Jr., Eugene Brown, Virdin Brown, Dorothy Canter, Ph.D., Thomas Cavanaugh, Donald Field, Ph.D., Glenn Haas, Charles Howell, III, Neil Johannssen, Ellen Harvey Kelly, G. Robert Kerr, Betty Lilienthal, Thomas Markowsky, Robert Millard, F.I. Nebhut, Jr., John Oakes, Jerome Paige, Ph.D., Toby Pitts, Virgil Rose, Alfred Runte, Ph.D., Marian Albright Schenck, M.H. Schwartz, Dolph Simons, Jr., Lowell Thomas, Jr., Nancy Wheat, Fred Williamson, Sr., Robin Winks, Ph.D.
Periodicals: *National Parks* (bimonthly magazine).
Other Information: In the fiscal year ending June 1994, the Association received $15,271,466, or 87% of total revenue, from direct and indirect public support in the form of gifts and grants awarded by foundations, businesses, affiliates, and individuals. (These grants included $338,247 from the Environmental Federation of America, $45,000 from the Bullitt Foundation, $15,000 from the American Conservation Association, $10,000 from the New-Land Foundation, $3,594 from the Environmental Federation of California.) $1,251,432, or 7%, from membership dues. $362,059, or 2%, from advertising revenues from *National Parks*. $239,247, or 1%, from special events. $192,138, or 1%, from royalties and licensing. $174,980, or 1%, from mailing list rentals. Other sources of revenue included dividends and interest from securities, interest on savings and other temporary cash investments, magazine sales, and other miscellaneous sources. The Association lost $97,903 on the sale of securities, and $15,555 on special fund-raising events (this loss does not include the $70,762 in donations that resulted from the events). The Association held $2,815,962, or 49% of assets, in securities. $1,460,875, or 25%, in loans and notes payable. The Association did not hold any land for conservation purposes.

National Peace Foundation

1835 K St., N.W., Suite 610
Washington, DC 20006   **Phone:**   (202) 223-1770
USA

Contact Person: Glen Morin, Secretary.   **Officers or Principals:** Stephen P. Strickland, President ($38,331); Frances A. Crowther, Treasurer ($36,239); Kathleen J. Lansing, Vice President ($32,421).
Mission or Interest: "Public education on the use of peace-making and conflict resolution theory and techniques in international and domestic conflict."
Accomplishments: In 1994 the Foundation spent $346,059 on its programs. The largest, with expenditures of $334,449, was public education. $11,610 was spent on government relations "consulting with congress and other government bodies on the U.S. Institute of Peace on peace education and conflict resolution programs."
Net Revenue: 1994 $563,614   ($204,795, or 36%, from government grants)   **Net Expenses:** $589,738   59%/32%/9%
Net Assets: (-$111,650)   **Citations:** 3:222
Tax Status: 501(c)(4)
Other Information: The Foundation received $204,795, or 36% of revenue, from government grants. $194,918, or 35%, from gifts and grants awarded by foundations, businesses, and individuals. $158,859, or 28%, from membership dues. The remaining revenue came from interest on savings and temporary cash investments, and other miscellaneous sources.

National People's Action

810 N. Milwaukee Ave.
Chicago, IL 60622   **Phone:**   (312) 243-3038
USA   **Fax:**   (312) 243-7044

Mission or Interest: A coalition of grassroots neighborhood organizations. Focus on issues including redlining, affordable housing, community reinvestment, economic development, crime, drugs, and environmental justice. The coalition provides educational activities, protests, and lobbying.

National Public Radio (NPR)

635 Massachusetts Ave., N.W.
Washington, DC 20001-3753   **Phone:**   (202) 414-2000
USA

Contact Person: Ray Dilley, Project Director.
Officers or Principals: Robert Edwards, Senior Host ($155,616); Robert Siegel, Senior Host ($107,492); Linda Wertheimer, Senior Host ($107,424); Noah Adams, Senior Host ($106,376); Scott Simon, Senior Host ($105,146).
Mission or Interest: "News and information programming, cultural programming, and member services."
Accomplishments: NPR originally planned to air the commentaries of death-row inmate Mumia Abu-Jamal. Under the threat of reduced funding from Congress, NPR canceled the commentaries, which then aired on Radio Pacifica. (For more information, see the Pacifica Foundation.) In the fiscal year ending September 1994, NPR spent $50,370,806 on its programs; $37,991,115 on radio programming, and $12,379,691 on distribution services such as satellite maintenance and replacement and program feeds.
Net Revenue: FY ending 9/94 $60,067,036   ($1,151,204, or 2%, from government grants)
Net Expenses: $58,422,353   86%/11%/2% **Net Assets:** $21,458,690 **Citations:**   3,962:8
Products or Services: Radio programming. NPR spent $350,954 on lobbying. Most of this was lobbying on behalf of NPR's tax exempt status and continuation of its subsidies.
Tax Status: 501(c)(3)
Board of Directors or Trustees: David Anderson, Anthony Dean, Regina Dean, Joseph Dembo, Patricia Diaz Dennis, Eric DeWeese, Catherine Fraser, Joan Harris, Karen Holp, William Kovach, Thomas Livingston, Larmar Marchese, Carl Matthusen, Jack Mitchell, Delores Wharton, Lucien Wulsin.
Other Information: Affiliated with the 501(c)(3) NPR Foundation. The two affiliates had combined net revenues of $60,344,890, net expenses of $58,448,451, and net assets of $21,701,446. The Foundation received $31,261,598, or 52% of revenue, from radio programming related services. $19,972,415, or 33%, from gifts and grants awarded by foundations, businesses, affiliates, and individuals. (These grants included $1,000,000 from the John D. and Catherine T. MacArthur Foundation, $1,000,000 over two years from the Ford Foundation, $405,000 from the Henry J. Kaiser Family Foundation, $135,000 from the Joyce Foundation, $75,000 from the Florence and John Schumann Foundation, $50,000 from the Town Creek Foundation, $25,000 from the Bullitt Foundation, $20,000 from the New Prospect Foundation, $10,000 from the Bydale Foundation, and $400 from the Haymarket People's Fund. In 1995 NPR received $37,600 from the Tides Foundation.) $4,085,468, or 7%, from "distribution interconnection." $1,151,204, or 2%, from government grants. $808,802, or 1% from interest on savings and temporary cash investments. The remaining revenue came from studio rental and tape publishing, the sale of cassette tapes, the sale of inventory, capital gains, and other miscellaneous sources. NPR lost $49,810 from rental income.

National Puerto Rican Coalition (NPRC)

1700 K St., N.W., Suite 500
Washington, DC 20006   **Phone:**   (202) 223-3915
USA

Contact Person: Maria Swanson, Assistant.   **Officers or Principals:** Louis Nunez, President ($110,864); Roberto Nazario, Managing Director ($49,419); William Perez, Member Services ($42,366); Eric Munoz, Chairperson; Amalia Betanzos, Vice Chairperson; Lillian Escobar-Haskins, Treasurer; Maria Elena Girone, Secretary.
Mission or Interest: Promote the advancement of Puerto Rican people in the U.S., and promote cultural awareness and understanding.
Accomplishments: In 1993 the Coalition spent $791,675 on its programs. The largest program, with expenditures of $257,069, was public affairs. This consisted of working with the general public and communicating through press releases, newsletters, promotional materials, and the media. Included the biennial Life Achievement Awards honoring Puerto Ricans who have made significant contributions to American society. $253,477 was spent on public policy "to study, research and analyze the conditions of the Puerto Rican people in housing, labor, health, education, human resources, economic development and other related areas." Other programs include membership development and community economic development.
Net Revenue: 1993 $1,258,436   ($1,200,455, or 5%, from government grants) **Net Expenses:** $1,223,339   65%/30%/6%
Net Assets: $321,728 **Citations:**   11:195
Products or Services: Networking, research, publications, and lobbying. The NPRC spent $119,029 on lobbying, $41,660 on grassroots lobbying and $77,369 on the direct lobbying of legislators. This was an increase of 30% over the previous year.
Tax Status: 501(c)(3)
Board of Directors or Trustees: Amalia Betanzos, Joan Figueroa (Puerto Rican Legal Defense and Education Fund), Maria Elena Girone (Puerto Rican Family Inst.), Hon. Efrain Gonzalez (NY State Sen.), Eric Munoz, M.D., Jose Gonzalez (Inter American University of Puerto Rico), Migdalia Rivera (Latino Inst.), Hipolito Roldan (Hispanic Housing Development), Damaso Seda, Christine Torres-Matrullo, Ph.D., Edwin Vargas, Jr. (Hartford Fed. of Teachers), Tonio Burgos, Hon. Fernando Ferrer (Pres., Borough of the Bronx), Rep. Louis Gutierrez (D-IL), Bishop Roberto Gonzalez (Archdiocese of Boston), Luis Angel Irene (Circulo de Puerto Rico), Rep. Jose Serrano (D-NY), Ivette Torres (Consumers Union), Magdalena Torres, Lydia Valencia (Congreso Boricua de NJ), Rep. Nydia Velasquez (D-NY), Jose Villamil, Olga Wagenheim.
Periodicals: Newsletter.
Other Information: The Coalition received $1,135,012, or 90% of revenue, from gifts and grants awarded by foundations, businesses, and individuals. (These grants included $340,000 from the Ford Foundation.) $65,443, or 5%, from government grants. $20,965, or 2%, from membership dues. $19,990, or 2%, from interest on savings and temporary cash investments. $17,026 net, or 1%, from special fund-raising events.

National Puerto Rican Forum

31 E. 32nd St., 4th Floor
New York, NY 10016
USA

Phone: (212) 685-2311
Fax: (212) 689-5034

Contact Person: Hector E. Velasquez, President.   **Officers or Principals:** Hector E. Velasquez, President ($89,158); Betzaida Ferrer, Center Manager ($44,778); Amanda P. Caballers, Center Manager ($44,651); Aixa Beauchamp, Chairperson; Dr. Sara E. Melendez, Pete Spinella, Vice Chairs; Eric Soto, Treasurer/Secretary.
Mission or Interest: Educational and social services for Puerto Rican Americans. Programs include English language skills, job preparation, dropout prevention, adult education, and technical assistance for community groups.
Accomplishments: In the fiscal year ending June 1994 the Forum spent $1,362,995 on its programs.
Net Revenue: FY ending 6/94 $1,709,344 ($1,420,550, or 83%, from government grants)
Net Expenses: $1,752,423 78%/19%/3% **Net Assets:** (-$1,177,690) **Citations:** 3:222
Tax Status: 501(c)(3)
Board of Directors or Trustees: Emilio Bermiss (NY City Mission Society), Mary Ann Brigantti-Hughes (Asst. Attorney General, NY), Angel Louis Cuevas (Agency for Child Development, Human Resources Administration, NY), Jean Hodge (Director, Station Services, WCBS-TV), Gloria Rodriguez (Pres., MAPA Development Resources), Mario Torres (V.P., Community Affairs and Affirmative Action, Battery Park City Authority).
Other Information: The Forum received $1,420,550, or 83% of revenue, from government grants. $197,712, or 12%, from gifts and grants awarded by foundations, businesses, and individuals. $89,012, or 5%, from special fund-raising events. The remaining revenue came from other miscellaneous sources.

National Rainbow Coalition

1700 K St., N.W., Suite 800
Washington, DC 20006
USA

Phone: (202) 728-1180
Fax: (202) 728-1192
E-Mail: jackson@rainbow.org
Web-Page: http://www.rainbow.org/rainbow

Contact Person: Rev. Jesse Jackson, Sr., President.
Officers or Principals: Angela Jordan Davis, Chair; Hon. Salima Siler Marriott, Secretary; Francisco L. Borges, Treasurer.
Mission or Interest: Works to unite Americans of all races and build consensus in civil rights, economic justice, environmental justice, labor policy, health care, and other areas of public life. Advocates statehood for the District of Columbia.
Accomplishments: 250,000 members and 20 church affiliates.
Products or Services: "JAX-FAX" weekly update.
Tax Status: For-profit membership organization.
Board of Directors or Trustees: Dr. Marry Frances Berry (U.S. Commission on Civil Rights), Emma Chappell (Pres., United Bank of Philadelphia), Rep. Cleo Fields (D-LA), Willie Gary, Rev. H. Beecher Hicks, Patricia Ireland (Pres., NOW), Rep. Charles Rangel (D-NY), Ron Richardson (Intl. V.P., Hotel and Restaurant Employees Union), Dennis Rivera (Pres., National Health and Human Service Employees Union), William Shack (National Association of Minority Auto Dealers), Rep. Louis Stokes (D-OH), Pierre Sutton (Pres., National Association of Black Owned Broadcasters), Rep. Nydia Velasquez (D-NY), Daisy Wood (Pres., National Pan-Hellenic Council), James Zogby (Pres., Arab American Institute).
Periodicals: *Rainbow Hope* (newsletter).
Other Information: Founded in 1984 by the Rev. Jesse Jackson after his Presidential campaign.

National Rural Letter Carriers' Association (NRLCA)

1630 Duke St., 4th Floor
Alexandria, VA 22314
USA

Phone: (703) 684-5545
Fax: (703) 548-8735

Contact Person: Sharon Delarme, Chairman.
Officers or Principals: William R. Brown, President ($119,698); Leo J. Root, Director, Labor Relations ($114,018); Scottie B. Hicks, Vice President ($111,366); Roger W. Moreland, Secretary/Treasurer ($108,045).
Mission or Interest: Labor union representing approximately 85,000 letter carriers.
Net Revenue: 1994 $8,515,076 **Net Expenses:** $8,184,261 **Net Assets:** $2,707,937
Products or Services: Labor organizing and representation, annual convention, political action committee.
Tax Status: 501(c)(5)
Board of Directors or Trustees: Vilas Smith, Lawrence Adams, Augustus Baffa.
Periodicals: *National Rural Letter Carrier* (bimonthly newsletter).
Other Information: The Association received $4,041,270, or 47% of gross revenue, from membership dues. $3,751,928, or 44%, from program services, including insurance premiums from union members, and annual convention dues. $673,405, or 8%, from administrative fees. The remaining revenue came from interest on savings and temporary cash investments, advertising, and other miscellaneous sources.

National Security News Service (NSNS)

1730 Rhode Island Ave., Suite 1102
Washington, DC 20036
USA

Phone: (202) 466-4310

Contact Person: Wayne T. Jacquith, Founder.
Mission or Interest: News organization that monitors the military and national security apparatus. The Winston Foundation for World Peace (a financial contributor) refers to the Service as a "muckraking enterprise."
Accomplishments: The NSNS broke the story that Adm. Jeremy Michael Boorda was wearing commendation medals that he had not earned. When the story spread, the Admiral committed suicide, citing his desire to spare the Navy any embarrassment.
Tax Status: 501(c)(3)
Other Information: The Service was founded during the military build-up that preceded the Persian Gulf war. Founder Wayne Jacquith was previously the founding executive director of Physicians for Social Responsibility. In 1993 the Service received $20,000 from the J. Roderick MacArthur Foundation, and $10,000 from the Town Creek Foundation. In 1994, $17,000 from the Dear Creek Foundation, $10,000 from the Winston Foundation, and $5,000 from the Peace Development Fund.

National Training and Information Center (NTIC)

810 N. Milwaukee Ave.
Chicago, IL 60622   **Phone:**   (312) 243-3035
USA

Contact Person: Gale Cinotta, President.   **Officers or Principals:** Gale Cinotta, President ($70,502); Sheldon Trapp, Staff Director ($67,328), Ann-Marie Douglas, Administrator ($50,677); Bruce Gottschall, Secretary/Treasurer.
Mission or Interest: "Established in 1972 to provide community groups with the tools they need to effect community change. NTIC accomplishes this purpose through training, research, technical assistance, and consulting programs. The primary areas that these programs are operated for include housing and community reinvestment, anti-crime and drug prevention, utilities cost reduction, and leadership development."
Accomplishments: In 1994 NTIC spent $722,367 on its programs. The largest program, with expenditures of $323,178, was the Housing and Reinvestment Program which "provides leadership and organizational development expertise to low and moderate income groups engaged in neighborhood revitalization and activities aimed to eliminate redlining." $252,937 was spent on anti-crime and drug prevention programs. $146,252 was spent providing technical assistance to local nonprofit organizations.
Net Revenue: 1994 $1,206,417 ($262,874, or 21%, from government grants)
Net Expenses: $853,636 85%/15%/0% **Net Assets:** $1,333,283 **Citations:** 19:173
Products or Services: Community organization, leadership training and technical assistance.
Tax Status: 501(c)(3)
Board of Directors or Trustees: Paul Battle, Dr. Calvin Bradford, Rev. Roger Coughlin, Marilyn Evans, Joseph Fagan, John McKnight.
Other Information: The Center received $943,543, or 76% of revenue, from gifts and grants awarded by foundations, businesses, and individuals. (These grants included $12,000 from the Florence and John Schumann Foundation, and $3,500 from the New Prospect Foundation. In 1993, $270,000 from the Charles Stewart Mott Foundation.) $262,874, or 21%, from government grants. $16,672, or 1% from interest on savings and temporary cash investments. The remaining revenue came from training programs, consulting fees, sale of publications, rental income, and other miscellaneous sources.

National Wildlife Action (NWA)

1400 16th St., N.W.
Washington, DC 20036   **Phone:**   (202) 797-6817
USA

Contact Person: William W. Howard, Jr., Chairman.
Officers or Principals: Larry Schweiger, Secretary ($0); David H. Pardoe, Treasurer ($0).
Mission or Interest: Lobbying affiliate of the National Wildlife Federation.
Accomplishments: In the fiscal year ending August 1994, the organization spent $278,892 on its activities. The largest project, with expenditures of $116,425, lobbied in support of the North American Free Trade Agreement (NAFTA), which "provided an opportunity of rare magnitude for the conservation and environmental community to influence environmental decision making from Mexico to Canada." The organization hired former EPA Administrator, William K. Reilly, to lobby on behalf of NAFTA. $52,050, was spent to research and lobbying against various 'takings' and property rights ballot initiatives. These projects investigated how the public felt about regulatory measures which deprived land owners of the full use of their land, and legislation and ballot initiatives which would compensate land owners for this 'taking' of their property. "As private property rights is a very significant issue in American culture and a very emotional issue for many people, the NWA Board agreed to fund a contract to review polling and focus group research to better define the issue as it exists in the public mind and assist us to more effectively define and articulate our position on this issue." The results of the report were used to combat takings legislation. The Takings Project also focused on this issue. "What is at stake here is the ability of state and federal governments to enforce environmental regulations without having to compensate the violators." $35,000 was spent on the Center for Environmental Citizenship, a youth program for "student environmentalists." $29,950 was spent on Public Land Reform which sought to educate the public on the need for reforming the way public land is used, especially in regards to grazing on lands administered by the U.S. Forest Service and Bureau of Land Management.
Net Revenue: FY ending 8/94 $194,629 **Net Expenses:** $279,848 99%/1%/0% **Net Assets:** $184,284
Products or Services: Lobbying, polling, publications, and brochures.
Tax Status: 501(c)(4)

Board of Directors or Trustees: Christine Egan, Larry Green, Luke Danielson, Bill Eichbaum, Tom Dougherty.
Other Information: National Wildlife Action is affiliated with the 501(c)(3) National Wildlife Federation, and the 501(c)(3) National Wildlife Federation Endowment. The three affiliates had combined net revenues of $94,898,041, net expenses of $90,560,600, and net assets of $64,353,708. National Wildlife Action received $184,813, or 95% of revenue, from direct and indirect public support in the form of gifts and grants awarded by affiliates, foundations, businesses, and individuals. $9,465, or 5%, from interest on savings and temporary cash investments. The remaining revenue came from other miscellaneous sources.

National Wildlife Federation (NWF)

1400 16th St., N.W.
Washington, DC 20036   **Phone:** (202) 797-6800
USA

Contact Person: Jay D. Hair, President. **Officers or Principals:** Jay D. Hair, President ($323,602); William Howard, Executive Vice President ($193,466); Joel T. Thomas, Secretary ($148,180); Alric Clay, Senior Vice President of Constituent Services ($146,286); Francis A. DiCicco, Treasurer ($136,486); Robert Strohm, Vice President of Publications ($131,778); Alan Lamson, Vice President of Promotional Activities ($130,651); John Jensen, Vice President of Development ($117,076); Gene Stout, Chair; Carl Reidel, Gerald Barber, Thomas Warren, Robert Gardiner, Vice Chairmen.
Mission or Interest: Nature education, conservation and environmental advocacy.
Accomplishments: In the fiscal year ending August 1994, the Federation spent $73,235,536 on its programs. The largest program, with expenditures of $29,165,198, was the production of nature education materials which include books, games, records, and cards with nature/conservation themes. $11,224,530 was spent to produce and distribute magazines for the approximately 664,052 associate members. $9,135,779 was spent on the Ranger Rick membership program, which sent monthly *Ranger Rick* magazines to approximately 866,202 children ages 6-12. $3,179,097 was spent on regional resource centers and field staff operations that support NWF affiliates. $2,572,952 was spent on public information programs. $2,582,193 was spent on *Your Big Backyard*, educational magazines that are sent to 457,840 young children. Many other conservation and education programs. The Federation awarded $378,097 in grants to other organizations. The recipients of the largest grants included: Six grants totaling $70,000 for the center for Environmental Citizenship, $60,000 for Clinton Hill's Kids for Saving the Earth, two grants totaling $50,000 for the International Crane Foundation, and $30,000 for National Wildlife Action.
Net Revenue: FY ending 8/94 $84,513,071 ($42,900, or less than 1%, from government grants)
Net Expenses: $85,315,291 86%/5%/5% **Net Assets:** $12,421,334 **Citations:** 657:33
Products or Services: Numerous publications and educational materials, Environmental Publication Awards, Campership Scholarship Awards (to send disadvantaged urban youths to summer nature camp), and lobbying. The Federation spent $617,073 on lobbying, $70,417 on grassroots lobbying, and $546,656 on the direct lobbying of legislators. This was a 22% decrease from the year before.
Tax Status: 501(c)(3)
Board of Directors or Trustees: Jean Richardson, John Campanelli, John Lentz, James Carroll, Daryl Durham, Becky Scheibelhut, John Eichinger, Thomas Martine, Raymond Linder, Brian Pritchett, James Hemming, Paula Del Giudice, Jolyn Reeves.
Periodicals: *National Wildlife Magazine* (bimonthly), *International Wildlife Magazine* (bimonthly), *Ranger Rick* (monthly), *Your Big Backyard*.
Other Information: The Federation is affiliated with the 501(c)(3) National Wildlife Federation Endowment, and the 501(c)(4) National Wildlife Action. The three affiliates had combined net revenues of $94,898,041, net expenses of $90,560,600, and net assets of $64,353,708. The Federation received $29,052,910, or 34% of revenues from membership services. $28,929,216 net, or 34%, from the sale of inventory such as nature education materials. $19,606,022, or 23%, from direct and indirect public support in the form of gifts and grants awarded by foundations, affiliates, businesses, and individuals. (These grants included $4,209,992 from the affiliated National Wildlife Federation Endowment, $712,915 from the Environmental Federation of America, $128,000 from the Joyce Foundation, $9,000 from the Jessie Smith Noyes Foundation, $7,500 from the Bullitt Foundation, $7,500 from the American Conservation Association, $5,092 from the Environmental Federation of California.) $3,568,472, or 4%, from royalties. $1,153,370, or 1%, from registration fees for camps and summits. $809,662, or 1%, from dividends and interest from securities. The remaining revenue came from rental income, capital gains on the sale of securities, mailing list rentals, government grants, interest on savings and temporary cash investments, and other miscellaneous sources. Revenue was reduced by a loss of $901,617 on an investment.

National Wildlife Federation Endowment (NWF)

1400 16th St., N.W.
Washington, DC 20036   **Phone:** (202) 797-6800
USA

Contact Person: Susan Nickelson, Assistant Treasurer.
Officers or Principals: Dean L. Buntrock, Chair ($0); T. Halter Cunningham, Vice Chairman ($0); Eileen M. Johnson, Assistant Secretary ($0); Joel T. Thomas, Secretary; Francis A. Dicicco, Treasurer; John W. Jensen, Assistant Secretary. (Thomas, Dicicco, and Jensen are compensated by the National Wildlife Federation.)
Mission or Interest: "To provide long-term financial stability to the National Wildlife Federation."
Accomplishments: In the fiscal year ending August 1994, the Endowment spent $553,216 on its programs. The Endowment recieved $4,643,297 from the National Wildlife Federation, and then contributed $4,209,992 back to the Federation.

Net Revenue: FY ending 8/94 $10,190,341 **Net Expenses:** $4,965,461 11%/4%/0% **Net Assets:** $51,748,090
Tax Status: 501(c)(3)
Board of Directors or Trustees: Robert Gardiner (Maine Public Broadcasting Corp.), John Rainey.
Other Information: The Endowment is affiliated with the 501(c)(3) National Wildlife Federation, and the 501(c)(4) National Wildlife Action. The three affiliates had combined net revenues of $94,898,041, net expenses of $90,560,600, and net assets of $64,353,708. The Endowment also holds 50% ownership in a real estate company, Square 181, in Washington, DC. The Endowment received $4,750,516, or 47% of revenue, from direct and indirect public support in the form of gifts and grants awarded by affiliates, foundations, businesses, and individuals. (These grants included $4,643,297 from the affiliated National Wildlife Federation Endowment.) $1,986,585, or 19%, from dividends and interest from securities. $1,770,086 net, or 17%, from capital gains on the sale of securities. $1,666,184 net, or 16%, from rental income. The remaining revenue came from the sale of assets, and other miscellaneous sources. The Endowment's assets are held primarily in savings and temporary cash investments, 33% of total assets, securities, 29%, and land, buildings and equipment, 19%.

National Women's Law Center
11 Dupont Circle, N.W., Suite 800
Washington, DC 20036   **Phone:** (202) 588-5180
USA

Contact Person: Nancy Duff Campbell, Co-President.
Officers or Principals: Marcia Greenberger, Co-President ($93,810); Nancy Duff Campbell, Co-President ($93,810); Ellen Vargyas, Senior Counsel ($81,090); Ann Kolker, Director of Public Policy; Brooksley Born, Chair.
Mission or Interest: Litigation and advocacy on behalf of equality, education and employment, abortion rights, child and dependent care rights, the right of impoverished women to "secure equity."
Accomplishments: In the fiscal year ending June 1993, the Center spent $1,285,961 on its programs. The largest program, with expenditures of $368,844, was litigation, research, and technical assistance on behalf of general equal rights. $269,023 was spent on education and employment rights. $264,995 on abortion rights. $237,244 on "women and poverty" litigation and activities. $145,855 for child and dependent care rights and needs. Also operates the Women in Prison Project.
Net Revenue: FY ending 6/93 $1,575,220 ($24,999, or 2%, from government grants)
Net Expenses: $1,474,620 87%/7%/6% **Net Assets:** $584,804 **Citations:** 0:255
Products or Services: A Vision Beyond Survival: A Resource Guide for Incarcerated Women, other publications. Litigation, research, technical assistance and lobbying. The center spent $24,453 on lobbying, $1,359 on grassroots lobbying, and $23,094 on the direct lobbying of legislators. This was down 71% from the previous year.
Tax Status: 501(c)(3)
Board of Directors or Trustees: Elizabeth Coleman, Donna Varona, Elaine Jones, Judith Maynes, Gerald McEntee (AFSCME), Marilyn Monahan, Aida Waserstein, Iraline Barnes, Marna Tucker, Antonia Hernandez, Richard Beattie, Anita Hill.
Other Information: The Center is a member of the Washington Council of Agencies, National Society of Fundraising Executives, Women's Bar Association, Leadership Conference on Civil Rights, American Bar Association, and the American Society of Association Executives. The Center received $1,544,430, or 94% of gross revenue, from direct and indirect public support in the form of gifts and grants awarded by foundations, businesses, affiliates, and individuals. (These grants included $166,000 from the John Merck Fund, $60,000 from the Robert Sterling Clark Foundation, $25,000 from the General Service Foundation, and funding from the Jessie Smith Noyes Foundation. In 1994 these included $100,000 from the Rosenberg Foundation.) $56,713, or 4%, from interest on savings and temporary cash investments. $24,999, or 2%, from government grants. The remaining revenue came from rental income and other miscellaneous sources. The Center lost $75,229 on its annual dinner. This loss does not include the $209,451 in gifts that were received at this dinner, those are included under public support.

National Women's Mailing List
(see the Women's Information Exchange)

National Women's Political Caucus
1211 Connecticut Ave., N.W., Suite 425
Washington, DC 20036   **Phone:** (202) 785-1100
USA

Contact Person: Harriett Woods, President.
Officers or Principals: Harriett Woods, President ($41,989); Anita Perez Ferguson, Jean Cracium, Deanne Bonner, Linda Tangren, Pat Deal, Muriel Inabet, Vice Presidents ($0); Betty Lou Harmon, Treasurer; Linda Van Scoyoc, Secretary; Jane Macon, Counsel.
Mission or Interest: "Promotion of the election and appointment of women to public office throughout the United States through support of a membership organization with a network of projects."
Accomplishments: In 1994 the organization spent $257,693 on its programs.
Net Revenue: 1994 $627,134 **Net Expenses:** $748,268 34%/44%/22% **Net Assets:** $87,985 **Citations:** 2:231
Tax Status: 501(c)(4)
Board of Directors or Trustees: Fran Coleman, Jennifer Davis, Wesley Shipton-Hiatt, Sarah Lichtenstein, Peggy Shepard, Hazel Thomas, Nancy Zamora, Sharon Macha.
Other Information: The Caucus received $367,196, or 58% of revenue, from gifts and grants awarded by foundations, businesses, and individuals. (These grants included $5,000 from the Ms. Foundation for Women.) $212,452, or 34%, from membership dues. $27,601, or 4%, from list rentals. $14,672, or 2%, from meeting fees. $5,765, or 1%, from honoraria. The remaining revenue came from the sale of merchandise and interest on savings and temporary cash investments.

National Women's Political Caucus Leadership Development, Education and Research Fund

1211 Connecticut Ave., N.W., Suite 425
Washington, DC 20036   **Phone:**   (202) 785-1100
USA

Contact Person: Harriett Woods, President.
Officers or Principals: Harriett Woods, President ($14,369); Anita Perez Ferguson, Jean Cracium, Deane Bonner, Linda Tangren, Jeanne Fox, Muriel Inabnet, Vice Presidents ($0); Betty Lou Harmon, Treasurer; Lynda Van Scoyoc, Secretary.
Mission or Interest: "Provide leadership development workshops and training materials for women to develop their effectiveness as leaders in areas of public policy."
Accomplishments: In 1993 the Fund spent $171,943 on its programs.
Net Revenue: 1993 $332,893 **Net Expenses:** $326,032 53%/39%/9% **Net Assets:** $38,082 **Citations:** 2:234
Tax Status: 501(c)(3)
Board of Directors or Trustees: Fran Coleman, Wesley Shipton Hiatt, Peggy Shepard, Hazel Thomas, Nancy Zamora, Jennifer Davis, Sharon Macha.
Other Information: Affiliated with the 501(c)(4) National Women's Political Caucus at the same address. The Fund received $321,502, or 97% of revenue, from gifts and grants awarded by foundations, businesses, and individuals. $6,772, or 2%, from the sale of publications and educational materials. $4,698, or 1%, from interest on savings and temporary cash investments.

Native American Rights Fund (NARF)

1506 Broadway
Boulder, CO 80302   **Phone:**   (303) 447-8760
USA

Contact Person: John Echohawk, Executive Director.   **Officers or Principals:** Lare Aschenbrenner, Attorney ($135,874); John Echohawk, Executive Director ($117,663); Yvonne Knight, Litigation Management ($113,063); Kim Gottschalk, Litigation Management ($105,597); Don Miller, Attorney ($104,215); Walter Echo-Hawk, Attorney ($101,726); Clela Rorex, Treasurer; Ray Ramirez, Secretary; Marilyn Pourier, Development Director; Melody McCoy, Litigation Management.
Mission or Interest: Litigation and educational services "securing the rights of Indian clients."
Accomplishments: In the fiscal year ending September 1994, the Fund spent $4,670,161 on its programs; $4,341,324 on litigation and clients services (average case load of 200 clients) and $328,837 on the National Indian Law Library. The Fund collected $376,702 in legal fees and $35,000 in case settlements. NARF secured funding for future periods; by the end of the fiscal year it had received $1,924,083 in revenue designated for future periods. This included funds from the Rockefeller Foundation,$40,625; the John D. And Catherine T. MacArthur Foundation, $15,752; the Ford Foundation, $1,000,000; Carnegie Corporation, $112,028; U.S. Department of Health and Human Services, $278,642; U.S. Legal Services Corporation, $27,166.
Net Revenue: FY ending 9/94 $5,597,059 ($2,101,464, or 38%, from government grants)
Net Expenses: $6,208,683 75%/13%/11% **Net Assets:** $2,205,852 **Citations:** 58:132
Products or Services: Litigation, publications, research, and lobbying. NARF spent $84,949 on lobbying, $15,519 on grassroots lobbying and $69,430 on the direct lobbying of legislators. This was down 28% from $117,322 the previous year.
Tax Status: 501(c)(3)
Other Information: The Fund received $2,860,680, or 51% of revenue, from direct and indirect public support in the form of gifts and grants from foundations, companies, affiliates and individuals. (These grants included $1,200,000 over two years from the Ford Foundation, $30,000 from the General Service Foundation, $2,000 from the Liberty Hill Foundation, $500 from the Aaron and Martha Schecter Foundation, and $200 from the Compton Foundation.) $2,101,464, or 38%, from government grants. $411,702, or 7%, from legal fees and case settlements. $57,155 net, or 1%, from the sale of assets other than inventory. $51,951, or 1%, from interest on savings and temporary cash investments. $23,470 from mailing list rentals. The remaining revenue came from fund-raising events, publications, honoraria, and other miscellaneous sources. In addition to staff attorneys, they retained outside legal counsel. David Dornbusch, was compensated with $94,955; Nez Perce Tribe, $92,698; and Carl Ullman, $70,333. NARF retained two firms for consultation on hydro engineering matters, Chinook N.W. Inc., $80,352, and Entrix Inc., $75,192.

Natural Resources Defense Council (NRDC)

40 W. 20th St.
New York, NY 10011   **Phone:**   (212) 727-2700
USA   **Fax:**   (212) 727-1773

Contact Person: John H. Adams, Executive Director.
Officers or Principals: John H. Adams, Executive Director ($77,799); Frances Beinecke, Deputy Director ($28,204); Patricia Sullivan, Deputy Director; Judy Keefer, Financial Director; Frederick A. O. Schwartz, Chairman; Burks Lapham, Michael McIntosh, Adam Albright, Vice Chair; Henry R. Breck, Treasurer; Robert F. Kennedy, Jr., Attorney.
Mission or Interest: Litigation, research, education, and lobbying activities to protect the environment.
Accomplishments: NRDC's report "Intolerable Risk: Pesticides in Our Children's Food" created the 'Alar scare.' In the fiscal year ending June 1993, the Council spent $3,213,355 on its programs. The largest project, with expenditures of $1,203,542, was litigation. This litigation resulted in court-awarded attorney's fees of $342,112. $1,052,897 was spent on "scientific support and research of environmental issues and litigation." $684,279 for public education. $22,290 was spent on an intern program.

Net Revenue: FY ending 6/95 $3,127,295   **Net Expenses:** $4,188,960   77%/11%/13%   **Net Assets:** $10,755,439
Citations: 1,712:18
Products or Services: Litigation, educational materials, and lobbying. In the fiscal year ending June 1993, the Council spent $14,495 on lobbying, $467 on grassroots lobbying, and $14,028 on the direct lobbying of legislators. The amount spent on lobbying has been decreasing in recent years, down 64% from the previous year, down 75% from two years prior, and down 92% from $187,222 three years prior.
Tax Status: 501(c)(3)
Board of Directors or Trustees: Dr. Dean Abrahamson (Humphrey Inst., Univ. of MN), Richard Ayres, Dr. Eula Bingham (College of Medicine, Univ. of Cincinnati), Richard Cotton (Exec. V.P. & General Counsel, NBC), Robert Denham (Chair & CEO, Salomon), John Echohawk (Native American Rights Fund), Robert Fisher (Gap, Inc.), David Hahn-Baker, Francis Hatch, Jr. (Conservation Law Foundation), Alan Horn (Castle Rock Entertainment), Hamilton Kean (Natl. Westminster Bank), Charles Koob, Jonathan Larsen (*Village Voice*), Peter Morton (Hard Rock Cafe), Carol Noyes, John Oakes, Adebayo Ogunlesi (Dir., First Boston Corp.), Franklin Parker (Trust for Public Lands), Robert Redford (actor), Nathaniel Reed, Cruz Reynoso, John Robinson, Laurance Rockefeller, John Sheehan (United Steelworkers of America), James Gustave Speth, James Taylor, Frederick Terry, Jr., Thomas Troyer, Jacqueline Weld, Phyliss Wyeth.
Periodicals: *Amicus Journal* (quarterly).   **Internships:** Yes.
Other Information: The Council hired the Falls Church, Va firm of Craver, Matthews, Smith & Co., for fundraising consultation, and the Santa Fe, NM based consultant, Stephen Tukel, for public education. The firms were payed $36,999 and $31,500 respectively. In the fiscal year ending June 1993, the Council received $2,466,268, or 78% of total revenue, from gifts and grants awarded by foundations, businesses, and individuals. (These grants included $180,000 from the Charles Stewart Mott Foundation, $110,000 over two years from the Rockefeller Brothers Fund, $97,898 from the Environmental Federation of America, $75,000 from the Nathan Cummings Foundation, $55,000 from the Wallace Alexander Gerbode Foundation, $25,000 from the Winston Foundation, $20,000 from the Barbra Streisand Foundation, $15,000 from the Town Creek Foundation. In 1994 the Council received grants including $715,000 from the Pew Charitable Trusts, $350,000 from the Joyce Mertz-Gilmore Foundation, $324,445 from the Joyce Foundation, $150,000 from the Bullitt Foundation, $91,945 from the Environmental Federation of America, $75,000 from the American Conservation Association, $36,275 from the Environmental Federation of California, $35,000 from the Wallace Alexander Gerbode Foundation, $30,000 from the Cary Charitable Trust, $30,000 from the Robert Sterling Clark Foundation, $22,850 from the Tides Foundation, $20,000 from the James C. Penney Foundation, $20,000 from the Compton Foundation, $12,500 from the Beldon Fund, $31,000 from the Haymarket People's Fund, $1,500 from the Sierra Club, and $500 from the Aaron and Martha Schecter Foundation.) $342,112, or 11%, from court-awarded attorney's fees. $154,739, or 5%, from dividends and interest from securities. $27,649, or 1%, from interest on savings and temporary cash investments. The remaining revenue came from capital gains on the sale of securities, the sale of products, research contracts, special fundraising events, honoraria, mailing list rentals, royalties, and other miscellaneous sources.

Nature Conservancy
1815 N. Lynn St.
Arlington, VA 22209   **Phone:**   (703) 841-5300
USA   **Web-Page:** http://www.tnc.org

Contact Person: Lawrence Carpman, Communications Director. **Officers or Principals:** John Sawhill, President ($195,802); W. William Weeks, Vice President ($137,729); Niels Crone, Vice President ($123,839); Steven J. McCormick, Vice President ($122,679); Michael J. Coda, Vice President ($121,717); Geoffrey S. Barnard, Vice President ($121,600); Kelvin H. Taketa, Vice President ($116,196); Anita S. Attridge, Vice President ($112,700); Gregory L. Low, Vice President ($112,561); Bradford C. Northrup, Vice President ($111,714); John Cook, Vice President ($111,478); Michael Dennis, Vice President ($111,048); Robert E. Jenkins, Vice President ($108,957); John R. Flicker, Vice President ($108,885); Bruce R. Runnels, Vice President ($107,653); Charles R. Bassett, Vice President ($102,409); Lawrence Carpman, Communications Director ($102,357).
Mission or Interest: Environmental conservation. The protection and restoration of wildlife.
Accomplishments: The Nature Conservancy is the largest conservation organization in terms of assets. In the fiscal year ending June 1994, the Nature Conservancy had net assets of over $932 million, and total assets of over $1 billion. 736 employees and officers were paid over $30,000 each, and 125 firms or individuals were paid over $30,000 each for consulting, fund-raising, legal counsel, and other professional services. During that period the Conservancy spent $185,526,153 on its programs. The largest program, with expenditures of $116,060,153, was conservation and planning for "implementing protection plans and strategies to mitigate, prevent or slow the identified threats and stresses to plants, animals and ecological systems and communities through land and water protection actions." $23,975,000 was spent on stewardship and conservation of areas owned by the conservancy and others. $14,067,000 was spent on training and support to "development of non-governmental conservation partners." $13,946,000 was spent on biological information management. $12,656,000 was spent on communication and outreach for members and the general public. $4,822,000 was spent "implementing conservation programs in cooperation with domestic and international government offices and agencies." The Conservancy awarded $11,073,897 in grants to its partner organizations.
Net Revenue: FY ending 6/94 $306,679,337   ($28,167,119, or 9%, from government grants)
Net Expenses: $229,717,656   81%/8%/11%   **Net Assets:** $932,076,806   **Citations:** 2,272:11
Products or Services: Conservation, publications, contract services, lobbying. The Conservancy spent $793,793 on lobbying, $9,745 on grassroots lobbying and $784,048 on the direct lobbying of legislators. This was up 3% from the previous year, but down 5% from two years prior, and down 19% from three years prior.
Tax Status: 501(c)(3)
Board of Directors or Trustees: Peter Ashton, Carter Bales, David Cole, Ian Cumming, Louisa Duemling, William Dunvant Jr., Daniel Efroymson, Mary Fleming Finlay, David Pierpont Gardner, Wilbur Garrett, I. Lamond Godwin, Arturo Gomez-Pompa, Ralph Gutierrez, John Hanes Jr., Richard Heckert, Kate Ireland, Samuel Johnson, James Kennedy, Barbara Lipscomb, Alfredo Novoa Pena, Wendy Paulson, Leigh Perkins, John Pritzlaff Jr., Winthrop Rockefeller, H. Norman Schwarzkopf, John Seidl, John Sias, Daniel Simberloff, John Whitehead, Edward Wilson, Ward Woods, Gail Walling Yanney.

Periodicals: *Nature Conservancy* (monthly magazine).   **Internships:** Yes.
Other Information: The Nature Conservancy is affiliated with the 501(c)(4) Nature Conservancy Action Fund. The Nature Conservancy received $172,140,133, or 56% of total revenue, from gifts and grants awarded by foundations, businesses, and individuals. (These grants included $4,450,000 from the Pew Charitable Trusts, $1,152,418 from the Environmental Federation of America, $625,000 from the Philip D. Reed Foundation, $508,000 from the Cary Charitable Trust, $125,000 from the Charles Stewart Mott Foundation, $70,000 from the Compton Foundation, $50,000 from the Wallace Alexander Gerbode Foundation, $33,000 from the Wallace Genetic Foundation, $15,000 from the Tides Foundation, $15,000 from the New-Land Foundation, $5,000 from the Crestar Foundation, and $2,000 from the Liberty Hill Foundation.) $69,977,807, or 23%, from the sale of land to federal, state, and local governments for use as parks, recreational areas, and nature preserves. $28,167,119, or 9%, from government grants. (Combined, the Conservancy received $98,144,926 from various governments in grants and for purchased land.) $12,907,305, or 4%, from capital gains on the sale of securities. $8,720,344, or 3%, from fees for activities, such as meetings and lodging, on Conservancy lands. $7,890,637, or 3%, from dividends and interest from securities. $3,803,702, or 1%, from lease and royalty fees, such as grazing fees on Conservancy lands. The remaining revenue came from interest on savings and temporary cash investments, contract fees, rental income, special fund-raising events, the sale of inventory, preserve access fees, and other miscellaneous income. The Conservancy lost $2,244,835 on the sale of lands that were not "ecologically unique". The Nature Conservancy held most of its assets ($628,772,448, or 60%) in lands, buildings, and equipment. $279,649,754, or 27%, was held in stocks and bonds.

Nature Conservancy Action Fund
1815 N. Lynn St.
Arlington, VA 22209   **Phone:**   (703) 841-5300
USA

Contact Person: John Sawhill, President. **Officers or Principals:** M. Dennis, Vice President ($0); C. Baudler, Vice President ($0).
Mission or Interest: Lobbying affiliate of The Nature Conservancy.
Accomplishments: In the Fiscal year ending June 1995, the Action Fund did not spend any money on programs. All expenses incurred, $12,520, were for management and overhead.
Net Revenue: FY ending 6/95 $175,626 **Net Expenses:** $12,520 0%/100%/0% **Net Assets:** $582,588
Tax Status: 501(c)(4)
Other Information: The Action Fund received $154,475, or 88% of revenue, from gifts and grants awarded by foundations, affiliates, businesses, and individuals. $15,029, or 9%, from dividends and interest from securities. $6,122, or 3%, from interest on a note.

Neighbor to Neighbor Education Fund
2601 Mission St., Suite 400
San Francisco, CA 94110
USA

Mission or Interest: Health care reform, support of a 'Single Payer' system.
Other Information: In 1994 the Fund received $5,000 from the Angelina Fund, $4,464 from the Vanguard Public Foundation, $3,250 from the Haymarket People's Fund, $3,225 from the Liberty Hill Foundation, $2,500 from the Peace Development Fund, and $1,000 from the Aaron and Martha Schecter Private Foundation.

NETWORK: A National Catholic Social Justice Lobby
801 Pennsylvania Ave., S.E., Suite 460
Washington, DC 20003   **Phone:**   (202) 547-5556   **E-Mail:** HN5236@HANDSNET.ORG
USA   **Fax:**   (202) 547-5510

Contact Person: Kathy Thornton, RSM, National Coordinator.
Officers or Principals: Mary Elizabeth Clark, SSJ, President ($0); Louise Akers, SC, Vice President ($0); Richelle Friedman, PBVM, Catherine Pinkerton, CSJ, Lobbyists; Regina McKillip, OP, Organizer; Mary Ann Smith, Education Coordinator.
Mission or Interest: "Political lobbying goals are securing just access to economic resources, reordering federal budget priorities and transforming global relationships." According to Education Coordinator Mary Ann Smith, "A number of economic and political forces have contributed to the poverty we see at home and abroad: the Cold War, the Structural Adjustment Programs of the World Bank and IMF, the growth of communications and transportation industries, globalization of the market place, decline of organized labor and rapid population growth. In the midst of all these macro realities, we seem to have lost our sense of the Common Good. There has been little regard for people, especially those who are poor, and the environment."
Accomplishments: Successfully lobbied on behalf of voting rights, civil rights, the Family Leave Medical Act. "Educated and activated over 10,000 citizens on specific pieces of legislation." In 1995 the Network lobbied against Republicans' "unconscionable" budget cuts, against the Istook Amendment which would limit the lobbying by organizations that receive federal funds, against the use of landmines and arms sales, for increased funding and participation in the United Nations, for the International Monetary Fund and World Bank to redistribute wealth from the rich to the poor, and for a higher minimum wage. In 1994 the NETWORK spent $539,565 on its activities.
Net Revenue: 1994 $685,452 **Net Expenses:** $618,265 87%/8%/5% **Net Assets:** $277,107
Products or Services: Lobbying, A Ministry of Justice: A Handbook for Legislative Advocacy, and grassroots organizing.

Tax Status: 501(c)(4) **Annual Report:** Yes. **Employees:** 11
Board of Directors or Trustees: Rosie Castro, Mary Patricia Dewey, OP, Margaret Mary Fitzpatrick, SC, Marie Francios, Maria Gonzalez, Kathleen Hinga, SSJ, Loreta Jordan, Maryann Mason, Dolores Ann Morgan, Lillian Needham, SSJ, Elva Revilla, Kathy Thornton, RSM, Lynda Wright.
Periodicals: *NETWORK Connection* (bimonthly newsletter), and *NETWORKER* (monthly legislative update).
Internships: Yes, assisting in lobbying, organizing, and educational projects.
Other Information: Affiliated with the 501(c)(3) NETWORK Education Program. The two affiliates had combined net revenues of $734,953, net expenses of $661,281, and net assets of $284,212. NETWORK received $356,379, or 52% of revenue, from gifts and grants awarded by foundations, businesses, and individuals. $241,635, or 35%, from membership dues. $41,800, or 6%, from contracted services provided for the Education Program affiliate. $23,000, or 3%, from consultation fees. $11,267, or 2%, from workshop fees. $4,681, or 1%, from dividends and interest from securities. The remaining revenue came from interest on savings and temporary cash investments, and the sale of educational materials.

NETWORK Education Program

801 Pennsylvania Ave., S.E., Suite 460
Washington, DC 20003   **Phone:** (202) 547-5556   **E-Mail:** HN5236@HANDSNET.ORG
USA   **Fax:**   (202) 547-5510

Contact Person: Kathy Thornton, RSM, National Coordinator.   **Officers or Principals:** Rosie Castro, President ($0); Lynda Wright, Vice President ($0); Maria Gonzalez, Secretary ($0); Maryann Mason, Treasurer.
Mission or Interest: Educational affiliate of NETWORK.
Accomplishments: Provided educational services for 9,000 NETWORK members. In 1994 the Program spent $42,966 on its programs.
Net Revenue: 1994 $48,901 **Net Expenses:** $43,016 **Net Assets:** $7,105
Tax Status: 501(c)(3)
Other Information: Affiliated with the 501(c)(4) NETWORK. The two affiliates had combined net revenues of $734,953, net expenses of $661,281, and net assets of $284,212. The Program received $48,901, or 100% of revenue, from gifts and grants awarded by foundations, businesses, and individuals.

Network for Social Justice

209 E. 10th St., Suite 10
New York, NY 10003
USA

Contact Person: Seth Appel, Executive Director.
Officers or Principals: Mike Gordon, Director ($25,170); Seth Appel, Executive Director ($22,865).
Mission or Interest: Education services for youths to promote multi-culturalism.
Accomplishments: In 1994 the Network spent $200,835 on its programs. Services were provided to approximately 6,000 youngsters.
Net Revenue: 1994 $221,954 ($52,300, or 24%, from government grants) **Net Expenses:** $200,835 97%/3%/0%
Net Assets: $62,668
Tax Status: 501(c)(3)
Board of Directors or Trustees: Douglas Simmon, Audrey O'Connel.
Other Information: The Network received $160,954, or 73% of revenue, from fees received for programs. $52,300, or 24%, from government grants. $8,700, or 4%, from membership dues.

Network in Solidarity with the People of Guatemala (NISGUA)

1500 Massachusetts Ave., N.W., Suite 241
Washington, DC 20005   **Phone:** (202) 223-6474   **E-Mail:** nisgua@igc.apc.org
USA   **Fax:**   (202) 223-8221

Contact Person: Lael Parish, National Coordinator.
Officers or Principals: F. Michael Willis, Executive Director ($17,527); George Garry, Former National Organizer ($16,041); Patricia Geier, President ($0); Erinn McIntyre, Vice President; Bob Stix, Treasurer; Nancy Lorence, Secretary.
Mission or Interest: Promote awareness of the civil war in Guatemala, the United State's role in it, and lobbies U.S. foreign policy. Consistently supports the Marxist URNG (Guatemalan National Revolutionary Unity) guerillas in Guatemala, and opposes the United States' support of the military-backed government. Focus on "labor, Mayan, women's and campesino issues."
Accomplishments: Hosted 1992 Nobel Peace Prize Laureate, Rigoberta Menchu for a special speaking engagement attended by 1,200 people. Organized speaking tours of Guatemalan grassroots leaders, who visited 45 communities across the U.S. This tour raised $20,000 for "popular movement groups" in Guatemala. Lobbied for a U.S. foreign policy toward Guatemala that "improves respect for human rights and pressures the military to be accountable to the elected civilian authorities." Awarded $14,884 in grants, mostly to human rights groups in Guatemala, and to unions to assist in labor organizing and human rights programs.
Net Revenue: 1993 $155,190 **Net Expenses:** $141,446 71%/10%/20% **Net Assets:** $34,521
Products or Services: Books, magazines, videos, calendars, publications, conferences, speakers, more. Rapid Response Network that provides fast alerts on human rights issues.

Tax Status: 501(c)(4)   **Annual Report:** No.   **Employees:** 2
Board of Directors or Trustees: Frank Cummings, Craig Eisendrath, Barbara Gault, Joe Gorin, David Loeb, Karen Musalo, Ann Peters, Sebastian Quinac, Sunny Robinson.
Periodicals: *Report on Guatemala* (quarterly magazine), *Solidarity Update* (monthly newsletter).
Internships: Yes.
Other Information: Affiliated with the Fund for Popular Education. The Network received $129,121, or 83% of revenue, from gifts and grants awarded by foundations and individuals. (These grants included $250 from the Vanguard Public Foundation. In 1994 the Network received $30,000 from the Peace Development Fund.) $10,919, or 7%, from the sale and rental of educational materials. $5,939, or 4%, from the Rigoberta Menchu speaking event. $5,085, or 3%, from membership dues. The remaining revenue came from delegation fees, subscriptions, interest on savings and other temporary cash investments.

Network of Educators on the Americas (NECA)

P.O. Box 73038
Washington, DC 20056-3038   **Phone:**   (202) 806-7277   **E-Mail:** necadc@aol.com
USA   **Fax:**   (202) 806-7663

Contact Person: Deborah Menkart, Executive Director.   **Officers or Principals:** Deborah Menkart, Executive Director ($18,354); Lynda Tredway, President ($0); Connie Chubb, Treasurer ($0); M. Catherine Long, Secretary.
Mission or Interest: Promotes and distributes classroom plans and materials to promote the teaching of anti-sexist, anti-racist and multicultural education for grades K-12.
Accomplishments: In the fiscal year ending June 1994, over 100 teachers attended their in-service workshops and seminars. Over 100 teachers used their resource center for research. They distributed over 40,000 catalogs of publications and materials, "Teaching for Change." A grant from the Funding Exchange's Paul Robeson Fund made it possible for NECA to distribute subsidized copies of If the Mango Tree Could Speak: A Documentary about Children and War in Central America, to more than eighty schools.
Net Revenue: FY ending 6/94 $136,087   **Net Expenses:** $158,218 80%/20%/0%   **Net Assets:** $101,926
Products or Services: Offers staff development training in the District of Columbia public schools. Numerous books, teaching plans, videos and other materials. Teaching for Change includes A People's History of the United States by Howard Zinn, Lies My Teacher Told Me: Everything Your American History Textbook got Wrong by James Loewen, and other books on subjects such as: anti-bias and equity, language diversity, Latin America and the Caribbean, parent involvement and more.
Tax Status: 501(c)(3)
Board of Directors or Trustees: Trish Ahern, Patricia Bradford, Margarita Chamorro, Don Clausen, Michael Cohen, Marcy Fink, Evie Frankl, Sue Goodwin, Dollye Virginia McClain, Linda Cole McKay, E. Ethelbert Miller, Marie Moll, Rick Reinhard, Sandra Richardson, Carol Robledo, Sarah Sehnert, Renee Shea, Jenice Leilani View, Sandra Rogers-Green.
Other Information: The Network was supported mostly by the sale of its products. $116,411, or 86% of revenue, came from the sale of products and services. $16,419, or 12%, from gifts and grants awarded by foundations, companies and individuals. $2,278 net, or 2%, from a special fund-raising dance. The remaining revenue came from interest on savings and temporary cash investments.

Networking for Democracy

3411 W. Diversey, Suite 1
Chicago, IL 60647   **Phone:**   (312) 384-8827
USA

Contact Person: Carl Davidson, President.
Officers or Principals: Ivan Handler, Vice President ($0); Alynne Romo, Secretary ($0).
Mission or Interest: "Provides public education as well as donations to tax exempt organizations" to provide for wider participation in public policy.
Accomplishments: In 1993 the organization spent $42,046 on its programs, including $22,150 in grants for other organizations.
Net Revenue: 1993 $36,513   **Net Expenses:** $42,046   **Net Assets:** $1,459
Tax Status: 501(c)(3)
Other Information: The organization received $36,513, or 100% of revenue, from gifts and grants awarded by foundations, businesses, and individuals.

New Age Patriot

P.O. Box 419
Dearborn Heights, MI 48127   **Phone:**   (313) 563-3192   **E-Mail:** bwcain@aol.com
USA

Contact Person: Bruce Cain.
Mission or Interest: Magazine of drug legalization (and re-legalization), environmental and social reform.
Accomplishments: Organizer and participant in "The 4th Annual International Drug Policy Day" held in April 1995. The activities took place at 30 sites around the world. *New Age Patriot* was represented at the Ann Arbor, MI site, known as the "Hash Bash."
Tax Status: For profit.
Periodicals: *New Age Patriot* (quarterly magazine).

New Directions for News

School of Journalism
University of Missouri
Columbia, MO 65203
USA

Phone: (573) 882-1110   **E-Mail:** jourjgw@muccmail.missouri.edu
Fax: (573) 884-4735

Contact Person: Jean Gaddy Wilson
Mission or Interest: "New Directions for News seeks to become America's most important journalistic think tank, fostering innovation in the delivery of news and information in the service of a democratic society. It serves by: Bringing together innovative thinkers in news and related fields. Employing creativity, technology and research to develop journalism and its future. Acting as a nonprofit clearinghouse for new ideas and practical solutions. Providing the news industry a catalyst for change in an increasingly diverse society."
Tax Status: 501(c)(3)   **Employees:** 6 full-time, 4 part-time.
Board of Directors or Trustees: Sara Bentley (*Statesman-Journal*), Frank Daniels, III, Robert Danzig (Hearst Corp.), Frank Denton (*Wisconsin State Journal*), Colleen Dishon, William Hillard, Robert Ingle (Knight-Ridder New Media Center), Alejandro Junco de la Vega (*El Norte*), Karen Jurgonson (*USA Today*), Dorothy Jurney, David Lipman (Pulitzer Publishing Co.), Monica Lozano (*La Opinion*), R. Dean Mills (School of Journalism, Univ. of MO, Columbia), William Morris, III (Morris Communications Corp.), Ted Nail (*The Daily News*), Steven Newhouse (*The Jersey Journal*), Tom O'Donnell (Sun-Sentinel Co.), Kevin Peterson (*Calgary Herald*), Peter Prichard, John Seigenthaler (Freedom Forum First Amendment Center), James Shelledy (*Salt Lake Tribune*), Esther Thorson (School of Journalism, Univ. of MO, Columbia), William Woeslendiek (Annenberg School of Communication, USC), David Zeeck (*The News Tribune*).

New Environment Association / New Environment Institute

270 Fenway Dr.
Syracuse, NY 13224
USA

Phone: (315) 446-8009   **E-Mail:** hs38@mailbox.syr.edu

Contact Person: Harry Schwarzlander.
Mission or Interest: "The Association is an affiliation of people interested in learning and cooperating to create a sane, humane, ecological future. It promotes exploration of how to reorganize society so that its persistent problems will be resolved, and participatory projects which can demonstrate their value and practical utility. Ultimate goal is new communities which are humanly and environmentally sound." Although global in focus, its activities center around Syracuse.
Accomplishments: "Initiation and operation of two cooperative gardens; operation of a food buying club and initiation of several more; running a rototilling and lawn care service; initiating neighborhood recycling programs; running an internship program, construction of a solar food dehydrator, conducting a large number of workshops, study groups, and retreats...The Association has established its own library, has established a land trust, and incorporated its educational and service arm, the New Environment Institute."
Tax Status: 501(c)(3) (New Environment Institute)   **Annual Report:** No.   **Employees:** All volunteer.
Periodicals: *New Environment Bulletin* (monthly newsletter).
Internships: No.

New-Land Foundation

1114 Avenue of the Americas
New York, NY 10036-7798
USA

Phone: (212) 479-6086

Contact Person: Robert Wolf, President.   **Officers or Principals:** Renee Schwartz, Secretary/Treasurer ($0); Constance Harvey, Vice President ($0); Hal Harvey, Vice President ($0).
Mission or Interest: Grant-making private foundation that awards money to, among other things, environmental and civil rights groups.
Accomplishments: In 1994 the Foundation awarded $1,541,192 in grants. The recipients of the largest grants included: ten grants totaling $126,784 for the Sigmund Freud Museum, $125,000 for the Alaska Conservation Foundation, two grants totaling $50,000 for the Anna Freud Center, two grants totaling $45,000 for the NAACP Legal Defense and Education Fund, $40,000 for the Institute for Policy Studies, $35,000 for Green Seal, two grants totaling $30,000 for the Sierra Club Legal Defense Fund, $30,000 for the Center for Reproductive Law and Policy, and $28,000 for American Wildlands. Other recipients included the ACLU Foundation, Alliance for Justice, Center for Constitutional Rights, Choice in Dying, Council for a Livable World, Equal Employment Council, Environmental Defense Fund, Federation of American Scientists, Institute for Defense and Disarmament, League of Conservation Voters Educational Fund, Parliamentarians for Global Action, Planned Parenthood of America, NARAL Foundation, Nature Conservancy, Ploughshares Fund, Union of Concerned Scientists, and others.
Net Revenue: 1994 $1,751,016   **Net Expenses:** $1,954,695   **Net Assets:** $21,491,022
Tax Status: 501(c)(3)
Board of Directors or Trustees: Anna Frank Loeb, Joan Harvey, Al Solnit, Joseph Harvey.
Other Information: The New-Land Foundation received $816,153, or 47% of revenue, from capital gains on the sale of securities. $642,929, or 37%, from dividends and interest from securities. $290,824, or 17%, from a bequest from the estate of Joseph Buttinger. The remaining revenue came from other miscellaneous sources. The Foundation held most of its assets, $13,528,136 or 63%, in corporate stock.

New Prospect / *The American Prospect: A Journal for the Liberal Imagination*
6 University Rd.
Cambridge, MA 02138   **Phone:** (617) 547-2850   **E-Mail:** tap@epn.org
USA   **Web-Page:** http://epn.org/prospect.html

Contact Person: Jonathan Cohn, Executive Editor.   **Officers or Principals:** Robert Kuttner, Paul Starr, Editors; Hugh A. Westbrook, Chairman; Deborah Stone, Senior Editor.
Mission or Interest: Journal founded in 1989 by columnist Robert Kuttner, Princeton professor and Pulitzer prize winner Paul Starr, and Harvard professor Robert B. Reich, President Clinton's Secretary of Labor. Dedicated to "the rehabilitation of practical idealism and positive liberal thought."
Accomplishments: Circulation of 13,000. Read by President Clinton, who praised an *American Prospect* article in an interview that appeared in *Rolling Stone*. Winner of the 1994 Alternate Press Award for General Excellence (for publications with circulation under 15,000). Recent authors included John Kenneth Galbraith, Kathleen Sullivan, Lester Thurow (MIT), Pulitzer prize winning author J. Anthony Lukas, Robert Putnam, Randall Kennedy, Stanley Greenberg (President Clinton's pollster), and columnist E. J. Dionne. The average *American Prospect* reader is male, 52 years old, has a graduate degree, and an income of $106,233.
Tax Status: 501(c)(3)
Board of Directors or Trustees: Prof. Alan Blinder (Princeton), Prof. Alan Brinkley (CUNY), Prof. Walter Dellinger (Duke Law School), Jeff Faux (Economic Policy Institute), Prof. Arlie Hochschild (UC, Berkeley), Stephen Holmes (Univ. of Chicago), Prof. Christopher Jencks (Northwestern Univ.), Prof. Sheila Kamerman (Columbia Univ.), Prof. Steven Kelman (Kennedy School), Alice Munnell (Federal Reserve Bank of Boston), Karen Paget, Prof. Cass Sunstein (Univ. of Chicago), Lester Thurow (MIT), Prof. William Julius Wilson (Univ. of Chicago), Shoshana Zuboff (Harvard Business School). Board of Sponsors includes: Kenneth Arrow (1972 Nobel Laureate, Economics), Daniel Bell (author, Cultural Contradictions of Capitalism), Kenneth Clark (CUNY), Marian Wright Edelman (Children's Defense Fund), John Kenneth Galbraith, Sidney Harman (former Under Secretary of Commerce), Albert Hirschman, Prof. Charles Lindblom (Yale Univ.), Arthur Schlesinger, Jr., Prof. Fritz Stern (Columbia Univ.), James Tobin (1981 Nobel Laureate, Economics), Shirley Williams (Harvard Univ.).
Periodicals: *The American Prospect* (bimonthly journal).
Other Information: In 1994 New Prospect received $35,000 from the Joyce Foundation, $10,000 from the Florence and John Schumann Foundation.

New Prospect Foundation
1420 Sheridan Rd., Suite 9A
Wilmette, IL 60091   **Phone:** (708) 256-2343
USA

Contact Person: Frances Lehman, President.
Mission or Interest: Grant-making foundation that focuses on leftist groups and charitable causes in the Chicago area.
Accomplishments: In 1994 the Foundation awarded $806,913 in grants. The recipients of the largest grants included: $210,000 for WBEZ, Chicago, $45,000 for Business and Professional People for the Public Interest, $20,000 for National Public Radio, $20,000 for the Chicago United Way/Crusade of Mercy, $15,000 for the Jewish Council on Urban Affairs, $17,500 for the New Israel Fund, $15,000 for Planned Parenthood of the Chicago area, $15,000 for the Jewish Fund for Justice, $14,500 for the Roger Baldwin Foundation of the ACLU, $10,648 for the Donors Forum of Chicago, $10,500 for the Chicago Lawyers' Committee for Civil Rights Under Law, $10,000 for the AIDS Foundation of Chicago, and $10,000 for the National Abortion and Reproductive Rights Action League Foundation. Other Chicago area advocacy groups receiving grants included: the Chicago Abortion Fund, Chicago Foundation for Women, Chicago Legal Aid to Incarcerated Mothers, the Crossroads Fund, Illinois Council Against Handgun Violence, Illinois NARAL Fund, the Public Welfare Coalition, and others.
Net Revenue: 1994 $1,844,300 **Net Expenses:** $918,026 **Net Assets:** $11,278,882
Tax Status: 501(c)(3)
Board of Directors or Trustees: Kenneth and Lucy Lehman, Kay and Stanley Schlozman, Paul Lehman, Ronna Stamm.
Other Information: The Foundation received $795,903, or 43% of revenue, from capital gains on the sale of assets. $513,323, or 28%, from gifts and grants awarded by foundations, businesses, and individuals. $238,902, or 13%, from interest on savings and temporary cash investments. $223,480, or 12%, from dividends and interest from securities. $72,692, or 4%, from investment partnerships. The Foundation held $6,034,194, or 53% of assets, in corporate stocks. $2,599,226, or 23%, in corporate bonds.

New River Free Press
P.O. Box 846
Blacksburg, VA 24063   **Phone:** (540) 951-7320   **E-Mail:** anderson@math.vt.edu
USA   **Fax:**   (540) 951-2013

Contact Person: Susan Anderson.
Officers or Principals: Mariann Caine, Kim Kipling, Don Mackler, Bret Nelson, Ruth Steinberger, Beth Wellington, Staff.
Mission or Interest: "*The New River Free Press* is a community-based alternative newsmonthly. The Free Press provides news and commentary about citizens' struggles for social justice, peace, and a healthy environment. We strive to promote solidarity and to show the connections between regional, national, and global issues. We encourage individuals to play an active role in creating a more just society."

Accomplishments: Publishing since 1982. Circulation is 7,000. The *Free Press*'s Community Calender posts announcements for meetings and events held by leftist organizations.
Tax Status: 501(c)(3) **Annual Report:** Yes. **Employees:** All volunteer.
Periodicals: *New River Free Press* (monthly newspaper).
Internships: Yes, for students at local universities.

New Union Party
621 W. Lake St., Suite 210
Minneapolis, MN 55408   **Phone:** (612) 823-2593   **E-Mail:** nup@delphi.com
USA   **Fax:**   same

Contact Person: Brian McNeill, Correspondence Secretary. **Officers or Principals:** Jeff Miller, Editor; Tom Dalby, Treasurer.
Mission or Interest: Marxist organization promoting the complete ownership of the means of production by the workers. "To achieve this new economic system, the workers need to unite in one rank-and-file controlled union...In addition to organizing industrially, the workers will need a political party to spread the idea of social ownership and to gain the support of the majority at the polls. When this is achieved, the workers will assume control of their workplaces and manage them democratically through the New Unions. An elected Congress of delegates from each industry will plan and manage the national economy and will replace the present political congress as the nation's government."
Accomplishments: The New Union Party has published its newspaper *The New Unionist* each month since 1974. *The New Unionist* currently has a circulation of 10,000. Articles originally published in *The New Unionist* are frequently reprinted in other journals of the Left. The New Union Party has actively participated in many strikes in the Upper Midwest, particularly in the Austin, MN, Hormel Strike in 1985. Greenhaven Press has used their articles in its Opposing Viewpoints Series of college texts.
Products or Services: Organizing, agitation and advocacy of a "peaceful, democratic revolution, rather than the reform of the capitalist system."
Tax Status: Nonprofit.
Periodicals: *New Unionist* (monthly newspaper).
Internships: No.

New World Foundation
100 E. 85th St.
New York, NY 10028   **Phone:** (212) 249-1023
USA

Contact Person: Colin Greer, President.   **Officers or Principals:** Colin Greer, President ($150,053); Elena B. McCormick, Assistant Treasurer ($78,567); Patricia Coleman, Assistant Secretary ($55,486).
Mission or Interest: Grant-making foundation that focuses on peace, equal rights, education, health and environmental quality, community organizing, and other awards and fellowships.
Accomplishments: In the fiscal year ending September 1994, the Foundation awarded $1,546,700 in grants. The recipients of the largest awards were: $100,000 for the Federation of Southern Cooperatives, $92,000 for the Tides Foundation, $82,500 for Southerners for Economic Justice, $65,000 for the Center for Constitutional Rights, $45,000 for the Center for Third World Organizing, $25,000 each for the Institute for Alternative Journalism, Public Media Center, ACLU Foundation, Vanguard Foundation, Silicon Valley Toxics Coalition, Southwest Community Resources, Martin Luther King Legacy Association, National Farmworker Ministers, Riverside Church, San Francisco Foundation, Louisiana Consumer Education Fund, Environmental Health Coalition, National Coalition of Education Activists, and Rethinking Schools, $20,000 each for the National Religious Partnership for the Environment, Carolina Alliance for Fair Employment, Southern Empowerment Project, North Carolina Occupational Safety and Health Project, Women's Project, Committee Against Anti-Asian Violence, and the Center for Democratic Renewal.
Net Revenue: FY ending 9/94 $2,902,293 **Net Expenses:** $2,985,429 **Net Assets:** $22,327,864
Tax Status: 501(c)(3)
Other Information: The Foundation received $1,270,879, or 44% of revenue, from capital gains on the sale of securities. $976,686, or 34%, from gifts and grants awarded by foundations, businesses, and individuals. (These grants included $484,551 from the Fowey Light Fund, $102,500 from the Angelina Fund, $95,000 from the Bauman Family Foundation, $46,781 from the Tides Foundation, $30,000 from the Public Welfare Foundation, $25,000 from the Charles H. Revson Foundation, $10,000 from the Spencer Charitable Fund, and $5,000 from the Funding Exchange.) $507,586, or 17%, from dividends and interest from securities. $113,359, or 4%, from rental income. $21,000, or 1%, from consultation fees. The remaining revenue came from management fees and publication sales. The Foundation held $15,425,086, or 69% of assets, in corporate stock.

New York Lawyers for the Public Interest
30 W. 21st St., 9th Floor
New York, NY 10010   **Phone:** (212) 727-2270
USA   **Fax:**   (212) 727-2997

Contact Person: Joan Vermuelen, Executive Director.
Officers or Principals: Joan Vermuelen, Executive Director ($80,911); John A. Gresham, Senior Litigation Counsel ($66,068); Sam Sue, Staff Attorney ($44,812); Herbert Semmel, Litigation Director; Charles R. Hager, Chair.

Mission or Interest: Pursues litigation on behalf of the disabled and others, primarily against state and local governments, to guarantee their clients' rights and to receive increased social services.

Accomplishments: In the fiscal year ending May 1994, the organization spent $638,224 on its programs. Litigation included: The American Association of Physicians and Surgeons v. Clinton suit to force the administration to release documents used by the President's task force in drafting his health care reform bill. DIA v. NYC Department of Personnel to compel New York City "to establish goals and timetables for the hiring and promotion of people with disabilities." Mason Tenders District Council Welfare Fund v. Donaghey to force coverage of HIV/AIDS treatment by union funded health care plans. Rivera v. NYC Housing Authority class action suit to force the city to "make sufficient housing stock accessible to people with disabilities." Polkabla v. Commission on the Blind and Visually Handicapped to challenge the agency's "decision to deny services and training to maximize employability." The organization spent $6,592 on litigation expenses and received $171,190 in court-awarded attorney's fees.

Net Revenue: FY ending 5/94 $910,332 ($400,101, or 44%, from government grants) **Net Expenses:** $861,403   76%/24%/0%
Net Assets: $465,633 **Citations:** 3:222
Tax Status: 501(c)(3)
Board of Directors or Trustees: Molly Boast, Sharon Bowen, David Brodsky, Louis Craco, Robert Crotty, Mark Cunha, Juan Figueroa (Puerto Rican Legal Defense and Education Fund), Martin Flumenbaum, Max Friedman, Martin Gold, Stuart Gold, Deborah Greenberg (Columbia Law School), Jonathan Greenblatt, Allan Gropper, John Hall, Kenneth Handal, Alvin Hellerstein, Anne Hilker, Christopher Hu, Maria Imperial (Victim Services), Wilhelm Joseph, Jr. (Legal Services for New York City), Robert Kaufman, Douglas Kraus, Ogden Lewis, Mitchell Lowenthal, Patricia Martone, Joseph McDonald, Daniel Murdock, Ellen Nadler, Michael Nissan, Stuart Parker, James Rayhill, Timothy Rogers, Gerald Rosenberg, Alan Rothstein (Association of the Bar of the City of New York), Michael Schwartz, William Snipes, Louise Sommers, Kent Stauffer (Chase Manhattan Bank), Sidney Stein, Alexander Sussman, Peter Ward, Napoleon Williams, Jr.
Other Information: The Lawyers used the New York City firm Vantage Consulting Group for fund raising; the firm was paid $53,106. The Lawyers received $400,101, or 44% of revenue, from government grants. $295,146, or 32%, from gifts and grants awarded by foundations, businesses, and individuals. (These grants included $20,000 from the Joyce Mertz-Gilmore Foundation, $20,000 from the Mary Flagler Cary Charitable Trust, and $500 from the Stewart R. Mott Charitable Trust.) $177,190, or 19%, from court-awarded attorney's fees. $8,859, or 1%, from interest on savings and temporary cash investments. $7,566 net, or 1%, from special fund raising events. The remaining revenue came from other miscellaneous sources.

Newspaper Guild
8611 Second Ave.
Silver Spring, MD 20910   **Phone:**   (301) 585-2990
USA

Contact Person: Charles Dale, President.
Officers or Principals: Charles Dale, President ($94,356); Linda Foley, Secretary/Treasurer ($88,874); Michael Bocking, Canadian Director ($67,689); Carol Rothman, International Chair; John Edgington, Secretary/Treasurer.
Mission or Interest: Union representing approximately 30,000 newspaper workers. Affiliated with the AFL-CIO.
Net Revenue: FY ending 3/95 $5,128,764 **Net Expenses:** $5,164,492 **Net Assets:** $7,248,318
Products or Services: Collective bargaining, strike benefits, seminars, labor organizing, more. Awards the annual Heywood Broun Award for outstanding journalistic achievement.
Tax Status: 501(c)(5)
Board of Directors or Trustees: Carol Przbyszewski, David Mulcahy, Larry Hatfield, Patricia Bell, Richard Brandow, Thomas Thibeault, Russ Cain, Connie Knox, Eugene Jones, Patricia Nuttall, Lela Garlington, Jack Norman, Georgia Chisolm.
Periodicals: *Guild Reporter* (monthly newsletter).
Other Information: The Guild paid $190,635 to affiliates. $100,275 of that was paid to the AFL-CIO. The Guild received $5,163,781 from membership dues. $86,406 from interest on savings and temporary cash investments. $36,997 from dividends and interest on securities. Net revenue was decreased by a loss of $167,084 on rental properties.

Nicaragua Solidarity Network of Greater New York
339 Lafayette St.
New York, NY 10012   **Phone:**   (212) 674-9499   **E-Mail:** nicanet@blythe.org
USA   **Fax:**   (212) 674-9139

Contact Person: David L. Wilson.
Officers or Principals: "Volunteer collective, with no officers."
Mission or Interest: "Build awareness of and support for the grassroots and left movements in Nicaragua and the rest of Latin America and the Caribbean region."
Accomplishments: In 1987 they lead a campaign that generated 25,000 postcards against U.S. aid to the Nicaraguan Contras. In 1988, in just two weeks, they generated 3,700 mailgrams opposing Contra aid. In 1989 and 1990 they organized the local reception of televised addresses by then-Nicaraguan President Daniel Ortega. Their newsletter has been cited in many publications, including *The Nation* and *Extra!*. A founding member of the Campaign for Real Equitable Economic Development (CREED) coalition.
Net Revenue: Average annual income under $25,000.
Tax Status: None. **Annual Report:** No. **Employees:** 0
Periodicals: *Weekly News Update on the Americas* (weekly).

Internships: Yes. Interns usually work 7-8 hours a week conducting research for the *Weekly News Update*. Interns need language skills (Spanish, Portuguese, French or Creole).

Other Information: Founded in 1985 as an umbrella organization for the fifteen or so Nicaragua solidarity groups in the New York city metropolitan area. The Network received $1,000 from the North Star Fund in the fiscal year ending June 1994.

Norman Foundation

147 E. 48th St.
New York, NY 10017   **Phone:**   (212) 230-9800
USA

Contact Person: Andrew E. Norman, Chairman. **Officers or Principals:** Frank A. Weil, President; Lucinda W. Bunnen, Vice President; Nancy N. Lassalle, Secretary; Phyllis Eckhaus, Assistant Secretary.

Mission or Interest: Grant-making foundation that awards money to civil rights, feminist, labor, and other organizations.

Accomplishments: (Note: grants listed here are from 1993, while revenues, expenses, assets, and other financial information is from 1991.) In 1993 the Foundation awarded $1,197,000 in grants. Recipients included; $25,000 each for the Farm Labor Research Project, ECO Action, and the Environmental Health Network, $20,000 each for the Asian American Legal Defense and Education Fund, Southern Organizing Committee for Economic and Social Justice, HIV Law Project, Center for Democratic Renewal, Coalition for Humane Immigration Rights of Los Angeles, Disability Rights Education and Defense Fund, Equity Institute, Grassroots Leadership, Institute on Violence, NOW Legal Defense and Education Fund, Prairie Fire Rural Action, Seventh Generation Fund, Center for Population Education, Center for Third World Organizing, and Rural Advancement Foundation International, and $15,000 each for the Center for Community Action, Center for Women's Economic Alternatives, El Rescate Legal Services, Fair Employment Council of Greater Washington, Federation of Southern Cooperatives, National Immigration, Refugee and Citizenship Forum, Environmental and Economic Justice Project, Labor/Community Strategy Center, and the Legal Aid Society.

Net Revenue: 1991 $1,760,860 **Net Expenses:** $1,593,181 **Net Assets:** $23,224,595

Tax Status: 501(c)(3)

Board of Directors or Trustees: Belinda Reusch, Melissa Bunnen, Robert Bunnen, Jr., Alice Franklin, Andrew Franklin, Deborah Harrington, Diana Turner, Honor Lassalle, Philip Lassalle, Abigail Norman, Margaret Norman, Sarah Norman, Amanda Weil, Sandison Weil, William Weil.

Other Information: In 1991, the Foundation received $950,834, or 54% of revenue, from dividends and interest from securities. $756,348, or 43%, from capital gains on the sale of securities. $35,957, or 2%, from interest on savings and temporary cash investments. The remaining revenue came from a $5,000 gift from Dorothy Norman, and other miscellaneous investments. The Foundation's largest holding, $8,817,585, or 38% of assets, was in the Norman Weil Funds Investment Partnership. $4,713,022, or 20%, was held in corporate stock. $4,432,652, or 19%, in government obligations. A "Listerine royalty" was valued at $235,000.

Norman Lear Foundation

9720 Wilshire Blvd., 3rd Floor
Beverly Hills, CA 90212   **Phone:**   (310) 550-1254
USA

Contact Person: Murray Neidorf, Chief Financial Officer.

Officers or Principals: Norman Lear, President ($0); Murray Neidorf, Chief Financial Officer ($0); Lyn Lear, Secretary ($0).

Mission or Interest: Grant-making foundation funded by television producer Norman Lear.

Accomplishments: In the fiscal year ending November 1993, the Foundation awarded $150,200 in grants. Recipients included; $25,000 each for the Concern Foundation and the Center for Addiction and Substance Abuse at Columbia University, $15,000 for Interns for Peace Now, $10,000 each for the Humanitas Prize, and the Black United Fund of Oregon, $5,000 for the Center for Reproductive Law and Policy, $3,000 for the Gay and Lesbian Alliance, $1,000 for Americans for Peace Now, $1,000 for Planned Parenthood, $1,500 for the National Lesbian and Gay Journalists Association, $1,000 for the Center for Media and Values (now the Center for Media Literacy), $1,000 for the Hollywood Policy Center Foundation, $5,000 for the NAACP Legal Defense Fund, and others.

Net Revenue: FY ending 11/93 $39,090 **Net Expenses:** $154,083 **Net Assets:** $623,149

Tax Status: 501(c)(3)

Other Information: Norman Lear is best known as the producer of television's "All in the Family", "The Jeffersons", "Good Times", and others. In addition to his Foundation, he has historically supported the North Star Fund and People for the American Way. The Foundation received $33,106, or 85% of its revenue, from dividends and interest from securities. $5,984, or 15%, from interest on savings and temporary cash investments. The largest portion of assets was held in corporate stocks, and the largest holding of stock was in Time Warner Inc., 182,000 shares with a market value (as of 11/93) of $192,920.

North American Coalition on Religion and Ecology (NACRE)

5 Thomas Circle, N.W.
Washington, DC 20005   **Phone:**   (202) 462-2591
USA

Contact Person: Don Conroy, President.

Officers or Principals: Jan Hartke, Chairman ($0); Carolyn Gutwoski, Secretary ($0); Bruce Anderson, Past Chairman ($0).

Mission or Interest: "On-going support to churches for eco-ministry and population." An inter-religious effort to connect the religious community with the environmental movement.
Accomplishments: In 1994 NACRE spent $102,556 on its programs. The main program was the Caring for Creation Initiative, a "grassroots stewardship and habitat program."
Net Revenue: 1994 $146,259 **Net Expenses:** $152,526 67%/33%/0% **Net Assets:** $998
Tax Status: 501(c)(3)
Periodicals: *Eco-Letter* (newsletter).
Other Information: NACRE received $142,842, or 98% of revenue, from gifts and grants awarded by foundations, businesses, and individuals. $2,184, or 1%, from program service fees, such as conference presentations. $1,007 net, or 1%, from the sale of inventory. The remaining revenue came from interest on savings and temporary cash investments.

North American Congress on Latin America (NACLA)

475 Riverside Dr., Suite 454
New York, NY 10115   **Phone:**   (212) 870-3146   **E-Mail:** nacla@igc.apc.org
USA   **Fax:**   (212) 870-3305

Contact Person: Pierre La Ramée, Executive Director.
Mission or Interest: Provides information and analysis on both U.S. foreign policy toward Latin America and political, social and economic conditions within the region. NACLA has consistently supported Cuba's Fidel Castro, and has challenged U.S. "imperialism" and involvement in Latin American.
Accomplishments: NACLA's magazine, *NACLA Report on the Americas*, has a circulation of approximately 10,000 in 72 countries. NACLA founder Brady Tyson served in the Carter Administration as an advisor to the U.S. Delegation to the United Nations Human Rights Commission in Geneva.
Net Revenue: FY ending 11/94 $394,925 **Net Expenses:** $351,766 78%/19%/2%
Tax Status: 501(c)(3) **Annual Report:** Yes. **Employees:** 4
Board of Directors or Trustees: Prof. Maria Josefa Canino (Rutgers Univ.), Josh DeWind (Social Science Research Council), Prof. Marc Edelman (Hunter College/CUNY), Pastor Richard Edwards (United Methodist Church), Mark Fried (Oxfam Canada), Fred Goff (DataCenter), Susan Lowes (*Monthly Review*), Donna Nevel, Prof. Marifeli Perez-Stable (SUNY), Don Reasoner (General Board of Global Ministries), Dr. Klaudia Rivera (El Barrio Popular Education Program), George Vickers (Washington Office on Latin America), Prof. Steven Volk (Oberlin College), Susan Wood (Intl. Womens' Health Coalition), Peter Yarrow.
Periodicals: *NACLA Report on the Americas* (bimonthly magazine).
Internships: Yes. Semester-long internships for students with a background in Latin American or Caribbean studies, and or writing and editing skills.
Other Information: "NACLA was founded in 1966, in response to the U.S. invasion of the Dominican Republic - and to the disinformation campaign that accompanied it." NACLA received $194,409, or 49% of revenue, from gifts and grants awarded by foundations, businesses, and individuals. (These grants included $16,000 from the North Star Foundation, and $2,000 from the Aaron and Martha Schecter Charitable Foundation.) $143,309, or 36% of revenue, from Subscriptions. $34,891, or 9%, from the sale of literature. $10,887, or 3%, from advertising revenues. The remaining revenue came from royalties, mailing list rentals, and other miscellaneous sources.

North American Man - Boy Love Association (NAMBLA)

P.O. Box 174, Middletown Station
New York, NY 10018   **Phone:**   (212) 807-8578   **E-Mail:** falcor14@ix.netcom.com
USA

Mission or Interest: "For over 17 years, the North American Man-Boy Love Association has spoken out for the dignity and humanity of men and boys who are erotically attracted to one another. While strongly opposed to sexual coercion and child abuse in any form, NAMBLA distinguishes between love and abuse, challenging all laws and customs which fail to make that distinction." Argues that children have the same right to consensual sexual activity as adults.
Accomplishments: Poet Allen Ginsberg said, "Attacks on NAMBLA stink of politics, witch hunting for profit, humorlessness, vanity, anger and ignorance...I'm a member of NAMBLA because I love boys too. Everybody does, who has a little humanity." NAMBLA claims 1,500 members. NAMBLA contingents have marched in Gay Pride parades in Boston, New York, and San Francisco, as well as the "March on Washington." The Association has been featured on Donahue, Sally Jessie Raphael, Sonia Live, and Jerry Springer shows. NAMBLA is active in the International Pedophile and Children's Emancipation Group. The Association sends out a newsletter to over 250 pedophiles imprisoned for "consensual relationships with youth." The Association distributes, but does not produce, *gayme* (pronounced 'game') magazine. *Gayme* contains photos of shirtless boys and totally nude young men, who, although often look younger, "are at least 18 years of age, except in the case of some historical photographs."
Products or Services: "NAMBLA Topics," brief booklets on various topics.
Tax Status: Unincorporated association. Applying for 501(c)(3).
Periodicals: *NAMBLA Bulletin* (quarterly magazine), *gayme* (magazine).
Other Information: NAMBLA was an active member of the International Lesbian and Gay Association, until the ILGA sought reinstatement as an observer organization at the United Nations. The United States adopted a law withholding funds from the UN if organizations connected with it condone pedophilia or have member groups holding this position. "The guiding light behind this particular piece of legislation was anti-gay senator Jesse Helms." In July 1994 the ILGA voted by more than 80% to expel NAMBLA.

North Star Fund

666 Broadway, Fifth Floor
New York, NY 10012   **Phone:** (212) 460-5511
USA   **Fax:** (212) 982-9272

Contact Person: Miriam Hernandez, Office Manager.
Officers or Principals: Betty Kapetanakis, Associate Director ($49,716), Jose Luis Morin, Executive Director, ($41,208), Miriam Hernandez, Office Manager ($34,097); Susan Davidoff, Development Director.
Mission or Interest: Philanthropic organization concentrating on community-based groups in New York.
Accomplishments: In the fiscal year ending June 1994, the Fund awarded $1,100,771 in grants. The recipients of the largest grants were; four grants totaling $185,000 for People for the American Way, $190,734 for the Manic-Depressive Illness Foundation, $50,000 for the Jerusalem Foundation, $25,000 each for the ACLU Southern California Foundation, Columbia Journalism Review, the Environmental Media Association, and the Thomas Jefferson Center for Protection of Free Expression. The remaining grants averaged about $3,383 and were awarded to 170 organizations, including; Black Veterans for Social Justice, Campaign for Peace and Democracy, Center for Immigrants Rights, Circle of Sistahs, Citizen Soldier, DYKE TV, Gay Asian and Pacific Islander Men of NY, Greek American Labor Council, Hell's Kitchen AIDS Project, Institute for Democratic Socialism, Irish Gay and Lesbian Organization, Labor at the Crossroads, Lesbian Avengers, NY Marxist School/Brecht Forum, Patrice Lumumba Coalition, Stonewall 25, Students Organizing Students, Nicaraguan Solidarity Network of Greater NY, NY Committee in Solidarity with the People of El Salvador.
Net Revenue: FY ending 6/94 $1,275,307 **Net Expenses:** $1,451,587 88%/7%/5% **Net Assets:** $285,858
Products or Services: Grants, Finding the Grassroots: A Directory of NYC Activist Organizations.
Tax Status: 501(c)(3)
Other Information: The North Star Fund is located at the same address as the Funding Exchange and Common Giving Fund. The Fund received $1,263,888, or 99% of revenue, from gifts and grants awarded by foundations, businesses and individuals. (These grants included $10,000 from the Angelina Fund, and $4,500 from the New World Foundation. Norman and Francis Lear have been major supporters over the years. In the fiscal year ending April 1995, the North Star Fund received $766,046 from the Common Giving Fund.) The remaining revenue came from interest on savings and temporary cash investments. The North Star Fund had a loan or note payable to the Funding Exchange valued at $203,150.

Northeast Action

186 Hampshire St., 3rd Floor
Cambridge, MA 02139   **Phone:** (617) 547-1922
USA

Contact Person: Tim Costello.
Mission or Interest: Community coalition of organized labor and citizens' groups.
Accomplishments: Created the Massachusetts Jobs Task Force with other community organizations.

Northeast Citizen Action Resource Center (NECARC)

621 Farmington Ave.
Hartford, CT 06105   **Phone:** (203) 231-2410   **E-Mail:** kdmk62a@prodigy.com
USA   **Fax:** (203) 231-2419

Contact Person: Lynne Ide, President. **Officers or Principals:** Lynne Ide, President ($0); Judith Maslen, Secretary/Treasurer ($0).
Mission or Interest: Promotes and assists the building of grassroots and community-based coalitions and advocacy organizations.
Accomplishments: In 1992 the Center spent $409,449 on its programs. $254,589 was awarded in grants. The recipients of the largest grants included; $72,758 for the Commonwealth Institute, $40,000 for the Commonwealth Education Fund, $35,200 for the Center for Connecticut's Future, $30,300 for the Grassroots Education Fund, $25,000 for Ocean State Action, $24,000 for Maine Citizen Leadership, and $20,831 for the Connecticut Citizen Research Group.
Net Revenue: 1992 $608,288 **Net Expenses:** $481,705 85%/8%/7% **Net Assets:** $156,141
Products or Services: Grants, technical and organizational assistance, and lobbying. The Center spent $14,000 on grassroots lobbying.
Tax Status: 501(c)(3)
Board of Directors or Trustees: Karen Scharff, George Christie.
Other Information: The Center received $581,020, or 96% from gifts and grants awarded by foundations, businesses, and individuals. (These grants included $165,000 from the MacArthur Foundation, $52,500 from the New World Foundation, $40,000 from the Florence and John Schumann Foundation, $35,000 from the Arca Foundation, $35,000 from Citizen Vote, $25,000 from the Catholic Campaign for Human Development, $25,000 from the Ottinger Fund, $25,000 from the Rockefeller Foundation, $25,000 from the Fund 2000, $20,000 from the Stern Family Fund, $20,000 from the Angelina Fund, $15,000 from the Partnership for Democracy, $4,500 from the Lead Paint Outreach program, and $3,000 from the Haymarket Fund.) $21,864, or 4%, from conference fees. The remaining revenue came from interest on savings and temporary cash investments, and consulting fees.

Northwest Coalition Against Malicious Harassment

P.O. Box 16776
Seattle, WA 98116   **Phone:** (206) 233-9136
USA   **Fax:** (206) 233-0611

Contact Person: Bill Wassmuth, Executive Director.
Officers or Principals: Bill Wassmuth, Executive Director ($41,191); Jeannette Pai-Espinosa, President ($0); Nalani M. Askov, Jack Lang y Marquez, Dan Noelle, Vice Presidents ($0); Cherie Berthon, Secretary; Jesse Vialpando, Treasurer; Bob Lamb, Advisor; Eric Ward, Associate Director; Alice Gregory, Development Director; Gretchen Henry, Office Manager.
Mission or Interest: Monitors the activities of white supremacists and informs the public of these activities. Conducts research into these organizations, their participants, and their goals.
Accomplishments: In 1994 the Coalition spent $225,500 on its programs. The largest program, with expenditures of $80,000, was monitoring incidents of harassment and the activities of hate groups in the region. $75,500 was spent on public education, including approximately fifty presentations and training sessions, an annual conference with an attendance of 350, and a newsletter sent to 5,000 subscribers. $60,000 for community organizing and technical assistance. $10,000 was spent networking with like-minded individuals and groups.
Net Revenue: 1994 $315,751 **Net Expenses:** $283,481 80%/16%/5% **Net Assets:** $147,014
Products or Services: Coalition building, educational materials, lobbying. The Coalition spent $6,649 on grassroots lobbying.
Tax Status: 501(c)(3)
Board of Directors or Trustees: Jesse Berain, David Della (WA State Commission on Asian American Affairs), Bill Douglas (Kootenai County Prosecuting Attorney), Jorge Espinosa (Portland Community College), Kathleen Eymann (Coos County Is Colorful), Dan Gargan (Affiliated Tribes), Ted George (Racism Committee, Port Gamble S'Klallam and Suquamish Tribes), Judith Kahn (American Jewish Committee), Chris Kaufmann (Montana Human Rights Network), Skip Kuck (Kootenai County Task Force on Human Relations), Merritt Long (Exec. Dir., WA Human Rights Commission), Gwen Morgan-Jones (Wyoming Church Coalition), Chelsea Kesselheim (Wyoming Church Coalition), Anne MacIntyre (Exec. Dir., Montana Human Rights Commission), R. Terry Marsh (Housing Dir., Urban League of Metropolitan Seattle), Idaho Purce (NAACP), Lt. Sue Rahr (King County Police), Marshall Sauceda (Chair, Eugene Human Rights Commission, Univ. of Oregon Office of Multicultural Affairs), Marvin Stern (Anti-Defamation League of B'nai B'rith), Dan Stutesman (American Friends Service Committee, Lesbian/Gay Program), William Tynan (Chief of Police, Univ. of WY), Franklin Whitworth (Ground Zero), Kathy Yamamoto (Idaho Education Assoc.), Karen Yoshitomi (Japanese American Citizen's League), Cathy Wihlborg (Helena Human Rights Task Force).
Periodicals: Quarterly newsletter.
Other Information: The Coalition received $292,902, or 93% of revenue, from direct and indirect public support in the form of gifts and grants awarded by foundations, affiliates, businesses, and individuals. (These grants included $10,000 from the Ms. Foundation for Women, $5,000 from the Deer Creek Foundation.) $22,849, or 7%, from program services including the annual conference, presentations, and honoraria.

Northwest Coalition for Alternatives to Pesticides (NCAP)

P.O. Box 1393
Eugene, OR 97440-1393   **Phone:**   (503) 344-5044
USA

Contact Person: Jim Barngrover, Vice President.   **Officers or Principals:** Jennifer Curtis, President ($0); Jim Barngrover, Vice President ($0); Becky Casstevens, Treasurer ($0); Joanne Jewell, Secretary.
Mission or Interest: Gathers and disseminates information on the uses of pesticide and herbicides, their harmful effects, and alternatives to their use.
Accomplishments: 2,500 copies of the Coalition's journal is printed for each issue. In 1994 the Coalition spent $216,600 on its programs.
Net Revenue: 1994 $406,228 ($2,766, or 1%, from government grants) **Net Expenses:** $238,152 91%/1%/8%
Net Assets: $207,883
Products or Services: Research, education, and lobbying. The Coalition spent $896 on lobbying, $179 on grassroots lobbying and $717 on the direct lobbying of legislators. This was a 110% increase over the previous year.
Tax Status: 501(c)(3)
Board of Directors or Trustees: Dan Ford, Theresa Strolberg, Samantha McCarthy, Dahinda Meda, Jay Sherrerd, Bruce Jennings, Debbie Pickering, Jude Duryea.
Periodicals: *Journal of Pesticide Reform* (quarterly journal).
Other Information: The Coalition received $358,018, or 88% of revenue, from direct and indirect public support in the form of gifts and grants awarded by foundations, affiliates, businesses, and individuals. (These grants included $30,000 from the Jessie Smith Noyes Foundation, $25,000 from the Bullitt Foundation, and $20,000 from the Deer Creek Foundation.) $27,712, or 7%, from membership dues. $9,461, or 2%, from sales of reprinted articles. $6,230, or 2%, from the sale of inventory. $3,811, or 1%, from journal subscriptions. $2,766, or 1%, from government grants. The remaining revenue came from special fund-raising events, interest on savings and temporary cash investments, dividends and interest from securities, and other miscellaneous sources.

NPR Foundation

635 Massachusetts Ave., N.W.
Washington, DC 20001   **Phone:**   (202) 414-2000
USA

Contact Person: Delano Lewis, Director.   **Officers or Principals:** Barbara Hall, Director ($118,104); Delano Lewis, Director ($105,022). (Compensation paid by National Public Radio.)

Mission or Interest: Foundation that raises funds for National Public Radio.
Accomplishments: In the fiscal year ending September 1993, the foundation raised $242,756 after spending $26,098 on fund raising.
Net Revenue: FY ending 9/94 $268,854 **Net Expenses:** $26,098 0%/0%/100% **Net Assets:** $242,756
Tax Status: 501(c)(3)
Board of Directors or Trustees: David Chamberlain, William Poorvu, Paul Prosperi, Thomas Baer, Elizabeth Bagley, J. P. Bolduc, David Brokaw, Bob Burkett, Hon. Dick Clark, Christopher Clouser, Norman Cohn, Richard Donahue, Patricia Duff, Harold Evans, Peter Francese, Sidney Harman, John Herrmann, Jr., Jean Kahn, Susan King, Pat Kluge, Kenneth Lehman, Barbara Linhart, Frank Mankiewicz, Cyrus McKinnon, Philip Merrill, Jane Peyrouse, Sandra Seltzer Pressman, Billye Proctor-Shaw, Susan Rose, Jonah Shacknai, Samuel Shawhan, Stanley Shuman, Jennifer Stanley, Calvin Trillin, Jan Green Turner, William Wasserman, Jr., Carl Matthusen, Joan Harris.
Other Information: Affiliated with the 501(c)(3) National Public Radio. The two affiliates had combined net revenues of $60,344,890, net expenses of $58,448,451, and net assets of $21,701,446. The Foundation received $258,746, or 96% of revenue, from gifts and grants awarded by foundations, businesses, and individuals. $10,108, or 4%, from capital gains on the sale of securities.

Nuclear Age Peace Foundation

1622 Anacapa St.
Santa Barbara, CA 93101   **Phone:** (805) 965-3443
USA

Contact Person: David Krieger, President.
Officers or Principals: David Krieger, President ($84,653); Frank Kelly, Vice President ($5,000).
Mission or Interest: "International educational organization dedicated to: teaching peace; achieving a nuclear-weapons-free world; promoting non-violent resolution of conflicts within and between nations; strengthening international law; and creating a world order based on liberty, justice and human dignity for all."
Accomplishments: Founded in 1982, the Foundation is recognized by the United Nations as a Peace Messenger organization and has consultative status with the United Nations Economic and Social Council. In 1994 the Foundation spent $253,109 on its programs.
Net Revenue: 1994 $279,241 **Net Expenses:** $333,096 76%/10%/14% **Net Assets:** $664,602
Products or Services: Educational activities, books and pamphlets. The Foundation awards two annual scholarships, the Lena Chang Scholarship Awards, to minority students who can demonstrate both financial need and academic excellence.
Tax Status: 501(c)(3)
Other Information: The Foundation received $307,951 in gifts and grants awarded by foundations, businesses, and individuals. This was more than net revenues because of an "unrealized loss" of $68,275, and a loss of $18,356 from the depreciation of rental property. Other sources of revenue included: $30,066 from dividends and interest from securities, a capital gain of $25,255 on the sale of securities, $1,691 from special fund-raising events, and $909 from the sale of inventory.

Nuclear Control Institute

1000 Connecticut Ave., N.W., Suite 704
Washington, DC 20036   **Phone:** (202) 822-8444
USA

Mission or Interest: Monitors government and industry programs that contribute to the spread of nuclear weapons.
Accomplishments: Nuclear Oversight project.
Tax Status: 501(c)(3)
Other Information: In 1993 the Institute received $130,000 over two years from the Rockefeller Brothers Fund.

Nuclear Information and Resource Service (NIRS)

1424 16th St., N.W., Suite 601
Washington, DC 20036   **Phone:** (202) 328-0002
USA

Contact Person: Michael Mariotte, Executive Director. **Officers or Principals:** Michael Mariotte, Executive Director ($39,000).
Mission or Interest: "Providing up-to-date information and organizing assistance to individuals and groups who are working to replace nuclear power with safe and more economical alternatives."
Accomplishments: In the fiscal year ending January 1994, the Service spent $217,207 on its programs.
Net Revenue: FY ending 1/94 $288,573 **Net Expenses:** $269,202 **Net Assets:** $51,574
Products or Services: Conferences, publications, teacher's manual, and other information.
Tax Status: 501(c)(3)
Board of Directors or Trustees: Gary Ferdman, Bob Backus, David Horowitz, Bill Jordan, Kay Drey, Kathleen Welch, Rosemary Vietor.
Other Information: The Service received $287,841, or 99% of revenue from direct and indirect public support in the form of gifts and grants awarded by foundations, companies, and individuals. (These grants included $35,000 from the Rockefeller Family Fund, $15,000 from the C.S. Fund.) The remaining revenue came from the sale of teacher's manuals and interest on savings and temporary cash investments.

Nuclear Weapons Freeze of Santa Cruz
P.O. Box 8163
Santa Cruz, CA 95061   **Phone:**   (408) 458-9975
USA

Contact Person: Barry Van Driel, Executive Director. **Officers or Principals:** Barry Van Driel, Executive Director ($17,160); Julie Aquiar, Director ($0); Janet Bryer, Director ($0); Chris Woldemar, Director.
Mission or Interest: Supports the elimination of nuclear weapons, and peace through conflict resolution rather than military force.
Accomplishments: Approximately 2,500 members. In 1992 the organization spent $56,922 on its programs. $45,943 was spent to produce and distribute *The Monthly Planet*, which had a monthly print run of 12,000 copies per issue.
Net Revenue: 1992 $98,341 **Net Expenses:** $97,623 **Net Assets:** (-$7,020)
Tax Status: 501(c)(3)
Periodicals: *The Monthly Planet* (monthly tabloid).
Other Information: The organization received $36,686, or 37% of revenue, from program services. $30,740, or 31%, from membership dues. $25,157, or 26%, from gifts and grants awarded by foundations, businesses, and individuals. $4,537 net, or 5%, from special fund-raising events. The remaining revenue came from various miscellaneous sources.

off our backs: a women's newsjournal
2337 B 18th St., N.W.
Washington, DC 20009   **Phone:**   (202) 234-8072   **E-Mail:** 73613.1256@compuserve.com
USA   **Fax:**   (202) 234-8092

Contact Person: Jennie Ruby, Office Manager.
Mission or Interest: A radical feminist publication. "A newsjournal by, for and about women. It has been published continuously since 1970 and is run by collective where all decisions are made by consensus."
Accomplishments: Circulation of approximately 22,000.
Employees: 1   **Periodicals:** *off our backs* (monthly tabloid).   **Internships:** Yes.
Other Information: Features the cartoon, "Dykes to Watch Out For."

Office and Professional Employees International Union (OPEIU)
265 W. 14th St., Suite 610
New York, NY 10011   **Phone:**   (212) 675-3210
USA   **Fax:**   (212) 727-3466

Contact Person: C. M. Goodwin, Secretary/Treasurer.
Officers or Principals: C. M. Goodwin, Secretary/Treasurer ($104,358); J. Kelly, Business Manager ($6,841); N. Griffith, Board ($2,581); A. Merchant, President; E. Walker, Secretary; W. Mulryan, Vice President.
Mission or Interest: Union representing approximately 135,000 members. Member of the AFL-CIO.
Net Revenue: 1993 $4,420,942 **Net Expenses:** $4,676,427 **Net Assets:** $1,118,145
Tax Status: 501(c)(5)
Periodicals: *White Collar* (quarterly newsletter), and *Research News* (quarterly magazine).
Other Information: The Union received $3,910,629, or 88% of revenue, from membership dues. $445,940, or 10%, from reimbursed administrative expenses. The remaining revenue came from interest on savings and temporary cash investments, and other miscellaneous sources.

Office of the Americas
8124 W. 3rd St., Suite 201
Los Angeles, CA 90048   **Phone:**   (213) 852-9808
USA

Contact Person: Blase Bonpane, Executive Director. **Officers or Principals:** Theresa Bonpane, Financial Officer ($36,224); Blase Bonpane, Executive Director ($34,413); Joyce Norman, Secretary ($0).
Mission or Interest: "Promotion of international understanding and peace, especially in Latin America, by educational programs. Promotion of international exchange of representatives from countries in the western hemisphere."
Accomplishments: In the fiscal year ending June 1994 the Office spent $78,195 on its programs.
Net Revenue: FY ending 6/94 $90,473 **Net Expenses:** $100,234 78%/12%/10% **Net Assets:** $6,388
Tax Status: 501(c)(3)
Board of Directors or Trustees: Edward Asner (actor), Martin Sheen (actor), Linda Tumulty, Haskell Wexler.
Other Information: The Office received $85,288, or 94% of revenue, from gifts and grants awarded by foundations, businesses, and individuals. $5,184, or 6%, from the sale of items from a thrift shop operated by the Office.

Oil, Chemical and Atomic Workers International Union (OCAW)
P.O. Box 281200
Lakewood, CO 80228   **Phone:**   (303) 987-2229
USA   **Fax:**   (303) 987-1967

Contact Person: Robert E. Wages, President.
Mission or Interest: 100,000 member union. Affiliated with the AFL-CIO.
Accomplishments: President Wage was elected to the AFL-CIO's Executive Council in 1995. Wage has been an advocate of building a labor party in the United States. Maintains a Political Education committee.
Tax Status: 501(c)(5)
Periodicals: *OCAW Reporter* (bimonthly).
Other Information: In the year between July 1993 and June 1994 the Union received $2,898,000 from the U.S. Department of Health and Human Services' Superfund Worker Training Program.

One World Fund
793 Turnpike St.
North Andover, MA 01845
USA

Contact Person: Dr. Josephine Murray, Trustee. **Officers or Principals:** Dr. Josephine Murray, Trustee ($0).
Mission or Interest: Grant-making foundation that awards money for the arts, civil rights, environmental, peace, population control, and other areas.
Accomplishments: In 1994 the Fund awarded $169,050 in grants. The recipients of the largest grants included: $10,000 each for the Tides Foundation and Development Gap, $2,500 each for the Planned Parenthood Federation of America, Union of Concerned Scientists, and World Wildlife Fund, and $1,000 each for the ACLU, Earth Action, FACT, Grassroots International, and Population Institute. Other recipients included Action for Smoking and Health, Association of Forest Service Employees for Environmental Ethics, Earth Island Institute, Fund for Animals, Fund for the Homeless, Fund for Peace, Northeast Coalition vs. Nuclear Pollution, People for the Ethical Treatment of Animals, and Physicians for Human Rights.
Net Revenue: 1994 $2,226,281 **Net Expenses:** $233,050 **Net Assets:** $5,638,355
Tax Status: 501(c)(3)
Other Information: The Fund received $2,057,900, or 92% of revenue, from gifts of stock. $143,450, or 6%, from dividends and interest from securities. $22,619, or 1%, from interest on savings and temporary cash investments. The remaining revenue came from capital gains on the sale of securities. The Fund held $5,451,875, or 97% of assets in corporate stock. The remaining assets were held in cash.

One World Movement
P.O. Box 423
Notre Dame, IN 46556   **Phone:**   (219) 272-2024
USA

Contact Person: Susan Kiang, Secretary. **Officers or Principals:** John Kiang, Founder and Director.
Mission or Interest: "To achieve a world unity with a world government for a permanent peace on earth and general happiness of mankind through a world revolution to eliminate national independence, national sovereignty, and nationalism...A world revolution is called primarily for a quick and complete sweep of independence of the nation, national sovereignty, and nationalism, since they are the main stumbling blocks on the way of the group expansion to merge all nations into a single group."
Accomplishments: Published One World in 1984, and a revised and updated edition in 1992. Also published The Early One World Movement in 1992. The book One World was given to various public figures and Nobel Prize winners, many of them responded favorably. Two-time winner, the late Dr. Linus Pauling (Peace Prize in 1962 and Chemistry in 1954) said, "John Kiang has written a plea to the people of all countries on earth to work together to achieve the goal of a permanent peace on earth and the achievement of a society in which every person has the opportunity to lead a good life. His argument is presented in detail, and is supported by many references and footnotes...The principal message is that war has now ruled itself out - a war in which the existing nuclear weapons were used would with little doubt mean the end of our civilization, and possibly the end of the human race...The time has come now for the people of the world to join together in eliminating the evil of war and in building the world of the future. Everyone should read this book and heed its message."
Products or Services: Books.
Tax Status: 501(c)(3) **Annual Report:** No. **Employees:** 4

Open Space Institute (OSI)
666 Broadway, 9th Floor
New York, NY 10012   **Phone:**   (212) 505-7480
USA

Contact Person: Christopher J. Elliman, President. **Officers or Principals:** Peter R. Borrelli, Executive Vice President ($87,360); Jacqueline M. Tiso, Assistant Treasurer ($56,775); Christopher J. Elliman, President ($55,000); John H. Adams, Chairman; Katherine O. Roberts, J. Matthew Davidson, Vice Chairpersons; Edward A. Ames, Treasurer; Patricia F. Sullivan, Secretary.
Mission or Interest: Environmental protection and conservation. Assisting grassroots organizations.
Accomplishments: In 1993 the Institute spent $1,268,460 on its programs. The largest program, with expenditures of $780,517, was land preservation. OSI preserves land by holding it or selling the land to government agencies for use as parks or to private conservationists. $260,764 was spent assisting other environmental organizations engaged in local activities, including litigation and public education. $227,179 was spent assisting grassroots organizations with grants, technical, legal and administrative assistance.

Net Revenue: 1993 $2,092,430 ($168,754, or 8%, from government grants) **Net Expenses:** $1,605,373   79%/14%/7%
Net Assets: $4,103,937 **Citations:** 12·191
Tax Status: 501(c)(3)
Board of Directors or Trustees: Jerome Aron, Gilman Burke, Paul Elston, James Figg, III, Samuel Huber, Felix Kaufman, John Kidde, W. Barnabas McHenry, Eliza Reed, Stuart Root.
Other Information: OSI received $1,771,747, or 85% of revenue, from gifts and grants awarded by foundations, businesses, and individuals. $168,754, or 8%, from government grants. $84,387, or 4%, from interest on savings and temporary cash investments. $36,428, or 2%, from management fees. The remaining revenue came from rental income, investment income, and other miscellaneous sources.

Operative Plasterers' and Cement Masons' International Association
1125 17th St., N.W.
Washington, DC 20036   **Phone:** (202) 393-6569
USA   **Fax:**   (202) 393-2514

Contact Person: Dominic A. Martell, President.   **Officers or Principals:** Dominic A. Martell, President ($90,370); Arthur DiGregorio, Vice President ($76,541); Charles M. Axle, Jr., Richard R. Howard, Vice Presidents ($75,525); Robert Beam, Orlando J. Balotta, Michael Canuso, Michael J. Gannon, Vice Presidents.
Mission or Interest: Union representing approximately 58,000 members. Member of the AFL-CIO.
Net Revenue: 1994 $5,635,767 **Net Expenses:** $5,308,863 **Net Assets:** $6,959,543
Tax Status: 501(c)(5)
Periodicals: *Plaster and Cement Mason* (monthly newsletter).
Other Information: The union received $5,253,590, or 93% of total revenue, from membership dues. $344,195, or 6%, from dividends and interest from securities. The remaining revenue came from various miscellaneous sources. The union lost $17,438 on the sale of securities.

Organization for a New Equality
364 Boylston St.
Boston, MA 02116   **Phone:** (617) 445-7249
USA

Contact Person: Leslie Belay, Executive Vice President.
Officers or Principals: Leslie Belay, Executive Vice President ($39,033); Lillian Curley, Managing Director ($22,363); Jennifer Davis, Director of Communications ($18,404); Rev. Charles Stith, President; Dr. Niathan Allen, Chairman; William A. Jackson, Treasurer; Rev. Joseph E. Washington, Secretary; Rev. Dogba Bass, Educational Consultant.
Mission or Interest: Working for the elimination of racism and sexism.
Net Revenue: 1993 $422,434 **Net Expenses:** $351,554 **Net Assets:** $212,905
Tax Status: 501(c)(3)
Board of Directors or Trustees: Judge Joyce London Alexander, Dr. Niathan Allen, Rev. Emmanuel Cleaver, Rev. Charles Coverdale, Rev. Howard Creecy, Jr., Samuel Foster, II, Jesse Hill, Hassan Minor, Ph.D. (President's Office, Howard Univ.), Mildred Prothrow, Deborah Prothow-Smith, M.D. (Harvard School of Public Health), Thomas Saltonstall, Rev. Charles Stith, Rev. Joseph Washington, Arnett Waters, Percy Wilson (Coca Cola Africa), Leonard Zakim (Anti-Defamation League of B'nai B'rith).
Internships: Yes, fellowships for college students with an academic focus on public policy.
Other Information: The Organization received $356,079, or 84% of revenue, from gifts and grants awarded by foundations, businesses, and individuals. $64,099 net, or 15%, from special fund-raising events including a Medal of Hope Awards Dinner, Annual Awards Luncheon, and a St. Botolph's Fundraiser. $2,025, or 1%, from interest on savings and temporary cash investments. The remaining revenue came from the sale of inventory.

Other Americas Radio, The
P.O. Box 85
Santa Barbara, CA 93102   **Phone:** (805) 569-5381
USA

Contact Person: Eric Schwartz, Executive Producer.
Mission or Interest: Radio programing heard through various outlets around the country. They report on topics such as the environment and worldwide covert actions.
Accomplishments: Won the Corporation for Public Broadcasting award for documentary excellence in 1990 for the series "Pollution Solutions."
Products or Services: Audio cassettes of their programs.

Out on the Screen
8455 Beverly Blvd., Suite 309
Los Angeles, CA 90048   **Phone:** (213) 951-1247   **E-Mail:** outscreen@aol.com
USA   **Fax:**   (213) 951-0721

Contact Person: Morgan Rumpf, Executive Director.   **Officers or Principals:** Kelly Kay, President; Dilys Tosteson Garcia, Vice President; Gilbert Pierson, Secretary; Robert Berman, Treasurer.

Mission or Interest: "To present and promote films and videos by and or about gay men and lesbians to the communities of Southern California."

Accomplishments: Annually presents "Outfest: The Los Angeles Gay and Lesbian Film Festival." Festival sponsors included movie studios - MCA/Universal, Sony Pictures, New Line Cinema, television producers - Grub Street Productions (producers of NBC's "Wings" and "Frasier"), government support from the City of Los Angeles Cultural Affairs Department, and nonprofit organizations such as the Gay and Lesbian Alliance Against Defamation, J. Paul Getty Trust Fund for the Visual Arts, the AIDS Project of Los Angeles, and the Human Rights Campaign Fund.

Products or Services: "Outfest" catalog.

Tax Status: 501(c)(3)   **Annual Report:** No.   **Employees:** 6

Board of Directors or Trustees: Robert Berman (AIDS Service Center), Russell Blackstone, Bruce Cohen (Producer, Amblin Entertainment), Amy Goldstein, Roberta Grossman, Eric Gutierrez, Marcus Hu, Mitchell Kohn, Yoram Mandel, Maricel Pagulayan, Michelle Paymar, Gilbert Pierson, Alan Poul, Adam Shulman (Agency for the Performing Arts).

Internships: Three paid summer internships through the Getty Foundation, and other non-paid positions.

Other Information: Formerly the Gay and Lesbian Media Coalition.

Oxfam America

26 West St.
Boston, MA 02111
USA

Phone: (217) 482-1211   **E-Mail:** oxfamusa@igc.apc.org
Fax: (217) 728-2495

Contact Person: John Hammock, Executive Director.

Officers or Principals: John Hammock, Executive Director ($82,000); Sherry Adams, Director of Operations ($71,548); Joel Charney, Director of Policy ($62,437); Hubert Sapp, Manager of U.S. Programs.

Mission or Interest: Awards grants to aid in the development of self-help in the U.S. and worldwide. Advocates national and international policies to alleviate hunger.

Accomplishments: In the fiscal year ending October 1994, Oxfam spent $10,397,017 on its programs. $201,500 in grants went to U.S. programs and $5,869,623 went to overseas programs. Grants go towards development in the third world, and programs that remove barriers to development, such as the problem of un-mapped land mines. Other grants go towards improving the status of women, literacy, democratic participation and health care access. $355,025 was spent on development and support for these grants. $1,318,128 was spent on education projects "to provide and promote a better understanding of poverty and third world problems." $413,558 was spent to study and promote changing policies of the United States, the World Bank, and the United Nations "in ways that benefit the communities which Oxfam assists."

Net Revenue: FY ending 10/94 $14,452,325   **Net Expenses:** $14,140,704   74%/7%/19%   **Net Assets:** $6,635,540

Citations: 61:130

Products or Services: Grants, technical assistance, education programs, policy advocacy. In 1991 Oxfam spent $47,893 on lobbying.

Tax Status: 501(c)(3)

Board of Directors or Trustees: Liz Aberdale, Dr. Walden Bello (Food First), Dr. J. Larry Brown (Center for Hunger, Poverty, and Nutrition Policy, Tufts Univ.), Dr. Lata Chatterjee (Dept. of Geography, Boston Univ.), Boona Cheema (Berkeley Oakland Support Services), Ben Cohen (Ben & Jerry's Ice Cream), Barbara Fiorito, Robert Forrester (Coopers & Lybrand), Lloyd Byron Greig, M.D., Prof. Mel King (Urban Planning, MIT), Richard Levins (Dept. of Population Sciences, Harvard School of Public Health), George Lythcott, M.D., Michael MacLeod (Public Interest Data), Ellen Nissenbaum (Center on Budget & Policy Priorities), Sutti Oritz (Boston Univ.), Barbara Thomas Slayter (Clark Univ.), Sanford Ungar (American Univ.), Janet Walker (American Federation of Government Employees), Hon. Alan Wheat (former Rep., D-MO), Dessima Williams (Brandeis Univ.).

Other Information: Oxfam received $13,590,790, or 94% of revenue, from gifts and grants awarded by foundations, affiliates, businesses, and individuals. (These grants included $50,000 from the Tides Foundation, $10,300 from the Haymarket People's Fund, $5,000 from the New Prospect Foundation, $5,000 from the Peace Development Fund, $2,050 from the Vanguard Public Foundation, $1,000 from the Peace Development Fund, $300 from the Vanguard Public Foundation, and $200 from the Ruth Mott Fund.) $358,084, or 2%, from rental income. $351,818, or 2%, from the sale of inventory. The remaining revenue came from interest on savings and temporary cash investments and other program services. Revenues were partially offset by a loss on the sale of securities.

Pacifica Foundation

3729 W. Cahuenga Blvd.
North Hollywood, CA 91604
USA

Phone: (818) 985-8800
Fax: (818) 985-8802

Contact Person: David Salniker, Executive Director.

Officers or Principals: David Salniker, Executive Director ($54,900); Patricia Scott, Interim Executive Director ($51,850); Richard Bunce, Development Director ($50,027); Marci Baulsir, General Manager, KPFA-FM; Gail Christian, National Program Director; Jack O'Dell, Chair; Cecilia McCall, Vice Chair; Janis Hazel, Secretary; June Makela, Treasurer.

Mission or Interest: Operates five FM, "non-commercial educational radio stations, and a news service." Provides radio programming for other stations and outlets, college radio stations are frequent carriers of Pacifica programming. Programing topics include African-American affairs and history, feminism, environmentalism, and foreign policy.

Accomplishments: Pacifica co-sponsored the 1996 Media and Democracy Congress in San Francisco. Topics included strengthening independent journalism, grappling with new technology, and responding to threats from the Right. Other sponsors included the Center for Media Education, Fairness and Accuracy in Media, *The Progressive*, Political Research Associates, and *Utne Reader*. Radio Pacifica featured commentaries by death row convict Mumia Abu-Jamal. These commentaries were originally going to be broadcast by National Public Radio, but NPR backed down in the face of criticism. Abu-Jamal was convicted of killing Daniel Faulkner, a Philadelphia police officer in 1982. Faulkner was found dead, shot several times with Abu-Jamal's gun and bullets, while Abu-Jamal was found wounded by Faulkner's gun. Abu-Jamal's supporters claim that he did not receive a fair trial and was railroaded because of his political activism, and that there were numerous irregularities and unreliable witnesses. Abu-Jamal's commentaries were published in full in Live from Death Row (Addison-Wesley, 1995). In the fiscal year ending September 1994, the Foundation spent $4,763,300 on its programming and projects.
Net Revenue: FY ending 9/94 $7,191,591 ($1,097,835, or 15%, from government grants)
Net Expenses: $7,522,069 63%/20%/17% **Net Assets:** $5,463,009 **Citations:** 25:166
Products or Services: Radio programming, broadcasting, audio tapes, and lobbying. The Foundation spent $31,150 directly lobbying congress. "The purpose of the visits was to correct mis-information about Pacifica Foundation that had been circulating to congressional representatives." The lobbying was set up by Podesta Associates. Tapes of previous programming feature Prof. Noam Chomsky, radical historian Howard Zinn, columnist Molly Ivins, author Gore Vidal, Rev. Jesse Jackson, Black Panther Party leader Eldridge Cleaver, Physicians for Social Responsibility and Women's Action for New Directions founder Dr. Helen Caldicott, author Ken Kesey, Children's Defense Fund president Marion Wright Edelman, Barbara Ehrenriech, and many others.
Tax Status: 501(c)(3)
Board of Directors or Trustees: Leonor Lizardo, Roberta Brooks, Ambose Lane, Frank Millspaugh, Roger Scarbrough, Moneim Fadali, Alexis Gonzalez, Linda Mabalot.
Other Information: The Foundation received $4,781,032, or 66% of revenue, from gifts and grants awarded by foundations, businesses, and individuals. (These grants included $15,000 from the Town Creek Foundation, $5,000 from the General Service Foundation, $300 from the Haymarket People's Fund, $150 from the Compton Foundation, and $100 from the Stewart R. Mott Charitable Trust. In 1995 these included $37,600 from the Tides Foundation.) $1,097,835, or 15%, from government grants. $747,617, or 10%, from sub-carrier royalties. $191,090 net , or 3%, from special fund-raising events. $112,955, or 2%, from radio news fees paid by radio stations for a ½ hour newscast. $79,616, or 1%, from the sale of audio tapes. The remaining revenue came from mailing list rentals, dividends and interest from securities, interest on savings and temporary cash investments, rental income, folio advertising, and other miscellaneous sources.

Palestine Aid Society (PAS)
2025 I St., N.W., Suite 1020
Washington, DC 20006   **Phone:**   (202) 728-9425
USA

Contact Person: Taleb Salhab, Executive Director. **Officers or Principals:** Taleb Salhab, Executive Director ($26,000); George Zahr, President ($0); Rabia Shafie, Vice President ($0); Sahar Al Bazzaz, Staff.
Mission or Interest: Human rights monitoring and aid for Palestinians.
Accomplishments: In 1994 the Society spent $116,756 on its programs. The largest program, with expenditures of $72,473, was the distribution of information at their national convention. Grants were awarded, including: $14,510 for the Union of Health Care Committees, $6,033 for the Hebron Red Crescent Society, $5,740 for the Society of In'ash El-Usra, $5,000 for the Palestinian Federation of Women's Actions Committees. $12,500 in donated medical equipment was given away. $500 was spent on the Women's Studies Center.
Net Revenue: 1994 $162,249 **Net Expenses:** $162,141 72%/19%/9% **Net Assets:** $11,507
Tax Status: 501(c)(3)
Board of Directors or Trustees: Fairuz Lutfi, Linda Ramadan, Najwa Jardali, Tawfiq Barqawi, Noel Saleh, Emil Qadi, Bushra Karaman.
Periodicals: *PAS Newsletter*.
Other Information: The Society received $91,228, or 56% of revenue, from gifts and grants awarded by foundations, businesses, and individuals. $69,627, or 43%, from program services, including special events, convention fees, and other sources. $1,205, or 1%, from membership fees. The remaining revenue came from interest on savings and temporary cash investments.

Parents, Families and Friends of Lesbians and Gays (PFFLAG)
1101 14th St., N.W., Suite 1030
Washington, DC 20005   **Phone:**   (202) 638-4200
USA

Contact Person: Sandra Gillis, Executive Director. **Officers or Principals:** Sandra Gillis, Executive Director ($49,208); Mitzi Henderson, President ($0); Jon Wallman, Treasurer ($0); Eileen Durgin Clinchard, Vice President; Judith Tuuri-Ulseth.
Mission or Interest: "Operates programs to assist families and friends of people with AIDS, straight spouses, and youth, and support parents, families and friends of gays and lesbians."
Accomplishments: In the fiscal year ending September 1994, PFFLAG spent $720,021 on its programs. One of its programs initiated during this period was "Project Open Mind" which assists chapters with leadership training.
Net Revenue: FY ending 9/94 $914,316 **Net Expenses:** $910,566 79%/21%/0% **Net Assets:** $25,467 **Citations:** 245:68

Products or Services: Local support groups, telephone help lines, peer counseling, and publications.
Tax Status: 501(c)(3)
Other Information: PFFLAG received $682,455, or 75% of revenue, from gifts and grants awarded by foundations, businesses, and individuals. (These grants included $30,000 from the Joyce Mertz-Gilmore Foundation, and $3,200 from the Haymarket People's Fund.) $144,881, or 16%, from chapters' support. $44,249, or 5%, from the sale of publications. $33,670, or 4%, from membership dues. The remaining revenue came from rental income, and interest on savings and temporary cash investments.

Parents, Families and Friends of Lesbian and Gays, Washington DC Metropolitan Area (PFFLAG)
P.O. Box 28009
Washington, DC 20038
USA

Contact Person: Catherine Tuerk, President. **Officers or Principals:** Catherine Tuerk, President ($0); Jeanne Talpers, Vice President ($0); Sabina Cooper, Treasurer ($0); Shally Schwab, Secretary.
Mission or Interest: Washington, DC chapter of the national PFFLAG. Support group for parents and gay persons. AIDS support group.
Accomplishments: Approximately 3,500 members. In the fiscal year ending June 1994 the organization spent $27,226 on its programs. It paid $1,155 in dues to the national organization.
Net Revenue: FY ending 6/94 $25,657 **Net Expenses:** $30,292 **Net Assets:** $16,346
Tax Status: 501(c)(3)
Board of Directors or Trustees: Kevin Blass, Joanne Cate, Laurie Coburn, Ede Denenberg, Sarah Eveland, Shirley Goodman, Joyce Goodman, Ken Goodman, Ron Griesse, Maureen Healy, Suzi Kilbourne, James Nelson, Beverly Southerland, George Spiegel, Betty Sullivan, Bill Van Stone, John Walker, Barbara Warner, Seema Weinberg.
Other Information: The organization received $19,741, or 77% of revenues, from gifts or grants awarded by foundations, businesses, and individuals. $4,372, or 17%, from program service fees. $1,016 net, or 4%, from special fund-raising events. $528, or 2%, from investments income.

Parents for Rock and Rap (PFRR)
P.O. Box 53
Libertyville, IL 60048
USA

Mission or Interest: Organization fighting any censorship of music videos or recordings.
Accomplishments: PFRR won one of the first Hugh M. Hefner First Amendment Awards.
Periodicals: Newsletter.
Other Information: Parents for Rock and Rap is led by the mother of a band member from Rage Against the Machine, a band known for its communist advocacy.

Parliamentarians for Global Action
211 E. 43rd St., Suite 1604
New York, NY 10017 **Phone:** (212) 687-7755
USA

Mission or Interest: To strengthen multilateral and peacekeeping institutions.
Other Information: In 1993 the Parliamentarians received $200,000 over two years from the Carnegie Corporation, $50,000 from the Winston Foundation, $10,000 from the Town Creek Foundation. In 1994 the Parliamentarians received $60,000 from the Winston Foundation, $10,000 from the Ploughshares Fund, $10,000 from the Bydale Foundation, $5,000 from the New-Land Foundation.

Partisan Review
236 Bay State Rd.
Boston, MA 02215 **Phone:** (617) 353-4260
USA **Fax:** (617) 353-7444

Contact Person: William Phillips, President/Editor in Chief.
Officers or Principals: William Phillips, President/Editor in Chief ($30,275); Edith Kurzweil, Treasurer/Editor ($24,667); Helen Hazen, Clerk ($0); Steven Marcus, Associate Editor; Jane Uscilka, Managing Editor; Joanna S. Rose, Chairman.
Mission or Interest: Quarterly journal of Marxist social and literary criticism. Publishes non-fiction, fiction, poetry, book reviews and more.
Accomplishments: Distribution of approximately 8,500 copies per issue. During the first half of the century *Partisan Review* was a central point of non-sectarian radical and socialist criticism. In the fiscal year ending August 1994 *Partisan Review* spent $281,754 on its publication and distribution.
Net Revenue: FY ending 8/94 $337,530 ($21,600, or 6%, from government grants) **Net Expenses:** $326,684 86%/14%/0%
Net Assets: $19,036
Tax Status: 501(c)(3)

Periodicals: *Partisan Review* (quarterly journal).
Other Information: Affiliated with Boston University. Sidney Hook, a one time frequent contributor to *Partisan Review*, summed up its importance as "It was almost entirely literary and aesthetic, with a political stance reactive against the excesses of Stalinism but lacking a sense of the important problems created by the crisis of Marxism, the bankruptcy and criminality of Leninism and Stalinism, and the development of the New Deal and the Welfare State. The editors regarded the basic questions of education, law, philosophy, economics, and social thought as academic and boring...They were revolutionists not concerned with such superficial, quotidian questions as job and pension plans, labor legislation, unemployment insurance, or educational reform...they were revolutionists who for all their criticism of reformism, never took risks, never joined a picket line, did not get involved in any kind of political life, never reached out to trade-union members, or made attempts to win over the general public to the revolutionary cause through contributions to the mass media...Their undoubted merit was that they provided an opportunity for gifted young men and women, many of whom did not share their political views, to develop modernist literary themes in the pages of *Partisan Review*." The *Review* received $244,674, or 72% of revenue, from gifts and grants awarded by foundations and individuals. $70,347, or 21%, from sales and subscriptions. $21,600, or 6%, from government grants. The remaining revenue came from interest on savings and temporary cash investments. The publication of the *Review* cost $281,754, while revenues from its sale were only $70,347, requiring a subsidization of $211,407. This comes to a subsidization of $24.90 per subscriber/newsstand purchaser per year.

Pathfinder International

9 Galen St.
Watertown, MA 02172   **Phone:**   (617) 924-7200
USA

Contact Person: Daniel E. Pellegsom, President.   **Officers or Principals:** Daniel E. Pellegsom, President ($185,312); Doug Hubor, Director, Medical Services ($168,560); Claudia Ford, Vice President ($150,637); Carol L. Gibbs, Vice President, Finance ($114,790); Turkiz Gakgal, Vice President, Asia/near East ($108,536); Gerald Rosenthal, Development ($103,958).
Mission or Interest: Helps fund new and strategic birth control programs and population control programs in Asia, Latin America and Africa.
Accomplishments: In the fiscal year ending June 1994, the organization spent $36,131,024 on its programs. Most of this, $24,633,104, was awarded in grants to organizations outside of the United States. $18,876,326 went to programs in Asia. $8,967,331 went to Latin America, and $8,287,367 went to Africa.
Net Revenue: FY ending 6/94 $40,357,264   ($37,150,472, or 92%, from government grants)
Net Expenses: $40,337,990 90%/10%/1% **Net Assets:** $2,398,990 **Citations:** 2:231
Tax Status: 501(c)(3)
Board of Directors or Trustees: Timothy Armbruster, Ph.D. (Morris Goldseker Foundation), Dr. Nicolaas Biegman (Permanent Rep. of the Netherlands to the United Nations), J. Bayard Boyle, Jr., Holly Carter, James Epstein, Sarah Epstein, Henry Foster, Jr. M.D., Walter Gamble, M.D., Patrick Grant, Mary Hewlett, Meacham Hitchcock, Jennifer Kahrl, Kristina Kiehl, Dr. Oladapo Ladipo (South to South Cooperation in Reproductive Health), Mary Lindsay, Katherine Marshall, Jennifer Rosoff (Pres., Alan Guttmacher Inst.), Steven Sinding, Ph.D. (Director of Population Studies, Rockefeller Found.), Normand Smith, III, J.D., Paul Todd, Jr., Joseph Wheeler, Hon. Andrew Young (Chair, Law International).
Other Information: Pathfinder International received $37,150,472, or 92% of total revenue from government grants. (Most of these grants came from the United States Agency for International Development, USAID.) $3,141,124, or 8%, from gifts and grants awarded by foundations, businesses, and individuals. (These included $500,000 from the William and Flora Hewlett Foundation, $30,000 from the Compton Foundation, $20,000 from the General Service Foundation, and $500 from the Stewart R. Mott Charitable Trust.) The remaining revenue came from dividends and interest from securities, and interest on savings and temporary cash investments. The organization lost $32,062 on the sale of securities.

Pax Christi USA

348 E. 10th St.
Erie, PA 16503   **Phone:**   (814) 453-4955   **E-Mail:** paxchristi@igc.apc.org
USA   **Fax:**   (814) 452-4784

Contact Person: Mary Lou Kownacki, OSB, National Coordinator.
Officers or Principals: Bishop of Richmond, Walter F. Sullivan, President; Mary Carter Warren, Chair; Colleen McHenry-Connell, Treasurer; Cindy Pile, Executive Committee Member-at-Large.
Mission or Interest: "National Catholic peace movement." Research, education, and lobbying to promote peace and justice.
Accomplishments: Pax Christi published a statement on current public policies, "A Catholic Covenant of Compassion," in *The New York Times* that rejects "policies that would balance our national budget on the backs of those who are poor...policies which allocate exorbitant funds for the military while denying adequate funds for education, housing and the environment...government sanctioned death by capitol punishment...policies which institutionalize fear or deny the basic human rights of any member of society...policies which would close our borders to people from other countries, subject immigrants to harsh and discriminatory policies, and deny foreign aid to the people of countries in need." The statement, however, affirms "the development of affordable housing, equal access to education, universal health care, safe neighborhoods and full employment with a livable income...policies which empower and celebrate all people...a social structure that honors the value of every human life and fosters a supportive environment for children and families...policies which advocate our responsibility as stewards of creation."

Products or Services: Sells prayer cards, such as "Jesus Was a Victim of the Death Penalty: A Prayer to Abolish the Death Penalty." Catalog of greeting cards and gifts.

Tax Status: 501(c)(3)

Board of Directors or Trustees: David Atwood, Jim Burns, Ligory Fernandes, Margaret Gaffney, Bishop of Detroit Thomas Gumbleton, Elrik Fredrick-Harteis, Kathleen McInnis, RSM, Antonia Malone, Matthew Smith.

Periodicals: *Catholic Peace Voice* (quarterly newsletter).

Other Information: Co founded by Eileen Egan in the 1960's. Eileen was a "back door" lobbyist at the Vatican II council, and pressed for, among other things, a condemnation of indiscriminate warfare and the killing of civilians. Egan describes the basis of her faith as "we have to be transformed to be other Christs. And that transformation can only come by grace, and grace comes from prayer and surrender to God." In 1994 Pax Christi received $2,500 from the Peace Development Fund.

Pax World Services

1111 16th St., N.W.
Washington, DC 20036   **Phone:** (202) 293-7290
USA

Officers or Principals: Charlotte Rhoads, Past President ($40,880); Charles Demere, Chair ($0); Larry Ekin, President ($0); Joan Baker, Vice Chair; Robert McCan, Treasurer; Tom Veblen, Secretary.

Mission or Interest: International peace and understanding through citizen diplomacy and international institutions.

Accomplishments: In 1994 the organization spent $410,843 on its programs. The largest program, with expenditures of $203,289, was "Friendship Tours" that provided tours of troubled regions abroad to practice citizen diplomacy. $106,043 was spent "promoting understanding of the role of international institutions in encouraging and maintaining world peace." $57,360 was spent on a "Support the United Nations" campaign. $44,151 was spent supporting "community-based development efforts focussing on agro-forestry, agricultural research, and seed distribution. The organization awarded $19,193 in grants, mostly to organizations outside of the U.S.

Net Revenue: 1994 $548,772 **Net Expenses:** $480,330 86%/11%/3% **Net Assets:** $81,147 **Citations:** 0:255

Tax Status: 501(c)(3)

Board of Directors or Trustees: Rita Clark, Diana Dajani, Gregory Davis, Louise Diamond, Joseph Eldridge, Allison Herrick, Thomas Jones, Don Kruse, Phoebe Lansdale, Lucille Levin, Doug Nelson, Mary Jane Paterson, Eddy Perez, Christine Tucker.

Other Information: Pax World Services received $328,448, or 60% of revenue, from direct and indirect public support in the form of gifts and grants awarded by foundations, businesses, affiliates, and individuals. (These grants included $1,250 from the Foundation for Middle East Peace, and $100 from the Compton Foundation.) $154,473, or 28%, from Friendship Tour fees. $61,670, or 11%, from a "Peace Awards" event. The remaining revenue came from the sale of inventory, capital gains on the sale of securities, and interest on savings and temporary cash investments.

Peace Action

1819 H St., N.W., Suite 420
Washington, DC 20006   **Phone:** (202) 862-9740   **E-Mail:** paexcc@igc.apc.org
USA   **Fax:**   (202) 862-9762

Contact Person: Gordon Clark.

Officers or Principals: Monica Green, Executive Director ($36,889); Steven Brion-Meisels, Jan Sanders, Co-Chairs.

Mission or Interest: "Peace Action (formerly SANE/FREEZE) works to promote global security by redirecting federal spending priorities away from military and defense systems spending toward domestic needs, by stopping conventional weapons trafficking, and by promoting global nuclear disarmament."

Accomplishments: Founded in 1957. They currently have over 50,000 members. In 1993 they spent $348,238 on their efforts to influence the public and office holders. During the 1994 election, their political action committee was mostly successful. Two of the top three senate races they supported were won by the Democrats, Ted Kennedy (D-MA) and Chuck Robb (D-VA). Their support of Robb was more an effort to keep Republican Oliver North out of the Senate.

Net Revenue: 1993 $684,168 **Net Expenses:** $700,401 50%/18%/33% **Net Assets:** (-$207,484) **Citations:** 178:88

Products or Services: Networking, publications, speaking tours, and lobbying.

Tax Status: 501(c)(4) **Annual Report:** Yes. **Employees:** 14

Board of Directors or Trustees: Olivia Abelson, Dot Baker, Joan Bolte, Lois Booth, Kay Bridgeford, Beth Broadway, Acie Byrd, Elizabeth Ainsley Campbell, Norm Cohen, Judy Feinstein, Al Fishman, JoAnn Fuller, Mark Harrison, Michael Keller, Walter Kendall, Barbara Kopit, Judy Lerner, Don Macaulay, Darlene McNight, Jane Milliken, Virginia Morgan, Shirley Romaine, Robert Schwartz, Angelina Smith, Glen Stassen, Susan Strong, Sylvia Temmer, William Towe, Ester Webb, Cora Weiss.

Periodicals: *Peace Action* (quarterly newsletter).

Internships: Yes. Internships are available with the Peace Economy Campaign, the Nuclear Disarmament Campaign, the Arms Trade Campaign, and the Grassroots Development Program.

Other Information: Peace Action was formerly called SANE/FREEZE. They have a 501(c)(3) research and education affiliate, Peace Action Education Fund at the same address. The organization received $513,714, or 75% of revenue, from gifts and grants awarded by foundations, companies, and individuals. (These included $500 from the Haymarket People's Fund, $400 from the Bread and Roses Community Fund.) $77,446, or 11%, from membership dues. $30,072, or 4%, from mailing list rentals. $21,390, or 3%, from special fund-raising events. The remaining revenue came from the sale of publications, book royalties, and other miscellaneous sources. In 1994 the two affiliates had combined net revenues of approximately $1,215,267, and net expenses of $1,118,556.

Peace Action Education Fund

1819 H St., N.W., Suite 425
Washington, DC 20006   **Phone:** (202) 862-9740   **E-Mail:** paexec@igc.apc.org
USA   **Fax:**   (202) 862-9762

Contact Person: Gordon Clark.   **Officers or Principals:** Frances D. Teplitz, Executive Director ($28,233); Marcus Raskin, Chair ($0); Duane Shank, Secretary/Treasurer ($0).
Mission or Interest: Research and educational affiliate of Peace Action (formerly SANE/FREEZE).
Accomplishments: In 1994 the Fund spent $280,884 on its programs. These included programs on both nuclear and conventional weapons disarmament, research on federal budget priorities and economic conversion from military to peace economies, and international outreach. The Fund awarded $74,892 in grants, mostly to state affiliates.
Net Revenue: 1994 $460,999 **Net Expenses:** $393,427 71%/12%/17% **Net Assets:** $77,195
Products or Services: Conferences, reports, lobbying. In 1994 the Fund spent $8,053 on grassroots lobbying. This was an increase of 23% over the previous year, but down 39% from 1992.
Tax Status: 501(c)(3)
Board of Directors or Trustees: Andrea Ayvazian (Comunitas), Monica Green (Peace Action), Mary Price, Ria Pugeda (Tides Found.), Carlotta Scott (Office of Rep. Ron Dellums, D-CA), Elizabeth Anisley Campbell.
Other Information: Marcus Raskin and Duane Shank are both affiliated with the Institute for Policy Studies. The Peace Action Education Fund is affiliated with the 501(c)(4) Peace Action at the same address. In 1994 the two affiliates had combined net revenues of approximately $1,215,267, and net expenses of $1,118,556. The Fund received $453,750, or 98% of revenue, from gifts and grants awarded by foundations, businesses, and individuals. (These grants included $16,617 from the Peace Development Fund, $10,000 from the Winston Foundation, $2,000 from the Stewart R. Mott Charitable Trust.) $4,281, or 1%, from interest on savings and temporary cash investments. The remaining revenue came from various miscellaneous sources.

Peace Action Education Fund, New Jersey

40 Witherspoon
Princeton, NJ 08542   **Phone:** (609) 924-5024
USA

Contact Person: Robert Moore, Executive Director.
Officers or Principals: Robert Moore, Executive Director ($34,917); Patricia Cox, Associate Director ($15,945); Rev. Leslie Smith, Chairperson ($0); Darlene McKnight, Dr. George Temmer, Vice Chair; Stuart Brown, Treasurer; Gale Colby, Secretary.
Mission or Interest: Supports peaceful conflict resolution, against nuclear weapons.
Accomplishments: In 1994 the Fund spent $52,420 on its programs. These included a day long Children's Peace Fair, and various events and presentations in New Jersey.
Net Revenue: 1994 $81,897 **Net Expenses:** $71,669 **Net Assets:** $40,894
Products or Services: Awards the Lock Peace Prize.
Tax Status: 501(c)(3)
Other Information: Affiliated with the 501(c)(4) Coalition for Peace Action. The Fund was formerly called the Nuclear Disarmament Education Fund. The Fund received $53,738, or 66% of revenue, from gifts and grants awarded by foundations, businesses, and individuals. $14,786, or 18%, from program service revenues. $12,867 net, or 16%, from special fund-raising events. The remaining revenue came from investment income.

Peace and Justice Action League of Spokane

310 W. 5th Ave.
Spokane, WA 99204   **Phone:** (509) 838-7870
USA   **Fax:**   same

Contact Person: Lewis R. Nelson, Co-Director.   **Officers or Principals:** Lewis R. Nelson, Co-Director ($9,900); Nancy J. Nelson, Co-Director ($9,900); Betsey Heberer, Store Manager ($8,448); Chuck Armsbury, Chairperson.
Mission or Interest: "Peace and Justice" issues, such as poverty, racism, militarism, institutional violence, trade issues, and U.S. involvement in Latin America and Haiti.
Accomplishments: Approximately 350 members. In 1995 the League hosted four large Hiroshima-Nagasaki commemorative events. Recently began anti-racism programs. In 1993 the League spent $48,658 on its programs. The largest program, with expenditures of $22,426, was a Global Folk Art Bazaar that sells handmade crafts to "support low income individuals in the local community and in developing countries and to educate consumers about economic and social conditions." $14,710 was spent on public forums covering various issues. $9,022 was spent on a monthly newsletter and various bulletins.
Net Revenue: 1993 $68,984 **Net Expenses:** $57,427 85%/11%/4% **Net Assets:** $49,380
Products or Services: Public forums, arts and crafts, publications, and lobbying. The League spent $4,750 on lobbying. $2,000 was spent lobbying against NAFTA. $1,000 was spent lobbying congress to close the School of the Americas, a military academy that trains Latin American soldiers. $1,000 for lobbying against state and federal death penalty laws. $750 lobbying for policies "that would relieve hunger domestically and internationally."
Tax Status: 501(c)(3)
Board of Directors or Trustees: Chuck Armsbury, Gary Barlow, Doug Hockin, Teresa McCann, Alan McFarland, Mary Pat Truethart.

Periodicals: *Handful of Salt* (monthly newsletter).
Other Information: Founded in 1975. "Loosely" affiliated with the Fellowship of Reconciliation. The League received $31,492, or 46% of revenue, from the sale of inventory. $22,985, or 33%, from direct and indirect public support in the form of gifts and grants awarded by foundations, businesses, affiliates, and individuals. $11,871, or 17%, from membership dues. $2,539, or 4%, from special fund-raising events. The remaining revenue came from interest on savings and temporary cash investments, and honoraria.

Peace and Justice Center

21 Church St.
Burlington, VT 05401   **Phone:** (802) 863-8326   **E-Mail:** pjc@together.org
USA   **Fax:**   (802) 863-2532

Contact Person: Ellen Kahler.
Officers or Principals: Wendy Coe, Treasurer; Gene Bergman, Robin Lloyd, Ted Lewis, Tom Ragland, Jon Seely, Editors.
Mission or Interest: "Works for a just, peaceful and ecologically healthy world through education, advocacy, training and non-violent action."
Accomplishments: Their newsletter has a circulation of 1,500. Conducted diversity training for nonprofit groups and city government departments. The director of their Racial Justice & Equity Project joined the "Million Man March' in Washington, DC. Mobilized Vermonters to oppose state and federal budget cuts.
Net Revenue: FY ending 10/94 $165,939 **Net Expenses:** $185,076 77%/22%/1% **Net Assets:** $51,395
Products or Services: Technical assistance and small grants to grassroots organizations. A nonprofit Peace and Justice Store that sells a variety of items. Proceeds from the sales of certain items are dedicated to certain projects; i.e. proceeds from the sale of "Gay Java" go to gay and lesbian rights programs.
Tax Status: 501(c)(3) **Annual Report:** No. **Employees:** 7
Board of Directors or Trustees: Richard Kemp, Ed Everts, Crystal Holzer, Peter Duval, Robert Bensing, Donald Donnelly, Orin Langalle, Nancy Farrell, Marsha Mason, Christopher Myott, Sr. Marlene Perrotte, Chris Wood, Tom Mansfield, Judith Joseph.
Periodicals: *Peace & Justice News* (bimonthly).
Internships: Yes.
Other Information: They were formerly called the Peace & Justice Coalition. This name change was completed during the November 18, 1995 meeting following a fourteen-month restructuring process. The Center received $103,722, or 63% of revenue, from gifts and grants awarded by foundations, companies and individuals. (These grants included $7,000 from the Haymarket People's Fund, $2,500 from the Peace Development Fund, $1,500 from the Peace Development Fund, $1,000 from the Vanguard Public Foundation.) $55,145 net, or 33%, from the sale of inventory. $3,596, or 3%, from program services, including the sale of publications and goods. $3,347 net, or 2%, from special fund-raising events. The remaining revenue came from interest on savings and temporary cash investments.

Peace Development Fund (PDF)

44 N. Prospect St.
Amherst, MA 01004   **Phone:** (413) 256-8306   **E-Mail:** pdfeast@igc.apc.org
USA   **Fax:**   (413) 256-8871

Contact Person: Dana Gillette, Office Manager.
Officers or Principals: Ravi Khanna, Executive Director ($41,800); Elizabeth Rankin, Secretary ($30,034); Tawna Sanchez, Chair.
Mission or Interest: Foundation providing financial awards and technical assistance to "peace and justice" organizations.
Accomplishments: Since its founding in 1981, PDF has funded over 2,000 groups nationwide. In the fiscal year ending June 1994 they awarded $1,190,810 in grants. Recipients of the largest grants were: four grants totaling $93,045 for the National Commission for Economic Conversion and Disarmament, three grants totaling $92,500 for the Center for Economic Conversion, $30,000 for the Network in Solidarity with the People of Guatemala, $23,500 for the Helsinki Citizens' Assembly, $20,000 each for the Maine Peace Fund, Silicon Valley Toxics Coalition, St. Louis Economic Conversion Project, and Minnesota Jobs With Peace, $17,600 for Citizen Alert, $17,500 for Educators for Social Responsibility, $17,300 each for the Labor/Community Strategy Center and Native Americans for a Clean Environment, $15,000 each for Call to Action-Labor's Agenda for Economic Conversion, Carolina Alliance for Fair Employment of WRP, Long Island Alliance for Peaceful Alternatives, New Mexico Alliance, Peace Action of Washington, San Diego Economic Conversion Council and Tri-Valley CAREs, $11,374 for the Amazon Project, $10,000 each for the Lambi Fund of Haiti, North Dakota Peace Coalition and ASECSA (Guatemalan community organizing).
Net Revenue: FY ending 6/94 $2,272,165 **Net Expenses:** $1,956,961 $84%/10%/7% **Net Assets:** $446,438
Products or Services: Grants and technical assistance. Video tapes. Lobbying - in the fiscal year ending 6/94 they spent $29,763 on lobbying, $4,500 on grassroots lobbying and $25,263 on the direct lobbying of legislators. This was a large reduction, down 84%, from the previous year when they spent $162,000 on lobbying.
Tax Status: 501(c)(3) **Annual Report:** Yes. **Employees:** 10
Board of Directors or Trustees: Faye Brown, Kathy Flewellen (National African-American Network), Atanacio Gonzalez (Equal Rights Congress), Paul Haible, Noha Shaath Ismail (American Arab Anti-Discrimination League), Jennifer Ladd (Class Action), Robin Lloyd (Green Valley Film and Art Center), Karimah Nonyameko, Marla Painter (Rural Alliance for Military Accountability), Prof. Emeritus Alan Rabinowitz (Univ. of WA), Hubert Ellis Sapp (OXFAM), N. Jean Sindab (National Council of Churches), Abbot Stranahan (Needmor Fund).

Internships: Yes, unpaid.
Other Information: The Fund received $2,210,383, or 97% of revenue, from gifts and grants awarded by foundations, businesses, and individuals. (These grants included $500,000 over two years from the John D. and Catherine T. MacArthur Foundation, $35,000 from the Joyce Mertz-Gilmore Foundation, $15,000 from the Jessie Smith Noyes Foundation, $14,000 from the Haymarket People's Fund, $5,000 from the Aaron and Martha Schecter Foundation, $1,000 from the Stewart R. Mott Charitable Trust, $1,000 from the Vanguard Public Foundation. In 1994-95, $180,750 from the Tides Foundation) $52,004, or 2%, from reimbursements paid by other organizations for administrative services. The remaining revenue came from interest on savings and temporary cash investments.

Peace Resource Project

P.O. Box 1122
Arcata, CA 95518   **Phone:**   (707) 822-4229
USA   **Fax:**   (707) 822-6202

Contact Person: Gabriel Day, Owner.
Mission or Interest: Produce and sell fund-raising products (buttons, shirts, stickers, etc.) for "grassroots peace, environmental, and pro-choice groups use for promoting themselves within their community."
Products or Services: Catalog of products.
Tax Status: For profit. **Employees:** 6

PeaceNet

(see the Institute for Global Communications)

Pennsylvania Environmental Council

1211 Chestnut St.
Philadelphia, PA 19107   **Phone:**   (215) 563-0250
USA

Contact Person: Joanne Denworth, Executive Director.   **Officers or Principals:** Joanne Denworth, Executive Director ($62,308); Patrick Starr, Program Director ($53,773); Andy Johnson, Program Director ($48,632).
Mission or Interest: Environmental education projects in Pennsylvania.
Accomplishments: In the fiscal year ending June 1994, the Council spent $734,155 on its projects.
Net Revenue: FY ending 6/94 $952,416   **Net Expenses:** $935,453   78%/15%/7%   **Net Assets:** $116,636
Citations: 30:157
Products or Services: Consulting, seminars, conferences, and lobbying. The Council spent $20,487 on the direct lobbying of legislators. This was a 118% increase over the previous year.
Tax Status: 501(c)(3)
Board of Directors or Trustees: Betty Ross (PA League of Women Voters), Maurice Goddard (National Wildlife Found.), Patricia Imperato (PA Resources Council), Melissa Parker (Environmental Law Inst.), Karen Pitcairn (Clean Air Council), many others from the Pennsylvania environmental, academic, and business communities.
Other Information: The Council received $471,272, or 49% of revenue, from gifts and grants awarded by foundations, businesses, and individuals. $325,975, or 34%, from consulting and other service fees. $96,234 net, or 10%, from special fund-raising events. $51,454, or 5%, from membership dues. $5,215, or 1%, from seminars and conferences. The remaining revenue came from interest on savings and temporary cash investments, and other miscellaneous sources.

Pennsylvanians for Modern Courts

1717 Arch St., Suite 3700
Philadelphia, PA 19103   **Phone:**   (215) 994-5196
USA

Contact Person: Ellen Mattleman Kaplan, Associate Director.
Officers or Principals: Lynn A. Marks, Executive Director ($77,569); Ellen Mattleman Kaplan, Associate Director ($34,817); Hon. Edmund B. Spaeth, Jr., Chairman ($0); Frederick L. Voight, Treasurer.
Mission or Interest: "To study and affect reform of the judicial system of Pennsylvania through education and increased public awareness."
Accomplishments: In the fiscal year ending June 1994, the organization spent $108,884 on its projects.
Net Revenue: FY ending 6/94 $228,989   **Net Expenses:** $180,630   60%/24%/16%   **Net Assets:** $67,847
Tax Status: 501(c)(3)
Board of Directors or Trustees: Hon. Arlin Adams, Jeffrey Burdge, Constance Clayton, Ph.D., Francis Haas, Jr., Ernest Jones (Greater Philadelphia Urban Affairs Coalition), Leon Holt, Jr., John Murray, Jr. (Duquesne Univ.), Nancy Neuman.
Other Information: Affiliated with the 501(c)(4) Pennsylvanians for Modern Courts Fund. Executive director Lynn Marks is also a director for the Women's Law Project. The organization received $221,510, or 97% of revenue, from gifts and grants awarded by foundations, businesses, and individuals. $6,646, or 3%, from expense reimbursements from the lobbying affiliate. The remaining revenue came from interest on savings and temporary cash investments.

People Against Racist Terror (PART)

P.O. Box 1990
Burbank, CA 91507   **Phone:**   (310) 288-5003   **E-Mail:** mnovicktt@igc.apc.org
USA

Contact Person: Michael Novick.
Mission or Interest: "Resisting racism, sexism and colonialism, educating young people, exposing and opposing organized white supremacist and neo-Nazi groups and their links to institutionalized oppressive political and economic power." PART researches and publishes "organized white supremacist connections to anti-abortion violence, law enforcement, gay-bashing, anti-immigrant hysteria and the Christian Right," as well as solutions to these problems. Also anti-Zionist.
Accomplishments: Publishing their journal *Turning the Tide* on a shoe-string budget since 1986. Hosted many rallies and educational events in Southern California. Worked at building various coalitions. Recent issues of *Turning the Tide* have focused on: "Pat Buchanan: Point Man for Fascism," militias and their roots in American history, the case of Mumia Abu-Jamal (a black man convicted of killing a police officer in Philadelphia whose supporters claim he was railroaded - for more information see the Pacifica Foundation) and other "political prisoners," connections between police and white supremacist organizations, and more.
Products or Services: Networking, organizing and publications.
Tax Status: Unincorporated. **Employees:** 0
Periodicals: *Turning the Tide: A Journal of Anti-Racist Activism, Research & Education* (quarterly journal).
Internships: No.
Other Information: Novick is the author of White Lies, White Power: The Fight Against White Supremacy and Reactionary Violence (Common Courage Press, 1995). He is an adult education teacher, active in United Teachers Los Angeles. PART is an affiliate of the Center for Democratic Renewal.

People for the American Way (PAW)

2000 M St., N.W., Suite 400
Washington, DC 20036   **Phone:**   (202) 467-4999
USA

Contact Person: Arthur J. Kropp, President. **Officers or Principals:** Arthur J. Kropp, President ($147,760); D. Bollier ($92,341); Mike Hudson, Vice President ($82,822); Frieda King, Secretary; Demetra Green, Treasurer; Rev. Dr. David Ramage, Jr., Chairman.
Mission or Interest: Organization dedicated to maintaining a wall of separation between church and state. Opposed to censorship and considers parents objecting to certain school-provided educational materials to be censorship. Supports feminism, gay rights, and abortion rights. Strongly opposed to the 'Religious Right.'
Accomplishments: In 1994 PAW spent $4,015,735 on its programs. The largest program, with expenditures of $1,048,360, is membership and public information. $885,097 was spent responding to state and local concerns. $545,924 was spent on research. $365,584 was spent on media communications, including press conferences, press releases, and op-eds. $253,224 was spent on management and program development, including long and short-term strategic planning. $224,223 was spent on a legal defense fund. Other projects included public policy research and analysis, The Art Save Project, Voter/Citizen Project, Race Relations/Intolerance Project, and others.
Net Revenue: 1994 $5,768,956 **Net Expenses:** $5,918,922 68%/18%/14% **Net Assets:** $711,791 **Citations:** 707:30
Tax Status: 501(c)(3)
Board of Directors or Trustees: David Altschul (Warner Bros. Records), James Autry (author), Alec Baldwin (actor), Rev. Dr. Charles Bergstrom, Fr. Robert Brooks (Bishop's Staff Officer, Washington Office of the Episcopal Church), Blair Brown (actress), Don Cameron (National Education Association), Julius Chambers (Chancellor, North Carolina Central Univ.), Hon. Fr. Robert Drinan (former Rep., D-MA), James Gibson (Urban Inst.), Andrew Heiskell (Chairman Emeritus, New York Public Library), Norman Lear (television producer), Anthony Podesta (founding president), Thomas Pollock (Chair, MCA/Universal), Rabbi David Saperstein (Union of American Hebrew Congregations), Rev. William Schulz (Exec. Dir., Amnesty Int'l), Rev. Charles Stith (Organization for a New Equality), Margery Tabankin (Streisand Foundation), Cynthia Ann Telles Ph.D. (UCLA School of Medicine), Kathleen Turner (actress), and others.
Other Information: People for the American Way is affiliated with the 501(c)(4) People for the American Way Action Fund at the same address. Arthur Kropp is president of both, and was paid a combined $164,178. The two affiliates had combined net revenues of $7,189,602, net expenses of $7,493,393, and net assets of $1,474,347. The organization hired the Washington, DC, firm of O'Brien, McConnell & Co., for consulting; the firm was paid $66,000. Other hired consultants included Sandy Horwitt, Margo Fox, Susan Glickman, and John Buchanan. PAW received $5,481,184, or 95% of revenue, from gifts and grants awarded by foundations, businesses, and individuals. (These grants included $185,000 from the North Star Fund, $85,000 from the Deer Creek Foundation, $75,000 from the Nathan Cummings Foundation, $50,000 from the Joyce Foundation, $35,000 from the Robert Sterling Clark Foundation, $35,000 from the Joyce Mertz-Gilmore Foundation, $5,000 from the New Prospect Foundation, $1,000 from the Tides Foundation, $900 from the Stewart R. Mott Charitable Trust, $750 from the Aaron and Martha Schecter Private Foundation, $500 from the Haymarket People's Fund, and $150 from the Compton Foundation. In 1995, $50,000 from the Rockefeller Foundation.) $112,520, or 2%, from "in-kind contributions." $49,314, or 1%, from sub-lease income. $47,694, or 1%, from interest on savings and temporary cash investments. $39,241, or 1%, from mailing list rentals. $39,155, or 1%, from the sale of books and publications. The remaining income came from other miscellaneous sources.

People for the American Way Action Fund

2000 M. St., N.W., Suite 400
Washington, DC 20036   **Phone:**   (202) 467-4999
USA

Contact Person: Arthur J. Kropp, President. **Officers or Principals:** Arthur J. Kropp, President ($16,418); Frieda King, Secretary ($1,349); Michael Hudson, Vice President ($0); Demetra Green, Treasurer; Rev. Dr. David Ramage, Jr., Chairman.

Mission or Interest: Lobbying affiliate of People for the American Way.

Accomplishments: In 1994 the Fund spent $942,510 on its programs.

Net Revenue: 1994 $1,420,646 **Net Expenses:** $1,574,471 60%/13%/27% **Net Assets:** $762,556 **Citations:** 707:29

Tax Status: 501(c)(4)

Board of Directors or Trustees: James Autry (author), Rev. Dr. Charles Bergstrom, Fr. Robert Brooks (Bishop's Staff Officer, Washington Office of the Episcopal Church), Don Cameron (National Education Association), Arthur Chotin (American Financial Printers), Hon. Fr. Robert Drinan (former Rep., D-MA), Timothy Dyk, Katherine Mountcastle, Clyde Shorey, Margery Tabankin (Barbra Streisand Found).

Periodicals: *Forum* (quarterly newsletter).

Other Information: People for the American Way Action Fund is affiliated with the 501(c)(3) People for the American Way at the same address. Arthur Kropp is president of both, and was paid a combined $164,178. The two affiliates had combined net revenues of $7,189,602, net expenses of $7,493,393, and net assets of $1,474,347. The Action Fund received $1,395,283, or 98% of revenue, from gifts and grants awarded by foundations, businesses, and individuals. $21,152, or 1%, from interest on savings and temporary cash investment. The remaining revenue came from mailing list rentals, and the sale of books and materials.

People for the Ethical Treatment of Animals (PETA)

P.O. Box 42516

Washington, DC 20015-0516	**Phone:** (301) 770-7444	
USA	**Fax:** (301) 770-8969	**Web-Page:** http://envirolink.org/arrs/peta

Contact Person: Tracy Skalitzky, Personnel Assistant.   **Officers or Principals:** Scott Anderson, Director, Membership Development ($55,902); Jeff Kerr, Director, Finance ($45,000); Jeanne Roush, Executive Director ($44,944); Alex Pacheco, President; Ingrid Newkirk, Vice President; Linda Tyrell, Secretary/Treasurer.

Mission or Interest: Animal rights organization that believes animals "are not ours to eat, wear, experiment on, or use for entertainment."

Accomplishments: Persuaded factories to alter their smoke stacks so that birds and bats could not fly in. The "rescue of eleven chimpanzees in Buckshire." Convinced cosmetics company Loreal to stop testing on animals.

Net Revenue: FY ending 7/94 $11,647,866 **Net Expenses:** $11,520,211 80%/5%/16% **Net Assets:** $5,723,020

Citations: 1,208:20

Products or Services: Various educational and outreach activities. In the fiscal year ending July 1994 they spent $2,829,212 on seminars, publications and guides, many targeted to teachers and the educational system. They spent $2,312,916 on the research, investigation, evidence gathering, law enforcement liaison, and "rescuing" of animals. $3,484,777 was spent on international grassroots efforts to "inform the public how animals are abused in, among other places, the meat, clothing, testing, and entertainment industries." Various t-shirts, videos, and household products that have not been tested on animals. They also spent $8,546 on lobbying at the grassroots level, up from $1,896 the year before, but down from $126,761 two years prior. PETA also awards grants to other animal rights organizations and activists. They spent $780,263, including six grants totaling $71,100 for the Animal Rights Law Clinic at Rutgers University.

Tax Status: 501(c)(3) **Annual Report:** No.

Periodicals: *Animal Times* (bimonthly newsletter).

Other Information: PETA employed Public Interest Communications of Falls Church, VA, and paid them $359,962. PETA received $10,669,618, or 92% of revenue, from direct and indirect public support in the form of gifts and grants awarded by foundations, companies and individuals. (These grants included $500 from the One World Fund, $200 from the Animal Welfare Institute, and $37 from the Environmental Federation of California.) $494,801 net, or 4%, from the sale of inventory. $184,029, or 2%, from dividends and interest from securities. $99,016, or 1%, from mailing list rentals. The remaining revenue came from program services, interest on savings and temporary cash investments, net rental income, net income from special events, and other miscellaneous sources.

People Organized in Defense of Earth and Her Resources (PODER)

55 N. IH 35, Suite 205B

Austin, TX 78702	**Phone:** (512) 472-9921
USA	

Contact Person: Susan Almanza.

Officers or Principals: Research and community education on the effects of high tech industries and the environment. Focus on the Austin, TX area.

Mission or Interest: PODER research results "suggest that the City of Austin has encouraged industrial development in the poorer minority East Austin neighborhoods while aggressively discouraging similar development in the more affluent and predominantly white West section of the city...Most of the pollution has disproportionately occurred in census tracts and zip codes closest to the industrial cluster - where the proportions of people of color are among the highest in Austin."

Other Information: Received a grant from the Poverty and Race Research Action Council.

People United to Lead the Struggle for Equality (PULSE)
180 19th St., N.E.
Miami, FL 33132   **Phone:** (305) 635-0309
USA

Contact Person: Nathaniel J. Wilcox, Executive Director. **Officers or Principals:** Rev. Rommie Loudd, President ($0); Woodward Vaught, Vice President ($0); William Wallace, Treasurer ($0); Egertha Steward, Secretary.
Mission or Interest: Work to improve the community, end racism, and promote equality.
Accomplishments: In the fiscal year ending June 1993, PULSE spent $55,873 on its programs. The largest program, with expenditures of $27,937, was the Committee to End Discrimination. This Committee "met with the Attorney General, Miami Chief of Police, FBI, and other law enforcement officials to ensure justice in racially sensitive trials involving police officers." $13,968 was spent on the Fair Jobs Committee which helped the homeless find employment in the hurricane Andrew relief efforts and met with the Chamber of Commerce to promote more minority employment. $13,968 was spent on the Education Committee which sought to improve community schools.
Net Revenue: FY ending 6/93 $60,005 **Net Expenses:** $65,733 **Net Assets:** $9,866
Tax Status: 501(c)(3)
Other Information: Pulse received $42,577, or 71% of revenue, from gifts and grants awarded by foundations, businesses, and individuals. $17,428, or 29%, from membership dues.

People's Culture
P.O. Box 5224
Kansas City, KS 66119   **Phone:** (913) 342-6379   **E-Mail:** fwhitehe@kumc.edu
USA

Contact Person: Fred Whitehead.
Mission or Interest: Newsletter collecting, analyzing, and disseminating information for the Left. Focus on organized labor, culture and history.
Accomplishments: "Have continued publication since 1991, in spite of the collapse of the Left." Stan Rosen, Professor of Labor and Industrial Relations, University of Illinois and Vice President of the Worker's Education Local, says of *People's Culture*, "The history and culture of organized labor is all too often forgotten or suppressed by the major cultural institutions of America. We need to support publications that recognize the cultural contributions of workers and union members."
Products or Services: Back issues, other pamphlets and publications.
Periodicals: *People's Culture* (quarterly).
Other Information: Published by Fred Whitehead, a prolific writer and editor. His description of his work: "My perspective is that of the great heritage of Midwestern U.S. radicalism, from the Populists to (socialist leader Eugene) Debs, to the present."

People's Fund
1325 Nu'uanu Ave., Suite 207
Honolulu, HI 96817   **Phone:** (808) 526-2441
USA   **Fax:**   same

Contact Person: Rick Rothschiller, Exec. Director. **Officers or Principals:** Richard Rothschiller, Executive Director ($30,000); Danny Li, President ($0); Ku'umealoha Gomes, Vice President ($0); Carl Varady, Secretary; Joe Nedelkovitsch, Treasurer.
Mission or Interest: Provide financial grants and technical support to grassroots organizations in Hawaii that are working for "fundamental progressive social change."
Accomplishments: Since their founding in 1972 they have awarded more than $700,000 in grants to hundreds of activist organizations working on "peace, economic equality, racism, women's rights, gay, lesbian and bisexual rights, youth, the environment, human rights, etc." In the fiscal year ending June 1994, they awarded $29,292 in grants. Top recipients were; $2,300 for the Free Association, $2,000 for the Surfing Education Association and First Friday, $1,900 for Environment Hawaii, $1,800 for the Education Committee on Breast Cancer and the Environment and the Indigenous Peoples Literary Network, and $1,662 for MiCasa Third World Solar Project. The remaining 24 grants averaged $676.
Net Revenue: FY ending 6/94 $54,180 **Net Expenses:** $75,303 **Net Assets:** $25,458
Products or Services: Grants, booklets.
Tax Status: 501(c)(3) **Annual Report:** Yes, a biannual report. **Employees:** 1
Board of Directors or Trustees: Ibrahim Aoude, Setsu Okubo, Frank Peterson, Rachel Saiki, Pete Wilcox, Yoon Bok-Dong.
Periodicals: *The People's Fund* (semiannual newsletter). **Internships:** Yes.
Other Information: They are an associate member of the Funding Exchange. Their maximum grants are set at $2,000. The Fund received $51,876, or 96% of revenue, from gifts and grants awarded by foundations, companies, affiliates, and individuals. (These grants included $3,000 from the Tides Foundation.) The remaining revenue came from investments and miscellaneous sources.

People's Institute for Survival and Beyond
1444 N. Johnson St.
New Orleans, LA 70116   **Phone:** (504) 944-2354
USA

Contact Person: Charles Mills, President.
Officers or Principals: Crystal Jones, Vice President ($0); La Vaun Ishes, Secretary/Treasurer ($0)
Mission or Interest: "Conducts 'undoing racism' workshops and consultations as educational development events in many states."
Participants included nonprofit, religious organizations, government agencies, colleges, schools, social service agencies, United Ways and others.
Accomplishments: In 1994 the Institute spent $111,471 on its programs. The Institute also awarded $2,846 in grants to the Welfare Rights Organization, and others.
Net Revenue: 1994 $251,847 **Net Expenses:** $237,933 47%/53%/0% **Net Assets:** $20,656
Tax Status: 501(c)(3)
Other Information: The Institute received $228,863, or 91% of revenues, from workshop fees and training seminars. $22,984, or 9% from gifts and grants awarded by foundations, businesses, and individuals.

Philip D. Reed Foundation

570 Lexington Ave., Room 923
New York, NY 10022   **Phone:**   (212) 836-3330
USA

Contact Person: Patricia Anderson, Secretary. **Officers or Principals:** Patricia Anderson, Secretary ($9,600); Philip D. Reed, Jr., Chairman/President ($0); Harold A. Segall, Vice President ($0); Kathryn R. Smith, Trustee.
Mission or Interest: Grant-making foundation that includes money for environmental, population control, and family planning organizations.
Accomplishments: In the fiscal year ending June 1994 the Foundation awarded $1,645,000 in grants. The largest grants included: $550,000 for the Nature Conservancy (NJ), $75,000 for the Nature Conservancy (CA), $50,000 for the Planned Parenthood Federation of America, $30,000 for the Environmental Defense Fund, and $20,000 for Population Communications International.
Net Revenue: FY ending 6/94 $1,610,886 **Net Expenses:** $1,749,712 **Net Assets:** $5,304,784
Tax Status: 501(c)(3)
Other Information: The Foundation received $1,337,396, or 83% of revenue, from capital gains on the sale of securities. $268,308, or 17%, from dividends and interest from securities. The remaining revenue came from interest on savings and temporary cash investments.

Physicians for Human Rights

100 Boylston St., Suite 702
Boston, MA 02116   **Phone:**   (617) 695-0041
USA

Contact Person: Eric Stover, Executive Director. **Officers or Principals:** Eric Stover, Executive Director ($69,290); Susannah Sirkin, Deputy Director ($63,960); Gina Vanderloop, Development Director ($35,825); H. Jack Geiger, M.D., President; Carola Eisenberg, M.D., Vice President; Dr. Charles Clements, Secretary; Dr. Robert Cook-Deegan, Treasurer.
Mission or Interest: "To use the knowledge and skills of the medical and forensic sciences to investigate and prevent violations of human rights and international law."
Accomplishments: In the fiscal year ending June 1994, the organization spent $600,702 on its programs.
Net Revenue: FY ending 6/94 $1,224,138 **Net Expenses:** $1,061,614 57%/18%/25% **Net Assets:** $591,521
Citations: 233:72
Tax Status: 501(c)(3)
Board of Directors or Trustees: Dr. John Constable, Dr. Paul Epstein, Dr. Holly Atkinson, Dr. Robert Kirschner, Dr. Jennifer Leaning, Dr. Kevin Cahill, Dr. Jane Shaller, Dr. M. Roy Schwarz, Dr. Kim Thorburn, Philippe Villers (Families USA), Ambassador J. Kenneth Blackwell, Aryeh Neir (The Open Society).
Other Information: The organization received $1,048,476, or 86% of revenue, from gifts and grants awarded by foundations, businesses, and individuals. (These grants included $350,000 from the Joyce Mertz-Gilmore Foundation, $300,000 over three years from the John D. and Catherine T. MacArthur Foundation, $60,000 from the John Merck Fund, $25,000 from the American Foundation for AIDS Research, $20,000 from the J. Roderick MacArthur Foundation, $7,000 from the General Service Foundation, and $500 from the One World Fund.) $140,552, or 11%, from membership dues. $27,955, or 2%, from interest on savings and temporary cash investments. The remaining income came from the sale of reports and other miscellaneous sources.

Physicians for Social Responsibility (PSR)

1101 14th St., N.W., Suite 700
Washington, DC 20005   **Phone:**   (202) 898-0150
USA   **Fax:**   (202) 898-0172

Contact Person: Julia Moore, Executive Director. **Officers or Principals:** Julia Moore, Executive Director ($80,866); Robert K. Musil, Program Director ($64,842); Patricia Moore, Development Director ($57,637).
Mission or Interest: Education and advocacy "concerning the medical and environmental consequences of nuclear weapons use, production and testing, toxic substances in the environment, hand gun use, and other public health, violence, and environmental issues."

Accomplishments: Over 12,000 members and 150 chapters. In 1994 PSR spent $1,611,657 on its programs. The largest program, with expenditures of $886,411, was research and public education. $564,080 was spent on developing PSR chapters nationwide. $161,166 was spent on media and public policy advocacy.
Net Revenue: 1994 $2,146,501 **Net Expenses:** $2,144,986 75%/10%/15% **Net Assets:** $388,238 **Citations:** 255:64
Products or Services: Research, publications, and lobbying. PSR spent $104,950 on lobbying, a 12% decrease from the previous year.   **Tax Status:** 501(c)(3)
Board of Directors or Trustees: (All are M.D.'s) Herbert Abrams, Sidney Alexander, Elizabeth Bowen, Charles Clements, George Ellsworth, Cathey Falvo, Paul Fisher, John Goldenring, Adam Goldstein, Alan Lockwood, Michael McCally, Kirsten Meisinger, Robert Morris, Willard Osibin, David Rothstein, Timothy Takaro, Reed Tuckson, Robert Wesley Jr., Peter Wilk, Gregg Wilkinson.
Periodicals: *PSR Reports.*
Other Information: Founded by Dr. Helen Caldicott, who also founded the Women's Action for Nuclear Disarmament (now Women's Action for New Directions). PSR received $1,331,003, or 62% of revenue, from gifts and grants awarded by foundations, businesses, and individuals. (These grants included $50,000 from the Joyce Foundation, $50,000 from the Nathan Cummings Foundation, $40,000 from the Winston Foundation, $25,000 from the Deer Creek Foundation, and $500 from the Stewart R. Mott Charitable Trust.) $680,428, or 32%, from membership dues. $55,818, or 3%, from an annual meeting. $42,075, or 2%, from credit-card fees (for use of a PSR credit card). $26,071, or 1%, from interest on savings and temporary cash investments. The remaining revenue came from mailing list rentals, and the sale of inventory.

Physicians for Social Responsibility, Berkeley
2288 Fulton St.
Berkeley, CA 94704
USA

Contact Person: Pearl Leonard, Secretary.   **Officers or Principals:** Robert Gould, M.D., President ($0); Kathryn Smick, M.D., Vice President ($0); Ephraim Kahn, M.D., Treasurer.
Mission or Interest: Educate the profession and public about the dangers of nuclear weapons.
Accomplishments: In 1994 the organization spent $32,895 on its programs. $11,842 was spent on lectures and speakers. Another $11,842 for the production and distribution of a newsletter. $9,211 was spent developing its speakers bureau.
Net Revenue: 1994 $47,088 **Net Expenses:** $47,533 78%/22%/0% **Net Assets:** $36,960
Products or Services: Meetings, lectures, publications, and lobbying. The organization spent $439 on lobbying. PSR sent out "Legislative Alert" postcards to interested parties notifying them of pending legislation.
Tax Status: 501(c)(3) **Periodicals:** *PSR Newsletter.*
Other Information: The organization received $34,479, or 73% of revenue, from gifts and grants awarded by foundations, businesses, and individuals. $10,879, or 23%, from membership dues. $1,564, or 3%, from dividends and interest from securities. The remaining revenue came from interest on savings and temporary cash investments.

Physicians for Social Responsibility, Boston
11 Garden St.
Cambridge, MA 02138
USA

Contact Person: George Ellsworth, President.   **Officers or Principals:** John Butler, Treasurer.
Mission or Interest: "To provide educational films and seminars dealing with human health and the environment. To understand the medical consequences of nuclear war."
Accomplishments: In 1994 the organization spent $111,750 on its programs.
Net Revenue: 1994 $135,620 **Net Expenses:** $146,116 76%/17%/7% **Net Assets:** $60,668 **Tax Status:** 501(c)(3)
Other Information: In 1994 the organization received $120,548, or 89% of revenue, from gifts and grants awarded by foundations, businesses, and individuals. $9,166, or 7%, from membership dues. $4,357, or 3%, from royalties. The remaining revenue came from interest on savings and temporary cash investments.

Physicians for Social Responsibility, Los Angeles
1316 Third St. Promenade, Suite B-1
Santa Monica, CA 90401   **Phone:**   (310) 458-2694   **E-Mail:** psrsm@psr.org
USA   **Fax:**   (310) 458-7925

Contact Person: Jonathan Parfrey, Executive Director.   **Officers or Principals:** Dr. Jimmy Hara ($0), Dr. Robert Wesley, Jr., ($0), Co-Presidents; Dr. Sol Londe, Treasurer ($0); Dr. William Perkins, Secretary.
Mission or Interest: Advocates; the elimination of weapons of mass destruction, reducing violence and its causes, protecting public health through addressing environmental degradation.
Accomplishments: Los Angeles chapter of the 1985 Nobel Peace Prize-winning organization, International Physicians for the Prevention of Nuclear War. Produced the award-winning film "Race to Oblivion." Organized symposia on nuclear war, the environment, and violence. In 1994 the chapter spent $101,840 on programs. These programs included $11,590 in grants and honoraria to various physicians and activists, including $1,000 for anti-gun strategist Josh Sugerman.
Net Revenue: 1994 $115,773 **Net Expenses:** $150,025 68%/32%/0% **Net Assets:** $140,497
Products or Services: Symposia, films, videos, and voter education programs.
Tax Status: 501(c)(3) **Annual Report:** No. **Employees:** 1 paid, 2 volunteer.
Board of Directors or Trustees: Helen Caldicott, M.B., Charles Clements, M.D., Anne Ehrlich, Ph.D., Daniel Ellsberg, Ph.D., Robert Livingston, M.D., Reed Tuckson, M.D.
Periodicals: Quarterly newsletter.   **Internships:** Yes.

Other Information: Affiliated with the national Physicians for Social Responsibility, and International Physicians for the Prevention of Nuclear War. The Los Angeles chapter absorbed the Orange County chapter in 1994. The Los Angeles chapter received $95,862, or 83% of revenue, from direct and indirect public support in the form of gifts and grants awarded by foundations, affiliates, businesses, and individuals. $9,981, or 9%, from membership dues. $5,861, or 5%, from program service revenues. $4,069, or 3%, from interest on savings and temporary cash investments.

Physicians for Social Responsibility, New York
475 Riverside Dr. Suite 826
New York, NY 10115
USA

Officers or Principals: E. Allen, M.D., President ($0); C. Weinstein, M.D., Vice President ($0); R. Kirsch, M.D., Treasurer ($0); W. Perron, Secretary.
Net Revenue: 1994 $51,176   **Net Expenses:** $64,284   **Net Assets:** $346,072   **Tax Status:** 501(c)(3)

Physicians for Social Responsibility, Philadelphia
704 N. 23rd St.
Philadelphia, PA 19130   **Phone:** (215) 765-8703
USA

Contact Person: Sandy Dempsey, Executive Director.
Officers or Principals: Sandy Dempsey, Executive Director ($35,569); Robert Garfield, M.D., President ($0); Ken Ginsburg, M.D., Vice President ($0); Jacob Kriger, DDS, Treasurer; Edward Aguilar, Secretary.
Mission or Interest: Educating the medical community and general public on the "etiology and epidemiology of violence in society and the increasingly prominent threat it poses to the security of individuals and the community at large as well as the medical community."
Accomplishments: In 1994 the Physicians spent $9,511 on its programs.
Net Revenue: 1994 $129,836 **Net Expenses:** $134,055 7%/93%/0% **Net Assets:** $6,868
Tax Status: 501(c)(3)
Other Information: The organization received $121,691, or 94% of revenue, from gifts and grants awarded by foundations, businesses, and individuals. $6,859, or 5%, from program service revenues. $1,286, or 1%, from interest on savings and temporary cash investments.

Physicians for Social Responsibility, Portland
921 S.W., Morrison, Suite 500
Portland, OR 97205   **Phone:** (503) 274-2720
USA

Contact Person: Charles Grossman, M.D., President.   **Officers or Principals:** Charles Grossman, M.D., President ($0); Dick Belsey, M.D., Bonnie Reagan, Vice Presidents ($0); Robert A. McFarlane, Treasurer.
Mission or Interest: Affiliate of the national Physicians for Social Responsibility. Public education that supports; opposition to nuclear weapons, gun control, addressing domestic violence.
Accomplishments: The Physicians distribute 1,100 copies of a newsletter monthly. Held a public forum in cooperation with other community organizations to address domestic violence. 1994 the organization spent $35,207. Awarded $1,070 in grants. Recipients included: $330 for KBOO Radio, $300 for the Central Oregon Environmental Center, $50 for Ceasefire Oregon, $50 for the Oregon Peace Institute, and others.
Net Revenue: 1994 $56,586 **Net Expenses:** $53,067 **Net Assets:** $27,215
Products or Services: Monthly meetings, speakers bureau, publications, more.
Tax Status: 501(c)(3)   **Periodicals:** Newsletter.
Other Information: The organization received $44,146, or 78% of revenue, from gifts and grants awarded by foundations, affiliates, companies and individuals.

Pig Iron Press
26 North Phelps St.
P.O. Box 237
Youngstown, OH 44501   **Phone:** (216) 747-6932
USA   **Fax:**   (216) 747-0599

Contact Person: Jim Villani, Editor.
Mission or Interest: Publishing since 1975. Publishes works of poetry, fiction, literary nonfiction, art, photography, and cartoons. Often publishes books in series based on themes.
Products or Services: Numerous publications. Buttons. Kenneth Patchen Competition awarded annually to fiction and poetry manuscripts in alternating years; fiction in even years and poetry in odd. Winners receive $100, and their work will be published in a run of 1,000, with 50 copies of the finished volume for the author.

Planned Parenthood Federation of America
810 7th Ave.
New York, NY 10019   **Phone:** (212) 541-7800
USA

Contact Person: Susan M. Lamontagne, Vice President, Media Relations.
Officers or Principals: Dr. Pamela Maraldo, former President ($251,538); Robert E. Bason, Vice President, Development ($189,000); Jane M. Johnson, Interim Co-President ($165,300); Dan Weintraub, Vice President, International ($160,438); Eve W. Paul, Vice President, Legal ($159,268); Jill Corbin, Vice President, Insurance ($125,010); Barbara Snow, Vice President Communications ($121,085); Rita J. Menitoff, Vice President, Health Care Delivery System ($120,615); Jacqueline S. Jackson, Ph.D., Chairperson; R. Lucia Riddle, First Vice Chairperson; Joe Louis Barrow, Jr., Second Vice Chairperson; G. F. Gay LeBreton, Treasurer; Duane Dowell, M.D., Secretary; Diana Zuckerman, National Policy Director.
Mission or Interest: "We believe that the ability to regulate one's own fertility is a basic human right essential to the emotional, physical, social and economic well-being of the individual, the family, the community, the nation, and the world. Therefore, the purpose of the Federation shall be: To provide leadership: In making effective means of voluntary fertility regulation, including contraception, abortion, sterilization, and infertility services, available and fully accessible to all as a central element of reproductive health care...in achieving, through informed individual choice, a U.S. population of stable size in an optimum environment...To support and assist efforts to achieve similar goals in the United States and throughout the world."
Accomplishments: In the fiscal year ending June 1995 the Federation spent $29,716,619 on its programs. The largest program, with expenditures of $20,959,351, was grants and services for affiliates. $4,799,458 was spent on "service to the field of family planning." $3,957,810 for international assistance and family planning. In 1994, the Federation received a grant from the U.S. Commerce Department's National Telecommunications and Information Administration in the amount of $300,000 for Planned Parenthood and its affiliates to set up a "national on-line information system." In 1993 Federation leadership met with representatives of the China Family Planning Association.
Net Revenue: FY ending 6/95 $39,915,912 ($920,308, or 2%, from government grants)
Net Expenses: $41,146,189 72%/10%/14% **Net Assets:** $18,603,627 **Citations:** 232:73
Products or Services: Family planning services, contraception, abortion services, conferences, training sessions, and lobbying. The Federation spent $150,218 on lobbying; $24,427 on grassroots lobbying, and $125,791 directly lobbying legislators.
Tax Status: 501(c)(3)
Board of Directors or Trustees: Sharon Allison, Betty Lou Anderson, Thomas Borman, Almeda Dake, Annette Cumming, Lee Lee Doyle, Ph.D., Thomas Davis Jr., Ph.D., Alfred Dietsch, Paul Drisgula, Lisa Henry-Reid, M.D., Nancy Gleason, Felice Gonzales, Ann Hamilton, Siri Kjos, M.D., Mark Munger, Feelie Lee, Ph.D., Ellen Offner, Betty Olinger, Ed.D., R.N., Alfred Poindexter, III, M.D., Nancy Powers, Mary Rauh, Kenneth Edlin, M.D., R. Barrett Richards, John Romo, Allan Rosenfield, M.D., Mary Shallenberger, Barbara Singhaus, Doris Vasquez, Don Wineberg, Alma Young, MSW, Ed.D.
Other Information: Founded by Margaret Sanger (1879-1966). Sanger was an early advocate of birth control, abortion, and eugenics. Like many other Progressives of her time, Sanger supported the eugenics movement (the select breeding of humans) for several reasons. Sanger, a socialist, thought that eugenics and birth control, properly applied, would limit the growth of the working class. By limiting the number of workers, wages would be driven up, and the class war predicted by Karl Marx could be averted. Sanger also sought to eliminate the "unfit" in society. Sanger sought compulsory birth control to weed out the physically and mentally unfit "human weeds" and create a "race of thoroughbreds." Affiliated with the 501(c)(3) Alan Guttmacher Institute, 501(c)(3) International Planned Parenthood Federation, the 501(c)(4) Planned Parenthood Action Fund, and the for-profit Planned Protection Insurance Company. (Planned Parenthood is also affiliated with hundreds of 501(c)(3) affiliates nationwide. These affiliates typically offer birth control devices, medical attention, abortion procedures, and informational services. While some might maintain that these activities are political in and of themselves, it is beyond the scope of The Left Guide to provide information on all of these local affiliates. However, The Left Guide has attempted to provide information on the various 501(c)(4) affiliates nationwide because of these affiliates' direct political activity.) The Federation employed the Falls Church, VA, firms of Craver Matthews Smith & Co., and Public Interest Communications for fund raising and solicitation. The two firms were paid $745,226 and $989,122 respectively. The Los Angeles firm of Factor Direct was employed for telemarketing and paid $772,838. Production Solutions of Falls Church was employed and paid $1,074,871 for mailing work. National Policy Director Diana Zuckerman was previously a senior policy analyst for the Clinton administration. Former Vice President for Public Policy, Ann Lewis (sister of Rep. Barney Frank, D-MA), left to join the Clinton-Gore re-election campaign as Deputy Campaign Manager. The Federation received $31,014,747, or 78% of revenue, from gifts and grants awarded by foundations, businesses, affiliates, and individuals. (These grants included $300,000 from the William and Flora Hewlett Foundation, $100,000 from the Robert Sterling Clark Foundation, $75,000 from the F. M. Kirby Foundation, $50,000 from the Philip D. Reed Foundation, $38,175 from the Nathan Cummings Foundation, $35,000 from the General Service Foundation, $35,000 from the Deer Creek Foundation, $20,000 from the Stewart R. Mott Charitable Trust, $15,000 from the Compton Foundation, $10,000 from the New-Land Foundation, $5,000 from the New World Foundation, $2,500 from the One World Fund, and $1,500 from the Haymarket People's Fund.) $6,524,047, or 16%, from service fees paid by affiliates. $494,746, or 1%, from dividends and interest from securities. $308,720, or 1%, from capital gains on the sale of stock. The remaining revenue came from mailing list rentals, royalties, and the sale of publications.

Planned Parenthood Action Fund

810 7th Ave.
New York, NY 10019   **Phone:** (212) 541-7800
USA

Contact Person: Dr. Pamela Maraldo, President. **Officers or Principals:** Jacqueline S. Jackson, Ph.D., Chairperson ($0); Sharon Allison, Vice Chairperson ($0); Annette P. Cumming, Secretary ($0); Mark Gorman, Director of Finance; Paul Williams, Treasurer.
Mission or Interest: Public education and lobbying affiliate of Planned Parenthood.
Accomplishments: In the fiscal year ending June 1994, the Fund spent $191,051 on its programs.
Net Revenue: FY ending 6/94 $557,143 **Net Expenses:** $367,113 52%/10%/23% **Net Assets:** (-$330,332)
Citations: 2:231

Tax Status: 501(c)(4)

Other Information: Affiliated with the Planned Parenthood Federation of America. The Fund awarded $10,000 in grants to affiliates nationwide, and made payments of $57,275 to various affiliates. The Fund received $557,143, or 100% of revenue, from gifts and grants awarded by foundations, businesses, and individuals.

Planned Parenthood Advocates of Michigan
P.O. Box 19104
Lansing, MI 48901   **Phone:**   (517) 482-1080
USA

Contact Person: Charlotte Wenham, President.   **Officers or Principals:** Charlotte Wenham, President ($0); Olivia Maynard, Vice President ($0); James Richardson, Secretary ($0); Musette Bell, Treasurer.
Mission or Interest: Lobbying affiliate of Planned Parenthood in Michigan.
Accomplishments: In 1994 the Advocates spent $39,172 on its programs. The largest program, with expenditures of $19,563, was grassroots lobbying, such as information regarding political candidates. $12,944 was spent on organizational development. Other programs provided information and lobbied legislators directly.
Net Revenue: 1994 $38,718 **Net Expenses:** $60,487 **Net Assets:** $9,518
Tax Status: 501(c)(4)
Other Information: The Advocates received $35,797, or 92% of revenue, from gifts and grants awarded by foundations, businesses, and individuals. $1,904, or 5%, from expense reimbursements. $476 net, or 1%, from the sale of inventory. The remaining revenue came from royalties and interest on savings and temporary investments.

Planned Parenthood Affiliates of Ohio
16 E. Broad St., Suite 915
Columbus, OH 43215
USA

Contact Person: Carole Rogers, Public Affairs Director.
Mission or Interest: Ohio lobbying affiliate of Planned Parenthood.
Accomplishments: In 1994 the Affiliates spent $62,794 on its programs.
Net Revenue: 1994 $60,794 **Net Expenses:** $63,122 98%/2%/0% **Net Assets:** $38,754
Tax Status: 501(c)(4)
Other Information: The Affiliates received $48,636, or 80% of revenue, from membership dues. $11,185, or 18%, from an "Action Fund." $973, or 1%, from interest on savings and temporary cash investments.

Planned Parenthood Affiliates of Washington
2211 E. Madison
Seattle, WA 98112   **Phone:**   (206) 328-7730
USA

Contact Person: Gwen Chaplin, President.   **Officers or Principals:** Susan Edgar, Vice President ($0); Susan Meicher, Treasurer ($0); Christine Charbonneau, Legislative Chair ($0).
Mission or Interest: Washington state lobbying affiliate of Planned Parenthood.
Accomplishments: In 1994 the Affiliates spent $75,877 on its programs. The largest program, with expenditures of $62,659, was "information and education to affiliate groups and the public." $13,218 was spent lobbying public officials "to influence public policy in Washington to ensure universal access to reproductive healthcare."
Net Revenue: 1994 $95,028 **Net Expenses:** $91,541 **Net Assets:** $19,422
Tax Status: 501(c)(4)
Other Information: The Affiliate received $94,781, or 99.6% of revenue, from membership dues. The remaining revenue came from investment income and other miscellaneous sources.

Planned Parenthood Pennsylvania Advocates
1514 N. 2nd St.
Harrisburg, PA 17102   **Phone:**   (717) 234-3024
USA   **Fax:**   (717) 234-3032

Contact Person: Liz Hrenda-Roberts, Executive Director.   **Officers or Principals:** Susanne Wean, President ($0); Maggie Leigh Groff, Vice President ($0); Joan Coombs, Secretary ($0), Linda Shorey, Treasurer.
Mission or Interest: "To achieve maximum public and governmental support for reproductive health care, including family planning, by maintaining a state-wide environment in which organizations and concerned individuals can effectively function to assure that every Pennsylvanian has access to reproductive health care...activities shall include legislative efforts, and political activity."

Accomplishments: In 1994 the Advocates spent $31,556 on its programs. $19,536 on lobbying and $12,020 on "assistance to organizations and individuals interested in assuring that everyone in Pennsylvania has access to comprehensive reproductive health care."
Net Revenue: 1994 $33,141 **Net Expenses:** $31,556 **Net Assets:** (-$5,308)
Tax Status: 501(c)(4)
Board of Directors or Trustees: Pat Brogan, Kim Evert, Felicia Gaines, Linda Hahn, Betsy Magley, Nancy Osgood, Deb Reed, Frances Sheehan, Marti King-Pringle, others.
Other Information: Planned Parenthood Pennsylvania Advocates received $20,580, or 62% of revenue, from its lobbying services. $6,951, or 21%, from its telemarketing campaign. $5,549, or 17%, from gifts and grants. The remaining revenue came from interest and expense reimbursements.

Planned Parenthood Public Affairs, North Carolina
100 S. Boylan
Raleigh, NC 27603   **Phone:** (919) 833-7534
USA

Contact Person: Janet Colm, Staff Representative. **Officers or Principals:** Waltye Rasulala, Chair ($0); Ted Arrington, Vice Chair ($0); Gwyn Pearce, Secretary ($0); Ellen Olson, Treasurer.
Mission or Interest: "To preserve and broaden reproductive freedom through legislation, public education, and litigation in North Carolina."
Accomplishments: In 1993 the organization spent $47,046 on its programs.
Net Revenue: 1993 $31,832 **Net Expenses:** $47,046 **Net Assets:** $1,842
Tax Status: 501(c)(4)
Board of Directors or Trustees: Ted Arrington, Barbara Barnes, Pat Chamings, Jewel Cooper, Margo Evans, Sylvia Gelblum, Rob Glesener.
Other Information: The organization received $32,269, or 99.6% of total revenue, from membership dues. The remaining revenue came from investment income. The organization lost $471 on the sale of assets.

Planned Parenthood - World Population, Los Angeles
1920 Marengo St.
Los Angeles, CA 90033   **Phone:** (213) 223-4462
USA

Contact Person: Suellen Wood, Executive Director. **Officers or Principals:** Vallorie Saulsberry, MD, Physician ($93,254); Suellen Wood, Executive Director ($79,999); Tom Linkis, Technician ($70,452).
Mission or Interest: Provides family planning services, including examinations, counseling, birth control, sterilization, and abortions.
Accomplishments: In the fiscal year ending June 1994, the organization spent $6,714,221 on its programs.
Net Revenue: FY ending 6/94 $7,472,124 ($2,793,669, or 37%, from government grants)
Net Expenses: $8,335,202 81%/15%/4% **Net Assets:** $6,736,306 **Citations:** 1:240
Products or Services: Reproductive health services and lobbying. The organization spent $60,372 on lobbying.
Tax Status: 501(c)(3)
Board of Directors or Trustees: B. Boyd Hight, Geraldine Hurley, Kenneth Anderson, Rosalie Mendez, Robert Given, Lea Ann King, Sue Allen, Lynne Alschuler, William Bell, Mickey Bodek, Ann Fair Brahagan, John Brinsley, Sue Bunzel, Marissa Castro, John Chiang, Diane Cooke, Connie Destito, LCSW, Tamra Dickerson, Ruth Fisher, Bishop Oliver Garver, Jr., Carolyn Gold, Ellie Goldman, Peggy Elliot Goldwyn, Richard Greenberg, A. Zellerbach Haber, Susan Harbert, Susan Humphreville, Patricia Ann Kinaga, Rev. James Lawson, Carol Massey, Mrs. Franklin Murphy, Julene Perez, Judith Reichman-Cates, M.D., Barbara Rosenstein, Keith Russell, M.D., James Smith, Pamela Robinson Spektor, Dyan Sublett, Jeffrey Tamkin, Douglas Thomson, Kimmy Tokeshi, Kathleen Torres, MPH., Mary-Jane Wagle, Lynda Jenner Whaley, Karen Williams, Betty Wilson.
Other Information: The organization hired the Los Angeles firm of Diversity Search Partners for a personnel search to fill the position of Executive Director. The firm was paid $52,031. Planned Parenthood's World Population office received $2,793,669, or 37% of total revenue, from government grants. $2,620,391, or 35%, from gifts and grants awarded by foundations, businesses, and individuals. $1,773,447, or 24%, from clinics and consulting fees. $254,380, or 3%, from interest on savings and temporary cash investments. The remaining revenue came from dividends and interest from securities, and other miscellaneous sources. The organization lost $12,215 on the sale of securities.

Ploughshares Fund
Fort Mason, Building B, Suite 330
San Francisco, CA 94123   **Phone:** (415) 775-2244
USA

Contact Person: Sally Lilienthal, President. **Officers or Principals:** Deborah Bain, Development Director ($43,925); Karen Harris, Executive Director ($38,095); Lewis H. Butler, Chair ($0); Thomas C. Layton, Secretary; Patricia F. Sullivan, Treasurer.
Mission or Interest: "Funds organizations and individuals whose work fosters nuclear arms reduction, global cooperation and public participation in the debate about world security."

Accomplishments: In the fiscal year ending June 1994, the Fund spent $134,631 on educational speaking and other projects involving arms control. This included $43,448 in grants to individuals. The Fund awarded $1,488,877 in grants to organizations. Recipients of the largest grants included; $45,000 for the Council for a Livable World, two grants totaling $42,579 for the Union of Concerned Scientists, $40,000 for the 20/20 Vision National Project, $35,000 each for the Institute for Science and International Security, Women's Action for New Directions, and the Wisconsin Project on Nuclear Arms Control, $30,000 each for Nautilus Pacific Research, the Project on Demilitarization and Democracy, the British American Security Information Council, the National Commission on Economic Conversion and Disarmament, and the Pacific Institute for Studies in Development, Environment, and Security.
Net Revenue: FY ending 6/94 $1,974,691 **Net Expenses:** $1,822,398 89%/6%/5% **Net Assets:** $2,351,769
Products or Services: Grants and lobbying. In the fiscal year ending June 1994 the Fund spent $164,000 on lobbying; $44,000 on grassroots lobbying and $120,000 on the direct lobbying of legislators. This was 47% more than the year before, but down 22% from $210,000 three years prior.
Tax Status: 501(c)(3)
Board of Directors or Trustees: Christina Desser, Anne Ehrlich, Angela Foster, Mary LeCron Foster, Donald Fraser, Hal Harvey, Richard Nealey, David Holloway, Lynda Palevsky, Michael Parker, William Matson Roth, Barry Traub.
Other Information: The Fund received $1,835,527, or 93% of revenue, from gifts and grants awarded by foundations, businesses, and individuals. (These grants included $25,000 from the Compton Foundation, $15,000 from the New-Land Foundation, $5,000 from the Angelina Fund, $5,000 from the Aaron and Martha Schecter Foundation, $2,500 from the New Prospect Foundation, $1,000 from the Stewart R. Mott Charitable Trust, $1,000 from the Vanguard Public Foundation.) $74,649, or 4%, from dividends and interest from securities. $64,515, or 3%, from capital gains on the sale of securities.

Political Research Associates (PRA)

120 Beacon St., Suite 202
Cambridge, MA 02143   **Phone:** (617) 661-9313   **E-Mail:** publiceye@igc.apc.org
USA   **Fax:** (617) 661-0059   **Web-Page:** http://www.publiceye.org/pra/

Contact Person: Jean Hardisty, President. **Officers or Principals:** Jean Hardisty, Ph.D., President ($25,655); Deborah Bright, Treasurer ($0); Lucy Williams, Clerk ($0); Chip Berlet, Senior Analyst; Peter Snoad, Deputy Director; Surina Khan, Associate Analyst; Judith Glaubman, Researcher/Office Manager; Francine Almash, Information Specialist.
Mission or Interest: Research and analysis on the political Right. "PRA has 15 years' experience tracking authoritarian and anti-democratic movements and trends. We have detailed information on every facet of these movements - from their ideologies and hidden agendas to their financing, tactics and links to each other...In the U.S., there is an identifiable right-wing agenda. Its roots lie in the lynchings of Blacks in the South by the Ku Klux Klan, the ideological principles of the John Birch Society, and the McCarthy hearings of the 1950's. Central to that agenda is white supremacism, preservation of rigidly traditional religious and family structures, and defense of U.S. military hegemony."
Accomplishments: PRA co-sponsored the 1996 Media and Democracy Congress in San Francisco. Topics included strengthening independent journalism, grappling with new technology, and responding to threats from the Right. Other sponsors included the Center for Media Education, Pacifica Foundation, *The Progressive*, Fairness and Accuracy in Reporting, and *Utne Reader*. Following the bombing of the federal building in Oklahoma City, PRA and researcher Chip Berlet were much in demand from news organizations for information regarding the militia movement that was linked to the bombing suspects. In the first nine months of 1995, reported revenue was already $306,133, 79% more than the entire previous year. Suzanne Pharr, of the Arkansas Women's Project, said "PRA provides a lot of the invisible backbone of the work we do in our project to monitor racist, sexist and anti-gay and lesbian violence and the activities of neo-Nazis and the religious Right." In 1995 the PRA co-hosted a teach-in with the Astraea National Lesbian Action Foundation on the theme "Uniting for Democracy, Challenging the Right." In 1994 the PRA spent $114,317 on its projects.
Net Revenue: 1994 $170,588 **Net Expenses:** $178,581 69%/27%/9% **Net Assets:** $25,220
Products or Services: Numerous publications, reports, information packets, flyers, a library, speakers bureau, and staff support to answer questions. Books co-published with the South End Press include, EyesRight! Challenging the Right Wing Backlash, The Coors Connection: How the Coors Family Philanthropy Undermines Democratic Pluralism, and Old Nazis, the New Right, and the Republican Party.
Tax Status: 501(c)(3)
Board of Directors or Trustees: Rev. Sally Dries (United Church of Christ), Jean Entine (Boston Women's Fund), Dr. Robin Giles (Center for Health Services and Policy Research, Northwestern Univ.), Faith Smith (Native American Educational Services), Dr. Loretta Williams. The Advisory Board includes: Rita Arditti (Union Inst.), Ann Baker (National Center for the Pro-Choice Majority), Donna Bivens (Women's Theological Center), Sara Diamond, Ph.D., Fred Goff (Data Center), Beni Ivey (Center for Democratic Renewal), Maya Miller, Suzanne Pharr (Women's Project, Arkansas), Skipp Porteous (Inst. for First Amendment Studies), Barbara Simon (Inst. for First Amendment Studies), John Roberts (ACLU, MA), Mab Segrest (World Council of Churches), Alice Senturia (UNITE), Holly Sklar, Urvashi Vaid, Lucius Walker (Interreligious Foundation for Community Organizing), Leah Wise (Southern Regional Economic Justice Network), Louis Wolf (*CovertAction Quarterly*).
Periodicals: *The Public Eye* (quarterly newsletter). "*The Public Eye* represents the resurrection of a venerable newsletter of the 1970s and 1980s, published at various times by the Repression Information Project, Citizens in Defense of Civil Liberties, and the National Lawyers Guild Civil Liberties Committee, among others."
Other Information: Founded in 1981. Jean Hardisty was a former president of the Crossroads Fund. In 1994 PRA received $154,300, or 90% of revenue, from gifts and grants awarded by foundations, businesses, and individuals. $15,854, or 9%, from the sale of publications and services. The remaining revenue came from interest on savings and temporary cash investments.

Population Action International (PAI)

1120 19th St., N.W.
Washington, DC 20036   **Phone:**   (202) 659-1833
USA

Contact Person: J. Joseph Speidel, President.
Officers or Principals: J. Joseph Speidel, President ($150,200); Catherine Cameron, Vice President ($107,189); Patricia McGrath, Director of Development ($104,350); Robin Chandler Duke, Joseph Tydings, Victoria P. Sant, Robert B. Wallace, National Co-Chairs; William C. Edwards, Treasurer; Phyllis Tilson Piotrow, Secretary.
Mission or Interest: Committed to "universal access to voluntary family planning and reproductive health services, reproductive choices for women and men, and early stabilization of world population."
Accomplishments: In 1994 the organization spent $3,948,775 on its programs. PAI released studies on "the global gender gap in education...the unserved reproductive health needs of youth...the demographic, economic, and political factors contributing to global migration...how donor countries can finance the growing global demand for family planning..how population growth and consumption patterns must be modified if the carbon dioxide content of the atmosphere is to be stabilized." These studies received "broad media coverage." PAI "played a leadership role in preparations for the 1994 U.N. Conference on population in Cairo, especially in helping to persuade several donor nations to increase their funding commitments for international family planning, in building broad consensus on the key issues, in fostering a climate favorable to action on population and resource concerns, and in serving as a primary source of information for media stories." PAI also spent $1,204,529 on grants for 64 active projects in 20 countries.
Net Revenue: 1994 $4,504,308 **Net Expenses:** $4,576,514 86%/9%/4% **Net Assets:** $7,072,039 **Citations:** 122:107
Products or Services: Research, media relations, organizing, and lobbying. PAI spent $5,085 on the direct lobbying of legislators. This was a 43% decrease from the previous year.
Tax Status: 501(c)(3)
Board of Directors or Trustees: Vicki-Ann Assevero, Norman Borlaug, Sharon Camp, Marilyn Brant Chandler, A.W. Clausen, Philander Claxton, Jr., Barber Conable, J. Edward Day, William Draper, III, Henry Fowler, Bill Green, Kuval Gulhati, Julia Henderson, Lawrence Kegan, Deborah Leach, Frances Loeb, C. Payne Lucas, Edwin Martin, Paul McCloskey, Jr., Robert McNamara (Sec. of Defense, 1961-1968), Wendy Morgan, Russell Peterson, John Reinhardt, Yolanda Richardson, Thomas Roberts, Jr., Constance Spahn, Scott Spangler, Elmer Boyd Staats, Timothy Towell, Joseph Wheeler, Howard Williams, III.
Other Information: PAI received $4,142,063, or 92% of revenue, from direct and indirect public support in the form of gifts and grants awarded by foundations, businesses, individuals, and affiliates. (These grants included $40,000 from the Compton Foundation, $10,000 from the New-Land Foundation, $1,000 from the Stewart R. Mott Charitable Trust. In 1993, $655,000 from the Wallace Genetic Foundation, and in 1995, $343,000 from the Rockefeller Foundation.) $364,534, or 8%, from dividends and interest from securities. The remaining revenue came from publication sales.

Population Communication

1250 E. Walnut St.
Pasadena, CA 91106   **Phone:**   (818) 793-4750   **E-Mail:** popcommla@aol.com
USA   **Fax:**   (818) 793-4791

Contact Person: Robert W. Gillespie, President.   **Officers or Principals:** Robert W. Gillespie, President ($71,094); Dave Finnigan, Treasurer ($0); Ed Shuman, Secretary ($0); Edward Wortz, Chairman.
Mission or Interest: Population stabilization.
Accomplishments: Advocates for the United States to rejoin UNESCO. Recently added immigration matters to its area of inquiry. "Population Communication is designing health strategies to transfer the manual vacuum aspiration (abortion) technology to Pakistan, Indonesia, the Philippines and Egypt." In 1994 the organization spent $224,296 on its programs. The largest program, with expenditures of $204,964, obtained the signatures of 72 "heads of government" in support of a statement on population stabilization which was presented by President Soeharto of Indonesia to U.N. Secretary General Boutros Boutros-Ghali during the 50th anniversary celebrations at the United Nations. $14,070 was spent to "protest and develop population stabilization policies and programs" in India, Bangladesh, Thailand, Indonesia, Egypt, and Pakistan. $121,250 was awarded to individuals and organizations pursuing population stabilization.
Net Revenue: 1994 $286,971 **Net Expenses:** $281,783 80%/20%/0% **Net Assets:** $1,503,766
Products or Services: Various reports and publications.
Tax Status: 501(c)(3) **Annual Report:** Yes. **Employees:** 2
Board of Directors or Trustees: Lupe de la Vega, Prof. Murray Gell-Mann (CA Institute of Technology), Jack Mead, M.D., Malcolm Potts, Jennifer Daves (Media Director, Advocates for Youth), Sterling Franklin.
Internships: Yes, "the prospective intern must contact and convince the President of their passion for population studies in order to win an internship."
Other Information: Founded in 1977. Population Communication received $194,100, or 67% of total revenue, from gifts and grants awarded by foundations, businesses, and individuals. (These included $10,000 from the F. M. Kirby Foundation.) $63,712, or 22%, from dividends and interest from securities. $21,546, or 7%, from "Trust Deeds." $6,208, or 2%, from investment income. $3,217, or 1%, from interest on savings and temporary cash investments. The organization lost $1,812 on the sale of securities.

Population Communications International

777 United Nations Plaza
New York, NY 10017   **Phone:**   (212) 687-3366
USA   **Fax:**   (212) 661-4188

Contact Person: Mary Beth Powers, Executive Director.   **Officers or Principals:** William Ryerson, Executive Vice President ($130,305); Charles Scott, Director ($86,160); David O. Poindexter, President ($83,752); Irwin Fox, Chair.

Mission or Interest: "To assist international institutions, communications media, policy leaders and others to develop a better understanding of, and respond to, population problems." Assists governments and businesses outside the U.S. in developing entertainment programing that encourages birth control.

Accomplishments: In 1994 the organization spent $2,464,587 on its programs.

Net Revenue: 1994 $3,165,589 **Net Expenses:** $2,909,469 85%/7%/8% **Net Assets:** $463,385 **Citations:** 22:171

Tax Status: 501(c)(3)

Board of Directors or Trustees: Adam Albright, Cecile Guidote-Alvarez, Cely Favrot Arndt, Fred Cohen (King World Enterprises Intl.), Dr. Hans Fleisch, Steven Greenapple, Casey Herrick, Ernest Howell (Smith Barney), A. Scheffer Lang, Dr. Margaret McEvoy, Dr. Florence Manguyu, Richard Manoff, Nkwabi Ng'Wanakilala, Ing. Leopoldo Peralta, Randolph Rowland, Florence Sai, Jill Sheffield (Family Care Intl.), Ratan Tata, Dr, Charles Westoff (Princeton Univ.), Kenneth Henderson, Jack Howard.

Other Information: Population Communications International received $3,106,745, or 98% of revenue, from gifts and grants awarded by foundations, businesses, and individuals. (These grants included $20,000 from the Philip D. Reed Foundation, $20,000 from the Henry J. Kaiser Family Foundation.) $48,000, or 2%, from reimbursements for prior year's expenses related to the International Conference on Population and development in Cairo, Egypt.

Population Council

One Dag Hammarskjold Plaza
New York, NY 10017
USA

Phone: (212) 339-0500
Fax: (212) 755-6052

Contact Person: Margaret Catley-Carlson, President.   **Officers or Principals:** Margaret Catley-Carlson, President ($283,475); C. Wayne Bardin, Vice President, Center for Biomedical Research ($263,689); John Bongaarts, Vice President, Research ($201,049); George F. Brown, Vice President, Programs ($254,833); Paul Demeny, Distinguished Scholar ($182,798); Margaret McEvoy, Senior Associate ($181,653); Donald J. Abrams, Treasurer ($157,906); Monica Knorr, Secretary ($144,276); Shirley Alexander, Secretary ($122,177); John Townsend, Project Director ($113,040); McGeorge Bundy, Chair. [The Left Guide does not include expense accounts in compensation, and in most cases, these accounts are negligible. However, three employees of the Population Council had expense accounts over $100,000, and therefore are noteworthy. These employees, and their compensation including expense accounts, were; (the second figure is the expense account) John Townsend, Project Director ($263,131/$150,091); Peter Miller, Associate ($201,596/$114,829); John Skibiak, Associate ($186,474/$110,406).]

Mission or Interest: Conducts biomedical and social research in the areas of contraception, family planning, abortion, and population control. "Seeks to improve the well-being and reproductive health of current and future generations around the world and to help achieve a humane, equitable, and sustainable balance between people and resources...The Council analyzes population issues and trends; conducts research in the reproductive sciences, develops new contraceptives; works with public and private agencies to improve the quality and outreach of family planning and reproductive health services, help governments design and implement effective population policies, communicates the results of research in the population field to diverse audiences; and helps strengthen professional resources in developing countries through collaborative research and programs, technical exchange, awards, and fellowships."

Accomplishments: In 1994 the Council spent $37,760,445 on its programs. The largest expense, $18,689,744, was for their world-wide programs, with offices in Latin America and the Caribbean, West Asia and North Africa, South and East Asia, East and Southern Africa, and West and Central Africa. $14,072,187 was spent on the Center for Biomedical Research which develops new contraceptives. Products developed by the Center include the "Norplant" subdermal implants and three models of the "Copper T IU," and clinical tests of mifepristone (RU 486). $3,085,636 was spent on the Research Division, that studies population policies. $1,303,140 was spent on publications. $609,738 was spent on Distinguished Colleagues program that funds scholars and scientists. The Council awarded $7,297,876 in grants to organizations in the United States and abroad to conduct research, distribute publications, and test contraceptives and abortifacients. Grants recipients in the United States included: The Feminist Press for production of a book. The Health Research Association of the LAC/USC Medical center, Los Angeles, to test Norplant, Nestorone progestin implants, and vaginal rings that release morethindrone acetate and ethynylestradiol. Presidents and Fellows of Harvard College to support "gender, family, and population policy debates." Reproductive Health Services of St. Louis to study the "abortifacient effects of misoprostol administered intervaginally in the first trimester of pregnancy."

Net Revenue: 1994 $42,443,533 ($18,932,391, or 45%, from government grants) **Net Expenses:** $44,438,650 85%/14%/1%

Net Assets: $49,547,307 **Citations:** 475:43

Products or Services: The New Politics of Population: Conflict and Consensus in Family Planning, Finkle and McIntosh, eds., and other books.

Tax Status: 501(c)(3) **Employees:** 79 employees were paid in excess of $50,000. Total payroll and benefits for non-officers was $19,094,531.

Board of Directors or Trustees: Robert Ebert (Millbank Memorial Fund), Laura Chasin (Family Institute of Cambridge), Werner Holzer, Lucille Mathurin Mair (Permanent Rep. of Jamaica to the U.N.), Elizabeth McCormack (Rockefeller Family and Associates), Robert Millard (Managing Director, Lehman Bros.,), Frederick Sai (Pres., Intl. Planned Parenthood, London), Krister Stendahl (Professor and Dean Emeritus, Harvard Divinity School), Aminata Traore (Regional Coordinator, PROWWESS/AFRICA, United Nations Development Programme), others.

Periodicals: *Population and Development Review* (journal), *Studies in Family Planning* (journal).

Other Information: Chairman McGeorge Bundy was formerly Special Assistant to Presidents Kennedy and Johnson for National Security Affairs from 1961-1966. In 1994 the Council received $18,932,391, or 45% of revenue, from government grants. (These grants included $16,185,557 from the U.S. Aid for International Development, $2,746,833 from the U.S. National Institutes of Health, $1,926,182 from the U.N. Population Fund, $1,047,182 from the Swedish Intl. Development Authority, $927,719 from the World Bank, $437,193 from the Government of the Netherlands, $325,866 from the Canadian International Development Bank, $165,274 from the World Health Organization, $150,874 from the Asian Development Bank, $100,091 from the Australian International Development Assistance Bureau, $93,641 from the Arab Gulf Fund, $69,501 from the government of Finland, $27,631 from the U.N. Children Fund, and $4,481 from the U.N. Development Fund for Women.) $16,065,245, or 38%, from gifts and grants awarded by foundations, businesses, and individuals. (These grants included $1,717,090 from the Andrew W. Mellon Foundation, $1,520,895 from the Wyeth-Ayerst Laboratories, $1,449,476 from the Rockefeller Foundation, $1,118,718 from the Ford Foundation, $650,000 from the George G. Hecht Fund, $623,676 from the Buffett Foundation, $342,028 from Wellstart International, $311,679 from the John D. and Catherine T. MacArthur Foundation, $300,000 from the William and Flora Hewlett Foundation, $171,259 from the Pew Charitable Trusts, $88,788 from the John Merck Fund, $60,000 from the Compton Foundation, $49,395 from the South to South Cooperation in Reproductive Health, $23,176 from the General Service Foundation, $12,955 from the Association for Voluntary Surgical Contraception, $10,000 from the Playboy Foundation, and $250 from the Stewart R. Mott Charitable Trust.) $3,120,213, or 7%, from "payments received under licensing agreements." $2,106,726, or 5%, from capital gains on the sale of securities. $2,024,663, or 5%, from dividends and interest from securities. The remaining revenue came from the sale of publications, and other miscellaneous sources.

Population - Environment Balance
2000 P St., N.W., Suite 210
Washington, DC 20036   **Phone:** (202) 955-5700   **E-Mail:** uspop@balance.org
USA   **Fax:** (202) 955-6161

Contact Person: Maria Flynn, Assistant Secretary.   **Officers or Principals:** Mark W. Nowak, Executive Director ($44,346); Virginia Abernethy, President ($0); Lawrence W. Kown, Vice President ($0); David Durham, Esq., Secretary.
Mission or Interest: "Dedicated to maintaining and improving the quality of life in the U.S. through population stabilization."
Accomplishments: Testified before congressional committees and task forces regarding population and immigration policy.
Net Revenue: 1994 $350,264 **Net Expenses:** $388,455 80%/15%/5% **Net Assets:** (-$16,361)
Products or Services: Various educational programs to increase public awareness and support for population stabilization policies. In 1994 they spent $309,292 on these programs. Lobbying - they spent $8,554 in 1994, $3,507 on grassroots lobbying and $5,047 on the direct lobbying of legislators. This was down from $13,813 in the previous year.
Tax Status: 501(c)(3) **Annual Report:** No. **Employees:** 5
Board of Directors or Trustees: Thomas McKenna, Thomas McMahon.
Periodicals: *Balance Activist*.   **Internships:** Yes.
Other Information: Population-Environment Balance received $344,896, or 98% of revenue, from gifts and grants awarded by foundations, companies and individuals. $4,444 net, or 1%, from the sale of assets other than inventory. The remaining revenue came from interest on savings and temporary cash investments, and other miscellaneous sources.

Population Institute
107 2nd St., N.E.
Washington, DC 20002   **Phone:** (202) 544-3300
USA

Contact Person: Moyne Gross, Administrative Director.   **Officers or Principals:** Werner Fornos, President ($177,787); Harold Burdett, Editor ($70,584); Moyne Gross, Administrative Director ($59,905); Jack Brandenburg, Chair; Bettye J. Ward, Vice Chair; Suzanne Kellerman, Secretary; Van Crawford, Treasurer.
Mission or Interest: Promotes population control and family planning.
Accomplishments: In 1994 the Institute spent $1,370,350, on its programs. The largest program, with expenditures of $561,318, were international programs, including participation in the world conference on population issues. $556,088 was spent on public education and information services. $137,924 was spent recruiting, educating, and coordinating citizens who have an interest in issues involving world population. $78,459 for monitoring and analyzing legislative and executive matters pertaining to family planning assistance.
Net Revenue: 1994 $1,685,460 **Net Expenses:** $1,616,639 85%/8%/7% **Net Assets:** $1,210,920 **Citations:** 132:103
Products or Services: Research, conferences, organizing, and lobbying. The Institute spent $8,999 on lobbying.
Tax Status: 501(c)(3)
Board of Directors or Trustees: George Allen, Jack Brandenburg, H.E. Anwarul Karim Chowdhury (UNICEF), Betty Cogswell, Ph.D., Donald Collins, Van Crawford, Sally Epstein, James Fry, Jeane Greene, Dr. John Gulick, Russell Hemenway, H.E. John Karefa-Smart, M.D., Suzanne Kellerman, Victor Morgan, Anjum Niaz, Patricia Nielson, Nathan Schafer, Rosney Shaw, Mary-Jane Snyder, Phyllis Vineyard, Bettye Ward, Prof. Linda Williams (Cornell Univ.).
Periodicals: *Popline*.
Other Information: The Institute received $1,648,292, or 98% of revenue, from direct and indirect sources in the form of gifts and grants awarded by foundations, businesses, affiliates, and individuals. (These grants included $10,000 from the Compton Foundation, $7,500 from the New-Land Foundation, $5,000 from the Stewart R. Mott Charitable Trust, and $1,000 from the One World Fund.) $13,241, or 1%, from interest on savings and temporary cash investments. The remaining revenue came from speakers' fees, dividends and interest from securities, rental income, capital gains on the sale of securities, and other miscellaneous sources.

Population Resource Center

15 Roszel Rd,
Princeton, NJ 08540   **Phone:** (609) 452-2822   **E-Mail:** popresctr@aol.com
USA   **Fax:**   (609) 452-0010

Contact Person: Jane De Lung, President.   **Officers or Principals:** Oscar Harkavy, Ph.D., Chairman; Wayne H. Holtzman, Ph.D., Vice Chairman; Shelley E. Kossak, Vice President; Edna M. Friedman, Secretary.
Mission or Interest: Research and education on a variety of population matters; immigration, reproductive health, population growth control, demographics and more.
Accomplishments: In 1995 the Center hosted numerous conferences and presentations for and in cooperation with other organizations. Organized briefings for senate staffers, such as a meeting on child care and welfare reform attended by the staff of Senators Nancy Kassebaum (R-KS), Christopher Dodd (D-CT), and Edward Kennedy (D-MA). Hosted a briefing with the League of Women Voters for the League and the press on "Family Planning and Reproductive Health." Held a meeting on the World Bank and its population stabilization efforts (the World Bank makes over $200 million in loans for population control).
Net Revenue: 1995 $871,373 **Net Expenses:** $664,148 **Net Assets:** $734,209 **Citations:** 0:255
Products or Services: Numerous reports, conferences.
Tax Status: 501(c)(3)
Board of Directors or Trustees: Rep. Anthony Beilenson (D-CA), Henry Bienen, Ph.D. (Northwestern Univ.), Peter Carpenter (Mission and Values Inst.), Hodding Carter III (MainStreet TV Prod.), William Davis, Jr. (George Washington Univ.), Robert Diamond (Biothink), Arthur Graham (Free-Flow Packaging), Jean Hennessey (Dartmouth College), Wayne Holtszman, Ph.D. (Hogg Foundation for Mental Health), Elise Jones, Sen. Nancy Kassebaum (R-KS), Mark Kirk (House Committee on International Relations), M. Faith Mitchell, Ph.D. (National Academy of Sciences), Rep. John Porter (R-IL), S. Bruce Schearer, Ph.D. (Synergos Inst.), Steven Sindig, Ph.D. (Rockefeller Found.), Donald Straus, Arthur Taylor (Muhlenberg College), Marta Tienda, Ph.D. (Univ. of Chicago), Charles Westoff, Ph.D. (Princeton Univ.).
Other Information: The Center has a Washington DC office: 1725 K St., N.W., Suite 1102, Washington, DC 20006, (202) 467-5030, fax (202) 467-5034, "prc@capaccess.org". In 1995 the Center received $707,399, or 81% of revenue, from gifts and grants awarded by foundations, businesses, and individuals. (In 1994 these grants included $180,000 from the William and Flora Hewlett Foundation, $25,000 from the Robert Sterling Clark Foundation, and $5,000 from the Henry J. Kaiser Family Foundation.) $123,000, or 14%, from donated services (expert presenters and reviewers). $21,465, or 2%, from investment income. $11,449, or 1%, from capital gains on the sale of securities. The remaining revenue came from rental income, and fees for services.

Population Services International

1120 19th St., N.W., Suite 600
Washington, DC 20036   **Phone:** (202) 785-0072
USA

Other Information: In 1994 the organization received $386,000 from the William and Flora Hewlett Foundation, $106,667 from the Henry J. Kaiser Family Foundation, $20,000 from the Compton Foundation.

Post Amerikan

P.O. Box 3452
Bloomington, IL 61702   **Phone:** (309) 828-4473
USA

Contact Person: Sherrin Fitzer.
Mission or Interest: "To provide information and analysis that is screened out or down played by establishment news sources: an alternative to corporate media." Alternative community bimonthly newspaper focusing on various left-wing causes. Prints notices on groups and community activities of interest to progressives in the Bloomington area.
Accomplishments: Founded in 1971, "we are the oldest alternative paper in the country."
Tax Status: "Non-profit worker-run collective." **Annual Report:** No. **Employees:** All volunteer.
Periodicals: *Post Amerikan* (bimonthly newspaper).

Poverty and Race Research Action Council (PRRAC)

1711 Connecticut Ave., N.W., Suite 207
Washington, DC 20009   **Phone:** (202) 387-9887   **E-Mail:** prrac@aol.com
USA   **Fax:**   (202) 387-0764

Contact Person: Chester Hartman, Executive Director.
Officers or Principals: Chester Hartman, Executive Director ($70,730); John Charles Boger, Chair; John Powell, Secretary; Phyllis Holmen, Treasurer; Steven D. White, Assistant Director; Louisa Clark, Office Manager.
Mission or Interest: Focuses on the issues of racial discrimination and poverty. Concerned with 'environmental justice' and the disproportionate incidence of hazardous materials in minorities' neighborhoods.
Accomplishments: Awarded $74,100 in grants to other organizations. Recipients included; $10,000 for Arizona Toxics Information, $3,000 each for the Massachusetts Coalition for the Homeless, and the Sugar Law Center, $2,500 for the Labor / Community Strategy Center, and $1,000 for the Center for Democratic Renewal. Ex-Board member Betsy Julian is now Assistant Secretary for Housing and Equal Opportunity at Housing and Urban Development under the Clinton administration.
Net Revenues: 1994 $463,848 **Net Expenses:** $426,960 75%/16%/9% **Net Assets:** $232,809
Tax Status: 501(c)(3)

Periodicals: *Poverty & Race* (bimonthly newsletter).
Other Information: In 1994-95, the Council received $60,000 from the Bauman Family Foundation. Individual contributors include author Jonathan Kozol. In 1994 the Council received $441,683, or 95% of revenue, from gifts and grants.

Preamble Center for Public Policy

1727 21St., N.W.
Washington, DC 20009   **Phone:** (202) 265-3263   **E-Mail:** preamble@rtk.net
USA   **Fax:**   (202) 265-3647   **Web-Page:** http://www.igc.apc.org/preamble/

Contact Person: Scott Nova, Director.   **Officers or Principals:** Patricia Bauman, Chair; Kalle Makalou; Michelle Sforza-Roderick.
Mission or Interest: Public policy organization created to counter pro-free market policy. "A partnership of activists, academics, foundations and progressive elected officials founded in 1996 to promote basic structural and institutional changes in the status quo...Preamble seeks to challenge and offer constructive alternatives to prevailing myths about the superiority of market solutions, the desirability and inevitability of global market power, and the hyper-individualism of 'every man for himself' in a cold, cruel world."
Accomplishments: Although newly founded, Preamble has already produced several papers and studies, including: "False Choices: Is Security the Price We Pay for Economic Growth?", "Countering Corporate Downsizing: A Survey of Proposals to Halt Layoffs and Job Degradation", and "Corporate Irresponsibility: There Ought to Be Some Laws - A Study of the Political and Policy Implications of Public Attitudes Toward Corporate America."
Tax Status: 501(c)(3) status pending
Internships: Yes.
Other Information: Initially called the Preamble Collaborative. "Launched" by Patricia Bauman and John Bryant of the Bauman Family Foundation.

Prison Legal News (PLN)

P.O. Box 1684
Lake Worth, FL 33460   **Phone:** (407) 547-9716
USA   **Web-Page:** http://weber.u.washington.edu/~lursa/PLN/pln.html

Contact Person: Rollin Wright, Publisher.   **Officers or Principals:** Paul Wright, Dan Pens, Co-editors.
Mission or Interest: Monthly newspaper written by incarcerated felons for incarcerated felons. "Reports on court decisions affecting prisoners and contains information designed to help prisoners vindicate their rights in the judicial system."
Accomplishments: "Prison Legal News is the only un-censored, prisoner edited, written and produced national publication. We have published monthly since May 1990." They claim a circulation of over 2,000. Among their subscribers are attorneys general in 25 states, the 6th U.S. Circuit Court in Cincinnati and the New York Public Library. PLN is even distributed overseas. PLN is indexed by the Department of Justice and the Criminal Justice Periodicals Index.
Tax Status: 501(c)(3)   **Annual Report:** No.   **Employees:** All volunteer.
Periodicals: *Prison Legal News* (monthly newspaper).
Internships: No.
Other Information: Prison Legal News was created by two avowed Communists, Ed Mead, convicted for bombings he carried out as a member of the George Jackson Brigade, and Paul Wright, convicted of first degree murder. Mead has been released and ordered to stay away from PLN, a ban that he is fighting with the help of the ACLU. Dan Pens, a convicted rapist, is now co-editor. Wright and Pen are incarcerated at the Washington State Reformatory in Monroe. Publication and subscriptions are handled by Wright's father in Florida.

Prison Life

P.O. Box 537
Stone Ridge, NY 12484   **Phone:** (914) 687-0300   **E-Mail:** code3com@aol.com
USA   **Fax:**   (914) 687-4099

Contact Person: Richard Stratton, Editor/Publisher.
Officers or Principals: Richard Stratton, Editor/Publisher; Kim Wozencraft, Executive Editor; Annie Nocenti, Editor-at-large.
Mission or Interest: Magazine focusing on incarcerated criminals and the American legal system. "The drug war and the prison boom, our rights as Americans, and the future of our nation...are on the line."
Accomplishments: Editor Richard Stratton has spoken at numerous forums on various aspects of the penal system. Recently he spoke at the 25th reunion of the Harvard Law School's Prisoners Legal Assistance Project on a symposium on the privatization of prisons, which Stratton refers to as, "the latest permutation of American capitalism." In addition to articles, *Prison Life* publishes an extensive resource listing for prisoners' legal rights and social services.
Tax Status: For profit.
Periodicals: *Prison Life* (monthly magazine).
Other Information: Editor/Publisher Richard Stratton was a prep school student at Wellesley High School. He was later convicted of brokering "loads of Colombian pot and Lebanese hash...The marijuana underground that nourished my wayward designs was my chosen field not just because the pay was good - I did it because I believe the laws against marijuana are wrong." *Prison Life* is published by Joint Venture Media of Texas.

Prisoners Rights Union

P.O. Box 1019
Sacramento, CA 95812-1019   **Phone:** (916) 441-4214
USA

Officers or Principals: Gary Diamond, Chairperson ($0); Gina S. Berry, Vice Chairperson ($0); Frank Prantil, Secretary ($0); Carol Hart, M.D., Treasurer.
Mission or Interest: Provides assistance and information about the rights of prisoners to prisoners, their families, and others - both in and outside of California.
Accomplishments: In 1993 the Union spent $155,700 on their programs. Of this, $70,163 was spent on litigation costs. $70,259 was received in legal fees.
Net Revenue: 1993 $159,792 **Net Expenses:** $172,885 90%/10%/0% **Net Assets:** (-$55,715)
Products or Services: Publications, seminars, litigation, educational activities.
Tax Status: 501(c)(3)
Board of Directors or Trustees: Paul Comiskey, Esq., Luis Talamantez, Monique Olivier, Susan Brown-Kelly, Sharon Cammesa (Public Defender), Corey Weinstein, M.D., Mark Grimes (Justice Foundation), Fred Stephens, Deborah Garlin, Esq., Isaac Cubillos (La Prenza).
Other Information: The Union received $101,388, or 63% of revenue, from program services including legal fees received. $29,913, or 19%, from grants awarded by foundations and individuals. $11,142, or 7%, from membership dues. $6,713 net, or 4%, from fund-raising events. The remaining revenue came from interest on savings and temporary cash investments, rental income, and miscellaneous sources.

Pro Choice Resource Center

174 E. Boston Post Rd.
Mamaroneck, NY 10543   **Phone:** (914) 381-3792
USA

Contact Person: Nancy M. Yanofsky, Executive Director.
Mission or Interest: Provides training and technical assistance to abortion rights organizations. Develops materials and strategies.
Tax Status: 501(c)(3)
Other Information: Founded in 1990. A project of the New York State Council of Churches. In 1994 the Center received $38,100 from the Robert Sterling Clark Foundation, $30,000 from the Rockefeller Family Fund, $25,000 from the Tides Foundation, $25,000 from the General Service Foundation, $20,000 from the Jessie Smith Noyes Foundation, $10,000 from the Ms. Foundation for Women.

Progressive, The

409 E. Main St.
Madison, WI 53703   **Phone:** (608) 257-4626
USA   **Fax:** (608) 257-3373

Contact Person: Matthew Rothschild, Editor.
Officers or Principals: Joy E. Wallin, Publisher; Ruth Conniff, Managing Editor; Mary Sheridan, Chairman.
Mission or Interest: *The Progressive* is a monthly magazine of left-wing news and opinion.
Accomplishments: 30,000 paid subscribers. Contributing writers include Kate Clinton, Susan Douglas, Will Durst, Molly Ivins, and others. The Editorial Advisory Board includes: Ben Bagdikian, Jean Bathke Elshtain, Francis Flaherty, John Kenneth Galbraith, John B. Judis, Barbara Koeppel, Colman McCarthy, Daniel Schorr, Lawrence Walsh, and others.
Products or Services: Magazine, t-shirts and paraphernalia.
Tax Status: 501(c)(3)
Board of Directors or Trustees: Warren Randy, Brady Williamson, Terri Terry.

Periodicals: *The Progressive* (monthly magazine).
Other Information: Founded in 1909 by Robert M. La Follette. La Follette ran for President in 1924 on the Progressive Party ticket. Previous editors included Erwin Knoll (1973-1994), and Morris H. Rubin (1940-1973). In 1994 *The Progressive* recieved $10,000 from the Deer Creek Foundation, and $2,000 from the Peace Development Fund.

Progressive Foundation
518 C St., N.E.
Washington, DC 20002   **Phone:**   (202) 546-4482   **E-Mail:** info@dlccpi.org
USA   **Fax:**   (202) 544-5014   **Web-Page:** http://www.dlcppi.org/

Contact Person: Robert Shapiro, Economic Advisor.
Officers or Principals: Robert Shapiro, Economic Advisor ($59,217); Seymour Martin Lipset, President ($6,000); Linda Peek, Secretary ($0); Doug Ross, Director, Third Way Project; Dr. Debra S. Knopman, Director, Center for Environmental Economics.
Mission or Interest: "Research, study and analysis of certain solutions to a broad array of domestic and international issues." Affiliated with the Democratic Leadership Council and Progressive Policy Institute. Works through various projects, such as the "Third Way Project...an effort to develop and promote a new public philosophy and policy agenda to replace discredited liberalism as the counterweight to an ascendant conservatism." The Center for Environmental Economics is a project that "is developing a 'second generation' of environmental policies to replace outdated command-and-control laws and regulations."
Accomplishments: In 1994 the Foundation spent $191,189 on its programs.
Net Revenue: 1994 $319,191 **Net Expenses:** $254,912 75%/15%/0% **Net Assets:** $471,777
Tax Status: 501(c)(3)
Board of Directors or Trustees: William Marshall.
Other Information: Affiliated with the 501(c)(4) Democratic Leadership Council at the same address. The Progressive Foundation shares equipment and staff with the Democratic Leadership Council. The Foundation received $308,500, or 97% of revenue, from gifts and grants awarded by foundations, businesses, and individuals. (These grants included $1,000 from the Tides Foundation.) $10,390, or 3%, from interest on savings and temporary cash investments.

Progressive Periodicals Directory
P.O. Box 120574
Nashville, TN 37212
USA

Mission or Interest: Publishes a directory that reviews about 600 "social concerns" periodicals. Subjects include the environment, labor, peace, health, human rights, religion and culture. Includes price and subscription information.

Progressive Policy Institute (PPI)
518 C St., N.E.
Washington, DC 20002   **Phone:**   (202) 547-0001   **E-Mail:** info@dlcppi.org
USA   **Fax:**   (202) 544-5014   **Web-Page:** http://www.dlcppi.org

Contact Person: Robert J. Shapiro. **Officers or Principals:** David Kendall, Senior Analyst.
Mission or Interest: In-house think tank for the Democratic Leadership Council. A public policy institute that advocating proposals that rely more on markets, yet have the same goals as social-welfare programs. This approach is closely identified with the moderate wing of the Democratic Party. The Institute is a part of the Democratic Leadership Council associated with "New Democrats" such as President Clinton. "PPI was founded to promote ideas that spring from the progressive tradition of American politics. Though often labeled 'centrist,' PPI does not seek simple compromise between left and right: Halfway between 'trickle down' and 'tax and spend' is a meaningless place. Rather, PPI ideas are aimed at transcending a gridlocked, increasingly irrelevant ideological debate between right and left that threatens to cripple America's capacity to respond to the challenges of the next century."
Accomplishments: The Progressive Policy Institute's work has been featured in *The Wall Street Journal*. In an article on eliminating the federal income tax mortgage deduction, Robert Shapiro was quoted as saying that because of this deduction, "As a country, we're substantially overinvesting in housing relative to its economic value...We tie up as large a share of our capital pool in housing as in more productive assets such as capital equipment." Analyst David Kendall co-authored an op-ed on health care reform through individual tax credits for health care purchases. Prof. Richard McKenzie of the University of California, Irvine, in a study of Washington think tanks, found that the PPI and affiliated Democratic Leadership Council received the most attention, and therefore greatest impact, per dollars spent. (McKenzie notes that his research corresponded with the election and early administration of President Clinton, a former Chairman of the DLC, and that it is therefore not unusual that the DLC-PPI would receive much greater attention.)
Tax Status: Incorporated under the 501(c)(4) Democratic Leadership Council.
Other Information: A part of the 501(c)(4) Democratic Leadership Council (see the separate listing) and affiliated with the 501(c)(3) Progressive Foundation at the same address. In 1992 Robert Shapiro was an advisor to President Clinton's first Presidential campaign.

Progressive Review
1739 Connecticut Ave., N.W., Suite 2
Washington, DC 20009   **Phone:**   (202) 232-5544   **E-Mail:** ssmith@igc.apc.org
USA   **Fax:**   (202) 234-6222   **Web-Page:** http://emporium.turnpike.net/P/ProRev

Contact Person: Sam Smith, Editor.
Mission or Interest: Monthly newsletter of progressive politics.
Accomplishments: The *Progressive Review* began publishing as the *Capitol East Gazette*, when it focused on anti-Vietnam War efforts and local politics in the D.C. area. In 1969 the name was changed to the *DC Gazette*. The *DC Gazette* covered entertainment and culture as well, featuring television critic Tom Shales (now with the *Washington Post*) and movie critic Joel Siegel. The arts section spun off into the *Washington Review of the Arts*. Editor Sam Smith helped start the D.C. statehood movement in the pages of the *Gazette* in the 1970's. In 1984, in reaction to the Reagan administration, it was renamed the *Progressive Review*. The *Review* won a national Alternative Press Award in 1992. The *Utne Reader* said "In a spirited and compelling style, editor Sam Smith gently weaves messages about community and individual empowerment through coverage of politics." Sam Smith served for a while as a vice president of Americans for Democratic Action. He has also written several books, including Shadows of Hope: A Freethinkers Guide to Politics in the Time of Clinton in 1993, which was well received by the *Washington Post*, *Washington Times*, and the alternative weekly, *The City Paper*.
Tax Status: For profit.
Periodicals: *The Progressive Review* (monthly newsletter).

Progressive Way
1212 Broadway, Suite 830
Oakland, CA 94612   **Phone:**   (510) 839-6768
USA

Contact Person: James Shattuck, Executive Director.   **Officers or Principals:** James Shattuck, Executive Director ($35,000); Gillian Vialet, Chairperson ($0); Cecile Isaacs, Treasurer ($0).
Mission or Interest: Works with member organizations to run workplace fund-raising drives for the benefit of progressive causes.
Accomplishments: In 1994 the Progressive Way spent $135,912 on its programs, including $73,891 in grants. The recipients of the largest grants included: $4,964 each for the Community Action Board, Gray Panthers of Berkeley, Instituto Laboral de la Raza, Legal Aid Society of Santa Cruz, MOVE, World Institute on Disability, and the Extra Share Program, $3,098 for the Gay and Lesbian Alliance Against Defamation, $2,527 for the Bay Area Black Women's Health Project, $2,519 for the Black Coalition on AIDS, $1,923 for Women Empowering Women, $1,620 for the Coalition on Homelessness, $1,036 for the Center for Economic Conversion, and $1,013 for the Women's Foundation. Other recipients included: California Rural Legal Assistance, California SANE/FREEZE, Chinese Progressive Association, Coalition for Immigrants and Refugees Rights and Services, General Assistance Advocacy Project, West County Toxics Coalition, and more.
Net Revenue: 1994 $153,019 **Net Expenses:** $157,141   86%/11%/3% **Net Assets:** $3,211
Tax Status: 501(c)(3)
Other Information: The foundation received $122,353, or 80% of revenue, from gifts and grants awarded by foundations, businesses, and individuals. (These grants included $15,000 from the McKay Foundation.) $23,200, or 15%, from membership dues. $7,039, or 5%, from special fund-raising events. The remaining revenue came from interest on savings and temporary cash investments.

Project Equus
P.O. Box 6989
Denver, CO 80206   **Phone:**   (303) 388-0219
USA

Contact Person: Robin Duxbury.   **Officers or Principals:** Jaime Jackson.
Mission or Interest: "To provide education to the public about the rights of horses; to support legislation that protects horses; to conduct undercover horse abuse investigations...Project Equus challenges current training methods of horses - the organization bases its philosophy on what is natural for horses and therefore uses wild horses as its model for what should and should not be done to domestic horses."
Accomplishments: "Undercover investigations have forced several abusive horse trainers out of business!"
Tax Status: 501(c)(3) pending **Annual Report:** No. **Employees:** 1
Internships: Yes, for skilled equestrians who can assist in undercover investigations.
Other Information: The organization is newly founded and hopes to produce periodicals and an annual report soon.

Project Nishma
1225 15th St., N.W.
Washington, DC 20005   **Phone:**   (202) 462-4268
USA

Contact Person: Thomas Smerling, Secretary/Treasurer.
Officers or Principals: Thomas Smerling, Secretary/Treasurer ($68,542); Theodore R. Mann, President ($0).
Mission or Interest: Promotion of peace in the Middle East compatible with Israel's security needs.
Accomplishments: In the fiscal year ending June 1995 the Project spent $188,464 on its programs.
Net Revenue: FY ending 6/95 $229,715 **Net Expenses:** $245,627   77%/6%/17% **Net Assets:** $76,508
Products or Services: Articles and educational materials, lobbying. The Project spent $6,095 on lobbying, $5,409 on grassroots lobbying, and $686 on the direct lobbying of legislators.

Tax Status: 501(c)(3)
Board of Directors or Trustees: Edward Sanders, Henry Rasorsky.
Other Information: The Project received $226,180, or 98% of revenue, from gifts and grants awarded by foundations, businesses, and individuals. (These grants included $45,000 from the Nathan Cummings Foundation.) $3,535, or 2%, from interest on savings and temporary cash investments.

Psychologists for Social Responsibility

2607 Connecticut Ave., N.W., 2nd Floor
Washington, DC 20008   **Phone:**   (202) 745-7084
USA

Contact Person: Milton Schwebel, Ph.D., President.   **Officers or Principals:** Michael Wessels, Ph.D., Chairman ($0); Susan McKay, Ph.D., Secretary ($0); Sandra McPherson, Treasurer ($0).
Mission or Interest: Works for peace and to prevent nuclear war through the promotion of a sound psychological environment.
Accomplishments: In 1994 the organization spent $27,605 on its programs.
Net Revenue: 1994 $37,961 **Net Expenses:** $37,590 **Net Assets:** $12,684
Tax Status: 501(c)(3)
Periodicals: Newsletter.
Other Information: The organization received $19,591, or 51% of revenue, from gifts and grants awarded by foundations, businesses, and individuals. $17,086, or 45%, from membership dues. $770, or 2%, from program services. The remaining revenue came from investment income.

Public Citizen

215 Pennsylvania Ave., S.E.
Washington, DC 20003   **Phone:**   (202) 546-4996   **E-Mail:** EBarrett@essential.org
USA   **Fax:**   (202) 547-7392

Contact Person: Joan Claybrook, President.
Officers or Principals: Joan Claybrook, President ($25,037); Larry Bostian, Secretary ($0); Linda Beaver, Treasurer ($0).
Mission or Interest: Founded in 1971 by Ralph Nader, Public Citizen litigates and lobbies for legislation that supports the environment, consumer protection, and workplace protection.
Accomplishments: In the fiscal year ending September 1994, the organization spent $3,967,275 on its programs. Public Citizen received $33,170 in court-awarded attorney's fees.
Net Revenue: FY ending 9/94 $7,195,447 **Net Expenses:** $5,613,042 71%/2%/27% **Net Assets:** $5,399,915
Citations: 1,728:16
Tax Status: 501(c)(4)
Board of Directors or Trustees: Paul Gikas, Joseph Page.
Periodicals: *Public Citizen* (bimonthly newsletter).
Other Information: Public Citizen is affiliated with the 501(c)(3) Public Citizen Foundation. Joan Claybrook is the president of both, and received combined compensation of $71,043 from the two affiliates. The two affiliates had combined net revenues of $10,987,234, net expenses of $8,951,610, and net assets of $6,220,260. The two affiliates received a combined $196,001 in court-awarded attorney's fees. Public Citizen received $3,110,796, or 43% of revenue from gifts and grants awarded by foundations, businesses, and individuals. (These grants included $60,000 from the Tides Foundation, and $25,000 from the C.S. Fund.) $3,085,809, or 43%, from the sale of inventory. $329,941, or 5%, from the "Buyers Up" program. $291,375 net, or 4%, from rental income. $220,078, or 3%, from mailing list rentals. The remaining revenue came from interest on savings and temporary cash investments, court-awarded attorney's fees, capital gains on the sale of securities, and other miscellaneous sources.

Public Citizen Foundation

215 Pennsylania Ave, S.E.
Washington, DC 20003   **Phone:**   (202) 546-4996   **E-Mail:** EBarrett@essential.org
USA   **Fax:**   (202) 547-7392

Contact Person: Joan Claybrook, President.
Officers or Principals: Sidney Wolfe, Health Research ($76,605); Cornish Hitchcock, Litigation ($73,635); Paul Levy, David Vladek, Litigation ($71,128); Larry Bostian, Secretary; Linda Beaver, Treasurer; Robert Fellmeth, Chair.
Mission or Interest: Founded by Ralph Nader, the Public Citizen Foundation provides research and litigation on issues pertaining to the environment, consumer affairs, organized labor, public health, corporate responsibility, and occupational safety.
Accomplishments: In the fiscal year ending September 1994, the Foundation spent $3,129,869 on its programs. The largest program, with expenditures of $1,101,194, was the production and distribution of publications. $865,478 was spent on litigation and related activities. The Foundation received $162,831 in court-awarded attorney's fees for these activities. $598,443 was spent on health research. During the health care reform debate, the Foundation favored a Canadian-style, or single-payer,' system. Other programs included energy research and the publication of two periodicals, PC Texas and Congress Watch.
Net Revenue: FY ending 9/94 $3,791,787 **Net Expenses:** $3,338,568 94%/4%/2% **Net Assets:** $820,345
Citations: 1,728:16

Products or Services: Litigation, research, publications, and lobbying. The Foundation spent $26,803 on lobbying, $4,679 on grassroots lobbying, and $22,124 on the direct lobbying of legislators. This was down 51% from two years prior, and down 66% from $79,623 three years prior.
Tax Status: 501(c)(3)
Board of Directors or Trustees: Adolph Reed, Jr., Morris Dees, Jr. (Southern Poverty Law Center), Jim Hightower, Anthony Mazzocchi.
Periodicals: *Public Citizen* (bimonthly newsletter).
Other Information: The Public Citizen Foundation is affiliated with the 501(c)(4) Public Citizen. Joan Claybrook is the president of both, and received combined compensation of $71,043 from the two affiliates. The two affiliates had combined net revenues of $10,987,234, net expenses of $8,951,610, and net assets of $6,220,260. The two affiliates received a combined $196,001 in court-awarded attorney's fees. The Foundation received $2,986,762, or 79% of revenue, from gifts and grants awarded by foundations, businesses, and individuals. (These grants included $25,000 from the Rockefeller Family Fund, $25,000 from the Joyce Mertz-Gilmore Foundation, $10,000 from the Deer Creek Foundation, $500 from the Aaron and Martha Schecter Private Foundation.) $481,894, or 13%, from the sale of inventory. $162,831, or 4%, from court awarded attorney's fees. $135,689, or 4%, from mailing list rentals. The remaining revenue came from interest on savings and temporary cash investments, fees for the "Health Clearinghouse," and other miscellaneous activities.

Public Concern Foundation / *Washington Spectator*

P.O. Box 20065, London Terrace Station
New York, NY 10011   **Phone:**   (212) 741-2365
USA

Contact Person: Phillip Frazer, Publisher.
Officers or Principals: Phillip Frazer, Publisher ($49,500); Hamilton Fish, President ($25,700); Rhoda Dreyfus, Vice President ($0); Janet Michaud, Secretary; Peggy Cafritz, Treasurer; Ben A. Franklin, Editor; Tristram Coffin, Founding Editor.
Mission or Interest: Publishes the *Washington Spectator*, a bimonthly newsletter on "subjects of interest to progressives in the nation's capitol."
Accomplishments: Circulation of approximately 41,000. In 1994 the Foundation spent $472,426 on its projects. $312,517 of that went to publishing the *Washington Spectator*. Other programs included membership expenses.
Net Revenue: 1994 $697,308 **Net Expenses:** $666,990 71%/25%/4% **Net Assets:** $662,143 **Citations:** 2:231
Tax Status: 501(c)(3)
Board of Directors or Trustees: Roger Craver, Margaret Coffin, Nancy Larrick Crosby, William Elwood, Gloria Emerson, Erica Hunt, John Leonard, Frederic Melcher, Ruth Shikes, Kurt Vonnegut.
Periodicals: *Washington Spectator* (bimonthly newsletter).
Other Information: The Foundation received $418,560, or 60% of revenue, from membership dues. $191,323, or 27%, from gifts and grants awarded by foundations, businesses, and individuals. $55,724, or 8%, from mailing list rentals. $27,574, or 4%, from dividends and interest from securities. The remaining revenue came from interest on savings and temporary cash investments, and the sale of single copies.

Public Counsel

601 S. Ardmore
Los Angeles, CA 90005   **Phone:**   (213) 385-2977
USA   **Fax:**   (213) 385-9089

Contact Person: Steve Nissen, Executive Director.   **Officers or Principals:** Steve Nissen, Executive Director ($134,141); Kenneth Babcock, Attorney ($79,256); Virginia Weisz, Attorney ($77,188); Margaret Levy, President; Robin Meadow, Vice President; Joseph D. Mandel, Community Representative; Lawrence E. May, Secretary; Walter Cochran-Bond, Treasurer.
Mission or Interest: Public interest civil legal advocacy on behalf of the poor.
Accomplishments: In the fiscal year ending August 1994, the organization spent $1,408,787 on its programs.
Net Revenue: FY ending 8/94 $2,051,545 ($52,500, or 3%, from government grants) **Net Expenses:** $1,878,387 75%/25%/0%
Net Assets: $1,360,002 **Citations:** 223:75
Tax Status: 501(c)(3)
Board of Directors or Trustees: Enrique Baray (Senior V.P., Univision Network and Television Group), Gordon Bava, Paula Bennett, Morgan Chu, Wanda Denson-Low (Asst. General Counsel, Hughes Aircraft), Lori Huff Dillman, David Fields, Josie Gonzalez, David Henri, Stanley Iezman, Leslie LoBaugh, Joseph Luevanos, Denise MacRae, Marc Marmaro, Gregory Mazares (Litigation Sciences), Dean Gerald McLaughlin (Loyola Law School), Stephan Owens, Susan Erburu Reardon, Michael Soloff, John Stamper, Sally Suchil (Asst. General Counsel, MGM), Geoffrey Thomas, Pat Bowers Thomas, Carolyn Thorp, Thomas Unterman (Times Mirror Co.), Michael Waldorf, Michael White, Dan Wolf (V.P., Walt Disney Pictures and Television), Karen Wong, Bert Tigerman, Anthony Barash.
Other Information: Affiliated with the Los Angeles County Bar Association and the Beverly Hills Bar Association. Public Counsel received $1,640,608, or 80% of revenue, from gifts and grants awarded by foundations, businesses, and individuals. (These grants included $90,000 from the Rosenberg Foundation, $5,000 from the Barbra Streisand Foundation, and $5,000 from the Liberty Hill Foundation.) $333,750 net, or 16%, from special fund-raising events. $52,500, or 3%, from government grants. $22,289, or 1%, from litigation settlements. The remaining revenue came from interest on savings and temporary cash investments.

Public Employees for Environmental Responsibility (PEER)
810 1st St., N.E., Suite 680
Washington, DC 20002
USA

Contact Person: Jeff DeBonis, Founder/Executive Director.
Accomplishments: DeBonis called for a Congressional hearing into links between the militia movement, the Wise Use movement, and for "increased protections against violence aimed at subverting federal laws and thwarting public land protection."
Other Information: Executive Director DeBonis was also the founder of the Association of Forest Service Employees for Environmental Ethics in 1989. Prior to that he had worked in the Peace Corps in El Salvador in reforestation and soil conservation, and as a consultant for the U.S. Agency for International Development (USAID) working on logging damage to Ecuadoran rain forests. In 1994 the organization received $50,000 from the Florence and John Schumann Foundation, $30,000 from the Rockefeller Family Fund, $30,000 from the Deer Creek Foundation, $20,000 from the Bullitt Foundation, $10,000 from the C.S. Fund, $10,000 from the Compton Foundation, $5,000 from the New Land Foundation.

Public Health Institute
853 Broadway, Suite 2014
New York, NY 10003   **Phone:** (212) 674-3322
USA

Contact Person: Les Leopold, Co Director.
Mission or Interest: Build connections between organized labor and grassroots organizations on issues related to the environment, health, and safety issues.
Accomplishments: Directed such projects as "Global Warming Watch."
Tax Status: 501(c)(3)
Other Information: Affiliated with the Labor Institute at the same address. Founded in 1985. In 1994 the Institute received $45,000 from the Bauman Family Foundation, $40,000 from the Nathan Cummings Foundation, and $25,000 from the Jessie Smith Noyes Foundation.

Public Media Center
466 Green St., Suite 300
San Francisco, CA 94133
USA

Mission or Interest: Public media campaigns on behalf of public interest organizations.
Accomplishments: Worked with Forests Forever, conducted "AIDS Discrimination Strategy Development" project.
Other Information: In 1994 the Center received $437,483 from the Henry J. Kaiser Family Foundation, $400,000 from the Florence and John Schumann Foundation, $75,000 from the Rosenberg Foundation, $25,000 from the New World Foundation, $20,000 from the Angelina Fund, $10,000 from the Joyce Mertz-Gilmore Foundation, $2,875 from the Vanguard Public Foundation.

Puerto Rican Legal Defense and Education Fund (PRLDEF)
99 Hudson St.
New York, NY 10013-2815   **Phone:** (212) 219-3360
USA   **Fax:**   (212) 431-4276

Contact Person: Juan A. Figueroa, President.   **Officers or Principals:** Juan A. Figueroa, President/General Counsel ($123,182); Ken Kimerling, Associate Counsel ($85,604); Arthur Baer, Associate Counsel ($63,149); Olga Perez, Associate Counsel; Elsa Rios, Director, Education; Benito Romano, Chairperson; Alba J. Rovira-Paoli, Esq., Anna Carbonell, Vice Chairpersons; William F. Callejo, Esq., Secretary; Martin Zuckerman, Esq., Treasurer.
Mission or Interest: Litigation and education to ensure that Puerto Ricans and Latinos in the United States are guaranteed voting rights "by maximizing the number of districts in which they have ability to elect representatives of their own choice," education rights through "bilingual education and the fair distribution of resources for education," and Latina rights. They address poverty and "economic justice" by playing "a more active role in addressing inequities in the areas of economic development, employment and housing discrimination, and credit redlining."
Net Revenue: FY ending 6/94 $1,313,304 ($11,428, or 1%, from government grants)
Net Expenses: $1,405,607 79%/13%/8% **Net Assets:** $564,702 **Citations:** 13:190
Products or Services: PRLDEF provides litigation services. In the fiscal year ending June 1994 they spent $695,856 on these services. They spent $205,116 on education services, including $22,199 on scholarships and grants. Advocacy work on behalf of the community cost $210,782. They host an annual banquet and the Salsa Disco Fund Raiser.
Tax Status: 501(c)(3) **Employees:** 20
Board of Directors or Trustees: David R. Jones, Esq. (Pres./CEO, Community Service Society of NY), Prof. Wilfredo Caraballo (Seton Hall Univ. School of Law), Luis Alvarez (Pres., National Urban Fellows), Prof. Maria Josefa Canino-Arroyo (Rutgers Univ.), Diana Correa (Columbia Law School), Ricardo Fernandez (Pres., Herbert H. Lehman College), Prof. Rev. Joseph Fitzpatrick, S.J. (Fordham Univ.), Miguel Garcia, Jr., (Pres., New Directions in Community Revitalizations), Harold Lewis, Jr., Esq., (Mercer Univ. School of Law), Idelisse Malave, Esq. (V.P., Ms. Foundation), Lisa Quiroz (Dir., Education Programs, Time Magazine), Jose Reynoso (Manager, Financial Planning and Analysis, Times Mirror Co.), Celina Romany, Esq. (Univ. of Puerto Rico Law School), Nathan Quinones (Chancellor Emeritus, New York City Board of Education).

Internships: Yes, summer legal internships.

Other Information: The Fund received $907,753, or 69% of revenue, from gifts and grants awarded by foundations, companies and individuals. (In 1993 the Fund received $450,000 over three years from the Carnegie Corporation. In 1995, $800,000 from the Rockefeller Foundation.) $180,611, or 14%, from court-awarded attorney's fees. $105,959 net, or 8%, from special fund-raising events, an annual banquet and a "Salsa Disco Fund Raiser." $74,104, or 6%, from educational services. $21,951, or 2%, from dividends and interest from securities. The remaining income came from capital gains on the sale of securities, and interest on savings and temporary cash investments.

Quixote Center

3502 Varnum St.
Brentwood, MD 20722   **Phone:** (301) 699-0042   **E-Mail:** Quixote @igc.apc.org
USA   **Fax:**   (301) 864-2182

Contact Person: William R. Callahan, President.   **Officers or Principals:** William R. Callahan, President ($20,650); Dolores Pomerleau, Secretary/Treasurer ($20,650); Maureen Fiedler, Vice President ($19,222).
Mission or Interest: Catholic organizations seeking the "transformation of Church structures" to be more democratic. Provides humanitarian aid to foreign countries.
Accomplishments: Launched the "Equal Justice USA" project which supports death-row prisoner Mumia Abu-Jamal. Jamal was convicted, some say unfairly, of killing a police officer. (For more information on Abu-Jamal, see the Pacifica Foundation.) In the fiscal year ending June 1995, the Center spent $845,615 on its programs. The largest program, with expenditures of $315,809, was humanitarian aid to Nicaragua through a network of church organizations. This program included $87,133 in grants to organizations in Nicaragua. $169,943 was spent on "Priests for Equality," a network of priests and others promoting equality for women within the Church. $153,149 was spent on the "Equal Justice" project. $96,424 was spent on "Catholics Speak Out," a program to "work for justice in the church." $77,291 was spent on "Haiti Reborn," providing humanitarian aid to Haiti. The Center awarded grants to organizations in the United States as well. These included; five grants totaling $10,701 for the Black United Fund, $8,500 for the Funding Exchange, two grants totaling $5,897 for the Nicaraguan Cultural Alliance, and $250 for Global Demobilization.
Net Revenue: FY ending 6/95 $1,041,708 **Net Expenses:** $1,051,319 80%/12%/8% **Net Assets:** $156,154
Citations: 15:182
Products or Services: Humanitarian aid, reports, and lobbying. The Center spent $77 on the direct lobbying of legislators. The amount the Center spent on lobbying has decreased over the years, down 69% from the previous year, down 94% from two years prior, and down 99% from $6,125 three years prior.
Tax Status: 501(c)(3)
Board of Directors or Trustees: Ann Neele.
Periodicals: *Rocinante* (quarterly newsletter).
Other Information: In 1991 the Center absorbed Priests for Equality, a separate organization which is now a project of the Center. The Center received $882,253, or 85% of revenue, from gifts and grants awarded by foundations, businesses, and individuals. (These grants included $500 from the Haymarket People's Fund.) $147,988 net, or 14%, from the sale of inventory. The remaining revenue came from mailing list rentals, rental income, interest on savings and temporary cash investments, and other miscellaneous sources.

Rainforest Alliance

65 Blecker St.
New York, NY 10012   **Phone:**   (212) 677-1900
USA

Contact Person: Daniel R. Katz, Executive Director.
Officers or Principals: Daniel R. Katz, Executive Director ($55,000); Michael Goulding, Project Director ($46,000); Richard Donovan, Project Director ($44,000); Labeeb M. Abboud, Chairman; Marin Kreider, Vice President/Treasurer.
Mission or Interest: Research and educational alliance dedicated to preserving the world's rainforests.
Accomplishments: In the fiscal year ending June 1994, the Alliance spent $1,026,049 on its programs. The largest project, with expenditures of $252,755, was the Smart Wood Project which pursued "conservation of the rainforests by providing economic incentives for the adoption of improved timber harvesting and management practices that do not degrade the forests." $176,045 on communications. $151,811 on the Eco-Ok Banana Program to bring together banana growers and other interested parties to "transform the banana industry so that it is less environmentally damaging." Other projects included a Conservation Media Center, and biodiversity management models for fish in the Amazon river. The Alliance awarded $59,813 in grants to community-based conservation groups in tropical nations.
Net Revenue: FY ending 6/94 $1,182,892 ($54,475, or 5%, from government grants)
Net Expenses: $1,280,172 80%/8%/11% **Net Assets:** (-$17,806) **Citations:** 28:161
Tax Status: 501(c)(3)
Board of Directors or Trustees: Chrys Fisher, Dr. Alison Jolly, Paul Kopperl, Dr. Thomas Lovejoy, Robert von Mehren, Rev. James Parks Morton, Dr. Ghillean Prance, Dr. Anna Curtenius Roosevelt, Patricia Scharlin, Dr. Judith Sulzberger, Martin Tandler, Tensie Whelan, Chris Willie, Lawrence Wirth, Mrs. William Ziff.
Other Information: The Alliance received $883,792, or 75% of revenue, from gifts and grants awarded by foundations, businesses, and individuals. (These grants included $205,302 from the Environmental Federation of America, $8,559 from the Environmental Federation of California.) $131,409 net, or 11%, from special fund-raising events. $79,762, or 7%, from royalties. $54,475, or 5%, from government grants. $28,843, or 2%, from membership dues. The remaining revenue came from lecture fees, the sale of inventory, and interest on savings and temporary cash investments.

Rainforest Foundation

270 Lafayette St., Suite 1205
New York, NY 10012
USA

Contact Person: Larry Cox, Executive Director.   **Officers or Principals:** Larry Cox, Executive Director ($32,000); Trudie Styler, President ($0); Gordon Sumner, Vice President ($0); Jeffrey Hollender, Treasurer.
Mission or Interest: Foundation created by rock musician Sting to preserve the Amazon rainforests and the indigenous people living there.
Accomplishments: In the fiscal year ending August 1993, the Foundation spent $874,151 on its programs. The largest of these programs, with expenditures of $570,903, was educating the public about the rainforests and the indigenous population. $145,129 was spent on the "demarcation of an area of the Brazilian rainforest." $100,000 was spent providing medical assistance and medical supplies to indigenous people. Other programs included funding an Indian Center, and other charitable programs benefiting indigenous people.
Net Revenue: FY ending 8/93 $1,193,359 **Net Expenses:** $1,109,214   79%/9%/13% **Net Assets:** $224,189
Citations: 56:135
Tax Status: 501(c)(3)
Board of Directors or Trustees: Miles Copeland, Jonathan Rose, Rose Styron, Stephen Viederman, Joshua Mailman, Sandy Pittman.
Other Information: The Foundation received $1,210,410, or 99.6% of total revenue, from gifts and grants awarded by foundations, businesses, and individuals. The remaining revenue came from interest on savings and temporary cash investments. The Foundation lost $21,241 hosting special fund-raising events (this does not include the $982,161 received in contributions at these events.) These special events included a Carnegie Hall event, a children's event, and a Houston event.

Redwood Cultural Work

1222 Preservation Parkway
Oakland, CA 94612   **Phone:**   (415) 428-9191
USA

Contact Person: Susan Freudlich, Executive Director.   **Officers or Principals:** Susan Freudlich, Executive Director ($50,172); Helen Cohen, President ($0); Hugh Vasquez, Secretary ($0); Susanne Dyckman, Treasurer.
Mission or Interest: Promotes concerts, festivals, and recordings of various kinds of music, including the traditional music of many cultures, to promote diversity.
Accomplishments: In 1994 the organization spent $442,941 on its programs, $189,741 for recordings and $253,200 for live performances.
Net Revenue: 1994 $821,241 ($144,517, or 18%, from government grants) **Net Expenses:** $528,660   84%/9%/7%
Net Assets: (-$337,086)
Tax Status: 501(c)(3)
Board of Directors or Trustees: Dulce Arguelles, Ginny Berson, Charmaine Curtis, Carrie Koeturius, Nell Myhand, Gus Newport.
Other Information: Redwood Cultural Work received $332,271, or 40% of revenue, from "debt restructuring." $144,517, or 18%, from government grants. $130,367, or 15%, from gifts and grants awarded by foundations, businesses, and individuals. (These grants included $500 from the Vanguard Public Foundation.) $124,335 net, or 15%, from the sale of recordings and products. $87,226, or 11%, from ticket sales. The remaining revenue came from interest on savings and temporary cash investments.

Religious Coalition for Reproductive Choice

1025 Vermont Ave., N.W., Suite 1130
Washington, DC 20005   **Phone:**   (202) 628-7700
USA   **Fax:**   (202) 628-7716

Contact Person: Laurie Shepard.
Officers or Principals: Ann Thompson Cook, Executive Director ($39,000); Rev. Katherine Hancock Ragsdale, President ($0); Rev. Elenora Giddings Ivory, Vice President ($0); Donna Gary, Treasurer; Nancy Hunt Wirth, Secretary.
Mission or Interest: Lobbying affiliate of the Religious Coalition for Reproductive Choice Educational Fund.
Net Revenue: 1994 $692,066 **Net Expenses:** $689,722   74%/6%/18% **Net Assets:** $63,770 **Citations:** 0:255
Tax Status: 501(c)(4) **Annual Report:** Yes.
Board of Directors or Trustees: Jean Stewart Berg, Kelly Bower, Dorothy Chapman, Sonya Chung, Faith Adams Johnson, Laia Katz; Rabbi Lynne Lansberg, Rebecca Richards, Jerald Scott, Sandra Sorensen, Beverly Stripling.
Internships: Yes.
Other Information: They are affiliated with the 501(c)(3) Religious Coalition for Reproductive Choice Educational Fund at the same address. For more information see Religious Coalition for Reproductive Choice Educational Fund. The 501(c)(3) and 501(c)(4) affiliates combined in 1994 had revenues of $1,270,729, expenditures of $1,225,914, assets of $165,849, and Executive Director Ann Thompson Cook was paid $60,000. The Coalition received $692,066, or 96% of revenue, from gifts and grants awarded by foundations, companies and individuals. (These grants included $40,000 from the Jessie Smith Noyes Foundation.) $16,559, or 2%, from income derived from the Coalition's mailing list. $8,477, or 1%, from a fund-raising conference. The remaining revenue came from dividends and interest from securities, sales of publications, and other miscellaneous sources.

Religious Coalition for Reproductive Choice Educational Fund

1025 Vermont Ave., N.W., Suite 1130
Washington, DC 20005   **Phone:**   (202) 628-7700
USA   **Fax:**   (202) 628-7716

Contact Person: Laurie Shepard.
Officers or Principals: Ann Thompson Cook, Executive Director ($21,000); Rev. Katherine Hancock Ragsdale, President ($0); Rev. Elenora Giddings Ivory, Vice President ($0); Donna Gary, Treasurer; Nancy Hunt Wirth, Secretary.
Mission or Interest: Research and educational organization devoted to the right to have an abortion based on "the teachings of our religious traditions, by our faith communities, by our own innate sense of what is holy and sacred."
Accomplishments: Successfully launched a pro-choice billboard campaign. In 1994 they spent $186,027 on media outreach, education and training. Included in this was a national conference in Pensacola, FL. They spent $42,269 providing information regarding public policy and abortion. Continued programs to ensure that the Coalition's work builds "a multicultural, anti-racist organization." To this end they spent $164,510 on programs designed as an outreach to communities of color through their "Women of Color Partnership."
Net Revenue: 1994 $552,593   **Net Expenses:** $536,192   73%/9%/15%   **Net Assets:** $102,079   **Citations:**   0:260
Products or Services: Numerous publications describing religious affirmations of abortion. Research and educational materials. Bumper stickers, t-shirts, and buttons. Grants to state affiliates. Payments to affiliates totaled $15,214 in 1994.
Tax Status: 501(c)(3)   **Annual Report:** Yes.
Board of Directors or Trustees: Jean Stewart Berg, Kelly Bower, Dorothy Chapman, Sonya Chung, Faith Adams Johnson, Laia Katz; Rabbi Lynne Lansberg, Rebecca Richards, Jerald Scott, Sandra Sorensen, Beverly Stripling.
Internships: Yes.
Other Information: The Coalition is made up member organizations representing Protestants, Catholics, Jews, Universalists and Humanists. Their Women of Color Partnership includes, among others; AFSCME, NAACP Legal Fund, NARAL, National Council of Negro Women, NOW, National Council of Churches, National Urban League, and Planned Parenthood Federation of America. They are affiliated with the 501(c)(4) Religious Coalition for Reproductive Choice at the same address. They share a Board of Directors. The 501(c)(3) and 501(c)(4) affiliates combined had revenues of $1,270,729, expenditures of $1,225,914, assets of $165,849, and Executive Director Ann Thompson Cook was paid $60,000. They were formerly called the Religious Coalition for Abortion Rights. Although expressly religious, their mission statement makes no reference to God. God is referred to three time in their 1994 annual report, and two of these references are to an anti-abortion publication they refer to as "the 'Army of God' anti-abortion terrorist manual." The only other mention of God is in the President's message; "We are for women, and for men and children and families, who struggle to do God's will in the face of the very real challenges of our everyday lives." There is also no mention of the Bible, Torah, Talmud or Koran. The Fund received $539,226, or 98% of revenues, from gifts and grants awarded by foundations, companies and individuals. (These grants included $25,000 from the Robert Sterling Clark Foundation, $10,000 from the Ms. Foundation, and $500 from the Haymarket People's Fund.) $6,472, or 1%, from fund-raising conferences. The remaining revenue came from interest on savings and temporary cash investments, literature sales, and other miscellaneous sources.

Religious Task Force on Central America

1747 Connecticut Ave., N.W.
Washington, DC 20009   **Phone:**   (202) 387-7652
USA

Contact Person: Lee Miller, Director.
Officers or Principals: Margaret A. Swedish, Director ($18,500); Lee Miller, Director ($18,500).
Mission or Interest: "Education, news, theology, cultural information, history related to U.S. foreign policy, the Church and Central America."
Accomplishments: In the fiscal year ending September 1994, the Task Force spent $55,796 on its programs.
Net Revenue: FY ending 9/94 $71,291   **Net Expenses:** $75,400   **Net Assets:** $13,061
Products or Services: Meetings, conferences, newsletter, and lobbying. The Task Force spent $632 on lobbying.
Tax Status: 501(c)(3)
Board of Directors or Trustees: Louise Akers, SC (Leadership Conference of Religious Women), Marie Dennis (Maryknoll Fathers and Brothers), Amy Hoey, RSM (Sisters of Mercy), James Hug, SJ (Center of Concern), Ted Keating, SM (Conference of Major Superiors of Men), Joseph Lapauw, CICM (Missionhurst), Patricia McCann, RSM (Sisters of Mercy), Robert McChesney, SJ (Intl. and Refugee Services, Jesuit Conference), Lou McNeil (U.S. Catholic Mission Assoc.), Patricia Murphy, SSND (Central America Committee), Tom Quigley (U.S. Catholic Conference), Susan Thompson (Columbian Fathers Justice and Peace Office).
Periodicals: *Central American Report* (bimonthly newsletter).
Other Information: The Task Force received $55,463, or 78% of revenue, from gifts and grants awarded by foundations, businesses, and individuals. $15,533, or 22% of revenue, from program service fees. The remaining revenue came from investment income.

Resist

1 Summer St.
Somerville, MA 02143   **Phone:**   (617) 925-4185
USA   **Fax:**   (617) 925-8060

Contact Person: Louis Kampf, President.   **Officers or Principals:** Nancy Wechsler, Secretary/Treasurer ($28,477); Nancy Moriz, Director ($25,201); Robin Carton, Director ($11,080); Louis Kampf, President; Tess Ewing, Vice President.
Mission or Interest: Focusing on peace and justice issues, resisting "illegitimate authority," world peace, racial harmony, and "dissidents in the U.S. and other countries." Small grants (a maximum of $1,000), and subsidized loans for grassroots social-change organizations.
Accomplishments: Since its founding, *Resist* has awarded over 3,200 grants. In 1995 *Resist* spent $210,451 on its programs. $173,894 was spent assisting grassroots organizations, including $110,053 in grants. Grant recipients include: $1,000 each for the Committee in Solidarity with Central American People, Cuba Information Project, Guatemala Human Rights Commission, U.S./Guatemala Labor Education Project, Border Rights Coalition, Clergy and Laity Concerned, Institute for the Study of the Religious Right, National Lawyers Guild-Los Angeles, Center for Popular Economics, Share the Wealth, Lesbians and Gays Against Intervention, Boston Mobilization for Survival, Honor Our Neighbors' Origins and Rights, Coalition for New Priorities, Citizen Soldier, Women Against Military Madness, Committee to End the Marion Lockdown, Prison Law Project/National Lawyers Guild, Prisoners with AIDS-Rights Advocacy Group, Connecticut NARAL, National Network of Abortion Funds, Committee Opposed to Militarism and the Draft, and others. $36,557 was spent producing and distributing *Resist* to approximately 4,600 subscribers.
Net Revenue: 1995 $291,011 **Net Expenses:** $210,451 74%/12%/14% **Net Assets:** $294,450
Tax Status: 501(c)(3) **Annual Report:** Yes.
Board of Directors or Trustees: Frank Brodhead, Pam Chamberlain, Connie Chan, Bell Chevigny, Noam Chomsky (MIT), Kate Cloud, Norm Fruchter, Larry Goldsmith, Mitchell Goodman, Kenneth Hale, Oscar Hernandez, Frank Joyce, Louis Kampf, Hans Koning, Paul Lauter, Marc Miller, Richard Ohmann, Wayne O'Neil, Carlos Otero, Grace Paley, Roxanna Pastor, Merble Reagon, Henry Rosemont, Carol Schachet, Renae Scott, Cheryl Smith, Amy Swerdlow, Ken Tangvik, Rene Valle, George Vickers, Nancy Wechsler, Fran White.
Periodicals: *Resist* (bimonthly newsletter).
Other Information: Founded in 1967 to support draft resistance and oppose the Vietnam War. In 1995 *Resist* received $246,179, or 85% of total revenue, from gifts and grants awarded by foundations, businesses, and individuals. (In 1994 these grants included $6,200 from the Tides Foundation, $1,000 from the Haymarket People's Fund, $1,000 from the Aaron and Martha Schecter Private Foundation, and $250 from the Vanguard Public Foundation.) $28,545, or 10%, from interest on savings and temporary cash investments. $15,483, or 5%, from other investment sources. The remaining revenue came from the sale of inventory, refunded grants, and other miscellaneous sources.

Rex Foundation

P.O. Box 2204
San Anselmo, CA 94979
USA

Contact Person: Robert H. Weir, President.
Officers or Principals: Robert H. Weir, President ($0); Carolyn A. Garcia, Secretary/Treasurer ($0).
Mission or Interest: Philanthropic foundation created by the late Grateful Dead guitarist, Jerry Garcia. Grants are made to help the environment, the poor, the arts, and other areas.
Accomplishments: In the fiscal year ending August 1994, the Foundation awarded $1,259,100 in grants. The recipients included: $10,000 each for the Northcoast Environmental Center, ACLU Foundation of Northern California, AIDS Task Force of Alabama, Bread & Roses Community Fund, and Earth Communications Office, $5,000 each for the Men's Resource Center of Western Massachusetts, Citizens for Environmental Justice, Earth Conservation Corps., Environmental Defense Fund, and Humane Farming Association, $2,500 for the Peace Brigades International, and $1,000 for the Crossroads Community Fund.
Net Revenue: FY ending 8/94 $1,463,660 **Net Expenses:** $1,451,905 **Net Assets:** $108,392
Tax Status: 501(c)(3)
Board of Directors or Trustees: John Perry Barlow, Bernard Bildman, Harold Kant, Bill Walton, Michael Hart, Diane Blagman, David Grisman, Earl Smith, Hale Milgrim, John Scher, Jon McIntire.
Other Information: In 1995, following the death of Grateful Dead leader Jerry Garcia, Ben & Jerry's Homemade, the ice cream manufacturer, agreed to donate 50 cents from each sale of Cherry Garcia flavor ice cream and yogurt from its 120 scoop shops to the Rex Foundation. This lasted from the time of his death until his funeral. The Foundation received $1,374,730, or 94% of revenue, from concert proceeds. In addition to raising funds, these concerts featured information tables from many of the organizations who received grants. $82,102, or 6%, from gifts and grants awarded by foundations, businesses, and individuals. The remaining revenue came from merchandising items at the concerts.

Richard and Rhoda Goldman Fund

One Lombard St., Suite 303
San Francisco, CA 94111   **Phone:** (415) 788-1090
USA

Contact Person: Duane Silverstein, Executive Director. **Officers or Principals:** Duane Silverstein, Executive Director; Richard Nathaniel Goldman, President; Rhoda Frances Haas Goldman, Secretary/Treasurer.
Mission or Interest: Grant-making foundation that focuses on the environment, abortion rights, overpopulation, and civic activities in the San Francisco area.
Accomplishments: In 1993 the Foundation awarded $5,451,933 in grants. Recipients included; $100,000 for the National Abortion and Reproductive Rights Action League Foundation, $100,000 for the Reproductive Health Technologies Project, $50,000 each for the Natural Resources Defense Council, Tides Foundation, Zero Population Growth, and Sierra Club Foundation, $30,000 each for the Youth Law Center and Pesticide Action Network, and $25,000 each for Consumer Action, American Communications Foundation, and EarthAction.

Robert Sterling Clark Foundation

101 Park Ave.
New York, NY 10178   **Phone:**   (212) 696-6051
USA

Contact Person: Margaret C. Ayers, Executive Director.   **Officers or Principals:** Margaret C. Ayers, Executive Director ($172,387); Darcy H. Hector ($70,100); Laura Wolff ($58,612); Winthrop R. Munyon, President; Richardson Pratt Jr., Treasurer; Miner D. Crary, Secretary; Marion E. Mulhall, Assistant Treasurer.
Mission or Interest: Grant-making foundation focusing on civil liberties, abortion rights, and the arts.
Accomplishments: In the fiscal year ending October 1994 the Foundation awarded $3,504,780 in grants. The recipients of the largest grants included: $130,000 for the ACLU, $115,000 for the Center for Reproductive Law and Policy, $100,000 for the Planned Parenthood Federation of America, $80,000 for the National Abortion and Reproductive Rights League, $75,000 for the New York Civil Liberties Foundation, and $60,000 each for Catholics for a Free Choice, Ms. Foundation for Women, National Abortion Federation, National Women's Law Center, and the Women's Legal Defense Fund.
Net Revenue: FY ending 10/94 $6,952,909 **Net Expenses:** $4,532,036 **Net Assets:** $74,179,710
Tax Status: 501(c)(3)
Board of Directors or Trustees: Philip Svigals, John Romans.
Other Information: The Foundation received $4,298,525, or 62% of revenue, from capital gains on the sale of assets. $2,654,384, or 38%, from dividends and interest from securities. The Foundation held $65,091,117, or 88% of assets, in corporate stock.

Robert Wood Johnson Foundation

U.S. Route 1 and College Road, Box 2316
Princeton, NJ 08543-2316   **Phone:** (609) 452-8701
USA   **Fax:**   (609) 452-1865

Contact Person: Edward H. Robbins, Proposal Manager.
Officers or Principals: Steven Alfred Schroeder, M.D., President; Sidney Frederick Wentz, Chairman; Joshua Warren Wood, III, Secretary; Richard Clyde Reynolds, M.D., Andrew Richard Green, Executive Vice Presidents.
Mission or Interest: Grant-making foundation that focuses on health care and health-care reform.
Accomplishments: According to the Capital Research Center, there existed a special relationship between the Robert Wood Johnson Foundation and the Clinton Health Care Task Force headed by Hillary Rodham Clinton. In the last decade the Foundation has funded numerous health care reform projects in various states. Projects were funded that emphasized health data collection, the graduation of more primary care physicians, use of managed care, community ratings, and price controls on insurance rates and physicians fees.
 While governor of Arkansas, Bill Clinton presided over Arkansas Project Access, a reform proposal funded by the Foundation. Former Surgeon General, and then-Arkansas Director of Health, Dr. Jocelyn Elders worked on this project, as did White House Domestic Policy Advisor, Carol Rasco, who was named as a co-defendant in the lawsuit <u>AAPS v. Hillary Rodham Clinton</u> that forced the White House to open the Health Care Task Force documents to the public. Others associated with the President's health care reform efforts were also affiliated in some way with the Robert Woods Johnson Foundation. Foundation president Dr. Steven Schroeder was a leader of the Clintons' Health Policy Transitional Team, and was key in identifying private sector personnel who served on the Health Care Task Force. Dr. Henry Foster, Clinton's failed nominee for Surgeon General, is a Foundation consultant and former senior advisor. Judt Feder, Assistant Secretary for Planning and Evaluation at Health and Human Services, was a Foundation program director, consultant, and grantee. Philip Lee, Assistant Secretary of Health was a Foundation advisor, grantee, and consultant. Bruce Vladeck, Administrator of the Health Care Financing Administration (the agency responsible for granting states Medicaid waivers for reform efforts), was a former Foundation official. In 1994 the Foundation awarded $157,421,745 in grants. Most grants went to hospitals and universities for health care-related research. Grant recipients included: $2,800,000 for the Rock the Vote Education Fund, $305,396 for Concerned Parents for Head Start, $292,000 for the Alan Guttmacher Institute, $260,650 for the Committee for a Responsible Federal Budget, $175,000 for the National Black Women's Health Project, and $156,193 for the Economic and Social Research Institute.
Net Assets: 1994 $3,658,591,856
Tax Status: 501(c)(3) **Annual Report:** Yes.
Board of Directors or Trustees: Dr. Edward Andrews, Jr., James Edward Burke, Robert Campbell, David Clare, Leighton Eggertsen Cluff, M.D., Rheba DeTornyay, Lawrence Foster, Peter Goodwin, Linda Griego, John Heldrich, John Horan, Frank Karel, III, Thomas Kean, Jack Owen, Franklin Delano Raines, Norman Rosenberg, M.D., John Hyslop Steele, ScD.
Other Information: The Foundation was created in 1936 by Robert Wood Johnson, founder of Johnson & Johnson, the world's largest health and medical products conglomerate. Johnson died in 1968, leaving the Foundation approximately $1 billion in Johnson & Johnson stock. The Foundation is not affiliated with Johnson & Johnson. In 1994 the Foundation received $241,544 from the Henry J. Kaiser Family Foundation.

Rockefeller Brothers Fund

1290 Avenue of the Americas, Suite 3450
New York, NY 10104   **Phone:** (212) 373-4200
USA   **Fax:**   (212) 315-0996

Contact Person: Benjamin R. Shute, Jr., Secretary/Treasurer.
Officers or Principals: Colin Goetze Campbell, President; Russell Alexander Phillips, Jr., Executive Vice President; Abby Milton Rockefeller O'Neill, Chairman; Steven Clark Rockefeller, Vice Chairman; Benjamin R. Shute, Jr., Secretary/Treasurer.
Mission or Interest: "The fund seeks to achieve its major objective of improving the well-being of all people through support of efforts in the United States and abroad that contribute ideas, develop leaders, and encourage institutions in the transition to global interdependence and that counter world trends of resource depletion, militarization, protectionism, and isolation which now threaten to move humankind everywhere further away from cooperation, trade and economic growth, arms restraint, and conservation." Grants are made in five general areas: 1) "One World" efforts which include environmental and peace organizations, 2) promotion of the nonprofit sector, 3) Education, 4) New York City projects, and 5) Special concerns.
Accomplishments: In 1993 the Fund awarded $11,843,240 in grants. About 40% of the funding went to environmental organizations. Some of the top recipients included: $300,000 for the Asian Cultural Council, $225,000 for the Southern Environmental Law Center, $200,000 for the Environmental Defense Fund, $150,000 for the Centre for Environmental Studies Foundation, $150,000 for the Environmental Management and Law Association, $130,000 for the Nuclear Control Institute, $120,000 for Friends of the Earth (France), $110,000 for the Natural Resources Defense Council, $100,000 for the Center for Strategic and International Studies, $75,000 for the Conservation Law Foundation, $75,000 for the Foundation for International Environmental Law, $60,000 for the New York AIDS Coalition, and others.
Net Assets: 1993 $374,329,834
Tax Status: 501(c)(3)
Board of Directors or Trustees: Catharine Broderick, David Callard, Jonathan Fanton, Neva Goodwin (Executive Director, Tufts Univ., Center for the Study of Global Development Change), Kenneth Lipper, William Henry Luers (Inst. For East-West Studies), Jessica Tuchman Mathews (World Resources Institute), Richard Dean Parsons (Trustee, Howard Univ.), Joseph Pierson, David Rockefeller, Richard Gilder Rockefeller, Stephen Frederick Starr (Council on Foreign Relations).
Other Information: The Brothers Fund was established by the five grandsons of John Davison Rockefeller (1839-1937), founder of the Standard Oil Trust and the first billionaire in history. The five grandsons were Nelson Rockefeller, John Rockefeller, Laurence Rockefeller, Winthrop Rockefeller, and David Rockefeller. The fund is affiliated with the Asian Cultural Council in New York.

Rockefeller Family Fund

1290 Avenue of the Americas, Suite 3450
New York, NY 10104   **Phone:**   (212) 373-4252
USA   **Fax:**   (212) 315-0996

Contact Person: Donald K. Ross, Director.   **Officers or Principals:** Richard Gilder Rockefeller, President; Wendy Gordon Rockefeller, Barbara Rockefeller, Peter M. O'Neill, Dana Chasin, Clare Pierson Buden, Anne Bartley, Vice Presidents; Bevis Longstreth, Chairman; Leah A. D'Angelo, Treasurer; Donald K. Ross, Secretary.
Mission or Interest: Philanthropy that awards grants in five areas; "citizen education and participation, increasing voter participation and working for campaign finance reform; economic justice for women, enhancing the economic status of women by providing them with equitable employment opportunities and improving their work lives; the environment, emphasizing the reduction of military pollution, the conservation of natural resources and the protection of health as affected by the environment; institutional responsiveness, supporting projects to influence public opinion and private institutions on issues of social concern; and self-sufficiency for groups working within the fund's program areas."
Accomplishments: In 1994 the Fund awarded $1,916,000 in grants. The recipients of the largest grants included: $75,000 for the Campaign for an Environmental Economy, $50,000 each for the Center for Community Change and the Western Ancient Forests Campaign, $45,000 for the Wilderness Society, $35,000 each for the National Center for Fair and Open Testing, the Environmental Action Foundation, Environmental Support Center, Mineral Policy Center, and the Nuclear Information and Resource Center, $30,000 each for the Center for Responsive Politics, Equal Rights Advocates, National Committee on Pay Equity, Pro Choice Center, Environmental Strategies, Government Accountability Project, Military Toxics Campaign Fund, Public Employees for Environmental Responsibility, Boston Women's Health Book Collective, Federation of American Scientists Fund, and the Center for Media Education.
Net Assets: 1994 $44,000,000   **Tax Status:** 501(c)(3)
Board of Directors or Trustees: Hope Aldrich (editor, *Santa Fe Reporter*), Nancy Anderson, Laura Spelman Rockefeller Chasin (delegate, International Physicians for the Prevention of Nuclear War), Sandra Ferry, Jon Lewis Hagler (African-American Inst.), David Kaiser, Prof. Bruce Mazlish (MIT), Alida Messinger, Charles Mott, Hilda Ochoa, Mary Louise Pierson, David Rockefeller (Hon. Chair, Center for Inter-American Relations, Dir., Council on Foreign Relations), Diana Newell-Rowan Rockefeller, Laurance Spelman Rockefeller, Lisenne Rockefeller, Steven Clark Rockefeller, Loren Ross, Abby Rockefeller Simpson, James Sligar, Jeremy Waletzky, Lucy Aldrich Rockefeller Waletzky.
Other Information: Established in 1967 by the Rockefeller family.

Rockefeller Foundation

420 5th Ave.
New York, NY 10018   **Phone:**   (212) 869-8500
USA   **Fax:**   (212) 764-3468

Contact Person: Lynda Mullen, Secretary.
Officers or Principals: Peter Carl Goldmark, Jr., President; John Robert Evans, Chairman; Rosalie J. Wolfe, Treasurer; Alberta Bean Arthurs, Director, Arts and Humanities; Al Binger, Director, Global Environment; Sally Ferris, Director, Administration; Robert W. Herdt, Director, Agricultural Sciences; Robert Swan Lawrence, Director, Health Services; Julia I. Lopez, Director, Equal Opportunity; Steven W. Sinding, Director, Population Sciences; Angela Glover Blackwell, Danielle Paris, Hugh B. Price, Vice Presidents.

Mission or Interest: "To promote the well-being of mankind throughout the world." Funds the arts and humanities, civic and public affairs (including civil rights, economic development, economic policy, gay and lesbian issues, law and justice, women's affairs, and more), education, the environment, health (includes AIDS/HIV research, public health issues, medical research, and more), international affairs, scientific research, and social services.

Accomplishments: In 1995 recipients included; $1,762,360 for the Population Council, $1,550,000 for the World Health Organization's vaccine program, $1,283,250 for the United Nations Population Fund, $1,000,000 for the Children's Defense Fund, $800,000 for the Puerto Rican Legal Defense and Education Fund, $631,250 for the National Council of La Raza, $500,000 for Human Rights Watch, $450,000 for the Center on Budget and Policy Priorities, $343,000 for Population Action International, $241,700 for the Brookings Institution, $225,000 for the Midwest Center for Labor Research, $185,000 for the Carter Center, $151,000 for the International Center for Research on Women, $150,030 for the International Planned Parenthood Federation - London, $127,500 for the Alan Guttmacher Institute, $125,000 for the Center for Community Change, $113,200 for the Youth Law Center, $68,640 for the Federation of American Scientists Fund, $65,000 for the Earth Times Foundation, $61,860 for the China Population Information and Research Center, $60,000 each for the Foundation for Independent Video and Film, and the NAACP Legal Defense Fund, $52,797 for the Economic Policy Institute, $50,000 each for the Women U.S.A. Fund, People for the American Way, Arms Control Association, and Esperanza Peace and Justice Center, $49,510 for the National Council of Churches, $45,000 for the Foundation for the Study of Independent Social Ideas, $41,200 for the Highlander Research and Education Center, $30,000 for the Council on Foreign Relations, $27,500 for the Communications Consortium Media Center, $25,880 for the World Resources Institute, $25,000 for the Union of Concerned Scientists, $18,100 for the International Physicians for the Prevention of Nuclear War, $15,000 for the African-American Institute, $8,000 for the Feminist Press, $7,000 for the Centre for Development and Population Activities, and $3,190 for Advocates for Youth,

Net Expenses: 1995 est. $190,000,000 **Net Assets:** $2,540,171,000
Tax Status: 501(c)(3)
Board of Directors or Trustees: Alan Alda (actor), Johnnetta Cole (Pres., Spelman College), Robert Coles, David de Ferranti, Daniel Garcia, Ronald Goldsberry (Ford Motor Co.), Prof. Stephen Jay Gould (Harvard Univ.), Linda Hill, Karen Nicholson Horn, Alice Stone Ilchman, Richard Hampton Jenrette (Duke Endowment), Wyatt Thomas Johnson, Jr. (Dir., Trilateral Commission), Pasquale Pesce, Kenneth Prewitt (Dir., Center for the Advanced Study of Behavioral Sciences), Alvaro Umana.
Other Information: The Foundation was established in 1913 by John Davison Rockefeller (1839-1937), the founder of the Standard Oil Trust. The foundation is now independent of the Rockefeller family.

Rocky Mountain Institute (RMI)

1739 Snowmass Creek Rd.
Snowmass, CO 81654-9199   **Phone:**   (303) 927-3851
USA   **Fax:**   (303) 927-4178

Contact Person: Amory Lovins, Vice President.   **Officers or Principals:** Hunter Lovins, President ($45,201); Amory Lovins, Vice President/Treasurer ($45,001); Michael Stranahan, Chair.
Mission or Interest: Promotes energy conservation and the use of renewable energy sources. Advocates Amory Lovins' concept of a "soft energy path" to promote peace, the environment, and a sustainable culture. "We found that by combining advanced technology, creative use of market forces, aikido politics, and Jeffersonian community organizing, we can solve many problems at once without making new ones, and we can usually protect the environment not at a cost but at a profit."
Accomplishments: The Institute has worked with numerous public utilities to reduce energy use and promote conservation. Researched and tested elements of a "hyper car," an automobile that is ultra-light and highly fuel efficient. The hyper car would use a hybrid drive system; that is, it would use fuel to run a generator, which would in turn power the electric motors that would drive the wheels. Other projects include windows that would let in light, but not heat, and an ultraviolet light system for disinfecting water in the third world. "We've already cut the energy bill in the United States by about $160 billion a year."
Net Revenue: 1994 $1,615,662 ($36,750, or 2%, from government grants) **Net Expenses:** $1,858,138 85%/6%/9%
Net Assets: $313,903 **Citations:** 54:137
Tax Status: 501(c)(3) **Employees:** 40
Board of Directors or Trustees: Myron Curzan, John Denver (singer), Michael Edesess, John Fox, Dana Jackson (Land Stewardship Project), James Mills, Carol Noyes, Peter Schwartz (Global Business Network), Bardyl Tirana, Joanna Underwood (INFORM). Special Advisors were; Thomas Barron, David Brower (Earth Island Institute), and the Very Rev. James Parks Morton (Cathedral of St. John the Divine).
Periodicals: Newsletter.
Other Information: Amory Lovins' best known book is Soft Energy Path: Toward a Durable Peace. Lovins was encouraged to abandon his studies as a physicist at Oxford by David Brower, founder of the Earth Island Institute, League of Conservation Voters, and Friends of the Earth. Brower says of Lovins, "Amory set a standard by inventing the soft energy path, which challenged everything. He said that America had too much energy, that the hydro-nuclear-coal-electric grid was silly, often unnecessary, heavily subsidized by taxpayers, dangerous, and uneconomical, that the peaceful atom was a myth masking a bloated war machine. This shook some of us, but Amory had the figures to back himself up." Amory Lovins founded the Rocky Mountain Institute with his wife, Hunter, in 1982. Today, Lovins says "I'm not nearly so concerned about the depletion of nonrenewable resources such as oil or copper as about the depletion of things that ought to be renewable but are being mined, such as topsoil, biodiversity, social tolerance, traditional culture, civic virtue, and morality." Owns 100% of the for-profit publishing and consulting company, Rocky Mountain Institute Research Associates. In 1994 the Research Associates had total income of $1,977,869 and assets of $2,615,564. In 1994 the Institute received $1,132,244, or 70% of revenue, from gifts and grants awarded by foundations, businesses, and individuals. (These grants included $150,000 from the William and Flora Hewlett Foundation, $80,000 from the Joyce Mertz-

Gilmore Foundation, $25,000 from the Compton Foundation, $15,000 from the New-Land Foundation.) $161,126, or 10%, from interest on loans made by the Institute to its for-profit affiliate, Rocky Mountain Institute Research Associates. These unsecured loans were made at an interest rate of 8%; and at the end of the year were valued at $2,075,000. $114,201, or 7%, from consulting fees. $84,629, or 5%, from royalties. $40,940, or 3%, from publication sales. $21,388, or 1%, from the sale of assets. $17,628, or 1%, from interest on savings and temporary cash investments. The remaining revenue came from dividends and interest from securities, and other miscellaneous sources. Among the Institute's assets was staff housing, originally valued at $190,000. The Institute had received loans from the John D. and Catherine T. MacArthur Foundation in 1992 and 1993. The loans were $1,000,000 and $500,000 respectively, with an annual interest rate of 5%. In 1994 the Institute received an interest-free loan from the Joyce Mertz-Gilmore Foundation of $500,000.

Rocky Mountain Peace Center

1523 6th St.
Boulder, CO 80302   **Phone:**   (303) 444-6523
USA

Mission or Interest: Peace activism with a focus on Latin America. Anti-nuclear weapons.
Other Information: In 1994 the Center received $8,080 from the Chinook Fund, and $500 from the Vanguard Public Foundation.

Rosenberg Foundation

47 Kearny St., Suite 804
San Francisco, CA 94108-5528   **Phone:**   (415) 421-6105
USA

Contact Person: Kirke Wilson, Executive Director.   **Officers or Principals:** Kirke Wilson, Executive Director ($122,226); Benton W. Dial, President ($0); Robert E. Friedman, Vice President ($0); S. Donley Ritchey, Treasurer.
Mission or Interest: Philanthropic foundation that focuses on California. Grants are awarded to organizations that support the well-being of children, specifically "children that are minority, low-income, or immigrant." Two categories of organizations have priority: Groups focusing on the changing population of California who "promote the full social, economic, and cultural integration of immigrants, as well as minorities, into a pluralistic society," and groups that help rural and urban children in poverty. A third priority was added in 1993 for groups favoring child support reform.
Accomplishments: In 1994 the Foundation awarded $1,705,685 in grants. The recipients of the largest grants were: $150,000 for Children Now, $100,000 for the National Women's Law Center, $95,000 for the Center for Law and Social Policy, $85,000 for the Harriett Buhai Center for Family Law, $75,000 each for the Accountable Reinvestment Center, the ACLU Foundation of Northern California, and the Public Media Center, and $65,000 for Multicultural Education, Training and Advocacy. The Foundation also conducted educational efforts regarding California's Proposition 187, which the Foundation thought would hurt undocumented immigrant children. This Proposition passed in 1994 and sought to end social services for illegal immigrants.
Net Revenue: 1994 $225,995   **Net Expenses:** $2,269,998   **Net Assets:** $35,356,504
Tax Status: 501(c)(3)
Board of Directors or Trustees: Phyllis Cook (Jewish Community Federation), Judge Thelton Henderson (U.S. District Court, Northern Calif.), Bill Ong Hing (Stanford Univ., School of Law), Herma Hill Kay, Leslie Luttgens.
Other Information: The Foundation received $1,659,195 in revenue from capital gains on the sale of securities, and $1,434,923 from interest and dividends from securities. These two sources were 99% of gross revenues, however a loss of $2,895,778, mostly from a "change in unrealized appreciation" on assets, brought net revenues down to $225,995. $22,976,403, or 65% of assets, was held in corporate stock.

Rural Southern Voice for Peace (RSVP)

1898 Hannah Branch Rd.
Burnsville, NC 28714   **Phone:**   (704) 675-5933   **E-Mail:** rsvp@igc.apc.org
USA   **Fax:**   (704) 675-9335

Contact Person: Jennifer Morgan, Office Manager.   **Officers or Principals:** David Grant, Director ($14,785); Edwin King, Chairman ($0); Michael Appleby, Vice Chairman ($0); Ward McAllister, Treasurer; Claire Twose, Secretary.
Mission or Interest: "Networking and training in organizational development, planning, community outreach and non-violence." Developed and uses the "Listening Project" to teach conflict resolution.
Accomplishments: In 1994 RSVP spent $75,940 on its programs. $43,858 was spent on training and development serving approximately 995 individuals in 34 organizations. $32,083 was spent producing the quarterly *Voices*.
Net Revenue: 1994 $102,407   **Net Expenses:** $99,207 77%/9%/14%   **Net Assets:** $75,004
Tax Status: 501(c)(3) **Annual Report:** No. **Employees:** 3
Board of Directors or Trustees: Taylor Barnhill, Leigh Dudasik, Jeanette Lewis, Glenda McDowell, Jana McGrane, Virginia Sexton, Lorrie Streifel, Bill Thomsen, William Whiteside.
Periodicals: *Voices* (quarterly journal).
Internships: No.
Other Information: RSVP received $91,069, or 89% of revenue, from gifts and grants awarded by foundations, businesses, and individuals. (These grants included $1,250 from the Vanguard Public Foundation, $200 from the Haymarket People's Fund.) $7,722, or 8%, from honoraria and fees. $1,244, or 1%, from travel reimbursements. The remaining revenue came from interest and other miscellaneous sources.

Rush Watch Weekly
P.O. Box 1176
Langhorne, PA 19047   **Phone:** (610) 861-5540
USA

Mission or Interest: Weekly newsletter dedicated to countering the assertions and agenda of conservative radio host Rush Limbaugh.
Periodicals: *Rush Watch Weekly* (weekly newsletter).

Ruth Mott Fund
1726 Genesee Towers
Flint, MI 48502   **Phone:** (810) 232-3180
USA   **Fax:**   (810) 232-3272

Contact Person: Deborah Tuck, Executive Director.
Officers or Principals: Deborah Tuck, Executive Director ($77,514); Robert Stix, Program Director ($30,000); Maryanne Mott, President ($0); Joseph R. Robinson, Chair; Dudley Cocke, Vice Chair; Virginia M. Sullivan, Secretary/Treasurer.
Mission or Interest: Foundation that awards grants in the following areas; the arts, the environment, health issues, and peace and security.
Accomplishments: In the fiscal year ending November 1994, the Fund awarded $1,660,810 in grants. The recipients of the top grants included; $50,000 each for the Inlands Empire Public Lands Council, the Mineral Policy Center, Montana Wilderness Association, and American Friends Service Committee, $30,000 each for the Center to Prevent Handgun Violence and the Food Research and Action Center, and $25,000 each for the Alaska Conservation Foundation, Clean Water Fund, Native Americans for a Clean Environment, Association for Children for Enforcement of Support, Children's Defense Fund, Farmworkers Network for Environmental and Economic Justice, Center for Defense Information, Government Accountability Project, North American Congress on Latin America, Vietnam Veterans of America Foundation, Washington Office of Latin America, and the Wisconsin Project on Nuclear Arms Control.
Net Revenue: FY ending 11/94 $1,944,324 **Net Expenses:** $2,058,387 **Net Assets:** $1,980,416
Tax Status: 501(c)(3)
Board of Directors or Trustees: Ruth Mott (Founder), Brooks Bollman, III, Leslie Dunbar, Jean Fairfax, Donna Metcalf, Melissa Patterson, Herman Warsh.
Other Information: The Fund received $1,835,227, or 94% of revenue, from gifts and grants awarded by foundations, businesses, and individuals. $117,378, or 6%, from interest on savings and temporary cash investments. The Fund incurred a loss of $8,396 on the sale of assets. The Fund held $1,960,439, or 99% of its assets, in savings and temporary cash investments.

Sacred Earth Network
267 East St.
Petersham, MA 01366-9710   **Phone:** (508) 724-3443   **E-Mail:** sacredearth@igc.apc.org
USA   **Fax:**   (508) 724-3436

Contact Person: William Pfeiffer, Executive Director.   **Officers or Principals:** William Pfeiffer, Executive Director ($21,500); D. Chapman, Treasurer ($16,950); Ivan Ussach, Director ($9,000); Diane Depuydt, Secretary.
Mission or Interest: "To educate, train and assist small green groups in the former Soviet Union relative to environmental related activities and issues." Promotion of 'Deep Ecology.'
Accomplishments: In 1994 the Network spent $189,043 on its programs. Hosts the Deep Ecology Clearinghouse.
Net Revenue: 1994 $242,738 **Net Expenses:** $202,450 93%/0%/7% **Net Assets:** $59,479
Tax Status: 501(c)(3)
Board of Directors or Trustees: Kay Grindland, Francis Macy.
Periodicals: Newsletter.
Other Information: The Network received $242,738, or 98% of revenue, from direct and indirect public support in the form of gifts and grants from foundations, companies, affiliates and individuals. (These grants included $8,000 from the New-Land Foundation.) $4,860, or 2%, from program services. The remaining revenue came from interest on savings and temporary cash investments.

Safe Energy Communication Council (SECC)
1717 Massachusetts Ave., N.W., Suite 805
Washington, DC 20036   **Phone:** (202) 483-8491
USA

Contact Person: Scott Denman, Executive Director.
Officers or Principals: Scott Denman, Executive Director ($42,000); Andrew Schwartzman, President ($0).
Mission or Interest: Advocates "safe and economical energy alternatives to help alleviate the greenhouse effect." Opposed to nuclear energy. Works with other organizations to "respond to the campaigns of the nuclear energy industry," and to promote their own agendas in a media-wise way.
Accomplishments: In 1994 SECC spent $287,641 on its programs. The largest program, with expenditures of $72,263, was education and organization. $72,209 was spent on workshops and technical assistance for teaching media skills. $60,225 was spent on energy outreach that was "raising the awareness of the Potential for success of demand-side management (conservation and limitation) and renewable resources." $46,817 on press projects to "improve national and local press coverage of nuclear and alternative energy development issues." $36,127 on research. The Council awarded a $10,412 grant to the Media Access Project.

Net Revenue: 1994 $320,743 **Net Expenses:** $323,840 89%/8%/3% **Net Assets:** $21,252
Products or Services: Research, outreach, and media relations. Although the Council did not engage in lobbying in 1994, in 1993 it spent $547, $616 in 1992, and $3,125 in 1991.
Tax Status: 501(c)(3)
Board of Directors or Trustees: Tina Hobson, Chris Bedford, David Lapp, Roni Lieberman, Anna Aurilio, Dena Leibman, Herb Gunther, Gasby Greely, Michael Mariotte.
Other Information: The Council received $305,841, or 95% of revenue, from direct and indirect public support in the form of gifts and grants awarded by foundations, businesses, affiliates, and individuals. (These grants included $75,000 from the Joyce Mertz-Gilmore Foundation, $35,000 from the Nathan Cummings Foundation, $30,000 from the Florence and John Schumann Foundation, $10,000 from the Joyce Foundation, $6,739 from the Environmental Federation of America.) $7,320, or 2%, from workshop fees. $4,742, or 1%, from interest on savings and temporary cash investments. The remaining revenue came from the sale of publications and honoraria.

Salzberg Equal Justice Foundation

122 State St., Suite 608
Madison, WI 53703   **Phone:**   (608) 251-4616
USA

Contact Person: Harry E. Salzberg, Chairperson.
Officers or Principals: Heidi M. Salzberg, Vice President ($0); Harry E. Salzberg, Chairperson ($0).
Mission or Interest: Foundation that awards grants for human rights organizations with a focus on Latin America.
Accomplishments: In 1994 the Foundation awarded $14,550 in grants. The recipients were $12,000 for the Center for Human Rights and Constitutional Law, $2,000 for the Arcato Sister City Project, $350 for the Columbia Support Network, and $200 for the Wisconsin Coordinating Council on Nicaragua.
Net Revenue: 1994 $34,914 **Net Expenses:** $36,942 **Net Assets:** $8,673
Tax Status: 501(c)(3)
Board of Directors or Trustees: Daniel Kesselbrenner, Dana Cooley, Peter Schey, David Schwab.
Other Information: The Foundation received $34,500, or 99% of revenue, from gifts or grants awarded by foundations, businesses, and individuals. $414, or 1%, from expense reimbursements.

San Francisco Organizing Project

25 Taylor St., Suite 705
San Francisco, CA 94102   **Phone:**   (415) 474-7833
USA

Contact Person: Don A. Stahlhut, Executive Director.   **Officers or Principals:** Don A. Stahlhut, Executive Director ($48,139); Ernest W. Walker, Organizer ($38,283); Tom Barton, Chairperson ($0); Mary Liz de Jong, Secretary/Treasurer.
Mission or Interest: Community organizing, public housing tenant organizing, and nonprofit organization training. Areas include "housing, child care, health care, unemployment, transportation, community safety, neighborhood stability and immigration rights."
Accomplishments: In the fiscal year ending June 1994, the Project spent $145,251 on its programs.
Net Revenue: FY ending 6/94 $229,761 **Net Expenses:** $188,500 77%/17%/6% **Net Assets:** $41,597
Tax Status: 501(c)(3)
Board of Directors or Trustees: Louise Dutra, Rafael Espinoza (Hotel Employees & Restaurant Employees Union), Edith Wellin, Martha Quinn.
Other Information: The Project received $177,784, or 77% of revenue, from gifts and grants awarded by foundations, businesses, and individuals. (These grants included $30,000 from the Campaign for Human Development, $12,000 from the MacKay Foundation.) $51,394, or 22%, from government grants. The remaining revenue came from interest on savings and temporary cash investments.

San Francisco Women's Centers

3543 18th St.
San Francisco, CA 94110
USA

Accomplishments: Prison Integrated Health Project, Girls After School Academy, Venceremos Brigade project.
Other Information: In 1994 the Centers received $17,750 from the Vanguard Public Foundation, and $5,000 from the Ms. Foundation for Women.

Save the Whales

P.O. Box 2397
Venice, CA 90291   **Phone:**   (408) 899-9957
USA

Contact Person: Maris Sidenstecker, President.
Officers or Principals: Maris Sidenstecker, President ($0); Maris Sidenstecker, II, Treasurer/Secretary ($0).

Mission or Interest: "To educate children and adults about marine mammals, their environment, and their preservation."
Accomplishments: "Save the Whales' attorneys and scientific experts stopped the U.S. Navy from detonating 268 ship shock' detonations (underwater explosions set off to test hull integrity of new naval cruisers) for five years." Save the Whales estimates that these ship shocks' would have killed or injured 10,000 marine mammals. Save the Whales supports a rescue boat that rescues entangled marine mammals from fishing nets off the coast of Southern California. In 1994 the organization spent $13,202 to publish and distribute its newsletter. $32,593 was spent on the touring "Whale on Wheels" education program, providing hands-on educational materials. "Whales on Wheels has educated over 90,000 students since 1991.
Net Revenue: 1994 $66,734 **Net Expenses:** $99,981 **Net Assets:** $39,015
Tax Status: 501(c)(3) **Employees:** 2
Board of Directors or Trustees: Michele Levin, Mary Cunningham, Hon. Richard Kossow (retired judge).
Periodicals: *Save the Whales* (quarterly newsletter).
Other Information: Save the Whales was founded by Maris Sidenstecker in 1977 when she was fourteen years old. The organization received $50,121, or 75% of revenue, from grants awarded by foundations, companies and individuals. (These grants included $150 from People for the Ethical Treatment of Animals.) $10,555, or 16%, from membership dues. $3,580 net, or 5%, from the sale of inventory. The remaining revenue came from program service fees and investment income.

Scenic America

21 DuPont Circle, N.W.
Washington, DC 20036   **Phone:** (202) 833-4300
USA   **Fax:**   (202) 833-4304

Contact Person: Sally Oldham, President.   **Officers or Principals:** Sally Oldham, President ($90,072).
Mission or Interest: Environmental and conservation organization devoted to protecting and restoring America's scenic landscapes. Activities include cleaning up "visual pollution" such as billboards, and working with local activists and citizens to control growth.
Accomplishments: In the fiscal year ending March 1995, Scenic America spent $417,068 on its programs. These programs included working with state and local activists, developing and advocating public policy, membership development and services, and technical assistance to planners and elected officials "in relation to all aspects of sign and billboard control and various other forms of aesthetic regulation." America's Scenic Byways Project.
Net Revenue: FY ending 3/95 $480,310 **Net Expenses:** $503,281 83%/8%/9% **Net Assets:** $120,515
Citations: 81:117
Products or Services: Various handbooks, technical assistance, and lobbying. Scenic America spent $2,650 on the direct lobbying of public officials.
Tax Status: 501(c)(3)
Board of Directors or Trustees: Madeline Appel, James Benkard, Ann Franks Boren, Mation Fuller Brown, Charles Clusen (American Conservation Assoc.), Christopher Duerksen, Louise Dunlap, Ronald Lee Fleming (Townscape Inst.), Ann Harter, David Hartig, Roberta Henderson, Grant Jones, William Jonson, Ellen Kelly, Karl Kruse, Spencer Lee, Winsome Dunn McIntosh, Edward McMahon (Conservation Fund), Frederick Middleton, III (Southern Environmental Law Center), Robert Peck (Federal Communications Commission), Barbara Sandford, Carroll Shaddock, Kathryn Whitmire (Jr. Achievement).
Periodicals: *Sign Control News* (bimonthly newsletter).
Other Information: Scenic America received $363,310, or 76% of revenue, from gifts and grants awarded by foundations, businesses, and individuals. (These grants included $45,000 from the American Conservation Association, $6,288 from the Environmental Federation of America, $314 from the Environmental Federation of California.) $69,021, or 14%, from contract revenues. $19,262, or 4%, from membership dues. $14,921, or 3%, from the sale of publications. $5,798, or 1%, from interest on savings and temporary cash investments. The remaining revenue came from reimbursed expenses, payments from affiliates, and other miscellaneous sources.

Sea Shepherd Conservation Society (SSCS)

3107A Washington Blvd.
Marina del Rey, CA 90292   **Phone:** (310) 301-7325   **E-Mail:** seashpherd@aol.com
USA   **Fax:**   (310) 574-3161

Contact Person: Lisa Distefano.
Officers or Principals: Paul Watson, President ($0); Rose Waldron, Secretary ($0); Carrol Vogel, Treasurer ($0).
Mission or Interest: "The enforcement of international regulations protecting marine wildlife and the investigation and documentation of violations." Committed to ending all whaling. The Society's methods are direct, often violent, and effective.
Accomplishments: "Stopped commercial seal hunt in Canada; sank nine illegal whaling boats; ended pirate whaling operations in the Atlantic; rammed dolphin and shark-killer boats, driftnetters, and confiscated nets." Most rammings and sinkings resulted in no injuries. "In 1986 Sea Shepherd agents enforced the IWC moratorium on commercial whaling by sinking half the Icelandic whaling fleet and destroying their only whale processing factory." Chased Costa Rican poachers away using paint ball guns and a civil war-era cannon firing blanks. Painted baby seals with a harmless dye to make their pelts commercially worthless. Promoted alternatives to sealing; such as using molted hairs from seal pups in sweaters and insulation. "The seals seem to actually enjoy the brushing which relieved the itching of the molting stage." In the fiscal year ending April 1994, the Society spent $449,452 on its programs.
Net Revenue: FY ending 4/94 $784,813 **Net Expenses:** $529,678 85%/11%/5% **Net Assets:** $674,068

Products or Services: Educational materials and campaigns, newsletter, t-shirts, hats, and other paraphernalia.
Tax Status: 501(c)(3) **Employees:** 3
Periodicals: *Sea Shepherd Log* (newsletter).   **Internships:** Yes.
Other Information: The Society was founded in 1979 by Captain Paul Watson, one of the original founders of Greenpeace. Watson now refers to Greenpeace as "run by lawyers, accountants and bureaucrats...Greenpeace is just another trans-national corporation that I have to deal with...we, the voluntary visionaries, were purged by people who were paid employees (of Greenpeace)." Sea Shepherd ships are crewed by volunteers, and their work is documented on film and video. The activities of Sea Shepherds, including the ramming and sinking of illegal fishing and whaling vessels, are, in the opinion of the Society, sanctioned under the United Nations World Charter for Nature. They say that this has withstood the test of court scrutiny in Canada. The Society received $941,274, or 99.7% of total revenue, from gifts and grants awarded by foundations and individuals. (These grants included $1,000 from People for the Ethical Treatment of Animals, and $961 from the Tides Foundation.) The remaining revenue came from the sale of merchandise. These revenues were offset by a loss of $158,371 on the sale of assets; namely the "UN Resolution" ship and the "C. Amory" ship. $344,954, or 51% of the Society's assets were held in ships and equipment. $327,378, or 49%, was held in cash. After the sale of the two ships, the Society's asset schedule shows they still own two ships, the "Edward Abbey" and the "Whales 4 Ever." The Edward Abbey was named after the novelist, whose book The Monkey Wrench Gang described the sabotaging of equipment used by industries that the environmentalists opposed. Abbey died in 1989.

Service Employees International Union (SEIU)

1313 L St., N.W.
Washington, DC 20005   **Phone:**   (202) 898-3200
USA   **Fax:**   (202) 898-3304

Mission or Interest: Union representing workers in the service industries, such as janitorial and maintenance workers. Member of the AFL-CIO.
Accomplishments: Approximately 850,000 members. In 1995 Union President John J. Sweeney was elected President of the AFL-CIO. While at SEIU he built his reputation as an effective labor organizer and strategist.
Tax Status: 501(c)(5)
Periodicals: *Union* (monthly newsletter), *Update* (quarterly newsletter).
Other Information: Founded in 1921. In the year between July 1993 and June 1994, the Union received $628,000 from the U.S. Department of Health and Human Services' Superfund Worker Training Program.

Sex Information and Education Council of the United States (SIECUS)

130 W. 42nd St., Suite 2500
New York, NY 10036   **Phone:**   (212) 819-9770
USA   **Fax:**   (212) 819-9776

Contact Person: Debra Hafner, Executive Director.
Mission or Interest: Research, development, analysis, and promotion of comprehensive sexuality education. Opposes abstinence-only sex education programs.
Accomplishments: Over 4,000 members. Produces materials opposing the 'Religious Right.'
Tax Status: 501(c)(3)
Periodicals: *SIECUS Report* (journal).
Other Information: Founded in 1964. In 1994 SIECUS received $60,000 from the Robert Sterling Clark Foundation, $20,275 from the Henry J. Kaiser Family Foundation, $10,000 from the Compton Foundation.

Sierra Club

730 Polk St.
San Francisco, CA 94109   **Phone:**   (415) 776-2211
USA   **Fax:**   (415) 776-0350

Contact Person: Carl Pope, Executive Director.   **Officers or Principals:** Deborah Sorondo, Assistant Secretary ($112,735); J. Michael McCloskey, Chairman ($111,136); Carl Pope, Executive Director ($95,864); J. Robert Cox, President; Joni Bosh, Vice President; Richard Cellarius, Secretary; Denny Shaffer, Treasurer.
Mission or Interest: Environmental organization engaged in lobbying, research, legal activities, policy development, network building, and outdoor programs.
Accomplishments: In 1994 the Club spent $33,163,539 on it programs. The largest program, with expenditures of $10,741,679, was for studying and influencing public policy. $9,750,043 was spent supporting and funding the Club's 63 volunteer chapters and 400 member groups. $8,332,702 was spent producing books and publications. $4,339,115 was spent on outdoor activities. The Club awards grants to other environmental organizations. Recipients of the largest grants include: three grants totaling $17,800 for the National Audubon Society, six grants totaling $16,185 for the Wilderness Society, three grants totaling $16,000 for the Greater Yellowstone Coalition, and $10,000 for the Sierra Club Legal Defense Fund.
Net Revenue: 1994 $40,036,791 **Net Expenses:** $41,141,034 81%/10%/9% **Net Assets:** $12,150,748
Citations: 5,241:4
Products or Services: Catalogue, books, magazine, outdoor programs, grants.

Tax Status: 501(c)(4)

Periodicals: *Sierra* (monthly magazine).
Other Information: The Sierra Club is affiliated with the 501(c)(3) Sierra Club Foundation. The two affiliates together had combined net revenues of $48,309,221, net expenses of $49,079,241, and net assets of $23,952,500. The Club received $15,076,900, or 38% of revenue, from membership dues. $12,020,206, or 30%, from gifts and grants awarded by foundations, affiliates, businesses, and individuals. (These grants included $5,206,000 from the Sierra Club Foundation, $5,000 from the Global Environment Project Institute, $5,000 from Friends of the Earth.) $5,305,865, or 13%, from program service fees, including outings and lodgings. $2,583,024, or 6%, from advertising revenue. $2,215,407, or 6%, from royalties. $1,961,870 net, or 5%, from the sale of inventory. The remaining revenue came from publication sales, capital gains on the sale of securities, dividends and interest from securities, and interest on savings and temporary cash investments.

Sierra Club Foundation

220 Sansome St., Suite 1100
San Francisco, CA 94104   **Phone:**   (415) 291-1800
USA

Contact Person: Stephen W. Stevick, Executive Director.   **Officers or Principals:** Stephen W. Stevick, Executive Director ($99,000); Eugene Ho, Finance Director ($52,000); Mohammad Sheikh, Controller ($45,300); Patricia Dunbar, President; Robert B. Flint, Jr., Treasurer; Michael Loeb, Secretary; Cynthia Frank, Administration Manager.
Mission or Interest: Provides grants to environmental organizations. Supports "charitable, educational, scientific, literary, and endeavors that enhance the natural environment."
Accomplishments: In 1994 the Foundation awarded $6,166,851 in grants. The majority of the grants went to 501(c)(4) lobbying organizations. The largest of these grants, $5,206,000, went to the Foundation's 501(c)(4) lobbying affiliate, the Sierra Club.
Net Revenue: 1994 $8,272,430 ($6,000, or less than 1%, from government grants) **Net Expenses:** $7,938,207 78%/13%/9%
Net Assets: $11,801,752 **Citations:** 5,241:4
Products or Services: Grants and lobbying. The Foundation spent $5,778 on lobbying; $3,226 on grassroots lobbying and $2,552 on the direct lobbying of legislators. This was down 80% from 1992 (the Foundation did not lobby in 1993), and down 88% from $50,000 in 1991.
Tax Status: 501(c)(3)
Board of Directors or Trustees: Bert Fingerhut, Mary Jane Brock, Patricia Dunbar, Richard Cellarius, Marlene Fluharty, Allan Brown, Robert Flint, Jr., Alan Weeden, Janice McCoy Miller, Roy Miller, Peggy Wayburn, J. Fred Weintz, Jr., Harry Dalton, J. Robert Cox, Gary Torre.
Other Information: The Foundation is affiliated with the 501(c)(4) Sierra Club. The two affiliates together had combined net revenues of $48,309,221, net expenses of $49,079,241, and net assets of $23,952,500. The Foundation employed the Albuquerque, NM, firm of Rodey, Dickason, Sloan, Akin and Robb as legal counsel, the firm was paid $171,504. The Foundation received $8,001,744, or 93% of total revenue, from gifts and grants from foundations, businesses, affiliates, and individuals. (These grants included $200,000 from the Joyce Foundation, $148,760 from the Environmental Federation of America, $130,000 from the Nathan Cummings Foundation, $47,056 from the Environmental Federation of California, $24,600 from the Compton Foundation, $40,000 from the Bullitt Foundation, $20,000 from the Tides Foundation, $7,500 from the Beldon Fund, and $500 from the Haymarket People's Fund.) $518,000, or 6%, from dividends and interest from securities. $86,487, or 1%, from rental income. Total revenue was reduced by losses of $339,801 on securities and other investments.

Sierra Club Legal Defense Fund (SCLDF)

180 Montgomery St., Suite 1400
San Francisco, CA 94104   **Phone:**   (415) 627-6700
USA

Contact Person: Victor Sher, President.   **Officers or Principals:** Vawter Parker, Vice President ($137,134); Laurens Silver, Attorney ($114,157); Michael Sherwood, Attorney ($109,824); William Curtiss, Attorney ($105,072); Victor Sher, President ($104,936); Stephan Volker, Attorney ($100,672); Leslie Fox, Vice President; Frank Varenchik, Vice President; Hon. LaDoris H. Cordell, Chair; Cynthia Wayburn, Vice Chair; H. Donald Harris, Jr., Treasurer.
Mission or Interest: Litigation and educational activities to protect the environment.
Accomplishments: In the fiscal year ending July 1994, the Fund spent $7,891,960 on its programs. $6,936,023 was spent on its litigation. In addition, they claim program services donated by attorneys valued at $676,147 was not included in this figure. They received $2,819,949 in court-awarded attorney's fees. At least $2,480,175, or about 88%, of these awards were paid by governments at various levels, and ultimately by the taxpayers. $955,937 was spent on informational and educational materials. Law suits pending included: Intervention against the timber industry's attempts in federal district court to remove the tri-state marbled murrelets from the endangered species list. Represented several groups seeking to compel the U.S. Fish and Wildlife Service to publish overdue decisions regarding the placement of four species (the coastal cactus wren, Laguna Mountains skipper butterfly, San Diego fairy shrimp, and the Cuyamaca Lake downingia) on the endangered species list. Brought suit against the State of Louisiana for the failure of the Secretary of the Department of Natural Resources to comply with regulations in the issuing of permits for extensive canal dredging - the permits were issued without the required preparation of long-term management plans. Sixty-seven other suits were pending.

Net Revenue: FY ending 7/94 $11,126,486 **Net Expenses:** $10,180,188 78%/6%/16% **Net Assets:** $6,495,640
Citations: 343:54
Products or Services: Litigation, educational materials, lobbying. In the fiscal year ending July 1994, the Fund spent $114,156 on lobbying, $5,255 for grassroots lobbying and $108,901 for the direct lobbying of law makers. The Fund created the Sutherland Fellowship Fund whose purpose is to "enable minority and economically disadvantaged lawyers the means to engage in public interest litigation."
Tax Status: 501(c)(3) **Annual Report:** Yes.
Board of Directors or Trustees: Paul Brower, William Brinton, Donald Carmichael, Daniel Greenberg, Louise Gund, Barbara Haas, Alan Sieroty, Michael Traynor, Francis Wheat.
Other Information: The Sierra Club Legal Defense Fund is not affiliated with the Sierra Club or the Sierra Club Foundation, although those two often employ it for legal action. The Defense Fund, when it began, worked almost exclusively for the Sierra Club, but the organizations were never affiliated by incorporation. The Fund received $7,798,733, or 70% of revenue, from gifts and grants awarded by foundations, companies, affiliates and individuals. (These grants included $255,000 from the Bullitt Foundation for 1993-1994, $149,372 from the Environmental Federation of America, $50,000 from the American Conservation Association, $45,099 from the Environmental Federation of California, $30,000 from the New-Land Foundation, $20,000 from the Town Creek Foundation, $20,000 from the General Service Foundation, $15,000 from the New World Foundation, $10,000 from the Sierra Club, $10,000 from the C.S. Fund, and $1,300 from the Sierra Club Legal Defense Fund.) $2,819,949, or 25%, from court-awarded attorney's fees. $213,305, or 2%, from dividends and interest from securities. $195,090 net, or 2%, from the sale of assets other than inventory. The remaining revenue came from interest on savings and temporary cash investments, and the sale of books, t-shirts, etc. The Fund contracted Whitney Associates of Los Angeles for consultation on direct mail fundraising and compensated them $84,000. The firm of Douglas Gould and Co. of Mamaroneck, NY, was paid $49,200 for public relations.

Social Ecology Project

P.O. Box 111
Burlington, VT 05402   **E-Mail:** bookchin@igc.apc.org
USA

Contact Person: Murray Bookchin.   **Officers or Principals:** Janet Biehl.
Mission or Interest: Publishes *Green Perspectives* and distributes "social ecology" literature.
Periodicals: *Green Perspectives* (newsletter).

Social Investment Forum

1612 K St., N.W., Suite 600
Washington, DC 20006   **Phone:** (617) 451-3669
USA

Contact Person: Carla Mortensen, Board Member.   **Officers or Principals:** Carla Mortensen, Board Member ($30,416); Steve Schueth, Chair ($0); Alisa Gravitz, Vice Chair ($0); Elizabeth Glenshaw, Secretary; David Berge, Treasurer.
Mission or Interest: Professional organization of 'socially responsible' investors. Members include fund managers, institutional investors, analysts and individual investors.
Net Revenue: 1994 $134,483 **Net Expenses:** $177,913 **Net Assets:** (-$37,915)
Products or Services: Annual resource guide of members.
Tax Status: 501(c)(6)
Board of Directors or Trustees: Margaret Cheap, Patricia Farrar, George Gay, Peter Kinder, Patrick McVeigh, Greg Ramm, Raeann Skenadore, Howard Shapiro.
Periodicals: Newsletter.

Social Policy Corporation

25 W. 43rd St., Suite 620
New York, NY 10036   **Phone:** (212) 274-1139   **E-Mail:** social@igc.apc.org
USA   **Fax:** (212) 431-3251

Contact Person: David Dyssegaard Kallick, Editor.   **Officers or Principals:** Audrey Gartner, Secretary/Treasurer ($14,400); Alan Gartner, President ($0); Frank Riessmann, Vice President/Founder ($0).
Mission or Interest: Publishes *Social Policy* magazine "covering key progressive political and social movements as they develop...focusing on a progressive alternative to liberalism." Educational events on various social issues.
Accomplishments: Published articles by Jonathan Kozol, Barbara Ehrenreich, and many others. In 1994 the Corporation spent $97,394 on its programs. Hosted a special forum on the dangers of a balanced federal budget. Issued "The Balanced Budget Movement is a Threat to Our Economy" policy statement signed by founder Frank Reissman, Prof. Noam Chomsky (MIT), Jeff Faux (Economic Policy Institute), S.M. Miller (Poverty and Race Research Action Council), Chester Hartman (Poverty and Race Research Action Council), and others.
Net Revenue: 1994 $95,498 **Net Expenses:** $132,652 73%/27%/0% **Net Assets:** $34,593
Tax Status: 501(c)(3) **Annual Report:** No. **Employees:** 3
Periodicals: *Social Policy* (quarterly magazine).
Other Information: The Corporation received $55,904, or 59% of revenue, from magazine subscriptions. $32,450, or 34%, from gifts and grants awarded by foundations, businesses, and individuals. (These grants included $7,500 from the New World Foundation.) $3,965, or 4%, from reprints. $2,532, or 3%, from royalties. $647, or 1%, from interest on savings and temporary cash investments.

Social Workers' National Research and Education Fund

750 1st St., N.E., Suite 700
Washington, DC 20002   **Phone:**   (202) 336-8203
USA

Contact Person: Ann A. Abbott, President.   **Officers or Principals:** Ann A. Abbott, President ($0); Virginia E. Jacobson, First Vice President ($0); Jay J. Cayner, Second Vice President ($0); Terry Mizrahi, Secretary ($0); Eugene Hickey, Treasurer.
Mission or Interest: Research and education organization promoting and expanding the work of social workers.
Accomplishments: In the fiscal year ending June 1994, the Fund spent $838,837 on its programs. The largest program, with expenditures of $217,695, was the maintenance of a national library. $137,165 was spent on a curriculum model. $124,663 was spent addressing the issues of violence. $48,102 was spent on family preservation, and $29,892 on the Global Family Media Initiative. Other programs included work on the "diverse aging population", a peace curriculum guide, a special assembly on violence, a children's education program, and other research.
Net Revenue: FY ending 6/93 $1,176,276 ($477,890, or 41%, from government grants)
Net Expenses: $1,164,354 72%/0%/28% **Net Assets:** $454,120
Products or Services: Scholarships for social-work students "who have demonstrated a commitment to Native American or Hispanic populations; who work with public or voluntary nonprofit agencies, or with local grassroots groups; who demonstrate commitment to work with other disenfranchised or under-served groups in the United States." The Fund spent $26,279 on lobbying, $5,000 on grassroots lobbying and $21,279 on the direct lobbying of legislators.
Tax Status: 501(c)(3)
Board of Directors or Trustees: Prof. Mary Ann Bromley (Rhode Island College), Prof. Julio Morales (Univ. of CT), Prof. Ruth Brandwein (SUNY at Stony Brook), Prof. Gloria Bonilla-Santiago (Rutgers Univ.), Lydia Durbin (Dir., Placement Services, Family and Children Services of Delaware), Marjorie Hammock (Chief, Social Work Services, South Carolina Dept. of Corrections), Carolyne Brown (NAACP Jobs Program), Hilda Patricia Curran (Michigan Jobs Commission), Prof. Barbara Bacon (Loyola Univ. of Chicago), Bonnie Limbird (Children's Hospital, Univ. of Arkansas), Judy Walruff (Flinn Found.), Kenneth Lee (Social Work Services, Tripler Army Medical Center), Marsena Buck (Stanislaus County Dept. of Social Services, CA), Dean Frances Caple (School of Social Work, USC), Shirley Cox (UNLV), Prof. Ramon Salcido (USC), Alicia Smalley, Sharon Jones, Joanne Tenery.
Other Information: Affiliated with the 501(c)(6) National Association of Social Workers. The Fund received $618,513, or 53% of revenue, from gifts and grants awarded by foundations, affiliates, businesses, and individuals. $477,890, or 41%, from government grants. $31,269, or 3%, from interest on savings and temporary cash investments. The remaining revenue came from various "miscellaneous" sources.

Socialist Labor Party

111 W. Evelyn Ave., Suite 209
Sunnyvale, CA 94086   **Phone:**   (408) 245-2047   **E-Mail:** thepeople@igc.apc.org
USA   **Fax:**   (408) 245-2049

Contact Person: Robert Bills, National Secretary.
Officers or Principals: Donna Bills, Ken Boettcher, Genevieve Gunderson, Nathan Karp, Jim Parker.
Mission or Interest: The Socialist Labor Party was founded in 1891. Publishes the monthly newsletter, *The People*, which aims to be the "Truthful Recorder of Labor's Struggles! Unflinching Advocate of Labor's Rights! Intrepid Foes of Labor's Oppressors!" Promotes class awareness and the complete ownership of the means of production by workers.
Periodicals: *The People* (monthly newsletter).

Society for Animal Protective Legislation

P.O. Box 3719, Georgetown Station
Washington, DC 20007
USA

Contact Person: John Gleiber, Executive Secretary.
Officers or Principals: John Gleiber, Executive Secretary ($12,480); Madeleine Bemelmans, President ($0); John F. Kullberg, Vice President ($0); Christine Stevens, Secretary; Roger L. Stevens, Treasurer.
Mission or Interest: "Passage of legislation to protect animals."
Accomplishments: In 1994 the Society spent $76,836 on its lobbying.
Net Revenue: 1994 $70,429 **Net Expenses:** $98,618 **Net Assets:** $3,115
Tax Status: 501(c)(4)
Board of Directors or Trustees: Hope Ryden, William MacBlair, Jr.
Other Information: The Society received $59,103, or 84% of revenue, from gifts and grants awarded by foundations, businesses, and individuals. $8,465, or 12%, from capital gains on the sale of securities. $2,861, or 4%, from investment income.

Society for Ecological Restoration (SER)

1207 Seminole Highway, Suite B
Madison, WI 53711   **Phone:**   (608) 262-9547   **E-Mail:** ser@vms2.macc.wisc.edu
USA   **Fax:**   (608) 265-8557

Contact Person: Laura Lee Hoefs, Office Manager. **Officers or Principals:** Laura Lee Hoefs, Office Manager ($19,960); Robin Kurzer, Administrative Assistant ($18,609); Don Falk, Executive Director ($16,250); Andre Clewell, President; Nikita Lopoukhine, Vice President; John Rodman, Secretary; Dr. William Halvorson, Treasurer.
Mission or Interest: Promotes ecological restoration "as a means of sustaining the diversity of life on Earth and reestablishing an ecologically healthy relationship between nature and culture."
Accomplishments: 500 people attended their conference where environmental professionals exchanged information. Hosted regional conferences.
Net Revenue: 1994 $213,900 **Net Expenses:** $259,093 91%/9%/0% **Net Assets:** $34,444
Products or Services: Publications, conferences.
Tax Status: 501(c)(3) **Employees:** 4
Board of Directors or Trustees: Leslie Sauer (Andropogon Associates), George Gann-Matzen (Ecohorizons), Steve Packard (The Nature Conservancy), Deborah Keammerer (Keammerer Ecological Consultants), Deborah Hillyard, Dennis Martinez (American Indian Culture Center), Ariel Lugo (Institute of Tropical Forestry).
Periodicals: *Restoration Ecology* (quarterly journal), *Restoration and Management Notes* (semi-annual journal), and *SER News* (quarterly newsletter).
Other Information: The Society received $134,493, or 63% of revenue, from membership dues. $55,558, or 26%, from conference and workshop revenues. $11,660, or 5%, from gifts and grants awarded by foundations and individuals. The remaining revenue came from the net sales of publications, an Awards Program, interest on savings and temporary cash investments, and other miscellaneous sources.

Society for Humanistic Judaism

28611 W. Twelve Mile Rd.
Farmington Hills, MI 48334   **Phone:**   (810) 478-7610   **E-Mail:** SHJM@netcom.com
USA   **Fax:**   (810) 478-3159

Contact Person: Bonnie Cousens, Executive Director.
Officers or Principals: Bonnie Cousens, Executive Director ($0); Dana Wolfe Naimark, President ($0); E. Ronald Milan, Vice President ($0); Rick Naimark, Treasurer; Jane Goldhamer, Secretary; Rabbi Sherwin Wine, Rabbinic Advisor.
Mission or Interest: "To celebrate Jewish identity and culture consistent with a humanistic philosophy of life...a realistic view of Jewish history...ethics that rely on human judgement rather than supernatural guidance."
Accomplishments: 1,500 members. Hosted a colloquium in 1995 that brought together Jewish artists, writers and scholars including Charles Silberman, Norman Cantor, Anne Roiphe, Yehuda Bauer, among others. In the fiscal year ending April 1995, the Society spent $169,264 on its programs. The largest program, with expenditures of $62,415, was the publication and distribution of a quarterly journal to 3,000 individuals. The second largest program, at $55,438, was to develop leadership and train Humanistic Jewish rabbis.
Net Revenue: FY ending 4/95 $175,281 **Net Expenses:** $191,594 88%/12%/0% **Net Assets:** $15,460
Products or Services: Publications, colloquium, special ceremonies, more.
Tax Status: 501(c)(3)
Board of Directors or Trustees: Michael Beltzman, Harold Black, Lucie Brandon, Helen Bussell, Len Cherlin, Jay Cohen, Toby Dorfman, Jeanne Franklin, Esther Friedman, Shari Gelber, James Goldstein, Adelle Heller, Ron Hirsch, Alan Jacobs, Elaine Kamienny, Ed Klein, Irvine Margolses, Jutta Organek, Ben Pivnick, Anne Rossen, Earl Shiffman, Helen Svoboda, Henrietta Wexler.
Periodicals: *Humanistic Judaism* (quarterly journal).
Internships: Yes.
Other Information: Affiliated with the International Institute for Secular Humanistic Judaism and the International Federation of Secular Human Jews. The society received $75,279, or 43% of revenue, from membership dues. $75,077, or 43%, from gifts and grants awarded by foundations, companies and individuals. $19,824, or 11%, from program services, including the sale of publications, conference fees, and holiday services. The remaining revenue came from interest on savings and temporary cash investments, and other miscellaneous sources.

Sojourners

2401 15th St., N.W.
Washington, DC 20009   **Phone:**   (202) 328-8842
USA

Contact Person: James E. Wallis, President. **Officers or Principals:** James E. Wallis, President ($24,000); Scot DeGraf, Director ($24,000); Joseph Roos, Secretary/Treasurer ($23,917); Karen Lattea, Director ($23,917).
Mission or Interest: "A monthly magazine on faith, politics and culture to advocate church renewal and encourage the faith of its readers." Liberal and 'liberation' theology.
Accomplishments: In 1994 *Sojourners* spent $942,487 on its programs. $851,565 was spent on the magazine. $90,922 was spent on outreach.
Net Revenue: 1994 $1,170,974 **Net Expenses:** $1,099,251 86%/1%/13% **Net Assets:** (-$105,541) **Citations:** 295:58
Tax Status: 501(c)(3)
Periodicals: *Sojourners* (monthly magazine).
Other Information: The magazine received $567,052, or 47% of total revenue, from membership fees. $540,003, or 45%, from gifts and grants awarded by foundations, businesses, and individuals. $33,155, or 3%, from advertising revenue. $32,900 net, or 3%, from rental income. $22,176, or 2%, from honoraria. $9,933, or 1%, from subscriptions. The remaining revenue came from interest on savings and temporary cash investments, and other miscellaneous sources. The magazine lost $35,155 on the sale of inventory, and $1,000 on the sale of assets.

South Coast Foundation
611 S. Elm St.
Arroyo Grande, CA 93420
USA

Contact Person: Franklin Cook, Vice President.
Officers or Principals: Kathleen Cook, President ($24,000); Jason Hebel, Secretary/Treasurer ($0).
Mission or Interest: Grant-making foundation that gives primarily to South African organizations.
Accomplishments: In 1994 the Foundation awarded $104,278 in grants. Recipients included: $25,000 for South African Freedom Through Education, $23,200 for the Institute for Social and Economic Studies, $6,000 for the American Friends Service Committee, $5,000 for DataCenter, and $3,500 for Global Exchange.
Net Revenue: 1994 $181,913 **Net Expenses:** $170,566 **Net Assets:** $2,178,838
Tax Status: 501(c)(3)
Other Information: The Foundation received $86,146, or 47% of revenue, from dividends and interest from securities. $77,884, or 43%, from capital gains on the sale of securities. $10,718, or 6%, from gifts and grants awarded by foundations, businesses, and individuals. $5,816, or 3%, from interest income. The remaining revenue came from interest on savings and temporary cash investments, and other miscellaneous sources. The Foundation held $1,983,170, or 91% of its assets, in corporate stock.

South Dakota Peace and Justice Center
P.O. Box 405
Watertown, SD 57201   **Phone:**   (605) 882-2822
USA   **Fax:**   same

Contact Person: Jeanne Koster, Director.
Officers or Principals: Legia Spicer, Director ($21,923); Jeanne Koster, Director ($11,610); Mike Sprong, President; Jeff Moser, Vice President; Charles Fullen Kamp, Secretary/Treasurer; Charlie Garriott, Director.
Mission or Interest: Interfaith organization focusing on various 'peace and justice' issues, including ending racism, opposing capital punishment, immigrants rights, Martin Luther King Jr. Day observances, environmental issues, nuclear weapons issues, hunger and more.
Accomplishments: The Center's newsletter was distributed to 850 people and an annual meeting was attended by 75. In 1994 the Center spent $48,432 on its programs. The largest program, with expenditures of $15,216, was "undoing racism and reconciliation work" that included working with "four reconciliation committees composed of both native and non-native people." $12,108 was spent on a capital punishment task force. Another $12,108 was spent on local community issues.
Net Revenue: 1994 $57,788 **Net Expenses:** $56,978 **Net Assets:** $715
Products or Services: Community activism and lobbying. The Center spent $3,828 on the direct lobbying of legislators.
Tax Status: 501(c)(3) **Annual Report:** Yes. **Employees:** 2
Periodicals: *South Dakota Sun* (bimonthly newsletter).
Internships: Yes, unpaid.
Other Information: The Center received $49,021, or 85% of revenue, from gifts and grants awarded by foundations, businesses, and individuals. (These grants included $3,500 from the Peace Development Fund.) $6,606, or 11%, from membership dues. $1,000, or 2%, from a loan made by a member. $819, or 1%, from the sale of inventory. The remaining revenue came from program services and investment income.

South and Meso-American Indian Rights Center (SAIIC)
P.O. Box 28703
Oakland, CA 94612   **Phone:**   (510) 834-4263   **E-Mail:** saiic@igc.apc.org
USA   **Fax:**   (510) 834-4264   **Web-Page:** http://www.igc.apc.org/saiic.html

Contact Person: Amalia Dixon, Director.   **Officers or Principals:** Leticia Valdez, Administrative Coordinator; Andrew Bartlett, Development Coordinator; Marc Becker, Communications Coordinator.
Mission or Interest: "Promote peace, social justice, and the full participation of Indian peoples in decision making processes affecting their lives." Of particular interest is the imposition of state and national borders and nationalities on indigenous people. Especially in Latin America, tribal communities were bisected by nation-states, and communities were conscripted and force to fight against each other in wars not of their own making. SAIIC is devoted to linking indigenous people without respect to these imposed divisions.
Products or Services: Videos, audio tapes, directory and resource guide, speakers bureau, library, and online resources.
Tax Status: 501(c)(3) **Annual Report:** No. **Employees:** 3
Board of Directors or Trustees: Nilo Cayuqueo, Wara Alderete, Alejandro Amaru Argumedo, Guillermo Delgado, Xihuanel Huerta, Carlos Maibeth, Gina Pacaldo, Marcos Yoc.
Periodicals: *Abya Yala News* (quarterly journal).   **Internships:** Yes.
Other Information: The organization was previously called the South and Meso American Indian Information Center. "Information" was changed to "Rights" but the group maintained the acronym SAIIC.

South North Communication Network
P.O. Box 410150
San Francisco, CA 94141   **Phone:**   (415) 621-8981
USA

Contact Person: Barbara Johnson.
Mission or Interest: "Educate the public about the U.S.'s role in Nicaragua and Central America."
Periodicals: *Barricada International* (monthly).

Southern Appalachian Labor School

P.O. Box 127
Kincaid, WV 25119   **Phone:** (304) 442-3157
USA

Contact Person: John David, Director.
Officers or Principals: Helen M. Powell, Chair ($0); Bob Wilson, Vice Chair ($0); Sharon Rose, Secretary ($0).
Mission or Interest: Grassroots organizing concerned with health care, environment, welfare reform, and other issues.
Accomplishments: In 1994 the School spent $89,144 on its programs. The largest program, with expenditures of $25,985, held health care reform workshops for approximately 300 people. $17,991 was spent providing assistance to other nonprofit organizations. Other programs focused on the environment and affordable housing. The School awarded $37,208 in grants to small nonprofit organizations. All awards were $2,000 or less.
Net Revenue: 1994 $116,365 **Net Expenses:** $95,116 94%/6%/0% **Net Assets:** $159,838
Tax Status: 501(c)(3)
Other Information: The School received $114,152, or 98% of revenue, from gifts and grants awarded by foundations, businesses, and individuals. (These grants included $7,500 from the Appalachian Community Fund.) $2,171, or 2%, from interest on savings and temporary cash investments. The remaining revenue came from rental income.

Southern California Library for Social Studies and Research (SCL)

6120 S. Vermont Ave.
Los Angeles, CA 90044   **Phone:** (213) 759-6063
USA   **Fax:** (213) 759-2252

Contact Person: Sarah Cooper.
Officers or Principals: Donna Wilkinson, President; Eric Gordon, Secretary; Leo Baefsky, Treasurer.
Mission or Interest: "The roots of the Library go back to the 1930's, when Los Angeles activist Emil Freed began collecting labor and Left literature. Later, in the politically repressive 1950's, the collection mushroomed when Freed began rescuing materials that fearful activists were consigning to their backyard incinerators...Today, the Library is a major resource for people's movements of the twentieth century - the labor, Left, civil rights, women's, gay and lesbian movements, and many struggles for progressive social change in Southern California."
Accomplishments: An all-day conference on the Los Angeles Police Department in 1991 following the Rodney King incident. Programs on the Chicano/Latino community, and the Black Panther Party.
Products or Services: "Picking up the Torch: Immigrant Labor in Los Angeles" video, "We Built This City: A Labor History Tour of Los Angeles" map, 30th anniversary journal and more.
Tax Status: 501(c)(3) **Employees:** 4
Board of Directors or Trustees: J. Marx Ayres, Ruth Abraham, Leo Baefsky, Sydney Brisker, Myrna Donahoe, Sue Kunitomi Embrey, Muriel Goldsmith, Eric Gordon, Joe Hicks, Shirley Magidson, August Maymudes, Rena Maymudes, Pat Oliansky, Peter Olney, Sherman Pearl, Susan Philips, Gary Phillips, John Shannon, Keith Skotnes, Stuart Timmons, Rodolfo Torres, Donna Wilkinson, Goetz Wolff, Irene Wolt.
Periodicals: *Heritage* (newsletter).
Internships: Yes, usually library science students.
Other Information: "Four murals adorn the library building: A Vietnam Solidarity mural by Renee Mederos, one of Cuba's foremost public artists, 'Women and the Labor Movement in California,' the 'Wall of Honor' mural by Eva Cockcroft, and 'Labor Solidarity has No Borders' by Mike Alewitz."

Southern Empowerment Project (SEP)

343 Ellis Ave.
Maryville, TN 37804   **Phone:** (423) 984-6500   **E-Mail:** souempower@igc.apc.org
USA   **Fax:** (423) 984-9916

Contact Person: Walter Davis, Recruiter/Trainer. **Officers or Principals:** June Rostan, Coordinator; Howard White, Chair; Lynn Chaney, Secretary; James Lawrence, Sarah Scott, Executives at Large; John McCoy, Vice Chair.
Mission or Interest: Grassroots anti-poverty organization. "A multi-racial association of member-run, member-based organizations. The mission of SEP is to recruit and train a pool of community leaders to become organizers to help citizen organizations in the South solve problems by challenging racism and social injustice." Holds training sessions for activists and citizens.
Accomplishments: Since 1987 the SEP has trained over 150 community organizers. Offered training programs nationally in cooperation with the Center for Third World Organizing.
Products or Services: Six-week training program. Maintains a job bank for organizers and activists. Books, including: Home Grown Organizing by Melanie Zuercher, Organizing for Social Change by Kim Bobo et al, Organizing the Movement by Gary Delgado, and others.
Tax Status: 501(c)(3) **Annual Report:** Yes. **Employees:** 4

Board of Directors or Trustees: Hannah Cureton and Brenda Erwin (Charlotte Organizing Project), Linda Vice and Lynn Chaney (Community Farm Alliance), Howard White and Elnora Yarbrough (Just Organized Neighborhoods Area Headquarters), Earl Wilson and Joe Newsome (Kentuckians for the Commonwealth), John McCoy and James Lawrence (NC, A. Philip Randolph Institute), Mike Easter and Betty Anderson (Save Our Cumberland Mountains), Sarah Scott and Ruth Ragland (Solutions to Issues of Concern to Koxvillians), Margaret Fogle and Gladys Montgomery (South Carolina United Action), Jack Caudill and June Willis (West Virginia Organizing Project).
Periodicals: *Southern Empowerment Project Newsletter* (bimonthly newsletter).
Internships: Yes.
Other Information: In 1994 Sep received $40,000 from the Florence and John Schumann Foundation, and $20,000 from the New World Foundation. Other grants came from the Campaign for Human Development, Commission on Religion in Appalachia, Evangelical Lutheran Church in America, French American Charitable Trust, Fund for Southern Communities, Fund of Four Directions, Charles Stewart Mott Foundation, New World Foundation, Presbyterian Church USA, and the Unitarian Universalist Veatch Program at Shelter Rock.

Southern Environmental Law Center
201 W. Main St., Suite 14
Charlottesville, VA 22902   **Phone:**   (804) 977-4090
USA

Contact Person: Frederick S. Middleton, III, President.
Officers or Principals: Frederick S. Middleton, III, President ($153,172); Lark Hayes, Director, North Carolina Office ($84,009); James K. Gilliam ($77,705); Dr. Dennis W. Barnes, Vice President; Deaderick C. Montague, Chairman.
Mission or Interest: Public interest law firm that litigates on behalf of environmental and conservation concerns.
Accomplishments: In the fiscal year ending March 1995, the Center spent $1,599,403 on its programs. The largest program, with expenditures of $415,844, was energy conservation "to advocate increased reliance on cost-effective conservation measures that will result in lower electric bills and a cleaner environment." $383,856 was spent on coastal concerns and wetlands. $351,868 was spent on water and toxic pollution concerns. $319,880 was spent on public land management issues. $127,955 was spent on growth management and scenic resources. The Center received $62,638 in court-awarded legal fees, at least $18,097 of that came from taxpayers following a lawsuit against the U.S. Corps of Engineers. Litigation included: Environmental Defense Fund et. al. v. Tidwell et. al. (East Dismal Swamp) which sought to "secure an interpretation of the normal silviculture exemption of the Clean Water Act which more fully protects wetland values and functions." Friends of Hatteras Island v. North Carolina Coastal Resources Commission and Cape Hatteras Water Association Inc. that sought to "require state agency to protect maritime forest and wetlands in the Buxton Woods Coastal Reserve." The Wilderness Society, Sierra Club, et. al. v. John E. Alcock as Regional Forester of the Southern Region of the U.S. Forest Service that sought to "ensure that the U.S. Forest Service plan protects biological diversity and eliminate below cost timber sales in the Cherokee National Forest."
Net Revenue: FY ending 3/95 $2,506,939 **Net Expenses:** $1,944,175 82%/5%/13% **Net Assets:** $1,629,438
Citations: 70:122
Products or Services: Litigation and lobbying. The Center spent $1,876 on lobbying conducted by staff attorney Katherine Slaughter.
Tax Status: 501(c)(3)
Board of Directors or Trustees: Mary Bailey, Marion Cowell, J. Stephen Dockery, III, Georgia Herbert, Dr. Charles Lupton, Jr., Stephen O'Day, John Scott, Jr., Terence Sieg, W. Lawrence Wallace, William Want, Branford Wyche, Jane Hurt Yarn.
Other Information: The Center has a North Carolina Office, 137 E. Franklin St., Suite 404, Chapel Hill, NC 27514. The Center received $2,342,605, or 93% of revenue, from gifts and grants awarded by foundations, businesses, and individuals. (These grants included $300,000 from the Lyndhurst Foundation, $275,000 from the Energy Foundation, $140,000 from the Pew Charitable Trust, $100,000 from the Public Welfare Foundation, $100,000 from the Hillsdale Foundation, $90,000 from the Educational Foundation of America, $90,000 from the Mary Reynolds Babcock, $80,000 from the W. Alton Jones Foundation, $75,000 from the Rockefeller Brothers Foundation, $60,000 from the Joyce Mertz-Gilmore Foundation, $50,000 from the Prince Charitable Trusts, $50,000 from the Merck Family Fund, $50,000 Moriah Foundation, $30,000 from the Turner Foundation, $30,000 from the Bryan Family Foundation, $25,000 from the Janirve Foundation, $25,000 from the Maclellan Foundation, $25,000 from the Jessie Smith Noyes Foundation, $20,000 from the Curtis and Edith Munson Foundation, $15,000 from the Town Creek Foundation, $12,500 from the American Conservation Association, $11,500 from the Friendship Fund, $10,000 from the Flagler Foundation, and $5,000 from the New Land Foundation.) $62,638, or 2%, from court-awarded attorneys fees. $42,975, or 2%, from membership dues. $39,282, or 2%, from interest on savings and temporary cash investments. $19,439, or 1%, from fees reimbursed by clients.

Southern Organizing Committee for Economic and Social Justice (SOC)
P.O. Box 10518
Atlanta, GA 30310   **Phone:**   (404) 755-2855   **E-Mail:** socejp@igc.apc.org
USA

Contact Person: Connie Tucker, Executive Director.   **Officers or Principals:** Anne Braden, Co-Chair.
Mission or Interest: Grassroots civil rights and peace organization.
Accomplishments: Environmental justice forum entitled "Peace in the Streets," and a public forum on the "Crisis Black Youth Force."

Tax Status: 501(c)(3)
Periodicals: *Southern Fight-Back* (quarterly newsletter).
Other Information: Founded in the mid 1970s. In 1994 the Committee received $26,500 from the Jessie Smith Noyes Foundation, $7,000 from the Appalachian Community Fund, $500 the Jessie Smith Noyes Foundation, $500 from the Peace Development Fund, and $200 from the Haymarket People's Fund.

Southern Poverty Law Center

400 Washington Ave.
Montgomery, AL 36101   **Phone:**   (334) 264-0286
USA

Contact Person: Joann Chancellor, Secretary/Treasurer.   **Officers or Principals:** Morris Dees, Jr., Chief Trial Counsel ($175,809); Richard Cohen, Legal Director ($163,650); Eddie Ashworth, Executive Director ($161,259); Joseph Levin, President ($155,519); Joann Chancellor, Secretary/Treasurer; Joe Roy, *Klanwatch* Chief Investigator.
Mission or Interest: Litigation against racist organizations and hate groups and educating the poor on their legal rights. Publishes *Klanwatch*, a newsletter that monitors the activities of hate groups, with a new focus on hate groups operating within the national militia movement.
Accomplishments: The Center uses its litigation to prosecute those they see as agitators of violence. Most notably, in 1989, they filed and won a lawsuit against neo-Nazi Tom Metzger for the murder of an Ethiopian immigrant in Portland by a 'skinhead' gang. Although Metzger took no part in the physical murder, nor directed anyone to attack the Ethiopian immigrant or any other *specific* individual, the Center and the jury maintained that his speech and activities were sufficiently instigative. The Center is trying this approach against an anti-abortion activist, seeking to prove that he created a "climate" of violence which resulted in another abortion opponent killing a Florida doctor who performed abortions. Dees and the Center have become the most frequently cited sources on the militia and patriot movements in the United States. *Klanwatch* publishes the activities of hate groups and racially motivated murders, assaults, arsons, threats, cross burnings, intimidation, harassment, vandalism, and subsequent legal developments. *Klanwatch* publishes the results of these criminal investigations even when they turn out to be non-racially or hate-motivated, or a hoax. In the December 1994 issue of *Klanwatch*, a leader of the Michigan Militia was named as meeting with an Aryan Nation leader in Tennessee. The charge was disproved, and subsequent distribution of that issue deleted the reference. In the fiscal year ending July 1995, the Center spent $8,777,637 on its programs. The largest program, with expenditures of $7,146,303, was "educating the economically and educationally deprived of their rights under the Constitution and Bill of Rights and promoting racial and ethnic tolerance through educating teachers and students to respect other's rights." $1,631,334 was spent on litigation and legal services.
Net Revenue: FY ending 7/95 $17,188,114 **Net Expenses:** $12,106,514 73%/7%/20% **Net Assets:** $60,984,362
Citations: 938:24
Tax Status: 501(c)(3)
Board of Directors or Trustees: Patricia Clark, Frances Green, Hon. Rufus Huffman, Howard Mandell, Jack Watson, Jr.
Periodicals: *Klanwatch* (monthly newsletter).
Other Information: Established in 1971. The Center was founded by Morris Dees, a direct mail marketer who served as National Finance Director for George McGovern's 1972 Presidential campaign. Dees was a part of the defense team for Joan Little, a black female prisoner (convicted of breaking and entering) who was accused of killing a white prison guard with an ice pick and escaping following a sexual encounter that she maintained was rape. In the 1970's the case was a cause celebre with the far Left. The Communist Party USA, through its National Alliance Against Racist and Political Repression, took an active part on Little's defense committee, and communist activist Angela Davis served as constant companion and spokesperson for Little. Dees was removed from the Little defense team and charged with suborning perjury from a witness. The charge against Dees was later dropped. The Southern Poverty Law Center is a member of the National Coalition to Abolish the Death Penalty. The Center received $14,195,698, or 83% of revenue, from gifts and grants awarded by foundations, businesses, and individuals. (These grants included $4,100 from the Haymarket People's Fund, $650 from the Vanguard Public Foundation, $500 from the Stern Family of Nevada Foundation, $500 from the New Prospect Foundation, and $400 from the Stewart R. Mott Charitable Trust.) $1,843,119, or 11%, from dividends and interest from securities. $848,788, or 5%, from capital gains on the sale of securities. The remaining revenue came from interest on savings and temporary cash investments, the sale and rental of educational materials, rental income, and other miscellaneous sources. The Center held $56,558,238, or 90% of total assets, in securities.

Southerners for Economic Justice (SEJ)

P.O. Box 240
Durham, NC 27702   **Phone:**   (919) 956-2117
USA   **Fax:**   (919) 956-2177

Contact Person: Cynthia D. Brown, Executive Director.
Officers or Principals: Susan Perry-Cole, Chair; Cynthia D. Brown, Executive Director; Isaiah Madison, Vice President; Ray Eurquhart, Treasurer; Denise Crawford, Secretary; James Ferguson, General Counsel.
Mission or Interest: "SEJ is committed to helping unemployed poor and working people develop their capacity to shape the policies and institutions that affect their lives." Works in partnership with organized labor, churches, and grassroots organizations.
Accomplishments: Executive director Cynthia Brown was elected to the Durham City Council. She traveled to the Fourth U.N. Conference on Women in Beijing, paid for by the Ms. Foundation for Women. SEJ has published several books and articles. Formed three independent grassroots organizations, Schlage Workers for Justice, North Carolinians Against Racist and Religious Violence ("the only group monitoring hate crime activity in the state"), and the Carolina Alliance for Fair Employment. "Helped ensure the passage of ten occupational safety and health bills in the 1992 NC Legislature." Recently, SEJ has called attention to the fact that "the United States government sits on the verge of declaring war on the poor. Under the banner of reducing the deficit and cutting taxes, Congress is in the process of devising a budget that will 'cut taxes on the rich and raise them on the poor'."

Products or Services: Betrayal of Trust: Stories of Working North Carolinians, book which Julian Bond called "A compelling expose of the glaring absence of civil rights in the Southern workplace in the 1980's."
Tax Status: 501(c)(3) **Annual Report:** Yes. **Employees:** 6
Board of Directors or Trustees: Joe Alvarez (ACTWU), Hon. Julian Bond (former State Senator, GA-D), Constance Curry, Michael Dixon (Youth for Social Change), Hon. Billy Freemont, Barbara Prear, Renee Lynch, Tony Jefferies (Youth for Social Change), Estellalah Rasheed, James Sessions (Highlander Center), Pearl Shelby, Dr. Carol Stack (UC, Berkeley), Mary Joyce Carlson (Teamsters).
Periodicals: *Common Good* (monthly newsletter).   **Internships:** Yes, unpaid.
Other Information: Founded in 1976. In 1994 the organization received $82,500 from the New World Foundation, $20,000 from the Angelina Fund, $8,000 from the Tides Foundation, $7,500 from the Ms. Foundation for Women, $7,500 from the Abelard Foundation.

Southerners on New Ground (SONG)

P.O. Box 3912
Louisville, KY 40201   **Phone:**   (502) 896-2070
USA

Mission or Interest: Focus on lesbian and homosexual issues as they relate to class and race issues.
Periodicals: *SONG* (newsletter).

Southpaw Books

P.O. Box 155
Conway, MA 01341   **Phone:**   (413) 369-4406
USA

Contact Person: Eugene Povirk.
Mission or Interest: Specialize in used, rare and out of print books on: social reform, labor, radicalism, African American studies, and women's studies.
Accomplishments: They have over 15,000 books and a similar number of paper items (magazines, pamphlets, etc.).
Products or Services: They issue several catalogs and help individuals develop collections. They also purchase materials.
Tax Status: For profit.

Southwest Environmental Center (SEC)

1494A S. Solano Dr.
Las Cruces, NM 88001   **Phone:**   (505) 522-5552
USA

Contact Person: Kevin Bixby, Executive Director.
Mission or Interest: "Dedicated to protecting the environment in southern New Mexico and surrounding areas through public education and activism."
Accomplishments: The SEC bid on land leases for publicly-owned land with the intention of preserving it. Although the SEC placed a higher bid than the ranchers (who usually pay only 52¢ an acre), the ranchers were allowed to match the SEC's bid under "preferential rights." The New Mexico Land Office then declared the SEC's bids invalid and awarded the leases to the ranchers at the original low prices. The SEC says this proves that so called 'public lands' are really only open to certain privileged groups and industries. Worked to protect species such as the silvery minnow.
Products or Services: Nature tours, natural history walks, other educational materials.
Tax Status: 501(c)(3)
Board of Directors or Trustees: Daryl Smith (NM Dept. of Health), Michael Lilley (Pastors for Peace), Greg Vogel (Western Environmental Management Corp.).
Periodicals: *The Mesquite Grill* (quarterly newsletter).
Other Information: Funding included a grant from the McCune Foundation.

SouthWest Organizing Project (SWOP)

211 10th St., S.W.
Albuquerque, NM 87102   **Phone:**   (505) 247-8832
USA

Contact Person: Jeanne Gauna, Director.   **Officers or Principals:** Louis Head, Grants Administrator.
Mission or Interest: Addresses environmental problems as a part of a broader agenda for social, racial, and economic justice.
Tax Status: 501(c)(3)
Other Information: In 1994 the Project received $25,000 from the Jessie Smith Noyes Foundation. In 1995, $300 from Resist.

Southwest Research and Information Center (SRIC)

105 Stanford, S.E.
Albuquerque, NM 87106   **Phone:**   (505) 262-1862
USA   **Fax:**   (505) 262-1864

Contact Person: Don Hancock, Administrator.
Officers or Principals: David Benavides, President ($0); Linda Velarde, Vice President ($0); Anne Albrink, Secretary ($0); Annette Aguayo, Office Manager.
Mission or Interest: "SRIC exists to provide timely, accurate information to the public on matters that affect the environment, human health, and communities in order to protect natural resources, promote citizen participation, and ensure environmental and social justice now and for the future generations."
Accomplishments: They will celebrate their 25th anniversary in 1996. Staff member Lynda Taylor is on the Board of Directors for the Border Environment Cooperation Commission (BECC) which was created as the result of side agreements on NAFTA. Their quarterly magazine, *The Workbook*, has a circulation of 3,000. SRIC has worked extensively on uranium mining and milling issues related to UMTRA and the Uranium Miners Compensation Act. Works on nuclear waste policy issues at the national level.
Net Revenue: 1994 $510,093 ($165,817, or 33%, from government grants) **Net Expenses:** $481,447 84%/16%/1%
Net Assets: $388,715
Products or Services: Numerous publications and educational materials. Sponsors an environmental scholarship contest for students in New Mexico, the Navajo nation, and El Paso, Texas. Provides technical assistance to community activist groups on water, mining, oil and gas issues in the Southwest. Lobbying - in 1994 they spent $8,777 on lobbying, $6,477 at the grassroots level and $2,300 on the direct lobbying of legislators. They also award some grants to other grassroots organizations; four grants totaling $7,143 in 1994.
Tax Status: 501(c)(3) **Employees:** 9
Board of Directors or Trustees: Peter Montague, Ph.D. (Environmental Research Found.), Katherine Montague (Columbia Univ. Medical Center), Wilfred Rael, Gaurav Rajen, Ph.D., Mary Anne Tsosie.
Periodicals: *The Workbook* (quarterly magazine).
Internships: Yes. Interns help produce *The Workbook* or work on other projects, e.g. mining, border issues, nuclear waste.
Other Information: In addition to government grants in 1994, SRIC received two grants from the EPA in 1995 to support citizen participation in mining, oil and gas waste issues. The Center received $246,848, or 48% of revenue, from foundations, companies, and individuals. (These grants included $25,000 from the Florence and John Schumann Foundation, $10,000 from the New-Land Foundation, $2,000 from the Tides Foundation, $1,500 from the Jessie Smith Noyes Foundation, and $1,500 from the Beldon Fund.) $165,817, or 33%, from government grants. $81,110, or 16%, from consulting fees. $6,826, or 1%, from dividends and interest from securities. $6,710, or 1%, from the sale of publications. The remaining revenue came from rental income and other miscellaneous sources.

Southwest Voter Registration Education Project

403 E. Commerce, Suite 220
San Antonio, TX 78205   **Phone:**   (210) 222-0224
USA

Contact Person: Andrew Hernandez, President.
Officers or Principals: Richard Martinez, Executive Director ($22,309); Andrew Hernandez, President ($6,803); Juan J. Maldonado, Chairperson ($0); Hon. Manny Aragon, Vice Chairperson; Arnold Flores, Treasurer; Lucy Valeno, Secretary.
Mission or Interest: To provide voter registration services and public education with an emphasis on Hispanic voters. Conferences to educate southwestern voters on redistricting and reapportionment procedures.
Net Revenue: FY ending 6/94 $218,192 **Net Expenses:** $179,616 **Net Assets:** (-$90,719)
Tax Status: 501(c)(3)
Board of Directors or Trustees: Dora Olivo, Hon. Gloria Molina (Chair, County Board of Supervisors, Los Angeles).
Other Information: The Education Project is affiliated with the Southwest Voter Research Institute. The Project received $190,712, or 87% of revenue, from gifts and grants awarded by foundations, businesses, and individuals. $21,496 net, or 10%, from special fund-raising events. $5,984, or 3%, from conference registration fees.

St. Louis Journalism Review

8380 Olive Blvd.
St. Louis, MO 63132   **Phone:**   (314) 991-1699
USA   **Fax:**   (314) 997-1898

Contact Person: Charles L. Klotzer, Editor/Publisher.   **Officers or Principals:** Ed Bishop, Editor.
Mission or Interest: "Critique primarily of St. Louis area media, but also of national and international media. Coverage of events ignored by the media."
Accomplishments: Circulation of approximately 6,500.
Tax Status: 501(c)(3)
Periodicals: *St. Louis Journalism Review* (monthly).
Other Information: Founded in 1970. In 1996 the Review plans to move to the Webster University in St. Louis. However, it will remain "completely independent" and will be managed by "a public body." Charles Klotzer will remain involved in all areas, but Ed Bishop will become the new editor.

Stewart R. Mott Charitable Trust

515 Madison Ave., Suite 720
New York, NY 10022   **Phone:**   (212) 421-5200
USA

Contact Person: Stewart R. Mott, Trustee.   **Officers or Principals:** Kappy Jo Wells, Trustee.
Mission or Interest: Grant-making philanthropy that focuses on abortion rights, population concerns, civil liberties, lesbian and gay rights, and the environment.
Accomplishments: In 1994 the Trust awarded $207,730 in grants. The recipients of the largest grants were: $60,000 for the Fund for Constitutional Government, $20,000 for the Planned Parenthood Federation of America, $10,000 each for the Ms. Foundation for Women and the Project on Government Oversight, $6,000 for the International Center, $5,000 each for the ACLU, Voters for Choice Education Fund, and the Population Institute,$4,000 for the Citizens' Research Fund, $3,000 for the Center for International Policy, $2,500 for the Center for Reproductive Law and Policy, $2,000 each for the Earth Action Alerts Network, Council for a Livable World, Fairness and Accuracy in Reporting, Federation of American Scientists Fund, Help Abolish Legal Tyranny, National Committee for Radiation Victims, PeaceAction Education Fund, Public Education Center, and the 7th Generation Fund for Indians.
Net Revenue: 1994 $797,562 **Net Expenses:** $612,074 **Net Assets:** $9,182,337
Tax Status: 501(c)(3)
Other Information: The Trust received $668,228, or 84% of revenue, from capital gains on the sale of assets. $71,847, or 9%, from interest on savings and temporary cash investments. $57,481, or 7%, from dividends and interest from securities.   The Trust held $7,075,194, or 77% of assets, in corporate stock.

Student Action Corps for Animals

P.O. Box 15588
Washington, DC 20003
USA

Mission or Interest: Students' animal rights organization.
Net Revenue: 1992   less than $25,000   **Tax Status:** 501(c)(3)

Student Environmental Action Coalition (SEAC)

P.O. Box 1168
Chapel Hill, NC 27514   **Phone:**   (919) 967-4600
USA

Contact Person: Miya Yoshitani, National Office Representative.
Mission or Interest: Youth-run environmental organization that educates, trains, and builds networks in the pursuit of environmental and social justice.
Tax Status: 501(c)(3)
Periodicals: *Threshold* (eight times a year newsletter).
Other Information: In 1994 the Coalition received $26,500 from the Jessie Smith Noyes Foundation.

Students Organizing Students

1600 Broadway, Suite 404
New York, NY 10019   **Phone:**   (212) 977-6710
USA

Contact Person: Dion Thompson, Executive Director.
Officers or Principals: Anna Bondac, Development Director ($20,833); Dion Thompson, Executive Director ($20,005); Anna Marie Nieves, Program Director ($17,658); Karla Jackson-Brewer, President; Kica Matos, Secretary; Sara Rios, Treasurer.
Mission or Interest: Provides leadership training and organization for college and high school students.
Accomplishments: In the fiscal year ending June 1994, the organization spent $120,952 on its programs. The largest program, with expenditures of $58,315, provided skills training. The program discussed "important issues to identify (the students') leadership potential." $39,059 was spent on field organization to "educate and activate peer young women to raise their community's awareness about health issues." $17,298 was spent to "recruit and select applicants at the high school and college levels to develop skills in fundraising, media development and program development." Other programs strengthened chapter affiliates.
Net Revenue: FY ending 6/94 $162,678 **Net Expenses:** $209,154 58%/16%/26% **Net Assets:** $7,367
Tax Status: 501(c)(3)
Board of Directors or Trustees: Jane Xiaonan Agbontaen, Kathy Engel, Gwendolen Hardwick, Wubnesh Hylton, Karla Jackson-Brewer, Kica Matos, Lynn Michau, Kathlees Peratis, Evelyn Maria Rivera, Alexandra Stanton, Jenny Warburg, Kim McGillicuddy,
Other Information: Students Organizing Students received $162,341, or 99.8% of revenue, from gifts and grants awarded by foundations, businesses, and individuals. (These grants included $15,000 from the North Star Fund, $10,000 from the Ms. Foundation for Women, $10,000 from the Tides Foundation, $500 from the Haymarket People's Fund.) The remaining revenue came from interest on savings and temporary cash investments. The Organization has historically received support from the Funding Exchange, Ms. Foundation for Women, Tides Foundation, the Public Welfare Foundation and others.

Support Coalition

P.O. Box 11284
Eugene, OR 97440   **Phone:** (503) 345-9106   **E-Mail:** dendron@efn.org
USA   **Fax:**   same

Contact Person: David Oaks, Co-Coordinator.   **Officers or Principals:** Janet Foner, David Oaks, Co-Coordinator.
Mission or Interest: "Revitalize the psychiatric survivors' liberation movement."
Accomplishments: "Broke the silence about forced electroshock, federal violence initiative, and forced psychiatric drugging." In 1995, following a "Zap Back Campaign" which included e-mail, letters, faxes, and protests, directed at the U.S. Department of Health and Human Services (DHSS), Assistant Secretary Dr. Philip Lee wrote the Support Coalition saying that the issue of forced electroshock therapy was being handled by a sub-agency, the U.S. Center for Mental Health Services (CMHS). CMHS director Dr. Bernie Arons announced that the matter was being reviewed.
Products or Services: Publications, protests, and campaigns to influence public officials.
Tax Status: Applying for 501(c)(3).   **Annual Report:** No.   **Employees:** 1
Periodicals: *Dendron News* (quarterly).
Other Information: They are an alliance of thirty groups promoting human rights in, and alternatives to, psychiatry.

Sustainable America (SA)

350 5th Ave., Suite 3112
New York, NY 10118-3199   **Phone:** (212) 239-4221   **E-Mail:** sustamer@igc.apc.org
USA   **Fax:**   (212) 239-3670

Contact Person: Kim Chaloner, Program Assistant.   **Officers or Principals:** Elaine Gross, Executive Director
Mission or Interest: Promotion of an environmentally sustainable economy. "To create an infrastructure for Sustainable America member groups that increases the prevalence, effectiveness, and the scale of a variety of policy and development strategies that are the building blocks for sustainable economic development models in urban and rural communities in the U.S." Addresses issues such as "workplace/community organizing, fair trade, investment/credit, sectoral strategies, sustainable technologies, transportation, environmental issues, and tax policy."
Tax Status: 501(c)(3)   **Annual Report:** No.   **Employees:** 2
Board of Directors or Trustees: Amy Dean (South Bay Labor Council), Steve Kest (ACORN), Bill Fletcher (Service Employees' Intl. Union), Mark Ritchie (IATP), Joel Rogers (Center on Wisconsin Strategy), Omowale Satterwhite (Community Development Institute), Daniel Swinney (MCLR), Cynthia Ward (Northeast Action), Angie Wright (Ensley Forum), Dave Zwick (Clean Water Action).
Periodicals: *SA Talks* (newsletter).   **Internships:** Yes.
Other Information: Founded November 1995. Formerly located in Madison, Wisconsin.

Synergetic Society

1825 N. Lake Shore Dr.
Chapel Hill, NC 27514   **Phone:** (919) 942-2994
USA

Contact Person: N. Art Coulter, M.D.   **Officers or Principals:** Mary Keller Cox, President; James Young, Treasurer.
Mission or Interest: "To abolish war" through "a new way of thinking called 'Tracking'."
Accomplishments: Described a new way of thinking in a book, Synergetics: An Adventure in Human Development (Prentice Hall 1976) by N. Arthur Coulter, M.D.
Tax Status: 501(c)(3)   **Employees:** All volunteer.
Periodicals: *Change* (journal).   **Internships:** No.

Synergos Institute

100 E. 85th St.
New York, NY 10028   **Phone:** (212) 517-4900
USA   **Fax:**   (212) 517-4815

Contact Person: Judith Factor, Development Director.   **Officers or Principals:** S. Bruce Schearer, Director ($182,022); David Winder, Program Director ($118,791); Judith Factor, Development Director ($83,162); Peggy Dulany, President; Michaela Walsh, Chair; James Sligar, Secretary: Kenneth H. Wanderer, Treasurer.
Mission or Interest: Works with partners throughout the world to overcome poverty through "community-led partnerships."
Accomplishments: In the fiscal year ending August 1994, the Institute spent $1,109,265 on its programs. The largest program, with expenditures of $318,037, "collaborated with partner groups in the U.S., Japan, Europe and in the Southern Hemisphere countries, enlisting the support of the public, the private sector and opinion-makers on behalf of participatory efforts to overcome poverty." $289,535 was spent to research and document the results of these programs. The Institute awarded $92,503 in grants to individuals and organizations, mostly abroad.
Net Revenue: FY ending 8/94 $1,812,454   **Net Expenses:** $1,493,249 74%/19%/7%   **Net Assets:** $563,977
Citations: 0:255

Tax Status: 501(c)(3)
Board of Directors or Trustees: Etienne Allard, P. Michael Timpane, Elizabeth McCormack, Ellen Johnson Sirleaf (UN Development Programme), Adele Simmons, Ph.D. (John D. & Catherine T. MacArthur Found.), Nadine Hack, Isaac Shapiro, John Watts, Jacqueline deChollet, Maria Elena Lagomasino.
Other Information: The Institute received $1,791,767, or 99% of revenue, from gifts and grants awarded by foundations, businesses, and individuals. (These grants included $600,000 over three years from the John D. and Catherine T. MacArthur Foundation, $10,000 from the Compton Foundation). $14,053, or 1%, from investment income. The remaining revenue came from interest on savings and temporary cash investments, and dividends and interest from securities.

Syracuse Cultural Workers

P.O. Box 6367
Syracuse, NY 13217   **Phone:**   (315) 474-1132
USA   **Fax:**   (315) 475-1277

Contact Person: Dik Cool, President.
Officers or Principals: Dik Cool, President; Susan Gaynes, Vice President; Amy Bartell, Secretary.
Mission or Interest: "Product sales of posters, cards, calendars, design services and catalogs to educate people of cultural and social change...posters, calendars, etc., depicting environmental, world peace and unjust social conditions aid in the awareness and education of people." "Carry It On Peace Calendar" a multicultural calendar "addressing social issues and celebrating diversity."

Teamsters for a Democratic Union Foundation

P.O. Box 10128
Detroit, MI 48210   **Phone:**   (313) 842-2600
USA

Contact Person: Ken Paff, National Organizer.   **Officers or Principals:** Ken Paff, National Organizer ($3,769); Dan Campbell, Joe Fahey, Diana Kilmury, Michael Savwoir, Co-Chairs ($0).
Mission or Interest: Supports union democracy at the Teamsters. Works to organize the rank and file.
Accomplishments: Since 1976 they have promoted rank and file mobilization and education. In 1991"a new reform leadership backed by TDU was elected to top office in the Union, opening a new era of revitalization for the nation's largest private-sector union." They distribute their newsletter, *Convoy Dispatch* to over 60,000 readers.
Net Revenue: 1994 $310,403 **Net Expenses:** $261,870 **Net Assets:** $148,926
Products or Services: Annual convention. Organizational training and materials.
Tax Status: 501(c)(5)
Board of Directors or Trustees: Peter Camarata, Bilal Chaka, Chuck Crawley, Patricia Franks, Lisa Hopper, Tom Rose, Michael Ruscigno, Sally Smith, Patrick McBride, Lucio Reyes, Michael Turnure.
Periodicals: *Convoy Dispatch* (nine times a year).
Other Information: The Foundation received $119,140, or 38% of revenue, from membership dues. $76,060, or 25%, from the annual convention. $57,949, or 19%, from gifts and grants awarded by foundations, affiliates, and individuals. (These grants included $500 from the Bread and Roses Community Fund.) $19,253, or 6%, from the sale of literature and promotional items. The remaining revenue came from interest on savings and temporary cash investments, special events, and other miscellaneous sources.

Tenants' and Workers' Support Committee

3805 Mt. Vernon Ave., Suite 5
Alexandria, VA 22305   **Phone:**   (703) 684-5697   **E-Mail:** shenfan@aol.com
USA   **Fax:**   (703) 684-5714

Contact Person: Jon Liss, Director.   **Officers or Principals:** Jesse Taylor, Jr., President; Juana Vega, Vice President.
Mission or Interest: "Leadership development. Struggle for Latino and African-American low wage peoples rights as workers and tenants. Struggle for community power."
Accomplishments: "Formed the nation's only housing cooperative from bankrupt (Resolution Trust Corp.) S&L properties. This placed $8 million + of property under community control. Prevented evictions of 6,000 low-income residents."
Products or Services: Monthly "Broken English" video.
Tax Status: 501(c)(3) **Employees:** 3
Internships: Yes, mostly geared to women who are currently members.
Other Information: Formerly called the Tenants' Support Committee. Information published in English and Spanish.

Tennessee Environmental Council (TEC)

1700 Hayes St., Suite 101
Nashville, TN 37203   **Phone:**   (615) 321-5075   **E-Mail:** christl@edge.net
USA   **Fax:**   (615) 321-5082   **Web-Page:** http://www.nol.com/~nol/tec.html

Contact Person: Christl Peacock, Office Administrator.

Officers or Principals: Alan D. Jones, Executive Director; Marion Fowlkes, President; Clifford S. Russell, Treasurer.
Mission or Interest: "A statewide environmental coalition of over 1,500 individual members and 43 member organizations, educating and advocating for the protection of Tennessee's environment and public health."
Accomplishments: TEC settled two Clean Water Act citizen suits in 1995 which resulted in fines of $1,362,500 levied on the Dana Corporation and Harman Automotive Inc. A new endowment was started with money from the settlements to make grants to environmental organizations. Created a dialogue between the staff of the Tennessee Valley Authority and environmentalists. TEC helped stop a bill that would have protected environmental audits from disclosure during legal proceedings. In 1993 the Council spent $139,809 on its programs.
Net Revenue: 1993 $219,539 **Net Expenses:** $211,996 66%/11%/23% **Net Assets:** $62,991
Products or Services: Litigation, publications, coalition building, lobbying. The Council spent $9,357 on lobbying. This was an 82% increase over the previous year.
Tax Status: 501(c)(3)
Board of Directors or Trustees: Doug Cameron (Vanderbilt Inst. for Public Policy), Eleanor Cooper, David Crockett (Chattanooga City Councilman), Hamp Dobbins, Jr., Prof. Maurice Houston Field (Univ. of TN, Martin), Jenny Freeman, Judith Ideker, Sandra Kurtz, Chester McConnell (Wildlife Management Inst.), Kathryn McCoy (TN Energy Education Network), Juli Mosley, Daphne Murdock, John Noel, III, Jill Norvell (Univ. of Memphis), Robert Schreiber (Dean Witter Reynolds), Christine Sherman (Stop Trashing Our Premises), John Stone, III, Barry Sulkin, Ann Tidwell, Byron Trauger, Connie Whitehead, Patrick Willard (Office of State Rep. Bill Purcell, House Majority Leader).
Periodicals: *Protect* (quarterly newsletter).
Other Information: The Council received $78,310, or 36% of revenue, from special fund-raising events. $63,006, or 29%, from direct and indirect public support in the form of gifts and grants awarded by foundations, businesses, individuals, and affiliates. (These grants included $10,000 from the Beldon Fund.) $61,912, or 28%, from program service fees. $15,069, or 7%, from membership dues. The remaining revenue came from interest on savings and temporary cash investments.

Third Wave

185 Franklin St., 3rd Fl.
New York, NY 10013   **Phone:** (212) 925-3400   **E-Mail:** 3Wave@nyo.com
USA   **Fax:**   (212) 925-3427

Mission or Interest: Dedicated to "young feminist activism for social change."

Third World Viewpoint

328 Flatbush Ave., Box 171
Brooklyn, NY 11238   **Phone:** (718) 451-1213
USA

Mission or Interest: Quarterly review of Third World revolutionary movements. Considers the plight of African-Americans in the U.S. as part of this revolutionary struggle.
Periodicals: *Third World Viewpoint* (quarterly magazine).

Thorne Ecological Institute (TEI)

5398 Manhattan Circle, Suite 120
Boulder, CO 80303   **Phone:** (303) 499-3647
USA   **Fax:**   (303) 499-8340

Contact Person: Andre Mallinger.   **Officers or Principals:** Susan Q. Foster, Executive Director ($41,121); John Peters, Chair; Jonathan Horne, Treasurer; Hilary Renner, Secretary; Oakleigh Thorne, Founder.
Mission or Interest: Teaches "the principles of ecology to achieve environmental, economic and social balance."
Accomplishments: One of the first environmental organizations, TEI has been a nonprofit organization since 1954. They pioneered the use of the environmental impact statements before they were required by law. Played a lead role in the establishment of the Denver Audubon Society, the Colorado field office of the Nature Conservancy, the Balarat Outdoor Education Center for Denver Public Schools, and the Aspen Center for Environmental Studies. 1994 programs included a Wildlife Symposium, $15,074; the Watershed Ecological Workshop, $16,630; the Prairie Wetlands-EPA Conference, $17,601; and others.
Net Revenue: 1994 $234,112 ($39,183, or 17%, from government grants) **Net Expenses:** $243,460 65%/26%/9%
Net Assets: $20,014
Products or Services: Numerous educational programs and workshops. Publications and proceedings from conferences. Front Range Natural Science School, a summer environmental studies day camp. The camp has been offered for 38 years now and reaches up to 700 children a year. In 1994 TEI spent $57,665 on Front Range.
Tax Status: 501(c)(3) **Annual Report:** Yes, yearly prospectus. **Employees:** 1-3 staff members, up to 50 contractors/teachers per year.
Board of Directors or Trustees: Carl Crookham (Denver Public Schools), Bettie Willard, Pam Hill, Mike Flanagan, others.
Internships: Yes. Unpaid opportunities as teaching assistants with the Front Range Natural Science School. Other positions.
Other Information: Thorne Ecological Institute is a member of the Chatfield Environmental Education Resource System (CHEERS), a partnership of government agencies, other nonprofits and businesses in the Chatfield Basin of Colorado. The Institute received $96,100, or 41% of revenue, from program services, including workshops, classes and symposiums. $56,357 net, or 24%, from special fund-raising events. $42,204, or 18%, from gifts and grants awarded by foundations, companies and individuals. $39,183, or 17%, from government grants. The remaining revenue came from interest on savings and temporary cash investments.

Three Rivers Community Fund
100 N. Braddock Ave. Suite 207
Pittsburgh, PA 15208   **Phone:**   (412) 243-9250
USA   **Fax:**   (412) 243-0504

Contact Person: Anne Hawkins.   **Officers or Principals:** Cynthia Vanda, President; Nancy Bernstein, Vice President; Ellie Siegal, Treasurer; Bill Wekselman, Secretary.
Mission or Interest: Philanthropy that awards grants to grassroots organizations in southwest Pennsylvania. An affiliate of the Funding Exchange.
Accomplishments: Since 1991 the Fund has distributed over $100,000. 1996 recipients include: $1,500 each for the Alliance for Progressive Action, Citizens Budget Campaign, Pittsburgh Coalition to Counter Hate Groups, $1,000 each for Chain of Hope, Strength Inc., Alle-Kiski Homeless Project, and the Haitian Solidarity Committee.
Tax Status: 501(c)(3)   **Annual Report:** No.   **Employees:** 1
Board of Directors or Trustees: Marvin Bellin, M.D., Fran Gialamas, Sara Hartman, Carrie Leanna, Barbara Mackey, Lisa Scales, Zinna Scott, Carol Wharton Titus, Gina Wilson.
Periodicals: *The Bridge* (quarterly newsletter). **Internships:** Yes, unpaid.
Other Information: In 1994 the Fund received $2,000 from the Vanguard Public Foundation.

Threepenny Review
P.O. Box 9131
Berkeley, CA 94709   **Phone:**   (510) 849-4545
USA   **Fax:**   (510) 849-4551

Contact Person: Wendy Lesser President.
Officers or Principals: Wendy Lesser, President/Chairman ($10,000); Richard Rizzo, Secretary/Treasurer ($0).
Mission or Interest: Magazine of culture, arts, the media, and politics.
Accomplishments: In 1994 the Review spent $110,869 on production.
Net Revenue: 1994 $213,514   ($44,313, or 21%, from government grants)   **Net Expenses:** $173,710   64%/29%/7%
Net Assets: $83,764
Tax Status: 501(c)(3)
Board of Directors or Trustees: Gregory Farnham, Nina Gillman, Susan Gillman, John Kadvany, Arthur Lubow, Katherine Ogden.
Periodicals: *Threepenny Review* (quarterly journal).
Other Information: The Review received $80,304, or 38%, from gifts and grants awarded by foundations, businesses, and individuals. $63,472, or 30%, from subscriptions. $44,313, or 21%, from government grants. $10,914, or 5%, from advertising sales. $4,826, or 2%, from bookstore sales. $4,675, or 2%, from mailing list rentals. The remaining revenue came from interest on savings and temporary cash investments, single copy sales, and other miscellaneous sources. The journal cost $110,869 to produce, and brought in $87,337 in revenues (subscriptions, advertising, mailing lists, and other sales). The *Threepenny Review* required subsidization of $23,532.

Tides Foundation
P.O. Box 29903
San Francisco, CA 94129   **Phone:**   (415) 561-6400   **E-Mail:** outreach@igc.apc.org
USA   **Web-Page:** http://www.igc.org/

Contact Person: Ellen Friedman, Vice President.   **Officers or Principals:** Robert Fuller, Project Director ($104,375); Mary Kelly, Project Director ($94,850); Drummond Pike, President ($85,000); Wade Rathke, Chairman; Louise Brotsky, Ellen Friedman, Vice Presidents; Michael Kieschnick, Treasurer; Lynda Palevsky, Secretary.
Mission or Interest: Grant-making foundation that concentrates on grassroots organizations and organizing. Projects and areas of funding include the Military Toxics Project, People and the Planet: Rethinking Population Project, Solar and Renewable Energy Project, People Organizing to Demand Environmental Rights, more. Maintains computer networks through the Institute for Global Communications (see the separate listing for the Institute for Global Communications.)
Accomplishments: In the fiscal year ending April 30, 1995, the Foundation awarded $11,361,220 in grants. The largest grants included: $370,500 for the Fidelity Investments Charitable Gifts Fund, $265,000 for the Southern Rural Development Initiative, $260,100 for Friends of the Earth, $180,750 for the Peace Development Fund, $174,475 for the Threshold Foundation, $159,300 for Essential Information, $97,500 for the Citizens Fund, $91,500 for the Brooklyn In Touch Information Center, $91,500 for the Community Resource Exchange, $84,000 for A Territory Resource Foundation, $78,945 for Oxfam America, $77,896 for the Center for Third World Organizing, $75,000 for the Families USA Foundation, $75,605 for the Western States Center, $75,000 for the Chinook Learning Center, $64,689 for the Asian Women's Shelter, $60,000 for Public Citizen Foundation, $59,500 for Classical Action, $53,111 for Grassroots International, $52,012 for the Body-Mind Centering Association, $50,000 for the Greenhouse Crisis Foundation, $50,000 for the Berkeley Oakland Support Services, $50,000 for Native Action, $50,000 for the ACLU, $48,000 for the New York Community Foundation, $46,900 for the Environmental Working Group, $45,000 for the Pro Choice Resource Center, $45,000 for the Western Organization of Resource Councils, and $40,000 for Lighthawk. The Foundation also awarded a very small percentage of its grants to some conservative and free-market organizations, including $50,000 for the Foundation for Teaching Economics, $25,000 for Hillsdale College, $50,000 for the Institute for Contemporary Studies, and $25,000 for the Philanthropy

Roundtable. The Foundation also awarded grants for lobbying to Arizona Community Protection ($20,000), Handgun Control ($19,832), Heart of America Northwest ($12,457), Tsunami Fund ($4,724), Washington Citizens For Fairness ($3,499), Support Our Communities ($2,500), and the Western States Center ($105). The Foundation also spent $20,698,797 on its own educational efforts. These included the Institute for Global Communications (IGC) and its computer networks.

Net Revenue: FY ending 4/95 $45,029,673 ($297,770, or 1%, from government grants) **Net Expenses:** $35,494,027 90%/9%/1% **Net Assets:** $44,786,995

Products or Services: The IGC offers numerous computer services, including web page creating and e-mail mailing lists. Grants, computer network and lobbying. The Foundation spent $225,240 on grassroots lobbying. This was an increase of 188% over the previous year.

Tax Status: 501(c)(3)

Board of Directors or Trustees: Richard Boone, Mary Mountcastle, Charles Savitt, Andrea Kydd, Susan Carmichael.

Periodicals: *Ground Work* (magazine) formerly called *Greenletter*.

Internships: Yes.

Other Information: The Foundation owns full control of a for-profit corporation, Highwater Inc. - a subsidiary that is developing a location for a new office. The Foundation also has connections to the Working Assets Funding Service, a for-profit corporation that offers long distance and credit card services and devotes a portion of the profits to leftist organizations. President Drummond Pike serves as a shareholder and director of Working Assets, and Treasurer Michael Kieschnick is President and Chief Operating Officer of Working Assets. The Foundation holds 10,525 shares of Working Assets as a result of gifts made by these two officers. The Foundation employed the Washington DC firms of Greer, Margolis & Associates for program consultation, Communications Consortium Media Center for program consultation, and the Los Angeles firm of Laufer Associates for marketing and public relations (overall the Foundation spent $319,939 on public relations). These firms were paid $449,880, $227,353, and $83,670 respectively. The Foundation received $36,187,331, or 81%, from gifts and grants awarded by foundations, businesses, and individuals. (These grants included $425,500 from the Joyce Mertz-Gilmore Foundation, $310,000 from the Nathan Cummings Foundation, $125,000 from the Joyce Foundation, $92,000 from the New World Foundation, $77,500 from the General Service Foundation, $72,054 from the Rosenberg Foundation, $50,000 from the James C. Penney Foundation, $40,000 from the Florence and John Schumann Foundation, $38,430 from the Compton Foundation, $30,000 from the Columbia Foundation, $27,500 from the Deer Creek Foundation, $25,000 from the Ms. Foundation for Women, $20,000 from the J. Roderick MacArthur Foundation, $18,679 from Greenpeace, $18,000 from the Abelard Foundation, $15,500 from the Vanguard Public Foundation, $15,000 from the Henry J. Kaiser Family Foundation, $13,750 from the Joyce Foundation, $10,000 from the One World Fund, $10,000 from the C.S. Fund, $5,250 from the Beldon Fund, $5,000 from the New Prospect Foundation, $1,000 from the Peace Development Fund, and $1,000 from the Sierra Club.) $2,191,865, or 5%, from the Institute for Global Communications' network access fees. $1,738,327, or 4%, from dividends and interest from securities. $1,603,622, or 4%, from the sale of publications and other materials. $1,342,593, or 3%, from private contract fees. $469,228, or 1%, from capital gains on the sale of securities. $481,761, or 1%, from conference fees. $440,736, or 1%, from project fees. $297,770, or 1%, from government grants. The remaining revenue came from contract management fees, and rental income. The Foundation held $33,501,537, or 64% of its assets, in securities.

Tikkun
(see the Institute for Labor and Mental Health)

Toward Freedom (TF)
209 College St.
Burlington, VT 05401
USA

Phone: (802) 658-2523   **E-Mail:** TFmag@aol.com
Fax: (802) 658-3738

Contact Person: Mike Reilly, Administrator.   **Officers or Principals:** Greg Guma, Editor; Robin Lloyd, Dave Dellinger, Co-Chairs; Sandra Baird, Vice Chair; Anthony Chavez, Secretary; Chris Lloyd, Treasurer.

Mission or Interest: "An international news, analysis and advocacy journal. TF seeks to strengthen and extend human justice and liberties in every Sphere. Believing that freedom of the imagination is the basis for a just world, TF opposes all forms of domination that repress human potential to reason, work creatively, and dream." Editor Greg Guma states, "the threat (to free speech) today isn't mainly government but rather gigantic private institutions, transnational entities with enormous economic and information power at their disposal. Protecting free speech therefore requires affirmative actions. Failure to fulfill this responsibility leaves the power to inform - and to censor - in the hands of a few."

Accomplishments: Publishing since 1952. Sponsors and co-sponsors conferences on human rights, co-sponsored the Vermont International Film Festival. Many of the contributors to TF have had books published, including essays previously included in TF. Some of these titles include The People's Republic: Vermont and the Sanders Revolution (New England Press) by Greg Guma, and Ecological Democracy (South End Press) by Roy Morrison.

Tax Status: 501(c)(3) **Annual Report:** No. **Employees:** 2

Board of Directors or Trustees: J.R. Deep Ford, Susan Meeker-Lowry, Kristin Peterson-Ishaq, Wolfsong. Advisors are; Terry Allen, Amiri Baraka, Dennis Brutus, Paul DuBois, Lawrence Ferlinghetti, Allen Ginsberg, Joanne Landy, Francis Moore Lappé, Robert Nichols, Grace Paley, Brian Tokar, Anne Waldman, Brian Wilson.

Periodicals: *Toward Freedom* (eight times a year magazine).

Internships: Yes, unpaid, for college credit.

Other Information: Reduced rate low-income subscriptions available. Unsolicited manuscripts welcome. Listings for progressive organization events provided in the calendar section.

Town Creek Foundation

P O Box 159
Oxford, MD 21654
USA

Contact Person: Edmund A. Stanley, Jr., President.   **Officers or Principals:** Philip E.L. Dietz, Jr., Treasurer ($2,250); Lisa Stanley, Director ($1,750); Betsy Taylor, Director ($1,750); Edmund A. Stanley, Jr., President; Jennifer Stanley, Vice President.
Mission or Interest: Grant-making foundation that gives mostly to environmental and conservation organizations.
Accomplishments: In 1993 the Foundation awarded $1,315,000 in grants. Recipients of the largest grants included: $100,000 for the Wilderness Society, $75,000 for the Chesapeake Bay Foundation, $60,000 for WETA Public Television, $50,000 for National Public Radio, $35,000 for the National Audubon Society, $25,000 each for American Rivers and the Center for Marine Conservation, and $20,000 each for the Citizens Clearinghouse for Hazardous Wastes, Living on Earth, Natural Resources Council of Maine, and the Sierra Club Legal Defense Fund. Other organizations receiving grants include: Center for Defense Information, Center for Economic Conversion, Center for Investigative Reporting, Center for Policy Alternatives, Educators for Social Responsibility, Greenpeace Fund, Pacifica Foundation, Parliamentarians for Global Action, and Physicians for Social Responsibility.
Net Revenue: 1993 $1,956,001 **Net Expenses:** $1,523,354 **Net Assets:** $29,824,803
Tax Status: 501(c)(3)
Other Information: The Foundation received $1,440,367, or 74% of revenue, from dividends and interest from securities. $513,893, or 26%, from capital gains on the sale of securities. The remaining revenue came from interest on savings and temporary cash investments. The Foundation holds $26,512,447, or 89% of assets, in corporate stocks and bonds.

TRANET

P.O. Box 567
Rangeley, ME 04970   **Phone:**   (207) 864-2252   **E-Mail:** tranet@igc.apc.org
USA

Contact Person: Bill Ellis, General Coordinator.
Officers or Principals: Peter Thibeault, President ($0); Allan Philbrick, Secretary/Treasurer ($0); David Green, Director ($0).
Mission or Interest: Global clearinghouse for replacing the "Global Competitive Economic System" with "Cooperative Community Economics." Emphasis on the building of small, autonomous, self sufficient communities built around learning centers. Works with activists working for peace, the environment, feminism, human rights, and other causes.
Net Revenue: 1994 $14,726 **Net Expenses:** $16,288 100%/0%/0% **Net Assets:** $6,025
Products or Services: Recently created the Coalition for Cooperative Community Economics, or 3CE, a network of individuals and organizations that are changing the world by changing their own lifestyles.
Tax Status: 501(c)(3) **Employees:** 7 volunteers.
Periodicals: *TRANET* (bimonthly newsletter). **Internships:** Yes.
Other Information: TRANET was started at the 1976 U.N. Conference on Human Settlements. A group of citizens from around the world gathered in a non-governmental forum called HABITAT. For ten days the forum met and exchanged ideas and decided to form a 'transnational network', or TRANET. They state that cooperative economics are not new. The competitive, profit-based economy is a recent European imposition unknown to the rest of the world until recently. They draw on many sources and thinkers to construct the theory behind their self-sufficient, sustainable, "Gaian" communities. The organization received $13,178, or 89% of revenue, from membership dues. $1,357, or 9%, from gifts and grants awarded by foundations and individuals. The remaining revenue came from interest on savings and temporary cash investments.

TransAfrica

1744 R St., N.W.
Washington, DC 20009   **Phone:**   (202) 797-2301
USA

Contact Person: Randall Robinson, Executive Director.   **Officers or Principals:** Randall Robinson, Executive Director ($41,980); William Lucy, Chairman ($0); Dr. Mary Francis Berry, Secretary ($0); Dr. James Davis, Treasurer.
Mission or Interest: Lobbies for a "more progressive foreign policy towards the nations of Africa and the Caribbean."
Accomplishments: In 1994 TransAfrica spent $231,819 on its activities, a 119% increase from the previous year.
Net Revenue: 1994 $18,681 **Net Expenses:** $340,298 68%/18%/14% **Net Assets:** $335,549 **Citations:** 42:143
Tax Status: 501(c)(4)
Board of Directors or Trustees: Jean Sindab (Program Director, Natl. Council of Churches), Wade Henderson, Quincy Jones (Quincy Jones Entertainment), Rep. Donald Payne (D-NJ), Bishop John Hurst Adams (Bishop of SC), Dr. William (Bill) Cosby (actor), Earl Graves (Black Enterprise Magazine), Dr. Dorothy Height (Natl. Council of Negro Women), Ernest Lofton (UAW), William Lucy (AFSCME), Dr. Pearl Robinson (Tufts Univ.), Rep. Maxine Waters (D-CA), Willie Baker.
Other Information: Affiliated with the 501(c)(3) TransAfrica Forum at the same address. The two affiliates had combined net revenues of $1,312,479, net expenses of $1,389,645, and net assets of $1,824,136. Randall Robinson served as executive director of both, receiving a combined $79,480. TransAfrica received $12,049, or 64% of revenue, from gifts and grants received by foundations, businesses, and individuals. $4,214, or 23%, from special fund-raising events. The remaining revenue came from membership dues and interest on savings and temporary cash investments.

TransAfrica Forum
1744 R St., N.W.
Washington, DC 20009   **Phone:**   (202) 797-2301
USA

Contact Person: Randall Robinson, Executive Director.   **Officers or Principals:** Randall Robinson, Executive Director ($37,500); Edward Lewis, Chairman ($0), Dr. Sylvia Hill, Treasurer ($0); Harriet Michel, Secretary.
Mission or Interest: Research and education "promoting more progressive foreign policy towards the nations of Africa and the Caribbean."
Accomplishments: In 1994 the Forum spent $686,020 on its projects.
Net Revenue: 1994 $1,293,798 **Net Expenses:** $1,049,347 65%/17%/18% **Net Assets:** $1,488,587 **Citations:** 42:145
Tax Status: 501(c)(3)
Board of Directors or Trustees: Emelda Cathcart (Dir., Corporate Contributions, Time-Warner), Dr. Locksley Edmondson (Cornell Univ.), Donna Brown Guillaume, Hon. A. Leon Higginbotham, Jr., Dr. Sylvia Hill (Univ., DC), Dr. Edmond Keller (UCLA), Bertram Lee (Pres., WKYS Radio), Peter Bynoe, Prof. Charles Ogletree (Harvard Law School), James Joseph (Pres., Council on Foundations).
Other Information: Affiliated with the 501(c)(4) TransAfrica at the same address. The Forum transferred $370,167 to TransAfrica for the use of facilities and other reimbursement arrangements payable, and co-signed a mortgage with it. The two affiliates had combined net revenues of $1,312,479, net expenses of $1,389,645, and net assets of $1,824,136. Randall Robinson served as executive director of both, receiving a combined $79,480. The Forum received $1,107,202, or 86% of revenue, from gifts and grants awarded by foundations, businesses, and individuals. (In 1993 the Forum received $75,000 from the Carnegie Corporation.) $135,263 net, or 10%, from special fund-raising events. $47,486, or 4%, from rental income. The remaining revenue came from interest on savings and temporary cash investments, and the sale of subscriptions.

Transport Workers Union of America
80 West End Ave.
New York, NY 10023   **Phone:**   (212) 873-6000
USA

Contact Person: H. Hall, President.
Officers or Principals: H. Hall, President ($155,353); John Kerrigan, Secretary/Treasurer ($146,751); F. McCann, Executive Vice President ($143,252); E. Koziatek, Vice President ($116,763); P. Gaynor, Vice President ($112,948); L. Martin, Vice President ($109,232); M. O'Brien, Vice President ($104,156); G. Roberts, Vice President ($101,958); M. Bakalo, Vice President ($101,726).
Mission or Interest: Member of the AFL-CIO.
Accomplishments: In the fiscal year ending August 1994 the Union paid $374,000 in dues to the AFL-CIO.
Net Revenue: FY ending 8/94 $12,880,969 **Net Expenses:** $8,730,129 **Net Assets:** $37,493,171
Tax Status: 501(c)(5)
Other Information: The Union received $11,130,294, or 85% of total revenue, from membership dues. $1,142,475, or 9%, from dividends and interest from securities. $360,249, or 3%, from interest on savings and temporary cash investments. $213,995, or 2%, from reimbursed expenses. The remaining revenue came from investment income, the sale of supplies, and other miscellaneous sources.

Traprock Peace Center
Woolman Hill, Keets Rd.
Deerfield, MA 01342   **Phone:**   (413) 773-7427
USA

Contact Person: Jack Seery, Executive Director.   **Officers or Principals:** Jack Seery, Executive Director ($17,845); Leslie Fraser, President ($0); Sunny Miller, Vice President ($0); Karen Young, Treasurer.
Mission or Interest: Grant-making and other educational activities directed towards "community outreach by teaching nonviolent alternatives for solving personal, national and international conflicts."
Accomplishments: In 1994 the Center spent $177,168 on its programs. This included $141,005 in grants. These grants included: $77,600 for the National Voting Rights Institute, $28,518 for the Working Group on Electoral Democracy, $19,400 for the Worker Ownership Resource Center, $3,744 for the Gun Buy Back Campaign, $3,618 for the Pioneer Valley Pro Democracy, $2,433 for Full Moon Rising, $1,867 for the Sri Lanka Women's Dance Troop, $1,183 for Networking for Democracy, $611 for the Amherst Middle East Education Committee, $600 for MA ALERT, $485 for the War Tax Refusers' Support Group, $446 for the Pioneer Valley Coalition to Lift the Cuban Embargo, $257 for Friends of Student Refugees, and $243 for Feminist Aid to Central America. The Center also made loans to the Institute for Community economics and the Western Massachusetts Enterprise Fund. At the end of the year these notes receivable were worth $10,101 and $10,097 respectively.
Net Revenue: 1994 $185,720 **Net Expenses:** $218,459 81%/19%/1% **Net Assets:** $90,029
Products or Services: Peace education activities and grants. In 1994 the Center did not engage in lobbying, but it has in the past, spending $2,822 in 1992.
Tax Status: 501(c)(3)
Board of Directors or Trustees: Rich Trenholm, Jamie Babson, Jolayne Hinkel, Cora Reiser, Ginny Schneider.
Other Information: The Center received $170,667, or 92% of revenue, from gifts and grants awarded by foundations, businesses, and individuals. (These grants included $80,000 from the Florence and John Schumann Foundation, $7,500 from the New World Foundation.) $12,390, or 7%, from program service fees. $2,663, or 1%, from dividends and interest from securities.

TreePeople

12601 Mulholland Dr
Beverly Hills, CA 90272   **Phone:**   (818) 753-4600
USA   **Fax:**   (818) 753-4625

Contact Person: Andy Lipkis, Executive Director.   **Officers or Principals:** Andy Lipkis, Executive Director ($75,000); Artha Kass ($65,005); Diane Hunt ($39,501); Joanie Aitken ($39,501).
Mission or Interest: Environmental organization that teaches protection and stewardship. Focus is on trees and forestry.
Accomplishments: In the fiscal year ending June 1994, TreePeople spent $1,098,698 on its programs. The largest program, with expenditures of $543,246, was education and outreach. This included a newsletter and other literature, speeches, and presentations at public events. $249,220 was spent on 'Citizen Forestry' programs which included mountain and urban plantings, "gang diversion programs", and forestry training classes. $157,478 was spent on school programs that reached approximately 120,000 children. $148,754 was spent recruiting and supporting volunteers.
Net Revenue: FY ending 6/94 $1,723,982 ($181,957, or 11%, from government grants)
Net Expenses: $1,641,300 67%/6%/27% **Net Assets:** $749,245 **Citations:** 39:145
Tax Status: 501(c)(3)
Board of Directors or Trustees: Gary Barr, Paul Bergman (UCLA School of Law), Jerry Daniel, Marlene Grossman, David Hagen, Marshall Herskovitz, Chris Howell, Winnie Huang, Dr. Leon Lipkis, Dan Pearlman, Darry Sragow, Tony Thomas (Witt-Thomas-Harris Prod.), Teddy Zee (Exec. V.P., Columbia Pictures), David Zucker (Zucker Bros. Prod.).
Periodicals: Bimonthly newsletter.
Other Information: TreePeople received $1,217,588, or 71% of revenue, from gifts and grants awarded by foundations. (These grants included $41,987 from the Environmental Federation of California, $6,000 from the Barbra Streisand Foundation, and $100 from the Compton Foundation.) $204,121 net, or 12%, from special fund raising events. $181,957, or 11%, from government grants. $102,500, or 6%, from program service fees. The remaining revenue came from the sale of assets, dividends and interest from savings and temporary cash investments, the sale of inventory, and other miscellaneous sources.

Trial Lawyers for Public Justice Foundation (TLPJ Foundation)

1717 Massachusetts Ave., N.W., Suite 800
Washington, DC 20036   **Phone:**   (202) 797-8600
USA   **Fax:**   (202) 232-7203

Contact Person: Kye Briesath, Deputy Director.   **Officers or Principals:** Marjorie Spitz, Development Director ($52,500); Arthur Bryant, Executive Director; Michael Withey, President; William Snead, President-Elect; Fred Baron, Vice President; William A. Rossbach, Treasurer; Nicole Schultheis, Secretary.
Mission or Interest: "A national public interest law firm that marshals the skills and resources of trial lawyers to create a more just society."
Accomplishments: Won a New Hampshire Supreme Court decision that allowed TLPJ to sue Ford Motor Co. for negligence for not providing airbags in a car involved in a fatal accident, when TLPJ believes that the technology was available and should have been provided. Won the largest Clean Water Act settlement. Won a "pesticide-free environment for a woman with multiple chemical sensitivity." Forced the University of Bridgeport to reinstate its women's gymnastics team. Won the largest property damage class-action settlement in U.S. history. In the past TLPJ has worked with the American Civil Liberties Union, Alliance for Justice, Environmental Action, NOW Legal Defense Fund, National Wildlife Federation, Public Citizen, and others. In 1994 the Foundation spent $957,715 on its programs. The Foundation awarded a grant of $475,000 to its lobbying affiliate, the Trial Lawyers for Public Justice.
Net Revenue: 1994 $854,663 **Net Expenses:** $1,253,567 76%/11%/12% **Net Assets:** $635,192 **Citations:** 4:217
Products or Services: Publications, litigation, brochures, "Working Together for Public Justice"- a guide for public interest organizations, and more. Annual award for "Trial Lawyer of the Year."
Tax Status: 501(c)(3) **Annual Report:** No. **Employees:** 17
Board of Directors or Trustees: Joan Claybrook (Public Citizen), and numerous other trial lawyers.
Periodicals: *Public Justice* (quarterly newsletter).   **Internships:** Yes.
Other Information: Affiliated with the 501(c)(4) Trial Lawyers for Public Justice at the same address. The Foundation received $519,856, or 61% of revenue, from membership dues. $239,410, or 28%, from gifts and grants awarded by foundations, businesses, and individuals. $50,075, or 6%, from events and conferences. $19,823, or 2%, from interest on savings and temporary cash investments. The remaining revenue came from the "Airbag Clearinghouse" and other miscellaneous sources.

Triangle AIDS Network

P.O. Box 12279
Beaumont, TX 77726   **Phone:**   (409) 832-8338
USA

Contact Person: Sherridan Futt, Executive Director.   **Officers or Principals:** Sherridan Futt, Executive Director ($35,525); Steve Bean, President ($0); Jeff McManus, Vice President ($0); Patsy Brumfield, Treasurer; Evonne Mondy, Secretary.
Mission or Interest: AIDS education and support for people with AIDS.
Accomplishments: In 1994 the Network spent $471,615 on its programs. It produced approximately 25,000 pieces of printed material.

Net Revenue: 1994 $511,707 ($349,600, or 68%, from government grants) **Net Expenses:** $552,939 85%/13%/2%
Net Assets: $90,326 **Citations:** 0:255
Tax Status: 501(c)(3)
Board of Directors or Trustees: Corky Cullins, Mary Williams, Joann Benjamin, Susan Oliver, Tamara Duncan, Jim Courville, Don Kelly, Davis Franklin, Deborah Washington, Nathan Wright.
Other Information: The Network received $349,600, or 68% of revenue, from government grants. $157,523, or 31%, from gifts and grants awarded by foundations, businesses, and individuals. $3,794 net, or 1%, from special fund-raising events. The remaining revenue came from membership dues and dividends and interest from securities.

Trilateral Commission
345 E. 46th St.
New York, NY 10017   **Phone:** (212) 661-1180
USA

Contact Person: Charles B. Heck, President.   **Officers or Principals:** Charles B. Heck, President ($147,000); Christina Hanophy, Treasurer ($67,501); Peter White, Secretary ($58,501); Marshall Hornblower, Assistant Secretary.
Mission or Interest: "Analysis and discussion toward developing cooperative solutions to common world problems." Emphasis on the United Nations and international governmental organizations, and collective action.
Accomplishments: In the fiscal year ending June 1994 the Commission spent $489,830 on its programs. These included the publication of papers and task force reports.
Net Revenue: FY ending 6/94 $556,491 **Net Expenses:** $664,809 74%/19%/7% **Net Assets:** $51,535
Citations: 267:61
Tax Status: 501(c)(3)
Other Information: The Commission received $543,180, or 98% of revenue, from gifts and grants awarded by foundations, businesses, and individuals. $5,609, or 1%, from subscription revenue. $5,434, or 1%, from the sale of publications. The remaining revenue came from interest on savings and temporary cash investments, royalties, and other miscellaneous sources.

Trust for Public Land
116 New Montgomery St., 4th Floor
San Francisco, CA 94105   **Phone:** (415) 495-4014
USA

Contact Person: Mary Morelli, Director of National Development.
Officers or Principals: Martin Rosen, President ($156,398); Robert McIntyre, Senior Vice President/Treasurer ($104,253); Ralph W. Benson, Executive Vice President ($101,137); F. Jerome Tone, Chairman; Christopher G. Sawyer, Vice Chairman; Nelson J. Lee, Secretary; Corey Brown, Director of Government Affairs.
Mission or Interest: The Trust purchases, preserves, and gives or sells land in order to insure its preservation for future generations. Most of the land is awarded to various governments and government agencies, but some is awarded to nonprofit organizations as well. Works with other land trusts and instructs them on how to do the same.
Accomplishments: Since its founding, the Trust has preserved over half a million acres of land, including a key role in preserving Walden Woods in Massachusetts. In the fiscal year ending March 1995, the Trust awarded approximately 10,152 acres of land valued at $73,394,054 to various organizations (almost entirely governments and agencies), and in return received $66,823,369; so the net amount awarded was $6,570,685. The Trust often purchases land with below market-rate loans payable, and loans the money for sales at market rates.
Net Revenue: FY ending 3/95 $27,304,653 ($1,847,334, or 7%, from government grants) **Net Expenses:** $26,486,923 87%/10%/3% **Net Assets:** $27,871,868 **Citations:** 226:74
Products or Services: The purchase, maintenance, and conveyance of land, technical assistance for government and nonprofit agencies, and lobbying. The Trust spent $263,312 on lobbying; $54,696 on grassroots lobbying, and $208,616 on the direct lobbying of legislators. This was a decrease of 51% from the previous year.
Tax Status: 501(c)(3)
Board of Directors or Trustees: John Baird, Eugene Barth, Sara Brown, Robert Carlson, George Denny, William Evarts, Jr., Douglas Ferguson, Eugene Lee, Charles Peterson, Douglass Raff, Marie Ridder, Nancy Russell, James Sano.
Other Information: Established in 1973. The Trust is a member of the Environmental Federation of America. The Trust received $20,295,032, or 74% of net revenue, from gifts and grants awarded by foundations, businesses, and individuals. (These included $75,000 from the Mary Flagler Cary Charitable Trust, $40,000 from the Bullitt Foundation, $37,655 from the Environmental Federation of America, $34,266 from the Environmental Federation of California, $20,000 from the Joyce Mertz-Gilmore Foundation, $5,000 from the New-Land Foundation, $5,000 from the Rex Foundation, $5,000 from the American Conservation Association, $2,259 from the Environmental Federation of California, and $1,000 from the Compton Foundation.) $1,847,334, or 7%, from government grants. (The Trust also received $65,422,869 in payment from various federal, state, and local governments and agencies. Combined with the grants and reimbursed fees, this is a total of $68,238,932 from taxpayer-funded sources for the fiscal year.) $1,524,539, or 6%, from dividends and interest from securities. $1,386,705, or 5%, from fees for technical assistance. $968,729, or 4%, from reimbursements by public agencies for "certain costs incurred in helping them acquire open space and park lands." $307,826, or 1%, from interest on savings and temporary cash investments. $150,254, or 1%, from the sale of securities. The Trust held $18,688,295, or 28% of total assets, in land holdings. $18,217,995, or 27%, in investment securities. $17,835,544, or 27%, in savings and temporary cash investments.

Twentieth Century Fund

41 E. 70th St.
New York, NY 10021   **Phone:**   (212) 535-4441   **E-Mail:** xxthfund@ix.netcom.com
USA   **Web-Page:** http://epn.org/tcf.html

Contact Person: Richard C. Leone, President.
Officers or Principals: Richard C. Leone, President ($221,063); Beverly Goldberg, Vice President ($87,967); Michelle Miller, Vice President ($74,690); Gregory Anrig, Carol Starmack, Vice Presidents; Elliot D. Sclar, Project Director; Brewster C. Denny, Chairman; Rep. James A. Leach (R-IA), Vice Chairman; Charles V. Hamilton, Secretary; Richard Ravitch, Treasurer.
Mission or Interest: "Policy oriented studies of economic, political, and social issues."
Accomplishments: In the fiscal year ending June 1994, the Fund spent $744,145 on programs and awarded grants of $11,500 for two public television stations. Projects that have resulted in books or other publication were; American Energy Policy, Benjamin V. Cohen and the Spirit of the New Deal, Concentration of Media Ownership, Defense Conversion, Future of American Cities, Future of Capitalism, Privacy, Abortion and the Supreme Court, Public Policy Strategies for America's Homeless, Race, Poverty and Politics, The Wage Crunch, Arms Control, Virtues and Limits of Markets, and others. The fund works in partnership with the Council on Foreign Relations and the Carnegie Corporation in support of the Center for Preventive Action. Projects on economics have included Robert Kuttner, James K. Galbraith, Elliot Sclar, Orley Ashenfelter, and Cecelia Rouse. The Fund also conducts the "New Federalist Papers Project."
Net Revenue: FY ending 6/94 $4,626,337 **Net Expenses:** $3,082,261 **Net Assets:** $49,990,683
Products or Services: Recent books include: Top Heavy: A Study of the Increasing Inequality of Wealth in America by Edward Wolff, Utopia Lost: The United Nations and World Order by Rosemary Righter, Ecological Disaster: Cleaning Up the Hidden Legacy of the Soviet Regime by Murray Feshbash, and many others, often published by other publishing companies including MIT Press, Brookings Institution, Princeton University Press, and others.
Tax Status: 501(c)(3)
Board of Directors or Trustees: H. Brandt Ayers (*Anniston Star*), Peter Berle (National Audubon Society), Hon. Jose Cabranes (U.S. Court of Appeals), Joseph Califano Jr. (Center on Addiction and Substance Abuse), Alexander Capron (Univ. of S. California), Hodding Carter, III (Main ST. T.V. Productions), Edward David, Jr., Lewis Kaden, P. Michael Pitfield (Senate of Canada), Harvey Sloane (Leukemia Society of America), Theodore Sorensen (Presidential Special Counsel, 1961-64), Shirley Williams (Kennedy School of Government, Harvard Univ.), William Julius Wilson (Univ. of Chicago).
Other Information: The Fund was endowed by liberal businessman Edward A. Filene (1860-1937). Filene took over his father's chain of women's specialty stores, but was removed from control when his management policies, which gave employees "near absolute power," caused a rift between himself and the other shareholders. Filene used his money to create the Co-operative League in 1919. In 1922 the League was renamed the Twentieth Century Fund. Following the stock-market crash of 1929, the Fund began to focus more on economics. Later, with the rise of communism, the Fund focused more on foreign policy and security. Filene was an impassioned champion of the New Deal. The Fund played a large role in the institution of the New Deal. The Fund's study, Stock Market Control, was an acknowledged source for portions of the Fletcher-Rayburn Bill, later the Securities Exchange Act of 1934. Other influential works from the Fund included; Asian Drama, by the 1974 co-winner of the Nobel Prize in economics, socialist, and father of modern population policy, Gunnar Myrdal. Performing Arts - The Economic Dilemma by William Baumol and William Bowen, whose themes "remain the most effective justification for maintaining public support for the arts." Past trustees included Albert Shanker, Vernon E. Jordan, Jr., Michael Harrington, John Kenneth Galbraith, Arthur Burns, Robert J. Oppenheimer, Benjamin V. Cohen, Adolpf A. Berle, Jr., and Paul H. Douglas. The Fund received $2,528,173, or 55% of revenue, from dividends and interest from securities. $1,926,082, or 42%, from capital gains on the sale of securities. $53,984, or 1%, from the sale of publications. $38,381, or 1%, from royalties. The remaining revenue came from other miscellaneous sources.

Union of Concerned Scientists (UCS)

Two Brattle Square
Cambridge, MA 02238-9105   **Phone:**   (617) 547-5552   **E-Mail:** menu@ucsusa.org
USA   **Fax:**   (617) 864-9405   **Web-Page:** http://www.ucsusa.org

Officers or Principals: Howard Ris, Vice President ($92,718); Robert Bland, Development Director ($77,351); Robert Pollard, Nuclear Safety Engineer ($75,276); Alden Meyer, Legislative Director; Warren Leon, Deputy Director for Programs; Jonathan Dean, Arms Advisor; Henry Kendall, Chairman; Lynda Dreyfuss, Secretary; Jennifer Cummings-Saxton, Secretary.
Mission or Interest: Advocates public policy that addresses technology and its effects on national security and the environment. "Two common threads - global sustainability and global security - wind their way through UCS's programs, weaving them together into a unified vision: achieving a secure and sustainable world without sacrificing the environment of tomorrow."
Accomplishments: UCS pioneered "new analytic techniques" to demonstrate "the breadth of renewable energy resources in 12 Midwestern states." Minnesota and Nebraska enacted legislation to develop renewable energy technologies due in part to these efforts. In 1994 they spent $821,807 on this renewable energy program. With research and advocacy they persuaded the California Air Resources Board to uphold the state's zero-emission vehicle mandate requiring that electric cars be offered for sale beginning in 1998. They spent $440,922 on transportation policy programs. Lobbied congress to spend more money on arms control and monitoring. "In response to an urgent appeal from UCS, the Department of Defense agreed to provide funds to improve controls on fissile material in the former Soviet Union." $509,986 was spent on arms control programs, and $737,756 was spent on global resources programs.
Net Revenue: FY ending 9/94 $4,603,212 **Net Expenses:** $4,024,102 80%/4%/16% **Net Assets:** $1,954,049
Citations: 239:70

Products or Services: Research and educational programs. Numerous books and publication. Speakers Bureau (can be reached on e-mail at speakers@ucscsa.org). Links with other organizations, such as the National Religious Partnership for the Environment, as well as other scientists. Lobbying - spent $185,923 on the direct lobbying of legislators. This was down from $208,337 the year before, and from $220,754 two years prior. They contracted Joe Caves to act as their legislative advocate. He was compensated $42,000.
Tax Status: 501(c)(3) **Annual Report:** Yes. **Employees:** 50
Board of Directors or Trustees: Prof. Sallie Chisholm (MIT), Alvin Duskin (Chair, Trinity Flywheel Batteries), Prof. Thomas Eisner (Cornell Univ.), Prof. Emeritus James Fay (MIT), Prof. Daniel Fisher (Harvard Univ.), Prof. Kurt Gottfried (Cornell Univ.), James Hoyte (Assoc. V.P., Harvard Univ.), Leonard Meeker (former legal advisor to the U.S. Department of State), Hon. Claudine Schneider (former member of U.S. Congress), Adele Simmons (Pres., John D. & Catherine T. MacArthur Found.), Ellyn Weiss (former Assistant Attorney General for Environmental Protection, MA), Prof. Emeritus Victor Weisskopf (MIT).
Periodicals: *Nucleus* (quarterly magazine).   **Internships:** Yes.
Other Information: Established in 1969. They have a Washington office and a West Coast office; 1616 P St., N.W., Suite 310, Washington, DC 20036, voice (202) 332-0900, fax (202) 332-0905 and 2397 Shattuck Ave., Suite 203, Berkeley, CA 94704, voice (510) 843-1872, fax (510) 843-3785. Their Cambridge headquarters recently installed solar powered electrical cells on the roof. The PV panels provide 2 kilowatts under bright sun conditions and up to 600 watts on cloudy days. This project was jointly funded by UCS with Cambridge Electric and the Electric Power Research Institute. The Union received $4,422,860, or 96% of revenue, from gifts and grants awarded by foundations, companies and individuals. (These grants included $295,000 from the Joyce Foundation, $170,000 from the Joyce Mertz-Gilmore Foundation, $50,000 from the Wallace Genetic Foundation, $42,579 from the Ploughshares Fund, $35,755 from the Environmental Federation of America, $35,000 from the Winston Foundation for World Peace, $10,000 from the Compton Foundation, $10,000 from the New-Land Foundation, $2,500 from the One World Fund, $1,000 from the Aaron and Martha Schecter Foundation, and $869 from the Environmental Federation of California. In 1995, $25,000 from the Rockefeller Foundation.) $101,058, or 2%, from the renting and leasing of mailing lists and labels. $52,697, or 1%, from interest on savings and temporary cash investments. The remaining revenue came from royalties, honoraria, and other sources of miscellaneous income.

Union of Needletrades, Industrial and Textile Employees (UNITE)

Mission or Interest: UNITE was recently created by merging the International Ladies' Garment Workers' Union and the Amalgamated Clothing and Textile Workers Union. For more information, see these two unions' separate entries.
Other Information: An organizer for UNITE testifying before legislative hearings in California said, "On the one hand, (garment) industry leaders and their government supporters claim that they want to clean up sweatshops...and even deplore the flagrant violation of labor standards that prevail in at least one-third of the region's garment factories. Yet when it comes to one solution that will surely work: the empowerment of the workers through unionization, the industry and government supporters recoil in horror, because this will drive up costs! You can't have it both ways. Sweatshops will not disappear without a rise in labor costs."

Unitarian Universalist Service Committee
130 Prospect St.
Cambridge, MA 02139-1845   **Phone:** (617) 868-6600
USA   **Fax:** (617) 868-7102

Contact Person: Steve Schick. **Officers or Principals:** Dr. Richard S. Scobie, Executive Director ($97,824); Linda Chadwick, Director of Administration and Finance ($60,365); Louis V. Witherite, Director of International Programs ($60,050); Dorothy Smith Patterson, President; Jewel Graham, Vice President; Warner Henderson, Treasurer; Neil H. Shadle, Secretary.
Mission or Interest: "To seek a more just and humane society by...providing experiences that promote self-determination and human freedom...resisting and changing oppressive institutions and practices...educating and mobilizing individuals and groups for service and action...bringing occasional emergency relief where human dignity and rights are violated."
Accomplishments: In the fiscal year ending March 1995, the Committee spent $2,561,342 on its programs. The largest program, with expenditures of $575,705, was the domestic agenda. This included a program to "develop, design, and implement programs which will contribute to ending childhood poverty and hunger and insure the human rights of all children." Another goal was to "develop, design, and implement programs which will promote volunteer and professional public policy advocacy and service." The remaining programs focused on international efforts in Asia and Latin America. These programs included: Issues related to the environmental cleanup of abandoned U.S. military bases in the Philippines. Women's rights, including human rights and "reproductive rights" in India, Philippines, Nicaragua, Haiti, El Salvador, Guatemala, and Mexico. Earthquake relief for women in India. Support for a "peasants' movement" in Haiti and a book documenting human rights abuses. Lobbied in the U.S. on behalf of welfare programs and against block grants, against the 1995 Balanced Budget Amendment, and met with Rep. Jim McDermott (D-WA, one of congress' strongest supporters of the Clinton health-care plan) on health-care reform. Awarded grants for emergency relief at home and abroad.
Net Revenue: FY ending 3/95 $3,275,384 **Net Expenses:** $3,353,490 76%/6%/17% **Net Assets:** $4,674,816
Citations: 25:167
Products or Services: Educational activities, organization, grants. Spent $8,475 on lobbying. This was down 76% from $34,738 the year before.
Tax Status: 501(c)(3)
Board of Directors or Trustees: Nancy Bartlett, Albert Boyce, William Brach, Richard Fuhrman, Kwasi Harris, Olivia Holmes, Mary-Ella Holst, Margaret Sanstad.
Other Information: Affiliated with Unitarian Universalist Association. The Committee received $3,154,869, or 96% of revenue, from direct and indirect public support in the form of gifts and grants awarded by foundations, affiliates, businesses, and individuals. $95,910, or 3%, from dividends and interest on securities. The remaining revenue came from the sale of goods, mortgage interest, interest on savings and temporary cash investments, and other miscellaneous sources.

United Action for Animals

P.O. Box 635, Lenox Hill Station
New York, NY 10021   **Phone:**   (212) 249-9178
USA

Contact Person: Julie Van Ness, President.
Officers or Principals: Julie Van Ness, President ($37,595); Melanie Darby, Secretary/Treasurer ($0).
Mission or Interest: "To educate the public through publications, direct mail, and advertising to apply alternative methods in medical research other than cruelty to animals and the utilization of the same."
Accomplishments: In 1994 United Action for Animals spent $138,341 on its programs.
Net Revenue: 1994 $212,973 **Net Expenses:** $169,820 81%/8%/11% **Net Assets:** $157,223
Tax Status: 501(c)(3)
Board of Directors or Trustees: Joy Milke, Anna Briggs, Marion Jo Dix, Virginia Dungan, Marilyn Mason.
Other Information: The organization received $211,577, or 99% of total revenue, from gifts and grants awarded by foundations, businesses, and individuals. $2,437, or 1%, from interest on savings and temporary cash investments. The remaining revenue came from dividends and interest from securities, and other miscellaneous sources.

United Brotherhood of Carpenters and Joiners of America (UBC)

101 Constitution Ave., N.W.
Washington, DC 20001   **Phone:**   (202) 546-6206
USA

Contact Person: Sigurd Lucassen, President.   **Officers or Principals:** Sigurd Lucassen, President ($192,964); Paschel McGuinness, 1st Vice President ($174,381); James Bledsoe, Treasurer ($167,679); James Patterson, Secretary ($167,679); Salvatore Pelliccio, Executive Board ($125,051); Douglas Banes, Executive Board ($125,051); James Slebiska, Executive Board ($125,051); Armando Vergara, Executive Board ($125,051); James Smith, Executive Board ($125,051); William Michalowski, Executive Board ($125,051); Fred E. Carter, Executive Board ($125,051); Patrick Mattei, Executive Board ($125,051).
Mission or Interest: Union representing approximately 500,000 workers. "To organize workers in the carpentry industry for better working conditions and advancement." A member of the AFL-CIO.
Accomplishments: In 1994 the Union spent $1,466,756 on labor organizing. It paid $3,762,761 to affiliates, including $1,867,550 to the AFL-CIO. It made $4,911,000 in loans to locals and regional councils. $40,000 in strike benefits was paid.
Net Revenue: 1994 $57,789,431 ($8,040,038, or 14%, from government grants) **Net Expenses:** $50,354,472
Net Assets: $149,398,824
Tax Status: 501(c)(5)
Board of Directors or Trustees: Jose Collado, William Nipper, Michael Draper, H. Paul Johnson.
Periodicals: *Carpenter* (bimonthly newsletter).
Other Information: The Union received $40,525,805, or 69% of total revenue, from membership dues. $8,040,038, or 14%, from government grants. (These included $3,723,000 from the U.S. Department of Health and Human Services' Superfund Worker Training Program.) $7,037,147, or 12%, from dividends and interest from securities. $1,474,693, or 2%, from reimbursed expenses. $659,498, or 1%, or interest on savings and temporary cash investments. $346,536, or 1%, from rental income. The remaining revenue came from program service fees, the sale of inventory, advertising, legal settlements, and other miscellaneous sources. The Union had full ownership of four real estate companies valued at $10,943,896.

United Farm Workers National Union (UFW)

P.O. Box 62
Keene, CA 93531   **Phone:**   (805) 822-5571
USA   **Fax:**   (805) 822-6103

Contact Person: Arturo S. Rodriguez, President.
Officers or Principals: Efren Barajas, National Vice President ($19,126); Dolores Huerta, Vice President ($10,689); Arturo S. Rodriguez, President ($9,524); David M. Martinez, Secretary/Treasurer; Irv Hershenbaum, Cecilia Ruiz, Vice Presidents.
Mission or Interest: Union representing approximately 50,000 members "to unite under its banner all individuals employed as agricultural and related laborers, regardless of race, creed, sex or nationality." Member of the AFL-CIO.
Accomplishments: Since its founding in 1962 (when it was called the National Farm Workers Association), the UFW has worked to organize migrant and farm laborers. In 1965 the Union found its most effective tool, the consumer boycott. A successful boycott of California grapes led to the first ever collective bargaining agreement for farm workers. In 1972 it joined the AFL-CIO. In 1975 California Governor Jerry Brown signed the Agriculture Labor Relations Act, "written in part by Cesar Chavez and members of his legal staff." The union provides organizing, anti-pesticide advocacy, legal aid, and Radio Campesina, a network of radio stations focusing on the needs of farm workers. The Union's 'get out the vote' effort on behalf of California Assemblyman Mike Machado (D-Linden) during a recall election in 1995 is widely credited with helping the assemblyman keep his seat. The Union successfully beat back an effort to prevent the renaming of San Francisco's Army Street after Cesar Chavez.
Net Revenue: 1994 $2,960,922 **Net Expenses:** $3,488,351 **Net Assets:** $3,012,546
Products or Services: "Wrath of Grapes" video.
Tax Status: 501(c)(5)

Internships: Yes, in the areas of legal action, public action, administration and public relations.

Other Information: Affiliated with the Cesar Chavez Foundation at the same address. The Union was founded by Cesar Chavez (1928-1993). Vice President Dolores Huerta is an Honorary Chair of the Democratic Socialists of America, and was a featured speaker at the National Organization for Women's Washington DC abortion rights rally in 1995. The Union received $1,705,685, or 57% of total revenue, from gifts and grants awarded by foundations, unions, and individuals. (These grants included $750 from the Vanguard Foundation.) $898,245, or 30%, from membership dues. (It is unusual for a 501(c)(5) labor union to receive more in gifts and grants than in membership dues.) $195,494, or 6%, from membership services. $114,479, or 4%, from interest on savings and temporary cash investments. $44,331 net, or 1%, from the sale of inventory. The remaining revenue came from the sale of assets, and other miscellaneous revenue. The Union lost $53,746 on an investment.

United Food and Commercial Workers International Union (UFCW)

1775 K St., N.W.
Washington, DC 20006   **Phone:** (202) 223-3111
USA

Contact Person: Douglas H. Dority, President.

Officers or Principals: Douglas H. Dority, President ($276,683); Gerald R. Menapace, Secretary/Treasurer ($222,712); Carl C. Huber, Vice President ($192,026); David T. Barry, Vice President ($192,022); Jay H. Foreman, Executive Vice President ($192,022); Robert B. Novicoff, Vice President ($177,716); Jory P. McChesney, Vice President ($139,271); Joseph E. Hansen, Vice President ($139,239); Walter A. Sauter, Vice President ($137,464); Gary R. Nebeker, Vice President ($128,989); Willie L. Baker, Jr., Vice President ($128,989); Patricia A. Scarcelli, Vice President ($128,989); Beth S. Shulman, Vice President ($128,989); Dwayne Carman, Vice President ($128,832); Robert A. Petronella, Vice President ($128,832); Sean Harrigan, Vice President ($128,832); Sarah P. Amos, Vice President ($128,832); Ronald Preston, Vice President ($128,832); Larry L. Kolman, Vice President ($128,832); Frank R. Dininger, Vice President ($128,832); Robert Morand, Vice President ($125,014); Thomas Kukovica, Vice President ($121,634); Marvin Hrubes, Vice President ($115,282); Douglas L. Couttee, Vice President ($108,331).

Mission or Interest: Labor union representing approximately 1,350,000 workers in 600 locals. "To organize all workers for economic, moral and social advancement of their conditions and status." Affiliated with the AFL-CIO.

Accomplishments: In the fiscal year ending April 1995, the Union paid $32,047,863 in benefits to members, including $9,585,405 in strike benefits and assistance. The Union paid $6,774,122 to affiliates, including $4,649,152 to the AFL-CIO.

Net Revenue: FY ending 4/95 $124,159,094 ($65,808, or less than 1%, from government grants.) **Net Expenses:** $122,476,952 **Net Assets:** (-$53,613,384)

Tax Status: 501(c)(5)

Periodicals: *UFCW Leadership Update* (monthly newsletter) and *UFCW Action* (bimonthly newsletter).

Other Information: The Union received $115,871,091, or 93% of total revenue, from membership dues. $2,786,086, or 2%, from a reduction in a "legal judgement estimate." $1,902,890, or 2%, from dividends and interest from securities. $1,725,079, or 1%, from the sale of assets. $1,080,517, or 1%, from gifts and grants. The remaining revenue came from program service fees, interest on savings and temporary cash investments, government grants, capital gains on the sale of securities, and other miscellaneous sources.

United Garment Workers of America (UGW)

P.O. Box 239
Hermitage, TN 37076   **Phone:** (615) 889-9221
USA   **Fax:**   (615) 885-3102

Contact Person: Dave Johnson, President.

Officers or Principals: Dave Johnson, President ($59,450); Timothy Fitzpatrick, Treasurer ($59,450); Evelyn Forsythe, General Auditor ($41,069).

Mission or Interest: Union with approximately 25,000 members. Member of the AFL-CIO.

Net Revenue: FY ending 6/94 $1,383,119 **Net Expenses:** $1,407,237 **Net Assets:** $2,286,663

Tax Status: 501(c)(5)

Board of Directors or Trustees: Tom Agan, Charles Boyd, Regina Lucero, Hattie Scruggs, Perseus Tosco, Anne Ozipko.

Periodicals: *The Garment Worker* (monthly newsletter).

Other Information: The union received $1,244,208, or 89% of total revenue, from membership dues. $79,362, or 6%, from "label fees charged in order to obtain the right to use the union label." $61,592, or 4%, from interest on savings and temporary cash investments. The remaining revenue came from rental income, and other miscellaneous sources.

United Nations Association of the USA (UNA-USA)

485 5th Ave.
New York, NY 10017   **Phone:** (212) 697-3232
USA   **Fax:**   (212) 682-9185

Contact Person: J. Tessitore, Director.

Officers or Principals: E. Luck, President ($198,000); R. Cwerman, Vice President ($107,430); N. Hunt, Director ($80,000); S. Dimoff, Executive Director; Thomas B. Morgan, CEO; John C. Whitehead, Chair of the Association; William J. vanden Huevel, Chair, Board of Governors; Louis Perlmutter, Chair, Executive Committee; Elliot Richardson, Cyrus Vance, Co-Chairs, National Council.

Mission or Interest: Research and educational activities "dedicated to strengthening the United Nations system and to enhancing U.S. participation in international institutions through various publications and educational exchanges with other nonprofit organizations." Global policy study in the areas of economics and development, peace keeping policy, and the environment. Special focus on youth and "preparing young people for global leadership through the study and discussion of multilateral issues."

Accomplishments: 23,000 members nationwide, 170 community-based chapters and divisions. In 1993 the Association spent $2,525,144 on its programs. Top projects included $399,095 spent on Congressional Affairs, $254,208 on the Washington Office, and $230,381 on the "Membership Ford Grant." Other projects included; *The Interdependent*, issues before the General Assembly, "Quadrilateral Studies," "The New World Order," narcotics project, security project, and others. $10,700 was spent on grants to local chapters and divisions. The Association held two fund-raising receptions; The UNA Ball to honor permanent representatives to the United Nations, and a Washington Concert and Dinner to honor the Ambassadors accredited to the U.S. and the Organization of American States. These special events cost $247,371 and raised net $491,791.

Net Revenue: 1993 $6,704,958 **Net Expenses:** $4,814,659 52%/15%/29% **Net Assets:** $3,730,095 **Citations:** 34:154
Products or Services: Publications, seminars, research, special events, more.
Tax Status: 501(c)(3)
Board of Directors or Trustees: Peter Adriance (Baha'is of the U.S.), Christopher Brody, Anne Bryant (American Assn. of University Women), Edison Dick (National Capital Area Division), Prof. Rodolfo de la Garza (Univ. of TX), Patrick Gerschel, Maurice Greenberg (Chair, American International Group), Mary Grefe (Iowa Peace Inst.), August Heckscher, William Hensley (NANA), Ruth Hinerfeld, Ramesh Krishnamurthy, Leilynne Lau, Estelle Linzer, John Luke, Jr., Amb. Donald McHenry (Foreign Service School, Georgetown Univ.), Ken Miller (Vice Chair, C.S. First Boston Corp.), William Miller, Prof. James Nafziger, Leo Nevas, William Norman (Exec. Vice Pres., Natl. Railroad Passenger Corp.), Henry Picker, Shirley Quisenberry, Arthur Ross, William Rouhana, Jr., Betty Sandford, Jack Sheinkman (Pres., Amalgated Clothing & Textile Workers Union), Michael Sonnenfeldt, Hon. Cyrus Vance (Sec. of State, 1977-1979), Edwin Wesely, Hon. Richard Williamson, Hon. Milton Wolf.
Periodicals: *The Interdependent.*
Other Information: Founded in 1943 as the American Association for the United Nations (AAUN), it was first led by Eleanor Roosevelt. In 1964 the AAUN merged with the U.S. Committee for the United Nations, creating the UNA-USA. The Association has a Washington, DC office to provide information and advice to federal policy makers; 1010 Vermont Ave., N.W., Suite 904, Washington, DC 20005, voice (202) 347-5004, fax (202) 628-5945. The Association received $6,704,958, or 81% of revenue, from grants awarded by foundations, companies and individuals. (These grants included $5,000 from the Ploughshares Fund, and $200 from the Compton Foundation.) $1,048,772, or 13%, from membership dues. $491,793, or 6%, from program services. The remaining revenue came from interest on savings and temporary cash investments. The Association paid several consultants, including, Burson Marsteller of New York city ($560,931), Frederick Marketing Group of Morris Township, NJ ($75,000), Washington, Inc, of the District of Columbia ($54,232), George Trescher Associates of New York city ($52,555), and Bud Pomeranz of Oakhurst, NJ ($36,250).

United States Catholic Conference (USCC)

3211 4th St., N.E.
Washington, DC 20005   **Phone:**   (202) 541-3184
USA   **Fax:**   (202) 541-3339

Contact Person: Timothy Collins, Deputy Executive Director. **Officers or Principals:** Rev. James H. Garland, Chairman; Rev. Joseph R. Hacala, Jr.; James Cardinal Hickey, Advisor.
Mission or Interest: Operates the Campaign for Human Development (CHD), a program that collects money from American Catholics and distributes it to various anti-poverty and community organizations. The CHD also funds numerous abortion rights and homosexuals' rights organizations.
Accomplishments: Since its foundation, the CHD has collected and distributed over $230 million. In 1995 the CHD celebrated its 25th anniversary in Chicago. Speakers included Marxist Prof. Cornel West (Harvard), Dolores Huerta (United Farmworkers of America), Bertha Lewis (Brooklyn ACORN), Winona LaDuke (Indigenous Women's Network), William Greider (political editor, *Rolling Stone*), Rep. Marcy Kaptur (D-OH), Pablo Eisenberg (Center for Community Change), and Si Kahn (Grassroots Leadership). In 1994 CHD distributed $7,851,000. Recipients included; $436,000 for fourteen ACORN affiliates, $70,000 for the Farm Labor Research Project, $50,000 each for the White Earth Land Recovery Project, and National Alliance of HUD Tenants, $45,000 for the Southwest Network for Environmental and Economic Justice, $40,000 for the Tennessee Industrial Renewal Network, $35,000 each for the Center for Community Advocacy, Center for Community Action, and People Acting in Community Together, $30,000 each for the Idaho Rural Council, and Center for Women's Economic Alternatives, $25,000 each for Grassroots Leadership, Hotel Workers Organizing Project, Direct Action for Rights and Equality, and the Northwest Organizing Project, $24,000 for Montana People's Action, $21,000 for the AFDC Coalition, $20,000 for the Western Colorado Congress, $15,000 for the Environmental Health Coalition, and $10,000 for Esperanza Unida.
Tax Status: Nonprofit.
Other Information: Member of the National Coalition to Abolish the Death Penalty.

United States Justice Foundation (USJF)

2091 E. Valley Parkway, Suite 1C
Escondido, CA 92027   **Phone:**   (619) 741-8086
USA   **Fax:**   (619) 741-9548

Contact Person: Gary G. Kreep, Executive Director. **Officers or Principals:** Gary G. Kreep, Executive Director ($96,000); Norman Olney, Treasurer ($0); Stewart Mollrich, Secretary ($0).

Mission or Interest: "To protect the civil, constitutional, property, and human rights of the American public...represents individuals or groups before Courts or other arbitrators in matters where the rights of such individuals or groups and the rights of others may be imperiled by the lack of such representation."

Accomplishments: "Filed lawsuits which generated publicity over illegal psychological testing of students in California. Publicity lead to parent revolt over the testing program and its ultimate de-funding." In 1994 the Foundation spent $776,401 on its programs.

Net Revenue: 1994 $1,704,116 **Net Expenses:** $1,808,777 43%/10%/47% **Net Assets:** (-$177,276) **Citations:** 11:195

Tax Status: 501(c)(3) **Employees:** 3

Periodicals: Newsletter. **Internships:** Yes.

Other Information: The Foundation contracted the McLean, VA, firm of Bruce W. Eberle and Associates to provide "creative" services. The firm was paid $175,458. The Justice Foundation received $1,623,915, or 95% of revenue, from gifts and grants awarded by foundations, businesses, and individuals. $79,268, or 5%, from mailing list rentals. The remaining revenue came from the sale of newsletters, interest on savings and temporary cash investments, and dividends and interest from securities.

United States Public Interest Research Group (USPIRG)

215 Pennsylvania Ave., S.E.
Washington, DC 20003 **Phone:** (202) 546-9707 **E-Mail:** pirg@pirg.org
USA **Fax:** (202) 546-2461

Contact Person: Gene Karpinski, President.

Officers or Principals: Gene Karpinski, President ($34,615); Douglas Phelps, Chair ($0); David Wood, Secretary ($0).

Mission or Interest: Lobbying division of USPIRG. "Direct and grassroots lobbying on a wide variety of consumer, environmental, energy and government reform issues and producing consumer surveys and investigative reports."

Accomplishments: In the fiscal year ending June 1994, the organization spent $286,620 on its programs.

Net Revenue: FY ending 6/94 $361,265 **Net Expenses:** $328,321 82%/15%/3% **Net Assets:** $285,242

Tax Status: 501(c)(4)

Board of Directors or Trustees: Maureen Kirk, Jay Halfon, Britta Ipri, Janet Domenitz, Alleia Grouppe, Samara Rifkin, Diane Brown, Adjay Harris.

Periodicals: *Citizen Agenda* (quarterly newsletter).

Other Information: Affiliated with 501(c)(3) United States Public Interest Research Group Education Fund at the same address. The organizations were started by Ralph Nader. The two national affiliates together had net revenues of $668,247, net expenses of $572,903, and net assets of $406,397. Gene Karpinski served as president of both and was paid a combined $39,057. USPIRG received $348,253, or 97% of revenue, from gifts and grants awarded by foundations, businesses, and individuals. $6,426, or 2%, from the sale of inventory. $6,086, or 1%, from interest on savings and temporary cash investments.

United States Public Interest Research Group Education Fund (USPIRG)

215 Pennsylvania Ave., S.E.
Washington, DC 20003 **Phone:** (202) 546-9707 **E-Mail:** pirg@pirg.org
USA **Fax:** (202) 546-2461

Contact Person: Paul Orum, Project Coordinator. **Officers or Principals:** Paul Orum, Project Coordinator ($31,877); Gene Karpinski, President ($4,442); Maureen Kirk, Chair ($0); David Wood, Secretary.

Mission or Interest: Research and education division of USPIRG. Pursues open government, consumer protection, environmental issues, and health issues.

Accomplishments: In the fiscal year ending June 1994, the Fund spent $237,007 on its programs. The largest program, with expenditures of $83,070, was Open Government, which included information on campaign financing and voter registration. $51,641 was spent on Toxics Right To Know, "enhancement of public participation in the prevention of toxic pollution." $35,465 was spent on environmental programs, including "issues such as solid waste, toxics, pesticides, global warming and ozone depletion." $31,963 on consumer education about product safety issues. Other projects included energy research and research on toxins. The Fund awarded $90,600 in grants to member PIRG's.

Net Revenue: FY ending 6/94 $306,982 **Net Expenses:** $244,582 97%/2%/1% **Net Assets:** $121,155

Tax Status: 501(c)(3)

Board of Directors or Trustees: Jay Halfon, Britta Ipri, Janet Domenitz, Alleia Grouppe, Samara Rifkin, Diane Brown, Adjay Harris.

Other Information: The Fund is affiliated with 501(c)(4) United States Public Interest Research Group at the same address. The organizations were started by Ralph Nader. The two national affiliates together had net revenues of $668,247, net expenses of $572,903, and net assets of $406,397. Gene Karpinski served as president of both and was paid a combined $39,057. The Fund received $299,787, or 98% of revenue, from direct and indirect public support in the form of gifts and grants awarded by foundations, businesses, affiliates, and individuals. (These grants included $40,250 from the Environmental Federation of America, $25,000 from the Rockefeller Family Fund, $25,000 from the Florence and John Schumann Foundation, $12,000 from the Tides Foundation, $10,000 from the Beldon II Fund.) $7,195, or 2%, from interest on savings and temporary cash investments.

United States Student Association

815 15th St., N.W., Suite 838
Washington, DC 20005 **Phone:** (202) 347-8772
USA

Contact Person: S. Leyton, President.   **Officers or Principals:** S. Leyton, President ($16,000); T. Cornelius, Vice President ($16,000); A. Johnson, Secretary ($0); M.K. Cullen, Treasurer.
Mission or Interest: Lobbying organization representing the interests of college students. Includes various caucuses such as the National Lesbian, Gay, Bisexual People of Color Caucus.
Accomplishments: In the fiscal year ending September 1993, the Association spent $245,020 on its programs. The largest program, costing $148,458, was the conferences and congress, which served as a forum for student associations. $82,874 was spent on field organization. $13,688 was spent on voter registration.
Net Revenue: FY ending 9/93 $394,208 **Net Expenses:** $381,916 64%/36%/1% **Net Assets:** (-$5,565)
Tax Status: 501(c)(4)
Other Information: The Association is affiliated with the 501(c)(3) United States Student Association Foundation at the same address. The Student Association received $152,337, or 39% of revenue, from membership dues. $126,042, or 32%, from program services. $56,545, or 14%, from royalties. The remaining revenue came from reimbursed expenses, publications, rental income, interest on savings and temporary cash investments, and other miscellaneous sources.

University Conversion Project

P.O. Box 748
Cambridge, MA 02142
USA

Mission or Interest: Seeks an end to military-funded research on campus.
Other Information: In 1993 the Project received $5,000 from the C.S. Fund.

Utne Reader

1624 Harmon Place, Suite 330
Minneapolis, MN 55403   **Phone:** (612) 338-5040   **E-Mail:** editor@utne.com
USA   **Fax:**   (612) 338-6043   **Web-Page:** http://www.utne.com

Contact Person: Eric Utne, President/Editor in Chief. **Officers or Principals:** Eric Utne, President/Editor in Chief; Hugh Delehanty, Editor; Craig Cox, Managing Editor; Marilyn Berlin Snell, Executive Editor; Joshua Glenn, Associate Editor.
Mission or Interest: Bimonthly journal of the "best of the alternative press." Reprints articles from other sources, including *Mother Jones*, *Rolling Stone*, *The Nation*, national daily newspapers, specialty journals (such as art and music criticism), and other sources. Features an on-line version of the *Utne Reader*, *The Utne Lens*, at "http://www.utne.com".
Accomplishments: Has an audited average paid circulation of 305,033. The median *Utne* subscriber is forty-one years old, female, attended graduate school, and has a household income of $75,500. *The New York Times* called it "one of the most distinctive voices in magazine journalism." *USA Today* said it is "arguably the best magazine published today." The *Utne Reader* attracts advertising from major corporations. The journal has been profitable since 1991.
Products or Services: Presents awards to other publications for outstanding journalism in several areas.
Tax Status: For profit.   **Periodicals:** *Utne Reader* (bimonthly journal).

Vanguard Public Foundation

383 Rhode Island St., Suite 301
San Francisco, CA 94103   **Phone:** (415) 487-2111
USA   **Fax:**   (415) 487-2124

Contact Person: Hari Dillon, Executive Director. **Officers or Principals:** Hari Dillon, Executive Director ($46,800); G. Flannery, Director ($41,375); Dan Geiger, Development Director ($37,776); M. Lynn, Director.
Mission or Interest: Foundation that awards grants to grassroots organizations. Also holds workshops on 'socially responsible giving.'
Accomplishments: In the fiscal year ending June 1994 the Foundation spent $1,380,600 on its programs, this included $1,083,035 in grants. The recipients of the largest grants included: $162,691 for the Indigenous Environmental Network, $74,548 for the Fund for a Free South Africa, $32,870 for the Funding Exchange, $11,000 for the Center for Immigrants Rights, $10,000 each for Barrios Unidos, California Coalition to End Barrio Warfare, and the Center for Human Development, Earth Connections, $9,661 for the Center for Health Care Innovation, $8,550 for the National Coalition of Education Activists, $8,000 each for the Chico Peace and Justice Center, Legal Services for Prisoners with Children, and the Fund for Southern Communities, $6,000 each for the Appalachian Community Fund, the Astraea National Lesbian Fund, Bread and Roses Community Fund, Crossroads Fund, Global Fund for Women, $5,700 for Health Care Reform Education Fund, $5,000 each for the Quixote Center (for an "Emergency Publicity Campaign in support of Mumia Abu-Jamal) and the Mountain Lion Foundation, $4,464 for Neighbor to Neighbor, $3,000 for the Chinook Fund, and many others.
Net Revenue: FY ending 6/94 $1,676,073 **Net Expenses:** $1,557,869 89%/6%/5% **Net Assets:** $348,813
Tax Status: 501(c)(3)
Board of Directors or Trustees: Jannen Antoine, Jane Baker, Nancy Feinstein, David Matchett, Carol Snow, Yvette Radford, Peter Stern, Holly Badgley Stern, Magdalena Avila, Kimo Campbell, Nancy Campbell, Kitty Kelly Epstein, Paul Kivel, Rob McKay, Walter Riley.
Other Information: The Foundation received $1,605,878, or 96% of revenue, from gifts and grants awarded by foundations, businesses, and individuals. (These grants included $25,000 from the New World Foundation, $25,000 from the Angelina Fund, $20,600 from the McKay Foundation.) $48,052 net, or 3%, from special fund-raising events. The remaining revenues came from returned grants, interest on savings and temporary cash investments, workshop fees, and other miscellaneous sources.

Vietnam Veterans Against the War Anti-Imperialist
P.O. Box 95172
Seattle, WA 98145   **Phone:**   (206) 324-5007   **E-Mail:** vvawai@igc.apc.org
USA   **Fax:**   (206) 324-3983

Mission or Interest: "We are part of a network of anti-imperialist veterans who are proud of our resistance to U.S. aggression around the world. In the 1970s, to be a Vietnam vet was to be against the war. That proud legacy must be carried forward today."
Periodicals: *Storm Warning* (quarterly newsletter).
Other Information: Vietnam Veterans is a membership organization. Free memberships are available to imprisoned and homeless or unemployed vets.

Village Voice / *VLS* / VV Publishing Corp.
36 Cooper Square
New York, NY 10003-7118   **Phone:**   (212) 475-3300
USA

Contact Person: Karen Durbin, Editor-in-Chief.   **Officers or Principals:** Karen Durbin, Editor-in-Chief; Doug Simmons, Managing Editor; Richard Goldstein, Executive Editor; David Schneiderman, Publisher.
Mission or Interest: A weekly newspaper distributed free in New York City. *The Village Voice* publishes articles and reviews that represent a leftist view. Publishes the new *VLS*, Voice Literary Supplement, a supplement included in the *Village Voice* and sold as a stand-alone publication.
Accomplishments: Paid circulation of approximately 135,900. The average *Village Voice* reader is 31 years old, male, has a college degree, is single/separated/divorced, and has a household income of $42,300.
Tax Status: For profit.   **Periodicals:** *Village Voice* (weekly tabloid), *VLS* (ten times a year magazine).

Violence Policy Center (VPC)
2000 P St., N.W., Suite 200
Washington, DC 20036   **Phone:**   (202) 822-8200
USA   **Fax:**   (202) 822-8205

Contact Person: Susan Glick.   **Officers or Principals:** Josh Sugarman, Executive Director.
Mission or Interest: Research and education on violence with a focus on the role of firearms in society. Works closely with the media. "The reality of firearms violence is that it stems not from 'guns in the wrong hands,' but from the virtually unregulated distribution of an inherently dangerous consumer product of which specific categories - such as handguns and assault weapons - are particularly prone to misuse."
Accomplishments: Josh Sugarman is considered a leading strategist for the gun control movement. His efforts have focused attention on assault weapons and he was instrumental in the effort to place Constitutional Second Amendment rights in the context of states' rights rather than individual rights. His articles have appeared in *Mother Jones* and other publications.
Citations: 77:119
Products or Services: Numerous studies including; "Assault Weapons and Accessories in America", "More Gun Dealers than Gas Stations", "National Rifle Association: Money, Firepower & Fear", "Concealed Carry: The Criminal's Companion", and others.
Tax Status: 501(c)(3)
Other Information: In 1994 the Center was awarded $130,000 from the Joyce Foundation.

Visual Studies Workshop / *Afterimage*
31 Prince St.
Rochester, NY 14607   **Phone:**   (716) 442-8676   **E-Mail:** afterimg@servtech.com
USA   **Fax:**   (716) 442-1992

Contact Person: Karen van Meenen, Managing Editor.   **Officers or Principals:** Michael Starenko, Editor.
Mission or Interest: "We strive to present new and alternative work and to provide a forum for emerging writers and theorists through news articles, essays, feature articles and book, catalog, exhibition, festival and conference reviews. Our 'Notices' section is an invaluable resource for makers to find venues for their work, and for academics and producers to find employment."
Accomplishments: "In an era of increasing federal cutbacks to the arts, *Afterimage* has survived and approaches its 25th anniversary, serving the academic and artistic communities concerned with media arts and cultural studies. In the spring of 1995, we published a special issue on the tactics and media foundations of Right-wing and fundamentalist organizations." The Visual Studies Workshop receives funding from the National Endowment for the Arts and the New York State Council on the Arts.
Tax Status: 501(c)(3)   **Annual Report:** No.   **Employees:** 2 full time, 1 part time.
Periodicals: *Afterimage* (bimonthly tabloid journal).
Internships: Yes, "we welcome unpaid (for credit) interns interested in journalism, media arts, cultural studies, and alternative publishing."

Voice for Animals
P.O. Box 120095
San Antonio, TX 78212
USA

Contact Person: Lee Ann Evans, Treasurer.
Mission or Interest: Animal rights organization.
Net Revenue: 1992 less than $25,000   **Tax Status:** 501(c)(3)

Voices for Haiti

P.O. Box 29615
Washington, DC 20017   **Phone:** (202) 319-5544   **E-Mail:** voices4haiti@igc.apc.org
USA   **Fax:**   (202) 319-6090

Contact Person: Jenny Russell, Coordinator.
Mission or Interest: "A coalition of individuals and 75 national and local organizations committed to advocating for a U.S. policy towards Haiti that supports democracy, human rights, and equitable development." Supports Haitian leader Jean-Bertrand Aristide.
Accomplishments: "Published a comprehensive critique of U.S. elections assistance to Haiti...sponsored NGO briefings by officials from the U.S. and Haitian governments, the World Bank, and the Inter-American Development Bank."
Tax Status: 501(c)(4)
Board of Directors or Trustees: Marx Aristide (Washington Office on Haiti), Angie Berryman (American Friends Service Committee), Max Blanchet (Bay Area Haitian American Council), Marie Dennis (Maryknoll Justice and Peace Office), John Engle (Beyond Borders), Rev. Anne Hall (Seattle Voices for Haiti), Wes Hare (Christian Peacemaker Teams), Judith Kelly (Witness for Peace), Jim Matlack (American Friends Service Committee), Nancy McDonald (Pax Christi, FL), Tim McElwee (Church of the Brethren), Lisa McGowan (Development GAP), Linda Gray McKay (Unitarian Universalist Service Committee), Julie Meyer (Lambi Fund of Haiti), Alix Pharuns (Quixote Center), Cinny Poppen (Chicago Coalition for Democracy in Haiti), Marie Racine (Univ. of DC), Bill Ramsey (St. Louis Voice for Haiti), Paul Scire (Witness for Peace), Lydia Williams (Oxfam American), Scott Wright (Ecumenical Program on Central America and the Caribbean).
Periodicals: *Voices for Haiti Speaking Out* (bimonthly newsletter).

Volunteers for Peace (VFP)

43 Tiffany Rd.
Belmont, VT 05730   **Phone:** (802) 259-2759   **E-Mail:** vfpusa@igc.apc.org
USA   **Fax:**   (802) 259-2922

Contact Person: Peter Colwell, Executive Director.   **Officers or Principals:** Peter Colwell, Executive Director ($19,109); Tom Sherman, Treasurer ($0); Scott Simpson, Secretary ($0); Kerry Jacox.
Mission or Interest: Coordinates the placement of volunteers in workcamps worldwide. These workcamps are meant to provide a bridge between citizens and serve as "a microcosm of a world where nations join together to improve life for everyone."
Accomplishments: Since 1981 their programs have exchanged over 1,000 workcamp volunteers. "In the 1980's, many of these exchanges were with Eastern European countries and with Russia. The citizen diplomacy that we fostered was influential in the end of the Cold War."
Net Revenue: 1994 $179,741 **Net Expenses:** $175,292 82%/18%/0% **Net Assets:** $45,538
Products or Services: International Workcamp Directory, an annual guide to available workcamps. The exchange of volunteers for these workcamps. In 1994 they spent $142,898 on this program. Some examples from the Directory: Nijmegen, Netherlands - "Its basic idea is that most of women's problems are caused by the position of women in society. The work will consist of painting walls. A big part of the camp will be used for studying the feminist background of Saffier, the feminist way of giving psychological assistance, and the role of women in society." Cheng Rai, Thailand - "Since a market economy has permeated, breaking their self sufficiency, this village has been getting poorer, so most of the females experience prostitution, AIDS spreads more, and the forest is disappearing rapidly. You'll plant fruit trees and teaks with local people for their self generation and enlightenment of environmental and AIDS protection."
Tax Status: 501(c)(3) **Annual Report:** Yes. **Employees:** 3
Periodicals: *International Workcamper Newsletter* (annual).
Internships: Yes, internships are arranged by participants volunteering for multiple workcamps.
Other Information: They are a member of the Coordinating Committee for International Voluntary Service, CCIVS, at UNESCO in Paris. The organization received $142,680, or 79% of revenue from program services, including placement fees, air fare receipts, train tickets, host insurance payments, and royalties. $35,534, or 20%, from membership fees. The remaining revenue came from interest on savings and temporary cash investments.

Wallace Alexander Gerbode Foundation

470 Columbus Ave., Suite 209
San Francisco, CA 94133   **Phone:** (415) 391-0911
USA

Contact Person: Thomas C. Layton, Executive Director.
Officers or Principals: Thomas C. Layton, Executive Director ($125,494); Merylee Smith Bingham, Administrative Assistant ($37,531); Maryanna G. Stockholm, President/Chairman ($0); Frank A. Gerbode, M.D., Vice President/Vice Chairman; Charles M. Stockholm, Treasurer; Joan Richardson, Secretary.
Mission or Interest: Foundation that awards grants for the arts and humanities, public policy, abortion rights, "right to die projects," education, the environment, and the philanthropic process.

Accomplishments: In 1993 the Foundation awarded $1,512,731 in grants. The top recipients included: $79,800 for the Philanthropic Ventures Foundation's "Death with Dignity" public education project, two grants totaling $55,000 for the Natural Resources Defense Council, $50,000 for the Nature Conservancy, $28,000 for the Reproductive Health Technologies Project, $25,000 for the Earth Island Institute, $20,524 for the Center for Community Change, and $20,000 for the ACLU Foundation of Northern California,
Net Revenue: 1993 $7,782,315 **Net Expenses:** $2,265,218 **Net Assets:** $46,355,959
Tax Status: 501(c)(3)
Other Information: The Foundation received $6,246,084, or 80% of revenue, from capital gains on the sale of securities. $1,504,707, or 19%, from dividends and interest from securities. The remaining revenue came from gifts and grants, interest on savings and temporary cash investments, and other miscellaneous sources. The Foundation held $36,068,826, or 78% of assets, in corporate stocks. $8,263,875, or 18%, in corporate bonds.

Wallace Genetic Foundation

7 Charles Lane
Rye Brook, NY 10573   **Phone:** (914) 937-5992
USA

Contact Person: Stanley Rosenberg, Assistant Secretary.   **Officers or Principals:** Stanley Rosenberg, Assistant Secretary ($31,860); Jean W. Douglas, Director ($0); Robert B. Wallace, Director ($0).
Mission or Interest: Foundation that awards grants to groups concerned with agriculture, the environment, and population growth.
Accomplishments: In 1993 the Foundation awarded $3,276,475 in grants. The recipients of the largest grants included: $655,000 for Population Action International, $132,500 for the Henry A. Wallace Institute for Alternative Agriculture, $100,000 for the Institute for Alternative Agriculture, $95,000 for the Policy Sciences Center, $71,640 for the Arizona Nature Conservancy, $60,000 for the Natural Resources Defense Council, and $50,000 each for the WorldWatch Institute, and the Union of Concerned Scientists.
Net Revenue: 1993 $4,566,607 **Net Expenses:** $3,535,196 **Net Assets:** $133,985,981
Tax Status: 501(c)(3)
Other Information: The Foundation received $2,022,209, or 44% of revenue, from dividends and interest from securities. $1,794,400, or 39%, from capital gains on the sale of assets. $665,000, or 15%, from gifts and grants awarded by foundations, businesses, and individuals. $84,998, or 2%, from interest on savings and temporary cash investments. The Foundation held $131,208,561, or 98% of assets, in corporate stock. $112,114,782, or 85% of corporate stock and 84% of assets, was held in Pioneer Hi-Bred International.

War and Peace Foundation for Education

32 Union Square, E.
New York, NY 10003   **Phone:** (212) 777-4210
USA

Contact Person: Selma Brackman.
Mission or Interest: Anti-war and disarmament organization.
Net Revenue: 1993 $1,445 **Net Expenses:** $151 **Net Assets:** $1,294
Tax Status: 501(c)(3)
Other Information: The Foundation received $1,439, or 99.9% of revenue, from gifts and grants. The remaining revenue came from interest on savings and temporary cash investments.

War Resisters League (WRL)

339 Lafayette St.
New York, NY 10012   **Phone:** (212) 228-0450   **E-Mail:** wrl@igc.apc.org
USA   **Fax:** (212) 228-6193   **Web-Page:** http://www.nonviolence.org/~nvweb

Contact Person: Ruth Benn.
Officers or Principals: Ralph DiGia, Secretary/Treasurer ($0); Betty Winkler, Chris Ney, Coordinators.
Mission or Interest: "Advocates Gandhian nonviolence as the method for creating a democratic society free of war, racism, sexism and human exploitation." Lobbying affiliate of the War Resisters League.
Accomplishments: Founded in 1923, "a leader for 70 years in nonviolent direct action, including rallies, and civil disobedience actions." In 1994 WRL spent $78,161 on its programs, all of which went to the 501(c)(3) War Resisters League in the form of grants.
Net Revenue: 1994 $23,342 **Net Expenses:** $78,161 100%/0%/0% **Net Assets:** $311,698
Tax Status: 501(c)(4) **Annual Report:** Yes. **Employees:** 2 full time, 1part time.
Board of Directors or Trustees: Murray Rosenblith, Melissa Jameson.
Internships: Yes.
Other Information: Affiliated with the 501(c)(3) War Resisters League at the same address. The League received $25,980 from gifts and grants awarded by foundations and individuals. $4,562 from interest on savings and temporary cash investments. Revenue was offset by a loss of $7,200 from the sale of securities.

War Resisters League (WRL)

339 Lafayette St
New York, NY 10012   **Phone:** (212) 228-0450   **E-Mail:** wrl@igc.apc.org
USA   **Fax:**   (212) 228-6193   **Web-Page:** http://www.nonviolence.org/~nvweb

Contact Person: Ruth Benn, Director.
Officers or Principals: David McReynolds; Jessie Heiwa, YouthPeace Coordinator; Judith Mahoney Pasternak, Editor.
Mission or Interest: "Advocates Gandhian nonviolence as the method for creating a democratic society free of war, racism, sexism and human exploitation." Research and education affiliate of War Resisters League.
Accomplishments: Albert Einstein said, "The War Resisters League...is indispensable for the preparation of a fundamental change in public opinion, a change that, under present-day circumstances, is absolutely necessary if humanity is to survive." Sponsored an Enola Gay Action Coalition to focus attention on the Smithsonian Institutions's exhibit. YouthPeace program that includes opposition to 'war toys.' Their bimonthly magazine has a circulation of 8,000.
Net Revenue: FY ending 3/95 $317,027 **Net Expenses:** $238,788
Products or Services: Nonviolent activism, "Books That Make a Difference" catalog containing publications, clothing, posters and other paraphernalia promoting pacifism, civil disobedience, feminism, disarmament, socialism, and more. "Nothing But the Truth," a calendar featuring the courtroom statements of Susan B. Anthony, Gandhi, Nelson Mandela, Leonard Peltier, and Mumia Abu-Jamal.
Tax Status: 501(c)(3) **Annual Report:** Yes. **Employees:** 2 full time, 1 part time.
Board of Directors or Trustees: Murray Rosenblith, Melissa Jameson.
Periodicals: *Nonviolent Activist* (bimonthly magazine).   **Internships:** Yes.
Other Information: Affiliated with the 501(c)(4) War Resisters League at the same address. The League drew criticism from some of its members for attending a state-sponsored conference in Libya. The League defended its action saying that it was protesting the U.S. government's ban on travel to Libya.

Washington Office on Africa

110 Maryland Ave., N.E.
Washington, DC 20002   **Phone:** (202) 546-7961
USA

Contact Person: Cheryl Countess, Executive Director.   **Officers or Principals:** Cheryl Countess, Executive Director ($18,500).
Mission or Interest: "To assist the people of Africa in eliminating racial discrimination, injustice and violations of human rights and to promote the U.S. policies which are supportive of those goals."
Accomplishments: In 1994 the Office spent $21,442 on its programs.
Net Revenue: 1994 $123,500 **Net Expenses:** $116,120 18%/82%/0% **Net Assets:** $7,583
Tax Status: 501(c)(3)
Board of Directors or Trustees: Earl Shinholster (NAACP), Ntsiki Langford (Episcopal Church), Rev. Bernice Powell Jackson (United Church of Christ, Commission for Racial Justice), Bill Dyer (Missionaries of Africa), Jennifer Davis (American Committee on Africa), Barbara Green (Presbyterian Church, USA), Dan Hoffman (Christian Church, Africa Office), Mary Jernigan (Reformed Church in America), Mervin Keeney (Church of the Brethren), Rev. Archie LeMone (Progressive National Baptist Convention), Erich Mathias (United Church of Christ), Terence Miller (Maryknoll Fathers & Brothers, Justice and Peace Office), Pastor Daniel Olson (Evangelical Lutheran Church), Diane Porter (Episcopal Church, Coalition for Human Needs), Father Stephen Price (Society for African Missions), Anna Rhee (United Methodist Church, Global Ministries), Doreen Tilghman (United Methodist Church), Jon Chapman (Presbyterian Church, USA), Mark Brown (Evangelical Lutheran Church).
Periodicals: Newsletter.
Other Information: The Office received $108,389, or 88% of revenue, from gifts and grants awarded by foundations, businesses, and individuals. $7,359, or 6%, from the sale of publications and subscriptions. $2,582, or 2%, from special projects. The remaining revenue came from interest on savings and temporary cash investments, and other miscellaneous sources.

Washington Office on Haiti

110 Maryland Ave., N.E., Room 310
Washington, DC 20002   **Phone:** (202) 319-4464
USA   **Fax:**   (202) 319-6052

Contact Person: Mary Healy, RSM, Director.   **Officers or Principals:** Mary Healy, RSM, Director ($13,077); Jeane Alce, M.D., President ($0); Laurent Pierre-Philipe, M.D. ($0); Theresa Patterson, Secretary.
Mission or Interest: Collects, prepares, and disseminates information concerning conditions in Haiti.
Accomplishments: In 1994 the Office spent $98,823 on its programs.
Net Revenue: 1994 $104,274 **Net Expenses:** $122,585 81%/8%/11% **Net Assets:** $6,075
Tax Status: 501(c)(3)
Board of Directors or Trustees: Jeff Duaime, CSSp, Bernard Fils-Amie, Peggy Heiner (United Methodist Church), Kimberly Bell, Rep. John Conyers (D-MI), Worth Cooley-Prost, Wilfred Suprena, Andre Vainqueur, Esmerelda Brown, Carolyn Waller, James Healy, CSSp, Edward Kelly, CSSp, Paul Farmer, M.D., Cynthia Johnson.
Other Information: The Office received $92,596, or 89% of revenue, from gifts and grants awarded by foundations, businesses, and individuals. (These grants included $5,500 from the Peace Development Fund.) $6,324, or 6%, from the sale of inventory. $5,081, or 5%, from a fund raising dinner. The remaining revenue came from interest on savings and temporary cash investments.

Washington Office on Latin America

400 C St., N.E.
Washington, DC 20002   **Phone:** (202) 544-8045
USA   **Fax:** (202) 546-5288

Contact Person: George Vickers Executive Director.   **Officers or Principals:** George Vickers Executive Director ($57,240);
Sally Yudelman, Chair ($0); Roma Knee, Treasurer ($0); Cheryl Morden, Secretary; Peter Hakim, Vice Chair.
Mission or Interest: Research and dissemination of information regarding human rights and political conditions in Latin America.
Accomplishments: In the 1980's the Office consistently opposed U.S. efforts against the Sandinistas in Nicaragua and the FMLN
guerillas in El Salvador. In 1994 the Office spent $409,162 on its programs.
Net Revenue: 1994 $580,471 **Net Expenses:** $582,464 70%/23%/7% **Net Assets:** $50,871 **Citations:** 38:147
Products or Services: Research, publications, testimony, and lobbying. The Office spent $1,423 on lobbying, $844 on grassroots
and $579 on the direct lobbying of legislators. This was down 67% from the previous year.
Tax Status: 501(c)(3)
Board of Directors or Trustees: Rev. Oscar Bolioli (National Council of Churches), Tom Carothers (Carnegie Endowment for
Peace), Marie Dennis (Maryknoll Justice and Peace), Joe Eldridge (Lawyers Com. For Human Rights), Richard Erstad (AFSC),
Seamus Finn, Lisa Fuentes, Robert Goldman (American Univ.), Cynthia McClintock (George Washington Univ.), Mara Miller,
Richard Newfarmer (World Bank), Barbara Pessoa (United Methodist Church), Daniel Salcedo (AAAS), Thomas Quigley (U.S.
Catholic Conference).
Periodicals: *Latin America Update* (bimonthly magazine).
Other Information: The Office received $547,985, or 94% of revenue, from gifts and grants received by foundations, businesses,
and individuals. (These grants included $460,000 from the Joyce Mertz-Gilmore Foundation, $75,000 from the General Services
Foundation, $1,750 from the Stewart R. Mott Charitable Trust.) $20,285 net, or 3%, from an annual dinner. $9,172, or 2%, from
interest on savings and temporary cash investments. The remaining revenue came from the sale of publications and other
miscellaneous sources.

Washington Rural Organizing Project

P.O. Box 146
Spokane, WA 99210   **Phone:** (509) 326-5733
USA

Contact Person: Joe Chrastil, Staff Director.   **Officers or Principals:** Joe Chrastil, Staff Director ($4,210); Yvonne Smith, Sam
Oh Happy, Co-Chairs ($0); David King, Secretary/Treasurer ($0).
Mission or Interest: Develop leadership skills for rural advocates.
Accomplishments: In the fiscal year ending June 1993, the organization spent $13,079 on its projects. This included advocating
the expansion of low-income housing.
Net Revenue: FY ending 6/93 $15,945 **Net Expenses:** $18,321 **Net Assets:** $7,260
Tax Status: 501(c)(4)
Board of Directors or Trustees: Leonel Barajas, Sr. Maurita Bernet, Sergio Campos, Taleah Edmonds, Cynthia Reichelt, Maria
Zavala.
Other Information: The Project received $13,352, or 85% of revenue, from gifts and grants awarded by foundations, businesses,
and individuals. $2,350, or 14%, from program service revenues. $243, or 1%, from investment income.

Washington Toxics Coalition

4516 University Way, N.E.
Seattle, WA 98105   **Phone:** (206) 632-1545
USA

Contact Person: David Mann, President.
Officers or Principals: Joey Corcoran, President ($0); Don Bollinger, Treasurer ($0); Dave Coffman, Secretary ($0).
Mission or Interest: "To reduce society's reliance on toxic chemicals...(and) reliance on hazardous compounds in industry,
agriculture, homes, and public lands."
Accomplishments: In 1994 the Coalition spent $234,874 on its programs. The largest program, with expenditures of $82,623, was
the Industrial Toxics Project. $60,039 was spent on the Home Safe Home project which distributed printed information at fairs,
events, conferences, and on request. An estimated 25,000 items were distributed. $54,203 for pesticide reform issues that "works
with individuals, local citizen organizations, public agency staff and elected officials by providing information on the toxicity of
pesticides, model programs, alternative management strategies, and information about how to reduce reliance on pesticides." $34,060
on education and information services that met over 3,500 requests for information.
Net Revenue: 1994 $337,816 ($8,759, or 3%, from government grants) **Net Expenses:** $284,429 83%/3%/14%
Net Assets: $72,880
Tax Status: 501(c)(3)
Board of Directors or Trustees: Jean Day, Chris Luboff, John Perkins, David Stitzel.
Periodicals: Newsletter.
Other Information: The Coalition received $273,106, or 81% of revenue, from gifts and grants awarded by foundations, businesses,
and individuals. (These grants included $70,000 from the Bullitt Foundation, $10,000 from the Beldon Fund.) $34,375, or 10%,
from contract services provided for agencies. $12,078 net, or 4%, from the sale of inventory. $8,759, or 3%, from government
grants. $6,878, or 2%, from fees and contracts from government agencies. The remaining revenue came from interest on savings
and temporary cash investments.

Welfare Research

113 State St.
Albany, NY 12207   **Phone:**   (518) 432-2576
USA

Contact Person: Virginia Hayes Sibbison, Executive Director.
Officers or Principals: Virginia Hayes Sibbison, Executive Director ($97,316); William J. Coutu, Financial Manager ($57,880); Joseph M. Sullivan, President ($0); James R. Dumpson, Ph.D., Vice President; Maurice O. Hunt, Treasurer.
Mission or Interest: Studies, projects, and research in the area of welfare delivery and human services.
Accomplishments: In 1994 the organization spent $536,356 on its projects.
Net Revenue: 1994 $675,492 ($356,390, or 53% from government grants) **Net Expenses:** $674,986   79%/21%/0%
Net Assets: (-$115,076) **Citations:** 38:147
Tax Status: 501(c)(3)
Board of Directors or Trustees: Joseph Erazo, Prof. David Fanshel, DSW (Columbia School of Social Work), Peter Hughes (former Deputy Provost, NYU Medical Center), William Johnson, Jr. (Mayor, Rochester, NY). Horace Morris (United Way of NYC), Nancy Perlmen (former Exec. Dir., Center for Women in Government), Mary Ann Quaranta, DSW (Dean, Grad. School of Social Service Fordham Univ.), Assoc. Prof. Charles Trent, DSW (Yeshiva Univ.).
Other Information: Welfare Research received $356,390, or 53% of revenue, from government grants. $315,941, or 47%, from direct and indirect public support in the form of gifts and grants awarded by foundations, businesses, and individuals. The remaining revenue came from dividends and interest from securities.

Welfare Warriors

P.O. Box 116
Schnectady, NY 12301
USA

Mission or Interest: Promotes the right to receive government-provided, taxpayer-funded, welfare. Emphasis on women's rights to receive Aid to Families with Dependent Children (AFDC). "Welfare reform provides cheap, forced labor for corporations unwilling to pay family supporting wages that fathers demand."

Western Colorado Congress

P.O. Box 472
Montrose, CO 81402   **Phone:**   (970) 249-1978
USA

Contact Person: William Hiatt, President.
Officers or Principals: William Hiatt, President ($0); John Kierwaw, Vice President ($0); Syril Whitlock, Secretary ($0).
Mission or Interest: "Citizens' advocacy organization...on issues of mutual concern to the Western slope of Colorado."
Accomplishments: In 1994 the Congress spent $188,957 on its programs.
Net Revenue: 1994 $245,943 **Net Expenses:** $251,630 75%/11%/13% **Net Assets:** $42,013
Products or Services: Public policy advocacy and lobbying. The Congress spent $12,961 on lobbying, $40 on grassroots and $12,921 on the direct lobbying of legislators. This was down 10% from the previous year.
Tax Status: 501(c)(3)
Other Information: The Congress received $150,401, or 61% of revenue from grants awarded by foundations, businesses, and individuals. (These grants included $20,000 from the Tides Foundation, $20,000 from the Campaign for Human Development, $10,000 from the Beldon Fund, $10,000 from the Abelard Foundation, $5,000 from the New-Land Foundation, and $4,000 from the Chinook Fund.) $51,595, or 21%, from membership dues. $26,511, or 11%, from fund-raising activities. $12,202, or 5%, from donations. $4,268, or 2%, from interest on savings and temporary cash investments. The remaining revenue came from miscellaneous sources.

Western Organization of Resource Councils

2401 Montana Ave., Suite 301
Billings, MT 59101   **Phone:**   (406) 252-9672
USA

Contact Person: Patrick Sweeney, Regional Director.   **Officers or Principals:** Patrick Sweeney, Regional Director ($38,136); Darlene Medlar, Chair ($0); Pennie Vance, Vice Chair ($0); Mabel Dobbs, Secretary/Treasurer.
Mission or Interest: Provides news, research, lobbying and technical support for grassroots organizations. Involved with environmental, agriculture, energy use impact, and mining impact issues.
Accomplishments: In 1995 the Organization spent $237,344 on its programs. The largest program, with expenditures of $129,217, was the production of the "High Plains News Service," a weekly 14 minute news program broadcast on over 50 community and public radio stations. $97,314 was spent on research and analysis. $10,813 was spent on leadership and staff development, which included sessions with over 500 people in six states.
Net Revenue: 1995 $398,980 **Net Expenses:** $389,930 61%/35%/4% **Net Assets:** $49,979

Products or Services: "High Plains News Service" radio programming.
Tax Status: 501(c)(4)
Board of Directors or Trustees: Don Vig, Duane Lee, Shirley Effling, Jeannie Costello, Fred Wetlaufer, Robert McFarlane, Deborah Hanson, Richard Parks, Bob Hansing.
Periodicals: Quarterly newsletter.
Other Information: The Organization received $380,003, or 95% of revenue, from gifts and grants awarded by foundations, businesses, and individuals. (These grants included $15,000 from the Tides Foundation.) $13,100, or 3%, from training and consultation fees. $3,496, or 1%, from the sale of publications. The remaining revenue came from radio station fees, and producer training fees.

Western States Center
522 S.W. 5th Ave., Suite 1390
Portland, OR 97204   **Phone:**   (503) 228-8866   **E-Mail:** weststatctr@igc.apc.org
USA   **Fax:**   (503) 228-1965

Contact Person: Jeff Malachowsky, Executive Director.   **Officers or Principals:** Jeff Malachowsky, Executive Director ($42,578); Sharon Gary-Smith, President ($0); Kath Donaldson, Secretary ($0); Dan Petegorsky, Treasurer.
Mission or Interest: Promotes economic and environmental justice. Tracks the 'Wise Use' movement. Trains grassroots leaders and organizations.
Accomplishments: In 1994 the Center spent $805,418 on its projects. The largest project, with expenditures of $247,426, was the Community Leadership Training Program which "develops effective grassroots leaders and organizations, particularly in low-income communities and communities of color throughout our eight state region." $213,142 on the Western Progressive Leadership Network that "develops statewide progressive strategies, coalitions, leadership and public policies, and provides public education and research resources for these citizens." $147,696 on the Money in Western Politics Research Program that tracks and analyzes campaign contributions. Other coalition building and educational efforts.
Net Revenue: 1994 $992,757 **Net Expenses:** $992,757 81%/14%/5% **Net Assets:** $41,943 **Citations:** 29:159
Tax Status: 501(c)(3)
Other Information: The Center received $909,625, or 92% of revenue, from gifts and grants awarded by foundations, businesses, and individuals. (These grants included $100,000 from the Florence and John Schumann Foundation, $75,000 from the Bauman Family Foundation, $70,000 from the Bullitt Foundation, $51,105 from the Tides Foundation, $20,000 from the Jessie Smith Noyes Foundation, $7,500 from the Beldon Fund, $7,000 from the Deer Creek Foundation, and $5,000 from the Global Environment Project Institute. $77,252 came from individual contributors.) $43,397, or 4%, from Community Leadership Training Program fees. $16,436, or 2%, from Western Progressive Leadership Network fees. $8,512, or 1%, from Money in Western Politics Research Program fees. The remaining revenue came from dividends and interest from securities, interest from savings and temporary cash investments, expense reimbursements, and product sales.

Wieboldt Foundation
53 W. Jackson Blvd., Suite 838
Chicago, IL 60604   **Phone:**   (312) 786-9377
USA   **Fax:**   (312) 786-9232

Contact Person: Regina McGraw, Executive Director.
Officers or Principals: Carmen Prieto, Program Director ($48,236); Regina McGraw, Executive Director ($35,583).
Mission or Interest: Grant-making foundation that concentrates on community development and grassroots organizing in the Chicago area.
Accomplishments: In 1994 the Foundation awarded $703,950 in grants. The recipients of the largest grants included: $25,000 for the Pilsen Resurrection Development Corporation, $20,000 each for the Kenwood Oakland Community Organization and the Logan Square Neighborhood Association, $16,500 for the Center for Neighborhood Technology, and $15,000 each for Chicago ACORN, Chicago Video Project, Community Media Workshop, Developing Communities Project, Greater Grand Crossing Organizing Committee, Midwest Center for Labor Research, Near Northwest Neighborhood Network, Organization of the Northeast, South Suburban Action Conference, and the Westside Schools and Communities Organizing for Restructuring and Planning.
Net Revenue: 1994 $1,778,432 **Net Expenses:** $1,039,957 **Net Assets:** $17,591,830
Products or Services: Bestows annual awards for "excellence in community organizing."
Tax Status: 501(c)(3)
Board of Directors or Trustees: Anita Darrow, John Darrow, Jennifer Corrigan, T. Lawrence Doyle, Diane Glenn, Jacquelyne Grimshaw (Center for Neighborhood Technology), Nydia Hohf, Carol Larson, Henry Mendoza, Mary Sample, Anne Wieboldt, Nancy Wieboldt, John Kretzmann, Benjamin Kendrick.
Other Information: The Foundation received $1,191,610, or 67% of revenue, from capital gains on the sale of securities. $574,226, or 32%, from dividends and interest from securities. $9,908, or 1%, from program related revenues. The remaining revenues came from interest on savings and temporary cash investments. The Foundation held $11,633,242, or 66% of assets, in corporate stock. $4,724,840, or 29%, in government obligations.

Wilderness Society
900 17th St., N.W.
Washington, DC 20006   **Phone:**   (202) 833-2300
USA

Contact Person: Bennett Beach, Deputy Vice President, Public Affairs.

Officers or Principals: G. Jon Roush, President ($113,654); Mary F. Hanley, Vice President ($104,875); Rebecca Wodder, Vice President ($103,375); James J. Gillespie, Executive Vice President/CFO ($103,125); Mark Shaffer, Vice President ($101,500); Christopher Elliman, Chair; Thomas A. Barron, Vice Chairman; Edward A. Ames, Secretary; Bert Fingerhut, Treasurer.
Mission or Interest: Wilderness conservation and environmental education.
Accomplishments: In the fiscal year ending June 1994, the Society spent $10,845,681 on its programs. The largest program, with expenditures of $4,082,198, was membership services, including information referrals, coalition building, "action alerts," and education services for the general public. $4,007,968 was spent on conservation programs, protecting "wild lands, wild animals and wild and scenic rivers within the public ownership through the administrative processes established for their study, public review and congressional designation, assuring their permanent protection under the Wilderness Act and Scenic River Act and other land protection systems...designation of new parks and wildlife refuges, preventing over-cutting of national forests, unnecessary abuses to wild areas from ill-conceived pipelines, fossil fuel extraction, dams, roads and similar destructive development." $2,755,515 was spent on public education.
Net Revenue: FY ending 6/94 $15,478,131 **Net Expenses:** $14,571,493 74%/11%/15% **Net Assets:** $5,543,143
Citations: 776:25
Products or Services: Research information, coalition building, conservation, and lobbying. The Institute spent $194,191 on lobbying, $18,644 on grassroots lobbying and $175,527 on the direct lobbying of legislators. This was a decrease of 20% from the year before, and a decrease of 52% from two years prior.
Tax Status: 501(c)(3)
Board of Directors or Trustees: John Glover, Charles Wilkinson (Univ. of CO), Nancy Roen, Arsenio Milian, Amy Vedder, Cynthia Wayburn, John Bierwirth, William Evers, Stephen Griffith, Walter Minnick, Gilman Ordway, Caroline Getty, Mitchell Rogovin, Hansjorg Wyss.
Periodicals: *Wilderness Magazine* (quarterly magazine).
Other Information: Earth First! co-founder Dave Foreman was a lobbyist for the Wilderness Society prior to founding Earth First! The Society hired the Washington, DC firms of Outreach Affiliates to do telemarketing, and Chlopak, Leonard, Schecter for consulting. The firms were paid $848,755 and $380,339 respectively. The Society received $14,328,276, or 93% of revenue, from direct and indirect public support in the form of gifts and grants awarded by foundations, businesses, affiliates, and individuals. (These grants included $150,000 from the Bullitt Foundation for 1993-94, $137,626 from the Environmental Federation of America, $100,000 from the Town Creek Foundation, $50,000 from the Florence and John Schumann Foundation, $50,000 from the American Conservation Association, $45,000 from the Rockefeller Family Fund, $30,000 from the Merck Family Fund, $25,000 from the Compton Foundation, $11,185 from the Sierra Club, $5,000 from the Global Environment Project Institute, $5,000 from the Sierra Club, $3,001 from the Environmental Federation of California, $1,000 from the Crestar Foundation, and $500 from the New Prospect Foundation.) $407,523 or 3%, from dividends and interest from securities. $371,052, or 2%, from the sale of items bearing the Society's insignia. $219,346, or 1%, from credit card royalties. The remaining revenue came from mailing list rentals, and magazine subscriptions. The Wilderness Society held $6,280,320, or 56% of total assets, in securities. Only $311,352, or 3%, was held in land, buildings, and equipment.

Windstar Foundation

2317 Snowmass Creek Road
Snowmass, CO 81654   **Phone:**   (303) 927-4777
USA

Contact Person: Steve Blomeke, Executive Vice President.   **Officers or Principals:** Steve Blomeke, Executive Vice President ($71,100); John Katzenberger, Director ($61,000); Richard Johnson, Director, Research ($43,333); John Denver, President; Dr. Jay D. Hair, Chair; Beth Miller, Vice Chair; Joel T. Thomas, Secretary/Treasurer.
Mission or Interest: Environmental organization founded by singer John Denver.
Accomplishments: In the fiscal year ending November 1993, the Foundation spent $753,917 on its programs. The largest program, with expenditures of $473,513, was the Aspen Global Change Institute which brings together scientists to "synthesize what is known about how human activities impact earth systems." $151,221 was spent on Choices, an annual symposium bringing together "scientists, environmentalists, and members from around the world...to raise consciousness and discuss ways to improve the environment." $61,531 for membership services. Other programs include membership development, and other environmental and agricultural educational activities.
Net Revenue: FY ending 11/93 $987,548 ($499,915, or 51%, from government grants)
Net Expenses: $1,043,781 72%/28%/0% **Net Assets:** $419,517 **Citations:** 9:202
Products or Services: Presents the annual Windstar Award and Windstar Youth Award.
Tax Status: 501(c)(3)
Board of Directors or Trustees: Cheryl Charles, William Howard, Pat Robles.
Other Information: The Foundation received $499,915, or 51% of revenue, from government grants. $149,053, or 15%, from the Choice program. $130,563, or 13%, from membership dues. $84,406, or 9%, from gifts and grants awarded by foundations, businesses, and individuals. $58,194, or 6%, from royalty income. $35,071, or 4%, from rental income. $10,442 net, or 1%, from the sale of inventory. The remaining revenue came from consultation fees, reimbursements, interest on savings and temporary cash investments, special fund-raising events, and other miscellaneous sources.

Winston Foundation for World Peace

2040 S St., N.W., Suite 201
Washington, DC 20009-1157   **Phone:**   (202) 483-4215   **E-Mail:** winstonfoun@igc.apc.org
USA   **Fax:**   (202) 483-4219

Contact Person: Monica Dorbandt, Administrative Assistant.   **Officers or Principals:** John M. Tirman, Ph.D., Executive Director ($93,000); Bevis Longstreth, President ($0); William Zabel, Secretary ($0); Roy H. Carlin, Treasurer.
Mission or Interest: Grant-making foundation created in 1986 to campaign for the prevention of nuclear war. With the end of the Cold War the focus had broadened to conflict prevention in general. Grants are awarded in the areas of Cooperative Security, Conflict Prevention and Reconciliation, and Non-Proliferation of Weapons.
Accomplishments: In October 1994 the Foundation helped organize a symposium "Democracy at Home and Abroad," hosted by *Mother Jones* magazine. Speakers included Undersecretary of State Timothy Wirth and Clinton White House advisor Mort Halperin. The symposium was broadcast on C-Span. In 1993 the Foundation awarded $918,391 in grants. Recipients included: three grants totaling $85,000 for Search for Common Ground, two grants totaling $55,000 for the UN Non-governmental Organization Committee on Disarmament, $50,000 for the Center for War, Peace and the News Media, $40,000 for the Balkans Peace Project, $15,000 for the Union of Concerned Scientists, $15,000 for the Peace Action Education Fund, $25,000 for the Foundation for National Progress, $15,000 for the Arms Control Association, $15,000 for the Federation of American Scientists, $20,000 for the Wisconsin Project on Nuclear Arms Control, $15,000 for the Data Center, $15,000 for the Institute for Alternative Journalism, $25,000 for the Campaign for Peace and Democracy, $25,000 for Physicians for Social Responsibility, $25,000 for the Natural Resource Development Council, and $9,891 for Greenpeace.
Net Revenue: 1993 $1,131,232 **Net Expenses:** $1,125,651 **Net Assets:** $9,880,358
Products or Services: Grants, fellowships, and symposiums.
Tax Status: 501(c)(3) **Annual Report:** Yes.
Board of Directors or Trustees: John Adams (Natural Resources Defense Council), Robert Allen (Henry P. Kendall Found.), Leslie Dunbar (Field Found.), Melinda Scrivner, Albert Sims (College Board), Alice Tepper Marlin (Council on Economic Priorities).
Internships: No, but fellowships are awarded to students. In 1994 they awarded a fellowship to a graduate student in Journalism to investigate arms transfers for *Mother Jones* magazine.
Other Information: The Winston Foundation managed the grant-making activities of the CarEth Foundation for four years ending in 1994. Foundation executive director John Tirman was previously an editor and director of communications with the Union of Concerned Scientists, and an energy reporter for Time magazine. The Foundation received $702,644, or 62% of revenue from the sale of assets. $373,646, or 33%, from dividends and interest from securities. $54,301, or 5%, from consulting fees from the Kendall Foundation and the CarEth Foundation. The remaining revenue came from interest on savings and temporary cash investments.

Wisconsin Community Fund (WCF)

122 State St., Suite 508
Madison, WI 53703   **Phone:** (608) 251-6834
USA   **Fax:**   (608) 251-6846

Contact Person: Steve Starkey, Executive Director.
Officers or Principals: Steve Starkey, Executive Director; Tom Hecht, President; Kevin Bonds, Treasurer; James Hill, Secretary; John Adekoje, Development Administrator; Terry Johnson, Administrative Assistant.
Mission or Interest: Raises and disburses money to "progressive groups working for democracy, justice and social equality." Also provides technical support for grassroots organizations.
Accomplishments: Has awarded over $550,000 in grants to organizations in Wisconsin. Through a program with Lotus Software's philanthropy department they have given $350,000 worth of free Lotus software to nonprofits. For the fiscal year ending June 1994 they awarded $103,708 in cash and non-cash grants. Top grant recipients were; $5,000 to Honor our Neighbor's Origins and Rights, $5,000 to The United (gay and lesbians' rights), $5,000 to The Holton Youth Center, $4,800 for Down River Alliance (anti-nuclear power), $4,150 for Welfare Rights Organizing Committee. Steve Starkey won The United's "Man of The Year" award for 1995.
Net Revenue: FY ending 6/94 $222,303 **Net Expenses:** $217,902 59%/20%/21% **Net Assets:** (-$3,919)
Products or Services: Grants and technical support.
Tax Status: 501(c)(3) **Annual Report:** Yes. **Employees:** 3
Board of Directors or Trustees: Cris Derrick, Becky Glass, Bobbie Griffin, Dale Johnson.
Periodicals: *Wisconsin Community Fund* (quarterly newsletter).
Other Information: They are a member of The Funding Exchange network. They maintain a wide base of financial support. Despite strong support for gay rights and abortion, they receive funding from several Catholic sources, including Milwaukee Catholic Social Services, Madison and Monona Knights of Columbus, and the Diocese of LaCrosse. Numerous other individuals, labor unions and community organizations contribute. The Fund received $221,317, or 99.5% of revenue from gifts and grants from foundations, companies and individuals. (These grants included $33,000 from the Funding Exchange, $2,000 from the Vanguard Public Foundation.) The remaining revenue came from program services and interest on savings and temporary cash investments.

Witness for Peace

2201 P St., N.W., Suite 109
Washington, DC 20037   **Phone:** (202) 797-1160
USA

Contact Person: Leigh Carter, Executive Director.   **Officers or Principals:** Leigh Carter, Executive Director ($27,093); Betsy Crites, Chairman ($0); Phyllis Taylor, Vice Chair ($0); Bill Webber, Treasurer.
Mission or Interest: Establishes connections with, and sends volunteers to, various Latin American countries to serve as "witnesses to peace." These witnesses cooperate nonviolently with organizations, individuals, and governments and provide testimony of their experiences to influence public policy and opinion in the United States. Worked in Nicaragua during the war between the Sandinistas and Contras, and is currently working in Guatemala.
Accomplishments: In 1993 Witness for Peace spent $456,663 on its programs. This included $10,075 in grants to chapters around the country.

Net Revenue: 1993 $858,903   **Net Expenses:** $779,044   59%/17%/24%   **Net Assets:** $14,346   **Citations:** 120:108
Products or Services: Educational materials, grassroots organizing, media outreach, and lobbying. In 1993 the organization spent $5,082 on grassroots lobbying. This was down 35% from the previous year, and down 81% from $26,921 in 1990.
Tax Status: 501(c)(3)
Board of Directors or Trustees: Anne Barstow, Mary Peter Bruce, Louis Chase, Judy Kading, Anna Lee Utech, David Harris, Stephen Mathison-Bowie, Nancy Gwin, Ken Roberts, Rabbi Myra Soifer.
Periodicals: *Newsbrief* (newsletter).
Other Information: Witness for Peace received $694,556, or 81% of revenue, from gifts and grants awarded by foundations, businesses and individuals. (These grants included $2,500 from the Peace Development Fund, and $500 from the Aaron and Martha Schecter Private Foundation.) $158,660, or 18%, from delegation fees. The remaining revenue came from interest on savings and temporary cash investments, and miscellaneous sources.

Woman's National Democratic Club (WNDC)

1526 New Hampshire Ave., N.W.
Washington, DC 20036   **Phone:**   (202) 232-7363
USA   **Fax:**   (202) 986-2791

Contact Person: Barbara Zelenko, President.
Officers or Principals: Barbara Zelenko, President ($0); Alice Rowen, Josie Bass, Julie Johnstone, Marina Streznewski, Sadie Gold, Sara Rau, Vice Presidents ($0); Anne Goodrich, Secretary; June Bashkin, Assistant Secretary; Joan Chase, Treasurer.
Mission or Interest: Educational, cultural, and social club women in the Democrat Party.
Net Revenue: FY ending 6/95 $901,723   **Net Expenses:** $1,029,307   **Net Assets:** $1,433,286
Products or Services: Reference library, travel events, panel discussions, and an annual award for outstanding Democratic woman.
Tax Status: 501(c)(7)
Board of Directors or Trustees: Harriet Beaubien, Sandra Bieri, Dorothy Dillon, Jane Freeman, Peggy Gidez, Bernice Jacobson, Ruth Knee, Amanda MacKenzie, Mary Muromcew, Adelaide Newburger, Carol Parker, Marelyn Tank.
Periodicals: *WNDC News* (monthly newsletter).
Other Information: The Club received $419,334 net, or 47% of revenue, from the sale of inventory. $405,965, or 45%, from membership dues. $29,062, or 3%, from interest on savings and temporary cash investments. $27,615, or 3%, from gifts and grants awarded by foundations, businesses, and individuals. $6,410 net, or 1%, from rental income received from a restaurant. The remaining revenue came from other miscellaneous sources. $1,551,652, or 72% of total assets, were held in land, buildings and equipment held for use and investments. Among the equipment held and counted as assets by the club were; marble tiles, wrought iron, fine arts, a Steinway piano, sarouk rugs, a Kronos time clock, and china, silverware and glassware which was originally valued at over $29,000.

Women Against Military Madness (WAMM)

310 E. 38th St., Suite 225
Minneapolis, MN 55409   **Phone:**   (612) 827-5364
USA   **Fax:**   (612) 827-6433

Contact Person: Lucia Wilkes, Co-Director.   **Officers or Principals:** Daniella Maus, Co-Director.
Mission or Interest: "Teach positive nonviolent approaches for dealing with anger and conflict." World peace organization. "We have empowerment groups to facilitate action to demand policy and priority shifts of the U.S. government."
Accomplishments: In 1994 WAMM spent $78,377 on its programs.
Net Revenue: 1994 $98,592   **Net Expenses:** $97,293   81%/6%/13%   **Net Assets:** $7,078
Tax Status: 501(c)(3)
Other Information: A member of the Minnesota Peace and Justice Coalition. WAMM received $98,466, or 99.9% of revenue, from direct and indirect public support, in the form of gifts and grants awarded by foundations, businesses, affiliates, and individuals. The remaining revenue came from interest on savings and temporary cash investments.

Women Employed / Women Employed Institute

22 W. Monroe St., Suite 1400
Chicago, IL 60603   **Phone:**   (312) 782-3902   **E-Mail:** mujer@one.org
USA   **Fax:**   (312) 782-5249

Contact Person: Liz Libby, Marketing Coordinator.
Officers or Principals: Anne Ladky, Executive Director; Edith F. Canter, Chair.
Mission or Interest: "To empower women to improve their economic status and remove barriers to economic equity through advocacy, direct service, and public education." Opposed to discrimination against women in the workplace, supports affirmative action.
Accomplishments: 1,600 members. Organized the Coalition for Equal Opportunity "to educate the public and policy makers regarding the need for affirmative action." "Leader in Chicago Area Partnerships, a coalition of corporate, government and social service agencies which promotes the improvement of equal opportunity policy and practices. Disseminated information sheets on the wage gap, affirmative action, sexual harassment prevention, welfare reform, school-to-work transition, and employment rights to over 5,000 men and women nationwide."
Products or Services: "Organizing Kit to Fight Anti-Affirmative Action Measures at the Grassroots Level," other publications, fact sheets, and kits.

Tax Status: 501(c)(4) / Institute 501(c)(3)   **Annual Report:** Yes.   **Employees:** 12
Board of Directors or Trustees: Joni Alvarez, Shauna Babcock, Suzy Bangs, Deborah Minor Bennett, Sarah Bornstein, Alice Birkett, Sandra Bowen, Gloria Castillo, Vicki Curtis, Regina Dove, Shelley Freeman, Jill Garcia, Linda Impastato, Fern Josephs, Karen Latimer, Sillisa McClure, Cherie McDowell, Patricia McKiernan, Lucy Moynihan, Joy Muench, Sheila O'Donnell, Joan Perkins, Monique Sattler, Janet Schumacher, Jennifer Jane Smith, Terry Soto, Elizabeth Turley.

Women and Foundations / Corporate Philanthropy (WAF/CP)

322 8th Ave., 7th Floor
New York, NY 10001   **Phone:**   (212) 463-9934
USA   **Fax:**   (212) 463-9417

Contact Person: Walteen Grady Truely, President.   **Officers or Principals:** Walteen Grady Truely, President ($67,275); Rochelle Ritacco, Director of Membership ($60,228); Chakrauarity Maridula, Program Director ($40,627); Judith Simpson, Chair; Valeria Lee, Vice Chair; John Kostishack, Treasurer; Ruth Goins, Secretary.
Mission or Interest: Provides information and referrals to match corporate and foundation philanthropy with feminist organizations.
Accomplishments: In 1993 the organization spent $409,535 on its programs. The largest program, with expenditures of $297,036, was the "Far from Done" project which included regional seminars and data on the status of females. Also part of this program was $50,134 in grants. Grant recipients included; $21,600 for BIHA Women in Action, $12,833 for the Minnesota Coalition for Battered Women, $10,800 for Women Helping Offenders, and others.
Net Revenue: 1993 $596,715 **Net Expenses:** $589,621 69%/20%/10% **Net Assets:** $311,581 **Citations:** 0:255
Products or Services: Directory of Women's Funds, guide.
Tax Status: 501(c)(3)
Board of Directors or Trustees: Elizabeth Boris (Aspen Inst.), Stephanie Clohesy (W.K. Kellogg Found.), Elouise Cobell (Montana Community Found.), John Foster-Bey (John D. And Catherine T. MacArthur Found.), Ellen Friedman (Tides Found.), Mario Griffin (Levi Strauss Found.), Wenda Weekes Moore (W.K. Kellogg Found.), Marianne Philbin (Chicago Foundation for Women), Aida Rodriguez (Rockefeller Found.), Ruth Shack (Dade Community Found.), Margaret Smith (Kresge Found.), Marie Wilson (Ms. Foundation for Women), June Zeitlin (Ford Found.).
Other Information: The organization received $525,461, or 88% of revenue, from gifts and grants awarded by foundations, businesses, and individuals. (These grants included $7,000 from the Ms. Foundation for Women, $4,500 from the Wallace Alexander Gerbode Foundation, $2,000 from the Jessie Smith Noyes Foundation.) $35,115, or 6%, from conference fees. $16,952, or 3%, from interest on savings and temporary cash investments. $15,440, or 3%, from membership dues. The remaining revenue came from publication sales and training reimbursements. In 1994 the organization received $2,500 from the Robert Sterling Clark Foundation.

Women in Community Service (WICS)

1900 N. Beauregard St., Suite 103
Alexandria, VA 22311   **Phone:**   (703) 671-0500
USA

Contact Person: Vera Ford, Assistant Executive Director.   **Officers or Principals:** Ruth Herman, Executive Director ($81,627); Vera Ford, Assistant Executive Director ($59,938); John Hughes, Director of Finance and Administration ($53,630); Gertrude Peele, President; Sandy Goldberg, Vice President; Patricia Smuck, Secretary; Beverly K. Garrett, Treasurer.
Mission or Interest: "To provide recruitment of youths for the Job Corps." Works with Job Corp members to help them find employment, and match them with mentors. Special programs for women, including low income women, imprisoned women, and women recovering from substance abuse. Facilitates workshops for Job Corps staff and students "dealing with critical topics such as 'sexual harassment', 'homophobia', 'cultural diversity', and more."
Accomplishments: In the fiscal year ending September 1994, WICS spent $4,815,259 on its programs. The largest program, with expenditures of $4,307,610, was the recruitment of youths for the Job Corps and "to provide services for returning Corps members."
Net Revenue: FY ending 9/94 $5,045,231 ($4,430,979, or 88%, from government grants)
Net Expenses: $4,972,961 97%/3%/0% **Net Assets:** $581,614 **Citations:** 115:109
Tax Status: 501(c)(3)
Board of Directors or Trustees: Emma Bromon, Inez Galvan, Dorothy Henderson, Brenda Jarmon, Diane Kessler, Joan Lucas, Barbara Rabkin, Loretta Tyson, Emily Vallez, Sharon Van Slyke.
Other Information: WIC received $4,430,979, or 88% of revenue, from government grants. $569,201, or 11%, from gifts and grants awarded by foundations, businesses, and individuals. $26,618, or 1%, from fees for educational courses that "are aimed at raising the sensitivity level of the recruiters and counselors toward the youths they assist." The remaining revenue came from interest on savings and temporary cash investments, the sale of publications, and other miscellaneous sources.

Women Judges' Fund for Justice (WJFJ)

733 15th St., N.W., Suite 700
Washington, DC 20005   **Phone:**   (202) 783-2073
USA   **Fax:**   (202) 783-0930

Contact Person: Esther K. Ochsman, Executive Director.
Officers or Principals: Esther K. Ochsman, Executive Director ($34,874); Hon. Gina L. Hale, President ($0); Hon. Elizabeth Lacy, Vice President ($0); Hon. Carolyn Miller Parr, Secretary; Hon. Susan M. Moiseev, Treasurer.
Mission or Interest: Seeks to improve the administration of justice with an emphasis on issues that affect women. Operates state-level programs. Focus on abortion rights.

Accomplishments: In the abbreviated fiscal year from January to September 1995, the Fund spent $149,118 on its programs. The largest program, with expenditures of $63,139 was the publication of a manual for "judicial administration on the introduction of expert testimony on the effects of battering. $28,306 was spent on gathering data and presenting a roundtable discussion for the benefit of "judiciary considering sentencing of offenders who are pregnant substance abusers." $26,332 was spent on financial assistance to states "wishing to present WJFJ developed judicial education curricula on family violence, sentencing pregnant substance abusers, and bioethical (abortion) issues." Other programs included abortion rights, Women in Custody, Children and Violence, Non-Traditional Families, and more.

Net Revenue: FY running 1/95 to 9/95 $188,032 ($103,889, or 55%, from government grants)

Net Expenses: $194,523 77%/19%/4% **Net Assets:** $134,129

Products or Services: Educational programs for states, publications, and lobbying. The Fund spent $52 lobbying the U.S. Senate Appropriations Committee by sending letters encouraging continued funding for the State Justice Institute.

Tax Status: 501(c)(3)

Board of Directors or Trustees: Hon. Betty Barteau (Court of Appeals, IN), Hon. Judith Billings (Court of Appeals, UT), Hon. Betty Weinberg Ellerin (Pres., National Association of Women Judges, Assoc. Justice, Supreme Court of NY), Hon. Susan Finlay (ex officio, South Bay Municipal Court), Hon. Kathleen Gearin (Second Judicial District Court, MN), Hon. Ernestine Gray (Chief Justice, Orleans Parish Juvenile Court), Hon. Peggy Hora (San Leandro-Hayward Municipal Court), Hon. Noel Kramer (Associate Judge, DC Superior Court), Hon. Cindy Lederman (Dade County Court, 11th Judicial District, Juvenile Justice Center), Hon. Rose Norma Shapiro (U.S. District Court, PA), Marna Tucker.

Other Information: Affiliated with the 501(c)(6) National Association of Women Judges. The Fund received $103,889, or 55% of revenue, from government grants. $78,802, or 42%, from gifts and grants awarded by foundations, businesses, affiliates, and individuals. (In 1994 these grants included $30,000 from the Jessie Smith Noyes Foundation, $20,000 from the General Service Foundation.) $4,278, or 2%, from interest on savings and temporary cash investments. $1,063, or 1%, from the sale of publications.

Women USA Fund

845 3rd Ave., 15th Floor
New York, 10022   **Phone:**   (212) 759-7982
USA

Contact Person: Susan Davis, Executive Director.   **Officers or Principals:** Susan Davis, Executive Director ($66,040); Brownie Lebdetter, President ($0); Hon. Maxine Waters, Vice President ($0); Bella S. Abzug, Secretary; Mim Kelber, Treasurer.

Mission or Interest: "Encouraging greater widespread understanding and awareness of current social, economic, legal, political, cultural, educational and other issues affecting the condition and status of women."

Accomplishments: Launched the Women's Environment and Development Program (WEDO) in response to the exclusion of women from the early preparatory stages for the U.N.'s Earth Summit in Rio. "Pioneered the development of new advocacy techniques for women from the U.S. and other countries to participate in global public education and policy activities." Organized a caucus in the early stages of the U.N. International Conference on Population and Development in Cairo and the Fourth World Conference on Women in Beijing. Following the Beijing Conference, Bella Abzug created a 12-point "Contract With American Women", which Abzug considers "the mirror-opposite of the Gingrich 'Contract'." The Contract contains provisions for "equal pay for work of comparable value" and strengthening affirmative action, among others. In 1994 WEDO worked with Greenpeace USA and Women's Health Networks, to advance the thesis that breast cancer is linked to environmental causes. Held a conference with the Foundation for a Compassionate Society on environmental hazards. In 1994 the Fund spent $859,683 on its projects. The largest project, with expenditures of $290,807, was participation in the Fourth World Conference on Women in Beijing.

Net Revenue: 1994 $1,680,763 **Net Expenses:** $960,946 89%/11%/0% **Net Assets:** $1,102,063 **Citations:** 1:240

Products or Services: Women and Government: New Ways to Power (1994, Praeger Publishing).

Tax Status: 501(c)(3)

Other Information: The Fund received $1,659,134, or 99% of revenue, from gifts and grants awarded by foundations, businesses, the United Nations, and individuals. (These grants included $675,000 from the Ford Foundation, $100,000 from the MacArthur Foundation, $51,000 from the World Bank, $50,000 from the Henry J. Kaiser Family Foundation, $35,000 from the Jesse Smith Noyes Foundation, $25,000 from the Barbra Streisand Foundation, $15,000 from the Rockefeller Foundation, $5,342 from the Ford Foundation in China, $5,000 from the Ms. Foundation for Women, and $1,500 from the Foundation for a Compassionate Society. The Fund also received at least $85,000 from United Nations agencies. In 1995, $50,000 from the Rockefeller Foundation.) $17,786, or 1%, from dividends and interest from securities. The remaining revenue came from the sale of inventory.

Women Work! The National Network for Women's Employment

1625 K St., N.W., Suite 300
Washington, DC 20006   **Phone:**   (202) 467-6346   **E-Mail:** ww@imssys.imssys.com
USA   **Fax:**   (202) 467-5366

Contact Person: Jill W. Miller, Executive Director.

Officers or Principals: Jill W. Miller, Executive Director ($61,382); Rubie Coles, Co-Executive Director ($59,046); Olivia G. White, President; Sandy Nelson, President-Elect; Olga C. Chavez, Treasurer; Sara Ann Swida, Secretary; Gilda Nardone, Vice President, Long Range Planning; Cynthia Fobbs Morton, Vice President, Multi-Ethnic/Multi-Cultural Women.

Mission or Interest: "Dedicated to empowering women from diverse backgrounds and assisting them to achieve economic self-sufficiency through job readiness, education, training and employment." Runs programs funded by the Department of Labor. "Leading and or participating in coalitions that focus on Job training, vocational education, welfare reform, pay equity, minimum wage, and health care."

Accomplishments: "Network members include more than 1,300 education, training, and employment programs." In the fiscal year ending June 1995, the Network spent $623,122 on its programs. The largest program, with expenditures of $506,207, was information gathering and dissemination under U.S. Department of Labor grants. Other programs included training sessions, the production and distribution of studies on low wage jobs, and coalition building and participation.
Net Revenue: FY ending 6/95 $788,486 ($650,000, or 82%, from government grants) **Net Expenses:** $804,600 77%/22%/1%
Net Assets: $16,606
Products or Services: Catalog of publications, video tapes, "nation-wide information system", and lobbying. The Network spent $7,038 on grassroots lobbying.
Tax Status: 501(c)(3) **Annual Report:** No. **Employees:** 10
Board of Directors or Trustees: Andrea Chastain (Kansas City Community College), Mary Ann Eisenreich (Carlow College), Pat Thompson (YWCA), Jane Pease (ME Centers for Women, Work and Community), Irene Navero Hammel (Queens Women's Network), Joyce Blackburn, Loydia Webber (GA Dept. of Technical and Adult Education), Sherry Montgomery (Lincoln Land Community College), Patty McGuire, Cheryl Parks Hill, Sharon Kearnes (Miles Community College), Joanne Durkee (Mt. Diablo Adult Education), Sandy Nelson (Chemeketa Community College).
Other Information: Formerly called the National Displaced Homemakers Network. Women Work! received $650,000, or 82% of revenue, from government grants. $60,486, or 8%, from the sale of and subscriptions to publications. $45,985, or 6%, from gifts and grants awarded by foundations, businesses, and individuals. $13,386, or 2%, from fees for the management information systems. $11,961, or 2%, from membership dues. The remaining revenue came from video sales, and other miscellaneous sources.

Women's Action Alliance

370 Lexington Ave., Suite 603
New York City, NY 10017   **Phone:**   (212) 532-8330
USA   **Fax:**   (212) 779-2846

Contact Person: Karen R. Amaranth, Executive Director.
Officers or Principals: Chris Kirk, Project Director ($67,789); Karen R. Amaranth, Executive Director ($64,902); Cynthia Brewster, Controller ($52,476); Kay Ellen Consolver, Esq., Chair; Elaine Allen, Treasurer; Miori Tsubota, Esq., Secretary.
Mission or Interest: "Self determination for all women and girls through the creation, testing, and implementation of innovative program models through community-based organizations...Current projects provide public education and promote...female self esteem, equity in education and the workplace, substance abuse prevention, prenatal and maternal self care, breast cancer early detection, domestic violence and sexual harassment prevention.
Accomplishments: Conducted the National Women's Survey and distributed the results at the Non-Governmental Organizations Forum of the United Nations' Fourth World Conference on Women in Beijing, China. Produced "Listen to Us/Escúchanos" a bilingual documentary of their Multicultural Prenatal Drug and Alcohol Prevention Project. In 1994 the largest program was the Women's Alcohol and Drug Education Project, for which theyspent $830,632.
Net Revenue: FY ending 6/94 $1,027,769 ($887,066, or 86%, came from government grants)
Net Expenses: $1,069,879 83%/16%/1% **Net Assets:** $99,665 **Citations:** 0:255
Products or Services: Surveys, publications, conferences. Annual "Celebration of Leadership in Action" honoring outstanding role models for women and girls. Catalog of merchandise.
Tax Status: 501(c)(3) **Annual Report:** No. **Employees:** 6
Board of Directors or Trustees: Anne Biancardi (Chemical Bank), Cate Boeth (IBM Corp.), Brenda Clarke, Gwendolyn Evans (Prudential Insurance & Financial Services), Carolyn Fikke (Prudential Securities), Jane Lattes (American Museum of Natural History), Joyce Perry Jacobs (Newark Community School of the Arts).
Periodicals: *Women in Action* (quarterly newsletter).
Internships: Yes, unpaid, in the summer, fall or spring.
Other Information: The Alliance received $887,066, or 86% of revenue, from government grants. $116,213, or 11%, from gifts and grants awarded by foundations, individuals and companies. $2,316, or less than 1%, from the sale of publications. $2,338 from interest on savings and temporary cash investments. $19,836, or 2%, from "miscellaneous" sources.

Women's Action for New Directions Education Fund (WAND)

691 Massachusetts Ave.
Arlington, MA 02174   **Phone:**   (617) 643-4880
USA   **Fax:**   (617) 643-6744

Contact Person: Edie Allen, Vice President. **Officers or Principals:** Arlene Victor, President ($0); Peggy Kerry, Treasurer ($0); Dr. Helen Caldicott, Founder ($0); Edie Allen, Vice President; Sayre Sheldon, Clerk.
Mission or Interest: "To educate women to reduce violence and militarism and redirect resources to human and environmental needs."
Accomplishments: In the fiscal year ending June 1994, the Fund spent $143,946 on its programs.
Net Revenue: FY ending 6/94 $178,914 **Net Expenses:** $221,579 65%/18/17% **Net Assets:** $49,978
Tax Status: 501(c)(3)
Board of Directors or Trustees: Barbara Green, Henrietta Turnquest.

Other Information: Affiliated with the 501(c)(4) Women's Action for New Directions. Previously called Women's Action for Nuclear Disarmament. Founded by Dr. Helen Caldicott who also founded Physicians for Social Responsibility. The organization also has a Washington, DC office. 110 Maryland Ave., N.E., Washington, DC 20002, (202) 543-8505, fax (202) 673-6469. The Fund received $177,106, or 99% of revenue, from gifts and grants awarded by foundations, businesses, and individuals. (These grants included $35,000 from the Ploughshares Fund, $15,000 from the Town Creek Foundation, $10,000 from the Compton Foundation.) $1,626, or 1%, from interest on savings and temporary cash investments. The remaining revenue came from the sale of materials.

Women's Economic Agenda Project (WEAP)

518 17th St., Suite 200
Oakland, CA 94612   **Phone:**   (510) 451-7379
USA

Contact Person: Ethel Long-Scott, Executive Director.   **Officers or Principals:** Sonja Blutgarten, President ($0); Gloria Sandoval Vice President ($0); Janece Boyd, Secretary ($0); Kim Argula, Treasurer; Ethel Long-Scott, Executive Director.
Mission or Interest: Provides job and economic training for women and minorities. Provides education and advocacy on welfare issues.
Accomplishments: In 1994 WEAP spent $93,386 on its programs. These included: Workshops and presentations reaching over 300 organizations. Appearances on over 50 local and national media outlets. Participated in a Workshop for the Center on Social Welfare Policy and Law at Georgetown University, state hearings on welfare reform, testimony on gender and racism before a traveling United Nations Delegation, and addressed a NOW conference on "Who Speaks for Victims." Received a contract from the city of Oakland to evaluate "deficiencies" in hiring.
Net Revenue: 1994 $104,693 ($14,999, or 14%, from government contracts) **Net Expenses:** $112,489 83%/10%/7%
Net Assets: (-$29,441)
Tax Status: 501(c)(3)
Board of Directors or Trustees: Dorothy Amador, Maria Ayala, Octavia Tebeaux-Edgley, Linda Lemaster, Judy Pantoja, Angela Hatfield, Antionette Nicholas, Jeraleen Thornton-Peterson, Dee Petty.
Other Information: The Project received $77,951, or 74% of revenue, from gifts and grants awarded by foundations, businesses, and individuals. (These grants included $28,000 from the San Francisco Foundation, $10,000 from the Abelard Foundation, $7,500 from the Tides Foundation, $5,000 from the McKay Foundation.) $14,999, or 14%, from a contract with the city of Oakland. $5,744, or 5%, from training fees for job training programs. $4,450, or 4%, from rental income. $950, or 1%, from honoraria. The remaining revenue came from membership dues, interest on savings and temporary cash investments, the sale of inventory, and other miscellaneous sources.

Women's Health Action and Mobilization (WHAM!)

P.O. Box 733
New York, NY 10009   **Phone:**   (212) 560-7177   **E-Mail:** wham@listproc.net
USA

Officers or Principals: No officers, they are a "non-hierarchical organization".
Mission or Interest: "A direct action group committed to demanding, securing, and defending absolute reproductive freedom and quality health care for ALL women." Operates several action groups, including Church Ladies for Choice, and the New York Clinic Defense Task Force.
Tax Status: Informal "neighborhood association." **Annual Report:** No. **Employees:** None.
Board of Directors or Trustees: "None!"
Periodicals: *Frontlines*, and *The Urban Herbalist*.
Internships: "Unpaid, minimally supervised."

Women's Information Exchange

P.O. Box 68
Jenner, CA 95450   **Phone:**   (707) 632-5763   **E-Mail:** wie@wco.com
USA   **Fax:**   (707) 632-5589   **Web-Page:** http://www.electrapages.com

Contact Person: Jill Lippitt.   **Officers or Principals:** Deborah Brecher.
Mission or Interest: Provide networking and computer services for feminist organizations.
Accomplishments: They currently link 70 individuals and 10 organizations.
Products or Services: Computer services and networks. They offer mailing lists through their affiliate, the National Women's Mailing List.
Tax Status: For profit. **Annual Report:** No. **Employees:** 2
Other Information: They are affiliated with the National Women's Mailing List at the same address.

Women's International League for Peace and Freedom (WILPF)

1213 Race St.
Philadelphia, PA 19107   **Phone:**   (215) 563-7110   **E-Mail:** wilpfnat@igc.apc.org
USA   **Fax:**   (215) 563-5527

Contact Person: Pamela Jones Burnley, Administrative Director.   **Officers or Principals:** Pamela Jones Burnley, Administrative Director ($26,266); Jean Gore, President ($0); Susan Constantine, Ruth Graves, Jean Roland-Pender, Peggy Brozicevic, Vice Presidents ($0); Kathleen Tranchina, Secretary; Ruth Graves, Treasurer; Paula Tasso, United Nations Representative..
Mission or Interest: "To stop war, end economic inequality, fight racism, sexism and militarism through peace and freedom educational programs."
Accomplishments: In 1994 the League spent $116,173 on its programs. The largest program, with expenditures of $76,871, was "public education on peace and freedom in foreign countries." $29,745 was spent on "public education on peace, social welfare and race relations issues through peace curricula, educational seminars, literature, and a monthly newsletter." $9,557 to operate an office and lobby in Washington, DC. The League awarded $64,079 in grants to its affiliates in Geneva, Switzerland, and the Jane Addams Peace Association.
Net Revenue: 1994 $378,587 **Net Expenses:** $403,176 29%/65%/6% **Net Assets:** $60,339
Products or Services: Posters depicting recipients of corporate welfare, or "Wealthfare."
Tax Status: 501(c)(4)
Board of Directors or Trustees: Mary Fagan Bates, Ione Biggs, Judy Botwin, Peggy Brozicevic, Agnes Bryant, Betty Burkes, Susan Constantine, Donna Cooper, Carol Cutler, Madeline Duckles, Lynn Furay, Ruth Graves, Audley Green, Minnie Hoch, Barbara Howard, Betty Jallings, Ethel Jensen, Barbara Oskoui, Ann Chalmers Pendell, Jean Roland-Pender, Jackie Sparkman, Jan Strout, Kathleen Tranchina, Mary Zepernick.
Periodicals: *Peace and Freedom* (monthly newsletter).
Other Information: In 1994 the League received $204,897, or 53% of total revenue, from gifts and grants awarded by foundations, businesses, and individuals. $139,801, or 36%, from membership dues. $24,035, or 6%, from the sale of literature. $9,805, or 3%, from newsletter subscriptions. $5,158, or 1%, from interest on savings and temporary cash investments. The League realized a lost of $5,109 on long-term investments.

Women's International Network (WIN)
187 Grant St.
Lexington, MA 02173   **Phone:** (617) 862-9431
USA   **Fax:**   same

Contact Person: Fran Hosken, President.
Officers or Principals: Fran Hosken, President ($0); Caroline Hosken, Clerk ($0); Helen Rigelow, Director ($0).
Mission or Interest: To encourage cooperation and communication between women around the world. Conducts research on issues such as health, the environment, violence, female genital mutilation, and United Nations projects of interest to women. Fran Hosken states "Women around the world are uniting on their own issues and demanding to be heard on their own rights. Times are changing...in the greatest of social revolutions: the revolution for women's rights - women, who are still the largest and most oppressed majority in literally all societies."
Accomplishments: In 1987 Fran Hosken was awarded the Humanist Heroine Award from the American Humanist Association's Feminist Caucus. In 1994 the Network, although a private foundation, made no grants. $20,474 was spent producing and distributing its publications.
Net Revenue: 1994 $73,739 **Net Expenses:** $63,812 **Net Assets:** $96,615
Products or Services: Childbirth Picture Book (in English, Arabic, French, Somali, and Spanish), and the Hosken Report: Sexual Mutilation of Females.
Tax Status: 501(c)(3)
Periodicals: *WIN News* (quarterly newsletter).
Other Information: Founded in 1975. The Network received $40,133, or 54% of revenue, from the sale of publications. $31,300, or 42%, from gifts and grants awarded by foundations and individuals. (This included $25,000 from the Wallace Genetic Foundation, the rest came from individuals.) $2,356, or 4%, from interest on savings and temporary cash investments.

Women's Law Fund
3214 Prospect Ave.
Cleveland, OH 44115   **Phone:** (216) 431-4850
USA   **Fax:**   (216) 391-8176

Contact Person: Caryn Groedel, Executive Director.
Officers or Principals: Caryn Groedel, Executive Director ($0); Jane Picker, President ($0); Aldona Cytraus, Treasurer ($0).
Mission or Interest: Foundation that awards grants to organizations fighting sex discrimination.
Accomplishments: In the fiscal year ending May 1994, the Fund spent a total of $22,489, all on administrative expenses.
Net Revenue: FY ending 5/94 $8,585 **Net Expenses:** $22,489 **Net Assets:** $50,826
Tax Status: 501(c)(3)
Board of Directors or Trustees: Joan Farragher, Ranelle Gamble, Marie Graff, Pamela Hultin, Janice Jacobs, Denise Knecht, Grace Kudukis, Anne Lukas (Notre Dame College), Phyllis Melnick, Lana Moresky (County Auditor's Office, Cleveland), Christine Patronik-Holder, Alice Rickel, Hon. Linda Rocker, Karen Sawka, Gilda Spears, Ellen Spielman, Mercedes Spotts, Marilyn Tobocman.
Other Information: The Fund received $7,388, or 86% of revenue, from gifts and grants awarded by foundations, businesses, and individuals. $1,131, or 14%, from interest on savings and temporary cash investments. The remaining revenue came from seminar income. Besides running a deficit that year, the Fund's assets were reduced from $119,433 to $50,826 by an unrealized depreciation on their library.

Women's Law Project

125 S. 9th St., Suite 401
Philadelphia, PA 19107   **Phone:**   (215) 928-9801
USA

Contact Person: Linda Wharton, Managing Attorney.   **Officers or Principals:** Carol E. Tracy, Director ($62,083); Linda Wharton, Managing Attorney ($56,011); Dabney Miller, Programs and Development ($49,371); Susan Frietsche, Staff Attorney; Amy E. Wilkinson, Chair; Thomas Zemaitis, Secretary; Kelly Moylan, Treasurer.
Mission or Interest: Education, advocacy, and litigation on behalf of women's rights. Maintains various working groups such as the Working Group for the Legal Rights of Lesbian and Gay Parents.
Accomplishments: In the fiscal year ending June 1994, the Foundation spent $366,034 on its programs. The largest program, with expenditures of $158,953, was the general protection of women's rights. $116,247 was spent protecting abortion rights. $53,365 was spent on education and advocacy. Other programs included prison litigation, child support, parenting rights, and substance abuse. As part of the programs, the Project paid $1,903 to Pennsylvanians for Choice. The Law Project spent $2,115 on litigation costs, and received $20,455 in court-awarded attorneys' fees.
Net Revenue: FY ending 6/94 $274,376 **Net Expenses:** $428,084 86%/7%/7% **Net Assets:** $67,752
Tax Status: 501(c)(3)
Board of Directors or Trustees: Heather Burns, Louise Cerasoli-Kepler, Robin Coward (PA Liquor Control Board), Ellie DiLapi, Frank Finch III, Ann Freedman (Rutgers-Camden Law School), Susan Frietsche, Judy Greenwood, Phoebe Haddon, Seth Kreimer (School of Law, University of PA), Arline Jolles Lotman, Lynn Marks (Pennsylvanians for Modern Courts), Mary McLaughlin, Karlyn Messinger, Joann Mitchell (Princeton Univ.), Sarah Wiggins Mitchell, Barbara Penny, Anu Rao, Robert Schwartz (Juvenile Law Center), Martha Swartz, Peter Vaughan (School of Social Work, Univ. of PA), Sherri Williams-Nehy.
Other Information: The Women's Law Project received $213,993, or 78% of revenue, from direct and indirect public support in the form of gifts and grants awarded by foundations, affiliates, businesses, and individuals. (These grants included $63,000 from Women's Way, $15,000 from the Ms. Foundation for Women, $15,000 from the Robert Sterling Clark Foundation, and $10,450 from the Bread and Roses Community Fund.) $34,563 net, or 13%, from special fund-raising events. $20,455, or 7%, from court awarded attorney's fees. $5,365, or 2%, from interest on savings and temporary cash investments.

Women's Legal Defense Fund (WLDF)

1875 Connecticut Ave., N.W., Suite 700
Washington, DC 20009   **Phone:**   (202) 986-2600
USA   **Fax:**   (202) 686-9448

Contact Person: Judith Lichtman, President.   **Officers or Principals:** Judith Lichtman, President ($89,476); Debra L. Ness, Executive Vice President ($83,273); Nina Robbins, Development Director ($76,016); Donna Lenhoff, General Counsel; Ellen Malcolm, Chair; Pauline Schneider, Vice Chair; Chris Sale, Treasurer; Judy Langford Carter, Secretary.
Mission or Interest: Through publications, conferences, litigation and lobbying, "increased the public's understanding of the status of women in society and of the public policies needed to enable women's full and equal participation in work and family. Advocated for such public policies."
Accomplishments: In the fiscal year ending March 1994, WLDF spent $1,294,140 on its programs. The largest set of programs, with expenditures of $435,112, were the Employment Programs. These programs "carried out activities to ensure women's fair treatment on the job, including participation as amicus or as counsel in selected litigation." Issues involved sexual harassment and family leave. $275,221 was spent on public education and advocacy which provided membership services to approximately 3,000 members and contributors. $220,331 was spent on Women's Health programs, which focused on abortion rights and other issues involved in the health care reform debate. Other programs dealt with "Family Economic Security" issues, such as child support, and litigation.
Net Revenue: FY ending 3/94 $1,547,272 **Net Expenses:** $1,565,508 83%/6%/12% **Net Assets:** $206,041
Citations: 0:255
Products or Services: Custody Handbook, other publications, litigation, and lobbying. The Fund spent $65,007 on lobbying, $1,189 on grassroots lobbying and $63,818 on the direct lobbying of legislators. The amount spent on lobbying declined over the years, down 15% from one year prior, 38% from two, and down 56% from $148,408 three years prior.
Tax Status: 501(c)(3)
Board of Directors or Trustees: Nancy Buc, Sara-Ann Determan, Cassandra Flipper (The Nature Company Group), Douglas Fraser, Perry Granoff (Inst. For Family Interaction), Nikki Heidepriem, Antonia Hernandez (Mexican-American Legal Defense & Education Fund), Lowell Douglass Johnston, Patricia King (Georgetown Univ. Law Center), Ellen Malcolm (EMILY's List), Paulette Meyer, Judith Scott (Int'l. Brotherhood of Teamsters).
Other Information: The Fund hired the DC firm of PR Solutions for media and public relations, and paid the firm $33,000. The Fund is a member of, or paid event fees to, the Human Rights Campaign Fund, Leadership Conference on Civil Rights, and the National Abortion Rights Action League. The Fund Received $1,373,758, or 87% of gross revenue, from direct and indirect public support in the form of gifts and grants from foundations, businesses, affiliates, and individuals. (These grants included $75,000 from the Rosenberg Foundation, $60,000 from the Robert Sterling Clark Foundation, $30,000 from the Jessie Smith Noyes Foundation, $20,000 from the General Service Foundation, and $250 from the Stewart R. Mott Charitable Trust.) $185,099, or 12%, from membership dues. The remaining revenue came from interest on savings and temporary cash investments, publications, honoraria, and rents. The Fund lost $29,631 on special fund-raising events.

Women's Project

2224 Main St.
Little Rock, AR 72206   **Phone:**   (501) 372-5113
USA

Contact Person: Susan Pharr.
Mission or Interest: Works for social and economic justice.
Tax Status: 501(c)(3)
Periodicals: *Transformation* (newsletter).
Other Information: In 1994 the Project received $20,000 from the New World Fund, and $5,167 from the American Federation for AIDS Research. Other donors included the Astraea National Lesbian Action Foundation.

Women's Research and Education Institute (WREI)

1700 18th St., Suite 400
Washington, DC 20009   **Phone:**   (202) 328-7070
USA

Contact Person: Betty P. Dooley, Executive Director.
Officers or Principals: Betty P. Dooley, Executive Director ($85,477); Cindy Costello, Research Associate ($65,360); Jean Stapleton, President ($0); Dorothy Gregg, Vice President; Esther Coopersmith, Treasurer; Dorothy Height, Secretary.
Mission or Interest: "Monitors, analyzes and researches changes in the status of women in America and serves as a national information source and clearinghouse for information relating to women."
Accomplishments: In 1994 the Institute spent $657,762 on its programs. The largest program, with expenditures of $136,889, was stipends paid for fellowships for graduate students to work in the offices of members of the Congressional Caucus for Women's Issues and U.S. Congressional Committees to perform research on women's issues. $91,063 was spent on a Women in the Military project. $84,995 for fellowships for women from Eastern European countries. Other programs included: Women and Health Care, Women and Mental Health, the Fourth U.N. Conference on Women in Beijing, and others.
Net Revenue: 1994 $687,540 ($123,857, or 17%, from government grants) **Net Expenses:** $811,087 81%/15%/4%
Net Assets: (-$36,322) **Citations:** 0:255
Products or Services: *The American Woman*, annual journal on the status of women. Although WREI did not engage in lobbying in 1994, in 1993 it spent $101 on lobbying.
Tax Status: 501(c)(3)
Board of Directors or Trustees: Martina Bradford (AT&T), Hon. Juanita Kreps (Duke Univ.), Margaret Heckler (former Secretary, Health and Human Services, 1983-85), Matina Horner, Carolyn Forrest (UAW), Lindy Boggs, Evelyn Dubrow (Intl. Ladies Garment Workers Union), Denisl Ferguson, Joann Heffernan Heisen (Johnson & Johnson), Helen Wiederhorn (Ford Motor Co.), Alma Rangel, Annette Strauss, Celia Torres, Paquita Vivo, State Sen. Diane Watson (CA).
Periodicals: *The American Woman* (annual journal).
Other Information: The Institute received $564,919, or 79% of total revenue, from gifts and grants awarded by foundations, businesses, and individuals. $123,857, or 17%, from government grants. $12,035, or 2%, from the sale of publications. $7,126, or 1% from the sale of *The American Woman*. The remaining revenue came from conference registration fees, interest on savings and temporary cash investments, dividends and interest from securities, royalties, mailing list rentals, and other miscellaneous sources.

Women's Resource Center of New York

2315 Broadway, Suite 306
New York, NY 10024   **Phone:**   (212) 875-8533
USA

Contact Person: Christine Merser, President.
Officers or Principals: Joslyn Levy, Director ($27,100); Christine Merser, President ($10,833).
Mission or Interest: Provides "Women-focused services, resources, issues and events in the New York area."
Accomplishments: In the fiscal year ending February 1994, the Center spent $102,842 on its programs. $38,472 was spent producing a college handbook. $29,951 was spent on a finance seminar. The Center hosted a Women's Film Festival. "This years film festival dealt with relationships, lesbian issues, aging, disabilities, domestic violence, substance abuse and mixed racial heritage."
Net Revenue: FY ending 2/94 $285,445 **Net Expenses:** $290,188 **Net Assets:** $47,777
Tax Status: 501(c)(3)
Board of Directors or Trustees: Polly Carpenter, Shawn Grain Carter, Tina Cohoe, Martha Davis, Vicki Gershwin, Jane Gould (former Director, Barnard College Women's Center), Bernice Kanner (Bloomberg Business News), Mary Mitchell, Debra Osofsky Esq. (Air Line Pilot Assoc.), Jody Owen, Hal Peller, Alexandra Lally Peters, Susan Soros (Pres., Bard Graduate Center), Patrice Tanaka, Manisha Thakor, Arleatha Williams (Assoc. V.P., Prudential Securities).
Periodicals: Newsletter.
Other Information: The Center received $261,577, or 92% of revenue, from gifts and grants awarded by foundations, businesses, and individuals. (These grants included $50,000 from the Dobkin Family Foundation, $31,500 from the Istel Foundation, $20,000 from the Open Society Fund, and $10,000 from the Avon Products Foundation.) $20,760, or 7%, from membership dues. $2,946, or 1%, from the film festival. The remaining revenue came from interest on savings and temporary cash investments.

Women's Review / *Women's Review of Books*
Wellesley College Center for Research on Women
Wellesley, MA 02181   Phone: (617) 283-2087
USA   Fax: (617) 283-3645

Contact Person: Karin Christianson.   **Officers or Principals:** Anita McClellan, Advertising Manager ($52,474); Linda Gardiner, Editor in Chief ($36,587); Ellen Cantarow, Senior Editor; Martha Nichols, Associate Editor; Kathleen Hobson, Assistant Editor.
Mission or Interest: "We review books by and about women, in all areas, trade, scholarly and small press, from a variety of feminist perspectives."
Accomplishments: Published monthly since 1983. Monthly print run of approximately 13,000, readership of approximately 45,000, "making us one of the largest literary reviews in existence." Reviewers include some of the 'best known women writing today - Patricia Williams, Barbara Kingsower, Alix Kates Shulman, Carolyn Heilsman, etc." In the fiscal year ending June 1995 the Review spent $234,891 on the production and distribution of the *Women's Review of Books*. The *Review* received $355,447 in revenue from subscriptions, single copy sales, royalties, mailing list rentals, and advertising, and required no subsidization that year.
Net Revenue: FY ending 6/95 $361,549 **Net Expenses:** $377,618 62%/36%/1% **Net Assets:** $27,886
Tax Status: 501(c)(3) **Annual Report:** Yes. **Employees:** 6
Board of Directors or Trustees: Margaret Anderson, Robin Becker, Marsha Darling, Carol Gilligan, Sandra Harding, Nancy Hartsock, Carolyn Heilbrun, Evelyn Fox Keller, Jean Baker Miller, Ruth Perry (MIT), Peggy Phelan, Helene Vivienne Wenzel.
Periodicals: *The Women's Review of Books* (monthly journal).
Internships: No.
Other Information: The Review received $182,465, or 50% of revenue, from subscriptions. $153,997, or 43%, from advertising revenues. $13,113, or 4%, from mailing list rentals. $5,201, or 1%, from single copy sales. $3,410, or 1%, from gifts and grants awarded by foundations, businesses, and individuals. The remaining revenue came from the sale of donated items, royalties, and interest on savings and temporary cash investments.

Women's Way
1233 Locust St., 3rd Floor
Philadelphia, PA 19107   Phone: (215) 985-3322
USA

Contact Person: Constance G. Beresin, President.   **Officers or Principals:** Constance G. Beresin, President ($70,452); Linda Davenport, Director ($42,401); Barbara Kincaid, Director, Gift Planning ($40,624); Liz Werthan, Chair; Veronica McPherson, Vice Chair; Jean Young, Treasurer; Sally Simmons, Secretary.
Mission or Interest: "Women's Way is a fundraising coalition. It's purpose is to raise funds to be distributed to organizations in the Delaware Valley, serving women and children." These organizations pursue abortion rights, rights litigation, social services, tenants' advocacy, and more. Also provides technical assistance and referrals for coalition members.
Accomplishments: In the fiscal year ending June 1994, the organization spent $2,081,623 on its programs. $1,698,775 was awarded in grants to coalition members. The largest grants included; $991,010 for William Penn Foundation grants, $63,000 each for CHOICE, Community Women's Education Project, Domestic Abuse Project, Elizabeth Blackwell Health Center for Women, OPTIONS, Tenants' Action Group, Women Against Abuse, Women's Law project, and Women Organized Against Rape, $40,742 for the Supportive Older Women's Net work, and $38,029 for the Women's Alliance for Job Equity.
Net Revenue: FY ending 6/94 $2,388,743 **Net Expenses:** $2,354,117 88%/4%/8% **Net Assets:** $664,606
Tax Status: 501(c)(3)
Board of Directors or Trustees: Lila Booth, Rochelle Caplan (City of Philadelphia, Dept. of Human Services), Miriam Diamond, Molly Finn, Lois Fogg, Ellen Fischer, Vanessa Grant Jackson (Women Organized Against Rape), Ellen Greenlee, Eric Hoffman, Ann Hosage Moss, Robert Kimmel, Vicki Kramer, Kelly Lee, Mark Lipowicz, Lucille Mason, Patricia McInerney, Veronica Michael, Tracy Monroe, Evelyn Montalvo, Colleen O'Connell, Maria Pajil-Battle, Carole Phillips, Carol Ray (Women Against Abuse), Barbara Rosenberg, Ellen Rubin, Linda Seigel, Lisa Shulock (CHOICE), Sally Simmons (Women's Alliance for Job Equity).
Other Information: The organization received $2,393,621, or 99% of gross revenue, from direct and indirect public support in the form of gifts and grants awarded by foundations, affiliates, businesses, and individuals. The remaining revenue came from interest on savings and temporary cash investments. Women's Way lost $33,013 on its annual fund-raising dinner (this did not include the $312,385 in gifts and grants that were received at this dinner).

WomensNet
(see the Institute for Global Communications)

Womyn's Press
P.O. Box 562
Eugene, OR 97440   Phone: (541) 302-8146   **E-Mail:** womynprs@efn.org
USA

Contact Person: J.R. David.   **Officers or Principals:** N. Bruckner.
Mission or Interest: "Eclectic feminist newspaper dedicated to the voices of womyn, especially those not heard in the mainstream press: young women, old women, women of size, women of color, lesbian women, Jewish women, alternative spiritualities."
Accomplishments: "Continuously published for 25 years - the second oldest feminist publication in the U.S.!"
Tax Status: Oregon nonprofit. **Annual Report:** No. **Employees:** All volunteer.
Periodicals: *Womyn's Press* (bimonthly newspaper).
Internships: Yes.

Woodstock Institute
407 S. Dearborn, Suite 550
Chicago, IL 60605   **Phone:** (312) 427-8070
USA

Contact Person: Malcolm Bush, President.
Officers or Principals: Malcolm Bush, President ($68,500); Daniel Immergluck, Vice President ($42,840); Kathryn Tholin, Vice President ($39,718); Sokoni Karanja, Chair; Mary Nelson, Vice Chair; James Capraro, Secretary; Elizabeth Hollander, Treasurer.
Mission or Interest: Supports community reinvestment, and low income housing development.
Accomplishments: The Institute's study of the Small Business Administration's "LowDoc" (low-documentation) program was the subject of an August 8, 1995 *Wall Street Journal* article. The Institute's study found that in one major metropolitan area, San Antonio, the SBA's loan program was disproportionately helping non-minorities, and were going to businesses in higher-than-median income areas. In 1994 the Institute spent $274,685 on its programs. The largest program, with expenditures of $248,359, was technical assistance to neighborhood groups, nonprofits, and government agencies to develop community reinvestment programs. $26,326 was spent on research and support for coalitions to "increase the availability of low cost housing in low income neighborhoods."
Net Revenue: 1994 $444,986 **Net Expenses:** $458,545 60%/40%/0% **Net Assets:** $135,883
Tax Status: 501(c)(3)
Board of Directors or Trustees: Ronald Grzywinski, Stanley Hallett, John McKnight, Alexander Polikoff, David Ramage, Lawrence Rosser, Sandra Scheinfeld, Richard Shealey, Richard Harinack.
Other Information: The Institute received $412,392, or 93% of revenue, from gifts and grants awarded by foundations, businesses, and individuals. (These grants included $10,000 from the Wiebolt Foundation.) $18,514, or 4%, from the sale of assets. $7,780, or 2%, on interest from savings and temporary cash investments. $6,300, or 1%, from contract service fees.

Workers Defense League
218 W. 40th St., Suite 203
New York, NY 10018   **Phone:** (212) 730-7412
USA

Contact Person: Henry Fleischman, Chairman.   **Officers or Principals:** Leon Lynch, President ($0); Henry Fleischman, Chairman ($0); Noreen Connell, Vice President ($0); Lenore Miller, Secretary; Larry Cary, Treasurer.
Mission or Interest: Provide employee rights information, referrals, and legal consultation to workers.
Accomplishments: In the fiscal year ending June 1994, the League spent $41,380 on its programs. The largest program, with expenditures of $22,759, was "caller assistance" which dealt with work related problems and gave referrals to the "appropriate agencies" for assistance. $6,207 was spent on an educational and advocacy "Anti-Strike Breaking Project." $6,207 was spent on a Workers Rights program which provided speakers and literature. $6,207 was spent on a legal clinic that gave free information and advice.
Net Revenue: FY ending 6/94 $103,203 **Net Expenses:** $74,399 56%/31%/14% **Net Assets:** $190,548
Tax Status: 501(c)(3)
Board of Directors or Trustees: Morris Milgram, Patricia Sexton, William Stern, Alice Wolfson.
Other Information: The League received $50,303 net, or 49%, from special fund raising events. $49,589, or 48%, from gifts and grants awarded by foundations and individuals. $3,311, or 3%, from interest on savings and temporary cash investments.

Working From the Heart
1309 Merchant Lane
McLean, VA 22101   **Phone:** (703) 827-2742
USA

Contact Person: Jacqueline McMakin, President.   **Officers or Principals:** Jacqueline McMakin, President ($14,200); Sonya Dyer, former Treasurer ($14,000); Susan Gardiner, Treasurer/Vice President ($3,700).
Mission or Interest: Vocational mentoring to help individuals move toward "meaningful work" in the areas of activism, peace, and human rights.
Accomplishments: In the fiscal year ending July 1994 the organization spent $45,630 on its programs. These included a number of scholarships.
Net Revenue: FY ending 7/94 $77,413 **Net Expenses:** $80,673 **Net Assets:** $39,156
Tax Status: 501(c)(3)
Other Information: The organization received $65,338, or 84% of revenue, from program service fees. $10,350, or 13%, from gifts and grants awarded by foundations, businesses, and individuals. $880 net, or 1%, from the sale of inventory. The remaining revenue came from an IRS refund, and investment income.

Working Partnerships USA
2102 Almaden Rd., Suite 100
San Jose, CA 95125   **Phone:** (408) 269-7872
USA

Contact Person: Toby Rogers.
Mission or Interest: Promotion of leftist public policy through community and workplace organizing.

World Conference on Religion and Peace (WCRP)

777 United Nations Plaza
New York, NY 10017   **Phone:**   (212) 697-2163
USA

Contact Person: Dr. William F. Vendley. **Officers or Principals:** Dr. William F. Vendley, Secretary General ($95,403).
Mission or Interest: Inter-religious organization promoting world peace.
Accomplishments: In 1994 the WCRP spent $617,136 on its programs.
Net Revenue: 1994 $890,870 ($10,000, or 1%, from government grants) **Net Expenses:** $892,377 69%/30%/1%
Net Assets: $98,967 **Citations:** 0:255
Tax Status: 501(c)(3)
Board of Directors or Trustees: Dr. Elizabeth Bowen, Rev. Joan Campbell, Dr. Diana Eck, Rev. Rainer Lingscheid, Imam Deen Mohammed, Rabbi Alexander Schindler, and many representatives from outside the U.S.
Other Information: The WCRP received $872,663, or 99%, from gifts and grants awarded by foundations, businesses, and individuals. $10,000, or 1%, from government grants. The remaining revenue came from interest on savings and temporary cash investments, and other miscellaneous sources.

World Coordinating Council for Nicaragua (WCCN)

P.O. Box 1534
Madison, WI 53701   **Phone:**   (608) 257-7904   **E-Mail:** wccn@igc.apc.org
USA

Mission or Interest: Addresses poverty in Nicaragua, particularly that caused by the World Bank, International Monetary Fund, and U.S. AID. WCCN promotes community development, co-ops, and small business coupled with social spending to promote economic growth, as opposed to austerity measures, foreign loans, and exports.

World Federalist Association (WFA)

418 7th St., S.E.
Washington, DC 20003   **Phone:**   (202) 546-3950
USA   **Fax:**   (202) 546-3950

Contact Person: Tim Barner, Executive Director.   **Officers or Principals:** John Anderson, President ($0); Robert Stuart, Senior Vice President ($0); Dale Hiller, Chair ($0); Betty Anderson, Vice President.
Mission or Interest: "The abolition of war through just and enforceable world law." Also concerned with environmental matters.
Accomplishments: In 1993 the Association spent $353,161 on its programs.
Net Revenue: 1993 $1,116,546 **Net Expenses:** $620,154 57%/36%/7% **Net Assets:** $1,649,919 **Citations:** 58:133
Products or Services: Publications, lobbying. In 1993 the Association spent $48,000 on lobbying, an increase of 9% over the previous year.
Tax Status: 501(c)(3)
Board of Directors or Trustees: Paul Anderson, Yul Anderson, Sue Bailey, Lakshmi Bharadwaj, Lowell Blankfort, Tom Butterworth, Michael Chalfee, Chris Currie, Steve Damours, Lynn Elling, Jeffrey Epstein, Tim Evered, John Ewbank, Ian Gaynor, Desta Girma, Morton Gladstone, Avery Glasser, Mike Gravel, Joy Harbeson, Erling Helland, Richard Hudson, Eric Johnson, Sr. Pat Kenoyer, Ramesh Krishnamurthy, Myron Kronisch, Paul Malmberg, Thesil Morlan, Arnold Peterson, Harry Petrequin, Richard Ponzio, Floyd Ramp, Randy Robinson, Richard Robinson, Barbara Rhode, Jeanette Short, Sohini Sinha, Judy Snyder, Ira Straus, Ben Subedi, Jon Trevathan, Lesley Vann, Raymond Watts.
Periodicals: *World Federalist* (magazine).
Other Information: The Association received $586,741, or 53% of revenue, from gifts and grants awarded by foundations, businesses, and individuals. (In 1994 these included $1,300 from the Compton Foundation.) $273,371, or 24%, from program services. $132,570, or 12%, from dividends and interest from securities. $72,192, or 6%, from membership dues. $44,314, or 4%, from direct mail contributions. $7,358, or 1%, from interest on savings and temporary cash investments.

World Federalist Association of Pittsburgh

339 Boulevard of the Allies
Pittsburgh, PA 15222   **Phone:**   (412) 471-7852
USA

Contact Person: Earl James, Executive Director.   **Officers or Principals:** Earl James, Executive Director ($34,940).
Mission or Interest: "Educating members and the public on the principle of world peace through world law."
Accomplishments: In the fiscal year ending March 1994, the Association spent $89,526 on its programs.
Net Revenue: FY ending 3/94 $124,088 **Net Expenses:** $121,654 74%/25%/2% **Net Assets:** $132,548
Tax Status: 501(c)(3)
Other Information: The Association received $123,229, or 95% of gross revenue, from gifts and grants awarded by foundations, businesses, and individuals. $3,272, or 2%, from membership dues. $3,110, or 2%, from dividends and interest from securities. The remaining revenue came from interest on savings and temporary cash investments. The Association lost $5,841 on an investment.

World Peace Foundation
One Eliot Square
Cambridge, MA 02138   **Phone:**   (617) 491-5085
USA

Contact Person: Robert I. Rotberg, Executive Director. **Officers or Principals:** Robert I. Rotberg, Executive Director ($80,408); John W. Holmes, Acting Executive Director/Secretary ($55,826); Theresa Daranski, Assistant Treasurer ($41,213).
Mission or Interest: Private foundation that conducts seminars and programs focusing on world peace.
Accomplishments: In the fiscal year ending June 1994, the Foundation spent $223,210 on its programs, and awarded a grant of $15,000 to the publishers of *International Organization*, a scholarly journal formerly published by the World Peace Foundation. Programs included a Central America program, United States and Europe program, arms control and other programs.
Net Revenue: FY ending 6/94 $475,735 **Net Expenses:** $357,352 **Net Assets:** $3,025,996
Tax Status: 501(c)(3)
Board of Directors or Trustees: Peter Bell (Edna McConnell Clark Found.), Lincoln Bloomfield (MIT), Adam Chayes (Harvard Law School), Earl Foell, Milton Katz (Intl. Legal Studies), Judith Keenan (Headmistress, Commonwealth School), Donald McHenry (School of Foreign Service, Georgetown Univ.), Rosemarie Rogers (Tufts Univ.), Frederick G.P. Thorne, Richard Ullman (Princeton Univ.), Richard Wiley.
Other Information: The Foundation received $232,978, or 49% of revenue, from the Edward Ginn Trust. $120,378, or 25%, from dividends and interest from securities. $118,215, or 25%, from capital gains on the sale of securities. The remaining revenue came from interest on savings and temporary cash investments, and other miscellaneous sources.

World Population Society
1050 17th St., N.W., Suite 1050
Washington, DC 20036   **Phone:**   (202) 898-1303
USA   **Fax:**   (202) 861-0621

Contact Person: Philander Claxton, President. **Officers or Principals:** Philander Claxton, President ($31,248); Frank H. Oram, Executive Director ($0); Otto Schaler, Treasurer ($0); Page Wilson, First Vice President.
Mission or Interest: "Population policy development in less developed countries." Promotes birth control and family planning to ease overpopulation.
Accomplishments: In 1994 the Society spent $47,486 on its programs.
Net Revenue: 1994 $41,622 **Net Expenses:** $49,139 **Net Assets:** $31,597
Tax Status: 501(c)(3)
Other Information: The Society has received funding from the U.S. Agency for International Development; $49,607 in 1990, $25,500 in 1991, $20,100 in 1992, and $103,974 in 1993. In 1994 the Society received $40,259, or 97% of revenue, from gifts and grants. $1,363, or 3%, from investment income.

World Wildlife Fund (WWF)
1250 24th St., N.W.
Washington, DC 20037   **Phone:**   (202) 293-4800
USA

Contact Person: Kathryn Fuller, President. **Officers or Principals:** Kathryn Fuller, President ($228,335); James Leape, Senior Vice President ($160,125); Natalie Waugh, Vice President, Development ($127,928); Bruce Bunting, Vice President, Asia Program ($112,551); Lawrence J. Amon, Vice President, Finance ($111,590); John Noble, General Counsel ($107,156); Mark Rovner, Vice President, Public Affairs ($105,688); Gary Hartshorn, Vice President, Research and Development ($103,757); Roger W. Sant, Chairman; Lawrence S. Huntington, Chairman of the Executive Committee; Hunter Lewis, Treasurer; Edward P. Bass, Secretary.
Mission or Interest: Environmental protection and conservation worldwide. "The stakes have never been higher...The rich natural diversity of our planet is critically important. When we alter its fragile balance, we threaten our survival...Every hour of every day, hundreds of acres of irreplaceable rain forests are bulldozed, logged and burned off the face of the earth, destroying the livelihood of local peoples, wiping out entire species, choking the atmosphere and hastening global warming. We are only now discovering the enormity of our loss."
Accomplishments: "WWF is the foremost international conservation organization in the world, with affiliate organizations or representatives in more than 50 countries and a membership of more than 1,000,000 in the U.S. alone." WWF scientist Theo Colborn is a coauthor of Our Stolen Future, a book which alleges that synthetic chemicals may duplicate the effects of the hormone estrogen in males, lowering fertility and intelligence. Our Stolen Future is in its fifth printing. In the fiscal year ending June 1995, the Fund spent $54,962,352 on its programs. The largest program, with expenditures of $39,688,821, was conservation, the conservation of "nature-the diversity of species, communities, ecosystems, and ecological processes" through creating and preserving habitat, "effective models to reconcile human needs with the conservation of nature and working to integrate conservation into the actions, programs and policies of government agencies, major development institutions, and the private sector," protecting endangered species, and focusing on "global threats" such as carbon emissions and toxins. These programs included $10,583,963 in grants. These grants were awarded for efforts worldwide; $706,239 to Africa, $3,118,880 to Asia, $5,357,593 to Latin America and the Caribbean, and $1,401,249 to Europe, North America, and general worldwide efforts. $7,808,827 was spent on membership programs to "cultivate WWF's members' support and to give them the information they need to better understand the complexities of our global environment, to motivate them to pursue more environmentally sensitive lifestyles, to take action in their communities, and to spread the word to others about the importance of such efforts." $7,464,704 was spent on public education.

Net Revenue: FY ending 6/95 $67,725,579   ($19,807,492, or 29%, from government grants)   **Net Expenses:** $63,597,284   86%/5%/8%   **Net Assets:** $44,837,732   **Citations:**   763:28
Products or Services: Educational materials and curriculum, school projects, exhibits, books, directories, publications, and lobbying. The Fund spent $201,851 on lobbying, $94,330 on grassroots lobbying and $107,521 on the direct lobbying of legislators. This was a decrease of 14% from the previous year.
Tax Status: 501(c)(3)
Board of Directors or Trustees: Nancy Abraham, Barbara Cox Anthony, George Crowell, Joseph Cullman, III, Jared Diamond, Marshall Field, Lynn Foster, Julio Gutierrez Trujillo, C. Wolcott Henry, III, Milicent Johnsen, Thomas Kean, Frederick Krehbiel, William Lake, Cruz Matos, Scott McVay, Paul Miller, Jr., Gordon Orians, Arthur Ortenberg, James Ottaway, Jr., Anne Pattee, Singleton Rankin, William Reilly (former EPA Director), Gerald Rupp, Roque Sevilla, Margaret Taylor, John Terborgh, Rodney Wagner, Robert Waterman, Jr.
Other Information: The Fund received $43,145,540, or 64% of revenue, from gifts and grants awarded by foundations, affiliates, businesses, and individuals. (These grants included $731,749 from the Environmental Federation of America, $200,000 from the Pew Charitable Trusts, $157,000 from the Joyce Foundation, $20,000 from the General Service Foundation, $20,000 from the Bauman Family Foundation, $15,000 from the American Conservation Association, $14,567 from the Environmental Federation of California, $10,000 from the Global Environment Project Institute, $2,500 from the One World Fund, $1,200 from the Haymarket People's Fund, and $1,000 from the Compton Foundation. In 1993 the Fund received $300,000 from the Ford Foundation.) $19,807,492, or 29%, from government grants. $1,632,145, or 2%, from dividends and interest from securities. $1,114,825, or 2%, from royalties. $1,079,809, or 2%, from capital gains on the sale of securities. $688,972, or 1%, from mailing list rentals. The remaining revenue came from travel programs, interest on savings and temporary cash investments, and other miscellaneous sources.

World Without War Council (WWWC)
1730 Martin Luther King, Jr. Way
Berkeley, CA 94709   **Phone:**   (510) 845-1992   **E-Mail:** wwwc@igc.apc.org
USA   **Fax:**   (510) 845-5721

Contact Person: Robert Pickus, President.   **Officers or Principals:** Robert Pickus, President ($20,833); Fred Stevens, Assistant Secretary/Treasurer ($14,294); Kale Williams, Chairman ($0); Philip Siegelman, Secretary/Treasurer.
Mission or Interest: Working toward a world that resolves conflict through peaceful and lawful means. Works with nonprofit organizations and governmental agencies. "Perhaps the most apt analogy would be that of a management-consultant agency for enterprises that do not yet exist...Our initial task, therefore, involves conceiving programs, relationships, structures, that do not yet exist, and then persuading those who could help bring them into existence, to do so."
Accomplishments: In the fiscal year ending June 1994, the Council spent $60,000 on its "Reestablishing and Extending the Idea of the Common Good" program. The program seeks to build American leadership by building up our intellectual base to support the things that unite us, rather than "emphasizing the diversity and this or that ethnic heritage above what holds us together." The Common Good program held numerous conferences and featured 20 scholars. 100-150 community, academic, and organizational leaders attended these events. The Council spent $10,567 on their leadership training activities. The eleven participants attended seminars and conferences, and met with leaders in the field. They spent $7,000 to produce a directory of peace organizations, the "Organization Map Project."
Net Revenue: FY ending 6/94 $52,748   **Net Expenses:** $110,551   **Net Assets:** (-$5,333)
Products or Services: World Affairs Organizations in Northern California directory. Conferences, seminars, networking activities, publications, more.
Tax Status: 501(c)(3)   **Annual Report:** No.   **Employees:** 7
Board of Directors or Trustees: Allan Blackman, Paul Ekman, James Finn, Kent Hill, Ted Lobman, John Meermans, Byron Miller, Dan Seeger, Art Siegal, Kurt Taylor Gaubatz, George Weigel.
Internships: Yes, through their Americans and World Affairs Fellows Program.
Other Information: WWWC grew out of earlier peace efforts, namely Acts for Peace (1958-1961) and Turn Toward Peace (1961-1966). Turn Toward Peace fell apart over strategy opposing the war in Vietnam. On one side were the predominately Marxist radicals who not only opposed the U.S.'s actions, but supported Communist North Vietnam. "Its dominant spirit was not anti-war -- not once during all the Vietnam years did it criticize Hanoi's war policies." On the other side was what became the World Without War Council. WWWC's strategy has always been to appeal to "mainstream American life; toward a defense of democratic values against anti-democratic currents." The Council received $52,438, or 99% of its revenue, from gifts and grants awarded by foundations, companies and individuals. The remaining revenue came from investments.

Worldwatch Institute
1776 Massachusetts Ave., N.W.
Washington, DC 20036   **Phone:**   (202) 452-1999
USA

Contact Person: Lester Brown, President.
Officers or Principals: Christopher Flavin, Vice President ($67,980); Blondeen Gravely, Vice President ($58,147); Reah Janise Kauffman, Secretary ($55,110); Lester R. Brown, President ($54,450); Barbara Fallin, Assistant Treasurer.
Mission or Interest: Public policy organization concerned with population, the environment, and third world development.
Accomplishments: Worldwatch's annual *State of the World*, the Institute's guide to environmental and human conditions, is standard course material on college campuses nationwide. In 1994 the Institute spent $1,788,834 on its programs.

Net Revenue: 1994 $2,098,099 **Net Expenses:** $2,218,605 84%/18%/2% **Net Assets:** $2,013,854 **Citations:** 344:53
Tax Status: 501(c)(3)
Board of Directors or Trustees: Orville Freeman, Carlo Cipolla, Edward Cornish (World Future Society), Herman Daly (Inst. For Public Affairs, Univ. of MD), Mahbub ul Haq (United Nations Dept. of Population), Hazel Henderson, Lynne Gallagher, Anne-Marie Holenstein, Abd-El Rahman Khane, Hunter Lewis (Cambridge Assoc.), Larry Minear, Andrew Rice.
Periodicals: *World Watch* (bimonthly magazine), and *State of the World* (annual).
Other Information: The Institute received $1,999,586, or 88% of gross revenue, from gifts and grants awarded by foundations, businesses, and individuals. (These grants included $35,000 from the Nathan Cummings Foundation.) $170,151, or 7%, from royalties. $98,870, or 4%, from interest on savings and temporary cash investments. The Institute lost net $170,508 on the sale of inventory, including books and magazine subscriptions.

Worldwide Network
1331 H St., N.W., Suite 903
Washington, DC 20005   **Phone:**   (202) 347-1514
USA

Contact Person: Waafas Ofosu-Amaah, Executive Director.
Officers or Principals: Waafas Ofosu-Amaah, Executive Director ($28,100); Elie Garcia McComie, Executive Director ($13,500); Kathryn Cameron Porter, Chairperson ($0); Julia Panourgia Clones, Treasurer.
Mission or Interest: Network of women concerned about the environment, third world development, and the status of women.
Accomplishments: In 1993 the Network spent $159,853 on its programs. The largest program, with expenditures of $102,223, was various international meetings and assemblies on environmental issues and how these issues relate to women. $48,700 was spent on publications and reports. $8,930 was spent publishing a directory of women worldwide involved in environmental issues.
Net Revenue: 1993 $189,684 **Net Expenses:** $269,226 59%/41%/0% **Net Assets:** (-$7,194)
Products or Services: Directory of Women in Environment, meetings.
Tax Status: 501(c)(3)
Periodicals: *Worldwide News* (bimonthly newsletter).
Other Information: The Network received $154,543, or 87% of revenue, from gifts and grants awarded by foundations, businesses, and individuals. $6,555, or 3%, from dividends and interest from securities. $6,053, or 3%, from membership dues. $4,646, or 3%, from the sale of publications. $4,574, or 3%, from luncheons and meeting fees. The remaining revenue came from interest on savings and temporary cash investments, and capital gains on the sale of assets.

Young Communist League (YCL)
(see the Communist Party USA)

Young Women's Project
923 F St., N.W., 3rd Floor
Washington, DC 20004   **Phone:**   (202) 393-0461
USA

Contact Person: Nadia Moritz, Executive Director.
Mission or Interest: Develops and supports young women leaders and organizations concerned about abortion rights and violence issues.
Tax Status: 501(c)(3)
Other Information: Founded in 1989. In 1994 the Project received $5,000 from the Jessie Smith Noyes Foundation.

Z Magazine
(see the Institute for Social and Cultural Communications)

Zero Population Growth (ZPG)
1400 16th St., N.W., Suite 320
Washington, DC 20036   **Phone:**   (202) 332-2220
USA

Contact Person: Susan Weber, Executive Director. **Officers or Principals:** Susan Weber, Executive Director ($78,358); Dianne Sherman, Communications Director ($53,213); Dianne Dillon-Ridgley, President ($0); Chet Atkins, Edwin F. Leach, II, Vice Presidents; Alden Meyer, Treasurer; Eugene Kuscher, Secretary.
Mission or Interest: Founded in the 1960's by The Population Bomb author Paul Ehrlich. The organization advocates zero population growth, and an eventual reduction in the number of humans. The organization educates the public about the benefits of zero population growth, and maintaining a balance between population, the environment and resources.
Accomplishments: In 1994 ZPG spent $2,205,394 on its programs. The largest program, with expenditures of $727,579, was media and public information. $671,707 was spent on membership services, such as newsletters and updates, for its approximately 53,000 members. $278,342 was spent on public outreach and field services, such as information and technical assistance to a network of activists at the state and local level. $273,800 was spent on public policy research and advocacy. $253,966 was spent to train teachers and develop curriculum materials for grades K-12. Approximately 290,000 K-12 students were reached through these programs.
Net Revenue: 1994 $2,856,754 **Net Expenses:** $2,778,907 79%/10%/11% **Net Assets:** $543,327 **Citations:** 146:96

Products or Services: Publications, educational materials, teacher's materials, and lobbying. ZPG spent $7,232 on lobbying, $425 on grassroots lobbying and $6,807 on the direct lobbying of legislators. Lobbying expenditures have been decreasing over the last few years, down 16% from 1993, 41% from 1992, and down 56% from $16,522 in 1991.

Tax Status: 501(c)(3)

Board of Directors or Trustees: Ken Bilby, Jeffrey Bloomberg, Don Hutson, Tom Kring, John Lazarus.

Periodicals: *ZPG Reporter* (newsletter).

Other Information: Affiliated with the Zero Population Growth Foundation. The organization received $1,676,915, or 59% of revenue, from direct and indirect public support in the form of gifts and grants awarded by foundations, affiliates, businesses, and individuals. (These grants included $50,000 from the Richard and Rhoda Goldman Fund, $5,000 from the Compton Foundation). $1,068,962, or 37%, from membership dues. $50,717, or 2%, from the sale of inventory. $43,328, or 2%, from mailing list rentals. The remaining revenue came from interest on savings and temporary cash investments, royalties, and honoraria.

STATUS UNKNOWN

The organizations listed in this section were identified as being left-of-center policy advocates. However, they did not respond to our questionnaires nor did we receive any notification from the Postal Service that their address had changed. The organizations may be defunct, temporarily inactive, or simply not responsive to the public's interest. Readers may pursue them, but The Left Guide can not verify any of these groups' aims, responses, or operations. If users of The Left Guide can provide any information about these groups, we would be happy to include it in future editions. We have listed their address and, when available, their phone number and a contact person.

9 to 5, National Association for Working
Women
614 Superior Ave., N.W.
Cleveland, OH 44113

A Distribution
P.O. Box 2361
Landover Hills, MD 20784

Abalone Alliance
2940 16th St., Suite 310
San Francisco, CA 94103

Abortion Research Notes
8307 Whitman Dr.
Bethesda, MD 20817

Action for Animals
4207 Arroyzelo Ave.
Oakland, CA 94611

Action Linkage Network
P.O. Box 684
Bangor, ME 04401

Activists for Protective Animal Legislation
P.O. Box 11743
Costa Mesa, CA 92627

Africa Network
P.O. Box 5366
Evanston, IL 60204

Africa News
P.O. Box 3851
Durham, NC 27702

African American Coalition for Crisis in
Education
P.O. Box 851
Tuskegee, AL 36088

African World
60 Platinum Circle
Northhampton, MA 01060-3663

Africare
440 R St., N.W.
Washington, DC 20001

Afro-American Cultural Foundation
221 Cleveland Dr.
Croton, NY 10520-2414

After the Fall
2161 Massachusetts Ave.
Cambridge, MA 02140

Against the Current
7012 Michigan Ave.
Detroit, MI 48210

Air and Waste Management Association
P.O. Box 2861
Pittsburgh, PA 15230

Akwesasne Notes
P.O. Box 196
Rooseveltown, NY 13683

Al Fajr Palestinian Weekly
16 Cromwell St.
Hempstead, NY 11550

Alaska Coalition for the Homeless
P.O. Box 100940
Anchorage, AK 99510

Alaska Public Interest Research Group
P.O. Box 220411
Anchorage, AK 99522

Albanian Affairs Study Group
P.O. Box 912
New York, NY 10008

Albert Einstein Institution
1430 Massachusetts Ave., N.W., 5th Floor
Cambridge, MA 02138

All-Nations Women's League
39-55 51st St., Suite 2E
New York, NY 11377

All-Peoples Congress
P.O. Box 1819
New York, NY 10159

All Points of View
P.O. Box 321
San Antonio, TX 78292

Alliance for Animals
111 King St.
Madison, WI 53703

Alliance for Cultural Democracy
P.O. Box 7591
Minneapolis, MN 55407

Alliance for Progress
888 Grand Concourse
Bronx, NY 10452

Alliance of Atomic Veterans
P.O. Box 32
Topok, AZ 86436

Alternative News Collective
84 Massachusetts Ave.
Cambridge, MA 02139

Alternative Orange
126T Shine Center
Syracuse University
Syracuse, NY 13244

Alternative Press Center
P.O. Box 33109
Baltimore, MD 21218

Alternative Press Review
P.O. Box 1446
Columbia, MO 65205

Alternative Press Syndicate
P.O. Box 3323
Madison, WI 53704

Alternatives
1800 30th St.
Boulder, CO 80301

Alternatives to Animal Research
175 W. 12th St., Suite 16G
New York, NY 10011

Always Causing Legal Unrest
P.O. Box 2085
Rancho Cordova, CA 95741

American Association of Public Welfare
Attorneys
810 1st St., N.E., Suite 500
Washington, DC 20002
Jennifer Small, President

American Association of State Social Work
Boards
400 S. Ridge Pky., Suite B
Culpeper, VA 22701
Frances Byrd Goddard, Executive Director
(703) 829-6880, fax (703) 829-0142

American Baptist Church Peace Concerns
Program
P.O. Box 851
Valley Forge, PA 19482-2451

American Environment
1400 16th St., N.W., Box 24
Washington, DC 20036-2266

American Federation for Aging Research
1414 Avenue of the Americas
New York, NY 10019

American Humane Association
P.O. Box 1266
Denver, CO 80201

American Indian Defense News
P.O. Box 3121
Hutchinson, KS 67504

American Indian Liberation Crusade
4009 S. Halldale Ave.
Los Angeles, CA 90062

American Institute of Cooperation
50 F St., N.W., Suite 900
Washington, DC 20001

American Middle East Understanding
475 Riverside Dr., Suite 241
New York, NY 10015

American Movement for World Government
1F Adrian Court
Peekskill, NY 10566

American Oceans Campaign
725 Arizona Ave.
Santa Monica, CA 90401

American Peace Network
610 Ethan Allen Ave.
Takoma Park, MD 20712-5425

American Peace Test
135 Albert Ave., Apt. 16
Las Vegas, NV 89109

American Public Health Association
1015 15th St., N.W.
Washington, DC 20005

American Public Works Association
106 W. 11th St., Suite 1800
Kansas City, MO 64105-1806
William Bertera, Executive Director

American Solidarity Movement
853 Broadway, Suite 801
New York, NY 10003

American-Spanish Committee
P.O. Box 119
New York, NY 10013

Americans Against Animal Mistreatment
P.O. Box 904
Wilmington, DE 19899

Americans for a Safe Future
16830 Ventura Blvd., Suite Y
Encino, CA 91436

Amicus
40 W. 20th St.
New York, NY 10011

Anarchist Activist Center
7146 Remmet Ave., Suite 120
Canoga Park, CA 91303

Anarchist Archives Project
P.O. Box 1323
Cambridge, MA 02238

Anarchist Labor League
659 37th Ave., Suite A
San Francisco, CA 94121

Anarchy: Journal of Desire Armed
P.O. Box 1446
Columbia, MO 65205

Angola Foundation
5113 Georgia Ave., N.W.
Washington, DC 20011

Animal Activist Alert
2100 L St., N.W.
Washington, DC 20037

Animal Agenda
P.O. Box 25881
Baltimore, MD 21224

Animal Defense League
11300 Nacogdoches Rd.
San Antonio, TX 78217-2318

Animal Legal Defense Fund
1363 Lincoln Ave.
San Rafael, CA 94901

Animal Liberation
319 W. 74th St.
New York, NY 10023

Animal Rights League of America
P.O. Box 474
New Albany, OH 43054

Anti-Fascist Working Group
P.O. Box 10491
Detroit, MI 48210

Anti-Racist Action
P.O. Box 11211
Chicago, IL 60611

Anti-War Activist
P.O. Box 30061
New York, NY 10011

Aprovecho Institute
80574 Hazeltine Rd.
Cottage Grove, OR 97424

Arctic to Amazonia Alliance
P.O. Box 73
Strattford, VT 05072

Art Paper
P.O. Box 77348
Atlanta, GA 30357

Arthur Morgan School
1901 Hannah Branch Rd.
Burnsville, NC 28714

Artists Contributing to the Solution (ACTS)
1727 N. Spring St.
Los Angeles, CA 90012

Artists for Social Responsibility
Johnson State College, Building 52
Johnson, VT 05656

Artpolice
3131 lst Ave., S.
Minneapolis, MN 55408

Asian American Task Force
1122 Keeler Ave.
Berkeley, CA 94708

Association for a Democratic Workplace
P.O. Box 2092
Jasper, OR 97438-0299

Association for Humanist Sociology
899 10th Ave.
New York, NY 10019

Association for Humanistic Psychology
45 Franklin St., Suite 315
San Francisco, CA 94102

Association for the Advancement of Policy
Research and Development in the Third
World
P.O. Box 70257
Washington, DC 20024

Association for Transarmament Studies
3636 Lafayette Ave.
Omaha, NE 68131

Association for Voluntary Surgical
Contraception
79 Madison Ave., 7th Fl.
New York, NY 10016-7802
Hugo Hoogenboom, Executive Director
(212) 561-8095, fax (212) 599-0959

Association of Corporate Environmental
Officers
9690 Deereco Rd., Suite 250
Timonium, MD 21093

Association of Gay and Lesbian
Psychiatrists
24 Olmstead St.
Jamaica Plain, MA 02401
Marshall Forstein, M.D., President
(617) 522-1267

Association of Gay and Lesbian
Psychiatrists
1732 S.E. Ash
Portland, OR 97214

Association of Reproductive Health
Professionals
2401 Pennsylvania Ave., N.W., Suite 350
Washington, DC 20037-1718
Dennis J. Barbour, J.D., President
(202) 466-3825, fax (202) 466-3826

Association of Sierra Club Members for
Environmental Ethics
P.O. Box 1591
Davis, CA 95617
David Orr

Association of Transpersonal Psychology
P.O. Box 3049
Stanford, CA 94305

Association of Veterinarians for Animal
Rights
530 E. Putnam Ave.
Greenwich, CT 06830

Association to Unite the Democracies
P.O. Box 75920
Washington, DC 20013

Atlanta Art Papers
P.O. Box 77348
Atlanta, GA 30357

Atlantic Center for the Environment
55 S. Main St.
Ipswich, MA 01938
Lawrence Morris, President

Audubon Society
1719 Christina Dr.
Los Altos, CA 94024

Austin United Support Group
711 4th Ave., N.E.
Austin, MN 55912

Baba Yaga News
P.O. Box 330
South Lee, MA 01260

Bank Check
1847 Berkeley Way
Berkeley, CA 94703

Baptist Joint Committee on Public Affairs
200 Maryland Ave., N.E.
Washington, DC 20002

Baptist Peace Fellowship
499 Patterson St.
Memphis, TN 38111

Barricade Books
P.O. Box 1401
Secaucus, NJ 07076

Basic Foundation
P.O. Box 47012
St. Petersburg, FL 33743

Batterers' Group
412 Dayton St.
Yellow Springs, OH 45387-1706

Bayou La Rose
P.O. Box 5464
Tacoma, WA 98415

Beltane Papers
1333 Lincoln St., Suite 240
Bellingham, WA 98226

Berkeley Women's Law Journal
2120 Berkeley Way
Berkeley, CA 94720

Bertha Capen Reynolds Society
P.O. Box 20563
New York, NY 10023

Black Cat Collective
P.O. Box 1191
Newark, NJ 07101

Black Film Review
110 S St., N.W.
Washington, DC 20001

Black Liberation Radio
333 N. 12th St.
Springfield, IL 62702

Black Organization of Students
101 Washington St.
Newark, NJ 07102

Black Panther
P.O. Box 519
Berkeley, CA 94701

Black Panther National Committee
P.O. Box 16330
Jersey City, NJ 07306

Black Scholar
P.O. Box 2869
Oakland, CA 94609

Black United Front
709 Park Ave.
Greensboro, NC 27405

Black Women's United Front
3611 Dunbar
Dallas, TX 75215

Blacklist Mailorder Books
475 Valencia St.
San Francisco, CA 94103

Blacks Against Nukes
3728 New Hampshire Ave., N.W., Suite 202
Washington, DC 20010

Blast
P.O. Box 7075
Minneapolis, MN 55407

BLK
P.O. Box 8392
Los Angeles, CA 90083

Blue Mountain Environmental Organization
921 Germans Rd.
Lehighton, PA 18235

Blueprint for Social Justice
P.O. Box 12
Loyola University
New Orleans, LA 70118

Bolerium Books
2141 Mission St., Suite 300
San Francisco, CA 94110

Bolton Institute for a Sustainable Future
4 Linden Square
Wellesley, MA 02181-4709

Boston Review
33 Harrison Ave.
Boston, MA 02111

Boston Women's Teachers Group
P.O. Box 102
Cambridge, MA 02142

Brecht Forum
122 W. 27th St.
New York, NY 10001

Broomstick
3543 18th St., Suite 3
San Francisco, CA 94110

Bunny Huggers Gazette
P.O. Box 601
Temple, TX 76503

California Abortion Rights Action League,
North (CARAL)
330 Townsend St., Suite 204
San Francisco, CA 94107

California Communities Against Toxics
3813 W. 50th St.
Rosamond, CA 93560

Campaign for a New Tomorrow
P.O. Box 27798
Washington, DC 20038

Campaign for Peace and Democracy
P.O. Box 1640
New York, NY 10025

Campaign for Responsible Technology
408 Hyland Ave.
Somerville, MA 02144

Campaign to End Homophobia
P.O. Box 819
Cambridge, MA 02139

Campus Environmental Audit
1600 Oak St.
Santa Monica, CA 90405

Campus Green Network
724 Hillcrest Dr.
Thousand Oaks, CA 91359

CarEth Foundation
2040 S St., N.W., Suite 201
Washington, DC 20009

Carnegie Institute of Washington
5241 Broad Branch Rd., N.W., Suite 173
Washington, DC 20015-4376

Catalyst
P.O. Box 1308
Montpelier, VT 05601
Susan Meeker-Lowry, Director

Catholic Agitator
632 N. Brittania St.
Los Angeles, CA 90033

Catholic Peace Fellowship
339 Lafayette St.
New York, NY 10012

Caucus for a New Political Science
Political Science Dept.
Columbia University
New York, NY 10027

Caucus for Social Theory and Art Education
123 Education Bldg.
Florida State University
Tallahassee, FL 32306

Center for Anti-Violence Education
421 5th Ave.
Brooklyn, NY 11215

Center for Communal Studies
8600 University Blvd.
Evansville, IN 47712

Center for Environmental Education
881 Alma Real Dr., Suite 300
Pacific Palisades, CA 90272

Center for International Affairs
1737 Cambridge St.
Cambridge, MA 02138

Center for International Security and Arms
Control
320 Galez St.
Stanford University
Stanford, CA 94305-6165

Center for Lesbian and Gay Studies
CUNY Graduate Center
33 W. 42nd St.
New York, NY 10036
Martin Duberman, Executive Officer
(212) 642-2924, fax (212) 642-2642

Center for Marxist Education
550 Massachusetts Ave., 2nd Fl.
Cambridge, MA 02139

Center for New Creation
3339 Mansfield Rd.
Falls Church, VA 22041-1709

Center for Peace and Conflict Studies
5229 Cass, Suite 101
Detroit, MI 48202

Center for Peace and Life Studies
2010 W. CR Rd., 1270 N
Muncie, IN 47303

Center for Policy Analysis on Palestine
2435 Virginia Ave., N.W.
Washington, DC 20037

Center for Policy Research
1720 Emerson St.
Denver, CO 80218

Center for Policy Research
2700 Virginia Ave., N.W.
Washington, DC 20037

Center for Population Options' Media
Project
3733 Motor Ave., Suite 204
Los Angeles, CA 90034
Jennifer Daves, Director
(310) 559-5700, fax (310) 599-5784

Center for Post-Soviet Studies
2 Wisconsin Circle, Suite 410
Chevy Chase, MD 20815

Center for Psychology in the Public Interest
21 W. Euclid Ave.
Haddonfield, NJ 08033

Center for Rural Studies
2305 S. Irving
Minneapolis, MN 55405

Center for the Study of the Americas
2288 Fulton St., Suite 103
Berkeley, CA 94704

Center for Theology and Public Policy
4500 Massachusetts Ave., N.W.
Washington, DC 20016

Center for Watershed Protection
1020 Elden St., Suite 205
Herndon, VA 22070

Center for Workers Education
P.O. Box 25015
Providence, RI 02905

Center on Social Welfare Policy and Law
275 7th Ave., 6th Fl.
New York, NY 10001-6708

Center on War, Peace and the News Media
10 Washington Place
New York, NY 10003

Central America Information Center
P.O. Box 50211
San Diego, CA 92105

Central America Monitor
464 19th St.
Oakland, CA 94612

Central America Resource Center
P.O. Box 2327
Austin, TX 78768

Central America Solidarity Association
1151 Massachusetts Ave.
Cambridge, MA 02138

Central American Education Project
P.O. Box 40601
San Francisco, CA 94140

Central American Information Center
P.O. Box 50211
San Diego, CA 92165

Central American Refugee Center
3112 Mt. Pleasant St., N.W.
Washington, DC 20010

Central American Refugee Defense Fund
14 Beacon St., Suite 506
Boston, MA 02108

Central Park
P.O. Box 1446
New York, NY 10023

Changing Men
306 N. Brooks
Madison, WI 53715

Charles H. Kerr Publishing Co.
1740 W. Greenleaf
Chicago, IL 60626

Chicago ACORN
117 W. Harrison St., 2nd Fl.
Chicago, IL 60605

Children's Creative Response
P.O. Box 271
Nyack, NY 10960

Christian Children's Fund
203 E. Carey
Richmond, VA 23261

Citizen-Labor Energy Coalition
1300 Connecticut Ave., N.W.
Washington, DC 20036

Citizens Awareness Network
P.O. Box 83
Shelbourne Falls, MA 01370

Citizens Environmental Coalition
33 Central Ave.
Albany, NY 12210

Citizens for Change
P.O. Box 256
Thiensville, WI 53092

Citizens Global Action
P.O. Box 19742
Portland, OR 97219

Clare Foundation
1871 9th St.
Santa Monica, CA 90404

Clearinghouse on Women's Issues
P.O. Box 70603
Friendship Heights, MD 20813

Cleis Press
P.O. Box 8933
Pittsburgh, PA 15221

Coalition for Clean Air
901 Wilshire Blvd., Suite 350
Santa Monica, CA 90401

Coalition for Fair Trade and Social Justice
518 17th St., Suite 200
Oakland, CA 94612

Coalition for Indian Rights
1083 Barona Rd.
Lakeside, CA 92040

Coalition for Nuclear Disarmament
40 Witherspoon
Princeton, NJ 08542

Coalition for Palestinian Rights
P.O. Box 2316
Cambridge, MA 02238

Coalition for Prisoners' Rights
P.O. Box 1911
Santa Fe, NM 87504

Coalition for the Rights of the Homeless
Montebello A-0
Garden Hills, PR 00966

Coalition to Abolish the Fur Trade
1510 Monroe
Memphis, TN 38104

Coalition to End Nuclear Power/Weapons
77 Homewood Ave.
Allendale, NJ 07401

COINTELPRO Survivors
P.O. Box 632
Ft Bragg, CA 95437

Colombian Human Rights Committee
P.O. Box 3130
Washington, DC 20010

Colombian Human Rights Information
Committee
P.O. Box 40155
San Francisco, CA 94140

Colorado National Abortion Rights Action
League
1210 E. Colfax, Suite 203
Denver, CO 80218

Colorado Women's Agenda
1245 E. Colfax, Suite 319
Denver, CO 80218

Columbia Lesbian, Bisexual and Gay
Coalition
303 Earl Hall
New York, NY 10027
(212) 854-1488

Columbiana
Chesaw Rt., Box 83-F
Oroville, WA 98844

Committee Against Anti-Asian Violence
191 E. 3rd St.
New York, NY 10009

Committee for a New Korea Policy
33 Central Ave.
Albany, NY 12210

Committee for Environmentally Effective
Packaging
601 13th St., N.W., Suite 510S
Washington, DC 20005
James Benfield, Executive Director

Committee for Human Rights in Grenada
P.O. Box 20714
New York, NY 10025

Committee for Nuclear Responsibility
P.O. Box 421993
San Francisco, CA 94142

Committee in Support of Irish Political
Prisoners
P.O. Box 24744
Detroit, MI 48224

Committee of Correspondence
11 John St., Suite 506
New York, NY 10038

Committee to Abolish Sport Hunting
P.O. Box 44
Tompkins Cove, NY 10986

Committee to Expose Patriarchy
8319 Fulham Ct.
Richmond, VA 23227

Committee to Support the Revolution in
Peru
P.O. Box 1246
Berkeley, CA 94701

Common Ground
1115 Orchard Park Rd.
West Seneca, NY 14224

Communist Labor Party
P.O. Box 3524
Chicago, IL 60654

Communitarian Network
2130 H St., N.W., Suite 714
Washington, DC 20052

Communities
Rt. 1, Box 155
Rutledge, MO 63563

Community Action in Latin America
731 State St.
Madison, WI 53703

Computer Bridge Alliance
3931 Brooklyn Ave., N.E.
Seattle, WA 98105

Concerned Citizens of Delaware Valley
P.O. Box 47
Bryn Mawr, PA 19010

Conference on Critical Legal Studies
C.U.N.Y., OBrien Hall
Buffalo, NY 14260

Conflict Resolution Center International
7514 Kensington St.
Pittsburgh, PA 15221

Congress of National Black Churches
1225 I St., N.W.
Washington, DC 20005

Conscience and Military Tax Campaign
4534 ½ University Way, N.E.
Seattle, WA 98105

Contact II Magazine
P.O. Box 451
New York, NY 10004

Cook Brothers Educational Fund
3102 8th Ave., N.E.
Olympia, WA 98506

Coordinating Body of Indigenous Peoples'
Organizations
1011 Orleans St.
New Orleans, LA 70116

Corporate Crime Reporter
P.O. Box 18384
Washington, DC 20036

Council Democracy and Secular Humanism
P.O. Box 5
Buffalo, NY 14215

Council Israeli-Palestine Peace
4816 Cornell Ave.
Downers Grove, IL 60515

Council of International Fellowship
P.O. Box 376
Morgantown, WV 26507
Marcia Pops, President
(304) 291-7254, fax (304) 291-7273

Council on American-Soviet Friendship
P.O. Box 14461
Minneapolis, MN 55414

*Counter*punch
1601 Connecticut Ave., N.W.
Washington, DC 20009

Creating Our Future
2669 Le Conte Ave.
Berkeley, CA 94709-1024

Crestar
P.O. Box 27182
Richmond, VA 23270-0001

Critical Sociology
Department of Sociology
University of Oregon
Eugene, OR 97403

Critique of Anthropology
P.O. Box 5096
Newbury Park, CA 91359

Crossing Press
P.O. Box 1048
Freedom, CA 95019

Crossroad Support Network
3021 W. 63rd St.
Chicago, IL 60629

Crossroads
427 E. 140th St.
Bronx, NY 10454

Crusade to Abolish War and Armaments by
World Law
174 Majestic Ave.
San Francisco, CA 94112

Cuba Information Project
198 Broadway, Suite 800
New York, NY 10038

Cultural Diversity at Work
13751 Lake City Way, N.E.
Seattle, WA 98125

Custody Action for Lesbian Mothers
P.O. Box 281
Narberth, PA 19072
Rosalie Davies, Coordinator
(215) 667-7508

D.C. Committee Against Racsim
P.O. Box 18291
Washington, DC 20036

Daily Citizen
P.O. Box 57365
Washington, DC 20036

Daughters of Bilitis
1151 Massachusetts Ave.
Cambridge, MA 02138

Daybreak
P.O. Box 315
Williamville, NY 14321

Death Penalty Information Center
1606 20th St., 2nd Fl.
Washington, DC 20009

DeLeonist Society of the U.S.
P.O. Box 22055
San Francisco, CA 94122

Democratic Socialist Report
2121 Waylife Ct.
Alva, FL 33920

Desktop Assistance
324 Fuller Ave., Suite C2
Helena, MT 59601-5029

Dialectics Workshop
53 Hickory Hill
Tappan, NY 10983

Dialogue
P.O. Box 71221
New Orleans, LA 70172

Dickey Endowment for International
Understanding
4 Webster Terrace
Hanover, NH 03755

Direct Action Rights and Equality
340 Lockwood St.
Providence, RI 02907

Disciples Peace Fellowship
P.O. Box 1986
Indianapolis, IN 46206

Discussion Bulletin
P.O. Box 1564
Grand Rapids, MI 49501

Draft and Military Project
P.O. Box 8726
Silver Spring, MD 20907

Dumpster Times
P.O. Box 8044
Akron, OH 44308

Dyke Review
584 Castro St., Suite 456
San Francisco, CA 94114

Earth 2000
P.O. Box 24
Shillington, PA 19607

Earth Promise
P.O. Box 2189
Glen Rose, TX 76043

Earth Protection Group
P.O. Box 2833
Malibu, CA 90265

Earth Regeneration Society
1442A Walnut St., Suite 57
Berkeley, CA 94709
Alden Bryant, President

Earth Society Foundation
11 W. 42nd St., Suite 3100
New York, NY 10036
Hans Janitschek, President

East Timor Action Network
P.O. Box 1182
White Plains, NY 10602

East-West Bridges for Peace
P.O. Box 710
Norwich, VT 05055

East/West Journal
P.O. Box 52372
Boulder, CO 80321

Eco-Justice Project and Network
Taylor Hall
Cornell University
Ithaca, NY 14853

Ecologist
55 Hayward St.
Cambridge, MA 02142

EcoSocialist Review
1608 N. Milwaukee, 4th Fl.
Chicago, IL 60647

Education and Action for Animals
2605 Voorhees Ave.
Redondo Beach, CA 90278

Educators Against Racism and Apartheid
164-04 Goethals Ave.
Jamaica, NY 11432

Eight Day Center for Justice
205 W. Monroe
Chicago, IL 60606

El Salvador Media Projects
335 W. 38th St., 5th Fl.
New York, NY 10018

Emergency Response Network
P.O. Box 11395
Fresno, CA 93773

Environmental Action Coalition
625 Broadway, 2nd Floor
New York, NY 10012
Stephen Richardson, Executive Director

Environmental Advocacy Trust
133 S.W. Second Ave., Suite 302
Portland, OR 97204

Environmental Alternatives
P.O. Box 3940
Quincy, CA 95971

Environmental Council
2900 N.E. Indian River Dr.
Jensen Beach, FL 34957

Environmental Defense Center
906 Garden St., Suite 2
Santa Barbara, CA 93101

Environmental Fund of Washington
1402 3rd Ave., Suite 825
Seattle, WA 98105

Environmental Health Institute
725 North St.
Pittsfield, MA 01201

Environmental Technology Seminar
P.O. Box 391
Bethpage, NY 11714
Jean Wood, President

Equal Rights Congress
4167 S. Normandy Ave.
Los Angeles, CA 90037

Evergreen International
P.O. Box 3
Salt Lake City, UT 84110

Fag Rag
P.O. Box 311
Boston, MA 02215

Fair Budget Action Campaign
P.O. Box 31151
Seattle, WA 98103

Family Planning International Assistance
810 7th Ave.
New York, NY 10019
Dr. Daniel Weintraub, Vice President
(212) 261-4762, fax (212) 247-6274

Federalist Caucus
P.O. Box 19482
Portland, OR 97219

Federation for an Egalitarian Community
P.O. Box 426
Louisa, VA 23095

Federation of Egalitarian Communities
P.O. Box FB4
Tecumseh, MO 65760

Federation of Former Jewish Fighters
12 E. 31st St.
New York, NY 10016

Fellowship Racial Economic Equality
P.O. Box 2183
Chapel Hill, NC 27514

Feminist Alternative
5700 S.W. 67th Ave.
Miami, FL 33143

Feminist Bookstore News
P.O. Box 882554
San Francisco, CA 94188

Feminist Collections
728 State St.
Madison, WI 53706

Feminist Issues
Transaction
Rutgers University
New Brunswick, NJ 08903

Feminist Teacher
Indiana University
Bloomington, IN 47405

Feminists Against Pornography
2147 O St., N.W., Suite 305
Washington, DC 20009

Feminists for Animal Rights
P.O. Box 10017, N. Berkeley Station
Berkeley, CA 94709

Final Call
734 W. 79th St.
Chicago, IL 60620

Financial Democracy Campaign
1315 Alexander
Houston, TX 77008

Financial Democracy Campaign
739 8th St., S.E.
Washington, DC 20003

Financial Democracy Campaign
2009 Chapel Hill
Durham, NC 27707

Firebrand Books
141 The Commons
Ithaca, NY 14850

First Amendment Coalition of Texas
1104 West Ave., Suite 101
Austin, TX 78701

First Amendment Congress
2301 S. Gaylord St.
Denver, CO 80208

Florida Coalition for Peace and Justice
P.O. Box 2486
Orlando, FL 32802

Focus on Animals
P.O. Box 150
Trumbull, CT 06611

Foreign Bases Project
P.O. Box 150753
Brooklyn, NY 11215

Foreign Policy Association
729 Seventh Ave.
New York, NY 10019

Foresight Institute
10108 Hemlock Dr., Box 13267
Overland Park, KS 66212

Foundation for a Compassionate Society
227 Congress Ave.
Austin, TX 78701-4021

Foundation for International Community
Assistance
2504 E. Elm St.
Tucson, AZ 85716

Fourth Freedom Forum
803 N. Main St.
Goshen, IN 46526

Freedom Coalition
P.O. Box 12266
Gainesville, FL 32604

Freedom from Hunger Foundation
1644 DaVinci Ct.
P.O. Box 2000
Davis, CA 95617

Freedom Information Service
P.O. Box 3568
Jackson, MS 39207

Freedom Now
1671 N. Claremont
Chicago, IL 60647

Freedom of Expression Foundation
5220 S. Marina Pacifica
Long Beach, CA 90803

Freedom Socialist Party
5018 S. Rainier Ave.
Seattle, WA 98118

Freedomways
799 Broadway, Suite 542
New York, NY 10003

Freethinker Forum
P.O. Box 14447
St. Louis, MO 63178

Friends Committee on Unity with Nature
7700 Clarks Lake Rd.
Chelsea, MI 48118

Friends of Brazil
7303 23rd Ave., N.E.
Seattle, WA 98115

Friends of Irish Freedom
3634 Tibbett
Bronx, NY 10463

Friends of Solidarity
13814 Hidden Glen Lane
Gaithersburg, MD 20878

Friends of the Filipino People
P.O. Box 2125
Durham, NC 27702

Friends of the Rainbow Warrior
P.O. Box 96099
Washington, DC 20090-6099

Friends of UNEP
2013 Q St., N.W.
Washington, DC 20009

Front Page
P.O. Box 25642
Raleigh, NC 27611

Frontlash
815 16th St., N.W.
Washington, DC 20006

Frontline Coalition
4614 Cathi Dr., Suite B
Indianapolis, IN 46217

Fund for Free Expression
485 5th Ave.
New York, NY 10017

Fund for New Priorities
171 Madison Ave.
New York, NY 10016

Gaia Press
P.O. Box 466
El Cerrito, CA 94530

Gateway Green Alliance
P.O. Box 8094
St Louis, MO 63156

Gay and Lesbian Advocates and Defenders
P.O. Box 218
Boston, MA 02112

Gay and Lesbian Anti-Violence Project
208 W. 13th St.
New York, NY 10011

Gay and Lesbian Educators
837 Earp St.
Philadelphia, PA 19147

Gay Media Task Force
71-426 Estellita Dr.
Rancho Mirage, CA 92270

Gay Officers' Action League
510 E. 20th St., Apt. 11C
New York, NY 10009
Peter Guardino

Gay Veterans Association
346 Broadway, Suite 814
New York, NY 10013

General Assistance Rights Union
126 Hyde St., Suite 102
San Francisco, CA 94117
Brian Russell

Generation After
P.O. Box 14
Brooklyn, NY 11229

Generations for Peace
1315 S.W. Park Ave.
Portland, OR 97201

Gentle Survivalist
P.O. Box 4004
St. George, UT 84770

Global Action and Information Network
740 Front St., Suite 355
Santa Cruz, CA 95060
Bill Leland, Director

Global Action Plan for the Earth
449A Route 28A
West Hurley, NY 12491

Global Concerns Center
2131 W. Berwyn Ave.
Chicago, IL 60625

Global Cooperation for a Better World
866 UN Plaza
New York, NY 10017

Global Education Association
475 Riverside Dr., Suite 570
New York, NY 10115

Global Exchange
2017 Mission St., Suite 303
San Francisco, CA 94110

Global Family
112 Jordan Ave.
San Anselmo, CA 94960

Global Justice
University of Denver
Denver, CO 80206

Global Options
P.O. Box 40601
San Francisco, CA 94140

Global Warming International Center
1 Heritage Plaza
P.O. Box 5275
Woodridge, IL 60517
Dr. Sinyan Shen, Director

Grassroots Coalition for Environmental and
Economic Justice
P.O. Box 1319
Clarksville, MD 21029

Great Atlantic Radio Conspiracy
2748 Maryland Ave.
Baltimore, MD 21218

Greater Ecosystem Alliance
P.O. Box 2813
Bellingham, WA 98227
Mitch Friedman, Executive Director

Green Century Funds
29 Temple Place, Suite 200
Boston, MA 02111

Green Committees of Correspondence
P.O. Box 30208
Kansas City, MO 64112

Green Earth Foundation
P.O. Box 327
El Verano, CA 95433

Green Letter
P.O. Box 14141
San Francisco, CA 94114

Green Line
P.O. Box 144
Asheville, SC 28802

Green Mountain Post Films
P.O. Box 229
Turners Falls, MA 01376

Ground Zero
7135 S.W. 36th St.
Portland, OR 97219

Ground Zero Center for Nonviolent Action
16159 Clear Creek Rd., N.W.
Poulsbo, WA 98370

Group Research Report
733 15th St., N.W., Suite 202
Washington, DC 20005

Guatemala Information and Documentation
918 S. George Mason Dr.
Arlington, VA 22204

Guatemala News and Information Bureau
P.O. Box 28594
Oakland, CA 94604

Guatemala Solidarity Committee
147 N.W. 80th St.
Seattle, WA 98117

Haiti Communications Project
11 Inman St.
Cambridge, MA 02139

Haiti News
131 N. Main St.
Sharon, MA 02067

Haitian Patriotic Union
3900 Yuma St., N.W.
Washington, DC 20016

Halt
1319 F St., N.W., Suite 300
Washington, DC 20004

Hands Off Cuba
P.O. Box 13202
Denver, CO 80201

Hands Off!
111 E. 14th St., Suite 132
New York, NY 10003

Harvard Women's Law Journal
Harvard Law School
Cambridge, MA 02138

Hawaii Union of Socialists
P.O. Box 11208
Honolulu, HI 96828

Haymarket People's Fund
42 Seaverns Ave.
Boston, MA 02130

Healing Woman
P.O. Box 3038
Moss Beach, CA 94038

Hispanic Federation of New York City
545 8th Ave.
New York, NY 10018

HKH Foundation
c/o Blue Mountain Center
Blue Mountain Lake, NY 12812

Holistic Education Review
39 Pearl St.
Brandon, VT 05733

Hollywood Urban Projects
1760 N. Gower St.
Hollywood, CA 90028

Homosexual Information Center
115 Monroe
Bossier City, LA 71111-4539
(318) 742-4709

Horn of Africa
P.O. Box 803
Summit, NJ 07901

Human Economy Center
P.O. Box 14, Department of Economics
Mankato State University
Mankato, MN 56001

Hypatia
601 N. Morton St.
Bloomington, IN 47404

Hysteria
P.O. Box 8581
Bridgeport, CT 06605

Immigration Working Group
P.O. Box 3606
Oakland, CA 94609

Impact Visuals
24 W. 25th, 12th Fl.
New York, NY 10010

Incite Information
P.O. Box 326
Arlington, VA 22210

Independent Action
1511 K St., N.W., Suite 619
Washington, DC 20005

Indian Report
245 2nd St., N.E.
Washington, DC 20002

Indigenous People's Network
226 Blackman Hill Rd.
Berkshire, NY 13736

Indigenous World Association
275 Grand View Ave., Suite 103
San Francisco, CA 94114

INFACT
P.O. Box 3223
South Pasadena, CA 91031

Infected Faggot Perspectives
P.O. Box 26246
Los Angeles, CA 90026

Inland Empire Public Lands Council
P.O. Box 2174
Spokane, WA 99210

Inner-City Scholarship Fund
1011 1st Ave.
New York, NY 10022

Institute for Arts of Democracy
RR 1, Box Blackfox
Brattleboro, VT 05301-9801

Institute for Cooperative Community
Development
2500 North River Rd.
Manchester, NH 03106

Institute for Lesbian Studies
P.O. Box 25568
Chicago, IL 60625-0568

Institute for Palestine Studies
P.O. Box 25697
Washington, DC 20007

Institute for Social Justice
1024 Elysian Fields Ave.
New Orleans, LA 70117

Institute for Space and Security Studies
5115 S. A1A Highway
Melbourne Beach, FL 32951

Institute for the Human Environment
41 Sutter, Suite 510
San Francisco, CA 94104

Institute of Women Today
7315 S. Yale Ave.
Chicago, IL 60621

Institute on Women and Technology
P.O. Box 9338
North Amherst, MA 01059
H. Patricia Hynes, Director

Interfaith Action for Economic Justice
110 Maryland Ave., N.E.
Washington, DC 20002

Interfaith Impact for Justice and Peace
110 Maryland Ave., N.E.
Washington, DC 20002

Interfaith Task Force
3370 S. Irving
Englewood, CO 80110
Terry Brown, Executive Director
(303) 789-0501

International Action Center
39 W. 14th St., Suite 206
New York, NY 10011

International Black Women's Congress
1081 Bergen St.
Newark, NJ 07112

International Center for Peace and Justice
50 Oak St., Room 503
San Francisco, CA 94102

International Clearinghouse on the Military
and the Environment
P.O. Box 150753
Brooklyn, NY 11215
John Miller, Contact

International Committee Against Racism
P.O. Box 904
Brooklyn, NY 11202

International Communist Current
P.O. Box 288
New York, NY 10018

International Ecology Society
1471 Barclay St.
St. Paul, MN 55106-1405
R. J. F. Kramer, President

International Forum on Globalization
P.O. Box 12218
San Francisco, CA 94112

International Foundation for Ethical
Research
53 W. Jackson Blvd., Suite 1552
Chicago, IL 60604

International Fund for Animal Welfare
411 Main St.
Yarmouth Port, MA 02675

International Labor Office
1828 L St., N.W., Suite 801
Washington, DC 20036

International League for Human Rights
432 S. Park Ave., Suite 1103
New York, NY 10016

International Planned Parenthood Federation
902 Broadway, 10th Fl.
New York, NY 10010

International Review of Third World Culture
P.O. Box 1785
Palm Springs, CA 92263

International Socialist Organization
P.O. Box 16085
Chicago, IL 60616

Into the Night
1980 65th St., Suite 3D
Brooklyn, NY 11204

Investor Responsibility Research Center
1755 Massachusetts Ave., N.W., Suite 600
Washington, DC 20005

Irish Republican Clubs
243 Mount Hope
Albany, NY 12202

Isolated Woman
P.O. Box 140710
Dallas, TX 75214

Issues in Radical Therapy
1404 Wicklow
Boulder, CO 80303

Jesuit Social Ministries
1424 16th St., N.W., Suite 300
Washington, DC 20036

Jewish Affairs
235 W. 23rd St., 7th Fl.
New York, NY 10011

Jewish Committee on the Middle East
P.O. Box 18367
Washington, DC 20036

Jewish Currents
22 E. 17th St., Suite 601
New York, NY 10003

Jewish Peace Fellowship
P.O. Box 271
Nyack, NY 10960

JHIN
26740 Via Linda St.
Malibu, CA 90265-4452

Journal of Palestine Studies
2120 Berkeley Way
Berkeley, CA 94720

Journal of Women's History
c/o Department of History, Ballantine Hall
Indiana University
Bloomington, IN 47405

Jump Cut
P.O. Box 865
Berkeley, CA 94701

Justice and Peace News Notes
Maryknoll Peace Office
Marynoll, NY 10545

Justice for Women
100 Witherspoon St.
Louisville, KY 40202

Kalamazoo Animal Liberation League
P.O. Box 3295
Kalamazoo, MI 49003

Keystone Socialist
2208 South St.
Philadelphia, PA 19146

Korean Institute for Human Rights
6110 Executive Blvd.
Rockville, MD 20852

La Raza Unida Party
483 5th St.
San Fernando, CA 91340

Labor Committee on the Middle East
P.O. Box 421546
San Francisco, CA 94142

Labor History
P.O. Box 1236
Washington, CT 06793

Labor Militant
P.O. Box 39462
Chicago, IL 60639

Labor-Farm Party
1618 Jennifer St.
Madison, WI 53704

Lakota Times
P.O. Box 2180
Rapid City, SD 57709

Lamb of Hope Project
P.O. Box 5412
Pasadena, CA 77508

Lambda Book Report
1625 Connecticut Ave., N.W.
Washington, DC 20009

Land Educational Association Foundation
3368 Oak Ave.
Stevens Point, WI 54481

Last Gasp Bookstore
777 Florida St.
San Francisco, CA 94110

Latin American Video Archive
124 Washington Place
New York, NY 10014

League for a Revolutionary Party
P.O. Box 3573
New York, NY 10008

League for Lesbian/Gay Prisoners
1202 E. Pike St., Suite 1044
Seattle, WA 98122

League of United Latin American Citizens
433 W. Santa Clara
Santa Ana, CA 92707

League of United Latin American Citizens
2100 M St., N.W., Suite 602
Washington, DC 20037-1207

Left Bank Distribution
4142 Brooklyn, N.E., Suite 201
Seattle, WA 98105

Left Business Observer
250 W. 85th St., Suite 7J
New York, NY 10024

Lesbian Activist Bureau
P.O. Box 1485
Cincinnati, OH 45201

Lesbian Connection
P.O. Box 811
East Lansing, MI 48826

Lesbian Contradiction
584 Castro St., Suite 263
San Francisco, CA 94114

Lesbian Ethics
P.O. Box 4723
Albuquerque, NH 87196

Lesbian Feminist Liberation
208 W. 13th St.
New York, NY 10011
(212) 924-2657

Lesbian-Feminist Liberation League
243 W. 20th St.
New York, NY 10011

Lesbian Interest Press
P.O. Box 761
Utica, NY 13503

Liberty Union Party
183 Western Ave.
Brattleboro, VT 05301

Libyan Human Rights Commission
P.O. Box 2762
Eugene, OR 97402

Lies of Our Times
145 W. 4th St.
New York, NY 10012

Love and Rage Newspaper
P.O. Box 853
New York, NY 10009

Lutheran Peace Fellowship
1710 11th Ave.
Seattle, WA 98122-2420

Mad Woman
1514 Holly Hill Dr.
Champaign, IL 61821-2002

Madison Edge
P.O. Box 845
Madison, WI 53701

Madison Environmental Support Alliance
218 Liberty St.
Oneida, NY 13421

Madison Insurgent
P.O. Box 704
Madison, WI 53701

Maine Coalition for the Homeless
P.O. Box 2
Alfred, ME 04002

Maine Progressive
387 Gorham Rd.
Scarborough, ME 04074

Markle Foundation
75 Rockefeller Plaza
New York, NY 10025

Marxism and Black Liberation
P.O. Box 7696
Chicago, IL 60680

Maryknoll Justice and Peace
P.O. Box 29132
Washington, DC 20017

Massachusetts Tenants Resource Center
14 Beacon St., Suite 719
Boston, MA 02108

Match
P.O. Box 3488
Tucson, AZ 85722

Media Action Alliance
P.O. Box 391
Circle Pines, MN 55014

Media Action Research Center
1962 S. Shenandoah
Los Angeles, CA 90034

Media Fund for Human Rights
P.O. Box 8185
Universal City, CA 91608
R. J. Curry, Executive Director
(818) 902-1476

Media Network
800 Riverside Dr., Suite 2E
New York, NY 10032

Media Network
39 W. 14th St., Suite 403
New York, NY 10011

MediCuba
1870 Wyoming Ave., N.W., Suite 604
Washington, DC 20009

Meeting Ground
P.O. Box 808
Elkton, MD 21922

Men of All Colors Together
P.O. Box 1518
New York, NY 10023

Men's Anti-Rape Resource Center
P.O. Box 73559
Washington, DC 20056

Mennonite Central Committee
21 S. 12th St.
Akron, PA 17501

Mental Health Client Action Network
P.O. Box 962
Santa Cruz, CA 95061

MetroDC Environmental Network
645 Morris Place, N.E.
Washington, DC 20002

Micro Associates
P.O. Box 3596
Arlington, VA 22205

Middle East Crisis Committee
P.O. Box 8993
New Haven, CT 06532

Middle East International
1700 17th St., N.W., Suite 306
Washington, DC 20009

Middle East Watch
485 5th Ave., 3rd Fl.
New York, NY 10017

Middle Passage Press
5517 Secrest Dr.
Los Angeles, CA 90043-2029

Midwest Treaty Network
731 State St.
Madison, WI 53703

Millennial Prophecy Report
P.O. Box 34021
Philadelphia, PA 19101

Minnesota Center for Environmental
Advocacy
26 E. Exchange St., Suite 206
St. Paul, MN 55101-2264

Missouri Alliance for Choice Education
Fund
P.O. Box 603
Jefferson City, MO 65102

Montana Wilderness Association Legal and
Educational Fund
P.O. Box 635
Helena, MT 59624

Montanans for a Healthy Future
P.O. Box 2135, MTS
Clancy, MT 59634

Monthly Planet
P.O. Box 8463
Santa Cruz, CA 95061

Mount Diablo Peace Center
65 Eckley Lane
Walnut Creek, CA 94596

Movement Support Network
666 Broadway, 7th Fl.
New York, NY 10012

Multicultural Publishing Exchange
2280 Grass Valley Hwy., Suite 181
Auburn, CA 95603
Rennie Mau, President

Multicultural Review
10 Bay St.
Westport, CT 06880

Naiad Press
P.O. Box 10543
Tallahassee, FL 32302

Namebase Newsline
P.O. Box 680635
San Antonio, TX 78268

Namibia Information Service
P.O. Box 43234
Washington, DC 20010

Nashville Coalition for the Homeless
2012 21st Ave., S.
Nashville, TN 37212-4313

National Abortion Rights Action League,
Missouri (NARAL)
393 N. Euclid, Suite 310
St. Louis, MO 63108

National Abortion Rights Action League
P.O. Box 908
Durham, NC 27702

National Alliance of Black Feminists
202 S. State St., Suite 1024
Chicago, IL 60604

National Anti-Hunger Coalition
1875 Connecticut Ave., N.W., Suite 540
Washington, DC 20009-5728
Michele Tingling-Clemmons
(202) 986-2200

National Association Against Fraud in
Psychiatry
P.O. Box 5012
Reno, NV 89513

National Association of Black Journalists
11600 Sunrise Valley Dr.
Reston, VA 22091-1412

National Association of Environmental
Professionals
5165 MacArthur Blvd., N.W.
Washington, DC 20016-3315
Susan Eisenberg, Executive Director

National Association of Media Women
157 W. 126th St.
New York, NY 10027

National Association of Psychiatric
Survivors
P.O. Box 618
Sioux Falls, SD 57101

National Association of Puerto Rican
Hispanic Social Workers
P.O. Box 651
Brentwood, NY 11717
Sonia Palacio-Grottola, ACSW, President
(516) 864-1536, fax (202) 336-8310

National Black Media Coalition
38 New York Ave., N.E.
Washington, DC 20002

National Black Political Assembly
401 Broadway
Gary, IN 46402

National Black Survival Fund
P.O. Box 3885
Lafayette, LA 70502-3885
Rev. A. J. McKnight, CS, Chairman
(318) 232-7672

National Black Women's Health Project
1237 Abernathy Dr., S.W.
Atlanta, GA 30310

National Camp for a Peace Tax Fund
2121 Decatur Place, N.W.
Washington, DC 20008

National Chicana Foundation
1005 S. Alamo
San Antonio, TX 78207

National Coalition
36 E. 12th St., 6th Fl.
New York, NY 10003

National Committee for an Effective
Congress
10 E. 39th St., Suite 601
New York, NY 10016

National Committee for Sexual Civil
Liberties
98 Olden Lane
Princeton, NJ 08540
Dr. Arthur C. Warner, Chairman
(609) 924-1950

National Conference of Black Political
Scientists
P.O. Box 560, M.S.U.
Baltimore, MD 21239

National Education Service Center
2100 M St., N.W., Suite 602
Washington, DC 20037-1207

National Federation of Parents and Friends
of Gays
8020 Eastern Ave., N.W.
Washington, DC 20012
Eugene Baker, Executive Secretary
(202) 726-3223

National Gay Alliance for Young Adults
P.O. Box 190712
Dallas, TX 75219
(817) 381-0343

National Gay Youth Network
P.O. Box 846
San Francisco, CA 94101-0846
M. Nulty, Executive Officer

National Health Law Program
2639 S. LaCienega Blvd.
Los Angeles, CA 90034

National Institute Against Prejudice
31 South Greene St.
Baltimore, MD 21201

National Latina Health Organization
P.O. Box 7567
Oakland, CA 94601

National League for Social Understanding
4470-107 Sunset Blvd., Suite 293
Los Angeles, CA 90027
Rev. Jerome Stevens, President
(213) 664-6422

National Multi-Cultural Institute
3006 Connecticut Ave., N.W., Suite 438
Washington, DC 20008

National Neighbors
3130 Mayfield Rd.
Cleveland Heights, OH 44118

National Network for Immigrant Rights
310 8th St., Suite 307
Oakland, CA 94607

National Network for Social Work Managers
6501 N. Federal Hwy., Suite 5
Boca Raton, FL 33487
Harold Benson, Jr., Executive Director
(407) 997-7560, fax (407) 241-6746

National Network of Women's Funds
1821 University Ave., Suite 409N
Saint Paul, MN 55104

National Organization for Women, San
Francisco
3543 18th St.
San Francisco, CA 94110
Elizabeth Toledo, President

National Organization for Women, Virginia
P.O. Box 25831
Richmond, VA 23260-5831

National People's Campaign
2489 Mission St., Suite 28
San Francisco, CA 94110

National Puerto Rican Coalition
1700 K St., N.W., Suite 500
Washington, DC 20006

National Registry of Environmental
Professionals
P.O. Box 2068
Glenview, IL 60025
Richard A. Young, Executive Director

National Safety Council
1019 19th St., N.W., Suite 401
Washington, DC 20036

National Sharecroppers Fund
2124 Commonwealth Ave.
Charlotte, NC 28205

National Student Campaign Against Hunger
and Homelessness
29 Temple Pl.
Boston, MA 02111
Jennifer Coken, Director
(617) 292-4823, fax (617) 292-8057

National Tree Society
P.O. Box 10808
Bakersfield, CA 93389
Gregory W. Davis, President

National Women's Health Network
1325 G St., N.W.
Washington, DC 20005

National Women's Party
144 Constitution Ave., N.E.
Washington, DC 20002

Native Resource Coalition
P.O. Box 93
Porcupine, SD 57772

Natural Rights Center
156 Drakes Lane
P.O. Box 90
Summertown, TN 38483-0090
Albert K. Bates, Director

Nature, Society and Thought
116 Church St., S.E.
Minneapolis, MN 55455

Negative Population Growth
P.O. Box 1206
210 The Plaza
Teaneck, NJ 07666
Donald Mann, President
(201) 837-3555, fax (201) 837-0288

New Afrikan Network for Political Prisoners
P.O. Box 90604
Washington, DC 20090

New Afrikan Peoples Organization
P.O. Box 11464
Atlanta, GA 30310

New Age
P.O. Box 53275
Boulder, CO 80321

New Alliance Party
500 Greenwich St., Suite 201
New York, NY 10013

New Call to Peacemaking
P.O. Box 500
Akron, PA 17501

New Dimensions Radio
P.O. Box 410510
San Francisco, CA 94141

New Environment Bulletin
902 Second Ave.
Liverpool, NY 13088

New Internationalist
P.O. Box 1143
Lewiston, NY 14092

New Pages
P.O. Box 438
Grand Blanc, MI 48439

New People Magazine
P.O. Box 47490
Oak Park, MI 48237

New Politics
P.O. Box 98
Brooklyn, NY 11231

New York Public Interest Group
9 Murray St.
New York, NY 10007

New York Transfer News Service
235 E. 87th St., Suite 12-J
New York, NY 10138

News and Letters
59 E. Van Buren, Suite 707
Chicago, IL 60605

Nicaragua Center for Community Action
2140 Shattuck, Suite 2063
Berkeley, CA 94704

Nicaragua Information Center
P.O. Box 1004
Berkeley, CA 94701

Nicaragua Interfaith Coalition Action
942 Market St., 7th Fl.
San Francisco, CA 94102

Nicaragua Network Education Fund
1247 E St., N.W.
Washington, DC 20003

Nonviolence International
P.O. Box 39127
Washington, DC 20016

Nonviolence Network
210 S. 1st St.
Marshall, MN 56258

North American Coalition on Religion and
Freedom
5 Thomas Circle, N.W.
Washington, DC 20005
Dr. Donald B. Conroy, President

North Carolinans Against Racist Violence
P.O. Box 240
Durham, NC 27702

North Coast Express
P.O. Box 1226
Occidental, CA 95465

North Star Network
P.O. Box 9887
Berkeley, CA 94709

Northeast Indian Quarterly
300 Caldwell Hall
Columbia University
Ithaca, NY 14853

Northern Indiana Skin Heads
P.O. Box 737
Whiting, IN 46394

Northland Poster Collective
1613 E. Lake St.
Minneapolis, MN 55407

NST
116 Church St., S.E.
Minneapolis, MN 55455

Nuclear Free America
325 E. 25th St.
Baltimore, MD 21218

Nuclear Resister
P.O. Box 43383
Tucson, AZ 85733

Oklahoma Coalition for the Homeless
9119 N. Hudson Ave.
Oklahoma City, OK 73114

Older Women's League
666 11th St., N.W., Suite 700
Washington, DC 20001

On the Issues
P.O. Box 3000
Danville, IL 07834

One, Inc.
1130 Arlington Ave.
Los Angeles, CA 90019
W. Dorr Legg, Secretary/Treasurer
(213) 735-5252

One World Now
P.O. Box 1145
Houston, TX 77251

Operation PUSH
930 E. 50th St.
Chicago, IL 60615

Oral History of the American Left
70 Washington Square
New York, NY 10012

Organization for a New Equality
364 Boylston St., 3rd Fl.
Boston, MA 02116-3805

Ottinger Foundation
256 N. Pleasant St.
Amherst, MA 01002

Overground Railroad
722 Monroe
Evanston, IL 60202

Ozone Action
1621 Connecticut Ave., N.W.
Washington, DC 20009

Pacific News Service
450 Mission St., Suite 506
San Francisco, CA 94105

Palestine Affairs Center
1730 K St., N.W., Suite 703
Washington, DC 20006

Palestine Center for Non-Violence
P.O. Box 39127
Washington, DC 20016

Palestine Research and Education Center
9522-A Lee Highway
Fairfax, VA 22031

Palestinian Human Rights Campaign
6902 N. Clark St., Suite 2-A
Chicago, IL 60626

Paper
2040 N. Milwaukee Ave.
Chicago, IL 60647

Paper Tiger Television
339 Lafayette St.
New York, NY 10012

Partisan Defense Committee
P.O. Box 77462
San Francisco, CA 94609

Pathfinder Press
410 West St.
New York, NY 10014

PAWS
P.O. Box 1037
Lynwood, WA 98046

Peace Activists East and West
113 Meadow St.
Amherst, MA 01002

Peace and Freedom Party
P.O. Box 422644
San Francisco, CA 94142

Peace Brigades International
333 Valencia St., Suite 330
San Francisco, CA 94103

Peace for Cuba
36 E. 12th St., 6th Fl.
New York, NY 10003

Peace in Central America Coalition
P.O. Box 41762
Tucson, AZ 85717

Peace Links
747 8th St., S.E.
Washington, DC 20003

Peace PAC
110 Maryland Ave., N.E.
Washington, DC 20002

Peace Research Network
P.O. Box 13127
Minneapolis, MN 55414

Peace USA
P.O. Box 200596
Austin, TX 78720-0596

Peacemaker
P.O. Box 627
Garverville, CA 95440

Peaceworkers
3149 Plymouth Rd.
Lafayette, CA 94549

Pennsylvania Environmental Network
P.O. Box 131
Wallacetown, PA 16876

Penny Resistance
8319 Fulham Ct.
Richmond, VA 23277

People Animals Network
3827 Carroll Ave.
Dayton, OH 45405

People for Open Space
116 New Montgomery St., Suite 640
San Francisco, CA 94105

People's Anti-War Mobilization
P.O. Box 1819
New York, NY 10159

People's Institute for Survival
144 N. Johnson St.
New Orleans, LA 70116

People's Resource of Southwest Ohio
P.O. Box 6366
Cincinnati, OH 45206

People's Culture
P.O. Box 5224
Kansas City, KS 66119

People's Tribune
P.O. Box 477113
Chicago, IL 60647

Perennial Books
P.O. Box 814
Montague, MA 01351

Performing Artists for World Peace
P.O. Box 1050
Volcano, HI 96785-1050

Pesticide Action Network
116 New Montgomery, Suite 810
San Francisco, CA 94105

Philippine Action Group
1631 Balard St.
Carson, CA 90745

Planet Well
P.O. Box 254
Tallahassee, FL 32302

Political Affairs
235 W. 23rd St.
New York, NY 10011

Political Prisoners Unite
272 Hutton St., Suite 21
Jersey City, NJ 07307
(201) 420-9434

Practice
500 Greenwich St., Suite 201
New York, NY 10013

Prairie Fire Organizing Committee
P.O. Box 14422
San Francisco, CA 94114

Praxis International
238 Main St., Suite 501
Cambridge, MA 02142

Presbyterian Hunger Program
100 Witherspoon St.
Louisville, KY 40202-1396
(502) 569-5827

Presbyterian Peace Fellowship
P.O. Box 271
Nyack, NY 10960

Prevailing Winds Research
P.O. Box 23511
Santa Barbara, CA 93121

Prison Activist Resource Center
P.O. Box 3201
Berkeley, CA 94703
(516) 845-8813

Processed World
41 Sutter St., Suite 1829
San Francisco, CA 94123

Progressive Action Center
1443 Gorsuch Ave.
Baltimore, MD 21218

Progressive Labor Party
231 W. 29th St., Suite 502
New York, NY 10001

Progressive Librarians Guild
330 W. 42nd St., 4th Fl.
New York, NY 10036

Proutist Universal
P.O. Box 56466
Washington, DC 20011

Proutist Universal Women
P.O. Box 114
Northampton, MA 01061

Prozac Survivors Support Group
1758 Alamos
Clovis, CA 93612

Public Interest Research Foundation of New
Jersey
11 N. Willow St.
Trenton, NJ 08608

Public Law Education Institute
1601 Connecticut Ave., N.W., Suite 450
Washington, DC 20009
Thomas P. Alder, President

Public Welfare Foundation
2600 Virginia Ave., N.W.
Washington, DC 20037

Publications Exchange
8306 Mills Dr., Suite 241
Miami, FL 33182

Quayle Quarterly
P.O. Box 8593
Bridgeport, CT 06605

Queer Women/Men Support for Prisoners
380 Bleeker St., Suite 134
New York, NY 10014

Questionable Cartoons
160 Sixth Ave.
New York, NY 10013

Quixote
1812 Marshall
Houston, TX 77098

Race Traitor
P.O. Box 603
Cambridge, MA 02140

Radical American
One Summer St.
Somerville, MA 02143

Radical Historians' Organization
445 W. 59th St., Suite 4312
New York, NY 10019

Radical History Review
70 S. Washington Square
New York, NY 10012

Radical Philosophy Association
1443 Gorsuch Ave.
Baltimore, MD 21218

Radical Teacher
P.O. Box 102
Cambridge, MA 01242

Radical Women
523-A Valencia St.
San Francisco, CA 94110

Rain
P.O. Box 30097
Eugene, OR 97403

Rainforest Action Network
450 Sansome St., Suite 700
San Francisco, CA 94111

Raise the Stakes
P.O. Box 31251
San Francisco, CA 94131

Raza United Party
4500 Highland Terrace
Austin, TX 78731

Realist
P.O. Box 1230
Venice, CA 90294

RECON
P.O. Box 14602t
Philadelphia, PA 19134

Refuse and Resist
305 Madison Ave., Suite 1166
New York, NY 10165

Regeneration
P.O. Box 24115
St Louis, MO 63130

Religion and Socialism Committee
P.O. Box 80
Camp Hill, PA 17001

Religious Task Force on Central America
1747 Connecticut Ave., N.W.
Washington, DC 20009

Renaissance Universal
9738 42nd Ave., Suite 1-F
Corona, NY 11368

Rene Dubos Center for Human
Environments
100 E. 85th St.
New York, NY 10028
Ruth A. Eblen, Executive Director

Reproductive Freedom Project
132 W. 43rd St.
New York, NY 10036

Research Group for Socialism and
Democracy
33 W. 42nd St.
New York, NY 10036

Resource Center for Non-Violence
515 Broadway
Santa Cruz, CA 95060

Resource Cycling
P.O. Box 10540
Portland, OR 97210

Resource Policy Institute
1745 Selby, Suite 11
Los Angeles, CA 90024
Dr. Arthur H. Purcell, Executive Director

Results
236 Massachusetts Ave., N.E., Suite 300
Washington, DC 20002

Revitalization Corps.
P.O. Box 1625
Hartford, CT 06101
Edward Coll, Director
(203) 249-7523

Revolutionary Communist Party
P.O. Box 3486, Merchant Market
Chicago, IL 60654

Revolutionary Political Organization
P.O. Box 15914
New Orleans, LA 70175

RFD
RR 1, Box 84-A
Liberty, TN 37095

Rhode Island Right to Housing
103 Ring St.
Providence, RI 02909

Right to Choose
P.O. Box 33
Old Bethpage, NY 11804

Rock and Roll Confidential
P.O. Box 341305
Los Angeles, CA 90034

RSVP
821 Highway Ave.
Manhattan Beach, CA 90266

Sacramento Peace Center
414 T St.
Sacramento, CA 95814-6914

Sage: Journal of Black Women
P.O. Box 42741
Atlanta, GA 30311

Sage Woman
P.O. Box 641
Point Arena, CA 95468

Saharan Peoples Support Committee
217 E. Lehr Ave.
Ada, OH 45810

San Francisco Greens
2940 16th St., Suite 314
San Francisco, CA 94103

Santa Monica AIDS Project
309 Santa Monica Blvd., #224
Santa Monica, CA 90401

Science and Society
445 W. 59th St., Suite 4331
New York, NY 10019

Science for Democratic Action
6935 Laurel Ave.
Takoma Park, MD 20912

Seamless Garment Network
109 Pickwick Dr.
Rochester, NY 14618

Seattle Community Catalyst
5031 University Way, N.E.
Seattle, WA 98105

Senior Action in a Gay Environment
208 W. 13th St.
New York, NY 10011
Arlene Kochman, Executive Director
(212) 741-2247, fax (212) 366-1947

Sequoia
942 Market St., Suite 707
San Francisco, CA 94102

Seventh Generation Fund
P.O. Box 4569
Arcata, CA 95521-8569

Shelterforce
439 Main St.
Orange, NJ 07050

Sing Out!
P.O. Box 5253
Bethlehem, PA 18015

Sinister Wisdom
P.O. Box 3252
Berkeley, CA 94703

Slingshot
700 Eshelman Hall
University of California
Berkeley, CA 94720

Soapbox Junction
P.O. Box 597996
Chicago, IL 60659

SOAR
210 Delaware St., S.E., Suite 603E
Minneapolis, MN 55455

Social Activist Professors' Defense Fund
19329 Monte Vista Dr.
Detroit, MI 48221

Social Anarchism
2743 Maryland Ave.
Baltimore, MD 21218

Social Legislation Information Service
440 1st St., N.W., Suite 310
Washington, DC 20001
Marjorie Kopp, Editor
(202) 638-2952

Socialism and Democracy
33 W. 42nd St.
New York, NY 10036

Socialism and Sexuality
1608 N. Milwaukee
Chicago, IL 60647

Socialist Action
3455 Army St., Suite 308
San Francisco, CA 94110

Socialist Party USA
516 W. 25th St., Suite 404
New York, NY 10001

Socialist Workers Party
410 West St.
New York, NY 10014

Society Against Vivisection
P.O. Box 10206
Costa Mesa, CA 92627

Solidarity/Solidaridad
24 E. Wall St.
Bethlehem, PA 18018

South Asia Bulletin
History Deptartment
SUNY
Albany, NY 12222

South Coast Foundation
1563 Solano Ave., #354
Berkeley, CA 94707

South End Press
P.O. Box 741
Monroe, ME 04951

Southern Africa Media Center
149 9th St., S.E.
San Francisco, CA 94103

Southern Conference Education Fund
3210 W. Broadway
Louisville, KY 40211

Southern Echo
P.O. Box 10433
Jackson, MS 39289

Southwest Network for Environmental and
Economic Justice
P.O. Box 7399
Alburquerque, NM 87194

Sovereignty
1154 West Logan St.
Freeport, IL 61032
(815) 232-8737

Sovereignty Network
HCO4, Box 9880
Palmer, AK 99642

Spartacist League
P.O. Box 1377
New York, NY 10116

Spartacist Youth League
P.O. Box 3118
New York, NY 10008

Speak Out!
2215 Market St., Suite 520
San Francisco, CA 94114

Stop War Toys Campaign
P.O. Box 1093
Norwich, CT 06360

Student Action Union
P.O. Box 456
New Brunswick, NJ 08903

Student Coalition Against Apartheid
P.O. Box 18291
Washington, DC 20036

Student Press Service News Report
1221 Massachusetts Ave., N.W., Suite B
Washington, DC 20005

Synergy
P.O. Box 185411
New York, NY 10025

Syracuse Cultural Workers
P.O. Box 6367
Syracuse, NY 13217

Syracuse Peace Council
924 Burnet Ave.
Syracuse, NY 13203

Talkin' Union
P.O. Box 5349
Takoma Park, MD 20912

Tangent Group
115 Monroe St.
Bossier City, LA 71111
Don Slater
(318) 742-4709

Task Force Against Nuclear Pollution
P.O. Box 564
Greenbelt, MD 20768

Task Force Indonesia
7538 Newberry Lane
Lanham-Seabrook, MD 20706

Territory Resource
603 Stewart, Suite 221
Seattle, WA 98101

Texas Civil Liberties Union
P.O. Box 3629
Austin, TX 78764
Jay Jacobson

Thesmorphia
5856 College Ave.
Oakland, CA 94618

Third World Newsreel
335 W. 38th St., 5th Floor
New York, NY 10018

Third World Resources
464 19th St.
Oakland, CA 94612

Third World Women's Alliance
346 W. 20th St.
New York, NY 10011

Threshold
Drawer CU
Bisbee, AZ 85603
John P. Milton, President

Time Dollar Network
P.O. Box 142160
Washington, DC 20015

Times Change Press
P.O. Box 1380
Ojai, CA 93023

Town Hall
123 W. 43rd St.
New York, NY

Transitions Abroad
P.O. Box 3000, Dept TRA
Denville, NJ 07834

Tribe: An American Gay Journal
234 E. 25th St.
Baltimore, MD 21218

Tribune
777 United Nations Plaza
New York, NY 10017

Trivia
P.O. Box 606
North Amherst, MA 01059

U. S. - China Peoples Friendship
50 Oak St., Suite 502
San Francisco, CA 94102

U. S. Hands Off Cuba Coalition
3181 Mission St., Suite 120
San Francisco, CA 94110

U. S. Marxist-Leninist Organization
3942 N. Central Ave.
Chicago, IL 60634

U. S.- Cuba Labor Exchange
P.O. Box 39188
Redford, MI 48239

Union Democratic Communications
Media Arts
University of Arizona
Tucson, AZ 85721

Union of Radical Political Economists
Economics Deptartment
University of California, Riverside
Riverside, CA 92521

Union Settlement Association
237 E. 104th St.
New York, NY 10029
Eugene Sklar, Executive Director
(212) 360-8823, fax (212) 360-8835

Uniquest Foundation
1 Lawson Rd.
Berkeley, CA 94707

Unitarian Universalist Veatch Program at
Shelter Rock
48 Shelter Rock Rd.
Manhasset, NY 11030

United Activists for Animal Rights
P.O. Box 2448
Riverside, CA 92516

United Front Against Fascism
5018 Rainier Ave., S.
Seattle, WA 98118

United Methodist Church Board of Church
and Society
100 Maryland Ave., N.E.
Washington, DC 20002

United Native Americans
2434 Faria Ave.
Pinole, CA 94564

United States Committee for the United
Nations Environment Program
2013 Q St., N.W.
Washington, DC 20009
Richard A. Hellman, President

United States Committee of the International
Council on Social Welfare
1600 Duke St., Suite 300
Alexandria, VA 22314-3421
(703) 683-8080

United States Pacifist Party
5729 S. Dorchester Ave.
Chicago, IL 60637

Unity and Thought
P.O. Box 1313
Newark, NJ 07101

Universal Proutist Labour Federation
P.O. Box 56466
Washington, DC 20011

Urban Initiatives
530 W. 25th St.
New York, NY 10001
Gianni Longo, President

Vencermos Brigade
P.O. Box 673
New York, NY 10035

Vermont Coalition for the Homeless
P.O. Box 1616
Burlington, VT 05402

Veterans Advocate
2001 S St., N.W., Suite 610
Washington, DC 20009

Veterans Education Project
P.O. Box 416
Amherst, MA 01004

Veterans for Peace
P.O. Box 1314
Jamaica Plain, MA 02130

Veterans of the Abraham Lincoln Brigade
799 Broadway, Suite 227
New York, NY 10003

Virginians Against Handgun Violence
P.O. Box 267
Luray, VA 22835

Virginians for Animal Rights
P.O. Box 17265
Richmond, VA 23226

Volunteers of America
3939 N. Causeway Blvd.
Metairie, LA 70002
Clint Cheveallier, President

War Research Information Service
P.O. Box 748
Cambridge, MA 02142

Warsh-Mott Legacy
469 Bohemian Hwy.
Freestone, CA 95472

Washington Association of Churches
4759 15th Ave., N.E.
Seattle, WA 98105

Washington Free Press
1463 E. Republican St.
Seattle, WA 98112

Way of Mountain Learning Center
P.O. Box 542
Silverton, CO 81433
Dolores LaChapelle

Weekly Alternative News Monitor
P.O. Box 587
Olean, NY 14760

West Virginia Citizens Research Group
1324 E. Virginia St.
Charleston, WV 25301

Western Socialist Conference
1519 E. 17th St.
Oakland, CA 94606

Whole Earth Review
P.O. Box 38
Sausalito, CA 94966

Wild Earth
P.O. Box 455
Richmond, VA 05477

Windward Foundation
55 Windward Lane
Klickitat, WA 98628
(509) 369-2000

Wisconsin Light
1843 N. Palmer
Milwaukee, WI 53212

Wiser Woman
P.O. Box 1053
Bellevue, ID 83313

Womankind Books
5 Kivy St.
Huntington, NY 11746

Women Activists
2310 Barbour Rd.
Falls Church, VA 22043

Women Against Imperialism
3543 18th St., Suite 14
San Francisco, CA 94110

Women Against Pornography
321 W. 47th St.
New York, NY 10036

Women and Revolution
P.O. Box 1377
New York, NY 10116

Women and Therapy
Psychology Deptartment
University of Vermont
Burlington, VT 05405

Women for Racial and Economic Equality
198 Broadway, Suite 606
New York, NY 10028

Women of All Red Nations
4511 N. Hermitage
Chicago, IL 60640

Women Strike for Peace
110 Maryland Ave., N.E.
Washington, DC 20002

Women Who Masturbate
P.O. Box 3690
Minneapolis, MN 55403

Women's Health Action and Mobilization
P.O. Box 733
New York, NY 10009

Women's Institute for Freedom of the Press
3306 Ross Place, N.W.
Washington, DC 20008

Women's International League of Peace and
Freedom
1213 Race St.
Philadelphia, PA 19107

Women's Media Project
1333 H St., N.W., 11th Floor
Washington, DC 20005

Women's Rights Law Reporter
15 Washington St.
Newark, NJ 07102

Women's Studies International Forum
660 White Plains Rd.
Tarrytown, NY 10591

Women's Studies Quarterly
311 E. 94th St.
New York, NY 10128

Workers Unity Organization
P.O. Box 23001
St Louis, MO 63108

World Citizens, Inc.
3721 48th Ave., S.
Minneapolis, MN 55406

World Constitution and Parliament
Association
1480 Hoyt St., Suite 31
Lakewood, CO 80215

World Future Society
7910 Woodmont Ave., Suite 450
Bethesda, MD 20814

World Hunger Action Newsletter
AFSC, 15 Rutherford Place
New York, NY 10003

World Peace One
5135 Dearborn St.
Pittsburgh, PA 15224-2432
Timothy L. Cimino, Executive Director
(412) 362-4990

World Peace One
7114 Idlewild
St. Louis, MO 63136

World Society to Protect Animals
P.O. Box 190
Boston, MA 02130

Wyoming Against Homelessness
930 Western Hills Blvd.
Cheyenne, WY 82009

Year Left
English Deptartment
State University of New York
Stony Brook, NY 11794

Yellow Silk
P.O. Box 6374
Albany, CA 94706

Youth International Party
P.O. Box 392
New York, NY 10013

NO FORWARDING ADDRESS

The organizations listed in this section were identified as left-of-center political activists. However, mail sent to their last known address was returned, marked as "No Forwarding Address." We suspect that some of these organizations are no longer in existence, some reorganized under different names, and others moved but their forwarding order expired or their new address is not available. We have listed their last known address and, when available, a contact person. One use of this section is to update correspondence and referral files. If users of The Left Guide can provide valid addresses or the status of these organizations, we would be pleased to contact them for the next edition.

Access: Networking in the Public Interest
50 Beacon St.
Boston, MA 02100

Across Frontiers
P.O. Box 2383
Berkeley, CA 94702

Action for Corporate Accountability
3255 S. Hennepin Ave., Suite 255
Minneapolis, MN 55408-9986

Action Linkage
5825 Telegraph Ave., Suite 45
Oakland, CA 94609

Activists for Independent Socialist Politics
P.O. Box 78241
San Francisco, CA 94107

Adapt
12 Broadway
Denver, CO 80203

African American Student Association
10 Clover Place
Brooklyn, NY 11238

African and Caribbean Resource Center
P.O. Box 1606
Brooklyn, NY 11202

African National Congress
801 Second Ave., Suite 405
New York, NY 10017

African People's Socialist Party
P.O. Box 27295
Oakland, CA 94605

Afrikan Universal Library
437 19th St.
Oakland, CA 94612

Agencia Nueva Nicaragua
1260 National Press Bldg.
Washington, DC 20045

All-African Peoples Revolutionary Party
1738 A St., S.E.
Washington, DC 20003

All-Peoples Congress
146 W. 25th St.
New York, NY 10001

Alliance for a Clean Rural Environment
1155 15th St., N.W., Suite 900
Washington, DC 20005
John Thorne, Director

Alliance of Native Americans
P.O. Box 30392
Los Angeles, CA 90030

Alliance of Third World Journalists
P.O. Box 43208
Washington, DC 20010

Alternative Radio
1814 Spruce
Boulder, CO 80302

Alternative Youth Brigade
P.O. Box 90537
Santa Barbara, CA 93190

Alternative Energy Resources Organization
44 North Last Chance Gulch, Suite 9
Helena, MT 35001

Alternative Index
P.O. Box 326
Westmoreland, KS 66549

American Agri-Women
1342 West San Jose
Fresno, CA 93711

American Association of University Women
Education Fund
2401 Virginia Ave., N.W.
Washington, DC 20037

American Committee on U.S. - Soviet
Relations
201 Massachusetts Ave., N.E., Suite 5
Washington, DC 20002

American Committee to Protect Foreign
Born
175 Fifth Ave., Suite 712
New York, NY 10010

American Council on the Environment
1301 20th St., N.W.
Washington, DC 20036
John Gullett, Executive Officer

American Indian Movement
710 Clayton St., Suite 1
San Francisco, CA 94117

American Psychological Association
1200 17th St., N.W.
Washington, DC 20036

American Visions
P.O. Box 53219
Boulder, CO 80322

Anarchist Association of America
P.O. Box 840
Washington, DC 20044

Anarchist Youth Federation
P.O. Box 8972
Denver, CO 80201

Animal Advocates
P.O. Box 6887
Pittsburgh, PA 15212

Animal Political Action Committee
P.O. Box 2706
Washington, DC 20077

Animal Rights Information and Education
Service
P.O. Box 332
Rowayton, CT 06853

Animal Rights Mobilization
P.O. Box 1553
Williamsport, PA 17703

Anthropology Resource Center
P.O. Box 90
Cambridge, MA 02138

Anti-Racist Literature Project
P.O. Box 2902
Brooklyn, NY 11202

Anti-Warrior
48 Shattuck Ave., Suite 129
Berkeley, CA 94704

Anti-Racist Action
P.O. Box 7471
Minneapolis, MN 55407

Antipode
3 Cambridge Center
Cambridge, MA 02142

Architects for Social Responsibility
225 Lafayette St., Suite 205
New York, NY 10012

Arizona Right to Choose
3602 E. Campbell
Phoenix, AZ 85018

Arms Control Media Project
2001 S St., N.W., Suite 300
Washington, DC 20009

Association of Black Sociologists
P.O. Box 302
Washington, DC 20059

Association of World Citizens
110 Sutter St., Suite 708
San Francisco, CA 94104

Association of Black Psychologists
P.O. Box 29292
Washington, DC 20002

Athletes United for Peace
116 Johnson
Highland Park, NJ 08904

Austin Men's Center
1611 W. 6th St.
Austin, TX 78703

Bertrand Russell Society
RD #1, Box 409
Coopersburg, PA 18036

Big Apple Dyke News
192 Spring St., Suite 15
New York, NY 10012

Bill of Rights Association
P.O. Box 1061
Santa Cruz, CA 95061
Maestro Malik, President

Bill of Rights Foundation
523 S. Plymouth Ct., Suite 800
Chicago, IL 60605

Black Consciousness Movement
410 Central Park West, Suite 3C
New York, NY 10025

Black Panther Militia
2636 Martin Luther King Dr.
Milwaukee, WI 53712

Black Vanguard Resource Center
P.O. Box 6289
Norfolk, VA 23508

Black Women Organized for Action
P.O. Box 15072
San Francisco, CA 94115

Black Women's Network
P.O. Box 12072
Milwaukee, WI 53212

Brazil Network
P.O. Box 2738
Washington, DC 20013

Buffalo Soldier
481 Auzerias Ave.
San Jose, CA 95126

Bulletin of Municipal Foreign Policy
17931 Sky Park Cr., Suite F
Irvine, CA 92714

California Community Foundation
3580 Wilshire Blvd., Suite 1660
Los Angeles, CA 90010

California Prisoners' Union
1909 6th St.
Sacramento, CA 95814

Campaign for Political Rights
201 Massachusetts Ave., N.E.
Washington, DC 20002

Campaign for Sovereignty
P.O. Box 132
Red Rock, OK 74651

Campaign for World Government
552 Lincoln Ave., Suite 202
Winnetka, IL 60093

Campus Anti-Repression Network
P.O. Box 12006
Washington, DC 20005

Casa Chile
P.O. Box 3620
Berkeley, CA 94703

CEED Institute
1807 2nd St., Studio 2
Santa Fe, NM 87501

Center for American-Soviet Dialogue
615 2nd Ave., Suite 110
Seattle, WA 98104

Center for Democratic Alternatives
1739 Connecticut Ave., N.W.
Washington, DC 20009

Center for Dispute Resolution
1337 Ocean Ave.
Santa Monica, CA 90401

Center for National Policy
317 Massachusetts Ave., N.E.
Washington, DC 20002

Center for New National Security
1016 Prince St., Suite 5
Alexandria, VA 22314

Center for the Study of Public Policy
124 Mount Auburn St.
Cambridge, MA 02138

Central America Bulletin
P.O. Box 4797
Berkeley, CA 94704

Central America Peace Campaign
4556 University Way, N.E.
Seattle, WA 98105

Central America Research Institute
347 Dolores St., Suite 327
San Francisco, CA 94110

Chicago Friends of Albania
P.O. Box 87436
Chicago, IL 60680

Children as Peacemakers Foundation
950 Battery St.
San Francisco, CA 94111

Chile Democratico
P.O. Box 497
New York, NY 10025

Chile Information Network
P.O. Box 20179
New York, NY 10025

Christian Action Network
P.O. Box 836
Teaneck, NJ 07666

Christianity and Crisis
537 W. 121st St.
New York, NY 10027

Church and State
8120 Fenton St.
Silver Spring, MD 20910

Civilian-Based Defense Association
P.O. Box 31616
Omaha, NE 68131

Clergy and Laity Concerned
198 Broadway, Suite 305
New York, NY 10038

Co-op America
2100 M St., N.W., Suite 310
Washington, DC 20063

Coalition for a National Healthcare System
49 Corwin Ave.
Rochester, NY 14609

Coalition for a New Foreign Policy
712 G St., S.E.
Washington, DC 20003

Coalition for Corporate Accountability
57 ½ North Court St.
Athens, OH 45701

Coalition for the Homeless
500 Eighth Ave.
New York, NY 10018

Colorado Coalition to Abolish the Death Penalty
P.O. Box 300552
Denver, CO 80203
James Sunderland

Committee for Artists' Rights
5 West Grand
Chicago, IL 60610

Committee for Non-Intervention in Honduras
P.O. Box 641
New York, NY 10032

Committee for Responsible Genetics
186 South St., 4th Fl.
Boston, MA 02111

Committee in Support of Solidarity
48 E. 21st St., 3rd Fl.
New York, NY 10010

Committee of Black Gay Men
P.O. Box 7209
Chicago, IL 60680

Committee on Israeli Censorship
P.O. Box 3034
Chicago, IL 60654

Committee to Defend Reproductive Rights
25 Taylor St., Suite 704
San Francisco, CA 94102

Concerned Citizens for Nuclear Safety
712 Calle Grillo
Santa Fe, NM 87501

Connexions
4228 Telegraph Ave.
Oakland, CA 94609

Conscience and Military Tax Campaign
44 Bellhaven Rd.
Bellport, NY 11713

Conservation Law Foundation of New England
3 Joy St.
Boston, MA 02108-1497

Crusade for Justice
1567 Downing St.
Denver, CO 80218

Cuba Resource Center
P.O. Box 206
New York, NY 10025

Death Penalty Focus
P.O. Box 806
San Francisco, CA 94101

Disability Rag
P.O. Box 14560
Louisville, KY 40201

Disarm Education Fund
36 E. 12th St., 6th Fl.
New York, NY 10003

Earth Keeper
P.O. Box 242
Whittier, NC 28789

Education for the People
1801 18th St., N.W.
Washington, DC 20009

Educators Committee on Central America
P.O. Box 371107
San Diego, CA 92137

El Estiliano
P.O. Box 1409
Cambridge, MA 02238

Elmwood Institute
P.O. Box 5765
Berkeley, CA 94705

Empowerment Project
1653 18th St., Suite 3
Santa Monica, CA 90404

Energy Conservation Coalition
235 Pennsylvania Ave., S.E.
Washington, DC 20003

Environmental Data Research Institute
797 Elmwood Ave.
Rochester, NY 14620

Environmental Exchange
1930 18th St., N.W., Suite 24
Washington, DC 20009

Environmental News Network
1442-A Walnut St., Suite 81
Berkeley, CA 94709

Environmental Task Force
1012 14th St., N.W., 15th Fl.
Washington, DC 20005

Environment and Democracy Campaign
224 E. 7th St., Rm. 11
New York, NY 10009

Feminist Alliance Against Rape
P.O. Box 21033
Washington, DC 20009

Feminist Institute
P.O. Box 30563
Bethesda, MD 20824

Feminist Writers Guild
P.O. Box 14055
Chicago, IL 60614

Feminists Fighting Pornography
P.O. Box 1483
New York, NY 10156

Fighting Woman News
P.O. Box 1459
New York, NY 10163

Filipino American Political Association
3250 Wilshire Blvd.
Los Angeles, CA 90010

Firearms Policy Project
1834 18th St., N.W.
Washington, DC 20009

First National Development Institute
69 Kelly Rd.
Falmouth, VA 22405

Food First News
145 9th St.
San Francisco, CA 94103

Forward Motion
P.O. Box 1884
Jamaica Plain, MA 02130

Foundation for Change, Inc.
1841 Broadway
New York, NY 10023

Fourth International Tendency
27 W. Union Square, Suite 208
New York, NY 10003

Free Press
1066 N. High St.
Columbus, OH 12201

Free World Government Earthbank
P.O. Box 332146
Miami, FL 33233

Freedom Now!
P.O. Box 28191
Washington, DC 20038

Friends of Palestinian Prisoners
P.O. Box 15288
Washington, DC 20003

Fund for Human Rights
84 5th Ave.
New York, NY 10011

Fund for Open Information and
Accountability
P.O. Box 02-2397
Brooklyn, NY 11202

Gaia Pacific: The Art of Activism
P.O. Box 53
Del Mar, CA 92014

Gay and Lesbian Defense Committee
P.O. Box 225
Somerville, MA 02144

Gay and Lesbian Democrats of America
114 15th St., N.E.
Washington, DC 20002

Gay and Lesbians Against Defamation
80 Varick St., Suite 3-E
New York, NY 10013

Gay Community News
62 Berkeley St.
Boston, MA 02116

Gay Fathers Coalition
418 W. 51st St.
New York, NY 10019

Gay Press Association
P.O. Box A
New York, NY 10011

Gay Rights National Lobby
P.O. Box 1892
Washington, DC 20013

Genesis 2
99 Bishop Allen Dr.
Cambridge, MA 02139

Genewatch
19 Garden St.
Cambridge, MA 02138

Georgia Environmental Project
429 Moreland Ave.
Atlanta, GA 30307

Grandmothers for Peace
909 12th St., Suite 118
Sacramento, CA 95814

Grassroots Leadership
P.O. Box 9586
Charlotte, NC 28299

Gray Panther Network
311 S. Juniper St., Suite 601
Philadelphia, PA 19107

Green Age
P.O. Box 1262
York, PA 17405

Green and Rainbow Activists for a
Democratic Society
P.O. Box 5194
New York, NY 10185

Green Party Organizing Caucus
P.O. Box 39
Huntington, NY 11743

Greensboro Justice Fund
P.O. Box 15726
Durham, NC 27704

Guatemala Solidarity Front
P.O. Box 25770
Chicago, IL 60625

Hag Rag Intergalactic Lesbians
P.O. Box 1171
Madison, WI 53701

Health Policy Advisory Center
17 Murray St.
New York, NY 10007

Hemp Council
P.O. Box 2096
Pahoa, HI 96778

High Performance
240 S. Broadway, 5th Floor
Los Angeles, CA 90012

Honduras Information Center
One Summer St.
Somerville, MA 02143

Honduras Information Network
536 E. Hoyt Ave.
St. Paul, MN 55101

Human Environment Center
1001 Connecticut Ave., N.W., Suite 82
Washington, DC 20036

Indian Rights Association
1601 Market St.
Philadelphia, PA 19103

Industrial Crisis Institute
649 E. 19th St.
Brooklyn, NY 11230

Industrial Union Party
P.O. Box 80
New York, NY 10159

Informe Columbiano
P.O. Box 1017
New York, NY 10156

Institute for Gaean Economics
64 Main St.
Montpelier, VT 05602

Institute for Social Service Alternatives
P.O. Box 1144
New York, NY 10025

Institute for Social Therapy
216 W. 102nd St, Suite 2C
New York, NY 10025

Institute for Soviet-American Relations
1608 New Hampshire Ave., N.W.
Washington, DC 20009

Institute of Black Studies
6372 Delmar Blvd.
St Louis, MO 63130

International Animal Rights Alliance
P.O. Box 1836
Boston, MA 02205

International Defenders of Animals
P.O. Box 112
Urbana, MO 65767

International Defense and Aid Fund
P.O. Box 17
Cambridge, MA 02138

International Green Party
P.O. Box 2413
Fullerton, CA 92631

International Jewish Peace Union
P.O. Box 20854
New York, NY 10009

Interrace Magazine
P.O. Box 15566
Beverly Hills, CA 90209

Interracial Books for Children
1841 Broadway
New York, NY 10023

Jacobin Books
P.O. Box 416, Van Brunt
Brooklyn, NY 11215

John Herling's Labor Letter
1411 K St., N.W.
Washington, DC 20005

Katipunan
P.O. Box 2759
Oakland, CA 94602

Kindred Spirits Journal
P.O. Box 542
Lewisburg, PA 17837

Korean Information Center
1314 14th St., N.W.
Washington, DC 20005

La Raza Unida
917 N. Waterloo Rd.
Jefferson, WI 53549

Labor Network on Central America
P.O. Box 28014
Oakland, CA 94604

Labor Party Advocates
P.O. Box 1510
Highland Park, NJ 08904

Latin American Perspectives
275 S. Beverly Dr.
Beverly Hills, CA 90212

Law Students Civil Rights Council
52 Fairlie St., Suite 350
Atlanta, GA 30303

Lawyers Committee on Nuclear Policy
225 Lafayette St.
New York, NY 10012

League for Industrial Democracy
181 Hudson St., Suite 3A
New York, NY 10013

Left Green Network
P.O. Box 366
Iowa City, IA 52244

Left Uncensored
1202 E. Pike, Suite 1094
Seattle, WA 98122

Lesbian Resource Center
1208 E. Pine Street
Seattle, WA 98122
Cherie Larson, Director

Lesbian Separatist Conference
P.O. Box 3065
Madison, WI 53704

Lesbian Tide
8855 Cattaragus Ave.
Los Angeles, CA 90034

Liberation League
P.O. Box 13851
New Orleans, LA 70185

Marxist-Leninist Books
3232 Grove St.
Oakland, CA 94609

Marxist-Leninist League
P.O. Box 19074
Sacramento, CA 95819

Marxist-Leninist Party, USA
P.O. Box 11942
Chicago, IL 60611

Mattachine Midwest
P.O. Box 924
Chicago, IL 60690

Media Network on Southern Africa
1208 W. 13th St.
New York, NY 10011

Middle East Justice Network
P.O. Box 558
Cambridge, MA 02238

Mideast Peace Coalition
P.O. Box 121013
Nashville, TN 37212

Militarism Resource Project
P.O. Box 13416
Philadelphia, PA 19101

Mill Hunk Herald
916 Middle St.
Pittsburgh, PA 15212

Millstream Fund
2275 Research Blvd., Suite 250
Rockville, MD 20850

Minority Research Center
117 R St., N.E.
Washington, DC 20002

Minority Rights Group
35 Claremont Ave.
New York, NY 10027

Mobilization for Survival
45 John St., Suite 811
New York, NY 10038

Modern Times Books
968 Valencia St
San Francisco, CA 94110

Mozambique Support Network
343 S. Dearborn, Suite 316
Chicago, IL 60604

National Alliance Against Racist Political
Repression
126 W. 119th St., Suite 101
New York, NY 10026

National Anti-Imperialist Movement
P.O. Box 5555
New York, NY 10027

National Association for Puerto Rican Civil
Rights
175 E. 116th St.
New York, NY 10029

National Association of Atomic Veterans
P.O. Box 707
Eldon, MO 65026

National Bisexual Network
584 Castro St., Suite 442
San Francisco, CA 94114

National Black Network
1350 Avenue of Americas
New York, NY 10019

National Black United Front
P.O. Box 470665
Brooklyn, NY 11247

National Center Policy Alternatives
2000 Florida Ave., N.W.
Washington, DC 20009

National Central American Health Rights
853 Broadway, Suite 416
New York, NY 10003

National Child Rights Alliance
P.O. Box 431
Greenfield, MA 01302

National Coalition of Universities in the
Public Interest
1801 18th St., N.W.
Washington, DC 20009

National Committee Against English Only
98 Wadsworth, Suites 127-17
Lakewood, CO 80225

National Conference of Black Lawyers
405 Hilgard
Los Angeles, CA 90024

National Council of American-Soviet
Friendship
101 Madison Ave.
New York, NY 10016

National Network in Solidarity with the
Nicaraguan People
P.O. Box 450
New York, NY 10012

National Organization for Women, Ohio
4207 Lorain Ave.
Cleveland, OH 44113

National Organization of Men Against
Sexism
798 Pennsylvania Ave., Box 5
Pittsburg, PA 15221

National Organization of Socially
Responsible Organizations
1925 K St., Suite 310
Washington, DC 20006

National Pledge of Resistance
4228 Telegraph, Suite 100
Berkeley, CA 94609

National Reporter
P.O. Box 21279
Washington, DC 21279

National Resistance Committee
P.O. Box 42488
San Francisco, CA 94142

National Student Action Center
P.O. Box 15599
Washington, DC 20003

National War Tax Resistance Coordinating
Committee
P.O. Box 85810
Seattle, WA 85810

Native American Solidarity Committee
3418 22nd St.
San Francisco, CA 94110

Nature/Technology Alliance
P.O. Box 8005
Baytown, TX 77522

Navaho Nation Today
P.O. Box 643
Window Rock, AZ 86515

Nerve Center
1917 E. 29th St.
Oakland, CA 94606

New Day Films
22 Riverside Dr.
Wayne, NJ 07470

New England Green Alliance
P.O. Box 703
White River Junction, VT 05001

New International News Service
4662 Landis St.
San Diego, CA 92105

New Jewish Agenda
64 Fulton St., Suite 1100
New York, NY 10028

New Liberation News Service
P.O. Box 325
Cambridge, MA 02142

New Options
P.O. Box 19324
Washington, DC 20036

New Outlook
150 5th Ave., Suite 911
New York, NY 10011

New Party
324 Belleville Ave.
Bloomfield, NJ 07003

New World Rising
Box 33, 77 Ives St.
Providence, RI 02906

New York CIRCUS
P.O. Box 37
New York, NY 10108

New York Marxist School
79 Leonard St.
New York, NY 10013

New York On-Line Computer Network
P.O. Box 829
Brooklyn, NY 11202

Nicaraguan Perspectives
P.O. Box 2929
Berkeley, CA 94618

North American Coalition for Human Rights
in Korea
110 Maryland Ave., N.E.
Washington, DC 20002

North American Farm Alliance
P.O. Box 176
Ames, IA 50010

North Star News
P.O. Box 622
Arcata, CA 95521

Northeast South African Solidarity Network
P.O. Box 1322 NW
New Haven, CT 06505

Northern Sun Alliance
1519 E. Franklin Ave.
Minneapolis, MN 55404

Nurses Alliance to Prevent Nuclear War
225 Lafayette St., Suite 613
New York, NY 10012

OEF International
1815 H St., N.W., 11th Fl.
Washington, DC 20005

One Hundredth Monkey Project
504-A Emerson St.
Palo Alto, CA 94301

Organization for a Marxist-Lenin Workers
Party
P.O. Box 5830
Chicago, IL 60680

Organization of Chinese-American Citizens
2025 I St., N.W., Suite 926
Washington, DC 20006

Organization of Chinese-American Women
1300 N St., N.W., Suite 100
Washington, DC 20005

Organization to Stop Sexism and Racism
P.O. Box 471012
Charlotte, NC 32604

Outlook
2940 16th St., Suite 319
San Francisco, CA 94103

Outrageous Woman
P.O. Box 23
Somerville, MA 02143

Pacific Concerns Resource Center
P.O. Box 27692
Honolulu, HI 96827

Palestine Academic Freedom Network
P.O. Box 53353
Washington, DC 20009

Palestine Human Rights Information Center
4753 N. Broadway, Suite 930
Chicago, IL 60640

Palestine Solidarity Committee
P.O. Box 372
New York, NY 10272

Pan African Congress
8809 Joy Rd.
Detroit, MI 48204

Pan Africanist Congress of Azania
211 E. 43rd St., Suite 703
New York, NY 10017

Paraguay Watch
P.O. Box 21128
Washington, DC 20009

Paying for Peace
P.O. Box 5946
Takoma Park, MD 20913

Peace and Solidarity Project
P.O. Box 20555
Oakland, CA 94620

Peace Education Network
3125 E. Ocean Blvd.
Long Beach, CA 90803

Peace Resource Center of Santa Barbara
P.O. Box 91757
Santa Barbara, CA 93190-1757

People for Social Responsibility University
358 N. Pleasant St., Suite 307
Amherst, MA 01002

People of Color News Collective
700 Eshelman Hall
Berkeley, CA 94720

People United to Save Humanity
127 N. Paulina St.
Chicago, IL 60612

Philippine Resource Center
P.O. Box 40090
Berkeley, CA 94704

Physicians Forum
220 S. State St., Suite 1926
Chicago, IL 60604

Planetary Citizens
P.O. Box 1509
Mt. Shasta, CA 96067

Planners Network
1901 Q St., N.W.
Washington, DC 20009

Pledge of Resistance
P.O. Box 53411
Washington, DC 20009

Practical Anarchy
P.O. Box 173
Madison, WI 53701

Progressive Student Network
P.O. Box 1027
Iowa City, IA 52244

Proletariat
P.O. Box 12247-D
San Francisco, CA 94112

Prout Institute
P.O. Box 2667
Santa Cruz, CA 95063

Public Interest Computer Association
1025 Connecticut Ave., N.W., Suite 1015
Washington, DC 20036

Puerto Rico Independence and Socialism
3543 18th St., Suite 17
San Francisco, CA 94110

Radioactive Waste Campaign
7 West St.
Warwick, NY 10990

Rational Feminist
P.O. Box 28253
St. Petersburg, FL 33709

Red Bass
2425 Burgundy St.
New Orleans, LA 70117

Red Flag / Bandera Roja
P.O. Box 30735
Los Angeles, CA 90060

Redwood Records Culture and Education
Fund
478 W. MacArthur Blvd.
Oakland, CA 94609

Religious Socialism
45 Thornton St.
Roxbury, MA 01908

Reproductive Health Technology Project
1601 Connecticut Ave., N.W., Suite 801
Washington, DC 20009

Republic of New Afrika
P.O. Box 465
Jackson, MS 39205

Rethinking Marxism
P.O. Box 85
Newton Center, MA 02159

Revolutionary Socialist League
P.O. Box 1288
New York, NY 10016

Sassafras
158 Cliff St.
Norwich, CT 06360

Science as Culture
72 Spring St.
New York, NY 10012

Science for the People
897 Main St.
Cambridge, MA 02139

Science Resource Center
897 Main St.
Cambridge, MA 02139

Skins and Punks Against Racism
P.O. Box 119002, Suite 222
San Diego, CA 92111

Social Concept
1266 Boulevard
New Haven, CT 06511

Social Revolutionary Anarchists
P.O. Box 11966
Salt Lake City, UT 84147

Social Text
P.O. Box 1474
New York, NY 10011

Socialist Review
2940 16th St., Suite 102
San Francisco, CA 94103

Sojourner: The Women's Forum
1050 Commonwealth Ave.
Boston, MA 02215

Solidarity
70121 Michigan Ave.
Detroit, MI 43210

Solstice
1110 E. Market, Suite 16E
Charlottesville, VA 22901

Southern Africa Resource Project
P.O. Box 5420
Santa Monica, CA 90405

Southern Africa Support and Information
802 N. Homewood Ave, 2nd Fl.
Pittsburgh, PA 15208

Southern Regional Council
60 Watson St., N.W.
Atlanta, GA 30303

Soviet-American Exchange Center
345 Franklin St., Suite 520
San Francisco, CA 94102

Student Anti-Apartheid Movement
198 Broadway
New York, NY 10038

Student Press Law Center
800 18th St., N.W., Suite 300
Washington, DC 20006

Student Pugwash
1638 R St., N.W., Suite 32
Washington, DC 20009

Students United for Peace
630 14th St., Suite 6
Sacramento, CA 95814

Subconscious Soup
P.O. Box 421272
Kissimmee, FL 34742

Subtext
1408 18th Ave.
Seattle, WA 98122

Subversive Agent
P.O. Box 11835
Minneapolis, MN 55411

Three Continents Press
1901 Pennsylvania Ave., N.W.
Washington, DC 20006

Too Far
P.O. Box 40185
Berkeley, CA 94704

Trade Union Action and Democracy
7917 S. Exchange, Suite 211
Chicago, IL 60617

Tradeswoman
P.O. Box 40664
San Francisco, CA 94140

Trident Information Network
P.O. Box 181
New Haven, CT 06501

Twenty-First Century Party
1600 Wilson Blvd., Suite 707
Arlington, VA 22209

U. S. Farmers Association
P.O. Box 496
Hampton, IA 50441

U. S. Peace Council
11 John St., Suite 804
New York, NY 10038

U. S. - Vietnam Friendship Association
P.O. Box 5043
San Francisco, CA 94101

Underground Beat
1718 N St., N.W., Suite 154
Washington, DC 20036

United Anarchist Front
P.O. Box 3941
Fullerton, CA 92634

Vietnam Generation
10301 Proctor St.
Silver Spring, MD 20901

Vox Summary
P.O. Box 8151
Kansas City, MO 64112

Washington Blade
724 9th St., N.W., 8th Fl.
Washington, DC 20001

Web Collective, The
P.O. Box 40890
San Francisco, CA 91110

Without Prejudice
2025 I St., N.W., Suite 1020
Washington, DC 20006

Womanews
P.O. Box 220
New York, NY 10014

Women for Guatemala
P.O. Box 322
Concordia, KS 66901

Women of Power
P.O. Box 827
Cambridge, MA 02238

Womenstruggle
P.O. Box 54115
Minneapolis, MN 55454

Workers League
P.O. Box 5174
Southfield, MI 48086

Workers Solidarity Alliance
P.O. Box 40400
San Francisco, CA 94140

Workers World Party
46 W. 21st St.
New York, NY 10010

Worker's Advocate
P.O. Box 8706
Emeryville, CA 94662

Working Classics
298 Ninth Ave.
San Francisco, CA 94118

Working People's News
P.O. Box 1870
New York, NY 10014

Workplace Democracy
111 Draper
Amherst, MA 01003

World Association of Electroshock
Survivors
P.O. Box 14743
Austin, TX 78761

World Government Organizations Coalition
260 16th St., S.E., Suite 1
Washington, DC 20003

World Peace Foundation
22 Batterymarch St.
Boston, MA 02109

World Perspectives
P.O. Box 3074
Madison, WI 53704

World Policy Institute
777 United Nations Plaza
New York, NY 10017

World Socialist Party
P.O. Box 405
Boston, MA 02272

World Women for Animal Rights
616 6th St., Suite 2
Brooklyn, NY 11213

Young Socialist Alliance
P.O. Box 211
New York, NY 10011

Youth Against War and Fascism
46 W. 21st St.
New York, NY 10010

Zimbabwe African National Union
211 E. 43rd St., Suite 902
New York, NY 10017

Zimbabwe Support Committee
P.O. Box 181
Bronx, NY 10453

DEFUNCT

The organizations listed here have been confirmed to no longer exist. The last known address and contact person are listed. The organizations of the political Left have been operating for decades. In that time period literally thousands have been created and then dissolved. It is beyond the scope of The Left Guide to list all of these. This section lists the organizations that have been confirmed to have dissolved in the last few years.

Conservatory for Native Culture
RFD 2, Box 330
Brooks, ME 04921

Council for Economic Action
One International Place, 17th Fl.
Boston, MA 02110

Foundation for Social Justice in South Africa
39 Old Ridgebury Rd., Suite F3300
Danbury, CT 06817

John Brown Anti-Klan Committee
220 9th St., Suite 443
San Francisco, CA 94103
Founder Linda Evans is currently serving 30 years in prison for participating in the 1983 bombing of the U.S. Capitol building and for purchasing guns using false identification.

Minnesota Human Rights Foundation
1619 Dayton Ave., Suite 327
St. Paul, MN 55104

Minnesota Peace and Justice Coalition
1929 5th St., S.
Minneapolis, MN 55454

Mothers Embracing Nuclear Disarmament
5017 San Joaquin Dr.
San Diego, CA 92109

Nuclear Times
P.O. Box 401
Boston, MA 02215

Religious Coalition for a Moral Drug Policy
3421 M St., N.W., Suite 351
Washington, DC 20007

Sipapu
RR 1, Box 216
Winters, CA 95694

Ventana Newsletter
339 Lafayette St.
New York, NY 10012

PERIODICALS

This section contains the names and addresses of the periodicals offered by organizations listed in the **Profiles** section of this guide. For more information, the researcher should refer to the corresponding profile.

$50+ Club News
Association for Union Democracy (AUD)
500 State St., 2nd Fl.
Brooklyn, NY 11217

AAP
Boston Reproductive Rights Network
P.O. Box 686
Cambridge, MA 02130

AARP Bulletin
American Association of Retired Persons
601 E St., N.W.
Washington, DC 20049

ABG Light
Aluminum, Brick and Glass Workers
International Union
3362 Hollenberg Dr.
Bridgeton, MO 63044

Abya Yala News
South and Meso-American Indian Rights
Center
P.O. Box 28703
Oakland, CA 94612

Access
Fund for Peace
1511 K St., N.W., Suite 643
Washington, DC 20005

ACLU News
American Civil Liberties Union, Ohio
Foundation
1226 W. 6th St., Suite 200
Cleveland, OH 44113

ACOA Action News
American Committee on Africa
17 John St., 12th Fl.
New York, NY 10038

Action Agenda
Media Watch
P.O. Box 618
Santa Cruz, CA 95061-0618

Action Alerts
EarthAction
30 Cottage St.
Amherst, MA 01002

Action Line
Montana People's Action
208 E. Main St.
Missoula, MT 59802

ActiVate for Animals
American Anti-Vivisection Society
801 Old York Rd., Suite 204
Jenkintown, PA 19046

ADA Today
Americans for Democratic Action
1625 K St., N.W., Suite 210
Washington, DC 20005

ADC Times
American-Arab Anti-Discrimination
Committee
4201 Connecticut Ave., N.W., Suite 500
Washington, DC 20008

Advice
Center for the Study of Commercialism
1875 Connecticut Ave., N.W., Suite 300
Washington, DC 20009

Advocate
Association of Trial Lawyers of America
1050 31st St., N.W.
Washington, DC 20007

*Advocate, The: The National Gay & Lesbian
Newsmagazine*
6922 Hollywood Blvd., Suite 1000
Los Angeles, CA 90028

AFL-CIO News
American Federation of Labor
815 16th St., N.W.
Washington, DC 20006

Africa Report
African-American Institute
833 United Nations Plaza
New York, NY 10017

AFSCME Leader
American Federation of State, County and
Municipal Employees
1625 L St., N.W.
Washington, DC 20036

Afterimage
Visual Studies Workshop
31 Prince St.
Rochester, NY 14607

AFT Action
American Federation of Teachers
555 New Jersey Ave., N.W.
Washington, DC 20001

AFTRA Magazine
American Federation of Television and Radio
Artists
260 Madison Ave.
New York, NY 10016

Agenda
National Council of La Raza
1111 19th St., N.W., Suite 1000
Washington, DC 20036

Agenda
220 S. Main St.
Ann Arbor, MI 48104

AGLBIC Newsletter
Association for Gay, Lesbian, and Bisexual
Issues in Counseling
P.O. Box 216
Jenkintown, PA 19046

AIM: America's Intercultural Magazine
7308 S. Eberhart
Chicago, IL 60619

AK PIRG Advocate
Alaska Public Interest Research Group
P.O. Box 220411
Anchorage, AK 99522

ALERT: Focus on Central America
Committee in Solidarity with the People of El
Salvador
19 W. 21st St.
New York, NY 10010

Alliance, The
National Center on Education and the
Economy
700 11th St., N.W., Suite 750
Washington, DC 20001

ALLY
Alliance for Animals
661 Massachusetts Ave.
Arlington, MA 02174

Alternative Press Index
Alternative Press Center
1443 Gorsuch Ave.
Baltimore, MD 21218

Alternative Trading News
Friends of the Third World
611 W. Wayne St.
Fort Wayne, IN 46802

American Educator
American Federation of Teachers
555 New Jersey Ave., N.W.
Washington, DC 20001

American Libraries
American Library Association
50 E. Huron St.
Chicago, IL 60611

American Prospect, The
New Prospect
6 University Rd.
Cambridge, MA 02138

American Teacher
American Federation of Teachers
555 New Jersey Ave., N.W.
Washington, DC 20001

American Woman, The
Women's Research and Education Institute
1700 18th St., Suite 400
Washington, DC 20009

Amicus Journal
Natural Resources Defense Council
40 W. 20th St.
New York, NY 10011

Ammo
International Union, United Automobile,
Aerospace and Agricultural Implement
Workers of America (UAW)
8000 E. Jefferson
Detroit, MI 48214

Amnesty Action
Amnesty International of the U.S.A.
322 Eighth Ave.
New York, NY 10001-4808

Animal People
P.O. Box 205
Shushan, NY 12873

Animal Rights Coalition News
Animal Rights Coalition
3255 Hennepin Ave., S., Suite 30
Minneapolis, MN 55408

Animal Times
People for the Ethical Treatment of Animals
(PETA)
P.O. Box 42516
Washington, DC 20015-0516

Animals' Agenda, The
Animal Rights Network
3201 Elliott St.
Baltimore, MD 21224

Anything That Moves
Bay Area Bisexual Network (BABN)
2404 California St., Box 24
San Francisco, CA 94115

Aquarian Alternatives
Aquarian Research Foundation
5620 Morton St.
Philadelphia, PA 19144

ARFF News
Animal Rights Foundation of Florida (ARFF)
P.O. Box 841154
Pembroke Pines, FL 33084

Arms Control Reporter
Institute for Defense and Disarmament
Studies
675 Massachusetts Ave.
Cambridge, MA 02139

Arms Control Today
Arms Control Association
1726 M St., N.W., Suite 201
Washington, DC 20036

ASH Smoking and Health Review
Action on Smoking and Health (ASH)
2013 H St., N.W.
Washington, DC 20006

Astraea Bulletin
Astraea National Lesbian Action Foundation
116E. 16th St., 7th Floor
New York, NY   10003

AV Magazine, The
American Anti-Vivisection Society (AAVS)
801 Old York Rd., Suite 204
Jenkintown, PA 19046

Balance Activist
Population - Environment Balance
2000 P St., N.W., Suite 210
Washington, DC 20036

Bank Check
International Rivers Network
1847 Berkeley Way
Berkeley, CA 94703

Barricada International
South North Communication Network
P.O. Box 410150
San Francisco, CA 94141

BCT News
Bakery, Confectionery and Tobacco Workers
Union
10401 Connecticut Ave.
Kensington, MD 20895

Berkeley Journal of Sociology
458A Barrows Hall / Department of
Sociology
Berkeley, CA 94705

*Between the Lines: For Lesbians, Gays,
Bisexuals & Friends*
1632 Church St.
Detroit, MI 48216

Bill of Rights in Action
Constitutional Rights Foundation
601 S. Kingsley
Los Angeles, CA 90005

Bill of Rights Journal
National Emergency Civil Liberties
Foundation
175 Fifth Ave., 8th Fl.
New York, NY 10010

Black Caucus Journal
National Association of Black Social Workers
(NABSW)
8436 W. McNichols
Detroit, MI 48221

Black Vet
Black Veterans for Social Justice
686 Fulton St.
Brooklyn, NY 11217

Body Politic, The
P.O. Box 2363
Binghamton, NY 13902

Booklist
American Library Association
50 E. Huron St.
Chicago, IL 60611

Books on Trial
National Coalition Against Censorship
275 Seventh Ave.
New York, NY 10001

BorderLines
Interhemispheric Resource Center
P.O. Box 4506
Albuquerque, NM 87196

Boycott Quarterly
Center for Economic Democracy
P.O. Box 30727
Seattle, WA 98103

Breaking Ground
Coalition on Homelessness and Housing in
Ohio (COHHIO)
1066 N. High St.
Columbus, OH 43201

Breakthrough
Global Education Associates
475 Riverside Dr., Suite 456
New York, NY 10115

Bridging the Gap
Government Accountability Project (GAP)
810 1st St., N.E., Suite 630
Washington, DC 20002

Bridge, The
Three Rivers Community Fund
100 N. Braddock Ave., Suite 207
Pittsburgh, PA 15208

Brookings Review
Brookings Institution
1775 Massachusetts Ave., N.W.
Washington, DC 20036

Bulletin of Concerned Asian Scholars
3239 9th St.
Boulder, CO 80304

Bulletin of the Atomic Scientists, The
Educational Foundation for Nuclear Science
6042 S. Kimbark Ave.
Chicago, IL 60637

Capital Eye
Center for Responsive Politics
1320 19th St., N.W., Suite 700
Washington, DC 20036

Capitalism, Nature, Socialism
Center for Political Ecology
P.O. Box 8467
Santa Cruz, CA 95061

Caribbean Newsletter
Friends for Jamaica
P.O. Box 20392
New York, NY 10025

Carpenter
United Brotherhood of Carpenters and Joiners
101 Constitution Ave., N.W.
Washington, DC 20001

Catering Industry Employee
Hotel Employees and Restaurant Employees
International Union
1219 26th St., N.W.
Washington, DC 20007

Catholic Peace Voice
Pax Christi USA
348 E. 10th St.
Erie, PA 16503

Catholic Worker, The
36 E. 1st St.
New York, NY 10003

CCCO News Notes
Central Committee for Conscientious
Objectors
1515 Cherry St.
Philadelphia, PA 19146

CDF Reports
Children's Defense Fund
25 E St., N.W.
Washington, DC 20001

CDI Military Almanac
Center for Defense Information
1500 Massachusetts Ave., N.W.
Washington, DC 20005

Censorship News
National Coalition Against Censorship
275 Seventh Ave.
New York, NY 10001

Central American Report
Religious Task Force on Central America
1747 Connecticut Ave., N.W.
Washington, DC 20009

Chalkline
Intl. Union of Bricklayers & Allied Craftsmen
815 15th St., N.W.
Washington, DC 20005

Change
Synergetic Society
1825 N. Lake Shore Dr.
Chapel Hill, NC 27514

Chemical Worker
International Chemical Workers Union
1655 W. Market St.
Akron, OH 44313

Choice Words
National Abortion and Reproductive Rights
Action League, Connecticut
135 Broad St.
Hartford, CT 06105

Church and State
Americans United for Separation of Church
and State
1816 Jefferson Place, N.W.
Washington, DC 20036

Church Women ACT
Church Women United
110 Maryland Ave., N.E.
Washington, DC 20002

Churchwoman Magazine
Church Women United
110 Maryland Ave., N.E.
Washington, DC 20002

Cineaste
200 Park Ave., S., Suite 1601
New York, NY 10003

CIR Reports
Center for Immigrants Rights
48 St. Marks Place
New York, NY 10003

cIRCular
Idaho Rural Council
110 West 31st St., Suite 200
Boise, ID 83701

Citizen Agenda
United States Public Interest Research Group
215 Pennsylvania Ave., S.E.
Washington, DC 20003

Citizen Alert Newsletter
Citizen Alert
P.O. Box 1681
Las Vegas, NV 89125

City Limits
City Limits Community Information Service
40 Prince St.
New York, NY 10012

Civil Rights Monitor
Leadership Conference Education Fund
1629 K St., N.W., Suite 1010
Washington, DC 20006

Clearinghouse Bulletin
Carrying Capacity Network
1325 G St., N.W., Suite 1003
Washington, DC 20005-3104

Climate Alert
Climate Institute
324 4th St., N.E.
Washington, DC 20002

CLUW News
Coalition of Labor Union Women
1126 16th St., N.W.
Washington, DC 20036

Common Cause
Common Cause
2030 M St.
Washington, DC 20036

Common Good
Southerners for Economic Justice
P.O. Box 240
Durham, NC 27702

Commonweal
Commonweal Foundation
15 Dutch St.
New York, NY 10038

Communist Voice
Communist Voice Organization
P.O. Box 13261, Harper Station
Detroit, MI 48213-0261

Community Change
Center for Community Change
1000 Wisconsin Ave., N.W.
Washington, DC 20007

Concerned Citizen
Concerned Citizens for Racially Free America
P.O. Box 320497
Birmingham, AL 35232

Connect
Center for Media Literacy
1962 S. Shenandoah St.
Los Angeles, CA 90034

Connecting the Dots
Earthsave Foundation
706 Frederick St.
Santa Cruz, CA 95062

Conscience
Catholics for a Free Choice
1436 U St., N.W., Suite 301
Washington, DC 20009

Consumer Reports
Consumers Union
101 Truman Ave.
Yonkers, NY 10703-1057

Convoy Dispatch
Teamsters for a Democratic Union
Foundation
P.O. Box 10128
Detroit, MI 48210

Coordinator's Report
Animal Rights International
P.O. Box 214, Planetarium Station
New York, NY 10024

Corporate Examiner
Interfaith Center on Corporate Responsibility
475 Riverside Dr., Suite 566
New York, NY 10115

Council on Economic Priorities Research Report
Council on Economic Priorities
30 Irving Place, 9th Fl.
New York, NY 10003-2386

Country Reports
Africa Faith and Justice Network
401 Michigan Ave., N.E., Suite 230
Washington, DC 20017

CovertAction Quarterly.
1500 Massachusetts Ave., N.W., Suite 732
Washington, DC 20005

CPSR Newsletter, The
Computer Professionals for Social Responsibility
P.O. Box 717
Palo Alto, CA 94302

CRA Reporter, The
Center for Community Change
1000 Wisconsin Ave., N.W.
Washington, DC 20007

Crisis: The Most Progressive Voice of Black America
National Association for the Advancement of Colored People
4805 Mt. Hope Dr.
Baltimore, MD 21215

CrossRoads
Institute for Social and Economic Studies
P.O. Box 2809
Oakland, CA 94609

Crossroads Fund Newsletter
Crossroads Fund
3411 W. Diversey Ave., Suite 20
Chicago, IL 60647-1245

Cuba Action
Cuba Information Project
198 Broadway, Suite 800
New York, NY 10038

Cuba Update
Center for Cuban Studies
124 W. 23rd St.
New York, NY 10011

Cultural Survival Quarterly
Cultural Survival
46 Brattle St.
Cambridge, MA 02138

CultureWatch
DataCenter
464 19th St.
Oakland, CA 94612

Daughters of Sarah
3801 N. Keeler
Chicago, IL 60641

Defense Monitor
Center for Defense Information
1500 Massachusetts Ave., N.W.
Washington, DC 20005

Democracy Backgrounder
Interhemispheric Resource Center
P.O. Box 4506
Albuquerque, NM 87196

Democratic Left
Democratic Socialists of America
180 Varick St., 12th Fl.
New York, NY 10038

Dendron News
Support Coalition
P.O. Box 11284
Eugene, OR 97440

Digest, The
Honor Our Neighbors Origins and Rights
2647 N. Stowell Ave.
Milwaukee, WI 53211

Dignity Report
Coalition for Human Dignity
P.O. Box 40344
Portland, OR 97240

Dispatcher
International Longshoremen's and Warehousemen's Union
1188 Franklin St.
San Francisco, CA 94109

Dissent
Foundation for the Study of Independent Social Ideas
521 5th Ave.
New York, NY 10175

Docket Report
The Nation Institute
72 5th Ave.
New York, NY 10011

Dollars & Sense
Economic Affairs Bureau
1 Summer St.
Somerville, MA 02143

E: The Environmental Magazine
Earth Action Network
28 Knight St.
Norwalk, CT 06851

Earth Day News
Earth Day USA
P.O. Box 470
Peterborough, NH 03458

Earth First!
Earth First!
P.O. Box 1415
Eugene, OR 97440

Earth Island Journal
Earth Island Institute
300 Broadway, Suite 28
San Francisco, CA 94133

Eco-Letter
North American Coalition on Religion and
Ecology
5 Thomas Circle, N.W.
Washington, DC 20005

Economic Notes
Labor Research Association
145 W. 28th St.
New York, NY 10001

EDF Letter
Environmental Defense Fund
257 S. Park Ave.
New York, NY 10010

Employee Advocate Newsletter and
Supplement
National Employment Lawyers Association
600 Harrison St., Suite 535
San Francisco, CA 94107

Enneagram Educator
National Catholic Reporter Publishing Co.
115 E. Armour Blvd.
Kansas City, MO 64111

Environmental Action
Environmental Action Foundation
6930 Carroll Ave., Suite 600
Takoma Park, MD 20912

Environmental Health Monthly
Citizens Clearinghouse for Hazardous Waste
119 Rowell Ct.
Falls Church, VA 22040

Environmental Law Reporter and *National*
Wetlands Newsletter
Environmental Law Institute
1616 P St., N.W.
Washington, DC 20036

Environmental Update
Friends of the Earth
1025 Vermont Ave., N.W., 3rd Floor
Washington, DC 20005

Everyone's Backyard
Citizens Clearinghouse for Hazardous Waste
119 Rowell Ct.
Falls Church, VA 22040

EXTRA!
Fairness and Accuracy in Reporting
130 W. 25th St.
New York, NY 10001

Factsheet Five
P.O. Box 170099
San Francisco, CA 94117

Family Planning Perspectives
Alan Guttmacher Institute
120 Wall St., 21st Fl.
New York, NY 10005

FARM Report
Farm Animals Reform Movement
10101 Ashburton Lane
Bethesda, MD 20817

FCNL Washington Newsletter
Friends Committee on National Legislation
245 Second St., N.E.
Washington, DC 20002-5795

Fednews, The
National Association of Government
Employees
159 Burgin Parkway
Quincy, MA 02169

Fellowship
Fellowship of Reconciliation
P.O. Box 271
Nyack, NY 10960

Feminist Majority Report
Fund For the Feminist Majority
8105 W. Third St., Suite 1
Los Angeles, CA 90048

Feminist Studies
c/o Women's Studies Program
University of Maryland
College Park, MD 20742

Fenton Communique
Fenton Communications
1606 20th St., N.W.
Washington, DC 20009

Fifth Estate Newspaper
4632 Second Ave.
Detroit, MI 48201

First Amendment Congress Newsletter
First Amendment Congress
2301 S. Gaylord
Denver, CO 80208

Flightlog
Association of Flight Attendants
1625 Massachusetts Ave., N.E., Suite 300
Washington, DC 20036

Focus
Carrying Capacity Network
1325 G St., N.W., Suite 1003
Washington, DC 20005-3104

Foodlines
Food Research and Action Center
1875 Connecticut Ave., N.W., Suite 540
Washington, DC 20009

Foreign Affairs
Council on Foreign Relations
58 E. 68th St.
New York, NY 10021

Foreign Policy
Carnegie Endowment for International Peace
2400 N St., N.W.
Washington, DC 20037

Forum
Educators for Social Responsibility
23 Garden St.
Cambridge, MA 02138

Forum
People for the American Way Action Fund
2000 M. St., N.W., Suite 400
Washington, DC 20036

Fourth World Journal
Fourth World Movement
7600 Willow Hill Dr.
Landover, MD 20785

Freedom to Read Foundation News
Freedom to Read Foundation
50 E. Huron St.
Chicago, IL 60611

Frontlines
Women's Health Action and Mobilization
P.O. Box 733
New York, NY 10009

Fur-Bearer Defenders, The
Fur-Bearer Defenders
P.O. Box 188950
Sacramento, CA 95818

Garment Worker, The
United Garment Workers of America
P.O. Box 239
Hermitage, TN 37076

Gay Community News
29 Stanhope St.
Boston, MA 02116

gayme
North American Man - Boy Love Association
P.O. Box 174, Middletown Station
New York, NY 10018

Global Report
Center for War / Peace Studies
218 East 18th St.
New York, NY 10003

Grassroots Fundraising Journal
Chardon Press
P.O. Box 11607
Berkeley, CA 94702

Green Guide for Everyday Life
Mothers and Others for a Livable Planet
40 W. 20th St., 9th Fl.
New York, NY 10011

Green Perspectives
Social Ecology Project
P.O. Box 111
Burlington, VT 05402

Green Politics
Greens/Green Party USA
P.O. Box 100
Blodgett Mills, NY 13738

Greenpeace Action
Greenpeace
1436 U St., N.W.
Washington, DC 20009

Greenpeace Magazine
Greenpeace Fund
1436 U St., N.W.
Washington, DC 20009

Greenwire
League of Conservation Voters Education
Fund
1707 L St., N.W., Suite 550
Washington, DC 20036

Ground Work
Tides Foundation
P.O. Box 29903
San Francisco, CA 94129

Groundwork
Groundwork for a Just World
11224 Kercheval
Detroit, MI 48214

Guild Reporter
Newspaper Guild
8611 Second Ave.
Silver Spring, MD 20910

Handful of Salt
Peace and Justice Action League of Spokane
310 W. 5th Ave.
Spokane, WA 99204

*Heresies: A Feminist Publication on Art and
Politics*
Heresies Collective
P.O. Box 1306
New York, NY 10013

Heritage
Southern California Library for Social Studies
and Research
6120 S. Vermont Ave.
Los Angeles, CA 90044

Highlights
American Association of Retired Persons
601 E. St., N.W.
Washington, DC 20049

Homesteader
Association of Community Organizations for
Reform Now
523 W. 15th St.
Little Rock, AR 72202

Hook-Up News and Views
National Hook-Up of Black Women
5117 S. University Ave.
Chicago, IL 60615

Human Ecologist, The
Human Ecology Action League
P.O. Box 49126
Atlanta, GA 30359

Humanist, The
American Humanist Association
7 Harwood Drive
P.O. Box 1188
Amherst, NY 14266

Humanistic Judaism
Society for Humanistic Judaism
28611 W. Twelve Mile Rd.
Farmington Hills, MI 48334

IBEW Journal
International Brotherhood of Electrical
Workers
1125 15th St., N.W.
Washington, DC 20005

IN CONTEXT
Context Institute
P.O. Box 11470
Bainbridge Island, WA 98110

In Defense of Animals
In Defense of Animals
131 Camino Alto, Suite E
Mill Valley, CA 94941

In Just Times
National Law Center on Homelessness and
Poverty
918 F St., N.W., Suite 412
Washington, DC 20004

Independent Political Action Bulletin
National Independent Politics Summit
P.O. Box 170610
Brooklyn, NY 11217

Independent, The
Foundation for Independent Video and Film
625 Broadway, 9th Fl.
New York, NY 10012

Indian Report, The
Friends Committee on National Legislation
245 Second St., N.E.
Washington, DC 20002-5795

Indigenous Women
Indigenous Women's Network
P.O. Box 174
Lake Elmo, MN 55042

Indochina Issues
Indochina Project
2001 S St., N.W., Suite 740
Washington, DC 20009

Industrial Worker
Industrial Workers of the World
1095 Market St.
San Francisco, CA 94103

INFORM
Church Women United
110 Maryland Ave., N.E.
Washington, DC 20002

INFORM Reports
INFORM
120 Wall St.
New York, NY 10005

Information Services Latin America
DataCenter
464 19th St.
Oakland, CA 94612

Infusion
Center for Campus Organizing
P.O. Box 748
Cambridge, MA 02142

Interdependent, The
United Nations Association of the USA
485 5th Ave.
New York, NY 0017

International Family Planning Perspectives
Alan Guttmacher Institute
120 Wall St., 21st Floor
New York, NY 10005

International Operating Engineer
International Union of Operating Engineers
1125 17th St., N.W.
Washington, DC 20036

International Policy Report
Center for International Policy
1755 Massachusetts Ave., N.W., Suite 312
Washington, DC 20036

International Wildlife Magazine
National Wildlife Federation
1400 16th St., N.W.
Washington, DC 20036

International Workcamper Newsletter
Volunteers for Peace
43 Tiffany Rd.
Belmont, VT 05730

IPPNW Report
International Physicians for the Prevention of
Nuclear War
126 Rogers St.
Cambridge, MA 02142

Irish Lobby
Irish National Caucus Foundation
413 E. Capitol St., S.E.
Washington, DC 20003

ISAR Report
International Society for Animal Rights
421 S. State St.
Clarks Summit, PA 18411

ISES News
American Solar Energy Society
2400 Central Ave., Unit G-1
Boulder, CO 80301

Issues Quarterly
National Council for Research on Women
530 Broadway, 10th Fl.
New York, NY 10012

Jobs With Peace Campaign Report
Jobs With Peace Educational Fund
38 Chauncey St., Suite 812
Boston, MA 02111

Journal of Pesticide Reform
Northwest Coalition for Alternatives to
Pesticides
P.O. Box 1393
Eugene, OR 97440-1393

Journal of Women's History
c/o Department of History, Ballantine Hall
Indiana University
Bloomington, IN 47405

Justice
International Ladies' Garment Workers'
Union
1710 Broadway
New York, NY 10019

Kids FACE Illustrated
Kids For A Clean Environment
P.O. Box 158254
Nashville, TN 37215

Klanwatch
Southern Poverty Law Center
400 Washington Ave.
Montgomery, AL 36101

Labor Notes
Labor Education and Research Project
7435 Michigan Ave.
Detroit, MI 48210

Labor Research Review
Midwest Center for Labor Research
3411 W. Diversey, Room 10
Chicago, IL 60647

Labor Unity
Amalgamated Clothing and Textile Workers
Union
1710 Broadway
New York, NY 10019

Labor Zionist Letters
275 7th Ave.
New York, NY 10001

Laborer, The
Laborers' International Union of North
America
905 16th St., N.W.
Washington, DC 20006

Lambda Update
Lambda Legal Defense and Education Fund
666 Broadway, 12th Fl.
New York, NY 10012

Latin America Update
Washington Office on Latin America
400 C St., N.E.
Washington, DC 20002

Law Reporter
Association of Trial Lawyers of America
Education Fund
1050 31st St., N.W.
Washington, DC 20007

Lead Inform
National Lead Information Center
1019 19th St., N.W., Suite 401
Washington, DC 20036

LEAF Briefs
Legal Environmental Assistance Foundation
1115 N. Gadsden St.
Tallahassee, FL 32303

Left Curve
Left Curve Publication
P.O. Box 472
Oakland, CA 94604

Legislative Report.
Idaho Women's Network
817 W. Franklin St.
Boise, ID 83702

Letter to Friends Around the World
Fourth World Movement
7600 Willow Hill Dr.
Landover, MD 20785

Liberal Opinion Week
P.O. Box 468
Vinton, IA 52349

Lifelines
National Coalition to Abolish the Death
Penalty
918 F St., N.W., Suite 601
Washington, DC 20004

Lilith
Lilith Publications
250 W. 57th St., Suite 2432
New York, NY 10107

Lumpen Times
Lumpen Media Group
2558 W. Armitage Ave.
Chicago, IL 60647

Lunatic Fringe
P.O. Box 7652
Santa Cruz, CA 95061

Machinist, The
International Association of Machinists and
Aerospace Workers
9000 Machinists Place
Upper Marlboro, MD 20772

Man Not Apart
Friends of the Earth
1025 Vermont Ave., N.W., 3rd Fl.
Washington, DC 20005

Maoist Sojourner
Maoist Internationalist Movement
P.O. Box 3576
Ann Arbor, MI 48106

Meander Quarterly
Affinity Group of Evolutionary Anarchists
P.O. Box 1402
Lawrence, KS 66044-8402

MediaFile
Media Alliance
814 Mission St., Suite 205
San Francisco, CA 94103

Mesechabe
Center for Gulf South History and Culture
1539 Crete St.
New Orleans, LA 70119

Mesquite Grill, The
Southwest Environmental Center
1494A S. Solano Dr.
Las Cruces, NM 88001

Middle East Children's Alliance News
Middle East Children's Alliance
905 Parker St.
Berkeley, CA 94710

Middle East Report
Middle East Research and Information Project
1500 Massachusetts Ave., N.W., Suite 119
Washington, DC 20005

MIM Notes
Maoist Internationalist Movement
P.O. Box 3576
Ann Arbor, MI 48106

Mind Matters Review
2040 Polk St., Box 234
San Francisco, CA 94109

Minnesota NOW Times
National Organization for Women, Minnesota
550 Rice St., Suite 106A
St. Paul, MN 55103

Modern Maturity
American Association of Retired Persons
601 E. St., N.W.
Washington, DC 20049

Mom's Apple Pie
Lavender Families Resource Network
P.O. Box 21567
Seattle, WA 98111

Monthly Planet, The
Nuclear Weapons Freeze of Santa Cruz
P.O. Box 8463
Santa Cruz, CA 95061

Monthly Review
Monthly Review Foundation
122 W. 27th St., 10th Fl.
New York, NY 10001

Mother Jones
Foundation for National Progress
731 Market St.
San Francisco, CA 94103

Mott Exchange
Charles Stewart Mott Foundation
1200 Mott Foundation Bldg.
Flint, MI 48502-1851

Ms.
230 Park Ave.
New York, NY 10169

Muckraker
Center for Investigative Reporting
568 Howard St., 5th Fl.
San Francisco, CA 94105

Multinational Monitor
Essential Information
P.O. Box 19405
Washington, DC 20036

NACLA Report on the Americas
North American Congress on Latin America
475 Riverside Dr., Suite 454
New York, NY 10115

NALC Activist
National Association of Letter Carriers of the
USA
100 Indiana Ave., N.W.
Washington, DC 20001

NAMBLA Bulletin
North American Man - Boy Love Association
P.O. Box 174, Middletown Station
New York, NY 10018

Nation, The
The Nation Company
72 5th Ave.
New York, NY 10011

National Campaign for a Peace Tax Fund
Newsletter
National Campaign for a Peace Tax Fund
2121 Decatur Place, N.W.
Washington, DC 20008

National Catholic Reporter
National Catholic Reporter Publishing Co.
115 E. Armour Blvd.
Kansas City, MO 64111

National Environmental Scorecard
League of Conservation Voters
1707 L St., N.W., Suite 550
Washington, DC 20036

National NOW Times
National Organization for Women
1000 16th St., N.W., Suite 700
Washington, DC 20036

National Parks
National Parks and Conservation Association
1776 Massachusetts Ave., N.W., Suite 200
Washington, DC 20036

National Rural Letter Carrier
National Rural Letter Carriers' Association
1630 Duke St., 4th Fl.
Alexandria, VA 22314

National Voter, The
League of Women Voters
1730 M St., N.W.
Washington, DC 20036

National Wildlife Magazine
National Wildlife Federation
1400 16th St., N.W.
Washington, DC 20036

NationAlerts
The Nation Company
72 5th Ave.
New York, NY 10011

Nature Conservancy
Nature Conservancy
1815 N. Lynn St.
Arlington, VA 2209

NEA Today
National Education Association
1201 16th St., N.W.
Washington, DC 20036

Neighborhood Works, The
Center for Neighborhood Technology
2125 W. North Ave.
Chicago, IL 60647

NETWORK Connection
NETWORK: A National Catholic Social
Justice Lobby
801 Pennsylvania Ave., S.E., Suite 460
Washington, DC 20003

Network
Gray Panthers Project Fund
2025 Pennsylvania Ave., N.W., Suite 821
Washington, DC 20006

NETWORK
Gay and Lesbian Parents Coalition
International
P.O. Box 50360
Washington, DC 20091

NETWORKER
NETWORK: A National Catholic Social
Justice Lobby
801 Pennsylvania Ave., S.E., Suite 460
Washington, DC 20003

New Age Patriot
P.O. Box 419
Dearborn Heights, MI 48127

New Democrat, The
Democratic Leadership Council
518 C St., N.E.
Washington, DC 20002

New Environment Bulletin
New Environment Association
270 Fenway Dr.
Syracuse, NY 13224

New Physician
American Medical Student Association
1902 Association Dr.
Reston, VA 22091

New River Free Press
P.O. Box 846
Blacksburg, VA 24063

New Teamster, The
International Brotherhood of Teamsters
25 Louisiana Ave., N.W.
Washington, DC 20001

New Unionist
New Union Party
621 W. Lake St., Suite 210
Minneapolis, MN 55408

Newsbrief
Witness for Peace
2201 P St., N.W., Suite 109
Washington, DC 20037

Newsbriefs
Lawyers Committee for Human Rights
330 7th Ave.
New York, NY 10001

Newsletter
E. F. Schumacher Society
140 Jug End Road
Great Barrington, MA 01230

Newsletter of the Historians of American
Communism
Historians of American Communism
P.O. Box 1216
Washington, CT 06793

Newsprints
Essential Information
P.O. Box 19405
Washington, DC 20036

NFPRHA News
National Family Planning and Reproductive
Health Association
122 C St., N.W., Suite 380
Washington, DC 20001

NIWC Network News
National Institute for Women of Color
429 N St., S.W., Suite 805
Washington, DC 20024-3713

NNAF News
National Network of Abortion Funds
c/o CLPP, Hampshire College
Amherst, MA 01002

Nonviolent Activist
War Resisters League
339 Lafayette St.
New York, NY 10012

Northwest Conservation
Greater Ecosystem Alliance
P.O. Box 2813
Bellingham, WA 98227

Nucleus
Union of Concerned Scientists
Two Brattle Square
Cambridge, MA 02238-9105

Nutrition Action Healthletter
Center for Science in the Public Interest
1875 Connecticut Ave., N.W.
Washington, DC 20009

Objector
Central Committee for Conscientious
Objectors
1515 Cherry St.
Philadelphia, PA 19146

OCAW Reporter
Oil, Chemical and Atomic Workers
International Union
P.O. Box 281200
Lakewood, CO 80228

Ocean Alert
Earth Island Institute
300 Broadway, Suite 28
San Francisco, CA 94133

Ocean Magazine
Friends of the Earth
1025 Vermont Ave., N.W., 3rd Fl.
Washington, DC 20005

off our backs: a women's newsjournal
2337 B 18th St., N.W.
Washington, DC 20009

Omega Project Newsletter
Mind Matters Review
2040 Polk St., Box 234
San Francisco, CA 94109

On Display
NAMES Project Foundation
310 Townsend St., Suite 310
San Francisco, CA 94107

On Guard
Alternatives to Militarism
175 5th Ave., Suite 2135
New York, NY 10010

Open Secrets
Coalition on Political Assassinations
P.O. Box 772
Washington, DC 20044

Panama Update
Fellowship of Reconciliation
P.O. Box 271
Nyack, NY 10960

Partisan Review
236 Bay State Rd.
Boston, MA 02215

PAS Newsletter
Palestine Aid Society
2025 I St., N.W., Suite 1020
Washington, DC 20006

PEACE in Action
Foundation for a Peaceful Environment
Among Communities Everywhere
P.O. Box 1238
Garner, NC 27529

Peace & Democracy
Campaign for Peace and Democracy
P.O. Box 1640, Cathedral Station
New York, NY 10025

Peace & Justice News
Peace and Justice Center
21 Church St.
Burlington, VT 05401

Peace Action
Peace Action
1819 H St., N.W., Suite 420
Washington, DC 20006

Peace and Freedom
Women's International League for Peace and
Freedom
1213 Race St.
Philadelphia, PA 19107

People, The
Socialist Labor Party
111 W. Evelyn Ave., Suite 209
Sunnyvale, CA 94086

People's Culture
P.O. Box 5224
Kansas City, KS 66119

People's Fund, The
People's Fund
1325 Nu'uanu Ave., Suite 207
Honolulu, HI 96817

People's Weekly World
Communist Party USA
235 W. 23rd St.
New York, NY 10011

Pesticides and You
National Coalition Against the Misuse of
Pesticides
701 E. St., S.E., Suite 200
Washington, DC 20003

Place Matters
Center for Neighborhood Technology
2125 W. North Ave.
Chicago, IL 60647

Plant Shutdowns Monitor
DataCenter
464 19th St.
Oakland, CA 94612

Plaster and Cement Mason
Operative Plasterers' and Cement Masons'
International Association
1125 17th St., N.W.
Washington, DC 20036

PMLA
Modern Language Association of America
10 Astor Place
New York, NY 10003

Popline
Population Institute
107 2nd St., N.E.
Washington, DC 20002

Political Affairs
Communist Party USA
235 W. 23rd St.
New York, NY 10011

Population and Development Review
Population Council
One Dag Hammarskjold Plaza
New York, NY 10017

Positive Alternatives
Center for Economic Conversion
222 View St., Suite C
Mountain View, CA 94041

Post Amerikan
P.O. Box 3452
Bloomington, IL 61702

Postal Record
National Association of Letter Carriers
100 Indiana Ave., N.W.
Washington, DC 20001

Poverty & Race
Poverty and Race Research Action Council
1711 Connecticut Ave., N.W., Suite 207
Washington, DC 20009

Praying
National Catholic Reporter Publishing Co.
115 E. Armour Blvd.
Kansas City, MO 64111

Prison Legal News
P.O. Box 1684
Lake Worth, FL 33460

Prison Life
P.O. Box 537
Stone Ridge, NY 12484

Products Liability
Association of Trial Lawyers of America
Education Fund
1050 31st St., N.W.
Washington, DC 20007

Professional Negligence Law Reporter
Association of Trial Lawyers of America
Education Fund
1050 31st St., N.W.
Washington, DC 20007

Progressive Review
1739 Connecticut Ave., N.W., Suite 2
Washington, DC 20009

Progressive, The
409 E. Main St.
Madison, WI 53703

Prologue
Coalition on Political Assassinations
P.O. Box 772
Washington, DC 20044

Protect
Tennessee Environmental Council
1700 Hayes St., Suite 101
Nashville, TN 37203

PSR Newsletter
Physicians for Social Responsibility, Berkeley
2288 Fulton St.
Berkeley, CA 94704

PSR Reports
Physicians for Social Responsibility
1101 14th St., N.W., Suite 700
Washington, DC 20005

Public Citizen
Public Citizen
215 Pennsylvania Ave., S.E.
Washington, DC 20003

Public Employee Newspaper
American Federation of State, County and
Municipal Employees
1625 L St., N.W.
Washington, DC 20036

Public Eye, The
Political Research Associates
120 Beacon St., Suite 202
Cambridge, MA 02143

Public I, The
Center for Public Integrity
1634 I St., N.W., Suite 902
Washington, DC 20006

Public Interest Report
Federation of American Scientists
307 Massachusetts Ave., N.E.
Washington, DC 20002

Public Justice
Trial Lawyers for Public Justice Foundation
1717 Massachusetts Ave., N.W., Suite 800
Washington, DC 20036

Race Poverty and the Environment
Earth Island Institute
300 Broadway, Suite 28
San Francisco, CA 94133

Rachel's Hazardous Waste News
Environmental Research Foundation
P.O. Box 5036
Annapolis, MD 21403

Rainbow Hope
National Rainbow Coalition
1700 K St., N.W., Suite 800
Washington, DC 20006

Report from the Hill
League of Women Voters Education Fund
1730 M. St., N.W.
Washington, DC 20036

Report on Guatemala
Network in Solidarity with the People of
Guatemala
1500 Massachusetts Ave., N.W., Suite 241
Washington, DC 20005

*Report on Israeli Settlement in the Occupied
Territories*
Foundation for Middle East Peace
555 13th St., N.W., Suite 800
Washington, DC 20004

Reproductive Rights Network Newsletter
Boston Reproductive Rights Network
P.O. Box 686
Cambridge, MA 02130

Research News
Office and Professional Employees
International Union
265 W. 14th St., Suite 610
New York, NY 10011

Resist
1 Summer St.
Somerville, MA 02143

Resource Center Bulletin
Interhemispheric Resource Center
P.O. Box 4506
Albuquerque, NM 87196

Responsive Philanthropy
National Committee for Responsive
Philanthropy
2001 S St., N.W., Suite 620
Washington, DC 20009

Restoration and Management Notes
Society for Ecological Restoration
1207 Seminole Highway, Suite B
Madison, WI 53711

Restoration Ecology
Society for Ecological Restoration
1207 Seminole Highway, Suite B
Madison, WI 53711

Rights
National Emergency Civil Liberties
Foundation
175 Fifth Ave., 8th Fl.
New York, NY 10010

Robin
Forest Ecosystem Rescue Network
P.O. Box 672
Dahlonega, GA 30533-0672

Rocinante
Quixote Center
3502 Varnum St.
Brentwood, MD 20722

Rush Watch Weekly
P.O. Box 1176
Langhorne, PA 19047

SA Talks
Sustainable America
350 5th Ave., Suite 3112
New York, NY 10118-3199

Save the Whales
Save the Whales
P.O. Box 2397
Venice, CA 90291

Sea Shepherd Log
Sea Shepherd Conservation Society
3107A Washington Blvd.
Marina del Rey, CA 90292

Second Stone
Bailey Communications
P.O. Box 8340
New Orleans, LA 70182

Senior Citizen News
National Council of Senior Citizens
1331 F St., N.W.
Washington, DC 20004

SeniorWatch.
Families USA Foundation
1334 G St., N.W.
Washington, DC 20005

SER News
Society for Ecological Restoration
1207 Seminole Highway, Suite B
Madison, WI 53711

SIECUS Report
Sex Information and Education Council of the
United States
130 W. 42nd St., Suite 2500
New York, NY 10036

Sierra
Sierra Club
730 Polk St.
San Francisco, CA 94109

Sign Control News
Scenic America
21 DuPont Circle, N.W.
Washington, DC 20036

Skill
International Union, United Automobile,
Aerospace and Agricultural Implement
Workers of America (UAW)
8000 E. Jefferson
Detroit, MI 48214

Social Justice
Global Options
P.O. Box 40601
San Francisco, CA 94140

Social Policy
Social Policy Corporation
25 W. 43rd St., Suite 620
New York, NY 10036

Sojourners
2401 15th St., N.W.
Washington, DC 20009

Solar Energy
American Solar Energy Society
2400 Central Ave., Unit G-1
Boulder, CO 80301

Solar Today
American Solar Energy Society
2400 Central Ave., Unit G-1
Boulder, CO 80301

Solidarity
International Union, United Automobile,
Aerospace and Agricultural Implement
Workers of America (UAW)
8000 E. Jefferson
Detroit, MI 48214

Solidarity Update
Network in Solidarity with the People of
Guatemala
1500 Massachusetts Ave., N.W., Suite 241
Washington, DC 20005

SONG
Southerners on New Ground
P.O. Box 3912
Louisville, KY 40201

South Dakota Sun
South Dakota Peace and Justice Center
P.O. Box 405
Watertown, SD 57201

Southern Empowerment Project Newsletter
Southern Empowerment Project
343 Ellis Ave.
Maryville, TN 37804

Southern Exposure
Institute for Southern Studies
P.O. Box 531
Durham, NC 27702

Southern Fight-Back
Southern Organizing Committee for
Economic and Social Justice
P.O. Box 10518
Atlanta, GA 30310

St. Louis Journalism Review
8380 Olive Blvd.
St. Louis, MO 63132

State of the World
Worldwatch Institute
1776 Massachusetts Ave., N.W.
Washington, DC 20036

State Reproductive Health Monitor
Alan Guttmacher Institute
120 Wall St., 21st Floor
New York, NY 10005

Statement
National Coalition of 100 Black Women
38 W. 32nd St., Suite 1610
New York, NY 10001

Storm Warning
Vietnam Veterans Against the War Anti-
Imperialist
P.O. Box 95172
Seattle, WA 98145

Street Sheet
Coalition on Homelessness
126 Hyde St., Suite 102
San Francisco, CA 94102

Studies in Family Planning
Population Council
One Dag Hammarskjold Plaza
New York, NY 10017

SunWorld
American Solar Energy Society
2400 Central Ave., Unit G-1
Boulder, CO 80301

Synthesis/Regeneration
Greens/Green Party USA
P.O. Box 100
Blodgett Mills, NY 13738

Talkin' Basics
Coalition for Basic Human Needs
54 Essex St.
Cambridge, MA 02139

Tapori
Fourth World Movement
7600 Willow Hill Dr.
Landover, MD 20785

Task Force Quarterly
American Medical Student Association
1902 Association Dr.
Reston, VA 22091

Third Force
Center for Third World Organizing
1218 E 21st St.
Oakland, CA 94606

Third World Resources
DataCenter
464 19th St.
Oakland, CA 94612

Third World Viewpoint
328 Flatbush Ave., Box 171
Brooklyn, NY 11238

Threepenny Review
P.O. Box 9131
Berkeley, CA 94709

Threshold
Student Environmental Action Coalition
P.O. Box 1168
Chapel Hill, NC 27514

Tikkun
Institute for Labor and Mental Health
5100 Leona St.
Oakland, CA 94619

Toward Freedom
209 College St.
Burlington, VT 05401

Trade Union Advisor
Labor Research Association
145 W. 28th St.
New York, NY 10001

TRANET
P.O. Box 567
Rangeley, ME 04970

Transformation
Women's Project
2224 Main St.
Little Rock, AK 72206

Trial
Association of Trial Lawyers of America
1050 31st St., N.W.
Washington, DC 20007

Tribune
International Women's Tribune Centre
777 United Nations Plaza
New York, NY 10017

Turning the Tide
People Against Racist Terror
P.O. Box 1990
Burbank, CA 91507

UFCW Action
United Food and Commercial Workers
International Union
1775 K St., N.W.
Washington, DC 20006

UFCW Leadership Update
United Food and Commercial Workers
International Union
1775 K St., N.W.
Washington, DC 20006

U.N. Reform Campaigner
Campaign for U.N. Reform
713 D St., S.E.
Washington, DC 20003

Union
Service Employees International Union
1313 L St., N.W.
Washington, DC 20005

Union Democracy
Association for Union Democracy
500 State St., 2nd Fl.
Brooklyn, NY 11217

Unioncraft
National Organization of Industrial Trade
Unions
148-06 Hillside Ave.
Jamaica, NY 11435

United States of ACORN
Association of Community Organizations for
Reform Now
523 W. 15th St.
Little Rock, AR 72202

Update
Service Employees International Union
1313 L St., N.W.
Washington, DC 20005

Update
National Coalition Against Domestic
Violence
P.O. Box 18749
Denver, CO 80218-0749

Urban Herbalist, The
Women's Health Action and Mobilization
P.O. Box 733
New York, NY 10009

Usual Suspects, The
Desert Moon Periodicals
1226 A Calle de Comercio
Santa Fe, NM 87505

Utne Reader
1624 Harmon Place, Suite 330
Minneapolis, MN 55403

Village Voice
VV Publishing Corp.
36 Cooper Square
New York, NY 10003-7118

VISTA
Earth Communications / Radio For Peace
International
P.O. Box 20728
Portland, OR 97220

VLS
VV Publishing Corp.
36 Cooper Square
New York, NY 10003-7118

Voice
National Coalition Against Domestic
Violence
P.O. Box 18749
Denver, CO 80218-0749

Voice for Choice
Feminist Women's Health Center
106 East E St.
Yakima, WA 98901

Voice of Reason, The
Americans for Religious Liberty
P.O. Box 6656
Silver Springs, MD 20906

Voices
Rural Southern Voice for Peace
1898 Hannah Branch Rd.
Burnsville, NC 28714

Voices for Haiti Speaking Out
Voices for Haiti
P.O. Box 29615
Washington, DC 20017

Washington Memo
Alan Guttmacher Institute
120 Wall St., 21st Fl.
New York, NY 10005

Washington Report on Middle East Affairs
American Educational Trust
P.O. Box 53062
Washington, DC 20009

Washington Spectator
Public Concern Foundation
P.O. Box 20065, London Terrace Station
New York, NY 10011

Weekly News Update on the Americas
Nicaragua Solidarity Network of Greater New
York
339 Lafayette St.
New York, NY 10012

White Collar
Office and Professional Employees
International Union
265 W. 14th St., Suite 610
New York, NY 10011

WIC Newsletter
Center on Budget and Policy Priorities
777 N. Capitol St., N.E., Suite 705
Washington, DC 20002

Wilderness Magazine
Wilderness Society
900 17th St., N.W.
Washington, DC 20006

WIN News
Women's International Network
187 Grant St.
Lexington, MA 02173

Wisconsin Community Fund Newsletter
Wisconsin Community Fund
122 State St., Suite 508
Madison, WI 53703

WNDC News
Woman's National Democratic Club
1526 New Hampshire Ave., N.W.
Washington, DC 20036

Women in Action
Women's Action Alliance
370 Lexington Ave., Suite 603
New York City, NY 10017

WomenWise
Concord Feminist Health Center
38 S. Main St.
Concord, NH 03301

Women's Research Network News
National Council for Research on Women
530 Broadway, 10th Fl.
New York, NY 10012

Women's Review of Books, The
Women's Review
Wellesley College Center for Research on
Women
Wellesley, MA 02181

Womyn's Press
P.O. Box 562
Eugene, OR 97440

Workbook, The
Southwest Research and Information Center
105 Stanford, S.E.
Albuquerque, NM 87106

World Federalist
World Federalist Association
418 7th St., S.E.
Washington, DC 20003

World Goodwill Newsletter
Lucius Trust and Arcane School
120 Wall St., 24th Floor
New York, NY 10005

World Watch
Worldwatch Institute
1776 Massachusetts Ave., N.W.
Washington, DC 20036

Worldwide News
Worldwide Network
1331 H St., N.W., Suite 903
Washington, DC 20005

Youth Law News
National Center for Youth Law
114 Sansome St., Suite 900
San Francisco, CA 94104-3820

Z Magazine
Institute for Social and Cultural
Communications
18 Millfield St.
Woods Hole, MA 02543

ZPG Reporter
Zero Population Growth
1400 16th St., N.W., Suite 320
Washington, DC 20036

OTHER INFORMATION SOURCES

This section contains additional sources of information on left-of-center organizations. Several publications serve specific needs. Some are general guides to organizations of all types, political and non-political; others are specific guides to left-of-center organizations published by both the Left and Right.

OTHER INFORMATION SOURCES

The Activist's Almanac, 1993, A Fireside Book Published by Simon & Schuster, 1230 Avenue of the Americas, New York, NY 10020, (212) 245-6400. Softbound, 431 pp.
     Written by David Walls. This directory lists 105 organizations, including eleven conservative or free-market organizations. The listings include contact information, annual budget, tax status, and an in-depth history and description of the organization.

Capital Research Center, 727 15th St., N.W., Suite 800, Washington, DC 20005, (202) 393-2600.
     Conservative non-profit organization that researches corporate philanthropy with an emphasis on corporate contributions to left-of-center organizations. Publishes an annual guide, Patterns of Corporate Philanthropy, and several newsletters, including *Organization Trends*.

Encyclopedia of Associations, 31st Edition, 1996, Gale Research Co., 835 Penobscott Building, Detroit, MI 48226-4094, (313) 961-2242. Three volumes, soft-bound.
     Lists over 23,000 organizations. Listed associations cover all parts of the political spectrum.

Foundation Directory, 18th Edition, 1996, The Foundation Center, 79 5th Ave., New York, NY 10003, (800) 424-9836. Hardbound.
     Publication of the Foundation Center that includes over 7,500 of the largest philanthropic foundations in the United States. Listed foundations all have assets of over $1 million. Lists assets, total amount of grants awarded in the most recent year, areas of interest that awards are made in, and the recipients of the largest grants.

Guide to the American Left, 17th Edition, Editorial Research Services, P.O. Box 2047, Olathe, KS 66061, (913) 829-0609. Plastic-comb softbound.
     Written and published by Laird Wilcox. Lists name and addresses of over 1,400 organizations and publications. Organizations include "Liberal, Socialist, Radical, Revolutionary, Feminist, Gay, Anti-Nuclear, Environmental, Ethnic (minority) Nationalist, and others." Contains a bibliography of note-worthy books by and about the Left.

Historians of American Communism, P.O. Box 1216, Washington, CT 06793.
     Nonprofit organization serving as a clearinghouse for scholars of American Communism.

Macrocosm USA: Possibilities for a New Progressive Era, 1st Edition, 1992, Macrocosm USA, P.O. Box 969, Cambria, CA 93428, (805) 927-8030. Softbound, 422pp.
     A handbook of "environmental, political, and social solutions." Contains 200 full-text articles, and 5,000 listings of "progressive organizations, periodicals, media outlets, businesses, publishers and reference sources."

TRANET, P.O. Box 567, Rangeley, ME 04970, (207) 864-2252.
     Bimonthly newsletter that lists organizations working for peace, the environment, feminism, human rights, and cooperative economics.

GEOGRAPHIC LISTING

This section contains a listing of the organizations from the **Profiles** section, listed by the states and the District of Columbia. There are no organizations listed for four states; Nebraska, Mississippi, North Dakota, and Wyoming.

ALABAMA

Concerned Citizens for Racially Free America
Southern Poverty Law Center

ALASKA

Alaska Public Interest Research Group

ARIZONA

Advocates for the Disabled
Lesbian and Gay Public Awareness Project

ARKANSAS

Arkansas Coalition for Choice
Association of Community Organizations for Reform Now
Center on War and the Child
Women's Project

CALIFORNIA

Action for Grassroots Empowerment and Neighborhood
        Development Alternatives (AGENDA)
Advocate: The National Gay & Lesbian Newsmagazine
AIDS Action League
Alliance for Survival
American Civil Liberties Union, San Diego and Imperial
        Counties Foundation (ACLU)
American Civil Liberties Union, Southern California
        Foundation (ACLU)
American Civil Liberties Union, Northern California
        Foundation (ACLU)
American Civil Liberties Union, Northern California (ACLU)
Archives on Audio
Ark Trust
Asian Immigrant Women Advocates
Barbra Streisand Foundation
Bay Area Bisexual Network
Bay Area Physicians for Human Rights
Berkeley Community Law Center
Berkeley Journal of Sociology (*BJS*)
Bound Together Books
C.S. Fund
California Women's Law Center
Center for Community Advocacy
Center for Economic Conversion
Center for Investigative Reporting (CIR)
Center for Law in the Public Interest
Center for Media Literacy (CML)
Center for Political Ecology
Center for Socialist History
Center for Third World Organizing (CTWO)
Cesar E. Chavez Foundation
Chardon Press
Chinese for Affirmative Action
Chinese Progressive Association
Christic Institute
Coalition for Clean Air
Coalition of California Welfare Rights Organizations

Coalition on Homelessness (COH)
Columbia Foundation
Committee for Nuclear Responsibility (CNR)
Committee to Bridge the Gap (CBG)
Communities for a Better Environment
Compton Foundation
Computer Professionals for Social Responsibility (CPSR)
Constitutional Rights Foundation
DataCenter
Directors Guild of America
Disability Rights Education and Defense Fund
Earth Day 2000
Earth Day Resources
Earth Island Institute (EII)
Earth Trust Foundation
Earthsave Foundation
Education 1st!
El Rescate
El Rescate Legal Services
Environmental Federation of California
Environmental Health Coalition
Equal Rights Advocates (ERA)
Evangelicals for Social Action, Fresno
Factsheet Five
Feminist Majority Foundation
Filipinos for Affirmative Action
Film Arts Foundation
First Amendment Foundation
Foundation for Global Community
Foundation for National Progress / *Mother Jones*
Foundation for the Study of Individual and World Peace
Friends Committee on Legislation of California (FCL)
Fund For the Feminist Majority
Fur-Bearer Defenders
Gay and Lesbian Alliance Against Defamation, Los Angeles
Gay and Lesbian Media Coalition
Gayshine Press
Global Exchange
Global Fund for Women
Global Options
Greenbelt Alliance
Henry J. Kaiser Family Foundation
Hollywood Policy Center Foundation (HPC)
Humane Farming Action Fund
Humane Farming Association
In Defense of Animals (IDA)
Income Rights Project (IRP)
Industrial Workers of the World (IWW)
Institute for Economic Democracy
Institute for Global Communications (IGC)
Institute for Labor and Mental Health / *Tikkun*
Institute for Social and Economic Studies / *CrossRoads*
Institute for the Study of the Religious Right (ISRR)
International Gay and Lesbian Human Rights Commission
International Longshoremen's and Warehousemen's Union
International Rivers Network
La Raza Centro Legal
Labor / Community Strategy Center
Left Curve Publication
Legal Aid Society of San Francisco
Liberty Hill Foundation
Light Party, The
Lucius and Eva Eastman Fund
Lunatic Fringe
Macrocosm USA

(California continued)

McKay Foundation
Media Alliance
Media Watch
Meiklejohn Civil Liberties Institute
Mexican Americans Legal Defense and Education Fund
Middle East Children's Alliance (MECA)
Middle Passage Foundation
Mind Matters Review
NAMES Project Foundation
National Association for the Advancement of Colored People,
    California (NAACP)
National Center for Lesbian Rights (NCLR)
National Center for Youth Law
National Clearinghouse on Marital and Date Rape
National Employment Lawyers Association (NELA)
National Network of Grantmakers
Neighbor to Neighbor Education Fund
Norman Lear Foundation
Nuclear Age Peace Foundation
Nuclear Weapons Freeze of Santa Cruz
Office of the Americas
Other Americas Radio, The
Out on the Screen
Pacifica Foundation
Peace Resource Project
People Against Racist Terror (PART)
Physicians for Social Responsibility, Los Angeles
Physicians for Social Responsibility, Berkeley
Planned Parenthood - World Population, Los Angeles
Ploughshares Fund
Population Communication
Prisoners Rights Union
Progressive Way
Public Counsel
Public Media Center
Redwood Cultural Work
Rex Foundation
Richard and Rhoda Goldman Fund
Rosenberg Foundation
San Francisco Organizing Project
San Francisco Women's Centers
Save the Whales
Sea Shepherd Conservation Society (SSCS)
Sierra Club
Sierra Club Foundation
Sierra Club Legal Defense Fund (SCLDF)
Socialist Labor Party
South and Meso-American Indian Rights Center (SAIIC)
South Coast Foundation
South North Communication Network
Southern California Library for Social Studies and Research
Threepenny Review
Tides Foundation
TreePeople
Trust for Public Land
United Farm Workers National Union (UFW)
United States Justice Foundation (USJF)
Vanguard Public Foundation
Wallace Alexander Gerbode Foundation
Women's Information Exchange
Women's Economic Agenda Project (WEAP)
Working Partnerships USA
World Without War Council (WWWC)

COLORADO

American Civil Liberties Union, Colorado Foundation
American Solar Energy Society (ASES)
Animal Rights Mobilization
Bulletin of Concerned Asian Scholars
Center for Legal Advocacy
Chinook Fund
Colorado Coalition for the Homeless
Denver - Havana Friendship / Sister City Project
First Amendment Congress
General Service Foundation
National Coalition Against Domestic Violence (NCADV)
Native American Rights Fund (NARF)
Oil, Chemical and Atomic Workers International Union Project
    Equus
Rocky Mountain Institute
Rocky Mountain Peace Center
Thorne Ecological Institute (TEI)
Western Colorado Congress
Windstar Foundation

CONNECTICUT

Action for Corporate Accountability
Agent Orange Victims International
Angelina Fund
Center for Medicare Advocacy
Earth Action Network / *E: The Environmental Magazine*
Historians of American Communism
National Abortion and Reproductive Rights Action League,
    Connecticut (NARAL)
National Organization for Women, Connecticut (NOW)
Northeast Citizen Action Resource Center (NECARC)

DELAWARE

American Civil Liberties Union, Delaware Foundation

DISTRICT OF COLUMBIA

50 Years is Enough: U.S. Network for Global Economic
    Justice
A. Philip Randolph Educational Fund
Action on Smoking and Health (ASH)
Advocacy Institute
Advocates for Highway and Auto Safety
Advocates for Youth
Africa Faith and Justice Network
African-American Labor Center
AIDS Action Council
AIDS Action Foundation
Alliance for Acid Rain Control
Alliance for Justice
Alliance to End Childhood Lead Poisoning
American Association of Retired Persons (AARP)
American Civil Liberties Union, National Capital Area Fund
American Educational Trust (AET)
American Federation of Labor and Congress of Industrial
    Organizations (AFL-CIO)
American Federation of State, County and Municipal
    Employees (AFSCME)

(District of Columbia continued)

American Federation of Teachers (AFT)
American Federation of Teachers Educational Foundation
American Institute for Free Labor Development
American Postal Workers Union
American Public Welfare Association
American-Arab Anti-Discrimination Committee (ADC)
Americans for Democratic Action (ADA)
Americans for the Environment (AFE)
Americans United for Separation of Church and State
Americans United Research Foundation
Animal Welfare Institute (AWI)
Arms Control Association
Asia Pacific Center for Justice and Peace
Asian-American Free Labor Institute
Association of Flight Attendants (AFA)
Association of Trial Lawyers of America Education Fund
Association of Trial Lawyers of America (ATLA)
Association on Third World Affairs
Bank Information Center (BIC)
Bauman Family Foundation
Beldon Fund
Brookings Institution
Campaign for U.N. Reform
Carnegie Endowment for International Peace / *Foreign Policy*
Carrying Capacity Network (CCN)
Catholics for a Free Choice (CFFC)
Center for a New Democracy (CND)
Center for Clean Air Policy
Center for Community Change
Center for Defense Information (CDI)
Center for International Environmental Law (CIEL)
Center for International Policy (CIP)
Center for Law and Social Policy
Center for Policy Alternatives
Center for Public Integrity
Center for Responsive Politics
Center for Science in the Public Interest (CSPI)
Center for Teaching Peace
Center for the Study of Commercialism (CSC)
Center for Women Policy Studies (CWPS)
Center on Budget and Policy Priorities
Center to Prevent Handgun Violence
Children's Defense Fund (CDF)
Church Women United (CWU)
Citizen Action
Citizens for Tax Justice
Citizens Fund
Clean Water Action
Clean Water Fund
Climate Institute
Coalition for the Homeless
Coalition of Black Trade Unionists
Coalition of Labor Union Women (CLUW)
Coalition on Political Assassinations
Coalition to Stop Gun Violence
Committee for National Health Insurance
Common Cause
Community for Creative Non-Violence
Concern
Council for a Livable World Education Fund
Council for a Livable World
CovertAction Quarterly (CAQ)
Democratic Leadership Council (DLC)
Democratic National Committee (DNC)

Earthkind USA
Economic Policy Institute (EPI)
Ecostewards Alliance
Educational Fund to End Gun Violence
Ending Men's Violence Network
Environmental and Energy Study Institute (EESI)
Environmental Federation of America
Environmental Investigation Agency
Environmental Law Institute
Environmental Media Services
Environmental Support Center
Episcopal Peace Fellowship (EPF)
Essential Information
Families USA
Families USA Foundation
Federally Employed Women
Federation of American Scientists (FAS)
Federation of American Scientists Fund
Fenton Communications
Focus Project
Food Research and Action Center (FRAC)
Foundation for Middle East Peace
Foundation on Economic Trends
Free Trade Union Institute
Freedom of Expression Foundation
Friends Committee on National Legislation (FCNL)
Friends of the Earth
Fund for Peace
Fund for Popular Education
Fund for the Center for Community Change
Gay and Lesbian Parents Coalition International (GLPCI)
Government Accountability Project (GAP)
Gray Panthers Project Fund
Greenpeace
Greenpeace Fund
Greenpeace International
Guatemala Partners
Handgun Control, Inc. (HCI)
Health Security Action Council
Hotel Employees and Restaurant Employees International
        Union (HERE)
Human Rights Campaign Fund
Immigration and Refugee Services of America (IRSA)
Indochina Project
Institute for Policy Studies (IPS)
Institute for Social Justice
Institute for Women, Law and Development
Institute for Women's Policy Research (IWPR)
International Brotherhood of Electrical Workers (IBEW)
International Brotherhood of Teamsters (IBT)
International Center for Research on Women (ICRW)
International Union of Bricklayers and Allied Craftsmen
International Union of Operating Engineers (IUOE)
Irish National Caucus Foundation
Judge David L. Bazelon Center for Mental Health Law
Labor Council for Latin American Advancement
Labor Institute of Public Affairs
Laborers' International Union of North America (LIUNA)
Lawyers Alliance for World Security
Lawyers' Committee for Civil Rights Under Law
Leadership Conference Education Fund
Leadership Conference on Civil Rights (LCCR)
League of Conservation Voters Education Fund
League of Conservation Voters (LCV)
League of Women Voters Education Fund (LWVEF)

(District of Columbia continued)

League of Women Voters
Legal Services Corporation
Management Assistance Group (MAG)
Mexican American Women's National Association (MANA)
Middle East Policy Council
Middle East Research and Information Project (MERIP)
Mineral Policy Center
National Abortion and Reproductive Rights Action League
    Foundation (NARAL)
National Abortion and Reproductive Rights Action League
National Abortion Federation (NAF)
National AIDS Fund
National Air Traffic Controllers Association (NATCA)
National Alliance to End Homelessness
National Association of Community Action Agencies
National Association of Letter Carriers of the USA
National Campaign for a Peace Tax Fund
National Center for Economic Alternatives
National Center on Education and the Economy (NCEE)
National Coalition Against the Misuse of Pesticides
National Coalition for the Homeless
National Coalition to Abolish the Death Penalty (NCADP)
National Committee for Responsive Philanthropy (NCRP)
National Committee on Pay Equity
National Conference of Puerto Rican Women
National Congress of American Indians (NCAI)
National Congress of American Indians Fund (NCAI Fund)
National Council of La Raza (NCLR)
National Council of Negro Women
National Council of Senior Citizens (NCSC)
National Education Association (NEA)
National Family Planning and Reproductive Health
    Association (NFPRHA)
National Gay and Lesbian Task Force Policy Institute
National Gay and Lesbian Task Force
National Institute for Women of Color
National Law Center on Homelessness and Poverty
National Lead Information Center
National Leadership Coalition for Health Care Reform
National Low Income Housing Coalition
National Organization for the Reform of Marijuana Laws
National Organization for Women (NOW)
National Organization for Women Foundation (NOW)
National Parks and Conservation Association
National Peace Foundation
National Public Radio (NPR)
National Puerto Rican Coalition (NPRC)
National Rainbow Coalition
National Security News Service (NSNS)
National Wildlife Action (NWA)
National Wildlife Federation (NWF)
National Wildlife Federation Endowment (NWF)
National Women's Law Center
National Women's Political Caucus
National Women's Political Caucus Leadership Development,
    Education and Research Fund
NETWORK: A National Catholic Social Justice Lobby
NETWORK Education Program
Network in Solidarity with the People of Guatemala Network
    of Educators on the Americas (NECA)
North American Coalition on Religion and Ecology (NACRE)
NPR Foundation
Nuclear Control Institute
Nuclear Information and Resource Service (NIRS)

off our backs: a women's newsjournal
Operative Plasterers' and Cement Masons' International
    Association
Palestine Aid Society (PAS)
Parents, Families and Friends of Lesbians and Gays (PFFLAG)
Parents, Families and Friends of Lesbian and Gays,
    Washington Metropolitan Area (PFFLAG)
Pax World Services
Peace Action
Peace Action Education Fund
People for the American Way (PAW)
People for the American Way Action Fund
People for the Ethical Treatment of Animals (PETA)
Physicians for Social Responsibility (PSR)
Population Action International (PAI)
Population - Environment Balance
Population Institute
Population Services International
Poverty and Race Research Action Council (PRRAC)
Preamble Center for Public Policy
Progressive Foundation
Progressive Policy Institute (PPI)
Progressive Review
Project Nishma
Psychologists for Social Responsibility
Public Citizen
Public Citizen Foundation
Public Employees for Environmental Responsibility (PEER)
Religious Coalition for Reproductive Choice Educational Fund
Religious Coalition for Reproductive Choice
Religious Task Force on Central America
Safe Energy Communication Council (SECC)
Scenic America
Service Employees International Union (SEIU)
Social Investment Forum
Social Workers' National Research and Education Fund
Society for Animal Protective Legislation
Sojourners
Student Action Corps for Animals
TransAfrica
TransAfrica Forum
Trial Lawyers for Public Justice Foundation
United Brotherhood of Carpenters and Joiners of America
United Food and Commercial Workers International Union
United States Catholic Conference
United States Public Interest Research Group
United States Public Interest Research Group Education Fund
United States Student Association
Violence Policy Center
Voices for Haiti
Washington Office on Africa
Washington Office on Haiti
Washington Office on Latin America
Wilderness Society
Winston Foundation for World Peace
Witness for Peace
Woman's National Democratic Club (WNDC)
Women Judges' Fund for Justice (WJFJ)
Women Work! The National Network for Women's
    Employment
Women's Legal Defense Fund (WLDF)
Women's Research and Education Institute (WREI)
World Federalist Association (WFA)
World Population Society
World Wildlife Fund (WWF)

(District of Columbia continued)
Worldwatch Institute
Worldwide Network
Young Women's Project
Zero Population Growth (ZPG)

FLORIDA

Aaron and Martha Schecter Private Foundation
American Civil Liberties Union, Florida Foundation (ACLU)
Animal Rights Foundation of Florida (ARFF)
Legal Environmental Assistance Foundation (LEAF)
People United to Lead the Struggle for Equality (PULSE)
Prison Legal News (PLN)

GEORGIA

Carter Center
Center for Democratic Renewal and Education
Citizens for Environmental Justice
Environmental Community Action (ECO Action)
Forest Ecosystem Rescue Network (FERN)
Fund for Southern Communities
Georgians for Choice
Global 2000
Human Ecology Action League (HEAL)
Martin Luther King, Jr., Center for Nonviolent Social Change
Southern Organizing Committee for Economic and Social
    Justice (SOC)

HAWAII

American Civil Liberties Union, Hawai'i Foundation
Earthtrust
People's Fund

IDAHO

Global Environment Project Institute (GEPI)
Idaho Rural Council (IRC)
Idaho Women's Network (IWN)
Idaho Women's Network Research and Education Fund

ILLINOIS

AIM: America's Intercultural Magazine
American Library Association (ALA)
Business and Professional People for the Public Interest
Center for Neighborhood Technology (CNT)
Chicago Animal Rights Coalition
Chicago Coalition for the Homeless
Citizens for a Better Environment
Coalition for New Priorities
Congress of Independent Unions
Crossroads Fund
Daughters of Sarah
Educational Foundation for Nuclear Science / *The Bulletin of
    the Atomic Scientists*

Federation for Industrial Retention and Renewal (FIRR)
Feminist Writers Guild
Freedom to Read Foundation
Illinois Peace Action Education Fund
Institute for Public Affairs / *In These Times*
International Foundation for Ethical Research
J. Roderick MacArthur Foundation
John D. and Catherine T. MacArthur Foundation
Joyce Foundation
Lumpen Media Group
Midwest Center for Labor Research
National Anti-Vivisection Society
National Hook-Up of Black Women
National Organization for Women, Chicago (NOW)
National People's Action
National Training and Information Center (NTIC)
Networking for Democracy
New Prospect Foundation
Parents for Rock and Rap (PFRR)
Post Amerikan
Wieboldt Foundation
Women Employed / Women Employed Institute
Woodstock Institute

INDIANA

Calumet Project for Industrial Jobs
Friends of the Third World
Journal of Women's History
One World Movement

IOWA

Liberal Opinion Week

KANSAS

Affinity Group of Evolutionary Anarchists
Leonard Peltier Defense Committee
People's Culture

KENTUCKY

Appalachia Science in the Public Interest (ASPI)
Kentucky Coalition
Southerners on New Ground (SONG)

LOUISIANA

American Civil Liberties Union, Louisiana Foundation
Arkansas Institute for Social Justice
Bailey Communications / *Second Stone*
Center for Gulf South History and Culture
Louisiana Environmental Action Network (LEAN)
National Council of Negro Women, New Orleans
People's Institute for Survival and Beyond

MAINE

American Civil Liberties Union, Maine Foundation (ACLU)
Common Courage Press
Forgotten Families of the Cold War
Maine Peace Fund
Maine People's Alliance
Maine People's Resource Center
Military Toxics Project
TRANET

MARYLAND

Advocates for Children and Youth
Advocates for the Homeless
Alternative Press Center
Americans for Religious Liberty
Animal Rights Network / *The Animals' Agenda*
Bakery, Confectionery and Tobacco Workers Union
Defenders of Animal Rights
Environmental Action
Environmental Action Foundation (EAF)
Environmental Research Foundation
Farm Animals Reform Movement (FARM)
Feminist Studies
Fourth World Movement
International Association of Machinists and Aerospace
Workers (IAM)
Jewish Peace Lobby
Merck Family Fund
National Association for the Advancement of Colored People
Newspaper Guild
Quixote Center
Town Creek Foundation

MASSACHUSETTS

AIDS Action Committee of Massachusetts
Alliance for Animals (AFA)
Boston Reproductive Rights Network
Center for Campus Organizing (CCO)
Center for Popular Economics (CPE)
Center for Public Representation
Central America Education Fund
Citizens to End Animal Suffering and Exploitation (CEASE)
Coalition for Basic Human Needs (CBHN)
Coalition for Environmentally Responsible Economies
Cultural Survival
Discount Foundation
E. F. Schumacher Society
EarthAction
Economic Affairs Bureau / *Dollars & Sense*
Educators for Social Responsibility (ESR)
FairTest: The National Center for Fair and Open Testing
Friends of the United Nations
Fund for a Free South Africa
Gay Community News (GCN)
Grassroots International
Haymarket People's Fund
Health Care for All
Institute for Defense and Disarmament Studies
Institute for First Amendment Studies
Institute for Peace and International Security (IPIS)

Institute for Social and Cultural Communications / *Z Magazine*
Institute on Women and Technology
International Physicians for the Prevention of Nuclear War
Jobs With Peace Educational Fund
John Merck Fund
Liberal Religious Charitable Society
Massachusetts Senior Action Council
National Association of Government Employees
National Environmental Law Center (NELC)
National Network of Abortion Funds (NNAF)
National Organization for Women, Boston (NOW)
New Prospect / *The American Prospect: A Journal for the
    Liberal Imagination*
Northeast Action
Northwest Coalition for Alternatives to Pesticides (NCAP)
One World Fund
Organization for a New Equality
Oxfam America
Partisan Review
Pathfinder International
Peace Development Fund (PDF)
Physicians for Human Rights
Physicians for Social Responsibility, Boston
Political Research Associates (PRA)
Resist
Sacred Earth Network
Southpaw Books
Traprock Peace Center
Union of Concerned Scientists (UCS)
Unitarian Universalist Service Committee
University Conversion Project
Women's Action for New Directions Education Fund (WAND)
Women's International Network (WIN)
Women's Review / *Women's Review of Books*
World Peace Foundation

MICHIGAN

Agenda
American Civil Liberties Union, Michigan Fund (ACLU)
Between the Lines: For Lesbians, Gays, Bisexuals & Friends
Charles Stewart Mott Foundation
Communist Voice Organization
Fifth Estate Newspaper
Fund for Equal Justice
Groundwork for a Just World
Guild Sugar Law Center
International Union, United Automobile, Aerospace and
        Agricultural Implement Workers of America (UAW)
Labor Education and Research Project
Labor Zionist Institute
Maoist Internationalist Movement (MIM)
National Association of Black Social Workers (NABSW)
New Age Patriot
Planned Parenthood Advocates of Michigan
Ruth Mott Fund
Society for Humanistic Judaism
Teamsters for a Democratic Union Foundation

MINNESOTA

Animal Rights Coalition

(Minnesota continued)

Gay and Lesbian Community Action
Headwaters Fund
Indigenous Women's Network
Minnesota Alliance for Progressive Action (MAPA)
Minnesota Civil Liberties Union Foundation
Minnesota Coalition for the Homeless
Minnesota Jobs With Peace Campaign
National Organization for Women, Minnesota (NOW)
New Union Party
Utne Reader
Women Against Military Madness (WAMM)

MISSOURI

Aluminum, Brick and Glass Workers International Union
American Civil Liberties Union, Western Missouri Foundation
American Civil Liberties Union, Eastern Missouri Fund
Deer Creek Foundation
National Catholic Reporter Publishing Co. / *National Catholic Reporter* (NCR)
New Directions for News
St. Louis Journalism Review

MONTANA

Montana Alliance for Progressive Policy (MAPP)
Montana People's Action
Montanans for Choice
Western Organization of Resource Councils

NEVADA

Citizen Alert

NEW HAMPSHIRE

Concord Feminist Health Center / *WomenWise*
Earth Day USA
National Abortion and Reproductive Rights Action League,
    New Hampshire (NARAL)

NEW JERSEY

American Civil Liberties Union, New Jersey (ACLU)
Animal Rights Law Clinic
Florence and John Schumann Foundation
Independent Publications
International Black Women's Congress
National Coalition for Sex Equity in Education
National Organization for Women, New Jersey
National Organization for Women, New Jersey Foundation
Peace Action Education Fund
Population Resource Center
Robert Wood Johnson Foundation

NEW MEXICO

American Indian Law Center

Desert Moon Periodicals
Interhemispheric Resource Center
LightHawk
SouthWest Organizing Project (SWOP)
Southwest Environmental Center (SEC)
Southwest Research and Information Center (SRIC)

NEW YORK

Abelard Foundation
Abortion Rights Mobilization (ARM)
Activists for Animals
Africa Fund
African-American Institute
AIDS Coalition to Unleash Power (ACT-UP!)
Alan Guttmacher Institute (AGI)
Alternative Media Information Center
Alternatives to Militarism
Amalgamated Clothing and Textile Workers Union (ACTWU)
American Civil Liberties Union, National (ACLU)
American Civil Liberties Union, National Foundation (ACLU)
American Committee on Africa (ACOA)
American Conservation Association
American Federation of Television and Radio Artists (AFTRA)
American Foundation for AIDS Research (AmFAR)
American Humanist Association (AHA) / *The Humanist*
Americans for Peace Now
Amnesty International of the U.S.A. (AIUSA)
Animal People
Animal Rights International (AIR)
Anti Defamation League Foundation (ADL)
Anti Defamation League of B'nai B'rith (ADL)
Asian American Legal Defense and Education Fund
Association for Union Democracy (AUD)
Astraea National Lesbian Action Foundation
Beauty Without Cruelty
Black Veterans for Social Justice
Body Politic, The
Bydale Foundation
Campaign for Peace and Democracy
Carnegie Corporation of New York
Carnegie Council on Ethics and International Affairs
Catholic Worker, The
Center for Constitutional Rights (CCR)
Center for Cuban Studies
Center for Environmental Information
Center for Immigrants Rights (CIR)
Center for Reproductive Law and Policy
Center for War / Peace Studies
Cineaste
Cinema Guild
City Limits Community Information Service / *City Limits*
Coalition for Free and Open Elections
Coalition for the Homeless
Committee for Truth in Psychiatry
Committee in Solidarity with the People of El Salvador
Common Giving Fund
Commonweal Foundation / *Commonweal*
Concerts for Human Rights Foundation
Consumers Union / *Consumer Reports*
Council on Economic Priorities
Council on Foreign Relations (CFR) / *Foreign Affairs*
Council on International Public Affairs
Cuba Information Project

(New York continued)

Democratic Socialists of America (DSA)
Design Industries Foundation Fighting AIDS
Disarm Education Fund
Earth Action
Environmental Defense Fund (EDF)
Episcopal Church Public Policy Network
EPL / Environmental Advocates
Fairness and Accuracy In Reporting (FAIR)
Fellowship of Reconciliation (FOR)
Feminist Press
Ford Foundation
Foundation for Independent Video and Film
Foundation for the Study of Independent Social Ideas / *Dissent*
Friends for Jamaica
Fund for Animals
Funding Exchange
Gay Men's Health Crisis (GMHC)
Global Committee of Parliamentarians on Population and
    Development
Global Education Associates
Greens/Green Party USA
Hempstead, NY 11550
Heresies Collective / *Heresies*
Hetrick-Martin Institute (HMI)
Human Rights Watch (HRW)
Human SERVE
Industrial Areas Foundation
INFORM
Institute for Democratic Socialism
Interfaith Center on Corporate Responsibility (ICCR)
Interfaith Hunger Appeal
International Ladies' Garment Workers' Union (ILGWU)
International League for Human Rights
International Publishers Co.
International Women's Health Coalition
International Women's Tribune Centre (IWTC)
James C. Penney Foundation
Jane Addams Peace Association
Jessie Smith Noyes Foundation
Jewish Fund for Justice
Joyce Mertz-Gilmore Foundation
Kitchen Table: Women of Color Press
Labor Institute
Labor Research Association
Labor Zionist Letters
Lambda Legal Defense and Education Fund
Lawyers Committee for Human Rights
Legal Action Center for the Homeless
Lesbian and Gay Immigration Rights Task Force (LGRITF)
Lesbian Herstory Educational Foundation
Lilith Publications / *Lilith*
Lucius Trust and Arcane School
MADRE
Media Coalition
Methodist Federation for Social Action / Methodist Federation
    Fund
Modern Language Association of America (MLA)
Monthly Review Foundation / *Monthly Review*
Mothers and Others for a Livable Planet
Ms.
Ms. Foundation for Education and Communication
Ms. Foundation for Women
Nathan Cummings Foundation
Nation Company, The / *The Nation*

Nation Institute, The
National Association for the Advancement of Colored People
    Legal Defense Fund (NAACP)
National Coalition Against Censorship (NCAC)
National Coalition of 100 Black Women
National Coalition of Education Activists
National Council for Research on Women (NCRW)
National Council of Churches (NCC)
National Emergency Civil Liberties Foundation
National Independent Politics Summit
National Labor Committee Education Fund in Support of
    Worker and Human Rights in Central America
National Lawyers Guild Foundation
National Network on Cuba
National Organization for Women, Nassau (NOW)
National Organization for Women Legal Defense and
    Education Fund (NOW)
National Organization of Industrial Trade Unions (NOITU)
National Puerto Rican Forum
Natural Resources Defense Council (NRDC)
Network for Social Justice
New Environment Association / New Environment Institute
New-Land Foundation
New World Foundation
New York Lawyers for the Public Interest
Nicaragua Solidarity Network of Greater New York
Norman Foundation
North American Congress on Latin America (NACLA)
North American Man - Boy Love Association (NAMBLA)
North Star Fund
Office and Professional Employees International Union
Open Space Institute (OSI)
Parliamentarians for Global Action
Philip D. Reed Foundation
Physicians for Social Responsibility, New York
Planned Parenthood Action Fund
Planned Parenthood Federation of America
Population Communications International
Population Council
Prison Life
Pro Choice Resource Center
Public Concern Foundation / *Washington Spectator*
Public Health Institute
Puerto Rican Legal Defense and Education Fund (PRLDEF)
Rainforest Alliance
Rainforest Foundation
Robert Sterling Clark Foundation
Rockefeller Brothers Fund
Rockefeller Family Foundation
Rockefeller Foundation
Sex Information and Education Council of the United States
Social Policy Corporation
Stewart R. Mott Charitable Trust
Students Organizing Students
Sustainable America
Synergos Institute
Syracuse Cultural Workers
Third Wave
Third World Viewpoint
Transport Workers Union of America
Trilateral Commission
Twentieth Century Fund
United Action for Animals
United Nations Association of the USA (UNA-USA)

(New York continued)

Village Voice / *VLS* / VV Publishing Corp.
Visual Studies Workshop / *Afterimage*
Wallace Genetic Foundation
War and Peace Foundation for Education
War Resisters League (WRL)
Welfare Research
Welfare Warriors
Women and Foundations / Corporate Philanthropy (WAF/CP)
Women USA Fund
Women's Action Alliance
Women's Health Action and Mobilization (WHAM!)
Women's Resource Center of New York
Workers Defense League
World Conference on Religion and Peace (WCRP)

NORTH CAROLINA

Acid Rain Foundation
Blue Ridge Environmental Defense League
Center for Reflection on the Second Law (CFRSL)
Center for Women's Economic Alternatives
Foundation for a Peaceful Environment Among Communities
	Everywhere (Foundation for PEACE)
Grassroots Leadership
Institute for Southern Studies (ISS)
Laddyslipper
National Abortion and Reproductive Rights Action League,
North Carolina (NARAL)
Planned Parenthood Public Affairs, North Carolina
Rural Southern Voice for Peace (RSVP)
Southerners for Economic Justice (SEJ)
Student Environmental Action Coalition (SEAC)
Synergetic Society

OHIO

American Civil Liberties Union, Ohio Foundation
Coalition on Homelessness and Housing in Ohio (COHHIO)
Environmental Health Watch (EHW)
Farm Labor Organizing Committee
Farm Labor Research Project (FLRP)
Institute for Environmental Education
International Chemical Workers Union (ICWU)
National Abortion and Reproductive Rights Action League,
	Ohio Education Foundation (NARAL)
National Abortion and Reproductive Rights Action League,
	Ohio (NARAL)
Pig Iron Press
Planned Parenthood Affiliates of Ohio
Women's Law Fund

OKLAHOMA

American Civil Liberties Union, Oklahoma Foundation

OREGON

American Civil Liberties Union, Oregon Foundation (ACLU)
Association of Forest Service Employees for Environmental
	Ethics

Coalition for Human Dignity
Earth Communications / Radio For Peace International (RFPI)
Earth First!
McKenzie River Gathering Foundation (MRG)
Physicians for Social Responsibility, Portland
Support Coalition
Western States Center
Womyn's Press

PENNSYLVANIA

American Anti-Vivisection Society (AAVS)
American Civil Liberties Union, Pennsylvania Foundation
American Friends Service Committee (AFSC)
Aquarian Research Foundation
Association for Gay, Lesbian, and Bisexual Issues in
	Counseling (AGLBIC)
Bread and Roses Community Fund
Central Committee for Conscientious Objectors
CHOICE
Education Law Center, PA (ELC-PA)
Evangelicals for Social Action (ESA)
Fund for an OPEN Society
International Society for Animal Rights (ISAR)
Juvenile Law Center
Letters for Animals
National Coalition Against Sexual Assault (NCASA)
National Federation of Independent Unions (NFIU)
Pax Christi USA
Pennsylvania Environmental Council
Pennsylvanians for Modern Courts
Physicians for Social Responsibility, Philadelphia
Planned Parenthood Pennsylvania Advocates
Rush Watch Weekly
Three Rivers Community Fund
Women's Law Project
Women's Way
Women's International League for Peace and Freedom
World Federalist Association of Pittsburgh

RHODE ISLAND

Coalition to Preserve Choice: 2 to 1

SOUTH CAROLINA

American Civil Liberties Union, South Carolina Foundation

SOUTH DAKOTA

South Dakota Peace and Justice Center

TENNESSEE

American Civil Liberties Union, Tennessee Foundation
Appalachian Community Fund
Highlander Research and Education Center
Kids For A Clean Environment (Kids FACE)
National Association for the Advancement of Colored People,
	Memphis Branch
National Health Care for the Homeless
Progressive Periodicals Directory
Southern Empowerment Project (SEP)
Tennessee Environmental Council (TEC)
United Garment Workers of America (UGW)

TEXAS

American Atheist General Headquarters
American Atheists
Children's Alliance for Protection of the Environment
Esperanza Peace and Justice Center
First Amendment Coalition of Texas
International Center for the Solution of Environmental
        Problems (ICSEP)
Live Oak Fund for Change
Mujeres Project
People Organized in Defense of Earth and Her Resources
Southwest Voter Registration Education Project
Triangle AIDS Network
Voice for Animals

UTAH

American Civil Liberties Union, Utah Foundation (ACLU)

VERMONT

American Civil Liberties Union, Vermont Foundation
Peace and Justice Center
Social Ecology Project
Toward Freedom (TF)
Volunteers for Peace (VFP)

VIRGINIA

Alliance for Environmental Education
American Civil Liberties Union, Virginia (ACLU)
American Civil Liberties Union, Virginia Foundation (ACLU)
American Medical Student Association Foundation
American Medical Student Association (AMSA)
Appalachian Peace Education Center (APEC)
Brethren Peace Fellowship
Center for New Creation
Center on National Labor Policy
CIABASE
Citizens Clearinghouse for Hazardous Waste (CCHW)
Guatemala Information Documentation
National Federation of Societies for Clinical Social Work
National Organization for Women, Virginia (NOW)
National Rural Letter Carriers' Association (NRLCA)
Nature Conservancy
Nature Conservancy Action Fund
New River Free Press
Southern Environmental Law Center
Tenants' and Workers' Support Committee
Women in Community Service (WICS)
Working From the Heart

WASHINGTON

American Civil Liberties Union, Washington Endowment Fund
American Civil Liberties Union, Washington Foundation
Bullitt Foundation
Center for Economic Democracy / *Boycott Quarterly*
Context Institute / *IN CONTEXT*
Earthstewards Network
EduComics

Environmental Fund of Washington
Feminist Women's Health Center (FWHC)
Greater Ecosystem Alliance
Institute for Consumer Responsibility
Japanese American Citizens League
Lavender Families Resource Network
National Campaign for Freedom of Expression (NCFE)
Northwest Coalition Against Malicious Harassment
Peace and Justice Action League of Spokane
Planned Parenthood Affiliates of Washington
Vietnam Veterans Against the War Anti-Imperialist
Washington Rural Organizing Project
Washington Toxics Coalition

WEST VIRGINIA

Southern Appalachian Labor School

WISCONSIN

American Civil Liberties Union, Wisconsin Foundation
Campaign for a Sustainable Milwaukee
Center for Alternative Mining Development Policy
Center for Public Representation, Wisconsin
Committee Against Registration and the Draft
Honor Our Neighbors Origins and Rights (HONOR)
Jobs With Peace, Milwaukee
Progressive, The
Salzberg Equal Justice Foundation
Society for Ecological Restoration (SER)
Wisconsin Community Fund (WCF)
World Coordinating Council for Nicaragua (WCCN)

KEYWORD INDEX

This index includes the organizations and publications mentioned in <u>The Left Guide</u>. Each reference has been indexed by its full name with the number of the page or pages on which it appears. In addition, each name has been cross-referenced by the keywords in its name. For example; the Environmental Defense Fund is listed as:

and under its commonly used acronym:

In each case the "◗" denotes the beginning of the group's name, while the first word on the line indicates where it is located alphabetically within the **Keyword Index**. The organization is listed in several places so researchers can find it even if they don't know its full name.

NOTES

NOTES